8th Workshop on Statistical Machine Translation

(WMT 2013)

Sofia, Bulgaria
8 - 9 August 2013

ISBN: 978-1-62748-986-7

Printed from e-media with permission by:

Curran Associates, Inc.
57 Morehouse Lane
Red Hook, NY 12571

Some format issues inherent in the e-media version may also appear in this print version.

Printed by Curran Associates, Inc. (2013)

For permission requests, please contact the Association for Computational Linguistics at the address below.

Association for Computational Linguistics
209 N. Eighth Street
Stroudsburg, Pennsylvania 18360

Phone: 1-570-476-8006
Fax: 1-570-476-0860

acl@aclweb.org

Additional copies of this publication are available from:

Curran Associates, Inc.
57 Morehouse Lane
Red Hook, NY 12571 USA
Phone: 845-758-0400
Fax: 845-758-2634
Email: curran@proceedings.com
Web: www.proceedings.com

Preface

The ACL 2013 Workshop on Statistical Machine Translation (WMT 2013) took place on Thursday and Friday, August 8–9, 2013 in Sofia, Bulgaria, immediately following the Conference of the Association for Computational Linguistics (ACL).

This is the eighth time this workshop has been held. The first time it was held at HLT-NAACL 2006 in New York City, USA. In the following years the Workshop on Statistical Machine Translation was held at ACL 2007 in Prague, Czech Republic, ACL 2008, Columbus, Ohio, USA, EACL 2009 in Athens, Greece, ACL 2010 in Uppsala, Sweden, EMNLP 2011 in Edinburgh, Scotland, and NAACL 2012 in Montréal, Canada.

The focus of our workshop was to use parallel corpora for machine translation. Recent experimentation has shown that the performance of SMT systems varies greatly with the source language. In this workshop we encouraged researchers to investigate ways to improve the performance of SMT systems for diverse languages, including morphologically more complex languages, languages with partial free word order, and low-resource languages.

Prior to the workshop, in addition to soliciting relevant papers for review and possible presentation, we conducted three shared tasks: a translation task, a quality estimation task, and a task to test automatic evaluation metrics. The results of the shared tasks were announced at the workshop, and these proceedings also include an overview paper for the shared tasks that summarizes the results, as well as provides information about the data used and any procedures that were followed in conducting or scoring the task. In addition, there are short papers from each participating team that describe their underlying system in greater detail.

Like in previous years, we have received a far larger number of submission than we could accept for presentation. This year we have received 32 full paper submissions and 46 shared task submissions. In total WMT-2013 featured 18 full paper oral presentations and 45 shared task poster presentations.

The invited talk was given by Andreas Eisele (Directorate-General for Translation at the European Commission, Luxembourg) entitled "Machine Translation at the European Commission: Serving the multilingual needs of the European Commission".

We would like to thank the members of the Program Committee for their timely reviews. We also would like to thank the participants of the shared task and all the other volunteers who helped with the evaluations.

Ondřej Bojar, Christian Buck, Chris Callison-Burch, Barry Haddow, Philipp Koehn, Christof Monz, Matt Post, Hervé Saint-Amand, Radu Soricut, and Lucia Specia

WMT 5-year Retrospective Best Paper Award

Each year WMT awards a 5-year Retrospective Best Paper Award. This year we selected the best paper from 2008's Workshop on Statistical Machine Translation, which was collocated with ACL in Columbus, Ohio. The goals of this retrospective award are to recognize high-quality work that has stood the test of time, and to highlight the excellent work that appears at WMT.

37 members of the WMT13 program committee voted on the best paper from a list of seven nominated papers. These were nominated by selecting the papers with the most non-self-citations in the ACL anthology network. This year the vote was very close, and was divided between several excellent papers. Ultimately, the program committee decided to award the WMT 5-year Retrospective Best Paper Award to:

Kevin Gimpel and Noah A. Smith. 2008. *Rich Source-Side Context for Statistical Machine Translation*. In Proceedings of the Workshop on Statistical Machine Translation. Pages 9-17.

In this paper, Gimpel and Smith used a variety of features, including surrounding words and part-of-speech tags, local syntactic structure, and other properties of the source language sentence to help predict each phrase's translation. They argued that source side features were easier to exploit than target side features, and that they were likely to make a bigger impact, since some target side features are already exploited via the language model. Gimpel and Smith empirically demonstrated the value of their model by augmenting the baseline Moses MT system and fielding an entry into the English-to-German shared task at WMT that year.

One of the program committee members, Preslav Nakov, commented that this work made an important contribution in the direction of context-aware SMT, which has been largely neglected in mainstream SMT research.

Congratulations to Kevin Gimpel and Noah Smith on their excellent work!

Organizers:

Ondřej Bojar (Charles University)
Christian Buck (University of Edinburgh)
Chris Callison-Burch (Johns Hopkins University)
Barry Haddow (University of Edinburgh)
Philipp Koehn (University of Edinburgh)
Christof Monz (University of Amsterdam)
Matt Post (Johns Hopkins University)
Hervé Saint-Amand (University of Edinburgh)
Radu Soricut (Google)
Lucia Specia (University of Sheffield)

Invited Talk:

Andreas Eisele (European Commission)

Program Committee:

Lars Ahrenberg (Linköping University)
Eleftherios Avramidis (German Research Center for Artificial Intelligence (DFKI))
Daniel Beck (University of Sheffield)
Nicola Bertoldi (FBK)
Arianna Bisazza (Fondazione Bruno Kessler)
Graeme Blackwood (IBM Research)
Phil Blunsom (University of Oxford)
Chris Brockett (Microsoft Research)
Bill Byrne (University of Cambridge)
Nicola Cancedda (Xerox Research Centre Europe)
Hailong Cao (Harbin Institute of Technology)
Marine Carpuat (National Research Council)
Francisco Casacuberta (Universitat Politécnica de Valencia)
Daniel Cer (Stanford University)
Boxing Chen (NRC)
Colin Cherry (NRC)
David Chiang (USC/ISI)
Steve DeNeefe (SDL Language Weaver)
John DeNero (Google)
Michael Denkowski (Carnegie Mellon University)
Markus Dreyer (SDL Language Weaver)
Kevin Duh (Nara Institute of Science and Technology)
Chris Dyer (Carnegie Mellon University)
Marc Dymetman (Xerox Research Centre Europe)
Stefano Faralli (Sapienza University of Rome)

Yang Feng (University of Sheffield)
Andrew Finch (NICT)
José A. R. Fonollosa (Universitat Politécnica de Catalunya)
Mikel Forcada (Universitat d'Alacant)
George Foster (NRC)
Alexander Fraser (University of Stuttgart)
Katya Garmash (University of Amsterdam)
Niyu Ge (IBM Research)
Ulrich Germann (University of Edinburgh)
Daniel Gildea (University of Rochester)
Cyril Goutte (National Research Council Canada)
Nizar Habash (Columbia University)
Jan Hajic (Charles University in Prague)
Keith Hall (Google Research)
Greg Hanneman (Carnegie Mellon University)
Christian Hardmeier (Uppsala universitet)
Xiaodong He (Microsoft Research)
Yifan He (New York University)
Kenneth Heafield (Carnegie Mellon University, University of Edinburgh)
John Henderson (MITRE)
Silja Hildebrand (CMU)
Hieu Hoang (University of Edinburgh)
Young-Sook Hwang (SKPlanet)
Gonzalo Iglesias (University of Cambridge)
Abe Ittycheriah (IBM)
Doug Jones (MIT Lincoln Laboratory)
Maxim Khalilov (TAUS Labs)
Roland Kuhn (National Research Council of Canada)
Shankar Kumar (Google)
Mathias Lambert (Amazon.com)
Qun Liu (Dublin City University)
Wolfgang Macherey (Google)
Daniel Marcu (SDL)
José B. Mariño (Polytechnic University of Catalonia)
Cettolo Mauro (FBK)
Arne Mauser (Google, Inc)
Shachar Mirkin (Xerox Research Centre Europe)
Dragos Munteanu (SDL Language Technologies)
Markos Mylonakis (Xerox Research Centre Europe)
Preslav Nakov (Qatar Computing Research Institute, Qatar Foundation)
Kemal Oflazer (Carnegie Mellon University - Qatar)
Sergio Penkale (Lingo24)
Chris Quirk (Microsoft Research)
Stefan Riezler (Heidelberg University)
Johann Roturier (Symantec)
Anoop Sarkar (Simon Fraser University)
Holger Schwenk (University of Le Mans)

Jean Senellart (SYSTRAN)
Hendra Setiawan (IBM T.J. Watson Research Center)
Kashif Shah (University of Sheffield)
Wade Shen (MIT)
Linfeng Song (ICT/CAS)
Felipe Sánchez-Martínez (Universitat d'Alacant)
Joerg Tiedemann (Uppsala University)
Christoph Tillmann (IBM Research)
Dan Tufis (Research Institute for Artificial Intelligence, Romanian Academy)
Masao Utiyama (NICT)
Josef van Genabith (Dublin City University)
David Vilar (DFKI)
Haifeng Wang (Baidu)
Taro Watanabe (NICT)
Hua Wu (Baidu)
Peng Xu (Google Inc.)
Francois Yvon (LIMSI/CNRS)
Richard Zens (Google)
Hao Zhang (Google)
Joy Ying Zhang (Carnegie Mellon University)
Liu Zhanyi (Baidu)

Table of Contents

Workshop Program

Thursday, August 8, 2013

9:00–9:10 Opening Remarks

Session 1: Shared Tasks and their Evaluation

10:30–11:00 Coffee

Session 2: Poster Session

11:00–12:30 Shared Task: Translation

Thursday, August 8, 2013 (continued)

Thursday, August 8, 2013 (continued)

Session 3: Invited Talk

Session 4: Quality Estimation

Session 5: Translation Models

Friday, August 9, 2013

Session 6: Learning

Session 7: Poster Session

Friday, August 9, 2013 (continued)

MT Quality Estimation: The CMU System for WMT'13
Silja Hildebrand and Stephan Vogel

LORIA System for the WMT13 Quality Estimation Shared Task
David Langlois and Kamel Smaili

LIG System for WMT13 QE Task: Investigating the Usefulness of Features in Word Confidence Estimation for MT
Ngoc Quang Luong, Benjamin Lecouteux and Laurent Besacier

DCU-Symantec at the WMT 2013 Quality Estimation Shared Task
Raphael Rubino, Joachim Wagner, Jennifer Foster, Johann Roturier, Rasoul Samad Zadeh Kaljahi and Fred Hollowood

LIMSI Submission for the WMT'13 Quality Estimation Task: an Experiment with N-Gram Posteriors
Anil Kumar Singh, Guillaume Wisniewski and François Yvon

11:00–12:30 Shared Task: Evaluation

Ranking Translations using Error Analysis and Quality Estimation
Mark Fishel

Are ACT's Scores Increasing with Better Translation Quality?
Najeh Hajlaoui

A Description of Tunable Machine Translation Evaluation Systems in WMT13 Metrics Task
Aaron Li-Feng Han, Derek F. Wong, Lidia S. Chao, Yi Lu, Liangye He, Yiming Wang and Jiaji Zhou

MEANT at WMT 2013: A tunable, accurate yet inexpensivesemantic frame based MT evaluation metric
Chi-kiu Lo and Dekai Wu

An Approach Using Style Classification Features for Quality Estimation
Erwan Moreau and Raphael Rubino

DCU Participation in WMT2013 Metrics Task
Xiaofeng Wu, Hui Yu and Qun Liu

12:30–14:00 Lunch Break

Friday, August 9, 2013 (continued)

Session 8: Reordering and Hierarchical Models

14:00–14:20 *Efficient Solutions for Word Reordering in German-English Phrase-Based Statistical Machine Translation*
Arianna Bisazza and Marcello Federico

14:20–14:40 *A Phrase Orientation Model for Hierarchical Machine Translation*
Matthias Huck, Joern Wuebker, Felix Rietig and Hermann Ney

14:40–15:00 *A Dependency-Constrained Hierarchical Model with Moses*
Yvette Graham

15:00–15:20 *Investigations in Exact Inference for Hierarchical Translation*
Wilker Aziz, Marc Dymetman and Sriram Venkatapathy

15:20–16:00 Coffee Break

Session 9: Alignment and Word Translation Models

16:00–16:20 *Evaluating (and Improving) Sentence Alignment under Noisy Conditions*
Omar Zaidan and Vishal Chowdhary

16:20–16:40 *Multi-Rate HMMs for Word Alignment*
Elif Eyigöz, Daniel Gildea and Kemal Oflazer

16:40–17:00 *Hidden Markov Tree Model for Word Alignment*
Shuhei Kondo, Kevin Duh and Yuji Matsumoto

17:00–17:20 *An MT Error-Driven Discriminative Word Lexicon using Sentence Structure Features*
Jan Niehues and Alex Waibel

Findings of the 2013 Workshop on Statistical Machine Translation

Ondřej Bojar
Charles University in Prague

Christian Buck
University of Edinburgh

Chris Callison-Burch
University of Pennsylvania

Christian Federmann
Saarland University

Barry Haddow
University of Edinburgh

Philipp Koehn
University of Edinburgh

Christof Monz
University of Amsterdam

Matt Post
Johns Hopkins University

Radu Soricut
Google

Lucia Specia
University of Sheffield

Abstract

We present the results of the WMT13 shared tasks, which included a translation task, a task for run-time estimation of machine translation quality, and an unofficial metrics task. This year, 143 machine translation systems were submitted to the ten translation tasks from 23 institutions. An additional 6 anonymized systems were included, and were then evaluated both automatically and manually, in our largest manual evaluation to date. The quality estimation task had four subtasks, with a total of 14 teams, submitting 55 entries.

1 Introduction

We present the results of the shared tasks of the Workshop on Statistical Machine Translation (WMT) held at ACL 2013. This workshop builds on seven previous WMT workshops (Koehn and Monz, 2006; Callison-Burch et al., 2007, 2008, 2009, 2010, 2011, 2012).

This year we conducted three official tasks: a translation task, a human evaluation of translation results, and a quality estimation task.[1] In the translation task (§2), participants were asked to translate a shared test set, optionally restricting themselves to the provided training data. We held ten translation tasks this year, between English and each of Czech, French, German, Spanish, and Russian. The Russian translation tasks were new this year, and were also the most popular. The system outputs for each task were evaluated both automatically and manually.

The human evaluation task (§3) involves asking human judges to rank sentences output by anonymized systems. We obtained large numbers of rankings from two groups: researchers (who contributed evaluations proportional to the number of tasks they entered) and workers on Amazon's Mechanical Turk (who were paid). This year's effort was our largest yet by a wide margin; we managed to collect an order of magnitude more judgments than in the past, allowing us to achieve statistical significance on the majority of the pairwise system rankings. This year, we are also clustering the systems according to these significance results, instead of presenting a total ordering over systems.

The focus of the quality estimation task (§6) is to produce real-time estimates of sentence- or word-level machine translation quality. This task has potential usefulness in a range of settings, such as prioritizing output for human post-editing, or selecting the best translations from a number of systems. This year the following subtasks were proposed: prediction of percentage of word edits necessary to fix a sentence, ranking of up to five alternative translations for a given source sentence, prediction of post-editing time for a sentence, and prediction of word-level scores for a given translation (correct/incorrect and types of edits). The datasets included English-Spanish and German-English news translations produced by a number of machine translation systems. This marks the second year we have conducted this task.

The primary objectives of WMT are to evaluate the state of the art in machine translation, to disseminate common test sets and public training data with published performance numbers, and to refine evaluation methodologies for machine translation. As before, all of the data, translations, and collected human judgments are publicly available.[2] We hope these datasets serve as a valuable resource for research into statistical machine translation, system combination, and automatic evaluation or prediction of translation quality.

[1]The traditional metrics task is evaluated in a separate paper (Macháček and Bojar, 2013).

[2]http://statmt.org/wmt13/results.html

2 Overview of the Translation Task

The recurring task of the workshop examines translation between English and five other languages: German, Spanish, French, Czech, and — new this year — Russian. We created a test set for each language pair by translating newspaper articles and provided training data.

2.1 Test data

The test data for this year's task was selected from news stories from online sources. A total of 52 articles were selected, in roughly equal amounts from a variety of Czech, English, French, German, Spanish, and Russian news sites:[3]

Czech: aktuálně.cz (1), CTK (1), deník (1), iDNES.cz (3), lidovky.cz (1), Novinky.cz (2)

French: Cyber Presse (3), Le Devoir (1), Le Monde (3), Liberation (2)

Spanish: ABC.es (2), BBC Spanish (1), El Periodico (1), Milenio (3), Noroeste (1), Primera Hora (3)

English: BBC (2), CNN (2), Economist (1), Guardian (1), New York Times (2), The Telegraph (1)

German: Der Standard (1), Deutsche Welle (1), FAZ (1), Frankfurter Rundschau (2), Welt (2)

Russian: AIF (2), BBC Russian (2), Izvestiya (1), Rosbalt (1), Vesti (1)

The stories were translated by the professional translation agency Capita, funded by the EU Framework Programme 7 project MosesCore, and by Yandex, a Russian search engine.[4] All of the translations were done directly, and not via an intermediate language.

2.2 Training data

As in past years we provided parallel corpora to train translation models, monolingual corpora to train language models, and development sets to tune system parameters. Some training corpora were identical from last year (Europarl[5], United Nations, French-English 10^9 corpus, CzEng), some were updated (News Commentary, monolingual data), and new corpora were added (Common Crawl (Smith et al., 2013), Russian-English parallel data provided by Yandex, Russian-English Wikipedia Headlines provided by CMU).

Some statistics about the training materials are given in Figure 1.

2.3 Submitted systems

We received 143 submissions from 23 institutions. The participating institutions and their entry names are listed in Table 1; each system did not necessarily appear in all translation tasks. We also included three commercial off-the-shelf MT systems and three online statistical MT systems,[6] which we anonymized.

For presentation of the results, systems are treated as either *constrained* or *unconstrained*, depending on whether their models were trained only on the provided data. Since we do not know how they were built, these online and commercial systems are treated as unconstrained during the automatic and human evaluations.

3 Human Evaluation

As with past workshops, we contend that automatic measures of machine translation quality are an imperfect substitute for human assessments. We therefore conduct a manual evaluation of the system outputs and define its results to be the principal ranking of the workshop. In this section, we describe how we collected this data and compute the results, and then present the official results of the ranking.

We run the evaluation campaign using an updated version of Appraise (Federmann, 2012); the tool has been extended to support collecting judgments using Amazon's Mechanical Turk, replacing the annotation system used in previous WMTs. The software, including all changes made for this year's workshop, is available from GitHub.[7]

This year differs from prior years in a few important ways:

- We collected about ten times more judgments that we have in the past, using judgments from both participants in the shared task and non-experts hired on Amazon's Mechanical Turk.

- Instead of presenting a total ordering of systems for each pair, we cluster them and report a ranking over the clusters.

[3]For more details see the XML test files. The `docid` tag gives the source and the date for each document in the test set, and the `origlang` tag indicates the original source language.

[4]`http://www.yandex.com/`

[5]As of Fall 2011, the proceedings of the European Parliament are no longer translated into all official languages.

[6]Thanks to Hervé Saint-Amand and Martin Popel for harvesting these entries.

[7]`https://github.com/cfedermann/Appraise`

Europarl Parallel Corpus

	Spanish ↔ English		French ↔ English		German ↔ English		Czech ↔ English	
Sentences	1,965,734		2,007,723		1,920,209		646,605	
Words	56,895,229	54,420,026	60,125,563	55,642,101	50,486,398	53,008,851	14,946,399	17,376,433
Distinct words	176,258	117,481	140,915	118,404	381,583	115,966	172,461	63,039

News Commentary Parallel Corpus

	Spanish ↔ English		French ↔ English		German ↔ English		Czech ↔ English		Russian ↔ English	
Sentences	174,441		157,168		178,221		140,324		150,217	
Words	5,116,388	4,520,796	4,928,135	4,066,721	4,597,904	4,541,058	3,206,423	3,507,249	3,841,950	4,008,949
Distinct words	84,273	61,693	69,028	58,295	142,461	61,761	138,991	54,270	145,997	57,991

Common Crawl Parallel Corpus

	Spanish ↔ English		French ↔ English		German ↔ English		Czech ↔ English		Russian ↔ English	
Sentences	1,845,286		3,244,152		2,399,123		161,838		878,386	
Words	49,561,060	46,861,758	91,328,790	81,096,306	54,575,405	58,870,638	3,529,783	3,927,378	21,018,793	21,535,122
Distinct words	710,755	640,778	889,291	859,017	1,640,835	823,480	210,170	128,212	764,203	432,062

United Nations Parallel Corpus

	Spanish ↔ English		French ↔ English	
Sentences	11,196,913		12,886,831	
Words	318,788,686	365,127,098	411,916,781	360,341,450
Distinct words	593,567	581,339	565,553	666,077

10^9 Word Parallel Corpus

	French ↔ English	
Sentences	22,520,400	
Words	811,203,407	668,412,817
Distinct words	2,738,882	2,861,836

Yandex 1M Parallel Corpus

	Russian ↔ English	
Sentences	1,000,000	
Words	24,121,459	26,107,293
Distinct words	701,809	387,646

CzEng Parallel Corpus

	Czech ↔ English	
Sentences	14,833,358	
Words	200,658,857	228,040,794
Distinct words	1,389,803	920,824

Wiki Headlines Parallel Corpus

	Russian ↔ English	
Sentences	514,859	
Words	1,191,474	1,230,644
Distinct words	282,989	251,328

Europarl Language Model Data

	English	Spanish	French	German	Czech
Sentence	2,218,201	2,123,835	2,190,579	2,176,537	668,595
Words	59,848,044	60,476,282	63,439,791	53,534,167	14,946,399
Distinct words	123,059	181,837	145,496	394,781	172,461

News Language Model Data

	English	Spanish	French	German	Czech	Russian
Sentence	68,521,621	13,384,314	21,195,476	54,619,789	27,540,749	19,912,911
Words	1,613,778,461	386,014,234	524,541,570	983,818,841	456,271,247	351,595,790
Distinct words	3,392,137	1,163,825	1,590,187	6,814,953	2,655,813	2,195,112

News Test Set

	English	Spanish	French	German	Czech	Russian
Sentences	3000					
Words	64,810	73,659	73,659	63,412	57,050	58,327
Distinct words	8,935	10,601	11,441	12,189	15,324	15,736

Figure 1: Statistics for the training and test sets used in the translation task. The number of words and the number of distinct words (case-insensitive) is based on the provided tokenizer.

ID	Institution
BALAGUR	Yandex (Borisov et al., 2013)
CMU CMU-TREE-TO-TREE	Carnegie Mellon University (Ammar et al., 2013)
CU-BOJAR, CU-DEPFIX, CU-TAMCHYNA	Charles University in Prague (Bojar et al., 2013)
CU-KAREL, CU-ZEMAN	Charles University in Prague (Bílek and Zeman, 2013)
CU-PHRASEFIX, CU-TECTOMT	Charles University in Prague (Galuščáková et al., 2013)
DCU	Dublin City University (Rubino et al., 2013a)
DCU-FDA	Dublin City University (Bicici, 2013a)
DCU-OKITA	Dublin City University (Okita et al., 2013)
DESRT	Università di Pisa (Miceli Barone and Attardi, 2013)
ITS-LATL	University of Geneva
JHU	Johns Hopkins University (Post et al., 2013)
KIT	Karlsruhe Institute of Technology (Cho et al., 2013)
LIA	Université d'Avignon (Huet et al., 2013)
LIMSI	LIMSI (Allauzen et al., 2013)
MES-*	Munich / Edinburgh / Stuttgart (Durrani et al., 2013a; Weller et al., 2013)
OMNIFLUENT	SAIC (Matusov and Leusch, 2013)
PROMT	PROMT Automated Translations Solutions
QCRI-MES	Qatar / Munich / Edinburgh / Stuttgart (Sajjad et al., 2013)
QUAERO	QUAERO (Peitz et al., 2013a)
RWTH	RWTH Aachen (Peitz et al., 2013b)
SHEF	University of Sheffield
STANFORD	Stanford University (Green et al., 2013)
TALP-UPC	TALP Research Centre (Formiga et al., 2013a)
TUBITAK	TÜBİTAK-BİLGEM (Durgar El-Kahlout and Mermer, 2013)
UCAM	University of Cambridge (Pino et al., 2013)
UEDIN, UEDIN-HEAFIELD	University of Edinburgh (Durrani et al., 2013b)
UEDIN-SYNTAX	University of Edinburgh (Nadejde et al., 2013)
UMD	University of Maryland (Eidelman et al., 2013)
UU	Uppsala University (Stymne et al., 2013)
COMMERCIAL-1,2,3	*Anonymized commercial systems*
ONLINE-A,B,G	*Anonymized online systems*

Table 1: Participants in the shared translation task. Not all teams participated in all language pairs. The translations from the commercial and online systems were not submitted by their respective companies but were obtained by us, and are therefore anonymized in a fashion consistent with previous years of the workshop.

3.1 Ranking translations of sentences

The ranking among systems is produced by collecting a large number of rankings between the systems' translations. Every language task had many participating systems (the largest was 19, for the Russian-English task). Rather than asking judges to provide a complete ordering over all the translations of a source segment, we instead randomly select five systems and ask the judge to rank just those. We call each of these a *ranking task*. A screenshot of the ranking interface is shown in Figure 2.

For each ranking task, the judge is presented with a source segment, a reference translation, and the outputs of five systems (anonymized and randomly-ordered). The following simple instructions are provided:

> *You are shown a source sentence followed by several candidate translations. Your task is to rank the translations from best to worst (ties are allowed).*

The rankings of the systems are numbered from 1 to 5, with 1 being the best translation and 5 being the worst. Each ranking task has the potential to provide 10 *pairwise rankings*, and fewer if the judge chooses any ties. For example, the ranking

{A:1, B:2, C:4, D:3, E:5}

provides 10 pairwise rankings, while the ranking

{A:3, B:3, C:4, D:3, E:1}

provides just 7. The absolute value of the ranking or the degree of difference is not considered.

We use the collected pairwise rankings to assign each system a score that reflects how highly that system was usually ranked by the annotators. The score for some system A reflects how frequently it was judged to be better than other systems when compared on the same segment; its score is the number of pairwise rankings where it was judged to be better, divided by the total number of non-tying pairwise comparisons. These scores were used to compute clusters of systems and rankings between them (§3.4).

3.2 Collecting the data

A goal this year was to collect enough data to achieve statistical significance in the rankings. We distributed the workload among two groups of judges: *researchers* and *Turkers*. The researcher group comprised partipants in the shared task, who were asked to contribute judgments on 300 sentences for each system they contributed. The researcher evaluation was held over three weeks from May 17–June 7, and yielded about 280k pairwise rankings.

The Turker group was composed of non-expert annotators hired on Amazon's Mechanical Turk (MTurk). A basic unit of work on MTurk is called a Human Intelligence Task (HIT) and included three ranking tasks, for which we paid $0.25. To ensure that the Turkers provided high quality annotations, this portion of the evaluation was begun after the researcher portion had completed, enabling us to embed controls in the form of high-consensus pairwise rankings in the Turker HITs. To build these controls, we collected ranking tasks containing pairwise rankings with a high degree of researcher consensus. An example task is here:

SENTENCE	504
SOURCE	*Vor den heiligen Stätten verbeugen*
REFERENCE	*Let's worship the holy places*
SYSTEM A	Before the holy sites curtain
SYSTEM B	Before we bow to the Holy Places
SYSTEM C	To the holy sites bow
SYSTEM D	Bow down to the holy sites
SYSTEM E	Before the holy sites pay

MATRIX

	A	B	C	D	E
A	-	0	0	0	3
B	5	-	0	1	5
C	6	6	-	0	6
D	6	8	5	-	6
E	0	0	0	0	-

Matrix entry $M_{i,j}$ records the number of researchers who judged System i to be better than System j. We use as controls pairwise judgments for which $|M_{i,j} - M_{j,i}| > 5$, i.e., judgments where the researcher consensus ran strongly in one direction. We rejected HITs from Turkers who encountered at least 10 of these controls and failed more than 50% of them.

There were 463 people who participated in the Turker portion of the manual evaluation, contributing 664k pairwise rankings from Turkers who passed the controls. Together with the researcher judgments, we collected close to a million pairwise rankings, compared to 101k collected last year: a ten-fold increase. Table 2 contains more detail.

Figure 2: Screenshot of the Appraise interface used in the human evaluation campaign. The annotator is presented with a source segment, a reference translation, and the outputs of five systems (anonymized and randomly-ordered) and has to rank these according to their translation quality, ties are allowed. For technical reasons, annotators on Amazon's Mechanical Turk received all three ranking tasks for a single HIT on a single page, one upon the other.

3.3 Annotator agreement

Each year we calculate annotator agreement scores for the human evaluation as a measure of the reliability of the rankings. We measured pairwise agreement among annotators using Cohen's kappa coefficient (κ) (Cohen, 1960), which is defined as

$$\kappa = \frac{P(A) - P(E)}{1 - P(E)}$$

where $P(A)$ is the proportion of times that the annotators agree, and $P(E)$ is the proportion of time that they would agree by chance. Note that κ is basically a normalized version of $P(A)$, one which takes into account how meaningful it is for annotators to agree with each other, by incorporating $P(E)$. The values for κ range from 0 to 1, with zero indicating no agreement and 1 perfect agreement.

We calculate $P(A)$ by examining all pairs of systems which had been judged by two or more judges, and calculating the proportion of time that they agreed that $A > B$, $A = B$, or $A < B$. In other words, $P(A)$ is the empirical, observed rate at which annotators agree, in the context of pairwise comparisons.

As for $P(E)$, it should capture the probability that two annotators would agree randomly. Therefore:

$$P(E) = P(\text{A>B})^2 + P(\text{A=B})^2 + P(\text{A<B})^2$$

Note that each of the three probabilities in $P(E)$'s definition are squared to reflect the fact that we are considering the chance that *two* annotators would agree by chance. Each of these probabilities is computed empirically, by observing how often annotators actually rank two systems as being tied.

Table 3 gives κ values for inter-annotator agreement for WMT11–WMT13 while Table 4 details intra-annotator agreement scores. Due to the change of annotation software, we used a slightly different way of computing annotator agreement scores. Therefore, we chose to re-compute values for previous WMTs to allow for a fair comparison. The exact interpretation of the kappa coefficient is difficult, but according to Landis and Koch (1977), 0–0.2 is slight, 0.2–0.4 is fair, 0.4–0.6 is moderate,

LANGUAGE PAIR	Systems	Rankings	Average
Czech-English	11	85,469	7,769.91
English-Czech	12	102,842	8,570.17
German-English	17	128,668	7,568.71
English-German	15	77,286	5,152.40
Spanish-English	12	67,832	5,652.67
English-Spanish	13	60,464	4,651.08
French-English	13	80,741	6,210.85
English-French	17	100,783	5,928.41
Russian-English	19	151,422	7,969.58
English-Russian	14	87,323	6,237.36
Total	148	942,840	6,370.54
WMT12	103	101,969	999.69
WMT11	133	63,045	474.02

Table 2: Amount of data collected in the WMT13 manual evaluation. The final two rows report summary information from the previous two workshops.

LANGUAGE PAIR	WMT11	WMT12	WMT13	$WMT13_r$	$WMT13_m$
Czech-English	0.400	0.311	0.244	0.342	0.279
English-Czech	0.460	0.359	0.168	0.408	0.075
German-English	0.324	0.385	0.299	0.443	0.324
English-German	0.378	0.356	0.267	0.457	0.239
Spanish-English	0.494	0.298	0.277	0.415	0.295
English-Spanish	0.367	0.254	0.206	0.333	0.249
French-English	0.402	0.272	0.275	0.405	0.321
English-French	0.406	0.296	0.231	0.434	0.237
Russian-English	—	—	0.278	0.315	0.324
English-Russian	—	—	0.243	0.416	0.207

Table 3: κ scores measuring inter-annotator agreement. The $WMT13_r$ and $WMT13_m$ columns provide breakdowns for researcher annotations and MTurk annotations, respectively. See Table 4 for corresponding intra-annotator agreement scores.

0.6–0.8 is substantial, and 0.8–1.0 is almost perfect. We find that the agreement rates are more or less the same as in prior years.

The WMT13 column contains both researcher and Turker annotations at a roughly 1:2 ratio. The final two columns break out agreement numbers between these two groups. The researcher agreement rates are similar to agreement rates from past years, while the Turker agreement are well below researcher agreement rates, varying widely, but often comparable to WMT11 and WMT12. Clearly, researchers are providing us with more consistent opinions, but whether these differences are explained by Turkers racing through jobs, the particularities that inform researchers judging systems they know well, or something else, is hard to tell. Intra-annotator agreement scores are also on par from last year's level, and are often much better. We observe better intra-annotator agreement for researchers compared to Turkers.

As a small test, we varied the threshold of acceptance against the controls for the Turker data alone and computed inter-annotator agreement scores on the datasets for the Russian–English task (the only language pair where we had enough data at high thresholds). Table 5 shows that higher thresholds do indeed give us better agreements, but not monotonically. The increasing κs suggests that we can find a segment of Turkers who do a better job and that perhaps a slightly higher threshold of 0.6 would serve us better, while the remaining difference against the researchers suggests there may be different mindsets informing the decisions. In any case, getting the best performance out of the Turkers remains difficult.

3.4 System Score

Given the multitude of pairwise comparisons, we would like to rank the systems according to a single score computed for each system. In re-

LANGUAGE PAIR	WMT11	WMT12	WMT13	WMT13$_r$	WMT13$_m$
Czech-English	0.597	0.454	0.479	0.483	0.478
English-Czech	0.601	0.390	0.290	0.547	0.242
German-English	0.576	0.392	0.535	0.643	0.515
English-German	0.528	0.433	0.498	0.649	0.452
Spanish-English	0.574	1.000	0.575	0.605	0.537
English-Spanish	0.426	0.329	0.492	0.468	0.492
French-English	0.673	0.360	0.578	0.585	0.565
English-French	0.524	0.414	0.495	0.630	0.486
Russian-English	—	—	0.450	0.363	0.477
English-Russian	—	—	0.513	0.582	0.500

Table 4: κ scores measuring intra-annotator agreement, i.e., self-consistency of judges, across for the past few years of the human evaluation. The WMT13$_r$ and WMT13$_m$ columns provide breakdowns for researcher annotations and MTurk annotations, respectively. The perfect inter-annotator agreement for Spanish-English is a result of there being very little data for that language pair.

thresh.	rankings	κ
0.5	16,605	0.234
0.6	9,999	0.337
0.7	3,219	0.360
0.8	1,851	0.395
0.9	849	0.336

Table 5: Agreement as a function of threshold for Turkers on the Russian–English task. The threshold is the percentage of controls a Turker must pass for her rankings to be accepted.

cent evaluation campaigns, we tweaked the metric and now arrived at a intuitive score that has been demonstrated to be accurate in ranking systems according to their true quality (Koehn, 2012).

The score, which we call EXPECTED WINS, has an intuitive explanation. If the system is compared against a randomly picked opposing system, on a randomly picked sentence, by a randomly picked judge, what is the probability that its translation is ranked higher?

Formally, the score for a system S_i among a set of systems $\{S_j\}$ given a pool of pairwise rankings summarized as win(A, B) — the number of times system A is ranked higher than system B — is defined as follows:

$$\text{score}(S_i) = \frac{1}{|\{S_j\}|} \sum_{j,j \neq i} \frac{\text{win}(S_i, S_j)}{\text{win}(S_i, S_j) + \text{win}(S_j, S_i)}$$

Note that this score ignores ties.

3.5 Rank Ranges and Clusters

Given the scores, we would like to rank the systems, which is straightforward. But we would also like to know, if the obtained system ranking is statistically significant. Typically, given the large number of systems that participate, and the similarity of the systems given a common training data condition and often common toolsets, there will be some systems that will be very close in quality.

To establish the reliability of the obtained system ranking, we use bootstrap resampling. We sample from the set of pairwise rankings an equal sized set of pairwise rankings (allowing for multiple drawings of the same pairwise ranking), compute the expected wins score for each system based on this sample, and rank each system. By repeating this procedure a 1,000 times, we can determine a range of ranks, into which system falls at least 95% of the time (i.e., at least 950 times) — corresponding to a p-level of $p \leq 0.05$.

Furthermore, given the rank ranges for each system, we can cluster systems with overlapping rank ranges.[8]

For all language pairs and all systems, Table 6 reports all system scores, rank ranges, and clusters. The official interpretation of these results is that systems in the same cluster are considered tied. Given the large number of judgements that we collected, it was possible to group on average about two systems in a cluster, even though the systems in the middle are typically in larger clusters.

[8]Formally, given ranges defined by start(S_i) and end(S_i), we seek the largest set of clusters $\{C_c\}$ that satisfies:

$$\forall S\ \exists C : S \in C$$
$$S \in C_a, S \in C_b \rightarrow C_a = C_b$$
$$C_a \neq C_b \rightarrow \forall S_i \in C_a, S_j \in C_b :$$
$$\text{start}(S_i) > \text{end}(S_j) \text{ or } \text{start}(S_j) > \text{end}(S_i)$$

Czech-English

#	score	range	system
1	0.607	1	UEDIN-HEAFIELD
2	0.582	2-3	ONLINE-B
	0.573	2-4	MES
	0.562	3-5	UEDIN
	0.547	4-7	ONLINE-A
	0.542	5-7	UEDIN-SYNTAX
	0.534	6-7	CU-ZEMAN
8	0.482	8	CU-TAMCHYNA
9	0.458	9	DCU-FDA
10	0.321	10	JHU
11	0.297	11	SHEF-WPROA

English-Czech

#	score	range	system
1	0.580	1-2	CU-BOJAR
	0.578	1-2	CU-DEPFIX
3	0.562	3	ONLINE-B
4	0.525	4	UEDIN
5	0.505	5-7	CU-ZEMAN
	0.502	5-7	MES
	0.499	5-8	ONLINE-A
	0.484	7-9	CU-PHRASEFIX
	0.476	8-9	CU-TECTOMT
10	0.457	10-11	COMMERCIAL-1
	0.450	10-11	COMMERCIAL-2
12	0.389	12	SHEF-WPROA

Spanish-English

#	score	range	system
1	0.624	1	UEDIN-HEAFIELD
2	0.595	2	ONLINE-B
3	0.570	3-5	UEDIN
	0.570	3-5	ONLINE-A
	0.567	3-5	MES
6	0.537	6	LIMSI-SOUL
7	0.514	7	DCU
8	0.488	8-9	DCU-OKITA
	0.484	8-9	DCU-FDA
10	0.462	10	CU-ZEMAN
11	0.425	11	JHU
12	0.169	12	SHEF-WPROA

English-Spanish

#	rank	range	system
1	0.637	1	ONLINE-B
2	0.582	2-4	ONLINE-A
	0.578	2-4	UEDIN
	0.567	3-4	PROMT
5	0.535	5-6	MES
	0.528	5-6	TALP-UPC
7	0.491	7-8	LIMSI
	0.474	7-9	DCU
	0.472	8-10	DCU-FDA
	0.455	9-11	DCU-OKITA
	0.446	10-11	CU-ZEMAN
12	0.417	12	JHU
13	0.324	13	SHEF-WPROA

German-English

#	rank	range	system
1	0.660	1	ONLINE-B
2	0.620	2-3	ONLINE-A
	0.608	2-3	UEDIN-SYNTAX
4	0.586	4-5	UEDIN
	0.584	4-5	QUAERO
	0.571	5-7	KIT
	0.562	6-7	MES
8	0.543	8-9	RWTH-JANE
	0.533	8-10	MES-REORDER
	0.526	9-10	LIMSI-SOUL
11	0.480	11	TUBITAK
12	0.462	12-13	UMD
	0.462	12-13	DCU
14	0.396	14	CU-ZEMAN
15	0.367	15	JHU
16	0.311	16	SHEF-WPROA
17	0.238	17	DESRT

English-German

#	rank	range	system
1	0.637	1-2	ONLINE-B
	0.636	1-2	PROMT
3	0.614	3	UEDIN-SYNTAX
	0.587	3-5	ONLINE-A
	0.571	4-6	UEDIN
	0.554	5-6	KIT
7	0.523	7	STANFORD
8	0.507	8	LIMSI-SOUL
9	0.477	9-11	MES-REORDER
	0.476	9-11	JHU
	0.460	10-12	CU-ZEMAN
	0.453	11-12	TUBITAK
13	0.361	13	UU
14	0.329	14-15	SHEF-WPROA
	0.323	14-15	RWTH-JANE

English-Russian

#	rank	range	system
1	0.641	1	PROMT
2	0.623	2	ONLINE-B
3	0.556	3-4	CMU
	0.542	3-6	ONLINE-G
	0.538	3-7	ONLINE-A
	0.531	4-7	UEDIN
	0.520	5-7	QCRI-MES
8	0.498	8	CU-KAREL
9	0.478	9-10	MES-QCRI
	0.469	9-10	JHU
11	0.434	11-12	COMMERCIAL-3
	0.426	11-13	LIA
	0.419	12-13	BALAGUR
14	0.331	14	CU-ZEMAN

French-English

#	rank	range	system
1	0.638	1	UEDIN-HEAFIELD
2	0.604	2-3	UEDIN
	0.591	2-3	ONLINE-B
4	0.573	4-5	LIMSI-SOUL
	0.562	4-5	KIT
	0.541	5-6	ONLINE-A
7	0.512	7	MES-SIMPLIFIED
8	0.486	8	DCU
9	0.439	9-10	RWTH
	0.429	9-11	CMU-T2T
	0.420	10-11	CU-ZEMAN
12	0.389	12	JHU
13	0.322	13	SHEF-WPROA

English-French

#	rank	range	system
1	0.607	1-2	UEDIN
	0.600	1-3	ONLINE-B
	0.588	2-4	LIMSI-SOUL
	0.584	3-4	KIT
5	0.553	5-7	PROMT
	0.551	5-8	STANFORD
	0.547	5-8	MES
	0.537	6-9	MES-INFLECTION
	0.533	7-10	RWTH-PB
	0.516	9-11	ONLINE-A
	0.499	10-11	DCU
12	0.427	12	CU-ZEMAN
13	0.408	13	JHU
14	0.382	14	OMNIFLUENT
15	0.350	15	ITS-LATL
16	0.326	16	ITS-LATL-PE

Russian-English

#	rank	range	system
1	0.657	1	ONLINE-B
2	0.604	2-3	CMU
	0.588	2-3	ONLINE-A
4	0.562	4-6	ONLINE-G
	0.561	4-6	PROMT
	0.550	5-7	QCRI-MES
	0.546	5-7	UCAM
8	0.527	8-9	BALAGUR
	0.519	8-10	MES-QCRI
	0.507	9-11	UEDIN
	0.497	10-12	OMNIFLUENT
	0.492	11-14	LIA
	0.483	12-15	OMNIFLUENT-C
	0.481	12-15	UMD
	0.476	13-15	CU-KAREL
16	0.432	16	COMMERCIAL-3
17	0.417	17	UEDIN-SYNTAX
18	0.396	18	JHU
19	0.215	19	CU-ZEMAN

Table 6: Official results for the WMT13 translation task. Systems are ordered by the expected win score. Lines between systems indicate clusters according to bootstrap resampling at p-level $p \leq .05$. This method is also used to determine the range of ranks into which system falls. Systems with grey background indicate use of resources that fall outside the constraints provided for the shared task.

4 Understandability of English→Czech

For the English-to-Czech translation, we conducted a variation of the "understandability" test as introduced in WMT09 (Callison-Burch et al., 2009) and used in WMT10. In order to obtain additional reference translations, we conflated this test with post-editing. The procedure was as follows:

1. **Monolingual editing** (also called blind editing). The first annotator is given just the MT output and requested to correct it. Given errors in MT outputs, some guessing of the original meaning is often inevitable and the annotators are welcome to try. If unable, they can mark the sentences as incomprehensible.
2. **Review**. A second annotator is asked to validate the monolingual edit given both the source and reference translations. Our instructions specify three options:
   (a) If the monolingual edit is an adequate translation and acceptably fluent Czech, confirm it without changes.
   (b) If the monolingual edit is adequate but needs polishing, modify the sentence and prefix it with the label 'OK:'.
   (c) If the monolingual edit is wrong, correct it. You may start from the original unedited MT output, if that is easier. Avoid using the reference directly, prefer words from MT output whenever possible.

The motivation behind this procedure is that we want to save the time necessary for reading the sentence. If the reviewer has already considered whether the sentence is an acceptable translation, they do not need to read the MT output again in order to post-edit it. Our approach is thus somewhat the converse of Aziz et al. (2013) who analyze post-editing effort to obtain rankings of MT systems. We want to measure the understandability of MT outputs and obtain post-edits at the same time.

Both annotation steps were carried out in the CASMACAT/Matecat post-editing user interface.[9], modified to provide the relevant variants of the sentence next to the main edit box. Screenshots of the two annotation phases are given in Figure 3 and Figure 4.

[9]http://www.casmacat.eu/index.php?n=Workbench

Occurrence	GOOD	ALMOST	BAD	EMPTY	Total
First	34.7	0.1	42.3	11.0	4082
Repeated	41.1	0.1	41.0	6.1	805
Overall	35.8	0.1	42.1	10.2	4887

Table 7: Distribution of review statuses.

Similarly to the traditional ranking task, we provided three consecutive sentences from the original text, each translated with a different MT system. The annotators are free to use this contextual information when guessing the meaning or reviewing the monolingual edits. Each "annotation HIT" consists of 24 sentences, i.e. 8 snippets of 3 consecutive sentences.

4.1 Basic Statistics on Editing

In total, 21 annotators took part in the exercise, 20 of them contributed to monolingual editing and 19 contributed to the reviews.

Connecting each review with the monolingual edit (some edits received multiple reviews), we obtain one data row. We collected 4887 data rows (i.e. sentence revisions) for 3538 monolingual edits, covering 1468 source sentences as translated by 12 MT systems (including the reference).

Not all MT systems were considered for each sentence, we preferred to obtain judgments for more source sentences.

Based on the annotation instructions, each data row has one of the four possible statuses: GOOD, ALMOST, BAD, and EMPTY. GOOD rows are those where the reviewer accepted the monolingual edit without changes, ALMOST edits were modified by the reviewer but they were marked as 'OK'. BAD edits were changed by the reviewer and no 'OK' mark was given. Finally, the status EMPTY is assigned to rows where the monolingual editor refused to edit the sentence. The EMPTY rows nevertheless contain the ("regular") post-edit of the reviewer, so they still provide a new reference translation for the sentence.

Table 7 summarizes the distribution of row statuses depending on one more significant distinction: whether the monolingual editor has seen the sentence before or not. We see that EMPTY and BAD monolingual edits together drop by about 6% absolute when the sentence is not new to the monolingual editor. The occurrence is counted as "repeated" regardless whether the annotator has previously seen the sentence in an editing or reviewing task. Unless stated otherwise, we exclude repeated edits from our calculations.

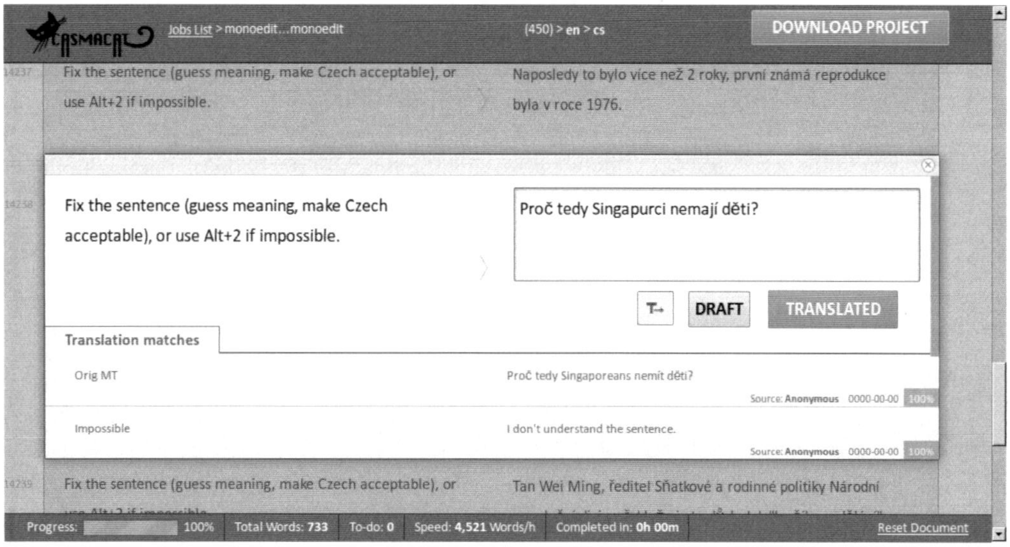

Figure 3: In this screen, the annotator is expected to correct the MT output given only the context of at most two neighbouring machine-translated sentences.

	ALMOST treated	Pairwise Comparisons	Agreement	κ
inter	separate	2690	56.0	0.270
	as BAD	2690	67.9	0.351
	as GOOD	2690	65.2	0.289
intra	separate	170	65.3	0.410
	as BAD	170	69.4	0.386
	as GOOD	170	71.8	0.422

Table 8: Annotator agreement when reviewing monolingual edits.

4.2 Agreement on Understandability

Before looking at individual system results, we consider annotator agreement in the review step. Details are given in Table 8. Given a (non-EMPTY) string from a monolingual edit, we would like to know how often two acceptability judgments by two different reviewers (inter-) or the same reviewer (intra-) agree. The repeated edits remain in this analysis because we are not interested in the origin of the string.

Our annotation setup leads to three possible labels: GOOD, ALMOST, and BAD. The agreement on one of three classes is bound to be lower than the agreement on two classes, so we also re-interpret ALMOST as either GOOD or BAD. Generally speaking, ALMOST is a positive judgment, so it would be natural to treat it as GOOD. However, in our particular setup, when the reviewer modified the sentence and *forgot* to add the label 'OK:', the item ended up in the BAD class. We conclude that this is indeed the case: the inter-annotator agreement appears higher if ALMOST is treated as BAD. Future versions of the reviewing interface should perhaps first ask for the yes/no judgment and only then allow to post-edit.

The κ values in Table 8 are the Fleiss' kappa (Fleiss, 1971), accounting for agreement by chance given the observed label distributions.

In WMT09, the agreements for this task were higher: 77.4 for inter-AA and 86.6 for intra-AA. (In 2010, the agreements for this task were not reported.) It is difficult to say whether the difference lies in the particular language pair, the different set of annotators, or the different user interface for our reviewing task. In 2009 and 2010, the reviewers were shown 5 monolingual edits at once and they were asked to judge each as acceptable or not acceptable. We show just one segment and they have probably set their minds on the post-editing rather than acceptability judgment. We believe that higher agreements can be reached if the reviewers first validate one or more of the edits and only then are allowed to post-edit it.

4.3 Understandability of English→Czech

Table 9 brings about the first main result of our post-editing effort. For each system (including the reference translation), we check how often a monolingual edit was marked OK or ALMOST by the subsequent reviewer. The average understandability across all MT systems into Czech is $44.2\pm1.6\%$. This is a considerable improvement compared to 2009 where the best systems produced about 32% understandable sentences. In

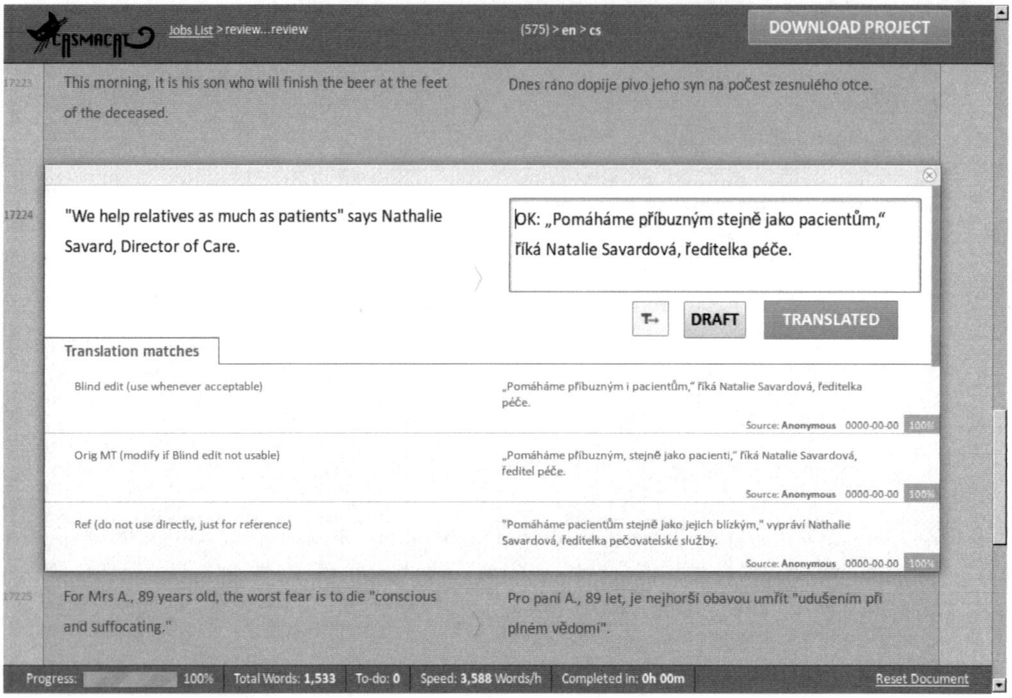

Figure 4: In this screen, the annotator is expected to validate the monolingual edit, correcting it if necessary. The annotator is expected to add the prefix 'OK:' if the correction was more or less cosmetic.

Rank	System	Total Observations	% Understandable
	Overall incl. ref.	4082	46.7±1.6
	Overall without ref.	3808	44.2±1.6
1	Reference	274±31	80.3±4.8
2-6	CU-ZEMAN	348±34	51.7±5.1
2-6	UEDIN	332±33	51.5±5.4
2-6	ONLINE-B	337±34	50.7±5.3
2-6	CU-BOJAR	341±35	50.7±5.2
2-7	CU-DEPFIX	350±34	48.0±5.3
6-10	COMMERCIAL-2	358±36	43.6±5.2
6-11	COMMERCIAL-1	316±34	41.5±5.5
7-12	CU-TECTOMT	338±34	39.4±5.2
8-12	MES	346±36	38.4±5.2
8-12	CU-PHRASEFIX	394±40	38.1±4.8
10-12	SHEF-WPROA	348±32	34.2±5.1
	2009 Reference		91
	2009 Best System		32
	2010 Reference		97
	2010 Best System		58

Table 9: Understandability of English→Czech systems. The ± values indicate empirical confidence bounds at 95%. Rank ranges were also obtained in the same resampling: in 95% of observations, the system was ranked in the given range.

2010, the best systems or system combinations reached 55%–58%. The test set across years and the quality of references and judgments also play a role. In our annotation setup, the references appear to be correctly understandable only to 80.3±4.8%.

To estimate the variance of these results due to the particular sentences chosen, we draw 1000 random samples from the dataset, preserving the dataset size and repeating some. The exact number of judgments per system can thus vary. We report the 95% empirical confidence interval after the '±' signs in Table 9 (the systems range from ±4.8 to ±5.5). When we drop individual blind editors or reviewers, the understandability judgments differ by about ±2 to ±4. In other words, the dependence on the test set appears higher than the dependence on the annotators.

The limited size of our dataset allows us only to separate two main groups of systems: those ranking 2–6 and those ranking worse. This rough grouping vaguely matches with WMT13 ranking results as given in Table 6. A somewhat surprising observation is that two automatic corrections ranked better in WMT13 ranking but score worse in understandability: CU-DEPFIX fixes some lost negation and some agreement errors of CU-BOJAR and CU-PHRASEFIX is a standard statistical post-editing of a transfer-based system CU-TECTOMT. A detailed inspection of the data is necessary to explain this.

5 More Reference Translations for Czech

Our annotation procedure described in Section 4 allowed us to obtain a considerable number of additional reference translations on top of official single reference.

Refs	1	2	3	4	5	6	7	8	9	10-16
Sents	233	709	174	123	60	48	40	27	25	29

Table 10: Number of source sentences with the given number of distinct reference translations.

In total, our edits cover 1468 source sentences, i.e. about a half of the official test set size, and provide 4311 unique references. On average, one sentence in our set has 2.94±2.17 unique reference translations. Table 10 provides a histogram.

It is well known that automatic MT evaluation methods perform better with more references, because a single one may not confirm a correct part of MT output. This issue is more severe for morphologically rich languages like Czech where about 1/3 of MT output was correct but not confirmed by the reference (Bojar et al., 2010). Advanced evaluation methods apply paraphrasing to smooth out some of the lexical divergence (Kauchak and Barzilay, 2006; Snover et al., 2009; Denkowski and Lavie, 2010). Simpler techniques such as lemmatizing are effective for morphologically rich languages (Tantug et al., 2008; Kos and Bojar, 2009) but they will lose resolution once the systems start performing generally well.

WMTs have taken the stance that a big enough test set with just a single reference should compensate for the lack of other references. We use our post-edited reference translations to check this assumption for BLEU and NIST as implemented in `mteval-13a` (international tokenization switched on, which is not the default setting).

We run many probes, randomly picking the test set size (number of distinct sentences) and the number of distinct references per sentence. Note that such test sets are somewhat artificially more diverse; in narrow domains, source sentences can repeat and even appear verbatim in the training data, and in natural test sets with multiple references, short sentences can receive several identical translations.

For each probe, we measure the Spearman's rank correlation coefficient ρ of the ranks proposed by BLEU or NIST and the manual ranks. We use the same implementation as applied in the WMT13 Shared Metrics Task (Macháček and Bojar, 2013). Note that the WMT13 metrics task still uses the WMT12 evaluation method ignoring ties, not the expected wins. As Koehn (2012) shows, the two methods do not differ much.

Overall, the correlation is strongly impacted by

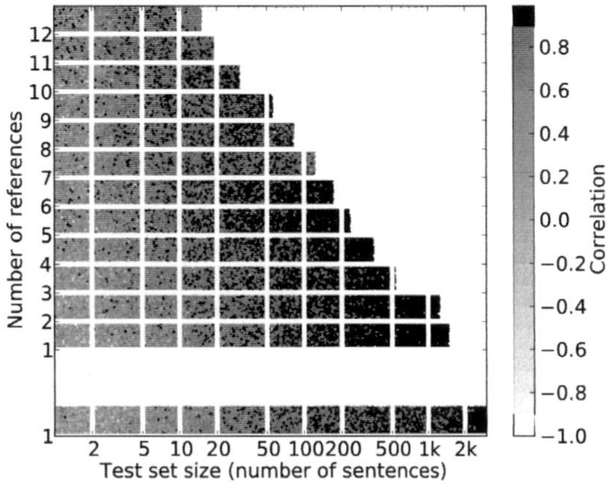

Figure 5: Correlation of BLEU and WMT13 manual ranks for English→Czech translation

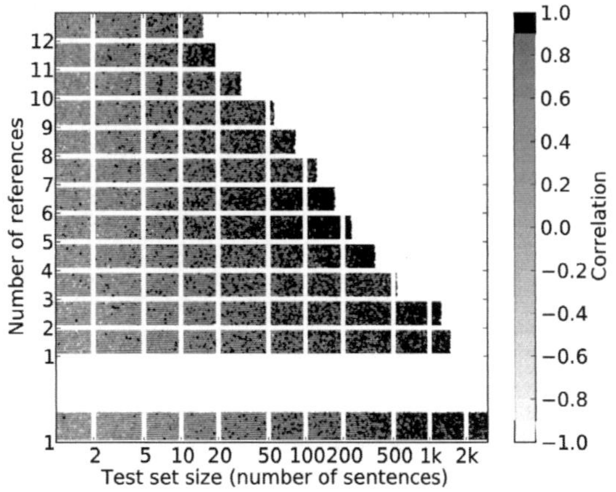

Figure 6: Correlation of NIST and WMT13 manual ranks for English→Czech translation

the particular choice of test sentences and reference translations. By picking sentences randomly, similarly or equally sized test sets can reach different correlations. Indeed, e.g. for a test set of about 1500 distinct sentences selected from the 3000-sentence official test set (1 reference translation), we obtain correlations for BLEU between 0.86 and 0.94.

Figure 5 plots the correlations of BLEU and the system rankings, Figure 6 provides the same picture for NIST. The upper triangular part of the plot contains samples from our post-edited reference translations, the lower rectangular part contains probes from the official test set of 3000 sentences with 1 reference translation.

To interpret the observations, we also calculate the average and standard deviation of correlations for each cell in Figures 5 and 6. Figures 7 and 8 plot the values for 1, 6, 7 and 8 references for

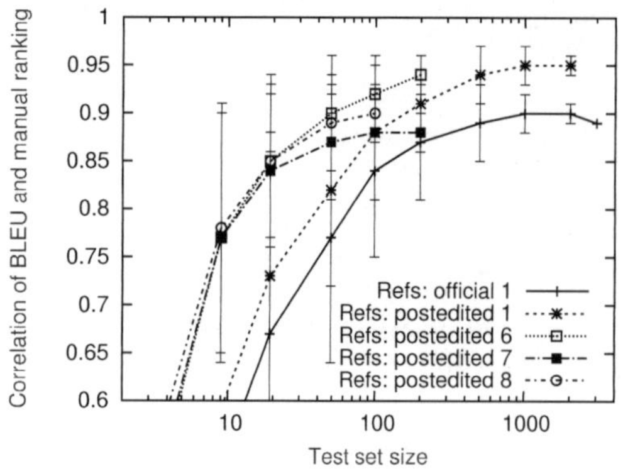

Figure 7: Projections from Figure 5 of BLEU and WMT13 manual ranks for English→Czech translation

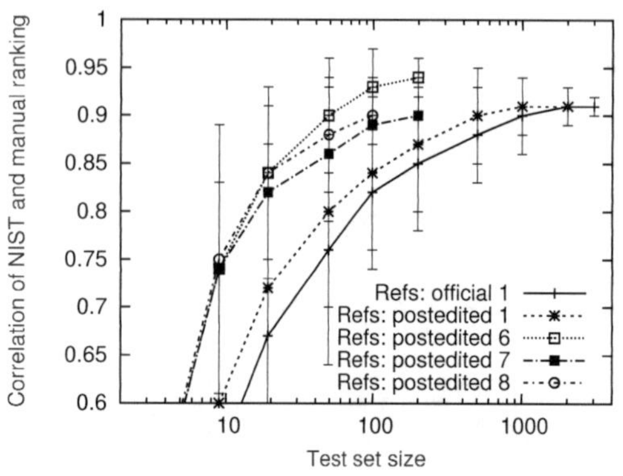

Figure 8: Projections from Figure 6 of NIST and WMT13 manual ranks for English→Czech translation

BLEU and NIST, resp. The projections confirm that the average correlations grow with test set size, the growth is however sub-logarithmic.

Starting from as few as a dozen of sentences, we see that using more references is better than using a larger test set. For BLEU, we however already seem to reach false positives at 7 references for one or two hundred sentences: larger sets with just one reference may correlate slightly better.

Using one reference obtained by post-editing seems better than using the official (independent) reference translations. BLEU is more affected than NIST by this difference even at relatively large test set size. Note that our post-edits are inspired by all MT systems, the good as well as the bad ones. This probably provides our set with a certain balance.

Overall, the best balance between the test set size and the number of references seems to lie somewhere around 7 references and 100 or 200 sentences. Creating such a test set could be even cheaper than the standard 3000 sentences with just one reference. However, the wide error bars remind us that even this setting can lead to correlations anywhere between 0.86 and 0.96. For other languages, data sets types or other MT evaluation methods, the best setting can be quite different and has to be sought for.

6 Quality Estimation Task

Machine translation quality estimation is the task of predicting a quality score for a machine translated text without access to reference translations. The most common approach is to treat the problem as a supervised machine learning task, using standard regression or classification algorithms. The second edition of the WMT shared task on quality estimation builds on the previous edition of the task (Callison-Burch et al., 2012), with variants to this previous task, including both sentence-level and word-level estimation, with new training and test datasets, along with evaluation metrics and baseline systems.

The motivation to include both sentence- and word-level estimation come from the different potential applications of these variants. Some interesting uses of sentence-level quality estimation are the following:

- Decide whether a given translation is good enough for publishing as is.
- Inform readers of the target language only whether or not they can rely on a translation.
- Filter out sentences that are not good enough for post-editing by professional translators.
- Select the best translation among options from multiple MT and/or translation memory systems.

Some interesting uses of word-level quality estimation are the following:

- Highlight words that need editing in post-editing tasks.
- Inform readers of portions of the sentence which are not reliable.
- Select the best segments among options from multiple translation systems for MT system combination.

The goals of this year's shared task were:

- To explore various granularity levels for the task (sentence-level and word-level).
- To explore the prediction of more objective scores such as edit distance and post-editing time.
- To explore the use of quality estimation techniques to replace reference-based MT evaluation metrics in the task of ranking alternative translations generated by different MT systems.
- To identify new and effective quality indicators (features) for all variants of the quality estimation task.
- To identify effective machine learning techniques for all variants of the quality estimation task.
- To establish the state of the art performance in the field.

Four subtasks were proposed, as we discuss in Sections 6.1 and 6.2. Each subtask provides specific datasets, annotated for quality according to the subtask (Section 6.3), and evaluates the system submissions using specific metrics (Section 6.6). When available, external resources (e.g. SMT training corpus) and translation engine-related resources were given to participants (Section 6.4), who could also use any additional external resources (no distinction between *open* and *close* tracks is made). Participants were also provided with a software package to extract quality estimation features and perform model learning (Section 6.5), with a suggested list of *baseline* features and learning method (Section 6.7). Participants could submit up to two systems for each subtask.

6.1 Sentence-level Quality Estimation

Task 1.1 Predicting Post-editing Distance This task is similar to the quality estimation task in WMT12, but with one important difference in the scoring variant: instead of using the post-editing effort scores in the [1-5] range, we use HTER (Snover et al., 2006) as quality score. This score is to be interpreted as the minimum edit distance between the machine translation and its manually post-edited version, and its range is [0, 1] (0 when no edit needs to be made, and 1 when all words need to be edited). Two variants of the results could be submitted in the shared task:

- **Scoring**: A quality score for each sentence translation in [0,1], to be interpreted as an HTER score; lower scores mean better translations.
- **Ranking**: A ranking of sentence translations for all source test sentences from best to worst. For this variant, it does not matter how the ranking is produced (from HTER predictions, likert predictions, or even without machine learning). The reference ranking is defined based on the true HTER scores.

Task 1.2 Selecting Best Translation This task consists in ranking up to five alternative translations for the same source sentence produced by multiple MT systems. We use essentially the same data provided to participants of previous years WMT's evaluation metrics task – where MT evaluation metrics are assessed according to how well they correlate with human rankings. However, reference translations produced by humans are not be used in this task.

Task 1.3 Predicting Post-editing Time For this task systems are required to produce, for each translation, the expected time (in seconds) it would take a translator to post-edit such an MT output. The main application for predictions of this type is in computer-aided translation where the predicted time can be used to select among different hypotheses or even to omit any MT output in cases where no good suggestion is available.

6.2 Word-level Quality Estimation

Based on the data of Task 1.3, we define Task 2, a word-level annotation task for which participants are asked to produce a label for each token that indicates whether the word should be changed by a post-editor or kept in the final translation. We consider the following two sets of labels for prediction:

- **Binary classification**: a keep/change label, the latter meaning that the token should be corrected in the post-editing process.
- **Multi-class classification**: a label specifying the edit action that should be performed on the token (keep as is, delete, or substitute).

6.3 Datasets

Task 1.1 Predicting post-editing distance For the training of models, we provided the WMT12 quality estimation dataset: 2,254 English-Spanish news sentences extracted from previous WMT translation task English-Spanish test sets (WMT09, WMT10, and WMT12). These were translated by a phrase-based SMT Moses system trained on Europarl and News Commentaries corpora as provided by WMT, along with their source sentences, reference translations, post-edited translations, and HTER scores. We used TERp (default settings: tokenised, case insensitive, etc., but capped to 1)[10] to compute the HTER scores. Likert scores in [1,5] were also provided, as participants may choose to use them for the ranking variant.

As test data, we use a subset of the WMT13 English-Spanish news test set with 500 sentences, whose translations were produced by the same SMT system used for the training set. To compute the true HTER labels, the translations were post-edited under the same conditions as those on the training set. As in any blind shared task, the HTER scores were solely used to evaluate the submissions, and were only released to participants after they submitted their systems.

A few variations of the training and test data were provided, including a version with cases restored and a version detokenized. In addition, we provided a number of engine-internal information from Moses for glass-box feature extraction, such as phrase and word alignments, model scores, word graph, n-best lists and information from the decoder's search graph.

Task 1.2 Selecting best translation As training data, we provided a large set of up to five alternative machine translations produced by different MT systems for each source sentence and ranked for quality by humans. This was the outcome of the manual evaluation of the translation task from WMT09-WMT12. It includes two language pairs: German-English and English-Spanish, with 7,098 and 4,592 source sentences and up to five ranked translations, totalling 32,922 and 22,447 translations, respectively.

As test data, a set of up to five alternative machine translations per source sentence from the WMT08 test sets was provided, with 365 (1,810) and 264 (1,315) source sentences (translations) for German-English and English-Spanish, respectively. We note that there was some overlap between the MT systems used in the training data and test datasets, but not all systems were the same, as different systems participate in WMT over the years.

Task 1.3 and Task 2 Predicting post-editing time and word-level edits For Tasks 1.3 and 2 we provides a new dataset consisting of 22 English news articles which were translated into Spanish using Moses and post-edited during a CASMACAT[11] field trial. Of these, 15 documents have been processed repeatedly by at least 2 out of 5 translators, resulting in a total of 1,087 segments. For each segment we provided:

- English source and Spanish translation.
- Spanish MT output which was used as basis for post-editing.
- Document and translator ID.
- Position of the segment within the document.

The metadata about translator and document was made available as we expect that translator performance and normalisation over document complexity can be helpful when predicting the time spend on a given segment.

For the training portion of the data we also provided:

- Time to post-edit in seconds (Task 1.3).
- Binary (Keep, Change) and multiclass (Keep, Substitute, Delete) labels on word level along with explicit tokenization (Task 2).

The labels in Task 2 are derived by computing WER between the original machine translation and its post-edited version.

6.4 Resources

For all tasks, we provided resources to extract quality estimation features when these were available:

- The SMT training corpus (WMT News and Europarl): source and target sides of the corpus used to train the SMT engines for Tasks 1.1, 1.3, and 2, and truecase models generated from these. These corpora can also be used for Task 1.2, but we note that some of the MT systems used in the datasets of this task were not statistical or did not use (only) the training corpus provided by WMT.

[10] `http://www.umiacs.umd.edu/~snover/terp/`

[11] `http://casmacat.eu/`

- Language models: n-gram language models of source and target languages generated using the SMT training corpora and standard toolkits such as SRILM Stolcke (2002), and a language model of POS tags for the target language. We also provided unigram, bigram and trigram counts.

- IBM Model 1 lexical tables generated by GIZA++ using the SMT training corpora.

- Phrase tables with word alignment information generated by scripts provided by Moses from the parallel corpora.

- For Tasks 1.1, 1.3 and 2, the Moses configuration file used for decoding or the code to re-run the entire Moses system.

- For Task 1.1, both English and Spanish resources for a number of advanced features such as pre-generated PCFG parsing models, topic models, global lexicon models and mutual information trigger models.

We refer the reader to the QUEST website[12] for a detailed list of resources provided for each task.

6.5 QUEST **Framework**

QUEST (Specia et al., 2013) is an open source framework for quality estimation which provides a wide variety of feature extractors from source and translation texts and external resources and tools. These range from simple, language-independent features, to advanced, linguistically motivated features. They include features that rely on information from the MT system that generated the translations (glass-box features), and features that are oblivious to the way translations were produced (black-box features).

QUEST also integrates a well-known machine learning toolkit, `scikit-learn`,[13] and other algorithms that are known to perform well on this task (e.g. Gaussian Processes), providing a simple and effective way of experimenting with techniques for feature selection and model building, as well as parameter optimisation through grid search.

From QUEST, a subset of 17 features and an SVM regression implementation were used as baseline for Tasks 1.1, 1.2 and 1.3. The software was made available to all participants.

[12] `http://www.quest.dcs.shef.ac.uk/`

[13] `http://scikit-learn.org/`

6.6 Evaluation Metrics

Task 1.1 Predicting post-editing distance Evaluation is performed against the HTER and/or ranking of translations using the same metrics as in WMT12. For the **scoring** variant of the task, we use two standard metrics for regression tasks: Mean Absolute Error (MAE) as a primary metric, and Root of Mean Squared Error (RMSE) as a secondary metric. To improve readability, we report these error numbers by first mapping the HTER values to the $[0, 100]$ interval, to be read as percentage-points of the HTER metric. For a given test set S with entries $s_i, 1 \leq i \leq |S|$, we denote by $H(s_i)$ the proposed score for entry s_i (hypothesis), and by $V(s_i)$ the reference value for entry s_i (gold-standard value):

$$\text{MAE} = \frac{\sum_{i=1}^{N} |H(s_i) - V(s_i)|}{|S|}$$

$$\text{RMSE} = \sqrt{\frac{\sum_{i=1}^{N} (H(s_i) - V(s_i))^2}{|S|}}$$

Both these metrics are non-parametric, automatic and deterministic (and therefore consistent), and extrinsically interpretable. For instance, a MAE value of 10 means that, on average, the absolute difference between the hypothesized score and the reference score value is 10 percentage points (i.e., 0.10 difference in HTER scores). The interpretation of RMSE is similar, with the difference that RMSE penalises larger errors more (via the square function).

For the **ranking** variant of the task, we use the DeltaAvg metric proposed in the 2012 edition of the task (Callison-Burch et al., 2012) as our main metric. This metric assumes that each reference test instance has an extrinsic number associated with it that represents its ranking with respect to the other test instances. For completeness, we present here again the definition of DeltaAvg.

The goal of the DeltaAvg metric is to measure how valuable a proposed ranking (which we call a *hypothesis* ranking) is, according to the true ranking values associated with the test instances. We first define a parametrised version of this metric, called DeltaAvg$[n]$. The following notations are used: for a given entry sentence s, $V(s)$ represents the function that associates an extrinsic value to that entry; we extend this notation to a set S, with $V(S)$ representing the average of all $V(s), s \in S$.

Intuitively, $V(S)$ is a quantitative measure of the "quality" of the set S, as induced by the extrinsic values associated with the entries in S. For a set of ranked entries S and a parameter n, we denote by S_1 the first quantile of set S (the highest-ranked entries), S_2 the second quantile, and so on, for n quantiles of equal sizes.[14] We also use the notation $S_{i,j} = \bigcup_{k=i}^{j} S_k$. Using these notations, we define:

$$\text{DeltaAvg}_V[n] = \frac{\sum_{k=1}^{n-1} V(S_{1,k})}{n-1} - V(S)$$

When the valuation function V is clear from the context, we write DeltaAvg$[n]$ for DeltaAvg$_V[n]$. The parameter n represents the number of quantiles we want to split the set S into. For instance, $n = 2$ gives DeltaAvg[2] = $V(S_1) - V(S)$, hence it measures the difference between the quality of the top quantile (top half) S_1 and the overall quality (represented by $V(S)$). For $n = 3$, DeltaAvg[3] = $(V(S_1)+V(S_{1,2})/2 - V(S) = ((V(S_1)-V(S))+(V(S_{1,2}-V(S)))/2$, hence it measures an average difference across two cases: between the quality of the top quantile (top third) and the overall quality, and between the quality of the top two quantiles ($S_1 \cup S_2$, top two-thirds) and the overall quality. In general, DeltaAvg$[n]$ measures an average difference in quality across $n-1$ cases, with each case measuring the impact in quality of adding an additional quantile, from top to bottom. Finally, we define:

$$\text{DeltaAvg}_V = \frac{\sum_{n=2}^{N} \text{DeltaAvg}_V[n]}{N-1}$$

where $N = |S|/2$. As before, we write DeltaAvg for DeltaAvg$_V$ when the valuation function V is clear from the context. The DeltaAvg metric is an average across all DeltaAvg$[n]$ values, for those n values for which the resulting quantiles have at least 2 entries (no singleton quantiles).

We present results for DeltaAvg using as valuation function V the HTER scores, as defined in Section 6.3. We also use Spearman's rank correlation coefficient ρ as a secondary metric.

Task 1.2 Selecting best translation The performance on the task of selecting the best translation from a pool of translation candidates is measured by comparing proposed (hypothesis) rankings against human-produced rankings. The metric used is Kendall's τ rank correlation coefficient, computed as follows:

$$\tau = \frac{|\text{concordant pairs}| - |\text{discordant pairs}|}{|\text{total pairs}|}$$

where a concordant pair is a pair of two translations for the same source segment in which the ranking order proposed by a human annotator and the ranking order of the hypothesis agree; in a discordant pair, they disagree. The possible values of τ range between 1 (where all pairs are concordant) and -1 (where all pairs are discordant). Thus a system with ranking predictions having a higher τ value makes predictions that are more similar to human judgements than a system with ranking predictions having a lower τ. Note that, in general, being able to predict rankings with an accuracy of $\tau = -1$ is as difficult as predicting rankings with an accuracy of $\tau = 1$, whereas a completely random ranking would have an expected value of $\tau = 0$. The range is therefore said to be symmetric.

However, there are two distinct ways of measuring rank correlation using Kendall's τ, related to the way *ties* are treated. They greatly affect how Kendall's τ numbers are to be interpreted, and especially the symmetry property. We explain the difference in detail in what follows.

Kendall's τ with ties penalised If the goal is to measure to what extent the difference in quality visible to a human annotator has been captured by an automatically produced hypothesis (recall-oriented view), then proposing a tie between t_1 and t_2 (t_1-equal-to-t_2) when the pair was judged (in the reference) as t_1-better-than-t_2 is treated as a failure-to-recall. In other words, it is as bad as proposing t_1-worse-than-t_2. Henceforth, we call this recall-oriented measure "Kendall's τ with ties penalised". This metric has the following properties:

- it is completely fair when comparing different methods to produce ranking hypotheses, because the denominator (number of total pairs) is the same (it is the number of non-tied pairs under the human judgements).
- it is non-symmetric, in the sense that a value of $\tau = -1$ is not as difficult to obtain as $\tau =$

[14] If the size $|S|$ is not divisible by n, then the last quantile S_n is assumed to contain the rest of the entries.

1 (simply proposing only ties gets a $\tau = -1$); hence, the sign of the τ value matters.

- the expected value of a completely random ranking is not necessarily $\tau = 0$, but rather depends on the number of ties in the reference rankings (i.e., it is test set dependent).

Kendall's τ with ties ignored If the goal is to measure to what extent the difference in quality signalled by an automatically produced hypothesis is reflected in the human annotation (precision-oriented view), then proposing t_1-equal-to-t_2 when the pair was judged differently in the reference does no harm the metric.

Henceforth, we call this precision-oriented measure "Kendall's τ with ties ignored". This metric has the following properties:

- it is not completely fair when comparing different methods to produce ranking hypotheses, because the denominator (number of total pairs) may not be the same (it is the number of non-tied pairs under each system's proposal).
- it is symmetric, in the sense that a value of $\tau = -1$ is as difficult to obtain as $\tau = 1$; hence, the sign of the τ value may not matter. [15]
- the expected value of a completely random ranking is $\tau = 0$ (test-set independent).

The first property is the most worrisome from the perspective of reporting the results of a shared task, because a system may fare very well on this metric simply because it choses not to commit (proposes ties) most of the time. Therefore, to give a better understanding of the systems' performance, for Kendall's τ with ties ignored we also provide the number of non-ties proposed by each system.

Task 1.3 Predicting post-editing time Submissions are evaluated in terms of Mean Average Error (MAE) against the actual time spent by post-editors (in seconds). By using a linear error measure we limit the influence of outliers: sentences that took very long to edit or where the measurement taken is questionable.

[15] In real life applications this distinction matters. Even if, from a computational perspective, it is as hard to get τ close to -1 as it is to get it close to 1, knowing the sign is the difference between selecting the best or the worse translation.

To further analyse the influence of extreme values, we also compute Spearman's rank correlation ρ coefficient which does not depend on the absolute values of the predictions.

We also give RMSE and Pearson's correlation coefficient r for reference.

Task 2 Predicting word-level scores The word-level task is primarily evaluated by macro-averaged F-measure. Because the class distribution is skewed – in the test data about one third of the tokens are marked as correct – we compute precision and recall and F_1 for each class individually. Consider the following confusion matrix for the two classes *Keep* and *Change*:

		predicted	
		(K)eep	(C)hange
expected	(K)eep	10	20
	(C)hange	30	40

For the given example we derive true-positive (tp), true-negative (tn), false-positive (fp), and false-negative (fn) counts:

$$tp_K = 10 \quad fp_K = 30 \quad fn_K = 20$$
$$tp_C = 40 \quad fp_C = 20 \quad fn_C = 30$$

$$\text{precision}_K = \frac{tp_K}{tp_K + fp_K} = 10/40$$

$$\text{recall}_K = \frac{tp_K}{tp_K + fn_K} = 10/30$$

$$F_{1,K} = \frac{2 \cdot \text{precision}_K \cdot \text{recall}_K}{\text{precision}_K + \text{recall}_K}$$

A single cumulative statistic can be computed by averaging the resulting F-measures (*macro averaging*) or by *micro averaging* in which case precision and recall are first computed by accumulating the relevant values for all classes (Özgür et al., 2005), e.g.

$$\text{precision} = \frac{tp_K + tp_C}{(tp_K + fp_K) + (tp_C + fp_C)}$$

The latter gives equal weight to each example and is therefore dominated by performance on the largest class while macro-averaged F-measure gives equal weight to each class.

The same setup is used to evaluate the performance in the multiclass setting. Please note that here the test data only contains 4% examples for class (D)elete.

ID	Participating team
CMU	Carnegie Mellon University, USA (Hildebrand and Vogel, 2013)
CNGL	Centre for Next Generation Localization, Ireland (Bicici, 2013b)
DCU	Dublin City University, Ireland (Almaghout and Specia, 2013)
DCU-SYMC	Dublin City University & Symantec, Ireland (Rubino et al., 2013b)
DFKI	German Research Centre for Artificial Intelligence, Germany (Avramidis and Popovic, 2013)
FBK-UEdin	Fondazione Bruno Kessler, Italy & University of Edinburgh, UK (Camargo de Souza et al., 2013)
LIG	Laboratoire d'Informatique Grenoble, France (Luong et al., 2013)
LIMSI	Laboratoire d'Informatique pour la Mécanique et les Sciences de l'Ingénieur, France (Singh et al., 2013)
LORIA	Lorraine Laboratory of Research in Computer Science and its Applications, France (Langlois and Smaili, 2013)
SHEF	University of Sheffield, UK (Beck et al., 2013)
TCD-CNGL	Trinity College Dublin & CNGL, Ireland (Moreau and Rubino, 2013)
TCD-DCU-CNGL	Trinity College Dublin, Dublin City University & CNGL, Ireland (Moreau and Rubino, 2013)
UMAC	University of Macau, China (Han et al., 2013)
UPC	Universitat Politecnica de Catalunya, Spain (Formiga et al., 2013b)

Table 11: Participants in the WMT13 Quality Estimation shared task.

6.7 Participants

Table 11 lists all participating teams submitting systems to any subtask in this shared task. Each team was allowed up to two submissions for each subtask. In the descriptions below participation in specific tasks is denoted by a task identifier: T1.1, T1.2, T1.3, and T2.

Sentence-level baseline system (T1.1, T1.3): QuEst was used to extract 17 system-independent features from the source and translation files and the SMT training corpus that were found to be relevant in previous work (same features as in the WMT12 shared task):

- number of tokens in the source and target sentences.
- average source token length.
- average number of occurrences of the target word within the target sentence.
- number of punctuation marks in source and target sentences.
- Language model probability of source and target sentences using language models provided by the task.
- average number of translations per source word in the sentence: as given by IBM 1 model thresholded so that $P(t|s) > 0.2$, and so that $P(t|s) > 0.01$ weighted by the inverse frequency of each word in the source side of the SMT training corpus.
- percentage of unigrams, bigrams and trigrams in frequency quartiles 1 (lower frequency words) and 4 (higher frequency words) in the source side of the SMT training corpus
- percentage of unigrams in the source sentence seen in the source side of the SMT training corpus.

These features are used to train a Support Vector Machine (SVM) regression algorithm using a radial basis function kernel within the SCIKIT-LEARN toolkit. The γ, ϵ and C parameters were optimized using a grid-search and 5-fold cross validation on the training set. We note that although the system is referred to as a "baseline", it is in fact a strong system. For tasks of the same type as 1.1 and 1.3, it has proved robust across a range of language pairs, MT systems, and text domains for predicting post-editing effort, as it has also been shown in the previous edition of the task (Callison-Burch et al., 2012).

The same features could be useful for a baseline system for Task 1.2. In our official results, however, the baseline for Task 1.2 is simpler than that: it proposes random ranks for each pair of alternative translations for a given source sentence, as we will discuss in Section 6.8.

CMU (T1.1, T1.2, T1.3): The CMU quality estimation system was trained on features based on language models, the MT system's distortion model and phrase table features, statistical word lexica, several sentence length statistics, source language word and bi-gram frequency statistics, n-best list agreement and diversity, source language parse, source-target word alignment and a dependency parse based cohesion penalty. These features were extracted using GIZA++, a forced alignment algorithm and the Stanford parser (de Marneffe et al., 2006). The prediction models were trained using four classifiers in the Weka toolkit (Hall et al., 2009): linear regression, M5P trees, multi layer perceptron and SVM regression. In addition to main system submission, a classic n-best list re-ranking approach was used for Task 1.2.

CNGL (T1.1, T1.2, T1.3, T2): CNGL systems are based on referential translation machines (RTM) (Biçici and van Genabith, 2013), parallel feature decay algorithms (FDA) (Bicici, 2013a), and machine translation performance predictor (MTPP) (Biçici et al., 2013), all of which allow to obtain language and MT system-independent predictions. For each task, RTM models were developed using the parallel corpora and the language model corpora distributed by the WMT13 translation task and the language model corpora provided by LDC for English and Spanish.

The sentence-level features are described in MTPP (Biçici et al., 2013); they include monolingual or bilingual features using n-grams defined over text or common cover link (CCL) (Seginer, 2007) structures as the basic units of information over which similarity calculations are made. RTMs use 308 features about coverage and diversity, IBM1, and sentence translation performance, retrieval closeness and minimum Bayes retrieval risk, distributional similarity and entropy, IBM2 alignment, character n-grams, and sentence readability. The learning models are Support Vector Machines (SVR) and SVR with partial least squares (SVRPLS).

The word-level features include CCL links, word length, location, prefix, suffix, form, context, and alignment, totalling 511K features for binary classification, and 637K for multiclass classification. Generalised linear models (GLM) (Collins, 2002) and GLM with dynamic learning (GLMd) were used.

DCU (T1.2): The main German-English submission uses six Combinatory Categorial Grammar (CCG) features: CCG supertag language model perplexity and log probability, the number of maximal CCG constituents in the translation output which are the highest-probability minimum number of CCG constituents that span the translation output, the percentage of CCG argument mismatches between each subsequent CCG supertags, the percentage of CCG argument mismatches between each subsequent CCG maximal categories and the minimum number of phrases detected in the translation output. A second submission uses the aforementioned CCG features combined with 80 features from QuEst as described in (Specia, 2011). For the CCG features, the C&C parser was used to parse the translation output. Moses was used to build the phrase table from the SMT training corpus with maximum phrase length set to 7. The language model of supertags was built using the SRILM toolkit. As learning algorithm, Logistic Regression as provided by the SCIKIT-LEARN toolkit was used. The training data was prepared by converting each ranking of translation outputs to a set of pairwise comparisons according to the approach proposed by Avramidis et al. (2011). The rankings were generated back from pairwise comparisons predicted by the model.

DCU-SYMC (T1.1): The DCU-Symantec team employed a wide set of features which included language model, n-gram counts and word-alignment features as well as syntactic features, topic model features and pseudo-reference features. The main learning algorithm was SVR, but regression tree learning was used to perform feature selection, reducing the initial set of 442 features to 96 features (DCU-Symantec alltypes) and 134

(DCU-Symantec combine). Two methods for feature selection were used: a best-first search in the feature space using regression trees to evaluate the subsets, and reading binarised features directly from the nodes of pruned regression trees.

The following NLP tools were used in feature extraction: the Brown English Wall-Street-Journal-trained statistical parser (Charniak and Johnson, 2005), a Lexical Functional Grammar parser (XLE), together with a hand-crafted Lexical Functional Grammar, the English ParGram grammar (Kaplan et al., 2004), and the TreeTagger part-of-speech tagger (Schmidt, 1994) with off-the-shelf publicly available pre-trained tagging models for English and Spanish. For pseudo-reference features, the Bing, Moses and Systran translation systems were used. The Mallet toolkit (McCallum, 2002) was used to build the topic models and features based on a grammar checker were extracted with LanguageTool.[16]

DFKI (T1.2, T1.3): DFKI's submission for Task 1.2 was based on decomposing rankings into pairs (Avramidis, 2012), where the best system for each pair was predicted with Logistic Regression (LogReg). For German-English, LogReg was trained with Stepwise Feature Selection (Hosmer, 1989) on two feature sets: *Feature Set 24* includes basic counts augmented with PCFG parsing features (number of VPs, alternative parses, parse probability) on both source and target sentences (Avramidis et al., 2011), and pseudo-reference METEOR score; the most successful set, *Feature Set 33* combines those 24 features with the 17 baseline features. For English-Spanish, LogReg was used with L2 Regularisation (Lin et al., 2007) and two feature sets were devised after scoring features with ReliefF (Kononenko, 1994) and Information Gain (Hunt et al., 1966). *Feature Set 431* combines 30 features with highest absolute Relief-F and Information Gain (15 from each). features with the highest

Task 1.3 was modelled using feature sets selected after Relief-F scoring of external black-box and glass-box features extracted from the SMT decoding process. The most successful submission (linear6) was trained with Linear Regression including the 17 features with highest positive Relief-F. Most prominent features include the alternative possible parses of the source and target sentence, the positions of the phrases with the lowest and highest probability and future cost estimate in the translation, the counts of phrases in the decoding graph whose probability or whether the future cost estimate is higher/lower than their standard deviation, counts of verbs and determiners, etc. The second submission (pls8) was trained with Partial Least Squares regression (Stone and Brooks, 1990) including more glass-box features.

FBK-Uedin (T1.1, T1.3):

The submissions explored features built on MT engine resources including automatic word alignment, n-best candidate translation lists, back-translations and word posterior probabilities. Information about word alignments is used to extract quantitative (amount and distribution of the alignments) and qualitative (importance of the aligned terms) features under the assumption that alignment information can help tasks where sentence-level semantic relations need to be identified (Souza et al., 2013). Three similar English-Spanish systems are built and used to provide pseudo-references (Soricut et al., 2012) and back-translations, from which automatic MT evaluation metrics could be computed and used as features.

All features were computed over a concatenation of several publicly available parallel corpora for the English-Spanish language pair such as Europarl, News Commentary, and MultiUN. The models were developed using supervised learning algorithms: SVMs (with feature selection step prior to model learning) and extremely randomized trees.

LIG (T2): The LIG systems are designed to deal with both binary and multiclass variants of the word level task. They integrate several features including: system-based (graph topology, language model, alignment context, etc.), lexical (Part-of-Speech tags), syntactic (constituent label, distance to the con-

[16] `http://www.languagetool.org/`

stituent tree root) and semantic (target and source polysemy count). Besides the existing components of the SMT system, feature extraction requires further external tools and resources, such as: TreeTagger (for POS tagging), Bekerley Parser trained with AnCora treebank (for generating constituent trees in Spanish), WordNet and BabelNet (for polysemy count), Google Translate. The feature set is then combined and trained using a Conditional Random Fields (CRF) learning method. During the labelling phase, the optimal threshold is tuned using a small development set split from the original training set. In order to retain the most informative features and eliminate the redundant ones, a Sequential Backward Selection algorithm is employed over the all-feature systems. With the binary classifier, the Boosting technique is applied to allow a number of sub feature sets to complement each other, resulting in the "stronger" combined system.

LIMSI (T1.1, T1.3): The two tasks were treated as regression problems using a simple elastic regression, a linear model trained with L_1 and L_2 regularisers. Regarding features, the submissions mainly aimed at evaluating the usefulness for quality estimation of n-gram posterior probabilities (Gispert et al., 2013) that quantify the probability for a given n-gram to be part of the system output. Their computation relies on all the hypotheses considered by a SMT system during decoding: intuitively, the more hypotheses a n-gram appears in, the more confident the system is that this n-gram is part of the correct translation, and the higher its posterior probability is. The feature set contains 395 other features that differs, in two ways, from the traditional features used in quality estimation. First, it includes several features based on large span continuous space language models (Le et al., 2011) that have already proved their efficiency both for the translation task and the quality estimation task. Second, each feature was expanded into two "normalized forms" in which their value was divided either by the source length or the target length and, when relevant, into a "ratio form" in which the feature value computed on the target sentence is divided by its value computed in the source sentence.

LORIA (T1.1): The system uses the 17 baseline features, plus several numerical and boolean features computed from the source and target sentences (Langlois et al., 2012). These are based on language model information (perplexity, level of back-off, intra-lingual triggers), translation table (IBM1 table, inter-lingual triggers). For language models, forward and backward models are built. Each feature gives a score to each word in the sentence, and the score of the sentence is the average of word scores. For several features, the score of a word depends on the score of its neighbours. This leads to 66 features. Support Vector Machines are used to learn a regression model. In training is done in a multi-stage procedure aimed at increasing the size of the training corpus. Initially, the training corpus with machine translated sentences provided by the task is used to train an SVM model. Then this model is applied to the post-edited and reference sentences (also provided as part of the task). These are added to the quality estimation training corpus using as labels the SVM predictions. An algorithm to tune the predicted scores on a development corpus is used.

SHEF (T1.1, T1.3): These submissions use Gaussian Processes, a non-parametric probabilistic learning framework for regression, along with two techniques to improve prediction performance and minimise the amount of resources needed for the problem: feature selection based on optimised hyperparameters and active learning to reduce the training set size (and therefore the annotation effort). The initial set features contains all black box and glass box features available within the QuEst framework (Specia et al., 2013) for the dataset at hand (160 in total for Task 1.1, and 80 for Task 1.3). The query selection strategy for active learning is based on the informativeness of the instances using Information Density, a measure that leverages between the variance among instances and how dense the region (in the feature space) where the instance is located is. To perform feature selection, following (Shah et al., 2013) features are ranked by the Gaussian Process algorithm according to their learned length scales, which can be interpreted as the relevance of such feature for the model. This information was used for feature selection by discarding the lowest ranked (least useful) ones. based on empirical results found in (Shah et al., 2013), the top 25 features for both models were selected and used to retrain the same regression algorithm.

UPC (T1.2): The methodology used a broad set of features, mainly available through the last version of the *Asiya* toolkit for MT evaluation (Gonzàlez et al., 2012)[17]. Concretely, 86 features were derived for the German-to-English and 97 features for the English-to-Spanish tasks. These features cover different approaches and include standard quality estimation features, as provided by the above mentioned *Asiya* and QUEST toolkits, but also a variety of features based on *pseudo-references*, explicit semantic analysis and specialised language models trained on the parallel and monolingual corpora provided by the WMT Translation Task.

The system selection task is approached by means of pairwise ranking decisions. It uses Random Forest classifiers with ties, expanding the work of 402013cFormiga et al.), from which a full ranking can be derived and the best system per sentence is identified. Once the classes are given by the Random Forest, one can build a graph by means of the adjacency matrix of the pairwise decision. The final ranking is assigned through a dominance scheme similar to Pighin et al. (2012).

An important remark of the methodology is the feature selection process, since it was noticed that the learner was sensitive to the features used. Selecting the appropriate set of features was crucial to achieve a good performance. The best feature combination was composed of: *i*) a baseline quality estimation feature set (Asiya or Quest) but not both of them, *ii*) Length Model, *iii*) Pseudo-reference aligned based features, and *iv*) adapted language models. However, within the *de-en* task, substituting Length Model and Aligned Pseudo-references by the features based on Semantic Roles could bring marginally better accuracy.

[17]`http://asiya.lsi.upc.edu/`

TCD-CNGL (T1.1) and **TCD-DCU-CNGL** (T1.3): The system is based on features which are commonly used for style classification (e.g. author identification). The assumption is that low/high quality translations can be characterised by some patterns which are frequent and/or differ significantly from the opposite category. Such features are intended to focus on striking patterns rather than to capture the global quality in a sentence, but they are used in conjunction with classical features for quality estimation (language modelling, etc.). This requires two steps in the training process: first the reference categories against which sentences will be compared are built, then the standard quality estimation model training stage is performed. Both datasets (Tasks 1.1 and 1.3) were used for both tasks. Since the number of features can be very high (up to 65,000), a combination of various heuristics for selecting features was used before the training stage (the submitted systems were trained using SVM with RBF kernels).

UMAC (T1.1, T1.2, T2): For Task 1.1, the feature set consists in POS sequences of the source and target languages, using 12 universal tags that are common in both languages. The algorithm is an enhanced version of the BLEU metric (EBLEU) designed with a modified length penalty and added recall factor, and having the precision and recall components grouped using the harmonic mean. For Task 1.2, in addition to the universal POS sequences of the source and target languages, features include the scores of length penalty, precision, recall and rank. Variants of EBLEU with different strategies for alignment are used, as well as a Naïve Bayes classification algorithm. For Task 2, the features used are unigrams (from previous 4th to following 3rd tokens), bigrams (from previous 2nd to following 2nd tokens), skip bigrams (previous and next token), trigrams (from previous 2nd to following 2nd tokens). The learning algorithms are Conditional Random Fields and Naïve Bayes.

6.8 Results

In what follows we give the official results for all tasks followed by a discussion that highlights the main findings for each of the tasks.

Task 1.1 Predicting post-editing distance

Table 12 summarises the results for the **ranking variant** of the task. They are sorted from best to worse using the DeltaAvg metric scores as primary key and the Spearman's rank correlation scores as secondary key.

The winning submissions for the ranking variant of Task 1.1 are CNGL SVRPLS, with a DeltaAvg score of 11.09, and DCU-SYMC alltypes, with a DeltaAvg score of 10.13. While the former holds the higher score, the difference is not significant at the $p \leq 0.05$ level as estimated by a bootstrap resampling test.

Both submissions are better than the baseline system by a very wide margin, a larger relative improvement than that obtained in the corresponding WMT12 task. In addition, five submissions (out of 12 systems) scored significantly higher than the baseline system (systems above the middle gray area), which is a larger proportion than that in last year's task (only 3 out of 16 systems), indicating that this shared task succeeded in pushing the state-of-the-art performance to new levels.

In addition to the performance of the official submission, we report results obtained by two oracle methods: the gold-label HTER metric computed against the post-edited translations as reference (Oracle HTER), and the BLEU metric (1-BLEU to obtain the same range as HTER) computed against the same post-edited translations as reference (Oracle HBLEU). The "Oracle HTER" DeltaAvg score of 16.38 gives an upperbound in terms of DeltaAvg for the test set used in this evaluation. It indicates that, for this set, the difference in post-editing effort between the top quality quantiles and the overall quality is 16.38 on average. The oracle based on HBLEU gives a lower DeltaAvg score, which is expected since HTER was our actual gold label. However, it is still significantly higher than the score of the winning submission, which shows that there is significant room for improvement even by the highest scoring submissions.

The results for the **scoring variant** of the task are presented in Table 13, sorted from best to worse by using the MAE metric scores as primary key and the RMSE metric scores as secondary key.

According to MAE scores, the winning submission is SHEF FS (MAE = 12.42), which uses feature selection and a novel learning algorithm for the task, Gaussian Processes. The baseline system is measured to have an MAE of 14.81, with six other submissions having performances that are not different from the baseline at a statistically significant level, as shown by the gray area in the middle of Table 13). Nine submissions (out of 16) scored significantly higher than the baseline system (systems above the middle gray area), a considerably higher proportion of submissions as compared to last year (5 out of 19), which indicates that this shared task also succeeded in pushing the state-of-the-art performance to new levels in terms of absolute scoring. Only one (6%) system scored significantly lower than the baseline, as opposed to 8 (42%) in last year's task.

For the sake of completeness, we also show oracles figures using the same methods as for the ranking variant of the task. Here the lowerbound in error (Oracle HTER) will clearly be zero, as both MAE and RMSE are measured against the same gold label used for the oracle computation. "Oracle HBLEU" is also not indicative in this case, as the although the values for the two metrics (HTER and HBLEU) are within the same ranges, they are not directly comparable. This explains the larger MAE/RMSE figures for "Oracle HBLEU" than those for most submissions.

Task 1.2 Selecting the best translation

Below we present the results for this task for each of the two Kendall's τ flavours presented in Section 6.6, for the German-English test set (Tables 14 and 16) and the English-Spanish test set (Tables 15 and 17). The results are sorted from best to worse using each of the Kendall's τ metric flavours.

For German-English, the winning submission is DFKI's logRegFss33 entry, for both Kendall's τ with ties penalised and ties ignored, with $\tau = 0.31$ (since this submission has no ties, the two metrics give the same τ value). A trivial baseline that proposes random ranks (with ties allowed) has a Kendall's τ with ties penalised of -0.12 (as this metric penalises the system's ties that were non-ties in the reference), and a Kendall's τ with ties ignored of 0.08. Most of the submissions performed better than this simple baseline. More interestingly perhaps is the comparison between the best submission and the performance by an ora-

System ID	DeltaAvg	Spearman ρ
• CNGL SVRPLS	11.09	0.55
• DCU-SYMC alltypes	10.13	0.59
SHEF FS	9.76	0.57
CNGL SVR	9.88	0.51
DCU-SYMC combine	9.84	0.59
CMU noB	8.98	0.57
SHEF FS-AL	8.85	0.50
Baseline bb17 SVR	8.52	0.46
CMU full	8.23	0.54
LIMSI	8.15	0.44
TCD-CNGL open	6.03	0.33
TCD-CNGL restricted	5.85	0.31
UMAC	2.74	0.11
Oracle HTER	16.38	1.00
Oracle HBLEU	15.74	0.93

Table 12: Official results for the ranking variant of the WMT13 Quality Estimation Task 1.1. The winning submissions are indicated by a • (they are significantly better than all other submissions according to bootstrap resampling (10k times) with 95% confidence intervals). The systems in the gray area are not different from the baseline system at a statistically significant level according to the same test. Oracle results that use human-references are also shown for comparison purposes.

System ID	MAE	RMSE
• SHEF FS	12.42	15.74
SHEF FS-AL	13.02	17.03
CNGL SVRPLS	13.26	16.82
LIMSI	13.32	17.22
DCU-SYMC combine	13.45	16.64
DCU-SYMC alltypes	13.51	17.14
CMU noB	13.84	17.46
CNGL SVR	13.85	17.28
FBK-UEdin extra	14.38	17.68
FBK-UEdin rand-svr	14.50	17.73
LORIA inctrain	14.79	18.34
Baseline bb17 SVR	14.81	18.22
TCD-CNGL open	14.81	19.00
LORIA inctraincont	14.83	18.17
TCD-CNGL restricted	15.20	19.59
CMU full	15.25	18.97
UMAC	16.97	21.94
Oracle HTER	0.00	0.00
Oracle HBLEU (1-HBLEU)	16.85	19.72

Table 13: Official results for the scoring variant of the WMT13 Quality Estimation Task 1.1. The winning submission is indicated by a • (it is significantly better than the other submissions according to bootstrap resampling (10k times) with 95% confidence intervals). The systems in the gray area are not different from the baseline system at a statistically significant level according to the same test. Oracle results that use human-references are also shown for comparison purposes.

German-English System ID	Kendall's τ with ties penalised
• DFKI logRegFss33	0.31
DFKI logRegFss24	0.28
CNGL SVRPLSF1	0.17
CNGL SVRF1	0.17
DCU CCG	0.15
UPC AQE+SEM+LM	0.11
UPC AQE+LeM+ALGPR+LM	0.10
DCU baseline+CCG	0.00
Baseline Random-ranks-with-ties	-0.12
UMAC EBLEU-I	-0.39
UMAC NB-LPR	-0.49
Oracle Human	1.00
Oracle BLEU (margin 0.00)	0.19
Oracle BLEU (margin 0.01)	0.05
Oracle METEOR-ex (margin 0.00)	0.23
Oracle METEOR-ex (margin 0.01)	0.06

Table 14: Official results for the Task 1.2 of the WMT13 Quality Estimation shared task for German-English, using as metric Kendall's τ with ties penalised. The winning submissions are indicated by a •. Oracle results that use human-references are also shown for comparison purposes.

English-Spanish System ID	Kendall's τ with ties penalised
• CNGL SVRPLSF1	0.15
CNGL SVRF1	0.13
DFKI logRegL2-411	0.09
DFKI logRegL2-431	0.04
UPC QQE+LeM+ALGPR+LM	-0.03
UPC AQE+LeM+ALGPR+LM	-0.06
CMU BLEUopt	-0.11
Baseline Random-ranks-with-ties	-0.23
UMAC EBLEU-A	-0.27
UMAC EBLEU-I	-0.35
CMU cls	-0.63
Oracle Human	1.00
Oracle BLEU (margin 0.00)	0.17
Oracle BLEU (margin 0.02)	-0.06
Oracle METEOR-ex (margin 0.00)	0.19
Oracle METEOR-ex (margin 0.02)	0.05

Table 15: Official results for the Task 1.2 of the WMT13 Quality Estimation shared task for English-Spanish, using as metric Kendall's τ with ties penalised. The winning submissions are indicated by a •. Oracle results that use human-references are also shown for comparison purposes.

German-English System ID	Kendall's τ with ties ignored	Nr. of non-ties / Nr. of decisions
• DFKI logRegFss33	0.31	882/882
DFKI logRegFss24	0.28	882/882
UPC AQE+SEM+LM	0.27	768/882
UPC AQE+LeM+ALGPR+LM	0.24	788/882
DCU CCG	0.18	862/882
CNGL SVRPLSF1	0.17	882/882
CNGL SVRF1	0.17	881/882
Baseline Random-ranks-with-ties	0.08	718/882
DCU baseline+CCG	0.01	874/882
UMAC NB-LPR	0.01	447/882
UMAC EBLEU-I	-0.03	558/882
Oracle Human	1.00	882/882
Oracle BLEU (margin 0.00)	0.22	859/882
Oracle BLEU (margin 0.01)	0.27	728/882
Oracle METEOR-ex (margin 0.00)	0.20	869/882
Oracle METEOR-ex (margin 0.01)	0.24	757/882

Table 16: Official results for the Task 1.2 of the WMT13 Quality Estimation shared task for German-English, using as metric Kendall's τ with ties ignored. The winning submissions are indicated by a •. Oracle results that use human-references are also shown for comparison purposes.

English-Spanish System ID	Kendall's τ with ties ignored	Nr. of non-ties / Nr. of decisions
• CMU cls	0.23	192/633
CNGL SVRPLSF1	0.16	632/633
CNGL SVRF1	0.13	631/633
DFKI logRegL2-411	0.13	610/633
UPC QQE+LeM+ALGPR+LM	0.11	554/633
UPC AQE+LeM+ALGPR+LM	0.08	554/633
UMAC EBLEU-A	0.07	430/633
DFKI logRegL2-431	0.04	633/633
Baseline Random-ranks-with-ties	0.03	507/633
UMAC EBLEU-I	0.02	407/633
CMU BLEUopt	-0.11	633/633
Oracle Human	1.00	633/633
Oracle BLEU (margin 0.00)	0.19	621/633
Oracle BLEU (margin 0.02)	0.26	474/633
Oracle METEOR-ex (margin 0.00)	0.25	623/633
Oracle METEOR-ex (margin 0.02)	0.28	517/633

Table 17: Official results for the Task 1.2 of the WMT13 Quality Estimation shared task for English-Spanish, using as metric Kendall's τ with ties ignored. The winning submissions are indicated by a •. Oracle results that use human-references are also shown for comparison purposes.

cle method that has access to human-created references. This oracle uses human references to compute BLEU and METEOR scores for each translation segment, and consequently computes rankings for the competing translations based on these scores. To reflect the impact of ties on the two versions of Kendall's τ metric we use, we allow these ranks to be tied if the difference between the oracle BLEU or METEOR scores is smaller than a margin (see lower section of Tables 14 and 16, with margins of 0 and 0.01 for the scores). For example, under a regime of BLEU with margin 0.01, a translation with BLEU score of 0.172 would get the same rank as a translation with BLEU score of 0.164 (difference of 0.008), but a higher rank than a translation with BLEU score of 0.158 (difference of 0.014). Not surprisingly, under the Kendall's τ with ties penalised the best Oracle BLEU or METEOR performance happens for a 0.0 margin (which makes ties possible only for exactly-matching scores), for a value of $\tau = 0.19$ and $\tau = 0.23$, respectively. Under the Kendall's τ with ties ignored, the Oracle BLEU performance for a 0.01 margin (i.e, translations under 1 BLEU point should be considered as having the same rank) achieves $\tau = 0.27$, while Oracle METEOR for a 0.01 margin achieves $\tau = 0.24$. These values are lower than the $\tau = 0.31$ of the winning submission without access to reference translations, suggesting that quality estimation models are capable of better modelling translation differences compared to traditional, human reference-based MT evaluation metrics.

For English-Spanish, under Kendall's τ with ties penalised the winning submission is CNGL's SVRPLSF1, with $\tau = 0.15$. Under Kendall's τ with ties ignored, the best scoring submission is CMU's cls with $\tau = 0.23$, but this is achieved by offering non-tie judgements only for 192 of the 633 total judgements (30% of them). As we discussed in Section 6.6, the "Kendall's τ with ties ignored" metric is weak with respect to comparing different submissions, since it favours systems that are do not commit to a given rank and rather produce a large number of ties. This becomes even clearer when we look at the performance of the oracle methods (Tables 15 and 17). Under Kendall's τ with ties penalised, "Oracle BLEU" (margin 0.00) achieves $\tau = 0.17$, while under Kendall's τ with ties ignored, "Oracle BLEU" (margin 0.02) has a $\tau = 0.26$. This results in 474 non-tie decisions (75% of them), and a better τ value compared to "Oracle BLEU" (margin 0.00), with a $\tau = 0.19$ under the same metric. The oracle values for both BLEU and METEOR are close to the τ values of the winning submissions, supporting the conclusion that quality estimation techniques can successfully replace traditional, human reference-based MT evaluation metrics.

Task 1.3 Predicting post-editing time

Results for this task are presented in Table 18. A third of the submissions was able to beat the baseline. Among these FBK-UEDIN's submission ranked best in terms of MAE, our main metric for this task, and also achieved the lowest RMSE.

Only three systems were able to beat our baseline in terms of MAE. Please note that while all features were available to the participants, our baseline is actually a competitive system.

The second-best entry, CNGL SVR, reached the highest Spearman's rank correlation, our secondary metric. Furthermore, in terms of this metric all four top-ranking entries, two by CNGL and FBK-UEDIN respectively, are significantly better than the baseline (10k bootstrap resampling test with 95% confidence intervals). As high ranking submissions also yield strong rank correlation to the observed post-editing time, we can be confident that improvements in MAE are not only due to better handling of extreme cases.

Many participants submitted two variants of their systems with different numbers of features and/or machine learning approaches. In Table 18 we can see these are grouped closely together giving rise to the assumption that the general pool of available features and thereby the used resources and strongest features are most relevant for a system's performance. Another hint in that direction is the observation the top-ranked systems rely on additional data and resources to generate their features.

Task 2 Predicting word-level scores

Results for this task are presented in Table 19 and 20, sorted by macro average F_1. Since this is a new task, we have yet to establish a strong baseline. For reference we provide a trivial baseline that predicts the dominant class – *(K)eep* – for every token.

The first observation in Table 19 is that this trivial baseline is difficult to beat in terms of accuracy. However, considering our main metric – macro-

System ID	MAE	RMSE	Pearson's r	Spearman's ρ
• FBK-UEDIN Extra	47.5	82.6	0.65	0.75
• FBK-UEDIN Rand-SVR	47.9	86.7	0.66	0.74
CNGL SVR	49.2	90.4	0.67	0.76
CNGL SVRPLS	49.6	86.6	0.68	0.74
CMU slim	51.6	84.7	0.63	0.68
Baseline bb17 SVR	51.9	93.4	0.61	0.70
DFKI linear6	52.4	84.3	0.64	0.68
CMU full	53.6	92.2	0.58	0.60
DFKI pls8	53.6	88.3	0.59	0.67
TCD-DCU-CNGL SVM2	55.8	98.9	0.47	0.60
TCD-DCU-CNGL SVM1	55.9	99.4	0.48	0.60
SHEF FS	55.9	103.1	0.42	0.61
SHEF FS-AL	64.6	99.1	0.57	0.60
LIMSI elastic	70.6	114.4	0.58	0.64

Table 18: Official results for the Task 1.3 of the WMT13 Quality Estimation shared-task. The winning submissions are indicated by a • (they are significantly better than all other submissions according to bootstrap resampling (10k times) with 95% confidence intervals). The systems in the gray area are not different from the baseline system at a statistically significant level according to the same test.

		Keep			Change			
System ID	Accuracy	Prec.	Recall	F_1	Prec.	Recall	F_1	Macro F_1
• LIG FS_BIN	0.74	0.79	0.86	0.82	0.56	0.43	0.48	0.65
• LIG BOOST_BIN	0.74	0.78	0.88	0.83	0.57	0.37	0.45	0.64
CNGL GLM	0.70	0.76	0.86	0.80	0.47	0.31	0.38	0.59
UMAC NB	0.56	0.82	0.49	0.62	0.37	0.73	0.49	0.55
CNGL GLMd	0.71	0.74	0.93	0.82	0.51	0.19	0.28	0.55
UMAC CRF	0.71	0.72	0.98	0.83	0.49	0.04	0.07	0.45
Baseline (one class)	0.71	0.71	1.00	0.83	0.00	0.00	0.00	0.42

Table 19: Official results for Task 2: binary classification on word level of the WMT13 Quality Estimation shared-task. The winning submissions are indicated by a •.

System ID	F_1 Keep	F_1 Substitute	F_1 Delete	Micro-F_1	Macro-F_1
• LIG FS_MULT	0.83	0.44	0.072	0.72	0.45
• LIG ALL_MULT	0.83	0.45	0.064	0.72	0.45
UMAC NB	0.62	0.43	0.042	0.52	0.36
CNGL GLM	0.83	0.18	0.028	0.71	0.35
CNGL GLMd	0.83	0.14	0.034	0.72	0.34
UMAC CRF	0.83	0.04	0.012	0.71	0.29
Baseline (one class)	0.83	0.00	0.000	0.71	0.28

Table 20: Official results for Task 2: multiclass classification on word level of the WMT13 Quality Estimation shared-task. The winning submissions are indicated by a •.

average F_1 – it is clear that all systems outperform the baseline. The winning systems by LIG for the binary task are also the top ranking systems on the multiclass task.

While promising results are found for the binary variant of the task where systems are able to achieve an F_1 of almost 0.5 for the relevant class – *Change*, the multiclass prediction variant of the task seem to suffer from its severe class imbalance. In fact, none of the systems shows good performance when predicting deletions.

6.9 Discussion

In what follows, we discuss the main accomplishments of this shared task starting from the goals we had previously identified for it.

Explore various granularity levels for the quality-prediction task The decision on which level of granularity quality estimation is applied depends strongly on the intended application. In Task 2 we tested binary word-level classification in a post-editing setting. If such annotation is presented through a user interface we imagine that words marked as incorrect would be hidden from the editor, highlighted as possibly wrong or that a list of alternatives would we generated.

With respect to the poor improvements over trivial baselines, we consider that the results for word-level prediction could be mostly connected to limitations of the datasets provided, which are very small for word-level prediction, as compared to successful previous work such as (Bach et al., 2011). Despite the limited amount of training data, several systems were able to predict dubious words (binary variant of the task), showing that this can be a promising task. Extending the granularity even further by predicting the actual editing action necessary for a word yielded less positive results than the binary setting.

We cannot directly compare sentence- and word-level results. However, since sentence-level predictions can benefit from more information available and therefore more signal on which the prediction is based, the natural conclusion is that, if there is a choice in the prediction granularity, to opt for the coarser one possible (i.e., sentence-level over word-level). But certain applications may require finer granularity levels, and therefore word-level predictions can still be very valuable.

Explore the prediction of more objective scores Given the multitude of possible applications for quality estimation we must decide which predicted values are both useful and accurate. In this year's task we have attempted to address the usefulness criterion by moving from the subjective, human judgement-based scores, to the prediction of scores that can be more easily interpreted for practical applications: post-editing distance or types of edits (word-level), post-editing time, and ranking of alternative translations.

The general promise of using objective scores is that predicting a value that is related to the use case will make quality estimation more applicable and yield lower deviance compared to the use of proxy metrics. The magnitude of this benefit should be sufficient to account for the possible additional effort related to collecting such scores.

While a direct comparison between the different types of scores used for this year's tasks is not possible as they are based on different datasets, if we compare last year's task on predicting 1-5 likert scores (and generating an overall ranking of all translations in the test set) with this year's Task 1.1, which is virtually the same, but using post-editing distance as gold-label, we see that the number of systems that outperform the baseline [18] is proportionally larger this year. We can also notice a higher relative improvement of these submissions over the baseline system. While this could simply be a consequence of progress in the field, it may also provide an indication that objective metrics are more suitable for the problem.

Particularly with respect to post-editing time, given that this label has a long tailed distribution and is not trivial to measure even in a controlled environment, the results of Task 1.3 are encouraging. Comparison with the better results seen on Tasks 1.1 and 1.2, however, suggests that, for Task 1.3, additional data processing, filtering, and modelling (including modelling translator-specific traits such as their variance in time) is required, as evidenced in (Cohn and Specia, 2013).

Explore the use of quality estimation techniques to replace reference-based MT evaluation metrics When it comes to the task of automatically ranking alternative translations generated by different MT systems, the traditional use of reference-based MT evaluation metrics is challenged by the findings of this task.

The top ranking quality estimation submissions

[18] The two baselines are exactly the same, and therefore the comparison is meaningful.

to Task 1.2 have performances that outperform or are at least at the same level with the ones that involve the use of human references. The most interesting property of these techniques is that, being reference-free, they can be used for any source sentences, and therefore are ready to be deployed for arbitrary texts.

An immediate application for this capability is a procedure by which MT system-selection is performed, based on the output of such quality estimators. Additional measurements are needed to determine the level of improvement in translation quality that the current performance of these techniques can achieve in a system-selection scenario.

Identify new and effective quality indicators Quality indicators, or features, are core to the problem of quality estimation. One significant difference this year with respect to previous year was the availability of QUEST, a framework for the extraction of a large number of features. A few submissions used these larger sets – as opposed to the 17 baseline features used in the 2012 edition – as their starting point, to which they added other features. Most features available in this framework, however, had already been used in previous work.

Novel families of features used this year which seems to have played an important role are those proposed by CNGL. They include a number of language and MT-system independent monolingual and bilingual similarity metrics between the sentences for prediction and corpora of the language pair under consideration. Based on standard regression algorithm (the same used by the baseline system), the submissions from CNGL using such feature families topped many of the tasks.

Another interesting family of features is that used by TCD-CNGL and TCD-DCU-CNGL for Tasks 1.1 and 1.3. These were borrowed from work on style or authorship identification. The assumption is that low/high quality translations can be characterised by some patterns which are frequent and/or differ significantly from patterns belonging to the opposite category.

Like in last year's task, the vast majority of the participating systems used external resources in addition to those provided for the task, particularly for linguistically-oriented features, such as parsers, part-of-speech taggers, named entity recognizers, etc. A novel set of syntactic features based on Combinatory Categorial Grammar (CCG) performed reasonably well in Task 1.2: with six CCG-based features and no additional features, the system outperformed the baseline system and also a second submission where the 17 baseline features were added. This highlights the potential of linguistically-motivated features for the problem.

As expected, different feature sets were used for different tasks. This is essential for Task 2, where word-level features are certainly necessary. For example, LIG used a number of lexical features such as part-of-speech tag, word-posterior probabilities, syntactic (constituent label, distance to the constituent tree root, and target and source polysemy count). For submissions where a sequence labelling algorithm such as a Conditional Random Fields was used for prediction, the interdependencies between adjacent words and labels was also modelled though features.

Pseudo-references, i.e., scores from standard evaluation metrics such as BLEU based on translations generated by an alternative MT system as "reference", featured in more than half of the submissions for sentence-level tasks. This is not surprising given their performance in previous work on quality estimation.

Identify effective machine learning techniques for all variants of the quality estimation task For the sentence-level tasks, standard regression methods such as SVR performed well as in the previous edition of the shared task, topping the results for the ranking variant of Task 1.1, both first and second place. In fact this algorithm was used by most submissions that outperformed the baseline. An alternative algorithm to SVR with very promising results and which was introduced for the problem this year is that of Gaussian Processes. It was used by SHEF, the winning submission in the scoring variant of Task 1.1, which also performed well in the ranking variant, despite its hyperparameters having been optimised for scoring only. Algorithms behave similarly for Task 1.3, with SVR performing particularly well.

For Task 1.2, logistic regression performed the best or among the best, along with SVR. One of the most effective approach for this task, however, appears to be one that is better tailored for the task, namely pair-wise decomposition for ranking. This approach benefits from transforming a k-way ranking problem into a series of simpler, 2-way ranking problems, which can be more accurately solved. Another approach that shows promise is that of ensemble of regressors, in which the output is the results combining the predictions of different regression models.

Linear-chain Conditional Random Fields are a popular model of choice for sequence labelling tasks and have been successfully used by several participants in Task 2, along with discriminatively trained Hidden Markov Models and Naïve Bayes.

As in the previous edition, feature engineering and feature selection prior to model learning were important components in many submissions. However, the role of individual features is hard to judge separately from the role of the machine learning techniques employed.

Establish the state of the art performance All four tasks addressed in this shared task have achieved a dual role that is important for the research community: (i) to make publicly available new data sets that can serve to compare different approaches and contributions; and (ii) to establish the present state-of-the-art performance in the field, so that progress can be easily measured and tracked. In addition, the public availability of the scoring scripts makes evaluation and direct comparison straightforward.

Many participants submitted predictions for several tasks. Comparison of the results shows that there is little overlap between the best systems when the predicted value is varied. While we did not formally require the participants to use similar systems across tasks, these results indicate that specialised systems with features selected depending on the predicted variable can in fact be beneficial.

As we mentioned before, compared to the previous edition of the task, we noticed (for Task 1.1) a larger relative improvement of scores over the baseline system, as well as a larger proportion of systems outperforming the baseline systems, which are a good indication that the field is progressing over the years. For example, in the scoring variant of Task 1.1, last year only 5 out of 20 systems (i.e. 25% of the systems) were able to significantly outperform the baseline. This year, 9 out 16 systems (i.e. 56%) outperformed the same baseline. Last year, the relative improvement of the winning submission with respect to the baseline system was 13%, while this year the relative improvement is of 19%.

Overall, the tables of results presented in Section 6.8 give a comprehensive view of the current state-of-the-art on the data sets used for this shared task, as well as indications on how much room there still is for improvement via figures from oracle methods. As a result, people interested in contributing to research in these machine translation quality estimation tasks will be able to do so in a principled way, with clearly established state-of-the-art levels and straightforward means of comparison.

7 Summary

As in previous incarnations of this workshop we carried out an extensive manual and automatic evaluation of machine translation performance, and we used the human judgements that we collected to validate automatic metrics of translation quality. We also refined last year's quality estimation task, asking for methods that predict sentence-level post-editing effort and time, rank translations from alternative systems, and pinpoint words in the output that are more likely to be wrong.

As in previous years, all data sets generated by this workshop, including the human judgments, system translations and automatic scores, are publicly available for other researchers to analyze.[19]

Acknowledgments

This work was supported in parts by the MosesCore, Casmacat, Khresmoi, Matecat and QTLaunchPad projects funded by the European Commission (7th Framework Programme), and by gifts from Google, Microsoft and Yandex.

We would also like to thank our colleagues Matouš Macháček and Martin Popel for detailed discussions.

References

Allauzen, A., Pécheux, N., Do, Q. K., Dinarelli, M., Lavergne, T., Max, A., Le, H.-S., and Yvon, F. (2013). LIMSI @ WMT13. In *Proceedings of the Eighth Workshop on Statistical Machine Translation*, pages 60–67, Sofia, Bulgaria. Association for Computational Linguistics.

Almaghout, H. and Specia, L. (2013). A CCG-based Quality Estimation Metric for Statistical Machine Translation. In *Proceedings of MT Summit XIV (to appear)*, Nice, France.

Ammar, W., Chahuneau, V., Denkowski, M., Hanneman, G., Ling, W., Matthews, A., Murray,

[19]http://statmt.org/wmt13/results.html

K., Segall, N., Lavie, A., and Dyer, C. (2013). The CMU machine translation systems at WMT 2013: Syntax, synthetic translation options, and pseudo-references. In *Proceedings of the Eighth Workshop on Statistical Machine Translation*, pages 68–75, Sofia, Bulgaria. Association for Computational Linguistics.

Avramidis, E. (2012). Comparative Quality Estimation: Automatic Sentence-Level Ranking of Multiple Machine Translation Outputs. In *Proceedings of 24th International Conference on Computational Linguistics*, pages 115–132, Mumbai, India.

Avramidis, E. and Popovic, M. (2013). Selecting feature sets for comparative and time-oriented quality estimation of machine translation output. In *Proceedings of the Eighth Workshop on Statistical Machine Translation*, pages 327–334, Sofia, Bulgaria. Association for Computational Linguistics.

Avramidis, E., Popović, M., Vilar, D., and Burchardt, A. (2011). Evaluate with confidence estimation: Machine ranking of translation outputs using grammatical features. In *Proceedings of the Sixth Workshop on Statistical Machine Translation*.

Aziz, W., Mitkov, R., and Specia, L. (2013). Ranking Machine Translation Systems via Post-Editing. In *Proc. of Text, Speech and Dialogue (TSD)*, Lecture Notes in Artificial Intelligence, Berlin / Heidelberg. Západočeská univerzita v Plzni, Springer Verlag.

Bach, N., Huang, F., and Al-Onaizan, Y. (2011). Goodness: A method for measuring machine translation confidence. In *Proceedings of the 49th Annual Meeting of the Association for Computational Linguistics: Human Language Technologies*, pages 211–219, Portland, Oregon, USA.

Beck, D., Shah, K., Cohn, T., and Specia, L. (2013). SHEF-Lite: When less is more for translation quality estimation. In *Proceedings of the Eighth Workshop on Statistical Machine Translation*, pages 335–340, Sofia, Bulgaria. Association for Computational Linguistics.

Biçici, E., Groves, D., and van Genabith, J. (2013). Predicting sentence translation quality using extrinsic and language independent features. *Machine Translation*.

Biçici, E. and van Genabith, J. (2013). CNGL-CORE: Referential translation machines for measuring semantic similarity. In **SEM 2013: The Second Joint Conference on Lexical and Computational Semantics*, Atlanta, Georgia, USA. Association for Computational Linguistics.

Bicici, E. (2013a). Feature decay algorithms for fast deployment of accurate statistical machine translation systems. In *Proceedings of the Eighth Workshop on Statistical Machine Translation*, pages 76–82, Sofia, Bulgaria. Association for Computational Linguistics.

Bicici, E. (2013b). Referential translation machines for quality estimation. In *Proceedings of the Eighth Workshop on Statistical Machine Translation*, pages 341–349, Sofia, Bulgaria. Association for Computational Linguistics.

Bílek, K. and Zeman, D. (2013). CUni multilingual matrix in the WMT 2013 shared task. In *Proceedings of the Eighth Workshop on Statistical Machine Translation*, pages 83–89, Sofia, Bulgaria. Association for Computational Linguistics.

Bojar, O., Kos, K., and Mareček, D. (2010). Tackling Sparse Data Issue in Machine Translation Evaluation. In *Proceedings of the ACL 2010 Conference Short Papers*, pages 86–91, Uppsala, Sweden. Association for Computational Linguistics.

Bojar, O., Rosa, R., and Tamchyna, A. (2013). Chimera – three heads for English-to-Czech translation. In *Proceedings of the Eighth Workshop on Statistical Machine Translation*, pages 90–96, Sofia, Bulgaria. Association for Computational Linguistics.

Borisov, A., Dlougach, J., and Galinskaya, I. (2013). Yandex school of data analysis machine translation systems for WMT13. In *Proceedings of the Eighth Workshop on Statistical Machine Translation*, pages 97–101, Sofia, Bulgaria. Association for Computational Linguistics.

Callison-Burch, C., Fordyce, C., Koehn, P., Monz, C., and Schroeder, J. (2007). (Meta-) evaluation of machine translation. In *Proceedings of the Second Workshop on Statistical Machine Translation (WMT07)*, Prague, Czech Republic.

Callison-Burch, C., Fordyce, C., Koehn, P., Monz, C., and Schroeder, J. (2008). Further meta-evaluation of machine translation. In *Proceedings of the Third Workshop on Statistical Machine Translation (WMT08)*, Colmbus, Ohio.

Callison-Burch, C., Koehn, P., Monz, C., Peterson, K., Przybocki, M., and Zaidan, O. F. (2010). Findings of the 2010 joint workshop on statistical machine translation and metrics for machine translation. In *Proceedings of the Fourth Workshop on Statistical Machine Translation (WMT10)*, Uppsala, Sweden.

Callison-Burch, C., Koehn, P., Monz, C., Post, M., Soricut, R., and Specia, L. (2012). Findings of the 2012 workshop on statistical machine translation. In *Proceedings of the Seventh Workshop on Statistical Machine Translation*, pages 10–51, Montréal, Canada. Association for Computational Linguistics.

Callison-Burch, C., Koehn, P., Monz, C., and Schroeder, J. (2009). Findings of the 2009 workshop on statistical machine translation. In *Proceedings of the Fourth Workshop on Statistical Machine Translation (WMT09)*, Athens, Greece.

Callison-Burch, C., Koehn, P., Monz, C., and Zaidan, O. (2011). Findings of the 2011 workshop on statistical machine translation. In *Proceedings of the Sixth Workshop on Statistical Machine Translation*, pages 22–64, Edinburgh, Scotland.

Camargo de Souza, J. G., Buck, C., Turchi, M., and Negri, M. (2013). FBK-UEdin participation to the WMT13 quality estimation shared task. In *Proceedings of the Eighth Workshop on Statistical Machine Translation*, pages 350–356, Sofia, Bulgaria. Association for Computational Linguistics.

Charniak, E. and Johnson, M. (2005). Coarse-to-fine n-best parsing and maxent discriminative reranking. In *Proceedings of the 43rd Annual Meeting on Association for Computational Linguistics*, pages 173–180. Association for Computational Linguistics.

Cho, E., Ha, T.-L., Mediani, M., Niehues, J., Herrmann, T., Slawik, I., and Waibel, A. (2013). The Karlsruhe Institute of Technology translation systems for the WMT 2013. In *Proceedings of the Eighth Workshop on Statistical Machine Translation*, pages 102–106, Sofia, Bulgaria. Association for Computational Linguistics.

Cohen, J. (1960). A coefficient of agreement for nominal scales. *Educational and Psychological Measurment*, 20(1):37–46.

Cohn, T. and Specia, L. (2013). Modelling Annotator Bias with Multi-task Gaussian Processes: An Application to Machine Translation Quality Estimation. In *Proceedings of the 51st Annual Meeting of the Association for Computational Linguistics (to appear)*.

Collins, M. (2002). Discriminative training methods for hidden markov models: theory and experiments with perceptron algorithms. In *Proceedings of the ACL-02 conference on Empirical methods in natural language processing - Volume 10*, EMNLP '02, pages 1–8, Stroudsburg, PA, USA. Association for Computational Linguistics.

de Marneffe, M.-C., MacCartney, B., and Manning, C. D. (2006). Generating typed dependency parses from phrase structure parses. In *Proceedings of LREC-06*, pages 449–454.

Denkowski, M. and Lavie, A. (2010). Meteor-next and the meteor paraphrase tables: improved evaluation support for five target languages. In *Proceedings of the Joint Fifth Workshop on Statistical Machine Translation and MetricsMATR*, WMT '10, pages 339–342, Stroudsburg, PA, USA. Association for Computational Linguistics.

Durgar El-Kahlout, I. and Mermer, C. (2013). TÜbtak-blgem german-english machine translation systems for w13. In *Proceedings of the Eighth Workshop on Statistical Machine Translation*, pages 107–111, Sofia, Bulgaria. Association for Computational Linguistics.

Durrani, N., Fraser, A., Schmid, H., Sajjad, H., and Farkas, R. (2013a). Munich-Edinburgh-Stuttgart submissions of OSM systems at WMT13. In *Proceedings of the Eighth Workshop on Statistical Machine Translation*, pages 120–125, Sofia, Bulgaria. Association for Computational Linguistics.

Durrani, N., Haddow, B., Heafield, K., and Koehn, P. (2013b). Edinburgh's machine translation systems for European language pairs. In *Proceedings of the Eighth Workshop on Statistical Machine Translation*, pages 112–119, Sofia, Bulgaria. Association for Computational Linguistics.

Eidelman, V., Wu, K., Ture, F., Resnik, P., and Lin, J. (2013). Towards efficient large-scale feature-rich statistical machine translation. In *Proceedings of the Eighth Workshop on Statistical Machine Translation*, pages 126–131, Sofia, Bulgaria. Association for Computational Linguistics.

Federmann, C. (2012). Appraise: An Open-Source Toolkit for Manual Evaluation of Machine Translation Output. *The Prague Bulletin of Mathematical Linguistics (PBML)*, 98:25–35.

Fleiss, J. L. (1971). Measuring nominal scale agreement among many raters. *Psychological Bulletin*, 76(5):378–382.

Formiga, L., Costa-jussà, M. R., Mariño, J. B., Fonollosa, J. A. R., Barrón-Cedeño, A., and Marquez, L. (2013a). The TALP-UPC phrase-based translation systems for WMT13: System combination with morphology generation, domain adaptation and corpus filtering. In *Proceedings of the Eighth Workshop on Statistical Machine Translation*, pages 132–138, Sofia, Bulgaria. Association for Computational Linguistics.

Formiga, L., Gonzàlez, M., Barrón-Cedeño, A., Fonollosa, J. A. R., and Marquez, L. (2013b). The TALP-UPC approach to system selection: Asiya features and pairwise classification using random forests. In *Proceedings of the Eighth Workshop on Statistical Machine Translation*, pages 357–362, Sofia, Bulgaria. Association for Computational Linguistics.

Formiga, L., Màrquez, L., and Pujantell, J. (2013c). Real-life translation quality estimation for mt system selection. In *Proceedings of MT Summit XIV (to appear)*, Nice, France.

Galuščáková, P., Popel, M., and Bojar, O. (2013). PhraseFix: Statistical post-editing of TectoMT. In *Proceedings of the Eighth Workshop on Statistical Machine Translation*, pages 139–145, Sofia, Bulgaria. Association for Computational Linguistics.

Gispert, A., Blackwood, G., Iglesias, G., and Byrne, W. (2013). N-gram posterior probability confidence measures for statistical machine translation: an empirical study. *Machine Translation*, 27:85–114.

Gonzàlez, M., Giménez, J., and Màrquez, L. (2012). A graphical interface for mt evaluation and error analysis. In *Proceedings of the ACL 2012 System Demonstrations*, pages 139–144, Jeju Island, Korea.

Green, S., Cer, D., Reschke, K., Voigt, R., Bauer, J., Wang, S., Silveira, N., Neidert, J., and Manning, C. D. (2013). Feature-rich phrase-based translation: Stanford University's submission to the WMT 2013 translation task. In *Proceedings of the Eighth Workshop on Statistical Machine Translation*, pages 146–151, Sofia, Bulgaria. Association for Computational Linguistics.

Hall, M., Frank, E., Holmes, G., Pfahringer, B., Reutemann, P., and Witten, I. H. (2009). The weka data mining software: an update. *SIGKDD Explor. Newsl.*, 11(1):10–18.

Han, A. L.-F., Wong, D. F., Chao, L. S., Lu, Y., He, L., Wang, Y., and Zhou, J. (2013). A description of tunable machine translation evaluation systems in WMT13 metrics task. In *Proceedings of the Eighth Workshop on Statistical Machine Translation*, pages 412–419, Sofia, Bulgaria. Association for Computational Linguistics.

Hildebrand, S. and Vogel, S. (2013). MT quality estimation: The CMU system for WMT'13. In *Proceedings of the Eighth Workshop on Statistical Machine Translation*, pages 371–377, Sofia, Bulgaria. Association for Computational Linguistics.

Hosmer, D. (1989). *Applied logistic regression*. Wiley, New York, 8th edition.

Huet, S., Manishina, E., and Lefèvre, F. (2013). Factored machine translation systems for Russian-English. In *Proceedings of the Eighth Workshop on Statistical Machine Translation*, pages 152–155, Sofia, Bulgaria. Association for Computational Linguistics.

Hunt, E., Martin, J., and Stone, P. (1966). *Experiments in Induction*. Academic Press, New York.

Kaplan, R., Riezler, S., King, T., Maxwell, J., Vasserman, A., and Crouch, R. (2004). Speed and accuracy in shallow and deep stochastic parsing. In *Proceedings of the Human Language Technology Conference and the 4th Annual Meeting of the North American Chapter of the Association for Computational Linguistics (HLT/NAACL 04)*.

Kauchak, D. and Barzilay, R. (2006). Paraphrasing for automatic evaluation. In *Proceedings of the main conference on Human Language Technology Conference of the North American Chapter of the Association of Computational Linguistics*, HLT-NAACL '06, pages 455–462, Stroudsburg, PA, USA. Association for Computational Linguistics.

Koehn, P. (2012). Simulating human judgment in machine translation evaluation campaigns. In *International Workshop on Spoken Language Translation (IWSLT)*.

Koehn, P. and Monz, C. (2006). Manual and automatic evaluation of machine translation between European languages. In *Proceedings of NAACL 2006 Workshop on Statistical Machine Translation*, New York, New York.

Kononenko, I. (1994). Estimating attributes: analysis and extensions of RELIEF. In *Proceedings of the European conference on machine learning on Machine Learning*, pages 171–182, Secaucus, NJ, USA. Springer-Verlag New York, Inc.

Kos, K. and Bojar, O. (2009). Evaluation of Machine Translation Metrics for Czech as the Target Language. *Prague Bulletin of Mathematical Linguistics*, 92:135–147.

Landis, J. R. and Koch, G. G. (1977). The measurement of observer agreement for categorical data. *Biometrics*, 33:159–174.

Langlois, D., Raybaud, S., and Smaïli, K. (2012). Loria system for the wmt12 quality estimation shared task. In *Proceedings of the Seventh Workshop on Statistical Machine Translation*, pages 114–119, Montréal, Canada.

Langlois, D. and Smaili, K. (2013). LORIA system for the WMT13 quality estimation shared task. In *Proceedings of the Eighth Workshop on Statistical Machine Translation*, pages 378–383, Sofia, Bulgaria. Association for Computational Linguistics.

Le, H. S., Oparin, I., Allauzen, A., Gauvain, J.-L., and Yvon, F. (2011). Structured output layer neural network language model. In *ICASSP*, pages 5524–5527.

Lin, C.-J., Weng, R. C., and Keerthi, S. S. (2007). Trust region Newton methods for large-scale logistic regression. In *Proceedings of the 24th international conference on Machine learning - ICML '07*, pages 561–568, New York, New York, USA. ACM Press.

Luong, N. Q., Lecouteux, B., and Besacier, L. (2013). LIG system for WMT13 QE task: Investigating the usefulness of features in word confidence estimation for MT. In *Proceedings of the Eighth Workshop on Statistical Machine Translation*, pages 384–389, Sofia, Bulgaria. Association for Computational Linguistics.

Macháček, M. and Bojar, O. (2013). Results of the WMT13 metrics shared task. In *Proceedings of the Eighth Workshop on Statistical Machine Translation*, pages 43–49, Sofia, Bulgaria. Association for Computational Linguistics.

Matusov, E. and Leusch, G. (2013). Omnifluent English-to-French and Russian-to-English systems for the 2013 Workshop on Statistical Machine Translation. In *Proceedings of the Eighth Workshop on Statistical Machine Translation*, pages 156–161, Sofia, Bulgaria. Association for Computational Linguistics.

McCallum, A. K. (2002). MALLET: a machine learning for language toolkit.

Miceli Barone, A. V. and Attardi, G. (2013). Pre-reordering for machine translation using transition-based walks on dependency parse trees. In *Proceedings of the Eighth Workshop on Statistical Machine Translation*, pages 162–167, Sofia, Bulgaria. Association for Computational Linguistics.

Moreau, E. and Rubino, R. (2013). An approach using style classification features for quality estimation. In *Proceedings of the Eighth Workshop on Statistical Machine Translation*, pages 427–432, Sofia, Bulgaria. Association for Computational Linguistics.

Nadejde, M., Williams, P., and Koehn, P. (2013). Edinburgh's syntax-based machine translation systems. In *Proceedings of the Eighth Workshop on Statistical Machine Translation*, pages 168–174, Sofia, Bulgaria. Association for Computational Linguistics.

Okita, T., Liu, Q., and van Genabith, J. (2013). Shallow semantically-informed PBSMT and HPBSMT. In *Proceedings of the Eighth Workshop on Statistical Machine Translation*, pages 175–182, Sofia, Bulgaria. Association for Computational Linguistics.

Özgür, A., Özgür, L., and Güngör, T. (2005). Text

categorization with class-based and corpus-based keyword selection. In *Proceedings of the 20th International Conference on Computer and Information Sciences*, ISCIS'05, pages 606–615, Berlin, Heidelberg. Springer.

Peitz, S., Mansour, S., Huck, M., Freitag, M., Ney, H., Cho, E., Herrmann, T., Mediani, M., Niehues, J., Waibel, A., Allauzen, A., Khanh Do, Q., Buschbeck, B., and Wandmacher, T. (2013a). Joint WMT 2013 submission of the QUAERO project. In *Proceedings of the Eighth Workshop on Statistical Machine Translation*, pages 183–190, Sofia, Bulgaria. Association for Computational Linguistics.

Peitz, S., Mansour, S., Peter, J.-T., Schmidt, C., Wuebker, J., Huck, M., Freitag, M., and Ney, H. (2013b). The RWTH aachen machine translation system for WMT 2013. In *Proceedings of the Eighth Workshop on Statistical Machine Translation*, pages 191–197, Sofia, Bulgaria. Association for Computational Linguistics.

Pighin, D., Formiga, L., and Màrquez, L. (2012). A graph-based strategy to streamline translation quality assessments. In *Proceedings of the Tenth Conference of the Association for Machine Translation in the Americas (AMTA'2012)*, San Diego, USA.

Pino, J., Waite, A., Xiao, T., de Gispert, A., Flego, F., and Byrne, W. (2013). The University of Cambridge Russian-English system at WMT13. In *Proceedings of the Eighth Workshop on Statistical Machine Translation*, pages 198–203, Sofia, Bulgaria. Association for Computational Linguistics.

Post, M., Ganitkevitch, J., Orland, L., Weese, J., Cao, Y., and Callison-Burch, C. (2013). Joshua 5.0: Sparser, better, faster, server. In *Proceedings of the Eighth Workshop on Statistical Machine Translation*, pages 204–210, Sofia, Bulgaria. Association for Computational Linguistics.

Rubino, R., Toral, A., Cortés Vaíllo, S., Xie, J., Wu, X., Doherty, S., and Liu, Q. (2013a). The CNGL-DCU-Prompsit translation systems for WMT13. In *Proceedings of the Eighth Workshop on Statistical Machine Translation*, pages 211–216, Sofia, Bulgaria. Association for Computational Linguistics.

Rubino, R., Wagner, J., Foster, J., Roturier, J., Samad Zadeh Kaljahi, R., and Hollowood, F. (2013b). DCU-Symantec at the WMT 2013 quality estimation shared task. In *Proceedings of the Eighth Workshop on Statistical Machine Translation*, pages 390–395, Sofia, Bulgaria. Association for Computational Linguistics.

Sajjad, H., Smekalova, S., Durrani, N., Fraser, A., and Schmid, H. (2013). QCRI-MES submission at WMT13: Using transliteration mining to improve statistical machine translation. In *Proceedings of the Eighth Workshop on Statistical Machine Translation*, pages 217–222, Sofia, Bulgaria. Association for Computational Linguistics.

Schmidt, H. (1994). Probabilistic part-of-speech tagging using decision trees. In *Proceedings of the International Conference on New Methods in Natural Language Processing*.

Seginer, Y. (2007). *Learning Syntactic Structure*. PhD thesis, University of Amsterdam.

Shah, K., Cohn, T., and Specia, L. (2013). An Investigation on the Effectiveness of Features for Translation Quality Estimation. In *Proceedings of MT Summit XIV (to appear)*, Nice, France.

Singh, A. K., Wisniewski, G., and Yvon, F. (2013). LIMSI submission for the WMT'13 quality estimation task: an experiment with n-gram posteriors. In *Proceedings of the Eighth Workshop on Statistical Machine Translation*, pages 396–402, Sofia, Bulgaria. Association for Computational Linguistics.

Smith, J., Saint-Amand, H., Plamada, M., Koehn, P., Callison-Burch, C., and Lopez, A. (2013). Dirt cheap web-scale parallel text from the Common Crawl. In *Proceedings of the 2013 Conference of the Association for Computational Linguistics (ACL 2013)*, Sofia, Bulgaria. Association for Computational Linguistics.

Snover, M., Dorr, B., Schwartz, R., Micciulla, L., and Makhoul, J. (2006). A study of translation edit rate with targeted human annotation. In *Proceedings of the 7th Biennial Conference of the Association for Machine Translation in the Americas (AMTA-2006)*, Cambridge, Massachusetts.

Snover, M., Madnani, N., Dorr, B. J., and Schwartz, R. (2009). Fluency, adequacy, or hter?: exploring different human judgments with a tunable mt metric. In *Proceedings of the Fourth Workshop on Statistical Machine Trans-*

lation, StatMT '09, pages 259–268, Stroudsburg, PA, USA. Association for Computational Linguistics.

Soricut, R., Bach, N., and Wang, Z. (2012). The SDL Language Weaver Systems in the WMT12 Quality Estimation Shared Task. In *Proceedings of the 7th Workshop on Statistical Machine Translation*, pages 145–151.

Souza, J. G. C. d., Espl-Gomis, M., Turchi, M., and Negri, M. (2013). Exploiting qualitative information from automatic word alignment for cross-lingual nlp tasks. In *The 51st Annual Meeting of the Association for Computational Linguistics - Short Papers (ACL Short Papers 2013)*.

Specia, L. (2011). Exploiting Objective Annotations for Measuring Translation Post-editing Effort. In *Proceedings of the 15th Conference of the European Association for Machine Translation*, pages 73–80, Leuven.

Specia, L., Shah, K., de Souza, J. G. C., and Cohn, T. (2013). QuEst - A Translation Quality Estimation Framework. In *Proceedings of the 51th Conference of the Association for Computational Linguistics (ACL), Demo Session*, Sofia, Bulgaria. Association for Computational Linguistics.

Stolcke, A. (2002). SRILM – An extensible language modeling toolkit. In *Proceedings of the 7th International Conference on Spoken Language Processing (ICSLP 2002)*, pages 901–904.

Stone, M. and Brooks, R. J. (1990). Continuum regression: cross-validated sequentially constructed prediction embracing ordinary least squares, partial least squares and principal components regression. *Journal of the Royal Statistical Society Series B Methodological*, 52(2):237–269.

Stymne, S., Hardmeier, C., Tiedemann, J., and Nivre, J. (2013). Tunable distortion limits and corpus cleaning for SMT. In *Proceedings of the Eighth Workshop on Statistical Machine Translation*, pages 223–229, Sofia, Bulgaria. Association for Computational Linguistics.

Tantug, A. C., Oflazer, K., and El-Kahlout, I. D. (2008). BLEU+: a Tool for Fine-Grained BLEU Computation. In (ELRA), E. L. R. A., editor, *Proceedings of the Sixth International Language Resources and Evaluation (LREC'08)*, Marrakech, Morocco.

Weller, M., Kisselew, M., Smekalova, S., Fraser, A., Schmid, H., Durrani, N., Sajjad, H., and Farkas, R. (2013). Munich-Edinburgh-Stuttgart submissions at WMT13: Morphological and syntactic processing for SMT. In *Proceedings of the Eighth Workshop on Statistical Machine Translation*, pages 230–237, Sofia, Bulgaria. Association for Computational Linguistics.

A Pairwise System Comparisons by Human Judges

Tables 21–30 show pairwise comparisons between systems for each language pair. The numbers in each of the tables' cells indicate the percentage of times that the system in that column was judged to be better than the system in that row, ignoring ties. Bolding indicates the winner of the two systems.

Because there were so many systems and data conditions the significance of each pairwise comparison needs to be quantified. We applied the Sign Test to measure which comparisons indicate genuine differences (rather than differences that are attributable to chance). In the following tables ⋆ indicates statistical significance at $p \le 0.10$, † indicates statistical significance at $p \le 0.05$, and ‡ indicates statistical significance at $p \le 0.01$, according to the Sign Test.

Each table contains final rows showing how likely a system would win when paired against a randomly selected system (the expected win ratio score) and the rank range according bootstrap resampling ($p \le 0.05$). Gray lines separate clusters based on non-overlapping rank ranges.

	UEDIN-HEAFIELD	ONLINE-B	MES	UEDIN	ONLINE-A	UEDIN-SYNTAX	CU-ZEMAN	CU-TAMCHYNA	DCU-FDA	JHU	SHEF-WPROA
UEDIN-HEAFIELD	–	.50	.48†	.43‡	.47†	.43‡	.44‡	.38‡	.32‡	.25‡	.26‡
ONLINE-B	.50	–	.46‡	.48†	.47†	.49	.44‡	.40‡	.39‡	.29‡	.27‡
MES	**.52†**	**.54‡**	–	.49	.47⋆	.44‡	.45‡	.42‡	.41‡	.27‡	.25‡
UEDIN	**.57‡**	**.52†**	**.51**	–	**.51**	.48†	.47‡	.42‡	.39‡	.28‡	.25‡
ONLINE-A	**.53†**	**.53†**	**.53⋆**	.49	–	.48	**.51**	.44‡	.42‡	.31‡	.30‡
UEDIN-SYNTAX	**.57‡**	**.51**	**.56‡**	**.52†**	**.52**	–	**.51**	.43‡	.41‡	.29‡	.26‡
CU-ZEMAN	**.56‡**	**.56‡**	**.55‡**	**.53‡**	.49	.49	–	.45‡	.42‡	.32‡	.29‡
CU-TAMCHYNA	**.62‡**	**.60‡**	**.58‡**	**.58‡**	**.56‡**	**.57‡**	**.55‡**	–	.46‡	.35‡	.32‡
DCU-FDA	**.68‡**	**.61‡**	**.59‡**	**.61‡**	**.58‡**	**.59‡**	**.58‡**	**.54‡**	–	.32‡	.32‡
JHU	**.75‡**	**.71‡**	**.73‡**	**.72‡**	**.69‡**	**.71‡**	**.68‡**	**.65‡**	**.68‡**	–	.46‡
SHEF-WPROA	**.74‡**	**.73‡**	**.75‡**	**.75‡**	**.70‡**	**.74‡**	**.71‡**	**.68‡**	**.68‡**	**.54‡**	–
score	.60	.58	.57	.56	.54	.54	.53	.48	.45	.32	.29
rank	1	2-3	2-4	3-5	4-7	5-7	6-7	8	9	10	11

Table 21: Head to head comparison, ignoring ties, for Czech-English systems

	CU-BOJAR	CU-DEPFIX	ONLINE-B	UEDIN	CU-ZEMAN	MES	ONLINE-A	CU-PHRASEFIX	CU-TECTOMT	COMMERCIAL-1	COMMERCIAL-2	SHEF-WPROA
CU-BOJAR	–	**.51**	.47†	.44‡	.42‡	.43‡	.48	.41‡	.37‡	.39‡	.38‡	.33‡
CU-DEPFIX	.49	–	.48⋆	.42‡	.43‡	.41‡	.47†	.42‡	.40‡	.40‡	.39‡	.34‡
ONLINE-B	**.53†**	**.52⋆**	–	.47‡	.44‡	.44‡	.44‡	.44‡	.44‡	.41‡	.36‡	.34‡
UEDIN	**.56‡**	**.58‡**	**.53‡**	–	.47†	.47‡	.48	.45‡	.44‡	.42‡	.43‡	.38‡
CU-ZEMAN	**.58‡**	**.57‡**	**.56‡**	**.53†**	–	.49	.49	.48†	.46‡	.47‡	.47‡	.35‡
MES	**.57‡**	**.59‡**	**.56‡**	**.53‡**	**.51**	–	.50	.47†	.46‡	.43‡	.44‡	.42‡
ONLINE-A	**.52**	**.53†**	**.56‡**	**.52**	**.51**	.50	–	**.52**	.47⋆	.47†	.47†	.46†
CU-PHRASEFIX	**.59‡**	**.58‡**	**.56‡**	**.55‡**	**.52†**	**.53†**	.48	–	.49	.48†	.49	.42‡
CU-TECTOMT	**.63‡**	**.60‡**	**.56‡**	**.56‡**	**.54‡**	**.54‡**	**.53⋆**	**.51**	–	.46‡	.46‡	.40‡
COMMERCIAL-1	**.61‡**	**.60‡**	**.59‡**	**.58‡**	**.53‡**	**.57‡**	**.53†**	**.52†**	**.54‡**	–	.49	.42‡
COMMERCIAL-2	**.62‡**	**.61‡**	**.64‡**	**.57‡**	**.53‡**	**.56‡**	**.53†**	**.51**	**.54‡**	**.51**	–	.43‡
SHEF-WPROA	**.67‡**	**.66‡**	**.66‡**	**.62‡**	**.65‡**	**.58‡**	**.54†**	**.58‡**	**.60‡**	**.58‡**	**.57‡**	–
score	.58	.57	.56	.52	.50	.50	.49	.48	.47	.45	.45	.38
rank	1-2	1-2	3	4	5-7	5-7	5-8	7-9	8-9	10-11	10-11	12

Table 22: Head to head comparison, ignoring ties, for English-Czech systems

	ONLINE-B	ONLINE-A	UEDIN-SYNTAX	UEDIN	QUAERO	KIT	MES	RWTH-JANE	MES-SZEGED-REORDER-SPLIT	LIMSI-NCODE-SOUL	TUBITAK	UMD	DCU	CU-ZEMAN	JHU	SHEF-WPROA	DESRT
ONLINE-B	–	.48	.44‡	.37‡	.44‡	.41‡	.42‡	.40‡	.35‡	.37‡	.32‡	.31‡	.31‡	.27‡	.23‡	.18‡	.16‡
ONLINE-A	**.52**	–	.47	.45†	.47	.43‡	.42‡	.41‡	.44‡	.40‡	.35‡	.36‡	.34‡	.31‡	.27‡	.25‡	.21‡
UEDIN-SYNTAX	**.56‡**	**.53**	–	.48	.46†	.48⋆	.46†	.46†	.45‡	.45‡	.35‡	.35‡	.34‡	.28‡	.25‡	.20‡	.19‡
UEDIN	**.63‡**	**.55†**	**.52**	–	**.51**	.46‡	.47†	.49	.44‡	.43‡	.39‡	.34‡	.35‡	.32‡	.28‡	.24‡	.22‡
QUAERO	**.56‡**	**.53**	**.54†**	.49	–	.49	**.52**	.44‡	.46‡	.44‡	.39‡	.38‡	.37‡	.30‡	.31‡	.25‡	.21‡
KIT	**.59‡**	**.57‡**	**.52⋆**	**.54‡**	**.51**	–	.45‡	**.51**	.43‡	.46‡	.37‡	.38‡	.41‡	.35‡	.31‡	.25‡	.21‡
MES	**.58‡**	**.58‡**	**.54†**	**.53†**	.48	**.55‡**	–	.49	.49	.46‡	.44‡	.37‡	.40‡	.34‡	.30‡	.26‡	.20‡
RWTH-JANE	**.60‡**	**.59‡**	**.54†**	**.51**	**.56‡**	.49	**.51**	–	.46‡	.50	.45‡	.46‡	.47†	.38‡	.33‡	.28‡	.20‡
MES-SZEGED-REORDER-SPLIT	**.65‡**	**.56‡**	**.55‡**	**.56‡**	**.54‡**	**.57‡**	**.51**	**.54‡**	–	**.53⋆**	.44‡	.41‡	.41‡	.36‡	.34‡	.31‡	.21‡
LIMSI-NCODE-SOUL	**.63‡**	**.60‡**	**.55‡**	**.57‡**	**.56‡**	**.54‡**	**.54‡**	.50	.47⋆	–	**.51**	.45‡	.43‡	.37‡	.34‡	.30‡	.22‡
TUBITAK	**.68‡**	**.65‡**	**.65‡**	**.61‡**	**.61‡**	**.63‡**	**.56‡**	**.55‡**	**.56‡**	.49	–	.48⋆	.49	.39‡	.41‡	.30‡	.25‡
UMD	**.69‡**	**.64‡**	**.65‡**	**.66‡**	**.62‡**	**.62‡**	**.63‡**	**.54‡**	**.59‡**	**.55‡**	**.52⋆**	–	.48⋆	.41‡	.40‡	.33‡	.27‡
DCU	**.69‡**	**.66‡**	**.66‡**	**.65‡**	**.63‡**	**.59‡**	**.60‡**	**.53†**	**.59‡**	**.57‡**	**.51**	**.52⋆**	–	.41‡	.38‡	.37‡	.25‡
CU-ZEMAN	**.73‡**	**.69‡**	**.72‡**	**.68‡**	**.70‡**	**.65‡**	**.66‡**	**.62‡**	**.64‡**	**.63‡**	**.61‡**	**.59‡**	**.59‡**	–	.44‡	.43‡	.29‡
JHU	**.77‡**	**.73‡**	**.75‡**	**.72‡**	**.69‡**	**.69‡**	**.70‡**	**.67‡**	**.66‡**	**.66‡**	**.59‡**	**.60‡**	**.62‡**	**.56‡**	–	.43‡	.30‡
SHEF-WPROA	**.82‡**	**.75‡**	**.80‡**	**.76‡**	**.75‡**	**.75‡**	**.74‡**	**.72‡**	**.69‡**	**.70‡**	**.70‡**	**.67‡**	**.63‡**	**.57‡**	**.57‡**	–	.41‡
DESRT	**.84‡**	**.79‡**	**.81‡**	**.78‡**	**.79‡**	**.79‡**	**.80‡**	**.80‡**	**.79‡**	**.78‡**	**.75‡**	**.73‡**	**.75‡**	**.71‡**	**.70‡**	**.59‡**	–
score	.66	.62	.60	.58	.58	.57	.56	.54	.53	.52	.48	.46	.46	.39	.36	.31	.23
rank	1	2-3	2-3	4-5	4-5	5-7	6-7	8-9	8-10	9-10	11	12-13	12-13	14	15	16	17

Table 23: Head to head comparison, ignoring ties, for German-English systems

	ONLINE-B	PROMT	UEDIN-SYNTAX	ONLINE-A	UEDIN	KIT	STANFORD	LIMSI-NCODE-SOUL	MES-REORDER	JHU	CU-ZEMAN	TUBITAK	UU	SHEF-WPROA	RWTH-JANE
ONLINE-B	–	**.55‡**	.50	.45⋆	.45‡	.34‡	.37‡	.37‡	.37‡	.32‡	.32‡	.33‡	.24‡	.21‡	.26‡
PROMT	.45‡	–	.48⋆	.50	.43‡	.40‡	.39‡	.36‡	.37‡	.31‡	.31‡	.32‡	.27‡	.24‡	.27‡
UEDIN-SYNTAX	.50	**.52⋆**	–	**.57†**	.45‡	.43‡	.38‡	.41‡	.39‡	.38‡	.33‡	.33‡	.26‡	.25‡	.22‡
ONLINE-A	**.55⋆**	.50	.43†	–	**.51**	.42†	.48	.41‡	.36‡	.44⋆	.44⋆	.38‡	.32‡	.27‡	.29‡
UEDIN	**.55‡**	**.57‡**	**.55‡**	.49	–	**.52**	.45‡	.45‡	.42‡	.43‡	.37‡	.34‡	.29‡	.27‡	.31‡
KIT	**.66‡**	**.60‡**	**.57‡**	**.58†**	.48	–	.48	.45‡	.42‡	.36‡	.39‡	.40‡	.30‡	.29‡	.26‡
STANFORD	**.63‡**	**.61‡**	**.62‡**	**.52**	**.55‡**	**.52**	–	.50	.44‡	.48	.44‡	.43‡	.34‡	.29‡	.32‡
LIMSI-NCODE-SOUL	**.63‡**	**.64‡**	**.59‡**	**.59‡**	**.55‡**	**.55‡**	.50	–	.44‡	.44‡	.44‡	.47†	.40‡	.34‡	.33‡
MES-REORDER	**.63‡**	**.63‡**	**.61‡**	**.64‡**	**.58‡**	**.58‡**	**.56‡**	**.56‡**	–	.50	.46‡	.49	.38‡	.37‡	.34‡
JHU	**.68‡**	**.69‡**	**.62‡**	**.56⋆**	**.57‡**	**.64‡**	**.52**	**.56‡**	.50	–	.48⋆	.45‡	.36‡	.37‡	.34‡
CU-ZEMAN	**.68‡**	**.69‡**	**.67‡**	**.56⋆**	**.63‡**	**.61‡**	**.56‡**	**.56‡**	**.54‡**	**.52⋆**	–	.48	.40‡	.33‡	.34‡
TUBITAK	**.67‡**	**.68‡**	**.67‡**	**.62‡**	**.66‡**	**.60‡**	**.57‡**	**.53†**	**.51**	**.55‡**	**.52**	–	.38‡	.40‡	.32‡
UU	**.76‡**	**.73‡**	**.74‡**	**.68‡**	**.71‡**	**.70‡**	**.66‡**	**.60‡**	**.62‡**	**.64‡**	**.60‡**	**.62‡**	–	.44‡	.46†
SHEF-WPROA	**.79‡**	**.76‡**	**.75‡**	**.73‡**	**.73‡**	**.71‡**	**.71‡**	**.66‡**	**.63‡**	**.63‡**	**.67‡**	**.60‡**	**.56‡**	–	.47†
RWTH-JANE	**.74‡**	**.73‡**	**.78‡**	**.71‡**	**.69‡**	**.74‡**	**.68‡**	**.67‡**	**.66‡**	**.66‡**	**.66‡**	**.68‡**	**.54†**	**.53†**	–
score	.63	.63	.61	.58	.57	.55	.52	.50	.47	.47	.46	.45	.36	.32	.32
rank	1-2	1-2	3	3-5	4-6	5-6	7	8	9-11	9-11	10-12	11-12	13	14-15	14-15

Table 24: Head to head comparison, ignoring ties, for English-German systems

	UEDIN-HEAFIELD	UEDIN	ONLINE-B	LIMSI-NCODE-SOUL	KIT	ONLINE-A	MES-SIMPLIFIEDFRENCH	DCU	RWTH	CMU-TREE-TO-TREE	CU-ZEMAN	JHU	SHEF-WPROA
UEDIN-HEAFIELD	–	.45‡	.46‡	.46‡	.42‡	.42‡	.34‡	.34‡	.29‡	.33‡	.31‡	.28‡	.24‡
UEDIN	**.55‡**	–	**.52⋆**	.43‡	.45‡	.46⋆	.40‡	.38‡	.33‡	.36‡	.33‡	.32‡	.23‡
ONLINE-B	**.54‡**	.48⋆	–	.49	.46‡	.44‡	.45‡	.40‡	.38‡	.34‡	.36‡	.31‡	.26‡
LIMSI-NCODE-SOUL	**.54‡**	**.57‡**	**.51**	–	**.52⋆**	.47	.45‡	.42‡	.38‡	.36‡	.34‡	.31‡	.28‡
KIT	**.58‡**	**.55‡**	**.54‡**	.48⋆	–	.47	.46‡	.44‡	.39‡	.38‡	.37‡	.33‡	.28‡
ONLINE-A	**.58‡**	**.54⋆**	**.56‡**	**.53**	**.53**	–	.47	.45†	.40‡	.40‡	.39‡	.34‡	.32‡
MES-SIMPLIFIEDFRENCH	**.66‡**	**.60‡**	**.55‡**	**.55‡**	**.54‡**	**.53**	–	.48⋆	.44‡	.40‡	.39‡	.39‡	.32‡
DCU	**.66‡**	**.62‡**	**.60‡**	**.58‡**	**.56‡**	**.55†**	**.52⋆**	–	.45‡	.45‡	.42‡	.41‡	.36‡
RWTH	**.71‡**	**.67‡**	**.62‡**	**.62‡**	**.61‡**	**.60‡**	**.56‡**	**.55‡**	–	.48⋆	.47†	.47⋆	.38‡
CMU-TREE-TO-TREE	**.67‡**	**.64‡**	**.66‡**	**.64‡**	**.62‡**	**.60‡**	**.60‡**	**.55‡**	**.52⋆**	–	.50	.48	.37‡
CU-ZEMAN	**.69‡**	**.67‡**	**.64‡**	**.66‡**	**.63‡**	**.61‡**	**.61‡**	**.58‡**	**.53†**	.50	–	.47†	.39‡
JHU	**.72‡**	**.68‡**	**.69‡**	**.69‡**	**.67‡**	**.66‡**	**.61‡**	**.59‡**	**.53⋆**	**.52**	**.53†**	–	.45‡
SHEF-WPROA	**.76‡**	**.77‡**	**.74‡**	**.72‡**	**.72‡**	**.68‡**	**.68‡**	**.64‡**	**.62‡**	**.63‡**	**.61‡**	**.55‡**	–
score	.63	.60	.59	.57	.56	.54	.51	.48	.43	.42	.42	.38	.32
rank	1	2-3	2-3	4-5	4-5	5-6	7	8	9-10	9-11	10-11	12	13

Table 25: Head to head comparison, ignoring ties, for French-English systems

	UEDIN	ONLINE-B	LIMSI-NCODE-SOUL	KIT	PROMT	STANFORD	MES	MES-INFLECTION	RWTH-PHRASE-BASED-JANE	ONLINE-A	DCU	CU-ZEMAN	JHU	OMNIFLUENT	ITS-LATL	ITS-LATL-PE
UEDIN	–	.49	.47⋆	.48	.50	.44‡	.41‡	.40‡	.47⋆	.39‡	.41‡	.35‡	.29‡	.30‡	.27‡	.24‡
ONLINE-B	**.51**	–	.46‡	.47⋆	.47†	.44‡	.49	.43‡	.43‡	.43‡	.38‡	.35‡	.36‡	.28‡	.25‡	.25‡
LIMSI-NCODE-SOUL	**.53⋆**	**.54‡**	–	.45‡	.48	.48	.45‡	.43‡	.44‡	.45†	.41‡	.32‡	.34‡	.30‡	.27‡	.27‡
KIT	**.52**	**.53⋆**	**.55‡**	–	.48	.46†	.45‡	.43‡	.45‡	.46⋆	.38‡	.30‡	.33‡	.31‡	.29‡	.29‡
PROMT	.50	**.53†**	**.52**	**.52**	–	.50	.48	**.52⋆**	.45‡	.47	.48⋆	.38‡	.36‡	.36‡	.34‡	.31‡
STANFORD	**.56‡**	**.56‡**	**.52**	**.54†**	.50	–	**.52**	.48	.44‡	.49	.44‡	.39‡	.34‡	.36‡	.30‡	.29‡
MES	**.59‡**	**.51**	**.55‡**	**.55‡**	**.52**	.48	–	**.52**	**.51**	.45⋆	.45‡	.36‡	.37‡	.34‡	.29‡	.29‡
MES-INFLECTION	**.60‡**	**.57‡**	**.57‡**	**.57‡**	.48⋆	**.52**	.48	–	**.54†**	**.51**	.46†	.37‡	.35‡	.31‡	.33‡	.31‡
RWTH-PHRASE-BASED-JANE	**.53⋆**	**.57‡**	**.56‡**	**.55‡**	**.55‡**	**.56‡**	.49	.46†	–	**.53**	.49	.38‡	.36‡	.34‡	.35‡	.31‡
ONLINE-A	**.61‡**	**.57‡**	**.55†**	**.54⋆**	**.53**	**.51**	**.55⋆**	.49	.47	–	.50	.45†	.38‡	.38‡	.39‡	.35‡
DCU	**.59‡**	**.62‡**	**.59‡**	**.62‡**	**.52⋆**	**.56‡**	**.55‡**	**.54†**	**.51**	.50	–	.42‡	.40‡	.40‡	.36‡	.35‡
CU-ZEMAN	**.65‡**	**.65‡**	**.68‡**	**.70‡**	**.62‡**	**.61‡**	**.64‡**	**.63‡**	**.62‡**	**.55†**	**.58‡**	–	.50	.42‡	.41‡	.37‡
JHU	**.71‡**	**.64‡**	**.66‡**	**.67‡**	**.64‡**	**.66‡**	**.63‡**	**.65‡**	**.64‡**	**.62‡**	**.60‡**	.50	–	.47‡	.42‡	.38‡
OMNIFLUENT	**.70‡**	**.72‡**	**.70‡**	**.69‡**	**.64‡**	**.64‡**	**.66‡**	**.69‡**	**.66‡**	**.62‡**	**.60‡**	**.58‡**	**.53‡**	–	.43‡	.42‡
ITS-LATL	**.73‡**	**.75‡**	**.72‡**	**.71‡**	**.66‡**	**.70‡**	**.71‡**	**.67‡**	**.65‡**	**.61‡**	**.64‡**	**.59‡**	**.58‡**	**.57‡**	–	.45‡
ITS-LATL-PE	**.76‡**	**.75‡**	**.73‡**	**.71‡**	**.69‡**	**.71‡**	**.71‡**	**.69‡**	**.69‡**	**.65‡**	**.65‡**	**.63‡**	**.62‡**	**.58‡**	**.55‡**	–
score	.60	.60	.58	.58	.55	.55	.54	.53	.53	.51	.49	.42	.40	.38	.35	.32
rank	1-2	1-3	2-4	3-4	5-7	5-8	5-8	6-9	7-10	9-11	10-11	12	13	14	15	16

Table 26: Head to head comparison, ignoring ties, for English-French systems

	UEDIN-HEAFIELD	ONLINE-B	UEDIN	ONLINE-A	MES	LIMSI-NCODE-SOUL	DCU	DCU-OKITA	DCU-FDA	CU-ZEMAN	JHU	SHEF-WPROA
UEDIN-HEAFIELD	–	.49	.42‡	.45⋆	.43‡	.40‡	.34‡	.43‡	.37‡	.34‡	.31‡	.15‡
ONLINE-B	**.51**	–	.49	.44‡	.46‡	.47†	.42‡	.39‡	.40‡	.37‡	.37‡	.16‡
UEDIN	**.58‡**	**.51**	–	**.55†**	.50	.47†	.43‡	.42‡	.39‡	.39‡	.35‡	.14‡
ONLINE-A	**.55⋆**	**.56‡**	.45†	–	.50	.44‡	.45†	.42‡	.42‡	.41‡	.37‡	.18‡
MES	**.57‡**	**.54‡**	.50	.50	–	.47†	.45‡	.41‡	.41‡	.40‡	.38‡	.15‡
LIMSI-NCODE-SOUL	**.60‡**	**.53†**	**.53†**	**.56‡**	**.53†**	–	.46‡	.45‡	.44‡	.43‡	.38‡	.18‡
DCU	**.66‡**	**.58‡**	**.57‡**	**.55†**	**.55‡**	**.54‡**	–	.44‡	.47†	.42‡	.41‡	.16‡
DCU-OKITA	**.57‡**	**.61‡**	**.58‡**	**.58‡**	**.59‡**	**.55‡**	**.56‡**	–	.49	.46‡	.46‡	.18‡
DCU-FDA	**.63‡**	**.60‡**	**.61‡**	**.58‡**	**.59‡**	**.56‡**	**.53†**	**.51**	–	.48⋆	.43‡	.18‡
CU-ZEMAN	**.66‡**	**.63‡**	**.61‡**	**.59‡**	**.60‡**	**.57‡**	**.58‡**	**.54‡**	**.52⋆**	–	.43‡	.18‡
JHU	**.69‡**	**.63‡**	**.65‡**	**.63‡**	**.62‡**	**.62‡**	**.59‡**	**.54‡**	**.57‡**	**.57‡**	–	.22‡
SHEF-WPROA	**.85‡**	**.84‡**	**.86‡**	**.82‡**	**.85‡**	**.82‡**	**.84‡**	**.82‡**	**.82‡**	**.82‡**	**.78‡**	–
score	.62	.59	.57	.57	.56	.53	.51	.48	.48	.46	.42	.16
rank	1	2	3-5	3-5	3-5	6	7	8-9	8-9	10	11	12

Table 27: Head to head comparison, ignoring ties, for Spanish-English systems

	ONLINE-B	ONLINE-A	UEDIN	PROMT	MES	TALP-UPC	LIMSI-NCODE	DCU	DCU-FDA	DCU-OKITA	CU-ZEMAN	JHU	SHEF-WPROA
ONLINE-B	–	.49	.45‡	.43‡	.38‡	.35‡	.34‡	.35‡	.37‡	.34‡	.33‡	.32‡	.23‡
ONLINE-A	**.51**	–	.49	.48	.38‡	.46⋆	.42‡	.41‡	.43‡	.38‡	.38‡	.37‡	.31‡
UEDIN	**.55‡**	**.51**	–	.49	.46†	.45‡	.43‡	.42‡	.36‡	.38‡	.38‡	.38‡	.26‡
PROMT	**.57‡**	**.52**	**.51**	–	.46‡	.48	.43‡	.43‡	.40‡	.37‡	.39‡	.34‡	.29‡
MES	**.62‡**	**.62‡**	**.54†**	**.54‡**	–	.46‡	.44‡	.44‡	.41‡	.40‡	.43‡	.36‡	.32‡
TALP-UPC	**.65‡**	**.54⋆**	**.55‡**	**.52**	**.54‡**	–	.50	.45‡	.44‡	.40‡	.40‡	.37‡	.32‡
LIMSI-NCODE	**.66‡**	**.58‡**	**.57‡**	**.57‡**	**.56‡**	.50	–	.46‡	**.51**	.48	.44‡	.45‡	.35‡
DCU	**.65‡**	**.59‡**	**.58‡**	**.57‡**	**.56‡**	**.55‡**	**.54‡**	–	.50	.48	.48	.45‡	.36‡
DCU-FDA	**.63‡**	**.57‡**	**.64‡**	**.60‡**	**.59‡**	**.56‡**	.49	.50	–	**.53⋆**	.49	.42‡	.32‡
DCU-OKITA	**.66‡**	**.62‡**	**.62‡**	**.63‡**	**.60‡**	**.60‡**	**.52**	**.52**	.47⋆	–	.50	.47†	.36‡
CU-ZEMAN	**.67‡**	**.62‡**	**.62‡**	**.61‡**	**.57‡**	**.60‡**	**.56‡**	**.52**	**.51**	.50	–	.46‡	.40‡
JHU	**.68‡**	**.63‡**	**.62‡**	**.66‡**	**.64‡**	**.63‡**	**.55‡**	**.55‡**	**.58‡**	**.53†**	**.54‡**	–	.37‡
SHEF-WPROA	**.77‡**	**.69‡**	**.74‡**	**.71‡**	**.68‡**	**.68‡**	**.65‡**	**.64‡**	**.68‡**	**.64‡**	**.60‡**	**.63‡**	–
score	.63	.58	.57	.56	.53	.52	.49	.47	.47	.45	.44	.41	.32
rank	1	2-4	2-4	3-4	5-6	5-6	7-8	7-9	8-10	9-11	10-11	12	13

Table 28: Head to head comparison, ignoring ties, for English-Spanish systems

	ONLINE-B	CMU	ONLINE-A	ONLINE-G	PROMT	QCRI-MES	UCAM-MULTIFRONTEND	BALAGUR	MES-QCRI	UEDIN	OMNIFLUENT-UNCNSTR	LIA	OMNIFLUENT-CNSTR	UMD	CU-KAREL	COMMERCIAL-3	UEDIN-SYNTAX	JHU	CU-ZEMAN
ONLINE-B	–	.40‡	.42‡	.41‡	.37‡	.37‡	.41‡	.33‡	.33‡	.37‡	.33‡	.33‡	.35‡	.38‡	.34‡	.33‡	.29‡	.28‡	.14‡
CMU	**.60**‡	–	.50	.46†	.43‡	.47†	.42‡	.42‡	.39‡	.43‡	.41‡	.41‡	.40‡	.38‡	.36‡	.30‡	.30‡	.29‡	.17‡
ONLINE-A	**.58**‡	.50	–	.50	**.51**	.43‡	.47⋆	.44‡	.40‡	.41‡	.43‡	.38‡	.40‡	.38‡	.38‡	.39‡	.34‡	.30‡	.19‡
ONLINE-G	**.59**‡	**.54**†	.50	–	**.55**†	.50	**.51**	.48	.42‡	.41‡	.44‡	.43‡	.46†	.40‡	.44‡	.36‡	.34‡	.33‡	.19‡
PROMT	**.63**‡	**.57**‡	.49	.45†	–	.43‡	.47†	.43‡	.47†	.47†	.43‡	.39‡	.44‡	.43‡	.37‡	.41‡	.40‡	.38‡	.25‡
QCRI-MES	**.63**‡	**.53**†	**.57**‡	.50	**.57**‡	–	.48	.46†	.47⋆	.45‡	.43‡	.45‡	.45‡	.38‡	.42‡	.37‡	.33‡	.40‡	.19‡
UCAM-MULTIFRONTEND	**.59**‡	**.58**‡	**.53**⋆	.49	**.53**†	**.52**	–	.47†	.48	.46‡	.46‡	.42‡	.45‡	.46‡	.45‡	.40‡	.39‡	.33‡	.17‡
BALAGUR	**.67**‡	**.58**‡	**.56**‡	**.52**	**.57**‡	**.54**†	**.53**†	–	.47†	.49	.45‡	**.53**⋆	.40‡	.44‡	.44‡	.41‡	.36‡	.33‡	.23‡
MES-QCRI	**.67**‡	**.61**‡	**.60**‡	**.58**‡	**.53**†	**.53**⋆	**.52**	**.53**†	–	.49	.47†	.47⋆	.43‡	.43‡	.44‡	.38‡	.42‡	.39‡	.17‡
UEDIN	**.63**‡	**.57**‡	**.59**‡	**.59**‡	**.53**†	**.55**‡	**.54**‡	**.51**	**.51**	–	.48	**.52**	.44‡	**.52**	.49	.42‡	.43‡	.35‡	.21‡
OMNIFLUENT-UNCNSTR	**.67**‡	**.59**‡	**.57**‡	**.56**‡	**.57**‡	**.57**‡	**.54**‡	**.55**‡	**.53**†	**.52**	–	**.51**	.46†	.48	.48	.44‡	.40‡	.39‡	.25‡
LIA	**.67**‡	**.59**‡	**.62**‡	**.57**‡	**.61**‡	**.55**‡	**.58**‡	.47⋆	**.53**⋆	.48	.49	–	**.51**	.49	.48	.50	.41‡	.39‡	.20‡
OMNIFLUENT-CNSTR	**.65**‡	**.60**‡	**.60**‡	**.54**†	**.56**‡	**.55**‡	**.55**‡	**.60**‡	**.57**‡	**.56**‡	**.54**†	.49	–	**.51**	.48	.47⋆	.40‡	.40‡	.25‡
UMD	**.62**‡	**.62**‡	**.62**‡	**.60**‡	**.57**‡	**.62**‡	**.54**‡	**.56**‡	**.57**‡	.48	**.52**	**.51**	.49	–	**.53**†	.42‡	.46‡	.42‡	.19‡
CU-KAREL	**.66**‡	**.64**‡	**.62**‡	**.56**‡	**.63**‡	**.58**‡	**.55**‡	**.56**‡	**.56**‡	**.51**	**.52**	**.52**	**.52**	.47†	–	.44‡	.40‡	.47⋆	.24‡
COMMERCIAL-3	**.67**‡	**.70**‡	**.61**‡	**.64**‡	**.59**‡	**.63**‡	**.60**‡	**.59**‡	**.62**‡	**.58**‡	**.56**‡	.50	**.53**⋆	**.58**‡	**.56**‡	–	**.51**	.44‡	.32‡
UEDIN-SYNTAX	**.71**‡	**.70**‡	**.66**‡	**.66**‡	**.60**‡	**.67**‡	**.61**‡	**.64**‡	**.58**‡	**.57**‡	**.60**‡	**.59**‡	**.60**‡	**.54**‡	**.60**‡	.49	–	.45‡	.25‡
JHU	**.72**‡	**.71**‡	**.70**‡	**.67**‡	**.62**‡	**.60**‡	**.67**‡	**.67**‡	**.61**‡	**.65**‡	**.61**‡	**.61**‡	**.60**‡	**.58**‡	**.53**⋆	**.56**‡	**.55**‡	–	.24‡
CU-ZEMAN	**.86**‡	**.83**‡	**.81**‡	**.81**‡	**.75**‡	**.81**‡	**.83**‡	**.77**‡	**.83**‡	**.79**‡	**.75**‡	**.80**‡	**.75**‡	**.81**‡	**.76**‡	**.68**‡	**.75**‡	**.76**‡	–
score	.65	.60	.58	.56	.56	.55	.54	.52	.51	.50	.49	.49	.48	.48	.47	.43	.41	.39	.21
rank	1	2-3	2-3	4-6	4-6	5-7	5-7	8-9	8-10	9-11	10-12	11-14	12-15	12-15	13-15	16	17	18	19

Table 29: Head to head comparison, ignoring ties, for Russian-English systems

	PROMT	ONLINE-B	CMU	ONLINE-G	ONLINE-A	UEDIN	QCRI-MES	CU-KAREL	MES-QCRI	JHU	COMMERCIAL-3	LIA	BALAGUR	CU-ZEMAN
PROMT	–	.44‡	.39‡	.47	.46⋆	.36‡	.37‡	.37‡	.32‡	.35‡	.28‡	.30‡	.32‡	.24‡
ONLINE-B	**.56**‡	–	.44‡	.41‡	.44†	.38‡	.37‡	.35‡	.33‡	.39‡	.33‡	.31‡	.35‡	.24‡
CMU	**.61**‡	**.56**‡	–	**.52**	.49	.47†	.43‡	.41‡	.39‡	.44‡	.44‡	.40‡	.35‡	.28‡
ONLINE-G	**.53**	**.59**‡	.48	–	.48	.50	.48	.46	.46⋆	.42‡	.38‡	.43‡	.38‡	.36‡
ONLINE-A	**.54**⋆	**.56**†	**.51**	**.52**	–	.47	.49	.49	.48	.44†	.38‡	.40‡	.40‡	.34‡
UEDIN	**.64**‡	**.62**‡	**.53**†	.50	**.53**	–	.49	.46†	.42‡	.39‡	.44‡	.41‡	.38‡	.29‡
QCRI-MES	**.63**‡	**.63**‡	**.57**‡	**.52**	**.51**	**.51**	–	.48	.45‡	.44‡	.42‡	.39‡	.40‡	.29‡
CU-KAREL	**.63**‡	**.65**‡	**.59**‡	**.54**	**.51**	**.54**†	**.52**	–	.50	.46†	.43‡	.40‡	.42‡	.34‡
MES-QCRI	**.68**‡	**.67**‡	**.61**‡	**.54**⋆	**.52**	**.58**‡	**.55**‡	.50	–	.48⋆	.47‡	.43‡	.45‡	.34‡
JHU	**.65**‡	**.61**‡	**.56**‡	**.58**‡	**.56**†	**.61**‡	**.56**‡	**.54**†	**.52**⋆	–	**.51**	.44‡	.44‡	.33‡
COMMERCIAL-3	**.72**‡	**.67**‡	**.56**‡	**.62**‡	**.62**‡	**.56**‡	**.58**‡	**.57**‡	**.53**‡	.49	–	**.52**	.48	.44‡
LIA	**.70**‡	**.69**‡	**.60**‡	**.57**‡	**.60**‡	**.59**‡	**.61**‡	**.60**‡	**.57**‡	**.56**‡	.48	–	.47†	.41‡
BALAGUR	**.68**‡	**.65**‡	**.65**‡	**.62**‡	**.60**‡	**.62**‡	**.60**‡	**.58**‡	**.55**‡	**.56**‡	**.52**	**.53**†	–	.41‡
CU-ZEMAN	**.76**‡	**.76**‡	**.72**‡	**.64**‡	**.66**‡	**.71**‡	**.71**‡	**.66**‡	**.66**‡	**.67**‡	**.56**‡	**.59**‡	**.59**‡	–
score	.64	.62	.55	.54	.53	.53	.52	.49	.47	.46	.43	.42	.41	.33
rank	1	2	3-4	3-6	3-7	4-7	5-7	8	9-10	9-10	11-12	11-13	12-13	14

Table 30: Head to head comparison, ignoring ties, for English-Russian systems

Results of the WMT13 Metrics Shared Task

Matouš Macháček and **Ondřej Bojar**
Charles University in Prague, Faculty of Mathematics and Physics
Institute of Formal and Applied Linguistics
machacekmatous@gmail.com and bojar@ufal.mff.cuni.cz

Abstract

This paper presents the results of the WMT13 Metrics Shared Task. We asked participants of this task to score the outputs of the MT systems involved in WMT13 Shared Translation Task. We collected scores of 16 metrics from 8 research groups. In addition to that we computed scores of 5 standard metrics such as BLEU, WER, PER as baselines. Collected scores were evaluated in terms of system level correlation (how well each metric's scores correlate with WMT13 official human scores) and in terms of segment level correlation (how often a metric agrees with humans in comparing two translations of a particular sentence).

1 Introduction

Automatic machine translation metrics play a very important role in the development of MT systems and their evaluation. There are many different metrics of diverse nature and one would like to assess their quality. For this reason, the Metrics Shared Task is held annually at the Workshop of Statistical Machine Translation (Callison-Burch et al., 2012). This year, the Metrics Task was run by different organizers but the only visible change is hopefully that the results of the task are presented in a separate paper instead of the main WMT overview paper.

In this task, we asked metrics developers to score the outputs of WMT13 Shared Translation Task (Bojar et al., 2013). We have collected the computed metrics' scores and use them to evaluate quality of the metrics.

The systems' outputs, human judgements and evaluated metrics are described in Section 2. The quality of the metrics in terms of system level correlation is reported in Section 3. Segment level correlation is reported in Section 4.

2 Data

We used the translations of MT systems involved in WMT13 Shared Translation Task together with reference translations as the test set for the Metrics Task. This dataset consists of 135 systems' outputs and 6 reference translations in 10 translation directions (5 into English and 5 out of English). Each system's output and the reference translation contain 3000 sentences. For more details please see the WMT13 main overview paper (Bojar et al., 2013).

2.1 Manual MT Quality Judgements

During the WMT13 Translation Task a large scale manual annotation was conducted to compare the systems. We used these collected human judgements for evaluating the automatic metrics.

The participants in the manual annotation were asked to evaluate system outputs by ranking translated sentences relative to each other. For each source segment that was included in the procedure, the annotator was shown the outputs of five systems to which he or she was supposed to assign ranks. Ties were allowed. Only sentences with 30 or less words were ranked by humans.

These collected rank labels were then used to assign each system a score that reflects how high that system was usually ranked by the annotators. Please see the WMT13 main overview paper for details on how this score is computed. You can also find inter- and intra-annotator agreement estimates there.

2.2 Participants of the Shared Task

Table 1 lists the participants of WMT13 Shared Metrics Task, along with their metrics. We have collected 16 metrics from a total of 8 research groups.

In addition to that we have computed the following two groups of standard metrics as baselines:

Metrics	Participant
METEOR	Carnegie Mellon University (Denkowski and Lavie, 2011)
LEPOR, NLEPOR	University of Macau (Han et al., 2013)
ACTA, ACTA5+6	Idiap Research Institute (Hajlaoui, 2013) (Hajlaoui and Popescu-Belis, 2013)
DEPREF-{ALIGN,EXACT}	Dublin City University (Wu et al., 2013)
SIMPBLEU-{RECALL,PREC}	University of Shefield (Song et al., 2013)
MEANT, UMEANT	Hong Kong University of Science and Technology (Lo and Wu, 2013)
TERRORCAT	German Research Center for Artificial Intelligence (Fishel, 2013)
LOGREGFSS, LOGREGNORM	DFKI (Avramidis and Popović, 2013)

Table 1: Participants of WMT13 Metrics Shared Task

- **Moses Scorer.** Metrics BLEU (Papineni et al., 2002), TER (Snover et al., 2006), WER, PER and CDER (Leusch et al., 2006) were computed using the Moses scorer which is used in Moses model optimization. To tokenize the sentences we used the standard tokenizer script as available in Moses Toolkit. In this paper we use the suffix *-MOSES to label these metrics.

- **Mteval.** Metrics BLEU (Papineni et al., 2002) and NIST (Doddington, 2002) were computed using the script `mteval-v13a.pl` [1] which is used in OpenMT Evaluation Campaign and includes its own tokenization. We use *-MTEVAL suffix to label these metrics. By default, `mteval` assumes the text is in ASCII, causing poor tokenization around curly quotes. We run `mteval` in both the default setting as well as with the flag `--international-tokenization` (marked *-INTL).

We have normalized all metrics' scores such that better translations get higher scores.

3 System-Level Metric Analysis

We measured the quality of system-level metrics' scores using the Spearman's rank correlation coefficient ρ. For each direction of translation we converted the official human scores into ranks. For each metric, we converted the metric's scores of systems in a given direction into ranks. Since there were no ties in the rankings, we used the simplified formula to compute the Spearman's ρ:

$$\rho = 1 - \frac{6 \sum d_i^2}{n(n^2 - 1)} \qquad (1)$$

[1] `http://www.itl.nist.gov/iad/mig/` `/tools/`

where d_i is the difference between the human rank and metric's rank for system i and n is number of systems. The possible values of ρ range between 1 (where all systems are ranked in the same order) and -1 (where the systems are ranked in the reverse order). A good metric produces rankings of systems similar to human rankings. Since we have normalized all metrics such that better translations get higher score we consider metrics with values of Spearman's ρ closer to 1 as better.

We also computed empirical confidences of Spearman's ρ using bootstrap resampling. Since we did not have direct access to participants' metrics (we received only metrics' scores for the complete test sets without the ability to run them on new sampled test sets), we varied the "golden truth" by sampling from human judgments. We have bootstrapped 1000 new sets and used 95 % confidence level to compute confidence intervals.

The Spearman's ρ correlation coefficient is sometimes too harsh: If a metric disagrees with humans in ranking two systems of a very similar quality, the ρ coefficient penalizes this equally as if the systems were very distant in their quality. Aware of how uncertain the golden ranks are in general, we do not find the method very fair. We thus also computed three following correlation coefficients besides the Spearman's ρ:

- **Pearson's correlation coefficient.** This coefficient measures the strength of the linear relationship between metric's scores and human scores. In fact, Spearman's ρ is Pearson's correlation coefficient applied to ranks.

- **Correlation with systems' clusters.** In the Translation Task (Bojar et al., 2013), the manual scores are also presented as clusters of systems that can no longer be significantly distinguished from one another given the available judgements. (Please see the WMT13 Overview paper for more details).

We take this cluster information as a "rank with ties" for each system and calculate its Pearson's correlation coefficient with each metric's scores.

- **Correlation with systems' fuzzy ranks.** For a given system the fuzzy rank is computed as an average of ranks of all systems which are not significantly better or worse than the given system. The Pearson's correlation coefficient of a metric's scores and systems' fuzzy ranks is then computed.

You can find the system-level correlations for translations into English in Table 2 and for translations out of English in Table 3. Each row in the tables contains correlations of a metric in each of the examined translation directions. The metrics are sorted by average Spearman's ρ correlation across translation directions. The best results in each direction are in bold.

As in previous years, a lot of metrics outperformed BLEU in system level correlation. The metric which has on average the strongest correlation in directions into English is METEOR. For the out of English direction, SIMPBLEU-RECALL has the highest system-level correlation. TERRORCAT achieved even a higher average correlation but it did not participate in all language pairs. The implementation of BLEU in `mteval` is slightly better than the one in Moses scorer (BLEU-MOSES). This confirms the known truth that tokenization and other minor implementation details can considerably influence a metric performance.

4 Segment-Level Metric Analysis

We measured the quality of metrics' segment-level scores using Kendall's τ rank correlation coefficient. For this we did not use the official WMT13 human scores but we worked with raw human judgements: For each translation direction we extracted all pairwise comparisons where one system's translation of a particular segment was judged to be (strictly) better than the other system's translation. Formally, this is a list of pairs (a, b) where a segment translation a was ranked better than translation b:

$$Pairs := \{(a, b) \mid r(a) < r(b)\} \quad (2)$$

where $r(\cdot)$ is human rank. For a given metric $m(\cdot)$, we then counted all concordant pairwise comparisons and all discordant pairwise comparisons. A concordant pair is a pair of two translations of the same segment in which the comparison of human ranks agree with the comparison of the metric's scores. A discordant pair is a pair in which the comparison of human ranks disagrees with the metric's comparison. Note that we totally ignore pairs where human ranks or metric's scores are tied. Formally:

$$Con := \{(a, b) \in Pairs \mid m(a) > m(b)\} \quad (3)$$

$$Dis := \{(a, b) \in Pairs \mid m(a) < m(b)\} \quad (4)$$

Finally the Kendall's τ is computed using the following formula:

$$\tau = \frac{|Con| - |Dis|}{|Con| + |Dis|} \quad (5)$$

The possible values of τ range between -1 (a metric always predicted a different order than humans did) and 1 (a metric always predicted the same order as humans). Metrics with higher τ are better.

The final Kendall's τs are shown in Table 4 for directions into English and in Table 5 for directions out of English. Each row in the tables contains correlations of a metric in given directions. The metrics are sorted by average correlation across the translation directions. Metrics which did not compute scores for systems in all directions are at the bottom of the tables.

You can see that in both categories, into and out of English, the strongest correlated segment-level metric is SIMPBLEU-RECALL.

4.1 Details on Kendall's τ

The computation of Kendall's τ has slightly changed this year. In WMT12 Metrics Task (Callison-Burch et al., 2012), the concordant pairs were defined exactly as we do (Equation 3) but the discordant pairs were defined differently: pairs in which one system was ranked better by the human annotator but in which the metric predicted a tie were considered also as discordant:

$$Dis := \{(a, b) \in Pairs \mid m(a) \leq m(b)\} \quad (6)$$

We feel that for two translations a and b of a segment, where a is ranked better by humans, a metric which produces equal scores for both translations should not be penalized as much as a metric which

Correlation coefficient	Spearman's ρ Correlation Coefficient						Pearson's	Clusters	Fuzzy Ranks
Directions	fr-en	de-en	es-en	cs-en	ru-en	Average	Average	Average	Average
Considered systems	12	22	11	10	17				
METEOR	.984 ± .014	.961 ± .020	**.979** ± .024	.964 ± .027	.789 ± .040	**.935** ± .012	**.950**	**.924**	**.936**
DEPREF-ALIGN	**.995** ± .011	**.966** ± .018	.965 ± .031	.964 ± .023	.768 ± .041	.931 ± .012	.926	.909	.924
UMEANT	.989 ± .011	.946 ± .018	.958 ± .028	**.973** ± .032	.775 ± .037	.928 ± .012	.909	.903	≀ .930
MEANT	.973 ± .014	.926 ± .021	.944 ± .038	**.973** ± .032	.765 ± .038	.916 ± .013	.901	.891	.918
SEMPOS	.938 ± .014	.919 ± .028	.930 ± .031	.955 ± .018	**.823** ± .037	.913 ± .012	≀ .934	≀ .894	.901
DEPREF-EXACT	.984 ± .011	.961 ± .017	.937 ± .038	.936 ± .027	.744 ± .046	.912 ± .015	≀ .924	≀ .892	.901
SIMPBLEU-RECALL	.978 ± .014	.936 ± .020	.923 ± .052	.909 ± .027	.798 ± .043	.909 ± .017	≀ .923	.874	.886
BLEU-MTEVAL-INTL	.989 ± .014	.902 ± .017	.895 ± .049	.936 ± .032	.695 ± .042	.883 ± .015	.866	.843	.874
BLEU-MTEVAL	.989 ± .014	.895 ± .020	.888 ± .045	.936 ± .032	.670 ± .041	.876 ± .015	.854	.835	.865
BLEU-MOSES	.993 ± .014	.902 ± .017	.879 ± .051	.936 ± .036	.651 ± .041	.872 ± .016	≀ .856	.826	.861
CDER-MOSES	**.995** ± .014	.877 ± .017	.888 ± .049	.927 ± .036	.659 ± .045	.869 ± .017	≀ .877	≀ .831	.859
SIMPBLEU-PREC	.989 ± .008	.846 ± .020	.832 ± .059	.918 ± .023	.704 ± .042	.858 ± .017	≀ .871	.815	.847
NLEPOR	.945 ± .022	.949 ± .025	.825 ± .056	.845 ± .041	.705 ± .043	.854 ± .018	≀ .867	.804	≀ .853
LEPOR V3.100	.945 ± .019	.934 ± .027	.748 ± .077	.800 ± .036	.779 ± .041	.841 ± .020	≀ .869	.780	≀ .850
NIST-MTEVAL	.951 ± .019	.875 ± .022	.769 ± .077	.891 ± .027	.649 ± .045	.827 ± .020	.852	.774	.824
NIST-MTEVAL-INTL	.951 ± .019	.875 ± .022	.762 ± .077	.882 ± .032	.658 ± .045	.826 ± .021	≀ .856	.774	≀ .826
TER-MOSES	.951 ± .019	.833 ± .023	.825 ± .077	.800 ± .036	.581 ± .045	.798 ± .021	.803	.733	.797
WER-MOSES	.951 ± .019	.672 ± .026	.797 ± .070	.755 ± .041	.591 ± .042	.753 ± .020	.785	.682	.749
PER-MOSES	.852 ± .027	.858 ± .025	.357 ± .091	.697 ± .043	.677 ± .040	.688 ± .024	.757	.637	.706
TERRORCAT	.984 ± .011	.961 ± .023	.972 ± .028	n/a	n/a	**.972** ± .012	**.977**	**.958**	**.959**

Table 2: System-level correlations of automatic evaluation metrics and the official WMT human scores when translating into English. The symbol "≀" indicates where the other averages are out of sequence compared to the main Spearman's ρ average.

Correlation coefficient	Spearman's ρ Correlation Coefficient						Pearson's	Clusters	Fuzzy Ranks
Directions	en-fr	en-de	en-es	en-cs	en-ru	Average	Average	Average	Average
Considered systems	14	14	12	11	12				
SIMPBLEU-RECALL	.924 ± .022	**.925** ± .020	.830 ± .047	.867 ± .031	.710 ± .053	**.851** ± .018	.844	.856	**.849**
LEPOR V3.100	.904 ± .034	.900 ± .027	.841 ± .049	.748 ± .056	**.855** ± .048	.850 ± .020	≀ **.854**	.833	.844
NIST-MTEVAL-INTL	**.929** ± .032	.846 ± .029	.797 ± .060	.902 ± .045	.771 ± .048	.849 ± .020	.808	≀ **.863**	≀ .845
CDER-MOSES	.921 ± .029	.867 ± .029	**.857** ± .058	.888 ± .024	.701 ± .059	.847 ± .019	.796	≀ .861	.843
NLEPOR	.919 ± .028	.904 ± .027	.852 ± .049	.818 ± .045	.727 ± .064	.844 ± .021	≀ .849	≀ .846	.840
NIST-MTEVAL	.914 ± .034	.825 ± .030	.780 ± .066	.916 ± .031	.723 ± .048	.832 ± .021	.794	≀ .851	.828
SIMPBLEU-PREC	.909 ± .026	.879 ± .025	.780 ± .071	.881 ± .035	.697 ± .051	.829 ± .020	≀ .840	≀ .852	.827
METEOR	.924 ± .027	.879 ± .030	.780 ± .060	**.937** ± .024	.569 ± .066	.818 ± .022	≀ .806	.825	.814
BLEU-MTEVAL-INTL	.917 ± .033	.832 ± .030	.764 ± .071	.895 ± .028	.657 ± .062	.813 ± .022	≀ .802	.821	.808
BLEU-MTEVAL	.895 ± .037	.786 ± .034	.764 ± .071	.895 ± .028	.631 ± .053	.794 ± .022	≀ .799	.809	.790
TER-MOSES	.912 ± .038	.854 ± .032	.753 ± .066	.860 ± .059	.538 ± .068	.783 ± .023	.746	.806	.778
BLEU-MOSES	.897 ± .034	.786 ± .034	.759 ± .078	.895 ± .028	.574 ± .057	.782 ± .022	≀ .802	.792	≀ .779
WER-MOSES	.914 ± .034	.825 ± .034	.714 ± .077	.860 ± .056	.552 ± .066	.773 ± .024	.737	≀ .796	.766
PER-MOSES	.873 ± .040	.686 ± .045	.775 ± .047	.797 ± .049	.591 ± .062	.744 ± .024	≀ .758	.747	.739
TERRORCAT	**.929** ± .022	**.946** ± .018	**.912** ± .041	n/a	n/a	**.929** ± .017	**.952**	**.933**	**.923**
SEMPOS	n/a	n/a	n/a	.699 ± .045	n/a	.699 ± .045	.717	.615	.696
ACTA5 ± 6	.809 ± .046	-.526 ± .034	n/a	n/a	n/a	.141 ± .029	.166	.196	.176
ACTA	.809 ± .046	-.526 ± .034	n/a	n/a	n/a	.141 ± .029	.166	.196	.176

Table 3: System-level correlations of automatic evaluation metrics and the official WMT human scores when translating out of English. The symbol "≀" indicates where the other averages are out of sequence compared to the main Spearman's ρ average.

Directions	fr-en	de-en	es-en	cs-en	ru-en	Average
Extracted pairs	80741	128668	67832	85469	151422	
SIMPBLEU-RECALL	**.193**	**.318**	**.279**	.260	.234	**.257**
METEOR	.178	.293	.236	**.265**	**.239**	.242
DEPREF-ALIGN	.161	.267	.234	.228	.200	.218
DEPREF-EXACT	.167	.263	.228	.227	.195	.216
SIMPBLEU-PREC	.154	.236	.214	.208	.174	.197
NLEPOR	.149	.240	.204	.176	.172	.188
SENTBLEU-MOSES	.150	.218	.198	.197	.170	.187
LEPOR V3.100	.149	.221	.161	.187	.177	.179
UMEANT	.101	.166	.144	.160	.108	.136
MEANT	.101	.160	.145	.164	.109	.136
LOGREGFSS-33	n/a	.272	n/a	n/a	n/a	.272
LOGREGFSS-24	n/a	.270	n/a	n/a	n/a	.270
TERRORCAT	.161	.298	.230	n/a	n/a	.230

Table 4: Segment-level Kendall's τ correlations of automatic evaluation metrics and the official WMT human judgements when translating into English.

Directions	en-fr	en-de	en-es	en-cs	en-ru	Average
Extracted pairs	100783	77286	60464	102842	87323	
SIMPBLEU-RECALL	**.158**	**.085**	**.231**	**.065**	**.126**	**.133**
SIMPBLEU-PREC	.138	.065	.187	.055	.095	.108
METEOR	.147	.049	.175	.058	.111	.108
SENTBLEU-MOSES	.133	.047	.171	.052	.095	.100
LEPOR V3.100	.126	.058	.178	.023	.109	.099
NLEPOR	.124	.048	.163	.048	.097	.096
LOGREGNORM-411	n/a	n/a	.136	n/a	n/a	.136
TERRORCAT	.116	.074	.186	n/a	n/a	.125
LOGREGNORMSOFT-431	n/a	n/a	.033	n/a	n/a	.033

Table 5: Segment-level Kendall's τ correlations of automatic evaluation metrics and the official WMT human judgements when translating out of English.

strongly disagrees with humans. The method we used this year does not harm metrics which often estimate two segments as equally good.

5 Conclusion

We carried out WMT13 Metrics Shared Task in which we assessed the quality of various automatic machine translation metrics. We used the human judgements as collected for WMT13 Translation Task to compute system-level and segment-level correlations with human scores.

While most of the metrics correlate very well on the system-level, the segment-level correlations are still rather poor. It was shown again this year that a lot of metrics outperform BLEU, hopefully one of them will attract a wider use at last.

Acknowledgements

This work was supported by the grants P406/11/1499 of the Grant Agency of the Czech Republic and FP7-ICT-2011-7-288487 (MosesCore) of the European Union.

References

Eleftherios Avramidis and Maja Popović. 2013. Machine learning methods for comparative and time-oriented Quality Estimation of Machine Translation output. In *Proceedings of the Eight Workshop on Statistical Machine Translation*.

Ondřej Bojar, Christian Buck, Chris Callison-Burch, Christian Federmann, Barry Haddow, Philipp Koehn, Christof Monz, Matt Post, Radu Soricut, and Lucia Specia. 2013. Findings of the 2013 workshop on statistical machine translation. In *Proceedings of the Eight Workshop on Statistical Machine Translation*.

Chris Callison-Burch, Philipp Koehn, Christof Monz, Matt Post, Radu Soricut, and Lucia Specia. 2012. Findings of the 2012 workshop on statistical machine translation. In *Proceedings of the Seventh Workshop on Statistical Machine Translation*, pages 10–51, Montréal, Canada, June. Association for Computational Linguistics.

Michael Denkowski and Alon Lavie. 2011. Meteor 1.3: Automatic Metric for Reliable Optimization and Evaluation of Machine Translation Systems. In *Proceedings of the EMNLP 2011 Workshop on Statistical Machine Translation*.

George Doddington. 2002. Automatic evaluation of machine translation quality using n-gram co-occurrence statistics. In *Proceedings of the second international conference on Human Language Technology Research*, HLT '02, pages 138–145, San Francisco, CA, USA. Morgan Kaufmann Publishers Inc.

Mark Fishel. 2013. Ranking Translations using Error Analysis and Quality Estimation. In *Proceedings of the Eight Workshop on Statistical Machine Translation*.

Najeh Hajlaoui and Andrei Popescu-Belis. 2013. Assessing the accuracy of discourse connective translations: Validation of an automatic metric. In *14th International Conference on Intelligent Text Processing and Computational Linguistics*, page 12. University of the Aegean, Springer, March.

Najeh Hajlaoui. 2013. Are ACT's scores increasing with better translation quality. In *Proceedings of the Eight Workshop on Statistical Machine Translation*.

Aaron Li-Feng Han, Derek F. Wong, Lidia S. Chao, Yi Lu, Liangye He, Yiming Wang, and Jiaji Zhou. 2013. A Description of Tunable Machine Translation Evaluation Systems in WMT13 Metrics Task. In *Proceedings of the Eight Workshop on Statistical Machine Translation*.

Gregor Leusch, Nicola Ueffing, and Hermann Ney. 2006. Cder: Efficient mt evaluation using block movements. In *In Proceedings of EACL*, pages 241–248.

Chi-Kiu Lo and Dekai Wu. 2013. MEANT @ WMT2013 metrics evaluation. In *Proceedings of the Eight Workshop on Statistical Machine Translation*.

Kishore Papineni, Salim Roukos, Todd Ward, and Wei jing Zhu. 2002. Bleu: a method for automatic evaluation of machine translation. pages 311–318.

Matthew Snover, Bonnie Dorr, Richard Schwartz, Linnea Micciulla, and John Makhoul. 2006. A study of translation edit rate with targeted human annotation. In *In Proceedings of Association for Machine Translation in the Americas*, pages 223–231.

Xingyi Song, Trevor Cohn, and Lucia Specia. 2013. BLEU deconstructed: Designing a better MT evaluation metric. March.

Xiaofeng Wu, Hui Yu, and Qun Liu. 2013. DCU Participation in WMT2013 Metrics Task. In *Proceedings of the Eight Workshop on Statistical Machine Translation*.

The Feasibility of HMEANT as a Human MT Evaluation Metric

Alexandra Birch
a.birch@ed.ac.uk

Barry Haddow
bhaddow@inf.ed.ac.uk

Ulrich Germann
ugermann@inf.ed.ac.uk

Maria Nadejde
maria.nadejde@gmail.com

Christian Buck
cbuck@lantis.de

Philipp Koehn
pkoehn@inf.ed.ac.uk

University of Edinburgh
10 Crichton Street
Edinburgh, EH8 9AB, UK

Abstract

There has been a recent surge of interest in semantic machine translation, which standard automatic metrics struggle to evaluate. A family of measures called MEANT has been proposed which uses semantic role labels (SRL) to overcome this problem. The human variant, HMEANT, has largely been evaluated using correlation with human contrastive evaluations, the standard human evaluation metric for the WMT shared tasks. In this paper we claim that for a human metric to be useful, it needs to be evaluated on intrinsic properties. It needs to be reliable; it needs to work across different language pairs; and it needs to be lightweight. Most importantly, however, a human metric must be discerning. We conclude that HMEANT is a step in the right direction, but has some serious flaws. The reliance on verbs as heads of frames, and the assumption that annotators need minimal guidelines are particularly problematic.

1 Introduction

Human evaluation is essential in machine translation (MT) research because it is the ultimate way to judge system quality. Furthermore, human evaluation is used to evaluate automatic metrics which are necessary for tuning system parameters. Unfortunately, there is no clear consensus on which evaluation strategy is best. Humans have been asked to judge if translations are correct, to grade them and to rank them. But it is often very difficult to decide how good a translation is, when there are so many possible ways of translating a sentence. Another problem is that different types of evaluation might be useful for different purposes. If the MT is going to be the basis of a human translator's work-flow, then post-editing effort seems like a natural fit. However, for people using MT for gisting, what we really want is some measure of how much meaning has been retained.

We clearly need a metric which tries to answer the question, how much of the meaning does the translation capture. In this paper, we explore the use of human evaluation metrics which attempt to capture the extent of this meaning retention. In particular, we consider HMEANT (Lo and Wu, 2011a), a metric that uses semantic role labels to measure how much of the "who, why, when, where" has been preserved. For HMEANT evaluation, annotators are instructed to identify verbs as heads of semantic frames. Then they attach role fillers to the heads and finally they align heads and role fillers in the candidate translation with those in a reference translation. In a series of papers, Lo and Wu (2010, 2011b,a, 2012) explored a number of questions, evaluating HMEANT by using correlation statistics to compare it to judgements of human adequacy and contrastive evaluations. Given the drawbacks of those evaluation measures, which we discuss in Sec. 2, they could just as well have been evaluating the human adequacy and contrastive judgements using HMEANT. Human evaluation metrics need to be judged on other intrinsic qualities, which we describe below.

The aim of this paper is to evaluate the effectiveness of HMEANT, with the goal of using it to judge the relative merits of different MT systems, for example in the shared task of the Workshop on Machine Translation.

In order to be useful, an MT evaluation metric must be *reliable*, be *language independent*, have *discriminatory power*, and be *efficient*. We address each of these criteria as follows:

Reliability We produce extensive IAA (Inter-annotator agreement) for HMEANT, breaking it down into the different stages of annotation. Our experimental results show that whilst the IAA for HMEANT is acceptable at the individual stages of the annotation, the compounding effect of disagreement at each stage of the pipeline greatly reduces the effective overall IAA — to 0.44 on role alignment for German, and, only slightly better, 0.59 for English. This raises doubts about the reliability of HMEANT in its current form.

Discriminatory Power We consider output of three types of MT system (Phrase-based, Syntax-based and Rule-based) to attempt to gain insight into the different types of semantic information preserved by the different systems. The Syntax-based system seems to have a slight edge overall, but since IAA is so low, this result has to be taken with a grain of salt.

Language Independence We apply HMEANT to both English and German translation outputs, showing that the guidelines can be adapted to the new language.

Efficiency Whilst HMEANT evaluation will never be as fast as, for example, the contrastive judgements used for the WMT shared task, it is still reasonably efficient considering the fine-grained nature of the evaluation. On average, annotators evaluated about 10 sentences per hour.

2 Related Work

Even though the idea that machine translation requires a semantic representation of the translated content is as old as the idea of computer-based translation itself (Weaver, 1955), it has not been until recently that people have begun to combine statistical models with semantic representations. Jones et al. (2012), for example, represent meaning as directed acyclic graphs and map these to PropBank (Palmer et al., 2005) style dependencies. To evaluate such approaches properly, we need evaluation metrics that capture the accuracy of the translation.

Current automatic metrics of machine translation, such as BLEU (Papineni et al., 2002), METEOR (Lavie and Denkowski, 2009) and TER (Snover et al., 2009b), which have greatly accelerated progress in MT research, rely on shallow surface properties of the translations, and only indirectly capture whether or not the translation preserves the meaning. This has meant that potentially more sophisticated translation models are pitted against the flatter phrase-based models, based on metrics which cannot reflect their strengths. Callison-Burch et al. (2011) provide evidence that automatic metrics are inconsistent with human judgements when comparing rule-based against statistical machine translation systems.

Automatic evaluation metrics are evaluated and calibrated based on their correlation with human judgements. However, after more than 60 years of research into machine translation, there is still no consensus on how to evaluate machine translation based on human judgements. (Hutchins and Somers, 1992; Przybocki et al., 2009).

One obvious approach is to ask annotators to rate translation candidates on a numerical scale. Under the DARPA TIDES program, the Linguistic Data Consortium (2002) developed an evaluation scheme that relies on two five-point scales representing fluency and adequacy. This was also the human evaluation scheme used in the annual MT competitions sponsored by NIST (2005).

In an analysis of human evaluation results for the WMT '07 workshop, however, Callison-Burch et al. (2007) found high correlation between fluency and adequacy scores assigned by individual annotators, suggesting that human annotators are not able to separate these two evaluation dimensions easily. Furthermore these absolute scores show low inter-annotator agreement. Instead of giving absolute quality assessments, annotators appeared to be using their ratings to rank translation candidates according to their overall preference for one over the other.

In line with these findings, Callison-Burch et al. (2007) proposed to let annotators rank translation candidates directly, without asking them to assign an absolute quality assessment to each candidate. This type of human evaluation has been performed in the last six Workshops on Statistical Machine Translation.

Although it is useful to have a score or a rank for a particular sentence, especially for evaluating automatic metrics, these ratings are necessarily a simplification of the real differences between translations. Translations can contain a large number of different types of errors of varying severity. Even if we put aside difficulties with selecting one preferred sentence, ranking judgements are difficult to generalise. Humans are shown five translations at a time, and there is a high cognitive cost to ranking these at once. Furthermore, these represent a subset of the competing systems, and these rankings must be combined with other annotators judgements on five other system outputs to compute an overall ranking. The methodology for interpreting the contrastive evaluations has been the subject of much recent debate in the community (Bojar et al., 2011; Lopez, 2012).

There has been some effort to overcome these problems. HTER (Snover et al., 2009a) is a metric which counts the number of edits needed by a human to convert the machine translation so as to convey the same meaning as the reference. This type of evaluation is of some use when one is using MT to aid human translation (although the relationship between number of edits and actual effort is not straightforward (Koponen, 2012)), but it is not so helpful when one's task is gisting. The number of edits need not correlate with the severity of the semantic differences between the two sentences. The loss of a negative, for instance, is only one edit away from the original, but the semantics change completely.

Alternatively, HyTER (Dreyer and Marcu, 2012) is an annotation tool which allows a user to create an exponential number of correct translations for a given sentence. These references are then efficiently exploited to compare with machine translation output. The authors argue that the current metrics fail simply because they have access to sets of reference translations which are simply too small. However, the fact is that even if one does have access to large numbers of translations, it is very difficult to determine whether the reference correctly captures the essential semantic content of the references.

The idea of using semantic role labels to evaluate machine translation is not new. Giménez and Màrquez (2007) proposed using automatically assigned semantic role labels as a feature in a combined MT metric. The main difference between this application of semantic roles and MEANT is that arguments for specific verbs are taken into account, instead of just applying the subset agent, patient and benefactor. This idea would probably help human annotators to handle sentences with passives, copulas and other constructions which do not easily match the most basic arguments. On the other hand, verb specific arguments are language dependent.

Bojar and Wu (2012), applying HMEANT to English-to-Czech MT output, identified a number of problems with HMEANT, and suggested a variety of improvements. In some respects, this work is very similar, except that our goal is to evaluate HMEANT along a range of intrinsic properties, to determine how useful the metric really is to evaluation campaigns such as the workshop on machine translation.

3 Evaluation with HMEANT

3.1 Annotation Procedure

The goal of the HMEANT metric is to capture essential semantic content, but still be simple and fast. There are two stages to the annotation, the first of which is semantic role labelling (SRL). Here the annotator is directed to select the actions, or frame heads, by marking all the verbs in the sentence except for auxilliaries and modals. The roles (or slot fillers) within the frame are then marked and each is linked with a unique action. Each role is given a type from an inventory of 11 (Table 1), and an action with its collection of corresponding roles is known as a *frame*. In the role annotation the idea is to get the annotator to recognise *who did what* to *who, when, where* and *why* in both the references and the MT outputs.

who	**what**	**whom**	**when**	**where**
agent	patient	benefactive	temporal	locative
why	**how**			
purpose	degree, manner, modal, negation, other			

Table 1: Semantic roles

The second stage in the annotation is alignment, where the annotators match elements of the SRL annotation in the reference with that in the MT output. The annotators link both actions and roles, and these alignments can be matched as "Correct" or "Partial" matches, depending on how well the action or role is translated. The guidelines for the annotators are deliberately minimalistic, with the argument being that non-experts can get started quickly. Lo and Wu (2011a) claim that unskilled annotators can be trained within 15 minutes.

In all such human evaluation, there is a tradeoff between simplicity and accuracy. Clearly when evaluating bad machine translation output, we do not want to label too much. However, sometimes having so little choice of semantic roles can lead to confusion and slow down the annotator when more complicated examples do not fit the scheme. Therefore, common exceptions need to be handled either in the roles provided, or in the annotator guidelines.

3.2 Calculation of Score

The overall HMEANT score for MT evaluation is computed as the f-score from the counts of matches of frames and their role fillers between the reference and the MT output. Unmatched frames are excluded from the calculation together with all their corresponding roles.

In recognition that preservation of some types of semantic relations may be more important than others for a human to understand a sentence, one may want to weight them differently in the computation of the HMEANT score. Lo and Wu (2012) train weights for each role filler type to optimise correlation with human adequacy judgements. As an unsupervised alternative, they suggest weighting roles according to their frequency as approximation to their importance.

Since the main focus of the current paper is the annotation of the actions, roles and alignments that HMEANT depends on, we do not explore such different weight-setting schemes, but set the weights uniformly, with the exception of a partial alignment, which is given a weight of 0.5. HMEANT is thus defined as follows:

$$F_i = \text{\# correct or partially correct fillers for PRED i in MT}$$

$$MT_i = \text{total \# fillers for PRED i in MT}$$

$$REF_i = \text{total \# fillers for PRED i in REF}$$

$$P = \sum_{matched\ i} \frac{F_i}{MT_i}$$

$$R = \sum_{matched\ i} \frac{F_i}{REF_i}$$

$$P_{total} = \frac{P_{correct} + 0.5 P_{partial}}{\text{total \# predicates in MT}}$$

$$R_{total} = \frac{P_{correct} + 0.5 P_{partial}}{\text{total \# predicates in REF}}$$

$$\text{HMEANT} = \frac{2 * P_{total} * R_{total}}{P_{total} + R_{total}}$$

3.3 Automating HMEANT

One of the main directions taken by the authors of HMEANT is in creating a fully automated version of the metric (MEANT) in (Lo et al., 2012). The metric combines shallow semantic parsing with a simple maximum weighted bipartite matching algorithm for aligning semantic frames. They use approximate matching schemes (Cosine and Jaccard similarity) for matching roles, with the latter producing better alignments (Tumuluru et al., 2012). They demonstrate that MEANT correlates with human adequacy judgements better than other commonly used automatic metrics. In this paper we focus on human evaluation, as it is essential for building better automatic metrics, and therefore a more fundamental problem.

4 Experimental Setup

4.1 Systems and Data Sets

We performed HMEANT evaluation on three systems selected from 2013 WMT evaluation[1]. The systems we selected were `uedin-wmt13`, `uedin-syntax` and `rbmt-3`, which were chosen to provide us with a high performing phrase-based system, a high performing syntax-based system and the top performing rule-based system, respectively. The cased BLEU scores of the three systems are shown in Table 2.

System	Type	de-en	en-de
`uedin-wmt13`	Phrase	26.6	20.1
`uedin-syntax`	Syntax	26.3	19.4
`rbmt-3`	Rule	18.8	16.5

Table 2: Cased BLEU on the full `newstest2013` test set for the systems used in this study

We randomly selected sentences from the en-de and de-en `newstest2013` tasks, and extracted the corresponding references and system outputs for these sentences. For the en-de task, 75% of our selected sentences were selected from the section of `newstest2013` that was originally in German, with the other 25% from the section that was originally in English. The sentence selection for the de-en task was performed in a similar manner. For presentation to the annotators, the sentences were split into segments of 12. We found that with practice, annotators could complete one of these segments in around 100-120 minutes. In total, with close to 70 hours of annotator effort, we evaluated 142 sentences of German, and 72 sentences of English. The annotation for each sentence includes 1 reference, 3 system outputs, and their corresponding alignments. Apart from 5 singly-annotated German sentences, and 1 singly-annotated English sentence, all sentences were annotated by exactly 2 annotators.

[1] `www.statmt.org/wmt13`

4.2 Annotation

The annotation for English was performed by 3 different annotators (E1, E2 and E3), and the German annotation by 2 annotators (D1 and D2). All the English annotators were machine translation researchers, with E1 and E2 both native English speakers whereas E3 is not a native speaker, but lives and works in an English-speaking country. The two German annotators were both native speakers of German, with no background in computational linguistics, although D2 is a teacher of German as a second language and has had linguistic training.

The HMEANT evaluation task was carried out following the framework described in Lo and Wu (2011a) and Bojar and Wu (2012). For each sentence in the evaluation set, the annotators were first asked to mark the semantic frames and roles (i.e., slot fillers within the frame) in a human reference translation of the respective sentence. They were then presented with the output of several machine translation systems for the same source sentence, one system at a time, with the reference translation and its annotations visible in the left half of the screen (cf. Fig. 1). For each system, the annotators were asked to annotate semantic frames and slot fillers in the translation first, and then align them with frame heads and slot fillers in the human reference translation. Annotations and alignment were performed with Edi-HMEANT[2], a web-based annotation tool for HMEANT that we developed on the basis of Yawat (Germann, 2008). The tool allows the alignment of slots from different semantic frames, and the alignment of slots of different types; however, such alignments are not considered in the computation of the final HMEANT score.

The annotation guidelines were essentially those used in Bojar and Wu (2012), with some additional English examples, and a complete set of German examples. For ease of comparison with prior work, we used the same set of semantic role labels as Bojar and Wu (2012), shown in Table 1. Given the restriction that the head of a frame can consist of only one word, a convention was made that all other verbs attached to the main verb such as modals, auxiliaries or separable particles for German verbs, would be labelled as *modal*. This was the only change we made to the HMEANT scheme.

[2]Edi-HMEANT is part of the *Edinburgh Multi-text Annotation and Alignment Tool Suite* (http://www.statmt.org/edimtaats).

5 Results and Discussion

5.1 Inter-Annotator Agreement

We first measured IAA on role identification, as in Lo and Wu (2011a), except that we use exact match on word spans as opposed to the approximate match employed in that reference. Whilst exact match is a harsher measure, penalising disagreements related to punctuation and articles, using any sort of approximate match would mean having to deal with N:M matches. IAA is defined as follows:

$$IAA = \frac{2 * P * R}{P + R}$$

Where P is defined as the number of labels (either heads, roles, or alignments) that match between annotators, divided by the total number of labels given by annotator 1. And R is defined the same way for annotator 2. This is similar to an F-measure (f1), where we consider one of the annotators as the gold standard. The IAA for role identification is shown in Table 3.

	Reference		Hypothesis	
Lang.	matches	f1	matches	f1
de	865	0.846	2091	0.737
en	461	0.759	1199	0.749

Table 3: IAA for role identification. This is calculated by considering exact endpoint matches on all spans (predicates and arguments).

The agreements in Table 3 are not too different from those reported in earlier work. We note that the IAA for the German annotators drops for the MT system outputs, but this may be because the English annotators (as MT researchers) are less bothered by bad MT output than their counterparts working on the German texts.

Next we looked at the IAA on role classification, the other IAA figure provided by Lo and Wu (2011a). We only considered roles where both annotators had marked the same span in the same frame, with the frame being identified by its action. The IAA for role classification is shown in Table 4.

Again, we show similar levels of IAA to those reported in (Lo and Wu, 2011a). Examining the disagreements in more detail, we produced counts of the most common role type disagreements, by

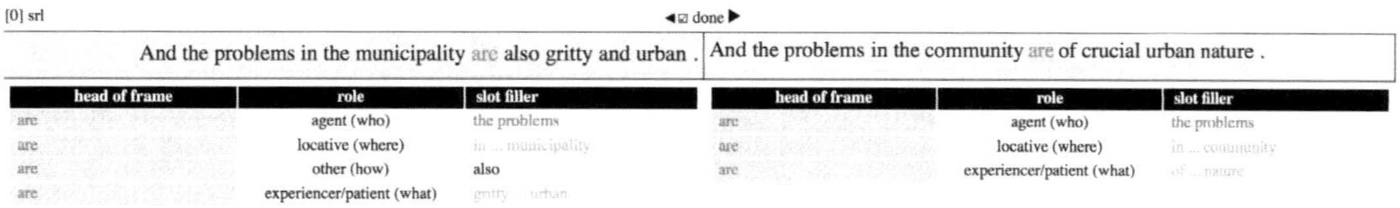

Figure 1: Example of a sentence pair annotated with Edi-HMEANT. The reference translation is on the left, the machine translation output on the right. Head and slot fillers for each semantic frame are marked by selecting spans in the text and automatically listed in tables below the respective sentences. Frames and slot fillers are aligned by clicking on table cells. The alignments of the semantic frames are highlighted: green (grey in black and white version) for *exact match* and grey (light grey) for *partial match*.

	Reference		Hypothesis	
Lang.	matches	f1	matches	f1
de	425	0.717	1050	0.769
en	245	0.825	634	0.826

Table 4: IAA for role classification. We only consider cases where annotators had marked the same span in the same frame.

Role 1	Role 2	Count
Agent	Experiencer-Patient	110
Degree-Extent	Modal	92
Beneficiary	Experiencer-Patient	45
Experiencer-Patient	Manner	26
Manner	Other	25

Table 5: Most common role type disagreements, for German

language. We show the top 5 disagreements in Tables 5 and 6. Essentially these show that the most common role types provide the most confusions.

In order to shed more light on the role type disagreements, we examined a random sample of 10 of the English annotations where the annotators had disagreed about "Agent" versus "Experiencer-Patient". In 7 of these cases, there was a definite correct answer, according to the annotation guidelines. Of the other 3, there were 2 cases of poor MT output making the semantic interpretation difficult, and one case of existential "there". Of the 7 cases where one annotator appears in error, 3 were passive, 1 was a copula, and 1 involved the verb "receive". For the other 2 there was no clear reason for the error. From this small sample, we suggest that passive constructions are still difficult to annotate semantically.

Role 1	Role 2	Count
Agent	Experiencer-Patient	44
Manner	Other	22
Degree-Extent	Temporal	12
Degree-Extent	Other	12
Beneficiary	Experiencer-Patient	11

Table 6: Most common role type disagreements, for English

The last of elements of the semantic frames to be considered for IAA are the actions, i.e. the frame heads or predicates. In this case identifying a match was straightforward as actions are identified by a single token. The IAA for action identification is shown in Table 7.

	Reference		Hypothesis	
Lang.	matches	f1	matches	f1
de	238	0.937	592	0.826
en	126	0.818	362	0.868

Table 7: IAA for action identification.

We see fairly high IAA for actions, which seems encouraging, but given the importance of actions in HMEANT, we probably need the scores to be higher. Most of the problems with the identification of actions centre around multiple-verb constructions and participles.

We now turn our attention to the second stage of the annotation process where the annotators marked alignments between slots and roles. These provide the relevant statistics for the calculation of the HMEANT score so it is important that they are annotated reliably.

Firstly, we consider the alignment of actions. In this case, we use pipelined statistics, in that if one annotator marks actions in the reference and hypothesis, then aligns them, whilst the other annotator does not mark the corresponding actions, we still count this as an action alignment mismatch. This creates a harsher measure on action alignment, but gives a better idea of the overall reliability of the annotation task. In Table 8 we show the IAA (as F1) on action alignments. Comparing Tables 8 and 7 we see that, for English at least, the

Lang.	matches	f1
de	300	0.655
en	275	0.769

Table 8: IAA for action alignment, collapsing partial and full alignment

agreement on action alignment is not much lower than that on action identification, indicating that if annotators agree on the actions then they generally agree on how they align. For German, however, the IAA on action alignment is a bit lower, apparently because one of the annotators was much stricter about which actions they aligned.

In order to calculate the IAA on role alignments, we only consider those alignments that connect two roles in aligned frames, of the same type, since these are the only role alignments that count for computing the HMEANT score. This means that if one of the annotators does not align the frames, then all the contained role alignments are counted as mismatches. We do not consider the spans when calculating the agreement on role alignments, meaning that if one annotator has an alignment between roles of type T in frame F, and the other annotator also aligns the same types of roles in the same frame, then they are considered as a match. This is done because it is only the counts of alignments that are relevant for HMEANT scoring. The IAA on the role alignments is quite

Lang.	matches	f1
de	448	0.442
en	506	0.596

Table 9: IAA for role alignment.

low, dipping below 0.5 for German. This is mainly because of the pipelining effect, where annotation disagreements at each stage are compounded. Since the final HMEANT score is computed essentially by counting role alignments, this level of IAA causes problems for this score calculation.

We computed HMEANT and BLEU scores for the hypotheses annotated by each annotator pair. The HMEANT scores were calculated as described in Section 3.2. The two metrics are calculated for each sentence (we apply +1 smoothing for BLEU), then averaged across all sentences. Table 10 shows the scores organised by annotator pair and system type. The agreement in the overall scores is not good, but really just reflects the compounded

Annotator Pair	System	BLEU	HMEANT (Annot. 1)	HMEANT (Annot. 2)
	Phrase	0.310	0.626 (2)	0.672 (3)
E1, E2	Syntax	0.291	0.635 (1)	0.730 (1)
	Rule	0.252	0.578 (3)	0.673 (2)
	Phrase	0.378	0.569 (1)	0.602 (3)
E1, E3	Syntax	0.376	0.553 (2)	0.627 (2)
	Rule	0.320	0.546 (3)	0.646 (1)
	Phrase	0.360	0.669 (2)	0.696 (3)
E2, E3	Syntax	0.362	0.751 (1)	0.739 (1)
	Rule	0.308	0.624 (3)	0.716 (2)
	Phrase	0.296	0.327 (1)	0.631 (3)
D1, D2	Syntax	0.321	0.312 (2)	0.707 (1)
	Rule	0.242	0.274 (3)	0.648 (2)

Table 10: Scores assigned by each annotator pair. The numbers in brackets after the HMEANT scores show the relative ranking assigned by each annotator.

agreement problems in the role alignments (Table 9). In no case do the annotators choose a consistent ranking of the 3 systems, and in 2 of the 4 annotator pairs, the annotators disagree about which is the top performing system.

5.2 Overall Scores

In this section we report the overall HMEANT scores of the three systems whose output we annotated. Our main focus on this paper was on the annotation task, so we do not wish to emphasise the scoring, but it is nevertheless an important end-product of the HMEANT annotation process. The overall scores (HMEANT and +1 smoothed sentence BLEU, averaged across sentences and annotators) are given in Table 11.

Language	System	BLEU	HMEANT
	Phrase	0.351	0.634
en	Syntax	0.344	0.667
	Rule	0.295	0.625
	Phrase	0.294	0.482
de	Syntax	0.302	0.517
	Rule	0.242	0.464

Table 11: Comparison of mean HMEANT and (smoothed sentence) BLEU for the three systems.

From the table we can observe that, whilst BLEU shows similar scores for the phrase-based and syntax-based systems, with lower scores for the rule-based system, HMEANT shows the syntax-based system as being ahead, with the other two showing similar performance. We would caution against reading too much into this, considering the relatively small number of sentences annotated, and the issues with IAA exposed in the previous section, but it is an encouraging results for syntax-based MT.

5.3 Discussion

Machine translation research needs a reliable method for evaluating and comparing different machine translation systems. The performance of HMEANT as shown in the previous section is disappointing. The fact that the final role IAA, in Table 9, is 0.442 for German and 0.596 for English, demonstrates that there are fundamental problems with the scheme. One of the areas of greatest confusion is between what seems like one of the easiest role types to distinguish: agent and patient. Here is an example of a passive where one annotator has marked "tea" wrongly as agent, and the other annotator correctly labelled it as patient:

Reference: In the kitchen, tea is prepared for the guests

ACTION prepared
LOCATIVE In the kitchen
AGENT / PATIENT tea
MODAL is
BENEFICIARY for the guests

We would argue that the most important change to HMEANT must be in creating more comprehensive annotation guidelines, with examples of difficult cases. Bojar and Wu (2012) listed a number of problems and improvements to HMEANT, which we largely agree with. We list the most important limitations of HMEANT that we have encountered:

- **Single Word Heads** Verbal predicates often consist of multiple words, which can be split. For example: "*Take* him *up* on his offer".

- **Heads being limited to verbs** The semantics of verbs can often be carried by an equivalent noun and should be allowed by HMEANT. For example "My father broke down and cried .", the verb "cried" is correctly paraphrased in "My father collapsed in tears ."

- **Copular Verbs** These do not fit in to the limited list of role types. For example forcing this sentence "The story is plausible", to have and agent and patient is confusing.

- **Prepositional Phrases attaching to a noun** These can greatly affect the semantics of a sentence, but HMEANT has no way of capturing this.

- **Semantics not on head** This frequently occurs with light verbs, for example "Bouson did the review of the paper" is equivalent to "Bouson reviewed the paper".

- **Hierarchy of frames** There are often frames which are embedded in other frames, for example in reported speech. It is not clear whether errors at the lowest level should be marked wrong just at that point, or whether they should be marked wrong all the way up the semantic tree. For example: "Arafat said 'Isreal suffocates such a hope in the germ' ". The frame headed by "said" is largely correct, but the reported speech is not. The patient role of the verb "said" could be aligned as correct, as the error is already captured in relation to the verb "suffocates".

- **No discourse markers** These are important for capturing the relationships between frames and should be labelled.

6 Conclusion

HMEANT represents an attempt to create a human evaluation for machine translation which directly measures the semantic content preserved by the MT. It partly succeeds. However we have cast doubt on the claim that HMEANT can be reliably annotated with minimal annotator training and guidelines. In the most extensive study of inter-annotator agreement yet performed for HMEANT, across two language pairs, we have shown that the disagreements between annotators make it difficult to reliably compare different MT systems with HMEANT scores.

Furthermore, the fact that HMEANT is restricted to annotating purely verbal predicates results in some important disadvantages. Ideally we need a more general definition of a frame, not restricted to purely verbal predicates, and we would like to be able to link frames. We should explore the feasibility of a semantic framework which attempts to overcome reliance on syntactic properties such as Universal Conceptual Cognitive Annotation (Abend and Rappoport, 2013).

7 Acknowledgements

The research leading to these results has received funding from the European Union Seventh Framework Programme (FP7/2007-2013) under grant agreement 287658 (EU BRIDGE).

References

Abend, Omri and Ari Rappoport. 2013. "Universal Conceptual Cognitive Annotation (UCCA)." *Proceedings of ACL.*

Bojar, Ondrej, Miloš Ercegovčević, Martin Popel, and Omar Zaidan. 2011. "A Grain of Salt for the WMT Manual Evaluation." *Proceedings of the Sixth Workshop on Statistical Machine Translation*, 1–11. Edinburgh, Scotland.

Bojar, Ondrej and Dekai Wu. 2012. "Towards a Predicate-Argument Evaluation for MT." *Proceedings of SSST*, 30–38.

Callison-Burch, Chris, Cameron Fordyce, Philipp Koehn, Christof Monz, and Josh Schroeder. 2007. "(Meta-) evaluation of machine translation." *Proceedings of the Second Workshop on Statistical Machine Translation*, 136–158. Prague, Czech Republic.

Callison-Burch, Chris, Philipp Koehn, Christof Monz, and Omar F Zaidan. 2011. "Findings of the 2011 workshop on statistical machine translation." *Proceedings of the Sixth Workshop on Statistical Machine Translation*, 22–64.

Dreyer, Markus and Daniel Marcu. 2012. "Hyter: Meaning-equivalent semantics for translation evaluation." *Proceedings of the 2012 Conference of the North American Chapter of the Association for Computational Linguistics: Human Language Technologies*, 162–171. Montréal, Canada.

Germann, Ulrich. 2008. "Yawat: Yet Another Word Alignment Tool." *Proceedings of the ACL-08: HLT Demo Session*, 20–23. Columbus, Ohio.

Giménez, Jesús and Lluís Màrquez. 2007. "Linguistic features for automatic evaluation of heterogenous mt systems." *Proceedings of the Second Workshop on Statistical Machine Translation*, StatMT '07, 256–264. Stroudsburg, PA, USA.

Hutchins, W. J. and H. L. Somers. 1992. *An introduction to machine translation*. Academic Press New York.

Jones, Bevan, Jacob Andreas, Daniel Bauer, Karl Moritz Hermann, and Kevin Knight. 2012. "Semantics-based machine translation with hyperedge replacement grammars." *Proceedings of COLING.*

Koponen, Maarit. 2012. "Comparing human perceptions of post-editing effort with post-editing operations." *Proceedings of the Seventh Workshop on Statistical Machine Translation*, 181–190. Montréal, Canada.

Lavie, Alon and Michael Denkowski. 2009. "The METEOR metric for automatic evaluation of machine translation." *Machine Translation.*

Linguistic Data Consortium. 2002. "Linguistic data annotation specification: Assessment of fluency and adequacy in Chinese-English translation." `http://projects.ldc.upenn.edu/TIDES/Translation/TranAssessSpec.pdf`.

Lo, Chi-kiu, Anand Karthik Tumuluru, and Dekai Wu. 2012. "Fully automatic semantic MT evaluation." *Proceedings of WMT*, 243–252.

Lo, Chi-kiu and Dekai Wu. 2010. "Evaluating machine translation utility via semantic role labels." *Proceedings of LREC*, 2873–2877.

Lo, Chi-kiu and Dekai Wu. 2011a. "MEANT : An inexpensive , high-accuracy , semi-automatic metric for evaluating translation utility via semantic frames." *Proceedings of ACL*, 220–229.

Lo, Chi-kiu and Dekai Wu. 2011b. "Structured vs. flat semantic role representations for machine translation evaluation." *Proceedings of SSST*, 10–20.

Lo, Chi-kiu and Dekai Wu. 2012. "Unsupervised vs. supervised weight estimation for semantic MT evaluation metrics." *Proceedings of SSST*, 49–56.

Lopez, Adam. 2012. "Putting human assessments of machine translation systems in order." *Proceedings of WMT*, 1–9.

NIST. 2005. "The 2005 NIST machine translation evaluation plan (MT-05)." `http://www.itl.nist.gov/iad/mig/tests/mt/2005/doc/mt05_evalplan.v1.1.pdf`.

Palmer, Martha, Daniel Gildea, and Paul Kingsbury. 2005. "The proposition bank: An annotated corpus of semantic roles." *Computational Linguistics*, 31(1):71–106.

Papineni, Kishore, Salim Roukos, Todd Ward, and Wei-Jing Zhu. 2002. "BLEU: a method for automatic evaluation of machine translation." *Proceedings of the Association for Computational Linguistics*, 311–318. Philadelphia, USA.

Przybocki, Mark, Kay Peterson, Sébastien Bronsart, and Gregory Sanders. 2009. "The NIST

2008 metrics for machine translation challengeoverview, methodology, metrics, and results." *Machine Translation*, 23(2):71–103.

Snover, Matthew, Nitin Madnani, Bonnie Dorr, and Richard Schwartz. 2009a. "Fluency, adequacy, or HTER? exploring different human judgments with a tunable MT metric." *Proceedings of the Workshop on Statistical Machine Translation at the Meeting of the European Chapter of the Association for Computational Linguistics (EACL-2009)*. Athens, Greece.

Snover, Matthew, Nitin Madnani, Bonnie Dorr, and Richard Schwartz. 2009b. "TER-plus: paraphrase, semantic, and alignment enhancements to translation edit rate." *Machine Translation*.

Tumuluru, Anand Karthik, Chi-kiu Lo, and Dekai Wu. 2012. "Accuracy and robustness in measuring the lexical similarity of semantic role fillers for automatic semantic MT evaluation." *Proceedings of PACLIC*, 574–581.

Weaver, Warren. 1955. "Translation." William N. Locke and Andrew D. Booth (eds.), *Machine Translation of Languages; Fourteen Essays*, 15–23. Cambridge, MA: MIT Press. Reprint of a memorandum written in 1949.

LIMSI @ WMT'13

Alexandre Allauzen[1,2], **Nicolas Pécheux**[1,2], **Quoc Khanh Do**[1,2], **Marco Dinarelli**[2], **Thomas Lavergne**[1,2], **Aurélien Max**[1,2], **Hai-Son Le**[3], **François Yvon**[1,2]
Univ. Paris-Sud[1] and LIMSI-CNRS[2]
rue John von Neumann, 91403 Orsay cedex, France
{firstname.lastname}@limsi.fr
Vietnamese Academy of Science and Technology[3], Hanoi, Vietnam
lehaison@ioit.ac.vn

Abstract

This paper describes LIMSI's submissions to the shared WMT'13 translation task. We report results for French-English, German-English and Spanish-English in both directions. Our submissions use n-code, an open source system based on bilingual n-grams, and continuous space models in a post-processing step. The main novelties of this year's participation are the following: our first participation to the Spanish-English task; experiments with source pre-ordering; a tighter integration of continuous space language models using artificial text generation (for German); and the use of different tuning sets according to the original language of the text to be translated.

1 Introduction

This paper describes LIMSI's submissions to the shared translation task of the Eighth Workshop on Statistical Machine Translation. LIMSI participated in the French-English, German-English and Spanish-English tasks in both directions. For this evaluation, we used n-code, an open source in-house Statistical Machine Translation (SMT) system based on bilingual n-grams[1], and continuous space models in a post-processing step, both for translation and target language modeling.

This paper is organized as follows. Section 2 contains an overview of the baseline systems built with n-code, including the continuous space models. As in our previous participations, several steps of data pre-processing, cleaning and filtering are applied, and their improvement took a non-negligible part of our work. These steps are summarized in Section 3. The rest of the paper is devoted to the novelties of the systems submitted this year. Section 4 describes the system developed for our first participation to the Spanish-English translation task in both directions. To translate from German into English, the impact of source pre-ordering is investigated, and experimental results are reported in Section 5, while for the reverse direction, we explored a text sampling strategy using a 10-gram SOUL model to allow a tighter integration of continuous space models during the translation process (see Section 6). A final section discusses the main lessons of this study.

2 System overview

n-code implements the bilingual n-gram approach to SMT (Casacuberta and Vidal, 2004; Mariño et al., 2006; Crego and Mariño, 2006). In this framework, translation is divided in two steps: a source reordering step and a (monotonic) translation step. Source reordering is based on a set of learned rewrite rules that non-deterministically reorder the input words. Applying these rules result in a finite-state graph of possible source reorderings, which is then searched for the best possible candidate translation.

2.1 Features

Given a source sentence $\mathbf{s}$ of I words, the best translation hypothesis $\hat{\mathbf{t}}$ is defined as the sequence of J words that maximizes a linear combination of feature functions:

$$\hat{\mathbf{t}} = \arg\max_{\mathbf{t},\mathbf{a}} \left\{ \sum_{m=1}^{M} \lambda_m h_m(\mathbf{a}, \mathbf{s}, \mathbf{t}) \right\} \qquad (1)$$

where λ_m is the weight associated with feature function h_m and $\mathbf{a}$ denotes an alignment between source and target phrases. Among the feature functions, the peculiar form of the translation model constitutes one of the main difference between the n-gram approach and standard phrase-based systems.

[1] http://ncode.limsi.fr/

In addition to the translation model (TM), *fourteen* feature functions are combined: a *target-language model*; four *lexicon models*; six *lexicalized reordering models* (Tillmann, 2004; Crego et al., 2011) aimed at predicting the orientation of the next translation unit; a "weak" distance-based *distortion model*; and finally a *word-bonus model* and a *tuple-bonus model* which compensate for the system preference for short translations. The four *lexicon models* are similar to the ones used in standard phrase-based systems: two scores correspond to the relative frequencies of the tuples and two lexical weights are estimated from the automatic word alignments. The weight vector λ is learned using the Minimum Error Rate Training framework (MERT) (Och, 2003) and BLEU (Papineni et al., 2002) measured on *nt09* (newstest2009) as the optimization criteria.

2.2 Translation Inference

During decoding, source sentences are represented in the form of word lattices containing the most promising reordering hypotheses, so as to reproduce the word order modifications introduced during the tuple extraction process. Hence, only those reordering hypotheses are translated and are introduced using a set of reordering rules automatically learned from the word alignments. Part-of-speech (POS) information is used to increase the generalization power of these rules. Hence, rewrite rules are built using POS, rather than surface word forms (Crego and Mariño, 2006).

2.3 SOUL rescoring

Neural networks, working on top of conventional n-gram back-off language models (BOLMs), have been introduced in (Bengio et al., 2003; Schwenk et al., 2006) as a potential means to improve discrete language models (LMs). As for our last year participation (Le et al., 2012c), we take advantage of the recent proposal of Le et al. (2011). Using a specific neural network architecture (the *Structured OUtput Layer* or SOUL model), it becomes possible to estimate n-gram models that use large vocabulary, thereby making the training of large neural network LMs (NNLMs) feasible both for target language models and translation models (Le et al., 2012a). We use the same models as last year, meaning that the SOUL rescoring was used for all systems, except for translating into Spanish. See section 6 and (Le et al., 2012c) for more details.

3 Corpora and data pre-processing

Concerning data pre-processing, we started from our submissions from last year (Le et al., 2012c) and mainly upgraded the corpora and the associated language-dependent pre-processing routines. We used in-house text processing tools for the tokenization and detokenization steps (Déchelotte et al., 2008). Previous experiments have demonstrated that better normalization tools provide better BLEU scores: all systems are thus built using the "true-case" scheme.

As German is morphologically more complex than English, the default policy which consists in treating each word form independently is plagued with data sparsity, which severely impacts both training (alignment) and decoding (due to unknown forms). When translating from German into English, the German side is thus normalized using a specific pre-processing scheme (Allauzen et al., 2010; Durgar El-Kahlout and Yvon, 2010) which aims at reducing the lexical redundancy by (i) normalizing the orthography, (ii) neutralizing most inflections and (iii) splitting complex compounds. All parallel corpora were POS-tagged with the TreeTagger (Schmid, 1994); in addition, for German, fine-grained POS labels were also needed for pre-processing and were obtained using the RFTagger (Schmid and Laws, 2008).

For Spanish, all the availaible data are tokenized using FreeLing[2] toolkit (Padró and Stanilovsky, 2012), with default settings and some added rules. Sentence splitting and morphological analysis are disabled except for *del* $\rightarrow$ *de el* and *al* $\rightarrow$ *a el*. Moreover, a simple "true-caser" based on upper-case word frequency is used, and the specific Spanish punctuation signs "¿" and "¡" are removed and heuristically reintroduced in a post-processing step. All Spanish texts are POS-tagged also using Freeling. The EAGLES tag set is however simplified by truncating the category label to the first two symbols, in order to reduce the sparsity of the reordering rules estimated by n-code.

For the CommonCrawl corpus, we found that many sentences are not in the expected language. For example, in the French side of the French-English version, most of the first sentences are in English. Therefore, foreign sentence pairs are filtered out with a MaxEnt classifier that uses n-grams of characters as features (n is between 1 and 4). This filter discards approximatively 10%

[2] http://nlp.lsi.upc.edu/freeling/

of the sentence pairs. Moreover, we also observe that a lot of sentence pairs are not translation of each other. Therefore, an extra sentence alignment step is carried out using an in-house implementation of the tool described in (Moore, 2002). This last step discards approximately 20% of the corpus. For the Spanish-English task, the same filtering is applied to all the available corpora.

4 System development for the Spanish-English task

This is our first participation to the Spanish-English translation task in both directions. This section provides details about the development of n-code systems for this language pair.

4.1 Data selection and filtering

The CommonCrawl and UN corpora can be considered as very noisy and out-of-domain. As described in (Allauzen et al., 2011), to select a subset of parallel sentences, trigram LMs were trained for both Spanish and English languages on a subset of the available News data: the Spanish (resp. English) LM was used to rank the Spanish (resp. English) side of the corpus, and only those sentences with perplexity above a given threshold were selected. Finally, the two selected sets were intersected. In the following experiments, the filtered versions of these corpora are used to train the translation systems unless explicitly stated.

4.2 Spanish language model

To train the language models, we assumed that the test set would consist in a selection of recent news texts and all the available monolingual data for Spanish were used, including the Spanish Gigaword, Third Edition. A vocabulary is first defined by including all tokens observed in the News-Commentary and Europarl corpora. This vocabulary is then expanded with all words that occur more than 10 times in the recent news texts (LDC-2007-2011 and news-crawl-2011-2012). This procedure results in a vocabulary containing 372k words. Then, the training data are divided into 7 sets based on dates or genres. On each set, a standard 4-gram LM is estimated from the vocabulary using absolute discounting interpolated with lower order models (Kneser and Ney, 1995; Chen and Goodman, 1998). The resulting LMs are then linearly interpolated using coefficients chosen so as to minimise the perplexity evaluated on the development set (*nt08*).

	Corpora	*BLEU*	
		dev nt11	*test nt12*
es2en	N,E	30.2	33.2
	N,E,C	30.6	33.7
	N,E,U	30.3	33.6
	N,E,C,U	30.6	33.7
	N,E,C,U (nf)	30.7	33.6
en2es	N,E	32.2	33.3
	N,E,C,U	32.3	33.6
	N,E,C,U (nf)	32.5	33.9

Table 1: BLEU scores achieved with different sets of parallel corpora. All systems are baseline n-code with POS factor models. The following shorthands are used to denote corpora, : "N" stands for News-Commentary, "E" for Europarl, "C" for CommonCrawl, "U" for UN and (nf) for non filtered corpora.

4.3 Experiments

All reported results are averaged on 3 MERT runs. Table 1 shows the BLEU scores obtained with different corpora setups. We can observe that using the CommonCrawl corpus improves the performances in both directions, while the impact of the UN data is less important, especially when combined with CommonCrawl. The filtering strategy described in Section 4.2 has a slightly positive impact of +0.1 BLEU point for the Spanish-to-English direction but yields a 0.2 BLEU point decrease in the opposite direction.

For the following experiments, all the available corpora are therefore used: News-Commentary, Europarl, filtered CommonCrawl and UN. For each of these corpora, a bilingual n-gram model is estimated and used by n-code as one individual model score. An additionnal TM is trained on the concatenation all these corpora, resulting in a total of 5 TMs. Moreover, n-code is able to handle additional "factored" bilingual models where the source side words are replaced by the corresponding lemma or even POS tag (Koehn and Hoang, 2007). Table 2 reports the scores obtained with different settings.

In Table 2, *big* denotes the use of a wider context for n-gram TMs ($n = 4, 5, 4$ instead of $3, 4, 3$ respectively for word-based, POS-based and lemma-based TMs). Using POS factored

	Condition	BLEU	
		dev nt11	*test nt12*
es2en	base	30.3	33.5
	pos	30.6	33.7
	big-pos	30.7	33.7
	big-pos-lem	30.7	33.8
en2es	base	32.0	33.4
	pos	32.3	33.6
	big-pos	32.3	33.8
	big-pos-pos+	32.2	33.4

Table 2: BLEU scores for different configuration of factored translation models. The *big* prefix denotes experiments with the larger context for n-gram translation models.

models yields a significant BLEU improvement, as well as using a wider context for n-gram TMs. Since Spanish is morphologically richer than English, lemmas are introduced only on the Spanish side. An additionnal BLEU improvement is achieved by adding factored models based on lemmas when translating from Spanish to English, while in the opposite direction it does not seem to have any clear impact.

For English to Spanish, we also experimented with a 5-gram target factored model, using the whole morphosyntactic EAGLES tagset, (*pos+* in Table 2), to add some syntactic information, but this, in fact, proved harmful.

As several tuning sets were available, experiments were carried out with the concatenation of *nt09* to *nt11* as a tuning data set. This yields an improvement between 0.1 and 0.3 BLEU point when testing on *nt12* when translating from Spanish to English.

4.4 Submitted systems

For both directions, the submitted systems are trained on all the available training data, the corpora CommonCrawl and UN being filtered as described previously. A word-based TM and a POS factored TM are estimated for each training set. To translate from Spanish to English, the system is tuned on the concatenation of the *nt09* to *nt11* datasets with an additionnal 4-gram lemma-based factored model, while in the opposite direction, we only use *nt11*.

	dev nt09	*test nt11*
en2de	15.43	15.35
en-mod2de	15.06	15.00

Table 3: BLEU scores for pre-ordering experiments with a n-code system and the approach proposed by (Neubig et al., 2012)

5 Source pre-ordering for English to German translation

While distorsion models can efficiently handle short range reorderings, they are inadequate to capture long-range reorderings, especially for language pairs that differ significantly in their syntax. A promising workaround is the source pre-ordering method that can be considered similar, to some extent, to the reordering strategy implemented in n-code; the main difference is that the latter uses one deterministic (long-range) reordering on top of conventional distortion-based models, while the former only considers one single model delivering permutation lattices. The pre-ordering approach is illustrated by the recent work of Neubig et al. (2012), where the authors use a discriminatively trained ITG parser to infer a single permutation of the source sentence.

In this section, we investigate the use of this pre-ordering model in conjunction with the bilingual n-gram approach for translating English into German (see (Collins et al., 2005) for similar experiments with the reverse translation direction). Experiments are carried out with the same settings as described in (Neubig et al., 2012): given the source side of the parallel data (*en*), the parser is estimated to modify the original word order and to generate a new source side (*en-mod*); then a SMT system is built for the new language pair (*en-mod* $\rightarrow$ *de*). The same reordering model is used to reorder the test set, which is then translated with the *en-mod* $\rightarrow$ *de* system.

Results for these experiments are reported in Table 3, where *nt09* and *nt11* are respectively used as development and test sets. We can observe that applying pre-ordering on source sentences leads to small drops in performance for this language pair.

To explain this degradation, the histogram of token movements performed by the model on the pre-ordered training data is represented in Figure 1. We can observe that most of the movements are in the range $[-4, +6]$ (92% of the total occur-

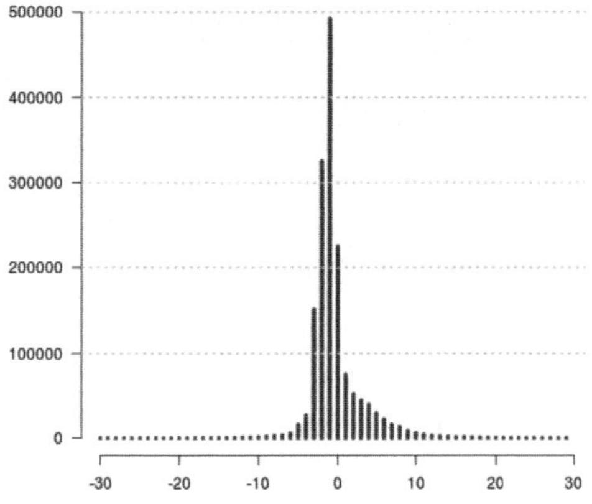

Figure 1: Histogram of token movement size versus its occurrences performed by the model *Neubig* on the source english data.

rences), which can be already taken into account by the standard reordering model of the baseline system. This is reflected also by the following statistics: surprisingly, only 16% of the total number of sentences are changed by the pre-ordering model, and the average sentence-wise Kendall's τ and the average displacement of these small parts of modified sentences are, respectively, 0.027 and 3.5. These numbers are striking for two reasons: first, English and German have in general quite different word order, thus our experimental condition should be somehow similar to the English-Japanese scenario studied in (Neubig et al., 2012); second, since the model is able to perform pre-ordering basically at any distance, it is surprising that a large part of the data remains unmodified.

6 Artificial Text generation with SOUL

While the context size for BOLMs is limited (usually up to 4-grams) because of sparsity issues, NNLMs can efficiently handle larger contexts up to 10-grams without a prohibitive increase of the overall number of parameters (see for instance the study in (Le et al., 2012b)). However the major bottleneck of NNLMs is the computation cost during both training and inference. In fact, the prohibitive inference time usually implies to resort to a two-pass approach: the first pass uses a conventional BOLM to produce a k-best list (the k most likely translations); in the second pass, the probability of a NNLM is computed for each hypothesis, which is then added as a new feature before the k-best list is reranked. Note that to produce the k-best list, the decoder uses a beam search strategy to prune the search space. Crucially, this pruning does not use the NNLMs scores and results in potentially sub-optimal k-best-lists.

6.1 Sampling texts with SOUL

In language modeling, a language is represented by a corpus that is approximated by a n-gram model. Following (Sutskever et al., 2011; Deoras et al., 2013), we propose an additionnal approximation to allow a tighter integration of the NNLM: a 10-gram NNLM is first estimated on the training corpus; texts then are sampled from this model to create an artificial training corpus; finally, this artificial corpus is approximated by a 4-gram BOLM.

The training procedure for the SOUL NNLM is the same as the one described in (Le et al., 2012c). To sample a sentence from the SOUL model, first the sentence length is randomly drawn from the empirical distribution, then each word of the sentence is sampled from the 10-gram distribution estimated with the SOUL model.

The convergence of this sampling strategy can be evaluated by monitoring the perplexity evolution *vs.* the number of sentences that are generated. Figure 2 depicts this evolution by measuring perplexity on the *nt08* set with a step size of 400M sampled sentences. The baseline BOLM (*std*) is estimated on all the available training data that consist of approximately 300M of running words. We can observe that the perplexity of the BOLM estimated on sampled texts (*generated texts*) decreases when the number of sample sentences increases, and tends to reach slowly the perplexity of the baseline BOLM. Moreover, when both BOLMs are interpolated, an even lower perplexity is obtained, which further decreases with the amount of sampled training texts.

6.2 Translation results

Experiments are run for translation into German, which lacks a GigaWord corpus. An artificial corpus containing 3 billions of running words is first generated as described in Section 6.1. This corpus is used to estimate a BOLM with standard settings, that is then used for decoding, thereby approximating the use of a NNLM during the first pass. Results reported in Table 4 show that adding generated texts improves the BLEU scores even when the SOUL model is added in a rescoring step. Also note that using the LM trained on the sampled corpus yields the same BLEU score that using the standard LM.

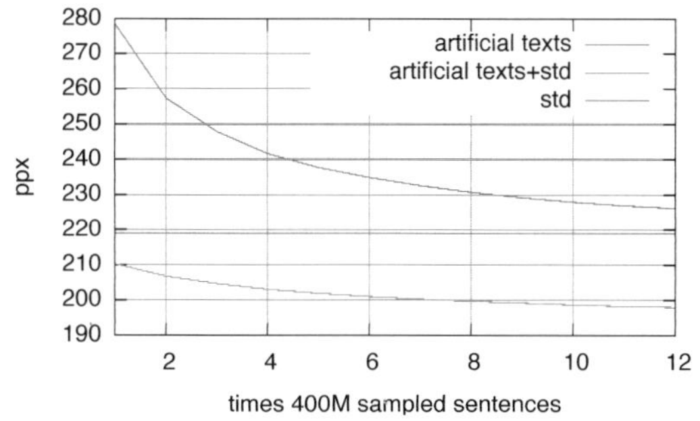

Figure 2: Perplexity measured on *nt08* with the baseline LM (*std*), with the LM estimated on the sampled texts (*generated texts*), and with the interpolation of both.

Therefore, to translate from English to German, the submitted system includes three BOLMs: one trained on all the monolingual data, one on artificial texts and a third one that uses the freely available *deWack* corpus[3] (1.7 billion words).

target LM	*BLEU*	
	dev nt09	test nt10
base	15.3	16.5
+genText	15.5	16.8
+SOUL	16.4	17.6
+genText+SOUL	16.5	17.8

Table 4: Impact of the use of sampled texts.

7 Different tunings for different original languages

As shown by Lembersky et al. (2012), the original language of a text can have a significant impact on translation performance. In this section, this effect is assessed on the French to English translation task. Training one SMT system per original language is impractical, since the required information is not available for most of parallel corpora. However, metadata provided by the WMT evaluation allows us to split the development and test sets according to the original language of the text. To ensure a sufficient amount of texts for each condition, we used the concatenation of newstest corpora for the years 2008, 2009, 2011, and 2012, leaving *nt10* for testing purposes.

Five different development sets have been created to tune five different systems. Experimental results are reported in Table 7 and show a drastic improvement in terms of BLEU score when translating back to the original English and a significant increase for original text in Czech and French. In this year's evaluation, Russian was introduced as a new language, so for sentences originally in this language, the baseline system was used. This system is used as our primary submission to the evaluation, with additional SOUL rescoring step.

[3]http://wacky.sslmit.unibo.it/doku.php

original language	baseline	adapted tuning
cz	22.31	23.83
en	36.41	39.21
fr	31.61	32.41
de	18.46	18.49
es	30.17	29.34
all	29.43	30.12

Table 5: BLEU scores for the French-to-English translation task measured on nt10 with systems tuned on development sets selected according to their original language (*adapted tuning*).

8 Conclusion

In this paper, we have described our submissions to the translation task of WMT'13 for the French-English, German-English and Spanish-English language pairs. Similarly to last year's systems, our main submissions use n-code, and continuous space models are introduced in a post-processing step, both for translation and target language modeling. To translate from English to German, we showed a slight improvement with a tighter integration of the continuous space language model using a text sampling strategy. Experiments with pre-ordering were disappointing, and the reasons for this failure need to be better understood. We also explored the impact of using different tuning sets according to the original language of the text to be translated. Even though the gain vanishes when adding the SOUL model in a post-processing step, it should be noted that due to time limitation this second step was not tuned accordingly to the original language. We therefore plan to assess the impact of using different tuning sets on the post-processing step.

Acknowledgments

This work was partially funded by the French State agency for innovation (OSEO), in the Quaero Programme.

References

Alexandre Allauzen, Josep M. Crego, İlknur Durgar El-Kahlout, and François Yvon. 2010. LIMSI's statistical translation systems for WMT'10. In *Proc. of the Joint Workshop on Statistical Machine Translation and MetricsMATR*, pages 54–59, Uppsala, Sweden.

Alexandre Allauzen, Gilles Adda, Hélène Bonneau-Maynard, Josep M. Crego, Hai-Son Le, Aurélien Max, Adrien Lardilleux, Thomas Lavergne, Artem Sokolov, Guillaume Wisniewski, and François Yvon. 2011. LIMSI @ WMT11. In *Proceedings of the Sixth Workshop on Statistical Machine Translation*, pages 309–315, Edinburgh, Scotland, July. Association for Computational Linguistics.

Yoshua Bengio, Réjean Ducharme, Pascal Vincent, and Christian Janvin. 2003. A neural probabilistic language model. *JMLR*, 3:1137–1155.

Francesco Casacuberta and Enrique Vidal. 2004. Machine translation with inferred stochastic finite-state transducers. *Computational Linguistics*, 30(3):205–225.

Stanley F. Chen and Joshua T. Goodman. 1998. An empirical study of smoothing techniques for language modeling. Technical Report TR-10-98, Computer Science Group, Harvard Un iversity.

Michael Collins, Philipp Koehn, and Ivona Kucerova. 2005. Clause restructuring for statistical machine translation. In *Proceedings of the 43rd Annual Meeting of the Association for Computational Linguistics (ACL'05)*, pages 531–540, Ann Arbor, Michigan.

Josep M. Crego and José B. Mariño. 2006. Improving statistical MT by coupling reordering and decoding. *Machine Translation*, 20(3):199–215.

Josep M. Crego, Franois Yvon, and Jos B. Mariño. 2011. N-code: an open-source Bilingual N-gram SMT Toolkit. *Prague Bulletin of Mathematical Linguistics*, 96:49–58.

Daniel Déchelotte, Gilles Adda, Alexandre Allauzen, Olivier Galibert, Jean-Luc Gauvain, Hlne Maynard, and Franois Yvon. 2008. LIMSI's statistical translation systems for WMT'08. In *Proc. of the NAACL-HTL Statistical Machine Translation Workshop*, Columbus, Ohio.

Anoop Deoras, Tomáš Mikolov, Stefan Kombrink, and Kenneth Church. 2013. Approximate inference: A sampling based modeling technique to capture complex dependencies in a language model. *Speech Communication*, 55(1):162 – 177.

Ilknur Durgar El-Kahlout and Franois Yvon. 2010. The pay-offs of preprocessing for German-English Statistical Machine Translation. In Marcello Federico, Ian Lane, Michael Paul, and Franois Yvon, editors, *Proceedings of the seventh International Workshop on Spoken Language Translation (IWSLT)*, pages 251–258.

Reinhard Kneser and Herman Ney. 1995. Improved backing-off for m-gram language modeling. In *Proceedings of the International Conference on Acoustics, Speech, and Signal Processing, ICASSP'95*, pages 181–184, Detroit, MI.

Philipp Koehn and Hieu Hoang. 2007. Factored translation models. In *Proceedings of the 2007 Joint Conference on Empirical Methods in Natural Language Processing and Computational Natural Language Learning (EMNLP-CoNLL)*, pages 868–876.

Hai-Son Le, Ilya Oparin, Alexandre Allauzen, Jean-Luc Gauvain, and François Yvon. 2011. Structured output layer neural network language model. In *Proceedings of ICASSP'11*, pages 5524–5527.

Hai-Son Le, Alexandre Allauzen, and François Yvon. 2012a. Continuous space translation models with neural networks. In *NAACL '12: Proceedings of the 2012 Conference of the North American Chapter of the Association for Computational Linguistics on Human Language Technology*.

Hai-Son Le, Alexandre Allauzen, and François Yvon. 2012b. Measuring the influence of long range dependencies with neural network language models. In *Proceedings of the NAACL-HLT 2012 Workshop: Will We Ever Really Replace the N-gram Model? On the Future of Language Modeling for HLT*, pages 1–10, Montréal, Canada.

Hai-Son Le, Thomas Lavergne, Alexandre Allauzen, Marianna Apidianaki, Li Gong, Aurélien Max, Artem Sokolov, Guillaume Wisniewski, and François Yvon. 2012c. Limsi @ wmt12. In *Proceedings of the Seventh Workshop on Statistical Machine Translation*, pages 330–337, Montréal, Canada.

Gennadi Lembersky, Noam Ordan, and Shuly Wintner. 2012. Language models for machine translation: Original vs. translated texts. *Comput. Linguist.*, 38(4):799–825, December.

José B. Mariño, Rafael E. Banchs, Josep M. Crego, Adrià de Gispert, Patrick Lambert, José A.R. Fonollosa, and Marta R. Costa-Jussà. 2006. N-gram-based machine translation. *Computational Linguistics*, 32(4):527–549.

Robert C. Moore. 2002. Fast and accurate sentence alignment of bilingual corpora. In *Proceedings of the 5th Conference of the Association for Machine Translation in the Americas on Machine Translation: From Research to Real Users*, AMTA '02, pages 135–144, Tiburon, CA, USA. Springer-Verlag.

Graham Neubig, Taro Watanabe, and Shinsuke Mori. 2012. Inducing a discriminative parser to optimize machine translation reordering. In *Proceedings of the 2012 Joint Conference on Empirical Methods in Natural Language Processing and Computational Natural Language Learning*, pages 843–853, Jeju Island, Korea, July. Association for Computational Linguistics.

Franz Josef Och. 2003. Minimum error rate training in statistical machine translation. In *ACL '03: Proc. of the 41st Annual Meeting on Association for Computational Linguistics*, pages 160–167.

Lluís Padró and Evgeny Stanilovsky. 2012. Freeling 3.0: Towards wider multilinguality. In *Proceedings of the Language Resources and Evaluation Conference (LREC 2012)*, Istanbul, Turkey, May. ELRA.

Kishore Papineni, Salim Roukos, Todd Ward, and Wei-Jing Zhu. 2002. BLEU: a method for automatic evaluation of machine translation. In *ACL '02: Proc. of the 40th Annual Meeting on Association for Computational Linguistics*, pages 311–318. Association for Computational Linguistics.

Helmut Schmid and Florian Laws. 2008. Estimation of conditional probabilities with decision trees and an application to fine-grained POS tagging. In *Proceedings of the 22nd International Conference on Computational Linguistics (Coling 2008)*, pages 777–784, Manchester, UK, August.

Helmut Schmid. 1994. Probabilistic part-of-speech tagging using decision trees. In *Proc. of International Conference on New Methods in Language Processing*, pages 44–49, Manchester, UK.

Holger Schwenk, Daniel Déchelotte, and Jean-Luc Gauvain. 2006. Continuous space language models for statistical machine translation. In *Proc. COLING/ACL'06*, pages 723–730.

Ilya Sutskever, James Martens, and Geoffrey Hinton. 2011. Generating text with recurrent neural networks. In Lise Getoor and Tobias Scheffer, editors, *Proceedings of the 28th International Conference on Machine Learning (ICML-11)*, ICML '11, pages 1017–1024, New York, NY, USA, June. ACM.

Christoph Tillmann. 2004. A unigram orientation model for statistical machine translation. In *Proceedings of HLT-NAACL 2004*, pages 101–104. Association for Computational Linguistics.

The CMU Machine Translation Systems at WMT 2013: Syntax, Synthetic Translation Options, and Pseudo-References

Waleed Ammar Victor Chahuneau Michael Denkowski Greg Hanneman Wang Ling Austin Matthews Kenton Murray Nicola Segall Yulia Tsvetkov Alon Lavie Chris Dyer*

Language Technologies Institute
Carnegie Mellon University
Pittsburgh, PA 15213 USA
*Corresponding author: cdyer@cs.cmu.edu

Abstract

We describe the CMU systems submitted to the 2013 WMT shared task in machine translation. We participated in three language pairs, French–English, Russian–English, and English–Russian. Our particular innovations include: a label-coarsening scheme for syntactic tree-to-tree translation and the use of specialized modules to create "synthetic translation options" that can both generalize beyond what is directly observed in the parallel training data and use rich source language context to decide how a phrase should translate in context.

1 Introduction

The MT research group at Carnegie Mellon University's Language Technologies Institute participated in three language pairs for the 2013 Workshop on Machine Translation shared translation task: French–English, Russian–English, and English–Russian. Our French–English system (§3) showcased our group's syntactic system with coarsened nonterminal types (Hanneman and Lavie, 2011). Our Russian–English and English–Russian system demonstrate a new multi-phase approach to translation that our group is using, in which **synthetic translation options** (§4) to supplement the default translation rule inventory that is extracted from word-aligned training data. In the Russian-English system (§5), we used a CRF-based transliterator (Ammar et al., 2012) to propose transliteration candidates for out-of-vocabulary words, and used a language model to insert or remove common function words in phrases according to an n-gram English language model probability. In the English–Russian system (§6), we used a conditional logit model to predict the most likely inflectional morphology of Russian lemmas, conditioning on rich source syntactic features (§6.1). In addition to being able to generate inflected forms that were otherwise unobserved in the parallel training data, the translations options generated in this matter had features reflecting their appropriateness given much broader source language context than usually would have been incorporated in current statistical MT systems.

For our Russian–English system, we additionally used a secondary "pseudo-reference" translation when tuning the parameters of our Russian–English system. This was created by automatically translating the Spanish translation of the provided development data into English. While the output of an MT system is not always perfectly grammatical, previous work has shown that secondary machine-generated references improve translation quality when only a single human reference is available when BLEU is used as an optimization criterion (Madnani, 2010; Dyer et al., 2011).

2 Common System Components

The decoder infrastructure we used was cdec (Dyer et al., 2010). Only the constrained data resources provided for the shared task were used for training both the translation and language models. Word alignments were generated using the Model 2 variant described in Dyer et al. (2013). Language models used modified Kneser-Ney smoothing estimated using KenLM (Heafield, 2011). Translation model parameters were discriminatively set to optimize BLEU on a held-out development set using an online passive aggressive algorithm (Eidelman, 2012) or, in the case of the French–English system, using the hypergraph MERT algorithm and optimizing towards BLEU (Kumar et al., 2009). The remainder of the paper will focus on our primary innovations in the various system pairs.

3 French-English Syntax System

Our submission for French–English is a tree-to-tree translation system that demonstrates several innovations from group's research on SCFG-based translation.

3.1 Data Selection

We divided the French–English training data into two categories: clean data (Europarl, News Commentary, UN Documents) totaling 14.8 million sentence pairs, and web data (Common Crawl, Giga-FrEn) totaling 25.2 million sentence pairs. To reduce the volume of data used, we filtered non-parallel and other unhelpful segments according to the technique described by Denkowski et al. (2012). This procedure uses a lexical translation model learned from just the clean data, as well as source and target n-gram language models to compute the following feature scores:

- French and English 4-gram log likelihood (normalized by length);
- French–English and English–French lexical translation log likelihood (normalized by length); and,
- Fractions of aligned words under the French–English and English–French models.

We pooled previous years' WMT news test sets to form a reference data set. We computed the same features. To filter the web data, we retained only sentence for which each feature score was no lower than two standard deviations below the mean on the reference data. This reduced the web data from 25.2 million to 16.6 million sentence pairs. Parallel segments from all parts of the data that were blank on either side, were longer than 99 tokens, contained a token of more than 30 characters, or had particularly unbalanced length ratios were also removed. After filtering, 30.9 million sentence pairs remained for rule extraction: 14.4 million from the clean data, and 16.5 million from the web data.

3.2 Preprocessing and Grammar Extraction

Our French–English system uses parse trees in both the source and target languages, so tokenization in this language pair was carried out to match the tokenizations expected by the parsers we used (English data was tokenized with the Stanford tokenizer for English and an in-house tokenizer for French that targets the tokenization used by the Berkeley French parser). Both sides of the parallel training data were parsed using the Berkeley latent variable parser.

Synchronous context-free grammar rules were extracted from the corpus following the method of Hanneman et al. (2011). This decomposes each tree pair into a collection of SCFG rules by exhaustively identifying aligned subtrees to serve as rule left-hand sides and smaller aligned subtrees to be abstracted as right-hand-side nonterminals. Basic subtree alignment heuristics are similar to those by Galley et al. (2006), and composed rules are allowed. The computational complexity is held in check by a limit on the number of RHS elements (nodes and terminals), rather than a GHKM-style maximum composition depth or Hiero-style maximum rule span. Our rule extractor also allows "virtual nodes," or the insertion of new nodes in the parse tree to subdivide regions of flat structure. Virtual nodes are similar to the A+B extended categories of SAMT (Zollmann and Venugopal, 2006), but with the added constraint that they may not conflict with the surrounding tree structure.

Because the SCFG rules are labeled with nonterminals composed from both the source and target trees, the nonterminal inventory is quite large, leading to estimation difficulties. To deal with this, we automatically coarsening the nonterminal labels (Hanneman and Lavie, 2011). Labels are agglomeratively clustered based on a histogram-based similarity function that looks at what target labels correspond to a particular source label and vice versa. The number of clusters used is determined based on spikes in the distance between successive clustering iterations, or by the number of source, target, or joint labels remaining. Starting from a default grammar of 877 French, 2580 English, and 131,331 joint labels, we collapsed the label space for our WMT system down to 50 French, 54 English, and 1814 joint categories.[1]

[1]Selecting the stopping point still requires a measure of intuition. The label set size of 1814 chosen here roughly corresponds to the number of joint labels that would exist in the grammar if virtual nodes were not included. This equivalence has worked well in practice in both internal and published experiments on other data sets (Hanneman and Lavie, 2013).

Extracted rules each have 10 features associated with them. For an SCFG rule with source left-hand side ℓ_s, target left-hand side ℓ_t, source right-hand side r_s, and target right-hand side r_t, they are:

- phrasal translation log relative frequencies $\log f(r_s \mid r_t)$ and $\log f(r_t \mid r_s)$;
- labeling relative frequency $\log f(\ell_s, \ell_t \mid r_s, r_t)$ and generation relative frequency $\log f(r_s, r_t \mid \ell_s, \ell_t)$;
- lexical translation log probabilities $\log p_{lex}(r_s \mid r_t)$ and $\log p_{lex}(r_t \mid r_s)$, defined similarly to Moses's definition;
- a rarity score $\frac{\exp(\frac{1}{c})-1}{\exp(1)-1}$ for a rule with frequency c (this score is monotonically decreasing in the rule frequency); and,
- three binary indicator features that mark whether a rule is fully lexicalized, fully abstract, or a glue rule.

Grammar filtering. Even after collapsing labels, the extracted SCFGs contain an enormous number of rules — 660 million rule types from just under 4 billion extracted instances. To reduce the size of the grammar, we employ a combination of lossless filtering and lossy pruning. We first prune all rules to select no more than the 60 most frequent target-side alternatives for any source RHS, then do further filtering to produce grammars for each test sentence:

- Lexical rules are filtered to the sentence level. Only phrase pairs whose source sides match the test sentence are retained.
- Abstract rules (whose RHS are all nonterminals) are globally pruned. Only the 4000 most frequently observed rules are retained.
- Mixed rules (whose RHS are a mix of terminals and nonterminals) must match the test sentence, and there is an additional frequency cutoff.

After this filtering, the number of completely lexical rules that match a given sentence is typically low, up to a few thousand rules. Each fully abstract rule can potentially apply to every sentence; the strict pruning cutoff in use for these rules is meant to focus the grammar to the most important general syntactic divergences between French and English. Most of the latitude in grammar pruning comes from adjusting the frequency cutoff on the mixed rules since this category of rule is by far the most common type. We conducted experiments with three different frequency cutoffs: 100, 200, and 500, with each increase decreasing the grammar size by 70–80 percent.

3.3 French–English Experiments

We tuned our system to the newstest2008 set of 2051 segments. Aside from the official newstest2013 test set (3000 segments), we also collected test-set scores from last year's newstest2012 set (3003 segments). Automatic metric scores are computed according to BLEU (Papineni et al., 2002), METEOR (Denkowski and Lavie, 2011), and TER (Snover et al., 2006), all computed according to MultEval v. 0.5 (Clark et al., 2011). Each system variant is run with two independent MERT steps in order to control for optimizer instability.

Table 1 presents the results, with the metric scores averaged over both MERT runs. Quite interestingly, we find only minor differences in both tune and test scores despite the large differences in filtered/pruned grammar size as the cutoff for partially abstract rules increases. No system is fully statistically separable (at $p < 0.05$) from the others according to MultEval's approximate randomization algorithm. The closest is the variant with cutoff 200, which is generally judged to be slightly worse than the other two. METEOR claims full distinction on the 2013 test set, ranking the system with the strictest grammar cutoff (500) best. This is the version that we ultimately submitted to the shared translation task.

4 Synthetic Translation Options

Before discussing our Russian–English and English–Russian systems, we introduce the concept of **synthetic translation options**, which we use in these systems. We provide a brief overview here; for more detail, we refer the reader to Tsvetkov et al. (2013).

In language pairs that are typologically similar, words and phrases map relatively directly from source to target languages, and the standard approach to learning phrase pairs by extraction from parallel data can be very effective. However, in language pairs in which individual source language words have many different possible translations (e.g., when the target language word could have many different inflections or could be surrounded by different function words that have no

System	Dev (2008) BLEU	METR	TER	Test (2012) BLEU	METR	TER	Test (2013) BLEU	METR	TER
Cutoff 100	22.52	31.44	59.22	27.73	33.30	53.25	28.34	* 33.19	53.07
Cutoff 200	22.34	31.40	59.21	* 27.33	33.26	53.23	* 28.05	* 33.07	53.16
Cutoff 500	22.80	31.64	59.10	27.88	* 33.58	53.09	28.27	* 33.31	53.13

Table 1: French–English automatic metric scores for three grammar pruning cutoffs, averaged over two MERT runs each. Scores that are statistically separable ($p < 0.05$) from both others in the same column are marked with an asterisk (*).

direct correspondence in the source language), we can expect the standard phrasal inventory to be incomplete, except when very large quantities of parallel data are available or for very frequent words. There simply will not be enough examples from which to learn the ideal set of translation options. Therefore, since phrase based translation can only generate input/output word pairs that were directly observed in the training corpus, the decoder's only hope for producing a good output is to find a fluent, meaning-preserving translation using incomplete translation lexicons. Synthetic translation option generation seeks to fill these gaps using secondary generation processes that produce possible phrase translation alternatives that are not directly extractable from the training data. By filling in gaps in the translation options used to construct the sentential translation search space, global discriminative translation models and language models can be more effective than they would otherwise be.

From a practical perspective, synthetic translation options are attractive relative to trying to build more powerful models of translation since they enable focus on more targeted translation problems (for example, transliteration, or generating proper inflectional morphology for a single word or phrase). Since they are translation options and not complete translations, many of them may be generated.

In the following system pairs, we use synthetic translation options to augment hiero grammar rules learned in the usual way. The synthetic phrases we include augment draw from several sources:

- transliterations of OOV Russian words (§5.3);
- English target sides with varied function words (for example, given a phrase that translates into *cat* we procedure variants like *the cat*, *a cat* and *of the cat*); and,
- when translating *into* Russian, we generate phrases by first predicting the most likely Russian lemma for a source word or phrase, and then, conditioned on the English source context (including syntactic and lexical features), we predict the most likely inflection of the lemma (§6.1).

5 Russian–English System

5.1 Data

We used the same parallel data for both the Russian–English and English Russian systems. Except for filtering to remove sentence pairs whose log length ratios were statistical outliers, we only filtered the Common Crawl corpus to remove sentence pairs with less than 50% concentration of Cyrillic characters on the Russian side. The remaining data was tokenized and lower-cased. For language models, we trained 4-gram Markov models using the target side of the bitext and any available monolingual data (including Gigaword for English). Additionally, we trained 7-gram language models using 600-class Brown clusters with Witten-Bell smoothing.[2]

5.2 Baseline System

Our baseline Russian–English system is a hierarchical phrase-based translation model as implemented in cdec (Chiang, 2007; Dyer et al., 2010). SCFG translation rules that plausibly match each sentence in the development and deftest sets were extracted from the aligned parallel data using the suffix array indexing technique of Lopez (2008). A Russian morphological analyzer was used to lemmatize the training, development, and test data, and the "noisier channel" translation approach of Dyer (2007) was used in the Russian–English system to let unusually inflected surface forms back off to per-lemma translations.

[2] http://www.ark.cs.cmu.edu/cdyer/ru-600/.

5.3 Synthetic Translations: Transliteration

Analysis revealed that about one third of the unseen Russian tokens in the development set consisted of named entities which should be transliterated. We used individual Russian-English word pairs in Wikipedia parallel headlines [3] to train a linear-chained CRF tagger which labels each character in the Russian token with a sequence of zero or more English characters (Ammar et al., 2012). Since Russian names in the training set were in nominative case, we used a simple rule-based morphological generator to produce possible inflections and filtered out the ones not present in the Russian monolingual corpus. At decoding, unseen Russian tokens are fed to the transliterator which produces the most probable 20 transliterations. We add a synthetic translation option for each of the transliterations with four features: an indicator feature for transliterations, the CRF unnormalized score, the trigram character-LM log-probability, and the divergence from the average length-ratio between an English name and its Russian transliteration.

5.4 Synthetic Translations: Function Words

Slavic languages like Russian have a large number of different inflected forms for each lemma, representing different cases, tenses, and aspects. Since our training data is rather limited relative to the number of inflected forms that are possible, we use an English language model to generate a variety of common function word contexts for each content word phrase. These are added to the phrase table with a feature indicating that they were not actually observed in the training data, but rather hallucinated using SRILM's `disambig` tool.

5.5 Summary

Table 5.5 summarizes our Russian-English translation results. In the submitted system, we additionally used MBR reranking to combine the 500-best outputs of our system, with the 500-best outputs of a syntactic system constructed similarly to the French–English system.

6 English–Russian System

The bilingual training data was identical to the filtered data used in the previous section. Word alignments was performed after lemmatizing the Russian side of the training corpus. An unpruned, modified Kneser-Ney smoothed 4-gram language model (Chen and Goodman, 1996) was estimated from all available Russian text (410 million words) using the KenLM toolkit (Heafield et al., 2013).

A standard hierarchical phrase-based system was trained with rule shape indicator features, obtained by replacing terminals in translation rules by a generic symbol. MIRA training was performed to learn feature weights.

Additionally, word clusters (Brown et al., 1992) were obtained for the complete monolingual Russian data. Then, an unsmoothed 7-gram language model was trained on these clusters and added as a feature to the translation system. Indicator features were also added for each cluster and bigram cluster occurence. These changes resulted in an improvement of more than a BLEU point on our held-out development set.

Table 2: Russian-English summary.

Condition	BLEU
Baseline	30.8
Function words	30.9
Transliterations	31.1

6.1 Predicting Target Morphology

We train a classifier to predict the inflection of each Russian word independently given the corresponding English sentence and its word alignment. To do this, we first process the Russian side of the parallel training data using a statistical morphological tagger (Sharoff et al., 2008) to obtain lemmas and inflection tags for each word in context. Then, we obtain part-of-speech tags and dependency parses of the English side of the parallel data (Martins et al., 2010), as well as Brown clusters (Brown et al., 1992). We extract features capturing lexical and syntactical relationships in the source sentence and train structured linear logistic regression models to predict the tag of each English word independently given its part-of-speech.[4] In practice, due to the large size of the corpora and of the feature space dimension, we were only able to use about 10% of the available bilingual data, sampled randomly from the Common Crawl corpus. We also restricted the

[3]We contributed the data set to the shared task participants at http://www.statmt.org/wmt13/wiki-titles.ru-en.tar.gz

[4]We restrict ourselves to verbs, nouns, adjectives, adverbs and cardinals since these open-class words carry most inflection in Russian.

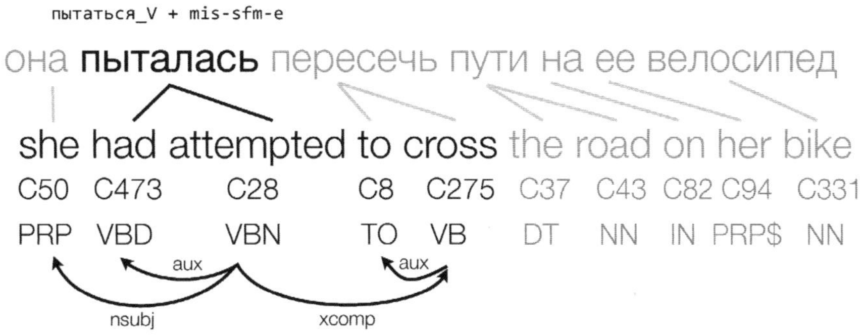

Figure 1: The classifier is trained to predict the verbal inflection mis-sfm-e based on the linear and syntactic context of the words aligned to the Russian word; given the stem пытаться (*pytat'sya*), this inflection paradigm produces the observed surface form пыталась (*pytalas'*).

set of possible inflections for each word to the set of tags that were observed with its lemma in the full monolingual training data. This was necessary because of our choice to use a tagger, which is not able to synthesize surface forms for a given lemma-tag pair.

We then augment the standard hierarchical phrase-base grammars extracted for the baseline systems with new rules containing inflections not necessarily observed in the parallel training data. We start by training a non-gappy phrase translation model on the bilingual data where the Russian has been lemmatized.[5] Then, before translating an English sentence, we extract translation phrases corresponding to this specific sentence and re-inflect each word in the target side of these phrases using the classifier with features extracted from the source sentence words and annotations. We keep the original phrase-based translation features and add the inflection score predicted by the classifier as well as indicator features for the part-of-speech categories of the re-inflected words.

On a held-out development set, these synthetic phrases produce a 0.3 BLEU point improvement. Interestingly, the feature weight learned for using these phrases is positive, indicating that useful inflections might be produced by this process.

7 Conclusion

The CMU systems draws on a large number of different research directions. Techniques such as MBR reranking and synthetic phrases allow different contributors to focus on different translation problems that are ultimately recombined into a single system. Our performance, in particular, on English–Russian machine translation was quite satisfying, we attribute our biggest gains in this language pair to the following:

- Our inflection model that predicted how an English word ought best be translated, given its context. This enabled us to generate forms that were not observed in the parallel data or would have been rare *independent of context* with precision.
- Brown cluster language models seem to be quite effective at modeling long-range morphological agreement patterns quite reliably.

Acknowledgments

We sincerely thank the organizers of the workshop for their hard work, year after year, and the reviewers for their careful reading of the submitted draft of this paper. This research work was supported in part by the U. S. Army Research Laboratory and the U. S. Army Research Office under contract/grant number W911NF-10-1-0533, by the National Science Foundation under grant IIS-0915327, by a NPRP grant (NPRP 09-1140-1-177) from the Qatar National Research Fund (a member of the Qatar Foundation), and by computing resources provided by the NSF-sponsored XSEDE program under grant TG-CCR110017. The statements made herein are solely the responsibility of the authors.

[5]We keep intact words belonging to non-predicted categories.

References

Waleed Ammar, Chris Dyer, and Noah A. Smith. 2012. Transliteration by sequence labeling with lattice encodings and reranking. In *NEWS workshop at ACL*.

Peter F. Brown, Peter V. deSouza, Robert L. Mercer, Vincent J. Della Pietra, and Jenifer C. Lai. 1992. Class-based n-gram models of natural language. *Computional Linguistics*, 18(4):467–479.

Stanley F. Chen and Joshua Goodman. 1996. An empirical study of smoothing techniques for language modeling. In *Proceedings of the 34th Annual Meeting of the Association for Computational Linguistics*, pages 310–318, Santa Cruz, California, USA, June. Association for Computational Linguistics.

David Chiang. 2007. Hierarchical phrase-based translation. *Computational Linguistics*, 33(2):201–228.

Jonathan H. Clark, Chris Dyer, Alon Lavie, and Noah A. Smith. 2011. Better hypothesis testing for statistical machine translation: Crontrolling for optimizer instability. In *Proceedings of the 49th Annual Meeting of the Association for Computational Linguistics: Short Papers*, pages 176–181, Portland, Oregon, USA, June.

Michael Denkowski and Alon Lavie. 2011. Meteor 1.3: Automatic metric for reliable optimization and evaluation of machine translation systems. In *Proceedings of the Sixth Workshop on Statistical Machine Translation*, pages 85–91, Edinburgh, Scotland, UK, July.

Michael Denkowski, Greg Hanneman, and Alon Lavie. 2012. The cmu-avenue french-english translation system. In *Proceedings of the NAACL 2012 Workshop on Statistical Machine Translation*.

Chris Dyer, Adam Lopez, Juri Ganitkevitch, Johnathan Weese, Ferhan Ture, Phil Blunsom, Hendra Setiawan, Vladimir Eidelman, and Philip Resnik. 2010. cdec: A decoder, alignment, and learning framework for finite-state and context-free translation models. In *Proc. of ACL*.

Chris Dyer, Kevin Gimpel, Jonathan H. Clark, and Noah A. Smith. 2011. The CMU-ARK German-English translation system. In *Proceedings of the Sixth Workshop on Statistical Machine Translation*.

Chris Dyer, Victor Chahuneau, and Noah A. Smith. 2013. A simple, fast, and effective reparameterization of IBM Model 2. In *Proc. of NAACL*.

Chris Dyer. 2007. The 'noiser channel': Translation from morphologically complex languages. In *Proceedings of WMT*.

Vladimir Eidelman. 2012. Optimization strategies for online large-margin learning in machine translation. In *Proceedings of the Seventh Workshop on Statistical Machine Translation*.

Michel Galley, Jonathan Graehl, Kevin Knight, Daniel Marcu, Steve DeNeefe, Wei Wang, and Ignacio Thayer. 2006. Scalable inference and training of context-rich syntactic translation models. In *Proceedings of the 21st International Conference on Computational Linguistics and 44th Annual Meeting of the ACL*, pages 961–968, Sydney, Australia, July.

Greg Hanneman and Alon Lavie. 2011. Automatic category label coarsening for syntax-based machine translation. In *Proceedings of SSST-5: Fifth Workshop on Syntax, Semantics, and Structure in Statistical Translation*, pages 98–106, Portland, Oregon, USA, June.

Greg Hanneman and Alon Lavie. 2013. Improving syntax-augmented machine translation by coarsening the label set. In *Proceedings of NAACL-HLT 2013*, pages 288–297, Atlanta, Georgia, USA, June.

Greg Hanneman, Michelle Burroughs, and Alon Lavie. 2011. A general-purpose rule extractor for SCFG-based machine translation. In *Proceedings of SSST-5: Fifth Workshop on Syntax, Semantics, and Structure in Statistical Translation*, pages 135–144, Portland, Oregon, USA, June.

Kenneth Heafield, Ivan Pouzyrevsky, Jonathan H. Clark, and Philipp Koehn. 2013. Scalable modified Kneser-Ney language model estimation. In *Proceedings of the 51st Annual Meeting of the Association for Computational Linguistics*, Sofia, Bulgaria, August.

Kenneth Heafield. 2011. KenLM: Faster and smaller language model queries. In *Proceedings of the Sixth Workshop on Statistical Machine Translation*, Edinburgh, Scotland, UK, July.

Shankar Kumar, Wolfgang Macherey, Chris Dyer, and Franz Och. 2009. Efficient minimum error rate training and minimum Bayes-risk decoding for translation hypergraphs and lattices. In *Proc. of ACL-IJCNLP*.

Adam Lopez. 2008. Tera-scale translation models via pattern matching. In *Proc. of COLING*.

Nitin Madnani. 2010. *The Circle of Meaning: From Translation to Paraphrasing and Back*. Ph.D. thesis, Department of Computer Science, University of Maryland College Park.

André F. T. Martins, Noah A. Smith, Eric P. Xing, Pedro M. Q. Aguiar, and Mário A. T. Figueiredo. 2010. Turbo parsers: Dependency parsing by approximate variational inference. In *Proceedings of the Conference on Empirical Methods in Natural Language Processing*.

Kishore Papineni, Salim Roukos, Todd Ward, and Wei-Jing Zhu. 2002. BLEU: A method for automatic evalution of machine translation. In *Proceedings of the 40th Annual Meeting of the Association for Computational Linguistics*, pages 311–318, Philadelphia, Pennsylvania, USA, July.

Serge Sharoff, Mikhail Kopotev, Tomaz Erjavec, Anna Feldman, and Dagmar Divjak. 2008. Designing and evaluating a russian tagset. In *Proc. of LREC*.

Matthew Snover, Bonnie Dorr, Richard Schwartz, Linnea Micciulla, and John Makhoul. 2006. A study of translation edit rate with targeted human annotation. In *Proceedings of the Seventh Conference of the Association for Machine Translation in the Americas*, pages 223–231, Cambridge, Massachusetts, USA, August.

Yulia Tsvetkov, Chris Dyer, Lori Levin, and Archna Batia. 2013. Generating English determiners in phrase-based translation with synthetic translation options. In *Proceedings of the Eighth Workshop on Statistical Machine Translation*.

Andreas Zollmann and Ashish Venugopal. 2006. Syntax augmented machine translation via chart parsing. In *Proceedings of the Workshop on Statistical Machine Translation*, pages 138–141, New York, New York, USA, June.

Feature Decay Algorithms for Fast Deployment of Accurate Statistical Machine Translation Systems

Ergun Biçici
Centre for Next Generation Localisation,
Dublin City University, Dublin, Ireland.
ergun.bicici@computing.dcu.ie

Abstract

We use feature decay algorithms (FDA) for fast deployment of accurate statistical machine translation systems taking only about half a day for each translation direction. We develop parallel FDA for solving computational scalability problems caused by the abundance of training data for SMT models and LM models and still achieve SMT performance that is on par with using all of the training data or better. Parallel FDA runs separate FDA models on randomized subsets of the training data and combines the instance selections later. Parallel FDA can also be used for selecting the LM corpus based on the training set selected by parallel FDA. The high quality of the selected training data allows us to obtain very accurate translation outputs close to the top performing SMT systems. The relevancy of the selected LM corpus can reach up to 86% reduction in the number of OOV tokens and up to 74% reduction in the perplexity. We perform SMT experiments in all language pairs in the WMT13 translation task and obtain SMT performance close to the top systems using significantly less resources for training and development.

1 Introduction

Statistical machine translation (SMT) is a data intensive problem. If you have the translations for the source sentences you are translating in your training set or even portions of it, then the translation task becomes easier. If some tokens are not found in your training data then you cannot translate them and if some translated word do not appear in your language model (LM) corpus, then it becomes harder for the SMT engine to find their correct position in the translation.

Current SMT systems also face problems caused by the proliferation of various parallel corpora available for building SMT systems. The training data for many of the language pairs in the translation task, part of the Workshop on Machine translation (WMT13) (Callison-Burch et al., 2013), have increased the size of the available parallel corpora for instance by web crawled corpora over the years. The increased size of the training material creates computational scalability problems when training SMT models and can increase the amount of noisy parallel sentences found. As the training set sizes increase, proper training set selection becomes more important.

At the same time, when we are going to translate just a couple of thousand sentences, possibly belonging to the same target domain, it does not make sense to invest resources for training SMT models over tens of millions of sentences or even more. SMT models like Moses already have filtering mechanisms to create smaller parts of the built models that are relevant to the test set.

In this paper, we develop parallel feature decay algorithms (FDA) for solving computational scalability problems caused by the abundance of training data for SMT models and LM models and still achieve SMT performance that is on par with using all of the training data or better. Parallel FDA runs separate FDA models on randomized subsets of the training data and combines the instance selections later. We perform SMT experiments in all language pairs of the WMT13 (Callison-Burch et al., 2013) and obtain SMT performance close to the baseline Moses (Koehn et al., 2007) system using less resources for training. With parallel FDA, we can solve not only the instance selection problem for training data but also instance selection for the LM training corpus, which allows us to train higher order n-gram language models and model the dependencies better.

Parallel FDA improves the scalability of FDA

and allows rapid prototyping of SMT systems for a given target domain or task. Parallel FDA can be very useful for MT in target domains with limited resources or in disaster and crisis situations (Lewis et al., 2011) where parallel corpora can be gathered by crawling and selected by parallel FDA. Parallel FDA also improves the computational requirements of FDA by selecting from smaller corpora and distributing the work load. The high quality of the selected training data allows us to obtain very accurate translation outputs close to the top performing SMT systems. The relevancy of the LM corpus selected can reach up to 86% reduction in the number of OOV tokens and up to 74% reduction in the perplexity.

We organize our work as follows. We describe FDA and parallel FDA models in the next section. We also describe how we extend the FDA model for LM corpus selection. In section 3, we present our experimental results and in the last section, we summarize our contributions.

2 Feature Decay Algorithms for Instance Selection

In this section, we describe the FDA algorithm, the parallel FDA model, and how FDA training instance selection algorithms can be used also for instance selection for language model corpora.

2.1 Feature Decay Algorithm (FDA)

Feature decay algorithms (Biçici and Yuret, 2011a) increase the diversity of the training set by decaying the weights of n-gram features that have already been included. FDAs try to maximize the coverage of the target language features for the test set. Translation performance can improve as we include multiple possible translations for a given word, which increases the diversity of the training set. A target language feature that does not appear in the selected training instances will be difficult to produce regardless of the decoding algorithm (impossible for unigram features). FDA tries to find as many training instances as possible to increase the chances of covering the correct target language feature by reducing the weight of the included features after selecting each training instance.

Algorithm 1 gives the pseudo-code for FDA. We improve FDA with improved scaling, where the score for each sentence is scaled proportional to the length of the sentence, which reduces the average length of the training instances.

Algorithm 1: The Feature Decay Algorithm

Input: Parallel training sentences $\mathcal{U}$, test set features $\mathcal{F}$, and desired number of training instances N.
Data: A priority queue $\mathcal{Q}$, sentence scores $\texttt{score}$, feature values $\texttt{fval}$.
Output: Subset of the parallel sentences to be used as the training data $\mathcal{L} \subseteq \mathcal{U}$.

foreach $f \in \mathcal{F}$ **do**
  $\texttt{fval}(f) \leftarrow \texttt{init}(f, \mathcal{U})$
foreach $S \in \mathcal{U}$ **do**
  $\texttt{score}(S) \leftarrow \frac{1}{|S|^s} \sum_{f \in \texttt{features}(S)} \texttt{fval}(f)$
  $\texttt{enqueue}(\mathcal{Q}, S, \texttt{score}(S))$
while $|\mathcal{L}| < N$ **do**
  $S \leftarrow \texttt{dequeue}(\mathcal{Q})$
  $\texttt{score}(S) \leftarrow \frac{1}{|S|^s} \sum_{f \in \texttt{features}(S)} \texttt{fval}(f)$
  if $\texttt{score}(S) \geq \texttt{topval}(\mathcal{Q})$ **then**
    $\mathcal{L} \leftarrow \mathcal{L} \cup \{S\}$
    foreach $f \in \texttt{features}(S)$ **do**
      $\texttt{fval}(f) \leftarrow \texttt{decay}(f, \mathcal{U}, \mathcal{L})$
  else
    $\texttt{enqueue}(\mathcal{Q}, S, \texttt{score}(S))$

The input to the algorithm consists of parallel training sentences, the number of desired training instances, and the source language features of the test set. The feature decay function (decay) is the most important part of the algorithm where feature weights are multiplied by $1/n$ where n is the count of the feature in the current training set. The initialization function (init) calculates the log of inverse document frequency (idf): $\texttt{init}(f, \mathcal{U}) = \log(|\mathcal{U}|/(1 + C(f, \mathcal{U})))$, where $|\mathcal{U}|$ is the sum of the number of features appearing in the training corpus and $C(f, \mathcal{U})$ is the number of times feature f appear in $\mathcal{U}$. Further experiments with the algorithm are given in (Biçici and Yuret, 2011a). We improve FDA with a scaling factor that prefers shorter sentences defined as: $|S|^s$, where s is the power of the source sentence length and we set it to 0.9 after optimizing it over the perplexity of the LM built over the selected corpus (further discussed in Section 2.3).

2.2 Parallel FDA Model

FDA model obtains a sorting over all of the available training corpus based on the weights of the features found on the test set. Each selected train-

Algorithm 2: Parallel FDA

Input: $\mathcal{U}$, $\mathcal{F}$, and N.
Output: $\mathcal{L} \subseteq \mathcal{U}$.

$\mathcal{U} \leftarrow$ `shuffle`$(\mathcal{U})$
$\boldsymbol{\mathcal{U}}, M \leftarrow$ `split`$(\mathcal{U}, N)$
$\boldsymbol{\mathcal{L}} \leftarrow \{\}$
$\boldsymbol{\mathcal{S}} \leftarrow \{\}$
foreach $\mathcal{U}_i \in \boldsymbol{\mathcal{U}}$ **do**
  $\mathcal{L}_i, \mathcal{S}_i \leftarrow$ `FDA`$(\mathcal{U}_i, \mathcal{F}, M)$
  `add`$(\boldsymbol{\mathcal{L}}, \mathcal{L}_i)$
  `add`$(\boldsymbol{\mathcal{S}}, \mathcal{S}_i)$
$\mathcal{L} \leftarrow$ `merge`$(\boldsymbol{\mathcal{L}}, \boldsymbol{\mathcal{S}})$

ing instance effects which feature weights will be decayed and therefore can result in a different ordering of the instances if previous instance selections are altered. This makes it difficult to parallelize the FDA algorithm fully. Parallel FDA model first shuffles the parallel training sentences, $\mathcal{U}$, and distributes them to multiple splits for running individual FDA models on them.

The input to parallel FDA also consists of parallel training sentences, the number of desired training instances, and the source language features of the test set. The first step shuffles the parallel training sentences and the next step splits into equal parts and outputs the split files and the adjusted number of instances to select from each, M. Since we split into equal parts, we select equal number of sentences, M, from each split. Then we run FDA on each file to obtain sorted files, $\boldsymbol{\mathcal{L}}$, together with their scores, $\boldsymbol{\mathcal{S}}$. `merge` combines k sorted lists into one sorted list in $O(Mk \log k)$ where Mk is the total number of elements in all of the input lists. [1] The obtained $\mathcal{L}$ is the new training set to be used for SMT experiments. We compared the target 2-gram feature coverage of the training sets obtained with FDA and parallel FDA and found that parallel FDA achieves close performance.

Parallel FDA improves the scalability of FDA and allows rapid prototyping of SMT systems for a given target domain or task. Parallel FDA also improves the computational requirements of FDA by selecting from smaller corpora and distributing the work load, which can be very useful for MT in disaster scenarios.

2.3 Instance Selection for the Language Model Corpus

The language model corpus is very important for improving the SMT performance since it helps finding the correct ordering among the translated tokens or phrases. Increased LM corpus size can increase the SMT performance where doubling the LM corpus can improve the BLEU (Papineni et al., 2002) by 0.5 (Koehn, 2006). However, although LM corpora resources are more abundant, training on large LM corpora also poses computational scalability problems and until 2012, LM corpora such as LDC Gigaword corpora were not fully utilized due to memory limitations of computers and even with large memory machines, the LM corpora is split into pieces, interpolated, and merged (Koehn and Haddow, 2012) or the LM order is decreased to use up to 4-grams (Markus et al., 2012) or low frequency n-gram counts are omitted and better smoothing techniques are developed (Yuret, 2008). Using only the given training data for building the LM is another option used for limiting the size of the corpus, which can also obtain the second best performance in Spanish-English translation task and in the top tier for German-English (Guzman et al., 2012; Callison-Burch et al., 2012). This can also indicate that prior knowledge of the test set domain and its similarity to the available parallel training data may be diminishing the gains in SMT performance through better language modeling or better domain adaptation.

For solving the computational scalability problems, there is a need for properly selecting LM training data as well. We select LM corpus with parallel FDA based on this observation:

> No word not appearing in the training set can appear in the translation.

It is impossible for an SMT system to translate a word unseen in the training corpus nor can it translate it with a word not found in the target side of the training set [2]. Thus we are only interested in correctly ordering the words appearing in the training corpus and collecting the sentences that contain them for building the LM. At the same time, we want to be able to model longer range dependencies more efficiently especially for morphologically rich languages (Yuret and Biçici,

[1] (Cormen et al., 2009), question 6.5-9. Merging k sorted lists into one sorted list using a min-heap for k-way merging.

[2] Unless the translation is a verbatim copy of the source.

2009). Therefore, a compact and more relevant LM corpus can be useful.

Selecting the LM corpus is harder. First of all, we know which words should appear in the LM corpus but we do not know which phrases should be there since the translation model may reorder the translated words, find different translations, and generate different phrases. Thus, we use 1-gram features for LM corpus selection. At the same time, in contrast with selecting instances for the training set, we are less motivated to increase the diversity since we want predictive power on the most commonly observed patterns. Thus, we do not initialize feature weights with the idf score and instead, we use the inverse of the idf score for initialization, which is giving more importance to frequently occurring words in the training set. This way of LM corpus selection also allows us to obtain a more controlled language and helps us create translation outputs within the scope of the training corpus and the closely related LM corpus.

We shuffle the LM corpus available before splitting and select from individual splits, to prevent extreme cases. We add the training set directly into the LM and also add the training set not selected into the pool of sentences that can be selected for the LM. The scaling parameter s is optimized over the perplexity of the training data with the LM built over the selected LM corpus.

3 Experiments

We experiment with all language pairs in both directions in the WMT13 translation task (Callison-Burch et al., 2013), which include English-German (en-de), English-Spanish (en-es), English-French (en-fr), English-Czech (en-cs), and English-Russian (en-ru). We develop translation models using the phrase-based Moses (Koehn et al., 2007) SMT system. We true-case all of the corpora, use 150-best lists during tuning, set the max-fertility of GIZA++ (Och and Ney, 2003) to a value between 8-10, use 70 word classes learned over 3 iterations with mkcls tool during GIZA++ training, and vary the language model order between 5 to 9 for all language pairs. The development set contains 3000 sentences randomly sampled from among all of the development sentences provided.

Since we do not know the best training set size that will maximize the performance, we rely on previous SMT experiments (Biçici and Yuret, 2011a; Biçici and Yuret, 2011b) to select the proper training set size. We choose close to 15 million words and its corresponding number of sentences for each training corpus and 10 million sentences for each LM corpus not including the selected training set, which is added later. This corresponds to selecting roughly 15% of the training corpus for en-de and 35% for ru-en, and due to their larger size, 5% for en-es, 6% for cs-en, 2% for en-fr language pairs. The size of the LM corpus allows us to build higher order models. The statistics of the training data selected by the parallel FDA is given in Table 1. Note that the training set size for different translation directions differ slightly since we run a parallel FDA for each.

	cs / en	de / en	es / en	fr / en	ru / en
words (#M)	186 / 215	92 / 99	409 / 359	1010 / 886	41 / 44
sents (#K)	867	631	841	998	709
words (#M)	13 / 15	16 / 17	23 / 21	26 / 22	16 / 18

Table 1: Comparison of the training data available and the selected training set by parallel FDA for each language pair. The size of the parallel corpora is given in millions (M) of words or thousands (K) of sentences.

After selecting the training set, we select the LM corpora using the words in the target side of the training set as the features. For en, es, and fr, we have access to the LDC Gigaword corpora, from which we extract only the story type news and for en, we exclude the corpora from Xinhua News Agency (xin_eng). The size of the LM corpora from LDC and the monolingual LM corpora provided by WMT13 are given in Table 2. For all target languages, we select 10M sentences with parallel FDA from the LM corpora and the remaining training sentences and add the selected training data to obtain the LM corpus. Thus the size of the LM corpora is 10M plus the number of sentences in the training set as given in Table 1.

#M	cs	de	en	es	fr	ru
LDC	-	-	3402	949	773	-
Mono	388	842	1389	341	434	289

Table 2: The size of the LM corpora from LDC and the monolingual language model corpora provided in millions (M) of words.

With FDA, we can solve not only the instance selection problem for the training data but also the instance selection problem for the LM training corpus and achieve close target 2-gram cover-

	$S \rightarrow en$					$en \rightarrow T$				
	cs-en	de-en	es-en	fr-en	ru-en	en-cs	en-de	en-es	en-fr	en-ru
WMT13	.2620	.2680	.3060	.3150	.2430	.1860	.2030	.3040	.3060	.1880
BLEUc	.2430	.2414	.2909	.2539	.2226	.1708	.1792	.2799	.2379	.1732
BLEUc diff	.0190	.0266	.0151	.0611	.0204	.0152	.0238	.0241	.0681	.0148
LM order	7	9	7	9	6	5	5	5	7	5
BLEUc, n	.2407, 5	.2396, 5	.2886, 8	.2532, 6	.2215, 9	.1698, 9	.1784, 9	.2794, 9	.2374, 9	.1719, 9

Table 3: Best BLEUc results obtained on the translation task together with the LM order used when obtaining the result compared with the best constrained Moses results in WMT12 and WMT13. The last row compares the BLEUc result with respect to using a different LM order.

age using about 5% of the available training data and 5% of the available LM corpus for instance for en. A smaller LM training corpus also allows us to train higher order n-gram language models and model the dependencies better and achieve lower perplexity as given in Table 5.

3.1 WMT13 Translation Task Results

We run a number of SMT experiments for each language pair varying the LM order used and obtain different results and sorted these based on the tokenized BLEU performance, BLEUc. The best BLEUc results obtained on the translation task together with the LM order used when obtaining the results are given in Table 3. We also list the top results from WMT13 (Callison-Burch et al., 2013) [3], which use phrase-based Moses for comparison [4] and the BLEUc difference we obtain. For translation tasks with en as the target, higher order n-gram LM perform better whereas for translation tasks with en as the source, mostly 5-gram LM perform the best. We can obtain significant gains in BLEU (+0.0023) using higher order LMs.

For all translation tasks except fr-en and en-fr, we are able to obtain very close results to the top Moses system output (0.0148 to 0.0266 BLEUc difference). This shows that we can obtain very accurate translation outputs yet use only a small portion of the training corpus available, significantly reducing the time required for training, development, and deployment of an SMT system for a given translation task.

We are surprised by the lower performance in en-fr or fr-en translation tasks and the reason is, we believe, due to the inherent noise in the GigaFrEn training corpus [5]. FDA is an instance selection tool and it does not filter out target sentences that are noisy since FDA only looks at the source sentences when selecting training instance pairs. Noisy instances may be caused by a sentence alignment problem and one way to fix them is to measure the sentence alignment accuracy by using a similarity score over word distributions such as the Zipfian Word Vectors (Biçici, 2008). Since noisy parallel corpora can decrease the performance, we also experimented with discarding the GigaFrEn corpus in the experiments. However, this decreased the results by 0.0003 BLEU in contrast to 0.004-0.01 BLEU gains reported in (Koehn and Haddow, 2012). Also, note that the BLEU results we obtained are lower than in (Koehn and Haddow, 2012), which may be an indication that our training set size was small for this task.

3.2 Training Corpus Quality

We measure the quality of the training corpus by the coverage of the target 2-gram features of the test set, which is found to correlate well with the BLEU performance achievable (Biçici and Yuret, 2011a). Table 4 presents the source (scov) and target (tcov) 2-gram feature coverage of both the parallel training corpora (train) that we select from and the training sets obtained with parallel FDA. We show that we can obtain coverages close to using all of the available training corpora.

3.3 LM Corpus Quality

We compare the perplexity of the LM trained on all of the available training corpora for the de-en language pair versus the LM trained on the parallel FDA training corpus and the parallel FDA LM corpus. The number of OOV tokens become 2098, 2255, and 291 respectively for English and 2143, 2555, and 666 for German. To be able to compare the perplexities, we take the OOV tokens into consideration during calculations. Tokenized LM

[3] We use the results from matrix.statmt.org.

[4] Phrase-based Moses systems usually rank in the top 3.

[5] We even found control characters in the corpora.

		cs-en	de-en	es-en	fr-en	ru-en	en-cs	en-de	en-es	en-fr	en-ru
train	scov	.70	.74	.85	.83	.66	.82	.82	.84	.87	.78
	tcov	.82	.82	.84	.87	.78	.70	.74	.85	.83	.66
FDA	scov	.70	.74	.85	.82	.66	.82	.82	.84	.84	.78
	tcov	.74	.75	.77	.78	.75	.59	.67	.78	.76	.61

Table 4: Source (scov) and target (tcov) 2-gram feature coverage comparison of the training corpora (train) with the training sets obtained with parallel FDA (FDA).

corpus has 247M tokens for en and 218M tokens for de. We assume that each OOV word in *en* or *de* contributes $\log(1/218M)$ to the log probability, which we round to -19. We also present results for the case when we handle OOV words better with a cost of -11 each in Table 5.

Table 5 shows that we reduce the perplexity with a LM built on the training set selected with parallel FDA, which uses only 15% of the training data for de-en. More significantly, the LM build on the LM corpus selected by the parallel FDA is able to decrease both the number of OOV tokens and the perplexity and allows us to efficiently model higher order relationships as well. We reach up to 86% reduction in the number of OOV tokens and up to 74% reduction in the perplexity.

		log OOV = -19			log OOV = -11		
ppl		train	FDA	FDA LM	train	FDA	FDA LM
en	3	763	774	203	431	419	187
	4	728	754	192	412	409	178
	5	725	753	191	410	408	176
	6	724	753	190	409	408	176
	7	724	753	190	409	408	176
de	3	1255	1449	412	693	713	343
	4	1216	1428	398	671	703	331
	5	1211	1427	394	668	702	327
	6	1210	1427	393	668	702	326
	7	1210	1427	392	668	702	326

Table 5: Perplexity comparison of the LM built from the training corpus (train), parallel FDA selected training corpus (FDA), and the parallel FDA selected LM corpus (FDA LM).

3.4 Computational Costs

In this section, we quantify how fast the overall system runs for a given language pair. The instance selection times are dependent on the number of training sentences available for the language pair for training set selection and for the target language for LM corpus selection. We give the average number of minutes it takes for the parallel FDA to finish selection for each direction and for each target language in Table 6.

time (minutes)	en-fr	en-ru
Parallel FDA train	50	18
Parallel FDA LM	66	50

Table 6: The average time in the number of minutes for parallel FDA to select instances for the training set or for the LM corpus for language pairs en-fr and en-ru.

Once the training set and the LM corpus are ready, the training of the phrase-based SMT model Moses takes about 12 hours. Therefore, we are able to deploy an SMT system for the target translation task in about half a day and still obtain very accurate translation results.

4 Contributions

We develop parallel FDA for solving computational scalability problems caused by the abundance of training data for SMT models and LM models and still achieve SMT performance that is on par with the top performing SMT systems. The high quality of the selected training data and the LM corpus allows us to obtain very accurate translation outputs while the selected the LM corpus results in up to 86% reduction in the number of OOV tokens and up to 74% reduction in the perplexity and allows us to model higher order dependencies.

FDA and parallel FDA raise the bar of expectations from SMT translation outputs with highly accurate translations and lowering the bar to entry for SMT into new domains and tasks by allowing fast deployment of SMT systems in about half a day. Parallel FDA provides a new step towards rapid SMT system development in budgeted training scenarios and can be useful in developing machine translation systems in target domains with limited resources or in disaster and crisis situations where parallel corpora can be gathered by crawling and selected by parallel FDA. Parallel FDA is also allowing a shift from general purpose SMT systems towards task adaptive SMT solutions.

Acknowledgments

This work is supported in part by SFI (07/CE/I1142) as part of the Centre for Next Generation Localisation (www.cngl.ie) at Dublin City University and in part by the European Commission through the QTLaunchPad FP7 project (No: 296347). We also thank the SFI/HEA Irish Centre for High-End Computing (ICHEC), Koç University, and Deniz Yuret for the provision of computational facilities and support.

References

Ergun Biçici and Deniz Yuret. 2011a. Instance selection for machine translation using feature decay algorithms. In *Proceedings of the Sixth Workshop on Statistical Machine Translation*, pages 272–283, Edinburgh, Scotland, July. Association for Computational Linguistics.

Ergun Biçici and Deniz Yuret. 2011b. RegMT system for machine translation, system combination, and evaluation. In *Proceedings of the Sixth Workshop on Statistical Machine Translation*, pages 323–329, Edinburgh, Scotland, July. Association for Computational Linguistics.

Ergun Biçici. 2008. Context-based sentence alignment in parallel corpora. In *Proceedings of the 9th International Conference on Intelligent Text Processing and Computational Linguistics (CICLing 2008), LNCS*, Haifa, Israel, February.

Chris Callison-Burch, Philipp Koehn, Christof Monz, Matt Post, Radu Soricut, and Lucia Specia. 2012. Findings of the 2012 workshop on statistical machine translation. In *Proceedings of the Seventh Workshop on Statistical Machine Translation*, pages 10–51, Montréal, Canada, June. Association for Computational Linguistics.

Chris Callison-Burch, Philipp Koehn, Christof Monz, Matt Post, Radu Soricut, and Lucia Specia. 2013. Findings of the 2013 workshop on statistical machine translation. In *Proceedings of the Eighth Workshop on Statistical Machine Translation*, pages 10–51. Association for Computational Linguistics, August.

Thomas H. Cormen, Charles E. Leiserson, Ronald L. Rivest, and Clifford Stein. 2009. *Introduction to Algorithms (3. ed.)*. MIT Press.

Francisco Guzman, Preslav Nakov, Ahmed Thabet, and Stephan Vogel. 2012. Qcri at wmt12: Experiments in spanish-english and german-english machine translation of news text. In *Proceedings of the Seventh Workshop on Statistical Machine Translation*, pages 298–303, Montréal, Canada, June. Association for Computational Linguistics.

Philipp Koehn and Barry Haddow. 2012. Towards effective use of training data in statistical machine translation. In *Proceedings of the Seventh Workshop on Statistical Machine Translation*, pages 317–321, Montréal, Canada, June. Association for Computational Linguistics.

Philipp Koehn, Hieu Hoang, Alexandra Birch, Chris Callison-Burch, Marcello Federico, Nicola Bertoldi, Brooke Cowan, Wade Shen, Christine Moran, Richard Zens, Chris Dyer, Ondrej Bojar, Alexandra Constantin, and Evan Herbst. 2007. Moses: Open source toolkit for statistical machine translation. In *Annual Meeting of the Assoc. for Computational Linguistics*, pages 177–180, Prague, Czech Republic, June.

Philipp Koehn. 2006. Statistical machine translation: the basic, the novel, and the speculative. Tutorial at EACL 2006.

William Lewis, Robert Munro, and Stephan Vogel. 2011. Crisis mt: Developing a cookbook for mt in crisis situations. In *Proceedings of the Sixth Workshop on Statistical Machine Translation*, pages 501–511, Edinburgh, Scotland, July. Association for Computational Linguistics.

Freitag Markus, Peitz Stephan, Huck Matthias, Ney Hermann, Niehues Jan, Herrmann Teresa, Waibel Alex, Hai-son Le, Lavergne Thomas, Allauzen Alexandre, Buschbeck Bianka, Crego Joseph Maria, and Senellart Jean. 2012. Joint wmt 2012 submission of the quaero project. In *Proceedings of the Seventh Workshop on Statistical Machine Translation*, pages 322–329, Montréal, Canada, June. Association for Computational Linguistics.

Franz Josef Och and Hermann Ney. 2003. A systematic comparison of various statistical alignment models. *Computational Linguistics*, 29(1):19–51.

Kishore Papineni, Salim Roukos, Todd Ward, and Wei-Jing Zhu. 2002. BLEU: a method for automatic evaluation of machine translation. In *Proceedings of 40th Annual Meeting of the Association for Computational Linguistics*, pages 311–318, Philadelphia, Pennsylvania, USA, July. Association for Computational Linguistics.

Deniz Yuret and Ergun Biçici. 2009. Modeling morphologically rich languages using split words and unstructured dependencies. In *Proceedings of the ACL-IJCNLP 2009 Conference Short Papers*, pages 345–348, Suntec, Singapore, August. Association for Computational Linguistics.

Deniz Yuret. 2008. Smoothing a tera-word language model. In *Proceedings of ACL-08: HLT, Short Papers*, pages 141–144, Columbus, Ohio, June. Association for Computational Linguistics.

CUni Multilingual Matrix in the WMT 2013 Shared Task

Karel Bílek **Daniel Zeman**
Charles University in Prague, Faculty of Mathematics and Physics,
Institute of Formal and Applied Linguistics
Malostranské náměstí 25, CZ-11800 Praha, Czechia
kb@karelbilek.com, zeman@ufal.mff.cuni.cz

Abstract

We describe our experiments with phrase-based machine translation for the WMT 2013 Shared Task. We trained one system for 18 translation directions between English or Czech on one side and English, Czech, German, Spanish, French or Russian on the other side. We describe a set of results with different training data sizes and subsets. For the pairs containing Russian, we describe a set of independent experiments with slightly different translation models.

1 Introduction

With so many official languages, Europe is a paradise for machine translation research. One of the largest bodies of electronically available parallel texts is being nowadays generated by the European Union and its institutions. At the same time, the EU also provides motivation and boosts potential market for machine translation outcomes.

Most of the major European languages belong to one of three branches of the Indo-European language family: Germanic, Romance or Slavic. Such relatedness is responsible for many structural similarities in European languages, although significant differences still exist. Within the language portfolio selected for the WMT shared task, English, French and Spanish seem to be closer to each other than to the rest.

German, despite being genetically related to English, differs in many properties. Its word order rules, shifting verbs from one end of the sentence to the other, easily create long-distance dependencies. Long German compound words are notorious for increasing out-of-vocabulary rate, which has led many researchers to devising unsupervised compound-splitting techniques. Also, uppercase/lowercase distinction is more important because all German nouns start with an uppercase letter by the rule.

Czech is a language with rich morphology (both inflectional and derivational) and relatively free word order. In fact, the predicate-argument structure, often encoded by fixed word order in English, is usually captured by inflection (especially the system of 7 grammatical cases) in Czech. While the free word order of Czech is a problem when translating to English (the text should be parsed first in order to determine the syntactic functions and the English word order), generating correct inflectional affixes is indeed a challenge for English-to-Czech systems. Furthermore, the multitude of possible Czech word forms (at least order of magnitude higher than in English) makes the data sparseness problem really severe, hindering both directions.

Most of the above characteristics of Czech also apply to Russian, another Slavic language. Similar issues have to be expected when translating between Russian and English. Still, there are also interesting divergences between Russian and Czech, especially on the syntactic level. Russian sentences typically omit copula in the present tense and there is also no direct equivalent of the verb "to have". Periphrastic constructions such as "there is XXX by him" are used instead. These differences make the Czech-Russian translation interesting as well. Interestingly enough, results of machine translation between Czech and Russian has so far been worse than between English and any of the two languages, language relatedness notwithstanding.

Our goal is to run one system under as similar conditions as possible to all eighteen translation directions, to compare their translation accuracies and see why some directions are easier than others. The current version of the system does not include really language-specific techniques: we neither split German compounds, nor do we address the peculiarities of Czech and Russian mentioned above.

In an independent set of experiments, we tried to deal with the data sparseness of Russian language with the addition of a backoff model with a simple stemming and some additional data; those experiments were done for Russian and Czech|English combinations.

2 The Translation System

Both sets of experiments use the same basic framework. The translation system is built around Moses[1] (Koehn et al., 2007). Two-way word alignment was computed using GIZA++[2] (Och and Ney, 2003), and alignment symmetrization using the *grow-diag-final-and* heuristic (Koehn et al., 2003). Weights of the system were optimized using MERT (Och, 2003). No lexical reordering model was trained.

For language modeling we use the SRILM toolkit[3] (Stolcke, 2002) with modified Kneser-Ney smoothing (Kneser and Ney, 1995; Chen and Goodman, 1998).

3 General experiments

In the first set of experiments we wanted to use the same setting for all language pairs.

3.1 Data and Pre-processing Pipeline

We applied our system to all the ten official language pairs. In addition, we also experimented with translation between Czech on one side and German, Spanish, French or Russian on the other side. Training data for these additional language pairs were obtained by combining parallel corpora of the officially supported pairs. For instance, to create the Czech-German parallel corpus, we identified the intersection of the English sides of Czech-English and English-German corpora, respectively; then we combined the corresponding Czech and German sentences.

We took part in the constrained task. Unless explicitly stated otherwise, the translation model in our experiments was trained on the combined News-Commentary v8 and Europarl v7 corpora.[4] Note that there is only News Commentary and no Europarl for Russian. We were also able to evaluate several combinations with large parallel corpora: the UN corpus (English, French and Spanish), the Giga French-English corpus and CzEng (Czech-English). We did not use any large corpus for Russian-English. Table 1 shows the sizes of the training data.

Corpus	SentPairs	Tkns lng1	Tkns lng2
cs-en	786,929	18,196,080	21,184,881
de-en	2,098,430	55,791,641	58,403,756
es-en	2,140,175	62,444,507	59,811,355
fr-en	2,164,891	70,363,304	60,583,967
ru-en	150,217	3,889,215	4,100,148
de-cs	657,539	18,160,857	17,788,600
es-cs	697,898	19,577,329	18,926,839
fr-cs	693,093	19,717,885	18,849,244
ru-cs	103,931	2,642,772	2,319,611
Czeng			
cs-en	14,833,358	204,837,216	235,177,231
UN			
es-en	11,196,913	368,154,702	328,840,003
fr-en	12,886,831	449,279,647	372,627,886
Giga			
fr-en	22,520,400	854,353,231	694,394,577

Table 1: Number of sentence pairs and tokens for every language pair in the parallel training corpus. Languages are identified by their ISO 639 codes: cs = Czech, de = German, en = English, es = Spanish, fr = French, ru = Russian. Every line corresponds to the respective version of EuroParl + News Commentary; the second part presents the extra corpora.

The News Test 2010 (2489 sentences in each language) and 2012 (3003 sentences) data sets[5] were used as development data for MERT. BLEU scores reported in this paper were computed on the News Test 2013 set

[1]http://www.statmt.org/moses/

[2]http://code.google.com/p/giza-pp/

[3]http://www-speech.sri.com/projects/srilm/

[4]http://www.statmt.org/wmt13/translation-task.html\#download

[5]http://www.statmt.org/wmt13/translation-task.html

(3000 sentences each language). We do not use the News Tests 2008, 2009 and 2011.

All parallel and monolingual corpora underwent the same preprocessing. They were tokenized and some characters normalized or cleaned. A set of language-dependent heuristics was applied in an attempt to restore the opening/closing quotation marks (i.e. "quoted" → “quoted”) (Zeman, 2012).

The data are then tagged and lemmatized. We used the Featurama tagger for Czech and English lemmatization and TreeTagger for German, Spanish, French and Russian lemmatization. All these tools are embedded in the Treex analysis framework (Žabokrtský et al., 2008).

The lemmas are used later to compute word alignment. Besides, they are needed to apply “supervised truecasing” to the data: we cast the case of the lemma to the form, relying on our morphological analyzers and taggers to identify proper names, all other words are lowercased. Note that guessing of the true case is only needed for the sentence-initial token. Other words can typically be left in their original form, unless they are uppercased as a form of HIGHLIGHTING.

3.2 Experiments

BLEU scores were computed by our system, comparing truecased tokenized hypothesis with truecased tokenized reference translation. Such scores must differ from the official evaluation—see Section 3.2.4 for discussion of the final results.

The confidence interval for most of the scores lies between ±0.5 and ±0.6 BLEU % points.

3.2.1 Baseline Experiments

The set of baseline experiments were trained on the supervised truecased combination of News Commentary and Europarl. As we had lemmatizers for the languages, word alignment was computed on lemmas. (But our previous experiments showed that there was little difference between using lemmas and lowercased 4-character “stems”.) A hexagram language model was trained on the monolingual version of the News Commentary + Europarl corpus (typically a slightly larger superset of the target side of the parallel corpus).

3.2.2 Larger Monolingual Data

Besides the monolingual halves of the parallel corpora, additional monolingual data were provided / permitted. Our experiments in previous years clearly showed that the Crawled News corpus (2007–2012), in-domain and large, contributed significantly to better BLEU scores. This year we included it in our baseline experiments for all language pairs: translation model on News Commentary + Europarl, language model on monolingual part of the two, plus Crawled News.

In addition there are the Gigaword corpora published by the Linguistic Data Consortium, available only for English (5th edition), Spanish (3rd) and French (3rd). Table 2 gives the sizes and Table 3 compares BLEU scores with Gigaword against the baseline. Gigaword mainly contains texts from news agencies and as such it should be also in-domain. Nevertheless, the crawled news are already so large that the improvement contributed by Gigaword is rarely significant.

Corpus	Segments	Tokens
newsc+euro.cs	830,904	18,862,626
newsc+euro.de	2,380,813	59,350,113
newsc+euro.en	2,466,167	67,033,745
newsc+euro.es	2,330,369	66,928,157
newsc+euro.fr	2,384,293	74,962,162
newsc.ru	183,083	4,340,275
news.all.cs	27,540,827	460,356,173
news.all.de	54,619,789	1,020,852,354
news.all.en	68,341,615	1,673,187,787
news.all.es	13,384,314	388,614,890
news.all.fr	21,195,476	557,431,929
news.all.ru	19,912,911	361,026,791
gigaword.en	117,905,755	4,418,360,239
gigaword.es	31,304,148	1,064,660,498
gigaword.fr	21,674,453	963,571,174

Table 2: Number of segments (paragraphs in Gigaword, sentences elsewhere) and tokens of additional monolingual training corpora. “newsc+euro” are the monolingual versions of the News Commentary and Europarl parallel corpora. “news.all” denotes all years of the Crawled News corpus for the given language.

Direction	Baseline	Gigaword
en-cs	0.1632	
en-de	0.1833	
en-es	0.2808	0.2856
en-fr	0.2987	0.2988
en-ru	0.1582	
cs-en	0.2328	0.2367
de-en	0.2389	0.2436
es-en	0.2916	0.2975
fr-en	0.2887	
ru-en	0.1975	0.2003
cs-de	0.1595	
cs-es	0.2170	0.2220
cs-fr	0.2220	0.2196
cs-ru	0.1660	
de-cs	0.1488	
es-cs	0.1580	
fr-cs	0.1420	
ru-cs	0.1506	

Table 3: BLEU scores of the baseline experiments (left column) on News Test 2013 data, computed by the system on tokenized data, versus similar setup with Gigaword. The difference was typically not significant.

Dir	Parallel	Mono	*BLEU*
en-es	news-euro	+gigaword	0.2856
en-es	news-euro-un	+gigaword	0.2844
en-es	un	un+gigaw.	0.2016
en-fr	giga	+gigaword	0.3106
en-fr	giga	+newsall	0.3037
en-fr	news-euro-un	+gigaword	0.3010
en-fr	news-euro	+gigaword	0.2988
en-fr	un	un	0.2933
es-en	news-euro	+gigaword	0.2975
es-en	news-euro-un	baseline	0.2845
es-en	un	un+news	0.2067
fr-en	news-euro-un	+gigaword	0.2914
fr-en	news-euro	baseline	0.2887
fr-en	un	un+news	0.2737

Table 4: BLEU scores with different parallel corpora.

3.2.3 Larger Parallel Data

Various combinations with larger parallel corpora were also tested. We do not have results for all combinations because these experiments needed a lot of time and resources and not all of them finished in time successfully.

In general the UN corpus seems to be of low quality or too much off-domain. It may help a little if used in combination with news-euro. If used separately, it always hurts the results.

The Giga French-English corpus gave the best results for English-French as expected, even without the core news-euro data. However, training the model on data of this size is extremely demanding on memory and time.

Finally, Czeng undoubtedly improves Czech-English translation in both directions. The news-euro dataset is smaller for this language pair, which makes Czeng stand out even more. See Table 4 for details.

3.2.4 Final Results

Table 5 compares our BLEU scores with those computed at `matrix.statmt.org`.

BLEU (without flag) denotes BLEU score computed by our system, comparing truecased tokenized hypothesis with truecased tokenized reference translation.

The official evaluation by `matrix.statmt.org` gives typically lower numbers, reflecting the loss caused by detokenization and new (different) tokenization.

3.2.5 Efficiency

The baseline experiments were conducted mostly on 64bit AMD Opteron quad-core 2.8 GHz CPUs with 32 GB RAM (decoding run on 15 machines in parallel) and the whole pipeline typically required between a half and a whole day.

However, we used machines with up to 500 GB RAM to train the large language models and translation models. Aligning the UN corpora with Giza++ took around 5 days. Giga French-English corpus was even worse and required several weeks to complete. Using such a large corpus without pruning is not practical.

4 Extra Experiments with Russian

In a separate set of experiments, we tried to take a basic Moses framework and change the setup a little for better results on morphologically rich languages.

Tried combinations were Russian-Czech and Russian-English.

Direction	$BLEU$	$BLEU_l$	$BLEU_t$
en-cs	0.1786	0.180	0.170
en-de	0.1833	0.179	0.173
en-es	0.2856	0.288	0.271
en-fr	0.3010	0.270	0.259
en-ru	0.1582	0.142	0.142
cs-en	0.2527	0.259	0.244
de-en	0.2389	0.244	0.230
es-en	0.2856	0.288	0.271
fr-en	0.2887	0.294	0.280
ru-en	0.1975	0.203	0.191
cs-de	0.1595	0.159	0.151
cs-es	0.2220	0.225	0.210
cs-fr	0.2220	0.191	0.181
cs-ru	0.1660	0.150	0.149
de-cs	0.1488	0.151	0.142
es-cs	0.1580	0.160	0.152
fr-cs	0.1420	0.145	0.137
ru-cs	0.1506	0.151	0.144

Table 5: Final BLEU scores. $BLEU$ is truecased computed by the system, $BLEU_l$ is the official lowercased evaluation by `matrix.statmt.org`. $BLEU_t$ is official truecased evaluation. Although lower official scores are expected, notice the larger gap in en-fr and cs-fr translation. There seems to be a problem in our French detokenization procedure.

4.1 Data

For the additional Russian-to-Czech systems, we used following parallel data:

- UMC 0.1 (Klyueva and Bojar, 2008) – tri-parallel set, consisting of news articles – 93,432 sentences
- data mined from movie subtitles (described in further detail below) – 2,324,373 sentences
- Czech-Russian part of InterCorp – a corpus from translation of fiction books (Čermák and Rosen, 2012) – 148,847 sentences

For Russian-to-English translation, we used combination of

- UMC 0.1 – 95,540 sentences
- subtitles – 1,790,209 sentences
- Yandex English-Russian parallel corpus [6] – 1,000,000 sentences
- wiki headlines from WMT website [7] – 514,859 sentences
- common crawl from WMT website – 878,386 sentences

Added together, Russian-Czech parallel data consisted of 2,566,615 sentences and English-Czech parallel data consisted of 4,275,961 sentences [8].

We also used 765 sentences from UMC003 as a devset for MERT training.

We used the following monolingual corpora to train language models. Russian:

- Russian sides of all the parallel data – 4,275,961 sentences
- News commentary from WMT website – 150,217 sentences
- News crawl 2012 – 9,789,861 sentences

For Czech:

- Czech sides of all the parallel data – 2,566,615 sentences
- Data downloaded from Czech news articles[9] – 1,531,403 sentences
- WebColl (Spoustová et al., 2010) – 4,053,223 sentences
- PDT [10] – 115,844 sentences
- Complete Czech Wikipedia – 3,695,172 sentences
- Sentences scraped from Czech social server okoun.cz – 580,249 sentences

For English:

- English sides of all the paralel data – 4,275,961 sentences
- News commentary from WMT website – 150,217 sentences

Table 6 and Table 7 shows the sizes of the training data.

[6] `https://translate.yandex.ru/corpus?lang=en`

[7] `http://www.statmt.org/wmt13/translation-task.html`

[8] some sentences had to be removed for technical reasons

[9] `http://thepiratebay.sx/torrent/7121533/`

[10] `http://ufal.mff.cuni.cz/pdt2.0/`

Corpus	SentPairs	Tok lng1	Tok lng2
cs-ru	2,566,615	19,680,239	20,031,688
en-ru	4,275,961	64,619,964	58,671,725

Table 6: Number of sentence pairs and tokens for every language pair.

Corpus	Sentences	Tokens
en mono	13,426,211	278,199,832
ru mono	13,701,213	231,076,387
cs mono	12,542,506	202,510,993

Table 7: Number of sentences and tokens for every language.

4.1.1 Tokenization, tagging

Czech and English data was tokenized and tagged using Morče tagger; Russian was tokenized and tagged using TreeTagger. TreeTagger also does lemmatization; however, we didn't use lemmas for alignment or translation models, since our experiments showed that primitive stemming got better results.

However, what is important to mention is that TreeTagger had problems with some corpora, mostly Common Crawl. For some reason, Russian TreeTagger has problems with "dirty" data—sentences in English, French or random non-unicode noise. It either slows down significantly or stops working at all. For this reason, we wrapped TreeTagger in a script that detected those hangs and replaced the erroneous Russian sentences with bogus, one-letter Russian sentences (we can't delete those, since the lines already exist in the opposite languages; but since the pair doesn't really make sense in the first place, it doesn't matter as much).

All the data are lowercased for all the models and we recase the letters only at the very end.

4.1.2 Subtitle data

For an unrelated project dealing with movie subtitles translation, we obtained data from OpenSubtitles.org for Czech and English subtitles. However, those data were not aligned on sentence level and were less structured—we had thousands of `.srt` files with some sort of metadata.

When exploiting the data from the subtitles, we made several observations:

- language used in subtitles is very different from the language used in news articles
- one of the easiest and most accurate sentence alignments in movie subtitles is the one based purely on the time stamps
- allowing bigger differences in the time stamps in the alignment produced more data, but less accurate
- the subtitles are terribly out of domain (as experiments with using *only* the subtitle data showed us), but adding the corpus mined from the subtitles *still* increases the accuracy of the translation
- allowing bigger differences in the time stamps and, therefore, more (albeit less accurate) data always led to better results in our tests.

In the end, we decided to pair as much subtitles as possible, even with the risk of some being misaligned, because we found out that this helped the most.

4.2 Translation model, language model

For alignment, we used primitive stemming that takes just first 6 letters from a word. We found out that using this "brute force" stemming—for reasons that will have to be explored in a further research—return better results than regular lemmatization, for both alignment and translation model, as described further.

For each language pair, we used a translation model with two translation tables, one of them as backoff model. More exactly, the primary translation is from a form to a combination of (lower case) form and tag, and the secondary backoff translation is from a "stem" described above to a combination of (lower case) form and tag.

We built two language models—one for tags and one for lower case forms.

The models were actually a mixed model using interpolate option in SRILM—we trained a different language model for each corpus, and then we mixed the language models using a small development set from UMC003.

4.3 Final Results

The final results from `matrix.statmt.org` are in the table Table 8. You might notice a sharp difference between lowercased and truecased BLEU—that is due to a technical error that we didn't notice before the deadline.

Direction	$BLEU_l$	$BLEU_t$
ru-cs	0.158	0.135
cs-ru	0.165	0.162
ru-en	0.224	0.174
en-ru	0.163	0.160

Table 8: Lowercased and cased BLEU scores

5 Conclusion

We have described two independent Moses-based SMT systems we used for the WMT 2013 shared task. We discussed experiments with large data for many language pairs from the point of view of both the translation accuracy and efficiency.

Acknowledgements

The work on this project was supported by the grant P406/11/1499 of the Czech Science Foundation (GAČR), and by the grant 639012 of the Grant Agency of Charles University (GAUK).

References

František Čermák and Alexandr Rosen. 2012. The case of InterCorp, a multilingual parallel corpus. *International Journal of Corpus Linguistics*, 13(3):411–427.

Stanley F. Chen and Joshua Goodman. 1998. An empirical study of smoothing techniques for language modeling. In *Technical report TR-10-98, Computer Science Group*, Harvard, MA, USA, August. Harvard University.

Natalia Klyueva and Ondřej Bojar. 2008. UMC 0.1: Czech-Russian-english multilingual corpus. In *International Conference Corpus Linguistics*.

Reinhard Kneser and Hermann Ney. 1995. Improved backing-off for m-gram language modeling. In *Proceedings of the IEEE International Conference on Acoustics, Speech and Signal Processing*, pages 181–184, Los Alamitos, California, USA. IEEE Computer Society Press.

Philipp Koehn, Franz Josef Och, and Daniel Marcu. 2003. Statistical phrase-based translation. In *NAACL '03: Proceedings of the 2003 Conference of the North American Chapter of the Association for Computational Linguistics on Human Language Technology*, pages 48–54, Morristown, NJ, USA. Association for Computational Linguistics.

Philipp Koehn, Hieu Hoang, Alexandra Birch, Chris Callison-Burch, Marcello Federico, Nicola Bertoldi, Brooke Cowan, Wade Shen, Christine Moran, Richard Zens, Chris Dyer, Ondřej Bojar, Alexandra Constantin, and Evan Herbst. 2007. Moses: Open Source Toolkit for Statistical Machine Translation. In *Proceedings of the 45th Annual Meeting of the Association for Computational Linguistics Companion Volume Proceedings of the Demo and Poster Sessions*, pages 177–180, Praha, Czechia, June. Association for Computational Linguistics.

Franz Josef Och and Hermann Ney. 2003. A systematic comparison of various statistical alignment models. *Computational Linguistics*, 29(1):19–51.

Franz Josef Och. 2003. Minimum error rate training in statistical machine translation. In *ACL '03: Proceedings of the 41st Annual Meeting on Association for Computational Linguistics*, pages 160–167, Morristown, NJ, USA. Association for Computational Linguistics.

Johanka Spoustová, Miroslav Spousta, and Pavel Pecina. 2010. Building a web corpus of czech. In *Proceedings of the Seventh International Conference on Language Resources and Evaluation (LREC'10)*, Valletta, Malta, may. European Language Resources Association (ELRA).

Andreas Stolcke. 2002. Srilm – an extensible language modeling toolkit. In *Proceedings of International Conference on Spoken Language Processing*, Denver, Colorado, USA.

Zdeněk Žabokrtský, Jan Ptáček, and Petr Pajas. 2008. TectoMT: Highly modular MT system with tectogrammatics used as transfer layer. In *ACL 2008 WMT: Proceedings of the Third Workshop on Statistical Machine Translation*, pages 167–170, Columbus, OH, USA. Association for Computational Linguistics.

Daniel Zeman. 2012. Data issues of the multilingual translation matrix. In *Proceedings of the Seventh Workshop on Statistical Machine Translation*, pages 395–400, Montréal, Canada. Association for Computational Linguistics.

Chimera – Three Heads for English-to-Czech Translation

Ondřej Bojar and **Rudolf Rosa** and **Aleš Tamchyna**
Charles University in Prague, Faculty of Mathematics and Physics
Institute of Formal and Applied Linguistics
Malostranské náměstí 25, Prague, Czech Republic
surname@ufal.mff.cuni.cz

Abstract

This paper describes our WMT submissions CU-BOJAR and CU-DEPFIX, the latter dubbed "CHIMERA" because it combines on three diverse approaches: TectoMT, a system with transfer at the deep syntactic level of representation, factored phrase-based translation using Moses, and finally automatic rule-based correction of frequent grammatical and meaning errors. We do not use any off-the-shelf system-combination method.

1 Introduction

Targeting Czech in statistical machine translation (SMT) is notoriously difficult due to the large number of possible word forms and complex agreement rules. Previous attempts to resolve these issues include specific probabilistic models (Subotin, 2011) or leaving the morphological generation to a separate processing step (Fraser et al., 2012; Mareček et al., 2011).

TectoMT (CU-TECTOMT, Galuščáková et al. (2013)) is a hybrid (rule-based and statistical) MT system that closely follows the analysis-transfer-synthesis pipeline. As such, it suffers from many issues but generating word forms in proper agreements with their neighbourhood as well as the translation of some diverging syntactic structures are handled well. Overall, TectoMT sometimes even ties with a highly tuned Moses configuration in manual evaluations, see Bojar et al. (2011).

Finally, Rosa et al. (2012) describes Depfix, a rule-based system for post-processing (S)MT output that corrects some morphological, syntactic and even semantic mistakes. Depfix was able to significantly improve Google output in WMT12, so now we applied it on an open-source system.

Our WMT13 system is thus a three-headed creature where, hopefully: (1) TectoMT provides missing word forms and safely handles some nonparallel syntactic constructions, (2) Moses exploits very large parallel and monolingual data, and boosts better lexical choice, (3) Depfix attempts to fix severe flaws in Moses output.

2 System Description

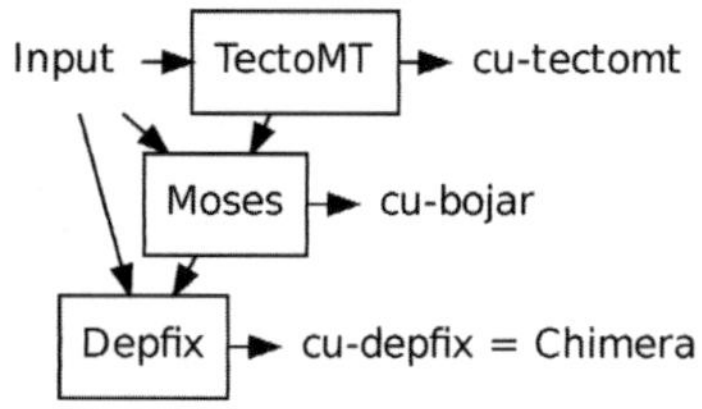

Figure 1: CHIMERA: three systems combined.

CHIMERA is a sequential combination of three diverse MT systems as depicted in Figure 1. Each of the intermediate stages of processing has been submitted as a separate primary system for the WMT manual evalution, allowing for a more thorough analysis.

Instead of an off-the-shelf system combination technique, we use TectoMT output as synthetic training data for Moses as described in Section 2.1 and finally we process its output using rule-based corrections of Depfix (Section 2.2). All steps directly use the source sentence.

2.1 Moses Setup for CU-BOJAR

We ran a couple of probes with reduced training data around the setup of Moses that proved successful in previous years (Bojar et al., 2012a).

2.1.1 Pre-processing

We use a stable pre-processing pipeline that includes normalization of quotation marks,[1] tokenization, tagging and lemmatization with tools

[1]We do not simply convert them to unpaired ASCII quotes but rather balance them and use other heuristics to convert most cases to the typographically correct form.

Case	recaser	lc→form	utc	stc
BLEU	9.05	9.13	9.70	**9.81**

Table 1: Letter Casing

included in the Treex platform (Popel and Žabokrtský, 2010).

This year, we evaluated the end-to-end effect of truecasing. Ideally, English-Czech SMT should be trained on data where only names are uppercased (and neither the beginnings of sentences, nor all-caps headlines or exclamations etc). For these experiments, we trained a simple baseline system on 1 million sentence pairs from CzEng 1.0.

Table 1 summarizes the final (case-sensitive!) BLEU scores for four setups. The standard approach is to train SMT lowercase and apply a recaser, e.g. the Moses one, on the output. Another option (denoted "lc→form") is to lowercase only the source side of the parallel data. This more or less makes the translation model responsible for identifying names and the language model for identifying beginnings of sentences.

The final two approaches attempt at "truecasing" the data, i.e. the ideal lowercasing of everything except names. Our simple unsupervised truecaser ("utc") uses a model trained on monolingual data (1 million sentences in this case, same as the parallel training data used in this experiment) to identify the most frequent "casing shape" of each token type when it appears within a sentence and then converts its occurrences at the beginnings of sentences to this shape. Our supervised truecaser ("stc") casts the case of the *lemma* on the form, because our lemmatizers for English and Czech produce case-sensitive lemmas to indicate names. After the translation, only deterministic uppercasing of sentence beginnings is needed.

We confirm that "stc" as we have been using it for a couple of years is indeed the best option, despite its unpleasingly frequent omissions of names (incl. "Spojené státy", "the United States"). One of the rules in Depfix tries to cast the case from the source to the MT output but due to alignment errors, it is not perfect in fixing these mistakes.

Surprisingly, the standard recasing worked worse than "lc→form", suggesting that two Moses runs in a row are worse than one joint search.

We consider using a full-fledged named entity recognizer in the future.

		Tokens [M]	
Corpus	Sents [M]	English	Czech
CzEng 1.0	14.83	235.67	205.17
Europarl	0.65	17.61	15.00
Common Crawl	0.16	4.08	3.63

Table 2: Basic Statistics of Parallel Data.

2.1.2 Factored Translation for Morphological Coherence

We use a quite standard factored configuration of Moses. We translate from "stc" to two factors: "stc" and "tag" (full Czech positional morphological tag). Even though tags on the target side make the data somewhat sparser (a single Czech word form typically represents several cases, numbers or genders), we do not use any back-off or alternative decoding path. A high-order language model on tags is used to promote grammatically correct and coherent output. Our system is thus less prone to errors in local morphological agreement.

2.1.3 Large Parallel Data

The main source of our parallel data was CzEng 1.0 (Bojar et al., 2012b). We also used Europarl (Koehn, 2005) as made available by WMT13 organizers.[2] The English-Czech part of the new Common Crawl corpus was quite small and very noisy, so we did not include it in our training data. Table 2 provides basic statistics of the data.

Processing large parallel data can be challenging in terms of time and computational resources required. The main bottlenecks are word alignment and phrase extraction.

GIZA++ (Och and Ney, 2000) has been the standard tool for computing word alignment in phrase-based MT. A multi-threaded version exists (Gao and Vogel, 2008), which also supports incremental extensions of parallel data by applying a saved model on a new sentence pair. We evaluated these tools and measured their wall-clock time[3] as well as the final BLEU score of a full MT system.

Surprisingly, single-threaded GIZA++ was considerably faster than single-threaded MGIZA. Using 12 threads, MGIZA outperformed GIZA++ but the difference was smaller than we expected.

Table 3 summarizes the results. We checked the difference in BLEU using the procedure by Clark et al. (2011) and GIZA++ alignments were indeed

[2] `http://www.statmt.org/wmt13/translation-task.html`

[3] Time measurements are only indicative, they were affected by the current load in our cluster.

Alignment	Wallclock Time	BLEU
GIZA++	71	**15.5**
MGIZA 1 thread	114	15.4
MGIZA 12 threads	**51**	15.4

Table 3: Rough wallclock time [hours] of word alignment and the resulting BLEU scores.

Corpus	Sents [M]	Tokens [M]
CzEng 1.0	14.83	205.17
CWC Articles	36.72	626.86
CNC News	28.08	483.88
CNA	47.00	830.32
Newspapers	64.39	1040.80
News Crawl	24.91	444.84
Total	215.93	3631.87

Table 4: Basic Statistics of Monolingual Data.

little but significantly better than MGIZA in three MERT runs.

We thus use the standard GIZA++ aligner.

2.1.4 Large Language Models

We were able to collect a very large amount of monolingual data for Czech: almost 216 million sentences, 3.6 billion tokens. Table 4 lists the corpora we used. CWC Articles is a section of the Czech Web Corpus (Spoustová and Spousta, 2012). CNC News refers to a subset of the Czech National Corpus[4] from the news domain. CNA is a corpus of Czech News Agency stories from 1998 to 2012. Newspapers is a collection of articles from various Czech newspapers from years 1998 to 2002. Finally, News Crawl is the monolingual corpus made available by the organizers of WMT13.

We created an in-domain language model from all the corpora except for CzEng (where we only used the news section). We were able to train a 4-gram language model using KenLM (Heafield et al., 2013). Unfortunately, we did not manage to use a model of higher order. The model file (even in the binarized trie format with probability quantization) was so large that we ran out of memory in decoding.[5] We also tried pruning these larger models but we did not have enough RAM.

To cater for a longer-range coherence, we trained a 7-gram language model only on the News Crawl corpus (concatenation of all years). In this case, we used SRILM (Stolcke, 2002) and pruned n-grams so that (training set) model perplexity does not increase more than 10^{-14}. The data for this LM exactly match the domain of WMT test sets.

Finally, we model sequences of morphological tags on the target side using a 10-gram LM estimated from CzEng. Individual sections of the corpus (news, fiction, subtitles, EU legislation, web pages, technical documentation and Navajo project) were interpolated to match WMT test sets from 2007 to 2011 best. This allows even out-of-domain data to contribute to modeling of overall sentence structure. We filtered the model using the same threshold 10^{-14}.

Table 5 summarizes the resulting LM files as used in CU-BOJAR and CHIMERA.

Token	Order	Sents [M]	Tokens [M]	ARPA.gz [GB]	Trie [GB]
stc	4	201.31	3430.92	28.2	11.8
stc	7	24.91	444.84	13.1	8.1
tag	10	14.83	205.17	7.2	3.0

Table 5: LMs used in CU-BOJAR.

2.1.5 Bigger Tuning Sets

Koehn and Haddow (2012) report benefits from tuning on a larger set of sentences. We experimented with a down-scaled MT system to compare a couple of options for our tuning set: the default 3003 sentences of newstest2011, the default and three more Czech references that were created by translating from German, the default and two more references that were created by post-editing a variant of our last year's Moses system and also a larger single-reference set consisting of several newstest years. The preliminary results were highly inconclusive: negligibly higher BLEU scores obtained lower manual scores. Unable to pick the best configuration, we picked the largest. We tune our systems on "bigref", as specified in Table 6. The dataset consists of 11583 source sentences, 3003 of which have 4 reference translations and a subset (1997 sents.) of which has 2 reference translations constructed by post-editing. The dataset does not include 2010 data as a heldout for other foreseen experiments.

2.1.6 Synthetic Parallel Data

Galuščáková et al. (2013) describe several possibilities of combining TectoMT and phrase-based approaches. Our CU-BOJAR uses one of the simpler but effective ones: adding TectoMT output on the test set to our training data. As a contrast to

[4] http://korpus.cz/

[5] Due to our cluster configuration, we need to pre-load language models.

English	Czech	# Refs	# Snts
newstest2011	official + 3 more from German	4	3003
newstest2011	2 post-edits of a system similar to (Bojar et al., 2012a)	2	1997
newstest2009	official	1	2525
newstest2008	official	1	2051
newstest2007	official	1	2007
Total		4	11583

Table 6: Our big tuning set (bigref).

CU-BOJAR, we also examine PLAIN Moses setup which is identical but lacks the additional synthetic phrase table by TectoMT.

In order to select the best balance between phrases suggested by TectoMT and our parallel data, we provide these data as two separate phrase tables. Each phrase table brings in its own five-tuple of scores, one of which, the phrase-penalty functions as an indicator how many phrases come from which of the phrase tables. The standard MERT is then used to optimize the weights.[6,7]

We use one more trick compared to Galuščáková et al. (2013): we deliberately overlap our training and tuning datasets. When preparing the synthetic parallel data, we use the English side of newstests 08 and 10–13. The Czech side is always produced by TectoMT. We tune on bigref (see Table 6), so the years 08, 11 and 12 overlap. (We could have overlapped also years 07, 09 and 10 but we had them originally reserved for other purposes.) Table 7 summarizes the situation and highlights that our setup is fair: we never use the target side of our final evaluation set newstest2013. Some test sets are denoted "*could have*" as including them would still be correct.

The overlap allows MERT to estimate how useful are TectoMT phrases compared to the standard phrase table not just in general but on the specific foreseen test set. This deliberate overfitting to newstest 08, 11 and 12 then helps in translating newstest13.

This combination technique in its current state is rather expensive as a new phrase table is required for every new input document. However, if we fix the weights for the TectoMT phrase table, we can avoid re-tuning the system (whether this would degrade translation quality needs to be empirically evaluated). Moreover, if we use a dynamic phrase table, we could update it with TectoMT outputs on the fly, thus bypassing the need to retrain the translation model.

[6]Using K-best batch MIRA (Cherry and Foster, 2012) did not work any better in our setup.

[7]We are aware of the fact that Moses alternative decoding paths (Birch and Osborne, 2007) with similar phrase tables clutter n-best lists with identical items, making MERT less stable (Eisele et al., 2008; Bojar and Tamchyna, 2011). The issue was not severe in our case, CU-BOJAR needed 10 iterations compared to 3 iterations needed for PLAIN.

	Used in		
Test Set	Training	Tuning	Final Eval
newstest07	*could have*	en+cs	–
newstest08	en+TectoMT	en+cs	–
newstest09	*could have*	en+cs	–
newstest10	en+TectoMT	*could have*	–
newstest11	en+TectoMT	en+cs	–
newstest12	en+TectoMT	en+cs	–
newstest13	en+TectoMT	–	en+cs

Table 7: Summary of test sets usage. "en" and "cs" denote the official English and Czech sides, resp. "TectoMT" denotes the synthetic Czech.

2.2 Depfix

Depfix is an automatic post-editing tool for correcting errors in English-to-Czech SMT. It is applied as a post-processing step to CU-BOJAR, resulting in the CHIMERA system. Depfix 2013 is an improvement of Depfix 2012 (Rosa et al., 2012).

Depfix focuses on three major types of language phenomena that can be captured by employing linguistic knowledge but are often hard for SMT systems to get right:

- morphological agreement, such as:
  - an adjective and the noun it modifies have to share the same morphological gender, number and case
  - the subject and the predicate have to agree in morphological gender, number and person, if applicable
- transfer of meaning in cases where the same meaning is expressed by different grammatical means in English and in Czech, such as:
  - a subject in English is marked by being a left modifier of the predicate, while in Czech a subject is marked by the nominative morphological case
  - English marks possessiveness by the preposition 'of', while Czech uses the genitive morphological case
  - negation can be marked in various ways in English and Czech
- verb-noun and noun-noun valency—see (Rosa et al., 2013)

Depfix first performs a complex lingustic anal-

System	BLEU	TER	WMT Ranking	
			Appraise	MTurk
CU-TECTOMT	14.7	0.741	0.455	0.491
CU-BOJAR	**20.1**	0.696	0.637	**0.555**
CU-DEPFIX	20.0	**0.693**	**0.664**	0.542
PLAIN Moses	19.5	0.713	–	–
GOOGLE TR.	–	–	0.618	0.526

Table 8: Overall results.

ysis of both the source English sentence and its translation to Czech by CU-BOJAR. The analysis includes tagging, word-alignment, and dependency parsing both to shallow-syntax ("analytical") and deep-syntax ("tectogrammatical") dependency trees. Detection and correction of errors is performed by rule-based components (the valency corrections use a simple statistical valency model). For example, if the adjective-noun agreement is found to be violated, it is corrected by projecting the morphological categories from the noun to the adjective, which is realized by changing their values in the Czech morphological tag and generating the appropriate word form from the lemma-tag pair using the rule-based generator of Hajič (2004).

Rosa (2013) provides details of the current version of Depfix. The main additions since 2012 are valency corrections and lost negation recovery.

3 Overall Results

Table 8 reports the scores on the WMT13 test set. BLEU and TER are taken from the evaluation web site[8] for the *normalized* outputs, case insensitive. The normalization affects typesetting of punctuation only and greatly increases automatic scores. "WMT ranking" lists results from judgments from Appraise and Mechanical Turk. Except CU-TECTOMT, the manual evaluation used non-normalized MT outputs. The figure is the WMT12 standard interpretation as suggested by Bojar et al. (2011) and says how often the given system was ranked better than its competitor across all 18.6k non-tying pairwise comparisons extracted from the annotations.

We see a giant leap from CU-TECTOMT to CU-BOJAR, confirming the utility of large data. However, CU-TECTOMT had something to offer since it improved over PLAIN, a very competitive baseline, by 0.6 BLEU absolute. Depfix seems to slightly worsen BLEU score but slightly improve TER; the manual evaluation is similarly indecisive.

[8] `http://matrix.statmt.org/`

System	# Tokens	% Tokens
All	22920	76.44
Moses	3864	12.89
TectoMT	2323	7.75
Other	877	2.92

Table 9: CHIMERA components that contribute "confirmed" tokens.

System	# Tokens	% Tokens
None	21633	79.93
Moses	2093	7.73
TectoMT	2585	9.55
Both	385	1.42
CU-BOJAR	370	1.37

Table 10: Tokens missing in CHIMERA output.

4 Combination Analysis

We now closely analyze the contributions of the individual engines to the performance of CHIMERA. We look at translations of the newstest2013 sets produced by the individual systems (PLAIN, CU-TECTOMT, CU-BOJAR, CHIMERA).

We divide the newstest2013 reference tokens into two classes: those successfully produced by CHIMERA (Table 9) and those missed (Table 10). The analysis can suffer from false positives as well as false negatives, a "confirmed" token can violate some grammatical constraints in MT output and an "unconfirmed" token can be a very good translation. If we had access to more references, the issue of false negatives would decrease.

Table 9 indicates that more than 3/4 of tokens confirmed by the reference were available in all CHIMERA components: PLAIN Moses, CU-TECTOMT alone but also in the subsequent combinations CU-BOJAR and the final CU-DEPFIX.

PLAIN Moses produced 13% tokens that TectoMT did not provide and TectoMT output roughly 8% tokens unknown to Moses. However, note that it is difficult to distinguish the effect of different model weights: PLAIN *might have* produced some of those tokens as well if its weights were different. The row "Other" includes cases where e.g. Depfix introduced a confirmed token that none of the previous systems had.

Table 10 analyses the potential of CHIMERA components. These tokens from the reference were *not* produced by CHIMERA. In almost 80% of cases, the token was not available in any 1-best output; it *may* have been available in Moses phrase tables or the input sentence.

TectoMT offered almost 10% of missed tokens, but these were not selected in the subsequent combination. The potential of Moses is somewhat lower (about 8%) because our phrase-based combination is likely to select wordings that score well in a phrase-based model. 385 tokens were suggested by both TectoMT and Moses alone, but the combination in CU-BOJAR did not select them, and finally 370 tokens were produced by the combination while they were *not* present in 1-best output of neither TectoMT nor Moses. Remember, all these tokens eventually did not get to CHIMERA output, so Depfix must have changed them.

4.1 Depfix analysis

Table 11 analyzes the performance of the individual components of Depfix. Each *evaluated* sentence was either *modified* by a Depfix component, or not. If it was *modified*, its quality could have been evaluated as better (*improved*), worse (*worsened*), or the same (*equal*) as before. Thus, we can evaluate the performance of the individual components by the following measures:[9]

$$precision = \frac{\#improved}{\#improved + \#worsened} \quad (1)$$

$$impact = \frac{\#modified}{\#evaluated} \quad (2)$$

$$useless = \frac{\#equal}{\#modified} \quad (3)$$

Please note that we make an assumption that if a sentence was modified by multiple Depfix components, they all have the same effect on its quality. While this is clearly incorrect, it is impossible to accurately determine the effect of each individual component with the evaluation data at hand. This probably skews especially the reported performance of "high-impact" components, which often operate in combination with other components.

The evaluation is computed on 871 hits in which CU-BOJAR and CHIMERA were compared.

The results show that the two newest components – Lost negation recovery and Valency model – both modify a large number of sentences. Valency model seems to have a slightly *negative* effect on the translation quality. As this is the only statistical component of Depfix, we believe that this is caused by the fact that its parameters were not tuned on the final CU-BOJAR system, as the tuning has to be done semi-manually and the final system was not available in advance. On the other hand, Lost negation recovery seems to have a highly positive effect on translation quality. This is to be expected, as a lost negation often leads to the translation bearing an opposite meaning to the original one, which is probably one of the most serious errors that an MT system can make.

Depfix component	Prc.	Imp.	Usl.
Aux 'be' agr.	–	1.4%	100%
No prep. without children	–	0.5%	100%
Sentence-initial capitalization	0%	0.1%	0%
Prepositional morph. case	0%	2.1%	83%
Preposition - noun agr.	40%	3.8%	70%
Noun number projection	41%	7.2%	65%
Valency model	48%	10.6%	66%
Subject - nominal pred. agr.	50%	3.8%	76%
Noun - adjective agr.	55%	17.8%	75%
Subject morph. case	56%	8.5%	57%
Tokenization projection	56%	3.0%	38%
Verb tense projection	58%	5.2%	47%
Passive actor with 'by'	60%	1.0%	44%
Possessive nouns	67%	0.9%	25%
Source-aware truecasing	67%	2.8%	50%
Subject - predicate agr.	68%	5.1%	57%
Pro-drop in subject	73%	3.4%	63%
Subject - past participle agr.	75%	6.3%	42%
Passive - aux 'be' agr.	77%	4.8%	69%
Possessive with 'of'	78%	1.5%	31%
Present continuous	78%	1.5%	31%
Missing reflexive verbs	80%	1.6%	64%
Subject categories projection	83%	3.7%	62%
Rehang children of aux verbs	83%	5.5%	62%
Lost negation recovery	90%	7.2%	38%

Table 11: Depfix components performance analysis on 871 sentences from WMT13 test set.

5 Conclusion

We have reached our chimera to beat Google Translate. We combined all we have: a deep-syntactic transfer-based system TectoMT, very large parallel and monolingual data, factored setup to ensure morphological coherence, and finally Depfix, a rule-based automatic post-editing system that corrects grammaticality (agreement and valency) of the output as well as some features vital for adequacy, namely lost negation.

Acknowledgments

This work was partially supported by the grants P406/11/1499 of the Grant Agency of the Czech Republic, FP7-ICT-2011-7-288487 (MosesCore) and FP7-ICT-2010-6-257528 (Khresmoi) of the European Union and by SVV project number 267 314.

[9] We use the term *precision* for our primary measure for convenience, even though the way we define it does not match exactly its usual definition.

References

Alexandra Birch and Miles Osborne. 2007. CCG Supertags in Factored Statistical Machine Translation. In *In ACL Workshop on Statistical Machine Translation*, pages 9–16.

Ondřej Bojar and Aleš Tamchyna. 2011. Improving Translation Model by Monolingual Data. In *Proc. of WMT*, pages 330–336. ACL.

Ondřej Bojar, Miloš Ercegovčević, Martin Popel, and Omar Zaidan. 2011. A Grain of Salt for the WMT Manual Evaluation. In *Proc. of WMT*, pages 1–11. ACL.

Ondřej Bojar, Bushra Jawaid, and Amir Kamran. 2012a. Probes in a Taxonomy of Factored Phrase-Based Models. In *Proc. of WMT*, pages 253–260. ACL.

Ondřej Bojar, Zdeněk Žabokrtský, Ondřej Dušek, Petra Galuščáková, Martin Majliš, David Mareček, Jiří Maršík, Michal Novák, Martin Popel, and Aleš Tamchyna. 2012b. The Joy of Parallelism with CzEng 1.0. In *Proc. of LREC*, pages 3921–3928. ELRA.

Colin Cherry and George Foster. 2012. Batch Tuning Strategies for Statistical Machine Translation. In *Proc. of NAACL/HLT*, pages 427–436. ACL.

Jonathan H. Clark, Chris Dyer, Alon Lavie, and Noah A. Smith. 2011. Better hypothesis testing for statistical machine translation: Controlling for optimizer instability. In *Proc. of ACL/HLT*, pages 176–181. ACL.

Andreas Eisele, Christian Federmann, Hervé Saint-Amand, Michael Jellinghaus, Teresa Herrmann, and Yu Chen. 2008. Using Moses to Integrate Multiple Rule-Based Machine Translation Engines into a Hybrid System. In *Proc. of WMT*, pages 179–182. ACL.

Alexander Fraser, Marion Weller, Aoife Cahill, and Fabienne Cap. 2012. Modeling Inflection and Word-Formation in SMT. In *Proc. of EACL 2012*. ACL.

Petra Galuščáková, Martin Popel, and Ondřej Bojar. 2013. PhraseFix: Statistical Post-Editing of TectoMT. In *Proc. of WMT13*. Under review.

Qin Gao and Stephan Vogel. 2008. Parallel Implementations of Word Alignment Tool. In *Software Engineering, Testing, and Quality Assurance for Natural Language Processing*, SETQA-NLP '08, pages 49–57. ACL.

Jan Hajič. 2004. *Disambiguation of rich inflection: computational morphology of Czech*. Karolinum.

Kenneth Heafield, Ivan Pouzyrevsky, Jonathan H. Clark, and Philipp Koehn. 2013. Scalable Modified Kneser-Ney Language Model Estimation. In *Proc. of ACL*.

Philipp Koehn and Barry Haddow. 2012. Towards Effective Use of Training Data in Statistical Machine Translation. In *Proc. of WMT*, pages 317–321. ACL.

Philipp Koehn. 2005. Europarl: A Parallel Corpus for Statistical Machine Translation. In *Machine Translation Summit X*, pages 79–86.

David Mareček, Rudolf Rosa, Petra Galuščáková, and Ondřej Bojar. 2011. Two-step translation with grammatical post-processing. In *Proc. of WMT*, pages 426–432. ACL.

Franz Josef Och and Hermann Ney. 2000. Improved Statistical Alignment Models. In *ACL*. ACL.

Martin Popel and Zdeněk Žabokrtský. 2010. TectoMT: Modular NLP Framework. In Hrafn Loftsson, Eirikur Rögnvaldsson, and Sigrun Helgadottir, editors, *IceTAL 2010*, volume 6233 of *Lecture Notes in Computer Science*, pages 293–304. Iceland Centre for Language Technology (ICLT), Springer.

Rudolf Rosa, David Mareček, and Ondřej Dušek. 2012. DEPFIX: A system for automatic correction of Czech MT outputs. In *Proc. of WMT*, pages 362–368. ACL.

Rudolf Rosa, David Mareček, and Aleš Tamchyna. 2013. Deepfix: Statistical Post-editing of Statistical Machine Translation Using Deep Syntactic Analysis. Bălgarska akademija na naukite, ACL.

Rudolf Rosa. 2013. Automatic post-editing of phrase-based machine translation outputs. Master's thesis, Charles University in Prague, Faculty of Mathematics and Physics, Praha, Czechia.

Johanka Spoustová and Miroslav Spousta. 2012. A High-Quality Web Corpus of Czech. In *Proc. of LREC*. ELRA.

Andreas Stolcke. 2002. SRILM – An Extensible Language Modeling Toolkit. In *Proc. Intl. Conf. on Spoken Language Processing*, volume 2, pages 901–904.

Michael Subotin. 2011. An exponential translation model for target language morphology. In *Proc. of ACL/HLT*, pages 230–238. ACL.

Yandex School of Data Analysis machine translation systems for WMT13

Alexey Borisov, Jacob Dlougach, Irina Galinskaya
Yandex School of Data Analysis
16, Leo Tolstoy street, Moscow, Russia
{alborisov, jacob, galinskaya}@yandex-team.ru

Abstract

This paper describes the English-Russian and Russian-English statistical machine translation (SMT) systems developed at Yandex School of Data Analysis for the shared translation task of the ACL 2013 *Eighth Workshop on Statistical Machine Translation*. We adopted phrase-based SMT approach and evaluated a number of different techniques, including data filtering, spelling correction, alignment of lemmatized word forms and transliteration. Altogether they yielded +2.0 and +1.5 BLEU improvement for ru-en and en-ru language pairs. We also report on the experiments that did not have any positive effect and provide an analysis of the problems we encountered during the development of our systems.

1 Introduction

We participated in the shared translation task of the ACL 2013 Workshop on Statistical Machine Translation (WMT13) for ru-en and en-ru language pairs. We provide a detailed description of the experiments carried out for the development of our systems.

The rest of the paper is organized as follows. Section 2 describes the tools and data we used. Our Russian→English and English→Russian setups are discussed in Section 3. In Section 4 we report on the experiments that did not have any positive effect despite our expectations. We provide a thorough analysis of erroneous outputs in Section 5 and draw conclusions in Section 6.

2 Tools and data

2.1 Tools

We used an open source SMT system Moses (Koehn et al., 2007) for all our experiments excluding the one described in Section 4.1 due to its performance constraints. To overcome the limitation we employed our in-house decoder.

Language models (LM) were created with an open source IRSTLM toolkit (Federico et al., 2008). We computed 4-gram LMs with modified Kneser-Ney smoothing (Kneser and Ney, 1995).

We used an open source MGIZA++ tool (Gao and Vogel, 2008) to compute word alignment.

To obtain part of speech (POS) tags we used an open source Stanford POS tagger for English (Toutanova et al., 2003) and an open source suite of language analyzers, FreeLing 3.0 (Carreras et al., 2004; Padró and Stanilovsky, 2012), for Russian.

We utilized a closed source free for non-commercial use morphological analyzer, Mystem (Segalovich, 2003), that used a limited dictionary to obtain lemmas.

We also made use of the in-house language recognizer based on (Dunning, 1994) and a spelling corrector designed on the basis of the work of Cucerzan and Brill (2004).

We report all results in case-sensitive BLEU (Papineni et al., 2002) using mt-eval13a script from Moses distribution.

2.2 Data

Training data

We used News Commentary and News Crawl monolingual corpora provided by the organizers of the workshop.

Bilingual training data comprised English-Russian parallel corpus release by Yandex[1], News Commentary and Common Crawl corpora provided by the organizers.

We also exploited Wiki Headlines collection of three parallel corpora provided by CMU[2] as a

[1] https://translate.yandex.ru/corpus
[2] http://www.statmt.org/wmt13/wiki-titles.ru-en.tar.gz

source of reliable data.

Development set

The newstest2012 test set (Callison-Burch et al., 2012) was divided in the ratio 2:1 into a tuning set and a test set. The latter is referred to as newstest2012-test in the rest of the paper.

3 Primary setups

3.1 Baseline

We built the baseline systems according to the instructions available at the Moses website[3].

3.2 Preprocessing

The first thing we noticed was that some sentences marked as Russian appeared to be sentences in other languages (most commonly English). We applied a language recognizer for both monolingual and bilingual corpora. Results are given in Table 1.

Corpus	Filtered out (%)
Bilingual	3.39
Monolingual (English)	0.41
Monolingual (Russian)	0.58

Table 1: Results of the language recognizer: percentage of filtered out sentences.

The next thing we came across was the presence of a lot of spelling errors in our training data, so we applied a spelling corrector. Statistics are presented in Table 2.

Corpus	Modified (%)
Bilingual (English)	0.79
Bilingual (Russian)	1.45
Monolingual (English)	0.61
Monolingual (Russian)	0.52

Table 2: Results of the spelling corrector: percentage of modified sentences.

3.3 Alignment of lemmatized word forms

Russian is a language with rich morphology. The diversity of word forms results in data sparseness that makes translation of rare words difficult. In some cases inflections do not contain any additional information and are used only to make an agreement between two words. E.g. ADJ + NOUN: красив[ая] арфа *(beautiful harp)*, красив[ое] пианино *(beautiful piano)*, красив[ый] рояль *(beautiful grand piano)*. These inflections reflect the gender of the noun words, that has no equivalent in English.

In this particular case we can drop the inflections, but for other categories they can still be useful for translation, because the information they contain appears in function words in English. On the other hand, most of Russian morphology is useless for word alignment.

We applied a morphological analyzer Mystem (Segalovich, 2003) to the Russian text and converted each word to its dictionary form. Next we computed word alignment between the original English text and the lemmatized Russian text. All the other steps were executed according to the standard procedure with the original texts.

3.4 Phrase score adjustment

Sometimes phrases occur one or two times in the training corpus. In this case the corresponding phrase translation probability would be overestimated. We used Good-Turing technique described in (Gale, 1994) to decrease it to some more realistic value.

3.5 Decoding

Minimum Bayes-Risk (MBR)

MBR decoding (Kumar and Byrne, 2004) aims to minimize the expected loss of translation errors. As it is not possible to explore the space of all possible translations, we approximated it with the 1,000 most probable translations. A minus smoothed BLEU score (Lin and Och, 2004) was used for the loss function.

Reordering constrains

We forbade reordering over punctuation and translated quoted phrases independently.

3.6 Handling unknown words

The news texts contained a lot of proper names that did not appear in the training data. E.g. almost 25% of our translations contained unknown words. Dropping the unknown words would lead to better BLEU scores, but it might had caused bad effect on human judgement. To leave them in Cyrillic was not an option, so we exploited two approaches: incorporating reliable data from Wiki Headlines and transliteration.

[3]http://www.statmt.org/moses/?n=moses.baseline

	newstest2012-test	newstest2013
Russian→English		
Baseline	28.96	21.82
+ Preprocessing	29.59	22.28
+ Alignment of lemmatized word forms	29.97	22.61
+ Good-Turing	30.31	22.87
+ MBR	30.45	23.21
+ Reordering constraints	30.54	23.33
+ Wiki Headlines	30.68	23.46
+ Transliteration	30.93	23.73
English→Russian		
Baseline	21.96	16.24
+ Preprocessing	22.48	16.76
+ Good-Turing	22.84	17.13
+ MBR and Reordering constraints	23.27	17.45
+ Wiki Headlines and Transliteration	23.54	17.80

Table 3: Experimental results in case-sensitive BLEU for Russian→English and English→Russian tasks.

Wiki Headlines

We replaced the names occurring in the text with their translations, based on the information in "guessed-names" corpus from Wiki Headlines.

As has been mentioned in Section 3.3, Russian is a morphologically rich language. This often makes it hard to find exactly the same phrases, so we applied lemmatization of Russian language both for the input text and the Russian side of the reference corpus.

Russian→English transliteration

We gained considerable improvement from incorporating Wiki Headlines, but still 17% of translations contained Cyrillic symbols.

We applied a transliteration algorithm based on (Knight and Graehl, 1998). This technique yielded us a significant improvement, but introduced a lot of errors. E.g. Джеймс Бонд *(James Bond)* was converted to *Dzhejms Bond*.

English→Russian transliteration

In Russian, it is a common practice to leave some foreign words in Latin. E.g. the names of companies: *Apple, Google, Microsoft* look inadmissible when either translated directly or transliterated.

Taking this into account, we applied the same transliteration algorithm (Knight and Graehl, 1998), but replaced an unknown word with its transliteration only if we found a sufficient number of occurrences of its transliterated form in the monolingual corpus. We used five for such number.

3.7 Experimental results

We summarized the gains from the described techniques for Russian→English and English→Russian tasks on Table 3.

4 What did not work

4.1 Translation in two stages

Frequently machine translations contain errors that can be easily corrected by human post-editors. Since human aided machine translation is cost-efficient, we decided to address this problem to the computer.

We propose to translate sentences in two stages. At the first stage a SMT system is used to translate the input text into a preliminary form (in target language). At the next stage the preliminary form is translated again with an auxiliary SMT system trained on the translated and the target sides of the parallel corpus.

We encountered a technical challenge, when we had to build a SMT system for the second stage. A training corpus with one side generated with the first stage SMT system was not possible to be acquired with Moses due to its performance constraints. Thereupon we utilized our in-house SMT decoder and managed to translate 2M sentences in time.

We applied this technique both for ru-en and en-ru language pairs. Approximately 20% of the sentences had changed, but the BLEU score remained the same.

4.2 Factored model

We tried to build a factored model for ru-en language pair with POS tags produced by Stanford POS tagger (Toutanova et al., 2003).

Unfortunately, we did not gain any improvements from it.

5 Analysis

We carefully examined the erroneous outputs of our system and compared it with the outputs of the other systems participating in ru-en and en-ru tasks, and with the commercial systems available online (Bing, Google, Yandex).

5.1 Transliteration

Russian→English

The standard transliteration procedure is not invertible. This means that a Latin word being transfered into Cyrillic and then transliterated back to Latin produces an artificial word form. E.g. Хавард Хальварсен / *Havard Halvarsen* was correctly transliterated by only four out of 23 systems, including ours. Twelve systems either dropped one of the words or left it in Cyrillic. We provide a list of typical mistakes in order of their frequency: *Khavard Khalvarsen, Khavard Khal'varsen, Xavard Xaljvarsen*. Another example: Мисс Уайэтт *(Miss Wyatt)* → *Miss Uayett* (all the systems failed).

The next issue is the presence of non-null inflections that most certainly would result in wrong translation by any straight-forward algorithm. E.g. Хайдельберг[а] *(Heidelberg)* → *Heidelberga.*

English→Russian

In Russian, most words of foreign origin are written phonetically. Thereby, in order to obtain the best quality we should transliterate the transcription, not the word itself. E.g. the French derived name *Elsie Monereau* ['elsi monə'rəʊ] being translated by letters would result in Элси Монереау while the transliteration of the transcription would result in the correct form Элси Монро.

5.2 Grammars

English and Russian make use of different grammars. When the difference in their sentence structure becomes fundamental the phrase-based approach might get inapplicable.

Word order

Both Russian and English are classified as subject-verb-object (SOV) languages, but Russian has rather flexible word order compared to English and might frequently appear in other forms. This often results in wrong structure of the translated sentence. A common mistake made by our system and reproduced by the major online services: не изменились и правила *(rules have not been changed either)* → *have not changed and the rules.*

Constructions

- **there is / there are** is a non-local construction that has no equivalent in Russian. In most cases it can not be produced from the Russian text. E.g. на столе стоит матрёшка *(there is a matryoshka doll on the table)* → *on the table is a matryoshka.*

- **multiple negatives** in Russian are grammatically correct ways to express negation (a single negative is sometimes incorrect) while they are undesirable in standard English. E.g. Там никто никогда не был *(nobody has ever been there)* being translated word by word would result in *there nobody never not was.*

5.3 Idioms

Idiomatic expressions are hard to discover and dangerous to translate literary. E.g. a Russian idiom была не была *(let come what may)* being translated word by word would result in *was not was.* Neither of the commercial systems we checked managed to collect sufficient statistic to translate this very popular expression.

6 Conclusion

We have described the primary systems developed by the team of Yandex School of Data Analysis for WMT13 shared translation task.

We have reported on the experiments and demonstrated considerable improvements over the respective baseline. Among the most notable techniques are data filtering, spelling correction, alignment of lemmatized word forms and transliteration. We have analyzed the drawbacks of our systems and shared the ideas for further research.

References

Chris Callison-Burch, Philipp Koehn, Christof Monz, Matt Post, Radu Soricut, and Lucia Specia. 2012. Findings of the 2012 workshop on statistical machine translation. In *Proceedings of the Seventh Workshop on Statistical Machine Translation (WMT12)*, pages 10–51, Montréal, Canada, June. Association for Computational Linguistics.

Xavier Carreras, Isaac Chao, Lluís Padró, and Muntsa Padró. 2004. FreeLing: An open-source suite of language analyzers. In *Proceedings of the 4th International Conference on Language Resources and Evaluation (LREC)*.

Silviu Cucerzan and Eric Brill. 2004. Spelling correction as an iterative process that exploits the collective knowledge of web users. In *Proceedings of Conference on Empirical Methods in Natural Language Processing (EMNLP)*, pages 293–300.

Ted Dunning. 1994. Statistical identification of language. Technical report, Computing Research Lab (CRL), New Mexico State University, Las Cruces, NM, USA.

Marcello Federico, Nicola Bertoldi, and Mauro Cettolo. 2008. IRSTLM: an open source toolkit for handling large scale language models. In *Proceedings of 9th Annual Conference of the International Speech Communication Association (INTERSPEECH)*, pages 1618–1621.

William Gale. 1994. Good-Turing smoothing without tears. *Journal of Quantitative Linguistics (JQL)*, 2:217–237.

Qin Gao and Stephan Vogel. 2008. Parallel implementations of word alignment tool. In *Proceedings of the 46th Annual Meeting of the Association for Computational Linguistics (ACL)*, pages 49–57.

Reinhard Kneser and Hermann Ney. 1995. Improved backing-off for m-gram language modeling. In *Proceedings of the International Conference on Acoustics, Speech, and Signal Processing (ICASSP)*, volume 1, pages 181–184.

Kevin Knight and Jonathan Graehl. 1998. Machine transliteration. *Computational Linguistics*, 24(4):599–612.

Philipp Koehn, Hieu Hoang, Alexandra Birch, Chris Callison-burch, Richard Zens, Rwth Aachen, Alexandra Constantin, Marcello Federico, Nicola Bertoldi, Chris Dyer, Brooke Cowan, Wade Shen, Christine Moran, and Ondřej Bojar. 2007. Moses: Open source toolkit for statistical machine translation. In *Proceedings of the 45th Annual Meeting of the Association for Computational Linguistics (ACL)*, pages 177–180.

Shankar Kumar and William Byrne. 2004. Minimum bayes-risk decoding for statistical machine translation. In *Proceedings of the Human Language Technology Conference of the North American Chapter of the Association for Computational Linguistics (HLT-NAACL)*, pages 163–171.

Chin-Yew Lin and Franz Josef Och. 2004. ORANGE: a method for evaluating automatic evaluation metrics for machine translation. In *Proceedings of the 20th international conference on Computational Linguistics (COLING)*, Stroudsburg, PA, USA. Association for Computational Linguistics.

Lluís Padró and Evgeny Stanilovsky. 2012. FreeLing 3.0: Towards wider multilinguality. In *Proceedings of the Language Resources and Evaluation Conference (LREC)*, Istanbul, Turkey, May.

Kishore Papineni, Salim Roukos, Todd Ward, and Wei jing Zhu. 2002. BLEU: a method for automatic evaluation of machine translation. In *Processings of the 41st Annual Meeting of the Association for Computational Linguistics (ACL)*, pages 311–318.

Ilya Segalovich. 2003. A fast morphological algorithm with unknown word guessing induced by a dictionary for a web search engine. In Hamid R. Arabnia and Elena B. Kozerenko, editors, *Proceedings of the International Conference on Machine Learning; Models, Technologies and Applications (MLMTA)*, pages 273–280, Las Vegas, NV, USA, June. CSREA Press.

Kristina Toutanova, Dan Klein, Christopher D. Manning, and Yoram Singer. 2003. Feature-rich part-of-speech tagging with a cyclic dependency network. In *Proceedings of the Human Language Technology Conference of the North American Chapter of the Association for Computational Linguistics (HLT-NAACL)*, pages 252–259.

The Karlsruhe Institute of Technology Translation Systems for the WMT 2013

Eunah Cho, Thanh-Le Ha, Mohammed Mediani, Jan Niehues, Teresa Herrmann, Isabel Slawik and Alex Waibel
Karlsruhe Institute of Technology
Karlsruhe, Germany
`firstname.lastname@kit.edu`

Abstract

This paper describes the phrase-based SMT systems developed for our participation in the WMT13 Shared Translation Task. Translations for English↔German and English↔French were generated using a phrase-based translation system which is extended by additional models such as bilingual, fine-grained part-of-speech (POS) and automatic cluster language models and discriminative word lexica (DWL). In addition, we combined reordering models on different sentence abstraction levels.

1 Introduction

In this paper, we describe our systems for the ACL 2013 Eighth Workshop on Statistical Machine Translation. We participated in the Shared Translation Task and submitted translations for English↔German and English↔French using a phrase-based decoder with lattice input.

The paper is organized as follows: the next section gives a detailed description of our systems including all the models. The translation results for all directions are presented afterwards and we close with a conclusion.

2 System Description

The phrase table is based on a GIZA++ word alignment for the French↔English systems. For the German↔English systems we use a Discriminative Word Alignment (DWA) as described in Niehues and Vogel (2008). For every source phrase only the top 10 translation options are considered during decoding. The SRILM Toolkit (Stolcke, 2002) is used for training SRI language models using Kneser-Ney smoothing.

For the word reordering between languages, we used POS-based reordering models as described in Section 4. In addition to it, tree-based reordering model and lexicalized reordering were added for German↔English systems.

An in-house phrase-based decoder (Vogel, 2003) is used to perform translation. The translation was optimized using Minimum Error Rate Training (MERT) as described in Venugopal et al. (2005) towards better BLEU (Papineni et al., 2002) scores.

2.1 Data

The Europarl corpus (EPPS) and News Commentary (NC) corpus were used for training our translation models. We trained language models for each language on the monolingual part of the training corpora as well as the News Shuffle and the Gigaword corpora. The additional data such as web-crawled corpus, UN and Giga corpora were used after filtering. The filtering work for this data is discussed in Section 3.

For the German↔English systems we use the news-test2010 set for tuning, while the news-test2011 set is used for the French↔English systems. For testing, news-test2012 set was used for all systems.

2.2 Preprocessing

The training data is preprocessed prior to training the system. This includes normalizing special symbols, smart-casing the first word of each sentence and removing long sentences and sentence pairs with length mismatch.

Compound splitting is applied to the German part of the corpus of the German→English system as described in Koehn and Knight (2003).

3 Filtering of Noisy Pairs

The filtering was applied on the corpora which are found to be noisy. Namely, the Giga English-French parallel corpus and the all the new web-crawled data . The operation was performed using an SVM classifier as in our past systems (Mediani et al., 2011). For each pair, the required lexica were extracted from Giza alignment of the corresponding EPPS and NC corpora. Furthermore, for the web-crawled data, higher precision classifiers were trained by providing a larger number of negative examples to the classifier.

After filtering, we could still find English sentences in the other part of the corpus. Therefore, we performed a language identification (LID)-based filtering afterwards (performed only on the French-English corpora, in this participation).

4 Word Reordering

Word reordering was modeled based on POS sequences. For the German↔English system, reordering rules learned from syntactic parse trees were used in addition.

4.1 POS-based Reordering Model

In order to train the POS-based reordering model, probabilistic rules were learned based on the POS tags from the TreeTagger (Schmid and Laws, 2008) of the training corpus and the alignment. As described in Rottmann and Vogel (2007), continuous reordering rules are extracted. This modeling of short-range reorderings was extended so that it can cover also long-range reorderings with non-continuous rules (Niehues and Kolss, 2009), for German↔English systems.

4.2 Tree-based Reordering Model

In addition to the POS-based reordering, we apply a tree-based reordering model for the German↔English translation to better address the differences in word order between German and English. We use the Stanford Parser (Rafferty and Manning, 2008) to generate syntactic parse trees for the source side of the training corpus. Then we use the word alignment between source and target language to learn rules on how to reorder the constituents in a German source sentence to make it match the English target sentence word order better (Herrmann et al., 2013). The POS-based and tree-based reordering rules are applied to each input sentence. The resulting reordered sentence variants as well as the original sentence order are encoded in a word lattice. The lattice is then used as input to the decoder.

4.3 Lexicalized Reordering

The lexicalized reordering model stores the reordering probabilities for each phrase pair. Possible reordering orientations at the incoming and outgoing phrase boundaries are monotone, swap or discontinuous. With the POS- and tree-based reordering word lattices encode different reordering variants. In order to apply the lexicalized reordering model, we store the original position of each word in the lattice. At each phrase boundary at the end, the reordering orientation with respect to the original position of the words is checked. The probability for the respective orientation is included as an additional score.

5 Translation Models

In addition to the models used in the baseline system described above, we conducted experiments including additional models that enhance translation quality by introducing alternative or additional information into the translation modeling process.

5.1 Bilingual Language Model

During the decoding the source sentence is segmented so that the best combination of phrases which maximizes the scores is available. However, this causes some loss of context information at the phrase boundaries. In order to make bilingual context available, we use a bilingual language model (Niehues et al., 2011). In the bilingual language model, each token consists of a target word and all source words it is aligned to.

5.2 Discriminative Word Lexicon

Mauser et al. (2009) introduced the Discriminative Word Lexicon (DWL) into phrase-based machine translation. In this approach, a maximum entropy model is used to determine the probability of using a target word in the translation.

In this evaluation, we used two extensions to this work as shown in (Niehues and Waibel, 2013). First, we added additional features to model the order of the source words better. Instead of representing the source sentence as a bag-of-words, we used a bag-of-n-grams. We used n-grams up to the order of three and applied count filtering to the features for higher order n-grams.

Furthermore, we created the training examples differently in order to focus on addressing errors of the other models of the phrase-based translation system. We first translated the whole corpus with a baseline system. Then we only used the words that occur in the N-Best List and not in the reference as negative examples instead of using all words that do not occur in the reference.

5.3 Quasi-Morphological Operations

Because of the inflected characteristic of the German language, we try to learn quasi-morphological operations that change the lexical entry of a known word form to the out-of-vocabulary (OOV) word form as described in Niehues and Waibel (2012).

5.4 Phrase Table Adaptation

For the French↔English systems, we built two phrase tables; one trained with all data and the other trained only with the EPPS and NC corpora. This is due to the fact that Giga corpus is big but noisy and EPPS and NC corpus are more reliable. The two models are combined log-linearly to achieve the adaptation towards the cleaner corpora as described in Niehues et al. (2010).

6 Language Models

The 4-gram language models generated by the SRILM toolkit are used as the main language models for all of our systems. For the English↔French systems, we use a good quality corpus as in-domain data to train in-domain language models. Additionally, we apply the POS and cluster language models in different systems. For the German→English system, we build separate language models using each corpus and combine them linearly before the decoding by minimizing the perplexity. Language models are integrated into the translation system by a log-linear combination and receive optimal weights during tuning by the MERT.

6.1 POS Language Models

For the English→German system, we use the POS language model, which is trained on the POS sequence of the target language. The POS tags are generated using the RFTagger (Schmid and Laws, 2008) for German. The RFTagger generates fine-grained tags which include person, gender, and case information. The language model is trained with up to 9-gram information, using the German side of the parallel EPPS and NC corpus, as well as the News Shuffle corpus.

6.2 Cluster Language Models

In order to use larger context information, we use a cluster language model for all our systems. The cluster language model is based on the idea shown in Och (1999). Using the MKCLS algorithm, we cluster the words in the corpus, given a number of classes. Then words in the corpus are replaced with their cluster IDs. Using these cluster IDs, we train n-gram language models as well as a phrase table with this additional factor of cluster ID. Our submitted systems have diversed range of the number of clusters as well as n-gram.

7 Results

Using the models described above we performed several experiments leading finally to the systems used for generating the translations submitted to the workshop. The results are reported as case-sensitive BLEU scores on one reference translation.

7.1 German→English

The experiments for the German to English translation system are summarized in Table 1. The baseline system uses POS-based reordering, DWA with lattice phrase extraction and language models trained on the News Shuffle corpus and Giga corpus separately. Then we added a 5-gram cluster LM trained with 1,000 word classes. By adding a language model using the filtered crawled data we gained 0.3 BLEU on the test set. For this we combined all language models linearly. The filtered crawled data was also used to generate a phrase table, which brought another improvement of 0.85 BLEU. Applying tree-based reordering improved the BLEU score, and the performance had more gain by adding the extended DWL, namely using both bag-of-ngrams and n-best lists. While lexicalized reordering gave us a slight gain, we added morphological operation and gained more improvements.

7.2 English→German

The English to German baseline system uses POS-based reordering and language models using parallel data (EPPS and NC) as shown in Table 2. Gradual gains were achieved by changing alignment from GIZA++ to DWA, adding a bilingual language model as well as a language model based on the POS tokens. A 9-gram cluster-based language model with 100 word classes gave us a

System	Dev	Test
Baseline	24.15	22.79
+ Cluster LM	24.18	22.84
+ Crawled Data LM (Comb.)	24.53	23.14
+ Crawled Data PT	25.38	23.99
+ Tree Rules	25.80	24.16
+ Extended DWL	25.59	24.54
+ Lexicalized Reordering	**26.04**	24.55
+ Morphological Operation	-	**24.62**

Table 1: Translation results for German→English

small gain. Improving the reordering using lexicalized reordering gave us gain on the optimization set. Using DWL let us have more improvements on our test set. By using the filtered crawled data, we gained a big improvement of 0.46 BLEU on the test set. Then we extended the DWL with bag of n-grams and n-best lists to achieve additional improvements. Finally, the best system includes lattices generated using tree rules.

System	Dev	Test
Baseline	17.00	16.24
+ DWA	17.27	16.53
+ Bilingual LM	17.27	16.59
+ POS LM	17.46	16.66
+ Cluster LM	17.49	16.68
+ Lexicalized Reordering	17.57	16.68
+ DWL	17.58	16.77
+ Crawled Data	18.43	17.23
+ Extended DWL	**18.66**	17.57
+ Tree Rules	18.63	**17.70**

Table 2: Translation results for English→German

7.3 French→English

Table 3 reports some remarkable improvements as we combined several techniques on the French→English direction. The baseline system was trained on parallel corpora such as EPPS, NC and Giga, while the language model was trained on the English part of those corpora plus News Shuffle. The newly presented web-crawled data helps to achieve almost 0.6 BLEU points more on test set. Adding bilingual language model and cluster language model does not show a significant impact. Further gains were achieved by the adaptation of in-domain data into general-theme phrase table, bringing 0.15 BLEU better on the test set. When we added the DWL feature, it notably improves the system by 0.25 BLEU points, resulting in our best system.

System	Dev	Test
Baseline	30.33	29.35
+ Crawled Data	30.59	29.93
+ Bilingual and Cluster LMs	30.67	30.01
+ In-Domain PT Adaptation	**31.17**	30.16
+ DWL	31.07	**30.40**

Table 3: Translation results for French→English

7.4 English→French

In the baseline system, EPPS, NC, Giga and News Shuffle corpora are used for language modeling. The big phrase tables tailored EPPC, NC and Giga data. The system also uses short-range reordering trained on EPPS and NC. Adding parallel and filtered crawl data improves the system. It was further enhanced by the integration of a 4-gram bilingual language model. Moreover, the best configuration of 9-gram language model trained on 500 clusters of French texts gains 0.25 BLEU points improvement. We also conducted phrase-table adaptation from the general one into the domain covered by EPPS and NC data and it helps as well. The initial try-out with lexicalized reordering feature showed an improvement of 0.23 points on the development set, but a surprising reduction on the test set, thus we decided to take the system after adaptation as our best English→French system.

System	Dev	Test
Baseline	30.50	27.77
+ Crawled Data	31.05	27.87
+ Bilingual LM	31.23	28.50
+ Cluster LM	31.58	28.75
+ In-Domain PT Adaptation	31.88	**29.12**
+ Lexicalized Reordering	**32.11**	28.98

Table 4: Translation results for English→French

8 Conclusions

We have presented the systems for our participation in the WMT 2013 Evaluation for English↔German and English↔French. All systems use a class-based language model as well as a bilingual language model. Using a DWL with source context improved the translation quality of English↔German systems. Also for these systems, we could improve even more with a tree-based reordering model. Special handling of OOV words improved German→English system, while for the inverse direction the language model with fine-grained POS tags was helpful. For English↔French, phrase table adaptation helps to avoid using wrong parts of the noisy Giga corpus.

9 Acknowledgements

This work was partly achieved as part of the Quaero Programme, funded by OSEO, French State agency for innovation. The research leading to these results has received funding from the European Union Seventh Framework Programme (FP7/2007-2013) under grant agreement n° 287658.

References

Teresa Herrmann, Jan Niehues, and Alex Waibel. 2013. Combining Word Reordering Methods on different Linguistic Abstraction Levels for Statistical Machine Translation. In *Proceedings of the Seventh Workshop on Syntax, Semantics and Structure in Statistical Translation*, Altanta, Georgia, USA, June. Association for Computational Linguistics.

Philipp Koehn and Kevin Knight. 2003. Empirical Methods for Compound Splitting. In *EACL*, Budapest, Hungary.

Arne Mauser, Saša Hasan, and Hermann Ney. 2009. Extending Statistical Machine Translation with Discriminative and Trigger-based Lexicon Models. In *Proceedings of the 2009 Conference on Empirical Methods in Natural Language Processing: Volume 1 - Volume 1*, EMNLP '09, Singapore.

Mohammed Mediani, Eunah Cho, Jan Niehues, Teresa Herrmann, and Alex Waibel. 2011. The kit english-french translation systems for iwslt 2011. In *Proceedings of the eight International Workshop on Spoken Language Translation (IWSLT)*.

Jan Niehues and Muntsin Kolss. 2009. A POS-Based Model for Long-Range Reorderings in SMT. In *Fourth Workshop on Statistical Machine Translation (WMT 2009)*, Athens, Greece.

Jan Niehues and Stephan Vogel. 2008. Discriminative Word Alignment via Alignment Matrix Modeling. In *Proc. of Third ACL Workshop on Statistical Machine Translation*, Columbus, USA.

Jan Niehues and Alex Waibel. 2012. Detailed Analysis of different Strategies for Phrase Table Adaptation in SMT. In *Proceedings of the American Machine Translation Association (AMTA)*, San Diego, California, October.

Jan Niehues and Alex Waibel. 2013. An MT Error-driven Discriminative Word Lexicon using Sentence Structure Features. In *Eighth Workshop on Statistical Machine Translation (WMT 2013)*, Sofia, Bulgaria.

Jan Niehues, Mohammed Mediani, Teresa Herrmann, Michael Heck, Christian Herff, and Alex Waibel. 2010. The KIT Translation system for IWSLT 2010. In Marcello Federico, Ian Lane, Michael Paul, and François Yvon, editors, *Proceedings of the seventh International Workshop on Spoken Language Translation (IWSLT)*, pages 93–98.

Jan Niehues, Teresa Herrmann, Stephan Vogel, and Alex Waibel. 2011. Wider Context by Using Bilingual Language Models in Machine Translation. In *Sixth Workshop on Statistical Machine Translation (WMT 2011)*, Edinburgh, UK.

Franz Josef Och. 1999. An efficient method for determining bilingual word classes. In *Proceedings of the ninth conference on European chapter of the Association for Computational Linguistics*, EACL '99, pages 71–76, Stroudsburg, PA, USA. Association for Computational Linguistics.

Kishore Papineni, Salim Roukos, Todd Ward, and Wei-Jing Zhu. 2002. Bleu: a Method for Automatic Evaluation of Machine Translation. Technical Report RC22176 (W0109-022), IBM Research Division, T. J. Watson Research Center.

Anna N. Rafferty and Christopher D. Manning. 2008. Parsing three German treebanks: lexicalized and unlexicalized baselines. In *Proceedings of the Workshop on Parsing German*, Columbus, Ohio.

Kay Rottmann and Stephan Vogel. 2007. Word Reordering in Statistical Machine Translation with a POS-Based Distortion Model. In *TMI*, Skövde, Sweden.

Helmut Schmid and Florian Laws. 2008. Estimation of Conditional Probabilities with Decision Trees and an Application to Fine-Grained POS Tagging. In *COLING 2008*, Manchester, Great Britain.

Andreas Stolcke. 2002. SRILM – An Extensible Language Modeling Toolkit. In *Proc. of ICSLP*, Denver, Colorado, USA.

Ashish Venugopal, Andreas Zollman, and Alex Waibel. 2005. Training and Evaluation Error Minimization Rules for Statistical Machine Translation. In *Workshop on Data-drive Machine Translation and Beyond (WPT-05)*, Ann Arbor, MI.

Stephan Vogel. 2003. SMT Decoder Dissected: Word Reordering. In *Int. Conf. on Natural Language Processing and Knowledge Engineering*, Beijing, China.

TÜBİTAK-BİLGEM German-English Machine Translation Systems for WMT'13

İlknur Durgar El-Kahlout and Coşkun Mermer
TÜBİTAK-BİLGEM
Gebze 41470, Kocaeli, TURKEY
{ilknur.durgar,coskun.mermer}@tubitak.gov.tr

Abstract

This paper describes TÜBİTAK-BİLGEM statistical machine translation (SMT) systems submitted to the Eighth Workshop on Statistical Machine Translation (WMT) shared translation task for German-English language pair in both directions. We implement phrase-based SMT systems with standard parameters. We present the results of using a big tuning data and the effect of averaging tuning weights of different seeds. Additionally, we performed a linguistically motivated compound splitting in the German-to-English SMT system.

1 Introduction

TÜBİTAK-BİLGEM participated for the first time in the WMT'13 shared translation task for the German-English language pairs in both directions. We implemented a phrase-based SMT system by using the entire available training data. In the German-to-English SMT system, we performed a linguistically motivated compound splitting. We tested different language model (LM) combinations by using the parallel data, monolingual data, and Gigaword v4. In each step, we tuned systems with five different tune seeds and used the average of tuning weights in the final system. We tuned our systems on a big tuning set which is generated from the last years' (2008, 2009, 2010, and 2012) development sets. The rest of the paper describes the details of our systems.

2 German-English

2.1 Baseline

All available data was tokenized, truecased, and the maximum number of tokens were fixed to 70 for the translation model. The Moses open SMT toolkit (Koehn et al., 2007) was used with MGIZA++ (Gao and Vogel, 2008) with the standard alignment heuristic *grow-diag-final* (Och and Ney, 2003) for word alignments. *Good-Turing* smoothing was used for phrase extraction. Systems were tuned on *newstest2012* with MERT (Och, 2003) and tested on *newstest2011*. 4-gram language models (LMs) were trained on the target side of the parallel text and the monolingual data by using SRILM (Stolcke, 2002) toolkit with Kneser-Ney smoothing (Kneser and Ney, 1995) and then binarized by using KenLM toolkit (Heafield, 2011). At each step, systems were tuned with five different seeds with lattice-samples. Minimum Bayes risk decoding (Kumar and Byrne, 2004) and *-drop-unknown* parameters were used during the decoding.

This configuration is common for all of the experiments decribed in this paper unless stated otherwise. Table 1 shows the number of sentences used in system training after the *clean-corpus* process.

Data	Number of sentences
Europarl	1908574
News-Commentary	177712
Commoncrawl	726458

Table 1: Parallel Corpus.

We trained two baseline systems in order to assess the effects of this year's new parallel data, *commoncrawl*. We first trained an SMT system by using only the training data from the previous WMT shared translation tasks that is *europarl* and *news-commentary* (**Baseline1**). As the second baseline, we also included the new parallel data *commoncrawl* only in the translation model (**Baseline2**). Then, we included *commoncrawl* corpus both to the translation model and the language model (**Baseline3**).

Table 2 compares the baseline results. For all

experiments throughout the paper, we present the minimum and the maximum BLEU scores obtained after five different tunes. As seen in the table, the addition of the *commoncrawl* corpus resultedin a 1.1 BLEU (Papineni et al., 2002) points improvement (on average) on the test set. Although **Baseline2** is slightly better than **Baseline3**, we used **Baseline3** and kept *commoncrawl* corpus in LMs for further experiments.

System	newstest12	newstest11
Baseline1	20.58|20.74	19.14|19.29
Baseline2	21.37|21.58	20.16|20.46
Baseline3	21.28|21.58	20.22|20.49

Table 2: Baseline Results.

2.2 Bayesian Alignment

In the original IBM models (Brown et al., 1993), word translation probabilities are treated as model parameters and the expectation-maximization (EM) algorithm is used to obtain the maximum-likelihood estimates of the parameters and the resulting distributions on alignments. However, EM provides a point-estimate, not a distribution, for the parameters. The Bayesian alignment on the other hand takes into account all values of the model parameters by treating them as multinomial-distributed random variables with Dirichlet priors and integrating over all possible values. A Bayesian approach to word alignment inference in IBM Models is shown to result in significantly less "garbage collection" and a much more compact alignment dictionary. As a result, the Bayesian word alignment has better translation performances and obtains significant BLEU improvements over EM on various language pairs, data sizes, and experimental settings (Mermer et al., 2013).

We compared the translation performance of word alignments obtained via Bayesian inference to those obtained via EM algorithm. We used a a Gibbs sampler for fully Bayesian inference in HMM alignment model, integrating over all possible parameter values in finding the alignment distribution by using **Baseline3** word alignments for initialization. Table 3 compares the Bayesian alignment to the EM alignment. The results show a slight increase in the development set *newstest12* but a decrease of 0.1 BLEU points on average in the test set *newstest11*.

System	newstest12	newstest11
Baseline3	21.28|21.58	20.22|20.49
Gibbs Sampling	21.36|21.59	19.98|20.40

Table 3: Bayesian Alignment Results.

2.3 Development Data in Training

Development data from the previous years (i.e. *newstest08*, *newstest09*, *newstest10*), though being a small set of corpus (7K sentences), is in-domain data and can positively affect the translation system. In order to make use of this data, we experimented two methods: i) adding the development data in the translation model as described in this section and ii) using it as a big tuning set for tuning the parameters more efficiently as explained in the next section.

Similar to including the *commoncrawl* corpus, we first add the development data both to the training and language models by concatenating it to the biggest corpus *europarl* (**DD(tm+lm)**) and then we removed this corpus from the language models (**DD(tm)**). Results in Table 4 show that including the development data both the tranining and language model increases the performance in development set but decreases the performance in the test set. Including the data only in the translation model shows a very slight improvement in the test set.

System	newstest12	newstest11
Baseline3	21.28|21.58	20.22|20.49
DD(tm+lm)	21.28|21.65	20.00|20.49
DD(tm)	21.23|21.52	20.26|20.49

Table 4: Development Sets Results.

2.4 Tuning with a Big Development Data

The second method of making use of the development data is to concatenate it to the tuning set. As a baseline, we tuned the system with *newstest12* as mentioned in Section 2.1. Then, we concatenated the development data of the previous years with the *newstest12* and built a big tuning set. Finally, we obtained a tuning set of 10K sentences. We excluded the *newstest11* as an internal test set to see the relative improvements of different systems. Table 5 shows the results of using a big tuning set. Tuning the system with a big tuning set resulted in a 0.13 BLEU points improvement.

System	newstest12	newstest11
newstest12	21.28|21.58	20.22|20.49
Big Tune	20.93|21.19	20.32|20.58

Table 5: Tuning Results.

2.5 Effects of Different Language Models

In this set of experiments, we tested the effects of different combinations of parallel and monolingual data as language models. As the baseline, we trained three LMs, one from each parallel corpus as *europarl*, *news-commentary*, and *commoncrawl* and one LM from the monolingual data *news-shuffled* (**Baseline3**). We then trained two LMs, one from the whole parallel data and one from the monolingual data (**2LMs**). Table 6 shows that using whole parallel corpora as one LM performs better than individual corpus LMs and results in 0.1 BLEU points improvement on the baseline. Finally, we trained Gigaword v4 (LDC2009T13) as a third LM (**3LMs**) which gives a 0.16 BLEU points improvement over the **2LMs**.

System	newstest12	newstest11
Baseline3	21.28|21.58	20.22|20.49
2LMs	21.46|21.70	20.28|20.57
3LMs	21.78|21.93	20.54|20.68

Table 6: Language Model Results.

2.6 German Preprocessing

In German, compounding is very common. From the machine translation point of view, compounds increase the vocabulary size with high number of the singletons in the training data and hence decrease the word alignment quality. Moreover, high number of out-of-vocabulary (OOV) words in tuning and test sets results in several German words left as untranslated. A well-known solution to this problem is compound splitting.

Similarly, having different word forms for a source side lemma for the same target lemma causes the lexical redundancy in translation. This redundancy results in unnecessary large phrase translation tables that overload the decoder, as a separate phrase translation entry has to be kept for each word form. For example, German definite determiner could be marked in sixteen different ways according to the possible combinations of genders, case and number, which are fused in six different tokens (e.g., der, das, die, den, dem, des). Except for the plural and genitive cases, all these forms are translated to the same English word "the".

In the German preprocessing, we aimed both normalizing lexical redundancy and splitting German compounds with corpus driven splitting algorithm based on Koehn and Knight (2003). We used the same compound splitting and lexical redundancy normalization methods described in Allauzen et al. (2010) and Durgar El-Kahlout and Yvon (2010) with minor in-house changes. We used only "addition" (e.g., -s, -n, -en, -e, -es) and "truncation" (e.g., -e, -en, -n) affixes for compound splitting. We selected minimum candidate length to 8 and minimum split length to 4. By using the Treetagger (Schmid, 1994) output, we included linguistic information in compound splitting such as not splitting named entities and foreign words (**CS1**). We also experimented adding # as a delimiter for the splitted words except the last word (e.g., Finanzkrisen is splitted as finanz# krisen) (**CS2**).

On top of the compound splitting, we applied the lexical redundancy normalization (**CS+Norm1**). We lemmatized German articles, adjectives (only positive form), for some pronouns and for nouns in order to remove the lexical redundancy (e.g., Bildes as Bild) by using the fine-grained part-of-speech tags generated by RFTagger (Schmid and Laws, 2008). Similar to **CS2**, We tested the delimited version of normalized words (**CS+Norm2**).

Table 7 shows the results of compound splitting and normalization methods. As a result, normalization on top of compounding did not perform well. Besides, experiments showed that compound word decomposition is crucial and helps vastly to improve translation results 0.43 BLEU points on average over the best system described in Section 2.5.

System	newstest12	newstest11
3LMs	21.78|21.93	20.54|20.68
CS1	22.01|22.21	20.63|20.89
CS2	22.06|22.22	20.74|20.99
CS+Norm2	21.96|22.16	20.70|20.88
CS+Norm1	20.63|20.76	22.01|22.16

Table 7: Compound Splitting Results.

2.7 Average of Weights

As mentioned in Section 2.1, we performed tuning with five different seeds. We averaged the five tuning weights and directly applied these weights during the decoding. Table 8 shows that using the average of several tuning weights performs better than each individual tuning (0.2 BLEU points).

System	newstest12	newstest11
CS2	22.06|22.22	20.74|20.99
Avg. of Weights	22.27	21.07

Table 8: Average of Weights Results.

2.8 Other parameters

In addition to the experiments described in the earlier sections, we removed the *-drop-unknown* parameter which gave us a 0.5 BLEU points improvement. We also included the monotone-at-punctuation, *-mp* in decoding. We handled out-of-vocabulary (OOV) words by lemmatizing the OOV words. Moreover, we added all development data in training after fixing the parameter weights as described in Section 2.7. Although each of these changes increases the translation scores each gave less than 0.1 BLEU point improvement. Table 9 shows the results of the final system after including all of the approaches except the ones described in Section 2.2 and 2.3.

System	newstest12	newstest11
Final System	22.59|22.77	21.86|21.93
Avg. of Weights	22.66	22.00
+ tune data in train	−−	22.09

Table 9: German-to-English Final System Results.

3 English-German

For English-to-German translation system, the baseline setting is the same as described in Section 2.1. We also added the items that showed positive improvement in the German to English SMT system such as using 2 LMs, tuning with five seeds and averaging tuning parameters, using *-mp*, and not using *-drop-unknown*. Table 10 shows the experimental results for English-to-German SMT systems. Similar to the German-to-English direction, tuning with a big development data outperforms the baseline 0.26 BLEU points (on average). Additionally, averaging the tuning weights of different seeds results in 0.2 BLEU points improvement.

System	newstest12	newstest11
Baseline	16.95|17.03	15.93|16.13
+ Big Tune	16.82|17.01	16.22|16.37
Avg. of Weights	16.99	16.47

Table 10: English to German Final System Results.

4 Final System and Results

Table 11 shows our official submission scores for German-English SMT systems submitted to the WMT'13.

System	newstest13
De-En	25.60
En-De	19.28

Table 11: German-English Official Test Submission.

5 Conclusion

In this paper, we described our submissions to WMT'13 Shared Translation Task for German-English language pairs. We used phrase-based systems with a big tuning set which is a combination of the development sets from last four years. We tuned the systems on this big tuning set with five different tunes. We averaged these five tuning weights in the final system. We trained 4-gram language models one from parallel data and one from monolingual data. Moreover, we trained a 4-gram language model with Gigaword v4 for German-to-English direction. For German-to-English, we performed a different compound splitting method instead of the Moses splitter. We obtained a 1.7 BLEU point increase for German-to-English SMT system and a 0.5 BLEU point increase for English-to-German SMT system for the internal test set *newstest2011*. Finally, we submitted our German-to-English SMT system with a BLEU score 25.6 and English-to-German SMT system with a BLEU score 19.3 for the official test set *newstest2013*.

References

Alexandre Allauzen, Josep M. Crego, İlknur Durgar El-Kahlout, and Francois Yvon. 2010. Limsi's statistical translation systems for wmt'10. In *Proceedings of the Fifth Workshop on Statistical Machine Translation*, pages 54–59.

Peter F. Brown, Stephen A. Della Pietra, Vincent J. Della Pietra, and Robert L. Mercer. 1993. The mathematics of statistical machine translation: Parameter estimation. *Computational Linguistics*, 19:263–311.

İlknur Durgar El-Kahlout and Francois Yvon. 2010. The pay-offs of preprocessing German-English statistical machine translation. In *Proceedings of the Seventh International Workshop on Spoken Language Translation (IWSLT)*, pages 251–258.

Qin Gao and Stephan Vogel. 2008. Parallel implementations of word alignment tool. In *Proceedings of ACL WSETQANLP*.

Kenneth Heafield. 2011. Kenlm: Faster and smaller language model queries. In *Proceedings of the Sixth Workshop on Statistical Machine Translation*, pages 187–197.

Reinhard Kneser and Hermann Ney. 1995. Improved backing-off for m-gram language modeling. In *Proceedings of the International Conference on Acoustics, Speech and Signal Processing*, pages 181–184.

Philipp Koehn and Kevin Knight. 2003. Emprical methods for compound splitting. In *Proceedings of European Chapter of the ACL (EACL)*, pages 187–194.

Philipp Koehn, Hieu Hoang, Alexandra Birch, Chris Callison-Burch, Marcello Federico, Nicola Bertoldi, Brooke Cowan, Wade Shen, Christine Moran, Richard Zens, Chris Dyer, Ondrej Bojar, Alexandra Constantin, and Evan Herbst. 2007. Moses: Open source toolkit for statistical machine translation. In *Proceedings of ACL Demo and Poster Session*, pages 177–180.

Shankar Kumar and William Byrne. 2004. Minimum bayes-risk decoding for statistical machine translation. In *Proceedings of HLT-NAACL*, pages 169–176.

Coşkun Mermer, Murat Saraçlar, and Ruhi Sarkaya. 2013. Improving statistical machine translation using bayesian word alignment and gibbs sampling. *IEEE Transactions on Audio, Speech and Language Processing*, 21:1090–1101.

Franz Josef Och and Hermann Ney. 2003. A systematic comparison of various statistical alignment models. *Computational Linguistics*, 1:19–51.

Franz Josef Och. 2003. Minimum error rate training in statistical machine translation. In *Proceedings of the 41st Annual Meeting of the Association for Computational Linguistics (ACL)*, pages 160–167.

Kishore Papineni, Salim Roukos, Todd Ward, and Wei-Jing Zhu. 2002. BLEU: A method for automatic evaluation of machine translation. In *Proceedings of the 41st Annual Meeting of the Association for Computational Linguistics (ACL)*, pages 311–318.

Helmut Schmid and Florian Laws. 2008. Estimation of conditional probabilities with decision trees and an application to fine-granined pos tagging. In *Proceedings of COLING*.

Helmut Schmid. 1994. Probabilistic part-of-speech tagging using decision trees. In *Proceedings of the International Conference on New Methods in Language Processing*.

Andreas Stolcke. 2002. SRILM - an extensible language modeling toolkit. In *Proceedings of the International Conference on Spoken Language Processing (ICSLP)*, pages 257–286.

Edinburgh's Machine Translation Systems for European Language Pairs

Nadir Durrani, Barry Haddow, Kenneth Heafield, and Philipp Koehn
School of Informatics
University of Edinburgh
Scotland, United Kingdom
{dnadir,bhaddow,kheafiel,pkoehn}@inf.ed.ac.uk

Abstract

We validated various novel and recently proposed methods for statistical machine translation on 10 language pairs, using large data resources. We saw gains from optimizing parameters, training with sparse features, the operation sequence model, and domain adaptation techniques. We also report on utilizing a huge language model trained on 126 billion tokens.

The annual machine translation evaluation campaign for European languages organized around the ACL Workshop on Statistical Machine Translation offers the opportunity to test recent advancements in machine translation in large data condition across several diverse language pairs.

Building on our own developments and external contributions to the Moses open source toolkit, we carried out extensive experiments that, by early indications, led to a strong showing in the evaluation campaign.

We would like to stress especially two contributions: the use of the new operation sequence model (Section 3) within Moses, and — in a separate unconstraint track submission — the use of a huge language model trained on 126 billion tokens with a new training tool (Section 4).

1 Initial System Development

We start with systems (Haddow and Koehn, 2012) that we developed for the 2012 Workshop on Statistical Machine Translation (Callison-Burch et al., 2012). The notable features of these systems are:

- Moses phrase-based models with mostly default settings
- training on all available parallel data, including the large UN parallel data, the French-English 10^9 parallel data and the LDC Gigaword data
- very large tuning set consisting of the test sets from 2008-2010, with a total of 7,567 sentences per language
- German–English with syntactic pre-reordering (Collins et al., 2005), compound splitting (Koehn and Knight, 2003) and use of factored representation for a POS target sequence model (Koehn and Hoang, 2007)
- English–German with morphological target sequence model

Note that while our final 2012 systems included subsampling of training data with modified Moore-Lewis filtering (Axelrod et al., 2011), we did not use such filtering at the starting point of our development. We will report on such filtering in Section 2.

Moreover, our system development initially used the WMT 2012 data condition, since it took place throughout 2012, and we switched to WMT 2013 training data at a later stage. In this section, we report cased BLEU scores (Papineni et al., 2001) on newstest2011.

1.1 Factored Backoff (German–English)

We have consistently used factored models in past WMT systems for the German–English language pairs to include POS and morphological target sequence models. But we did not use the factored decomposition of translation options into multiple mapping steps, since this usually lead to much slower systems with usually worse results.

A good place, however, for factored decomposition is the handling of rare and unknown source words which have more frequent morphological variants (Koehn and Haddow, 2012a). Here, we used only factored backoff for unknown words, giving gains in BLEU of +.12 for German–English.

1.2 Tuning with k-best MIRA

In preparation for training with sparse features, we moved away from MERT which is known to fall apart with many more than a couple of dozen features. Instead, we used k-best MIRA (Cherry and Foster, 2012). For the different language pairs, we saw improvements in BLEU of -.05 to +.39, with an average of +.09. There was only a minimal change in the length ratio (Table 1)

	MERT	k-best MIRA	Δ
de-en	22.11 (1.010)	22.10 (1.008)	–.01 (+.002)
fr-en	30.00 (1.023)	30.11 (1.026)	+.11 (±.003)
es-en	30.42 (1.021)	30.63 (1.020)	+.21 (–.001)
cs-en	25.54 (1.022)	25.49 (1.024)	–.05 (±.002)
en-de	16.08 (0.995)	16.04 (1.001)	–.04 (±.006)
en-fr	29.26 (0.980)	29.65 (0.982)	+.39 (±.002)
en-es	31.92 (0.985)	31.95 (0.985)	+.03 (±.000)
en-cs	17.38 (0.967)	17.42 (0.974)	+.04 (±.007)
avg	–	–	+.09

Table 1: Tuning with k-best MIRA instead of MERT (cased BLEU scores with length ratio)

1.3 Translation Table Smoothing with Kneser-Ney Discounting

Previously, we smoothed counts for the phrasal conditional probability distributions in the translation model with Good Turing discounting. We explored the use of Kneser-Ney discounting, but results are mixed (no difference on average, see Table 2), so we did not pursue this further.

	Good Turing	Kneser Ney	Δ
de-en	22.10	22.15	+.05
fr-en	30.11	30.13	+.02
es-en	30.63	30.64	+.01
cs-en	25.49	25.56	+.07
en-de	16.04	15.93	–.11
en-fr	29.65	29.75	+.10
en-es	31.95	31.98	+.03
en-cs	17.42	17.26	–.16
avg	–	–	±.00

Table 2: Translation model smoothing with Kneser-Ney

1.4 Sparse Features

A significant extension of the Moses system over the last couple of years was the support for large numbers of sparse features. This year, we tested this capability on our big WMT systems. First, we used features proposed by Chiang et al. (2009):

- phrase pair count bin features (bins 1, 2, 3, 4–5, 6–9, 10+)
- target word insertion features
- source word deletion features
- word translation features
- phrase length feature (source, target, both)

The lexical features were restricted to the 50 most frequent words. All these features together only gave minor improvements (Table 3).

	baseline	sparse	Δ
de-en	22.10	22.02	–.08
fr-en	30.11	30.24	+.13
es-en	30.63	30.61	–.02
cs-en	25.49	25.49	±.00
en-de	16.04	15.93	–.09
en-fr	29.65	29.81	+.16
en-es	31.95	32.02	+.07
en-cs	17.42	17.28	–.14
avg	–	–	+.04

Table 3: Sparse features

We also explored domain features in the sparse feature framework, in three different variations. Assume that we have three domains, and a phrase pair occurs in domain A 15 times, in domain B 5 times, and in domain C never.

We compute three types of domain features:

- binary indicator, if phrase-pairs occurs in domain (example: $\text{ind}_A = 1, \text{ind}_B = 1, \text{ind}_C = 0$)
- ratio how frequent the phrase pairs occurs in domain (example: $\text{ratio}_A = \frac{15}{15+5} = .75, \text{ratio}_B = \frac{5}{15+5} = .25, \text{ratio}_C = 0$)
- subset of domains in which phrase pair occurs (example: $\text{subset}_{AB} = 1$, other subsets 0)

We tested all three feature types, and found the biggest gain with the domain indicator feature (+.11, Table 4). Note that we define as domain the different corpora (Europarl, etc.). The number of domains ranges from 2 to 9 (see column #d).[1]

	#d	base.	indicator	ratio	subset
de-en	2	22.10	22.14 +.04	22.07 –.03	22.12 +.02
fr-en	4	30.11	30.34 +.23	30.29 +.18	30.15 +.04
es-en	3	30.63	30.88 +.25	30.64 +.01	30.82 +.19
cs-en	9	25.49	25.58 +.09	25.58 +.09	25.46 –.03
en-de	2	16.12[2]	16.14 +.02	15.96 –.16	16.01 –.11
en-fr	4	29.65	29.75 +.10	29.71 +.05	29.70 +.05
en-es	3	31.95	32.06 +.11	32.13 +.18	32.02 +.07
en-cs	9	17.42	17.45 +.03	17.35 –.07	17.44 +.02
avg.	-	–	+.11	+.03	+.03

Table 4: Sparse domain features

When combining the domain features and the other sparse features, we see roughly additive gains (Table 5). We use the domain indicator feature and the other sparse features in subsequent experiments.

[1]In the final experiments on the 2013 data condition, one domain (*commoncrawl*) was added for all language pairs.

	baseline	indicator	ratio	subset
de-en	22.10	22.18 +.08	22.10 ±.00	22.16 +.06
fr-en	30.11	30.41 +.30	30.49 +.38	30.36 +.25
es-en	30.63	30.75 +.12	30.56 –.07	30.85 +.22
cs-en	25.49	25.56 +.07	25.63 +.14	25.43 –.06
en-de	16.12	15.95 –.17	15.96 –.16	16.05 –.07
en-fr	29.65	29.96 +.31	29.88 +.23	29.92 +.27
en-es	31.95	32.12 +.17	32.16 +.21	32.08 +.23
en-cs	17.42	17.38 –.04	17.35 –.07	17.40 –.02
avg.	–	+.11	+.09	+.11

Table 5: Combining domain and other sparse features

1.5 Tuning Settings

Given the opportunity to explore the parameter tuning of models with sparse features across many language pairs, we investigated a number of settings. We expect tuning to work better with more iterations, longer n-best lists and bigger cube pruning pop limits. Our baseline settings are 10 iterations with 100-best lists (accumulating) and a pop limit of 1000 for tuning and 5000 for testing.

	base	25 it.	25it+1k-best	25it+pop5k
de-en	22.18	22.16 –.02	22.14 –.04	22.17 –.01
fr-en	30.41	30.40 –.01	30.44 +.03	30.49 +.08
es-en	30.75	30.91 +.16	30.86 +.11	30.81 +.06
cs-en	25.56	25.60 +.04	25.64 +.08	25.56 ±.00
en-de	15.96	15.99 +.03	16.05 +.09	15.96 ±.00
en-fr	29.96	29.90 –.06	29.95 –.01	29.92 –.04
en-es	32.12	32.17 +.05	32.11 –.01	32.19 +.07
en-cs	17.38	17.43 +.05	17.50 +.12	17.38 ±.00
avg	–	+.03	+.05	+.02

Table 6: Tuning settings (number of iterations, size of n-best list, and cube pruning pop limit)

Results support running tuning for 25 iterations but we see no gains for 5000 pops. There is evidence that an n-best list size of 1000 is better in tuning but we did not adopt this since these large lists take up a lot of disk space and slow down the MIRA optimization step (Table 6).

1.6 Smaller Phrases

Given the very large corpus sizes (up to a billion words of parallel data for French–English), the size of translation model and lexicalized reordering model becomes a challenge. Hence, we want to examine if restriction to smaller phrases is feasible without loss in translation quality. Results in Table 7 suggest that a maximum phrase length of 5 gives almost identical results, and only with a phrase length limit of 4 significant losses occur. We adopted the limit of 5.

	max 7	max 6	max 5	max 4
de-en	22.16	22.03 –.13	22.05 –.11	22.17 +.01
fr-en	30.40	30.30 –.10	30.39 –.01	30.23 –.17
es-en	30.91	30.80 –.09	30.86 –.05	30.81 –.10
cs-en	25.60	25.55 –.05	25.53 –.07	25.48 –.12
en-de	15.99	15.94 –.05	15.97 –.02	16.03 +.04
en-fr	29.90	29.97 +.07	29.89 –.01	29.77 –.13
en-es	32.17	32.13 –.04	32.27 +.10	31.93 –.24
en-cs	17.43	17.46 +.03	17.41 –.02	17.41 –.02
avg	–	–.05	–.03	–.09

Table 7: Maximum phrase length, reduced from baseline

1.7 Unpruned Language Models

Previously, we trained 5-gram language models using the default settings of the SRILM toolkit in terms of singleton pruning. Thus, training throws out all singletons n-grams of order 3 and higher. We explored whether unpruned language models could give better performance, even if we are only able to train 4-gram models due to memory constraints. At the time, we were not able to build unpruned 4-gram language models for English, but for the other language pairs we did see improvements of -.07 to +.13 (Table 8). We adopted such models for these language pairs.

	5g pruned	4g unpruned	Δ
en-fr	29.89	29.83	–.07
en-es	32.27	32.34	+.07
en-cs	17.41	17.54	+.13

Table 8: Language models without singleton pruning

1.8 Translations per Input Phrase

Finally, we explored one more parameter: the limit on how many translation options are considered per input phrase. The default for this setting is 20. However, our experiments (Table 9) show that we can get better results with a translation table limit of 100, so we adopted this.

	ttl 20	ttl 30	ttl 50	ttl 100
de-en	21.05	+.06	+.09	+.01
fr-en	30.39	–.02	+.05	+.07
es-en	30.86	±.00	–.03	–.07
cs-en	25.53	+.24	+.13	+.20
en-de	15.97	+.03	+.07	+.11
en-fr	29.83	+.14	+.19	+.13
en-es	32.34	+.08	+.10	+.07
en-cs	17.54	–.05	–.02	+.01
avg	–	+.06	+.07	+.07

Table 9: Maximal number translations per input phrase

1.9 Other Experiments

We explored a number of other settings and features, but did not observe any gains.

- Using HMM alignment instead of IBM Model 4 leads to losses of –.01 to –.27.
- An earlier check of modified Moore–Lewis filtering (see also below in Section 3) gave very inconsistent results.
- Filtering the phrase table with significance filtering (Johnson et al., 2007) leads to losses of –.19 to –.63.
- Throwing out phrase pairs with direct translation probability $\phi(\bar{e}|\bar{f})$ of less than 10^{-5} has almost no effect.
- Double-checking the contribution of the sparse lexical features in the final setup, we observe an average losses of –.07 when dropping these features.
- For the German–English language pairs we saw some benefits to using sparse lexical features over POS tags instead of words, so we used this in the final system.

1.10 Summary

We adopted a number of changes that improved our baseline system by an average of +.30, see Table 10 for a breakdown.

avg.	method
+.01	factored backoff
+.09	kbest MIRA
+.11	sparse features and domain indicator
+.03	tuning with 25 iterations
–.03	maximum phrase length 5
+.02	unpruned 4-gram LM
+.07	translation table limit 100
+.30	total

Table 10: Summary of impact of changes

Minor improvements that we did not adopt was avoiding reducing maximum phrase length to 5 (average +.03) and tuning with 1000-best lists (+.02).

The improvements differed significantly by language pair, as detailed in Table 11, with the biggest gains for English–French (+.70), no gain for English–German and no gain for English–German.

1.11 New Data

The final experiment of the initial system development phase was to train the systems on the new data, adding newstest2011 to the tuning set (now 10,068 sentences). Table 12 reports the gains on newstest2012 due to added data, indicating very clearly that valuable new data resources became available this year.

	baseline	improved	Δ
de-en	21.99	22.09	+.10
fr-en	30.00	30.46	+.46
es-en	30.42	30.79	+.37
cs-en	25.54	25.73	+.19
en-de	16.08	16.08	±.00
en-fr	29.26	29.96	+.70
en-es	31.92	32.41	+.49
en-cs	17.38	17.55	+.17

Table 11: Overall improvements per language pair

	WMT 2012	WMT 2013	Δ
de-en	23.11	24.01	+0.90
fr-en	29.25	30.77	+1.52
es-en	32.80	33.99	+1.19
cs-en	22.53	22.86	+0.33
ru-en	–	31.67	–
en-de	16.78	17.95	+1.17
en-fr	27.92	28.76	+0.84
en-es	33.41	34.00	+0.59
en-cs	15.51	15.78	+0.27
en-ru	–	23.78	–

Table 12: Training with new data (newstest2012 scores)

2 Domain Adaptation Techniques

We explored two additional domain adaptation techniques: phrase table interpolation and modified Moore-Lewis filtering.

2.1 Phrase Table Interpolation

We experimented with phrase-table interpolation using perplexity minimisation (Foster et al., 2010; Sennrich, 2012). In particular, we used the implementation released with Sennrich (2012) and available in Moses, comparing both the **naive** and **modified** interpolation methods from that paper. For each language pair, we took the alignments created from all the data concatenated, built separate phrase tables from each of the individual corpora, and interpolated using each method. The results are shown in Table 13

	baseline	naive	modified
fr-en	**30.77**	30.63 –.14	–
es-en*	33.98	33.83 –.15	**34.03** +.05
cs-en*	**23.19**	22.77 –.42	23.03 –.17
ru-en	**31.67**	31.42 –.25	31.59 –.08
en-fr	28.76	**28.88** +.12	–
en-es	34.00	34.07 +.07	**34.31** +.31
en-cs	15.78	**15.88** +.10	15.87 +.09
en-ru	23.78	**23.84** +.06	23.68 –.10

Table 13: Comparison of phrase-table interpolation (two methods) with baseline (on newstest2012). The baselines are as Table 12 except for the starred rows where tuning with PRO was found to be better. The modified interpolation was not possible in fr↔en as it uses to much RAM.

The results from the phrase-table interpolation are quite mixed, and we only used the technique for the final system in en-es. An interpolation based on PRO has recently been shown (Haddow, 2013) to improve on perplexity minimisation is some cases, but the current implementation of this method is limited to 2 phrase-tables, so we did not use it in this evaluation.

2.2 Modified Moore-Lewis Filtering

In last year's evaluation (Koehn and Haddow, 2012b) we had some success with modified Moore-Lewis filtering (Moore and Lewis, 2010; Axelrod et al., 2011) of the training data. This year we conducted experiments in most of the language pairs using MML filtering, and also experimented using *instance weighting* (Mansour and Ney, 2012) using the (exponential of) the MML weights. The results are show in Table 14

	base line	MML 20%	Inst. Wt	Inst. Wt (scale)
fr-en	**30.77**	–	–	–
es-en*	33.98	**34.26** +.28	33.85 –.13	33.98 ±.00
cs-en*	**23.19**	22.62 –.57	23.17 –.02	23.13 –.06
ru-en	**31.67**	31.58 –.09	31.57 –.10	31.62 –.05
en-fr	28.67	28.74 +.07	**28.81** +.17	28.63 –.04
en-es	34.00	34.07 +.07	**34.27** +.27	34.03 +.03
en-cs	15.78	15.37 –.41	15.87 +.09	**15.89** +.11
en-ru	23.78	22.90 –.88	**23.82** +.05	23.72 –.06

Table 14: Comparison of MML filtering and weighting with baseline. The MML uses monolingual news as in-domain, and selects from all training data after alignment.The weighting uses the MML weights, optionally downscaled by 10, then exponentiated. Baselines are as Table 13.

As with phrase-table interpolation, MML filtering and weighting shows a very mixed picture, and not the consistent improvements these techniques offer on IWSLT data. In the final systems, we used MML filtering only for es-en.

3 Operation Sequence Model (OSM)

We enhanced the phrase segmentation and reordering mechanism by integrating OSM: an operation sequence N-gram-based translation and reordering model (Durrani et al., 2011) into the Moses phrase-based decoder. The model is based on minimal translation units (MTUs) and Markov chains over sequences of operations. An operation can be (a) to jointly generate a bi-language MTU, composed from source and target words, or (b) to perform reordering by inserting gaps and doing jumps.

Model: Given a bilingual sentence pair $< F, E >$ and its alignment A, we transform it to

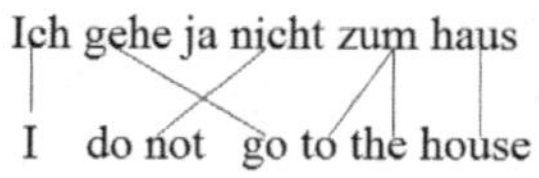

Figure 1: Bilingual Sentence with Alignments

sequence of operations $(o_1, o_2, \ldots, o_J)$ and learn a Markov model over this sequence as:

$$p_{osm}(F, E, A) = p(o_1^J) = \prod_{j=1}^{J} p(o_j | o_{j-n+1}, ..., o_{j-1})$$

By coupling reordering with lexical generation, each (translation or reordering) decision conditions on $n-1$ previous (translation and reordering) decisions spanning across phrasal boundaries thus overcoming the problematic phrasal independence assumption in the phrase-based model. In the OSM model, the reordering decisions influence lexical selection and vice versa. Lexical generation is strongly coupled with reordering thus improving the overall reordering mechanism.

We used the modified version of the OSM model (Durrani et al., 2013b) that additionally handles discontinuous and unaligned target MTUs[3]. We borrow 4 count-based supportive features, the *Gap*, *Open Gap*, *Gap-width* and *Deletion* penalties from Durrani et al. (2011).

Training: During training, each bilingual sentence pair is deterministically converted to a unique sequence of operations. Please refer to Durrani et al. (2011) for a list of operations and the conversion algorithm and see Figure 1 and Table 15 for a sample bilingual sentence pair and its step-wise conversion into a sequence of operation. A 9-gram Kneser-Ney smoothed operation sequence model is trained with SRILM.

Search: Although the OSM model is based on minimal units, phrase-based search on top of OSM model was found to be superior to the MTU-based decoding in Durrani et al. (2013a). Following this framework allows us to use OSM model in tandem with phrase-based models. We integrated the generative story of the OSM model into the hypothesis extension of the phrase-based Moses decoder. Please refer to (Durrani et al., 2013b) for details.

Results: Table 16 shows case-sensitive BLEU scores on newstest2012 and newstest2013 for fi-

[3]In the original OSM model these are removed from the alignments through a post-processing heuristic which hurts in some language pairs. See Durrani et al. (2013b) for detailed experiments.

Operation Sequence	Generation
Generate(Ich, I)	Ich ↓ I
Generate Target Only (do)	Ich ↓ I do
Insert Gap Generate (nicht, not)	Ich ☐ nicht ↓ I do not
Jump Back (1) Generate (gehe, go)	Ich gehe ↓ nicht I do not go
Generate Source Only (ja)	Ich gehe ja ↓ nicht I do not go
Jump Forward	Ich gehe ja nicht ↓ I do not go
Generate (zum, to the)	... gehe ja nicht zum ↓ ... not go to the
Generate (haus, house)	... ja nicht zum haus ↓ ... go to the house

Table 15: Step-wise Generation of Figure 1

LP	Baseline		+OSM	
newstest	2012	2013	2012	2013
de-en	23.85	26.54	24.11 +.26	26.83 +.29
fr-en	30.77	31.09	30.96 +.19	31.46 +.37
es-en	34.02	30.04	34.51 +.49	30.94 +.90
cs-en	22.70	25.70	23.03 +.33	25.79 +.09
ru-en	31.87	24.00	32.33 +.46	24.33 +.33
en-de	17.95	20.06	18.02 +.07	20.26 +.20
en-fr	28.76	30.03	29.36 +.60	30.39 +.36
en-es	33.87	29.66	34.44 +.57	30.10 +.44
en-cs	15.81	18.35	16.16 +.35	18.62 +.27
en-ru	23.75	18.44	24.05 +.30	18.84 +.40

Table 16: Results using the OSM Feature

nal systems from Section 1 and these systems augmented with the operation sequence model. The model gives gains for all language pairs (BLEU +.09 to +.90, average +.37, on newstest2013).

4 Huge Language Models

To overcome the memory limitations of SRILM, we implemented modified Kneser-Ney (Kneser and Ney, 1995; Chen and Goodman, 1998) smoothing from scratch using disk-based streaming algorithms. This open-source[4] tool is described fully by Heafield et al. (2013). We used it to estimate an unpruned 5–gram language model on web pages from ClueWeb09.[5] The corpus was preprocessed by removing spam (Cormack et al., 2011), selecting English documents, splitting sentences, deduplicating, tokenizing, and truecasing. Estimation on the remaining 126 billion tokens took 2.8 days on a single machine with 140 GB RAM (of which 123 GB was used at peak) and six hard drives in a RAID5 configuration. Statistics about the resulting model are shown in Table 17.

[4]http://kheafield.com/code/

[5]http://lemurproject.org/clueweb09/

1	2	3	4	5
393m	3,775m	17,629m	39,919m	59,794m

Table 17: Counts of unique n-grams (m for millions) for the 5 orders in the unconstrained language model

The large language model was then quantized to 10 bits and compressed to 643 GB with KenLM (Heafield, 2011), loaded onto a machine with 1 TB RAM, and used as an additional feature in unconstrained French–English, Spanish–English, and Czech–English submissions. This additional language model is the only difference between our final constrained and unconstrained submissions; no additional parallel data was used. Results are shown in Table 18. Improvement from large language models is not a new result (Brants et al., 2007); the primary contribution is estimating on a single machine.

	Constrained	Unconstrained	Δ
fr-en	31.46	32.24	+.78
es-en	30.59	31.37	+.78
cs-en	27.38	28.16	+.78
ru-en	24.33	25.14	+.81

Table 18: Gain on newstest2013 from the unconstrained language model. Our time on shared machines with 1 TB is limited so Russian–English was run after the deadline and German–English was not ready in time.

5 Summary

Table 19 breaks down the gains over the final system from Section 1 from using the operation sequence models (OSM), modified Moore-Lewis filtering (MML), fixing a bug with the sparse lexical features (Sparse-Lex Bugfix), and instance weighting (Instance Wt.), translation model combination (TM-Combine), and use of the huge language model (ClueWeb09 LM).

Acknowledgments

Thanks to Miles Osborne for preprocessing the ClueWeb09 corpus. The research leading to these results has received funding from the European Union Seventh Framework Programme (FP7/2007-2013) under grant agreement 287658 (EU BRIDGE) and grant agreement 288487(MosesCore).This work made use of the resources provided by the Edinburgh Compute and Data Facility[6]. The ECDF is partially supported by the eDIKT initiative[7]. This work also used the Extreme Science and Engineering Discovery Environment (XSEDE), which is supported by National Science Foundation grant number OCI-1053575. Specifically, Stampede was used under allocation TG-CCR110017.

[6]http://www.ecdf.ed.ac.uk/

[7]http://www.edikt.org.uk/

	System	2012	2013
	Spanish-English		
1.	Baseline	34.02	30.04
2.	1+OSM	34.51 +.49	30.94 +.90
3.	1+MML (20%)	34.38 +.36	30.38 +.34
4.	1+Sparse-Lex Bugfix	34.17 +.15	30.33 +.29
5.	1+2+3: OSM+MML	34.65 +.63	30.51 +.47
6.	**1+2+3+4**	34.68 +.66	30.59 +.55
7.	**6+ClueWeb09 LM**		31.37 +1.33
	English-Spanish		
1.	Baseline	33.87	29.66
2.	1+OSM	34.44 +.57	30.10 +.44
3.	1+TM-Combine	34.31 +44	29.76 +.10
4.	1+Instance Wt.	34.27 +.40	29.63 –.03
5.	1+Sparse-Lex Bugfix	34.20 +.33	29.86 +.20
6.	1+2+3: OSM+TM-Cmb.	34.63 +.76	30.21 +.55
7.	1+2+4: OSM+Inst. Wt.	34.58 +.71	30.11 +.45
8.	**1+2+3+5**	34.78 +.91	30.43 +.77
	Czech-English		
1.	Baseline	22.70	25.70
2.	1+OSM	23.03 +.33	25.79 +.09
3.	1+with PRO	23.19 +.49	26.08 +.38
4.	1+Sparse-Lex Bugfix	22.86 +.16	25.74 +.04
5.	**1+OSM+PRO**	23.42 +.72	26.23 +.53
6.	1+2+3+4	23.16 +.46	25.94 +.24
7.	**5+ClueWeb09 LM**		27.06 +.36
	English-Czech		
1.	Baseline	15.85	18.35
2.	**1+OSM**	16.16 +.31	18.62 +.27
	French-English		
1.	Baseline	30.77	31.09
2.	**1+OSM**	30.96 +.19	31.46 +.37
3.	**2+ClueWeb09 LM**		32.24 +1.15
	English-French		
1.	Baseline	28.76	30.03
2.	1+OSM	29.36 +.60	30.39 +.36
3.	1+Sparse-Lex Bugfix	28.97 +.21	30.08 +.05
4.	**1+2+3**	29.37 +.61	30.58 +.55
	German-English		
1.	**Baseline**	23.85	26.54
2.	1+OSM	24.11 +.26	26.83 +.29
	English-German		
1.	**Baseline**	17.95	20.06
2.	1+OSM	18.02 +.07	20.26 +.20
	Russian-English		
1.	Baseline	31.87	24.00
2.	**1+OSM**	32.33 +.46	24.33 +.33
	English-Russian		
1.	Baseline	23.75	18.44
2.	**1+OSM**	24.05 +.40	18.84 +.40

Table 19: Summary of methods with BLEU scores on newstest2012 and newstest2013. Bold systems were submitted, with the ClueWeb09 LM systems submitted in the unconstraint track. The German–English and English–German OSM systems did not complete in time for the official submission.

References

Axelrod, A., He, X., and Gao, J. (2011). Domain adaptation via pseudo in-domain data selection. In *Proceedings of the 2011 Conference on Empirical Methods in Natural Language Processing*, pages 355–362, Edinburgh, Scotland, UK. Association for Computational Linguistics.

Brants, T., Popat, A. C., Xu, P., Och, F. J., and Dean, J. (2007). Large language models in machine translation. In *Proceedings of the 2007 Joint Conference on Empirical Methods in Natural Language Processing and Computational Natural Language Learning (EMNLP-CoNLL)*, pages 858–867.

Callison-Burch, C., Koehn, P., Monz, C., Post, M., Soricut, R., and Specia, L. (2012). Findings of the 2012 workshop on statistical machine translation. In *Proceedings of the Seventh Workshop on Statistical Machine Translation*, pages 10–48, Montreal, Canada. Association for Computational Linguistics.

Chen, S. and Goodman, J. (1998). An empirical study of smoothing techniques for language modeling. Technical Report TR-10-98, Harvard University.

Cherry, C. and Foster, G. (2012). Batch tuning strategies for statistical machine translation. In *Proceedings of the 2012 Conference of the North American Chapter of the Association for Computational Linguistics: Human Language Technologies*, pages 427–436, Montréal, Canada. Association for Computational Linguistics.

Chiang, D., Knight, K., and Wang, W. (2009). 11,001 new features for statistical machine translation. In *Proceedings of Human Language Technologies: The 2009 Annual Conference of the North American Chapter of the Association for Computational Linguistics*, pages 218–226, Boulder, Colorado. Association for Computational Linguistics.

Collins, M., Koehn, P., and Kucerova, I. (2005). Clause restructuring for statistical machine translation. In *Proceedings of the 43rd Annual Meeting of the Association for Computational Linguistics (ACL'05)*, pages 531–540, Ann Arbor, Michigan. Association for Computational Linguistics.

Cormack, G. V., Smucker, M. D., and Clarke, C. L. (2011). Efficient and effective spam filtering and re-ranking for large web datasets. *Information retrieval*, 14(5):441–465.

Durrani, N., Fraser, A., and Schmid, H. (2013a). Model With Minimal Translation Units, But Decode With Phrases. In *The 2013 Conference of the North American Chapter of the Association for Computational Linguistics: Human Language Technologies*, Atlanta, Georgia, USA. Association for Computational Linguistics.

Durrani, N., Fraser, A., Schmid, H., Hoang, H., and Koehn, P. (2013b). Can Markov Models Over Minimal Translation Units Help Phrase-Based SMT? In *Proceedings of the 51st Annual Meeting of the Association for Computational Linguistics*, Sofia, Bulgaria. Association for Computational Linguistics.

Durrani, N., Schmid, H., and Fraser, A. (2011). A Joint Sequence Translation Model with Integrated Reordering. In *Proceedings of the 49th Annual Meeting of the Association for Computational Linguistics: Human Language Technologies*, pages 1045–1054, Portland, Oregon, USA.

Foster, G., Goutte, C., and Kuhn, R. (2010). Discriminative instance weighting for domain adaptation in statistical machine translation. In *Proceedings of the 2010 Conference on Empirical Methods in Natural Language Processing*, pages 451–459, Cambridge, MA. Association for Computational Linguistics.

Haddow, B. (2013). Applying pairwise ranked optimisation to improve the interpolation of translation models. In *Proceedings of the 2013 Conference of the North American Chapter of the Association for Computational Linguistics: Human Language Technologies*, pages 342–347, Atlanta, Georgia. Association for Computational Linguistics.

Haddow, B. and Koehn, P. (2012). Analysing the effect of out-of-domain data on smt systems. In *Proceedings of the Seventh Workshop on Statistical Machine Translation*, pages 175–185, Montreal, Canada. Association for Computational Linguistics.

Heafield, K. (2011). KenLM: Faster and smaller language model queries. In *Proceedings of the Sixth Workshop on Statistical Machine Translation*, pages 187–197, Edinburgh, Scotland. Association for Computational Linguistics.

Heafield, K., Pouzyrevsky, I., Clark, J. H., and Koehn, P. (2013). Scalable modified Kneser-Ney language model estimation. In *Proceedings of the 51st Annual Meeting of the Association for Computational Linguistics*, Sofia, Bulgaria.

Johnson, H., Martin, J., Foster, G., and Kuhn, R. (2007). Improving translation quality by discarding most of the phrasetable. In *Proceedings of the 2007 Joint Conference on Empirical Methods in Natural Language Processing and Computational Natural Language Learning (EMNLP-CoNLL)*, pages 967–975.

Kneser, R. and Ney, H. (1995). Improved backing-off for m-gram language modeling. In *Proceedings of the IEEE International Conference on Acoustics, Speech and Signal Processing*, pages 181–184.

Koehn, P. and Haddow, B. (2012a). Interpolated backoff for factored translation models. In *Proceedings of the Tenth Conference of the Association for Machine Translation in the Americas (AMTA)*.

Koehn, P. and Haddow, B. (2012b). Towards Effective Use of Training Data in Statistical Machine Translation. In *Proceedings of the Seventh Workshop on Statistical Machine Translation*, pages 317–321, Montréal, Canada. Association for Computational Linguistics.

Koehn, P. and Hoang, H. (2007). Factored Translation Models. In *Proceedings of the 2007 Joint Conference on Empirical Methods in Natural Language Processing and Computational Natural Language Learning (EMNLP-CoNLL)*, pages 868–876, Prague, Czech Republic. Association for Computational Linguistics.

Koehn, P. and Knight, K. (2003). Empirical methods for compound splitting. In *Proceedings of Meeting of the European Chapter of the Association of Computational Linguistics (EACL)*.

Mansour, S. and Ney, H. (2012). A Simple and Effective Weighted Phrase Extraction for Machine Translation Adaptation. In *Proceedings of IWSLT*.

Moore, R. C. and Lewis, W. (2010). Intelligent selection of language model training data. In *Proceedings of the ACL 2010 Conference Short Papers*, pages 220–224, Uppsala, Sweden. Association for Computational Linguistics.

Papineni, K., Roukos, S., Ward, T., and Zhu, W.-J. (2001). BLEU: a method for automatic evaluation of machine translation. Technical Report RC22176(W0109-022), IBM Research Report.

Sennrich, R. (2012). Perplexity minimization for translation model domain adaptation in statistical machine translation. In *Proceedings of the 13th Conference of the European Chapter of the Association for Computational Linguistics*, pages 539–549, Avignon, France. Association for Computational Linguistics.

Munich-Edinburgh-Stuttgart Submissions of OSM Systems at WMT13

Nadir Durrani[1], **Helmut Schmid**[2], **Alexander Fraser**[2],
Hassan Sajjad[3], **Richárd Farkas**[4]

[1]University of Edinburgh – dnadir@inf.ed.ac.uk

[2]Ludwig Maximilian University Munich – schmid,fraser@cis.uni-muenchen.de

[3]Qatar Computing Research Institute – hsajjad@qf.org.qa

[4]University of Szeged – rfarkas@inf.u-szeged.hu

Abstract

This paper describes Munich-Edinburgh-Stuttgart's submissions to the Eighth Workshop on Statistical Machine Translation. We report results of the translation tasks from German, Spanish, Czech and Russian into English and from English to German, Spanish, Czech, French and Russian. The systems described in this paper use OSM (Operation Sequence Model). We explain different pre-/post-processing steps that we carried out for different language pairs. For German-English we used constituent parsing for reordering and compound splitting as preprocessing steps. For Russian-English we transliterated the unknown words. The transliteration system is learned with the help of an unsupervised transliteration mining algorithm.

1 Introduction

In this paper we describe Munich-Edinburgh-Stuttgart's[1] joint submissions to the Eighth Workshop on Statistical Machine Translation. We use our in-house OSM decoder which is based on the operation sequence N-gram model (Durrani et al., 2011). The N-gram-based SMT framework (Mariño et al., 2006) memorizes Markov chains over sequences of minimal translation units (MTUs or tuples) composed of bilingual translation units. The OSM model integrates reordering operations within the tuple sequences to form a heterogeneous mixture of lexical translation and reordering operations and learns a Markov model over a sequence of operations.

Our decoder uses the beam search algorithm in a stack-based decoder like most sequence-based SMT frameworks. Although the model is based on minimal translation units, we use phrases during search because they improve the search accuracy of our system. The earlier decoder (Durrani et al., 2011) was based on minimal units. But we recently showed that using phrases during search gives better coverage of translation, better future cost estimation and lesser search errors (Durrani et al., 2013a) than MTU-based decoding. We have therefore shifted to phrase-based search on top of the OSM model.

This paper is organized as follows. Section 2 gives a short description of the model and search as used in the OSM decoder. In Section 3 we give a description of the POS-based operation sequence model that we test for our German-English and English-German experiments. Section 4 describes our processing of the German and English data for German-English and English-German experiments. In Section 5 we describe the unsupervised transliteration mining that has been done for the Russian-English and English-Russian experiments. In Section 6 we describe the sub-sampling technique that we have used for several language pairs. In Section 7 we describe the experimental setup followed by the results. Finally we summarize the paper in Section 8.

2 System Description

2.1 Model

Our systems are based on the OSM (Operation Sequence Model) that simultaneously learns translation and reordering by representing a bilingual

[1]Qatar Computing Research Institute and University of Szeged were partnered for RU-EN and DE-EN language pairs respectively.

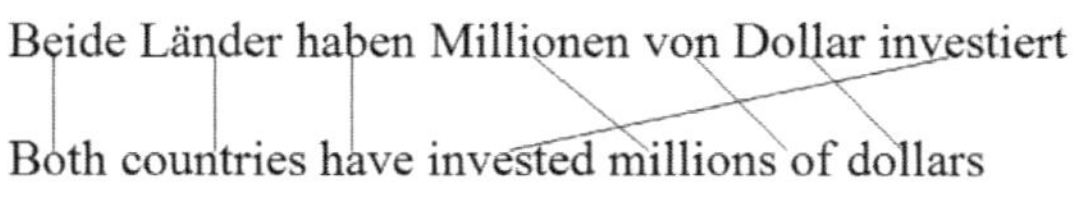

Figure 1: Bilingual Sentence with Alignments

sentence pair and its alignments as a unique sequence of operations. An operation either jointly generates source and target words, or it performs reordering by inserting gaps or jumping to gaps. We then learn a Markov model over a sequence of operations $o_1, o_2, \ldots, o_J$ that encapsulate MTUs and reordering information as:

$$p_{osm}(o_1, ..., o_J) = \prod_{j=1}^{J} p(o_j | o_{j-n+1}, ..., o_{j-1})$$

By coupling reordering with lexical generation, each (translation or reordering) decision depends on $n - 1$ previous (translation and reordering) decisions spanning across phrasal boundaries. The reordering decisions therefore influence lexical selection and vice versa. A heterogeneous mixture of translation and reordering operations enables us to memorize reordering patterns and lexicalized triggers unlike the classic N-gram model where translation and reordering are modeled separately.

2.2 Training

During training, each bilingual sentence pair is deterministically converted to a unique sequence of operations.[2] The example in Figure 1(a) is converted to the following sequence of operations:

Generate(Beide, Both) → Generate(Länder, countries) → Generate(haben, have) → Insert Gap → Generate(investiert, invested)

At this point, the (partial) German and English sentences look as follows:

Beide Länder haben ☐ investiert

Both countries have invested

The translator then jumps back and covers the skipped German words through the following sequence of operations:

Jump Back(1) → Generate(Millionen, millions) → Generate(von, of) → Generate(Dollar, dollars)

[2]Please refer to Durrani et al. (2011) for a list of operations and the conversion algorithm.

The generative story of the OSM model also supports discontinuous source-side cepts and source-word deletion. However, it doesn't provide a mechanism to deal with unaligned and discontinuous target cepts. These are handled through a 3-step process[3] in which we modify the alignments to remove discontinuous and unaligned target MTUs. Please see Durrani et al. (2011) for details. After modifying the alignments, we convert each bilingual sentence pair and its alignments into a sequence of operations as described above and learn an OSM model. To this end, a Kneser-Ney (Kneser and Ney, 1995) smoothed 9-gram model is trained with SRILM (Stolcke, 2002) while KenLM (Heafield, 2011) is used at runtime.

2.3 Feature Functions

We use additional features for our model and employ the standard log-linear approach (Och and Ney, 2004) to combine and tune them. We search for a target string E which maximizes a linear combination of feature functions:

$$\hat{E} = \arg\max_{E} \left\{ \sum_{j=1}^{J} \lambda_j h_j(o_1, ..., o_J) \right\}$$

where λ_j is the weight associated with the feature $h_j(o_1, ..., o_j)$. Apart from the main OSM feature we train 9 additional features: A target-language model (see Section 7 for details), 2 lexical weighting features, gap and open gap penalty features, two distance-based distortion models and 2 length-based penalty features. Please refer to Durrani et al. (2011) for details.

2.4 Phrase Extraction

Phrases are extracted in the following way: The aligned training corpus is first converted to an operation sequence. Each subsequence of operations that starts and ends with a translation operation, is considered a "phrase". The translation operations include *Generate Source Only (X)* operation which deletes unaligned source word. Such phrases may be discontinuous if they include reordering operations. We replace each subsequence of reordering operations by a discontinuity marker.

[3]Durrani et al. (2013b) recently showed that our post-processing of alignments hurt the performance of the Moses Phrase-based system in several language pairs. The solution they proposed has not been incorporated into the current OSM decoder yet.

During decoding, we match the source tokens of the phrase with the input. Whenever there is a discontinuity in the phrase, the next source token can be matched at any position of the input string. If there is no discontinuity marker, the next source token in the phrase must be to the right of the previous one. Finally we compute the number of uncovered input tokens within the source span of the hypothesized phrase and reject the phrase if the number is above a threshold. We use a threshold value of 2 which had worked well in initial experiments. Once the positions of all the source words of a phrase are known, we can compute the necessary reordering operations (which may be different from the ones that appeared in the training corpus). This usage of phrases allows the decoder to generalize from a seen translation "scored a goal – ein Tor schoss" (where scored/a/goal and schoss/ein/Tor are aligned, respectively) to "scored a goal – schoss ein Tor". The phrase can even be used to translate "er schoss heute ein Tor – he scored a goal today" although "heute" appears within the source span of the phrase "ein Tor schoss". Without phrase-based decoding, the unusual word translations "schoss–scored" and "Tor–goal" (at least outside of the soccer literature) are likely to be pruned.

The phrase tables are further filtered with threshold pruning. The translation options with a frequency less than x times the frequency of the most frequent translation are deleted. We use $x = 0.02$. We use additional settings to increase this threshold for longer phrases. The phrase filtering heuristic was used to speed up decoding. It did not lower the BLEU score in our small scale experiments (Durrani et al., 2013a), however we could not test whether this result holds in a large scale evaluation.

2.5 Decoder

The decoding framework used in the operation sequence model is based on Pharaoh (Koehn, 2004). The decoder uses beam search to build up the translation from left to right. The hypotheses are arranged in m stacks such that stack i maintains hypotheses that have already translated i many foreign words. The ultimate goal is to find the best scoring hypothesis, that translates all the words in the foreign sentence. During the hypothesis extension each extracted phrase is translated into a sequence of operations. The reordering operations (gaps and jumps) are generated by looking at the position of the translator, the last foreign word generated etc. (Please refer to Algorithm 1 in Durrani et al. (2011)). The probability of an operation depends on the $n-1$ previous operations. The model is smoothed with Kneser-Ney smoothing.

3 POS-based OSM Model

Part-of-speech information is often relevant for translation. The word "stores" e.g. should be translated to "Läden" if it is a noun and to "speichert" when it is a verb. The sentence "The small child cries" might be incorrectly translated to "Die kleinen Kind weint" where the first three words lack number, gender and case agreement.

In order to better learn such constraints which are best expressed in terms of part of speech, we add another OSM model as a new feature to the log-linear model of our decoder, which is identical to the regular OSM except that all the words have been replaced by their POS tags. The input of the decoder consists of the input sentence with automatically assigned part-of-speech tags. The source and target part of the training data are also automatically tagged and phrases with words and POS tags on both sides are extracted. The POS-based OSM model is only used in the German-to-English and English-to-German experiments.[4] So far, we only used coarse POS tags without gender and case information.

4 Constituent Parse Reordering

Our German-to-English system used constituent parses for pre-ordering of the input. We parsed all of the parallel German to English data available, and the tuning, test and blind-test sets. We then applied reordering rules to these parses. We used the rules for reordering German constituent parses of Collins et al. (2005) together with the additional rules described by Fraser (2009). These are applied as a preprocess to all German data (training, tuning and test data). To produce the parses, we started with the generative BitPar parser trained on the Tiger treebank with optimizations of the grammar, as described by (Fraser et al., 2013). We then performed self-training using the high quality Europarl corpus - we parsed it, and then retrained the parser on the output.

[4] This work is ongoing and we will present detailed experiments in the future.

Following this, we performed linguistically-informed compound splitting, using the system of Fritzinger and Fraser (2010), which disambiguates competing analyses from the high-recall Stuttgart Morphological Analyzer SMOR (Schmid et al., 2004) using corpus statistics (Koehn and Knight, 2003). We also split portmanteaus like German "zum" formed from "zu dem" meaning "to the". Due to time constraints, we did not address German inflection. See Weller et al. (2013) for further details of the linguistic processing involved in our German-to-English system.

5 Transliteration Mining/Handling OOVs

The machine translation system fails to translate out-of-vocabulary words (OOVs) as they are unknown to the training data. Most of the OOVs are named entities and simply passing them to the output often produces correct translations if source and target language use the same script. If the scripts are different transliterating them to the target language script could solve this problem. However, building a transliteration system requires a list of transliteration pairs for training. We do not have such a list and making one is a cumbersome process. Instead, we use the unsupervised transliteration mining system of Sajjad et al. (2012) that takes a list of word pairs for training and extracts transliteration pairs that can be used for the training of the transliteration system. The procedure of mining transliteration pairs and transliterating OOVs is described as follows:

We word-align the parallel corpus using GIZA++ in both direction and symmetrize the alignments using the grow-diag-final-and heuristic. We extract all word pairs which occur as 1-to-1 alignments (like Sajjad et al. (2011)) and later refer to them as the *list of word pairs*. We train the unsupervised transliteration mining system on the list of word pairs and extract transliteration pairs. We use these mined pairs to build a transliteration system using the Moses toolkit. The transliteration system is applied in a post-processing step to transliterate OOVs. Please refer to Sajjad et al. (2013) for further details on our transliteration work.

6 Sub-sampling

Because of scalability problems we were not able to use the entire data made available for building the translation model in some cases. We used modified Moore-Lewis sampling (Axelrod et al., 2011) for the language pairs es-en, en-es, en-fr, and en-cs. In each case we included the News-Commentary and Europarl corpora in their entirety, and scored the sentences in the remaining corpora (the selection corpus) using a filtering criterion, adding 10% of the selection corpus to the training data. We can not say with certainty whether using the entire data will produce better results with the OSM decoder. However, we know that the same data used with the state-of-the-art Moses produced worse results in some cases. The experiments in Durrani et al. (2013c) showed that MML filtering decreases the BLEU scores in es-en (news-test13: Table 19) and en-cs (news-test12: Table 14). We can therefore speculate that being able to use all of the data may improve our results somewhat.

7 Experiments

Parallel Corpus: The amount of bitext used for the estimation of the translation models is: de–en $\approx$ 4.5M and ru–en $\approx$ 2M parallel sentences. We were able to use all the available data for cs-to-en ($\approx$ 15.6M sentences). However, sub-sampled data was used for en-to-cs ($\approx$ 3M sentences), en-to-fr ($\approx$ 7.8M sentences) and es–en ($\approx$ 3M sentences).

Monolingual Language Model: We used all the available training data (including LDC Gigaword data) for the estimation of monolingual language models: en $\approx$ 287.3M sentences, fr $\approx$ 91M, es $\approx$ 65.7M, cs $\approx$ 43.4M and ru $\approx$ 21.7M sentences. All data except for ru-en and en-ru was true-cased. We followed the approach of Schwenk and Koehn (2008) by training language models from each sub-corpus separately and then linearly interpolated them using SRILM with weights optimized on the held-out dev-set. We concatenated the news-test sets from four years (2008-2011) to obtain a large dev-set[5] in order to obtain more stable weights (Koehn and Haddow, 2012).

Decoder Settings: For each extracted input phrase only 15-best translation options were used during decoding.[6] We used a hard reordering limit

[5]For Russian-English and English-Russian language pairs, we divided the tuning-set news-test 2012 into two halves and used the first half for tuning and second for test.

[6]We could not experiment with higher n-best translation options due to a bug that was not fixed in time and hindered us from scaling.

of 16 words which disallows a jump beyond 16 source words. A stack size of 100 was used during tuning and 200 for decoding the test set.

Results: Table 1 shows the uncased BLEU scores along with the rank obtained on the submission matrix.[7] We also show the results from human evaluation.

Lang	Evaluation			
	Automatic		Human	
	BLEU	Rank	Win Ratio	Rank
de-en	27.6	9/31	0.562	6-8
es-en	30.4	6/12	0.569	3-5
cs-en	26.4	3/11	0.581	2-3
ru-en	24.5	8/22	0.534	7-9
en-de	20.0	6/18		
en-es	29.5	3/13	0.544	5-6
en-cs	17.6	14/22	0.517	4-6
en-ru	18.1	6/15	0.456	9-10
en-fr	30.0	7/26	0.541	5-9

Table 1: Translating into and from English

8 Conclusion

In this paper, we described our submissions to WMT 13 in all the shared-task language pairs (except for fr-en). We used an OSM-decoder, which implements a model on n-gram of operations encapsulating lexical generation and reordering. For German-to-English we used constituent parsing and applied linguistically motivated rules to these parses, followed by compound splitting. We additionally used a POS-based OSM model for German-to-English and English-to-German experiments. For Russian-English language pairs we used unsupervised transliteration mining. Because of scalability issues we could not use the entire data in some language pairs and used only sub-sampled data. Our Czech-to-English system that was built from the entire data did better in both automatic and human evaluation compared to the systems that used sub-sampled data.

Acknowledgments

We would like to thank the anonymous reviewers for their helpful feedback and suggestions. We would like to thank Philipp Koehn and Barry Haddow for providing data and alignments. Nadir Durrani was funded by the European Union Seventh Framework Programme (FP7/2007-2013) under grant agreement n ° 287658. Alexander Fraser was funded by Deutsche Forschungsgemeinschaft grant Models of Morphosyntax for Statistical Machine Translation. Helmut Schmid was supported by Deutsche Forschungsgemeinschaft grant SFB 732. Richárd Farkas was partially funded by the Hungarian National Excellence Program (TÁMOP 4.2.4.A/2-11-1-2012-0001). This publication only reflects the authors' views.

[7] http://matrix.statmt.org/

References

Amittai Axelrod, Xiaodong He, and Jianfeng Gao. 2011. Domain adaptation via pseudo in-domain data selection. In *Proceedings of the 2011 Conference on Empirical Methods in Natural Language Processing*, pages 355–362, Edinburgh, Scotland, UK., July. Association for Computational Linguistics.

Michael Collins, Philipp Koehn, and Ivona Kucerova. 2005. Clause Restructuring for Statistical Machine Translation. In *ACL05*, pages 531–540, Ann Arbor, MI.

Nadir Durrani, Helmut Schmid, and Alexander Fraser. 2011. A Joint Sequence Translation Model with Integrated Reordering. In *Proceedings of the 49th Annual Meeting of the Association for Computational Linguistics: Human Language Technologies*, pages 1045–1054, Portland, Oregon, USA, June.

Nadir Durrani, Alexander Fraser, and Helmut Schmid. 2013a. Model With Minimal Translation Units, But Decode With Phrases. In *The 2013 Conference of the North American Chapter of the Association for Computational Linguistics: Human Language Technologies*, Atlanta, Georgia, USA, June. Association for Computational Linguistics.

Nadir Durrani, Alexander Fraser, Helmut Schmid, Hieu Hoang, and Philipp Koehn. 2013b. Can Markov Models Over Minimal Translation Units Help Phrase-Based SMT? In *Proceedings of the 51st Annual Meeting of the Association for Computational Linguistics*, Sofia, Bulgaria, August. Association for Computational Linguistics.

Nadir Durrani, Barry Haddow, Kenneth Heafield, and Philipp Koehn. 2013c. Edinburgh's Machine Translation Systems for European Language Pairs. In *Proceedings of the Eighth Workshop on Statistical Machine Translation*, Sofia, Bulgaria, August. Association for Computational Linguistics.

Alexander Fraser, Helmut Schmid, Richárd Farkas, Renjing Wang, and Hinrich Schütze. 2013. Knowledge sources for constituent parsing of German, a morphologically rich and less-configurational language. *Computational Linguistics - to appear*.

Alexander Fraser. 2009. Experiments in Morphosyntactic Processing for Translating to and from German. In *Proceedings of the EACL 2009 Fourth Workshop on Statistical Machine Translation*, pages 115–119, Athens, Greece, March.

Fabienne Fritzinger and Alexander Fraser. 2010. How to Avoid Burning Ducks: Combining Linguistic Analysis and Corpus Statistics for German Compound Processing. In *Proceedings of the ACL 2010 Fifth Workshop on Statistical Machine Translation*, Uppsala, Sweden.

Kenneth Heafield. 2011. KenLM: Faster and Smaller Language Model Queries. In *Proceedings of the Sixth Workshop on Statistical Machine Translation*, pages 187–197, Edinburgh, Scotland, United Kingdom, 7.

Reinhard Kneser and Hermann Ney. 1995. Improved backing-off for m-gram language modeling. In *In Proceedings of the IEEE International Conference on Acoustics, Speech and Signal Processing*, volume I, pages 181–184, Detroit, Michigan, May.

Philipp Koehn and Barry Haddow. 2012. Towards Effective Use of Training Data in Statistical Machine Translation. In *Proceedings of the Seventh Workshop on Statistical Machine Translation*, pages 317–321, Montréal, Canada, June. Association for Computational Linguistics.

Philipp Koehn and Kevin Knight. 2003. Empirical methods for compound splitting. In *Proceedings of the 10th Conference of the European Chapter of the Association for Computational Linguistics (EACL)*, pages 187–193, Morristown, NJ.

Philipp Koehn. 2004. Pharaoh: A Beam Search Decoder for Phrase-Based Statistical Machine Translation Models. In *AMTA*, pages 115–124.

José B. Mariño, Rafael E. Banchs, Josep M. Crego, Adrià de Gispert, Patrik Lambert, José A. R. Fonollosa, and Marta R. Costa-jussà. 2006. N-gram-Based Machine Translation. *Computational Linguistics*, 32(4):527–549.

Franz J. Och and Hermann Ney. 2004. The Alignment Template Approach to Statistical Machine Translation. *Computational Linguistics*, 30(1):417–449.

Hassan Sajjad, Alexander Fraser, and Helmut Schmid. 2011. An algorithm for unsupervised transliteration mining with an application to word alignment. In *Proceedings of the 49th Annual Meeting of the Association for Computational Linguistics: Human Language Technologies - Volume 1*, Portland, USA.

Hassan Sajjad, Alexander Fraser, and Helmut Schmid. 2012. A statistical model for unsupervised and semi-supervised transliteration mining. In *Proceedings of the 50th Annual Meeting of the Association for Computational Linguistics: Long Papers - Volume 1*, Jeju, Korea.

Hassan Sajjad, Svetlana Smekalova, Nadir Durrani, Alexander Fraser, and Helmut Schmid. 2013. QCRI-MES Submission at WMT13: Using Transliteration Mining to Improve Statistical Machine Translation. In *Proceedings of the Eighth Workshop on Statistical Machine Translation*, Sofia, Bulgaria, August. Association for Computational Linguistics.

Helmut Schmid, Arne Fitschen, and Ulrich Heid. 2004. SMOR: A German Computational Morphology Covering Derivation, Composition, and Inflection. In *Proceedings of the Fourth International Conference on Language Resources and Evaluation (LREC)*.

Holger Schwenk and Philipp Koehn. 2008. Large and Diverse Language Models for Statistical Machine Translation. In *International Joint Conference on Natural Language Processing*, pages 661–666, January 2008.

Andreas Stolcke. 2002. SRILM - An Extensible Language Modeling Toolkit. In *Intl. Conf. Spoken Language Processing*, Denver, Colorado.

Marion Weller, Max Kisselew, Svetlana Smekalova, Alexander Fraser, Helmut Schmid, Nadir Durrani, Hassan Sajjad, and Richárd Farkas. 2013. Munich-Edinburgh-Stuttgart Submissions at WMT13: Morphological and Syntactic Processing for SMT. In *Proceedings of the Eighth Workshop on Statistical Machine Translation*, Sofia, Bulgaria, August. Association for Computational Linguistics.

Towards Efficient Large-Scale Feature-Rich Statistical Machine Translation

Vladimir Eidelman[1], **Ke Wu**[1], **Ferhan Ture**[1], **Philip Resnik**[2], **Jimmy Lin**[3]
[1] Dept. of Computer Science [2] Dept. of Linguistics [3] The iSchool
Institute for Advanced Computer Studies
University of Maryland
`{vlad,wuke,fture,resnik,jimmylin}@umiacs.umd.edu`

Abstract

We present the system we developed to provide efficient large-scale feature-rich discriminative training for machine translation. We describe how we integrate with MapReduce using Hadoop streaming to allow arbitrarily scaling the tuning set and utilizing a sparse feature set. We report our findings on German-English and Russian-English translation, and discuss benefits, as well as obstacles, to tuning on larger development sets drawn from the parallel training data.

1 Introduction

The adoption of discriminative learning methods for SMT that scale easily to handle sparse and lexicalized features has been increasing in the last several years (Chiang, 2012; Hopkins and May, 2011). However, relatively few systems take full advantage of the opportunity. With some exceptions (Simianer et al., 2012), most still rely on tuning a handful of common dense features, along with at most a few thousand others, on a relatively small development set (Cherry and Foster, 2012; Chiang et al., 2009). While *more* features tuned on *more* data usually results in better performance for other NLP tasks, this has not necessarily been the case for SMT.

Thus, our main focus in this paper is to improve understanding into the effective use of sparse features, and understand the benefits and shortcomings of large-scale discriminative training. To this end, we conducted experiments for the shared translation task of the 2013 Workshop on Statistical Machine Translation for the German-English and Russian-English language pairs.

2 Baseline system

We use a hierarchical phrase-based decoder implemented in the open source translation system `cdec`[1] (Dyer et al., 2010). For tuning, we use Mr. MIRA[2] (Eidelman et al., 2013), an open source decoder agnostic implementation of online large-margin learning in Hadoop MapReduce. Mr. MIRA separates learning from the decoder, allowing the flexibility to specify the desired inference procedure through a simple text communication protocol. The decoder receives input sentences and weight updates from the learner, while the learner receives k-best output with feature vectors from the decoder.

Hadoop MapReduce (Dean and Ghemawat, 2004) is a popular distributed processing framework that has gained widespread adoption, with the advantage of providing scalable parallelization in a manageable framework, taking care of data distribution, synchronization, fault tolerance, as well as other features. Thus, while we could otherwise achieve the same level of parallelization, it would be in a more ad-hoc manner.

The advantage of online methods lies in their ability to deal with large training sets and high-dimensional input representations while remaining simple and offering fast convergence. With Hadoop streaming, our system can take advantage of commodity clusters to handle parallel large-scale training while also being capable of running on a single machine or PBS-managed batch cluster.

System design To efficiently encode the information that the learner and decoder require (source sentence, reference translation, grammar rules) in a manner amenable to MapReduce, i.e. avoiding dependencies on "side data" and large transfers across the network, we append the reference and

[1] `http://cdec-decoder.org`
[2] `https://github.com/kho/mr-mira`

per-sentence grammar to each input source sentence. Although this file's size is substantial, it is not a problem since after the initial transfer, it resides on Hadoop distributed file system, and MapReduce optimizes for data locality when scheduling mappers.

A single iteration of training is performed as a Hadoop streaming job. Each begins with a *map* phase, with every parallel mapper loading the same initial weights and decoding and updating parameters on a shard of the data. This is followed by a *reduce* phase, with a single reducer collecting final weights from all mappers and computing a weighted average to distribute as initial weights for the next iteration.

Parameter Settings We tune our system toward approximate sentence-level BLEU (Papineni et al., 2002),[3] and the decoder is configured to use cube pruning (Huang and Chiang, 2007) with a limit of 200 candidates at each node. For optimization, we use a learning rate of η=1, regularization strength of C=0.01, and a 500-best list for hope and fear selection (Chiang, 2012) with a single passive-aggressive update for each sentence (Eidelman, 2012).

Baseline Features We used a set of 16 standard baseline features: rule translation relative frequency $P(e|f)$, lexical translation probabilities $P_{lex}(\overline{e}|\overline{f})$ and $P_{lex}(\overline{f}|\overline{e})$, target n-gram language model $P(e)$, penalties for source and target words, passing an untranslated source word to the target side, singleton rule and source side, as well as counts for arity-0,1, or 2 SCFG rules, the total number of rules used, and the number of times the glue rule is used.

2.1 Data preparation

For both languages, we used the provided Europarl and News Commentary parallel training data to create the translation grammar necessary for our model. For Russian, we additionally used the Common Crawl and Yandex data. The data were lowercased and tokenized, then filtered for length and aligned using the GIZA++ implementation of IBM Model 4 (Och and Ney, 2003) to obtain one-to-many alignments in both directions and symmetrized sing the grow-diag-final-and method (Koehn et al., 2003).

[3]We approximate corpus BLEU by scoring sentences using a pseudo-document of previous 1-best translations (Chiang et al., 2009).

We constructed a 5-gram language model using SRILM (Stolcke, 2002) from the provided English monolingual training data and parallel data with modified Kneser-Ney smoothing (Chen and Goodman, 1996), which was binarized using KenLM (Heafield, 2011). The sentence-specific translation grammars were extracted using a suffix array rule extractor (Lopez, 2007).

For German, we used the 3,003 sentences in newstest2011 as our Dev set, and report results on the 3,003 sentences of the newstest2012 Test set using BLEU and TER (Snover et al., 2006). For Russian, we took the first 2,000 sentences of newstest2012 for Dev, and report results on the remaining 1,003. For both languages, we selected 1,000 sentences from the bitext to be used as an additional testing set (Test2).

Compound segmentation lattices As German is a morphologically rich language with productive compounding, we use word segmentation lattices as input for the German translation task. These lattices encode alternative segmentations of compound words, allowing the decoder to automatically choose which segmentation is best. We use a maximum entropy model with recommended settings to create lattices for the dev and test sets, as well as for obtaining the 1-best segmentation of the training data (Dyer, 2009).

3 Evaluation

This section describes the experiments we conducted in moving towards a better understanding of the benefits and challenges posed by large-scale high-dimensional discriminative tuning.

3.1 Sparse Features

The ability to incorporate sparse features is the primary reason for the recent move away from Minimum Error Rate Training (Och, 2003), as well as for performing large-scale discriminative training. We include the following sparse Boolean feature templates in our system in addition to the aforementioned baseline features: rule identity (for every unique rule in the grammar), rule shape (mapping rules to sequences of terminals and nonterminals), target bigrams, lexical insertions and deletions (for the top 150 unaligned words from the training data), context-dependent word pairs (for the top 300 word pairs in the training data), and structural distortion (Chiang et al., 2008).

	Dev	Test	Test2	5k	10k	25k	50k
en	75k	74k	27k	132k	255k	634k	1258k
de	74k	73k	26k	133k	256k	639k	1272k

Table 1: Corpus statistics in tokens for German.

	Dev	Test	Test2	15k
ru	46k	24k	24k	350k
en	50k	27k	25k	371k

Table 2: Corpus statistics in tokens for Russian.

Set	# features	Tune	Test	
		↑BLEU	↑BLEU	↓TER
de-en	16	22.38	22.69	60.61
+sparse	108k	23.86	**23.01**	**59.89**
ru-en	16	30.18	29.89	49.05
+sparse	77k	32.40	**30.81**	**48.40**

Table 3: Results with the addition of sparse features for German and Russian.

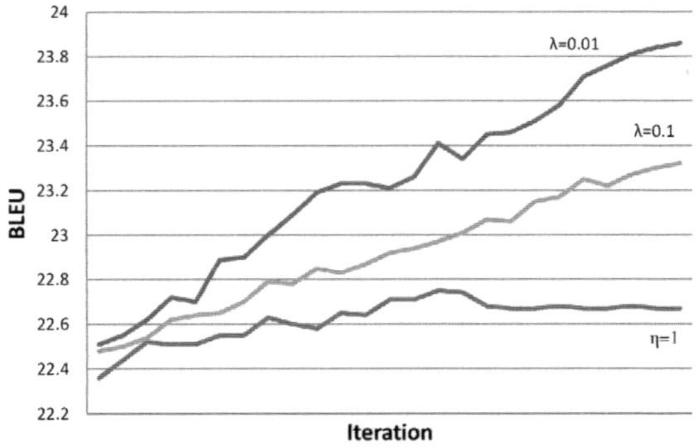

Figure 1: Learning curves for tuning when using a single step size (η) versus different per-feature learning rates.

All of these features are generated from the translation rules on the fly, and thus do not have to be stored as part of the grammar. To allow for memory efficiency while scaling the training data, we hash all the lexical features from their string representation into a 64-bit integer.

Altogether, these templates result in millions of potential features, thus how to select appropriate features, and how to properly learn their weights can have a large impact on the potential benefit.

3.2 Adaptive Learning Rate

The passive-aggressive update used in MIRA has a single learning rate η for all features, which along with α limits the amount each feature weight can change at each update. However, since the typical dense features (e.g., language model) are observed far more frequently than sparse features (e.g., rule identity), it has been shown to be advantageous to use an adaptive per-feature learning rate that allows larger steps for features that do not have much support (Green et al., 2013; Duchi et al., 2011). Essentially, instead of having a single parameter η,

$$\alpha \leftarrow \min\left(C, \frac{\text{cost}(y') - \mathbf{w}^\top(\mathbf{f}(y^+) - \mathbf{f}(y'))}{\|\mathbf{f}(y^+) - \mathbf{f}(y')\|^2}\right)$$

$$\mathbf{w} \leftarrow \mathbf{w} + \alpha\eta\left(\mathbf{f}(y^+) - \mathbf{f}(y')\right)$$

we instead have a vector Σ with one entry for each feature weight:

$$\Sigma^{-1} \leftarrow \Sigma^{-1} + \lambda \text{diag}\left(\mathbf{w}\mathbf{w}^\top\right)$$

$$\mathbf{w} \leftarrow \mathbf{w} + \alpha\Sigma^{1/2}\left(\mathbf{f}(y^+) - \mathbf{f}(y')\right)$$

In practice, this update is very similar to that of AROW (Crammer et al., 2009; Chiang, 2012).

Figure 1 shows learning curves for sparse models with a single learning rate, and adaptive learning with λ=0.01 and λ=0.1, with associated results on Test in Table 4.[4] As can be seen, using a single η produces almost no gain on Dev. However, while both settings using an adaptive rate fare better, the proper setting of λ is important. With λ=0.01 we observe 0.5 BLEU gain over λ=0.1 in tuning, which translates to a small gain on Test. Henceforth, we use an adaptive learning rate with λ=0.01 for all experiments.

Table 3 presents baseline results for both languages. With the addition of sparse features, tuning scores increase by 1.5 BLEU for German, leading to a 0.3 BLEU increase on Test, and 2.2 BLEU for Russian, with 1 BLEU increase on Test. The majority of active features for both languages are rule id (74%), followed by target bigrams (14%) and context-dependent word pairs (11%).

3.3 Feature Selection

As the tuning set size increases, so do the number of active features. This may cause practical problems, such as reduced speed of computation and memory issues. Furthermore, while some

[4]All sparse models are initialized with the same tuned baseline weights. Learning rates are local to each mapper.

Adaptive	# feat.	Tune	Test	
		↑BLEU	↑BLEU	↓TER
none	74k	22.75	22.87	60.19
λ=0.01	108k	23.86	**23.01**	**59.89**
λ=0.1	62k	23.32	22.92	60.09

Table 4: Results with different λ settings for using a per-feature learning rate with sparse features.

Set	# feat.	Tune	Test	
		↑BLEU	↑BLEU	↓TER
all	510k	32.99	22.36	59.26
top 200k	200k	32.96	22.35	59.29
all	373k	34.26	28.84	49.29
top 200k	200k	34.45	**28.98**	49.30

Table 5: Comparison of using all features versus top k selection.

sparse features will generalize well, others may not, thereby incurring practical costs with no performance benefit. Simianer et al. (2012) recently explored ℓ_1/ℓ_2 regularization for joint feature selection for SMT in order to improve efficiency and counter overfitting effects. When performing parallel learning, this allows for selecting a reduced set of the top k features at each iteration that are effective across all learners.

Table 5 compares selecting the top 200k features versus no selection for a larger German and Russian tuning set (§3.4). As can be seen, we achieve the same performance with the top 200k features as we do when using double that amount, while the latter becomes increasing cumbersome to manage. Therefore, we use a top 200k selection for the remainder of this work.

3.4 Large-Scale Training

In the previous section, we saw that learning sparse features on the small development set leads to substantial gains in performance. Next, we wanted to evaluate if we can obtain further gains by scaling the tuning data to learn parameters directly on a portion of the training bitext. Since the bitext is used to learn rules for translation, using the same parallel sentences for grammar extraction as well as for tuning feature weights can lead to severe overfitting (Flanigan et al., 2013). To avoid this issue, we used a jackknifing method to split the training data into $n = 10$ folds, and built a translation system on $n-1$ folds, while sampling sentences from the News Commentary portion of the held-out fold to obtain tuning sets from 5,000 to 50,000 sentences for German, and 15,000 sentences for Russian.

Results for large-scale training for German are presented in Table 6. Although we cannot compare the tuning scores across different size sets, we can see that tuning scores for all sets improve substantially with sparse features. Unfortunately, with increasing tuning set size, we see very little improvement in Test BLEU and TER with either feature set. Similar findings for Russian are presented in Table 7. Introducing sparse features improves performance on each set, respectively, but Dev always performs better on Test.

While tuning on Dev data results in better BLEU on Test than when tuning on the larger sets, it is important to note that although we are able to tune more features on the larger bitext tuning sets, they are not composed of the same genre as the Tune and Test sets, resulting in a domain mismatch.

This phenomenon is further evident in German when testing each model on Test2, which is selected from the bitext, and is thus closer matched to the larger tuning sets, but is separate from both the parallel data used to build the translation model and the tuning sets. Results on Test2 clearly show significant improvement using any of the larger tuning sets versus Dev for both the baseline and sparse features. The 50k sparse setting achieves almost 1 BLEU and 2 TER improvement, showing that there are significant differences between the Dev/Test sets and sets drawn from the bitext.

For Russian, we amplified the effects by selecting Test2 from the portion of the bitext that is separate from the tuning set, but is among the sentences used to create the translation model. The effects of overfitting are markedly more visible here, as there is almost a 7 BLEU difference between tuning on Dev and the 15k set with sparse features. Furthermore, it is interesting to note when looking at Dev that using sparse features has a significant negative impact, as the baseline tuned Dev performs

Tuning	Test	
	↑BLEU	↓TER
5k	22.81	59.90
10k	22.77	59.78
25k	22.88	59.77
50k	22.86	59.76

Table 8: Results for German with 2 iterations of tuning on Dev after tuning on larger set.

reasonably well, while the introduction of sparse features leads to overfitting the specificities of the Dev/Test genre, which are not present in the bitext.

We attempted two strategies to mitigate this problem: combining the Dev set with the larger bitext tuning set from the beginning, and tuning on a larger set to completion, and then running 2 additional iterations of tuning on the Dev set using the learned model. Results for tuning on Dev and a larger set together are presented in Table 7 for Russian and Table 6 for German. As can be seen, the resulting model improves somewhat on the other genre and strikes a middle ground, although it is worse on Test than Dev.

Table 8 presents results for tuning several additional iterations after learning a model on the larger sets. Although this leads to gains of around 0.5 BLEU on Test, none of the models outperform simply tuning on Dev. Thus, neither of these two strategies seem to help. In future work, we plan to forgo randomly sampling the tuning set from the bitext, and instead actively select the tuning set based on similarity to the test set.

4 Conclusion

We explored strategies for scaling learning for SMT to large tuning sets with sparse features. While incorporating an adaptive per-feature learning rate and feature selection, we were able to use Hadoop to efficiently take advantage of large amounts of data. Although discriminative training on larger sets still remains problematic, having the capability to do so remains highly desirable, and we plan to continue exploring methods by which to leverage the power of the bitext effectively.

Acknowledgments

This research was supported in part by the DARPA BOLT program, Contract No. HR0011-12-C-0015; NSF under awards IIS-0916043 and IIS-1144034. Vladimir Eidelman is supported by a NDSEG Fellowship.

References

S. Chen and J. Goodman. 1996. An empirical study of smoothing techniques for language modeling. In *ACL*.

Colin Cherry and George Foster. 2012. Batch tuning strategies for statistical machine translation. In *NAACL*.

David Chiang, Yuval Marton, and Philip Resnik. 2008. Online large-margin training of syntactic and structural translation features. In *EMNLP*.

D. Chiang, K. Knight, and W. Wang. 2009. 11,001 new features for statistical machine translation. In *NAACL-HLT*.

D. Chiang. 2012. Hope and fear for discriminative training of statistical translation models. *JMLR*, 13:1159–1187.

K. Crammer, A. Kulesza, and M. Dredze. 2009. Adaptive regularization of weight vectors. In *NIPS*.

J. Dean and S. Ghemawat. 2004. MapReduce: Simplified data processing on large clusters. In *OSDI*.

J. Duchi, E. Hazan, and Y. Singer. 2011. Adaptive subgradient methods for online learning and stochastic optimization. *JMLR*, 12:2121–2159.

C. Dyer, A. Lopez, J. Ganitkevitch, J. Weese, F. Ture, P. Blunsom, H. Setiawan, V. Eidelman, and P. Resnik. 2010. cdec: A decoder, alignment, and learning framework for finite-state and context-free translation models. In *ACL System Demonstrations*.

Chris Dyer. 2009. Using a maximum entropy model to build segmentation lattices for mt. In *Proceedings of NAACL-HLT*.

Vladimir Eidelman, Ke Wu, Ferhan Ture, Philip Resnik, and Jimmy Lin. 2013. Mr. MIRA: Open-source large-margin structured learning on map-reduce. In *ACL System Demonstrations*.

Vladimir Eidelman. 2012. Optimization strategies for online large-margin learning in machine translation. In *WMT*.

Jeffrey Flanigan, Chris Dyer, and Jaime Carbonell. 2013. Large-scale discriminative training for statistical machine translation using held-out line search. In *NAACL*.

S. Green, S. Wang, D. Cer, and C. Manning. 2013. Fast and adaptive online training of feature-rich translation models. In *ACL*.

Kenneth Heafield. 2011. KenLM: faster and smaller language model queries. In *WMT*.

Mark Hopkins and Jonathan May. 2011. Tuning as ranking. In *EMNLP*.

Tuning	# mappers	# features	Tune	Test		Test2	
			↑BLEU	↑BLEU	↓TER	↑BLEU	↓TER
Dev	120	16	22.38	**22.69**	60.61	29.31	54.26
5k	120	16	32.60	22.14	59.60	29.69	52.96
10k	120	16	33.16	22.06	59.43	29.93	52.37
Dev+10k	120	16	19.40	22.32	59.37	30.17	52.45
25k	300	16	32.48	22.21	59.54	30.03	51.71
50k	600	16	32.21	22.21	**59.39**	29.94	52.55
Dev	120	108k	23.86	**23.01**	59.89	29.65	53.86
5k	120	159k	33.70	22.26	59.26	30.53	51.84
10k	120	200k	34.00	22.12	59.24	30.51	51.71
Dev+10k	120	200k	19.62	22.42	59.17	30.26	52.21
25k	300	200k	32.96	22.35	59.29	30.39	52.14
50k	600	200k	32.86	22.40	**59.15**	30.54	51.88

Table 6: German evaluation with large-scale tuning, showing numbers of mappers employed, number of active features for best model, and test scores on Test and bitext Test2 domains.

Tuning	# mappers	# features	Tune	Test		Test2	
			↑BLEU	↑BLEU	↓TER	↑BLEU	↓TER
Dev	120	16	30.18	29.89	49.05	57.14	32.56
15k	200	16	34.65	28.60	49.63	59.64	30.65
Dev+15k	200	16	33.97	28.88	49.37	58.24	31.81
Dev	120	77k	32.40	**30.81**	**48.40**	52.90	36.85
15k	200	200k	35.05	28.34	49.69	59.81	30.59
Dev+15k	200	200k	34.45	28.98	49.30	57.61	32.71

Table 7: Russian evaluation with large-scale tuning, showing numbers of mappers employed, number of active features for best model, and test scores on Test and bitext Test2 domains.

Liang Huang and David Chiang. 2007. Forest rescoring: Faster decoding with integrated language models. In *ACL*.

Philipp Koehn, Franz Josef Och, and Daniel Marcu. 2003. Statistical phrase-based translation. In *NAACL*.

Adam Lopez. 2007. Hierarchical phrase-based translation with suffix arrays. In *EMNLP*.

Franz Och and Hermann Ney. 2003. A systematic comparison of various statistical alignment models. In *Computational Linguistics*.

Franz Josef Och. 2003. Minimum error rate training in statistical machine translation. In *ACL*.

K. Papineni, S. Roukos, T. Ward, and W.-J. Zhu. 2002. BLEU: a method for automatic evaluation of machine translation. In *ACL*.

P. Simianer, S. Riezler, and C. Dyer. 2012. Joint feature selection in distributed stochastic learning for large-scale discriminative training in SMT. In *ACL*.

M. Snover, B. Dorr, R. Schwartz, L. Micciulla, and J. Makhoul. 2006. A study of translation edit rate with targeted human annotation. In *AMTA*.

Andreas Stolcke. 2002. SRILM - an extensible language modeling toolkit. In *ICSLP*.

The TALP-UPC Phrase-based Translation Systems for WMT13: System Combination with Morphology Generation, Domain Adaptation and Corpus Filtering

Lluís Formiga*, **Marta R. Costa-jussà***, **José B. Mariño***
José A. R. Fonollosa*, **Alberto Barrón-Cedeño*†**, **Lluís Màrquez***

*TALP Research Centre
Universitat Politècnica de Catalunya
Barcelona, Spain

†Facultad de Informática
Universidad Politécnica de Madrid
Madrid, Spain

{lluis.formiga,marta.ruiz,jose.marino,jose.fonollosa}@upc.edu
{albarron, lluism}@lsi.upc.edu

Abstract

This paper describes the TALP participation in the WMT13 evaluation campaign. Our participation is based on the combination of several statistical machine translation systems: based on standard phrase-based Moses systems. Variations include techniques such as morphology generation, training sentence filtering, and domain adaptation through unit derivation. The results show a coherent improvement on TER, METEOR, NIST, and BLEU scores when compared to our baseline system.

1 Introduction

The TALP-UPC center (Center for Language and Speech Technologies and Applications at Universitat Politècnica de Catalunya) focused on the English to Spanish translation of the WMT13 shared task.

Our primary (contrastive) run is an internal system selection comprised of different training approaches (without CommonCrawl, unless stated): (a) Moses Baseline (Koehn et al., 2007b), (b) Moses Baseline + Morphology Generation (Formiga et al., 2012b), (c) Moses Baseline + News Adaptation (Henríquez Q. et al., 2011), (d) Moses Baseline + News Adaptation + Morphology Generation , and (e) Moses Baseline + News Adaptation + Filtered CommonCrawl Adaptation (Barrón-Cedeño et al., 2013). Our secondary run includes is the full training strategy marked as *(e)* in the previous description.

The main differences with respect to our last year's participation (Formiga et al., 2012a) are: *i)* the inclusion of the CommonCrawl corpus, using a sentence filtering technique and the system combination itself, and *ii)* a system selection scheme to select the best translation among the different configurations.

The paper is organized as follows. Section 2 presents the phrase-based system and the main pipeline of our baseline system. Section 3 describes the our approaches to improve the baseline system on the English-to-Spanish task (special attention is given to the approaches that differ from last year). Section 4 presents the system combination approach once the best candidate phrase of the different subsystems are selected. Section 5 discusses the obtained results considering both internal and official test sets. Section 6 includes conclusions and further work.

2 Baseline system: Phrase-Based SMT

Our contribution is a follow up of our last year participation (Formiga et al., 2012a), based on a factored Moses from English to Spanish words plus their Part-of-Speech (POS). Factored corpora augments words with additional information, such as POS tags or lemmas. In that case, factors other than surface (e.g. POS) are usually less sparse, allowing the construction of factor-specific language models with higher-order n-grams. Such language models can help to obtain syntactically more correct outputs.

We used the standard models available in Moses as feature functions: relative frequencies, lexical weights, word and phrase penalties, *wbe-msd-bidirectional-fe* reordering models, and two language models (one for surface and one for POS tags). Phrase scoring was computed using Good-Turing discounting (Foster et al., 2006).

As aforementioned, we developed five factored Moses-based independent systems with different approaches. We explain them in Section 3. As a final decision, we applied a system selection scheme (Formiga et al., 2013; Specia et al., 2010) to consider the best candidate for each sentence, according to human trained quality estimation (QE) models. We set monotone reordering of the punctuation signs for the decoding using the Moses wall feature.

We tuned the systems using the Moses MERT (Och, 2003) implementation. Our focus was on minimizing the BLEU score (Papineni et al., 2002) of the development set. Still, for exploratory purposes, we tuned configuration *(c)* using PRO (Hopkins and May, 2011) to set the initial weights at every iteration of the MERT algorithm. However, it showed no significant differences compared to the original MERT implementation.

We trained the baseline system using all the available parallel corpora, except for common-crawl. That is, European Parliament (EPPS) (Koehn, 2005), News Commentary, and United Nations. Regarding the monolingual data, there were more News corpora organized by years for Spanish. The data is available at the Translation Task's website[1]. We used all the News corpora to busld the language model (LM). Firstly, a LM was built for every corpus independently. Afterwards, they were combined to produce de final LM.

For internal testing we used the News 2011 and News 2012 data and concatenated the remaining three years of News data as a single parallel corpus for development.

We processed the corpora as in our participation to WMT12 (Formiga et al., 2012a). Tokenization and POS-tagging in both Spanish and English was obtained with FreeLing (Padró et al., 2010). Stemming was carried out with Snowball (Porter, 2001). Words were conditionally case folded based on their POS: proper nouns and adjectives were separated from other categories to determine whether a string should be fully folded (no special property), partially folded (noun or adjective) or not folded at all in (acronym).

Bilingual corpora was filtered with the *clean-corpus-n* script of Moses (Koehn et al., 2007a), removing those pairs in which a sentence was longer than 70. For the CommonCrawl corpus we used a more complex filtering step (cf. Section 3.3).

[1]http://www.statmt.org/wmt13/translation-task.html

Postprocessing included two special scripts to recover contractions and clitics. Detruecasing was done forcing the capitals after the punctuation signs. Furthermore we used an additional script in order to check the casing of output names with respect to the source. We reused our language models and alignments (with stems) from WMT12.

3 Improvement strategies

We tried three different strategies to improve the baseline system. Section 3.1 shows a strategy based on morphology simplification plus generation. Its aim is dealing with the problems raised by morphology-rich languages, such as Spanish. Section 3.2 presents a domain–adaptation strategy that consists of deriving new units. Section 3.3 presents an advanced strategy to filter the good bisentences from the CommonCrawl corpus, which might be useful to perform the domain adaptation.

3.1 Morphology generation

Following the success of our WMT12 participation (Formiga et al., 2012a), our first improvement is based on the morphology generalization and generation approach (Formiga et al., 2012b). We focus our strategy on simplifying verb forms only.

The approach first translates into Spanish simplified forms (de Gispert and Mariño, 2008). The final inflected forms are predicted through a morphology generation step, based on the shallow and deep-projected linguistic information available from both source and target language sentences.

Lexical sparseness is a crucial aspect to deal with for an open-domain robust SMT when translating to morphology-rich languages (e.g. Spanish) . We knew beforehand (Formiga et al., 2012b) that morphology generalization is a good method to deal with generic translations and it provides stability to translations of the training domain.

Our morphology prediction (generation) systems are trained with the WMT13 corpora (Europarl, News, and UN) together with noisy data (OpenSubtitles). This combination helps to obtain better translations without compromising the quality of the translation models. These kind of morphology generation systems are trained with a relatively short amount of parallel data compared to standard SMT training corpora.

Our main enhancement to this strategy is the

addition of source-projected deep features to the target sentence in order to perform the morphology prediction. These features are Dependency Features and Semantic Role Labelling, obtained from the source sentence through Lund Dependency Parser[2]. These features are then projected to the target sentence as explained in (Formiga et al., 2012b).

Projected deep features are important to predict the correct verb morphology from clean and fluent text. However, the projection of deep features is sentence-fluency sensitive, making it unreliable when the baseline MT output is poor. In other words, the morphology generation strategy becomes more relevant with high-quality MT decoders, as their output is more fluent, making the shallow and deep features more reliable classifier guides.

3.2 Domain Adaptation through pivot derived units

Usually the WMT Translation Task focuses on adapting a system to a news domain, offering an in-domain parallel corpus to work with. However this corpus is relatively small compared to the other corpora. In our previous participation we demonstrated the need of performing a more aggressive domain adaptation strategy. Our strategy was based on using in-domain parallel data to adapt the translation model, but focusing on the decoding errors that the out-of-domain baseline system makes when translating the in-domain corpus.

The idea is to identify the system mistakes and use the in-domain data to learn how to correct them. To that effect, we interpolate the translation models (phrase and lexical reordering tables) with a new adapted translation model with derived units. We obtained the units identifying the mismatching parts between the non-adapted translation and the actual reference (Henríquez Q. et al., 2011). This derivation approach uses the original translation as a pivot to find a word-to-word alignment between the source side and the target correction (word-to-word alignment provided by Moses during decoding).

The word-to-word monolingual alignment between output translation target correction was obtained combining different probabilities such as *i*)lexical identity, *ii*) TER-based alignment links,

[2]http://nlp.cs.lth.se/software/

Corpus		Sent.	Words	Vocab.	avg.len.
Original	EN	1.48M	29.44M	465.1k	19.90
	ES		31.6M	459.9k	21.45
Filtered	EN	0.78M	15.3M	278.0k	19.72
	ES		16.6M	306.8k	21.37

Table 1: Commoncrawl corpora statistics for WMT13 before and after filtering.

iii) lexical model probabilities, *iv*) char-based Levenshtein distance between tokens and *v*) filtering out those alignments from NULL to a stop word ($p = -\infty$).

We empirically set the linear interpolation weight as $w = 0.60$ for the baseline translation models and $w = 0.40$ for the derived units translations models. We applied the pivot derived units strategy to the News domain and to the filtered Commoncrawl corpus (cf. Section 5). The procedure to filter out the Commoncrawl corpus is explained next.

3.3 CommonCrawl Filtering

We used the CommonCrawl corpus, provided for the first time by the organization, as an important source of information for performing aggressive domain adaptation. To decrease the impact of the noise in the corpus, we performed an automatic pre-selection of the supposedly more correct (hence useful) sentence pairs: we applied the automatic quality estimation filters developed in the context of the FAUST project[3]. The filters' purpose is to identify cases in which the post-editions provided by casual users really improve over automatic translations.

The adaptation to the current framework is as follows. Example selection is modelled as a binary classification problem. We consider triples (*src*, *ref*, *trans*), where *src* and *ref* stand for the source-reference sentences in the CommonCrawl corpus and *trans* is an automatic translation of the source, generated by our baseline SMT system. A triple is assigned a positive label iff *ref* is a better translation from *src* than *trans*. That is, if the translation example provided by CommonCrawl is better than the output of our baseline SMT system.

We used four feature sets to characterize the three sentences and their relationships: *surface*, *back-translation*, *noise-based* and *similarity-based*. These features try to capture (*a*) the similarity between the different texts on the basis of

[3]`http://www.faust-fp7.eu`

diverse measures, (*b*) the length of the different sentences (including ratios), and (*c*) the likelihood of a source or target text to include noisy text.[4] Most of them are simple, fast-calculation and language-independent features. However, back-translation features require that *trans* and *ref* are back-translated into the source language. We did it by using the TALP es-en system from WMT12.

Considering these features, we trained linear Support Vector Machines using SVM^{light} (Joachims, 1999). Our training collection was the FFF^{+} corpus, with +500 hundred manually annotated instances (Barrón-Cedeño et al., 2013). No adaptation to CommonCrawl was performed. To give an idea, classification accuracy over the test partition of the FFF^{+} corpus was only moderately good ($\sim$70%). However, ranking by classification score a fresh set of over 6,000 new examples, and selecting the top ranked 50% examples to enrich a state-of-the-art SMT system, allowed us to significantly improve translation quality (Barrón-Cedeño et al., 2013).

For WMT13, we applied these classifiers to rank the CommonCrawl translation pairs and then selected the top 53% instances to be processed by the domain adaptation strategy. Table 1 displays the corpus statistics before and after filtering.

4 System Combination

We approached system combination as a *system selection* task. More concretely, we applied Quality Estimation (QE) models (Specia et al., 2010; Formiga et al., 2013) to select the highest quality translation at sentence level among the translation candidates obtained by our different strategies. The QE models are trained with human supervision, making use of no system-dependent features.

In a previous study (Formiga et al., 2013), we showed the plausibility of building reliable system-independent QE models from human annotations. This type of task should be addressed with a pairwise ranking strategy, as it yields better results than an absolute quality estimation approach (i.e., regression) for system selection. We also found that training the quality estimation models from human assessments, instead of automatic reference scores, helped to obtain better models for system selection for both *i)* mimicking the behavior of automatic metrics and *ii)* learning the human behavior when ranking different translation candidates.

For training the QE models we used the data from the WMT13 shared task on quality estimation (*System Selection Quality Estimation at Sentence Level* task[5]), which contains the test sets from other WMT campaigns with human assessments. We used five groups of features, namely: *i) QuestQE*: 17 QE features provided by the Quest toolkit[6]; *ii) AsiyaQE*: 26 QE features provided by the Asiya toolkit for MT evaluation (Giménez and Màrquez, 2010a); *iii)* LM (and LM-PoS) perplexities trained with monolingual data; *iv) PR*: Classical lexical-based measures -BLEU (Papineni et al., 2002), NIST (Doddington, 2002), and METEOR (Denkowski and Lavie, 2011)- computed with a pseudo-reference approach, that is, using the other system candidates as references (Soricut and Echihabi, 2010); and *v) PROTHER*: Reference based metrics provided by Asiya, including GTM, ROUGE, PER, TER (Snover et al., 2008), and syntax-based evaluation measures also with a pseudo-reference approach.

We trained a Support Vector Machine ranker by means of pairwise comparison using the SVM^{light} toolkit (Joachims, 1999), but with the "`-z p`" parameter, which can provide system rankings for all the members of different groups. The learner algorithm was run according to the following parameters: linear kernel, expanding the working set by 9 variables at each iteration, for a maximum of 50,000 iterations and with a cache size of 100 for kernel evaluations. The trade-off parameter was empirically set to 0.001.

Table 2 shows the contribution of different feature groups when training the QE models. For evaluating performance, we used the Asiya normalized linear combination metric ULC (Giménez and Màrquez, 2010b), which combines BLEU, NIST, and METEOR (with exact, paraphrases and synonym variants). Within this scenario, it can be observed that the quality estimation features (QuestQE and AsiyaQE) did not obtain good results, perhaps because of the high similarity between the test candidates (Moses with different configurations) in contrast to the strong difference between the candidates in training (Moses,

[4] We refer the interested reader to (Barrón-Cedeño et al., 2013) for a detailed description of features, process, and evaluation.

[5] http://www.quest.dcs.shef.ac.uk/wmt13_qe.html

[6] http://www.quest.dcs.shef.ac.uk

Features	Asiya ULC			
	WMT'11	WMT'12	AVG	WMT'13
QuestQE	60.46	60.64	60.55	60.06
AsiyaQE	61.04	60.89	60.97	60.29
QuestQE+AsiyaQE	60.86	61.07	60.96	60.42
LM	60.84	60.63	60.74	60.37
QuestQE+AsiyaQE+LM	60.80	60.55	60.67	60.21
QuestQE+AsiyaQE+PR	60.97	61.12	61.05	60.54
QuestQE+AsiyaQE+PR+PROTHER	61.05	61.19	61.12	60.69
PR	*61.24*	61.08	61.16	***61.04***
PR+PROTHER	61.19	61.16	61.18	60.98
PR+PROTHER+LM	61.11	*61.29*	***61.20***	61.03
QuestQE+AsiyaQE+PR+PROTHER+LM	60.70	60.88	60.79	60.14

Table 2: System selection scores (ULC) obtained using QE models trained with different groups of features. Results displayed for WMT11, WMT12 internal tests, their average, and the WMT13 test

EN→ES		BLEU	TER
wmt13	Primary	29.5	0.586
wmt13	Secondary	29.4	0.586

Table 4: Official automatic scores for the WMT13 English↔Spanish translations.

RBMT, Jane, etc.). On the contrary, the pseudo-reference-based features play a crucial role in the proper performance of the QE model, confirming the hypothesis that PR features need a clear dominant system to be used as reference. The PR-based configurations (with and without LM) had no big differences between them. We choose the best AVG result for the final system combination: *PR+PROTHER+LM*, which it is consistent with the actual WMT13 evaluated afterwards.

5 Results

Evaluations were performed considering different quality measures: BLEU, NIST, TER, and METEOR in addition to an informal manual analysis. This manifold of metrics evaluates distinct aspects of the translation. We evaluated both over the WMT11 and WMT12 test sets as internal indicators of our systems. We also give our performance on the WMT13 test dataset.

Table 3 presents the obtained results for the different strategies: (a) Moses Baseline (w/o commoncrawl) (b) Moses Baseline+Morphology Generation (w/o commoncrawl) (c) Moses Baseline+News Adaptation through pivot based alignment (w/o commoncrawl) (d) Moses Baseline + News Adaptation (b) + Morphology Generation (c) (e) Moses Baseline + News Adaptation (b) + Filtered CommonCrawl Adaptation.

The official results are in Table 4. Our primary (contrastive) run is the system combination strategy whereas our secondary run is the full training strategy marked as (e) on the system combination. Our primary system was ranked in the second cluster out of ten constrained systems in the official manual evaluation.

Independent analyzes of the improvement strategies show that the highest improvement comes from the CommonCrawl Filtering + Adaptation strategy (system e). The second best strategy is the combination of the morphology prediction system plus the news adaptation system. However, for the WMT12 test the News Adaptation strategy contributes to main improvement whereas for the WMT13 this major improvement is achieved with the morphology strategy. Analyzing the distance betweem each test set with respect to the News and CommonCrawl domain to further understand the behavior of each strategy seems an interesting future work. Specifically, for further contrasting the difference in the morphology approach, it would be nice to analyze the variation in the verb inflection forms. Hypothetically, the person or the number of the verb forms used may have a higher tendency to be different in the WMT13 test set, implying that our morphology approach is further exploited.

Regarding the system selection step (internal WMT12 test), the only automatic metric that has an improvement is TER. However, TER is one of

EN→ES		BLEU	NIST	TER	METEOR
wmt12	Baseline	32.97	8.27	49.27	49.91
wmt12	+ Morphology Generation	33.03	8.29	49.02	50.01
wmt12	+ News Adaptation	33.22	8.31	49.00	50.16
wmt12	+ News Adaptation + Morphology Generation	33.29	8.32	48.83	50.29
wmt12	+ News Adaptation + Filtered CommonCrawl Adaptation	**33.61**	**8.35**	48.82	**50.52**
wmt12	System Combination	33.43	8.34	**48.78**	50.44
wmt13	Baseline	29.02	7.72	51.92	46.96
wmt13	Morphology Generation	29.35	7.73	52.04	47.04
wmt13	News Adaptation	29.19	7.74	51.91	47.07
wmt13	News Adaptation + Morphology Generation	29.40	7.74	51.96	47.12
wmt13	News Adaptation + Filtered CommonCrawl Adaptation	29.47	7.77	51.82	47.22
wmt13	System Combination	**29.54**	**7.77**	**51.76**	**47.34**

Table 3: Automatic scores for English→Spanish translations.

the most reliable metrics according to human evaluation. Regarding the actual WMT13 test, the system selection step is able to overcome all the automatic metrics.

6 Conclusions and further work

This paper described the TALP-UPC participation for the English-to-Spanish WMT13 translation task. We applied the same systems as in last year, but enhanced with new techniques: sentence filtering and system combination.

Results showed that both approaches performed better than the baseline system, being the sentence filtering technique the one that most improvement reached in terms of all the automatic quality indicators: BLEU, NIST, TER, and METEOR. The system combination was able to outperform the independent systems which used morphological knowledge and/or domain adaptation techniques.

As further work would like to focus on further advancing on the morphology-based techniques.

Acknowledgments

This work has been supported in part by Spanish Ministerio de Economía y Competitividad, contract TEC2012-38939-C03-02 as well as from the European Regional Development Fund (ERDF/FEDER) and the European Community's FP7 (2007-2013) program under the following grants: 247762 (FAUST, FP7-ICT-2009-4-247762), 29951 (the International Outgoing Fellowship Marie Curie Action – IMTraP-2011-29951) and 246016 (ERCIM "Alain Bensoussan" Fellowship).

References

Alberto Barrón-Cedeño, Lluís Màrquez, Carlos A. Henríquez Q, Lluís Formiga, Enrique Romero, and Jonathan May. 2013. Identifying Useful Human Correction Feedback from an On-line Machine Translation Service. In *Proceedings of the Twenty-Third International Joint Conference on Artificial Intelligence*. AAAI Press.

Adrià de de Gispert and José B. Mariño. 2008. On the impact of morphology in English to Spanish statistical MT. *Speech Communication*, 50(11-12):1034–1046.

Michael Denkowski and Alon Lavie. 2011. Meteor 1.3: Automatic Metric for Reliable Optimization and Evaluation of Machine Translation Systems. In *Proceedings of the EMNLP 2011 Workshop on Statistical Machine Translation*.

George Doddington. 2002. Automatic evaluation of machine translation quality using n-gram co-occurrence statistics. In *Proceedings of the second international conference on Human Language Technology Research*, HLT '02, pages 138–145, San Francisco, CA, USA. Morgan Kaufmann Publishers Inc.

Lluis Formiga, Carlos A. Henríquez Q., Adolfo Hernández, José B. Mariño, Enric Monte, and José A. R. Fonollosa. 2012a. The TALP-UPC phrase-based translation systems for WMT12: Morphology simplification and domain adaptation. In *Proceedings of the Seventh Workshop on Statistical Machine Translation*, pages 275–282, Montréal, Canada, June. Association for Computational Linguistics.

Lluís Formiga, Adolfo Hernández, José B. Mariñ, and Enrique Monte. 2012b. Improving english to spanish out-of-domain translations by morphology generalization and generation. In *Proceedings of the AMTA Monolingual Machine Translation-2012 Workshop.*

Lluís Formiga, Lluís Màrquez, and Jaume Pujantell. 2013. Real-life translation quality estimation for mt system selection. In *Proceedings of 14th Machine Translation Summit (MT Summit)*, Nice, France, September. EAMT.

George Foster, Roland Kuhn, and Howard Johnson. 2006. Phrasetable smoothing for statistical machine translation. In *Proceedings of the 2006 Conference on Empirical Methods in Natural Language Processing*, EMNLP '06, pages 53–61, Stroudsburg, PA, USA. Association for Computational Linguistics.

Jesús Giménez and Lluís Màrquez. 2010a. Asiya: An Open Toolkit for Automatic Machine Translation (Meta-)Evaluation. *The Prague Bulletin of Mathematical Linguistics*, (94):77–86.

Jesús Giménez and Lluís Màrquez. 2010b. Linguistic measures for automatic machine translation evaluation. *Machine Translation*, 24(3-4):209–240, December.

Carlos A. Henríquez Q., José B. Mariño, and Rafael E. Banchs. 2011. Deriving translation units using small additional corpora. In *Proceedings of the 15th Conference of the European Association for Machine Translation.*

Mark Hopkins and Jonathan May. 2011. Tuning as ranking. In *Proceedings of the 2011 Conference on Empirical Methods in Natural Language Processing*, pages 1352–1362, Edinburgh, Scotland, UK., July. Association for Computational Linguistics.

Thorsten Joachims, 1999. *Advances in Kernel Methods – Support Vector Learning*, chapter Making large-Scale SVM Learning Practical. MIT Press.

P. Koehn, H. Hoang, A. Birch, C. Callison-Burch, M. Federico, N. Bertoldi, B. Cowan, W. Shen, C. Moran, R. Zens, et al. 2007a. Moses: Open source toolkit for statistical machine translation. In *Proceedings of the 45th Annual Meeting of the ACL on Interactive Poster and Demonstration Sessions*, pages 177–180. Association for Computational Linguistics.

Philipp Koehn, Hieu Hoang, Alexandra Birch, Chris Callison-Burch, Marcello Federico, Nicola Bertoldi, Brooke Cowan, Wade Shen, Christine Moran, Richard Zens, Chris Dyer, Ondrej Bojar, Alexandra Constantin, and Evan Herbst. 2007b. Moses: Open source toolkit for statistical machine translation. In *Proceedings of the 45th Annual Meeting of the Association for Computational Linguistics Companion Volume Proceedings of the Demo and Poster Sessions*, pages 177–180, Prague, Czech Republic, June. Association for Computational Linguistics.

Philipp Koehn. 2005. Europarl: A Parallel Corpus for Statistical Machine Translation. In *Machine Translation Summit.*

Franz J. Och. 2003. Minimum error rate training in statistical machine translation. In *Proceedings of the Annual Meeting of the Association for Computational Linguistics (ACL).*

Lluís Padró, Miquel Collado, Samuel Reese, Marina Lloberes, and Irene Castellón. 2010. Freeling 2.1: Five years of open-source language processing tools. In *Proceedings of 7th Language Resources and Evaluation Conference (LREC 2010)*, La Valletta, MALTA, May. ELRA.

Kishore Papineni, Salim Roukos, Todd Ward, and Wei-Jing Zhu. 2002. BLEU: a method for automatic evaluation of machine translation. In *Proceedings of the Annual Meeting of the Association for Computational Linguistics (ACL).*

M. Porter. 2001. Snowball: A language for stemming algorithms.

Matthew Snover, Bonnie Dorr, and Richard Schwartz. 2008. Language and Translation Model Adaptation using Comparable Corpora. In *Proceedings of the 2008 Conference on Empirical Methods in Natural Language Processing.*

Radu Soricut and Abdessamad Echihabi. 2010. Trustrank: Inducing trust in automatic translations via ranking. In *Proceedings of the 48th Annual Meeting of the Association for Computational Linguistics*, pages 612–621, Uppsala, Sweden, July. Association for Computational Linguistics.

Lucia Specia, Dhwaj Raj, and Marco Turchi. 2010. Machine Translation Evaluation Versus Quality Estimation. *Machine Translation*, 24:39–50, March.

PhraseFix: Statistical Post-Editing of TectoMT

Petra Galuščáková, Martin Popel, and Ondřej Bojar
Charles University in Prague, Faculty of Mathematics and Physics
Institute of Formal and Applied Linguistics
Malostranské náměstí 25, Prague, Czech Republic
{galuscakova,popel,bojar}@ufal.mff.cuni.cz

Abstract

We present two English-to-Czech systems that took part in the WMT 2013 shared task: TECTOMT and PHRASEFIX. The former is a deep-syntactic transfer-based system, the latter is a more-or-less standard statistical post-editing (SPE) applied on top of TECTOMT. In a brief survey, we put SPE in context with other system combination techniques and evaluate SPE vs. another simple system combination technique: using synthetic parallel data from TECTOMT to train a statistical MT system (SMT). We confirm that PHRASEFIX (SPE) improves the output of TECTOMT, and we use this to analyze errors in TECTOMT. However, we also show that extending data for SMT is more effective.

1 Introduction

This paper describes two submissions to the WMT 2013 shared task:[1] TECTOMT – a deep-syntactic tree-to-tree system and PHRASEFIX – statistical post-editing of TECTOMT using Moses (Koehn et al., 2007). We also report on experiments with another hybrid method where TECTOMT is used to produce additional (so-called *synthetic*) parallel training data for Moses. This method was used in CU-BOJAR and CU-DEPFIX submissions, see Bojar et al. (2013).

2 Overview of Related Work

The number of approaches to system combination is enormous. We very briefly survey those that form the basis of our work reported in this paper.

2.1 Statistical Post-Editing

Statistical post-editing (SPE, see e.g. Simard et al. (2007), Dugast et al. (2009)) is a popular method for improving outputs of a rule-based MT system. In principle, SPE could be applied to any type of *first-stage system* including a statistical one (Oflazer and El-Kahlout, 2007; Béchara et al., 2011), but most benefit could be expected from post-editing rule-based MT because of the complementary nature of weaknesses and advantages of rule-based and statistical approaches.

SPE is usually done with an off-the-shelf SMT system (e.g. Moses) which is trained on output of the first-stage system aligned with reference translations of the original source text. The goal of SPE is to produce translations that are better than both the first-stage system alone and the second-stage SMT trained on the original training data.

Most SPE approaches use the reference translations from the original training parallel corpus to train the second-stage system. In contrast, Simard et al. (2007) use human-post-edited first-stage system outputs instead. Intuitively, the latter approach achieves better results because the human-post-edited translations are closer to the first-stage output than the original reference translations. Therefore, SPE learns to perform the changes which are needed the most. However, creating human-post-edited translations is laborious and must be done again for each new (version of the) first-stage system in order to preserve its full advantage over using the original references.[2]

Rosa et al. (2013) have applied SPE on English→Czech SMT outputs. They have used the approach introduced by Béchara et al. (2011), but no improvement was achieved. However, their rule-based post-editing were found helpful.

Our SPE setting (called PHRASEFIX) uses TECTOMT as the first-stage system and Moses as the second-stage system. Ideally, TECTOMT pre-

[1] http://www.statmt.org/wmt13

[2] If more reference translations are available, it would be beneficial to choose such references for training SPE which are most similar to the first-stage outputs. However, in our experiments only one reference is available.

serves well-formed syntactic sentence structures, and the SPE (Moses) fixes low fluency wordings.

2.2 MT Output Combination

An SPE system is trained to improve the output of a single first-stage system. Sometimes, more (first-stage) systems are available, and we would like to combine them. In *MT output selection*, for each sentence one system's translation is selected as the final output. In *MT output combination*, the final translation of each sentence is a combination of phrases from several systems. In both approaches, the systems are treated as black boxes, so only their outputs are needed. In the simplest setting, all systems are supposed to be equally good/reliable, and the final output is selected by voting, based on the number of shared n-grams or language model scores. The number and the identity of the systems to be combined therefore do not need to be known in advance. More sophisticated methods learn parameters/weights specific for the individual systems. These methods are based e.g. on confusion networks (Rosti et al., 2007; Matusov et al., 2008) and joint optimization of word alignment, word order and lexical choice (He and Toutanova, 2009).

2.3 Synthetic Data Combination

Another way to combine several first-stage systems is to employ a standard SMT toolkit, e.g. Moses. The core of the idea is to use the n first-stage systems to prepare synthetic parallel data and include them in the training data for the SMT.

Corpus Combination (CComb) The easiest method is to use these n newly created parallel corpora as additional training data, i.e. train Moses on a concatenation of the original parallel sentences (with human-translated references) and the new parallel sentences (with machine-translated pseudo-references).

Phrase Table Combination (PTComb) Another method is to extract n phrase tables in addition to the original phrase table and exploit the Moses option of multiple phrase tables (Koehn and Schroeder, 2007). This means that given the usual five features (forward/backward phrase/lexical log probability and phrase penalty), we need to tune $5 \cdot (n+1)$ features. Because such MERT (Och, 2003) tuning may be unstable for higher n, several methods were proposed where the $n+1$ phrase tables are merged into a single one (Eisele et al., 2008; Chen et al., 2009). Another issue of phrase table combination is that the same output can be achieved with phrases from several phrase tables, leading to spurious ambiguity and thus less diversity in n-best lists of a given size (see Chen et al. (2009) for one possible solution). CComb does not suffer from the spurious ambiguity issue, but it does not allow to tune special features for the individual first-stage systems.

In our experiments, we use both CComb and PTComb approaches. In PTComb, we use TECTOMT as the only first-stage system and Moses as the second-stage system. We use the two phrase tables separately (the merging is not needed; $5 \cdot 2$ is still a reasonable number of features in MERT). In CComb, we concatenate English↔Czech parallel corpus with English↔"synthetic Czech" corpus translated from English using TECTOMT. A single phrase table is created from the concatenated corpus.

3 TECTOMT

TECTOMT is a **linguistically-motivated** tree-to-tree deep-syntactic translation system with transfer based on Maximum Entropy context-sensitive translation models (Mareček et al., 2010) and Hidden Tree Markov Models (Žabokrtský and Popel, 2009). It employs some rule-based components, but the most important tasks in the analysis-transfer-synthesis pipeline are based on statistics and machine learning. There are three main reasons why it is a suitable candidate for SPE and other hybrid methods.

- TECTOMT has quite **different distribution and characteristics of errors** compared to standard SMT (Bojar et al., 2011).
- TECTOMT is **not tuned for BLEU** using MERT (its development is rather driven by human inspection of the errors although different setups are regularly evaluated with BLEU as an additional guidance).
- TECTOMT uses deep-syntactic dependency language models in the transfer phase, but it does **not use standard n-gram language models** on the surface forms because the current synthesis phase supports only 1-best output.

The version of TECTOMT submitted to WMT 2013 is almost identical to the WMT 2012 version. Only a few rule-based components (e.g. detection of surface tense of English verbs) were refined.

Corpus	Sents	Tokens	
		Czech	English
CzEng	15M	205M	236M
^{tmt}(CzEng)	15M	197M	236M
Czech Web Corpus	37M	627M	–
WMT News Crawl	25M	445M	–

Table 1: Statistics of used data.

	BLEU	1-TER
TECTOMT	14.71±0.53	35.61±0.60
PHRASEFIX	17.73±0.54	35.63±0.65
Filtering	14.68±0.50	35.47±0.57
Mark Reliable Phr.	**17.87±0.55**	35.57±0.66
Mark Identities	**17.87±0.57**	**35.85±0.68**

Table 2: Comparison of several strategies of SPE. Best results are in bold.

4 Common Experimental Setup

All our systems (including TECTOMT) were trained on the CzEng (Bojar et al., 2012) parallel corpus (development and evaluation subsets were omitted), see Table 1 for statistics. We translated the English side of CzEng with TECTOMT to obtain "synthetic Czech". This way we obtained a new parallel corpus, denoted ^{tmt}(CzEng), with English ↔ synthetic Czech sentences. Analogically, we translated the WMT 2013 test set (newstest2013) with TECTOMT and obtained ^{tmt}(newstest2013). Our baseline SMT system (Moses) trained on CzEng corpus only was then also used for WMT 2013 test set translation, and we obtained ^{smt}(newstest2013). For all MERT tuning, newstest2011 was used.

4.1 Alignment

All our parallel data were aligned with GIZA++ (Och and Ney, 2003) and symmetrized with the "grow-diag-final-and" heuristics. This applies also to the synthetic corpora ^{tmt}(CzEng), ^{tmt}(newstest2013),[3] and ^{smt}(newstest2013).

For the SPE experiments, we decided to base alignment on (genuine and synthetic Czech) lemmas, which could be acquired directly from the TECTOMT output. For the rest of the experiments, we approximated lemmas with just the first four lowercase characters of each (English and Czech) token.

4.2 Language Models

In all our experiments, we used three language models on truecased forms: News Crawl as provided by WMT organizers,[4] the Czech side of CzEng and the Articles section of the Czech Web Corpus (Spoustová and Spousta, 2012).

We used SRILM (Stolcke, 2002) with modified Kneser-Ney smoothing. We trained 5-grams on CzEng; on the other two corpora, we trained 7-grams and pruned them if the (training set) perplexity increased by less than 10^{-14} relative. The domain of the pruned corpora is similar to the test set domain, therefore we trained 7-grams on these corpora. Adding CzEng corpus can then increase the results only very slightly – training 5-grams on CzEng is therefore sufficient and more efficient.

Each of the three LMs got its weight assigned by MERT. Across the experiments, Czech Web Corpus usually gained the largest portion of weights (40±17% of the total weight assigned to language models), WMT News Crawl was the second (32±15%), and CzEng was the least useful (15±7%), perhaps due to its wide domain mixture.

5 SPE Experiments

We trained a base SPE system as described in Section 2.1 and dubbed it PHRASEFIX.

First two rows of Table 2 show that the first-stage TECTOMT system (serving here as the baseline) was significantly improved in terms of BLEU (Papineni et al., 2002) by PHRASEFIX ($p < 0.001$ according to the paired bootstrap test (Koehn, 2004)), but the difference in TER (Snover et al., 2006) is not significant.[5] The preliminary results of WMT 2013 manual evaluation show only a minor improvement: TECTOMT=0.476 vs. PHRASEFIX=0.484 (higher means better, for details on the ranking see Callison-Burch et al. (2012)).

[3] Another possibility was to adapt TECTOMT to output source-to-target word alignment, but GIZA++ was simpler to use also due to different internal tokenization in TECTOMT and our Moses pipeline.

[4] The deep-syntactic LM of TECTOMT was trained only on this News Crawl data – `http://www.statmt.org/wmt13/translation-task.html` (sets 2007–2012).

[5] The BLEU and TER results reported here slightly differ from the results shown at `http://matrix.statmt.org/matrix/systems_list/1720` because of different tokenization and normalization. It seems that statmt.org disables the `--international-tokenization` switch, so e.g. the correct Czech quotes („*word*“) are not tokenized, hence the neighboring tokens are never counted as matching the reference (which is tokenized as " *word* ").

Despite of the improvement, PHRASEFIX's phrase table (synthetic Czech $\leftrightarrow$ genuine Czech) still contains many wrong phrase pairs that worsen the TECTOMT output instead of improving it. They naturally arise in cases where the genuine Czech is a too loose translation (or when the English-Czech sentence pair is simply misaligned in CzEng), and the word alignment between genuine and synthetic Czech struggles.

Apart from removing such garbage phrase pairs, it would also be beneficial to have some control over the SPE. For instance, we would like to generally prefer the original output of TECTOMT except for clear errors, so only reliable phrase pairs should be used. We examine several strategies:

Phrase table filtering. We filter out all phrase pairs with forward probability ≤ 0.7 and all singleton phrase pairs. These thresholds were set based on our early experiments. Similar filtering was used by Dugast et al. (2009).

Marking of reliable phrases. This strategy is similar to the previous one, but the low-frequency phrase pairs are not filtered-out. Instead, a special feature marking these pairs is added. The subsequent MERT of the SPE system selects the best weight for this indicator feature. The frequency and probability thresholds for marking a phrase pair are the same as in the previous case.

Marking of identities A special feature indicating the equality of the source and target phrase in a phrase pair is added. In general, if the output of TECTOMT matched the reference, then such output was probably good and does not need any post-editing. These phrase pairs should be perhaps slightly preferred by the SPE.

As apparent from Table 2, marking either reliable phrases or identities is useful in our SPE setting in terms of BLEU score. In terms of TER measure, marking the identities slightly improves PHRASEFIX. However, none of the improvements is statistically significant.

6 Data Combination Experiments

We now describe experiments with phrase table and corpus combination. In the training step, the source-language monolingual corpus that serves as the basis of the synthetic parallel data can be:

- the source side of the original parallel training corpus (resulting in ^{tmt}(CzEng)),
- a huge source-language monolingual corpus for which no human translations are available (we have not finished this experiment yet),
- the source side of the test set (resulting in ^{tmt}(newstest2013) if translated by TECTOMT or ^{smt}(newstest2013) if translated by baseline configuration of Moses trained on CzEng), or
- a combination of the above.

There is a trade-off in the choice: the source side of the test set is obviously most useful for the given input, but it restricts the applicability (all systems must be installed or available online in the testing time) and speed (we must wait for the slowest system and the combination).

So far, in PTComb we tried adding the full synthetic CzEng ("CzEng + ^{tmt}(CzEng)"), adding the test set ("CzEng + ^{tmt}(newstest2013)" and "CzEng + ^{smt}(newstest2013)"), and adding both ("CzEng + ^{tmt}(CzEng) + ^{tmt}(newstest2013)"). In CComb, we concatenated CzEng and full synthetic CzEng ("CzEng + ^{tmt}(CzEng)").

There are two flavors of PTComb: either the two phrase tables are used both at once as alternative decoding paths ("Alternative"), where each source span is equipped with translation options from any of the tables, or the synthetic Czech phrase table is used only as a back-off method if a source phrase is not available in the primary table ("Back-off"). The back-off model was applied to source phrases of up to 5 tokens.

Table 3 summarizes our results with phrase table and corpus combination. We see that adding synthetic data unrelated to the test set does bring only a small benefit in terms of BLEU in the case of CComb, and we see a small improvement in TER in two cases. Adding the (synthetic) translation of the test set helps. However, adding translated source side of the test set is helpful only if it is translated by the TECTOMT system. If our baseline system is used for this translation, the results even slightly drop.

Somewhat related experiments for pivot languages by Galuščáková and Bojar (2012) showed a significant gain when the outputs of a rule-based system were added to the training data of Moses. In their case however, the genuine parallel corpus was much smaller than the synthetic data. The benefit of unrelated synthetic data seems to vanish with larger parallel data available.

Training Data for Moses	Decoding Type	BLEU	1-TER
baseline: CzEng	—	18.52±0.57	36.41±0.66
^{tmt}(CzEng)	—	15.96±0.53	33.67±0.63
CzEng + ^{tmt}(CzEng)	CComb	18.57±0.57	36.47±0.64
CzEng + ^{tmt}(CzEng)	PTComb Alternative	18.42±0.58	36.47±0.65
CzEng + ^{tmt}(CzEng)	PTComb Back-off	18.38±0.57	36.25±0.65
CzEng + ^{tmt}(newstest2013)	PTComb Alternative	18.68±0.57	37.00±0.65
CzEng + ^{smt}(newstest2013)	PTComb Alternative	18.46±0.54	36.59±0.65
CzEng + ^{tmt}(CzEng) + ^{tmt}(newstest2013)	PTComb Alternative	**18.85±0.58**	**37.03±0.66**

Table 3: Comparison of several strategies used for Synthetic Data Combination (PTComb – phrase table combination and CComb – corpus combination).

	BLEU	Judged better
SPE	17.73±0.54	123
PTComb	**18.68±0.57**	**152**

Table 4: Automatic (BLEU) and manual (number of sentences judged better than the other system) evaluation of SPE vs. PTComb.

7 Discussion

7.1 Comparison of SPE and PTComb

Assuming that our first-stage system, TECTOMT, guarantees the grammaticality of the output (sadly often not quite true), we see SPE and PTComb as two complementary methods that bring in the goods of SMT but risk breaking the grammaticality. Intuitively, SPE feels less risky, because one would hope that the post-edits affect short sequences of words and not e.g. the clause structure. With PTComb, one relies purely on the phrase-based model and its well-known limitations with respect to grammatical constraints.

Table 4 compares the two approaches empirically. For SPE, we use the default PHRASEFIX; for PTComb, we use the option "CzEng + ^{tmt}(newstest2013)". The BLEU scores are repeated.

We ran a small manual evaluation where three annotators judged which of the two outputs was better. The identity of the systems was hidden, but the annotators had access to both the source and the reference translation. Overall, we collected 333 judgments over 120 source sentences. Of the 333 judgments, 17 marked the two systems as equally correct, and 44 marked the systems as incomparably wrong. Across the remaining 275 non-tying comparisons, PTComb won – 152 vs. 123.

We attribute the better performance of PTComb to the fact that, unlike SPE, it has direct access to the source text. Also, the risk of flawed sentence structure in PTComb is probably not too bad, but this can very much depend on the language pair. English→Czech translation does not need much reordering in general.

Based on the analysis of the better marked results of the PTComb system, the biggest problem is the wrong selection of the word and word form, especially for verbs. PTComb also outperforms SPE in processing of frequent phrases and subordinate clauses. This problem could be solved by enhancing fluency in SPE or by incorporating more training data. Another possibility would be to modify TECTOMT system to produce more than one-best translation as the correct word or word form may be preserved in sequel translations.

7.2 Error Analysis of TECTOMT

While SPE seems to perform worse, it has a unique advantage: it can be used as a feedback for improving the first stage system. We can either inspect the filtered SPE phrase table or differences in translated sentences.

After submitting our WMT 2013 systems, this comparison allowed us to spot a systematic error in TECTOMT tagging of latin-origin words:

source	*pancreas*
TECTOMT	*slinivek* [plural]
PHRASEFIX	*slinivky* [singular] *břišní*

The part-of-speech tagger used in TECTOMT incorrectly detects *pancreas* as plural, and the wrong morphological number is used in the synthesis. PHRASEFIX correctly learns that the plural form *slinivek* should be changed to singular *slinivky*, which has also a higher language model score. Moreover, PHRASEFIX also learns that the translation of *pancreas* should be two words (*břišní* means *abdominal*). TECTOMT currently uses a simplifying assumption of 1-to-1 correspondence between content words, so it is not able to produce the correct translation in this case.

Another example shows where PHRASEFIX recovered from a lexical gap in TECTOMT:

source	*people who are strong-willed*
TECTOMT	*lidé , kteří jsou silná willed*
PHRASEFIX	*lidí , kteří mají silnou vůli*

TECTOMT's primary translation model considers *strong-willed* an OOV word, so a back-off dictionary specialized for hyphen compounds is used. However, this dictionary is not able to translate *willed*. PHRASEFIX corrects this and also the verb *jsou = are* (the correct Czech translation is *mají silnou vůli = have a strong will*).

Finally, PHRASEFIX can also break things:

source	*You won't be happy here*
TECTOMT	*Nebudete šťastní tady*
PHRASEFIX	*Vy tady šťastní* [you here happy]

Here, PHRASEFIX damaged the translation by omitting the negative verb *nebudete = you won't*.

8 Conclusion

Statistical post-editing (SPE) and phrase table combination (PTComb) can be seen as two complementary approaches to exploiting the mutual benefits of our deep-transfer system TECTOMT and SMT.

We have shown that SPE improves the results of TECTOMT. Several variations of SPE have been examined, and we have further improved SPE results by marking identical and reliable phrases using a special feature. However, SMT still outperforms SPE according to BLEU and TER measures. Finally, employing PTComb, we have improved the baseline SMT system by utilizing additional data translated by the TECTOMT system. A small manual evaluation suggests that PTComb is on average better than SPE, though in about one third of sentences SPE was judged better. In our future experiments, we plan to improve SPE by applying techniques suited for monolingual alignment, e.g. feature-based aligner considering word similarity (Rosa et al., 2012) or extending the parallel data with vocabulary identities to promote alignment of the same word form (Dugast et al., 2009). Marking and filtering methods for SPE also deserve a deeper study. As for PTComb, we plan to combine several sources of synthetic data (including a huge source-language monolingual corpus).

Acknowledgements

This research is supported by the grants GAUK 9209/2013, FP7-ICT-2011-7-288487 (MosesCore) of the European Union and SVV project number 267 314. We thank the two anonymous reviewers for their comments.

References

Hanna Béchara, Yanjun Ma, and Josef van Genabith. 2011. Statistical post-editing for a statistical MT system. *MT Summit XIII*, pages 308–315.

Ondřej Bojar, Miloš Ercegovčević, Martin Popel, and Omar Zaidan. 2011. A Grain of Salt for the WMT Manual Evaluation. In *Proc. of WMT*, pages 1–11, Edinburgh, Scotland. ACL.

Ondřej Bojar, Zdeněk Žabokrtský, Ondřej Dušek, Petra Galuščáková, Martin Majliš, David Mareček, Jiří Maršík, Michal Novák, Martin Popel, and Aleš Tamchyna. 2012. The Joy of Parallelism with CzEng 1.0. In *Proc. of LREC*, pages 3921–3928, Istanbul, Turkey. ELRA.

Ondřej Bojar, Rudolf Rosa, and Aleš Tamchyna. 2013. Chimera – Three Heads for English-to-Czech Translation. In *Proc. of WMT*.

Chris Callison-Burch, Philipp Koehn, Christof Monz, Matt Post, Radu Soricut, and Lucia Specia. 2012. Findings of the 2012 Workshop on Statistical Machine Translation. In *Proc. of WMT*, Montreal, Canada. ACL.

Yu Chen, Michael Jellinghaus, Andreas Eisele, Yi Zhang, Sabine Hunsicker, Silke Theison, Christian Federmann, and Hans Uszkoreit. 2009. Combining Multi-Engine Translations with Moses. In *Proc. of WMT*, pages 42–46, Athens, Greece. ACL.

Loïc Dugast, Jean Senellart, and Philipp Koehn. 2009. Statistical Post Editing and Dictionary Extraction: Systran/Edinburgh Submissions for ACL-WMT2009. In *Proc. of WMT*, pages 110–114, Athens, Greece. ACL.

Andreas Eisele, Christian Federmann, Hervé Saint-Amand, Michael Jellinghaus, Teresa Herrmann, and Yu Chen. 2008. Using Moses to Integrate Multiple Rule-Based Machine Translation Engines into a Hybrid System. In *Proc. of WMT*, pages 179–182, Columbus, Ohio. ACL.

Petra Galuščáková and Ondřej Bojar. 2012. Improving SMT by Using Parallel Data of a Closely Related Language. In *Proc. of HLT*, pages 58–65, Amsterdam, Netherlands. IOS Press.

Xiaodong He and Kristina Toutanova. 2009. Joint Optimization for Machine Translation System Combination. In *Proc. of EMNLP*, pages 1202–1211, Singapore. ACL.

Philipp Koehn and Josh Schroeder. 2007. Experiments in Domain Adaptation for Statistical Machine Translation. In *Proc. of WMT*, pages 224–227, Prague, Czech Republic. ACL.

Philipp Koehn, Hieu Hoang, Alexandra Birch, Chris Callison-Burch, Marcello Federico, Nicola Bertoldi, Brooke Cowan, Wade Shen, Christine Moran, Richard Zens, Chris Dyer, Ondřej Bojar, Alexandra Constantin, and Evan Herbst. 2007. Moses: Open Source Toolkit for Statistical Machine Translation. In *Proc. of ACL*, pages 177–180, Prague, Czech Republic. ACL.

Philipp Koehn. 2004. Statistical Significance Tests for Machine Translation Evaluation. In *Proc. of EMNLP*, Barcelona, Spain.

David Mareček, Martin Popel, and Zdeněk Žabokrtský. 2010. Maximum entropy translation model in dependency-based MT framework. In *Proc. of MATR*, pages 201–206. ACL.

Evgeny Matusov, Gregor Leusch, Rafael E. Banchs, Nicola Bertoldi, Daniel Dechelotte, Marcello Federico, Muntsin Kolss, Young-Suk Lee, Jose B. Marino, Matthias Paulik, Salim Roukos, Holger Schwenk, and Hermann Ney. 2008. System Combination for Machine Translation of Spoken and Written Language. *IEEE*, 16(7):1222–1237.

Franz Josef Och and Hermann Ney. 2003. A systematic comparison of various statistical alignment models. *Comput. Linguist.*, 29(1):19–51.

Franz Josef Och. 2003. Minimum Error Rate Training in Statistical Machine Translation. In *Proc. of ACL*, Sapporo, Japan.

Kemal Oflazer and Ilknur Durgar El-Kahlout. 2007. Exploring different representational units in English-to-Turkish statistical machine translation. In *Proc. of WMT*, pages 25–32. ACL.

Kishore Papineni, Salim Roukos, Todd Ward, and Wei-Jing Zhu. 2002. BLEU: a method for automatic evaluation of machine translation. In *Proc. of ACL*, pages 311–318, Stroudsburg, PA, USA. ACL.

Rudolf Rosa, Ondřej Dušek, David Mareček, and Martin Popel. 2012. Using Parallel Features in Parsing of Machine-Translated Sentences for Correction of Grammatical Errors. In *Proc. of SSST*, pages 39–48, Jeju, Republic of Korea. ACL.

Rudolf Rosa, David Mareček, and Aleš Tamchyna. 2013. Deepfix: Statistical Post-editing of Statistical Machine Translation Using Deep Syntactic Analysis. Sofia, Bulgaria. ACL.

Antti-Veikko Rosti, Necip Fazil Ayan, Bing Xiang, Spyros Matsoukas, Richard Schwartz, and Bonnie Dorr. 2007. Combining Outputs from Multiple Machine Translation Systems. In *Proc. of NAACL*, pages 228–235, Rochester, New York. ACL.

Michel Simard, Cyril Goutte, and Pierre Isabelle. 2007. Statistical Phrase-Based Post-Editing. In *Proc. of NAACL*, pages 508–515, Rochester, New York. ACL.

Matthew Snover, Bonnie Dorr, Richard Schwartz, Linnea Micciulla, and John Makhoul. 2006. A study of translation edit rate with targeted human annotation. In *Proc. of Association for Machine Translation in the Americas*, pages 223–231.

Johanka Spoustová and Miroslav Spousta. 2012. A High-Quality Web Corpus of Czech. In *Proc. of LREC*, Istanbul, Turkey. ELRA.

Andreas Stolcke. 2002. SRILM – an extensible language modeling toolkit. In *Proc. of ICSLP*, pages 257–286.

Zdeněk Žabokrtský and Martin Popel. 2009. Hidden Markov Tree Model in Dependency-based Machine Translation. In *Proc. of IJCNLP*, pages 145–148, Suntec, Singapore.

Feature-Rich Phrase-based Translation: Stanford University's Submission to the WMT 2013 Translation Task

Spence Green, Daniel Cer, Kevin Reschke, Rob Voigt*, **John Bauer**
Sida Wang, Natalia Silveira†, **Julia Neidert** and **Christopher D. Manning**
Computer Science Department, Stanford University
*Center for East Asian Studies, Stanford University
†Department of Linguistics, Stanford University
{spenceg, cerd, kreschke, robvoigt, horatio, sidaw, natalias, jneid, manning}@stanford.edu

Abstract

We describe the Stanford University NLP Group submission to the 2013 Workshop on Statistical Machine Translation Shared Task. We demonstrate the effectiveness of a new adaptive, online tuning algorithm that scales to large feature and tuning sets. For both English-French and English-German, the algorithm produces feature-rich models that improve over a dense baseline and compare favorably to models tuned with established methods.

1 Introduction

Green et al. (2013b) describe an online, adaptive tuning algorithm for feature-rich translation models. They showed considerable translation quality improvements over MERT (Och, 2003) and PRO (Hopkins and May, 2011) for two languages in a research setting. The purpose of our submission to the 2013 Workshop on Statistical Machine Translation (WMT) Shared Task is to compare the algorithm to more established methods in an evaluation. We submitted English-French (En-Fr) and English-German (En-De) systems, each with over 100k features tuned on 10k sentences. This paper describes the systems and also includes new feature sets and practical extensions to the original algorithm.

2 Translation Model

Our machine translation (MT) system is Phrasal (Cer et al., 2010), a phrase-based system based on alignment templates (Och and Ney, 2004). Like many MT systems, Phrasal models the predictive translation distribution $p(e|f;w)$ directly as

$$p(e|f;w) = \frac{1}{Z(f)} \exp\left[w^\top \phi(e,f)\right] \quad (1)$$

where e is the target sequence, f is the source sequence, w is the vector of model parameters, $\phi(\cdot)$ is a feature map, and $Z(f)$ is an appropriate normalizing constant. For many years the dimension of the feature map $\phi(\cdot)$ has been limited by MERT, which does not scale past tens of features.

Our submission explores real-world translation quality for high-dimensional feature maps and associated weight vectors. That case requires a more scalable tuning algorithm.

2.1 Online, Adaptive Tuning Algorithm

Following Hopkins and May (2011) we cast MT tuning as pairwise ranking. Consider a single source sentence f with associated references $e^{1:k}$. Let d be a derivation in an n-best list of f that has the target $e = e(d)$ and the feature map $\phi(d)$. Define the linear model score $M(d) = w \cdot \phi(d)$. For any derivation d_+ that is better than d_- under a gold metric G, we desire pairwise agreement such that

$$G\left(e(d_+), e^{1:k}\right) > G\left(e(d_-), e^{1:k}\right) \iff M(d_+) > M(d_-)$$

Ensuring pairwise agreement is the same as ensuring $w \cdot [\phi(d_+) - \phi(d_-)] > 0$.

For learning, we need to select derivation pairs (d_+, d_-) to compute difference vectors $x_+ = \phi(d_+) - \phi(d_-)$. Then we have a 1-class separation problem trying to ensure $w \cdot x_+ > 0$. The derivation pairs are sampled with the algorithm of Hopkins and May (2011). Suppose that we sample s pairs for source sentence f_t to compute a set of difference vectors $\mathcal{D}_t = \{x_+^{1:s}\}$. Then we optimize

$$\ell_t(w) = \ell(\mathcal{D}_t, w) = -\sum_{x_+ \in \mathcal{D}_t} \log \frac{1}{1 + e^{-w \cdot x_+}} \quad (2)$$

which is the familiar logistic loss. Hopkins and May (2011) optimize (2) in a batch algorithm that alternates between candidate generation (i.e., n-best list or lattice decoding) and optimization (e.g., L-BFGS). We instead use AdaGrad (Duchi et al., 2011), a variant of stochastic gradient descent (SGD) in which the learning rate is adapted to the data. Informally, AdaGrad scales the weight updates according to the geometry of the data observed in earlier iterations. Consider a particular dimension j of w, and let scalars $v_t = w_{t,j}$, $g_t = \nabla_j \ell_t(w_{t-1})$, and $G_t = \sum_{i=1}^{t} g_i^2$. The AdaGrad update rule is

$$v_t = v_{t-1} - \eta\, G_t^{-1/2} g_t \tag{3}$$

$$G_t = G_{t-1} + g_t^2 \tag{4}$$

In practice, G_t is a diagonal approximation. If $G_t = I$, observe that (3) is vanilla SGD.

In MT systems, the feature map may generate exponentially many irrelevant features, so we need to regularize (3). The L_1 norm of the weight vector is known to be an effective regularizer in such a setting (Ng, 2004). An efficient way to apply L_1 regularization is the Forward-Backward splitting (FOBOS) framework (Duchi and Singer, 2009), which has the following two-step update:

$$w_{t-\frac{1}{2}} = w_{t-1} - \eta_{t-1} \nabla \ell_{t-1}(w_{t-1}) \tag{5}$$

$$w_t = \arg\min_w \frac{1}{2} \|w - w_{t-\frac{1}{2}}\|_2^2 + \eta_{t-1} r(w) \tag{6}$$

where (5) is just an unregularized gradient descent step and (6) balances the regularization term $r(w)$ with staying close to the gradient step.

For L_1 regularization we have $r(w) = \lambda ||w||_1$ and the closed-form solution to (6) is

$$w_t = \text{sign}(w_{t-\frac{1}{2}}) \Big[|w_{t-\frac{1}{2}}| - \eta_{t-1}\lambda \Big]_+ \tag{7}$$

where $[x]_+ = \max(x, 0)$ is the clipping function that in this case sets a weight to 0 when it falls below the threshold $\eta_{t-1}\lambda$.

Online algorithms are inherently sequential; this algorithm is no exception. If we want to scale the algorithm to large tuning sets, then we need to parallelize the weight updates. Green et al. (2013b) describe the parallelization technique that is implemented in Phrasal.

2.2 Extensions to (Green et al., 2013b)

Sentence-Level Metric We previously used the gold metric BLEU+1 (Lin and Och, 2004), which smoothes bigram precisions and above. This metric worked well with multiple references, but we found that it is less effective in a single-reference setting like WMT. To make the metric more robust, Nakov et al. (2012) extended BLEU+1 by smoothing both the unigram precision and the reference length. We found that this extension yielded a consistent +0.2 BLEU improvement at test time for both languages. Subsequent experiments on the data sets of Green et al. (2013b) showed that standard BLEU+1 works best for multiple references.

Custom regularization parameters Green et al. (2013b) showed that large feature-rich models overfit the tuning sets. We discovered that certain features caused greater overfitting than others. Custom regularization strengths for each feature set are one solution to this problem. We found that technique largely fixed the overfitting problem as shown by the learning curves presented in section 5.1.

Convergence criteria Standard MERT implementations approximate tuning BLEU by reranking the previous n-best lists with the updated weight vector. This approximation becomes infeasible for large tuning sets, and is less accurate for algorithms like ours that do not accumulate n-best lists. We approximate tuning BLEU by maintaining the 1-best hypothesis for each tuning segment. At the end of each epoch, we compute corpus-level BLEU from this hypothesis set. We flush the set of stored hypotheses before the next epoch begins. Although memory-efficient, we find that this approximation is less dependable as a convergence criterion than the conventional method. Whereas we previously stopped the algorithm after four iterations, we now select the model according to held-out accuracy.

3 Feature Sets

3.1 Dense Features

The baseline "dense" model has 19 features: the nine Moses (Koehn et al., 2007) baseline features, a hierarchical lexicalized re-ordering model (Galley and Manning, 2008), the (log) bitext count of each translation rule, and an indicator for unique rules.

The final dense feature sets for each language differ slightly. The En-Fr system incorporates a second language model. The En-De system adds a future cost component to the linear distortion model (Green et al., 2010).The future cost estimate allows the distortion limit to be raised without a decrease in translation quality.

3.2 Sparse Features

Sparse features do not necessarily fire on each hypothesis extension. Unlike prior work on sparse MT features, our feature extractors do not filter features based on tuning set counts. We instead rely on the regularizer to select informative features.

Several of the feature extractors depend on source-side part of speech (POS) sequences and dependency parses. We created those annotations with the Stanford CoreNLP pipeline.

Discriminative Phrase Table A lexicalized indicator feature for each rule in a derivation. The feature weights can be interpreted as adjustments to the associated dense phrase table features.

Discriminative Alignments A lexicalized indicator feature for the phrase-internal alignments in each rule in a derivation. For one-to-many, many-to-one, and many-to-many alignments we extract the clique of aligned tokens, perform a lexical sort, and concatenate the tokens to form the feature string.

Discriminative Re-ordering A lexicalized indicator feature for each rule in a derivation that appears in the following orientations: monotone-with-next, monotone-with-previous, non-monotone-with-next, non-monotone-with-previous. Green et al. (2013b) included the richer non-monotone classes swap and discontinuous. However, we found that these classes yielded no significant improvement over the simpler non-monotone classes. The feature weights can be interpreted as adjustments to the generative lexicalized re-ordering model.

Source Content-Word Deletion Count-based features for source content words that are "deleted" in the target. Content words are nouns, adjectives, verbs, and adverbs. A deleted source word is either unaligned or aligned to one of the 100 most frequent target words in the target bitext. For each deleted word we increment both the feature for the particular source POS and an aggregate feature for all parts of speech. We add similar but separate features for head content words that are either unaligned or aligned to frequent target words.

Inverse Document Frequency Numeric features that compare source and target word frequencies. Let idf$(\cdot)$ return the inverse document frequency of a token in the training bitext. Suppose a derivation $d = \{r_1, r_2, \ldots, r_n\}$ is composed of n translation rules, where $e(r)$ is the target side of the rule and $f(r)$ is the source side. For each rule

	Bilingual		Monolingual
	Sentences	*Tokens*	*Tokens*
En-Fr	5.0M	289M	1.51B
En-De	4.4M	223M	1.03B

Table 1: Gross corpus statistics after data selection and pre-processing. The En-Fr monolingual counts include French Gigaword 3 (LDC2011T10).

r that translates j source tokens to i target tokens we compute

$$q = \sum_i \text{idf}(e(r)_i) - \sum_j \text{idf}(f(r)_j) \quad (8)$$

We add two numeric features, one for the source and another for the target. When $q > 0$ we increment the target feature by q; when $q < 0$ we increment the target feature by $|q|$. Together these features penalize asymmetric rules that map rare words to frequent words and vice versa.

POS-based Re-ordering The lexicalized discriminative re-ordering model is very sparse, so we added re-ordering features based on source parts of speech. When a rule is applied in a derivation, we extract the associated source POS sequence along with the POS sequences from the previous and next rules. We add a "with-previous" indicator feature that is the conjunction of the current and previous POS sequences; the "with-next" indicator feature is created analogously. This feature worked well for En-Fr, but not for En-De.

4 Data Preparation

Table 1 describes the pre-processed corpora from which our systems are built.

4.1 Data Selection

We used all of the monolingual and parallel En-De data allowed in the constrained condition. We incorporated all of the French monolingual data, but sampled a 5M-sentence bitext from the approximately 40M available En-Fr parallel sentences. To select the sentences we first created a "target" corpus by concatenating the tuning and test sets (newstest2008–2013). Then we ran the feature decay algorithm (FDA) (Biçici and Yuret, 2011), which samples sentences that most closely resemble the target corpus. FDA is a principled method for reducing the phrase table size by excluding less relevant training examples.

4.2 Tokenization

We tokenized the English (source) data according to the Penn Treebank standard (Marcus et al., 1993) with Stanford CoreNLP. The French data was tokenized with packages from the Stanford French Parser (Green et al., 2013a), which implements a scheme similar to that used in the French Treebank (Abeillé et al., 2003).

German is more complicated due to pervasive compounding. We first tokenized the data with the same English tokenizer. Then we split compounds with the lattice-based model (Dyer, 2009) in cdec (Dyer et al., 2010). To simplify post-processing we added segmentation markers to split tokens, e.g., *überschritt ⇒ über #schritt*.

4.3 Alignment

We aligned both bitexts with the Berkeley Aligner (Liang et al., 2006) configured with standard settings. We symmetrized the alignments according to the grow-diag heuristic.

4.4 Language Modeling

We estimated unfiltered 5-gram language models using lmplz (Heafield et al., 2013) and loaded them with KenLM (Heafield, 2011). For memory efficiency and faster loading we also used KenLM to convert the LMs to a trie-based, binary format. The German LM included all of the monolingual data plus the target side of the En-De bitext. We built an analogous model for French. In addition, we estimated a separate French LM from the Gigaword data.[1]

4.5 French Agreement Correction

In French verbs must agree in number and person with their subjects, and adjectives (and some past participles) must agree in number and gender with the nouns they modify. On their own, phrasal alignment and target side language modeling yield correct agreement inflection most of the time. For verbs, we find that the inflections are often accurate: number is encoded in the English verb and subject, and 3rd person is generally correct in the absence of a 1st or 2nd person pronoun. However, since English does not generally encode gender, adjective inflection must rely on language modeling, which is often insufficient.

To address this problem we apply an automatic inflection correction post-processing step. First, we generate dependency parses of our system's output using BONSAI (Candito and Crabbé, 2009), a French-specific extension to the Berkeley Parser (Petrov et al., 2006). Based on these dependencies, we match adjectives with the nouns they modify and past participles with their subjects. Then we use *Lefff* (Sagot, 2010), a machine-readable French lexicon, to determine the gender and number of the noun and to choose the correct inflection for the adjective or participle.

Applied to our 3,000 sentence development set, this correction scheme produced 200 corrections with perfect accuracy. It produces a slight (−0.014) drop in BLEU score. This arises from cases where the reference translation uses a synonymous but differently gendered noun, and consequently has different adjective inflection.

4.6 German De-compounding

Split German compounds must be merged after translation. This process often requires inserting affixes (e.g., *s*, *en*) between adjacent tokens in the compound. Since the German compounding rules are complex and exception-laden, we rely on a dictionary lookup procedure with backoffs. The dictionary was constructed during pre-processing. To compound the final translations, we first lookup the compound sequence—which is indicated by segmentation markers—in the dictionary. If it is present, then we use the dictionary entry. If the compound is novel, then for each pair of words to be compounded, we insert the suffix most commonly appended in compounds to the first word of the pair. If the first word itself is unknown in our dictionary, we insert the suffix most commonly appended after the last three characters. For example, words ending with *ung* most commonly have an *s* appended when they are used in compounds.

4.7 Recasing

Phrasal includes an LM-based recaser (Lita et al., 2003), which we trained on the target side of the bitext for each language. On the newstest2012 development data, the German recaser was 96.8% accurate and the French recaser was 97.9% accurate.

5 Translation Quality Experiments

During system development we tuned on newstest2008–2011 (10,570 sentences) and tested

[1]The MT system learns significantly different weights for the two LMs: 0.086 for the primary LM and 0.044 for the Gigaword LM.

	#iterations	#features	tune	newstest2012	newstest2013†
Dense	10	20	30.26	31.12	–
Feature-rich	11	207k	32.29	31.51	29.00

Table 2: En-Fr BLEU-4 [% uncased] results. The tuning set is newstest2008–2011. (†) newstest2013 is the cased score computed by the WMT organizers.

	#iterations	#features	tune	newstest2012	newstest2013†
Dense	10	19	16.83	18.45	–
Feature-rich	13	167k	17.66	18.70	18.50

Table 3: En-De BLEU-4 [% uncased] results.

on newstest2012 (3,003 sentences). We compare the feature-rich model to the "dense" baseline.

The En-De system parameters were: 200-best lists, a maximum phrase length of 8, and a distortion limit of 6 with future cost estimation. The En-Fr system parameters were: 200-best lists, a maximum phrase length of 8, and a distortion limit of 5.

The online tuning algorithm used a default learning rate $\eta = 0.03$ and a mini-batch size of 20. We set the regularization strength λ to 10.0 for the discriminative re-ordering model, 0.0 for the dense features, and 0.1 otherwise.

5.1 Results

Tables 2 and 3 show En-Fr and En-De results, respectively. The "Feature-rich" model, which contains the full complement of dense and sparse features, offers a meager improvement over the "Dense" baseline. This result contrasts with the results of Green et al. (2013b), who showed significant translation quality improvements over the same dense baseline for Arabic-English and Chinese-English. However, they had multiple target references, whereas the WMT data sets have just one. We speculate that this difference is significant. For example, consider a translation rule that rewrites to a 4-gram in the reference. This event can increase the sentence-level score, thus encouraging the model to upweight the rule indicator feature.

More evidence of overfitting can be seen in Figure 1, which shows learning curves on the development set for both language pairs. Whereas the dense model converges after just a few iterations, the feature-rich model continues to creep higher. Separate experiments on a held-out set showed that generalization did not improve after about eight iterations.

6 Conclusion

We submitted a feature-rich MT system to WMT 2013. While sparse features did offer a measurable improvement over a baseline dense feature set, the gains were not as significant as those shown by Green et al. (2013b). One important difference between the two sets of results is the number of references. Their NIST tuning and test sets had four references; the WMT data sets have just one. We speculate that sparse features tend to overfit more in this setting. Individual features can greatly influence the sentence-level metric and thus become large components of the gradient. To combat this phenomenon we experimented with custom regularization strengths and a more robust sentence-level metric. While these two improvements greatly reduced the model size relative to (Green et al., 2013b), a generalization problem remained. Nevertheless, we showed that feature-rich models are now competitive with the state-of-the-art.

Acknowledgments This work was supported by the Defense Advanced Research Projects Agency (DARPA) Broad Operational Language Translation (BOLT) program through IBM. Any opinions, findings, and conclusions or recommendations expressed in this material are those of the author(s) and do not necessarily reflect the view of DARPA or the US government.

References

A. Abeillé, L. Clément, and A. Kinyon, 2003. *Building a treebank for French*, chapter 10. Kluwer.

E. Biçici and D. Yuret. 2011. Instance selection for machine translation using feature decay algorithms. In *WMT*.

M. Candito and B. Crabbé. 2009. Improving generative statistical parsing with semi-supervised word clustering. In *IWPT*.

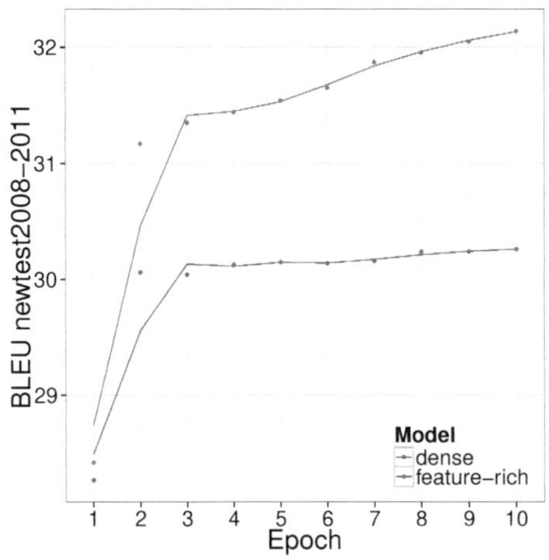

(a) En-Fr tuning

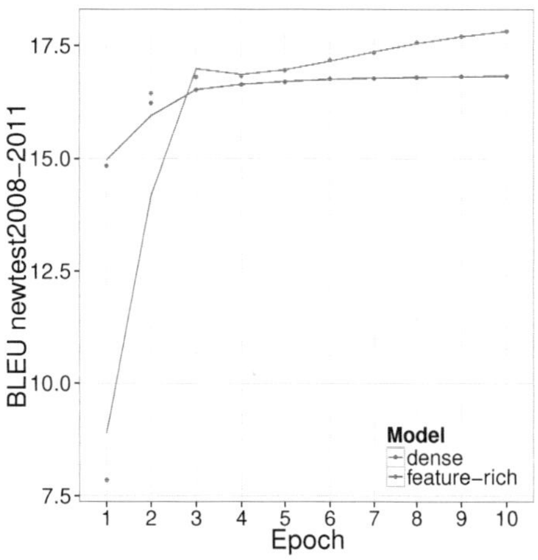

(b) En-De tuning

Figure 1: BLEU-4 [% uncased] Learning curves on newstest2008–2011 with loess trend lines.

D. Cer, M. Galley, D. Jurafsky, and C. D. Manning. 2010. Phrasal: A statistical machine translation toolkit for exploring new model features. In *HLT-NAACL, Demonstration Session*.

J. Duchi and Y. Singer. 2009. Efficient online and batch learning using forward backward splitting. *JMLR*, 10:2899–2934.

J. Duchi, E. Hazan, and Y. Singer. 2011. Adaptive subgradient methods for online learning and stochastic optimization. *JMLR*, 12:2121–2159.

C. Dyer, A. Lopez, J. Ganitkevitch, J. Weese, F. Ture, et al. 2010. `cdec`: A decoder, alignment, and learning framework for finite-state and context-free translation models. In *ACL System Demonstrations*.

C. Dyer. 2009. Using a maximum entropy model to build segmentation lattices for MT. In *NAACL*.

M. Galley and C. D. Manning. 2008. A simple and effective hierarchical phrase reordering model. In *EMNLP*.

S. Green, M. Galley, and C. D. Manning. 2010. Improved models of distortion cost for statistical machine translation. In *HLT-NAACL*.

S. Green, M-C. de Marneffe, and C. D. Manning. 2013a. Parsing models for identifying multiword expressions. *Computational Linguistics*, 39(1):195–227.

S. Green, S. Wang, D. Cer, and C. D. Manning. 2013b. Fast and adaptive online training of feature-rich translation models. In *ACL*.

K. Heafield, I. Pouzyrevsky, J. H. Clark, and P. Koehn. 2013. Scalable modified Kneser-Ney language model estimation. In *ACL, Short Papers*.

K. Heafield. 2011. KenLM: Faster and smaller language model queries. In *WMT*.

M. Hopkins and J. May. 2011. Tuning as ranking. In *EMNLP*.

P. Koehn, H. Hoang, A. Birch, C. Callison-Burch, M. Federico, N. Bertoldi, et al. 2007. Moses: Open source toolkit for statistical machine translation. In *ACL, Demonstration Session*.

P. Liang, B. Taskar, and D. Klein. 2006. Alignment by agreement. In *NAACL*.

C.-Y. Lin and F. J. Och. 2004. ORANGE: a method for evaluating automatic evaluation metrics for machine translation. In *COLING*.

L. V. Lita, A. Ittycheriah, S. Roukos, and N. Kambhatla. 2003. tRuEcasIng. In *ACL*.

M. Marcus, M. A. Marcinkiewicz, and B. Santorini. 1993. Building a large annotated corpus of English: The Penn Treebank. *Computational Linguistics*, 19:313–330.

P. Nakov, F. Guzman, and S. Vogel. 2012. Optimizing for sentence-level BLEU+1 yields short translations. In *COLING*.

A. Y. Ng. 2004. Feature selection, L_1 vs. L_2 regularization, and rotational invariance. In *ICML*.

F. J. Och and H. Ney. 2004. The alignment template approach to statistical machine translation. *Computational Linguistics*, 30(4):417–449.

F. J. Och. 2003. Minimum error rate training for statistical machine translation. In *ACL*.

S. Petrov, L. Barrett, R. Thibaux, and D. Klein. 2006. Learning accurate, compact, and interpretable tree annotation. In *ACL*.

B. Sagot. 2010. The Lefff, a freely available and large-coverage morphological and syntactic lexicon for French. In *LREC*.

Factored Machine Translation Systems for Russian-English

Stéphane Huet, Elena Manishina and Fabrice Lefèvre
Université d'Avignon, LIA/CERI, France
FirstName.LastName@univ-avignon.fr

Abstract

We describe the LIA machine translation systems for the Russian-English and English-Russian translation tasks. Various factored translation systems were built using MOSES to take into account the morphological complexity of Russian and we experimented with the romanization of untranslated Russian words.

1 Introduction

This paper presents the factored phrase-based Machine Translation (MT) systems (Koehn and Hoang, 2007) developed at LIA, for the Russian-English and English-Russian translation tasks at WMT'13. These systems use only data provided for the evaluation campaign along with the LDC English Gigaword corpus.

We summarize in Section 2 the resources used and the main characteristics of the systems based on the MOSES toolkit (Koehn et al., 2007). Section 3 reports experiments on the use of factored translation models. Section 4 describes the transliteration process used to improve the Russian to English task. Finally, we conclude in Section 5.

2 System Architecture

2.1 Pre-processing

The corpora available for the workshop were preprocessed using an in-house script that normalizes quotes, dashes, spaces and ligatures. Long sentences or sentences with many numeric or non-alphanumeric characters were also discarded. Since the Yandex corpus is provided as lowercased, we decided to lowercase all the other corpora. The same pipeline was applied to the LDC Gigaword; also only the documents classified as "story" were retained. Table 1 summarizes the used data and introduces designations that we follow in the remainder of this paper to refer to these corpora.

Russian is a morphologically rich language with nouns, adjectives and verbs inflected for case, number and gender. This property requires introducing morphological information inside the MT system to handle the lack of many inflectional forms inside training corpora. For this purpose, each corpus was previously tagged with Part-of-Speech (PoS) tags. The tagger TREETAGGER (Schmid, 1995) was selected for its good performance on several comparable tasks. The Russian tagger associates each word (e.g. ящика (*boxes*)) with a complex PoS including morphological information (e.g. "Ncmpnn" for "Noun Type=common Gender=masculine Number=plural Case=nominative Animate=no") and its lemma (e.g. ящик (*box*)). A description of the Russian tagset can be found in (Sharoff et al., 2008). The English tagger provides also a lemmatization and outputs PoS from the Penn Treebank tagset (Marcus et al., 1993) (e.g. "NNS" for "Noun plural").

In order to simplify the comparison of different setups, we used the tokenizer included in the TREETAGGER tool to process all the corpora.

2.2 Language Models

Kneser-Ney discounted LMs were built from monolingual corpora using the SRILM toolkit (Stolcke, 2002). 5-gram LMs were trained for words, 7-gram LMs for lemmas and PoS. A LM was built separately on each monolingual corpus: *mono-news-c* and *news-s*. Since *ldc* was too large to be processed as one file, it was split into three parts according to the original publication year of the document. These LMs were combined through linear interpolation. Weights were fixed by optimizing the perplexity on a corpus made of the WMT test sets from 2008 to 2011 for English and on the WMT 2012 test set for Russian (the

CORPORA	DESIGNATION	SIZE (SENTENCES)
English-Russian Bilingual training		
News Commentary v8	*news-c*	146 k
Common Crawl	*crawl*	755 k
Yandex	*yandex*	978 k
English Monolingual training		
News Commentary v8	*mono-news-c*	247 k
Shuffled News Crawl corpus (from 2007 to 2012)	*news-s*	68 M
LDC Gigaword	*ldc*	190 M
Russian Monolingual training		
News Commentary v8	*mono-news-c*	182 k
Shuffled News Crawl corpus (from 2008 to 2012)	*news-s*	20 M
Development		
newstest2012	*test12*	3,003

Table 1: Used bilingual and monolingual corpora

only available at that time).

2.3 Alignment and Translation Models

All parallel corpora were aligned using MGIZA++ (Gao and Vogel, 2008). Our translation models are phrase-based models (PBMs) built with MOSES using default settings. Weights of LM, phrase table and lexicalized reordering model scores were optimized on *test12*, thanks to the MERT algorithm (Gao and Vogel, 2008). Since only one development corpus was made available for Russian, we used a 3-fold cross-validation so that MERT is repeated three times for each translation model on a 2,000-sentence subsample of *test12*.

To recase the corpora, translation models were trained using a word-to-word translation model trained on the parallel corpora aligning lowercased and cased sentences of the monolingual corpora *mono-news-c* and *news-s*.

3 Experiments with Factored Translation Models

The evaluation was performed using case-insensitive BLEU and was computed with the `mteval-v13a.pl` script provided by NIST. The BLEU scores shown in the tables below are all averaged on the test parts obtained from the 3-fold cross validation process.

In the remainder of the paper, we employ the notation proposed by Bojar et al. (2012) to refer to factored translation models. For example, tW-W:tL-L+tP-P+gLaP-W, where "t" and "g" stand for "translation" and "generation", denotes a translation system with two decoding paths:

- a first one directly translates words to words (tW-W),
- a second one is divided into three steps:
  1. translation from lemmas to lemmas (tL-L),
  2. translation from PoS to PoS (tP-P) and
  3. generation of target words from target lemmas and PoS (gLaP-W).

3.1 Baseline Phrase-Based Systems

Table 2 is populated with the results of PBMs which use words as their sole factor. When LMs are built on *mono-news-c* and *news-s*, an improvement of BLEU is observed each time a training parallel corpus is used, both for both translation directions (columns 1 and 3). We can also notice an absolute increase of 0.4 BLEU score when the English LM is additionally trained on *ldc* (column 2).

3.2 Decomposition of factors

Koehn and Hoang (2007) suggested from their experiments for English-Czech systems that "it is beneficial to carefully consider which morphological information to be used." We therefore tested various decompositions of the complex Russian PoS tagset (P) output by TREETAGGER. We considered the grammatical category alone (C), morphological information restrained to case, number

	EN → RU	+LDC	RU → EN
news-c	26.52	26.82	19.89
+crawl	29.49	29.82	21.06
+yandex	31.08	**31.49**	**22.16**

Table 2: BLEU scores measured with standard PBMs.

Tagset	#tags	Examples
C	17	Af, Vm, P, C
M1	95	fsg, -s-, fsa, —
M2	380	fsg, -s-, fsa, что (*that*)
M3	580	fsg, -s-1ife, fsa3, что (*that*)
P	604	Afpfsg, Vmif1s-a-e, P-3fsa, C

Table 3: Statistics on Russian tagsets.

and gender (M1), the fields included in M1 along with additional information (lemmas) for conjunctions, particles and adpositions (M2), and finally the information included in M2 enriched with person for pronouns and person, tense and aspect for verbs (M3). Table 3 provides the number of tags and shows examples for each used tagset.

To speed up the training of translation models, we experimented with various setups for factor decomposition from *news-c*. The results displayed on Table 4 show that factors with morphological information lead to better results than a PBM trained on word forms (line 1) but that finally the best system is achieved when the complex PoS tag output by TREETAGGER is used without any decomposition (last line).

tW-W	19.89
tW-WaC	19.81
tW-WaM1	20.04
tW-WaCaM1	19.95
tW-WaM2	19.92
tW-WaCaM2	19.91
tW-WaM3	19.98
tW-WaCaM3	19.89
tW-WaP	**20.30**

Table 4: BLEU scores for EN→RU using *news-c* as training parallel corpus.

tL-W	29.23
tW-W	31.49
tWaP-WaP	31.62
tW-W:tL-W	31.69
tW-WaP	31.80
tW-WaP:tL-WaP	**31.89**

Table 5: BLEU scores for RU→EN using the three available parallel corpora.

3.3 Experimental Results for Factored Models

The many inflections for Russian induce a hight out-of-vocabulary rate for the PBMs, which generates many untranslated Russian words for Russian to English. We experimented with the training of a PMB on lemmatized Russian corpora (Table 5, line 1) but observed a decrease in BLEU score w.r.t. a PBM trained on words (line 2). With two decoding paths — one from words, one from lemmas (line 4) — using the MOSES ability to manage multiple decoding paths for factored translation models, an absolute improvement of 0.2 BLEU score was observed.

Another interest of factored models is disambiguating translated words according to their PoS. Translating a (word, PoS) pair results in an absolute increase of 0.3 BLEU (line 5), and of 0.4 BLEU when considering two decoding paths (last line). Disambiguating source words with PoS did not seem to help the translation process (line 3).

The Russian inflections are far more problematic in the other translation direction since morphological information, including case, gender and number, has to be induced from the English words and PoS, which are restrained for that language to the grammatical category and knowledge about number (singular/plural for nouns, 3rd person singular or not for verbs). Disambiguating translated Russian words with their PoS resulted in a dramatic increase of BLEU by 1.6 points (Table 6, last line vs line 3). The model that translates independently PoS and lemmas, before generating words, albeit appealing for its potential to deal with data sparsity, turned out to be very disappointing (first line). We additionally led experiments training generation models gLaP-W on monolingual corpora instead of the less voluminous parallel corpora, but we did not observed a gain in terms of BLEU.

tL-L+tP-P+gLaP-W	17.06
tW-W	22.16
tWaP-WaP	23.34
tWaP-LaP+gLaP-W	23.48
tW-LaP+gLaP-W	23.58
tW-WaP	**23.72**

Table 6: BLEU scores for EN→RU using the three available parallel corpora.

	BEFORE	AFTER
tW-WaP	31.80	32.15
tW-WaP:tL-WaP	31.89	**32.21**

Table 7: BLEU scores for RU → EN before and after transliteration.

4 Transliteration

Words written in Cyrillic inside the English translation output were transliterated into Latin letters. We decided to restrain the use of transliteration for the English to Russian direction since we found that many words, especially proper names, are intentionally used in Latin letters in the Russian reference.

Transliteration was performed in two steps. Firstly, untranslated words in Cyrillic are looked up in the *guessed-names.ru-en* file provided for the workshop and built from Wikipedia. Secondly, the remaining words are romanized with rules of the BGN/PCGN romanization method for Russian (on Geographic Names, 1994). Transliterating words in Cyrillic resulted in an absolute improvement of 0.3 BLEU for our two best factor-based system (Table 7, last column).

The factored model with the tW-WaP:tL-WaP translation path and a transliteration post-processing step is the final submission for the Russian-English workshop translation task, while the tW-WaP is the final submission for the other translation direction.

5 Conclusion

This paper presented experiments carried out with factored phrase-based translation models for the two-way Russian-English translation tasks. A minor gain was observed after romanizing Russian words (+0.3 BLEU points for RU → EN) and higher improvements using word forms, PoS integrating morphological information and lemma as factors (+0.4 BLEU points for RU → EN and +1.6 for EN → RU w.r.t. to a phrase-based restrained to word forms). However, these improvements were observed with setups which disambiguate words according to their grammatical category or morphology, while results integrating a generation step and dealing with data sparsity were disappointing. It seems that further work should be done to fully exploit the potential of this option inside MOSES.

References

Ondřej Bojar, Bushra Jawaid, and Amir Kamran. 2012. Probes in a taxonomy of factored phrase-based models. In *7th NAACL Workshop on Statistical Machine Translation (WMT)*, pages 253–260.

Qin Gao and Stephan Vogel. 2008. Parallel implementations of word alignment tool. In *Proceedings of the ACL Workshop: Software Engineering, Testing, and Quality Assurance for Natural Language Processing*, pages 49–57.

Philipp Koehn and Hieu Hoang. 2007. Factored translation models. In *Joint Conference on Empirical Methods in Natural Language Processing and Computational Natural Language Learning (EMNLP-CoNLL)*, pages 868—-876.

Philipp Koehn, Hieu Hoang, Alexandra Birch, Chris Callison-Burch, Marcello Federico, Nicola Bertoldi, Brooke Cowan, Wade Shen, Christine Moran, Richard Zens, Chris Dyer, Ondrej Bojar, Alexandra Constantin, and Evan Herbst. 2007. Moses: Open source toolkit for statistical machine translation. In *45th Annual Meeting of the Association for Computational Linguistics (ACL), Companion Volume*, pages 177–180.

Mitchell P. Marcus, Beatrice Santorini, and Mary Ann Marcinkiewicz. 1993. Building a large annotated corpus of English: The Penn Treebank. *Computational Linguistics*, 2:313–330.

U.S. Board on Geographic Names. 1994. Romanization systems and roman-script spelling conventions. Technical report, Defense Mapping Agency.

Helmut Schmid. 1995. Improvements in part-of-speech tagging with an application to german. In *ACL SIGDAT Workshop*, pages 47–50.

Serge Sharoff, Mikhail Kopotev, Tomaž Erjavec, Anna Feldman, and Dagmar Divjak. 2008. Designing and evaluating a russian tagset. In *6th International Conference on Language Resources and Evaluation (LREC)*, pages 279–285.

Andreas Stolcke. 2002. SRILM — an extensible language modeling toolkit. In *7th International Conference on Spoken Language Processing (ICSLP)*.

Omnifluent™ English-to-French and Russian-to-English Systems for the 2013 Workshop on Statistical Machine Translation

Evgeny Matusov, Gregor Leusch
Science Applications International Corporation (SAIC)
7990 Science Applications Ct.
Vienna, VA, USA
{evgeny.matusov,gregor.leusch}@saic.com

Abstract

This paper describes Omnifluent™ Translate – a state-of-the-art hybrid MT system capable of high-quality, high-speed translations of text and speech. The system participated in the English-to-French and Russian-to-English WMT evaluation tasks with competitive results. The features which contributed the most to high translation quality were training data sub-sampling methods, document-specific models, as well as rule-based morphological normalization for Russian. The latter improved the baseline Russian-to-English BLEU score from 30.1 to 31.3% on a held-out test set.

1 Introduction

Omnifluent Translate is a comprehensive multilingual translation platform developed at SAIC that automatically translates both text and audio content. SAIC's technology leverages hybrid machine translation, combining features of both rule-based machine and statistical machine translation for improved consistency, fluency, and accuracy of translation output.

In the WMT 2013 evaluation campaign, we trained and tested the Omnifluent system on the English-to-French and Russian-to-English tasks. We chose the En–Fr task because Omnifluent En–Fr systems are already extensively used by SAIC's commercial customers: large human translation service providers, as well as a leading fashion designer company (Matusov, 2012). Our Russian-to-English system also produces high-quality translations and is currently used by a US federal government customer of SAIC.

Our experimental efforts focused mainly on the effective use of the provided parallel and monolingual data, document-level models, as well using rules to cope with the morphological complexity of the Russian language. While striving for the best possible translation quality, our goal was to avoid those steps in the translation pipeline which would make a real-time use of the Omnifluent system impossible. For example, we did not integrate re-scoring of N-best lists with huge computationally expensive models, nor did we perform system combination of different system variants. This allowed us to create a MT system that produced our primary evaluation submission with the translation speed of 18 words per second[1]. This submission had a BLEU score of 24.2% on the Russian-to-English task[2], and 27.3% on the English-to-French task. In contrast to many other submissions from university research groups, our evaluation system can be turned into a fully functional, commercially deployable on-line system with the same high level of translation quality and speed within a single work day.

The rest of the paper is organized as follows. In the next section, we describe the core capabilities of the Omnifluent Translate systems. Section 3 explains our data selection and filtering strategy. In Section 4 we present the document-level translation and language models. Section 5 describes morphological transformations of Russian. In sections 6 we present an extension to the system that allows for automatic spelling correction. In Section 7, we discuss the experiments and their evaluation. Finally, we conclude the paper in Section 8.

2 Core System Capabilities

The Omnifluent system is a state-of-the-art hybrid MT system that originates from the AppTek technology acquired by SAIC (Matusov and Köprü, 2010a). The core of the system is a statistical search that employs a combination of multiple

[1]Using a single core of a 2.8 GHz Intel Xeon CPU.
[2]The highest score obtained in the evaluation was 25.9%

probabilistic translation models, including phrase-based and word-based lexicons, as well as reordering models and target n-gram language models. The retrieval of matching phrase pairs given an input sentence is done efficiently using an algorithm based on the work of (Zens, 2008). The main search algorithm is the source cardinality-synchronous search. The goal of the search is to find the most probable segmentation of the source sentence into non-empty non-overlapping contiguous blocks, select the most probable permutation of those blocks, and choose the best phrasal translations for each of the blocks at the same time. The concatenation of the translations of the permuted blocks yields a translation of the whole sentence. In practice, the permutations are limited to allow for a maximum of M "gaps" (contiguous regions of uncovered word positions) at any time during the translation process. We set M to 2 for the English-to-French translation to model the most frequent type of reordering which is the reordering of an adjective-noun group. The value of M for the Russian-to-English translation is 3.

The main differences of Omnifluent Translate as compared to the open-source MT system Moses (Koehn et al., 2007) is a reordering model that penalizes each deviation from monotonic translation instead of assigning costs proportional to the jump distance (4 features as described by Matusov and Köprü (2010b)) and a lexicalization of this model when such deviations depend on words or part-of-speech (POS) tags of the last covered and current word (2 features, see (Matusov and Köprü, 2010a)). Also, the whole input document is always visible to the system, which allows the use of document-specific translation and language models. In translation, multiple phrase tables can be interpolated linearly on the count level, as the phrasal probabilities are computed on-the-fly. Finally, various novel phrase-level features have been implemented, including binary topic/genre/phrase type indicators and translation memory match features (Matusov, 2012).

The Omnifluent system also allows for partial or full rule-based translations. Specific source language entities can be identified prior to the search, and rule-based translations of these entities can be either forced to be chosen by the MT system, or can compete with phrase translation candidates from the phrase translation model. In both cases, the language model context at the boundaries of the rule-based translations is taken into account. Omnifluent Translate identifies numbers, dates, URLs, e-mail addresses, smileys, etc. with manually crafted regular expressions and uses rules to convert them to the appropriate target language form. In addition, it is possible to add manual translation rules to the statistical phrase table of the system.

3 Training Data Selection and Filtering

We participated in the constrained data track of the evaluation in order to obtain results which are comparable to the majority of the other submissions. This means that we trained our systems only on the provided parallel and monolingual data.

3.1 TrueCasing

Instead of using a separate truecasing module, we apply an algorithm for finding the true case of the first word of each sentence in the target training data and train truecased phrase tables and a truecased language model[3]. Thus, the MT search decides on the right case of a word when ambiguities exist. Also, the Omnifluent Translate system has an optional feature to transfer the case of an input source word to the word in the translation output to which it is aligned. Although this approach is not always error-free, there is an advantage to it when the input contains previously unseen named entities which use common words that have to be capitalized. We used this feature for our English-to-French submission only.

3.2 Monolingual Data

For the French language model, we trained separate 5-gram models on the two GigaWord corpora AFP and APW, on the provided StatMT data for 2007–2012 (3 models), on the EuroParl data, and on the French side of the bilingual data. LMs were estimated and pruned using the IRSTLM toolkit (Federico et al., 2008). We then tuned a linear combination of these seven individual parts to optimum perplexity on WMT test sets 2009 and 2010 and converted them for use with the KenLM library (Heafield, 2011). Similarly, our English LM was a linear combination of separate LMs built for GigaWord AFP, APW, NYT, and the other parts, StatMT 2007–2012, Europarl/News Commentary, and the Yandex data, which was tuned for best perplexity on the WMT 2010-2013 test sets.

[3]Source sentences were lowercased.

3.3 Parallel Data

Since the provided parallel corpora had different levels of noise and quality of sentence alignment, we followed a two-step procedure for filtering the data. First, we trained a baseline system on the "good-quality" data (Europarl and News Commentary corpora) and used it to translate the French side of the Common Crawl data into English. Then, we computed the position-independent word error rate (PER) between the automatic translation and the target side on the segment level and only kept those original segment pairs, the PER for which was between 10% and 60%. With this criterion, we kept 48% of the original 3.2M sentence pairs of the common-crawl data.

To leverage the significantly larger Multi-UN parallel corpus, we performed perplexity-based data sub-sampling, similarly to the method described e. g. by Axelrod et al. (2011). First, we trained a relatively small 4-gram LM on the source (English) side of our development data and evaluation data. Then, we used this model to compute the perplexity of each Multi-UN source segment. We kept the 700K segments with the lowest perplexity (normalized by the segment length), so that the size of the Multi-UN corpus does not exceed 30% of the total parallel corpus size. This procedure is the only part of the translation pipeline for which we currently do not have a real-time solution. Yet such a real-time algorithm can be implemented without problems: we word-align the original corpora using GIZA++ahead of time, so that after sub-sampling we only need to perform a quick phrase extraction. To obtain additional data for the document-level models only (see Section 4), we also applied this procedure to the even larger Gigaword corpus and thus selected 1M sentence pairs from this corpus.

We used the PER-based procedure as described above to filter the Russian-English Common-crawl corpus to 47% of its original size. The baseline system used to obtain automatic translation for the PER-based filtering was trained on News Commentary, Yandex, and Wiki headlines data.

4 Document-level Models

As mentioned in the introduction, the Omnifluent system loads a whole source document at once. Thus, it is possible to leverage document context by using document-level models which score the phrasal translations of sentences from a specific document only and are unloaded after processing of this document.

To train a document-level model for a specific document from the development, test, or evaluation data, we automatically extract those source sentences from the background parallel training data which have (many) n-grams (n=2...7) in common with the source sentences of the document. Then, to train the document-level LM we take the target language counterparts of the extracted sentences and train a standard 3-gram LM on them. To train the document-level phrase table, we take the corresponding word alignments for the extracted source sentences and their target counterparts, and extract the phrase table as usual. To keep the additional computational overhead minimal yet have enough data for model estimation, we set the parameters of the n-gram matching in such a way that the number of sentences extracted for document-level training is around 20K for document-level phrase tables and 100K for document-level LMs.

In the search, the counts from the document-level phrase table are linearly combined with the counts from the background phrase table trained on the whole training data. The document-level LM is combined log-linearly with the general LM and all the other models and features. The scaling factors for the document-level LMs and phrase tables are not document-specific; neither is the linear interpolation factor for a document-level phrase table which we tuned manually on a development set. The scaling factor for the document-level LM was optimized together with the other scaling factors using Minimum Error Rate Training (MERT, see (Och, 2003)).

For English-to-French translation, we used both document-level phrase tables and document-level LMs; the background data for them contained the sub-sampled Gigaword corpus (see Section 3.3). We used only the document-level LMs for the Russian-to-English translation. They were extracted from the same data that was used to train the background phrase table.

5 Morphological Transformations of Russian

Russian is a morphologically rich language. Even for large vocabulary MT systems this leads to data sparseness and high out-of-vocabulary rate. To mitigate this problem, we developed rules for reducing the morphological complexity of the language, making it closer to English in terms of the used word forms. Another goal was to ease the translation of some morphological and syntactic phenomena in Russian by simplifying them; this included adding artificial function words.

We used the *pymorphy* morphological analyzer[4] to analyze Russian words in the input text. The output of *pymorphy* is one or more alternative analyses for each word, each of which includes the POS tag plus morphological categories such as gender, tense, etc. The analyses are generated based on a manual dictionary, do not depend on the context, and are not ordered by probability of any kind. However, to make some functional modifications to the input sentences, we applied the tool not to the vocabulary, but to the actual input text; thus, in some cases, we introduced a context dependency. To deterministically select one of the *pymorphy*'s analyses, we defined a POS priority list. Nouns had a higher priority than adjectives, and adjectives higher priority than verbs. Otherwise we relied on the first analysis for each POS.

The main idea behind our hand-crafted rules was to normalize any ending/suffix which does not carry information necessary for correct translation into English. Under normalization we mean the restoration of some "base" form. The *pymorphy* analyzer API provides inflection functions so that each word could be changed into a particular form (case, tense, etc.). We came up with the following normalization rules:

- convert all adjectives and participles to first-person masculine singular, nominative case;
- convert all nouns to the nominative case keeping the plural/singular distinction;
- for nouns in genitive case, add the artificial function word "of_" after the last noun before the current one, if the last noun is not more than 4 positions away;
- for each verb infinitive, add the artificial function word "to_" in front of it;
- convert all present-tense verbs to their infinitive form;
- convert all past-tense verbs to their past-tense first-person masculine singular form;
- convert all future-tense verbs to the artificial function word "will_" + the infinitive;
- For verbs ending with reflexive suffixes ся/сь, add the artificial function word "sya_" in front of the verb and remove the suffix. This is done to model the reflexion (e.g. "он умывался"– "он sya_ умывал" – "he washed himself", here "sya_" coresonds to "himself"), as well as, in other cases, the passive mood (e.g. "он вставляется" – "он sya_ вставлять"– "it is inserted").

An example that is characteristic of all these modifications is given in Figure 1.

It is worth noting that not all of these transformations are error-free because the analysis is also not always error-free. Also, sometimes there is information loss (as in case of the instrumental noun case, for example, which we currently drop instead of finding the right artificial preposition to express it). Nevertheless, our experiments show that this is a successful morphological normalization strategy for a statistical MT system.

6 Automatic Spelling Correction

Machine translation input texts, even if prepared for evaluations such as WMT, still contain spelling errors, which lead to serious translation errors. We extended the Omnifluent system by a spelling correction module based on Hunspell[5] – an open-source spelling correction software and dictionaries. For each input word that is unknown *both* to the Omnifluent MT system and to Hunspell, we add those Hunspell's spelling correction suggestions to the input which are in the vocabulary of the MT system. They are encoded in a lattice and assigned weights. The weight of a suggestion is inversely proportional to its rank in the Hunspell's list (the first suggestions are considered to be more probable) and proportional to the unigram probability of the word(s) in the suggestion. To avoid errors related to unknown names, we do not apply spelling correction to words which begin with an uppercase letter.

The lattice is translated by the decoder using the method described in (Matusov et al., 2008); the globally optimal suggestion is selected in the translation process. On the English-to-French task, 77 out of 3000 evaluation data sentences were translated differently because of automatic spelling correction. The BLEU score on these sentences improved from 22.4 to 22.6%. Manual analysis of the results shows that in around

[4] https://bitbucket.org/kmike/pymorphy

[5] http://hunspell.sourceforge.net

source	Обед проводился в отеле Вашингтон спустя несколько часов после совещания суда по делу
prep	Обед sya_ проводил в отель Вашингтон спустя несколько часы после совещание of_ суд по дело
ref	The dinner was held at a Washington hotel a few hours after the conference of the court over the case

Figure 1: Example of the proposed morphological normalization rules and insertion of artificial function words for Russian.

System	BLEU [%]	PER [%]
baseline	31.3	41.1
+ extended features	31.7	41.0
+ alignment combination	32.1	40.6
+ doc-level models	32.7	39.3
+ common-crawl/UN data	33.0	39.9

Table 1: English-to-French translation results (newstest-2012-part2 progress test set).

System	BLEU [%]	PER [%]
baseline (full forms)	30.1	38.9
morph. reduction	31.3	38.1
+ extended features	32.4	37.3
+ doc-level LMs	32.3	37.4
+ common-crawl data	32.9	37.1

Table 2: Russian-to-English translation results (newstest-2012-part2 progress test set).

70% of the cases the MT system picks the right or almost right correction. We applied automatic spelling correction also to the Russian-to-English evaluation submissions. Here, the spelling correction was applied to words which remained out-of-vocabulary after applying the morphological normalization rules.

7 Experiments

7.1 Development Data and Evaluation Criteria

For our experiments, we divided the 3000-sentence newstest-2012 test set from the WMT 2012 evaluation in two roughly equal parts, respecting document boundaries. The first part we used as a tuning set for N-best list MERT optimization (Och, 2003). We used the second part as a test set to measure progress; the results on it are reported below. We computed case-insensitive BLEU score (Papineni et al., 2002) for optimization and evaluation. Only one reference translation was available.

7.2 English-to-French System

The baseline system for the English-to-French translation direction was trained on Europarl and News Commentary corpora. The word alignment was obtained by training HMM and IBM Model 3 alignment models and combining their two directions using the "grow-diag-final" heuristic (Koehn, 2004). The first line in Table 1 shows the result for this system when we only use the standard features (phrase translation and word lexicon costs in both directions, the base reordering features as described in (Matusov and Köprü, 2010b) and the 5-gram target LM). When we also optimize the scaling factors for extended features, including the word-based and POS-based lexicalized reordering models described in (Matusov and Köprü, 2010a), we improve the BLEU score by 0.4% absolute. Extracting phrase pairs from three different, equally weighted alignment heuristics improves the score by another 0.3%. The next big improvement comes from using document-level language models and phrase tables, which include Gigaword data. Especially the PER decreases significantly, which indicates that the document-level models help, in most cases, to select the right word translations. Another significant improvement comes from adding parts of the Common-crawl and Multi-UN data, sub-sampled with the perplexity-based method as described in Section 3.3. The settings corresponding to the last line of Table 1 were used to produce the Omnifluent primary submission, which resulted in a BLEU score of 27.3 on the WMT 2013 test set.

After the deadline for submission, we discovered a bug in the extraction of the phrase table which had reduced the positive impact of the extended phrase-level features. We re-ran the optimization on our tuning set and obtained a BLEU score of 27.7% on the WMT 2013 evaluation set.

7.3 Russian-to-English System

The first experiment with the Russian-to-English system was to show the positive effect of the morphological transformations described in Section 5. Table 2 shows the result of the baseline system, trained using full forms of the Russian words on the News Commentary, truecased Yandex and Wiki Headlines data. When applying the morphological transformations described in Section 5 both in training and translation, we obtain a significant improvement in BLEU of 1.3% absolute. The out-of-vocabulary rate was reduced from 0.9 to 0.5%. This shows that the morphological reduction actually helps to alleviate the data sparseness problem and translate structurally complex constructs in Russian.

Significant improvements are obtained for Ru–En through the use of extended features, including the lexicalized and "POS"-based reordering models. As the "POS" tags for the Russian words we used the *pymorphy* POS tag selected deterministically based on our priority list, together with the codes for additional morphological features such as tense, case, and gender. In contrast to the En–Fr task, document-level models did not help here, most probably because we used only LMs and only trained on sub-sampled data that was already part of the background phrase table. The last boost in translation quality was obtained by adding those segments of the cleaned Common-crawl data to the phrase table training which are similar to the development and evaluation data in terms of LM perplexity. The BLEU score in the last line of Table 2 corresponds to Omnifluent's BLEU score of 24.2% on the WMT 2013 evaluation data. This is only 1.7% less than the score of the best BLEU-ranked system in the evaluation.

8 Summary and Future Work

In this paper we described the Omnifluent hybrid MT system and its use for the English-to-French and Russian-to-English WMT tasks. We showed that it is important for good translation quality to perform careful data filtering and selection, as well as use document-specific phrase tables and LMs. We also proposed and evaluated rule-based morphological normalizations for Russian. They significantly improved the Russian-to-English translation quality. In contrast to some evaluation participants, the presented high-quality system is fast and can be quickly turned into a real-time system. In the future, we intend to improve the rule-based component of the system, allowing users to add and delete translation rules on-the-fly.

References

Amittai Axelrod, Xiaodong He, and Jianfeng Gao. 2011. Domain Adaptation via Pseudo In-Domain Data Selection. In *International Conference on Emperical Methods in Natural Language Processing*, Edinburgh, UK, July.

Marcello Federico, Nicola Bertoldi, and Mauro Cettolo. 2008. IRSTLM: an open source toolkit for handling large scale language models. In *Proceedings of Interspeech*, pages 1618–1621.

Kenneth Heafield. 2011. KenLM: faster and smaller language model queries. In *Proceedings of the Sixth Workshop on Statistical Machine Translation*, pages 187–197, Edinburgh, Scotland, United Kingdom, July.

Philipp Koehn, Hieu Hoang, Alexandra Birch, Chris Callison-Burch, Marcello Federico, Nicola Bertoldi, Brooke Cowan, Wade Shen, Christine Moran, Richard Zens, Chris Dyer, Ondrej Bojar, Alexandra Constantin, and Evan Herbst. 2007. Moses: Open source toolkit for statistical machine translation. In *Annual Meeting of the Association for Computational Linguistics (ACL)*, Prague, Czech Republic. Association for Computational Linguistics.

Philipp Koehn. 2004. Pharaoh: a beam search decoder for phrase-based statistical machine translation models. In *6th Conference of the Association for Machine Translation in the Americas (AMTA 04)*, pages 115–124, Washington DC, September/October.

Evgeny Matusov and Selçuk Köprü. 2010a. AppTek's APT Machine Translation System for IWSLT 2010. In *Proc. of the International Workshop on Spoken Language Translation*, Paris, France, December.

Evgeny Matusov and Selçuk Köprü. 2010b. Improving Reordering in Statistical Machine Translation from Farsi. In *AMTA 2010: The Ninth Conference of the Association for Machine Translation in the Americas*, Denver, Colorado, USA, November.

Evgeny Matusov, Björn Hoffmeister, and Hermann Ney. 2008. ASR word lattice translation with exhaustive reordering is possible. In *Interspeech*, pages 2342–2345, Brisbane, Australia, September.

Evgeny Matusov. 2012. Incremental Re-training of a Hybrid English-French MT System with Customer Translation Memory Data. In *10th Conference of the Association for Machine Translation in the Americas (AMTA 12)*, San Diego, CA, USA, October-November.

Franz Josef Och. 2003. Minimum error rate training in statistical machine translation. In *41st Annual Meeting of the Association for Computational Linguistics (ACL)*, pages 160–167, Sapporo, Japan, July.

Kishore Papineni, Salim Roukos, Todd Ward, and Wei-Jing Zhu. 2002. BLEU: a method for automatic evaluation of machine translation. In *ACL '02: Proceedings of the 40th Annual Meeting on Association for Computational Linguistics*, pages 311–318, Morristown, NJ, USA. Association for Computational Linguistics.

Richard Zens. 2008. *Phrase-based Statistical Machine Translation: Models, Search, Training*. Ph.D. thesis, RWTH Aachen University, Aachen, Germany, February.

Pre-reordering for machine translation using transition-based walks on dependency parse trees

Antonio Valerio Miceli-Barone
Dipartimento di Informatica
Largo B. Pontecorvo, 3
56127 Pisa, Italy
miceli@di.unipi.it

Giuseppe Attardi
Dipartimento di Informatica
Largo B. Pontecorvo, 3
56127 Pisa, Italy
attardi@di.unipi.it

Abstract

We propose a pre-reordering scheme to improve the quality of machine translation by permuting the words of a source sentence to a target-like order. This is accomplished as a transition-based system that walks on the dependency parse tree of the sentence and emits words in target-like order, driven by a classifier trained on a parallel corpus. Our system is capable of generating arbitrary permutations up to flexible constraints determined by the choice of the classifier algorithm and input features.

1 Introduction

The dominant paradigm in statistical machine translation consists mainly of phrase-based system such as Moses (Koehn et.al.,2007). Different languages, however, often express the same concepts in different idiomatic word orders, and while phrase-based system can deal to some extent with short-distance word swaps that are captured by short segments, they typically perform poorly on long-distance (more than four or five words apart) reordering. In fact, according to (Birch et.al., 2008), the amount of reordering between two languages is the most predictive feature of phrase-based translation accuracy.

A number of approaches to deal with long-distance reordering have been proposed. Since an extuasive search of the permutation space is unfeasible, these approaches typically constrain the search space by leveraging syntactical structure of natural languages.

In this work we consider approaches which involve reordering the words of a source sentence in a target-like order as a preprocessing step, before feeding it to a phrase-based decoder which has itself been trained with a reordered training set. These methods also try to leverage syntax, typically by applying hand-coded or automatically induced reordering rules to a constituency or dependency parse of the source sentence. (Galley and Manning, 2008; Xu et.al., 2009; Genzel, 2010; Isozaki et.al., 2010) or by treating reordering as a global optimization problem (Tromble and Eisner, 2009; Visweswariah et.al., 2011). In order to keep the training and execution processes tractable, these methods impose hard constrains on the class of permutations they can generate.

We propose a pre-reordering method based on a walk on the dependency parse tree of the source sentence driven by a classifier trained on a parallel corpus.

In principle, our system is capable of generating arbitrary permutations of the source sentence. Practical implementations will necessarily limit the available permutations, but these constraints are not intrinsic to the model, rather they depend on the specific choice of the classifier algorithm, its hyper-parameters and input features.

2 Reordering as a walk on a dependency tree

2.1 Dependency parse trees

Let a sentence be a list of words $s \equiv (w_1, w_2, \ldots, w_n)$ and its dependency parse tree be a rooted tree whose nodes are the words of the sentence. An edge of the tree represents a syntactical dependency relation between a head (parent) word and a modifier (child) word. Typical dependency relations include *verb-subject*, *verb-object*, *noun-adjective*, and so on.

We assume that in addition to its head h_i and dependency relation type d_i each word is also annotated with a part-of-speech p_i and optionally a lemma l_i and a morphology m_i (e.g. grammatical case, gender, number, tense).

Some definitions require dependency parse trees to be *projective*, meaning that any complete subtree must correspond to a contiguous span of words in the sentence, however, we don't place such a requirement. In practice, languages with a substantially strict word ordering like English typically have largely projective dependencies, while languages with a more free word ordering like Czech can have substantial non-projectivity.

2.2 Reordering model

Given a sentence $s \in S$ with its dependency parse tree and additional annotations, we incrementally construct a reordered sentence s' by emitting its words in a sequence of steps. We model the reordering process as a non-deterministic transition system which traverses the parse tree:

Let the state of the system be a tuple $x \equiv (i, r, a, \ldots)$ containing at least the index of the current node i (initialized at the root), the list of emitted nodes r (initialized as empty) and the last transition action a (initialized as $null$). Additional information can be included in the state x, such as the list of the last K nodes that have been visited, the last K actions and a visit count for each node.

At each step we choose one of the following actions:

- $EMIT$: emit the current node. Enabled only if the current node hasn't already been emitted

$$\frac{i \notin r}{(i, r, a, \ldots) \overset{EMIT}{\rightarrow} (i, (r \mid i), EMIT, \ldots)}$$

- UP: move to the parent of the current node

$$\frac{h_i \neq null, \forall j\ a \neq DOWN_j}{(i, r, a, \ldots) \overset{UP}{\rightarrow} (h_i, r, UP, \ldots)}$$

- $DOWN_j$: move to the child j of the current node. Enabled if the subtree of j (including j) contains nodes that have not been emitted yet.

$$\frac{h_j = i,\ a \neq UP,\ \exists k \in subtree(i) : k \notin r}{(i, r, a, \ldots) \overset{DOWN_j}{\rightarrow} (j, r, DOWN_j, \ldots)}$$

The pre-conditions on the UP and DOWN actions prevent them from canceling each other, ensuring that progress is made at each step. The additional precondition on DOWN actions ensures that the process always halts at a final state where all the nodes have been emitted.

Let $T(s)$ be the set of legal traces of the transition system for sentence s. Each trace $\tau \in T(s)$ defines a permutation s_τ of s as the list of emitted nodes r of its final state.

We define the reordering problem as finding the trace τ^* that maximizes a scoring function Φ

$$\tau^* \equiv \arg\max_{\tau \in T(s)} \Phi(s, \tau) \tag{1}$$

Note that since the parse tree is connected, in principle any arbitrary permutation can be generated for a suitable choice of Φ, though the maximization problem (1) is NP-hard and APX-complete in the general case, by trivial reduction from the traveling salesman problem.

The intuition behind this model is to leverage the syntactical information provided by the dependency parse tree, as successfully done by (Xu et.al., 2009; Genzel, 2010; Isozaki et.al., 2010) without being strictly constrained by a specific type reordering rules.

2.3 Trace scores

We wish to design a scoring function Φ that captures good reorderings for machine translation and admits an efficient optimization scheme.

We chose a function that additively decomposes into local scoring functions, each depending only on a single state of the trace and the following transition action

$$\Phi(s, \tau) \equiv \sum_{t=1}^{|\tau|-1} \phi(s, x(\tau, t), x_a(\tau, t+1)) \tag{2}$$

We further restrict our choice to a function which is linear w.r.t. a set of elementary local feature functions $\{f_k\}$

$$\phi(s, x, a) \equiv \sum_{k=1}^{|F|} v_k f_k(s, x, a) \tag{3}$$

where $\{v_k\} \in \mathbb{R}^{|F|}$ is a vector of parameters derived from a training procedure.

While in principle each feature function could depend on the whole sentence and the whole sequence of nodes emitted so far, in practice we restrict the dependence to a fixed neighborhood of the current node and the last few emitted nodes. This reduces the space of possible permutations.

2.4 Classifier-driven action selection

Even when the permutation space has been restricted by an appropriate choice of the feature functions, computing an exact solution of the optimization problem (1) remains non-trivial, because at each step of the reordering generation process, the set of enabled actions depends in general on nodes emitted at any previous step, and this prevents us from applying typical dynamic programming techniques. Therefore, we need to apply an heuristic procedure.

In our experiments, we apply a simple greedy procedure: at each step we choose an action according to the output a two-stage classifier:

1. A three-class one-vs-all logistic classifier chooses an action among EMIT, UP or DOWN based on a vector of features extracted from a fixed neighborhood of the current node i, the last emitted nodes and additional content of the state.

2. If a DOWN action was chosen, then a one-vs-one voting scheme is used to choose which child to descend to: For each pair $(j, j') : j < j'$ of children of i, a binary logistic classifier assigns a vote either to j or j'. The child that receives most votes is chosen. This is similar to the max-wins approach used in packages such as LIBSVM (Chang and Lin, 2011) to construct a M-class classifier from $M(M-1)/2$ binary classifiers, except that we use a single binary classifier acting on a vector of features extracted from the pair of children (j, j') and the node i, with their respective neighborhoods.

We also experimented with different classification schemes, but we found that this one yields the best performance.

Note that we are not strictly maximizing a global linear scoring function as as defined by equations (2) and (3), although this approach is closely related to that framework.

This approach is related to transition-based dependency parsing such as (Nivre and Scholz, 2004; Attardi, 2006) or dependency tree revision(Attardi and Ciaramita, 2007).

3 Training

3.1 Dataset preparation

Following (Al-Onaizan and Papineni, 2006; Tromble and Eisner, 2009; Visweswariah et.al., 2011), we generate a source-side reference reordering of a parallel training corpus. For each sentence pair, we generate a bidirectional word alignment using GIZA++ (Och and Ney, 2000) and the "grow-diag-final-and" heuristic implemented in Moses (Koehn et.al.,2007), then we assign to each source-side word a integer index corresponding to the position of the leftmost target-side word it is aligned to (attaching unaligned words to the following aligned word) and finally we perform a stable sort of source-side words according to this index.

On language pairs where GIZA++ produces substantially accurate alignments (generally all European languages) this scheme generates a target-like reference reordering of the corpus.

In order to tune the parameters of the downstream phrase-based translation system and to test the overall translation accuracy, we need two additional small parallel corpora. We don't need a reference reordering for the tuning corpus since it is not used for training the reordering system, however we generate a reference reordering for the test corpus in order to evaluate the accuracy of the reordering system in isolation. We obtain an alignment of this corpus by appending it to the training corpus, and processing it with GIZA++ and the heuristic described above.

3.2 Reference traces generation and classifier training

For each source sentence s in the training set and its reference reordering s', we generate a minimum-length trace τ of the reordering transition system, and for each state and action pair in it we generate the following training examples:

- For the first-stage classifier we generate a single training examples mapping the local features to an EMIT, UP or DOWN action label
- For the second-stage classifier, if the action is $DOWN_j$, for each pair of children (k, k') : $k < k'$ of the current node i, we generate a positive example if $j = k$ or a negative example if $j = k'$.

Both classifiers are trained with the LIBLINEAR package (Fan et.al., 2008), using the L2-regularized logistic regression method. The regularization parameter C is chosen by two-fold cross-validation. In practice, subsampling of the training set might be required in order to keep memory usage and training time manageable.

3.3 Translation system training and testing

Once the classifiers have been trained, we run the reordering system on the source side of the whole (non-subsampled) training corpus and the tuning corpus. For instance, if the parallel corpora are German-to-English, after the reordering step we obtain *German'*-to-English corpora, where *German'* is German in an English-like word order. These reordered corpora are used to train a standard phrase-based translation system. Finally, the reordering system is applied to source side of the test corpus, which is then translated with the downstream phrase-based system and the resulting translation is compared to the reference translation in order to obtain an accuracy measure. We also evaluate the "monolingual" reordering accuracy of upstream reordering system by comparing its output on the source side of the test corpus to the reference reordering obtained from the alignment.

4 Experiments

We performed German-to-English and Italian-to-English reordering and translation experiments.

4.1 Data

The German-to-English corpus is Europarl v7 (Koehn, 2005). We split it in a 1,881,531 sentence pairs training set, a 2,000 sentence pairs development set (used for tuning) and a 2,000 sentence pairs test set. We also used a 3,000 sentence pairs "challenge" set of newspaper articles provided by the WMT 2013 translation task organizers.

The Italian-to-English corpus has been assembled by merging Europarl v7, JRC-ACQUIS v2.2 (Steinberger et.al., 2006) and bilingual newspaper articles crawled from news websites such as Corriere.it and Asianews.it. It consists of a 3,075,777 sentence pairs training set, a 3,923 sentence pairs development set and a 2,000 sentence pairs test set.

The source sides of these corpora have been parsed with Desr (Attardi, 2006). For both language pairs, we trained a baseline Moses phrase-based translation system with the default configuration (including lexicalized reordering).

In order to keep the memory requirements and duration of classifier training manageable, we subsampled each training set to 40,000 sentences, while both the baseline and reordered Moses system are trained on the full training sets.

4.2 Features

After various experiments with feature selection, we settled for the following configuration for both German-to-English and Italian-to-English:

- First stage classifier: current node i stateful features (emitted?, left/right subtree emitted?, visit count), curent node lexical and syntactical features (surface form w_i, lemma l_i, POS p_i, morphology m_i, DEPREL d_i, and pairwise combinations between lemma, POS and DEPREL), last two actions, last two visited nodes POS, DEPREL and visit count, last two emitted nodes POS and DEPREL, bigram and syntactical trigram features for the last two emitted nodes and the current node, all lexical, syntactical and stateful features for the neighborhood of the current node (left, right, parent, parent-left, parent-right, grandparent, left-child, right-child) and pairwise combination between syntactical features of these nodes.

- Second stage classifier: stateful features for the current node i and the the children pair (j, j'), lexical and syntactical features for each of the children and pairwise combinations of these features, visit count differences and signed distances between the two children and the current node, syntactical trigram features between all combinations of the two children, the current node, the parent h_i and the two last emitted nodes and the two last visited nodes, lexical and syntactical features for the two children left and right neighbors.

All features are encoded as binary one-of-n indicator functions.

4.3 Results

For both German-to-English and Italian-to-English experiments, we prepared the data as described above and we trained the classifiers on their subsampled training sets. In order to evaluate the classifiers accuracy in isolation from the rest of the system, we performed two-fold cross validation on the same training sets, which revealed an high accuracy: The first stage classifier obtains approximately 92% accuracy on both German and Italian, while the second stage classifier obtains approximately 89% accuracy on German and 92% on Italian.

	BLEU	NIST
German	57.35	13.2553
Italian	68.78	15.3441

Table 1: Monolingual reordering scores

	BLEU	NIST
de-en baseline	**33.78**	**7.9664**
de-en reordered	32.42	7.8202
it-en baseline	**29.17**	**7.1352**
it-en reordered	28.84	7.1443

Table 2: Translation scores

We applied the reordering preprocessing system to the source side of the corpora and evaluated the monolingual BLEU and NIST score of the test sets (extracted from Europarl) against their reference reordering computed from the alignment

To evaluate translation performance, we trained a Moses phrase-based system on the reordered training and tuning corpora, and evaluated the BLEU and NIST of the (Europarl) test sets. As a baseline, we also trained and evaluated Moses system on the original unreordered corpora.

We also applied our baseline and reordered German-to-English systems to the WMT2013 translation task dataset.

5 Discussion

Unfortunately we were generally unable to improve the translation scores over the baseline, even though our monolingual BLEU for German-to-English reordering is higher than the score reported by (Tromble and Eisner, 2009) for a comparable dataset.

Accuracy on the WMT 2013 set is very low. We attribute this to the fact that it comes form a different domain than the training set.

Since classifier training set cross-validation accuracy is high, we speculate that the main problem lies with the training example generation process: training examples are generated only from optimal reordering traces. This means that once the classifiers produce an error and the system strays away from an optimal trace, it may enter in a feature space that is not well-represented in the training set, and thus suffer from unrecoverable performance degradation. Moreover, errors occurring on nodes high in the parse tree may cause incorrect placement of whole spans of words, yielding a poor BLEU score (although a cursory examination of the reordered sentences doesn't reveal this problem to be prevalent). Both these issues could be possibly addressed by switching from a classifier-based system to a structured prediction system, such as averaged structured perceptron (Collins, 2002) or MIRA (Crammer, 2003; McDonald et.al., 2005).

Another possible cause of error is the purely greedy action selection policy. This could be addressed using a search approach such as beam search.

We reserve to investigate these approaches in future work.

References

Roy Tromble and Jason Eisner. 2009. Learning linear ordering problems for better translation. In *Proceedings of the 2009 Conference on Empirical Methods in Natural Language Processing*: Volume 2 - Volume 2 (EMNLP '09), Vol. 2. Association for Computational Linguistics, Stroudsburg, PA, USA, 1007-1016.

G. Attardi, M. Ciaramita. 2007. Tree Revision Learning for Dependency Parsing. In *Proc. of the Human Language Technology Conference 2007.*

Peng Xu, Jaeho Kang, Michael Ringgaard, and Franz Och. 2009. Using a dependency parser to improve SMT for subject-object-verb languages. *In Proceedings of Human Language Technologies: The 2009 Annual Conference of the North American Chapter of the Association for Computational Linguistics (NAACL '09).* Association for Computational Linguistics, Stroudsburg, PA, USA, 245-253.

Dmitriy Genzel. 2010. Automatically learning source-side reordering rules for large scale machine translation. In *Proceedings of the 23rd International Conference on Computational Linguistics (COLING '10).* Association for Computational Linguistics, Stroudsburg, PA, USA, 376-384.

Yaser Al-Onaizan and Kishore Papineni. 2006. Distortion models for statistical machine translation. In *Proceedings of the 21st International Conference on Computational Linguistics and the 44th annual meeting of the Association for Computational Linguistics (ACL-44).* Association for Computational Linguistics, Stroudsburg, PA, USA, 529-536.

Alexandra , Miles Osborne, and Philipp Koehn. 2008. Predicting success in machine translation. In *Proceedings of the Conference on Empirical Methods in Natural Language Processing (EMNLP '08).* Association for Computational Linguistics, Stroudsburg, PA, USA, 745-754.

	BLEU	BLEU (11b)	BLEU-cased	BLEU-cased (11b)	TER
de-en baseline	**18.8**	**18.8**	**17.8**	**17.8**	**0.722**
de-en reordered	18.1	18.1	17.3	17.3	0.739

Table 3: WMT2013 de-en translation scores

Philipp Koehn, Hieu Hoang, Alexandra Birch, Chris Callison-Burch, Marcello Federico, Nicola Bertoldi, Brooke Cowan, Wade Shen, Christine Moran, Richard Zens, Chris Dyer, Ondřej Bojar, Alexandra Constantin, and Evan Herbst. 2007. Moses: open source toolkit for statistical machine translation. In *Proceedings of the 45th Annual Meeting of the ACL on Interactive Poster and Demonstration Sessions (ACL '07)*. Association for Computational Linguistics, Stroudsburg, PA, USA, 177-180.

Hideki Isozaki, Katsuhito Sudoh, Hajime Tsukada, and Kevin Duh. 2010. Head finalization: a simple reordering rule for SOV languages. *In Proceedings of the Joint Fifth Workshop on Statistical Machine Translation and MetricsMATR (WMT '10)*. Association for Computational Linguistics, Stroudsburg, PA, USA, 244-251.

Michel Galley and Christopher D. Manning. 2008. A simple and effective hierarchical phrase reordering model. In *Proceedings of the Conference on Empirical Methods in Natural Language Processing (EMNLP '08)*. Association for Computational Linguistics, Stroudsburg, PA, USA, 848-856.

Karthik Visweswariah, Rajakrishnan Rajkumar, Ankur Gandhe, Ananthakrishnan Ramanathan, and Jiri Navratil. 2011. A word reordering model for improved machine translation. In *Proceedings of the Conference on Empirical Methods in Natural Language Processing (EMNLP '11)*. Association for Computational Linguistics, Stroudsburg, PA, USA, 486-496.

Giuseppe Attardi. 2006. Experiments with a multilanguage non-projective dependency parser. In *Proceedings of the Tenth Conference on Computational Natural Language Learning (CoNLL-X '06)*. Association for Computational Linguistics, Stroudsburg, PA, USA, 166-170.

Joakim Nivre and Mario Scholz. 2004. Deterministic dependency parsing of English text. In *Proceedings of the 20th international conference on Computational Linguistics (COLING '04)*. Association for Computational Linguistics, Stroudsburg, PA, USA, , Article 64 .

Franz Josef Och and Hermann Ney. 2000. Improved statistical alignment models. In *Proceedings of the 38th Annual Meeting on Association for Computational Linguistics (ACL '00)*. Association for Computational Linguistics, Stroudsburg, PA, USA, 440-447.

Chih-Chung Chang and Chih-Jen Lin. 2011. LIBSVM: A library for support vector machines. *ACM Trans. Intell. Syst. Technol.* 2, 3, Article 27 (May 2011), 27 pages.

Rong-En Fan, Kai-Wei Chang, Cho-Jui Hsieh, Xiang-Rui Wang, and Chih-Jen Lin. 2008. LIBLINEAR: A Library for Large Linear Classification. *J. Mach. Learn. Res.* 9 (June 2008), 1871-1874.

Philipp Koehn. 2005. Europarl: A Parallel Corpus for Statistical Machine Translation. *MT Summit 2005.*

Ralf Steinberger, Bruno Pouliquen, Anna Widiger, Camelia Ignat, Toma Erjavec, Dan Tufiş. 2006. The JRC-Acquis: A multilingual aligned parallel corpus with 20+ languages. In *Proceedings of the 5th International Conference on Language Resources and Evaluation (LREC'2006).*

Michael Collins. 2002. Discriminative training methods for hidden Markov models: theory and experiments with perceptron algorithms. In *Proceedings of the ACL-02 conference on Empirical methods in natural language processing - Volume 10 (EMNLP '02)*, Vol. 10. Association for Computational Linguistics, Stroudsburg, PA, USA, 1-8.

Ryan McDonald, Koby Crammer, and Fernando Pereira. 2005. Online large-margin training of dependency parsers. In *Proceedings of the 43rd Annual Meeting on Association for Computational Linguistics (ACL '05)*. Association for Computational Linguistics, Stroudsburg, PA, USA, 91-98.

Koby Crammer and Yoram Singer. 2003. Ultraconservative online algorithms for multiclass problems. *J. Mach. Learn. Res.* 3 (March 2003), 951-991.

Edinburgh's Syntax-Based Machine Translation Systems

Maria Nadejde, Philip Williams, and Philipp Koehn
School of Informatics, University of Edinburgh, Scotland, United Kingdom
maria.nadejde@gmail.com, P.J.Williams-2@sms.ed.ac.uk, pkoehn@inf.ed.ac.uk

Abstract

We present the syntax-based string-to-tree statistical machine translation systems built for the WMT 2013 shared translation task. Systems were developed for four language pairs. We report on adapting parameters, targeted reduction of the tuning set, and post-evaluation experiments on rule binarization and preventing dropping of verbs.

1 Overview

Syntax-based machine translation models hold the promise to overcome some of the fundamental problems of the currently dominating phrase-based approach, most importantly handling reordering for syntactically divergent language pairs and grammatical coherence of the output.

We are especially interested in string-to-tree models that focus syntactic annotation on the target side, especially for morphologically rich target languages (Williams and Koehn, 2011).

We have trained syntax-based systems for the language pairs

- English-German,
- German-English,
- Czech-English, and
- Russian-English.

We have also tried building systems for French-English and Spanish-English but the data size proved to be problematic given the time constraints. We give a brief description of the syntax-based model and its implementation within the Moses system. Some of the available features are described as well as some of the pre-processing steps. Several experiments are described and final results are presented for each language pair.

2 System Description

The syntax-based system used in all experiments is the Moses string-to-tree toolkit implementing GHKM rule extraction and Scope-3 parsing previously described in by Williams and Koehn (2012)

2.1 Grammar

Our translation grammar is a synchronous context-free grammar (SCFG) with phrase-structure labels on the target side and the generic non-terminal label X on the source side. In this paper, we write these rules in the form

$$\text{LHS} \rightarrow \text{RHS}_s \mid \text{RHS}_t$$

where LHS is a target-side non-terminal label and RHS_s and RHS_t are strings of terminals and non-terminals for the source and target sides, respectively. We use subscripted indices to indicate the correspondences between source and target non-terminals.

For example, a translation rule to translate the German *Haus* into the English *house* is

$$\text{NN} \rightarrow \textit{Haus} \mid \textit{house}$$

If our grammar also contains the translation rule

$$\text{S} \rightarrow \textit{das ist ein } \text{X}_1 \mid \textit{this is a } \text{NN}_1$$

then we can apply the two rules to an input *das ist ein Haus* to produce the output *this is a house*.

2.2 Rule Extraction

The GHKM rule extractor (Galley et al., 2004, 2006) learns translation rules from a word-aligned parallel corpora for which the target sentences are syntactically annotated. Given a string-tree pair, the set of minimally-sized translation rules is extracted that can explain the example and is consistent with the alignment. The resulting rules can be composed in a non-overlapping fashion in order to cover the string-tree pair.

Two or more minimal rules that are in a parent-child relationship can be composed together to obtain larger rules with more syntactic context. To avoid generating an exponential number of composed rules, several limitation have to be imposed.

One such limitation is on the size of the composed rules, which is defined as the number of non-part-of-speech, non-leaf constituent labels in the target tree (DeNeefe et al., 2007). The corresponding parameter in the Moses implementation is *MaxRuleSize* and its default value is 3.

Another limitation is on the depth of the rules' target subtree. The rule depth is computed as the maximum distance from its root node to any of its children, not counting pre-terminal nodes (parameter *MaxRuleDepth*, default 3).

The third limitation considered is the number of nodes in the composed rule, not counting target words (parameter *MaxNodes*, default 15).

These parameters are language-dependent and should be set to values that best represent the characteristics of the target trees on which the rule extractor is trained on. Therefore the style of the treebanks used for training the syntactic parsers will also influence these numbers. The default values have been set based on experiments on the English-German language pair (Williams and Koehn, 2012). It is worth noting that the German parse trees (Skut et al., 1997) tend to be broader and shallower than those for English. In Section 3 we present some experiments where we choose different settings of these parameters for the German-English language pair. We use those settings for all language pairs where the target language is English.

2.3 Tree Restructuring

The coverage of the extracted grammar depends partly on the structure of the target trees. If the target trees have flat constructions such as long noun phrases with many sibling nodes, the rules extracted will not generalize well to unseen data since there will be many constraints given by the types of different sibling nodes.

In order to improve the grammar coverage to generalize over such cases, the target tree can be restructured. One restructuring strategy is tree binarization. Wang et al. (2010) give an extensive overview of different tree binarization strategies applied for the Chinese-English language pair. Moses currently supports *left binarization* and *right binarization*.

By *left binarization* all the left-most children of a parent node *n* except the right most child are grouped under a new node. This node is inserted as the left child of *n* and receives the label $\bar{n}$. *Left binarization* is then applied recursively on all newly inserted nodes until the leaves are reached. *Right binarization* implies a similar procedure but in this case the right-most children of the parent node are grouped together except the left most child.

Another binarization strategy that is not currently integrated in Moses, but is worth investigating for different language pairs, is *parallel head binarization*.

The result of *parallel binarization* of a parse tree is a binarization forest. To generate a binarization forest node, both right binarization and left binarization are applied recursively to a parent node with more than two children. *Parallel head binarization* is a case of *parallel binarization* with the additional constraint that the head constituent is part of all the new nodes inserted by either left or right binarization steps.

In Section 3 we give example of some initial experiments carried out for the German-English language pair.

2.4 Pruning The Grammar

Decoding for syntax-based model relies on a bottom-up chart parsing algorithm. Therefore decoding efficiency is influenced by the following combinatorial problem: given an input sentence of length *n* and a context-free grammar rule with *s* consecutive non-terminals, there are $\binom{n+1}{s}$ ways to choose subspans, or *application contexts* (Hopkins and Langmead, 2010), that the rule can applied to. The asymptotic running time of chart parsing is linear in this number $O(n^s)$.

Hopkins and Langmead (2010) maintain cubic decoding time by pruning the grammar to remove rules for which the number of potential application contexts is too large. Their key observation is that a rule can have any number of non-terminals and terminals as long as the number of consecutive non-terminal pairs is bounded. Terminals act to anchor the rule, restricting the number of potential application contexts. An example is the rule $X \rightarrow WyYZz$ for which there are at most $O(n^2)$ application contexts, given that the terminals will have a fixed position and will play the role of anchors in the sentence for the non-terminal spans. The number of consecutive non-terminal pairs plus the number of non-terminals at the edge of a rule is referred to as the *scope* of the rule. The scope of a grammar is the maximum scope of any of its rules. Moses implements *scope-3 pruning* and therefore the resulting grammar can be parsed in cubic time.

2.5 Feature Functions

Our feature functions are unchanged from last year. They include the n-gram language model probability of the derivation's target yield, its word count, and various scores for the synchronous derivation. Our grammar rules are scored according to the following functions:

- $p(\text{RHS}_s|\text{RHS}_t, \text{LHS})$, the noisy-channel translation probability.
- $p(\text{LHS}, \text{RHS}_t|\text{RHS}_s)$, the direct translation probability.
- $p_{lex}(\text{RHS}_t|\text{RHS}_s)$ and $p_{lex}(\text{RHS}_s|\text{RHS}_t)$, the direct and indirect lexical weights (Koehn et al., 2003).
- $p_{pcfg}(\text{FRAG}_t)$, the monolingual PCFG probability of the tree fragment from which the rule was extracted. This is defined as $\prod_{i=1}^{n} p(r_i)$, where $r_1 \ldots r_n$ are the constituent CFG rules of the fragment. The PCFG parameters are estimated from the parse of the target-side training data. All lexical CFG rules are given the probability 1. This is similar to the p_{cfg} feature proposed by Marcu et al. (2006) and is intended to encourage the production of syntactically well-formed derivations.
- $exp(-1/count(r))$, a rule rareness penalty.
- $exp(1)$, a rule penalty. The main grammar and glue grammars have distinct penalty features.

3 Experiments

This section describes details for the syntax-based systems submitted by the University of Edinburgh. Additional post-evaluation experiments were carried out for the German-English language pair.

3.1 Data

We made use of all available data for each language pair except for the Russian-English where the *Commoncrawl* corpus was not used. Table 1 shows the size of the parallel corpus used for each language pair. The English side of the parallel corpus was parsed using the Berkeley parser (Petrov et al., 2006) and the German side of the parallel corpus was parsed using the BitPar parser (Schmid, 2004). For German-English, German compounds were split using the script provided with Moses. The parallel corpus was word-aligned using MGIZA++ (Gao and Vogel, 2008).

All available monolingual data was used for training the language models for each language

Lang. pair	Sentences	Grammar Size
en-de	4,411,792	31,568,480
de-en	4,434,060	55,310,162
cs-en	14,425,564	209,841,388
ru-en	1,140,359	7,946,502

Table 1: Corpus statistics for parallel data.

pair. 5-gram language models were trained using SRILM toolkit (Stolcke, 2002) with modified Kneser-Ney smoothing (Chen and Goodman, 1998) and then interpolated using weights tuned on the newstest2011 development set.

The feature weights for each system were tuned on development sets using the Moses implementation of minimum error rate training (Och, 2003). The size of the tuning data varied for different languages depending on the amount of available data. In the case of the the German-English pair a filtering criteria based on sentence level BLEU score was applied which is briefly described in Section 3.5. Table 2 shows the size of the tuning set for each language pair.

Lang. pair	Sentences
en-de	7,065
de-en	2,400
cs-en	10,068
ru-en	1,501

Table 2: Corpus statistics for tuning data.

3.2 Pre-processing

Some attention was given to pre-processing of the English side of the corpus prior to parsing. This was done to avoid propagating parser errors to the rule-extraction step. These particular errors arise from a mismatch in punctuation and tokenization between the corpus used to train the parser, the PennTree bank, and the corpus which is being parsed and passed on to the rule extractor. Therefore we changed the quotation marks, which appear quite often in the parallel corpora, to opening and closing quotation marks. We also added some PennTree bank style tokenization rules[1]. These rules split contractions such as *I'll*, *It's*, *Don't*, *Gonna*, *Commissioner's* in order to correctly separate the verbs, negation and possessives that are

[1]The PennTree bank tokenization rules considered were taken from `http://www.cis.upenn.edu/~treebank/tokenizer.sed`. Further examples of contractions were added.

	Grammar Size		BLEU			
Parameters	Full	Filtered	2009-40	2010-40	2011-40	Average
Depth=3, Nodes=15, Size=3	2,572,222	751,355	18.57	20.43	18.51	19.17
Depth=4, Nodes=20, Size=4	3,188,970	901,710	18.88	20.38	18.63	19.30
Depth=5, Nodes=20, Size=5	3,668,205	980,057	19.04	20.47	18.75	**19.42**
Depth=5, Nodes=30, Size=5	3,776,961	980,061	18.90	20.59	18.77	19.42
Depth=5, Nodes=30, Size=6	4,340,716	1,006,174	18.98	20.52	18.80	19.43

Table 3: Cased BLEU scores for various rule extraction parameter settings for German-English language pair. The parameters considered are *MaxRuleDepth*, *MaxRuleSize*, *MaxNodes*. Grammar sizes are given for the full extracted grammar and after filtering for the newstest2008 dev set.

		newstest2012			newstest2013		
System	Sentences	BLEU	Glue Rule	Tree Depth	BLEU	Glue Rule	Tree Depth
Baseline	5,771	23.21	5.42	4.03	26.27	4.23	3.80
Big tuning set	10,068	23.52	3.41	4.34	26.33	2.49	4.03
Filtered tuning set	2,400	**23.54**	3.21	4.37	**26.30**	2.37	4.05

Table 4: Cased BLEU scores for German-English systems tuned on different data. Scores are emphasized for the system submitted to the shared translation task.

parsed as separate constituents.

For German–English, we carried out the usual compound splitting (Koehn and Knight, 2003), but not pre-reordering (Collins et al., 2005).

3.3 Rule Extraction

Some preliminary experiments were carried out for the German-English language pair to determine the parameters for the rule extraction step: *MaxRuleDepth*, *MaxRuleSize*, *MaxNodes*. Table 3 shows the BLEU score on different test sets for various parameter settings. For efficiency reasons less training data was used, therefore the grammar sizes, measured as the total number of extracted rules, are smaller than the final systems (Table 1). The parameters on the third line *Depth=5, Nodes=20, Size=4* were chosen as the average BLEU score did not increase although the size of the extracted grammar kept growing. Comparing the rate of growth of the full grammar and the grammar after filtering for the dev set (the columns headed “Full” and “Filtered”) suggests that beyond this point not many more usable rules are extracted, even while the total number of rules stills increases.

3.4 Decoder Settings

We used the following non-default decoder parameters:

max-chart-span=25: This limits sub derivations to a maximum span of 25 source words. Glue rules are used to combine sub derivations allowing the full sentence to be covered.

ttable-limit=200: Moses prunes the translation grammar on loading, removing low scoring rules. This option increases the number of translation rules that are retained for any given source side RHS_s.

cube-pruning-pop-limit=1000: Number of hypotheses created for each chart span.

3.5 Tuning sets

One major limitation for the syntax-based systems is that decoding becomes inefficient for long sentences. Therefore using large tuning sets will slow down considerably the development cycle. We carried out some preliminary experiments to determine how the size of the tuning set affects the quality and speed of the system.

Three tuning sets were considered. The tuning set that was used for training the baseline system was built using the data from newstest2008-2010 filtering out sentences longer than 30 words. The second tuning set was built using all data from newstest2008-2011. The final tuning set was also built using the concatenation of the sets newstest2008-2011. All sentences in this set were decoded with a baseline system and the output was scored according to sentence-BLEU scores. We selected examples with high sentence-BLEU score in a way that penalizes excessively short examples[2]. Results of these experiments are shown in Table 4.

Results show that there is some gain in BLEU score when providing longer sentences during tuning. Further experiments should consider tuning the baseline with the newstest2008-2011 data, to eliminate variance caused by having different data sources. Although the size of the third tuning set is much smaller than that of the other tuning sets, the BLEU score remains the same as when using the largest tuning set. The *glue rule* number, which shows how many times the glue rule was applied, is lowest when tuning with the third data set. The *tree depth* number, which shows the depth of the resulting target parse tree, is higher for the third tuning set as compared to the baseline and similar to that resulted from using the largest tuning set. These numbers are all indicators of better utilisation of the syntactic structure.

Regarding efficiency, the baseline tuning set and the filtered tuning set took about a third of the time needed to decode the larger tuning set.

Therefore we could draw some initial conclusions that providing longer sentences is useful, but sentences for which some baseline system performs very poorly in terms of BLEU score can be eliminated from the tuning set.

3.6 Results

Table 5 summarizes the results for the systems submitted to the shared task. The BLEU scores for the phrase-based system submitted by the University of Edinburgh are also shown for comparison. The syntax-based system had BLEU scores similar to those of the phrase-based system for German-English and English-German language pairs. For the Czech-English and Russian-English language pairs the syntax-based system was 2 BLEU points behind the phrase-based system.

However, in the manual evaluation, the German–English and English–German syntax based systems were ranked higher than the phrase-based systems. For Czech–English, the syntax systems also came much closer than the BLEU score would have indicated.

The Russian-English system performed worse because we used much less of the available data for training (leaving out *Commoncrawl*) and therefore the extracted grammar is less reliable. Another reason was the mismatch in data formatting for the Russian-English parallel corpus. All the training data was lowercased which resulted in more parsing errors.

[2]Ongoing work by Eva Hasler. Filtered data set was provided in order to speed up experiment cycles.

	phrase-based		syntax-based	
	BLEU	manual	BLEU	manual
en-de	**20.1**	0.571	19.4	**0.614**
de-en	**26.6**	0.586	26.3	**0.608**
cs-en	**26.2**	**0.562**	24.4	0.542
ru-en	**24.3**	**0.507**	22.5	0.416

Table 5: Cased BLEU scores and manual evaluation scores ("expected wins") on the newstest2013 evaluation set for the phrase-based and syntax-based systems submitted by the University of Edinburgh.

3.7 Post-Submission Experiments

Table 6 shows results for some preliminary experiments carried out for the German-English language pair that were not included in the final submission. The baseline system is trained on all available parallel data and tuned on data from newstest2008-2010 filtered for sentences up to 30 words.

Tree restructuring — In one experiment the parse trees were restructured before training by *left binarization*. Tree restructuring is need to improve generalization power of rules extracted from flat structures such as base noun phrases with several children. The second raw in Table 6 shows that the BLEU score did not improve and more glue rules were applied when using *left binarization*. One reason for this result is that the rule extraction parameters *MaxRuleDepth*, *MaxRuleSize*, *MaxNodes* had the same values as in the baseline. Increasing this parameters should improve the extracted grammar since binarizing the trees will increase these three dimensions.

Verb dropping — A serious problem of German–English machine translation is the tendency to drop verbs, which shatters sentence structure. One cause of this problem is the failure of the IBM Models to properly align the German verb to its English equivalent, since it is often dislocated with respect to English word order. Further problems appear when the main verb is not reordered in the target sentence, which can result in lower lan-

		newstest2012			newstest2013		
System	Grammar size	BLEU	glue rule	tree depth	BLEU	glue rule	tree depth
Baseline	55,310,162	23.21	5.42	4.03	26.27	4.23	3.80
Left binarized	57,151,032	23.17	7.79	4.09	26.13	6.57	3.85
Realigned vb	53,894,112	23.26	4.88	4.19	26.26	3.73	3.96

Table 6: Cased BLEU scores for various German-English systems.

System	Vb drop rules	Vb Count nt2012	Vb Count nt2013
Baseline	1,038,597	9,216	8,418
Realigned verbs	391,231	9,471	8,614
Reference translation	-	9,992	9,207

Table 7: Statistics about verb dropping.

guage model scores and BLEU scores. However the syntax models handle the reordering of verbs better than phrase-based models.

In an experiment we investigated how the number of verbs dropped by the translation rules can be reduced. In order to reduce the number of verb dropping rules we looked at unaligned verbs and realigned them before rule extraction. An unaligned verb in the source sentence was aligned to the verb in the target sentence for which IBM model 1 predicted the highest translation probability. The third row in Table 6 shows the results of this experiment. While there is no change in BLEU score the number of glue rules applied is lower. Further analysis shows in Table 7 that the number of verb dropping rules in the grammar is almost three times lower and that there are more translated verbs in the output when realigning verbs.

4 Conclusion

We describe in detail the syntax-based machine translation systems that we developed for four European language pairs. We achieved competitive results, especially for the language pairs involving German.

Acknowledgments

The research leading to these results has received funding from the European Union Seventh Framework Programme (FP7/2007-2013) under grant agreement 287658 (EU BRIDGE) and grant agreement 288487 (MosesCore).

References

Chen, S. F. and Goodman, J. (1998). An empirical study of smoothing techniques for language modeling. Technical report, Harvard University.

Collins, M., Koehn, P., and Kucerova, I. (2005). Clause restructuring for statistical machine translation. In *Proceedings of the 43rd Annual Meeting of the Association for Computational Linguistics (ACL'05)*, pages 531–540, Ann Arbor, Michigan. Association for Computational Linguistics.

DeNeefe, S., Knight, K., Wang, W., and Marcu, D. (2007). What can syntax-based MT learn from phrase-based MT? In *Proceedings of the 2007 Joint Conference on Empirical Methods in Natural Language Processing and Computational Natural Language Learning (EMNLP-CoNLL 2007). June 28-30, 2007. Prague, Czech Republic.*

Galley, M., Graehl, J., Knight, K., Marcu, D., DeNeefe, S., Wang, W., and Thayer, I. (2006). Scalable inference and training of context-rich syntactic translation models. In *ACL-44: Proceedings of the 21st International Conference on Computational Linguistics and the 44th annual meeting of the Association for Computational Linguistics*, pages 961–968, Morristown, NJ, USA. Association for Computational Linguistics.

Galley, M., Hopkins, M., Knight, K., and Marcu, D. (2004). What's in a translation rule? In *HLT-NAACL '04*.

Gao, Q. and Vogel, S. (2008). Parallel implementations of word alignment tool. In *Software Engineering, Testing, and Quality Assurance for Natural Language Processing*, SETQA-NLP '08, pages 49–57, Stroudsburg, PA, USA. Association for Computational Linguistics.

Hopkins, M. and Langmead, G. (2010). SCFG decoding without binarization. In *Proceedings of the 2010 Conference on Empirical Methods in Natural Language Processing*, pages 646–655, Cambridge, MA. Association for Computational Linguistics.

Koehn, P. and Knight, K. (2003). Empirical methods for compound splitting. In *Proceedings of Meeting of the European Chapter of the Association of Computational Linguistics (EACL)*.

Koehn, P., Och, F. J., and Marcu, D. (2003). Statistical phrase-based translation. In *NAACL '03: Proceedings of the 2003 Conference of the North American Chapter of the Association for Computational Linguistics on Human Language Technology*, pages 48–54, Morristown, NJ, USA. Association for Computational Linguistics.

Marcu, D., Wang, W., Echihabi, A., and Knight, K. (2006). SPMT: statistical machine translation with syntactified target language phrases. In *EMNLP '06: Proceedings of the 2006 Conference on Empirical Methods in Natural Language Processing*, pages 44–52, Morristown, NJ, USA. Association for Computational Linguistics.

Och, F. J. (2003). Minimum error rate training in statistical machine translation. In *Proceedings of the 41st Annual Meeting on Association for Computational Linguistics - Volume 1*, ACL '03, pages 160–167, Morristown, NJ, USA. Association for Computational Linguistics.

Petrov, S., Barrett, L., Thibaux, R., and Klein, D. (2006). Learning accurate, compact, and interpretable tree annotation. In *Proceedings of the 21st International Conference on Computational Linguistics and the 44th annual meeting of the Association for Computational Linguistics*, ACL-44, pages 433–440, Stroudsburg, PA, USA. Association for Computational Linguistics.

Schmid, H. (2004). Efficient parsing of highly ambiguous context-free grammars with bit vectors. In *Proceedings of the 20th international conference on Computational Linguistics*, COLING '04, Stroudsburg, PA, USA. Association for Computational Linguistics.

Skut, W., Krenn, B., Brants, T., and Uszkoreit, H. (1997). An annotation scheme for free word order languages. In *Proceedings of the Fifth Conference on Applied Natural Language Processing (ANLP-97)*.

Stolcke, A. (2002). SRILM - an extensible language modeling toolkit. In *Intl. Conf. Spoken Language Processing, Denver, Colorado, September 2002.*

Wang, W., May, J., Knight, K., and Marcu, D. (2010). Re-structuring, re-labeling, and re-aligning for syntax-based machine translation. *Comput. Linguist.*, 36(2):247–277.

Williams, P. and Koehn, P. (2011). Agreement constraints for statistical machine translation into german. In *Proceedings of the Sixth Workshop on Statistical Machine Translation*, pages 217–226, Edinburgh, Scotland. Association for Computational Linguistics.

Williams, P. and Koehn, P. (2012). Ghkm rule extraction and scope-3 parsing in moses. In *Proceedings of the Seventh Workshop on Statistical Machine Translation*, pages 388–394, Montréal, Canada. Association for Computational Linguistics.

Shallow Semantically-Informed PBSMT and HPBSMT

Tsuyoshi Okita
Qun Liu
Josef van Genabith
Dublin City University
Glasnevin, Dublin 9, Ireland
{tokita,qliu,josef}@computing.dcu.ie

Abstract

This paper describes shallow semantically-informed Hierarchical Phrase-based SMT (HPBSMT) and Phrase-Based SMT (PBSMT) systems developed at Dublin City University for participation in the translation task between EN-ES and ES-EN at the Workshop on Statistical Machine Translation (WMT 13). The system uses PBSMT and HPBSMT decoders with multiple LMs, but will run only one decoding path decided before starting translation. Therefore the paper does not present a multi-engine system combination. We investigate three types of shallow semantics: (i) Quality Estimation (QE) score, (ii) genre ID, and (iii) context ID derived from context-dependent language models. Our results show that the improvement is 0.8 points absolute (BLEU) for EN-ES and 0.7 points for ES-EN compared to the standard PBSMT system (single best system). It is important to note that we developed this method when the standard (confusion network-based) system combination is ineffective such as in the case when the input is only two.

1 Introduction

This paper describes shallow semantically-informed Hierarchical Phrase-based SMT (HPBSMT) and Phrase-Based SMT (PBSMT) systems developed at Dublin City University for participation in the translation task between EN-ES and ES-EN at WMT 13. Our objectives are to incorporate several shallow semantics into SMT systems. The first semantics is the QE score for a given input sentence which can be used to select the decoding path either of HPBSMT or PBSMT. Although we call this a *QE* score, this score is not quite a standard one which does not have access to translation output information. The second semantics is genre ID which is intended to capture domain adaptation. The third semantics is context ID: this context ID is used to adjust the context for the local words. Context ID is used in a continuous-space LM (Schwenk, 2007), but is implicit since the context does not appear in the construction of a continuous-space LM. Note that our usage of the term *semantics* refers to meaning constructed by a sentence or words. The QE score works as a sentence level switch to select HPBSMT or PBSMT, based on the *semantics* of a sentence. The genre ID gives an indication that the sentence is to be translated by genre ID-sensitive MT systems, again based on *semantics* on a sentence level. The context-dependent LM can be interpreted as supplying the local context to a word, capturing *semantics* on a word level.

The architecture presented in this paper is substantially different from multi-engine system combination. Although the system has multiple paths, only one path is chosen at decoding when processing unseen data. Note that *standard* multi-engine system combination using these three semantics has been presented before (Okita et al., 2012b; Okita et al., 2012a; Okita, 2012). This paper also compares the two approaches.

The remainder of this paper is organized as follows. Section 2 describes the motivation for our approach. In Section 3, we describe our proposed systems, while in Section 4 we describe the experimental results. We conclude in Section 5.

2 Motivation

Model Difference of PBSMT and HPBSMT Our motivation is identical with a system combination strategy which would obtain a better translation if we can access more than two translations. Even though we are limited in the type of MT systems, i.e. SMT systems, we can access at least two systems, i.e. PBSMT and HPBSMT systems. The merit that accrues from accessing these two translation is shown in Figure 1. In this example between EN-ES, the skirts of the distribution shows that around 20% of the examples obtain the same BLEU score, 37% are better under PBSMT, and 42% under HPBSMT. Moreover, around 10% of sentences show difference of 10 BLEU points. Even a selection of outputs would improve the results. Unfortunately, some pitfall of system combination (Rosti et al., 2007) impact on the process when the number of available translation is only two. If there are only two inputs, (1) the mismatch of word order and word selection would yield a bad combination since system combination relies on monolingual word alignment (or TER-based alignment) which seeks identical words, and (2) Minimum Bayes Risk (MBR) decoding, which is a first step, will not work effectively since it relies on voting. (In fact, only selecting one of the translation outputs is even effective: this method is called system combination as well (Specia et al., 2010).) Hence, although the aim is similar, we do not use a system combination strategy, but we develop a semantically-informed SMT system.

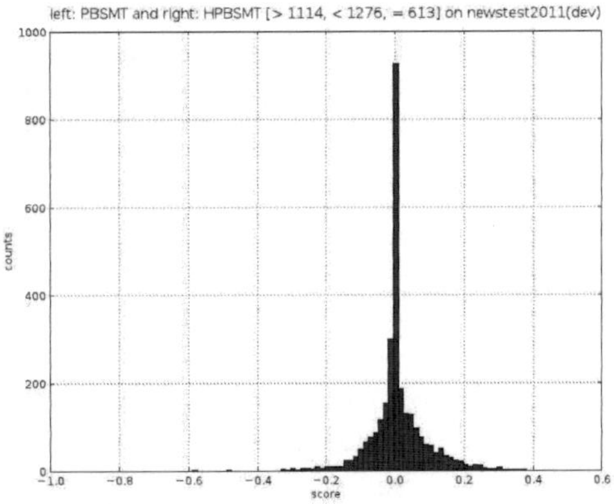

Figure 1: Figure shows the difference of sentence-based performance between PBSMT and HPBSMT systems.

Relation of Complexity of Source Sentence and Performance of HPBSMT and PBSMT It is interesting to note that PBSMT tends to be better than HPBSMT for European language pairs as the recent WMT workshop shows, while HPBSMT shows often better performance for distant language pairs such as EN-JP (Okita et al., 2010b) and EN-ZH in other workshops.

Under the assumption that we use the same training corpus for training PBSMT and HPBSMT systems, our hypothesis is that we may be able to predict the quality of translation. Note that although this is the analogy of quality estimation, the setting is slightly different in that in test phase, we will not be given a translation output, but only a source sentence. Our aim is to predict whether HPBSMT obtains better translation output than PBSMT or not. Hence, our aim does not require that the quality prediction here is very accurate compared to the standard quality estimation task. We use a feature set consisting of various characteristics of input sentences.

3 Our Methods: Shallow Semantics

Our system accommodates PBSMT and HPBSMT with multiple of LMs. A decoder which handles shallow semantic information is shown in Table 3.1.

3.1 QE Score

Quality estimation aims to predict the quality of translation outputs for unseen data (e.g. by building a regressor or a classifier) without access to references: the inputs are translation outputs and source sentences in a test phase, while in a training phase the corresponding BLEU or HTER scores are used. In this subsection, we try to build a regressor with the similar settings but without supplying the translation outputs. That is, we supply only the input sentences. (Since our method is not a quality estimation for a given translation output, *quality estimation* may not be an entirely appropriate term. However, we borrow this term for this paper.) If we can build such a regressor for PBSMT and HPBSMT systems, we would be able to select a better translation output without actually translating them for a given input sentence. Note that we translate the training set by PBSMT and HPBSMT in a training phase only to supply their BLEU scores to a regressor (since a regressor is a supervised learning method). Then, we use these regressors for a given unseen source sentence (which has no translation output attached) to predict their BLEU scores for PBSMT and HPBSMT.

Our motivation came from the comparison of a sequential learning system and a parser-based system. The typical decoder of the former is a

Viterbi decoder while that of the latter is a Cocke-Younger-Kasami (CYK) decoder (Younger, 1967). The capability of these two systems provides an intuition about the difference of PBSMT and HPBSMT: the CYK decoder-based system has some capability to handle syntactic constructions while the Viterbi decoder-based system has only the capability of learning a sequence. For example, the (context-free) grammar-based system has the capability of handling various difficulties caused by inserted clauses, coordination, long Multiword Expressions, and parentheses, while the sequential learning system does not (This is since this is what the aim of the context-free grammar-based system is.) These difficulties are manifest in input sentences.

```
Input: Foreign sent f=f_1,...,f_1f, language model,
translation model, rule table.
Output: English translation e

ceScore = predictQEScore(f_i)
if (ceScore == HPBSMTBetter)
  for span length l=1 to 1_f do
    for start=0..1_f-1 do
      genreID = predictGenreID(f_i)
      end = start + 1
      forall seq s of entries and words in span
[start,end] do
        forall rules r do
          if rule r applies to chart seq s then
            create new chart entry c
              with LM(genreID)
            add chart entry c to chart
  return e from best chart entry in span [0,1_f]
else:
  genreID = predictGenreID(f_i)
  place empty hypothesis into stack 0
  for all stacks 0...n-1 do
    for all hypotheses in stack do
      for all translation options do
        if applicable then
          create new hyp with LM(ID)
          place in stack
          recombine with existing hyp if
            possible
          prune stack if too big
  return e

predictQEScore()
predictGenreID()
predictContextID(word_i, word_i-1)
```

Table 1: Decoding algorithm: the main algorithm of PBSMT and HPBSMT are from (Koehn, 2010). The modification is related to predictQEScore(), predictGenreID(), and predictContextID().

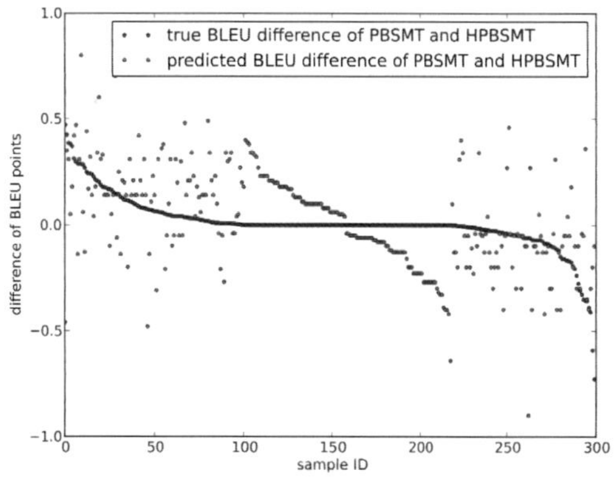

Figure 2: A blue line shows the true BLEU difference between PBSMT and HPBSMT (y-axis) where x-axis is the sample IDs reordered in descending order (blue), while green dots show the BLEU absolute difference (y-axis) of the typical samples where x-axis is shared with the above. This example is sampled 300 points from newstest2013 (ES-EN). Even if the regressor does not achieve a good performance, the bottom line of the overall performance is already really high in this tricky problem. Roughly, even if we plot randomly we could achieve around 80 - 90% of correctness. Around 50% of samples (middle of the curve) do not care (since the true performance of PBSMT and HPBSMT are even), there is a slope in the left side of the curve where random plot around this curve would achieve 15 - 20% among 25% of correctness (the performance of PBSMT is superior), and there is another slope in the right side of the curve where random plot would achieve again 15 - 20% among 25% (the performance of HPBSMT is superior). In this case, accuracy is 86%.

If we assume that this is one major difference between these two systems, the complexity of the input sentence will correlate with the difference of translation quality of these two systems. In this subsection, we assume that this is one major difference of these two systems and that the complexity of the input sentence will correlate with the difference of translation quality of these two systems. Based on these assumptions, we build a regressor for each system for a given input sentence where in a training phase we supply the BLEU score measured using the training set. One remark is that the BLEU score which we predict is only meaningful in a relative manner since we actually generate a translation output in preparation phase (there is a dependency to the mean of BLEU score in the training set). Nevertheless, this is still meaningful as a relative value if we want to talk about their difference, which is what we want in our settings to predict which system, either PBSMT or HPB-SMT, will generate a better output.

The main features used for training the regressor are as follows: (1) number of / length of inserted clause / coordination / multiword expressions, (2) number of long phrases (connection by 'of'; ordering of words), (3) number of OOV words (which let it lower the prediction quality), (4) number of / length of parenthesis, etc. We obtained these features using parser (de Marneffe et al., 2006) and multiword extractor (Okita et al., 2010a).

3.2 Genre ID

Genre IDs allow us to apply domain adaptation technique according to the genre ID of the testset. Among various methods of domain adaptation, we investigate unsupervised clustering rather than already specified genres.

We used (unsupervised) classification via Latent Dirichlet Allocation (LDA) (Blei et al., 2003) to obtain genre ID. LDA represents topics as multinomial distributions over the W unique word-types in the corpus and represents documents as a mixture of topics.

Let C be the number of unique labels in the corpus. Each label c is represented by a W-dimensional multinomial distribution ϕ_c over the vocabulary. For document d, we observe both the words in the document $w^{(d)}$ as well as the document labels $c^{(d)}$. Given the distribution over topics θ_d, the generation of words in the document is captured by the following generative model.

1. For each label $c \in \{1, \dots C\}$, sample a distribution over word-types $\phi_c \sim$ **Dirichlet**$(\cdot|\beta)$
2. For each document $d \in \{1, \dots, D\}$
   (a) Sample a distribution over its observed labels $\theta_d \sim$ **Dirichlet**$(\cdot|\alpha)$
   (b) For each word $i \in \{1, \dots, N_d^W\}$
      i. Sample a label $z_i^{(d)} \sim$ **Multinomial**(θ_d)
      ii. Sample a word $w_i^{(d)} \sim$ **Multinomial**(ϕ_c) from the label $c = z_i^{(d)}$

Using topic modeling (or LDA) as described above, we perform the in-domain data partitioning as follows, building LMs for each class, and running a decoding process for the development set, which will obtain the best weights for cluster i.

1. Fix the number of clusters C, we explore values from small to big.[1]
2. Do unsupervised document classification (or LDA) on the source side of the training, development and test sets.
3. Separate each class of training sets and build LM for each cluster i ($1 \leq i \leq C$).
4. Separate each class of development set (keep the original index and new index in the allocated separated dataset).
5. (Using the same class of development set): Run the decoder on each class to obtain the n-best lists, run a MERT process to obtain the best weights based on the n-best lists, (Repeat the decoding / MERT process several iterations. Then, we obtain the best weights for a particular class.)

For the test phase,

1. Separate each class of the test set (keep the original index and new index in the allocated separated dataset).
2. Suppose the test sentence belongs to cluster i, run the decoder of cluster i.
3. Repeat the previous step until all the test sentences are decoded.

3.3 Context ID

Context ID semantics is used through the reranking of the n-best list in a MERT process (Schwenk, 2007; Schwenk et al., 2012; Le et al., 2012). 2-layer ngram-HMM LM is a two layer version of the 1-layer ngram-HMM LM (Blunsom and Cohn, 2011) which is a nonparametric

[1]Currently, we do not have a definite recommendation on this. It needs to be studied more deeply.

Bayesian method using hierarchical Pitman-Yor prior. In the 2-layer LM, the hidden sequence of the first layer becomes the input to the higher layer of inputs. Note that such an architecture comes from the Restricted Boltzmann Machine (Smolensky, 1986) accumulating in multiple layers in order to build deep belief networks (Taylor and Hinton, 2009). Although a 2-layer ngram-HMM LM is inferior in its performance compared with other two LMs, the runtime cost is cheaper than these.

h_t denotes the hidden word for the first layer, $\bar{h}_t$ denotes the hidden word for the second layer, w_i denotes the word in output layer. The generative model for this is shown below.

$$h_t|\bar{h}_t \sim F(\bar{\phi}_{s_t}) \quad (1)$$

$$w_t|h_t \sim F(\phi_{s_t}) \quad (2)$$

$$w_i|w_{1:i-1} \sim \mathrm{PY}(d_i, \theta_i, G_i) \quad (3)$$

where α is a concentration parameter, θ is a strength parameter, and G_i is a base measure. Note that these terms belong to the hierarchical Pitman-Yor language model (Teh, 2006). We used a blocked inference for inference. The performance of 2-layer LM is shown in Table 3.

4 Experimental Settings

We used Moses (Koehn et al., 2007) for PBSMT and HPBSMT systems in our experiments. The GIZA++ implementation (Och and Ney, 2003) of IBM Model 4 is used as the baseline for word alignment: Model 4 is incrementally trained by performing 5 iterations of Model 1, 5 iterations of HMM, 3 iterations of Model 3, and 3 iterations of Model 4. For phrase extraction the grow-diag-final heuristics described in (Koehn et al., 2003) is used to derive the refined alignment from bidirectional alignments. We then perform MERT process (Och, 2003) which optimizes the BLEU metric, while a 5-gram language model is derived with Kneser-Ney smoothing (Kneser and Ney, 1995) trained with SRILM (Stolcke, 2002). For the HPBSMT system, the chart-based decoder of Moses (Koehn et al., 2007) is used. Most of the procedures are identical with the PBSMT systems except the rule extraction process (Chiang, 2005).

The procedures to handle three kinds of semantics are implemented using the already mentioned algorithm. We use libSVM (Chang and Lin, 2011), and Mallet (McCallum, 2002) for Latent Dirichlet Allocation (LDA) (Blei et al., 2003).

For the corpus, we used all the resources provided for the translation task at WMT13 for language model, that is parallel corpora (Europarl V7 (Koehn, 2005), Common Crawl corpus, UN corpus, and News Commentary) and monolingual corpora (Europarl V7, News Commentary, and News Crawl from 2007 to 2012).

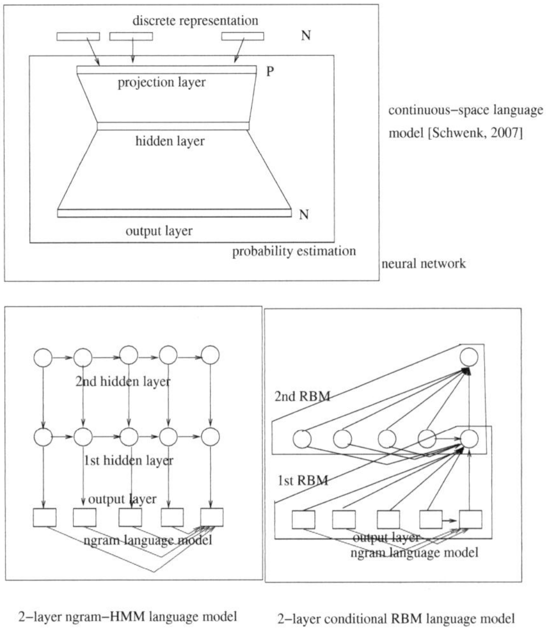

Figure 3: Figure shows the three kinds of context-dependent LM. The upper-side shows continuous-space language model (Schwenk, 2007). The lower-left shows ours, i.e. the 2-layer ngram-HMM LM. The lower-right shows the 2-layer conditional Restricted Boltzmann Machine LM (Taylor and Hinton, 2009).

Experimental results are shown in Table 2. The left-most column (*sem-inform*) shows our results. The *sem-inform* made a improvement of 0.8 BLEU points absolute compared to the PBSMT results in EN-ES, while the standard system combination lost 0.1 BLEU points absolute compared to the single worst. For ES-EN, the *sem-inform* made an improvement of 0.7 BLEU points absolute compared to the PBSMT results. These improvements over both of PBSMT and HPBSMT are statistically significant by a paired bootstrap test (Koehn, 2004).

5 Conclusion

This paper describes shallow semantically-informed HPBSMT and PBSMT systems developed at Dublin City University for participation in the translation task at the Workshop on Statistical Machine Translation (WMT 13). Our system has

EN-ES	sem-inform	PBSMT	HPBSMT	syscomb	aug-syscomb
BLEU	30.3	29.5	28.2	28.1	28.5
BLEU(11b)	30.3	29.5	28.2	28.1	28.5
BLEU-cased	29.0	28.4	27.1	27.0	27.5
BLEU-cased(11b)	29.0	28.4	27.1	27.0	27.5
NIST	7.91	7.74	7.35	7.35	7.36
Meteor	0.580	0.579	0.577	0.577	0.578
WER	53.7	55.4	59.3	59.2	58.9
PER	41.3	42.4	46.0	45.8	45.5
ES-EN	sem-inform	PBSMT	HPBSMT	syscomb	aug-syscomb
BLEU	31.1	30.4	23.1*	28.8	29.9
BLEU(11b)	31.1	30.4	23.1*	28.8	29.9
BLEU-cased	29.7	29.1	22.3*	27.9	28.8
BLEU-cased(11b)	29.7	29.1	22.3*	27.9	28.8
NIST	7.87	7.79	6.67*	7.40	7.71
Meteor	0.615	0.612	0.533*	0.612	0.613
WER	54.8	55.4	62.5*	59.3	56.1
PER	41.3	41.8	48.3*	45.8	41.9

Table 2: Table shows the score where "sem-inform" shows our system. Underlined figure shows the official score. "syscomb" denotes the confusion-network-based system combination using BLEU, while "aug-syscomb" uses three shallow semantics described in QE score (Okita et al., 2012a), genre ID (Okita et al., 2012b), and context ID (Okita, 2012). Note that the inputs for syscomb and aug-syscomb are the output of HPBSMT and PBSMT. HPBSMT from ES to EN has marked with *, which indicates that this is trained only with Europarl V7.

EN	2-layer ngram-HMM LM	SRI-LM
newstest12	130.4	140.3
newstest11	146.2	157.1
newstest10	156.4	166.8
newstest09	176.3	187.1

Table 3: Table shows the perplexity of context-dependent language models, which is 2-layer ngram HMM LM, and that of SRILM (Stolcke, 2002) in terms of newstest09 to 12.

PBSMT and HPBSMT decoders with multiple LMs, but our system will execute only one path, which is different from multi-engine system combination. We consider investigate three types of shallow semantic information: (i) a Quality Estimate (QE) score, (ii) genre ID, and (iii) a context ID through context-dependent language models. Our experimental results show that the improvement is 0.8 points absolute (BLEU) for EN-ES and 0.7 points for ES-EN compared to the standard PBSMT system (single best system). We developed this method when the standard (confusion network-based) system combination is ineffective such as in the case when the input is only two.

A further avenue would be the investigation of other semantics such as linguistic semantics, including co-reference resolution or anaphora resolution, hyper-graph decoding, and text understanding. Some of which are investigated in the context of textual entailment task (Okita, 2013b) and we would like to extend this to SMT task. Another investigation would be the integration of genre ID into the context-dependent LM. The preliminary work shows that such integration would decrease the overall perplexity (Okita, 2013a).

Acknowledgments

We thank Antonio Toral and Santiago Cortés Vaílo for providing parts of their processing data. This research is supported by the Science Foundation Ireland (Grant 07/CE/I1142) as part of the Centre for Next Generation Localisation (`http://www.cngl.ie`) at Dublin City University.

References

David Blei, Andrew Y. Ng, and Michael I. Jordan. 2003. Latent dirichlet allocation. *Journal of Machine Learning Research*, 3:9931022.

Phil Blunsom and Trevor Cohn. 2011. A hierarchical pitman-yor process hmm for unsupervised part of speech induction. *In Proceedings of Annual Meeting of the Association for Computational Linguistics (ACL11)*, pages 865–874.

Chih-Chung Chang and Chih-Jen Lin. 2011. LIBSVM: A library for support vector machines. *ACM Transactions on Intelligent Systems and Technology*, 2:27:1–27:27.

David Chiang. 2005. A hierarchical phrase-based model for statistical machine translation. *In Proceedings of the 43th Annual Meeting of the Association for Computational Linguistics (ACL-05)*, pages 263–270.

Marie-Catherine de Marneffe, Bill MacCartney, and Christopher D. Manning. 2006. Generating typed dependency parses from phrase structure parses. *In Proceedings of the Sixth International Conference on Language Resources and Evaluation (LREC-2006)*, pages 449–454.

Reinhard Kneser and Hermann Ney. 1995. Improved backing-off for n-gram language modeling. *In Proceedings of the IEEE International Conference on Acoustics, Speech and Signal Processing*, pages 181–184.

Philipp Koehn, Franz Och, and Daniel Marcu. 2003. Statistical phrase-based translation. *In Proceedings of the Human Language Technology Conference of the North American Chapter of the Association for Computationa Linguistics (HLT / NAACL 2003)*, pages 115–124.

Philipp Koehn, Hieu Hoang, Alexandra Birch, Chris Callison-Burch, Marcello Federico, Nicola Bertoldi, Brooke Cowan, Wade Shen, Christine Moran, Richard Zens, Chris Dyer, Ondrej Bojar, Alexandra Constantin, and Evan Herbst. 2007. Moses: Open source toolkit for Statistical Machine Translation. *In Proceedings of the 45th Annual Meeting of the Association for Computational Linguistics Companion Volume Proceedings of the Demo and Poster Sessions*, pages 177–180.

Philipp Koehn. 2004. Statistical significance tests for machine translation evaluation. *In Proceedings of Conference on Empirical Methods in Natural Language Processing (EMNLP 2004)*, pages 388–395.

Philipp Koehn. 2005. Europarl: A parallel corpus for statistical machine translation. *In Proceedings of the Machine Translation Summit*, pages 79–86.

Philipp Koehn. 2010. Statistical machine translation. *Cambridge University Press.*

Hai-Son Le, Thomas Lavergne, Alexandre Allauzen, Marianna Apidianaki, Li Gong, Aurelien Max, Artem Sokolov, Guillaume Wisniewski, and Francois Yvon. 2012. Limsi at wmt12. *In Proceedings of the Seventh Workshop on Statistical Machine Translation*, pages 330–337.

Andrew Kachites McCallum. 2002. Mallet: A machine learning for language toolkit. *http://mallet.cs.umass.edu.*

Franz Och and Hermann Ney. 2003. A systematic comparison of various statistical alignment models. *Computational Linguistics*, 29(1):19–51.

Franz Och. 2003. Minimum Error Rate Training in Statistical Machine Translation. *In Proceedings of the 41st Annual Meeting of the Association for Computational Linguistics*, pages 160–167.

Tsuyoshi Okita, Alfredo Maldonado Guerra, Yvette Graham, and Andy Way. 2010a. Multi-Word Expression sensitive word alignment. *In Proceedings of the Fourth International Workshop On Cross Lingual Information Access (CLIA2010, collocated with COLING2010), Beijing, China.*, pages 1–8.

Tsuyoshi Okita, Jie Jiang, Rejwanul Haque, Hala Al-Maghout, Jinhua Du, Sudip Kumar Naskar, and Andy Way. 2010b. MaTrEx: the DCU MT System for NTCIR-8. *In Proceedings of the MII Test Collection for IR Systems-8 Meeting (NTCIR-8)*, pages 377–383.

Tsuyoshi Okita, Raphaël Rubino, and Josef van Genabith. 2012a. Sentence-level quality estimation for mt system combination. *In Proceedings of ML4HMT Workshop (collocated with COLING 2012)*, pages 55–64.

Tsuyoshi Okita, Antonio Toral, and Josef van Genabith. 2012b. Topic modeling-based domain adaptation for system combination. *In Proceedings of ML4HMT Workshop (collocated with COLING 2012)*, pages 45–54.

Tsuyoshi Okita. 2012. Neural Probabilistic Language Model for System Combination. *In Proceedings of ML4HMT Workshop (collocated with COLING 2012)*, pages 65–76.

Tsuyoshi Okita. 2013a. Joint space neural probabilistic language model for statistical machine translation. *Technical Report at arXiv*, 1301(3614).

Tsuyoshi Okita. 2013b. Local graph matching with active learning for recognizing inference in text at ntcir-10. *NTCIR 10 Conference*, pages 499–506.

Antti-Veikko I. Rosti, Spyros Matsoukas, and Richard Schwartz. 2007. Improved word-level system combination for machine translation. *In Proceedings of the 45th Annual Meeting of the Association for Computational Linguistics*, pages 312–319.

Holger Schwenk, Anthony Rousseau, and Mohammed Attik. 2012. Large, pruned or continuous space language models on a gpu for statistical machine translation. *In NAACL-HLT workshop on the Future of Language Modeling for HLT*, pages 11–19.

Holger Schwenk. 2007. Continuous space language models. *Computer Speech and Language*, 21:492–518.

Paul Smolensky. 1986. Chapter 6: Information processing in dynamical systems: Foundations of harmony theory. *In Rumelhart, David E.; McLelland, James L. Parallel Distributed Processing: Explorations in the Microstructure of Cognition*, 1:194281.

Lucia Specia, D. Raj, and Marco Turchi. 2010. Machine translation evaluation versus quality estimation. *Machine Translation, Springer*, 24(1):39–50.

Andreas Stolcke. 2002. SRILM – An extensible language modeling toolkit. *In Proceedings of the International Conference on Spoken Language Processing*, pages 901–904.

Graham Taylor and Geoffrey Hinton. 2009. Factored conditional restricted boltzmann machines for modeling motion style. *In Proceedings of the 26th International Conference on Machine Learning (ICML)*, pages 1025–1032.

Yee Whye Teh. 2006. A hierarchical bayesian language model based on pitman-yor processes. *In Proceedings of the 44th Annual Meeting of the Association for Computational Linguistics (ACL-06), Prague, Czech Republic*, pages 985–992.

Daniel H. Younger. 1967. Recognition and parsing of context-free languages in time n3. *Information and Control*, 10(2):189208.

Joint WMT 2013 Submission of the QUAERO Project

*Stephan Peitz, *Saab Mansour, *Matthias Huck, *Markus Freitag, *Hermann Ney,
†Eunah Cho, †Teresa Herrmann, †Mohammed Mediani, †Jan Niehues, †Alex Waibel,
‡Alexandre Allauzen, ‡Quoc Khanh Do,
§Bianka Buschbeck, §Tonio Wandmacher
*RWTH Aachen University, Aachen, Germany
†Karlsruhe Institute of Technology, Karlsruhe, Germany
‡LIMSI-CNRS, Orsay, France
§SYSTRAN Software, Inc.
*surname@cs.rwth-aachen.de
†firstname.surname@kit.edu
‡firstname.lastname@limsi.fr §surname@systran.fr

Abstract

This paper describes the joint submission of the QUAERO project for the German→English translation task of the *ACL 2013 Eighth Workshop on Statistical Machine Translation* (WMT 2013). The submission was a system combination of the output of four different translation systems provided by RWTH Aachen University, Karlsruhe Institute of Technology (KIT), LIMSI-CNRS and SYSTRAN Software, Inc. The translations were joined using the RWTH's system combination approach. Experimental results show improvements of up to 1.2 points in BLEU and 1.2 points in TER compared to the best single translation.

1 Introduction

QUAERO is a European research and development program with the goal of developing multimedia and multilingual indexing and management tools for professional and general public applications (http://www.quaero.org). Research in machine translation is mainly assigned to the four groups participating in this joint submission. The aim of this submission was to show the quality of a joint translation by combining the knowledge of the four project partners. Each group develop and maintain their own different machine translation system. These single systems differ not only in their general approach, but also in the preprocessing of training and test data. To take advantage of these differences of each translation system, we combined all hypotheses of the different systems, using the RWTH system combination approach.

This paper is structured as follows. First, the different engines of all four groups are introduced. In Section 3, the RWTH Aachen system combination approach is presented. Experiments with different system selections for system combination are described in Section 4. This paper is concluded in Section 5.

2 Translation Systems

For WMT 2013, each QUAERO partner trained their systems on the parallel Europarl (EPPS), News Commentary (NC) corpora and the web-crawled corpus. All single systems were tuned on the newstest2009 *and* newstest2010 development set. The newstest2011 development set was used to tune the system combination parameters. Finally, on newstest2012 the results of the different system combination settings are compared. In this Section, all four different translation engines are presented.

2.1 RWTH Aachen Single System

For the WMT 2013 evaluation, RWTH utilized a phrase-based decoder based on (Wuebker et al., 2012) which is part of RWTH's open-source SMT toolkit Jane 2.1 [1]. GIZA++ (Och and Ney, 2003) was employed to train a word alignment, language models have been created with the SRILM toolkit (Stolcke, 2002).

After phrase pair extraction from the word-aligned parallel corpus, the translation probabilities are estimated by relative frequencies. The standard feature set also includes an n-gram language model, phrase-level IBM-1 and word-, phrase- and distortion-penalties, which are combined in log-linear fashion. Furthermore, we used an additional reordering model as described in (Galley and Manning, 2008). By this model six

[1] http://www-i6.informatik.rwth-aachen.de/jane/

additional feature are added to the log-linear combination. The model weights are optimized with standard Mert (Och, 2003a) on 200-best lists. The optimization criterion is BLEU.

2.1.1 Preprocessing

In order to reduce the source vocabulary size translation, the German text was preprocessed by splitting German compound words with the frequency-based method described in (Koehn and Knight, 2003). To further reduce translation complexity for the phrase-based approach, we performed the long-range part-of-speech based reordering rules proposed by (Popović et al., 2006).

2.1.2 Translation Model

We applied filtering and weighting for domain-adaptation similarly to (Mansour et al., 2011) and (Mansour and Ney, 2012). For filtering the bilingual data, a combination of LM and IBM Model 1 scores was used. In addition, we performed weighted phrase extraction by using a combined LM and IBM Model 1 weight.

2.1.3 Language Model

During decoding a 4-gram language model is applied. The language model is trained on the parallel data as well as the provided News crawl, the 10^9 French-English, UN and LDC Gigaword Fourth Edition corpora.

2.2 Karlsruhe Institute of Technology Single System

2.2.1 Preprocessing

The training data was preprocessed prior to the training. Symbols such as quotes, dashes and apostrophes are normalized. Then the first words of each sentence are smart-cased. For the German part of the training corpus, the hunspell[2] lexicon was used, in order to learn a mapping from old German spelling to new German writing rules. Compound-splitting was also performed as described in Koehn and Knight (2003). We also removed very long sentences, empty lines, and sentences which show big mismatch on the length.

2.2.2 Filtering

The web-crawled corpus was filtered using an SVM classifier as described in (Mediani et al., 2011). The lexica used in this filtering task were obtained from Giza alignments trained on the cleaner corpora, EPPS and NC. Assuming that this corpus is very noisy, we biased our classifier more towards precision than recall. This was realized by giving higher number of false examples (80% of the training data).

This filtering technique ruled out more than 38% of the corpus (the unfiltered corpus contains around 2.4M pairs, 0.9M of which were rejected in the filtering task).

2.2.3 System Overview

The in-house phrase-based decoder (Vogel, 2003) is used to perform decoding. Optimization with regard to the BLEU score is done using Minimum Error Rate Training (MERT) as described in Venugopal et al. (2005).

2.2.4 Reordering Model

We applied part-of-speech (POS) based reordering using probabilistic continuous (Rottmann and Vogel, 2007) and discontinuous (Niehues and Kolss, 2009) rules. This was learned using POS tags generated by the TreeTagger (Schmid, 1994) for short and long range reorderings respectively.

In addition to this POS-based reordering, we also used tree-based reordering rules. Syntactic parse trees of the whole training corpus and the word alignment between source and target language are used to learn rules on how to reorder the constituents in a German source sentence to make it match the English target sentence word order better (Herrmann et al., 2013). The training corpus was parsed by the Stanford parser (Rafferty and Manning, 2008). The reordering rules are applied to the source sentences and the reordered sentence variants as well as the original sequence are encoded in a word lattice which is used as input to the decoder.

Moreover, our reordering model was extended so that it could include the features of lexicalized reordering model. The reordering probabilities for each phrase pair are stored as well as the original position of each word in the lattice. During the decoding, the reordering origin of the words is checked along with its probability added as an additional score.

2.2.5 Translation Models

The translation model uses the parallel data of EPPS, NC, and the filtered web-crawled data. As word alignment, we used the Discriminative Word Alignment (DWA) as shown in (Niehues and Vo-

[2] http://hunspell.sourceforge.net/

gel, 2008). The phrase pairs were extracted using different source word order suggested by the POS-based reordering models presented previously as described in (Niehues et al., 2009).

In order to extend the context of source language words, we applied a bilingual language model (Niehues et al., 2011). A Discriminative Word Lexicon (DWL) introduced in (Mauser et al., 2009) was extended so that it could take the source context also into the account. For this, we used a bag-of-ngrams instead of representing the source sentence as a bag-of-words. Filtering based on counts was then applied to the features for higher order n-grams. In addition to this, the training examples were created differently so that we only used the words that occur in the n-best list but not in the reference as negative example.

2.2.6 Language Models

We build separate language models and combined them prior to decoding. As word-token based language models, one language model is built on EPPS, NC, and giga corpus, while another one is built using crawled data. We combined the LMs linearly by minimizing the perplexity on the development data. As a bilingual language model we used the EPPS, NC, and the web-crawled data and combined them. Furthermore, we use a 5-gram cluster-based language model with 1,000 word clusters, which was trained on the EPPS and NC corpus. The word clusters were created using the MKCLS algorithm.

2.3 LIMSI-CNRS Single System

2.3.1 System overview

LIMSI's system is built with *n*-code (Crego et al., 2011), an open source statistical machine translation system based on bilingual *n*-gram[3]. In this approach, the translation model relies on a specific decomposition of the joint probability of a sentence pair using the *n*-gram assumption: a sentence pair is decomposed into a sequence of bilingual units called *tuples*, defining a joint segmentation of the source and target. In the approach of (Mariño et al., 2006), this segmentation is a by-product of source reordering which ultimately derives from initial word and phrase alignments.

2.3.2 An overview of *n*-code

The baseline translation model is implemented as a stochastic finite-state transducer trained using a *n*-gram model of (source,target) pairs (Casacuberta and Vidal, 2004). Training this model requires to reorder source sentences so as to match the target word order. This is performed by a stochastic finite-state reordering model, which uses part-of-speech information[4] to generalize reordering patterns beyond lexical regularities.

In addition to the translation model, *eleven* feature functions are combined: a *target-language model*; four *lexicon models*; two *lexicalized reordering models* (Tillmann, 2004) aiming at predicting the orientation of the next translation unit; a 'weak' distance-based *distortion model*; and finally a *word-bonus model* and a *tuple-bonus model* which compensate for the system preference for short translations. The four *lexicon models* are similar to the ones use in a standard phrase based system: two scores correspond to the relative frequencies of the tuples and two lexical weights estimated from the automatically generated word alignments. The weights associated to feature functions are optimally combined using a discriminative training framework (Och, 2003b).

The overall search is based on a beam-search strategy on top of a dynamic programming algorithm. Reordering hypotheses are computed in a preprocessing step, making use of reordering rules built from the word reorderings introduced in the tuple extraction process. The resulting reordering hypotheses are passed to the decoder in the form of word lattices (Crego and Mario, 2006).

2.3.3 Continuous space translation models

One critical issue with standard *n*-gram translation models is that the elementary units are bilingual pairs, which means that the underlying vocabulary can be quite large, even for small translation tasks. Unfortunately, the parallel data available to train these models are typically order of magnitudes smaller than the corresponding monolingual corpora used to train target language models. It is very likely then, that such models should face severe estimation problems. In such setting, using neural network language model techniques seem all the more appropriate. For this study, we follow the recommendations of Le et al. (2012), who propose to factor the joint probability of a sentence pair by decomposing tuples in two (source and target) parts, and further each part in words. This yields a *word factored translation model* that

[3] `http://ncode.limsi.fr/`

[4] Part-of-speech labels for English and German are computed using the TreeTagger (Schmid, 1995).

can be estimated in a continuous space using the SOUL architecture (Le et al., 2011).

The design and integration of a SOUL model for large SMT tasks is far from easy, given the computational cost of computing n-gram probabilities. The solution used here was to resort to a two pass approach: the first pass uses a conventional back-off n-gram model to produce a k-best list; in the second pass, the k-best list is reordered using the probabilities of m-gram SOUL translation models. In the following experiments, we used a fixed context size for SOUL of $m = 10$, and used $k = 300$.

2.3.4 Corpora and data pre-processing

All the parallel data allowed in the constrained task are pooled together to create a single parallel corpus. This corpus is word-aligned using MGIZA++[5] with default settings. For the English monolingual training data, we used the same setup as last year[6] and thus the same target language model as detailed in (Allauzen et al., 2011).

For English, we also took advantage of our in-house text processing tools for the tokenization and detokenization steps (Dchelotte et al., 2008) and our system is built in "true-case". As German is morphologically more complex than English, the default policy which consists in treating each word form independently is plagued with data sparsity, which is detrimental both at training and decoding time. Thus, the German side was normalized using a specific pre-processing scheme (described in (Allauzen et al., 2010; Durgar El-Kahlout and Yvon, 2010)), which notably aims at reducing the lexical redundancy by (i) normalizing the orthography, (ii) neutralizing most inflections and (iii) splitting complex compounds.

2.4 SYSTRAN Software, Inc. Single System

In the past few years, SYSTRAN has been focusing on the introduction of statistical approaches to its rule-based backbone, leading to *Hybrid Machine Translation*.

The technique of *Statistical Post-Editing* (Dugast et al., 2007) is used to automatically edit the output of the rule-based system. A Statistical Post-Editing (SPE) module is generated from a bilingual corpus. It is basically a translation module by itself, however it is trained on rule-based translations and reference data. It applies corrections and adaptations learned from a phrase-based 5-gram language model. Using this two-step process will implicitly keep long distance relations and other constraints determined by the rule-based system while significantly improving phrasal fluency. It has the advantage that quality improvements can be achieved with very little but targeted bilingual data, thus significantly reducing training time and increasing translation performance.

The basic setup of the SPE component is identical to the one described in (Dugast et al., 2007). A statistical translation model is trained on the rule-based translation of the source and the target side of the parallel corpus. Language models are trained on each target half of the parallel corpora and also on additional in-domain corpora. Moreover, the following measures - limiting unwanted statistical effects - were applied:

- Named entities are replaced by special tokens on both sides. This usually improves word alignment, since the vocabulary size is significantly reduced. In addition, entity translation is handled more reliably by the rule-based engine.
- The intersection of both vocabularies (i.e. vocabularies of the rule-based output and the reference translation) is used to produce an additional parallel corpus (whose target is identical to the source). This was added to the parallel text in order to improve word alignment.
- Singleton phrase pairs are deleted from the phrase table to avoid overfitting.
- Phrase pairs not containing the same number of entities on the source and the target side are also discarded.
- Phrase pairs appearing less than 2 times were pruned.

The SPE language model was trained on 2M phrases from the news/europarl and Common-Crawl corpora, provided as training data for *WMT 2013*. Weights for these separate models were tuned by the Mert algorithm provided in the Moses toolkit (Koehn et al., 2007), using the provided news development set.

[5] `http://geek.kyloo.net/software`

[6] The fifth edition of the English Gigaword (LDC2011T07) was not used.

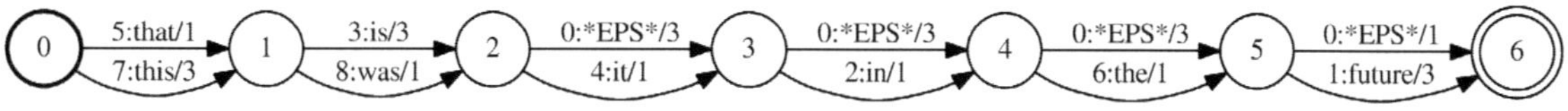

Figure 1: Confusion network of four different hypotheses.

3 RWTH Aachen System Combination

System combination is used to produce consensus translations from multiple hypotheses generated with different translation engines. First, a word to word alignment for the given single system hypotheses is produced. In a second step a confusion network is constructed. Then, the hypothesis with the highest probability is extracted from this confusion network. For the alignment procedure, each of the given single systems generates one confusion network with its own as primary system. To this primary system all other hypotheses are aligned using the METEOR (Lavie and Agarwal, 2007) alignment and thus the primary system defines the word order. Once the alignment is given, the corresponding confusion network is constructed. An example is given in Figure 1. The final network for one source sentence is the union of all confusion networks generated from the different primary systems. That allows the system combination to select the word order from different system outputs.

Before performing system combination, each translation output was normalized by tokenization and lowercasing. The output of the combination was then truecased based on the original truecased output.

The model weights of the system combination are optimized with standard Mert (Och, 2003a) on 100-best lists. We add one voting feature for each single system to the log-linear framework of the system combination. The voting feature fires for each word the single system agrees on. Moreover, a word penalty, a language model trained on the input hypotheses, a binary feature which penalizes word deletions in the confusion network and a primary feature which marks the system which provides the word order are combined in this log-linear model. The optimization criterion is 4BLEU-TER.

4 Experimental Results

In this year's experiments, we tried to improve the result of the system combination further by combining single systems tuned on different development sets. The idea is to achieve a more stable performance in terms of translation quality, if the single systems are not optimized on the same data set. In Table 1, the results of each provided single system tuned on newstest2009 and newstest2010 are shown. For RWTH, LIMSI and SYSTRAN, it seems that the performance of the single system depends on the chosen tuning set. However, the translation quality of the single systems provided by KIT is stable.

Table 1: Comparison of single systems tuned on newstest2009 and newstest2010. The results are reported on newstest2012.

single systems tuned on		newstest2012	
	newstest	BLEU	TER
KIT	2009	24.6	58.4
	2010	24.6	58.6
LIMSI	2009	22.5	61.5
	2010	22.6	59.8
SYSTRAN	2009	20.9	63.3
	2010	21.2	62.2
RWTH	2009	23.7	60.8
	2010	24.4	58.8

As initial approach and for the final submission, we grouped single systems with dissimilar approaches. Thus, KIT (phrase-based SMT) and SYSTRAN (rule-based MT) tuned their system on newstest2010, while RWTH (phrase-based SMT) and LIMSI (n-gram) optimized on newstest2009.

To compare the impact of this approach, all possible combinations were checked (Table 2). However, it seems that the translation quality can not be improved by this approach. For the test set (newstest2012), BLEU is steady around 25.6 points. Even if the single system with lowest BLEU are combined (KIT 2010, LIMSI 2009, SYSTRAN 2010, RWTH 2009), the translation quality in terms of BLEU is comparable with the combination of the best single systems (KIT 2009, LIMSI 2010, SYSTRAN 2010, RWTH 2010). However, we could gain 1.0 point in TER.

Due to the fact, that for the final submission the initial grouping was available only, we kept this

Table 2: Comparison of different system combination settings. For each possible combination of systems tuned on different tuning sets, a system combination was set up, re-tuned on newstest2011 and evaluated on newstest2012. The setting used for further experiments is set in boldface.

single systems				system combinations			
KIT	LIMSI	SYSTRAN	RWTH	newstest2011		newstest2012	
tuned on newstest				BLEU	TER	BLEU	TER
2009	2009	2009	2009	24.6	58.0	25.6	56.8
2010	2010	2010	2010	24.2	58.1	25.6	57.7
2010	2009	2009	2009	24.5	57.9	25.7	57.4
2009	2010	2009	2009	24.4	58.3	25.7	57.0
2009	2009	2010	2009	24.5	57.9	25.6	57.0
2009	2009	2009	2010	24.5	58.0	25.6	56.8
2009	2010	2010	2010	24.1	57.5	25.4	56.4
2010	2009	2010	2010	24.3	57.6	25.6	56.9
2010	2010	2009	2010	24.2	58.0	25.6	57.3
2010	2010	2010	2009	24.3	57.9	25.5	57.6
2010	2010	2009	2009	24.4	58.1	25.6	57.5
2009	2009	2010	2010	24.4	57.8	25.5	56.6
2009	2010	2010	2009	24.4	58.2	25.5	57.0
2009	2010	2009	2010	24.2	57.8	25.5	56.8
2010	2009	2009	2010	24.4	57.9	25.6	57.4
2010	**2009**	**2010**	**2009**	**24.4**	**57.7**	**25.6**	**57.4**

Table 3: Results of the final submission (boldface) compared with best single system on newstest2012.

	newstest2011		newstest2012	
	BLEU	TER	BLEU	TER
best single	23.2	60.9	24.6	58.4
system comb.	24.4	57.7	25.6	57.4
+ IBM-1	24.6	58.1	25.6	57.6
+ bigLM	**24.6**	**57.9**	**25.8**	**57.2**

combination. To improve this baseline further, two additional models were added. We applied lexical smoothing (*IBM-1*) and an additional language model (*bigLM*) trained on the English side of the parallel data and the News shuffle corpus. The results are presented in Table 3.

The baseline was slightly improved by 0.2 points in BLEU and TER. Note, this system combination was the final submission.

5 Conclusion

For the participation in the WMT 2013 shared translation task, the partners of the QUAERO project (Karlsruhe Institute of Technology, RWTH Aachen University, LIMSI-CNRS and SYSTRAN Software, Inc.) provided a joint submission. By joining the output of four different translation systems with RWTH's system combination, we reported an improvement of up to 1.2 points in BLEU and TER.

Combining systems optimized on different tuning sets does not seem to improve the translation quality. However, by adding additional model, the baseline was slightly improved.

All in all, we conclude that the variability in terms of BLEU does not influence the final result. It seems that using different approaches of MT in a system combination is more important (Freitag et al., 2012).

Acknowledgments

This work was achieved as part of the Quaero Programme, funded by OSEO, French State agency for innovation.

References

Alexandre Allauzen, Josep M. Crego, İlknur Durgar El-Kahlout, and François Yvon. 2010. LIMSI's statistical translation systems for WMT'10. In *Proc. of the Joint Workshop on Statistical Machine Translation and MetricsMATR*, pages 54–59, Uppsala, Sweden.

Alexandre Allauzen, Gilles Adda, Hélène Bonneau-Maynard, Josep M. Crego, Hai-Son Le, Aurélien Max, Adrien Lardilleux, Thomas Lavergne, Artem Sokolov, Guillaume Wisniewski, and François Yvon. 2011. LIMSI @ WMT11. In *Proceedings of the Sixth Workshop on Statistical Machine Translation*, pages 309–315, Edinburgh, Scotland, July. Association for Computational Linguistics.

Francesco Casacuberta and Enrique Vidal. 2004. Machine translation with inferred stochastic finite-state transducers. *Computational Linguistics*, 30(3):205–225.

Josep M. Crego and José B. Mario. 2006. Improving statistical MT by coupling reordering and decoding. *Machine Translation*, 20(3):199–215.

Josep M. Crego, Franois Yvon, and Jos B. Mario. 2011. N-code: an open-source Bilingual N-gram SMT Toolkit. *Prague Bulletin of Mathematical Linguistics*, 96:49–58.

Loïc Dugast, Jean Senellart, and Philipp Koehn. 2007. Statistical post-editing on systran's rule-based translation system. In *Proceedings of the Second Workshop on Statistical Machine Translation*, StatMT '07, pages 220–223, Stroudsburg, PA, USA. Association for Computational Linguistics.

Ilknur Durgar El-Kahlout and Franois Yvon. 2010. The pay-offs of preprocessing for German-English Statistical Machine Translation. In Marcello Federico, Ian Lane, Michael Paul, and Franois Yvon, editors, *Proceedings of the seventh International Workshop on Spoken Language Translation (IWSLT)*, pages 251–258.

Daniel Dchelotte, Gilles Adda, Alexandre Allauzen, Olivier Galibert, Jean-Luc Gauvain, Hlne Maynard, and Franois Yvon. 2008. LIMSI's statistical translation systems for WMT'08. In *Proc. of the NAACL-HTL Statistical Machine Translation Workshop*, Columbus, Ohio.

Markus Freitag, Stephan Peitz, Matthias Huck, Hermann Ney, Teresa Herrmann, Jan Niehues, Alex Waibel, Alexandre Allauzen, Gilles Adda, Bianka Buschbeck, Josep Maria Crego, and Jean Senellart. 2012. Joint wmt 2012 submission of the quaero project. In *NAACL 2012 Seventh Workshop on Statistical Machine Translation*, pages 322–329, Montreal, Canada, June.

Michel Galley and Christopher D. Manning. 2008. A simple and effective hierarchical phrase reordering model. In *Proceedings of the 2008 Conference on Empirical Methods in Natural Language Processing*, pages 847–855, Honolulu, Hawaii, October. Association for Computational Linguistics.

Teresa Herrmann, Jan Niehues, and Alex Waibel. 2013. Combining Word Reordering Methods on different Linguistic Abstraction Levels for Statistical Machine Translation. In *Proceedings of the Seventh Workshop on Syntax, Semantics and Structure in Statistical Translation*, Altanta, Georgia, USA, June. Association for Computational Linguistics.

Philipp Koehn and Kevin Knight. 2003. Empirical Methods for Compound Splitting. In *EACL*, Budapest, Hungary.

Philipp Koehn, Hieu Hoang, Alexandra Birch, Chris Callison-Burch, Marcello Federico, Nicola Bertoldi, Brooke Cowan, Wade Shen, Christine Moran, Richard Zens, Chris Dyer, Ondřej Bojar, Alexandra Constantine, and Evan Herbst. 2007. Moses: Open Source Toolkit for Statistical Machine Translation. pages 177–180, Prague, Czech Republic, June.

Alon Lavie and Abhaya Agarwal. 2007. METEOR: An Automatic Metric for MT Evaluation with High Levels of Correlation with Human Judgments. pages 228–231, Prague, Czech Republic, June.

Hai-Son Le, Ilya Oparin, Alexandre Allauzen, Jean-Luc Gauvain, and François Yvon. 2011. Structured output layer neural network language model. In *Proceedings of ICASSP'11*, pages 5524–5527.

Hai-Son Le, Alexandre Allauzen, and François Yvon. 2012. Continuous space translation models with neural networks. In *NAACL '12: Proceedings of the 2012 Conference of the North American Chapter of the Association for Computational Linguistics on Human Language Technology*.

Saab Mansour and Hermann Ney. 2012. A simple and effective weighted phrase extraction for machine translation adaptation. In *International Workshop on Spoken Language Translation*, pages 193–200, Hong Kong, December.

Sab Mansour, Joern Wuebker, and Hermann Ney. 2011. Combining Translation and Language Model Scoring for Domain-Specific Data Filtering. In *Proceedings of the International Workshop on Spoken Language Translation (IWSLT)*, San Francisco, CA, December.

José B. Mariño, Rafael E. Banchs, Josep M. Crego, Adrià de Gispert, Patrick Lambert, José A.R. Fonollosa, and Marta R. Costa-Jussà. 2006. N-gram-based machine translation. *Computational Linguistics*, 32(4):527–549.

Arne Mauser, Saša Hasan, and Hermann Ney. 2009. Extending Statistical Machine Translation with Discriminative and Trigger-based Lexicon Models. In *Proceedings of the 2009 Conference on Empirical Methods in Natural Language Processing: Volume 1 - Volume 1*, EMNLP '09, Singapore.

Mohammed Mediani, Eunah Cho, Jan Niehues, Teresa Herrmann, and Alex Waibel. 2011. The KIT English-French Translation Systems for IWSLT 2011. In *Proceedings of the Eighth International Workshop on Spoken Language Translation (IWSLT)*.

Jan Niehues and Muntsin Kolss. 2009. A POS-Based Model for Long-Range Reorderings in SMT. In *Fourth Workshop on Statistical Machine Translation (WMT 2009)*, Athens, Greece.

Jan Niehues and Stephan Vogel. 2008. Discriminative Word Alignment via Alignment Matrix Modeling. In *Proc. of Third ACL Workshop on Statistical Machine Translation*, Columbus, USA.

Jan Niehues, Teresa Herrmann, Muntsin Kolss, and Alex Waibel. 2009. The Universität Karlsruhe Translation System for the EACL-WMT 2009. In *Fourth Workshop on Statistical Machine Translation (WMT 2009)*, Athens, Greece.

Jan Niehues, Teresa Herrmann, Stephan Vogel, and Alex Waibel. 2011. Wider Context by Using Bilingual Language Models in Machine Translation. In *Sixth Workshop on Statistical Machine Translation (WMT 2011)*, Edinburgh, UK.

Franz Josef Och and Hermann Ney. 2003. A Systematic Comparison of Various Statistical Alignment Models. *Computational Linguistics*, 29(1):19–51, March.

Franz Josef Och. 2003a. Minimum Error Rate Training in Statistical Machine Translation. In *Proc. of the 41th Annual Meeting of the Association for Computational Linguistics (ACL)*, pages 160–167, Sapporo, Japan, July.

Franz Josef Och. 2003b. Minimum error rate training in statistical machine translation. In *ACL '03: Proc. of the 41st Annual Meeting on Association for Computational Linguistics*, pages 160–167.

M. Popović, D. Stein, and H. Ney. 2006. Statistical Machine Translation of German Compound Words. In *FinTAL - 5th International Conference on Natural Language Processing, Springer Verlag, LNCS*, pages 616–624.

Anna N. Rafferty and Christopher D. Manning. 2008. Parsing three German treebanks: lexicalized and unlexicalized baselines. In *Proceedings of the Workshop on Parsing German.*

Kay Rottmann and Stephan Vogel. 2007. Word Reordering in Statistical Machine Translation with a POS-Based Distortion Model. In *TMI*, Skövde, Sweden.

Helmut Schmid. 1994. Probabilistic Part-of-Speech Tagging Using Decision Trees. In *International Conference on New Methods in Language Processing*, Manchester, UK.

Helmut Schmid. 1995. Improvements in part-of-speech tagging with an application to German. In Evelyne Tzoukermann and SusanEditors Armstrong, editors, *Proceedings of the ACL SIGDAT-Workshop*, pages 47–50. Kluwer Academic Publishers.

Andreas Stolcke. 2002. SRILM – An Extensible Language Modeling Toolkit. In *Proc. Int. Conf. on Spoken Language Processing*, volume 2, pages 901–904, Denver, Colorado, USA.

Christoph Tillmann. 2004. A unigram orientation model for statistical machine translation. In *Proceedings of HLT-NAACL 2004*, pages 101–104. Association for Computational Linguistics.

Ashish Venugopal, Andreas Zollman, and Alex Waibel. 2005. Training and Evaluation Error Minimization Rules for Statistical Machine Translation. In *Workshop on Data-drive Machine Translation and Beyond (WPT-05)*, Ann Arbor, MI.

Stephan Vogel. 2003. SMT Decoder Dissected: Word Reordering. In *Int. Conf. on Natural Language Processing and Knowledge Engineering*, Beijing, China.

Joern Wuebker, Matthias Huck, Stephan Peitz, Malte Nuhn, Markus Freitag, Jan-Thorsten Peter, Saab Mansour, and Hermann Ney. 2012. Jane 2: Open source phrase-based and hierarchical statistical machine translation. In *International Conference on Computational Linguistics*, pages 483–491, Mumbai, India, December.

The RWTH Aachen Machine Translation System for WMT 2013

Stephan Peitz, Saab Mansour, Jan-Thorsten Peter, Christoph Schmidt, Joern Wuebker, Matthias Huck, Markus Freitag and Hermann Ney
Human Language Technology and Pattern Recognition Group
Computer Science Department
RWTH Aachen University
D-52056 Aachen, Germany
`<surname>@cs.rwth-aachen.de`

Abstract

This paper describes the statistical machine translation (SMT) systems developed at RWTH Aachen University for the translation task of the *ACL 2013 Eighth Workshop on Statistical Machine Translation* (WMT 2013). We participated in the evaluation campaign for the French-English and German-English language pairs in both translation directions. Both hierarchical and phrase-based SMT systems are applied. A number of different techniques are evaluated, including hierarchical phrase reordering, translation model interpolation, domain adaptation techniques, weighted phrase extraction, word class language model, continuous space language model and system combination. By application of these methods we achieve considerable improvements over the respective baseline systems.

1 Introduction

For the WMT 2013 shared translation task[1] RWTH utilized state-of-the-art phrase-based and hierarchical translation systems as well as an in-house system combination framework. We give a survey of these systems and the basic methods they implement in Section 2. For both the French-English (Section 3) and the German-English (Section 4) language pair, we investigate several different advanced techniques. We concentrate on specific research directions for each of the translation tasks and present the respective techniques along with the empirical results they yield: For the French→English task (Section 3.2), we apply a standard phrase-based system with up to five language models including a word class language model. In addition, we employ translation model interpolation and hierarchical phrase reordering. For the English→French task (Section 3.1), we train translation models on different training data sets and augment the phrase-based system with a hierarchical reordering model, a word class language model, a discriminative word lexicon and a insertion and deletion model. For the German→English (Section 4.3) and English→German (Section 4.4) tasks, we utilize morpho-syntactic analysis to preprocess the data (Section 4.1), domain-adaptation (Section 4.2) and a hierarchical reordering model. For the German→English task, an augmented hierarchical phrase-based system is set up and we rescore the phrase-based baseline with a continuous space language model. Finally, we perform a system combination.

2 Translation Systems

In this evaluation, we employ phrase-based translation and hierarchical phrase-based translation. Both approaches are implemented in *Jane* (Vilar et al., 2012; Wuebker et al., 2012), a statistical machine translation toolkit which has been developed at RWTH Aachen University and is freely available for non-commercial use.[2]

2.1 Phrase-based System

In the phrase-based decoder (source cardinality synchronous search, *SCSS*), we use the standard set of models with phrase translation probabilities and lexical smoothing in both directions, word and phrase penalty, distance-based distortion model, an n-gram target language model and three binary count features. Optional additional models used in this evaluation are the hierarchical reordering model (*HRM*) (Galley and Manning, 2008), a word class language model (*WCLM*) (Wuebker et

[1] `http://www.statmt.org/wmt13/translation-task.html`

[2] `http://www.hltpr.rwth-aachen.de/jane/`

al., 2012), a discriminative word lexicon (*DWL*) (Mauser et al., 2009), and insertion and deletion models (*IDM*) (Huck and Ney, 2012). The parameter weights are optimized with minimum error rate training (MERT) (Och, 2003). The optimization criterion is BLEU.

2.2 Hierarchical Phrase-based System

In hierarchical phrase-based translation (Chiang, 2007), a weighted synchronous context-free grammar is induced from parallel text. In addition to continuous *lexical* phrases, *hierarchical* phrases with up to two gaps are extracted. The search is carried out with a parsing-based procedure. The standard models integrated into our Jane hierarchical systems (Vilar et al., 2010; Huck et al., 2012c) are: phrase translation probabilities and lexical smoothing probabilities in both translation directions, word and phrase penalty, binary features marking hierarchical phrases, glue rule, and rules with non-terminals at the boundaries, four binary count features, and an n-gram language model. Optional additional models comprise IBM model 1 (Brown et al., 1993), discriminative word lexicon and triplet lexicon models (Mauser et al., 2009; Huck et al., 2011), discriminative reordering extensions (Huck et al., 2012a), insertion and deletion models (Huck and Ney, 2012), and several syntactic enhancements like preference grammars (Stein et al., 2010) and soft string-to-dependency features (Peter et al., 2011). We utilize the cube pruning algorithm for decoding (Huck et al., 2013) and optimize the model weights with MERT. The optimization criterion is BLEU.

2.3 System Combination

System combination is used to produce consensus translations from multiple hypotheses generated with different translation engines. First, a word to word alignment for the given single system hypotheses is produced. In a second step a confusion network is constructed. Then, the hypothesis with the highest probability is extracted from this confusion network. For the alignment procedure, one of the given single system hypotheses is chosen as primary system. To this primary system all other hypotheses are aligned using the METEOR (Lavie and Agarwal, 2007) alignment and thus the primary system defines the word order. Once the alignment is given, the corresponding confusion network is constructed. An example is given in Figure 1.

The model weights of the system combination are optimized with standard MERT on 100-best lists. For each single system, a factor is added to the log-linear framework of the system combination. Moreover, this log-linear model includes a word penalty, a language model trained on the input hypotheses, a binary feature which penalizes word deletions in the confusion network and a primary feature which marks the system which provides the word order. The optimization criterion is 4BLEU-TER.

2.4 Other Tools and Techniques

We employ GIZA++ (Och and Ney, 2003) to train word alignments. The two trained alignments are heuristically merged to obtain a symmetrized word alignment for phrase extraction. All language models (*LMs*) are created with the SRILM toolkit (Stolcke, 2002) and are standard 4-gram LMs with interpolated modified Kneser-Ney smoothing (Kneser and Ney, 1995; Chen and Goodman, 1998). The Stanford Parser (Klein and Manning, 2003) is used to obtain parses of the training data for the syntactic extensions of the hierarchical system. We evaluate in truecase with BLEU (Papineni et al., 2002) and TER (Snover et al., 2006).

2.5 Filtering of the Common Crawl Corpus

The new Common Crawl corpora contain a large number of sentences that are not in the labelled language. To clean these corpora, we first extracted a vocabulary from the other provided corpora. Then, only sentences containing at least 70% word from the known vocabulary were kept. In addition, we discarded sentences that contain more words from target vocabulary than source vocabulary on the source side. These heuristics reduced the French-English Common Crawl corpus by 5,1%. This filtering technique was also applied on the German-English version of the Common Crawl corpus.

3 French–English Setups

We trained phrase-based translation systems for French→English and for English→French. Corpus statistics for the French-English parallel data are given in Table 1. The LMs are 4-grams trained on the provided resources for the respective language (Europarl, News Commentary, UN, 10^9, Common Crawl, and monolingual News Crawl

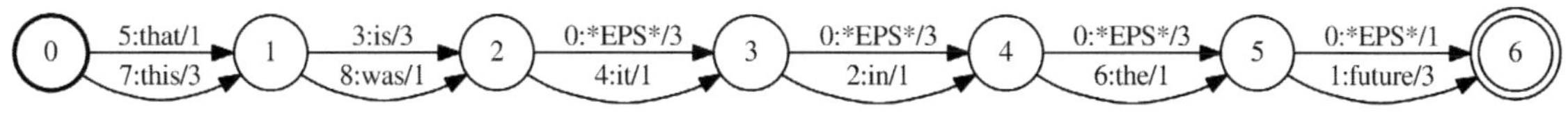

Figure 1: Confusion network of four different hypotheses.

Table 1: Corpus statistics of the preprocessed French-English parallel training data. *EPPS* denotes Europarl, *NC* denotes News Commentary, *CC* denotes Common Crawl. In the data, numerical quantities have been replaced by a single category symbol.

		French	English
EPPS + NC	Sentences	2.2M	
	Running Words	64.7M	59.7M
	Vocabulary	153.4K	132.2K
CC	Sentences	3.2M	
	Running Words	88.1M	80.9.0M
	Vocabulary	954.8K	908.0K
UN	Sentences	12.9M	
	Running Words	413.3M	362.3M
	Vocabulary	487.1K	508.3K
10^9	Sentences	22.5M	
	Running Words	771.7M	661.1M
	Vocabulary	1 974.0K	1 947.2K
All	Sentences	40.8M	
	Running Words	1 337.7M	1 163.9M
	Vocabulary	2 749.8K	2 730.1K

language model training data).[3]

3.1 Experimental Results English→French

For the English→French task, separate translation models (TMs) were trained for each of the five data sets and fed to the decoder. Four additional indicator features are introduced to distinguish the different TMs. Further, we applied the hierarchical reordering model, the word class language model, the discriminative word lexicon, and the insertion and deletion model. Table 2 shows the results of our experiments.

As a development set for MERT, we use newstest2010 in all setups.

3.2 Experimental Results French→English

For the French→English task, a translation model (*TM*) was trained on all available parallel data. For the baseline, we interpolated this TM with an in-domain TM trained on EPPS+NC and employed the hierarchical reordering model. Moreover, three language models were used: The first language model was trained on the English side of all available parallel data, the second one on EPPS and NC and the third LM on the News Shuffled data. The baseline was improved by adding a fourth LM trained on the Gigaword corpus (Version 5) and a 5-gram word class language model trained on News Shuffled data. For the WCLM, we used 50 word classes clustered with the tool *mkcls* (Och, 2000). All results are presented in Table 3.

4 German–English Setups

For both translation directions of the German-English language pair, we trained phrase-based translation systems. Corpus statistics for German-English can be found in Table 4. The language models are 4-grams trained on the respective target side of the bilingual data as well as on the provided News Crawl corpus. For the English language model the 10^9 French-English, UN and LDC Gigaword Fifth Edition corpora are used additionally.

4.1 Morpho-syntactic Analysis

In order to reduce the source vocabulary size for the German→English translation, the German text is preprocessed by splitting German compound words with the frequency-based method described in (Koehn and Knight, 2003). To further reduce translation complexity, we employ the long-range part-of-speech based reordering rules proposed by Popović and Ney (2006).

4.2 Domain Adaptation

This year, we experimented with filtering and weighting for domain-adaptation for the German-English task. To perform adaptation, we define a general-domain (GD) corpus composed from the news-commentary, europarl and Common Crawl corpora, and an in-domain (ID) corpus using a concatenation of the test sets (newstest{2008, 2009, 2010, 2011, 2012}) with the corresponding references. We use the test sets as in-domain

[3]The parallel 10^9 corpus is often also referred to as *WMT Giga French-English release 2.*

Table 2: Results for the English→French task (truecase). newstest2010 is used as development set. BLEU and TER are given in percentage.

English→French	newstest2008		newstest2009		newstest2010		newstest2011		newstest2012	
	BLEU	TER	BLEU	TER	BLEU	TER	BLEU	TER	BLEU	TER
TM:EPPS + HRM	22.9	63.0	25.0	60.0	27.8	56.7	28.9	54.4	27.2	57.1
TM:UN + HRM	22.7	63.4	25.0	60.0	28.3	56.4	29.5	54.2	27.3	57.1
TM:10^9 + HRM	23.5	62.3	26.0	59.2	29.6	55.2	30.3	53.3	28.0	56.4
TM:CC + HRM	23.5	62.3	26.2	58.8	29.2	55.3	30.3	53.3	28.2	56.0
TM:NC	21.0	64.8	22.3	61.6	25.6	58.7	26.9	56.6	25.7	58.5
+ HRM	21.5	64.3	22.6	61.2	26.1	58.4	27.3	56.1	26.0	58.2
+ TM:EPPS,CC,UN	23.9	61.8	26.4	58.6	29.9	54.7	31.0	52.7	28.6	55.6
+ TM:10^9	24.0	61.5	26.5	58.4	30.2	54.2	31.1	52.3	28.7	55.3
+ WCLM, DWL, IDM	24.0	61.6	26.5	58.3	30.4	54.0	31.4	52.1	28.8	55.2

Table 3: Results for the French→English task (truecase). newstest2010 is used as development set. BLEU and TER are given in percentage.

French→English	newstest2010		newstest2011		newstest2012	
	BLEU	TER	BLEU	TER	BLEU	TER
SCSS baseline	28.1	54.6	29.1	53.3	-	-
+ GigaWord.v5 LM	28.6	54.2	29.6	52.9	29.6	53.3
+ WCLM	29.1	53.8	30.1	52.5	29.8	53.1

(newswire) as the other corpora are coming from differing domains (news commentary, parliamentary discussions and various web sources), and on initial experiments, the other corpora did not perform well when used as an in-domain representative for adaptation. To check whether over-fitting occurs, we measure the results of the adapted systems on the evaluation set of this year (newstest2013) which was not used as part of the in-domain set.

The filtering experiments are done similarly to (Mansour et al., 2011), where we compare filtering using LM and a combined LM and IBM Model 1 (LM+M1) based scores. The scores for each sentence pair in the general-domain corpus are based on the bilingual cross-entropy difference of the in-domain and general-domain models. Denoting $H_{LM}(x)$ as the cross entropy of sentence x according to LM, then the cross entropy difference $DH_{LM}(x)$ can be written as:

$$DH_{LM}(x) = H_{LM_{ID}}(x) - H_{LM_{GD}}(x)$$

The bilingual cross entropy difference for a sentence pair (s, t) in the GD corpus is then defined by:

$$DH_{LM}(s) + DH_{LM}(t)$$

For IBM Model 1 (M1), the cross-entropy $H_{M1}(s|t)$ is defined similarly to the LM cross-entropy, and the resulting bilingual cross-entropy difference will be of the form:

$$DH_{M1}(s|t) + DH_{M1}(t|s)$$

The combined LM+M1 score is obtained by summing the LM and M1 bilingual cross-entropy difference scores. To perform filtering, the GD corpus sentence pairs are scored by the appropriate method, sorted by the score, and the n-best sentences are then used to build an adapted system.

In addition to adaptation using filtering, we experiment with weighted phrase extraction similar to (Mansour and Ney, 2012). We differ from their work by using a combined LM+M1 weight to perform the phrase extraction instead of an LM based weight. We use a combined LM+M1 weight as this worked best in the filtering experiments, making scoring with LM+M1 more reliable than LM scores only.

4.3 Experimental Results German→English

For the German→English task, the baseline is trained on all available parallel data and includes the hierarchical reordering model. The results of the various filtering and weighting experiments are summarized in Table 5.

Table 5: German-English results (truecase). BLEU and TER are given in percentage. Corresponding development set is marked with *. † labels the single systems selected for the system combination.

German→English	newstest2009		newstest2010		newstest2011		newstest2012		newstest2013	
	BLEU	TER	BLEU	TER	BLEU	TER	BLEU	TER	BLEU	TER
SCSS baseline	21.7	61.1	24.8*	58.9*	22.0	61.1	23.4	60.0	26.1	56.4
LM 800K-best	21.6	60.5	24.7*	58.3*	22.0	60.5	23.6	59.7	-	-
LM+M1 800K-best	21.4	60.5	24.7*	58.1*	22.0	60.4	23.7	59.2	-	-
(LM+M1)*TM	22.1	60.2	25.4*	57.8*	22.5	60.1	24.0	59.1	-	-
(LM+M1)*TM+GW	22.8	59.5	25.7*	57.2*	23.1	59.5	24.4	58.6	26.6	55.5
(LM+M1)*TM+GW†	22.9*	61.1*	25.2	59.3	22.8	61.5	23.7	60.8	26.4	57.1
SCSS baseline	22.6*	61.6*	24.1	60.1	22.1	62.0	23.1	61.2	-	-
CSLM rescoring†	22.0	60.4	25.1*	58.3*	22.4	60.2	23.9	59.3	26.0	56.0
HPBT†	21.9	60.4	24.9*	58.2*	22.3	60.3	23.6	59.6	25.9	56.3
system combination	-	-	-	-	23.4*	59.3*	24.7	58.5	27.1	55.3

Table 6: English-German results (truecase). newstest2009 was used as development set. BLEU and TER are given in percentage.

English→German	newstest2008		newstest2009		newstest2010		newstest2011		newstest2012	
	BLEU	TER	BLEU	TER	BLEU	TER	BLEU	TER	BLEU	TER
SCSS baseline	14.9	70.9	14.9	70.4	16.0	66.3	15.4	69.5	15.7	67.5
LM 800K-best	15.1	70.9	15.1	70.3	16.2	66.3	15.6	69.4	15.9	67.4
(LM+M1) 800K-best	15.8	70.8	15.4	70.0	16.2	66.2	16.0	69.3	16.1	67.4
(LM+M1) ifelse	16.1	70.6	15.7	69.9	16.5	66.0	16.2	69.2	16.3	67.2

Table 4: Corpus statistics of the preprocessed German-English parallel training data (Europarl, News Commentary and Common Crawl). In the data, numerical quantities have been replaced by a single category symbol.

	German	English
Sentences	4.1M	
Running Words	104M	104M
Vocabulary	717K	750K

For filtering, we use the 800K best sentences from the whole training corpora, as this selection performed best on the dev set among 100K,200K,400K,800K,1600K setups. Filtering seems to mainly improve on the TER scores, BLEU scores are virtually unchanged in comparison to the baseline. LM+M1 filtering improves further on TER in comparison to LM-based filtering.

The weighted phrase extraction performs best in our experiments, where the weights from the LM+M1 scoring method are used. Improvements in both BLEU and TER are achieved, with BLEU improvements ranging from +0.4% up-to +0.6% and TER improvements from -0.9% and up-to -1.1%.

As a final step, we added the English Gigaword corpus to the LM (+GW). This resulted in further improvements of the systems.

In addition, the system as described above was tuned on newstest2009. Using this development set results in worse translation quality.

Furthermore, we rescored the SCSS baseline tuned on newstest2009 with a continuous space language model (*CSLM*) as described in (Schwenk et al., 2012). The CSLM was trained on the europarl and news-commentary corpora. For rescoring, we used the newstest2011 set as tuning set and re-optimized the parameters with MERT on 1000-best lists. This results in an improvement of up to 0.8 points in BLEU compared to the baseline.

We compared the phrase-based setups with a hierarchical translation system, which was augmented with preference grammars, soft string-to-dependency features, discriminative reordering extensions, DWL, IDM, and discriminative reordering extensions. The phrase table of the hierarchical setup has been extracted from News Commentary and Europarl parallel data only (not from Common Crawl).

Finally, three setups were joined in a system combination and we gained an improvement of up to 0.5 points in BLEU compared to the best single system.

4.4 Experimental Results English→German

The results for the English→German task are shown in Table 6. While the LM-based filtering led to almost no improvement over the baseline, the LM+M1 filtering brought some improvements in BLEU. In addition to the sentence filtering, we tried to combine the translation model trained on NC+EPPS with a TM trained on Common Crawl using the *ifelse* combination (Mansour and Ney, 2012). This combination scheme concatenates both TMs and assigns the probabilities of the in-domain TM if it contains the phrase, else it uses the probabilities of the out-of-domain TM. Appling this method, we achieved further improvements.

5 Conclusion

For the participation in the WMT 2013 shared translation task, RWTH experimented with both phrase-based and hierarchical translation systems. Several different techniques were evaluated and yielded considerable improvements over the respective baseline systems as well as over our last year's setups (Huck et al., 2012b). Among these techniques are a hierarchical phrase reordering model, translation model interpolation, domain adaptation techniques, weighted phrase extraction, a word class language model, a continuous space language model and system combination.

Acknowledgments

This work was achieved as part of the Quaero Programme, funded by OSEO, French State agency for innovation.

References

Peter F. Brown, Stephen A. Della Pietra, Vincent J. Della Pietra, and Robert L. Mercer. 1993. The Mathematics of Statistical Machine Translation: Parameter Estimation. *Computational Linguistics*, 19(2):263–311, June.

Stanley F. Chen and Joshua Goodman. 1998. An Empirical Study of Smoothing Techniques for Language Modeling. Technical Report TR-10-98, Computer Science Group, Harvard University, Cambridge, Massachusetts, USA, August.

David Chiang. 2007. Hierarchical Phrase-Based Translation. *Computational Linguistics*, 33(2):201–228.

Michel Galley and Christopher D. Manning. 2008. A Simple and Effective Hierarchical Phrase Reordering Model. In *Proceedings of the 2008 Conference on Empirical Methods in Natural Language Processing*, pages 847–855, Honolulu, Hawaii, USA, October.

Matthias Huck and Hermann Ney. 2012. Insertion and Deletion Models for Statistical Machine Translation. In *Proceedings of the North American Chapter of the Association for Computational Linguistics - Human Language Technologies conference*, pages 347–351, Montréal, Canada, June.

Matthias Huck, Saab Mansour, Simon Wiesler, and Hermann Ney. 2011. Lexicon Models for Hierarchical Phrase-Based Machine Translation. In *Proceedings of the International Workshop on Spoken Language Translation (IWSLT)*, pages 191–198, San Francisco, California, USA, December.

Matthias Huck, Stephan Peitz, Markus Freitag, and Hermann Ney. 2012a. Discriminative Reordering Extensions for Hierarchical Phrase-Based Machine Translation. In *16th Annual Conference of the European Association for Machine Translation*, pages 313–320, Trento, Italy, May.

Matthias Huck, Stephan Peitz, Markus Freitag, Malte Nuhn, and Hermann Ney. 2012b. The RWTH Aachen Machine Translation System for WMT 2012. In *NAACL 2012 Seventh Workshop on Statistical Machine Translation*, pages 304–311, Montréal, Canada, June.

Matthias Huck, Jan-Thorsten Peter, Markus Freitag, Stephan Peitz, and Hermann Ney. 2012c. Hierarchical Phrase-Based Translation with Jane 2. *The Prague Bulletin of Mathematical Linguistics*, 98:37–50, October.

Matthias Huck, David Vilar, Markus Freitag, and Hermann Ney. 2013. A Performance Study of Cube Pruning for Large-Scale Hierarchical Machine Translation. In *Proceedings of the NAACL 7th Workshop on Syntax, Semantics and Structure in Statistical Translation*, pages 29–38, Atlanta, Georgia, USA, June.

Dan Klein and Christopher D. Manning. 2003. Accurate Unlexicalized Parsing. In *Proc. of the 41th Annual Meeting of the Association for Computational Linguistics (ACL)*, pages 423–430, Sapporo, Japan, July.

Reinhard Kneser and Hermann Ney. 1995. Improved Backing-Off for M-gram Language Modeling. In *Proceedings of the International Conference on Acoustics, Speech, and Signal Processing*, volume 1, pages 181–184, May.

Philipp Koehn and Kevin Knight. 2003. Empirical Methods for Compound Splitting. In *Proceedings of European Chapter of the ACL (EACL 2009)*, pages 187–194.

Alon Lavie and Abhaya Agarwal. 2007. METEOR: An Automatic Metric for MT Evaluation with High Levels of Correlation with Human Judgments. In *ACL 2007 Second Workshop on Statistical Machine Translation*, pages 228–231, Prague, Czech Republic, June.

Saab Mansour and Hermann Ney. 2012. A Simple and Effective Weighted Phrase Extraction for Machine Translation Adaptation. In *Proceedings of the International Workshop on Spoken Language Translation (IWSLT)*, pages 193–200, Hong Kong, December.

Saab Mansour, Joern Wuebker, and Hermann Ney. 2011. Combining Translation and Language Model Scoring for Domain-Specific Data Filtering. In *Proceedings of the International Workshop on Spoken Language Translation (IWSLT)*, pages 222–229, San Francisco, California, USA, December.

Arne Mauser, Saša Hasan, and Hermann Ney. 2009. Extending Statistical Machine Translation with Discriminative and Trigger-Based Lexicon Models. In *Proc. of the Conf. on Empirical Methods for Natural Language Processing (EMNLP)*, pages 210–218, Singapore, August.

Franz Josef Och and Hermann Ney. 2003. A Systematic Comparison of Various Statistical Alignment Models. *Computational Linguistics*, 29(1):19–51, March.

Franz Josef Och. 2000. mkcls: Training of word classes for language modeling. `http://www.hltpr.rwth-aachen.de/web/Software/mkcls.html`.

Franz Josef Och. 2003. Minimum Error Rate Training in Statistical Machine Translation. In *Proc. of the 41th Annual Meeting of the Association for Computational Linguistics (ACL)*, pages 160–167, Sapporo, Japan, July.

Kishore Papineni, Salim Roukos, Todd Ward, and Wei-Jing Zhu. 2002. Bleu: a Method for Automatic Evaluation of Machine Translation. In *Proceedings of the 41st Annual Meeting of the Association for Computational Linguistics*, pages 311–318, Philadelphia, Pennsylvania, USA, July.

Jan-Thorsten Peter, Matthias Huck, Hermann Ney, and Daniel Stein. 2011. Soft String-to-Dependency Hierarchical Machine Translation. In *International Workshop on Spoken Language Translation*, pages 246–253, San Francisco, California, USA, December.

Maja Popović and Hermann Ney. 2006. POS-based Word Reorderings for Statistical Machine Translation. In *International Conference on Language Resources and Evaluation*, pages 1278–1283, Genoa, Italy, May.

Holger Schwenk, Anthony Rousseau, and Mohammed Attik. 2012. Large, Pruned or Continuous Space Language Models on a GPU for Statistical Machine Translation. In *NAACL-HLT 2012 Workshop: Will We Ever Really Replace the N-gram Model? On the Future of Language Modeling for HLT*, pages 11–19, Montréal, Canada, June.

Matthew Snover, Bonnie Dorr, Richard Schwartz, Linnea Micciulla, and John Makhoul. 2006. A Study of Translation Edit Rate with Targeted Human Annotation. In *Proceedings of the 7th Conference of the Association for Machine Translation in the Americas*, pages 223–231, Cambridge, Massachusetts, USA, August.

Daniel Stein, Stephan Peitz, David Vilar, and Hermann Ney. 2010. A Cocktail of Deep Syntactic Features for Hierarchical Machine Translation. In *Conf. of the Association for Machine Translation in the Americas (AMTA)*, Denver, Colorado, USA, October/November.

Andreas Stolcke. 2002. SRILM – An Extensible Language Modeling Toolkit. In *Proc. of the Int. Conf. on Speech and Language Processing (ICSLP)*, volume 2, pages 901–904, Denver, Colorado, USA, September.

David Vilar, Daniel Stein, Matthias Huck, and Hermann Ney. 2010. Jane: Open Source Hierarchical Translation, Extended with Reordering and Lexicon Models. In *ACL 2010 Joint Fifth Workshop on Statistical Machine Translation and Metrics MATR*, pages 262–270, Uppsala, Sweden, July.

David Vilar, Daniel Stein, Matthias Huck, and Hermann Ney. 2012. Jane: an advanced freely available hierarchical machine translation toolkit. *Machine Translation*, 26(3):197–216, September.

Joern Wuebker, Matthias Huck, Stephan Peitz, Malte Nuhn, Markus Freitag, Jan-Thorsten Peter, Saab Mansour, and Hermann Ney. 2012. Jane 2: Open Source Phrase-based and Hierarchical Statistical Machine Translation. In *International Conference on Computational Linguistics*, pages 483–491, Mumbai, India, December.

The University of Cambridge Russian-English System at WMT13

Juan Pino Aurelien Waite Tong Xiao
Adrià de Gispert Federico Flego William Byrne
Department of Engineering, University of Cambridge, Cambridge, CB2 1PZ, UK
{jmp84,aaw35,tx212,ad465,ff257,wjb31}@eng.cam.ac.uk

Abstract

This paper describes the University of Cambridge submission to the Eighth Workshop on Statistical Machine Translation. We report results for the Russian-English translation task. We use multiple segmentations for the Russian input language. We employ the Hadoop framework to extract rules. The decoder is HiFST, a hierarchical phrase-based decoder implemented using weighted finite-state transducers. Lattices are rescored with a higher order language model and minimum Bayes-risk objective.

1 Introduction

This paper describes the University of Cambridge system submission to the ACL 2013 Eighth Workshop on Statistical Machine Translation (WMT13). Our translation system is HiFST (Iglesias et al., 2009), a hierarchical phrase-based decoder that generates translation lattices directly. Decoding is guided by a CYK parser based on a synchronous context-free grammar induced from automatic word alignments (Chiang, 2007). The decoder is implemented with Weighted Finite State Transducers (WFSTs) using standard operations available in the OpenFst libraries (Allauzen et al., 2007). The use of WFSTs allows fast and efficient exploration of a vast translation search space, avoiding search errors in decoding. It also allows better integration with other steps in our translation pipeline such as 5-gram language model (LM) rescoring and lattice minimum Bayes-risk (LMBR) decoding (Blackwood, 2010).

We participate in the Russian-English translation shared task in the Russian-English direction. This is the first time we train and evaluate a system on this language pair. This paper describes the development of the system.

The paper is organised as follows. Section 2 describes each step in the development of our system for submission, from pre-processing to post-processing and Section 3 presents and discusses results.

2 System Development

2.1 Pre-processing

We use all the Russian-English parallel data available in the constraint track. We filter out non Russian-English sentence pairs with the *language-detection* library.[2] A sentence pair is filtered out if the language detector detects a different language with probability more than 0.999995 in either the source or the target. This discards 78543 sentence pairs. In addition, sentence pairs where the source sentence has no Russian character, defined by the Perl regular expression [\x0400-\x04ff], are discarded. This further discards 19000 sentence pairs.

The Russian side of the parallel corpus is tokenised with the Stanford CoreNLP toolkit.[3] The Stanford CoreNLP tokenised text is additionally segmented with Morfessor (Creutz and Lagus, 2007) and with the TreeTagger (Schmid, 1995). In the latter case, we replace each token by its stem followed by its part-of-speech. This offers various segmentations that can be taken advantage of in hypothesis combination: CoreNLP, CoreNLP+Morfessor and CoreNLP+TreeTagger. The English side of the parallel corpus is tokenised with a standard in-house tokeniser. Both sides of the parallel corpus are then lowercased, so mixed case is restored in post-processing.

Corpus statistics after filtering and for various segmentations are summarised in Table 1.

[2]http://code.google.com/p/language-detection/
[3]http://nlp.stanford.edu/software/corenlp.shtml

Lang	Segmentation	# Tokens	# Types
RU	CoreNLP	47.4M	1.2M
RU	Morfessor	50.0M	0.4M
RU	TreeTagger	47.4M	1.5M
EN	Cambridge	50.4M	0.7M

Table 1: Russian-English parallel corpus statistics for various segmentations.

2.2 Alignments

Parallel data is aligned using the MTTK toolkit (Deng and Byrne, 2008). We train a word-to-phrase HMM model with a maximum phrase length of 4 in both source-to-target and target-to-source directions. The final alignments are obtained by taking the union of alignments obtained in both directions.

2.3 Rule Extraction and Retrieval

A synchronous context-free grammar (Chiang, 2007) is extracted from the alignments. The constraints are set as in the original publication with the following exceptions:

- phrase-based rule maximum number of source words: 9
- maximum number of source element (terminal or nonterminal): 5
- maximum span for nonterminals: 10

Maximum likelihood estimates for the translation probabilities are computed using MapReduce. We use a custom Hadoop-based toolkit which implements method 3 of Dyer et al. (2008). Once computed, the model parameters are stored on disk in the HFile format (Pino et al., 2012) for fast querying. Rule extraction and feature computation takes about 2h30. The HFile format requires data to be stored in a key-value structure. For the key, we use shared source side of many rules. The value is a list of tuples containing the possible targets for the source key and the associated parameters of the full rule. The query set of keys for the test set is all possible source phrases (including nonterminals) found in the test set.

During HFile querying we add other features. These include IBM Model 1 (Brown et al., 1993) lexical probabilities. Loading these models in memory doesn't fit well with the MapReduce model so lexical features are computed for each test set rather than for the entire parallel corpus. The model parameters are stored in a client-server based architecture. The client process computes the probability of the rule by querying the server process for the Model 1 parameters. The server process stores the model parameters completely in memory so that parameters are served quickly. This architecture allows for many low-memory client processes across many machines.

2.4 Language Model

We used the KenLM toolkit (Heafield et al., 2013) to estimate separate 4-gram LMs with Kneser-Ney smoothing (Kneser and Ney, 1995), for each of the corpora listed in Tables 2 (self-explanatory abbreviations). The component models were then interpolated with the SRILM toolkit (Stolcke, 2002) to form a single LM for use in first-pass translation decoding. The interpolation weights were optimised for perplexity on the *news-test2008*, *newstest2009* and *newssyscomb2009* development sets. The weights reflect both the size of the component models and the genre of the corpus the component models are trained on, e.g. weights are larger for larger corpora in the news genre.

Corpus	# Tokens
EU + NC + UN + CzEng + Yx	652.5M
Giga + CC + Wiki	654.1M
News Crawl	1594.3M
afp	874.1M
apw	1429.3M
cna + wpb	66.4M
ltw	326.5M
nyt	1744.3M
xin	425.3M
Total	7766.9M

Table 2: Statistics for English monolingual corpora.

2.5 Decoding

For translation, we use the HiFST decoder (Iglesias et al., 2009). HiFST is a hierarchical decoder that builds target word lattices guided by a probabilistic synchronous context-free grammar. Assuming $\mathbf{N}$ to be the set of non-terminals and $\mathbf{T}$ the set of terminals or words, then we can define the grammar as a set $\mathbf{R} = \{R\}$ of rules $R : N \rightarrow \langle\gamma,\alpha\rangle$ / p, where $N \in \mathbf{N}$, $\gamma, \alpha \in \{\mathbf{N} \cup \mathbf{T}\}^+$ and p the rule score.

HiFST translates in three steps. The first step is a variant of the CYK algorithm (Chappelier and Rajman, 1998), in which we apply hypothesis recombination without pruning. Only the source language sentence is parsed using the corresponding source-side context-free grammar with rules $N \to \gamma$. Each cell in the CYK grid is specified by a non-terminal symbol and position: (N, x, y), spanning s_x^{x+y-1} on the source sentence $s_1...s_J$.

For the second step, we use a recursive algorithm to construct word lattices with all possible translations produced by the hierarchical rules. Construction proceeds by traversing the CYK grid along the back-pointers established in parsing. In each cell (N, x, y) of the CYK grid, we build a target language word lattice $\mathcal{L}(N, x, y)$ containing every translation of s_x^{x+y-1} from every derivation headed by N. For efficiency, this lattice can use pointers to lattices on other cells of the grid.

In the third step, we apply the word-based LM via standard WFST composition with failure transitions, and perform likelihood-based pruning (Allauzen et al., 2007) based on the combined translation and LM scores.

We are using shallow-1 hierarchical grammars (de Gispert et al., 2010) in our experiments. This model is constrained enough that the decoder can build exact search spaces, i.e. there is no pruning in search that may lead to spurious undergeneration errors.

2.6 Features and Parameter Optimisation

We use the following standard features:

- language model
- source-to-target and target-to-source translation scores
- source-to-target and target-to-source lexical scores
- target word count
- rule count
- glue rule count
- deletion rule count (each source unigram, except for OOVs, is allowed to be deleted)
- binary feature indicating whether a rule is extracted once, twice or more than twice (Bender et al., 2007)

No alignment information is used when computing lexical scores as done in Equation (4) in (Koehn et al., 2005). Instead, the source-to-target lexical score is computed in Equation 1:

$$s(\mathbf{ru}, \mathbf{en}) = \frac{1}{(E+1)^R} \prod_{r=1}^{R} \sum_{e=0}^{E} p_{M1}(\mathbf{en}_e | \mathbf{ru}_r) \tag{1}$$

where **ru** are the terminals in the Russian side of a rule, **en** are the terminals in the English side of a rule, including the null word, R is the number of Russian terminals, E is the number of English terminals and p_{M1} is the IBM Model 1 probability.

In addition to these standard features, we also use provenance features (Chiang et al., 2011). The parallel data is divided into four subcorpora: the Common Crawl (CC) corpus, the News Commentary (NC) corpus, the Yandex (Yx) corpus and the Wiki Headlines (Wiki) corpus. For each of these subcorpora, source-to-target and target-to-source translation and lexical scores are computed. This requires computing IBM Model 1 for each subcorpus. In total, there are 28 features, 12 standard features and 16 provenance features.

When retrieving relevant rules for a particular test set, various thresholds are applied, such as number of targets per source or translation probability cutoffs. Thresholds involving source-to-target translation scores are applied separately for each provenance and the union of all surviving rules for each provenance is kept. This strategy gives slight gains over using thresholds only for the general translation table.

We use an implementation of lattice minimum error rate training (Macherey et al., 2008) to optimise under the BLEU score (Papineni et al., 2001) the feature weights with respect to the odd sentences of the *newstest2012* development set (*newstest2012.tune*). The weights obtained match our expectation, for example, the source-to-target translation feature weight is higher for the NC corpus than for other corpora since we are translating news.

2.7 Lattice Rescoring

The HiFST decoder is set to directly generate large translation lattices encoding many alternative translation hypotheses. These first-pass lattices are rescored with second-pass higher-order LMs prior to LMBR.

2.7.1 5-gram LM Lattice Rescoring

We build a sentence-specific, zero-cutoff stupid-backoff (Brants et al., 2007) 5-gram LMs estimated over the data described in section 2.4. Lattices obtained by first-pass decoding are rescored with this 5-gram LM (Blackwood, 2010).

2.7.2 LMBR Decoding

Minimum Bayes-risk decoding (Kumar and Byrne, 2004) over the full evidence space of the 5-gram rescored lattices is applied to select the translation hypothesis that maximises the conditional expected gain under the linearised sentence-level BLEU score (Tromble et al., 2008; Blackwood, 2010). The unigram precision p and average recall ratio r are set as described in Tromble et al. (2008) using the *newstest2012.tune* development set.

2.8 Hypothesis Combination

LMBR decoding (Tromble et al., 2008) can also be used as an effective framework for multiple lattice combination (Blackwood, 2010). We used LMBR to combine translation lattices produced by systems trained on alternative segmentations.

2.9 Post-processing

Training data is lowercased, so we apply truecasing as post-processing. We used the *disambig* tool provided by the SRILM toolkit (Stolcke, 2002). The word mapping model which contains the probability of mapping a lower-cased word to its mixed-cased form is trained on all available data. A Kneser-Ney smoothed 4-gram language model is also trained on the following corpora: NC, News Crawl, Wiki, afp, apw, cna, ltw, nyt, wpb, xin, giga. In addition, several rules are manually designed to improve upon the output of the *disambig* tool. First, casing information from pass-through translation rules (for OOV source words) is used to modify the casing of the output. For example, this allows us to get the correct casing for the word *Bundesrechnungshof*. Other rules are post-editing rules which force some words to their upper-case forms, such as *euro* $\rightarrow$ *Euro*. Post-editing rules are developed based on high-frequency errors on the *newstest2012.tune* development set. These rules give an improvement of 0.2 mixed-cased NIST BLEU on the development set.

Finally, the output is detokenised before submission and Cyrillic characters are transliterated. We assume for human judgment purposes that it is better to have a non English word in Latin alphabet than in Cyrillic (e.g. *uprazdnyayushchie*); sometimes, transliteration can also give a correct output (e.g. *Movember*), especially in the case of proper nouns.

3 Results and Discussion

Results are reported in Table 3. We use the internationalisation switch for the NIST BLEU scoring script in order to properly lowercase the hypothesis and the reference. This introduces a slight discrepancy with official results going into the English language. The *newstest2012.test* development set consists of even sentences from *newstest2012*. We observe that the CoreNLP system (A) outperforms the other two systems. The CoreNLP+Morfessor system (B) has a much smaller vocabulary but the model size is comparable to the system A's model size. Translation did not benefit from source side morphological decomposition. We also observe that the gain from LMBR hypothesis combination (A+B+C) is minimal. Unlike other language pairs, such as Arabic-English (de Gispert et al., 2009), we have not yet found any great advantage in multiple morphological decomposition or preprocessing analyses of the source text. 5-gram and LMBR rescoring give consistent improvements. 5-gram rescoring improvements are very modest, probably because the first pass 4-gram model is trained on the same data. As noted, hypothesis combination using the various segmentations gives consistent but modest gains over each individual system.

Two systems were submitted to the evaluation. System A+B+C achieved a mixed-cased NIST BLEU score of 24.6, which was the top score achieved under this measure. System A system achieved a mixed-cased NIST BLEU score of 24.5, which was the second highest score.

4 Summary

We have successfully trained a Russian-English system for the first time. Lessons learned include that simple tokenisation is enough to process the Russian side, very modest gains come from combining alternative segmentations (it could also be that the Morfessor segmentation should not be performed after CoreNLP but directly on untokenised data), and reordering between Russian and English is such that a shallow-1 grammar performs

Configuration	*newstest2012.tune*	*newstest2012.test*	*newstest2013*
CoreNLP(A)	33.65	32.36	25.55
+5g	33.67	32.58	25.63
+5g+LMBR	**33.98**	**32.89**	**25.89**
CoreNLP+Morfessor(B)	33.21	31.91	25.33
+5g	33.28	32.12	25.44
+5g+LMBR	33.58	32.43	25.78
CoreNLP+TreeTagger(C)	32.92	31.54	24.78
+5g	32.94	31.85	24.97
+5g+LMBR	33.12	32.12	25.05
A+B+C	**34.32**	**33.13**	**26.00**

Table 3: Translation results, shown in lowercase NIST BLEU. Bold results correspond to submitted systems.

competitively.

Future work could include exploring alternative grammars, applying a 5-gram Kneser-Ney smoothed language model directly in first-pass decoding, and combining alternative segmentations that are more diverse from each other.

Acknowledgments

The research leading to these results has received funding from the European Union Seventh Framework Programme (FP7-ICT-2009-4) under grant agreement number 247762. Tong Xiao was supported in part by the National Natural Science Foundation of China (Grant 61073140 and Grant 61272376) and the China Postdoctoral Science Foundation (Grant 2013M530131).

References

Cyril Allauzen, Michael Riley, Johan Schalkwyk, Wojciech Skut, and Mehryar Mohri. 2007. OpenFst: A general and efficient weighted finite-state transducer library. In *Proceedings of CIAA*, pages 11–23.

Oliver Bender, Evgeny Matusov, Stefan Hahn, Sasa Hasan, Shahram Khadivi, and Hermann Ney. 2007. The RWTH Arabic-to-English spoken language translation system. In *Proceedings of ASRU*, pages 396–401.

Graeme Blackwood. 2010. *Lattice rescoring methods for statistical machine translation*. Ph.D. thesis, Cambridge University Engineering Department and Clare College.

Thorsten Brants, Ashok C. Popat, Peng Xu, Franz J. Och, and Jeffrey Dean. 2007. Large language models in machine translation. In *Proceedings of EMNLP-ACL*, pages 858–867.

Peter F. Brown, Vincent J. Della Pietra, Stephen A. Della Pietra, and Robert L. Mercer. 1993. The mathematics of statistical machine translation: Parameter estimation. *Computational linguistics*, 19(2):263–311.

Jean-Cédric Chappelier and Martin Rajman. 1998. A generalized CYK algorithm for parsing stochastic CFG. In *Proceedings of TAPD*, pages 133–137.

David Chiang, Steve DeNeefe, and Michael Pust. 2011. Two easy improvements to lexical weighting. In *Proceedings of the 49th Annual Meeting of the Association for Computational Linguistics: Human Language Technologies*, pages 455–460, Portland, Oregon, USA, June. Association for Computational Linguistics.

David Chiang. 2007. Hierarchical phrase-based translation. *Computational Linguistics*, 33(2):201–228.

Mathias Creutz and Krista Lagus. 2007. Unsupervised models for morpheme segmentation and morphology learning. *ACM Transactions on Speech and Language Processing (TSLP)*, 4(1):3.

Adrià de Gispert, Sami Virpioja, Mikko Kurimo, and William Byrne. 2009. Minimum Bayes Risk Combination of Translation Hypotheses from Alternative Morphological Decompositions. In *Proceedings of HLT/NAACL, Companion Volume: Short Papers*, pages 73–76.

Adrià de Gispert, Gonzalo Iglesias, Graeme Blackwood, Eduardo R. Banga, and William Byrne. 2010. Hierarchical phrase-based translation with weighted finite state transducers and shallow-n grammars. In *Computational Linguistics*.

Yonggang Deng and William Byrne. 2008. Hmm word and phrase alignment for statistical machine translation. *IEEE Transactions on Audio, Speech, and Language Processing*, 16(3):494–507.

Chris Dyer, Aaron Cordova, Alex Mont, and Jimmy Lin. 2008. Fast, easy, and cheap: Construction of statistical machine translation models with

MapReduce. In *Proceedings of the Third Workshop on Statistical Machine Translation*, pages 199–207, Columbus, Ohio, June. Association for Computational Linguistics.

Kenneth Heafield, Ivan Pouzyrevsky, Jonathan H. Clark, and Philipp Koehn. 2013. Scalable modified Kneser-Ney language model estimation. In *Proceedings of the 51st Annual Meeting of the Association for Computational Linguistics*, Sofia, Bulgaria, August.

Gonzalo Iglesias, Adrià de Gispert, Eduardo R. Banga, and William Byrne. 2009. Hierarchical phrase-based translation with weighted finite state transducers. In *Proceedings of NAACL*, pages 433–441.

Reinhard Kneser and Hermann Ney. 1995. Improved backing-off for m-gram language modeling. In *Proceedings of ICASSP*, volume 1, pages 181–184.

Philipp Koehn, Amittai Axelrod, Alexandra Birch Mayne, Chris Callison-Burch, Miles Osborne, and David Talbot. 2005. Edinburgh system description for the 2005 iwslt speech translation evaluation. In *International Workshop on Spoken Language Translation*, volume 8.

Shankar Kumar and William Byrne. 2004. Minimum Bayes-risk decoding for statistical machine translation. In *Proceedings of HLT-NAACL*, pages 169–176.

Wolfgang Macherey, Franz Och, Ignacio Thayer, and Jakob Uszkoreit. 2008. Lattice-based minimum error rate training for statistical machine translation. In *Proceedings of the 2008 Conference on Empirical Methods in Natural Language Processing*, pages 725–734, Honolulu, Hawaii, October. Association for Computational Linguistics.

Kishore Papineni, Salim Roukos, Todd Ward, and Wei-Jing Zhu. 2001. BLEU: a method for automatic evaluation of machine translation. In *Proceedings of ACL*, pages 311–318.

Juan Pino, Aurelien Waite, and William Byrne. 2012. Simple and efficient model filtering in statistical machine translation. *The Prague Bulletin of Mathematical Linguistics*, 98(1):5–24.

Helmut Schmid. 1995. Improvements in part-of-speech tagging with an application to German. In *Proceedings of the ACL SIGDAT-Workshop*, pages 47–50.

Andreas Stolcke. 2002. SRILM–An Extensible Language Modeling Toolkit. In *Proceedings of ICSLP*, volume 3, pages 901–904.

Roy W. Tromble, Shankar Kumar, Franz Och, and Wolfgang Macherey. 2008. Lattice Minimum Bayes-Risk decoding for statistical machine translation. In *Proceedings of EMNLP*, pages 620–629.

Joshua 5.0: Sparser, better, faster, server

Matt Post[1] and **Juri Ganitkevitch**[2] and **Luke Orland**[1] and **Jonathan Weese**[2] and **Yuan Cao**[2]
[1]Human Language Technology Center of Excellence
[2]Center for Language and Speech Processing
Johns Hopkins University

Chris Callison-Burch
Computer and Information Sciences Department
University of Pennsylvania

Abstract

We describe improvements made over the past year to Joshua, an open-source translation system for parsing-based machine translation. The main contributions this past year are significant improvements in both speed and usability of the grammar extraction and decoding steps. We have also rewritten the decoder to use a sparse feature representation, enabling training of large numbers of features with discriminative training methods.

1 Introduction

Joshua is an open-source toolkit[1] for hierarchical and syntax-based statistical machine translation of human languages with synchronous context-free grammars (SCFGs). The original version of Joshua (Li et al., 2009) was a port (from Python to Java) of the Hiero machine translation system introduced by Chiang (2007). It was later extended to support grammars with rich syntactic labels (Li et al., 2010). Subsequent efforts produced Thrax, the extensible Hadoop-based extraction tool for synchronous context-free grammars (Weese et al., 2011), later extended to support pivoting-based paraphrase extraction (Ganitkevitch et al., 2012). Joshua 5.0 continues our yearly update cycle.

The major components of Joshua 5.0 are:

§3.1 *Sparse features.* Joshua now supports an easily-extensible sparse feature implementation, along with tuning methods (PRO and kbMIRA) for efficiently setting the weights on large feature vectors.

§3.2 *Significant speed increases.* Joshua 5.0 is up to six times faster than Joshua 4.0, and also does well against hierarchical Moses, where end-to-end decoding (including model loading) of WMT test sets is as much as three times faster.

§3.3 *Thrax 2.0.* Our reengineered Hadoop-based grammar extractor, Thrax, is up to 300% faster while using significantly less intermediate disk space.

§3.4 *Many other features.* Joshua now includes a server mode with fair round-robin scheduling among and within requests, a bundler for distributing trained models, improvements to the Joshua pipeline (for managing end-to-end experiments), and better documentation.

2 Overview

Joshua is an end-to-end statistical machine translation toolkit. In addition to the decoder component (which performs the actual translation), it includes the infrastructure needed to prepare and align training data, build translation and language models, and tune and evaluate them.

This section provides a brief overview of the contents and abilities of this toolkit. More information can be found in the online documentation (`joshua-decoder.org/5.0/`).

2.1 The Pipeline: Gluing it all together

The Joshua pipeline ties together all the infrastructure needed to train and evaluate machine translation systems for research or industrial purposes. Once data has been segmented into parallel training, development, and test sets, a single invocation of the pipeline script is enough to invoke this entire infrastructure from beginning to end. Each step is

[1] `joshua-decoder.org`

broken down into smaller steps (e.g., tokenizing a file) whose dependencies are cached with SHA1 sums. This allows a reinvoked pipeline to reliably skip earlier steps that do not need to be recomputed, solving a common headache in the research and development cycle.

The Joshua pipeline is similar to other "experiment management systems" such as Moses' Experiment Management System (EMS), a much more general, highly-customizable tool that allows the specification and parallel execution of steps in arbitrary acyclic dependency graphs (much like the UNIX `make` tool, but written with machine translation in mind). Joshua's pipeline is more limited in that the basic pipeline skeleton is hard-coded, but reduced versatility covers many standard use cases and is arguably easier to use.

The pipeline is parameterized in many ways, and all the options below are selectable with command-line switches. Pipeline documentation is available online.

2.2 Data preparation, alignment, and model building

Data preparation involves data normalization (e.g., collapsing certain punctuation symbols) and tokenization (with the Penn treebank or user-specified tokenizer). Alignment with GIZA++ (Och and Ney, 2000) and the Berkeley aligner (Liang et al., 2006b) are supported.

Joshua's builtin grammar extractor, Thrax, is a Hadoop-based extraction implementation that scales easily to large datasets (Ganitkevitch et al., 2013). It supports extraction of both Hiero (Chiang, 2005) and SAMT grammars (Zollmann and Venugopal, 2006) with extraction heuristics easily specified via a flexible configuration file. The pipeline also supports GHKM grammar extraction (Galley et al., 2006) using the extractors available from Michel Galley[2] or Moses.

SAMT and GHKM grammar extraction require a parse tree, which are produced using the Berkeley parser (Petrov et al., 2006), or can be done outside the pipeline and supplied as an argument.

2.3 Decoding

The Joshua decoder is an implementation of the CKY+ algorithm (Chappelier et al., 1998), which generalizes CKY by removing the requirement that the grammar first be converted to Chomsky Normal Form, thereby avoiding the complexities of explicit binarization schemes (Zhang et al., 2006; DeNero et al., 2009). CKY+ maintains cubic-time parsing complexity (in the sentence length) with Earley-style implicit binarization of rules. Joshua permits arbitrary SCFGs, imposing no limitation on the rank or form of grammar rules.

Parsing complexity is still exponential in the scope of the grammar,[3] so grammar filtering remains important. The default Thrax settings extract only grammars with rank 2, and the pipeline implements scope-3 filtering (Hopkins and Langmead, 2010) when filtering grammars to test sets (for GHKM).

Joshua uses cube pruning (Chiang, 2007) with a default pop limit of 100 to efficiently explore the search space. Other decoder options are too numerous to mention here, but are documented online.

2.4 Tuning and testing

The pipeline allows the specification (and optional linear interpolation) of an arbitrary number of language models. In addition, it builds an interpolated Kneser-Ney language model on the target side of the training data using KenLM (Heafield, 2011; Heafield et al., 2013), BerkeleyLM (Pauls and Klein, 2011) or SRILM (Stolcke, 2002).

Joshua ships with MERT (Och, 2003) and PRO implementations. Tuning with k-best batch MIRA (Cherry and Foster, 2012) is also supported via callouts to Moses.

3 What's New in Joshua 5.0

3.1 Sparse features

Until a few years ago, machine translation systems were for the most part limited in the number of features they could employ, since the line-based optimization method, MERT (Och, 2003), was not able to efficiently search over more than tens of feature weights. The introduction of discriminative tuning methods for machine translation (Liang et al., 2006a; Tillmann and Zhang, 2006; Chiang et al., 2008; Hopkins and May, 2011) has made it possible to tune large numbers of features in statistical machine translation systems, and open-

[2] `nlp.stanford.edu/~mgalley/software/stanford-ghkm-latest.tar.gz`

[3] Roughly, the number of consecutive nonterminals in a rule (Hopkins and Langmead, 2010).

source implementations such as Cherry and Foster (2012) have made it easy.

Joshua 5.0 has moved to a sparse feature representation internally. First, to clarify terminology, a feature as implemented in the decoder is actually a template that can introduce any number of actual features (in the standard machine learning sense). We will use the term *feature function* for these templates and *feature* for the individual, traditional features that are induced by these templates. For example, the (typically dense) features stored with the grammar on disk are each separate features contributed by the PHRASEMODEL feature function template. The LANGUAGEMODEL template contributes a single feature value for each language model that was loaded.

For efficiency, Joshua does not store the entire feature vector during decoding. Instead, hypergraph nodes maintain only the best cumulative score of each incoming hyperedge, and the edges themselves retain only the hyperedge delta (the inner product of the weight vector and features incurred by that edge). After decoding, the feature vector for each edge can be recomputed and explicitly represented if that information is required by the decoder (for example, during tuning).

This functionality is implemented via the following feature function interface, presented here in simplified pseudocode:

```
interface FeatureFunction:
  apply(context, accumulator)
```

The `context` comprises fixed pieces of the input sentence and hypergraph:

- the hypergraph edge (which represents the SCFG rule and sequence of tail nodes)
- the complete source sentence
- the input span

The `accumulator` object's job is to accumulate feature (name,value) pairs fired by a feature function during the application of a rule, via another interface:

```
interface Accumulator:
  add(feature_name, value)
```

The accumulator generalization[4] permits the use of a single feature-gathering function for two accumulator objects: the first, used during decoding, maintains only a weighted sum, and the second, used (if needed) during k-best extraction, holds onto the entire sparse feature vector.

For tuning large sets of features, Joshua supports both PRO (Hopkins and May, 2011), an inhouse version introduced with Joshua 4.0, and k-best batch MIRA (Cherry and Foster, 2012), implemented via calls to code provided by Moses.

3.2 Performance improvements

We introduced many performance improvements, replacing code designed to get the job done under research timeline constraints with more efficient alternatives, including smarter handling of locking among threads, more efficient (non string-based) computation of dynamic programming state, and replacement of fixed class-based array structures with fixed-size literals.

We used the following experimental setup to compare Joshua 4.0 and 5.0: We extracted a large German-English grammar from all sentences with no more than 50 words per side from Europarl v.7 (Koehn, 2005), News Commentary, and the Common Crawl corpora using Thrax default settings. After filtering against our test set (newstest2012), this grammar contained 70 million rules. We then trained three language models on (1) the target side of our grammar training data, (2) English Gigaword, and (3) the monolingual English data released for WMT13. We tuned a system using kbMIRA and decoded using KenLM (Heafield, 2011). Decoding was performed on 64-core 2.1 GHz AMD Opteron processors with 256 GB of available memory.

Figure 1 plots the end-to-end runtime[5] as a function of the number of threads. Each point in the graph is the minimum of at least fifteen runs computed at different times over a period of a few days. The main point of comparison, between Joshua 4.0 and 5.0, shows that the current version is up to 500% faster than it was last year, especially in multithreaded situations.

For further comparison, we took these models, converted them to hierarchical Moses format, and then decoded with the latest version.[6] We compiled Moses with the recommended optimization settings[7] and used the in-memory (SCFG) gram-

[4]Due to Kenneth Heafield.

[5]i.e., including model loading time and grammar sorting

[6]The latest version available on Github as of June 7, 2013

[7]With tcmalloc and the following compile flags: `--max-factors=1 --kenlm-max-order=5 debug-symbols=off`

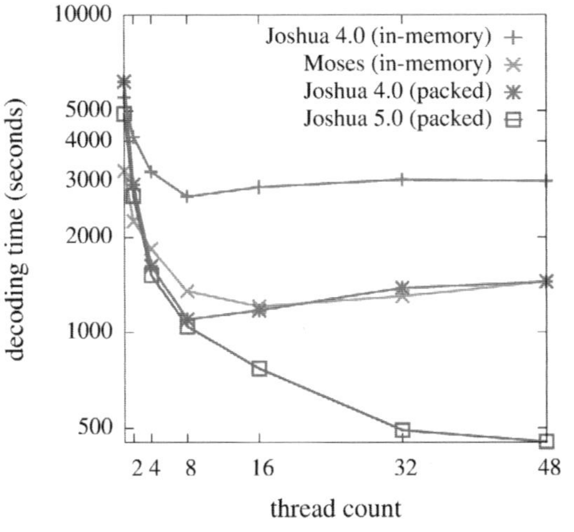

Figure 1: End-to-end runtime as a function of the number of threads. Each data point is the minimum of at least fifteen different runs.

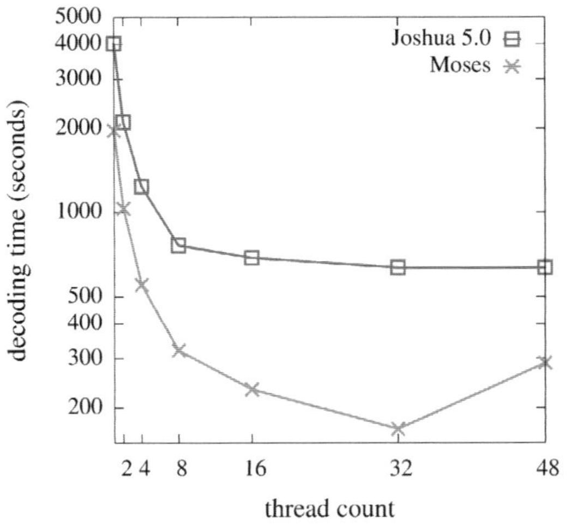

Figure 2: Decoding time alone.

mar format. BLEU scores were similar.[8] In this end-to-end setting, Joshua is about 200% faster than Moses at high thread counts (Figure 1).

Figure 2 furthers the Moses and Joshua comparison by plotting only decoding time (subtracting out model loading and sorting times). Moses' decoding speed is 2–3 times faster than Joshua's, suggesting that the end-to-end gains in Figure 1 are due to more efficient grammar loading.

3.3 Thrax 2.0

The Thrax module of our toolkit has undergone a similar overhaul. The rule extraction code was

[8] 22.88 (Moses), 22.99 (Joshua 4), and 23.23 (Joshua 5).

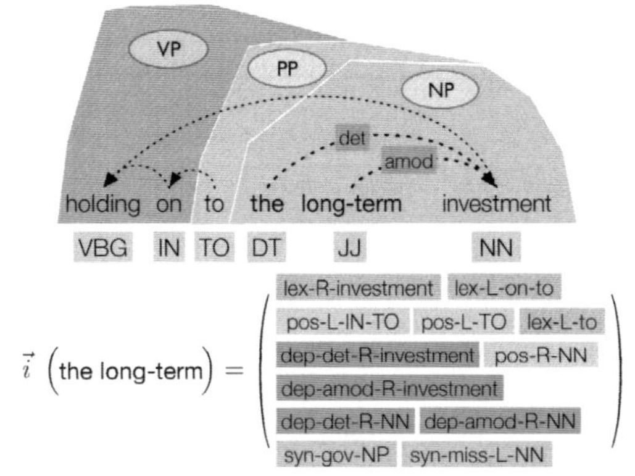

Figure 3: Here, position-aware lexical and part-of-speech n-gram features, labeled dependency links, and features reflecting the phrase's CCG-style label NP/NN are included in the context vector.

rewritten to be easier to understand and extend, allowing, for instance, for easy inclusion of alternative nonterminal labeling strategies.

We optimized the data representation used for the underlying map-reduce framework towards greater compactness and speed, resulting in a 300% increase in extraction speed and an equivalent reduction in disk I/O (Table 1). These gains enable us to extract a syntactically labeled German-English SAMT-style translation grammar from a bitext of over 4 million sentence pairs in just over three hours. Furthermore, Thrax 2.0 is capable of scaling to very large data sets, like the composite bitext used in the extraction of the paraphrase collection PPDB (Ganitkevitch et al., 2013), which counted 100 million sentence pairs and over 2 billion words on the English side.

Furthermore, Thrax 2.0 contains a module focused on the extraction of compact distributional signatures over large datasets. This *distributional* mode collects contextual features for n-gram phrases, such as words occurring in a window around the phrase, as well as dependency-based and syntactic features. Figure 3 illustrates the feature space. We then compute a bit signature from the resulting feature vector via a randomized locality-sensitive hashing projection. This yields a compact representation of a phrase's typical context. To perform this projection Thrax relies on the Jerboa toolkit (Van Durme, 2012). As part of the PPDB effort, Thrax has been used to extract rich distributional signatures for 175 million 1-to-4-gram phrases from the Annotated Gigaword corpus (Napoles et al., 2012), a parsed and pro-

Rules	Cs-En 112M		Fr-En 357M		De-En 202M		Es-En 380M	
	Space	Time	Space	Time	Space	Time	Space	Time
Joshua 4.0	120GB	112 min	364GB	369 min	211GB	203 min	413GB	397 min
Joshua 5.0	31GB	25 min	101GB	81 min	56GB	44 min	108GB	84 min
Difference	-74.1%	-77.7%	-72.3%	-78.0%	-73.5%	-78.3%	-73.8%	-78.8%

Table 1: Comparing Hadoop's intermediate disk space use and extraction time on a selection of Europarl v.7 Hiero grammar extractions. Disk space was measured at its maximum, at the input of Thrax's final grammar aggregation stage. Runtime was measured on our Hadoop cluster with a capacity of 52 mappers and 26 reducers. On average Thrax 2.0, bundled with Joshua 5.0, is up to 300% faster and more compact.

cessed version of the English Gigaword (Graff et al., 2003).

Thrax is distributed with Joshua and is also available as a separate download.[9]

3.4 Other features

Joshua 5.0 also includes many features designed to increase its usability. These include:

- A TCP/IP server architecture, designed to handle multiple sets of translation requests while ensuring fairness in thread assignment both across and within these connections.
- Intelligent selection of translation and language model training data using cross-entropy difference to rank training candidates (Moore and Lewis, 2010; Axelrod et al., 2011) (described in detail in Orland (2013)).
- A bundler for easy packaging of trained models with all of its dependencies.
- A year's worth of improvements to the Joshua pipeline, including many new features and supported options, and increased robustness to error.
- Extended documentation.

4 WMT Submissions

We submitted a constrained entry for all tracks except English-Czech (nine in total). Our systems were constructed in a straightforward fashion and without any language-specific adaptations using the Joshua pipeline. For each language pair, we trained a Hiero system on all sentences with no more than fifty words per side in the Europarl, News Commentary, and Common Crawl corpora. We built two interpolated Kneser-Ney language models: one from the monolingual News Crawl corpora (2007–2012), and another from the target side of the training data. For systems translating into English, we added a third language model built on Gigaword. Language models were combined linearly into a single language model using interpolation weights from the tuning data (newstest2011). We tuned our systems with kbMIRA. For truecasing, we used a monolingual translation system built on the training data, and finally detokenized with simple heuristics.

5 Summary

The 5.0 release of Joshua is the result of a significant year-long research, engineering, and usability effort that we hope will be of service to the research community. User-friendly packages of Joshua are available from `joshua-decoder.org`, while developers are encouraged to participate via `github.com/joshua-decoder/joshua`. Mailing lists, linked from the main Joshua page, are available for both.

Acknowledgments Joshua's sparse feature representation owes much to discussions with Colin Cherry, Barry Haddow, Chris Dyer, and Kenneth Heafield at MT Marathon 2012 in Edinburgh.

This material is based on research sponsored by the NSF under grant IIS-1249516 and DARPA under agreement number FA8750-13-2-0017 (the DEFT program). The U.S. Government is authorized to reproduce and distribute reprints for Governmental purposes. The views and conclusions contained in this publication are those of the authors and should not be interpreted as representing official policies or endorsements of DARPA or the U.S. Government.

[9] `github.com/joshua-decoder/thrax`

References

Amittai Axelrod, Xiaodong He, and Jianfeng Gao. 2011. Domain adaptation via pseudo in-domain data selection. In *Proceedings of EMNLP*, pages 355–362, Edinburgh, Scotland, UK., July.

J.C. Chappelier, M. Rajman, et al. 1998. A generalized CYK algorithm for parsing stochastic CFG. In *First Workshop on Tabulation in Parsing and Deduction (TAPD98)*, pages 133–137.

Colin Cherry and George Foster. 2012. Batch tuning strategies for statistical machine translation. In *Proceedings of NAACL-HLT*, pages 427–436, Montréal, Canada, June.

David Chiang, Yuval Marton, and Philip Resnik. 2008. Online large-margin training of syntactic and structural translation features. In *Proceedings of EMNLP*, Waikiki, Hawaii, USA, October.

David Chiang. 2005. A hierarchical phrase-based model for statistical machine translation. In *Proceedings of ACL*, Ann Arbor, Michigan.

David Chiang. 2007. Hierarchical phrase-based translation. *Computational Linguistics*, 33(2):201–228.

John DeNero, Adam Pauls, and Dan Klein. 2009. Asynchronous binarization for synchronous grammars. In *Proceedings of ACL*, Suntec, Singapore, August.

Michel Galley, Jonathan Graehl, Kevin Knight, Daniel Marcu, Steve DeNeefe, Wei Wang, and Ignacio Thayer. 2006. Scalable inference and training of context-rich syntactic translation models. In *Proceedings of ACL/COLING*, Sydney, Australia, July.

Juri Ganitkevitch, Yuan Cao, Jonathan Weese, Matt Post, and Chris Callison-Burch. 2012. Joshua 4.0: Packing, PRO, and paraphrases. In *Proceedings of the Workshop on Statistical Machine Translation*.

Juri Ganitkevitch, Chris Callison-Burch, and Benjamin Van Durme. 2013. Ppdb: The paraphrase database. In *Proceedings of HLT/NAACL*.

D. Graff, J. Kong, K. Chen, and K. Maeda. 2003. English gigaword. *Linguistic Data Consortium, Philadelphia*.

Kenneth Heafield, Ivan Pouzyrevsky, Jonathan H. Clark, and Philipp Koehn. 2013. Scalable modified Kneser-Ney language model estimation. In *Proceedings of ACL*, Sofia, Bulgaria, August.

Kenneth Heafield. 2011. KenLM: Faster and smaller language model queries. In *Proceedings of the Workshop on Statistical Machine Translation*, pages 187–197. Association for Computational Linguistics.

Mark Hopkins and Greg Langmead. 2010. SCFG decoding without binarization. In *Proceedings of EMNLP*, pages 646–655.

Mark Hopkins and Jonathan May. 2011. Tuning as ranking. In *Proceedings of EMNLP*.

Philipp Koehn. 2005. Europarl: A parallel corpus for statistical machine translation. In *MT summit*, volume 5.

Zhifei Li, Chris Callison-Burch, Chris Dyer, Juri Ganitkevitch, Sanjeev Khudanpur, Lane Schwartz, Wren Thornton, Jonathan Weese, and Omar Zaidan. 2009. Joshua: An open source toolkit for parsing-based machine translation. In *Proceedings of the Workshop on Statistical Machine Translation*, Athens, Greece, March.

Zhifei Li, Chris Callison-Burch, Chris Dyer, Juri Ganitkevitch, Ann Irvine, Sanjeev Khudanpur, Lane Schwartz, Wren N.G. Thornton, Ziyuan Wang, Jonathan Weese, and Omar F. Zaidan. 2010. Joshua 2.0: a toolkit for parsing-based machine translation with syntax, semirings, discriminative training and other goodies. In *Proceedings of the Workshop on Statistical Machine Translation*.

Percy Liang, Alexandre Bouchard-Côté, Dan Klein, and Ben Taskar. 2006a. An end-to-end discriminative approach to machine translation. In *Proceedings of ACL/COLING*.

Percy Liang, Ben Taskar, and Dan Klein. 2006b. Alignment by agreement. In *Proceedings of NAACL*, pages 104–111, New York City, USA, June.

Robert C. Moore and William Lewis. 2010. Intelligent selection of language model training data. In *Proceedings of ACL (short papers)*, pages 220–224.

Courtney Napoles, Matt Gormley, and Benjamin Van Durme. 2012. Annotated gigaword. In *Proceedings of AKBC-WEKEX 2012*.

F. J. Och and H. Ney. 2000. Improved statistical alignment models. In *Proceedings of ACL*, pages 440–447, Hong Kong, China, October.

Franz Och. 2003. Minimum error rate training in statistical machine translation. In *Proceedings of ACL*, Sapporo, Japan.

Luke Orland. 2013. Intelligent selection of translation model training data for machine translation with TAUS domain data: A summary. Master's thesis, Johns Hopkins University, Baltimore, Maryland, June.

Adam Pauls and Dan Klein. 2011. Faster and smaller n-gram language models. In *Proceedings of ACL*, pages 258–267, Portland, Oregon, USA, June.

Slav Petrov, Leon Barrett, Romain Thibaux, and Dan Klein. 2006. Learning accurate, compact, and interpretable tree annotation. In *Proceedings of ACL*, Sydney, Australia, July.

Andreas Stolcke. 2002. SRILM - an extensible language modeling toolkit. In *Seventh International Conference on Spoken Language Processing*.

Christoph Tillmann and Tong Zhang. 2006. A discriminative global training algorithm for statistical mt. In *Proceedings of ACL/COLING*, pages 721–728, Sydney, Australia, July.

Benjamin Van Durme. 2012. Jerboa: A toolkit for randomized and streaming algorithms. Technical Report 7, Human Language Technology Center of Excellence, Johns Hopkins University.

Jonathan Weese, Juri Ganitkevitch, Chris Callison-Burch, Matt Post, and Adam Lopez. 2011. Joshua 3.0: Syntax-based machine translation with the Thrax grammar extractor. In *Proceedings of the Workshop on Statistical Machine Translation*.

Hao Zhang, Liang Huang, Daniel Gildea, and Kevin Knight. 2006. Synchronous binarization for machine translation. In *Proceedings of HLT/NAACL*.

Andreas Zollmann and Ashish Venugopal. 2006. Syntax augmented machine translation via chart parsing. In *Proceedings of the Workshop on Statistical Machine Translation*, New York, New York.

The CNGL-DCU-Prompsit Translation Systems for WMT13

Raphael Rubino[†], Antonio Toral[†], Santiago Cortés Vaíllo[⋆], Jun Xie[§], Xiaofeng Wu[‡], Stephen Doherty[♭], Qun Liu[‡]
[†]NCLT, Dublin City University, Ireland
[⋆]Prompsit Language Engineering, Spain
[§]ICT, Chinese Academy of Sciences, China
[‡,♭]CNGL, Dublin City University, Ireland
[†,‡]{rrubino, atoral, xfwu, qliu}@computing.dcu.ie
[⋆]santiago@prompsit.com
[§]junxie@ict.ac.cn
[♭]stephen.doherty@dcu.ie

Abstract

This paper presents the experiments conducted by the Machine Translation group at DCU and Prompsit Language Engineering for the WMT13 translation task. Three language pairs are considered: Spanish-English and French-English in both directions and German-English in that direction. For the Spanish-English pair, the use of linguistic information to select parallel data is investigated. For the French-English pair, the usefulness of the small in-domain parallel corpus is evaluated, compared to an out-of-domain parallel data sub-sampling method. Finally, for the German-English system, we describe our work in addressing the long distance reordering problem and a system combination strategy.

1 Introduction

This paper presents the experiments conducted by the Machine Translation group at DCU[1] and Prompsit Language Engineering[2] for the WMT13 translation task on three language pairs: Spanish-English, French-English and German-English. For these language pairs, the language and translation models are built using different approaches and datasets, thus presented in this paper in separate sections.

In Section 2, the systems built for the Spanish-English pair in both directions are described. We investigate the use of linguistic information to select parallel data. In Section 3, we present the systems built for the French-English pair in both directions. The usefulness of the small in-domain parallel corpus is evaluated, compared to an out-of-domain parallel data sub-sampling method. In Section 4, for the German-English system, aiming at exploring the long distance reordering problem, we first describe our efforts in a dependency tree-to-string approach, before combining different hierarchical systems with a phrase-based system and show a significant improvement over three baseline systems.

2 Spanish-English

This section describes the experimental setup for the Spanish-English language pair.

2.1 Setting

Our setup uses the MOSES toolkit, version 1.0 (Koehn et al., 2007). We use a pipeline with the phrase-based decoder with standard parameters, unless noted otherwise. The decoder uses cube pruning (-cube-pruning-pop-limit 2000 -s 2000), MBR (-mbr-size 800 -mbr-scale 1) and monotone at punctuation reordering.

Individual language models (LMs), 5-gram and smoothed using a simplified version of the improved Kneser-Ney method (Chen and Goodman, 1996), are built for each monolingual corpus using IRSTLM 5.80.01 (Federico et al., 2008). These LMs are then interpolated with IRSTLM using the test set of WMT11 as the development set. Finally, the interpolated LMs are merged into one LM preserving the weights using SRILM (Stolcke, 2002).

We use all the parallel corpora available for this language pair: *Europarl* (EU), *News Commentary* (NC), *United Nations* (UN) and *Common Crawl* (CC). Regarding monolingual corpora, we use the freely available monolingual corpora (*Eu-*

[1]http://www.nclt.dcu.ie/mt/
[2]http://www.prompsit.com/

roparl, News Commentary, News 2007–2012) as well as the target side of several parallel corpora: *Common Crawl, United Nations* and 10^9 French–English corpus (only for English as target language). Both the parallel and monolingual data are tokenised and truecased using scripts from the MOSES toolkit.

2.2 Data selection

The main contribution in our participation regards the selection of parallel data. We follow the perplexity-based approach to filter monolingual data (Moore and Lewis, 2010) extended to filter parallel data (Axelrod et al., 2011). In our case, we do not measure perplexity only on word forms but also using different types of linguistic information (lemmas and named entities) (Toral, 2013).

We build LMs for the source and target sides of the domain-specific corpus (in our case NC) and for a random subset of the non-domain-specific corpus (EU, UN and CC) of the same size (number of sentences) of the domain-specific corpus. Each parallel sentence s in the non-domain-specific corpus is then scored according to equation 1 where $PP_{Isl}(s)$ is the perplexity of s in the source side according to the domain-specific LM and $PP_{Osl}(s)$ is the perplexity of s in the source side according to the non-domain-specific LM. $PP_{Itl}(s)$ and $PP_{O}tl(s)$ contain the corresponding values for the target side.

$$score(s) = \frac{1}{2} \times (PP_I sl(s) - PP_O sl(s)) + (PP_I tl(s) - PP_O tl(s)) \quad (1)$$

Table 1 shows the results obtained using four models: word forms (*forms*), forms and named entities (*forms+nes*), lemmas (*lem*) and lemmas and named entities (*lem+nes*). Details on these methods can be found in Toral (2013).

For each corpus we selected two subsets (see in bold in Table 1), the one for which one method obtained the best perplexity (top 5% of EU using forms, 2% of UN using lemmas and 50% of CC using forms and named entities) and a bigger one used to compare the performance in SMT (top 14% of EU using lemmas and named entities (*lem+nes*), top 12% of UN using forms and named entities and the whole CC). These subsets are used as training data in our systems.

As we can see in the table, the use of linguistic information allows to obtain subsets with lower perplexity than using solely word forms, e.g. 1057.7 (*lem+nes*) versus 1104.8 (*forms*) for 14% of EU. The only exception to this is the subset that comprises the top 5% of EU, where perplexity using word forms (957.9) is the lowest one.

corpus	size	forms	forms+nes	lem	lem+nes
EU	5%	**957.9**	987.2	974.3	1005.5
	14%	1104.8	1058.7	1111.6	**1057.7**
UN	2%	877.1	969.6	**866.6**	962.2
	12%	1203.2	**1130.9**	1183.8	1131.6
CC	50%	573.0	547.2	574.5	**546.4**
	100%	560.1	560.1	560.1	560.1

Table 1: Perplexities in data selection

2.3 Results

Table 2 presents the results obtained. Note that these were obtained during development and thus the systems are tuned on WMT's 2011 test set and tested on WMT's 2012 test set.

All the systems share the same LM. The first system (*no selection*) is trained with the whole NC and EU. The second (*small*) and third (*big*) systems use as training data the whole NC and subsets of EU (5% and 14%, respectively), UN (2% and 12%, respectively) and CC (50% and 100%, respectively), as shown in Table 1.

System	#sent.	BLEU	BLEUcased
no selection	2.1M	31.99	30.96
small	1.4M	33.12	32.05
big	3.8M	33.49	32.43

Table 2: Number of sentences and BLEU scores obtained on the WMT12 test set for the different systems on the EN–ES translation task.

The advantage of data selection is clear. The second system, although smaller in size compared to the first (1.4M sentence pairs versus 2.1M), takes its training from a more varied set of data, and its performance is over one absolute BLEU point higher.

When comparing the two systems that rely on data selection, one might expect the one that uses data with lower perplexity (*small*) to perform better. However, this is not the case, the third system (*big*) performing around half an absolute BLEU point higher than the second (*small*). This hints at the fact that perplexity alone is not an optimal metric for data selection, but size should also be considered. Note that the size of system 3's phrase table is more than double that of system 2.

3 French-English

This section describe the particularities of the MT systems built for the French-English language pair in both directions. The goal of the experimental setup presented here is to evaluate the gain of adding small in-domain parallel data into a translation system built on a sub-sample of the out-of-domain parallel data.

3.1 Data Pre-processing

All the available parallel and monolingual data for the French-English language pair, including the last versions of *LDC Gigaword* corpora, are normalised and special characters are escaped using the scripts provided by the shared task organisers. Then, the corpora are tokenised and for each language a true-case model is built on the concatenation of all the data after removing duplicated sentences, using the scripts included in MOSES distribution. The corpora are then true-cased before being used to build the language and the translation models.

3.2 Language Model

To build our final language models, we first build LMs on each corpus individually. All the monolingual corpora are considered, as well as the source or target side of the parallel corpora if the data are not already in the monolingual data. We build modified Kneser-Ney discounted 5-gram LMs using the SRILM toolkit for each corpus and separate the LMs in three groups: one in-domain (containing news-commentary and news crawl corpora), another out-of-domain (containing *Common Crawl*, *Europarl*, *UN* and 10^9 corpora), and the last one with *LDC Gigaword* LMs (the data are kept separated by news source, as distributed by *LDC*). The LMs in each group are linearly interpolated based on their perplexities obtained on the concatenation of all the development sets from previous WMT translation tasks. The same development corpus is used to linearly interpolate the in-domain and *LDC* LMs. We finally obtain two LMs, one containing out-of-domain data which is only used to filter parallel data, and another one containing in-domain data which is used to filter parallel data, tuning the translation model weights and at decoding time. Details about the number of n-grams in each language model are presented in Table 3.

	French		English	
	out	in	out	in
1-gram	4.0	3.3	4.2	10.7
2-gram	43.0	44.0	48.2	161.9
3-gram	54.2	61.8	63.4	256.8
4-gram	99.7	119.2	103.2	502.7
5-gram	136.4	165.0	125.4	680.7

Table 3: Number of n-grams (in millions) for the in-domain and out-of-domain LMs in French and English.

3.3 Translation Model

Two phrase-based translation models are built using MGIZA++ (Gao and Vogel, 2008) and MOSES[3], with the default alignment heuristic (*grow-diag-final*) and bidirectional reordering models. The first translation model is in-domain, built with the news-commentary corpus. The second one is built on a sample of all the other parallel corpora available for the French-English language pair. Both corpora are cleaned using the script provided with Moses, keeping the sentences with a length below 80 words. For the second translation model, we used the modified Moore-Lewis method based on the four LMs (two per language) presented in section 3.2. The sum of the source and target perplexity difference is computed for each sentence pair of the corpus. We set an acceptance threshold to keep a limited amount of sentence pairs. The kept sample finally contains $\sim$ 3.7M sentence pairs to train the translation model. Statistics about this data sample and the news-commentary corpus are presented in Table 4. The test set of WMT12 translation task is used to optimise the weights for the two translation models with the MERT algorithm. For this tuning step, the limit of target phrases loaded per source phrase is set to 50. We also use a reordering constraint around punctuation marks. The same parameters are used during the decoding of the test set.

	news-commentary	sample
tokens FR	4.7M	98.6M
tokens EN	4.0M	88.0M
sentences	156.5k	3.7M

Table 4: Statistics about the two parallel corpora, after pre-processing, used to train the translation models.

[3]Moses version 1.0

3.4 Results

The two translation models presented in Section 3.3 allow us to design three translation systems: one using only the in-domain model, one using only the model built on the sub-sample of the out-of-domain data, and one using both models by giving two decoding paths to Moses. For this latter system, the MERT algorithm is also used to optimise the translation model weights. Results obtained on the WMT13 test set, measured with the official automatic metrics, are presented in Table 5. The submitted system is the one built on the sub-sample of the out-of-domain parallel data. This system was chosen during the tuning step because it reached the highest BLEU scores on the development corpus, slightly above the combination of the two translation models.

	News-Com.	Sample	Comb.
	FR-EN		
BLEUdev	26.9	30.0	29.9
BLEU	27.0	30.8	30.4
BLEUcased	26.1	29.8	29.3
TER	62.9	58.9	59.3
	EN-FR		
BLEUdev	27.1	29.7	29.6
BLEU	26.6	29.6	29.4
BLEUcased	25.8	28.7	28.5
TER	65.1	61.8	62.0

Table 5: BLEU and TER scores obtained by our systems. BLEUdev is the score obtained on the development set given by MERT, while BLEU, BLEUcased and TER are obtained on the test set given by the submission website.

For both FR-EN and EN-FR tasks, the best results are reached by the system built on the sub-sample taken from the out-of-domain parallel data. Using only News-Commentary to build a translation model leads to acceptable BLEU scores, with regards to the size of the training corpus. When the sub-sample of the out-of-domain parallel data is used to build the translation model, adding a model built on *News-Commentary* does not improve the results. The difference between these two systems in terms of BLEU score (both cased sensitive and insensitive) indicates that similar results can be achieved, however it appears that the amount of sentence pairs in the sample is large enough to limit the impact of the small in-domain corpus parallel. Further experiments are still required to determine the minimum sample size needed to outperform both the in-domain system and the combination of the two translation models.

4 German-English

In this section we describe our work on German to English subtask. Firstly we describe the Dependency tree to string method which we tried but unfortunately failed due to short of time. Secondly we discuss the baseline system and the preprocessing we performed. Thirdly a system combination method is described.

4.1 Dependency Tree to String Method

Our original plan was to address the long distance reordering problem in German-English translation. We use Xie's Dependency tree to string method(Xie et al., 2011) which obtains good results on Chinese to English translation and exhibits good performance at long distance reordering as our decoder.

We use Stanford dependency parser[4] to parse the English side of the data and Mate-Tool[5] for the German side. The first set of experiments did not lead to encouraging results and due to insufficient time, we decide to switch to other decoders, based on statistical phrase-based and hierarchical approaches.

4.2 Baseline System

In this section we describe the three baseline system we used as well as the preprocessing technologies and the experiments set up.

4.2.1 Preprocessing and Corpus

We first use the normalisation scripts provided by WMT2013 to normalise both English and German side. Then we escape special characters on both sides. We use Stanford tokeniser for English and OpenNLP tokeniser[6] for German. Then we train a true-case model using with *Europarl* and *News-Commentary* corpora, and true-case all the corpus we used. The parallel corpus is filtered with the standard cleaning scripts provided with

[4] `http://nlp.stanford.edu/software/lex-parser.shtml`

[5] http://code.google.com/p/mate-tools/

[6] `http://opennlp.sourceforge.net/models-1.5/`

MOSES. We split the German compound words with jWordSplitter[7].

All the corpus provided for the shared task are used for training our translation models, while WMT2011 and WMT2012 test sets are used to tune the models parameters. For the LM, we use all the monolingual data provided, including *LDC Gigaword*. Each LM is trained with the SRILM toolkit, before interpolating all the LMs according to their weights obtained by minimizing the perplexity on the tuning set (WMT2011 and WMT2012 test sets). As SRILM can only interpolate 10 LMs, we first interpolate a LM with *Europarl*, *News Commentary*, *News Crawl* (2007-2012, each year individually, 6 separate parts), then we interpolate a new LM with this interpolated LM and *LDC Gigawords* (we kept the *Gigaword* subsets separated according to the news sources as distributed by *LDC*, which leads to 7 corpus).

4.2.2 Three baseline systems

We use the data set up described by the former subsection and build up three baseline systems, namely PB MOSES (phrase-based), Hiero MOSES (hierarchical) and CDEC (Dyer et al., 2010). The motivation of choosing Hierarchical Models is to address the German-English's long reorder problem. We want to test the performance of CDEC and Hiero MOSES and choose the best. PB MOSES is used as our benchmark. The three results obtained on the development and test sets for the three baseline system and the system combination are shown in the Table 6.

	Development	Test
PB MOSES	22.0	24.0
Hiero MOSES	22.1	24.4
CDEC	22.5	24.4
Combination	23.0	24.8

Table 6: BLEU scores obtained by our systems on the development and test sets for the German to English translation task.

From the Table 6 we can see that on development set, CDEC performs the best, and its much better than MOSES's two decoder, but on test set, Hiero MOSES and CDEC performs as well as each other, and they both performs better than PB Model.

[7]http://www.danielnaber.de/jwordsplitter/

4.3 System Combination

We also use a word-level combination strategy (Rosti et al., 2007) to combine the three translation hypotheses. To combine these systems, we first use the Minimum Bayes-Risk (MBR) (Kumar and Byrne, 2004) decoder to obtain the 5 best hypothesis as the alignment reference for the Confusion Network (CN) (Mangu et al., 2000). We then use IHMM (He et al., 2008) to choose the backbone build the CN and finally search for and generate the best translation.

We tune the system parameters on development set with Simple-Simplex algorithm. The parameters for system weights are set equal. Other parameters like language model, length penalty and combination coefficient are chosen when we see a good improvement on development set.

5 Conclusion

This paper presented a set of experiments conducted on Spanish-English, French-English and German-English language pairs. For the Spanish-English pair, we have explored the use of linguistic information to select parallel data and use this as the training for SMT. However, the comparison of the performance obtained using this method and the purely statistical one (i.e. perplexity on word forms) remains to be carried out. Another open question regards the optimal size of the selected data. As we have seen, minimum perplexity alone cannot be considered an optimal metric since using a larger set, even if it has higher perplexity, allowed us to obtain notably higher BLEU scores. The question is then how to decide the optimal size of parallel data to select.

For the French-English language pair, we investigated the usefulness of the small in-domain parallel data compared to out-of-domain parallel data sub-sampling. We show that with a sample containing $\sim 3.7M$ sentence pairs extracted from the out-of-domain parallel data, it is not necessary to use the small domain-specific parallel data. Further experiments are still required to determine the minimum sample size needed to outperform both the in-domain system and the combination of the two translation models.

Finally, for the German-English language pair, we presents our exploitation of long ordering problem. We compared two hierarchical models with one phrase-based model, and we also use a system combination strategy to further improve the translation systems performance.

Acknowledgments

The research leading to these results has received funding from the European Union Seventh Framework Programme FP7/2007-2013 under grant agreement PIAP-GA-2012-324414 (Abu-MaTran) and through Science Foundation Ireland as part of the CNGL (grant 07/CE/I1142).

References

Amittai Axelrod, Xiaodong He, and Jianfeng Gao. 2011. Domain adaptation via pseudo in-domain data selection. In *Proceedings of the Conference on Empirical Methods in Natural Language Processing*, EMNLP '11, pages 355–362, Stroudsburg, PA, USA. Association for Computational Linguistics.

Stanley F. Chen and Joshua Goodman. 1996. An empirical study of smoothing techniques for language modeling. In *Proceedings of the 34th annual meeting on Association for Computational Linguistics*, ACL '96, pages 310–318, Stroudsburg, PA, USA. Association for Computational Linguistics.

Chris Dyer, Jonathan Weese, Hendra Setiawan, Adam Lopez, Ferhan Ture, Vladimir Eidelman, Juri Ganitkevitch, Phil Blunsom, and Philip Resnik. 2010. cdec: A decoder, alignment, and learning framework for finite-state and context-free translation models. In *Proceedings of the ACL 2010 System Demonstrations*, pages 7–12. Association for Computational Linguistics.

Marcello Federico, Nicola Bertoldi, and Mauro Cettolo. 2008. IRSTLM: an open source toolkit for handling large scale language models. In *INTERSPEECH*, pages 1618–1621. ISCA.

Qin Gao and Stephan Vogel. 2008. Parallel implementations of word alignment tool. In *Software Engineering, Testing, and Quality Assurance for Natural Language Processing*, pages 49–57. Association for Computational Linguistics.

Xiaodong He, Mei Yang, Jianfeng Gao, Patrick Nguyen, and Robert Moore. 2008. Indirect-hmm-based hypothesis alignment for combining outputs from machine translation systems. In *Proceedings of the Conference on Empirical Methods in Natural Language Processing*, pages 98–107. Association for Computational Linguistics.

Philipp Koehn, Hieu Hoang, Alexandra Birch, Chris Callison-Burch, Marcello Federico, Nicola Bertoldi, Brooke Cowan, Wade Shen, Christine Moran, Richard Zens, Chris Dyer, Ondřej Bojar, Alexandra Constantin, and Evan Herbst. 2007. Moses: open source toolkit for statistical machine translation. In *Proceedings of the 45th Annual Meeting of the ACL on Interactive Poster and Demonstration Sessions*, ACL '07, pages 177–180, Stroudsburg, PA, USA. Association for Computational Linguistics.

Shankar Kumar and William Byrne. 2004. Minimum bayes-risk decoding for statistical machine translation. In *Proceedings of HLT-NAACL*, pages 169–176.

Lidia Mangu, Eric Brill, and Andreas Stolcke. 2000. Finding consensus in speech recognition: word error minimization and other applications of confusion networks. *Computer Speech & Language*, 14(4):373–400.

Robert C. Moore and William Lewis. 2010. Intelligent selection of language model training data. In *Proceedings of the ACL 2010 Conference Short Papers*, ACLShort '10, pages 220–224, Stroudsburg, PA, USA. Association for Computational Linguistics.

Antti-Veikko I Rosti, Necip Fazil Ayan, Bing Xiang, Spyros Matsoukas, Richard Schwartz, and Bonnie Dorr. 2007. Combining outputs from multiple machine translation systems. In *Human Language Technologies 2007: The Conference of the North American Chapter of the Association for Computational Linguistics*, pages 228–235.

Andreas Stolcke. 2002. Srilm - an extensible language modeling toolkit. In John H. L. Hansen and Bryan L. Pellom, editors, *INTERSPEECH*. ISCA.

Antonio Toral. 2013. Hybrid Selection of Language Model Training Data Using Linguistic Information and Perplexity. In *Proceedings of the Second Workshop on Hybrid Approaches to Machine Translation (HyTra)*, ACL 2013.

Jun Xie, Haitao Mi, and Qun Liu. 2011. A novel dependency-to-string model for statistical machine translation. In *Proceedings of the Conference on Empirical Methods in Natural Language Processing*, pages 216–226. Association for Computational Linguistics.

QCRI-MES Submission at WMT13: Using Transliteration Mining to Improve Statistical Machine Translation

Hassan Sajjad[1], **Svetlana Smekalova**[2], **Nadir Durrani**[3], **Alexander Fraser**[4], **Helmut Schmid**[4]
[1]Qatar Computing Research Institute – hsajjad@qf.org.qa
[2]University of Stuttgart – smekalsa@ims.uni-stuttgart.de
[3]University of Edinburgh – dnadir@inf.ed.ac.uk
[4]Ludwig-Maximilians University Munich – (fraser|schmid)@cis.uni-muenchen.de

Abstract

This paper describes QCRI-MES's submission on the English-Russian dataset to the Eighth Workshop on Statistical Machine Translation. We generate improved word alignment of the training data by incorporating an unsupervised transliteration mining module to GIZA++ and build a phrase-based machine translation system. For tuning, we use a variation of PRO which provides better weights by optimizing BLEU+1 at corpus-level. We transliterate out-of-vocabulary words in a post-processing step by using a transliteration system built on the transliteration pairs extracted using an unsupervised transliteration mining system. For the Russian to English translation direction, we apply linguistically motivated pre-processing on the Russian side of the data.

1 Introduction

We describe the QCRI-Munich-Edinburgh-Stuttgart (QCRI-MES) English to Russian and Russian to English systems submitted to the Eighth Workshop on Statistical Machine Translation. We experimented using the standard Phrase-based Statistical Machine Translation System (PSMT) as implemented in the Moses toolkit (Koehn et al., 2007). The typical pipeline for translation involves word alignment using GIZA++ (Och and Ney, 2003), phrase extraction, tuning and phrase-based decoding. Our system is different from standard PSMT in three ways:

- We integrate an unsupervised transliteration mining system (Sajjad et al., 2012) into the GIZA++ word aligner (Sajjad et al., 2011). So, the selection of a word pair as a correct alignment is decided using both translation probabilities and transliteration probabilities.

- The MT system fails when translating out-of-vocabulary (OOV) words. We build a statistical transliteration system on the transliteration pairs mined by the unsupervised transliteration mining system and transliterate them in a post-processing step.

- We use a variation of Pairwise Ranking Optimization (*PRO*) for tuning. It optimizes BLEU at corpus-level and provides better feature weights that leads to an improvement in translation quality (Nakov et al., 2012).

We participate in English to Russian and Russian to English translation tasks. For the Russian/English system, we present experiments with two variations of the parallel corpus. One set of experiments are conducted using the standard parallel corpus provided by the workshop. In the second set of experiments, we morphologically reduce Russian words based on their fine-grained POS tags and map them to their root form. We do this on the Russian side of the parallel corpus, tuning set, development set and test set. This improves word alignment and learns better translation probabilities by reducing the vocabulary size.

The paper is organized as follows. Section 2 talks about unsupervised transliteration mining and its incorporation to the GIZA++ word aligner. In Section 3, we describe the transliteration system. Section 4 describes the extension of PRO that optimizes BLEU+1 at corpus level. Section 5 and Section 6 present English/Russian and Russian/English machine translation experiments respectively. Section 7 concludes.

2 Transliteration Mining

Consider a list of word pairs that consists of either transliteration pairs or non-transliteration pairs. A non-transliteration pair is defined as a word pair where words are not transliteration of each other. They can be translation, misalignment, etc. Transliteration mining extracts transliteration pairs from the list of word pairs. Sajjad et al. (2012) presented an unsupervised transliteration mining system that trains on the list of word pairs and filters transliteration pairs from that. It models the training data as the combination of a transliteration sub-model and a non-transliteration sub-model. The transliteration model is a joint source channel model. The non-transliteration model assumes no correlation between source and target word characters, and independently generates a source and a target word using two fixed unigram character models. The transliteration mining model is defined as an interpolation of the transliteration model and the non-transliteration model.

We apply transliteration mining to the list of word pairs extracted from English/Russian parallel corpus and mine transliteration pairs. We use the mined pairs for the training of the transliteration system.

2.1 Transliteration Augmented-GIZA++

GIZA++ aligns parallel sentences at word level. It applies the IBM models (Brown et al., 1993) and the HMM model (Vogel et al., 1996) in both directions i.e. source to target and target to source. It generates a list of translation pairs with translation probabilities, which is called the t-table. Sajjad et al. (2011) used a heuristic-based transliteration mining system and integrated it into the GIZA++ word aligner. We follow a similar procedure but use the unsupervised transliteration mining system of Sajjad et al. (2012).

We define a transliteration sub-model and train it on the transliteration pairs mined by the unsupervised transliteration mining system. We integrate it into the GIZA++ word aligner. The probability of a word pair is calculated as an interpolation of the transliteration probability and the translation probability stored in the t-table of the different alignment models used by the GIZA++ aligner. This interpolation is done for all iterations of all alignment models.

2.1.1 Estimating Transliteration Probabilities

We use the algorithm for the estimation of transliteration probabilities of Sajjad et al. (2011). We modify it to improve efficiency. In step 6 of Algorithm 1 instead of taking all f that coocur with e, we take only those that have a word length ratio in range of 0.8-1.2.[1] This reduces $cooc(e)$ by more than half and speeds up step 9 of Algorithm 1. The word pairs that are filtered out from $cooc(e)$ won't have transliteration probability $p_{ti}(f|e)$. We do not interpolate in these cases and use the translation probability as it is.

Algorithm 1 Estimation of transliteration probabilities, **e**-to-**f** direction

1: unfiltered data ← list of word pairs
2: filtered data ←transliteration pairs extracted using unsupervised transliteration mining system
3: Train a transliteration system on the filtered data
4: **for all** e **do**
5: $nbestTI(e) \leftarrow$ 10 best transliterations for e according to the transliteration system
6: $cooc(e) \leftarrow$ set of all f that cooccur with e in a parallel sentence with a word length in ratio of 0.8-1.2
7: $candidateTI(e) \leftarrow cooc(e) \cup nbestTI(e)$
8: **for all** f **do**
9: $p_{moses}(f, e) \leftarrow$ joint transliteration probability of e and f according to the transliterator
10: Calculate conditional transliteration probability $p_{ti}(f|e) \leftarrow \frac{p_{moses}(f,e)}{\sum_{f' \in CandidateTI(e)} p_{moses}(f',e)}$

2.1.2 Modified EM Training

Sajjad et al. (2011) modified the EM training of the word alignment models. They combined the translation probabilities of the IBM models and the HMM model with the transliteration probabilities. Consider $p_{ta}(f|e) = f_{ta}(f,e)/f_{ta}(e)$ is the translation probability of the word alignment models. The interpolated probability is calculated by adding the smoothed alignment frequency $f_{ta}(f,e)$ to the transliteration probability weight by the factor λ. The modified translation probabilities is given by:

$$\hat{p}(f|e) = \frac{f_{ta}(f,e) + \lambda p_{ti}(f|e)}{f_{ta}(e) + \lambda} \quad (1)$$

where $f_{ta}(f,e) = p_{ta}(f|e) f_{ta}(e)$. $p_{ta}(f|e)$ is obtained from the original t-table of the alignment model. $f_{ta}(e)$ is the total corpus frequency of e. λ is the transliteration weight which is defined as the number of counts the transliteration model gets versus the translation model. The model is not

[1] We assume that the words with very different character counts are less likely to be transliterations.

very sensitive to the value of λ. We use $\lambda = 50$ for our experiments. The procedure we described of estimation of transliteration probabilities and modification of EM is also followed in the opposite direction **f**-to-**e**.

3 Transliteration System

The unsupervised transliteration mining system (as described in Section 2) outputs a list of transliteration pairs. We consider transliteration word pairs as parallel sentences by putting a space after every character of the words and train a PSMT system for transliteration. We apply the transliteration system to OOVs in a post-processing step on the output of the machine translation system.

Russian is a morphologically rich language. Different cases of a word are generally represented by adding suffixes to the root form. For OOVs that are named entities, transliterating the inflected forms generates wrong English transliterations as inflectional suffixes get transliterated too. To handle this, first we need to identify OOV named entities (as there can be other OOVs that are not named entities) and then transliterate them correctly. We tackle the first issue as follows: If an OOV word is starting with an upper case letter, we identify it as a named entity. To correctly transliterate it to English, we stem the named entity based on a list of suffixes (а, ом, ы, е, ой, у) and transliterate the stemmed form. For morphologically reduced Russian (see Section 6.1), we follow the same procedure as OOVs are unknown to the POS tagger too and are (incorrectly) not reduced to their root forms. For OOVs that are not identified as named entities, we transliterate them without any pre-processing.

4 PRO: Corpus-level BLEU

Pairwise Ranking Optimization (PRO) (Hopkins and May, 2011) is an extension of MERT (Och, 2003) that can scale to thousands of parameters. It optimizes sentence-level BLEU+1 which is an add-one smoothed version of BLEU (Lin and Och, 2004). The sentence-level BLEU+1 has a bias towards producing short translations as add-one smoothing improves precision but does not change the brevity penalty. Nakov et al. (2012) fixed this by using several heuristics on brevity penalty, reference length and grounding the precision length. In our experiments, we use the improved version of PRO as provided by Nakov et al. (2012). We call it *PROv1* later on.

5 English/Russian Experiments

5.1 Dataset

The amount of bitext used for the estimation of the translation model is $\approx$ 2M parallel sentences. We use newstest2012a for tuning and newstest2012b (tst2012) as development set.

The language model is estimated using large monolingual corpus of Russian $\approx$ 21.7M sentences. We follow the approach of Schwenk and Koehn (2008) by training domain-specific language models separately and then linearly interpolate them using SRILM with weights optimized on the held-out development set. We divide the tuning set newstest2012a into two halves and use the first half for tuning and second for test in order to obtain stable weights (Koehn and Haddow, 2012).

5.2 Baseline Settings

We word-aligned the parallel corpus using GIZA++ (Och and Ney, 2003) with 5 iterations of Model1, 4 iterations of HMM and 4 iterations of Model4, and symmetrized the alignments using the grow-diag-final-and heuristic (Koehn et al., 2003). We built a phrase-based machine translation system using the Moses toolkit. *Minimum error rate training (MERT)*, *margin infused relaxed algorithm (MIRA)* and *PRO* are used to optimize the parameters.

5.3 Main System Settings

Our main system involves a pre-processing step – unsupervised transliteration mining, and a post-processing step – transliteration of OOVs. For the training of the unsupervised transliteration mining system, we take the word alignments from our baseline settings and extract all word pairs which occur as 1-to-1 alignments (like Sajjad et al. (2011)) and later refer to them as a *list of word pairs*. The unsupervised transliteration mining system trains on the list of word pairs and mines transliteration pairs. We use the mined pairs to build a transliteration system using the Moses toolkit. The transliteration system is used in Algorithm 1 to generate transliteration probabilities of candidate word pairs and is also used in the post-processing step to transliterate OOVs.

We run GIZA++ with identical settings as described in Section 5.2. We interpolate for ev-

	GIZA++	TA-GIZA++	OOV-TI
MERT	23.41	23.51	23.60
MIRA	23.60	23.73	23.85
PRO	23.57	23.68	23.70
PROv1	23.65	23.76	23.87

Table 1: BLEU scores of English to Russian machine translation system evaluated on tst2012 using baseline GIZA++ alignment and transliteration augmented-GIZA++. OOV-TI presents the score of the system trained using TA-GIZA++ after transliterating OOVs

SYS	tst2012	tst2013
GIZA++	23.76	18.4
TA-GIZA++	23.87	18.5*

Table 2: BLEU scores of English to Russian machine translation system evaluated on tst2012 and tst2013 using baseline GIZA++ alignment and transliteration augmented-GIZA++ alignment and post-processed the output by transliterating OOVs. Human evaluation in WMT13 is performed on TA-GIZA++ tested on tst2013 (marked with *)

ery iteration of the IBM Model1 and the HMM model. We had problem in applying smoothing for Model4 and did not interpolate transliteration probabilities for Model4. The alignments are refined using the grow-diag-final-and heuristic. We build a phrase-based system on the aligned pairs and tune the parameters using *PROv1*. OOVs are transliterated in the post-processing step.

5.4 Results

Table 1 summarizes English/Russian results on tst2012. Improved word alignment gives up to 0.13 BLEU points improvement. PROv1 improves translation quality and shows 0.08 BLEU point increase in BLEU in comparison to the parameters tuned using PRO. The transliteration of OOVs consistently improve translation quality by at least 0.1 BLEU point for all systems.[2] This adds to a cumulative gain of up to 0.2 BLEU points.

We summarize results of our systems trained on GIZA++ and transliteration augmented-GIZA++ (TA-GIZA++) and tested on tst2012 and tst2013 in Table 2. Both systems use PROv1 for tuning and transliteration of OOVs in the post-processing step. The system trained on TA-GIZA++ performed better than the system trained on the baseline aligner GIZA++.

6 Russian/English Experiments

In this section, we present translation experiments in Russian to English direction. We morphologically reduce the Russian side of the parallel data in a pre-processing step and train the translation system on that. We compare its result with the Russian to English system trained on the un-processed parallel data.

[2]We see similar gain in BLEU when using operation sequence model (Durrani et al., 2011) for decoding and transliterating OOVs in a post-processing step (Durrani et al., 2013).

6.1 Morphological Processing

The linguistic processing of Russian involves POS tagging and morphological reduction. We first tag the Russian data using a fine grained tagset. The tagger identifies lemmas and the set of morphological attributes attached to each word. We reduce the number of these attributes by deleting some of them, that are not relevant for English (for example, gender agreement of verbs). This generates a morphologically reduced Russian which is used in parallel with English for the training of the machine translation system. Further details on the morphological processing of Russian are described in Weller et al. (2013).

6.1.1 POS Tagging

We use RFTagger (Schmid and Laws, 2008) for POS tagging. Despite the good quality of tagging provided by RFTagger, some errors seem to be unavoidable due to the ambiguity of certain grammatical forms in Russian. A good example of this is neuter nouns that have the same form in all cases, or feminine nouns, which have identical forms in singular genitive and plural nominative (Sharoff et al., 2008). Since Russian sentences have free word order, and the case of nouns cannot be determined on that basis, this imperfection can not be corrected during tagging or by post-processing the tagger output.

6.1.2 Morphological Reduction

English in comparison to Slavic group of languages is morphologically poor. For example, English has no morphological attributes for nouns and adjectives to express gender or case; verbs in English have no gender either. Russian, on the contrary, has rich morphology. It suffices to say that the Russian has 6 cases and 3 grammatical genders, which manifest themselves in different suffixes for nouns, pronouns, adjectives and some verb forms.

When translating from Russian into English, a lot of these attributes become meaningless and excessive. It makes sense to reduce the number of morphological attributes before the text is supplied for the training of the MT system. We apply morphological reduction to nouns, pronouns, verbs, adjectives, prepositions and conjunctions. The rest of the POS (adverbs, particles, interjections and abbreviations) have no morphological attributes and are left unchanged.

We apply morphological reduction to train, tune, development and test data. We refer to this data set as *morph-reduced* later on.

6.2 Dataset

We use two variations of the parallel corpus to build and test the Russian to English system. One system is built on the data provided by the workshop. For the second system, we preprocess the Russian side of the data as described in Section 6.1. Both the provided parallel corpus and the morph-reduced parallel corpus consist of 2M parallel sentences each. We use them for the estimation of the translation model. We use large training data for the estimation of monolingual language model – en $\approx$ 287.3M sentences. We follow the identical procedure of interpolated language model as described in Section 5.1. We use newstest2012a for tuning and newstest2012b (tst2012) for development.

6.3 System Settings

We use identical system settings to those described in Section 5.3. We trained the systems separately on GIZA++ and transliteration augmented-GIZA++ to compare their results. All systems are tuned using PROv1. The translation output is post-processed to transliterate OOVs.

6.4 Results

Table 3 summarizes results of Russian to English machine translation systems trained on the original parallel corpus and on the morph-reduced corpus and using GIZA++ and transliteration augmented-GIZA++ for word alignment. The system using TA-GIZA++ for alignment shows the best results for both tst2012 and tst2013. The improved alignment gives a BLEU improvement of up to 0.4 points.

Original corpus		
SYS	**tst2012**	**tst2013**
GIZA++	32.51	25.5
TA-GIZA++	33.40	25.9*
Morph-reduced		
SYS	**tst2012**	**tst2013**
GIZA++	31.22	24.30
TA-GIZA++	31.40	24.45

Table 3: Russian to English machine translation system evaluated on tst2012 and tst2013. Human evaluation in WMT13 is performed on the system trained using the original corpus with TA-GIZA++ for alignment (marked with *)

The system built on the morph-reduced data shows degradation in results by 1.29 BLEU points. However, the percentage of OOVs reduces for both test sets when using the morph-reduced data set compared to the original parallel corpus. We analyze the output of the system and find that the morph-reduced system makes mistakes in choosing the right tense of the verb. This might be one reason for poor performance. This implies that the morphological reduction is slightly damaging the data, perhaps for specific parts of speech. In the future, we would like to investigate this issue in detail.

7 Conclusion

In this paper, we described the QCRI-Munich-Edinburgh-Stuttgart machine translation systems submitted to the Eighth Workshop on Statistical Machine Translation. We aligned the parallel corpus using transliteration augmented-GIZA++ to improve the word alignments. We built a phrase-based system using the Moses toolkit. For tuning the feature weights, we used an improvement of PRO that optimizes for corpus-level BLEU. We post-processed the output of the machine translation system to transliterate OOV words.

For the Russian to English system, we morphologically reduced the Russian data in a preprocessing step. This reduced the vocabulary size and helped to generate better word alignments. However, the performance of the SMT system dropped by 1.29 BLEU points in decoding. We will investigate this issue further in the future.

Acknowledgments

We would like to thank the anonymous reviewers for their helpful feedback and suggestions. We would like to thank Philipp Koehn and Barry Haddow for providing data and alignments. Nadir Durrani was funded by the European Union Seventh Framework Programme (FP7/2007-2013) under grant agreement n ° 287658. Alexander Fraser was funded by Deutsche Forschungsgemeinschaft grant Models of Morphosyntax for Statistical Machine Translation. Helmut Schmid was supported by Deutsche Forschungsgemeinschaft grant SFB 732. This publication only reflects the authors views.

References

Peter F. Brown, Stephen A. Della Pietra, Vincent J. Della Pietra, and R. L. Mercer. 1993. The mathematics of statistical machine translation: parameter estimation. *Computational Linguistics*, 19(2).

Nadir Durrani, Helmut Schmid, and Alexander Fraser. 2011. A joint sequence translation model with integrated reordering. In *Proceedings of the 49th Annual Meeting of the Association for Computational Linguistics: Human Language Technologies*, Portland, USA.

Nadir Durrani, Helmut Schmid, Alexander Fraser, Hassan Sajjad, and Richárd Farkas. 2013. Munich-Edinburgh-Stuttgart submissions of OSM systems at WMT13. In *Proceedings of the Eighth Workshop on Statistical Machine Translation*, Sofia, Bulgaria.

Mark Hopkins and Jonathan May. 2011. Tuning as ranking. In *Proceedings of the Conference on Empirical Methods in Natural Language Processing*, Edinburgh, United Kingdom.

Philipp Koehn and Barry Haddow. 2012. Towards effective use of training data in statistical machine translation. In *Proceedings of the Seventh Workshop on Statistical Machine Translation*, Montréal, Canada.

Philipp Koehn, Franz J. Och, and Daniel Marcu. 2003. Statistical phrase-based translation. In *Proceedings of the Human Language Technology and North American Association for Computational Linguistics Conference*, Edmonton, Canada.

Philipp Koehn, Hieu Hoang, Alexandra Birch, Chris Callison-Burch, Marcello Federico, Nicola Bertoldi, Brooke Cowan, Wade Shen, Christine Moran, Richard Zens, Chris Dyer, Ondrej Bojar, Alexandra Constantin, and Evan Herbst. 2007. Moses: Open source toolkit for statistical machine translation. In *Proceedings of the 45th Annual Meeting of the Association for Computational Linguistics, Demonstration Program*, Prague, Czech Republic.

Chin-Yew Lin and Franz Josef Och. 2004. ORANGE: a method for evaluating automatic evaluation metrics for machine translation. In *Proceedings of the 20th international conference on Computational Linguistics*, Geneva, Switzerland.

Preslav Nakov, Francisco Guzmán, and Stephan Vogel. 2012. Optimizing for sentence-level BLEU+1 yields short translations. In *Proceedings of the 24th International Conference on Computational Linguistics*, Mumbai, India.

Franz J. Och and Hermann Ney. 2003. A systematic comparison of various statistical alignment models. *Computational Linguistics*, 29(1).

Franz J. Och. 2003. Minimum error rate training in statistical machine translation. In *Proceedings of the 41st Annual Meeting of the Association for Computational Linguistics*, Sapporo, Japan.

Hassan Sajjad, Alexander Fraser, and Helmut Schmid. 2011. An algorithm for unsupervised transliteration mining with an application to word alignment. In *Proceedings of the 49th Annual Conference of the Association for Computational Linguistics*, Portland, USA.

Hassan Sajjad, Alexander Fraser, and Helmut Schmid. 2012. A statistical model for unsupervised and semi-supervised transliteration mining. In *Proceedings of the 50th Annual Conference of the Association for Computational Linguistics*, Jeju, Korea.

Helmut Schmid and Florian Laws. 2008. Estimation of conditional probabilities with decision trees and an application to fine-grained pos tagging. In *Proceedings of the 22nd International Conference on Computational Linguistics - Volume 1*, Manchester, United Kingdom.

Holger Schwenk and Philipp Koehn. 2008. Large and Diverse Language Models for Statistical Machine Translation. In *International Joint Conference on Natural Language Processing*, Hyderabad, India.

Serge Sharoff, Mikhail Kopotev, Tomaz Erjavec, Anna Feldman, and Dagmar Divjak. 2008. Designing and evaluating a russian tagset. In *Proceedings of the Sixth International Conference on Language Resources and Evaluation.*

Stephan Vogel, Hermann Ney, and Christoph Tillmann. 1996. HMM-based word alignment in statistical translation. In *16th International Conference on Computational Linguistics*, Copenhagen, Denmark.

Marion Weller, Max Kisselew, Svetlana Smekalova, Alexander Fraser, Helmut Schmid, Nadir Durrani, Hassan Sajjad, and Richárd Farkas. 2013. Munich-Edinburgh-Stuttgart submissions at WMT13: Morphological and syntactic processing for SMT. In *Proceedings of the Eighth Workshop on Statistical Machine Translation*, Sofia, Bulgaria.

Tunable Distortion Limits and Corpus Cleaning for SMT

Sara Stymne Christian Hardmeier Jörg Tiedemann Joakim Nivre
Uppsala University
Department of Linguistics and Philology
firstname.lastname@lingfil.uu.se

Abstract

We describe the Uppsala University system for WMT13, for English-to-German translation. We use the Docent decoder, a local search decoder that translates at the document level. We add tunable distortion limits, that is, soft constraints on the maximum distortion allowed, to Docent. We also investigate cleaning of the noisy Common Crawl corpus. We show that we can use alignment-based filtering for cleaning with good results. Finally we investigate effects of corpus selection for recasing.

1 Introduction

In this paper we present the Uppsala University submission to WMT 2013. We have submitted one system, for translation from English to German. In our submission we use the document-level decoder Docent (Hardmeier et al., 2012; Hardmeier et al., 2013). In the current setup, we take advantage of Docent in that we introduce *tunable distortion limits*, that is, modeling distortion limits as soft constraints instead of as hard constraints. In addition we perform experiments on corpus cleaning. We investigate how the noisy Common Crawl corpus can be cleaned, and suggest an *alignment-based* cleaning method, which works well. We also investigate corpus selection for recasing.

In Section 2 we introduce our decoder, Docent, followed by a general system description in Section 3. In Section 4 we describe our experiments with corpus cleaning, and in Section 5 we describe experiments with tunable distortion limits. In Section 6 we investigate corpus selection for recasing. In Section 7 we compare our results with Docent to results using Moses (Koehn et al., 2007). We conclude in Section 8.

2 The Docent Decoder

Docent (Hardmeier et al., 2013) is a decoder for phrase-based SMT (Koehn et al., 2003). It differs from other publicly available decoders by its use of a different search algorithm that imposes fewer restrictions on the feature models that can be implemented.

The most popular decoding algorithm for phrase-based SMT is the one described by Koehn et al. (2003), which has become known as *stack decoding*. It constructs output sentences bit by bit by appending phrase translations to an initially empty hypothesis. Complexity is kept in check, on the one hand, by a beam search approach that only expands the most promising hypotheses. On the other hand, a dynamic programming technique called *hypothesis recombination* exploits the locality of the standard feature models, in particular the n-gram language model, to achieve a loss-free reduction of the search space. While this decoding approach delivers excellent search performance at a very reasonable speed, it limits the information available to the feature models to an n-gram window similar to a language model history. In stack decoding, it is difficult to implement models with sentence-internal long-range dependencies and cross-sentence dependencies, where the model score of a given sentence depends on the translations generated for another sentence.

In contrast to this very popular stack decoding approach, our decoder Docent implements a search procedure based on *local search* (Hardmeier et al., 2012). At any stage of the search process, its search state consists of a complete document translation, making it easy for feature models to access the complete document with its current translation at any point in time. The search algorithm is a stochastic variant of standard *hill climbing*. At each step, it generates a successor of the current search state by randomly applying one of a set of state changing operations to a random location in the document. If the new state has a better score than the previous one, it is accepted, else search continues from the previous state. The operations are designed in such a way that every state in the search space can be reached from every other state through a sequence of state operations. In the standard setup we use three operations: *change-phrase-translation* replaces the translation of a single phrase with another option from the phrase table, *resegment* alters the phrase segmentation of a sequence of phrases, and *swap-phrases* alters the output word order by exchanging two phrases.

In contrast to stack decoding, the search algorithm in Docent leaves model developers much greater freedom in the design of their feature functions because it gives them access to the translation of the complete document. On the downside, there is an increased risk of search errors because the document-level hill-climbing decoder cannot make as strong assumptions about the problem structure as the stack decoder does. In practice, this drawback can be mitigated by initializing the hill-climber with the output of a stack decoding pass using the baseline set of models without document-level features (Hardmeier et al., 2012). Since its inception, Docent has been used to experiment with document-level semantic language models (Hardmeier et al., 2012) and models to enhance text readability (Stymne et al., 2013b). Work on other discourse phenomena is ongoing. In the present paper, we focus on sentence-internal reordering by exploiting the fact that Docent implements distortion limits as soft constraints rather than strictly enforced limitations. We do not include any of our document-level feature functions.

3 System Setup

In this section we will describe our basic system setup. We used all corpora made available for English–German by the WMT13 workshop. We always concatenated the two bilingual corpora Europarl and News Commentary, which we will call EP-NC. We pre-processed all corpora by using the tools provided for tokenization and we also lower-cased all corpora. For the bilingual corpora we also filtered sentence pairs with a length ratio larger than three, or where either sentence was longer than 60 tokens. Recasing was performed as a post-processing step, trained using the resources in the Moses toolkit (Koehn et al., 2007).

For the language model we trained two separate models, one on the German side of EP-NC, and one on the monolingual News corpus. In both cases we trained 5-gram models. For the large News corpus we used entropy-based pruning, with 10^{-8} as a threshold (Stolcke, 1998). The language models were trained using the SRILM toolkit (Stolcke, 2002) and during decoding we used the KenLM toolkit (Heafield, 2011).

For the translation model we also trained two models, one with EP-NC, and one with Common Crawl. These two models were interpolated and used as a single model at decoding time, based on perplexity minimization interpolation (Sennrich, 2012), see details in Section 4. The translation models were trained using the Moses toolkit (Koehn et al., 2007), with standard settings with 5 features, phrase probabilities and lexical weighting in both directions and a phrase penalty. We applied significance-based filtering (Johnson et al., 2007) to the resulting phrase tables. For decoding we used the Docent decoder with random initialization and standard parameter settings (Hardmeier et al., 2012; Hardmeier et al., 2013), which beside translation and language model features include a word penalty and a distortion penalty.

Parameter optimization was performed using MERT (Och, 2003) at the document-level (Stymne et al., 2013a). In this setup we calculate both model and metric scores on the document-level instead of on the sentence-level. We produce k-best lists by sampling from the decoder. In each optimization run we run 40,000 hill-climbing iterations of the decoder, and sample translations with interval 100, from iteration 10,000. This procedure has been shown to give competitive results to standard tuning with Moses (Koehn et al., 2007) with relatively stable results (Stymne et al., 2013a). For tuning data we concatenated the tuning sets news-test 2008–2010 and newssyscomb2009, to get a higher number of documents. In this set there are 319 documents and 7434 sentences.

To evaluate our system we use newstest2012, which has 99 documents and 3003 sentences. In this article we give lower-case Bleu scores (Papineni et al., 2002), except in Section 6 where we investigate the effect of different recasing models.

Cleaning	Sentences	Reduction
None	2,399,123	
Basic	2,271,912	5.3%
Langid	2,072,294	8.8%
Alignment-based	1,512,401	27.0%

Table 1: Size of Common Crawl after the different cleaning steps and reduction in size compared to the previous step

4 Cleaning of Common Crawl

The Common Crawl (CC) corpus was collected from web sources, and was made available for the WMT13 workshop. It is noisy, with many sentences with the wrong language and also many non-corresponding sentence pairs. To make better use of this resource we investigated two methods for cleaning it, by making use of language identification and alignment-based filtering. Before any other cleaning we performed basic filtering where we only kept pairs where both sentences had at most 60 words, and with a length ratio of maximum 3. This led to a 5.3% reduction of sentences, as shown in Table 1.

Language Identification For language identification we used the off-the-shelf tool langid.py (Lui and Baldwin, 2012). It is a python library, covering 97 languages, including English and German, trained on data drawn from five different domains. It uses a naive Bayes classifier with a multinomial event model, over a mixture of byte n-grams. As for many language identification packages it works best for longer texts, but Lui and Baldwin (2012) also showed that it has good performance for short microblog texts, with an accuracy of 0.89–0.94.

We applied langid.py for each sentence in the CC corpus, and kept only those sentence pairs where the correct language was identified for both sentences with a confidence of at least 0.999. The total number of sentences was reduced by a further 8.8% based on the langid filtering.

We performed an analysis on a set of 1000 sentence pairs. Among the 907 sentences that were kept in this set we did not find any cases with the wrong language. Table 2 shows an analysis of the 93 sentences that were removed from this test set. The overall accuracy of langid.py is much higher than indicated in the table, however, since it does not include the correctly identified English and German sentences. We grouped the removed sentences into four categories, cases where both languages were correctly identified, but under the confidence threshold of 0.999, cases where both languages were incorrectly identified, and cases where one language was incorrectly identified. Overall the language identification was accurate on 54 of the 93 removed sentences. In 18 of the cases where it was wrong, the sentences were not translation correspondents, which means that we only wrongly removed 21 out of 1000 sentences. It was also often the case when the language was wrongly identified, that large parts of the sentence consisted of place names, such as “Forums about Conil de la Frontera - Cádiz.” – “Foren über Conil de la Frontera - Cádiz.”, which were identified as es/ht instead of en/de. Even though such sentence pairs do correspond, they do not contain much useful translation material.

Alignment-Based Cleaning For the alignment-based cleaning, we aligned the data from the previous step using GIZA++ (Och and Ney, 2003) in both directions, and used the intersection of the alignments. The intersection of alignments is more sparse than the standard SMT symmetrization heuristics, like grow-diag-final-and (Koehn et al., 2005). Our hypothesis was that sentence pairs with very few alignment points in the intersection would likely not be corresponding sentences.

We used two types of filtering thresholds based on alignment points. The first threshold is for the ratio of the number of alignment points and the maximum sentence length. The second threshold is the absolute number of alignment points in a sentence pair. In addition we used a third threshold based on the length ratio of the sentences.

To find good values for the filtering thresholds, we created a small gold standard where we manually annotated 100 sentence pairs as being corresponding or not. In this set the sentence pairs did not match in 33 cases. Table 3 show results for some different values for the threshold parameters. Overall we are able to get a very high precision on the task of removing non-corresponding sentences, which means that most sentences that are removed based on this cleaning are actually non-corresponding sentences. The recall is a bit lower, indicating that there are still non-corresponding sentences left in our data. In our translation system we used the bold values in Table 3, since it gave high precision with reasonable recall for the removal of non-corresponding sentences, meaning

Identification	Total	Wrong lang.	Non-corr	Corr	Languages identified
English and German < 0.999	15	0	7	8	
Both English and German wrong	6	2	2	2	2:na/es, 2:et/et, 1: es/an, 1:es/ht
English wrong	13	1	6	6	5: es 4: fr 1: br, it, de, eo
German wrong	59	51	3	5	51: en 3: es 2:nl 1: af, la, lb
Total	93	54	18	21	

Table 2: Reasons and correctness for removing sentences based on language ID for 93 sentences out of a 1000 sentence subset, divided into wrong lang(uage), non-corr(esponding) pairs, and corr(esponding) pairs.

Ratio align	Min align	Ratio length	Prec.	Recall	F	Kept
0.1	4	2	0.70	0.77	0.73	70%
0.28	**4**	**2**	**0.94**	**0.72**	**0.82**	**57%**
0.42	4	2	1.00	0.56	0.72	41%
0.28	2	2	0.91	0.73	0.81	59%
0.28	6	2	0.94	0.63	0.76	51%
0.28	4	1.5	0.94	0.65	0.77	52%
0.28	4	3	0.91	0.75	0.82	60%

Table 3: Results of alignment-based cleaning for different values of the filtering parameters, with precision, recall and F-score for the identification of erroneous sentence pairs and the percentage of kept sentence pairs

that we kept most correctly aligned sentence pairs.

This cleaning method is more aggressive than the other cleaning methods we described. For the gold standard only 57% of sentences were kept, but in the full training set it was a bit higher, 73%, as shown in Table 1.

Phrase Table Interpolation To use the CC corpus in our system we first trained a separate phrase table which we then interpolated with the phrase table trained on EP-NC. In this way we could always run the system with a single phrase table. For interpolation, we used the perplexity minimization for weighted counts method by Sennrich (2012). Each of the four weights in the phrase table, backward and forward phrase translation probabilities and lexical weights, are optimized separately. This method minimizes the cross-entropy based on a held-out corpus, for which we used the concatenation of all available News development sets.

The cross-entropy and the contribution of CC relative to EP-NC, are shown for phrase translation probabilities in both directions in Table 4. The numbers for lexical weights show similar trends. For each cleaning step the cross-entropy is reduced and the contribution of CC is increased. The difference between the basic cleaning and langid is very small, however. The alignment-based cleaning shows a much larger effect. After that cleaning step the CC corpus has a similar contribution to EP-NC. This is an indicator that the final cleaned CC corpus fits the development set well.

	$p(S\|T)$		$p(T\|S)$	
Cleaning	CE	IP	CE	IP
Basic	3.18	0.12	3.31	0.06
Langid	3.17	0.13	3.29	0.07
Alignment-based	3.02	0.47	3.17	0.61

Table 4: Cross-entropy (CE) and relative interpolation weights (IP) compared to EP-NC for the Common Crawl corpus, with different cleaning

Results In Table 5 we show the translation results with the different types of cleaning of CC, and without it. We show results of different corpus combinations both during tuning and testing. We see that we get the overall best result by both tuning and testing with the alignment-based cleaning of CC, but it is not as useful to do the extra cleaning if we do not tune with it as well. Overall we get the best results when tuning is performed including a cleaned version of CC. This setup gives a large improvement compared to not using CC at all, or to use it with only basic cleaning. There is little difference in Bleu scores when testing with either basic cleaning, or cleaning based on language ID, with a given tuning, which is not surprising given their small and similar interpolation weights. Tuning was, however, not successful when using CC with basic cleaning.

Overall we think that alignment-based corpus cleaning worked well. It reduced the size of the corpus by over 25%, improved the cross-entropy for interpolation with the EP-NC phrase-table, and

Tuning	Testing not used	basic	langid	alignment
not used	14.0	13.9	13.9	14.0
basic	14.2	14.5	14.3	14.3
langid	15.2	15.3	15.3	15.3
alignment	12.7	15.3	15.3	15.7

Table 5: Bleu scores with different types of cleaning and without Common Crawl

gave an improvement on the translation task. We still think that there is potential for further improving this filtering and to annotate larger test sets to investigate the effects in more detail.

5 Tunable Distortion Limits

The Docent decoder uses a hill-climbing search and can perform operations anywhere in the sentence. Thus, it does not need to enforce a strict distortion limit. In the Docent implementation, the distortion limit is actually implemented as a feature, which is normally given a very large weight, which effectively means that it works as a hard constraint. This could easily be relaxed, however, and in this work we investigate the effects of using soft distortion limits, which can be optimized during tuning, like other features. In this way long-distance movements can be allowed when they are useful, instead of prohibiting them completely. A drawback of using no or soft distortion limits is that it increases the search space.

In this work we mostly experiment with variants of one or two standard distortion limits, but with a tunable weight. We also tried to use separate soft distortion limits for left- and right-movement. Table 6 show the results with different types of distortion limits. The system with a standard fixed distortion limits of 6 has a somewhat lower score than most of the systems with no or soft distortion limits. In most cases the scores are similar, and we see no clear affects of allowing tunable limits over allowing unlimited distortion. The system that uses two mono-directional limits of 6 and 10 has slightly higher scores than the other systems, and is used in our final submission.

One possible reason for the lack of effect of allowing more distortion could be that it rarely happens that an operator is chosen that performs such distortion, when we use the standard Docent settings. To investigate this, we varied the settings of the parameters that guide the *swap-phrases* operator, and used the *move-phrases* operator instead of *swap-phrases*. None of these changes led to any

DL type	Limit	Bleu
No DL	–	15.5
Hard DL	6	15.0
One soft DL	6	15.5
	8	14.2
	10	15.5
Two soft DLs	4,8	15.5
	6,10	15.7
Bidirectional soft DLs	6,10	15.5

Table 6: Bleu scores for different distortion limit (DL) settings

improvements, however.

While we saw no clear effects when using tunable distortion limits, we plan to extend this work in the future to model movement differently based on parts of speech. For the English–German language pair, for instance, it would be reasonable to allow long distance moves of verb groups with no or little cost, but use a hard limit or a high cost for other parts of speech.

6 Corpus Selection for Recasing

In this section we investigate the effect of using different corpus combinations for recasing. We lower-cased our training corpus, which means that we need a full recasing step as post-processing. This is performed by training a SMT system on lower-cased and true-cased target language. We used the Moses toolkit to train the recasing system and to decode during recasing. We investigate the effect of using different combinations of the available training corpora to train the recasing model.

Table 7 show case sensitive Bleu scores, which can be compared to the previous case-insensitive scores of 15.7. We see that there is a larger effect of including more data in the language model than in the translation model. There is a performance jump both when adding CC data and when adding News data to the language model. The results are best when we include the News data, which is not included in the English–German translation model, but which is much larger than the other corpora. There is no further gain by using News in combination with other corpora compared to using only News. When adding more data to the translation model there is only a minor effect, with the difference between only using EP-NC and using all available corpora is at most 0.2 Bleu points. In our submitted system we use the monolingual News corpus both in the LM and the TM.

There are other options for how to treat recas-

TM	Language model				
	EP-NC	EP-NC-CC	News	EP-NC-News	EP-NC-CC-News
EP-NC	13.8	14.4	14.8	14.8	14.8
EP-NC-CC	13.9	14.5	14.9	14.8	14.8
News	13.9	14.5	14.9	14.9	14.9
EP-NC-News	13.9	14.5	14.9	14.9	14.9
EP-NC-CC-News	13.9	14.5	14.9	14.9	15.0

Table 7: Case-sensitive Bleu scores with different corpus combinations for the language model and translation model (TM) for recasing

ing. It is common to train the system on true-cased data instead of lower-cased data, which has been shown to lead to small gains for the English–German language pair (Koehn et al., 2008). In this framework there is still a need to find the correct case for the first word of each sentence, for which a similar corpus study might be useful.

7 Comparison to Moses

So far we have only shown results using the Docent decoder on its own, with a random initialization, since we wanted to submit a Docent-only system for the shared task. In this section we also show contrastive results with Moses, and for Docent initialized with stack decoding, using Moses, and for different type of tuning.

Previous research have shown mixed results for the effect of initializing Docent with and without stack decoding, when using the same feature sets. In Hardmeier et al. (2012) there was a drop of about 1 Bleu point for English–French translation based on WMT11 data when random initialization was used. In Stymne et al. (2013a), on the other hand, Docent gave very similar results with both types of initialization for German–English WMT13 data. The latter setup is similar to ours, except that no Common Crawl data was used.

The results with our setup are shown in Table 8. In this case we lose around a Bleu point when using Docent on its own, without Moses initialization. We also see that the results are lower when using Moses with the Docent tuning method, or when combining Moses and Docent with Docent tuning. This indicates that the document-level tuning has not given satisfactory results in this scenario, contrary to the results in Stymne et al. (2013a), which we plan to explore further in future work. Overall we think it is important to develop stronger context-sensitive models for Docent, which can take advantage of the document context.

Test system	Tuning system	Bleu
Docent (random)	Docent	15.7
Docent (stack)	Docent	15.9
Moses	Docent	15.9
Docent (random)	Moses	15.9
Docent (stack)	Moses	16.8
Moses	Moses	16.8

Table 8: Bleu scores for Docent initialized randomly or with stack decoding compared to Moses. Tuning is performed with either Moses or Docent. For the top line we used tunable distortion limits 6,10 with Docent, in the other cases a standard hard distortion limit of 6, since Moses does not allow soft distortion limits.

8 Conclusion

We have presented the Uppsala University system for WMT 2013. Our submitted system uses Docent with random initialization and two tunable distortion limits of 6 and 10. It is trained with the Common Crawl corpus, cleaned using language identification and alignment-based filtering. For recasing we used the monolingual News corpora.

For corpus-cleaning, we present a novel method for cleaning noisy corpora based on the number and ratio of word alignment links for sentence pairs, which leads to a large reduction of corpus size, and to small improvements on the translation task. We also experiment with tunable distortion limits, which do not lead to any consistent improvements at this stage.

In the current setup the search algorithm of Docent is not strong enough to compete with the effective search in standard decoders like Moses. We are, however, working on developing discourse-aware models that can take advantage of the document-level context, which is available in Docent. We also need to further investigate tuning methods for Docent.

References

Christian Hardmeier, Joakim Nivre, and Jörg Tiedemann. 2012. Document-wide decoding for phrase-based statistical machine translation. In *Proceedings of the 2012 Joint Conference on Empirical Methods in Natural Language Processing and Computational Natural Language Learning*, pages 1179–1190, Jeju Island, Korea.

Christian Hardmeier, Sara Stymne, Jörg Tiedemann, and Joakim Nivre. 2013. Docent: A document-level decoder for phrase-based statistical machine translation. In *Proceedings of the 51st Annual Meeting of the ACL, Demonstration session*, Sofia, Bulgaria.

Kenneth Heafield. 2011. KenLM: Faster and smaller language model queries. In *Proceedings of the Sixth Workshop on Statistical Machine Translation*, pages 187–197, Edinburgh, Scotland.

Howard Johnson, Joel Martin, George Foster, and Roland Kuhn. 2007. Improving translation quality by discarding most of the phrasetable. In *Proceedings of the 2007 Joint Conference on Empirical Methods in Natural Language Processing and Computational Natural Language Learning*, pages 967–975, Prague, Czech Republic.

Philipp Koehn, Franz Josef Och, and Daniel Marcu. 2003. Statistical phrase-based translation. In *Proceedings of the 2003 Human Language Technology Conference of the NAACL*, pages 48–54, Edmonton, Alberta, Canada.

Philipp Koehn, Amittai Axelrod, Alexandra Birch Mayne, Chris Callison-Burch, Miles Osborne, and David Talbot. 2005. Edinburgh system description for the 2005 IWSLT speech translation evaluation. In *Proceedings of the International Workshop on Spoken Language Translation*, Pittsburgh, Pennsylvania, USA.

Philipp Koehn, Hieu Hoang, Alexandra Birch, Chris Callison-Burch, Marcello Federico, Nicola Bertoldi, Brooke Cowan, Wade Shen, Christine Moran, Richard Zens, Chris Dyer, Ondrej Bojar, Alexandra Constantin, and Evan Herbst. 2007. Moses: Open source toolkit for statistical machine translation. In *Proceedings of the 45th Annual Meeting of the ACL, Demo and Poster Sessions*, pages 177–180, Prague, Czech Republic.

Philipp Koehn, Abhishek Arun, and Hieu Hoang. 2008. Towards better machine translation quality for the German-English language pairs. In *Proceedings of the Third Workshop on Statistical Machine Translation*, pages 139–142, Columbus, Ohio, USA.

Marco Lui and Timothy Baldwin. 2012. langid.py: An off-the-shelf language identification tool. In *Proceedings of the 50th Annual Meeting of the ACL, System Demonstrations*, pages 25–30, Jeju Island, Korea.

Franz Josef Och and Hermann Ney. 2003. A systematic comparison of various statistical alignment models. *Computational Linguistics*, 29(1):19–51.

Franz Josef Och. 2003. Minimum error rate training in statistical machine translation. In *Proceedings of the 42nd Annual Meeting of the ACL*, pages 160–167, Sapporo, Japan.

Kishore Papineni, Salim Roukos, Todd Ward, and Wei-Jing Zhu. 2002. BLEU: A method for automatic evaluation of machine translation. In *Proceedings of the 40th Annual Meeting of the ACL*, pages 311–318, Philadelphia, Pennsylvania, USA.

Rico Sennrich. 2012. Perplexity minimization for translation model domain adaptation in statistical machine translation. In *Proceedings of the 16th Annual Conference of the European Association for Machine Translation*, pages 539–549, Avignon, France.

Andreas Stolcke. 1998. Entropy-based pruning of backoff language models. In *Proceedings of the DARPA Broadcast News Transcription and Understanding Workshop*, pages 270–274, Landsdowne, Virginia, USA.

Andreas Stolcke. 2002. SRILM – an extensible language modeling toolkit. In *Proceedings of the Seventh International Conference on Spoken Language Processing*, pages 901–904, Denver, Colorado, USA.

Sara Stymne, Christian Hardmeier, Jörg Tiedemann, and Joakim Nivre. 2013a. Feature weight optimization for discourse-level SMT. In *Proceedings of the ACL 2013 Workshop on Discourse in Machine Translation (DiscoMT 2013)*, Sofia, Bulgaria.

Sara Stymne, Jörg Tiedemann, Christian Hardmeier, and Joakim Nivre. 2013b. Statistical machine translation with readability constraints. In *Proceedings of the 19th Nordic Conference on Computational Linguistics (NODALIDA'13)*, pages 375–386, Oslo, Norway.

Munich-Edinburgh-Stuttgart Submissions at WMT13: Morphological and Syntactic Processing for SMT

Marion Weller[1]**, Max Kisselew**[1]**, Svetlana Smekalova**[1]**, Alexander Fraser**[2]**,**
Helmut Schmid[2]**, Nadir Durrani**[3]**, Hassan Sajjad**[4]**, Richárd Farkas**[5]

[1]University of Stuttgart – (wellermn|kisselmx|smekalsa)@ims.uni-stuttgart.de

[2]Ludwig-Maximilian University of Munich – (schmid|fraser)@cis.uni-muenchen.de

[3]University of Edinburgh – dnadir@inf.ed.ac.uk

[4]Qatar Computing Research Institute – hsajjad@qf.org.qa

[5]University of Szeged – rfarkas@inf.u-szeged.hu

Abstract

We present 5 systems of the Munich-Edinburgh-Stuttgart[1] joint submissions to the 2013 SMT Shared Task: FR-EN, EN-FR, RU-EN, DE-EN and EN-DE. The first three systems employ inflectional generalization, while the latter two employ parser-based reordering, and DE-EN performs compound splitting. For our experiments, we use standard phrase-based Moses systems and operation sequence models (OSM).

1 Introduction

Morphologically complex languages often lead to data sparsity problems in statistical machine translation. For translation pairs with morphologically rich source languages and English as target language, we focus on simplifying the input language in order to reduce the complexity of the translation model. The pre-processing of the source-language is language-specific, requiring morphological analysis (FR, RU) as well as sentence reordering (DE) and dealing with compounds (DE). Due to time constraints we did not deal with inflection for DE-EN and EN-DE.

The morphological simplification process consists in lemmatizing inflected word forms and dealing with word formation (splitting portmanteau prepositions or compounds). This needs to take into account translation-relevant features (e.g. *number*) which vary across the different language pairs: while French only has the features *number* and *gender*, a wider array of features needs to be considered when modelling Russian (cf. table 6). In addition to morphological reduction, we also apply transliteration models learned from automatically mined transliterations to handle out-of-vocabulary words (OOVs) when translating from Russian.

Replacing inflected word forms with simpler variants (lemmas or the components of split compounds) aims not only at reducing the general complexity of the translation model, but also at decreasing the amount of out-of-vocabulary words in the input data. This is particularly the case with German compounds, which are very productive and thus often lack coverage in the parallel training data, whereas the individual components can be translated. Similarly, inflected word forms (e.g. adjectives) benefit from the reduction to lemmas if the full inflection paradigm does not occur in the parallel training data.

For EN-FR, a translation pair with a morphologically complex target language, we describe a two-step translation system built on non-inflected word stems with a post-processing component for predicting morphological features and the generation of inflected forms. In addition to the advantage of a more general translation model, this method also allows the generation of inflected word forms which do not occur in the training data.

2 Experimental setup

The translation experiments in this paper are carried out with either a standard phrase-based Moses system (DE-EN, EN-DE, EN-FR and FR-EN) or with an operation sequence model (RU-EN, DE-EN), cf. Durrani et al. (2013b) for more details. An operation sequence model (OSM) is a state-of-the-art SMT-system that learns translation and reordering patterns by representing a sentence pair and its word alignment as a unique sequence of operations (see e.g. Durrani et al. (2011), Durrani et al. (2013a) for more details). For the Moses systems we used the old train-model perl scripts rather than the EMS, so we did not perform Good-Turing smoothing; parameter tuning was carried out with *batch-mira* (Cherry and Foster, 2012).

[1]The language pairs DE-EN and RU-EN were developed in collaboration with the Qatar Computing Research Institute and the University of Szeged.

1	Removal of empty lines
2	Conversion of HTML special characters like *"* to the corresponding characters
3	Unification of words that were written both with an *æ* or with an *oe* to only one spelling
4	Punctuation normalization and tokenization
5	Putting together clitics and apostrophes like *l '* or *d '* to *l'* and *d'*

Table 1: Text normalization for FR-EN.

Definite determiners Indefinite determiners	*la / l' / les* → *le* *un / une* → *un*
Adjectives	Infl. form → lemma
Portmanteaus	e. g. *au* → *à le*
Verb participles inflected for gender and number ending in *ée/és/ées*	Reduced to non-inflected verb participle form ending in *é*
Clitics and apostrophized words are converted to their lemmas	*d'* → *de*, *qu'* → *que*, *n'* → *ne*, ...

Table 2: Rules for morphological simplification.

The development data consists of the concatenated news-data sets from the years 2008-2011. Unless otherwise stated, we use all constrained data (parallel and monolingual). For the target-side language models, we follow the approach of Schwenk and Koehn (2008) and train a separate language model for each corpus and then interpolate them using weights optimized on development data.

3 French to English

French has a much richer morphology than English; for example, adjectives in French are inflected with respect to gender and number whereas adjectives in English are not inflected at all. This causes data sparsity in coverage of French inflected forms. We try to overcome this problem by simplifying French inflected forms in a pre-processing step in order to adapt the French input better to the English output.

Processing of the training and test data The pre-processing of the French input consists of two steps: (1) normalizing not well-formed data (cf. table 1) and (2) morphological simplification.

In the second step, the normalized training data is annotated with Part-of-Speech tags (PoS-tags) and word lemmas using RFTagger (Schmid and Laws, 2008) which was trained on the French treebank (Abeillé et al., 2003). French forms are then simplified according to the rules given in table 2.

Data and experiments We trained a French to English Moses system on the preprocessed and simplified constrained parallel data.

Due to tractability problems with word alignment, the 10^9 French-English corpus and the UN corpus were filtered to a more manageable size. The filtering criteria are sentence length (between 15 and 25 words), as well as strings indicating that a sentence is neither French nor English, or otherwise not well-formed, aiming to obtain a subset of good-quality sentences. In total, we use 9M parallel sentences. For the English language model we use large training data with 287.3M true-cased sentences (including the LDC Giga-word data).

System	**BLEU** (cs)	**BLEU** (ci)
Baseline	29.90	31.02
Simplified French*	29.70	30.83

Table 3: Results of the French to English system (WMT-2012). The marked system (*) corresponds to the system submitted for manual evaluation. (cs: case-sensitive, ci: case-insensitive)

We compare two systems: a baseline with regular French text, and a system with the described morphological simplifications. Results for the WMT-2012 test set are shown in table 3. Even though the baseline is better than the simplified system in terms of BLEU, we assume that the translation model of the simplified system benefits from the overall generalization – thus, human annotators might prefer the output of the simplified system.

For the WMT-2013 set, we obtain BLEU scores of 29,97 (cs) and 31,05 (ci) with the system built on simplified French (*mes-simplifiedfrench*).

4 English to French

Translating into a morphologically rich language faces two problems: that of asymmetry of morphological information contained in the source and target language and that of data sparsity.

In this section we describe a two-step system designed to overcome these types of problems: first, the French data is reduced to non-inflected forms (stems) with translation-relevant morphological features, which is used to built the translation model. The second step consists of predicting all necessary morphological features for the translation output, which are then used to generate fully inflected forms. This two-step setup decreases the complexity of the translation task by removing language-specific features from the translation model. Furthermore, generating inflected forms based on word stems and morphological features allows to generate forms which do not occur in the parallel training data – this is not possible in a standard SMT setup.

The idea of separating the translation into two steps to deal with complex morphology was introduced by Toutanova et al. (2008). Fraser et al. (2012) applied this method to the language pair English-German with an additional special focus on word formation issues such as the splitting and merging of portmanteau prepositions and compounds. The presented inflection prediction systems focuses on nominal inflection; verbal inflection is not addressed.

Morphological analysis and resources The morphological analysis of the French training data is obtained using RFTagger, which is designed for annotating fine-grained morphological tags (Schmid and Laws, 2008). For generating inflected forms based on stems and morphological features, we use an extended version of the finite-state morphology FRMOR (Zhou, 2007). Additionally, we use a manually compiled list of abbreviations and named entities (names of countries) and their respective grammatical gender.

Stemming For building the SMT system, the French data (parallel and monolingual) is transformed into a stemmed representation. Nouns, i.e. the heads of NPs or PPs, are marked with inflection-relevant features: *gender* is considered as part of the stem, whereas *number* is determined by the source-side input: for example, we expect source-language words in plural to be translated by translated by stems with plural markup. This stem-markup is necessary in order to guarantee that the number information is not lost during translation. For a better generalization, portmanteaus are split into separate parts: *au* $\rightarrow$ *à+le* (meaning, "to the").

Predicting morphological features For predicting the morphological features of the SMT output (*number* and *gender*), we use a linear chain CRF (Lavergne et al., 2010) trained on data annotated with these features using n-grams of stems and part-of-speech tags within a window of 4 positions to each side of the current word. Through the CRF, the values specified in the stem-markup (*number* and *gender* on nouns) are propagated over the rest of the linguistic phrase, as shown in column 2 of table 4. Based on the stems and the morphological features, inflected forms can be generated using FRMOR (column 3).

Post-processing As the French data has been normalized, a post-processing step is needed in order to generate correct French surface forms: split portmanteaus are merged into their regular forms based on a simple rule set. Furthermore, apostrophes are reintroduced for words like *le, la, ne, ...* if they are followed by a vowel. Column 4 in table 4 shows post-processing including portmanteau formation. Since we work on lowercased data, an additional recasing step is required.

Experiments and evaluation We use the same set of reduced parallel data as the FR-EN system; the language model is built on 32M French sentences. Results for the WMT-2012 test set are given in table 5. Variant 1 shows the results for a small system trained only on a part of the training data (Europarl+News Commentary), whereas variant 2 corresponds to the submitted system. A small-scale analysis indicated that the inflection prediction system tends to have problems with subject-verb agreement. We trained a factored system using additional PoS-tags with number information which lead to a small improvement on both variants.

While the small model is significantly better than the baseline[2] as it benefits more from the generalization, the result for the full system is worse than the baseline[3]. Here, given the large amount of data, the generalization effect has less influence. However, we assume that the more general model from the inflection prediction system produces better translations than a regular model containing a large amount of irrelevant inflectional information, particularly when considering that it can produce well-formed inflected sequences that are inaccessible to the baseline. Even though this is not reflected in terms of BLEU, humans might prefer the inflection prediction system.

For the WMT-2013 set, we obtain BLEU scores of 29.6 (ci) and 28.30 (cs) with the inflection prediction system *mes-inflection* (marked in table 5).

5 Russian-English

The preparation of the Russian data includes the following stages: (1) tokenization and tagging and (2) morphological reduction.

Tagging and tagging errors For tagging, we use a version of RFTagger (Schmid and Laws, 2008)

[2]Pairwise bootstrap resampling with 1000 samples.

[3]However, the large inflection-prediction system has a slightly better NIST score than the baseline (7.63 vs. 7.61).

SMT-output with stem-markup in bold print	**predicted features**	**generated forms**	**after post-processing**	**gloss**
avertissement<**Masc**><**Pl**>[N]	Masc.Pl	avertissements	avertissements	*warnings*
sinistre[ADJ]	Masc.Pl	sinistres	sinistres	*dire*
de[P]	–	de	du	*from*
le[ART]	Masc.Sg	le		*the*
pentagone<**Masc**><**Sg**>[N]	Masc.Sg	pentagone	pentagone	*pentagon*
sur[P]	–	sur	sur	*over*
de[P]	–	de	d'	*of*
éventuel[ADJ]	Fem.Pl	éventuelles	éventuelles	*potential*
réduction<**Fem**><**Pl**>[N]	Fem.Pl	réductions	réductions	*reductions*
de[P]	–	de	du	*of*
le[ART]	Masc.Sg	le		*the*
budget<**Masc**><**Sg**>[N]	Masc.Sg	budget	budget	*budget*
de[P]	–	de	de	*of*
le[ART]	Fem.Sg	la	la	*the*
défense<**Fem**><**Sg**>[N]	Fem.Sg	défense	défense	*défense*

Table 4: Processing steps for the input sentence *dire warnings from pentagon over potential defence cuts.*

that has been developed based on data tagged with TreeTagger (Schmid, 1994) using a model from Sharoff et al. (2008). The data processed by TreeTagger contained errors such as wrong definition of PoS for adverbs, wrong selection of gender for adjectives in plural and missing features for pronouns and adverbs. In order to train RFTagger, the output of TreeTagger was corrected with a set of empirical rules. In particular, the morphological features of nominal phrases were made consistent to train RFTagger: in contrast to TreeTagger, where morphological features are regarded as part of the PoS-tag, RFTagger allows for a separate handling of morphological features and POS tags.

Despite a generally good tagging quality, some errors seem to be unavoidable due to the ambiguity of certain grammatical forms in Russian. A good example of this are neuter nouns that have the same form in all cases, or feminine nouns, which have identical forms in singular genitive and plural nominative (Sharoff et al., 2008). Since Russian has no binding word order, and the case of nouns cannot be determined on that basis, such errors cannot be corrected with empirical rules implemented as post-processing. Similar errors occur when specifying the case of adjectives, since the suffixes of adjectives are even less varied as compared to the nouns. In our application, we hope that this type of error does not affect the result due to the following suppression of a number of morphological attributes including the case of adjectives.

	System	BLEU (ci)	BLEU (cs)
1	Baseline	24.91	23.40
	InflPred	25.31	23.81
	InflPred-factored	25.53	24.04
2	Baseline	29.32	27.65
	InflPred*	29.07	27.40
	InflPred-factored	29.17	27.46

Table 5: Results for French inflection prediction on the WMT-2012 test set. The marked system (*) corresponds to the system submitted for manual evaluation.

Morphological reduction In comparison to Slavic languages, English is morphologically poor. For example, English has no morphological attributes for nouns and adjectives to express gender or case; verbs have no gender either. In contrast, Russian is morphologically very rich – there are e.g. 6 cases and 3 grammatical genders, which manifest themselves in different suffixes for nouns, pronouns, adjectives and some verb forms. When translating from Russian into English, many of these attributes are (hopefully) redundant and are therefore deleted from the training data. The morphological reduction in our system was applied to nouns, pronouns, verbs, adjectives, prepositions and conjunctions. The rest of the POS (adverbs, particles, interjections and abbreviations) have no morphological attributes. The list of the original and the reduced attributes is given in Table 6.

Transliteration mining to handle OOVs The machine translation system fails to translate out-of-vocabulary words (OOVs) as they are unknown to the training data. Most of the OOVs are named entities and transliterating them to the target language script could solve this problem. The transliteration system requires a list of transliteration pairs for training. As we do not have such a list, we use the unsupervised transliteration mining system of Sajjad et al. (2012) that takes a list of word pairs for

Part of Speech	Attributes RFTagger	Reduced attributes
Noun	Type Gender Number Case *nom,gen,dat,acc,instr,prep* Animate Case 2	Type Gender Number Case *gen,notgen*
Pronoun	Person Gender Number Case *nom,gen,dat,acc,instr,prep* Syntactic type Animated	Person Gender Number Case *nom,notnom*
Verb	Type VForm Tense Person Number Gender Voice Definiteness Aspect Case	Type VForm Tense Person Number Voice Aspect
Adjective	Type Degree Gender Number Case Definiteness	Type Degree
Preposition	Type Formation Case	
Conjunction	Type Formation	Type Formation

Table 6: Rules for simplifying the morphological complexity for RU.

training and extracts transliteration pairs that can be used for the training of the transliteration system. The procedure of mining transliteration pairs and transliterating OOVs is described as follows: We word-align the parallel corpus using GIZA++ and symmetrize the alignments using the *grow-diag-final-and* heuristic. We extract all word pairs which occur as 1-to-1 alignments (Sajjad et al., 2011) and later refer to them as a *list of word pairs*. We train the unsupervised transliteration mining system on the list of word pairs and extract transliteration pairs. We use these mined pairs to build a transliteration system using the Moses toolkit. The transliteration system is applied as a post-processing step to transliterate OOVs.

The morphological reduction of Russian (cf. section 5) does not process most of the OOVs as they are also unknown to the POS tagger. So OOVs that we get are in their original form. When transliterating them, the inflected forms generate wrong English transliterations as inflectional suffixes get transliterated too, specially OOV named entities. We solved this problem by stemming the OOVs based on a list of suffixes (а, ом, ы, е, ой, у) and transliterating the stemmed forms.

Original corpus

SYS	WMT-2012	WMT-2013
GIZA++	32.51	25.5
TA-GIZA++	33.40	25.9*

Morph-reduced

SYS	WMT-2012	WMT-2013
GIZA++	31.22	24.3
TA-GIZA++	31.40	24.45

Table 7: Russian to English machine translation system evaluated on WMT-2012 and WMT-2013. Human evaluation in WMT13 is performed on the system trained using the original corpus with TA-GIZA++ for alignment (marked with *).

Experiments and results We trained the systems separately on GIZA++ and transliteration augmented-GIZA++ (TA-GIZA++) to compare their results; for more details see Sajjad et al. (2013). All systems are tuned using PROv1 (Nakov et al., 2012). The translation output is post-processed to transliterate OOVs.

Table 7 summarizes the results of RU-EN translation systems trained on the original corpus and on the morph-reduced corpus. Using TA-GIZA++ alignment gives the best results for both WMT-2012 and WMT-2013, leading to an improvement of 0.4 BLEU points.

The system built on the morph-reduced data leads to decreased BLEU results. However, the percentage of OOVs is reduced for both test sets when using the morph-reduced data set compared to the original data. An analysis of the output showed that the morph-reduced system makes mistakes in choosing the right tense of the verb, which might be one reason for this outcome. In the future, we would like to investigate this issue in detail.

6 German to English and English to German

We submitted systems for DE-EN and EN-DE which used constituent parses for pre-reordering. For DE-EN we also deal with word formation issues such as compound splitting. We did not perform inflectional normalization or generation for German due to time constraints, instead focusing our efforts on these issues for French and Russian as previously described.

German to English German has a wider diversity of clausal orderings than English, all of which need to be mapped to the English SVO order. This is a difficult problem to solve during inference, as shown for hierarchical SMT by Fabienne Braune and Fraser (2012) and for phrase-based SMT by Bisazza and Federico (2012).

We syntactically parsed all of the source side sentences of the parallel German to English data available, and the tuning, test and blindtest sets. We then applied reordering rules to these parses. We use the rules for reordering German constituent parses of Collins et al. (2005) together with the additional rules described by Fraser (2009). These are applied as a preprocess to all German data.

For parsing the German sentences, we used the generative phrase-structure parser BitPar with optimizations of the grammar, as described by Fraser et al. (2013). The parser was trained on the Tiger Treebank (Brants et al., 2002) along with utilizing the Europarl corpus as unlabeled data. At the training of Bitpar, we followed the targeted self-training approach (Katz-Brown et al., 2011) as follows. We parsed the whole Europarl corpus using a grammar trained on the Tiger corpus and extracted the 100-best parse trees for each sentence. We selected the parse tree among the 100 candidates which got the highest *usefulness scores* for the reordering task. Then we trained a new grammar on the concatenation of the Tiger corpus and the automatic parses from Europarl.

The usefulness score estimates the value of a parse tree for the reordering task. We calculated this score as the similarity between the word order achieved by applying the parse tree-based reordering rules of Fraser (2009) and the word order indicated by the automatic word alignment between the German and English sentences in Europarl. We used the Kendall's Tau Distance as the similarity metric of two word orderings (as suggested by Birch and Osborne (2010)).

Following this, we performed linguistically-informed compound splitting, using the system of Fritzinger and Fraser (2010), which disambiguates competing analyses from the high-recall Stuttgart Morphological Analyzer SMOR (Schmid et al., 2004) using corpus statistics. We also split German portmanteaus like *zum* $\rightarrow$ *zu dem* (meaning *to the*).

system	BLEU (ci)	BLEU (cs)	system name
DE-EN (OSM)	27.60	26.12	*MES*
DE-EN (OSM) BitPar not self-trained	27.48	25.99	not submitted
DE-EN (Moses)	27.14	25.65	*MES-Szeged-reorder-split*
DE-EN (Moses) BitPar not self-trained	26.82	25.36	not submitted
EN-DE (Moses)	19.68	18.97	*MES-reorder*

Table 8: Results on WMT-2013 (blindtest)

English to German The task of mapping English SVO order to the different clausal orders in German is difficult. For our English to German systems, we solved this by parsing the English and applying the system of Gojun and Fraser (2012) to reorder English into the correct German clausal order (depending on the clause type which is detected using the English parse, see (Gojun and Fraser, 2012) for further details).

We primarily used the Charniak-Johnson generative parser (Charniak and Johnson, 2005) to parse the English Europarl data and the test data. However, due to time constraints we additionally used Berkeley parses of about 400K Europarl sentences and the other English parallel training data. We also left a small amount of the English parallel training data unparsed, which means that it was not reordered. For tune, test and blindtest (WMT-2013), we used the Charniak-Johnson generative parser.

Experiments and results We used all available training data for constrained systems; results for the WMT-2013 set are given in table 8. For the contrastive BitPar results, we reparsed WMT-2013.

7 Conclusion

We presented 5 systems dealing with complex morphology. For two language pairs with a morphologically rich source language (FR and RU), the input was reduced to a simplified representation containing only translation-relevant morphological information (e.g. number on nouns). We also used reordering techniques for DE-EN and EN-DE. For translating into a language with rich morphology (EN-FR), we applied a two-step method that first translates into a stemmed representation of the target language and then generates inflected forms based on morphological features predicted on monolingual data.

Acknowledgments

We would like to thank the anonymous reviewers for their helpful feedback and suggestions, Daniel Quernheim for providing Berkeley parses of some of the English data, Stefan Rüd for help with the manual evalution, and Philipp Koehn and Barry Haddow for providing data and alignments.

Nadir Durrani was funded by the European Union Seventh Framework Programme (FP7/2007-2013) under grant agreement n. 287658. Alexander Fraser was funded by Deutsche Forschungsgemeinschaft grant Models of Morphosyntax for Statistical Machine Translation and from the European Community's Seventh Framework Programme (FP7/2007-2013) under Grant Agreement n. 248005. Marion Weller was funded from the European Community's Seventh Framework Programme (FP7/2007-2013) under Grant Agreement n. 248005. Svetlana Smekalova was funded by Deutsche Forschungsgemeinschaft grant Models of Morphosyntax for Statistical Machine Translation. Helmut Schmid and Max Kisselew were supported by Deutsche Forschungsgemeinschaft grant SFB 732. Richárd Farkas was supported by the European Union and the European Social Fund through project FuturICT.hu (grant n. TÁMOP-4.2.2.C-11/1/KONV-2012-0013). This publication only reflects the authors' views.

References

A. Abeillé, L. Clément, and F. Toussenel. 2003. Building a treebank for french. In A. Abeillé, editor, *Treebanks*. Kluwer, Dordrecht.

Alexandra Birch and Miles Osborne. 2010. Lrscore for evaluating lexical and reordering quality in mt. In *Proceedings of ACL WMT and MetricsMATR*, Uppsala, Sweden.

Arianna Bisazza and Marcello Federico. 2012. Modified distortion matrices for phrase-based statistical machine translation. In *ACL*, pages 478–487.

Sabine Brants, Stefanie Dipper, Silvia Hansen, Wolfgang Lezius, and George Smith. 2002. The TIGER treebank. In *Proceedings of the Workshop on Treebanks and Linguistic Theories*.

Eugene Charniak and Mark Johnson. 2005. Coarse-to-fine n-best parsing and MaxEnt discriminative reranking. In *ACL*, pages 173–180, Ann Arbor, MI, June. Association for Computational Linguistics.

Colin Cherry and George Foster. 2012. Batch tuning strategies for statistical machine translation. In *Proceedings of the North American Chapter of the Association for Computational Linguistics (NAACL)*.

Michael Collins, Philipp Koehn, and Ivona Kučerová. 2005. Clause restructuring for statistical machine translation. In *Porceedings of ACL 2005*.

Nadir Durrani, Helmut Schmid, and Alexander Fraser. 2011. A Joint Sequence Translation Model with Integrated Reordering. In *Proceedings of ACL-HLT 2011*, Portland, Oregon, USA.

Nadir Durrani, Alexander Fraser, and Helmut Schmid. 2013a. Model With Minimal Translation Units, But Decode With Phrases. In *Proceedings of NAACL 2013*, Atlanta, Georgia, USA.

Nadir Durrani, Helmut Schmid, Alexander Fraser, Hassan Sajjad, and Richárd Farkas. 2013b. Munich-Edinburgh-Stuttgart Submissions of OSM Systems at WMT13. In *Proceedings of the Eighth Workshop on Statistical Machine Translation*, Sofia, Bulgaria.

Anita Gojun Fabienne Braune and Alexander Fraser. 2012. Long-distance reordering during search for hierarchical phrase-based SMT. In *Proceedings of EAMT 2012*.

Alexander Fraser, Marion Weller, Aoife Cahill, and Fabienne Cap. 2012. Modeling Inflection and Word-Formation in SMT. In *Proceedings of EACL 2012*, Avignon, France.

Alexander Fraser, Helmut Schmid, Richárd Farkas, Renjing Wang, and Hinrich Schütze. 2013. Knowledge sources for constituent parsing of German, a morphologically rich and less-configurational language. *Computational Linguistics - to appear*.

Alexander Fraser. 2009. Experiments in morphosyntactic processing for translating to and from German. In *EACL WMT*.

Fabienne Fritzinger and Alexander Fraser. 2010. How to avoid burning ducks: Combining linguistic analysis and corpus statistics for German compound processing. In *ACL WMT and Metrics MATR*.

Anita Gojun and Alexander Fraser. 2012. Determining the placement of German verbs in English-to-German SMT. In *Proceedings of EACL 2012*.

Jason Katz-Brown, Slav Petrov, Ryan McDonald, Franz Och, David Talbot, Hiroshi Ichikawa, Masakazu Seno, and Hideto Kazawa. 2011. Training a parser for machine translation reordering. In *Proceedings of EMNLP 2011*, Edinburgh, Scotland.

Thomas Lavergne, Olivier Cappé, and François Yvon. 2010. Practical very large scale CRFs. In *Proceedings of ACL 2010*, pages 504–513.

Preslav Nakov, Francisco Guzmán, and Stephan Vogel. 2012. Optimizing for sentence-level BLEU+1 yields short translations. Mumbai, India.

Hassan Sajjad, Alexander Fraser, and Helmut Schmid. 2011. An algorithm for unsupervised transliteration mining with an application to word alignment. In *Proceedings of ACL 2011*, Portland, USA.

Hassan Sajjad, Alexander Fraser, and Helmut Schmid. 2012. A statistical model for unsupervised and semi-supervised transliteration mining. In *Proceedings of ACL 2012*, Jeju, Korea.

Hassan Sajjad, Svetlana Smekalova, Nadir Durrani, Alexander Fraser, and Helmut Schmid. 2013. QCRI-MES Submission at WMT13: Using Transliteration Mining to Improve Statistical Machine Translation. In *Proceedings of the Eighth Workshop on Statistical Machine Translation*, Sofia, Bulgaria.

Helmut Schmid and Florian Laws. 2008. Estimation of conditional probabilities with decision trees and an application to fine-grained pos tagging. In *Proceedings of COLING 2008*, Stroudsburg, PA, USA.

Helmut Schmid, Arne Fitschen, and Ulrich Heid. 2004. SMOR: a German Computational Morphology Covering Derivation, Composition, and Inflection. In *Proceedings of LREC 2004*.

Helmut Schmid. 1994. Probabilistic part-of-speech tagging using decision trees. In *Proceedings of the International Conference on New Methods in Language Processing*.

Holger Schwenk and Philipp Koehn. 2008. Large and diverse language models for statistical machine translation. In *Proceedings of IJCNLP 2008*.

Serge Sharoff, Mikhail Kopotev, Tomaz Erjavec, Anna Feldman, and Dagmar Divjak. 2008. Designing and evaluating russian tagsets. In *Proceedings of LREC 2008*.

Kristina Toutanova, Hisami Suzuki, and Achim Ruopp. 2008. Applying Morphology Generation Models to Machine Translation. In *Proceedings of ACL-HLT 2008*.

Zhenxia Zhou. 2007. Entwicklung einer französischen Finite-State-Morphologie. Diploma Thesis, Institute for Natural Language Processing, University of Stuttgart.

Coping with the Subjectivity of Human Judgements in MT Quality Estimation

Marco Turchi **Matteo Negri** **Marcello Federico**
Fondazione Bruno Kessler, FBK-irst
Trento , Italy
{turchi|negri|federico}@fbk.eu

Abstract

Supervised approaches to NLP tasks rely on high-quality data annotations, which typically result from expensive manual labelling procedures. For some tasks, however, the subjectivity of human judgements might reduce the usefulness of the annotation for real-world applications. In Machine Translation (MT) Quality Estimation (QE), for instance, using human-annotated data to train a binary classifier that discriminates between *good* (useful for a post-editor) and *bad* translations is not trivial. Focusing on this binary task, we show that subjective human judgements can be effectively replaced with an automatic annotation procedure. To this aim, we compare binary classifiers trained on different data: the human-annotated dataset from the 7th Workshop on Statistical Machine Translation (WMT-12), and an automatically labelled version of the same corpus. Our results show that human labels are less suitable for the task.

1 Introduction

With the steady progress in the field of Statistical Machine Translation (SMT), the translation industry is now faced with the possibility of significant productivity increases (*i.e.* amount of publishable output per unit of time). One way to achieve this goal, in Computer Assisted Translation (CAT) environments, is the integration of (*precise, but often partial*) suggestions obtained through "fuzzy matches" from a Translation Memory (TM), with (*complete, but potentially less precise*) translations produced by an MT system. Such integration can loosely consist in presenting translators with unranked suggestions obtained from the MT and the TM, or rely on tighter combination strategies. For instance, MT and TM translations can be automatically ranked to ease the selection of the most suitable one for post-editing (He et al., 2010), or the TM can be used to constrain and improve MT suggestions (Ma et al., 2011). In all cases, the effectiveness of the integration is conditioned by: *i)* the quality of MT, and *ii)* the accuracy in automatically predicting such quality. Higher productivity increases depend on the capability of the MT system to output *useful* material that is close to be publishable "as is" (Denkowski and Lavie, 2012), and the capability to automatically identify and present to human translators only such suggestions.

Recognizing good translations falls in the scope of research on automatic MT Quality Estimation (QE), which addresses the problem of estimating the quality of a translated sentence at run-time, without access to reference translations (Specia et al., 2009; Soricut and Echihabi, 2010; Bach et al., 2011; Specia, 2011; Mehdad et al., 2012b). In recent years QE gained increasing interest in the MT community, resulting in several datasets available for training and evaluation (Callison-Burch et al., 2012), the definition of features showing good correlation with human judgements (Soricut et al., 2012), and the release of open-source software.[1]

The proposed solutions to the QE problem rely on supervised methods that strongly depend on the availability of labelled data. While early works (Blatz et al., 2003) exploited annotations obtained with automatic MT evaluation metrics like BLEU (Papineni et al., 2002), the current trend is to rely on human annotations, which seem to lead to more accurate models (Quirk, 2004; Specia et al., 2009). Along this direction, the QE task consists in predicting scores that reflect human quality judgements, by learning from manually annotated datasets (*e.g.* collections of *source-target* pairs la-

[1] http://www.quest.dcs.shef.ac.uk/

belled according to an n-point Likert scale or with real numbers in a given interval). Within this dominant supervised framework, **we explore different ways to obtain labelled data for training a binary QE classifier suitable for integration in a CAT tool**. Since, to the best of our knowledge, labelled data with binary judgements are currently not available, we consider two alternative options.

The first option is to adapt an existing dataset, checking whether it can be partitioned in a way that reflects the distinction between *good* (useful for the translator, suitable for post editing) and *bad* translations (that need complete rewriting).[2] To this aim we experiment with the QE data released within the 7th Workshop on Machine Translation (WMT-12). The corpus consists of *source-target* pairs annotated with manual QE labels (1-5 scores) indicating the post-editing needed to correct the translations. Besides explicit human judgements, the availability of post-edited translations makes also possible to calculate the actual HTER values (Snover et al., 2009), indicating the minimum edit distance between the machine translation and its manually post-edited version in the [0,1] interval.

The second option is to automatically re-annotate the same dataset, trying to produce labels that reflect an objective and more reliable binary distinction based on empirical observations.

Our analysis aims to answer the following questions:

1. Are human labels reliable and coherent enough to train accurate binary models?
2. Are arbitrarily-set thresholds useful to partition QE data for this task?
3. Is it possible to obtain reliable binary annotations from an automatic procedure?

Negative answers to the first two questions would respectively call into question: *i)* the intuitive idea that human labels are the most reliable for a supervised approach to binary QE, and *ii)* the possibility that thresholds on a single metric (*e.g.* the HTER) can be set to capture the subtle differences separating useful from useless translations. A positive answer to the third question would open to the possibility to create training datasets in a more coherent and replicable way compared to current data annotation methods. By answering these questions, this paper provides the following main contributions:

- We show that training a binary classifier on arbitrary partitions of an existing dataset is difficult. Our experiments with the WMT-12 corpus demonstrate that neither following standard indications (*e.g.* *"if more than 70% of the MT output needs to be edited, a translation from scratch is necessary"*)[3], nor considering arbitrary HTER thresholds, it is possible to obtain accurate binary classifiers suitable for integration in a CAT environment;
- We propose a replicable automatic (hence non subjective) method to re-annotate an existing dataset in a way that the resulting binary classifier outperforms those trained with human labels.
- We show that, with our method, a smaller amount of training data is sufficient to obtain similar or better performance compared to that of the human-annotated dataset used for comparison.

2 Binary QE for CAT environments

QE has been mainly addressed as a classification or regression task, where a quality score (respectively an integer or a real value) has to be automatically assigned to MT output sentences given their source (Specia et al., 2010). Casting the problem in this way, the integration of a QE component in a CAT environment makes possible to present translators with estimates of the expected quality of each MT suggestion. Such intuitive solution, however, disregards the fact that even precise QE scores would not alleviate translators from the effort of reading useless MT output (or at least the associated score).

A more effective alternative is to use the estimated QE scores to filter out poor MT suggestions, presenting only those worth for post-editing. Binary classification, however, has to confront with the problem of setting reasonable cut-off criteria. The arbitrary thresholds, used in several previous works (Quirk, 2004; Specia et al., 2010; Specia et al., 2011) are in fact hard to justify, and even harder to learn from human-labelled training data.

[2]In the remainder of the paper we will consider as "good" translations those for which post-editing requires a smaller effort than translation from scratch. Conversely, we will label as "bad" the translations that need complete rewriting.

[3]This was a guideline for the professional translators involved in the annotation of a previous version of the dataset used for the WMT-12 evaluation (see `http://www.statmt.org/wmt12/quality-estimation-task.html`).

On one side, for instance, there is no evidence that the 70% HTER threshold used in some datasets yields the optimal separation between acceptable and totally useless suggestions. Such arbitrary criterion, based on the raw count of post-editing operations, is likely to reflect a partial view on a complex problem, disregarding important aspects such as the distribution of the corrections in the MT output. However, in some cases, having the first 30% of words correctly translated might take less post-editing effort than having 50% of correctly translated terms scattered throughout the whole sentence. In these cases, a 70% HTER threshold would wrongly consider useless translations as positive instances and vice-versa.

On the other side, when arbitrary thresholds are used as annotation guidelines (Callison-Burch et al., 2012), the moderate agreement between human judges might make manual labels ill-suited to learn accurate models.

Under the constraints posed by a CAT environment, where only useful suggestions can lead to a significant productivity increase, the ideal model should maximize the number of true positives (useful translations recognized as good) minimizing, at the same time, the number of false positives (useless translations recognized as good). To this aim, the more the training data are partitioned according to objective criteria, the higher the expected reliability of the corresponding cut-off and, in turn, the higher the expected performance of the binary classifier.

Focusing on these issues, the following sections discuss various methods to obtain training data for binary QE geared to the integration in a CAT environment. Partitions based on human judgements from the WMT-12 dataset will be compared with an automatic method to re-annotate the same corpus. The suitability of the resulting training sets for binary classification will be assessed by measuring the performance of classifiers built from each training set. Metrics sensitive to the number of false positives will be used for this purpose.

3 Partitioning the WMT-12 dataset

Due to the lack of datasets annotated with explicit binary (good, bad) judgements about translation quality, the most intuitive way to obtain training data for our QE classifier is to adapt existing manually-labelled data. The reasonable size of the WMT-12 dataset makes it a good candidate for our purposes. The corpus consists of 2,254 English-Spanish news sentences (1,832 for training, 422 for test) produced by the Moses phrase-based SMT system (Koehn et al., 2007) trained on Europarl (Koehn, 2005) and News Commentaries corpora,[4] along with their source sentences, reference translations and post-edited translations. Training and test instances have been annotated by professional translators with scores (1 to 5) indicating the estimated post-editing effort (percentage of MT output that has to be corrected). According to the proposed scheme, the highest score indicates lowest effort (MT output requires little or no editing), while the lowest score indicates that the MT output needs to be translated from scratch. To cope with systematic biases among the annotators,[5] the judgements were combined in a final score obtained from their weighted average, resulting in a labelled dataset with real numbers in the [1, 5] interval as effort scores.

In order to obtain suitable data for binary QE, the WMT-12 training set (1,832 instances) has been partitioned in different ways, leaving the test set for evaluation (see Section 5). The goal, for each partition strategy, was to label as *bad* (the assigned label is -1) only the translations that *need complete rewriting*, keeping all the other translations as *good* instances (labelled with +1). Considering the averaged effort scores, the actual human judgements, and the HTER values calculated between the translations and the corresponding post-edited version, we experimented with the following three partition criteria.

Average effort scores (AES). Three partitions have been generated based on the effort scores of *2*, *2.5*, and *3*, labelling the WMT-12 training instances with scores below or equal to each threshold as negative examples (-1), and the instances with scores above the threshold as positive examples (+1). Partitions with thresholds below *2* were also considered, including the most intuitive partition with cut-off set to *1*. However, the resulting number of negative instances, if any, was too scarce, and the overall dataset too unbalanced, to make standard supervised learning methods effective The creation of highly unbalanced data is a recurring issue for all the partition meth-

[4] `http://www.statmt.org/wmt11/translation-task.html#download`

[5] Such biases support the idea that labelling translations with quality scores is *per se* a highly subjective task.

ods we applied to the WMT-12 corpus. Together with the low homogeneity of human labels (even for very poor translations the three judges do not agree in assigning the lowest score), in most of the cases the small number of low-quality translations in the dataset makes the negative class considerably smaller than the positive one. This can be observed in Table 1, which provides the total number of positive and negative instances for each partition method. For instance, with our lowest AES threshold (2) the total number of negative instances is 113, while the positive ones are 1,719. Although considering different cut-off criteria aims to make our investigation more complete, it's also worth remarking that the higher the threshold, the higher the distance of the resulting experimental setting from our target scenario. While *2*, as an effort score threshold, is likely to reflect a reasonable separation between useless and post-editable translations, higher values are in principle more appropriate for "soft" separations into worse *versus* better translations.

Human scores (HS). Five partitions have been generated using the actual labels assigned by the three annotators to each translation instead of the average effort scores. In particular, we considered the following score combinations ("X" stands for any integer between 1 and 5): *1-X-X*, *2-2-2*, *2-2-X*, *2-3-3*, *3-3-3*. Also in this case, as shown in Table 1, partitions based on lower scores lead to highly unbalanced datasets of limited usability, while those based on higher scores are increasingly more distant to our application scenario.[6]

HTER scores (HTER). Seven partitions have been generated considering the following HTER thresholds: *0.75*, *0.7*, *0.65*, *0.6*, *0.55*, *0.5*, *0.45*. In this case, being the HTER an error measure, training instances with scores above or equal to the threshold were labelled as negative examples (-1), while instances with lower scores were labelled as positive examples (+1). Similar to the other partition criteria, some of our threshold values reflect our task more closely than others, but result in more unbalanced datasets. In particular, thresholds around *0.7* substantially adhere to the WMT-12 annotation guidelines (as far as translations that need complete rewriting are concerned) and produce training data with fewer negative instances. Other thresholds, which is still worth exploring since we do not know the optimal cut-off value, are in principle less suitable to our task but produce more balanced training data.

	Training instances	
Average effort scores (AES)	*Positive*	*Negative*
2	1,719	113
2.5	1,475	357
3	1,194	638
Human scores (HS)	*Positive*	*Negative*
1-X-X	1,736	96
2-2-2	1,719	113
2-2-X	1,612	220
2-3-3	1,457	375
3-3-3	1,360	472
HTER scores (HTER)	*Positive*	*Negative*
0.75	1,798	34
0.7	1,786	46
0.65	1,756	76
0.6	1,708	124
0.55	1,653	179
0.5	1,531	301
0.45	1,420	412

Table 1: Number of positive/negative instances for each partition of the WMT-12 training set.

4 Re-annotating the WMT-12 dataset

As an alternative to partitioning methods, we investigated the possibility to re-annotate the WMT-12 training set with an automatic procedure.

4.1 Approach

Our approach, which does not involve subjective human judgements, is based on the observation of similarities and dissimilarities between an automatic translation (TGT), its post-edited version (PE) and the corresponding reference translation (RT). Such comparisons provide useful indications about the behaviour of a post-editor when correcting automatic translations and, in turn, about MT output quality.

Typically, the PE version of a good-quality TGT preserves some characteristics (*e.g.* lexical, structural) that indicate a moderate correction activity by the post editor. Conversely, in the PE version of a low-quality TGT, such characteristics are more difficult to observe, indicating an intense correction activity. At the two extremes, the PE of a perfect TGT preserves all its characteristics, while the PE of a useless TGT looses most of them. In the first case TGT and PE are iden-

[6] The partition most closely related to our task (*i.e.* 1-1-1) was impossible to produce since none of the examples was labelled with *1* by all the annotators. Even for *1-1-X*, the negative class contains only one example.

tical, and their similarity is the highest possible (*i.e.* $sim(TGT, PE) = 1$). In the second case, TGT and PE show a degree of similarity close to that of TGT and a completely rewritten translation featuring different lexical choices and structure. This is where reference translations come into play: considering RT as a good example of rewritten sentence,[7] for low-quality TGT we will have $sim(TGT, PE) \approx sim(TGT, RT)$.

In light of these considerations, we hypothesize that the automatic re-annotation of WMT-12 training data can take advantage of a classifier that learns a similarity threshold *T* such that:

- a PE sentence with $sim(TGT, PE) \leq T$ will be considered as a rewritten translation (hence TGT is useless, and the corresponding *source-TGT* pair a negative example to be labelled as "-1");
- a PE sentence with $sim(TGT, PE) > T$ will be considered as a real post-edition (hence TGT is useful for the post-editor, and the corresponding *source-TGT* pair a positive example to be labelled as "+1").

Based on this hypothesis, to perform our automatic re-annotation procedure we: 1) create a training set *Z* of positive and negative examples (*i.e.* [TGT, *correct_translation*] pairs, where *correct_translation* is either a post-editing or a rewritten translation); 2) design a feature set capable to capture different aspects of the similarity between TGT and *correct_translation*; 3) build a binary classifier using *Z*; 4) use the classifier to label the [TGT, PE] pairs as instances of post-editings or rewritings; 5) assess the quality of the resulting annotation.

4.2 Building the classifier

Training corpus. To build a classifier capable of labelling PE sentences as rewritten/post-edited material, we first created a set of positive and negative instances from the WMT-12 training set. For each tuple [source, TGT, PE, RT] of the dataset, one positive and one negative instance have been respectively obtained as the combination of [TGT, PE] and [TGT, RT]. Figure 1, which plots the distribution of positive and negative instances against HTER, shows a fairly good separation between the two classes. This indicates that our use of the references as examples of rewritten translations builds on a reasonable assumption.

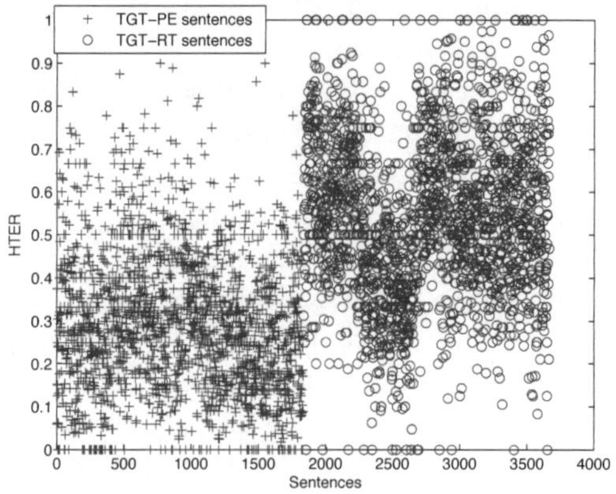

Figure 1: Distribution of [TGT, PE] and [TGT, RT] pairs plotted against the HTER.

Features. Crucial to our classification task, a number of features can be used to estimate sentence similarity. Differently from the binary QE task, where the possibility to catch common characteristics between two sentences is limited by language barriers, in our re-annotation task all the features are extracted by comparing two monolingual sentences (*i.e.* TGT and a *correct_translation*, either a PE or a RT). Although the problem of measuring sentence similarity can be addressed in many ways, the solutions should not overlook the specificities of the task. In our case, for instance, the scarce importance of the semantic aspect (TGT, PE and RT typically show a high semantic similarity) makes features used for other tasks (*e.g.* based on distributional similarity) less effective than shallow features looking at the surface form of the input sentences. Our problem presents some similarities with the plagiarism detection task, where subtle lexical and structural similarities have to be identified to spot suspicious plagiarized texts (Potthast et al., 2010). For this reason, part of our features (*e.g.* ROUGE scores) are inspired by research in such field (Chen et al., 2010), while others have been designed *ad-hoc*, based on the specific requirements of our task. The resulting feature set aims to capture text similarity by measuring word/n-gram matches, as well as the level of sparsity and density of the common words as a shallow indicator of structural similarity. In total, from each [TGT, *correct_translation*]

[7] Such assumption is supported by the fact that reference sentences are, by definition, free translations manually produced without any influence from the target.

pair, the following 22 features are extracted:

- Human-targeted Translation Error Rate – HTER. The editing operations considered are: shift, insertion, substitution and deletion.
- Number of words in common.
- Number of words in common, normalized by TGT length and *correct_translation* length (2 features).
- Number of words in TGT and in the *correct_translation* (2 features).
- Size of the longest common subsequence.
- Size of the longest common subsequence, normalized by TGT length.
- Aligned word density: total number of aligned words,[8] divided by the number of aligned blocks (more than 1 aligned word).
- Unaligned word density: total number of unaligned words, divided by the number of unaligned blocks (more than 1 unaligned word).
- Normalized number of aligned blocks: total number of aligned blocks, divided by TGT length.
- Normalized number of unaligned blocks: total number of unaligned blocks, divided by TGT length.
- Normalized density difference: difference between aligned word density and unaligned word density, divided by TGT length.
- Modified Lesk score (Lesk, 1986): sum of the squares of the length of n-gram matches, normalized by the product of the sentence lengths.
- ROUGE-1/2/3/4: n-gram recall with n=1,...,4 (4 features).[9]
- ROUGE-L: size of longest common subsequence, normalized by the *correct_translation* length.
- ROUGE-W: the ROUGE-L using different weights for consecutive matches of length L (default weight = *1.2*).
- ROUGE-S: the ROUGE-L allowing for the presence of skip-bigrams (pairs of words, even not adjacent, in their sentence order).
- ROUGE-SU: the extension of ROUGE-S adding unigrams as counting unit.

[8]Monolingual stem-to-stem exact matches between TGT and *correct_translation* are inferred by computing the HTER, as in (Blain et al., 2012).

[9]All ROUGE scores, described in (Lin, 2004), have been calculated using the software available at http://www.berouge.com.

To increase the capability of identifying similar sentences, all sentences are tokenized, lowercased and stemmed using the Snowball algorithm (Porter, 2001).

Classifier. On the resulting corpus, an SVM classifier has been trained using the LIBSVM toolbox (Chang and Lin, 2011). The selection of the kernel (linear) and the optimization of the parameters (C=0.8) were carried out through grid search in 5-fold cross-validation.

Labelling the dataset. Using the best parameter setting obtained, [TGT, PE] and [TGT, RT] pairs have been re-labelled as post-editings or rewritings through 5 rounds of cross-validation. The final label of each instance was set to the mode of the predictions produced by each cross-validation round. Since we assume that the quality of the target sentence can be inferred from the amount of correction activity done by the post-editor, the labels assigned to the [TGT, PE] pairs represent the result of our re-annotation of the corpus into positive and negative instances.

At the end of the process, of the 1,832 [TGT, PE] pairs of the WMT 2012 training set, 1.394 are labelled as examples of post-editing (TGT is useful), and 438 as examples of complete rewriting (TGT is useless). Compared to the distribution of positive and negative instances obtained with most of the partition methods described in Section 3, our automatic annotation produces a fairly balanced dataset. The resulting proportion of negative examples ($\sim$1:3) is similar to what could be reached only by partitions reflecting a "soft" separation into worse *versus* better translations rather than a strict separation into useless *versus* useful translations.[10] In Figure 2, the labelling results plotted against the HTER show that there is a quite clear separation between [TGT, PE] pairs marked as post-editings (lower HTER values) and pairs marked as rewritings (higher HTER values). Such separation corresponds to an HTER value around *0.4*, which is significantly lower than the threshold of *0.7* proposed by the WMT-12 guidelines as a criterion to label sentences for which "*a translation from scratch is necessary*". This confirms that our separation differs from those produced by partition methods based on human annotations or arbitrary HTER thresholds. Furthermore, our au-

[10]Such partitions are: average effort scores = 3, human scores = 3-3-3, HTER score = 0.45.

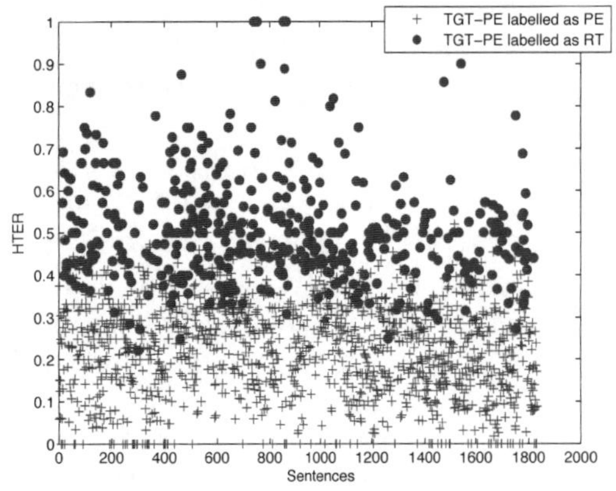

Figure 2: TGT-PE classification in post-editings and rewritings.

tomatic annotation procedure relies on the contribution of features designed to capture different aspects of the similarity between the TGT and a *correct_translation*, while some of the partition methods discussed in Section 3 rely on thresholds set on a single score (*e.g.* HTER). Considering the many facets of the binary QE problem, we expect that our features are more effective to deal with latent aspects disregarded by such thresholds.

5 Experiments and results

At this point, the question is: *are the automatically labelled data more suitable than partitions based on human labels to train a binary QE classifier?* To answer this question, all the proposed separations of the WMT-12 training set have been evaluated on different test sets. For each separation we trained a binary classifier able to assign a label (good or bad) to unseen *source-target* pairs. Since the classifiers use the same algorithm and feature set, differences in performance will mainly depend on the quality of the training data on which they are built. Using task-oriented metrics sensitive to the number of false positives, results highlighting such differences will indicate the best separation.

5.1 Experimental Setting

Binary QE classifier. Each separation of the WMT-12 training data was used to train a binary SVM classifier. Different kernels and parameters were optimized through a grid search in 5-fold cross-validation on each training set. Being the number of positive and negative training instances highly unbalanced, the best models were selected optimizing a metric that takes into account the number of true and false positives (see below).

Seventeen features proposed in (Specia et al., 2009) were extracted from each *source-target* pair. This feature set, fully described in (Callison-Burch et al., 2012), mainly takes into account the complexity of the source sentence (*e.g.* number of tokens, number of translations per source word) and the fluency of the target translation (*e.g.* language model probabilities). Results of the WMT 2012 QE task shown that these "baseline" features are particularly competitive in the regression task, with only few systems able to beat them. All the features are extracted using the Quest software[11] and the model files released by the organizers of the WMT 2013 workshop.

Test sets. To obtain different separations between good and bad translations, artificial test sets have been created using arbitrary thresholds on the HTER (the same used to partition the training set on a HTER basis) and the post-editing time (PET).[12] Two different datasets were split: *i)* the WMT-12 test (422 source, target, post-edited and reference sentences); *ii)* the WMT-13 training set for Task 1.3 (800 source, target and post-edited sentences labelled with PET). The first dataset, the most similar to the WMT-12 training set, should better reflect (and reward) the HTER-based partitions proposed in Section 3. The WMT-13 dataset contains sentences translated with a different configuration (data and parameters) of the SMT engine. This can result in different HTER-based partitions in good and bad, useful to test the portability of our automatic re-annotation method across different datasets. Finally, testing on data partitions based on PET allows us to check the stability of the automatic re-annotation method when evaluated on a test set divided according to a different concept of translation quality. In the end, the combination of different partition methods, thresholds and datasets results in 21 different test sets (see Table 2).

Evaluation metrics. F-score and accuracy are the classic evaluation metrics used in classification. In our evaluation, however, they would always result in high uninformative values due to the unbalanced nature of the test sets (positive instances $\gg$ negative instances). In order to bet-

[11] `http://www.quest.dcs.shef.ac.uk/`

[12] PET is the time spent by a post-editor to transform the target into a publishable sentence.

	Test instances	
WMT-12 HTER	*Positive*	*Negative*
0.45	289	133
0.5	319	103
0.55	352	70
0.6	371	51
0.65	386	36
0.70	398	24
0.75	406	16
WMT-13 Task 1.3 HTER	*Positive*	*Negative*
0.45	582	218
0.5	622	178
0.55	695	105
0.6	724	76
0.65	748	52
0.70	763	37
0.75	773	27
WMT-13 Task 1.3 PET	*Positive*	*Negative*
4	499	301
4.16*	517	283
4.50	554	246
5	594	206
6	659	141
7	698	102
8	727	73

Table 2: Number of positive and negative instances for each partition of the WMT-12 test set and WMT-13 training set. "*": Average PET computed on all the instances in the WMT-13 dataset.

ter understand the real quality of the classification, we hence opted for two task-oriented evaluation metrics sensitive to the number of false positives (the main issue in a CAT environment, where false positives and true positives should be respectively minimized and maximized). These are: *i)* the weighted combination of the false positive rate (FPR) and false discovery rate (FDR) (Benjamini and Hochberg, 1995), and *ii)* the weighed average of sensitivity and specificity (also called balanced/weighted accuracy). FPR measures the level of false positives, but does not provide information about the number of true positives. For this reason, we combined it with FDR (1-precision), which indirectly controls the level of true positives. FPR and FDR were equally weighted in the average; *lower values indicate good performance*. Furthermore, in our scenario it is desirable to have a classifier with high prediction accuracy over the minority class (specificity), while maintaining reasonable accuracy for the majority class (sensitivity). Weighted accuracy is useful in such situations. To better asses the performance on the minority (negative) class, we hence gave more importance to specificity (*0.7 vs 0.3*). As regards weighted accuracy *higher values in indicate better performance*. Penalizing majority voting classifiers, both metrics are particularly appropriate in our framework. Besides evaluation, the weighted average of FPR and FDR was also used to tune the parameters of the SVM classifier.

5.2 Results

Table 3 presents the results achieved by classifiers trained on different datasets, on the 21 splits produced from the test sets used for evaluation.

Although the total number of classifiers tested is 16 (15 resulting from partitions based on human labels, and 1 obtained with our automatic annotation method), most of them are not present in the table since they predict the majority class for all the test points. These are, in general, trained on highly unbalanced training sets where the number of negative samples is really small. However, it is interesting to note that increasing the number of instances in the negative class does not always result in a better classifier. For instance, the classifier built on an HTER separation with threshold at *0.55* performs majority voting even if it is built on a more balanced (but probably more noisy) training set than the classifier obtained with threshold at *0.6*. This suggests that the *quality* of the separation is as important as the actual proportion of positive and negative instances.

On all test sets, and for both the evaluation metrics used, the results achieved by the classifier built from the automatically annotated training set (*AA*) produces lower error rates (Weighted FPR-FDR) and higher accuracy (Weighted Accuracy), outperforming all the other classifiers. The effectiveness of the automatic annotation is confirmed by the fact that classifiers *3* (based on the average of effort scores - AES) and *3-3-3* (based on the actual human scores - HS), which are trained on more balanced training sets, achieve worse performances than the *AA* classifier.[13]

Results on the WMT-13 PET test set are not as good as in the other two test sets. This shows that test data labelled in terms of time are more difficult to be correctly classified compared to those based on the HTER. This can be explained considering the intrinsic differences between the HTER and the PET as approximations of the post-editing

[13]The distribution of positive/negative instances in the training sets is: 1194/638 for classifier *3*, 1360/472 for classifier *3-3-3*, 1394/438 for classifier *AA*.

Weighted FPR-FDR		Training: WMT-12 Separations						
		3	*2-2-X*	*2-3-3*	*3-3-3*	*0.5*	*0.6*	*AA*
		AES	*HS*	*HS*	*HS*	*HTER*	*HTER*	
Test: WMT-12 HTER	*0.45*	0.61	0.66	0.66	0.66	0.66	0.66	**0.55**
	0.5	0.57	0.62	0.62	0.62	0.62	0.62	**0.49**
	0.55	0.52	0.58	0.58	0.58	0.58	0.58	**0.42**
	0.6	0.5	0.56	0.56	0.56	0.56	0.56	**0.4**
	0.65	0.5	0.54	0.54	0.54	0.54	0.54	**0.39**
	0.7	0.49	0.53	0.53	0.53	0.53	0.53	**0.39**
	0.75	0.49	0.52	0.52	0.52	0.52	0.52	**0.35**
Test: WMT-13 HTER	*0.45*	0.59	0.63	0.63	0.64	0.64	0.63	**0.54**
	0.5	0.57	0.6	0.6	0.61	0.61	0.6	**0.5**
	0.55	0.51	0.56	0.56	0.57	0.57	0.56	**0.41**
	0.6	0.49	0.54	0.54	0.55	0.55	0.54	**0.37**
	0.65	0.47	0.53	0.53	0.53	0.53	0.53	**0.33**
	0.7	0.44	0.52	0.52	0.52	0.52	0.52	**0.29**
	0.75	0.44	0.52	0.52	0.52	0.52	0.52	**0.28**
Test: WMT-13 PET	*4*	0.61	0.68	0.68	0.69	0.69	0.68	**0.58**
	4.16	0.61	0.67	0.67	0.67	0.67	0.67	**0.56**
	4.5	0.58	0.65	0.64	0.65	0.65	0.65	**0.54**
	5	0.55	0.63	0.62	0.63	0.63	0.62	**0.51**
	6	0.49	0.58	0.58	0.58	0.58	0.58	**0.45**
	7	0.45	0.55	0.55	0.56	0.56	0.55	**0.43**
	8	0.45	0.54	0.54	0.54	0.54	0.54	**0.41**

Weighted Accuracy		Training: WMT-12 Separations						
		3	*2-2-X*	*2-3-3*	*3-3-3*	*0.5*	*0.6*	*AA*
		AES	*HS*	*HS*	*HS*	*HTER*	*HTER*	
Test: WMT-12 HTER	*0.45*	0.35	0.3	0.3	0.3	0.3	0.3	**0.41**
	0.5	0.35	0.3	0.3	0.3	0.3	0.3	**0.44**
	0.55	0.37	0.3	0.3	0.3	0.3	0.3	**0.48**
	0.6	0.37	0.3	0.3	0.3	0.3	0.3	**0.49**
	0.65	0.35	0.3	0.3	0.3	0.3	0.3	**0.47**
	0.7	0.35	0.3	0.3	0.3	0.3	0.3	**0.45**
	0.75	0.33	0.3	0.3	0.3	0.3	0.3	**0.49**
Test: WMT-13 HTER	*0.45*	0.33	0.31	0.31	0.3	0.3	0.31	**0.4**
	0.5	0.34	0.31	0.31	0.3	0.3	0.31	**0.42**
	0.55	0.35	0.31	0.31	0.3	0.3	0.31	**0.48**
	0.6	0.35	0.31	0.31	0.3	0.3	0.31	**0.51**
	0.65	0.36	0.3	0.3	0.3	0.3	0.3	**0.54**
	0.7	0.39	0.3	0.3	0.3	0.3	0.3	**0.56**
	0.75	0.38	0.3	0.3	0.3	0.3	0.3	**0.59**
Test: WMT-13 PET	*4*	0.37	0.3	0.31	0.3	0.3	0.3	**0.4**
	4.16	0.37	0.3	0.31	0.3	0.3	0.3	**0.4**
	4.5	0.37	0.3	0.31	0.3	0.3	0.3	**0.4**
	5	0.38	0.31	0.31	0.3	0.3	0.31	**0.41**
	6	0.41	0.31	0.31	0.3	0.3	0.31	**0.43**
	7	0.42	0.31	0.31	0.3	0.3	0.31	**0.44**
	8	0.4	0.31	0.31	0.3	0.3	0.31	**0.43**

Table 3: Weighted FPR-FDR (left table) and weighted Accuracy (right table) obtained by the binary QE classifiers trained on different separations of the WMT-12 training set. Several arbitrary partitions of the WMT-12 Test set and WMT-13 Training set are considered.

effort, as pointed out by several recent works (Specia, 2011; Koponen, 2012).

Comparing the results calculated with the two metrics, we note that weighted accuracy seems to be less sensible to small variations in terms of true and false negatives returned by the classifier, even if the specificity (accuracy on our minority class) is weighted more than sensitivity (accuracy on our majority class). This often results in scores very close (differences $\leq 10^{-3}$) to the accuracy obtained by majority voting classification (*0.3*).

Overall, our experiments demonstrate that the proposed automatic separation method is more effective than arbitrary partitions of datasets annotated with subjective human judgements.

5.3 Learning Curve

Our automatic re-annotation approach requires post-edited and reference sentences. Although all the datasets annotated for QE include post-edited sentences, this is not always true for the references. The cost of having both resources is in fact not negligible. For this reason, we investigated the minimal number of training data needed to re-annotate the WMT-12 training set without altering performance on binary classification. To this aim, we selected two of the test sets on which our re-annotation method produces classifiers with high performance results (*WMT-13 HTER 0.6* and *0.75*), and measured score variations with increasing amounts of data.

Nine subsets of the WMT-12 training set corpus were created (with 10%, 20%,..., 100% of the dataset) by sub-sampling sentences from a uniform distribution. The process was iterated 10 times. Then, for each subset, a new re-annotation process was run, the resulting training set was used to build the relative binary QE classifier, which was eventually evaluated on the test set in terms of weighted FPR-FDR. Figures 3 and 4 show the obtained learning curves. Each point is the average result of the 10 runs; the error bars show $\pm$1std.

As can be seen from both curves, performance results with 60% of the training data are already comparable with those obtained using the whole training data. Similar trends have been observed for several learning curves created with different test sets. This shows that, besides avoiding the use of human labelled data, our approach allows to drastically reduce the amount of training instances. Considering the high costs of collecting post-editions, and the fact that reference translations can be taken from parallel corpora, our solution represents a viable way to overcome the lack of training data for binary QE geared towards integration in a CAT environment.

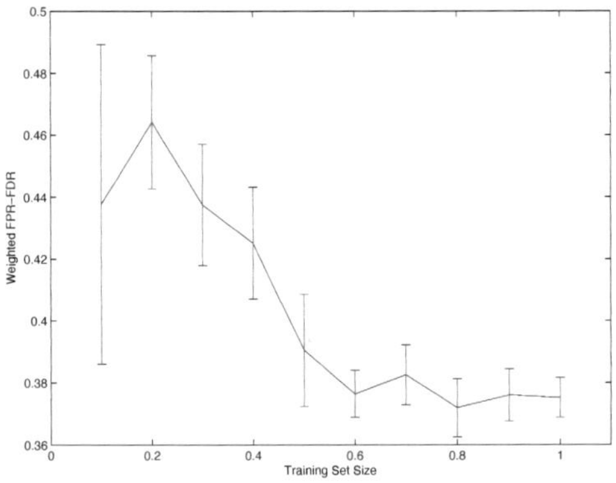

Figure 3: Learning curve for WMT-13 HTER *0.60*.

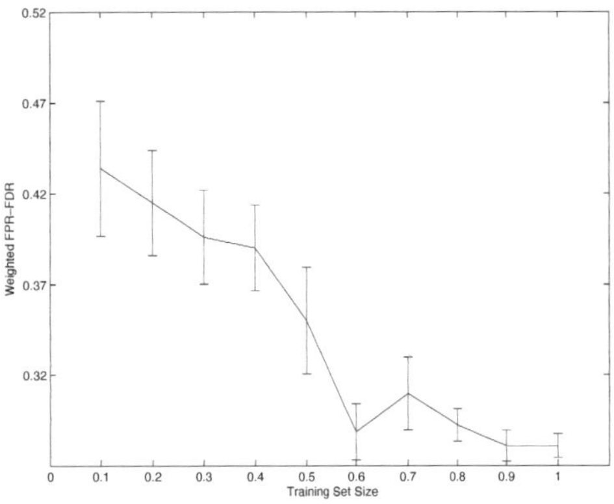

Figure 4: Learning curve for WMT-13 HTER *0.75*.

6 Conclusion

We presented a task-oriented analysis of the usefulness of human-labelled data for binary quality estimation. Our target scenario is computer-assisted translation, which calls for solutions to present human translators with *useful* MT suggestions (*i.e.* easier to correct than to rewrite from scratch). Within this framework, the integration of binary classifiers capable to distinguish "good" (useful) from "bad" (useless) suggestions would make possible to significantly increase translators' productivity. Such binary classifiers, however, need labelled training data (possibly of good quality) that are currently not available.

An intuitive solution to fill this gap is to take advantage of an existing dataset, adapting its manual annotations to our task. Exploring this solution (the first contribution of this paper) has to face problems related to the subjectivity of human judgements about translation quality, and the resulting variability in the annotation. In particular, our experiments with the WMT-12 dataset show that any adaptation (either based on human judgements or arbitrarily-set HTER thresholds) collides with the problem of setting reasonable partition criteria. Our results suggest that the subtle differences between useful and useless translations make subjective human judgements inadequate to learn effective models.

Instead of relying on manually-assigned quality labels, an alternative solution to the problem is to re-annotate an existing dataset. Proposing an automatic way to do that (the second contribution of this paper), we argue that reliable data separations into positive and negative examples can be obtained by measuring the similarities between: *i)* automatic translations and post-editings, and *ii)* automatic translations and their references. Our results demonstrate that binary classifiers built from training data produced with our supervised method are less prone to the misclassification of bad suggestions.

As in any supervised learning framework, the amount of data needed to obtain good results is of crucial importance. By analysing the demand of our automatic annotation method in terms of training data (the third contribution of this paper), we show that competitive results can be obtained with a fraction of the data needed by methods based on human labels. Our results indicate that a good-quality training set for binary classification can be obtained with 40% less instances of *[training, post_edited sentence, reference_sentence]*, totally avoiding manually-assigned quality judgements.

Our future works will address the improvement of the automatic annotation procedure using supervised methods suitable to learn from unbalanced training sets (*e.g.* one-class SVM, weighted random forests), and the integration of new features (*e.g.* GTM, meteor) to refine our classification of a *correct_sentence* into rewritten/post-edited. Then, to boost binary QE results on the resulting corpora, the "baseline" features used for experiments in this paper will be extended with new features explored in recent works (Mehdad et al., 2012a; de Souza et al., 2013; Turchi and Negri, 2013).

Acknowledgments

This work has been partially supported by the EC-funded project MateCat (ICT-2011.4.2-287688).

References

Nguyen Bach, Fei Huang, and Yaser Al-Onaizan. 2011. Goodness: a Method for Measuring Machine Translation Confidence. In *The 49th Annual Meeting of the Association for Computational Linguistics: Human Language Technologies, Proceedings of the Conference, 19-24 June, 2011, Portland, Oregon, USA*, pages 211–219. The Association for Computer Linguistics.

Yoav Benjamini and Yosef Hochberg. 1995. Controlling the False Discovery Rate: a Practical and Powerful Approach to Multiple Testing. *Journal of the Royal Statistical Society. Series B (Methodological)*, pages 289–300.

Frédéric Blain, Holger Schwenk, and Jean Senellart. 2012. Incremental Adaptation Using Translation Information and Post-Editing Analysis. In *International Workshop on Spoken Language Translation*, pages 234–241, Hong-Kong (China).

John Blatz, Erin Fitzgerald, George Foster, Simona Gandrabur, Cyril Goutte, Alex Kulesza, Alberto Sanchis, and Nicola Ueffing. 2003. Confidence Estimation for Machine Translation. Summer workshop final report, JHU/CLSP.

Chris Callison-Burch, Philipp Koehn, Christof Monz, Matt Post, Radu Soricut, and Lucia Specia. 2012. Findings of the 2012 Workshop on Statistical Machine Translation. In *Proceedings of the Seventh Workshop on Statistical Machine Translation (WMT'12)*, pages 10–51, Montréal, Canada.

Chih-Chung Chang and Chih-Jen Lin. 2011. LIBSVM: a Library for Support Vector Machines. *ACM Trans. Intell. Syst. Technol.*, 2(3):27:1–27:27, May.

Chien-Ying Chen, Jen-Yuan Yeh, and Hao-Ren Ke. 2010. Plagiarism Detection using ROUGE and WordNet. *Journal of Computing*, 2(3).

José G. C. de Souza, Miquel Esplà-Gomis, Marco Turchi, and Matteo Negri. 2013. Exploiting Qualitative Information from Automatic Word Alignment for Cross-lingual NLP Tasks. In *Proceedings of the 51st Annual Meeting of the Association for Computational Linguistics (ACL 2013)*.

Michael Denkowski and Alon Lavie. 2012. Challenges in Predicting Machine Translation Utility for Human Post-Editors. In *Proceedings of AMTA 2012*.

Yifan He, Yanjun Ma, Josef van Genabith, and Andy Way. 2010. Bridging SMT and TM with Translation Recommendation.

Philipp Koehn, Hieu Hoang, Alexandra Birch, Chris Callison-Burch, Marcello Federico, Nicola Bertoldi, Brooke Cowan, Wade Shen, Christine Moran, Richard Zens, et al. 2007. Moses: Open Source Toolkit for Statistical Machine Translation. In *Proceedings of the 45th Annual Meeting of the ACL on Interactive Poster and Demonstration Sessions*, pages 177–180. Association for Computational Linguistics.

Philip Koehn. 2005. Europarl: A parallel corpus for statistical machine translation. In *Proceedings of Machine Translation Summit X*, pages 79–86, Phuket, Thailand.

Maarit Koponen. 2012. Comparing Human Perceptions of Post-editing Effort with Post-editing Operations. In *Proceedings of the Seventh Workshop on Statistical Machine Translation*, pages 181–190. Association for Computational Linguistics.

Michael Lesk. 1986. Automated Sense Disambiguation Using Machine-readable Dictionaries: How to Tell a Pine Cone from an Ice Cream Cone. In *Proceedings of the 5th annual international conference on Systems documentation (SIGDOC86)*.

Chin-Yew Lin. 2004. ROUGE: A Package for Automatic Evaluation of Summaries. In *Proceedings of the ACL workshop on Text Summarization Branches Out.*, pages 74–81, Barcelona, Spain.

Yanjun Ma, Yifan He, Andy Way, and Josef van Genabith. 2011. Consistent Translation using Discriminative Learning: a Translation Memory-inspired Approach. *Proceedings of the 49th Annual Meeting of the Association for Computational Linguistics: Human Language Technologies*, pages 1239–1248.

Yashar Mehdad, Matteo Negri, and Marcello Federico. 2012a. Detecting semantic equivalence and information disparity in cross–lingual documents. In *Proceedings of the 50th Annual Meeting of the Association for Computational Linguistics (ACL'12)*, pages 120–124, Jeju Island, Korea.

Yashar Mehdad, Matteo Negri, and Marcello Federico. 2012b. Match without a Referee: Evaluating MT Adequacy without Reference Translations. In *Proceedings of the Seventh Workshop on Statistical Machine Translation*, WMT '12, pages 171–180, Stroudsburg, PA, USA. Association for Computational Linguistics.

Kishore Papineni, Salim Roukos, Todd Ward, and Wei-Jing Zhu. 2002. BLEU: a Method for Automatic Evaluation of Machine Translation. In *Proceedings of the 40th Annual Meeting on Association for Computational Linguistics*, ACL '02, pages 311–318, Stroudsburg, PA, USA. Association for Computational Linguistics.

M. Porter. 2001. Snowball: A language for stemming algorithms.

Martin Potthast, Alberto Barrón-Cedeño, Andreas Eiselt, Benno Stein, and Paolo Rosso. 2010. Overview of the 2nd International Competition on Plagiarism Detection. *Notebook Papers of CLEF*, 10.

Christopher B. Quirk. 2004. Training a Sentence-Level Machine Translation Confidence Measure. In *In Proceedings of LREC*.

Matthew Snover, Nitin Madnani, Bonnie J. Dorr, and Richard Schwartz. 2009. Fluency, Adequacy, or HTER?: Exploring Different Human Judgments with a Tunable MT Metric. In *Proceedings of the Fourth Workshop on Statistical Machine Translation*, StatMT '09, pages 259–268, Stroudsburg, PA, USA. Association for Computational Linguistics.

Radu Soricut and Abdessamad Echihabi. 2010. TrustRank: Inducing Trust in Automatic Translations via Ranking. In *Proceedings of the 48th Annual Meeting of the Association for Computational Linguistics*, ACL '10, pages 612–621, Stroudsburg, PA, USA. Association for Computational Linguistics.

Radu Soricut, Nguyen Bach, and Ziyuan Wang. 2012. The SDL language weaver systems in the WMT12 quality estimation shared task. In *Proceedings of the Seventh Workshop on Statistical Machine Translation (WMT'12)*, pages 145–151, Montréal, Canada.

Lucia Specia, Nicola Cancedda, Marc Dymetman, Marco Turchi, and Nello Cristianini. 2009. Estimating the Sentence-Level Quality of Machine Translation Systems. In *Proceedings of the 13th Annual Conference of the European Association for Machine Translation (EAMT'09)*, pages 28–35, Barcelona, Spain.

Lucia Specia, Dhwaj Raj, and Marco Turchi. 2010. Machine Translation Evaluation versus Quality Estimation. *Machine translation*, 24(1):39–50.

Lucia Specia, Najeh Hajlaoui, Catalina Hallett, and Wilker Aziz. 2011. Predicting machine translation adequacy. In *Proceedings of the 13th Machine Translation Summit*, pages 513–520, Xiamen, China, September.

Lucia Specia. 2011. Exploiting Objective Annotations for Measuring Translation Post-editing Effort. pages 73–80.

Marco Turchi and Matteo Negri. 2013. ALTN: Word Alignment Features for Cross-Lingual Textual Entailment. *Proceedings of the 7th International Workshop on Semantic Evaluation (SemEval 2013)*.

Online Polylingual Topic Models for Fast Document Translation Detection

Kriste Krstovski
School of Computer Science
University of Massachusetts Amherst
Amherst, MA, 01003
kriste@cs.umass.edu

David A. Smith
School of Computer Science
University of Massachusetts Amherst
Amherst, MA, 01003
dasmith@cs.umass.edu

Abstract

Many tasks in NLP and IR require efficient document similarity computations. Beyond their common application to exploratory data analysis, latent variable topic models have been used to represent text in a low-dimensional space, independent of vocabulary, where documents may be compared. This paper focuses on the task of searching a large multilingual collection for pairs of documents that are translations of each other. We present (1) efficient, online inference for representing documents in several languages in a common topic space and (2) fast approximations for finding near neighbors in the probability simplex. Empirical evaluations show that these methods are as accurate as—and significantly faster than—Gibbs sampling and brute-force all-pairs search.

1 Introduction

Statistical topic models, such as latent Dirichlet allocation (LDA) (Blei et al., 2003), have proven to be highly effective at discovering hidden structure in document collections (Hall et al., 2008, e.g.). Often, these models facilitate exploratory data analysis, by revealing which collocations of terms are favored in different kinds of documents or which terms and topics rise and fall over time (Blei and Lafferty, 2006; Wang and McCallum, 2006). One of the greatest advantages in using topic models to analyze and process large document collections is their ability to represent documents as probability distributions over a small number of topics, thereby mapping documents into a low-dimensional latent space—the T-dimensional probability simplex, where T is the number of topics. A document, represented by some point in this simplex, is said to have a particular "topic distribution".

Representing documents as points in a low-dimensional shared latent space abstracts away from the specific words used in each document, thereby facilitating the analysis of relationships between documents written using different vocabularies. For instance, topic models have been used to identify scientific communities working on related problems in different disciplines, e.g., work on cancer funded by multiple Institutes within the NIH (Talley et al., 2011). While vocabulary mismatch occurs within the realm of one language, naturally this mismatch occurs across different languages. Therefore, mapping documents in different languages into a common latent topic space can be of great benefit when detecting document translation pairs (Mimno et al., 2009; Platt et al., 2010). Aside from the benefits that it offers in the task of detecting document translation pairs, topic models offer potential benefits to the task of creating translation lexica, aligning passages, etc.

The process of discovering relationship between documents using topic models involves: (1) representing documents in the latent space by inferring their topic distributions and (2) comparing pairs of topic distributions to find close matches. Many widely used techniques do not scale efficiently, however, as the size of the document collection grows. Posterior inference by Gibbs sampling, for instance, may make thousands of passes through the data. For the task of comparing topic distributions, recent work has also resorted to comparing all pairs of documents (Talley et al., 2011).

This paper presents efficient methods for both

of these steps and performs empirical evaluations on the task of detected translated document pairs embedded in a large multilingual corpus. Unlike some more exploratory applications of topic models, translation detection is easy to evaluate. The need for bilingual training data in many language pairs and domains also makes it attractive to mitigate the quadratic runtime of brute force translation detection. We begin in §2 by extending the online variational Bayes approach of Hoffman et al. (2010) to polylingual topic models (Mimno et al., 2009). Then, in §3, we build on prior work on efficient approximations to the nearest neighbor problem by presenting theoretical and empirical evidence for applicability to topic distributions in the probability simplex and in §4, we evaluate the combination of online variational Bayes and approximate nearest neighbor methods on the translation detection task.

2 Online Variational Bayes for Polylingual Topic Models

Hierarchical generative Bayesian models, such as topic models, have proven to be very effective for modeling document collections and discovering underlying latent semantic structures. Most current topic models are based on Latent Dirichlet Allocation (LDA) (Blei et al., 2003). In some early work on the subject, Blei and Jordan (2003) showed the usefulness of LDA on the task of automatic annotation of images. Hall et al. (2008) used LDA to analyze historical trends in the scientific literature; Wei and Croft (2006) showed improvements on an information retrieval task. More recently Eisenstein et al. (2010) modeled geographic linguistic variation using Twitter data.

Aside from their widespread use on monolingual text, topic models have also been used to model multilingual data (Boyd-Graber and Blei, 2009; Platt et al., 2010; Jagarlamudi and Daumé, 2010; Fukumasu et al., 2012), to name a few. In this paper, we focus on the Polylingual Topic Model, introduced by Mimno et al. (2009). Given a multilingual set of aligned documents, the PLTM assumes that across an aligned multilingual document tuple, there exists a single, tuple-specific, distribution across topics. In addition, PLTM assumes that for each language–topic pair, there exists a distribution over words in that language β_l. As such, PLTM assumes that the multilingual corpus is created through a generative process where

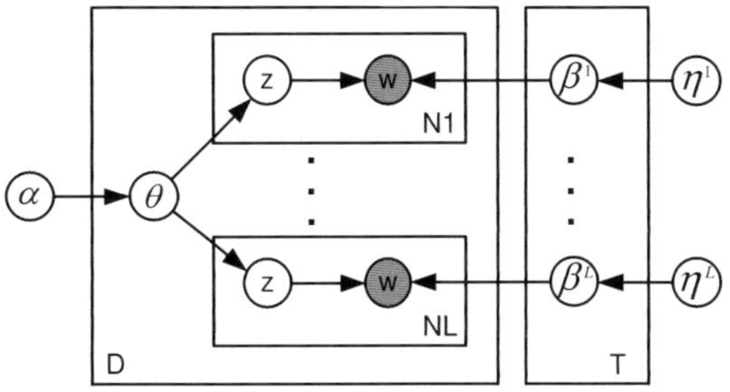

Figure 1: Polylingual topic model (PLTM)

first a document tuple is generated by drawing a tuple-specific distribution over topics θ^1 which, as it is the case with LDA, is drawn from a Dirichlet prior $\theta \sim Dir(\alpha)$. For each of the languages l in the tuple and for each of the N words w_n^l in the document the generative process: first chooses a topic assignment $z_n^l \sim Multinomial(\theta)$ which is then followed by choosing a word w_n^l from a multinomial distribution conditioned on the topic assignment and the language specific topics distribution over words $\beta_l \sim Dir(\eta_l)$. Both α and $\eta_{1,\dots,L}$ are symmetric priors, i.e. the priors are exchangeable Dirichlet distributions. Finally, each word is generated from a language- and topic-specific multinomial distribution β_t^l as selected by the topic assignment variable z_n^l:

$$w_n^l \sim p\left(w_n^l \mid z_n^l, \beta_n^l\right) \quad (1)$$

Figure 1 shows a graphical representation of the PLTM using plate notation. In their original work Mimno et al. (2009) used the Gibbs sampling approach as a posterior inference algorithm to assign topics distributions over their test collection. While more straightforward to implement, this sampling approach is inherently slow when applied to large collections which makes the original PLTM work practically infeasible to be used on real-world data sets.

In general, performing posterior inference over the latent variables of a Bayesian model is usually done with two of the three approximate approaches, Gibbs sampling, variational Bayes (VB) and expectation-propagation. While Gibbs Sampling is a variation of Markov Chain Monte Carlo method (MCMC) which generates a sample from the true posterior after converging to a stationary

[1]In the traditional LDA model θ is used to specify the document specific distribution over topics.

distribution; in VB, a set of free variational parameters characterizes a simpler family of probability distributions. These variational parameters are then optimized by finding the minimum Kullback-Leibler (KL) divergence between the variational distribution $q(\theta, z, \beta|\gamma, \phi, \lambda)$ and the true posterior $P(\theta, z, \beta|w, \alpha, \eta)$. From an algorithmic perspective, the variational Bayes approach follows the Expectation-Maximization (EM) procedure where for a given document, the E-step updates the per document variational parameters γ_d and ϕ_d while holding the per words-topic distribution parameter λ fixed. It then updates the variational parameter λ using the sufficient statistics computed in the E step. In order to converge to a stationary point, both approaches require going over the whole collection multiple times which makes their time complexity to grown linearly with the size of the data collection. The mere fact that they require continuous access to the whole collection makes both inference approaches impracticable to use on very large or streaming collections. To alleviate this problem, several algorithms have been proposed that draws from belief propagation (Zeng et al., 2012), the Gibbs sampling approach such as (Canini et al., 2009), variational Bayes (Hoffman et al., 2010) as well as a combination of the latter two (Hoffman et al., 2012) to name a few. In this paper we use Hoffman et al. (2010) approach. Hoffman et al. (2010) proposed a new inference approach called Online LDA which relies on the stochastic gradient descent to optimize the variational parameters. This approach can produce good estimates of LDA posteriors in a single pass over the whole collection.

2.1 Algorithmic Implementation

We now derive an online variational Bayes algorithm for PLTM to infer topic distributions over multilingual collections. Figure 2 shows the variational model and free parameters used in our approach. As in the case of Hoffman et al. (2010), our algorithm updates the variational parameters γ_d^l and ϕ_d^l on each batch of documents while the variational parameter λ is computed as a weighted average of the value on the previous batch and its approximate version $\tilde{\lambda}$. Averaging is performed using a decay function whose parameters control the rate at which old values of λ^l are forgotten. Within the E step of the VB approach, we compute the updates over the variational parameter ϕ_l

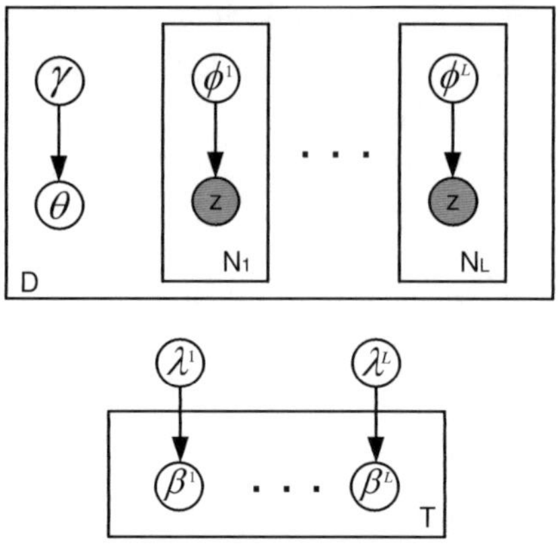

Figure 2: Graphical model representation of the free variational parameters for the online variational Bayes approximation of the PLTM posterior

for each language L present in our document tuple while the update on the γ parameter accumulates the language specific sufficient statistics:

$$\gamma_k^m = \alpha + \sum_l \sum_w \phi_{wk}^{ml} n_w^{ml} \quad (2)$$

We detail these steps in Algorithm 1.

2.2 Performance Analysis

To demonstrate the efficacy of online PLTM, we ran topic inference on a subset of the English-Spanish Europarl collection consisting of ~64k parallel speeches and compared the accuracy results vs. the training and inference speed against the original PLTM model using topic sets of T=50,100, 200 and 500. We explain in details the evaluation task and the performance metric used in §4. Shown in Figure 3 are the results of these comparisons. Our speed measurements were performed on Xeon quad processors with a clock speed of 2.66GHz and a total of 16GB of memory.

As we increase the number of topics we gain in accuracy over the evaluation task across both inference approaches. When we increase the number of topics from 50 to 500 the speed improvement obtained by Online VB PLTM drops by a factor of 2.9 within the training step and by a factor of 4.45 in the test step. Our total running time for the Online VB PLTM with T=500 approaches the running time of the Gibbs sampling approach with T=50. The gradual drop in speed improvement with the increase of the number topics is mostly attributed to the commutation of the

Algorithm 1 Online variational Bayes for PLTM

initialize λ_l randomly
obtain the t*th mini-batch of tuples* M_t
for $t = 1$ to ∞ **do**
  $\rho_t \leftarrow \left(\frac{1}{t_0+t}\right)^{\kappa}$
  E step:
  initialize γ_t randomly
  for each document tuple in mini-batch t
  for m in M_t **do**
    repeat
      for $l \in 1,\ldots$,L **do**
        $\phi_{wk}^{ml} \propto$
        $\exp\left\{E_q\left[\log \theta_k^m\right]\right\} *$
        $\exp\left\{E_q\left[\log \beta_{kw}^{ml}\right]\right\}$
      end for
      $\gamma_k^m = \alpha + \sum_l \sum_w \phi_{wk}^{ml}\, n_w^{ml}$
    until convergence
  end for
  M step:
  for $l \in 1,\ldots$,L **do**
    $\tilde{\lambda}_{kw}^{l} = \eta + D\sum_m \phi_{wk}^{ml} n_w^{ml}$
    $\lambda_{kw}^{lt} \leftarrow (1-\rho_t)\,\lambda_{kw}^{l(t-1)} + \rho_t \tilde{\lambda}_{kw}^{l}$
  end for
end for

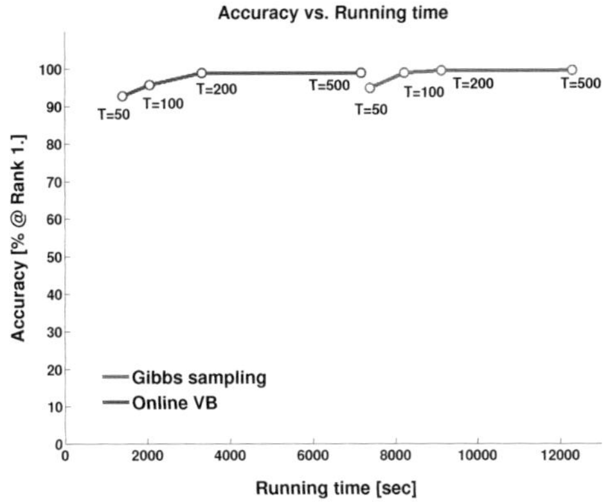

Figure 3: Speed vs. accuracy comparison between Online VB PLTM and Gibbs Sampling PLTM at T=50,100, 200 and 500. We used a Python implementation of Online VB and Mallet's Java implementation of PLTM with in-memory Gibbs Sampling using 1000 iterations.

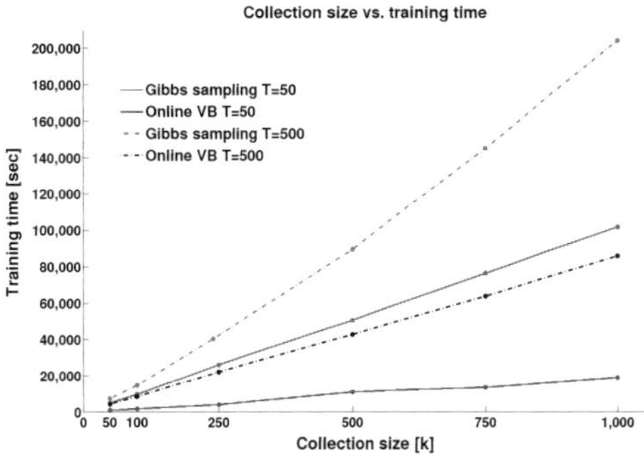

Figure 4: Collection size vs. training time comparison between Online VB PLTM and Gibbs Sampling PLTM using multilingual collections of 50k, 100k, 250k, 500k, 750k and 1M speech pairs.

digamma function (Asuncion et al., 2009) whose time complexity increases linearly with the number of topics.

While a multilingual collection of ~64k document pairs is considered relatively big, our goal of deriving the Online VB PLTM approach was to be able to utilize PLTM on very large multilingual collections. To analyze the potential of using Online VB PLTM on such collections we ran speed comparisons within the training step by creating multilingual collections of different lengths multiplying the original English-Spanish Europarl collection. Speed comparisons using collections of length 50K, 100K, 250K, 500K, 750K and 1M are shown in Figure 4. Training was performed with the number of topics T set to T=50 and T=500.

As we increase the collection size we observe the real benefit of using Online VB compared to Gibbs sampling. This is mostly attributed to the fact that the Gibbs sampling approach requires multiple iterations over the whole collection in order to achieve a convergence point. For collection sizes of 50k and 100k the training time for the Online VB PLTM with T=500 approaches the training time of Gibbs sampling with T=50 and as we increase the collection size this proximity dissipates.

In Figure 5 we show a sample set of the aligned topics extracted using Online VB PLTM with T=400 on the English-Spanish Europarl collection. For a given topic tuple words are ordered based on probability of occurrence within the given topic.

English	Spanish
1. animals	1. animales
2. animal	2. prohibición
3. disease	3. carne
4. export	4. fiebre
5. foot	5. aftosa
6. mouth	6. exportación
7. meat	7. comisión
8. feed	8. fischler
9. fischler	9. crisis
10. crisis	10. animal

English	Spanish
1. funds	1. millones
2. million	2. fondos
3. year	3. euros
4. fund	4. para
5. billion	5. irlanda
6. ireland	6. estructurales
7. structural	7. fondo
8. irish	8. irlandés
9. funding	9. total
10. budget	10. presupuesto

English	Spanish
1. health	1. productos
2. food	2. salud
3. products	3. alimentos
4. consumers	4. medicamentos
5. scientific	5. alimentaria
6. product	6. consumidores
7. risk	7. para
8. labeling	8. pública
9. medicines	9. genéticamente
10. gmos	10. enfermedades

English	Spanish
1. world	1. paises
2. problems	2. para
3. country	3. mundo
4. consequences	4. como
5. poverty	5. problemas
6. global	6. consecuencias
7. problem	7. este
8. much	8. importante
9. poor	9. mundial
10. third	10. pobreza

English	Spanish
1. tourism	1. turismo
2. sport	2. deporte
3. internet	3. internet
4. exploitation	4. explotación
5. television	5. televisión
6. football	6. fútbol
7. sports	7. juegos
8. games	8. infantil
9. film	9. menores
10. olympic	10. material

English	Spanish
1. immigration	1. inmigración
2. belgian	2. belga
3. western	3. europa
4. helsinki	4. paises
5. communist	5. occidental
6. democracies	6. helsinki
7. tradition	7. tradición
8. west	8. democracias
9. world	9. comunista
10. bolkestein	10. bolkestein

English	Spanish
1. palestinian	1. israelí
2. israel	2. oriente
3. middle	3. palestina
4. east	4. palestinos
5. israeli	5. autoridad
6. authority	6. palestino
7. peace	7. israelies
8. palestinians	8. medio
9. attacks	9. estado
10. united	10. sharon

English	Spanish
1. industry	1. industria
2. research	2. sector
3. sector	3. investigación
4. industrial	4. industrial
5. patent	5. innovación
6. innovation	6. marco
7. industries	7. industriales
8. technology	8. patente
9. technological	9. sectores
10. sixth	10. tecnología

Figure 5: Sample set of topics extracted from Europarl English-Spanish collection of 64k speeches using Online PLTM with T=400 ordered based on their probability of occurrence within the topic.

3 Approximate NN Search in the Probability Simplex

One of the most attractive applications for topic models has involved using the latent variables as a low-dimensional representation for document similarity computations (Hall et al., 2008; Boyd-Graber and Resnik, 2010; Talley et al., 2011). After computing topic distributions for documents, however, researchers in this line of work have almost always resorted to brute-force all-pairs similarity comparisons between topic distributions.

In this section, we present efficient methods for approximate near neighbor search in the probability simplex in which topic distributions live. Measurements for similarity between two probability distributions are information-theoretic, and distance metrics, typical for the metric space, are not appropriate (measurements such as Euclidean, cosine, Jaccard, etc.). Divergence metrics, such as Kullback-Leibler (KL), Jensen-Shannon (JS), and Hellinger distance are used instead. Shown in Figure 6 are the formulas of the divergence metrics along with the Euclidean distance. When dealing with a large data set of N documents, the $O(N^2)$ time complexity of all-pairs comparison makes the task practically infeasible. With some distance measures, however, the time complexity on near neighbor tasks has been alleviated using approximate methods that reduce the time complexity of each query to a sub-linear number of comparisons. For example, Euclidean distance (3) has been efficiently used on all-pairs comparison tasks in large data sets thanks to its approximate based versions developed using locality sensitive hashing (LSH) (Andoni et al., 2005) and k-d search trees (Friedman et al., 1977). In order to alleviate the all-pairs computational complexity in the probability simplex, we will use a reduction of the Hellinger divergence measure (4) to Euclidean distance and therefore utilize preexisting approximation techniques for the Euclidean distance in the probability simplex.

This reduction comes from the fact that both measurements have similar algebraic expressions. If we discard the square root used in the Euclidean distance, Hellinger distance (4) becomes equivalent to the Euclidean distance metric (3) between $\sqrt{p_i}$ and $\sqrt{q_i}$. The task of finding nearest neighbors for a given point (whether in the metric space or the probability simplex) involves ranking all nearest points discovered and as such not computing the square root function does not affect the overall ranking and the nearest neighbor discovery. Moreover, depending on its functional form, the Hellinger distance is often defined as square root over the whole summation. Aside from the Hellinger distance, we also approximate Jensen-Shannon divergence which is a symmetric version of the Kullback-Liebler divergence. For the JS approximation, we will use a constant factor relationship between the Jensen-Shannon divergence an Hellinger distance previously explored by (Topsøe, 2000). More specifically, we will be using its more concise form (7) also presented by

$$\text{Eu}(p,q) = \sqrt{\sum_{i=1}^{n}(p_i - q_i)^2} \quad (3)$$

$$\text{He}(p,q) = \sum_{i=1}^{n}\left(\sqrt{p(x_i)} - \sqrt{q(x_i)}\right)^2 \quad (4)$$

$$\text{KL}(p,q) = \sum_{i=1}^{n} p(x_i)\log\frac{p(x_i)}{q(x_i)} \quad (5)$$

$$\text{JS}(p,q) = \frac{1}{2}\text{KL}\left(p, \frac{p+q}{2}\right) + \frac{1}{2}\text{KL}\left(q, \frac{p+q}{2}\right) \quad (6)$$

$$\frac{1}{2}\text{He}(p,q) \leq \text{JS}(p,q) \leq 2\ln(2)\text{He}(p,q) \quad (7)$$

Figure 6: Distance measures and bounds

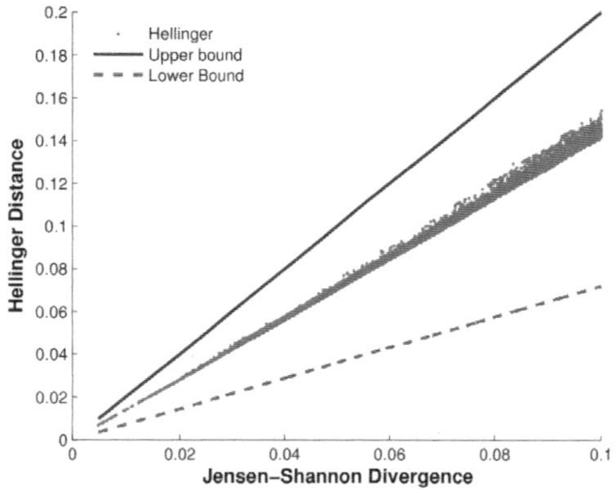

Figure 7: Empirical evidence of the bounds presented in Eq. 7 on 1 million document pairs—zoomed section where nearest neighbors reside. The lower bound is $He(p,q) = \frac{1}{2\ln(2)}JS(p,q)$ while the upper bound is $He(p,q) = 2JS(p,q)$.

(Guha et al., 2006). The constant factor relationship provides us with the theoretical guarantees necessary for this approximation.

In practice, we can often do much better than this theoretical bound. Figure 7 shows the empirical relation of JS and Hellinger on a translation-detection task. As will be described in §4, we computed the JS and Hellinger divergences between topic distributions of English and Spanish Europarl speeches for a total of 1 million document pairs. Each point in the figure represents one Spanish-English document pair that might or might not be translations of each other. In this figure we emphasize the lower left section of the plot where the nearest neighbors (i.e., likely translations) reside, and the relationship between JS and Hellinger is much tighter than the theoretical bounds and from pratical perspective as we will show in the next section. As a summary for the reader, using the above approaches, we will approximate JS divergence by using the Euclidean based representation of the Hellinger distance. As stated earlier, the Euclidean based representation is computed using well established approximation approaches and in our case we will use two such approaches: the Exact Euclidean LSH (E2LSH) (Andoni et al., 2005) and the k-d trees implementation within the Approximate Nearest Neighbor (ANN) library (Mount and Arya, 2010).

4 Efficient Approximate Translation Detection

Mapping multilingual documents into a common, language-independent vector space for the purpose of improving machine translation (MT) and performing cross-language information retrieval (CLIR) tasks has been explored through various techniques. Mimno et al. (2009) introduced polylingual topic models (PLTM), an extension of latent Dirichlet allocation (LDA), and, more recently, Platt et al. (2010) proposed extensions of principal component analysis (PCA) and probabilistic latent semantic indexing (PLSI). Both the PLTM and PLSI represent bilingual documents in the probability simplex, and thus the task of finding document translation pairs is formulated as finding similar probability distributions. While the nature of both works was exploratory, results shown on fairly large collections of bilingual documents (less than 20k documents) offer convincing argument of their potential. Expanding these approaches to much large collections of multilingual documents would require utilizing fast NN search for computing similarity in the probability simplex. While there are many other proposed approaches to the task of finding document translation pairs that represent documents in metric space, such as Krstovski and Smith (2011) which utilizes LSH for cosine distance, there is no evidence that they yield good results on documents of small lengths such as paragraphs and even sentences.

In this section, we empirically show how to utilize approaches that deal with representing documents in the probability simplex without a significant loss in accuracy while significantly improving the processing time. We use PLTM representations of bilingual documents. In addition, we show how the results as reported by Platt et al. (2010) can be obtained using the PLTM representation with a significant speed improvement.

As in (Platt et al., 2010) and (Mimno et al., 2009) the task is to find document translation pairs in a multilingual collection of documents by representing documents in the probability simplex and computing similarity between their probability distribution representation across all document pairs. For this experimental setup, accuracy is defined as the number of times (in percentage) that the target language document was discovered at rank 1 (i.e. % @Rank 1.) across the whole test collection.

4.1 Experimental Setup

We use Mallet's (McCallum, 2002) implementation of the PLTM to train and infer topics on the same data set used in Platt et al. (2010). That paper used the Europarl (Koehn, 2005) multilingual collection of English and Spanish sessions. Their training collection consists of speeches extracted from all Europarl sessions from the years 1996 through 1999 and the year 2002 and a development set which consists of speeches from sessions in 2001. The test collection consists of Europarl speeches from the year 2000 and the first nine months of 2003. While Platt et al. (2010) do offer absolute performance comparison between their JPLSA approach and previous results published by (Mimno et al., 2009), these performance comparisons are not done on the same training and test sets—a gap that we fill below.

We train PLTM models with number of topics T set to 50, 100, 200, and 500. In order to compare exactly the same topic distributions when computing speed vs. accuracy of various approximate and exhaustive all-pairs comparisons we focus only on one inference approach - the Gibbs sampling and ignore the online VB approach as it yields similar performance. For all four topic models, we use the same settings for PLTM (hyperparameter values and number of Gibbs sampling iterations) as in (Mimno et al., 2009)[2]. Topic distributions were then inferred on the test collection using the trained topics. We then performed all-pairs comparison using JS divergence, Hellinger distance, and approximate, LSH and kd-trees based, Hellinger distance. We measured the total time that it takes to perform exhaustive all-pairs comparison using JS divergence, the LSH and kd-trees version on a single machine consisting of a core 2 duo quad processors with a clock speed of 2.66GHz on each core and a total of 8GB of memory. Since the time performance of the E2LSH depends on the radius R of data set points considered for each query point (Indyk and Motwani, 1998), we performed measurements with different values of R. For this task, the all-pairs JS code implementation first reads both source and target sets of documents and stores them in hash tables. We then go over each entry in the source table and compute divergence against all target table entries.We refer to this code implementation as hash map implementation.

4.2 Evaluation Task and Results

Performance of the four PLTM models and the performance across the four different similarity measurements was evaluated based on the percentage of document translation pairs (out of the whole test set) that were discovered at rank one. This same approach was used by (Platt et al., 2010) to show the absolute performance comparison. As in the case of the previous two tasks, in order to evaluate the approximate, LSH based, Hellinger distance we used values of R=0.4, R=0.6 and R=0.8. Since in (Platt et al., 2010) numbers were reported on the test speeches whose word length is greater or equal to 100, we used the same subset (total of 14150 speeches) of the original test collection. Shown in Table 1 are results across the four different measurements for all four PLTM models. When using regular JS divergence, our PLTM model with 200 topics performs the best with 99.42% of the top one ranked candidate translation documents being true translations. When using approximate, kd-trees based, Hellinger distance, we outperform regular JS and Hellinger divergence across all topics and for T=500 we achieve the best overall accuracy of 99.61%. We believe that this is due to the small amount of error

[2]We start off by first replicating the results as in (Mimno et al., 2009) and thus verifying the functionality of our experimental setup.

Divergence	T=50	100	200	500
JS	94.27	98.48	99.42	99.33
He	94.30	98.45	99.40	99.31
He LSH R=0.4	93.95	97.46	98.27	98.01
He LSH R=0.6	94.30	98.46	99.40	99.31
He LSH R=0.8	94.30	98.45	99.34	99.31
He kd-trees	94.86	98.90	99.50	99.61

Table 1: Percentage of document pairs with the correct translation discovered at rank 1: comparison of different divergence measurements and different numbers T of PLTM topics.

Divergence	T=50	100	200	500
JS	7.8	4.6	2.4	1.0
He LSH R=0.4	511.5	383.6	196.7	69.7
He LSH R=0.6	142.1	105.0	59.0	18.6
He LSH R=0.8	73.8	44.7	29.5	16.3
He kd-trees	196.7	123.7	76.7	38.5

Table 2: Relative speed improvement between all-pairs JS divergence and approximate He divergence via kd-trees and LSH across different values of radius R. The baseline is brute-force all-pairs comparison with Jensen-Shannon and 500 topics.

in the search introduced by ANN, due to its approximate nature, which for this task yields positive results. On the same data set, (Platt et al., 2010) report accuracy of 98.9% using 50 topics, a slightly different prior distribution, and MAP instead of posterior inference.

Shown in Table 2 are the relative differences in time between all pairs JS divergence, approximate kd-trees and LSH based Hellinger distance with different value of R. Rather than showing absolute speed numbers, which are often influenced by the processor configuration and available memory, we show relative speed improvements where we take the slowest running configuration as a referent value. In our case we assign the referent speed value of 1 to the configuration with T=500 and all-pairs JS computation. Results shown are based on comparing running time of E2LSH and ANN against the all-pairs similarity comparison implementation that uses hash tables to store all documents in the bilingual collection which is significantly faster than the other code implementation.

For the approximate, LSH based, Hellinger distance with T=100 we obtain a speed improvement of 24.2 times compared to regular all-pairs JS divergence while maintaining the same performance compared to Hellinger distance metric and insignificant loss over all-pairs JS divergence. From Table 2 it is evident that as we increase the radius R we reduce the relative speed of performance since the range of points that LSH considers for a given query point increases. Also, as the number of topics increases, the speed benefit is reduced for both the LSH and k-d tree techniques.

5 Conclusion

Hierarchical Bayesian models, such as Polylingual Topic Models, have been shown to offer great potential in analyzing multilingual collections, extracting aligned topics and finding document translation pairs when trained on sufficiently large aligned collections. Online stochastic optimization inference allows us to generate good parameter estimates. By combining these two approaches we are able to infer topic distributions across documents in large multilingual document collections in an efficient manner. Utilizing approximate NN search techniques in the probability simplex, we showed that fast document translation detection could be achieved with insignificant loss in accuracy.

6 Acknowledgments

This work was supported in part by the Center for Intelligent Information Retrieval and in part by NSF grant #IIS-0910884. Any opinions, findings and conclusions or recommendations expressed in this material are those of the authors and do not necessarily reflect those of the sponsor.

References

Alexandr Andoni, Mayur Datar, Nicole Immorlica, Piotr Indyk, and Vahab Mirrokni. 2005. Locality-sensitive hashing using stable distributions. In G. Shakhnarovich, T. Darrell, and P. Indyk, editors, *Nearest Neighbor Methods in Learning and Vision: Theory and Practice*, pages 61–72. MIT Press.

Arthur Asuncion, Max Welling, Padhraic Smyth, and Yee Whye Teh. 2009. On smoothing and inference for topic models. In *Proceedings of the Twenty-Fifth Conference on Uncertainty in Artificial Intelligence*, UAI '09, pages 27–34, Arlington, Virginia, United States. AUAI Press.

David M. Blei and Michael I. Jordan. 2003. Modeling annotated data. In *Proceedings of the 26th annual international ACM SIGIR conference on Research and development in informaion retrieval*, SIGIR '03, pages 127–134, New York, NY, USA. ACM.

David M. Blei and John D. Lafferty. 2006. Dynamic topic models. In *Proceedings of the 23rd international conference on Machine learning*, ICML '06, pages 113–120, New York, NY, USA. ACM.

David M. Blei, Andrew Y. Ng, and Michael I. Jordan. 2003. Latent dirichlet allocation. *J. Mach. Learn. Res.*, 3:993–1022, March.

Jordan Boyd-Graber and David M. Blei. 2009. Multilingual topic models for unaligned text. In *Proceedings of the Twenty-Fifth Conference on Uncertainty in Artificial Intelligence*, UAI '09, pages 75–82, Arlington, Virginia, United States. AUAI Press.

Jordan Boyd-Graber and Philip Resnik. 2010. Holistic sentiment analysis across languages: multilingual supervised latent dirichlet allocation. In *Proceedings of the 2010 Conference on Empirical Methods in Natural Language Processing*, EMNLP '10, pages 45–55, Stroudsburg, PA, USA. Association for Computational Linguistics.

Kevin R. Canini, Lei Shi, and Thomas L. Griffiths. 2009. Online inference of topics with latent dirichlet allocation. In *Proceedings of the 12th International Conference on Artificial Intelligence and Statistics (AISTATS)*.

Jacob Eisenstein, Brendan O'Connor, Noah A. Smith, and Eric P. Xing. 2010. A latent variable model for geographic lexical variation. In *Proceedings of the 2010 Conference on Empirical Methods in Natural Language Processing*, EMNLP '10, pages 1277–1287, Stroudsburg, PA, USA. Association for Computational Linguistics.

J. H. Friedman, J. L. Bentley, and R. A. Finkel. 1977. An algorithm for finding best matches in logarithmic expected time. *ACM Transactions on Mathematical Software*, 3(3):209–226.

Kosuke Fukumasu, Koji Eguchi, and Eric Xing. 2012. Symmetric correspondence topic models for multilingual text analysis. In P. Bartlett, F.C.N. Pereira, C.J.C. Burges, L. Bottou, and K.Q. Weinberger, editors, *Advances in Neural Information Processing Systems 25*, pages 1295–1303.

Sudipto Guha, Andrew McGregor, and Suresh Venkatasubramanian. 2006. Streaming and sublinear approximation of entropy and information distances. In *ACM-SIAM Symposium on Discrete Algorithms*, pages 733–742.

David Hall, Daniel Jurafsky, and Christopher D. Manning. 2008. Studying the history of ideas using topic models. In *Proceedings of the Conference on Empirical Methods in Natural Language Processing*, EMNLP '08, pages 363–371, Stroudsburg, PA, USA. Association for Computational Linguistics.

Matthew Hoffman, David Blei, and Francis Bach. 2010. Online learning for latent dirichlet allocation. In J. Lafferty, C. K. I. Williams, J. Shawe-Taylor, R.S. Zemel, and A. Culotta, editors, *Advances in Neural Information Processing Systems 23*, pages 856–864.

Matt Hoffman, David M. Blei, and David M. Mimno. 2012. Sparse stochastic inference for latent dirichlet allocation. In John Langford and Joelle Pineau, editors, *Proceedings of the 29th International Conference on Machine Learning (ICML-12)*, pages 1599–1606, New York, NY, USA. ACM.

Piotr Indyk and Rajeev Motwani. 1998. Approximate nearest neighbors: towards removing the curse of dimensionality. In *Proceedings of the thirtieth annual ACM symposium on Theory of computing*, STOC '98, pages 604–613, New York, NY, USA. ACM.

Jagadeesh Jagarlamudi and Hal Daumé. 2010. Extracting multilingual topics from unaligned comparable corpora. In *Proceedings of the 32nd European conference on Advances in Information Retrieval*, ECIR'2010, pages 444–456, Berlin, Heidelberg. Springer-Verlag.

Philipp Koehn. 2005. Europarl: A parallel corpus for statistical machine translation. In *MT Summit*, pages 79–86.

Kriste Krstovski and David A. Smith. 2011. A minimally supervised approach for detecting and ranking document translation pairs. In *Proc. Workshop on Statistical MT*, pages 207–216.

Andrew Kachites McCallum, 2002. *MALLET: A Machine Learning for Language Toolkit*. `http://mallet.cs.umass.edu`.

David Mimno, Hanna M. Wallach, Jason Naradowsky, David A. Smith, and Andrew McCallum. 2009. Polylingual topic models. In *Proceedings of the 2009 Conference on Empirical Methods in Natural Language Processing: Volume 2 - Volume 2*, EMNLP '09, pages 880–889, Stroudsburg, PA, USA. Association for Computational Linguistics.

David M. Mount and Sunil Arya, 2010. *ANN: A Library for Approximate Nearest Neighbor Searching*. `http://www.cs.umd.edu/~mount/ANN/`.

John C. Platt, Kristina Toutanova, and Wen-tau Yih. 2010. Translingual document representations from discriminative projections. In *Proceedings of the 2010 Conference on Empirical Methods in Natural Language Processing*, EMNLP '10, pages 251–261, Stroudsburg, PA, USA. Association for Computational Linguistics.

Edmund Talley, David Newman, David Mimno, Bruce Herr, Hanna Wallach, Gully Burns, Miriam Leenders, and Andrew McCallum. 2011. Database of NIH grants using machine-learned categories and graphical clustering. *Nature Methods*, 8:443–444.

Flemming Topsøe. 2000. Some inequalities for information divergence and related measures of discrimination. *IEEE Trans. Information Theory*, 44(4):1602–1609.

Xuerui Wang and Andrew McCallum. 2006. Topics over time: a non-markov continuous-time model of topical trends. In *Proceedings of the 12th ACM SIGKDD international conference on Knowledge discovery and data mining*, KDD '06, pages 424–433, New York, NY, USA. ACM.

Xing Wei and W. Bruce Croft. 2006. Lda-based document models for ad-hoc retrieval. In *Proceedings of the 29th annual international ACM SIGIR conference on Research and development in information retrieval*, SIGIR '06, pages 178–185, New York, NY, USA. ACM.

Jia Zeng, Xiao-Qin Cao, and Zhi-Qiang Liu. 2012. Residual belief propagation for topic modeling. *CoRR*, abs/1204.6610.

Combining Bilingual and Comparable Corpora for Low Resource Machine Translation

Ann Irvine
Center for Language and Speech Processing
Johns Hopkins University

Chris Callison-Burch*
Computer and Information Science Dept.
University of Pennsylvania

Abstract

Statistical machine translation (SMT) performance suffers when models are trained on only small amounts of parallel data. The learned models typically have both low *accuracy* (incorrect translations and feature scores) and low *coverage* (high out-of-vocabulary rates). In this work, we use an additional data resource, *comparable corpora*, to improve both. Beginning with a small bitext and corresponding phrase-based SMT model, we improve coverage by using bilingual lexicon induction techniques to learn new translations from comparable corpora. Then, we supplement the model's feature space with translation scores estimated over comparable corpora in order to improve accuracy. We observe improvements between 0.5 and 1.7 BLEU translating Tamil, Telugu, Bengali, Malayalam, Hindi, and Urdu into English.

1 Introduction

Standard statistical machine translation (SMT) models (Koehn et al., 2003) are trained using large, sentence-aligned parallel corpora. Unfortunately, parallel corpora are not always available in large enough quantities to train robust models (Kolachina et al., 2012). In this work, we consider the situation in which we have access to only a small amount of bitext for a given low resource language pair, and we wish to supplement an SMT model with additional translations and features estimated using comparable corpora in the source and target languages. Assuming access to a small amount of parallel text is realistic, especially considering the recent success of crowdsourcing translations (Zaidan and Callison-Burch, 2011; Ambati, 2011; Post et al., 2012).

We frame the shortcomings of SMT models trained on limited amounts of parallel text[1] in terms of accuracy and coverage. In this context, coverage refers to the number of words and phrases that a model has any knowledge of at all, and it is low when the training text is small, which results in a high out-of-vocabulary (OOV) rate. Accuracy refers to the correctness of the translation pairs and their corresponding probability features that make up the translation model. Because the quality of unsupervised automatic word alignments correlates with the amount of available parallel text and alignment errors result in errors in extracted translation pairs, accuracy tends to be low in low resource settings. Additionally, estimating translation probabilities[2] over sparse training sets results in inaccurate feature scores.

Given these deficiencies, we begin with a baseline SMT model learned from a small parallel corpus and supplement the model to improve its accuracy and coverage. We apply techniques presented in prior work that use *comparable corpora* to estimate similarities between word and phrases. In particular, we build on prior work in bilingual lexicon induction in order to predict translations for OOV words, improving coverage. We then use the same corpora to estimate additional translation feature scores, improving model accuracy. We see improvements in translation quality between 0.5

*Performed while faculty at Johns Hopkins University

[1]We consider low resource settings to be those with parallel datasets of fewer than 1 million words. Most standard MT datasets contain tens or hundreds of millions of words.

[2]Estimating reordering probabilities over sparse data also leads to model inaccuracies; we do not tackle that here.

and 1.7 BLEU points translating the following low resource languages into English: Tamil, Telugu, Bengali, Malayalam, Hindi, and Urdu.

2 Previous Work

Prior work shows that a variety of signals, including distributional, temporal, topic, and string similarity, may inform bilingual lexicon induction (Rapp, 1995; Fung and Yee, 1998; Rapp, 1999; Schafer and Yarowsky, 2002; Koehn and Knight, 2002; Monz and Dorr, 2005; Huang et al., 2005; Schafer, 2006; Klementiev and Roth, 2006; Haghighi et al., 2008; Mimno et al., 2009; Mausam et al., 2010). Other work has used decipherment techniques to learn translations from monolingual and comparable data (Ravi and Knight, 2011; Dou and Knight, 2012; Nuhn et al., 2012). Daumé and Jagarlamudi (2011) use contextual and string similarity to mine translations for OOV words in a high resource language domain adaptation for a machine translation setting. Unlike most other prior work on bilingual lexicon induction, Daumé and Jagarlamudi (2011) use the translations in end-to-end SMT.

More recently, Irvine and Callison-Burch (2013) combine a variety of the techniques for estimating word pair similarity using source and target language comparable corpora. That work shows that only a small amount of supervision is needed to learn how to effectively combine similarity features into a single model for doing bilingual lexicon induction. In this work, because we assume access to a small amount of bilingual data, it is natural to take such a supervised approach to inducing new translations, and we directly apply that of Irvine and Callison-Burch (2013).

Klementiev et al. (2012) use comparable corpora to score an existing Spanish-English phrase table extracted from the Europarl corpus. In this work, we directly apply their technique for scoring an existing phrase table. However, unlike that work, our initial phrase tables are estimated from small parallel corpora for genuine low resource languages. Additionally, we include new translations discovered in comparable corpora.

Other prior work has mined supplemental parallel data from comparable corpora (Munteanu and Marcu, 2006; Abdul-Rauf and Schwenk, 2009; Smith et al., 2010; Uszkoreit et al., 2010; Smith et al., 2013). Such efforts are orthogonal and complementary to the approach that we take.

Language	Train Words (k)		Dev Types	Dev Tokens
	Sent	Dict	% OOV	% OOV
Tamil	335	77	44	25
Telugu	414	41	39	21
Bengali	240	7	37	18
Malayalam	263	151	6	3
Hindi	659	n/a	34	11
Urdu	616	116	23	6

Table 1: Information about datasets released by Post et al. (2012): thousands of words in the source language parallel sentences and dictionaries, and percent of development set word types (unique word tokens) and word tokens that are OOV (do not appear in either section of the training data).

Language	Web Crawls	Wikipedia
Tamil	0.1	4.4
Telugu	0.4	8.6
Bengali	2.7	3.3
Malayalam	0.1	3.7
Hindi	18.1	6.4
Urdu	285	2.5

Table 2: Millions of words of time-stamped web crawls and Wikipedia text, by language.

3 Using Comparable Corpora to Improve Accuracy and Coverage

After describing our bilingual and comparable corpora, we briefly describe the techniques proposed by Irvine and Callison-Burch (2013) and Klementiev et al. (2012). The contribution of this paper is the application and combination of these techniques in truly low resource translation conditions.

3.1 Datasets

Post et al. (2012) used Mechanical Turk to collect small parallel corpora for the following Indian languages and English: Tamil, Telugu, Bengali, Malayalam, Hindi, and Urdu. They collected both parallel sentence pairs and a dictionary of word translations.[3] We use all six datasets, which provide real low resource data conditions for six truly low resource language pairs. Table 1 shows statistics about the datasets.

Table 2 lists the amount of comparable data that we use for each language. Following both Klementiev et al. (2012) and Irvine and Callison-Burch (2013), we use time-stamped web crawls as well as interlingually linked Wikipedia documents. We use the time-stamped data to estimate temporal similarity and the interlingual Wikipedia links, which indicate documents about the same topic written in different languages, to estimate

[3]No dictionary was provided for Hindi.

topic similarity. We use both datasets in combination with a dictionary derived from the small parallel corpora to estimate contextual similarity.

3.2 Improving Coverage

In order to improve the coverage of our low resource translation models, we use bilingual lexicon induction techniques to learn translations for words which appear in our test sets but not in our training data (OOVs). Bilingual lexicon induction is the task of inducing pairs of words that are translations of one another from monolingual or comparable corpora. Irvine and Callison-Burch (2013) use a diverse set of features estimated over comparable corpora and a small set of known translations as supervision for training a discriminative classifier, which makes predictions (translation or not a translation) on test set words paired with all possible translations. Possible translations are taken from the set of all target words appearing in the comparable corpora. Candidates are ranked according to their classification scores. They achieve very good performance on the induction task itself compared with an unsupervised baseline that aggregates the same similarity features uniformly. In our setting, we have access to a small parallel corpus, which makes such a supervised approach to bilingual lexicon induction a natural choice.

We use the framework described in Irvine and Callison-Burch (2013) directly, and further details may be found there. In particular, we use the same feature set, which includes the temporal, contextual, topic, orthographic, and frequency similarity between a candidate translation pair. We derive translations to serve as positive supervision from our automatically aligned parallel text[4] and, like the prior work, use random word pairs as negative supervision. Figure 1 shows some examples of Bengali words, their correct translations, and the top-3 translations that this framework induces.

In our initial experiments, we add the highest ranked English candidate translation for each source language OOV to our phrase tables. Because all of the OOVs appear at least once in our comparable corpora,[5] we are able to mine translations for all of them. Adding these translations by definition improves the coverage of our MT models. Then, in additional sets of experiments, we also induce translations for source language words which are *low frequency* in the training data and supplement our SMT models with top-k translations, not just the highest ranked.

Source	Induced Translations	Correct Translation
গাণিতিকভাবে	mathematical equal ganitikovabe	mathematically
ফাংশন	function functions variables	function
অভিষেক	made goal earned	inauguration

Figure 1: Examples of OOV Bengali words, our top-3 ranked induced translations, and their correct translations.

3.3 Improving Accuracy

In order to improve the accuracy of our models, we use comparable corpora to estimate additional features over the translation pairs in our phrase tables and include those features in tuning and decoding. This approach follows that of Klementiev et al. (2012). We compute both phrasal features and lexically smoothed features (using word alignments, like the Moses lexical translation probabilities) for all of the following except orthographic similarity, for which we only use lexically smoothed features,[6] resulting in nine additional features: temporal similarity based on timestamped web crawls, contextual similarity based on web crawls and Wikipedia (separately), orthographic similarity using normalized edit distance, and topic similarity based on inter-lingually linked Wikipedia pages. Our hope is that by adding a diverse set of similarity features to the phrase tables, our models will better distinguish between good and bad translation pairs, improving accuracy.

4 Experiments

4.1 Experimental setup

We use the data splits given by Post et al. (2012) and, following that work, include the dictionaries in the training data and report results on the devtest set using case-insensitive BLEU and four references. We use the Moses phrase-based MT framework (Koehn et al., 2007). For each language, we extract a phrase table with a phrase limit of seven. In order to make our results comparable to those of Post et al. (2012), we follow that work and use

[4]GIZA++ intersection alignments over all training data.

[5]The Post et al. (2012) datasets are crowdsourced English translations of source Wikipedia text. Using Wikipedia as comparable corpora, we observe all OOVs at least once.

[6]Because the words within a phrase pair are often reordered, phrase-level orthographic similarity is unreliable.

Language	Top-1 Acc.	Top-10 Acc.
Tamil	4.5	10.2
Telugu	32.8	47.9
Bengali	17.9	29.8
Malayalam	12.9	23.0
Hindi	44.3	57.6
Urdu	16.1	33.8

Table 3: Percent of word types in a held out portion of the training data which are translated correctly by our bilingual lexicon induction technique. Evaluation is over the top-1 and top-10 outputs in the ranked lists for each source word.

the English side of the training data to train a language model. Using a language model trained on a larger corpus (e.g. the English side of our comparable corpora) may yield better results, but such an improvement is orthogonal to the focus of this work. Throughout our experiments, we use the batch version of MIRA (Cherry and Foster, 2012) for tuning the feature set.[7] We rerun tuning for all experimental conditions and report results averaged over three tuning runs (Clark et al., 2011).

Our baseline uses the bilingually extracted phrase pairs and standard translation probability features. We supplement it with the top ranked translation for each OOV to improve coverage (+ OOV Trans) and with additional features to improve accuracy (+Features). In Section 4.2, we make each modification separately and then together. Then we present additional experiments where we induce translations for low frequency words, in addition to OOVs (4.3), append top-k translations (4.4), vary the amount of training data used to induce the baseline model (4.5), and vary the amount of comparable corpora used to estimate features and induce translations (4.6).

4.2 Results

Before presenting end-to-end MT results, we examine the performance of the supervised bilingual lexicon induction technique that we use for translating OOVs. In Table 3, top-1 accuracy is the percent of source language words in a held out portion of the training data[8] for which the highest ranked English candidate is a correct translation.[9] Performance is lowest for Tamil and highest for Hindi. For all languages, top-10 accuracy is much higher than the top-1 accuracy. In Section 4.4, we explore appending the top-k translations for OOV words to our model instead of just the top-1.

Table 4 shows our results adding OOV translations, adding features, and then both. Additional translation features alone, which improve our models' accuracy, increase BLEU scores between 0.18 (Bengali) and 0.60 (Malayalam) points.

Adding OOV translations makes a big difference for some languages, such as Bengali and Urdu, and almost no difference for others, like Malayalam and Tamil. The OOV rate (Table 1) is low in the Malayalam dataset and high in the Tamil dataset. However, as Table 3 shows, the translation induction accuracy is low for both. Since few of the supplemental translations are correct, we don't observe BLEU gains. In contrast, induction accuracies for the other languages are higher, OOV rates are substantial, and we do observe moderate BLEU improvements by supplementing phrase tables with OOV translations.

In order to compute the *potential* BLEU gains that we could realize by correctly translating all OOV words (achieving 100% accuracy in Table 3), we perform an oracle experiment. We use automatic word alignments over the test sets to identify correct translations and append those to the phrase tables.[10] The results, in Table 4, show possible gains between 4.3 (Telugu and Bengali) and 0 (Malayalam) BLEU points above the baseline. Not surprisingly, the possible gain for Malayalam, which has a very low OOV rate, is very low. Our *+OOV Trans.* model gains between 0% (Tamil) and 38% (Urdu) of the potential improvement.

Using comparable corpora to improve both accuracy (+Features) and coverage (+OOV Trans.) results in translations that are better than applying either technique alone for five of the six languages. BLEU gains range from 0.48 (Bengali) to 1.39 (Urdu). We attribute the particularly good Urdu performance to the relatively large comparable corpora (Table 2). As a result, we have already begun to expand our web crawls for all languages. In Section 4.6, we present results varying the amount of Urdu-English comparable corpora used to induce translations and estimate additional features.

Table 4 also shows the Hiero (Chiang, 2005) and SAMT (Zollmann and Venugopal, 2006) results that Post et al. (2012) report for the same

[7]We experimented with MERT and PRO as well but saw consistently better baseline performance using batch MIRA.

[8]Described in Section 3.2. We retrain with all training data for MT experiments.

[9]Post et al. (2012) gathered up to six translations for each source word, so some have multiple correct translations

[10]Because the automatic word alignments are noisy, this oracle is conservative.

Experiment	Tamil BLEU	Tamil Diff.	Telugu BLEU	Telugu Diff.	Bengali BLEU	Bengali Diff.	Malayalam BLEU	Malayalam Diff.	Hindi BLEU	Hindi Diff.	Urdu BLEU	Urdu Diff.
Baseline	9.45		11.72		12.07		13.55		15.01		20.39	
+Features	9.77	+0.32	11.96	+0.24	12.25	+0.18	14.15	+0.60	15.34	+0.33	20.97	+0.58
+OOV Trans.	9.45	0.00	12.20	+0.48	**12.74**	+0.67	13.65	+0.10	15.59	+0.58	21.30	+0.91
+Feats & OOV	**9.98**	+0.53	**12.25**	+0.53	12.55	+0.48	**14.18**	+0.63	**16.08**	+1.07	**21.78**	+1.39
OOV Oracle	12.32	+2.87	16.04	+4.32	16.41	+4.34	13.55	0.00	17.72	+2.71	22.80	2.41
Hiero	9.81		12.46		12.72		13.72		15.53		19.53	
SAMT	9.85		12.61		13.53		14.28		17.29		20.99	

Table 4: BLEU performance gains that target coverage (+OOV Trans.) and accuracy (+Features), and both (+Feats & OOV). OOV oracle uses OOV translations from automatic word alignments. Hiero and SAMT results are reported in Post et al. (2012).

datasets. Both syntax-based models outperform the phrase-based MT baseline for each language except Urdu, where the phrase-based model outperforms Hiero. Here, we extend a phrase-based rather than a syntax-based system because it is simpler. However, our improvements may also apply to syntactic models (future work). Because our efforts have focused on the accuracy and coverage of translation pairs and have not addressed reordering or syntax, we expect that combining them with an SAMT grammar will result in state-of-the art performance.

4.3 Translations of Low Frequency Words

Given the positive results in Section 4.2, we hypothesize that mining translations for low frequency words, in addition to OOV words, may improve accuracy. For source words which only appear a few times in the parallel training text, the bilingually extracted translations in the standard phrase table are likely to be inaccurate. Therefore, we perform additional experiments varying the minimum source word training data frequency for which we induce additional translations. That is, if $freq(w_{src}) \leq M$, we induce a new translation for it and include that translation in our phrase table. Note that in the results presented in Table 4, $M = 0$. In these experiments, we include our additional phrase table features estimated over comparable corpora and hope that these scores will assist the model in choosing among multiple translation options for low frequency words, one or more of which is extracted bilingually and one of which is induced using comparable corpora. Table 5 shows the results when we vary M. As before, we average BLEU scores over three tuning runs.

In general, modest BLEU score gains are made as we supplement our phrase-based models with induced translations of low frequency words. The highest performance is achieved when M is between 5 and 50, depending on language. The largest gains are 0.5 and 0.3 BLEU points for Bengali and Urdu, respectively, at $M = 25$. This is not surprising; we also saw the largest relative gains for those two languages when we added OOV translations to our baseline model. With the addition of low frequency translations, our highest performing Urdu model achieves a BLEU score that is 1.7 points higher than the baseline.

Language	Base.	M: trans added for $freq(w_{src}) \leq M$: 0	1	5	10	25	50
Tamil	9.5	10.0	9.9	10.2	10.2	9.9	**10.2**
Telugu	11.7	12.3	12.2	12.3	**12.4**	12.3	11.9
Bengali	12.1	12.6	12.8	13.0	12.9	**13.1**	13.0
Malayalam	13.6	14.2	14.1	**14.2**	14.2	13.9	13.9
Hindi	15.0	16.1	16.1	16.2	**16.2**	16.0	15.8
Urdu	20.4	21.8	21.8	21.8	21.9	**22.1**	21.8

Table 5: Varying minimum parallel training data frequency of source words for which new translations are induced and included in the phrase-based model. In all cases, the top-1 induced translation is added to the phrase table and features estimated over comparable corpora are included (i.e. +Feats & Trans model).

In different data conditions, inducing translations for low frequency words may result in better or worse performance. For example, the size of the training set impacts the quality of automatic word alignments, which in turn impacts the reliability of translations of low frequency words. However, the experiments detailed here suggest that including induced translations of low frequency words will not hurt performance and may improve it.

4.4 Appending Top-K Translations

So far we have only added the top-1 induced translation for OOV and low frequency source words to our phrase-based model. However, the bilingual lexicon induction results in Table 3 show that accuracies in the top-10 ranked translations are, on average, nearly twice the top-1 accuracies. Here, we explore adding the top-k induced translations. We hope that our additional phrase table features estimated over comparable corpora will enable the

Language	Base.	k: top-k translations added				
		1	3	5	10	25
Tamil	9.5	10.0	**10.0**	9.8	10.0	10.0
Telugu	11.7	**12.3**	11.7	11.9	11.7	11.6
Bengali	12.1	12.6	12.6	12.6	12.7	**12.8**
Malayalam	13.6	14.2	14.2	14.2	**14.2**	14.1
Hindi	15.0	**16.1**	16.0	15.9	15.9	15.9
Urdu	20.4	21.8	**21.8**	21.7	21.5	21.6

Table 6: Adding top-k induced translations for source language OOV words, varying *k*. Features estimated over comparable corpora are included (i.e. +Feats & Trans model). The highest BLEU score for each language is highlighted. In many cases differences are less than 0.1 BLEU.

decoder to correctly choose between the k translation options. We induce translations for OOV words only ($M = 0$) and include all comparable corpora features.

Table 6 shows performance as we append the top-k ranked translations for each OOV word and vary k. With the exception of Bengali, using a k greater than 1 does not increase performance. In the case of Bengali, and additional 0.2 BLEU is observed when the top-25 translations are appended. In contrast, we see performance decrease substantially for other languages (0.7 BLEU for Telugu and 0.2 for Urdu) when the top-25 translations are used. Therefore, we conclude that, in general, the models do not sufficiently distinguish good from bad translations when we append more than just the top-1. Although using a k greater than 1 means that more correct translations are in the phrase table, it also increases the number of possible outputs over which the decoder must search.

4.5 Learning Curves over Parallel Data

In the experiments above, we only evaluated our methods for improving the accuracy and coverage of models trained on small amounts of bitext using the full parallel training corpora released by Post et al. (2012). Here, we apply the same techniques but vary the amount of parallel data in order to generate learning curves. Figure 2 shows learning cures for all six languages. In all cases, results are averaged over three tuning runs. We sample both parallel sentences and dictionary entries.

All six learning curves show similar trends. In all experimental conditions, BLEU performance increases approximately linearly with the log of the amount of training data. Additionally, supplementing the baseline with OOV translations improves performance more than supplementing the baseline with additional phrase table scores based on comparable corpora. However, in most cases, supplementing the baseline with both translations and features improves performance more than either alone. Performance gains are greatest when very little training data is used. The Urdu learning curve shows the most gains as well as the cleanest trends across training data amounts. As before, we attribute this to the relatively large comparable corpora available for Urdu.

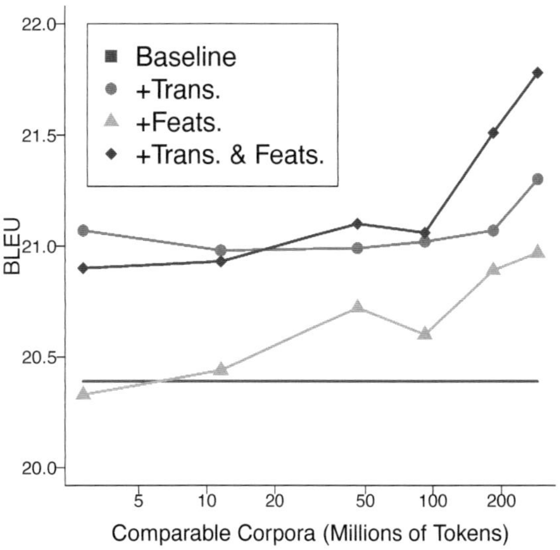

Figure 3: English to Urdu translation results using varying amounts of comparable corpora to estimate features and induce translations.

4.6 Learning Curves over Comparable Corpora

In our final experiment, we consider the effect of the amount of *comparable corpora* that we use to estimate features and induce translations. We present learning curves for Urdu-English because we have the largest amount of comparable corpora for that pair. We use the full amount of parallel data to train a baseline model, and then we randomly sample varying amounts of our Urdu-English comparable corpora. Sampling is done separately for the web crawl and Wikipedia comparable corpora. Figure 3 shows the results. As before, results are averaged over three tuning runs.

The phrase table features estimated over comparable corpora improve end-to-end MT performance more with increasing amounts of comparable corpora. In contrast, the amount of comparable corpora used to induce OOV translations does not impact the performance of the resulting MT system as much. The difference may be due

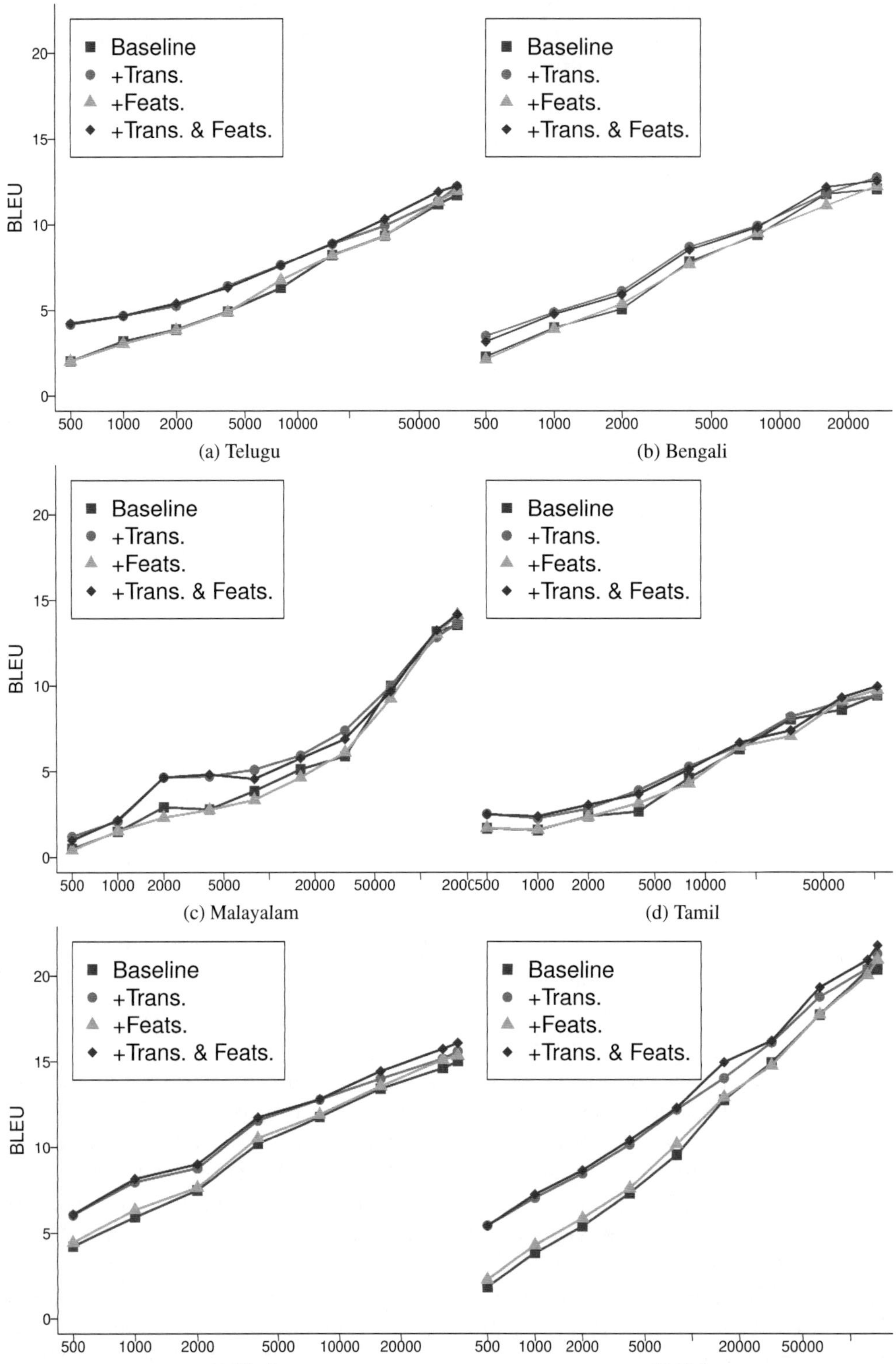

(a) Telugu (b) Bengali

(c) Malayalam (d) Tamil

(e) Hindi (f) Urdu

Figure 2: Comparison of learning curves over lines of parallel training data for four SMT systems: our baseline phrase-based model (baseline), model that supplements the baseline with translations of OOV words induced using our supervised bilingual lexicon induction framework (+Trans), model that supplements the baseline with additional phrase table features estimated over comparable corpora (+Feats), and a system that supplements the baseline with both OOV translations and additional features (+Trans & Feats).

to the fact that data sparsity is always more of an issue when estimating features over *phrase pairs* than when estimating features over *word pairs* because phrases appear less frequently than words in monolingual corpora. Our comparable corpora features are estimated over phrase pairs while translations are only induced for OOV words, not phrases. So, it makes sense that the former would benefit more from larger comparable corpora.

5 Conclusion

As Post et al. (2012) showed, it is reasonable to assume a small parallel corpus for training an SMT model even in a low resource setting. We have used comparable corpora to improve the accuracy and coverage of phrase-based MT models built using small bilingual corpora for six low resource languages. We have shown that our methods improve BLEU score performance independently and that their combined impact is nearly additive. Additionally, our results show that adding induced translations of low frequency words improves performance beyond what is achieved by inducing translations for OOVs alone. Finally, our results show that our techniques improve relative performance most when very little parallel training data is available.

6 Acknowledgements

This material is based on research sponsored by DARPA under contract HR0011-09-1-0044 and by the Johns Hopkins University Human Language Technology Center of Excellence. The views and conclusions contained in this publication are those of the authors and should not be interpreted as representing official policies or endorsements of DARPA or the U.S. Government.

References

Sadaf Abdul-Rauf and Holger Schwenk. 2009. On the use of comparable corpora to improve smt performance. In *Proceedings of the Conference of the European Association for Computational Linguistics (EACL)*.

Vamshi Ambati. 2011. *Active Learning for Machine Translation in Scarce Data Scenarios*. Ph.D. thesis, Carnegie Mellon University.

Colin Cherry and George Foster. 2012. Batch tuning strategies for statistical machine translation. In *Proceedings of the Conference of the North American Chapter of the Association for Computational Linguistics (NAACL)*.

David Chiang. 2005. A hierarchical phrase-based model for statistical machine translation. In *Proceedings of the Conference of the Association for Computational Linguistics (ACL)*.

Jonathan H. Clark, Chris Dyer, Alon Lavie, and Noah A. Smith. 2011. Better hypothesis testing for statistical machine translation: controlling for optimizer instability. In *Proceedings of the Conference of the Association for Computational Linguistics (ACL)*.

Hal Daumé, III and Jagadeesh Jagarlamudi. 2011. Domain adaptation for machine translation by mining unseen words. In *Proceedings of the Conference of the Association for Computational Linguistics (ACL)*.

Qing Dou and Kevin Knight. 2012. Large scale decipherment for out-of-domain machine translation. In *Proceedings of the Joint Conference on Empirical Methods in Natural Language Processing and Computational Natural Language Learning*.

Pascale Fung and Lo Yuen Yee. 1998. An IR approach for translating new words from nonparallel, comparable texts. In *Proceedings of the Conference of the Association for Computational Linguistics (ACL)*.

Aria Haghighi, Percy Liang, Taylor Berg-Kirkpatrick, and Dan Klein. 2008. Learning bilingual lexicons from monolingual corpora. In *Proceedings of the Conference of the Association for Computational Linguistics (ACL)*.

Fei Huang, Ying Zhang, and Stephan Vogel. 2005. Mining key phrase translations from web corpora. In *Proceedings of the Conference on Empirical Methods in Natural Language Processing (EMNLP)*.

Ann Irvine and Chris Callison-Burch. 2013. Supervised bilingual lexicon induction with multiple monolingual signals. In *Proceedings of the Conference of the North American Chapter of the Association for Computational Linguistics (NAACL)*.

Alexandre Klementiev and Dan Roth. 2006. Weakly supervised named entity transliteration and discovery from multilingual comparable corpora. In *Proceedings of the Conference of the Association for Computational Linguistics (ACL)*.

Alex Klementiev, Ann Irvine, Chris Callison-Burch, and David Yarowsky. 2012. Toward statistical machine translation without parallel corpora. In *Proceedings of the Conference of the European Association for Computational Linguistics (EACL)*.

Philipp Koehn and Kevin Knight. 2002. Learning a translation lexicon from monolingual corpora. In *ACL Workshop on Unsupervised Lexical Acquisition*.

Philipp Koehn, Franz Joseph Och, and Daniel Marcu. 2003. Statistical phrase-based translation. In *Proceedings of the Conference of the North American Chapter of the Association for Computational Linguistics (NAACL)*.

Philipp Koehn, Hieu Hoang, Alexandra Birch, Chris Callison-Burch, Marcello Federico, Nicola Bertoldi, Brooke Cowan, Wade Shen, Christine Moran, Richard Zens, Chris Dyer, Ondrej Bojar, Alexandra Constantin, and Evan Herbst. 2007. Moses: Open source toolkit for statistical machine translation. In *Proceedings of the Conference of the Association for Computational Linguistics (ACL)*.

Prasanth Kolachina, Nicola Cancedda, Marc Dymetman, and Sriram Venkatapathy. 2012. Prediction of learning curves in machine translation. In *Proceedings of the Conference of the Association for Computational Linguistics (ACL)*.

Mausam, Stephen Soderland, Oren Etzioni, Daniel S. Weld, Kobi Reiter, Michael Skinner, Marcus Sammer, and Jeff Bilmes. 2010. Panlingual lexical translation via probabilistic inference. *Artificial Intelligence*, 174:619–637, June.

David Mimno, Hanna Wallach, Jason Naradowsky, David Smith, and Andrew McCallum. 2009. Polylingual topic models. In *Proceedings of the Conference on Empirical Methods in Natural Language Processing (EMNLP)*.

Christof Monz and Bonnie J. Dorr. 2005. Iterative translation disambiguation for cross-language information retrieval. In *Proceedings of the Conference on Research and Developments in Information Retrieval (SIGIR)*.

Dragos Munteanu and Daniel Marcu. 2006. Extracting parallel sub-sentential fragments from non-parallel corpora. In *Proceedings of the Conference of the Association for Computational Linguistics (ACL)*.

Malte Nuhn, Arne Mauser, and Hermann Ney. 2012. Deciphering foreign language by combining language models and context vectors. In *Proceedings of the Conference of the Association for Computational Linguistics (ACL)*.

Matt Post, Chris Callison-Burch, and Miles Osborne. 2012. Constructing parallel corpora for six indian languages via crowdsourcing. In *Proceedings of the Workshop on Statistical Machine Translation (WMT)*.

Reinhard Rapp. 1995. Identifying word translations in non-parallel texts. In *Proceedings of the Conference of the Association for Computational Linguistics (ACL)*.

Reinhard Rapp. 1999. Automatic identification of word translations from unrelated English and German corpora. In *Proceedings of the Conference of the Association for Computational Linguistics (ACL)*.

Sujith Ravi and Kevin Knight. 2011. Deciphering foreign language. In *Proceedings of the Conference of the Association for Computational Linguistics (ACL)*.

Charles Schafer and David Yarowsky. 2002. Inducing translation lexicons via diverse similarity measures and bridge languages. In *Proceedings of the Conference on Natural Language Learning (CoNLL)*.

Charles Schafer. 2006. *Translation Discovery Using Diverse Similarity Measures*. Ph.D. thesis, Johns Hopkins University.

Jason R. Smith, Chris Quirk, and Kristina Toutanova. 2010. Extracting parallel sentences from comparable corpora using document level alignment. In *Proceedings of the Conference of the North American Chapter of the Association for Computational Linguistics (NAACL)*.

Jason Smith, Herve Saint-Amand, Magdalena Plamada, Philipp Koehn, Chris Callison-Burch, and Adam Lopez. 2013. Dirt cheap web-scale parallel text from the common crawl. In *Proceedings of the Conference of the Association for Computational Linguistics (ACL)*.

Jakob Uszkoreit, Jay M. Ponte, Ashok C. Popat, and Moshe Dubiner. 2010. Large scale parallel document mining for machine translation. In *Proceedings of the International Conference on Computational Linguistics (COLING)*.

Omar F. Zaidan and Chris Callison-Burch. 2011. Crowdsourcing translation: Professional quality from non-professionals. In *Proceedings of the Conference of the Association for Computational Linguistics (ACL)*.

Andreas Zollmann and Ashish Venugopal. 2006. Syntax augmented machine translation via chart parsing. In *Proceedings of the Workshop on Statistical Machine Translation (WMT)*.

Generating English Determiners in Phrase-Based Translation with Synthetic Translation Options

Yulia Tsvetkov **Chris Dyer** **Lori Levin** **Archna Bhatia**
Language Technologies Institute
Carnegie Mellon University
Pittspurgh, PA, 15213, USA
{ytsvetko, cdyer, lsl, archna}@cs.cmu.edu

Abstract

We propose a technique for improving the quality of phrase-based translation systems by creating synthetic translation options—phrasal translations that are generated by auxiliary translation and post-editing processes—to augment the default phrase inventory learned from parallel data. We apply our technique to the problem of producing English determiners when translating from Russian and Czech, languages that lack definiteness morphemes. Our approach augments the English side of the phrase table using a classifier to predict where English articles might plausibly be added or removed, and then we decode as usual. Doing so, we obtain significant improvements in quality relative to a standard phrase-based baseline and to a to post-editing complete translations with the classifier.

1 Introduction

Phrase-based translation works as follows. A set of candidate translations for an input sentence is created by matching contiguous spans of the input against an inventory of phrasal translations, reordering them into a target-language appropriate order, and choosing the best one according to a discriminative model that combines features of the phrases used, reordering patterns, and target language model (Koehn et al., 2003). This relatively simple approach to translation can be remarkably effective, and, since its introduction, it has been the basis for further innovations, including developing better models for distinguishing the good translations from bad ones (Chiang, 2012; Gimpel and Smith, 2012; Cherry and Foster, 2012; Eidelman et al., 2013), improving the identification of phrase pairs in parallel data (DeNero et al., 2008; DeNero and Klein, 2010), and formal generalizations to gapped rules and rich nonterminal types (Chiang, 2007; Galley et al., 2006). This paper proposes a different mechanism for improving phrase-based translation: the use of **synthetic translation options** to supplement the standard phrasal inventory used in phrase-based translation systems.

In the following, we argue that phrase tables acquired in usual way will be expected to have gaps in their coverage in certain language pairs and that supplementing these with synthetic translation options is *a priori* preferable to alternative techniques, such as post processing, for generalizing beyond the translation pairs observable in training data (§2). As a case study, we consider the problem of producing English definite/indefinite articles (*the*, *a*, and *an*) when translating from Russian and Czech, two languages that lack overt definiteness morphemes (§3). We develop a classifier that predicts the presence and absence of English articles (§4). This classifier is used to generate synthetic translation options that are used to augment phrase tables used the usual way (§5). We evaluate their performance relative to post-processing approach and to a baseline phrase-based system, finding that synthetic translation options reliably outperform the other approaches (§6). We then discuss how our approach relates to previous work (§7) and conclude by discussing further applications of our technique (§8).

2 Why Synthetic Translation Options?

Before turning to the problem of generating English articles, we give arguments for why synthetic translation options are a useful extension of standard phrase-based translation approaches, and why this technique might be better than some alternative proposals that been made for generalizing beyond translation examples directly observable in the training data.

In language pairs that are typologically similar (i.e., when both languages lexicalize the same kinds of semantic and syntactic information), words and phrases map relatively directly from source to target languages, and the standard approach to learning phrase pairs is quite effective.[1] However, in language pairs in which individual source language words have many different possible translations (e.g., when the target language word could have many different inflections or could be surrounded by different function words that have no direct correspondence in the source language), we can expect the standard phrasal inventory to be incomplete, except when very large quantities of parallel data are available or for very frequent words. There simply will not be enough examples from which to learn the ideal set of translation options. Therefore, since phrase based translation can only generate input/output word pairs that were directly observed in the training corpus, the decoder's only hope for producing a good output is to find a fluent, meaning-preserving translation using incomplete translation lexicons. Synthetic translation option generation seeks to fill these gaps using secondary generation processes that produce possible phrase translation alternatives that are not directly extractable from the training data. We hypothesize that by filling in gaps in the translation options, discriminative translation models will be more effective (leading to better translation quality).

The creation of synthetic translation options can be understood as a kind of translation or post-editing of phrasal units/translations. This raises a question: if we have the ability to post-edit a phrasal translation or retranslate a source phrase so as to fill in gaps in the phrasal inventory, we should be able to use the same technique to translate the sentence; why not do this? While the effectiveness of this approach will ultimately be assessed empirically, translation option generation is appealing because the translation option synthesizer need not produce only single-best guesses—

[1]When translating from a language with a richer lexical inventory to a simpler one, approximate matching or backing off to (e.g.) morphologically simpler forms likewise reliably produces good translations.

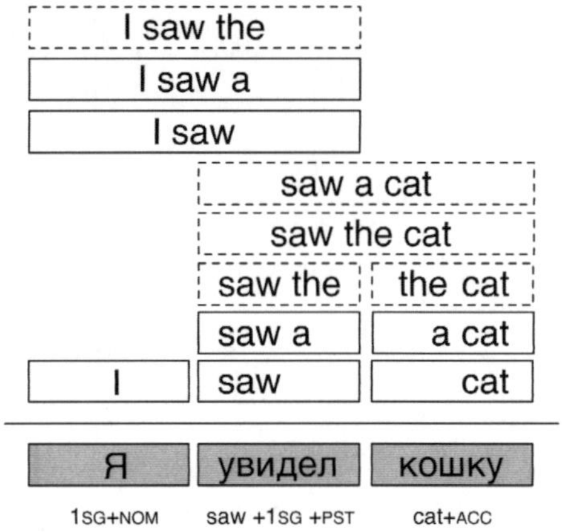

Figure 1: Russian-English phrase-based translation example. Since Russian lacks a definiteness morpheme the determiners *a*, *the* must be part of a translation option containing увидел or кошку in order to be present in the right place in the English output. Translation options that are in dashed boxes *should* exist but were not observed in the training data. This work seeks to produce such missing translation options *synthetically*.

if multiple possibilities appear to be equally good (say, multiple inflections of a translated lemma), then multiple translation options may be synthesized. Ultimately, of course, the global translation model must select one translation for every phrase it uses, but the decoder will have access to global information that it can use to pick better translation options.

3 Case Study: English Definite Articles

We now turn to a translation problem that we will use to assess the value of synthetic translation options: generating English in/definite articles when translating from Russian.

Definiteness is a semantic property of noun phrases that expresses information such as identifiability, specificity, familiarity and uniqueness (Lyons, 1999). In English, it is expressed through the use of article determiners and non-article determiners. Although languages may express definiteness through such morphemes, many languages use alternative mechanisms. For example they may use noncanonical word orders (Mohanan, 1994)[2] or different constructions such as existentials, differential object marking (Aissen, 2003), and the *ba* (把) construction in Chinese

[2]See pp. 11–12 for an example in Hindi, a language without articles.

(Chen, 2004). While these languages lack articles, they may use demonstratives and the quantifier *one* to emphasize definiteness and indefiniteness, respectively.

Russian and Czech are examples of languages that use non-lexical means to express definiteness. As such, in Russian to English translation systems, we expect that most Russian nouns should have at least three translation options—the bare noun, the noun preceded by *the*, and the noun preceded *a/an*.

Fig. 1 illustrates how the definiteness mismatch between Russian and English can result in "gaps" in the phrasal inventory learned from a relatively large parallel corpus. The Russian input should translate (depending on context) as either *I saw a cat* or *I saw the cat*; however, the phrase table we learned is only able to generate the former.[3]

4 Predicting English Definite Articles

Although English articles express semantic content, their use is largely predictable in context, both for native English speakers and for automated systems (Knight and Chander, 1994).[4] In this section we describe a classifier that uses local contextual features to predict whether an article belongs in a particular position in a sequence of words, and if so, whether it is definite or indefinite (the form of the indefinite article is deterministic given the pronunciation of the following word).

4.1 Model

The classifier takes an English word sequence $\mathbf{w} = \langle w_1, w_2, \ldots, w_{|\mathbf{w}|}\rangle$ with missing articles and an index i and predicts whether no article, a definite article, or an indefinite article should appear before w_i. We parameterize the classifier as a multiclass logistic regression:

$$p(y \mid \mathbf{w}, i) \propto \exp \sum_j \lambda_j h_j(y, \mathbf{w}, i),$$

where $h_j(\cdot)$ are feature functions, λ_j are the corresponding weights, and $y \in \{\mathtt{D}, \mathtt{I}, \mathtt{N}\}$ refer, respectively, to the outputs: definite article, indefinite article, and no article.[5]

4.2 Features

The English article system is extremely complex (as non-native English speakers will surely know!): in addition to a general placement rule that articles must precede a noun or its modifiers in an NP, multiple other factors can also affect article selection, including countability of the head noun, syntactic properties of an adjective modifying a noun (superlative, ordinal), discourse factors, general knowledge, etc. In this section, we define morphosyntactic features aimed at reflecting basic grammatical rules, we define statistical, semantic and shallow lexical features to capture additional regular and idiosyncratic usages of definite and indefinite articles in English. Below we provide brief details of the features and their motivation.

Lexical. Because training data can be constructed inexpensively (from any unannotated English corpus), n-gram indicator features, such as $[\![w_{i-1} y w_i w_{i+1} = \texttt{with}\ y\ \texttt{lot of}]\!]$, can be estimated reliably and capture construction-specific article use.

Morphosyntactic. We used part-of-speech (POS) tags produced by the Stanford POS tagger (Toutanova and Manning, 2000) to capture general article patterns. These are relevant features in the prediction of articles as we observe certain constraints regarding the use of articles in the neighborhood of certain POS tags. For example, we do not expect to predict an article following an adjective (JJ).

Semantic. We extract further information indicating whether a named entity, as identified by the Stanford NE Recognizer (Finkel et al., 2005) begins at w_i. These features are relevant as there

[3]The phrase table for this example was extracted from the WMT 2013 shared task training data consisting of 1.2M sentence pairs.

[4]An interesting contribution of this work is a discussion on lower and upper bounds that can be achieved by native English speakers in predicting determiners. 67% is a lower bound, obtained by guessing *the* for every instance. The upper bound was obtained experimentally, and was measured on noun phrases (NP) without context, in a context of 4 words (2 before and 2 after NP), and given full context. Human subjects achieved an accuracy of 94-96% given full context, 83-88% for NPs in a context of 4 words, and 79-80% for NPs without context. Since in the current state-of-the-art building an automated determiners prediction in a full context (representing meaning computationally) is not a feasible task, we view 83-88% accuracy as our goal, and 88% as an upper bound for our method.

[5]Realization of the classes `D` and `N` as lexical items is straightforward. To convert `I` into *a* or *an*, we use the CMU pronouncing dictionary (`http://www.speech.cs.cmu.edu/cgi-bin/cmudict`) and select *an* if w_i starts with a phonetic vowel.

is, in general, a constraint on the co-occurrence of articles with named entities which can help us predict the use of articles in such constructions. For example, proper nouns do not tend to co-occur with articles in English. Although there are some proper nouns that have an article included in them, such as *the Netherlands*, *the United States of America*, but these are fixed expressions and the model is easily able to capture such cases with lexical features.

Statistical. Statistical features capture probability of co-occurrences of a sample with each of the determiner classes, e.g., for $w_{i-1}yw_i$ we collect probabilities of $w_{i-1}\mathtt{I}w_i$, $w_{i-1}\mathtt{D}w_i$, and $w_{i-1}\mathtt{N}w_i$.[6]

4.3 Training and evaluation

We employ the `creg` regression modeling framework to train a ternary logistic regression classifier.[7] All features were computed for the target-side of the Russian-English TED corpus (Cettolo et al., 2012); from 117,527 sentences we removed 5K sentences used as tuning and test sets in the MT system. We extract statistical features from monolingual English corpora released for WMT-11 (Callison-Burch et al., 2011).

In the training corpus there are 65,075 `I` instances, 114,571 `D` instances, and 2,435,287 `N` instances. To create a balanced training set we randomly sample 65K instances from each set of collected instances.[8] This training set of feature vectors has 142,604 features and 285,210 parameters. To minimize the number of free parameters in our model we use ℓ_1 regularization. We perform 10-fold cross validation experiments with various feature combinations, evaluating the classifier accuracy for all classes and for each class independently. The performance of the classifier on individual classes and consolidated results for all classes are listed in Table 1.

We observe that morphosyntactic and lexical features are highly significant, reducing the error rate of statistical features by 25%. A combination of morphosyntactic, lexical, and statistical features is also helpful, reducing 13% more errors. Semantic features do not contribute to the classifier accuracy (we believe, mainly due to the feature sparsity).

Feature combination	All	I	D	N
Statistical	0.80	0.76	0.79	0.87
Lexical	0.82	0.79	0.80	0.87
Morphosyntactic	0.75	0.71	0.64	0.86
Semantic	0.35	0.99	0.02	0.04
Statistical+Lexical	0.85	0.83	0.82	0.89
+ Morphosyntactic	**0.87**	0.86	0.83	0.92
+ Semantic	0.87	0.86	0.83	0.92

Table 1: 10-fold cross validation accuracy of the classifier over all and by class.

5 Experimental Setup

Our experimental workflow includes the following steps. First, we select a phrase table PT_{source} from which we generate synthetic phrases. For each phrase pair $\langle f, e\rangle$ in PT_{source} we generate n synthetic variants of the target side phrase e which we then append to $PT_{baseline}$. We annotate both the original and synthetic phrases with additional translation features in $PT_{baseline}$.

For this language pair, we have several options for how to construct PT_{source}. The most straightforward way is to extract the phrasal inventory as usual; a second option is to extract phrases from training data from which definite articles have been removed (since we will rely on the classifier to reinsert them where they belong).

To synthesize phrases, we employ two different techniques: LM-based and classifier-based. We use a LM for one- or two-word phrases or an auxiliary classifier for longer phrases and create a new phrase in which we insert, remove or substitute an article between each adjacent pair of words in the original phrase. Such distinction between short and longer phrases has clear motivation: phrases without context may allow alternative, equally plausible options for article selection, therefore we can just rely on a LM, trained on large monolingual corpora, to identify phrases unobserved in MT training corpus. Longer context restricts determiners usage and statistical model decisions are less prone to generating ungrammatical synthetic phrases.

LM-based method is applied to phrases shorter than three words. These phrases are numerous, roughly 20% of a phrase table, and extracted from

[6] Although statistical features are *de rigeur* in NLP, they are arguably justified for this problem on linguistic grounds since human subjects use frequency-based in addition to their grammatical knowledge. For example, we say *He is at school* rather than *He is at the school*, but Americans say *He is in the hospital* while UK English speakers might prefer *He is in hospital*.

[7] https://github.com/redpony/creg

[8] Preliminary experiments indicated that the excess of `N` labels resulted in poor performance.

many sites in the training data. For each short (target) phrase we add all possible alternative entries observed in the LM and not observed in the original translation model. For example, for a short target phrase *a cat* we extract *the cat*.

We apply an auxiliary classifier to longer phrases, containing three or more words. Based on the classifier prediction, we use the maximally probable class to insert, remove or substitute an article between each adjacent pair of words in the original phrase. Synthetic phrases are generated by linguistically-informed features and can introduce alternative grammatically-correct translations of source phrases by adding or removing existing articles (since the English article selection in a local context is often ambiguous and not categorical). We add a synthetic phrase only if the phrase pair not observed in the original model.

We compare two possible applications of a classifier: one-pass and iterative prediction. With one-pass prediction we decide on the prediction for each position independently of other decisions. With iterative update we adopt the best first (greedy) strategy, selecting in each iteration the update-location in which the classifier obtains highest confidence score. In each iteration we incorporate a prediction in a target phrase, and in the next iteration the best first decision is made on an updated phrase. Iterative prediction stops when no updates are introduced.

Synthetic phrases are added to a phrase table with the five standard phrasal translation features that were found in the source phrase, and with several new features. First, we add a boolean feature indicating the origin of a phrase: synthetic or original. Second, we experiment with a posterior probability of a classifier averaged over all locations where it could be extracted from the training data. The next feature is derived from this score: it is a boolean feature indicating a confidence of the classifier: the feature value is 1 iff the average classifier score is higher than some threshold.

Consider again a phrase *I saw a cat* discussed in Section 1. Synthetic entry generation from the original phrase table entry is illustrated in Figure 2.

6 Translation Results

We now review the results of experiments using synthetic translation options in a machine translation system. We use the Moses toolkit (Koehn et al., 2007) to train a baseline phrase-based SMT system. Each configuration we compare has a different phrase table, with synthetic phrases generated with best-first or iterative strategies, from a phrase table with- or without-determiners, with variable number of translation features. To verify that system improvement is consistent, and is not a result of optimizer instability (Clark et al., 2011), we replicate each experimental setup three times, and then estimate the translation quality of the median MT system using the MultEval toolkit.[9]

The corpus is the same as in Section 4.3: the training part contains 112,527 sentences from Russian-English TED corpus, randomly sampled 3K sentences are used for tuning and a disjoint set of 2K sentences is used for test. We lowercase both sides, and use Stanford CoreNLP[10] tools to tokenize the corpora. We employ SRILM toolkit (Stolcke, 2002) to linearly interpolate the target side of the training corpus with the WMT English corpus, optimizing towards the MT tuning set. This LM is used in all experiments.

The rest of this section is organized as follows. First, we compare two approaches to the determiners classifier application. Then, we provide detailed description of experiments with synthetic phrases. We evaluate various aspects of synthetic phrases generation and summarize all the results in Table 3. In Table 5 we show examples of improved translations.

Classifier application: one-pass vs. iterative. First, as an intrinsic evaluation of the prediction strategy we remove definite and indefinite articles from the reference translations (2K test sentences) and then employ the determiners classifier to reproduce the original sentences. In Table 2 we report on the word error rate (WER) derived from the Levenshtein distance between the original sentences and the sentences (1) without articles, (2) with articles recovered using one-pass prediction, and (3) articles recovered using iterative prediction. The WER is averaged over all test sentences. Both one-pass and iterative approaches are effective in the task of determiners prediction, reducing the number of errors by 44%. The iterative approach yields slightly lower WER, hence we employ the iterative prediction in the future experiments with synthetic phrases.

[9] https://github.com/jhclark/multeval

[10] http://nlp.stanford.edu/software/corenlp.shtml

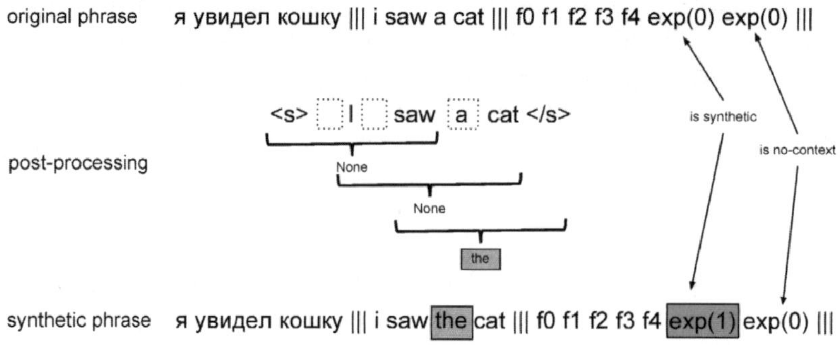

Figure 2: Synthetic entry generation example. The original parallel phrase has two additional boolean features (set to false) indicating that this is not a synthetic phrase and not a short phrase. We apply our determiners classifier to predict an article at each location marked with a dashed box. Based on a classifier prediction we derive a new phrase *I saw the cat*. Since corresponding parallel entry is not in the original phrase table, we set the synthetic indicator feature to 1.

Post-processing	WER
None	5.6%
One-pass	3.2%
Iterative	3.1%

Table 2: WER (lower is better) of reference translations without articles and of post-processed reference translations. Both one-pass and iterative approaches are effective in the task of determiners prediction.

MT output post-processing. We then evaluate the post-processing strategy directly on the MT output. We experiment with one-pass and iterative post-processing of two variants of the baseline system outputs: original output and the output without articles (we remove the articles prior to post-processing). The results are listed in Table 3. Interestingly, we do not obtain any improvements applying the determiners classifier in a conventional way of a MT output post-processing. It is the combination of linguistically-motivated features with synthetic phrases that contribute to the best performance.

LM-based synthetic phrases. As discussed above, LM-based (short) phrases are shorter than 3 tokens and their synthetic variants contain same words with articles inserted or deleted between each adjacent pair of words. The phrase table of the baseline system contains 2,441,678 phrase pairs. There are 518,453 original short phrases, and our technique yields 842,252 new synthetic entries which we append to the baseline phrase table. Table 3 shows the evaluation of the median SMT system (derived from three systems) with short phrases. In these systems the five phrasal translation features are the same as in the baseline systems. Improvement in the BLEU score (Papineni et al., 2002) is statistically significant ($p < .05$), compared to the baseline system

Classifier-generated synthetic phrases We apply classifier with the iterative prediction directly on the baseline phrase table entries and synthesize 944,145 new parallel phrases, increasing the phrase table size by 38%. The phrasal translation features in each synthetic phrase are the same as in the phrase it was derived from. The BLEU score of the median SMT system with synthetic phrases is $22.9 \pm .1$, the improvement is statistically significant ($p < .01$). Post-processing of a phrase table created from corpora without articles and adding synthetic phrases to the baseline phrase table yielded similar results.

Translation features for synthetic phrases In the following experiments we aim to establish the optimal set of translation features that should be used with synthetic phrases. We train several SMT systems, each containing synthetic phrases derived from the original phrase table by iterative classification, and with LM-based short phrases. Each synthetic phrase has five translation features as an original phrase it was derived from. The additional features that we evaluate are:

1. Boolean feature for LM-based synthetic phrases

MT System	BLEU
Baseline	$22.6 \pm .1$
MT output post-processing	
one-pass, MT output with articles	20.8
one-pass, MT output without articles	19.7
iterative, MT output with articles	22.6
iterative, MT output without articles	21.8
With synthetic phrases	
LM-based phrases	$22.9 \pm .1$
+ classifier-generated phrases	$22.9 \pm .1$
+ features 1,2	**23.0** $\pm .1$
+ features 1,2,3	$22.8 \pm .1$
+ features 1,2,3,4	$22.8 \pm .1$
+ feature 5	$22.9 \pm .1$

Table 3: Summary of experiments with MT output post-processing and with synthetic translation options in a phrase table. Post-processing of the MT output do not improve translations. Best performing system with synthetic phrases has five original phrase translation features and two additional boolean features indicating if the phrase is LM-based or not, is classifier-generated or not. All the synthetic systems are significantly better than the baseline system.

2. Boolean feature for classifier-generated synthetic phrases
3. Classifier confidence: posterior probability of the classifier averaged over all samples in a target phrase.
4. Boolean feature indicating a confidence of the classifier: the feature value is 1 iff the Feature 3 scores higher than some threshold. The threshold was set to 0.8, we did not experiment with other values.
5. Boolean feature for a synthetic phrase of any type: LM-based or classifier-generated

Table 3 details the change in the BLEU score of each experimental setup. The best performing system has five original phrase translation features and two additional boolean features indicating if the phrase is LM-based or not, is classifier-generated or not. Note that all the synthetic systems are significantly better than the baseline.

Czech-English. Our technique was developed using Russian-English system in the TED domain, so we want to see how our method generalizes to a different domain when translating from a different language. We therefore applied our most successful configuration to a Czech-English news translation task.[11] For training, we use the WMT Czech-English parallel corpus CzEng0.7; we tune using the WMT2011 test set and test on the WMT2012 test set. The LM is trained on the target side of the training corpus. Determiners classifier, re-trained on the English side of this corpus, with statistical, lexical, morphosyntactic and dependency features obtained an accuracy of 88%.

In Table 4, we report the results of evaluating the performance of the Russian-to-English and Czech-to-English MT systems with synthetic phrases. The results of both systems show a statistically significant ($p < .01$) improvement in terms of BLEU score.

	Russian	Czech
Baseline	$22.6 \pm .1$	$16.0 \pm .05$
Synthetic	**23.0** $\pm .1$	**16.2** $\pm .03$

Table 4: BLEU score of Russian-to-English and Czech-to-English MT systems with synthetic phrases and features 1 and 2 show a significant improvement.

Qualitative analysis. Table 5 shows some examples from the output of our Russian-to-English systems. Although both systems produce comprehensible translations, the system augmented with determiner classifier is more fluent. The first example represents a case where a singular count noun (*piece*) is present which requires an article. The baseline is not able to identify this requirement and hence does not insert the article *an* before the phrase *extraordinary engineering piece*. Our system, however, correctly identifies the construction requiring an article and thus provides an appropriate form of the article (*an*- Indefinite article for lexical items beginning with a vowel). Thus we see that our system is able to capture the linguistic requirement of the singular count nouns to co-occur with an article. In the second row, the lexical item *poor* is used as an adjective. The baseline has inserted an article in front of it, changing it to a noun. Our system, however, is able to maintain the status of *poor* as an adjective since it has the option not to insert an article. Thus we see that besides fluency, our system also does better in maintaining the grammatical category of a lexical item. In the third row, the phrase *three*

[11] Like Russian, Czech is a Slavic language that does not have definite or indefinite articles.

Source:	но тем не менее , это выдающееся произведение инженерного искусства .
Reference:	but nonetheless , it 's an extraordinary piece of engineering .
Baseline:	but nevertheless , it 's extraordinary engineering piece of art .
Ours:	but nevertheless , it 's an extraordinary piece of engineering art .
Source:	и по многим дефинициям она уже не бедная .
Reference:	and by many definitions she is no longer poor .
Baseline:	and in a lot definitions , it 's not a poor .
Ours:	and in a lot definitions she 's not poor .
Source:	нам нужно накормить три миллиарда городских жителей .
Reference:	we must feed three billion people in cities .
Baseline:	we need to feed the three billion urban hundreds of them .
Ours:	we need to feed three billion people in the city .

Table 5: Examples of translations with improved articles handling.

billion people refers to a nonidentifiable referent. The baseline inserts the definite article *the*. If a human subject reads this translation, it would mislead him/her to interpret the object *three billion people* as referring to a specific identifiable set. Our system, on the other hand, correctly selects the determiner class N and hence does not insert an article. Thus we see that our system does not just add fluency but it also captures a semantic distinction, namely **identifiability**, that a human subject makes when producing or interpreting a phrase.

7 Related Work

Automated determiner prediction has been found beneficial in a variety of applications, including postediting of MT output (Knight and Chander, 1994), text generation (Elhadad, 1993; Minnen et al., 2000), and more recently identification and correction of ESL errors (Han et al., 2006; De Felice and Pulman, 2008; Gamon et al., 2009; Rozovskaya and Roth, 2010). Our work on determiners extends previous studies in several dimensions. While all previous approaches were tested only on NP constructions, we evaluate our classifier on any sequence of tokens.

To the best of our knowledge, the only studies that directly address generation of synthetic phrase table entries was conducted by Chen et al. (2011) and Koehn and Hoang (2007). The former find semantically similar source phrases and produce "fabricated" translations by combining these source phrases with a set of their target phrases; however, they do not observe improvements. The later work integrates the synthesis of translation options into the decoder. While related in spirit, their method only supports a limited set of generative processes for producing the candidate set (lacking, for instance, the simple and effective phrase post-editing process we have used), and their implementation has been plagued by computational challenges.

Post-processing techniques have been extremely popular. These can be understood as using a translation model to generate a translation skeleton (or k-best skeletons) and then post-editing these in various ways. These have been applied to translation into morphologically rich languages, such as Japanese, German, Turkish, and Finnish (de Gispert et al., 2005; Suzuki and Toutanova, 2006; Suzuki and Toutanova, 2007; Fraser et al., 2012; Clifton and Sarkar, 2011; Oflazer and Durgar El-Kahlout, 2007).

8 Conclusions and future work

The contribution of this work is twofold. First, we propose a new supervised method to predict definite and indefinite articles. Our log-linear model trained on a linguistically-motivated set of features outperforms previously reported results, and obtains an upper bound of an accuracy achieved by human subjects given a context of four words. However, more important result of this work is the experimentally verified idea of improving phrase-based SMT via synthetic phrases. While we have focused on a limited problem in this paper, there are numerous alternative applications including translation into morphologically rich languages, as a method for incorporating (source) contextual information in making local translation decisions, enriching the target language lexicon using lexical translation resources, and many others.

Acknowledgments

We are grateful to Shuly Wintner for insightful suggestions and support. This work was supported in part by the U. S. Army Research Laboratory and the U. S. Army Research Office under contract/grant number W911NF-10-1-0533.

References

J. Aissen. 2003. Differential object marking: Iconicity vs. economy. *Natural Language and Linguistic Theory*, 21(3):435–483.

C. Callison-Burch, P. Koehn, C. Monz, and O. Zaidan. 2011. Findings of the 2011 workshop on statistical machine translation. In *Proceedings of the Sixth Workshop on Statistical Machine Translation*, pages 22–64, Edinburgh, Scotland, July. Association for Computational Linguistics.

M. Cettolo, C. Girardi, and M. Federico. 2012. WIT^3: Web inventory of transcribed and translated talks. In *Proceedings of the 16th Conference of the European Association for Machine Translation (EAMT)*, pages 261–268, Trento, Italy, May.

B. Chen, R. Kuhn, and G. Foster. 2011. Semantic smoothing and fabrication of phrase pairs for SMT. In *Proceedings of the International Workshop on Spoken Lanuage Translation (IWSLT-2011)*.

P. Chen. 2004. Identifiability and definiteness in chinese. *Linguistics*, 42(6):1129–1184.

C. Cherry and G. Foster. 2012. Batch tuning strategies for statistical machine translation. In *Proceedings of HLT-NAACL 2012*, volume 12, pages 34–35.

D. Chiang. 2007. Hierarchical phrase-based translation. *Computational Linguistics*, 33(2):201–228.

D. Chiang. 2012. Hope and fear for discriminative training of statistical translation models. *The Journal of Machine Learning Research*, 98888:1159–1187.

J. H. Clark, C. Dyer, A. Lavie, and N. A. Smith. 2011. Better hypothesis testing for statistical machine translation: Controlling for optimizer instability. In *In Proc. of ACL*.

A. Clifton and A. Sarkar. 2011. Combining morpheme-based machine translation with post-processing morpheme prediction. In *Proceedings of ACL*.

R. De Felice and S. G. Pulman. 2008. A classifier-based approach to preposition and determiner error correction in L2 English. In *Proceedings of the 22nd International Conference on Computational Linguistics-Volume 1*, pages 169–176. Association for Computational Linguistics.

A. de Gispert, J. B. Mariño, and J. M. Crego. 2005. Improving statistical machine translation by classifying and generalizing inflected verb forms. In *Proceedings of InterSpeech*.

J. DeNero and D. Klein. 2010. Discriminative modeling of extraction sets for machine translation. In *Proceedings of the 48th Annual Meeting of the Association for Computational Linguistics*, pages 1453–1463. Association for Computational Linguistics.

J. DeNero, A. Bouchard-Côté, and D. Klein. 2008. Sampling alignment structure under a Bayesian translation model. In *Proceedings of the Conference on Empirical Methods in Natural Language Processing*, pages 314–323. Association for Computational Linguistics.

V. Eidelman, Y. Marton, and P. Resnik. 2013. Online relative margin maximization for statistical machine translation. In *Proceedings of ACL*.

M. Elhadad. 1993. Generating argumentative judgment determiners. In *AAAI*, pages 344–349.

J. R. Finkel, T. Grenager, and C. Manning. 2005. Incorporating non-local information into information extraction systems by gibbs sampling. In *ACL '05: Proceedings of the 43rd Annual Meeting on Association for Computational Linguistics*, pages 363–370, Morristown, NJ, USA. Association for Computational Linguistics.

A. Fraser, M. Weller, A. Cahill, and F. Cap. 2012. Modeling inflection and word-formation in SMT. In *Proceedings of EACL*.

M. Galley, J. Graehl, K. Knight, D. Marcu, S. DeNeefe, W. Wang, and I. Thayer. 2006. Scalable inference and training of context-rich syntactic translation models. In *ACL-44: Proceedings of the 21st International Conference on Computational Linguistics and the 44th annual meeting of the Association for Computational Linguistics*, pages 961–968, Morristown, NJ, USA. Association for Computational Linguistics.

M. Gamon, J. Gao, C. Brockett, A. Klementiev, W. B. Dolan, D. Belenko, and L. Vanderwende. 2009. Using contextual speller techniques and language modeling for ESL error correction. *Urbana*, 51:61801.

K. Gimpel and N. A. Smith. 2012. Structured ramp loss minimization for machine translation. In *Proceedings of 2012 Conference of the North American Chapter of the Association for Computational Linguistics: Human Language Technologies HLT-NAACL 2012, Montreal, Canada*.

N.-R. Han, M. Chodorow, and C. Leacock. 2006. Detecting errors in English article usage by non-native speakers.

K. Knight and I. Chander. 1994. Automated postediting of documents. In *Proceedings of the National Conference on Artificial Intelligence*, pages 779–779, Seattle, WA.

P. Koehn and H. Hoang. 2007. Factored translation models. In *Proceedings of the 2007 Joint Conference on Empirical Methods in Natural Language Processing and Computational Natural Language Learning (EMNLP-CoNLL)*, pages 868–876, Prague, Czech Republic, June. Association for Computational Linguistics.

P. Koehn, F. J. Och, and D. Marcu. 2003. Statistical phrase-based translation. In *NAACL '03: Proceedings of the 2003 Conference of the North American Chapter of the Association for Computational Linguistics on Human Language Technology*, pages 48–54. Association for Computational Linguistics.

P. Koehn, H. Hoang, A. Birch, C. Callison-Burch, M. Federico, N. Bertoldi, B. Cowan, W. Shen, C. Moran, R. Zens, C. Dyer, O. Bojar, A. Constantin, and E. Herbst. 2007. Moses: Open source toolkit for statistical machine translation. In *Proceedings of the 45th Annual Meeting of the Association for Computational Linguistics Companion Volume Proceedings of the Demo and Poster Sessions*, pages 177–180, Prague, Czech Republic, June. Association for Computational Linguistics.

C. Lyons. 1999. *Definiteness*. Cambridge University Press.

G. Minnen, F. Bond, and A. Copestake. 2000. Memory-based learning for article generation. In *Proceedings of the 2nd workshop on Learning language in logic and the 4th conference on Computational natural language learning-Volume 7*, pages 43–48. Association for Computational Linguistics.

T. Mohanan. 1994. *Argument Structure in Hindi*. CSLI Publications.

K. Oflazer and I. Durgar El-Kahlout. 2007. Exploring different representational units in English-to-Turkish statistical machine translation. In *Proceedings of the Second Workshop on Statistical Machine Translation*, pages 25–32, Prague, Czech Republic, June. Association for Computational Linguistics.

K. Papineni, S. Roukos, T. Ward, and W.-J. Zhu. 2002. BLEU: a method for automatic evaluation of machine translation. In *ACL '02: Proceedings of the 40th Annual Meeting on Association for Computational Linguistics*, pages 311–318, Morristown, NJ, USA. Association for Computational Linguistics.

A. Rozovskaya and D. Roth. 2010. Training paradigms for correcting errors in grammar and usage. *Urbana*, 51:61801.

A. Stolcke. 2002. SRILM—an extensible language modeling toolkit. In *Procedings of International Conference on Spoken Language Processing*, pages 901–904.

H. Suzuki and K. Toutanova. 2006. Learning to predict case markers in Japanese. In *Proceedings of the 21st International Conference on Computational Linguistics and the 44th annual meeting of the Association for Computational Linguistics*, pages 1049–1056. Association for Computational Linguistics.

H. Suzuki and K. Toutanova. 2007. Generating case markers in machine translation. In *Proceedings of HLT-NAACL 2007*, pages 49–56.

K. Toutanova and C. D. Manning. 2000. Enriching the knowledge sources used in a maximum entropy part-of-speech tagger. In *Proceedings of the 2000 Joint SIGDAT conference on Empirical methods in natural language processing and very large corpora*, pages 63–70, Morristown, NJ, USA. Association for Computational Linguistics.

Dramatically Reducing Training Data Size Through Vocabulary Saturation

William D. Lewis
Microsoft Research
One Microsoft Way
Redmond, WA 98052
wilewis@microsoft.com

Sauleh Eetemadi
Microsoft Research
One Microsoft Way, Redmond, WA 98052
Michigan State University, East Lansing, MI 48824
saulehe@microsoft.com

Abstract

Our field has seen significant improvements in the quality of machine translation systems over the past several years. The single biggest factor in this improvement has been the accumulation of ever larger stores of data. However, we now find ourselves the victims of our own success, in that it has become increasingly difficult to train on such large sets of data, due to limitations in memory, processing power, and ultimately, speed (i.e., data to models takes an inordinate amount of time). Some teams have dealt with this by focusing on data cleaning to arrive at smaller data sets (Denkowski et al., 2012a; Rarrick et al., 2011), "domain adaptation" to arrive at data more suited to the task at hand (Moore and Lewis, 2010; Axelrod et al., 2011), or by specifically focusing on data reduction by keeping only as much data as is needed for building models *e.g.*, (Eck et al., 2005). This paper focuses on techniques related to the latter efforts. We have developed a very simple n-gram counting method that reduces the size of data sets dramatically, as much as 90%, and is applicable independent of specific dev and test data. At the same time it reduces model sizes, improves training times, and, because it attempts to preserve contexts for all n-grams in a corpus, the cost in quality is minimal (as measured by BLEU). Further, unlike other methods created specifically for data reduction that have similar effects on the data, our method scales to very large data, up to tens to hundreds of millions of parallel sentences.

1 Introduction

The push to build higher and higher quality Statistical Machine Translation systems has led the efforts to collect more and more data. The English-French (nearly) Gigaword Parallel Corpus (Callison-Burch et al., 2009), which we will refer to henceforth as EnFrGW, is the result of one such effort. The EnFrGW is a publicly available corpus scraped from Canadian, European and international Web sites, consisting of over 22.5M parallel English-French sentences. This corpus has been used regularly in the WMT competition since 2009.

As the size of data increases, BLEU scores increase, but the increase in BLEU is not linear in relation to data size. The relationship between data size and BLEU flattens fairly quickly, as demonstrated in Figure 1. Here we see that BLEU scores increase rapidly with small amounts of data, but they taper off and flatten at much larger amounts. Clearly, as we add more data, the value of the new data diminishes with each increase, until very little value is achieved through the addition of each new sentence. However, given that this figure represents samples from EnFrGW, can we be more efficient in the samples we take? Can we achieve near equivalent BLEU scores on much smaller amounts of data drawn from the same source, most especially better than what we can achieve through random sampling?

The focus of this work is three-fold. First, we seek to devise a method to reduce the size of training data, which can be run independently of particular dev and test data, so as to maintain the independence of the data, since we are not interested here in domain adaptation or selective tuning. Second, we desire an algorithm that is (mostly) quality preserving, as measured by BLEU, OOV rates, and human eval, ultimately resulting in decreased training times and reduced model sizes. Reduced

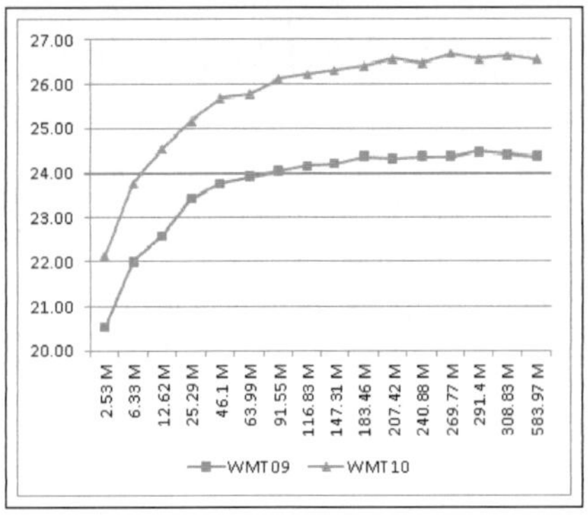

Figure 1: BLEU score increase as more data is added (in millions of words), random samples from EnFrGW

training times provide for greater iterative capacity, since we can make more rapid algorithmic improvements and do more experimentation on smaller data than we can on much larger data. Since we operate in a production environment, deploying smaller models is also desirable. Third, we require a method that scales to very large data. We show in the sections below the application of an algorithm at various settings to the 22.5M sentence EnFrGW corpus. Although large, 22.5M sentences does not represent the full total of the English-French data on the Web. We require an algorithm that can apply to even larger samples of data, on the order of tens to hundreds of millions of sentences.

2 Related Work

In statistical machine translation, selection, preparation and processing of parallel training data is often done to serve one of the following scenarios:

- Low Resource Languages: In languages with low parallel data availability, a subset of a monolingual corpus is selected for human translation ((Ananthakrishnan et al., 2010), (Eck et al., 2005) and (Haffari et al., 2009)).

- Mobile device deployment: For many languages, translation model sizes built on all available parallel data are too large to be hosted on mobile devices. In addition to translation model pruning, a common solution is selecting a subset of the data to be trained on ((Ananthakrishnan et al., 2010) and (Yasuda et al., 2008)).

- Quick turn-around time during development: A common motivation for training on a subset of a parallel corpus is to reduce training time during the development cycle of a statistical machine translation system ((Lin and Bilmes, 2011) and (Chao and Li, 2011a)).

- Noise reduction: Simple noise reduction techniques like sentence length and alpha numeric ratio are often used in data preparation. However, more sophisticated techniques have been developed to filter out noise from parallel data ((Denkowski et al., 2012a) and (Taghipour et al., 2010)).

- Domain Adaptation: Recently there has been significant interest in domain adaptation for statistical machine translation. One of the approaches to domain adaptation is selecting a subset of a data that is closer to the target domain ((Moore and Lewis, 2010), (Axelrod et al., 2011)).

- Improve translation quality: An interesting area of research is selecting a subset of the training data that is more suitable for statistical machine translation learning ((Okita, 2009)).

In comparison, the goal of this work is to efficiently reduce very large parallel data sets (in excess of tens of billions of tokens) to a desired size in a reasonable amount of time. In the related work referenced above two primary methods have been used.

1. Maximizing n-gram coverage with minimal data.

2. Filtering out noisy data based on sentence-pair based features.

One of the earliest and most cited works using the first method is (Eck et al., 2005). In this work, a greedy algorithm is developed to select a subset of the entire corpus that covers most n-grams with minimum number of words. In a later work by the same author, the algorithm was modified to give higher weight to more frequent words. Although this is a greedy algorithm and does not provide the optimum solution, its complexity is quadratic in the number of sentences. Hence it is not practical to run this algorithm over very large data sets.

Recently (Ananthakrishnan et al., 2010) introduced a new algorithm that is an improvement over (Eck et al., 2005). In this work discriminative training is used to train a maximum entropy pair-wise comparator with n-gram based features. The pair-wise comparator is used to select the highest scoring sentence followed by discounting features used for the sentence, which are drawn from the global pool of features. The complexity of this algorithm after training the pairwise comparator is $O(N \times K \times \log(F))$ where N is the number of sentences in the entire corpus, K is the number of sentences to be selected and F is the size of the feature space. Although this method works well for a constant K, its complexity is quadratic when K is a fraction of N. This method is reported to improve the BLEU score close to 1% over the work done by (Eck et al., 2005).

(Denkowski et al., 2012a) have developed relatively scalable algorithms that fit in the second category above. This algorithm automatically filters out noisy data primarily based on the following feature functions: normalized source and target language model scores, word alignment scores and fraction of aligned words. Sentences that don't score above a certain threshold (mean minus one or two standard deviations) for all their features are filtered out. In a similar work, (Taghipour et al., 2010) use an approach where they incorporate similar features based on translation table entries, word alignment models, source and target language models and length to build a binary classifier that filters out noisy data.

Our work incorporates both methods listed above in a scalable fashion where it selects a subset of the data that is less noisy with a reasonable n-gram representation of the superset parallel corpus. To put the scalability of our work in perspective we compiled Table 1, which shows the maximum size of the data sets reported in each of the relevant papers on the topic. Despite the public availability of parallel corpora in excess of tens of millions of sentence pairs, none of the related works, using the first method above, exceed couple of millions of sentences pairs. This demonstrates the importance of developing a scalable algorithm when addressing the data selection problem.

The careful reader may observe that an alternate strategy for reducing model sizes (*e.g.*, useful for the Mobile scenario noted above, but also in any scenario where space concerns are an issue), would be to reduce phrase table size rather than reduce training data size. A good example of work in this space is shown in (Johnson et al., 2007), who describe a method for phrase table reduction, sometimes substantial (>90%), with no impact on the resulting BLEU scores. The principal of our work versus theirs is where the data reductions occur: before or after training. The primary benefit of manipulating the training data directly is the impact on training performance. Further, given the increasing sizes of training data, it has become more difficult and more time consuming to train on large data, and in the case of very large data (say tens to hundreds of millions of sentence pairs), it may not even be possible to train models at all. Reduced training data sizes increases iterative capacity, and is possible in cases where phrase table reduction may not be (*i.e.*, with very big data).

Reference	Total Sentences
(Ananthakrishnan et al., 2010)	253K
(Eck et al., 2005)	123K
(Haffari et al., 2009)	1.8M[1]
(Lin and Bilmes, 2011)	1.2M[2]
(Chao and Li, 2011b)	2.3M

Table 1: Data Sizes for Related Systems

3 Vocabulary Saturation Filter (VSF)

The effects of more data on improving BLEU scores is clearly discernible from Figure 1: as more data is added, BLEU scores increase. However, the relationship between quantity of data and BLEU is not linear, such that the effects of more data diminishes with each increase in data size, effectively approaching some asymptote. One might say that the vocabulary of the phrase mappings derived from model training "saturate" as data size increases, since less and less novel information can be derived from each succeeding sentence of data added to training. It is this observation that led us to develop the Vocabulary Saturation Filter (VSF).

VSF makes the following very simple assumption: for any given vocabulary item v there is some point where the contexts for v—that is, the n-gram

[1]Sentence count was not reported. We estimated it based on 18M tokens.

[2]This is a very interesting work, but is only done for selecting speech data. The total number of sentences is not reported. We given a high-end estimate based on 128K selected tokens.

sequences that contain v—approach some level of saturation, such that each succeeding sentence containing v contributes few or no additional contexts, and thus has little impact on the frequency distributions over v. In other words, at a point where the diversity of contexts for v approach a maximum, there is little value in adding additional contexts containing v, *e.g.*, to translation models.

The optimal algorithm would then, for each $v \in V$, identify the number of unique contexts that contain v up to some threshold and discard all others. An exhaustive algorithm which sets thresholds for all n-gram contexts containing v, however, would take a large amount of time to run (minimally quadratic), and may also overrun memory limitations on large data sets.

For VSF, we made the following simplifying assumption: we set an arbitrary count threshold t for all vocabulary items. For any given v, when we reach t, we no longer need to keep additional sentences containing v. However, since each instance of v does not exist in isolation, but is rather contained within sentences that also contain other vocabulary items v, which, in turn, also need to be counted and thresholded, we simplified VSF even further with the following heuristic: for any given sentence s, if all $v \in V$ within s have *not* reached t, then the sentence is kept. This has the direct consequence that many vocabulary items will have frequencies above t in the output corpus.

The implementation of VSF is described in **Algorithm 1** below.

```
Input: ParallelCorpus, N, L
Output: SelectedCorpus
foreach sp ∈ ParallelCorpus do
    S ← EnumNgrams(sp.src, L);
    T ← EnumNgrams(sp.tgt, L);
    selected ← false;
    foreach (s, t) ∈ (S, T) do
        if SrcCnt[s]<N ∨ TgtCnt[t]<N
        then
            selected ← true;
        end
    end
    if selected then
        SelectedCorpus.Add(sp);
        foreach (s, t) ∈ (S, T) do
            SrcCnt[s]++;
            TgtCnt[t]++;
        end
    end
end
```

Algorithm 1: Pseudocode for implementing VSF. L: n-gram length, N: n-gram threshold.

VSF clearly makes a number of simplifying assumptions, many of which one might argue would reduce the value of the resulting data. Although easy to implement, it may not achieve the most optimal results. Assuming that VSF might be defective, we then looked into other algorithms attempting to achieve the same or similar results, such as those described in Section 2, and explored in-depth the algorithms described in (Eck et al., 2005).

4 An Alternative: (Eck et al., 2005)

In our pursuit of better and generic data reduction algorithms, we did a number of experiments using the algorithms described in (Eck et al., 2005). In the n-gram based method proposed by this work the weight of each function is calculated using Equation 1, where j is the n-gram length. In each iteration of the algorithm, the weight of each sentence is calculated and the sentence with the highest weight is selected. Once a sentence is selected, the n-grams in the sentence are marked as seen and have a zero weight when they appear in subsequent sentences. Therefore, the weights of all remaining sentences have to be recalculated before the next sentence can be selected. We refer to this algorithm henceforth as the Eck algorithm.

$$W_j\left(sentence\right) = \frac{\sum_{i=1}^{j}\left[\sum_{\substack{unseen\\ngrams}} Freq(ngram)\right]}{|sentence|} \quad (1)$$

To compare VSF against the Eck algorithm we selected the English-Lithuanian parallel corpus from JRC-ACQUIS (Steinberger et al., 2006). We selected the corpus for the following reasons:

- VSF performance on this particular data set was at its lowest compared to a number of other data sets, so there was room for improvement by a potentially better algorithm.
- With almost 50 million tokens combined (English and Lithuanian) we were able to optimize the Eck algorithm and run it on this data set in a reasonable amount of time. The experiments run by the original paper in 2005 were run on only 800,000 tokens.

Using the Eck algorithm with n-gram length set to one ($j \leftarrow 1$ in Equation 1) only 10% (5,020,194 tokens total) of the data is sorted, since all n-grams of size one have been observed by that point and the weight function for the remaining sentences returns zero. In other words, since there are no unseen unigrams after 10% of the data has been sorted, in Equation 1, the numerator becomes zero there after and therefore the remaining 90% of sentence pairs are not sorted. This must be taken into consideration when examining the comparison between unigram VSF and the Eck algorithm with n-gram length set to one in Figure 2. VSF with its lowest setting, that is threshold *t*=1, selects 20% of the data, so this chart may not be a fair comparison between the two algorithms.

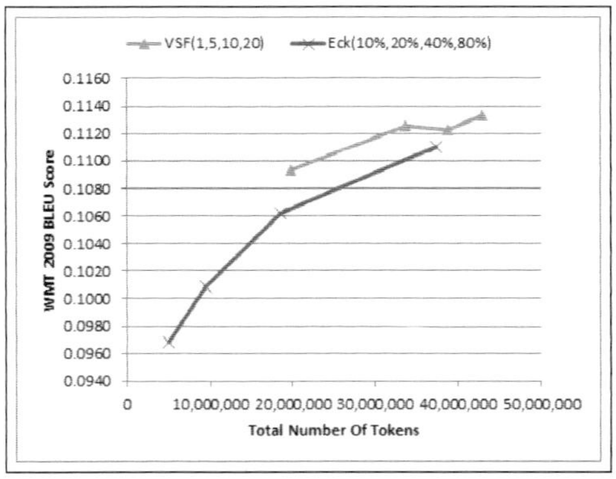

Figure 2: Unigram Eck vs. Unigram VSF

In an attempt to do a fairer comparison, we also tried n-grams of length two in the Eck algorithm, where 50% of the data can be sorted (since all unigrams and bigrams are observed by that point). As seen in Figure 3, the BLEU scores for the Eck and VSF systems built on the similar sized data score very closely on the WMT 2009 test set.[3]

Further exploring options using Eck, we developed the following two extensions to the Eck algorithm, none of which resulted in a significant gain in BLEU score over VSF with n-gram lengths set up to three.

- Incorporating target sentence n-grams in addition to source side sentence n-grams.
- Dividing the weight of an n-gram (its frequency) by a constant number each time a sentence that contains the n-gram is selected, as opposed to setting the weight of an n-gram to zero after it has been seen for the first time.[4]

In relatively small data sets there is not a significant difference between the two algorithms. The Eck algorithm does not scale to larger data sets and higher n-grams. Since a principal focus of our work is on scaling to very large data sets, and since Eck could not scale to even moderately sized data sets, we decided to continue our focus on VSF and improvements to that algorithm.

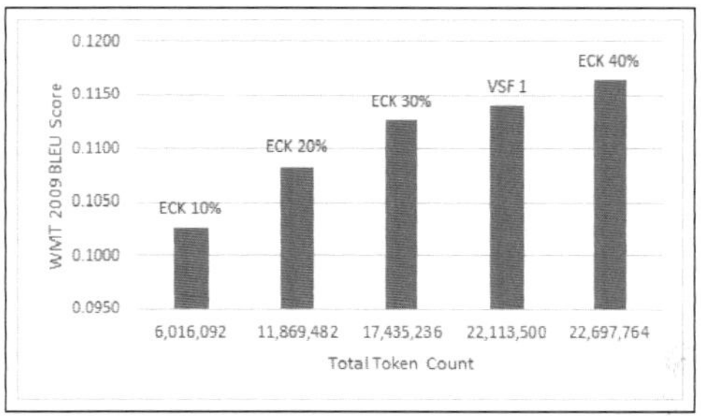

Figure 3: Bigram Eck vs. Unigram VSF

5 Data Order

Unlike the Eck algorithm, VSF is sensitive to the order of the input data due to the nature of the algorithm. Depending on the order of sentences in the input parallel corpus, VSF could select different subsets of the parallel corpus that would eventually (after training and test) result in different BLEU scores. To address this concern we use a feature function inspired by (Denkowski et al., 2012a) which is a normalized combined alignment score. This feature score is obtained by geometric averaging of the normalized forward and backward alignment scores which in turn are calculated using the process described in (Denkowski et al., 2012a). To keep the algorithm as scalable as possible we use radix sort. This ordering of the data ensures sentences with high normalized alignment scores appear first and sentences with low normalized alignment appear last. As a result, for each n-gram, VSF will choose the top-N highest scoring sentence pairs that contain that n-gram.

[3]The careful reader may note that there is no official WMT09 test set for Lithuanian, since Lithuanian is not (yet) a language used in the WMT competition. The test set mentioned here was created from a 1,000 sentence sample from the English-side of the WMT09 test sets, which we then manually translated into Lithuanian.

[4]Further details of the modifications to the Eck algorithm are not discussed here as they did not yield improvements over the baseline algorithm and the focus of our work presented here was shifted to improvements over VSF.

5.1 Data Ordering Complexity

Ordering the data based on normalized combined alignment score requires two steps. First, the normalized combined alignment score is computed for each sentence pair using an existing HMM alignment model. Next, sentence pairs are sorted based on the calculated score. The computational complexity of aligning a single sentence pair is $O\left(J + I^2\right)$ where J is the number of words in the source sentence and I is the number of words in the target sentence (Gao and Vogel, 2008). Therefore the complexity of calculating the combined alignment score would be $O\left(N \times (J^2 + I + I^2 + J)\right)$ or $O\left(N \times \max(I, J)^2\right)$ after simplification. Since radix sort is used for sorting the data, the data can be sorted in $O(d \times N)$ where d is the number of significant digits used for sorting. Since d is kept constant[5], the overall computational complexity for data ordering is $O\left(N + N \times \max(I, J)^2\right)$.

6 Experiments

6.1 The Machine Translation and Training Infrastructure

We used a custom-built tree-to-string (T2S) system for training the models for all experiments. The T2S system that we developed uses technology described in (Quirk et al., 2005), and requires a source-side dependency parser, which we have developed for English.[6] We trained a 5-gram French LM over the entire EnFrGW, which we used in all systems. We used Minimum Error Rate Training (MERT) (Och, 2003) for tuning the lambda values for all systems, tuned using the official WMT2010 dev data.

6.2 Test and Training Data

In all experiments, we used the EnFrGW corpus, or subsets thereof. [7] We used three test sets in all experiments, as well. Two consisted of the WMT 2009 and 2010 test sets, used in the WMT competitions in the respective years. The third consisted of 5,000 parallel English/French sentences sampled from logs of actual traffic received by our production service, Bing Translator (http://bing.com/translator), which were then manually translated. The first two test sets are publicly available, but are somewhat news focused. The third, which we will call ReqLog, consists of a mix of content and sources, so can be considered a truly "general" test set.

t =	Random	VSF	Ordered VSF
1	1.83 M	1.83 M	1.68 M
2	2.53 M	2.53 M	2.34 M
5	3.62 M	3.62 M	3.35 M
10	4.62 M	4.62 M	4.29 M
20	5.83 M	5.83 M	5.44 M
40	7.26 M	7.26 M	6.83 M
60	8.21 M	8.21 M	7.78 M
100	9.53 M	9.53 M	9.13 M
150	10.67 M	10.67 M	10.33 M
200	11.53 M	11.53 M	11.23 M
250	12.22 M	12.22 M	11.97 M
All	22.5 M		

Table 2: English-side Sentence Counts (in millions) for different thresholds for VSF, VSF after ordering the data based on normalized combined alignment score and random baselines.

To discern the effects of VSF at different degrees of "saturation", we tried VSF with different threshold values t, ranging from 1 to 250. For each t value we actually ran VSF twice. In the first case, we did no explicit sorting of the data. In the second case, we ranked the data using the method described in Section 5.

Finally, we created random baselines for each t, where each random baseline is paired with the relevant VSF run, controlled for the number of sentences (since t has no relevance for random samples). The different t values and the resulting training data sizes (sentence and word counts) are shown in Tables 2 and 3.

Since our interest in this study is scaling parallel data, for all trainings we used the same LM, which was built over all training data (the French side of the full EnFrGW). Because monolingual training scales much more readily than parallel,

[5] In experiments described in Section 6 five significant digits were used for radix sort.

[6] Further details about the decoders is beyond the scope of this paper. The reader is encouraged to refer to the sources provided for additional information.

[7] Because of some data cleaning filters we applied to the data, the actual full sized corpus we used consisted of slightly less data than that used in the WMT competitions. Every team has its own set of favorite data cleaning heuristics, and ours is no different. The filters applied to this data are focused mostly on noise reduction, and consist of a set of filters related to eliminating content that contains badly encoded characters, removing content that is too long (since there is little value in training on very long sentences), removing content where the ratio between numeric versus alphabetic characters is excessively large, deleting content where the script of the content is mostly not in latin1 (relevant for French), and some additional filters described in (Denkowski et al., 2012b). If the reader wishes additional material on data filtration, please see (Denkowski et al., 2012b) and (Lewis and Quirk, 2013).

$t=$	Random	VSF	Ordered VSF
1	46.1 M	64.52 M	65.74 M
2	63.99 M	87.41 M	88.12 M
5	91.55 M	121.3 M	120.86 M
10	116.83 M	151.53 M	149.95 M
20	147.31 M	186.99 M	184.14 M
40	183.46 M	228.14 M	224.29 M
60	207.42 M	254.89 M	250.68 M
100	240.88 M	291.45 M	287.02 M
150	269.77 M	322.5 M	318.33 M
200	291.4 M	345.37 M	341.69 M
250	308.83 M	363.44 M	360.32 M
All	583.97 M		

Table 3: English-side Word Counts for different thresholds for VSF, VSF after ordering the data based on normalized combined alignment score and random baselines.

$t=$	Random	VSF	Ordered VSF
1	1:07	2:17	1:56
2	1:33	2:55	2:39
5	2:15	4:05	3:47
10	2:43	4:49	4:50
20	3:23	5:25	5:14
40	4:12	6:16	5:56
60	4:45	6:41	7:15
100	5:31	7:32	7:55
150	6:07	8:20	8:18
200	6:36	8:31	8:52
250	7:30	9:19	9:11
All	13:12		

Table 4: Word alignment times (hh:mm) for different thresholds for VSF, VSF after model score ordering, and a random baseline

this seemed reasonable. Further, using one LM controls one parameter that would otherwise fluctuate across trainings. The result is a much more focused view on parallel training diffs.

6.3 Results

We trained models over each set of data. In addition to calculating BLEU scores for each resulting set of models in (Table 5), we also compared OOV rates (Table 6) and performance differences (Table 4). The former is another window into the "quality" of the resulting models, in that it describes vocabulary coverage (in other words, how much vocabulary is recovered from the full data). The latter gives some indication regarding the time savings after running VSF at different thresholds.

On the WMT09 data set, both sets of VSF models outperformed the relevant random baselines. On the WMT10 and ReqLog test sets, the pre-sorted VSF outperformed all random baselines, with the unsorted VSF outperforming most random baselines, except at t=60 and t=200 for WMT10. For the ReqLog, unsorted VSF drops below random starting at t=200. Clearly, the t=200 results show that there is less value in VSF as we approach the total data size.

The most instructive baseline, however, is the one built over all training data. It is quite obvious that at low threshold values, the sampled data is not a close approximation of the full data: not enough vocabulary and contextual information is preserved for the data to be taken as a proxy for the full data. However, with t values around 20-60 we recover enough BLEU and OOVs to make the datasets reasonable proxies. Further, because we see a relative reduction in data sizes of 32-44%, model size reductions of 27-39%, and performance improvements of 41-50% at these t values further argues for the value of VSF at these settings. Even at t=250, we have training data that is 54% of the full data size, yet fully recovers BLEU.

7 Discussion

VSF is a simple but effective algorithm for reducing the size of parallel training data, and does so independently of particular dev or test data. It performs as well as related algorithms, notably (Eck et al., 2005), but more importantly, it is able to scale to much larger data sets than other algorithms. In this paper, we showed VSF applied to the EnFrGW corpus. It should be noted, however, that we have also been testing VSF on much larger sets of English-French data. Two notable tests are one applied to 65.2M English-French sentence pairs and another applied to one consisting of 162M. In the former case, we were able to reduce the corpus size from 65.2M sentences/1.28B words[8] to 26.2M sentences/568M words. The BLEU score on this test was stable on the three test sets, as shown in Table 7. When applied to the 162M sentence/2.1B word data set, we were able to reduce the data size to 40.5M sentences/674M words. In this case, sorting the data using model scores produced the most desirable results, actually increasing BLEU by 0.90 on WMT09, but, unfortunately, showing a 0.40 drop on WMT10.

The fact that VSF runs in one pass is both an asset and a liability. It is an asset since the algorithm is able to operate linearly with respect to the size the data. It is a liability since the algorithm is

[8]Word counts based on the English-side, unwordbroken.

		WMT09			WMT10			ReqLog	
t =	Random	VSF	S+VSF	Random	VSF	S+VSF	Random	VSF	S+VSF
1	23.76	23.83	23.84	25.69	25.78	25.68	26.34	26.63	26.67
2	23.91	24.04	24.07	25.76	26.21	26.14	26.54	26.99	26.94
5	24.05	24.29	24.40	26.10	26.40	26.32	26.79	27.22	27.12
10	24.15	24.37	24.45	26.21	26.63	26.32	26.98	27.37	27.62
20	24.20	24.40	24.55	26.30	26.46	26.56	27.22	27.38	27.44
40	24.37	24.43	24.65	26.40	26.55	26.53	27.30	27.38	27.62
60	24.32	24.43	24.64	26.56	26.56	26.61	27.38	27.50	27.64
100	24.37	24.49	24.71	26.46	26.75	26.70	27.37	27.52	27.75
150	24.37	24.61	24.71	26.67	26.67	26.70	27.48	27.62	27.75
200	24.48	24.63	24.69	26.56	26.65	26.78	27.57	27.47	27.72
250	24.41	24.57	24.85	26.62	26.74	26.68	27.63	27.45	27.76
All	24.37			26.54			27.63		

Table 5: BLEU Score results for VSF, S+VSF (Sorted VSF), and Random Baseline at different thresholds *t*.

		WMT09			WMT10			ReqLog	
t =	Random	VSF	S+VSF	Random	VSF	S+VSF	Random	VSF	S+VSF
1	630	424	450	609	420	445	1299	973	1000
2	588	374	395	559	385	393	1183	906	919
5	520	343	347	492	350	356	1111	856	853
10	494	336	335	458	344	344	1092	837	848
20	453	335	335	432	339	341	1016	831	834
40	423	330	331	403	336	337	986	828	833
60	419	329	330	407	333	336	964	831	832
100	389	330	329	391	333	335	950	830	830
150	397	330	330	384	332	332	930	828	828
200	381	328	330	371	331	332	912	827	826
250	356	329	328	370	333	331	884	823	823
All	325			331			822		

Table 6: OOV rates for VSF, S+VSF (Sorted VSF), and Random Baseline at different thresholds *t*.

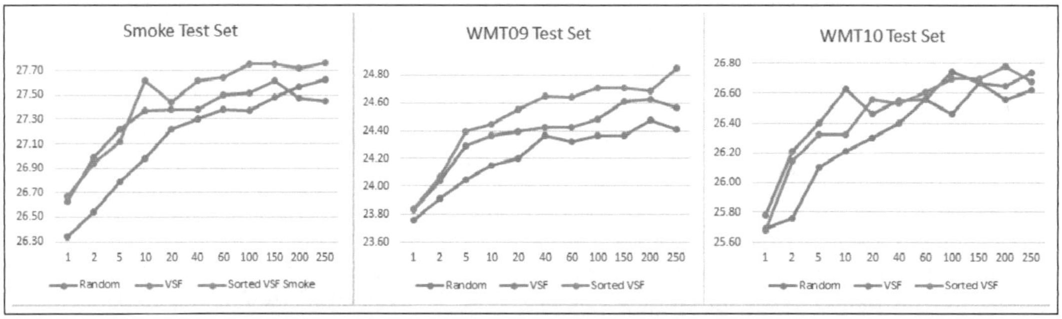

Figure 4: Comparative BLEU scores for two VSF implementations, against a randomly sampled baseline.

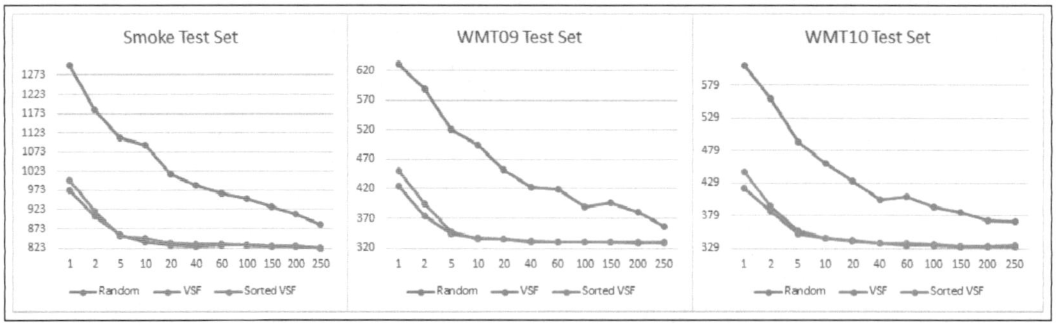

Figure 5: Comparative OOV rates for two VSF implementations, against a randomly sampled baseline.

	ReqLog	WMT09	WMT10
65.2 snts	32.90	26.77	29.05
VSF 26.2M snts	33.34	26.75	29.07

Table 7: VSF applied to a 65.2M sentence baseline system.

sensitive to the order of the data. The latter leads to issues of reproducibility: with poorly ordered data, one could easily arrive at a much less than optimal set of data. However, by adding an additional pass to build model scores, and then ranking the data by these scores, we address the serious issue of reproducibility. Further, the ranking tends to arrive at a better selection of data.

In an attempt to better understand the behavior of VSF and how VSF changes the n-gram distributions of vocabulary items in a sample as compared to the full corpus, we created log_2-scale scatter plots, as seen in Figure 6. In these plots, unigram frequencies of unfiltered data (*i.e.*, the full corpus, EnFrGW) are on the vertical axis, and unigram frequencies of the VSF filtered data are on the horizontal axis. The three plots show three different settings for *t*. There following observations can be made about these plots:

1. On the horizontal axis before we reach $log_2(t)$, all data points fall on the $x = y$ line.
2. As the threshold increases the scatter plot gets closer to the $x = y$ line.
3. VSF has the highest impact on the "medium" frequency unigrams, that is, those with a frequency higher than the threshold.

The third point speaks the most to the effects that VSF has on data: Very low frequency items, specifically those with frequencies below the threshold *t*, are unaffected by the algorithm, since we guarantee including all contexts in which they occur. Low frequency items are at the lower left of the plots, and their frequencies follow the $x = y$ line (point 1 above). Medium frequency items, however, specifically those with frequencies immediately above *t*, are the most affected by the algorithm. The "bulge" in the plots shows where these medium frequency items begin, and one can see plainly that their distributions are perturbed. The "bulge" dissipates as frequencies increase, until the effects diminish as we approach much higher frequencies. The latter is a consequence of a simplifying heuristic applied in VSF (as described in Section 3): *t* is not a hard ceiling, but rather a soft one. Vocabulary items that occur very frequently in a corpus will be counted many more times than *t*; for very high frequency items, their sampled distributions may approach those observed in the full corpus, and converge on the $x = y$ line. The authors suspect that the BLEU loss that results from the application of VSF is the result of the perturbed distributions for medium frequency items. Adjusting to higher *t* values decreases the degree of the perturbation, as noted in the second point, which likewise recovers some of the BLEU loss observed in lower settings.

8 Future Work

There are several future directions we see with work on VSF. Because one threshold *t* for *all* vocabulary items may be too coarse a setting, we first plan to explore setting *t* based on frequency, especially for vocabulary in the most affected mid-range (at and above t). If we set *t* based on unigrams falling into frequency buckets, rather than one setting for all unigrams, we may arrive earlier at a more distributionally balanced corpus, one that may better match the full corpus. That said, additional passes over the data come at additional cost.

Second, we plan to explore applying the VSF algorithm to higher order n-grams (all experiments thus far have been on unigrams). Preliminary experiments on bigram VSF, however, show that with even the lowest setting (*t*=1), we already preserve well over 50% of the data.

In this work we only experimented with sorting the data based on the normalized combined alignment score inspired by (Eck et al., 2005). A third direction for future work would be to consider ordering the data based on other feature functions presented in Eck, *e.g.*, source and target language model, alignment ratio, as well as and feature functions introduced in (Taghipour et al., 2010), or a combination of all of these feature functions.

In the fourth case, we plan to do more sophisticated statistical analysis of the effects of VSF on n-gram distributions and phrase-table entropy. We also plan to explore the interactions between VSF and data "diversity". For instance, VSF may have a greater positive impact on more narrowly focused domains than on those that are more generally focused.

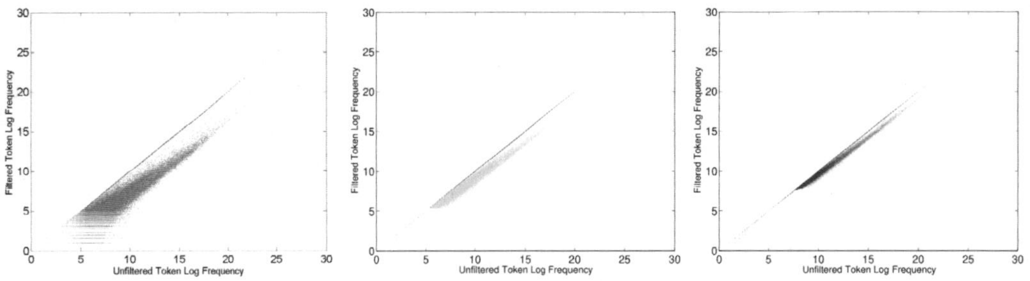

(a) VSF $t = 1$ (b) VSF $t = 40$ (c) VSF $t = 200$

Figure 6: log_2-scale Unigram Frequency scatter plot before VSF versus after VSF

References

S. Ananthakrishnan, R. Prasad, D. Stallard, and P. Natarajan. 2010. Discriminative sample selection for statistical machine translation. In *Proceedings of the 2010 Conference on Empirical Methods in Natural Language Processing*, page 626635.

A. Axelrod, X. He, and J. Gao. 2011. Domain adaptation via pseudo in-domain data selection. In *Proceedings of the 2011 Conference on Empirical Methods in Natural Language Processing*, page 355362.

Chris Callison-Burch, Philipp Koehn, Christof Monz, and Josh Schroeder. 2009. Findings of the 2009 Workshop on Statistical Machine Translation. In *Proceedings of the Fourth Workshop on Statistical Machine Translation*, pages 1–28, Athens, Greece, March. Association for Computational Linguistics.

W. Chao and Z. Li. 2011a. A graph-based bilingual corpus selection approach for SMT. In *Proceedings of the 25th Pacific Asia Conference on Language, Information and Computation*.

WenHan Chao and ZhouJun Li. 2011b. Improved graph-based bilingual corpus selection with sentence pair ranking for statistical machine translation. In *2011 23rd IEEE International Conference on Tools with Artificial Intelligence (ICTAI)*, pages 446 –451, November.

Michael Denkowski, Greg Hanneman, and Alon Lavie. 2012a. The CMU-Avenue French-English translation system. In *Proceedings of the NAACL 2012 Workshop on Statistical Machine Translation*.

Michael Denkowski, Greg Hanneman, and Alon Lavie. 2012b. The CMU-Avenue French-English Translation System. In *Proceedings of the NAACL 2012 Workshop on Statistical Machine Translation*.

M. Eck, S. Vogel, and A. Waibel. 2005. Low cost portability for statistical machine translation based in n-gram frequency and TF-IDF. In *International Workshop on Spoken Language Translation (IWSLT)*.

Qin Gao and Stephan Vogel. 2008. Parallel implementations of word alignment tool. In *Software Engineering, Testing, and Quality Assurance for Natural Language Processing*, page 4957.

G. Haffari, M. Roy, and A. Sarkar. 2009. Active learning for statistical phrase-based machine translation. In *Proceedings of Human Language Technologies: The 2009 Annual Conference of the North American Chapter of the Association for Computational Linguistics*, page 415423.

Howard Johnson, Joel D. Martin, George F. Foster, and Roland Kuhn. 2007. Improving translation quality by discarding most of the phrasetable. In *Proceedings of EMNLP*, pages 967–975.

William D. Lewis and Chris Quirk. 2013. Controlled Ascent: Imbuing Statistical MT with Linguistic Knowledge. In *Proceedings of the Second Hytra (Hybrid Approaches to Translation) Workshop*, Sofia, Bulgaria, August.

H. Lin and J. Bilmes. 2011. Optimal selection of limited vocabulary speech corpora. In *Proc. Interspeech*.

Robert C. Moore and William D. Lewis. 2010. Intelligent Selection of Language Model Training Data. In *Proceedings of the ACL 2010 Conference Short Papers*, Uppsala, Sweden, July.

Franz Josef Och. 2003. Minimum error rate training in statistical machine translation. In *Proceedings of the 41st ACL*, Sapporo, Japan.

T. Okita. 2009. Data cleaning for word alignment. In *Proceedings of the ACL-IJCNLP 2009 Student Research Workshop*, page 7280.

Chris Quirk, Arul Menezes, and Colin Cherry. 2005. Dependency tree translation: Syntactically informed phrasal smt. In *Proceedings of ACL 2005*.

Spencer Rarrick, Chris Quirk, and William D. Lewis. 2011. MT Detection in Web-Scraped Parallel Corpora. In *Proceedings of MT Summit XIII*, Xiamen, China, September.

Ralf Steinberger, Bruno Pouliquen, Anna Widiger, Camelia Ignat, Toma Erjavec, and Dan Tufi. 2006.

The JRC-Acquis: a multilingual aligned parallel corpus with 20+ languages. In *In Proceedings of the 5th International Conference on Language Resources and Evaluation (LREC'2006*, page 21422147.

K. Taghipour, N. Afhami, S. Khadivi, and S. Shiry. 2010. A discriminative approach to filter out noisy sentence pairs from bilingual corpora. In *2010 5th International Symposium on Telecommunications (IST)*, pages 537 –541, December.

K. Yasuda, R. Zhang, H. Yamamoto, and E. Sumita. 2008. Method of selecting training data to build a compact and efficient translation model. In *Proceedings of the Third International Joint Conference on Natural Language Processing*, volume 2, page 655660.

Multi-Task Learning for Improved Discriminative Training in SMT

Patrick Simianer and **Stefan Riezler**
Department of Computational Linguistics
Heidelberg University
69120 Heidelberg, Germany
{simianer,riezler}@cl.uni-heidelberg.de

Abstract

Multi-task learning has been shown to be effective in various applications, including discriminative SMT. We present an experimental evaluation of the question whether multi-task learning depends on a "natural" division of data into tasks that balance shared and individual knowledge, or whether its inherent regularization makes multi-task learning a broadly applicable remedy against overfitting. To investigate this question, we compare "natural" tasks defined as sections of the International Patent Classification versus "random" tasks defined as random shards in the context of patent SMT. We find that both versions of multi-task learning improve equally well over independent and pooled baselines, and gain nearly 2 BLEU points over standard MERT tuning.

1 Introduction

Multi-task learning is motivated by situations where a number of statistical models need to be estimated from data belonging to different tasks. It is assumed that the data are not completely independent of one another as they share some commonalities, yet they differ enough to counter a simple pooling of data. The goal of multi-task learning is to take advantage of commonalities among tasks by learning a shared model without neglecting individual knowledge. For example, Obozinski et al. (2010) present an optical character recognition scenario where data consist of samples of handwritten characters from several writers. While the styles of different writers vary, it is expected that there are also commonalities on a pixel- or stroke-level that are shared across writers. Chapelle et al. (2011) present a scenario where data from search engine query logs are available for different countries. While the rankings for some queries will have to be country-specific (they cite "football" as a query requiring different rankings in the US and the UK), a large fraction of queries will be country-insensitive. Wäschle and Riezler (2012b) present multi-task learning for statistical machine translation (SMT) of patents from different classes (so-called sections) according to the International Patent Classification (IPC)[1]. While the vocabulary may differ between the different IPC sections, specific legal jargon and a typical textual structure will be shared across IPC sections. As shown in the cited works, treating data from different writers, countries, or IPC classes as data from different tasks, and applying generic multi-task learning to the specific scenario, improves learning results over learning independent or pooled models.

The research question we ask in this paper is as follows: Is multi-task learning dependent on a "natural" task structure in the data, where shared and individual knowledge is properly balanced? Or can multi-task learning be seen as a general regularization technique that prevents overfitting irrespective of the task structure in the data?

We investigate this research question on the example of discriminative training for patent translation, using the algorithm for multi-task learning with ℓ_1/ℓ_2 regularization presented by Simianer et al. (2012). We compare multi-task learning on "natural" tasks given by IPC sections to multi-task learning on "random" tasks given by random shards and to baseline models trained on independent tasks and pooled tasks. We find that both versions of multi-task learning improve over independent or pooled training. However, differences between multi-task learning on IPC tasks and random tasks are small. This points to a more general regularization effect of multi-task learning and indicates a broad applicability of multi-task learning techniques. Another advantage of the ℓ_1/ℓ_2 reg-

[1] http://wipo.int/classifications/ipc/en/

ularization technique of Simianer et al. (2012) is a considerable efficiency gain due to parallelization and iterative feature selection that makes the algorithm suitable for big data applications and for large-scale training with millions of sparse features. Last but not least, our best result for multitask learning improves by nearly 2 BLEU points over the standard MERT baseline.

2 Related Work

Multi-task learning is an active area in machine learning, dating back at least to Caruana (1997). A regularization perspective was introduced by Evgeniou and Pontil (2004), who formalize the central idea of trading off optimality of parameter vectors for each task-specific model and closeness of these model parameters to the average parameter vector across models in an SVM framework. Equivalent formalizations replace parameter regularization by Bayesian prior distributions on the parameters (Finkel and Manning, 2009) or by augmentation of the feature space with domain independent features (Daumé, 2007). Besides SVMs, several learning algorithms have been extended to the multi-task scenario in a parameter regularization setting, e.g., perceptron-type algorithms (Dredze et al., 2010) or boosting (Chapelle et al., 2011). Further variants include different formalizations of norms for parameter regularization, e.g., ℓ_1/ℓ_2 regularization (Obozinski et al., 2010) or ℓ_1/ℓ_∞ regularization (Quattoni et al., 2009), where only the features that are most important across all tasks are kept in the model.

Early research on multi-task learning for SMT has investigated pooling of IPC sections, with larger pools improving results (Utiyama and Isahara, 2007; Tinsley et al., 2010; Ceauşu et al., 2011). Wäschle and Riezler (2012b) apply multitask learning to tasks defined as IPC sections and compare patent translation on independent tasks, pooled tasks, and multi-task learning, using samesized training data. They show small but statistically significant improvements for multi-task learning over independent and pooled training. Duh et al. (2010) introduce random tasks as n-best lists of translations and showed significant improvements by applying various multi-task learning techniques to discriminative reranking. Song et al. (2011) define tasks as bootstrap samples from the development set and show significant improvements for a bagging-based system combination over individual MERT training.

In this paper we apply the multi-task learning technique of Simianer et al. (2012) to tasks defined as IPC sections and to random tasks. Their algorithm can be seen as a weight-based backward feature elimination variant of Obozinski et al. (2010)'s gradient-based forward feature selection algorithm for ℓ_1/ℓ_2 regularization. The latter approach is related to the general methodology of using block norms to select entire groups of features jointly. For example, such groups can be defined as non-overlapping subsets of features (Yuan and Lin, 2006), or as hierarchical groups of features (Zhao et al., 2009), or they can be grouped by the general structure of the prediction problem (Martins et al., 2011). However, these approaches are concerned with grouping features within a single prediction problem whereas multitask learning adds an orthogonal layer of multiple task-specific prediction problems. By virtue of averaging selected weights after each epoch, the algorithm of Simianer et al. (2012) is related to McDonald et al. (2010)'s iterative mixing procedure. This algorithm is itself related to the bagging procedure of Breiman (1996), if random shards are considered from the perspective of random samples. In both cases averaging helps to reduce the variance of the per-sample classifiers.

3 Multi-task Learning for Discriminative Training in SMT

In multi-task learning, we have data points $\{(x_z^i, y_z^i), i = 1, \ldots, N_z, z = 1, \ldots, Z\}$, sampled from a distribution P_z on $X \times Y$. The subscript z indexes tasks and the superscript i indexes i.i.d. data for each task. For the application of discriminative ranking in SMT, the space X can be thought of as feature representations of n-best translations, and the space Y denotes corresponding sentence-level BLEU scores.[2] We assume that P_z is different for each task but that the P_z's are related as, for example, considered in Evgeniou and Pontil (2004). The standard approach is to fit an independent model involving a D-dimensional parameter vector $\mathbf{w}_z$ for each task z. In multi-task learning, we consider a Z-by-D matrix $\mathbf{W} = (\mathbf{w}_z^d)_{z,d}$ of stacked D-dimensional row vectors $\mathbf{w}_z$, and Z-dimensional column vectors $\mathbf{w}^d$ of weights associated with feature d across tasks. The central al-

[2]See Duh et al. (2010) for a similar formalization for the case of n-best reranking via multi-task learning.

gorithms in most multi-task learning techniques can be characterized as a form of regularization that enforces closeness of task-specific parameter vectors to shared parameter vectors, or promotes sparse models that only contain features that are shared across tasks. In this paper, we will follow the approach of Simianer et al. (2012), who formalize multi-task learning as a distributed feature selection algorithm using ℓ_1/ℓ_2 regularization. ℓ_1/ℓ_2 regularization can be described as penalizing weights $\mathbf{W}$ by the weighted ℓ_1/ℓ_2 norm, which is defined following Obozinski et al. (2010), as

$$\lambda \|\mathbf{W}\|_{1,2} = \lambda \sum_{d=1}^{D} \|\mathbf{w}^d\|_2.$$

Each ℓ_2 norm of a weight column $\mathbf{w}^d$ represents the relevance of the corresponding feature across tasks. The ℓ_1 sum of the ℓ_2 norms enforces a selection of features by encouraging several feature columns $\mathbf{w}^d$ to be $\mathbf{0}$ and others to have high weights across all tasks. This results in shrinking the matrix to the features that are useful across all tasks.

Simianer et al. (2012) achieve this behavior by the following weight-based iterative feature elimination algorithm that is wrapped around a stochastic gradient descent (SGD) algorithm for pairwise ranking (Shen and Joshi, 2005):

Algorithm 1 Multi-task SGD

Get data for Z tasks, each including S sentences; distribute to machines.
Initialize $\mathbf{v} \leftarrow \mathbf{0}$.
for epochs $t \leftarrow 0 \dots T-1$: **do**
  for all tasks $z \in \{1 \dots Z\}$: **parallel do**
    $\mathbf{w}_{z,t,0,0} \leftarrow \mathbf{v}$
    for all sentences $i \in \{0 \dots S-1\}$: **do**
      Decode i^{th} input with $\mathbf{w}_{z,t,i,0}$.
      for all pairs $j \in \{0 \dots P-1\}$: **do**
        $\mathbf{w}_{z,t,i,j+1} \leftarrow \mathbf{w}_{z,t,i,j} - \eta \nabla l_j(\mathbf{w}_{z,t,i,j})$
      end for
      $\mathbf{w}_{z,t,i+1,0} \leftarrow \mathbf{w}_{z,t,i,P}$
    end for
  end for
  Stack weights $\mathbf{W} \leftarrow [\mathbf{w}_{1,t,S,0}| \dots |\mathbf{w}_{Z,t,S,0}]^T$
  Select top K feature columns of $\mathbf{W}$ by ℓ_2 norm
  for $k \leftarrow 1 \dots K$ **do**
    $\mathbf{v}[k] = \frac{1}{Z} \sum_{z=1}^{Z} \mathbf{W}[z][k].$
  end for
end for
return v

The innermost loop of the algorithm computes an SGD update based on the subgradient ∇l_j of a pairwise loss function. ℓ_1/ℓ_2-based feature selection is done after each epoch of SGD training for each task in parallel. The ℓ_2 norm of the weights is computed for each feature column across tasks; features are sorted by this value; K top features are kept in the model; reduced weight vectors are mixed and the result is re-sent to each task-specific model to start another epoch of parallel training for each task.

We compare two different loss functions for pairwise ranking, one corresponding to the original perceptron algorithm (Rosenblatt, 1958), and an improved version called the margin perceptron (Collobert and Bengio, 2004). To create training data for a pairwise ranking setup, we generate preference pairs by ordering translations according to smoothed sentence-wise BLEU score (Nakov et al., 2012). Let each translation candidate in the n-best list be represented by a feature vector $\mathbf{x} \in \mathbb{R}^D$: For notational convenience, we denote by $\mathbf{x}_j$ a preference pair $\mathbf{x}_j = (\mathbf{x}_j^{(1)}, \mathbf{x}_j^{(2)})$ where $\mathbf{x}_j^{(1)}$ is ordered above $\mathbf{x}_j^{(2)}$ w.r.t. BLEU. Furthermore, we use the shorthand $\bar{\mathbf{x}}_j = \mathbf{x}_j^{(1)} - \mathbf{x}_j^{(2)}$ to denote a D-dimensional difference vector representing an input pattern. For completeness, a label $y = +1$ can be assigned to patterns $\bar{\mathbf{x}}_j$ where $\mathbf{x}_j^{(1)}$ is ordered above $\mathbf{x}_j^{(2)}$ ($y = -1$ otherwise), however, since the ordering relation is antisymmetric, we can consider an ordering in one direction and omit the label entirely.

The original perceptron algorithm is based on the following hinge loss-type objective function:

$$l_j(\mathbf{w}) = (-\langle \mathbf{w}, \bar{\mathbf{x}}_j \rangle)_+$$

where $(a)_+ = \max(0, a)$, $\mathbf{w} \in \mathbb{R}^D$ is a weight vector, and $\langle \cdot, \cdot \rangle$ denotes the standard vector dot product. Instantiating SGD to the stochastic subgradient

$$\nabla l_j(\mathbf{w}) = \begin{cases} -\bar{\mathbf{x}}_j & \text{if } \langle \mathbf{w}, \bar{\mathbf{x}}_j \rangle \leq 0, \\ 0 & \text{else.} \end{cases}$$

leads to the perceptron algorithm for pairwise ranking (Shen and Joshi, 2005).

Collobert and Bengio (2004) presented a version of perceptron learning that includes a margin term in order to control the capacity and thus the generalization performance. Their margin perceptron algorithm follows from applying SGD to the loss function

$$l_j(\mathbf{w}) = (1 - \langle \mathbf{w}, \bar{\mathbf{x}}_j \rangle)_+$$

with the following stochastic subgradient

$$\nabla l_j(\mathbf{w}) = \begin{cases} -\bar{\mathbf{x}}_j & \text{if } \langle \mathbf{w}, \bar{\mathbf{x}}_j \rangle < 1, \\ 0 & \text{else.} \end{cases}$$

Collobert and Bengio (2004) argue that the use of a margin term justifies not using an explicit regularization, thus making the margin perceptron an efficient and effective learning machine.

4 Experiments

4.1 Data & System Setup

For training, development and testing, we use data extracted from the PatTR[3] corpus for the experiments in Wäschle and Riezler (2012b). Training data consists of about 1.2 million German-English parallel sentences. We translate from German into English. German compound words were split using the technique of Koehn and Knight (2003). We use the SCFG decoder cdec (Dyer et al., 2010)[4] and build grammars using its implementation of the suffix array extraction method described in Lopez (2007). Word alignments are built from all parallel data using mgiza[5] and the Moses scripts[6]. SCFG models use the same settings as described in Chiang (2007). We built a modified Kneser-Ney smoothed 5-gram language model using the English side of the training data and performed querying with KenLM (Heafield, 2011)[7].

The International Patent Classification (IPC) categorizes patents hierarchically into 8 sections, 120 classes, 600 subclasses, down to 70,000 subgroups at the leaf level. The eight top classes (called sections) are listed in Table 1.

A	Human Necessities
B	Performing Operations, Transporting
C	Chemistry, Metallurgy
D	Textiles, Paper
E	Fixed Constructions
F	Mechanical Engineering, Lighting, Heating, Weapons
G	Physics
H	Electricity

Table 1: IPC top level **sections**.

Typically, a patent belongs to more than one section, with one section chosen as main classification. Our development and test sets for each of the classes, A to H, comprise 2,000 sentences each, originating from a patent with the respective class. These sets were built so that there is no overlap of development sets and test sets, and no overlap between sets of different classes. These eight test sets are referred to as *independent* test sets. Furthermore, we test on a combined set, called *pooled-cat*, that is constructed by concatenating the independent sets. Additionally we use two *pooled* sets for development and testing, each containing 2,000 sentences with all classes evenly represented.

Our tuning baseline is an implementation of hypergraph MERT (Kumar et al., 2009), directly optimizing IBM BLEU4 (Papineni et al., 2002). Furthermore, we present a regularization baseline by applying ℓ_1 regularization with clipping (Carpenter, 2008; Tsuruoka et al., 2009) to the standard pairwise ranking perceptron. All pairwise ranking methods use a smoothed sentence-wise BLEU+1 score (Nakov et al., 2012) to create gold standard rankings. Our multi-task learning experiments are based on pairwise ranking perceptrons that differ in their objective, corresponding either to the original *perceptron* or to the *margin-perceptron*. Both versions of the perceptron are used for *single-task tuning* and *multi-task tuning*. In the multi-task setting, we compare three different methods for defining a task: "natural" tasks given by *IPC* sections where each *independent* data set is considered as task; "random" tasks, defined by *sharding* where data is shuffled and split once, tasks are kept fixed throughout, and by *resharding* where after an epoch data is shuffled and new random tasks are constructed. In all cases a task/shard is defined to contain 2,000 sentences[8], resulting in eight shards for each setting. The number of features selected after each epoch was set to $K = 100,000$.

For all perceptron runs, the following meta parameters were fixed: A cube pruning pop limit of 200 and non-terminal span limit of 15; 100-best lists with unique entries; constant learning rate; multipartite pair selection. Single-task perceptron runs on *independent* and *pooled* tasks were done

[3] http://www.cl.uni-heidelberg.de/statnlpgroup/pattr

[4] https://github.com/redpony/cdec

[5] http://www.kyloo.net/software/doku.php/mgiza:overview

[6] http://www.statmt.org/moses/?n=Moses.SupportTools

[7] http://kheafield.com/code/kenlm/estimation/

[8] This number is determined by the size of the original development sets; variations of this size did not change results.

	single-task tuning		
	indep. ^{0}	pooled ^{1}	pooled-cat ^{2}
pooled test	–	51.18	51.22
A	54.92	^{02}55.27	^{0}55.17
B	51.53	51.48	^{01}51.69
C	^{12}56.31	^{2}55.90	55.74
D	49.94	^{0}50.33	^{0}50.26
E	^{1}49.19	48.97	^{1}49.13
F	^{12}51.26	51.02	51.12
G	^{1}49.61	49.44	49.55
H	49.38	49.50	^{01}49.67
average test	**51.52**	**51.49**	**51.54**

Table 2: BLEU4 results of MERT baseline using dense features for three different tuning sets: *independent* (separate tuning sets for each IPC class), *pooled* and *pooled-cat* (concatenated *independent* sets). Significant superior performance over other systems in the same row is denoted by prefixed numbers. The first row shows, e.g., that the result of *pooled* ^{1} is significantly better than *independent* ^{0}, and *pooled-cat* ^{2}.

	single-task tuning		
	indep. ^{0}	pooled ^{1}	pooled-cat ^{2}
pooled test	–	50.75	^{1} 52.08
A	^{1} 55.11	54.32	^{01} 55.94
B	^{1} 52.61	50.84	^{1} 52.57
C	56.18	56.11	^{01} 56.75
D	^{1} 50.68	49.48	^{01} 51.22
E	^{1} 50.27	48.69	^{1} 50.01
F	^{1} 51.68	50.71	^{1} 51.95
G	^{1} 49.90	49.06	^{01} 50.51
H	^{1} 50.48	49.16	^{1} 50.53
average test	**52.11**	**51.05**	**52.44**
model size	430,092.5	457,428	1,574,259

Table 3: BLEU4 results for standard *perceptron with ℓ_1 regularization* baseline using sparse rule features, tuned on *independent*, *pooled* and *pooled-cat* sets. Prefixed superscripts denote a significant improvement over the result in the same row indicated by the superscript.

for 15 epochs; multi-task perceptron runs used 10 epochs. Single-task tuning on *pooled-cat* data increases computation time by a factor of eight which makes this setup infeasible in practice. For the sake of comparison we performed 10 epochs in this setup.

MERT (with default parameters) is used to optimize the weights of 12 dense default features; eight translation model features, a word penalty, the passthrough weight, the language model (LM) score, and an LM out-of-vocabulary penalty. Perceptron training allows to add millions of sparse features which are directly derived from grammar rules: rule shape, rule identifier, bigrams in rule source and target. For a further explanation of these features see Simianer et al. (2012).

For testing we measured IBM BLEU4 on tokenized and lowercased data. Significance results were obtained by approximate randomization tests using the approach of Clark et al. (2011)[9] to account for optimizer instability. Tuning methods with a random component (MERT, randomized experiments) were repeated three times, scores reported in the tables are averaged over optimizer runs.

4.2 Experimental Results

In single-task tuning mode, systems are tuned on the eight *independent* data sets separately, the *pooled* data set, and the independent data sets concatenated (*pooled-cat*). Testing is done on each of the eight IPC sections separately, and on a *pooled test* set of 2,000 sentences where all sections are equally represented. Furthermore, we report **average test** results over runs for all independent data sets.

Results for the MERT baseline are shown in Table 2: Neither pooling nor concatenating independent sets leads to significant performance improvements on all sets with averaged scores being nearly identical.

Evaluation results obtained with the standard *perceptron* algorithm (Table 4) show improvements over MERT in *single-task tuning* mode. The gain on *pooled-cat* data shows that in contrast to MERT training on 12 dense features, discriminative training using large feature sets is able to benefit from large data sets. However, since the *pooled-cat* scenario increases computation time by a factor of 8, it is quite infeasible when used with large sets of sparse features. Single-task tuning on a small set of *pooled* data seems to show overfitting behavior.

Table 3 shows evaluation results for a regularization baseline that applies ℓ_1 *regularization with clipping* to the the single-task tuned standard perceptron in Table 4. We see gains in BLEU on independent and pooled-cat tuning data, but not on the small pooled data set.

Multi-task tuning for the standard perceptron is shown in the right half of Table 4. Because of parallelization, this scenario is as efficient as

[9] https://github.com/jhclark/multeval

	single-task tuning			multi-task tuning		
	indep. ^{0}	pooled ^{1}	pooled-cat ^{2}	IPC ^{3}	sharding ^{4}	resharding ^{5}
pooled test	–	51.33	^{1} 51.77	^{12} 52.56	^{12} 52.54	^{12} 52.60
A	54.79	54.76	^{01} 55.31	^{012} 56.35	^{012} 56.22	^{012} 56.21
B	^{12} 52.45	51.30	^{1} 52.19	^{012} 52.78	^{0123} 52.98	^{012} 52.96
C	^{2} 56.62	56.65	^{1} 56.12	^{01245} 57.76	^{012} 57.30	^{012} 57.44
D	^{1} 50.75	49.88	^{1} 50.63	^{01245} 51.54	^{012} 51.33	^{012} 51.20
E	^{1} 49.70	49.23	^{01} 49.92	^{012} 50.51	^{012} 50.52	^{012} 50.38
F	^{1} 51.60	51.09	^{1} 51.71	^{012} 52.28	^{012} 52.43	^{012} 52.32
G	^{1} 49.50	49.06	^{01} 49.97	^{012} 50.84	^{012} 50.88	^{012} 50.74
H	^{1} 49.77	49.50	^{01} 50.64	^{012} 51.16	^{012} 51.07	^{012} 51.10
average test	**51.90**	**51.42**	**52.06**	**52.90**	**52.84**	**52.79**
model size	366,869.4	448,359	1,478,049	100,000	100,000	100,000

Table 4: BLEU4 results for standard *perceptron* algorithm using sparse rule features, tuned in single-task mode on *independent*, *pooled*, and *pooled-cat* sets, and in multi-task mode on eight tasks taken from *IPC* sections or by random *(re)sharding*. Prefixed superscripts denote a significant improvement over the result in the same row indicated by the superscript.

	single-task tuning			multi-task tuning		
	indep. ^{0}	pooled ^{1}	pooled-cat ^{2}	IPC ^{3}	sharding ^{4}	resharding ^{5}
pooled test	–	51.33	^{1} 52.58	^{12} 52.98	^{12} 52.95	^{12} 52.99
A	^{1} 56.09	55.33	^{1} 55.92	^{01245}56.78	^{012} 56.62	^{012} 56.53
B	^{1} 52.45	51.59	^{1} 52.44	^{012}53.31	^{012} 53.35	^{012} 53.21
C	^{1} 57.20	56.85	^{01} 57.54	^{01}57.46	^{1} 57.42	^{1} 57.43
D	^{1} 50.51	50.18	^{01} 51.38	^{01245}52.14	^{0125} 51.82	^{012} 51.66
E	^{1} 50.27	49.36	^{01} 50.72	^{0124}51.13	^{012} 50.89	^{012} 51.02
F	^{1} 52.06	51.20	^{01} 52.61	^{01245}53.07	^{012} 52.80	^{012} 52.87
G	^{1} 50.00	49.58	^{01} 50.90	^{01245}51.36	^{012} 51.19	^{012} 51.11
H	^{1} 50.57	49.80	^{01} 51.32	^{012}51.57	^{012} 51.62	^{01} 51.47
average test	**52.39**	**51.74**	**52.85**	**53.35**	**53.21**	**53.16**
model size	423,731.5	484,483	1,697,398	100,000	100,000	100,000

Table 5: BLEU4 results for *margin-perceptron* algorithm using sparse rule features, tuned in single-task mode on *independent* tasks, and in multi-task mode on eight tasks taken from *IPC* sections or by random *(re)sharding*. Prefixed superscripts denote a significant improvement over the result in the same row indicated by the superscript.

single-task tuning on small data. We see improvements in BLEU over single-task tuning on small and large tuning data sets. Concerning our initial research questions, we see that the performance difference between "natural" tasks (IPC) and "random" tasks is not conclusive. However, multi-task learning using ℓ_1/ℓ_2 regularization consistently outperforms the standard perceptron under ℓ_1 regularization as shown in Table 3 and MERT tuning as shown in Table 2.

Table 5 shows the evaluation results of the *margin-perceptron* algorithm. Evaluation results on *single-task tuning* show that this algorithm improves over the standard perceptron (Table 4), even in its ℓ_1-regularized version (Table 3), on all tuning sets. Results for *multi-task tuning* show improvements over the same scenario for the standard perceptron (Table 4). This means that the improvements due to the orthogonal regularization techniques in example space and feature space, namely large-margin learning and multi-task learning, add up. A comparison between *single-task* and *multi-task tuning* modes of the margin-perceptron shows a gain for the latter scenarios. Differences between multi-task learning on *IPC* classes versus random *sharding* or *resharding* are again small, with the best overall result obtained by multi-task learning of the margin-perceptron on IPC classes.

Overall, our best multi-task learing result is nearly 2 BLEU points better than MERT training. The algorithm to achieve this result is efficient due to parallelization and due to iterative feature selection. As shown in the last rows of Tables 3-5 , the average size is around 400K features for independently tuned models and around 1.6M features for models tuned on pooled-cat data. In multi-task learning, models can be iteratively cut to 100K shared features whose weights are tuned in parallel.

5 Conclusion

We presented an experimental investigation of the question whether the power of multi-task learning depends on data structured along tasks that exhibit a proper balance of shared and individual knowledge, or whether its inherent feature selection and regularization makes multi-task learning a widely applicable remedy against overfitting. We compared multi-task patent SMT for "natural" tasks of IPC sections and "random" tasks of shards in distributed learning. Both versions of multi-task learning yield significant improvements over independent and pooled training, however, the difference between "natural" and "random" tasks is marginal. This is an indication for the usefulness of multi-task learning as a generic regularization tool. Considering also the efficiency gained by iterative feature selection, the ℓ_1/ℓ_2 regularization algorithm presented in Simianer et al. (2012) presents itself as an efficient and effective learning algorithm for general big data and sparse feature applications. Furthermore, the improvements by multi-task feature selection add up with improvements by large-margin learning, delivering overall improvements of nearly 2 BLEU points over the standard MERT baseline.

Our research question regarding the superiority of "natural" or "random" tasks was shown to be undetermined for the application of patent translation. The obvious question for future work is if and how a task division can be found that improves multi-task learning over our current results. Such an investigation will have to explore various similarity metrics and clustering techniques for IPC sub-classes (Wäschle and Riezler, 2012a), e.g., for the goal of optimizing clustering with respect to the ratio of between-cluster to within-cluster similarity for a given metric. However, the final criterion for the usefulness of a clustering is necessarily application specific (von Luxburg et al., 2012), in our case specific to patent translation performance. Nevertheless, we hope that the presented and future work will prove useful and generalizable for related multi-task learning scenarios.

Acknowledgments

The research presented in this paper was supported in part by DFG grant "Cross-language Learning-to-Rank for Patent Retrieval".

References

Leo Breiman. 1996. Bagging predictors. *Machine Learning*, 24:123–140.

Bob Carpenter. 2008. Lazy sparse stochastic gradient descent for regularized multinomial logistic regression. Technical report, Alias-i.

Rich Caruana. 1997. Multitask learning. *Journal of Machine Learning Research*, 28.

Alexandru Ceauşu, John Tinsley, Jian Zhang, and Andy Way. 2011. Experiments on domain adaptation for patent machine translation in the PLuTO project. In *Proceedings of the 15th Conference of the European Association for Machine Translation (EAMT 2011)*, Leuven, Belgium.

Olivier Chapelle, Pannagadatta Shivaswamy, Srinivas Vadrevu, Kilian Weinberger, Ya Zhang, and Belle Tseng. 2011. Boosted multi-task learning. *Machine Learning*.

David Chiang. 2007. Hierarchical phrase-based translation. *Computational Linguistics*, 33.

Jonathan Clark, Chris Dyer, Alon Lavie, and Noah Smith. 2011. Better hypothesis testing for statistical machine translation: Controlling for optimizer instability. In *Proceedings of the 49th Annual Meeting of the Association for Computational Linguistics (ACL'11)*, Portland, OR.

Ronan Collobert and Samy Bengio. 2004. Links between perceptrons, MLPs, and SVMs. In *Proceedings of the 21st International Conference on Machine Learning (ICML'04)*, Banff, Canada.

Hal Daumé. 2007. Frustratingly easy domain adaptation. In *Proceedings of the 45th Annual Meeting of the Association for Computational Linguistics (ACL'07)*, Prague, Czech Republic.

Mark Dredze, Alex Kulesza, and Koby Crammer. 2010. Multi-domain learning by confidence-weighted parameter combination. *Machine Learning*, 79:123–149.

Kevin Duh, Katsuhito Sudoh, Hajime Tsukada, Hideki Isozaki, and Masaaki Nagata. 2010. N-best reranking by multitask learning. In *Proceedings of the 5th Joint Workshop on Statistical Machine Translation and MetricsMATR*, Uppsala, Sweden.

Chris Dyer, Adam Lopez, Juri Ganitkevitch, Johnathan Weese, Ferhan Ture, Phil Blunsom, Hendra Setiawan, Vladimir Eidelman, and Philip Resnik. 2010. cdec: A decoder, alignment, and learning framework for finite-state and context-free translation models. In *Proceedings of the 48th Annual Meeting of the Association for Computational Linguistics (ACL'10)*.

Theodoros Evgeniou and Massimiliano Pontil. 2004. Regularized multi-task learning. In *Proceedings of the 10th ACM SIGKDD conference on knowledge discovery and data mining (KDD'04)*, Seattle, WA.

Jenny Rose Finkel and Christopher D. Manning. 2009. Hierarchical Bayesian domain adaptation. In *Proceedings of the Conference of the North American Chapter of the Association for Computational Linguistics - Human Language Technologies (NAACL-HLT'09)*, Boulder, CO.

Kenneth Heafield. 2011. KenLM: faster and smaller language model queries. In *Proceedings of the Sixth Workshop on Statistical Machine Translation (WMT'11)*, Edinburgh, UK.

Philipp Koehn and Kevin Knight. 2003. Empirical methods for compound splitting. In *Proceedings of the 10th conference on European chapter of the Association for Computational Linguistics (EACL'03)*, Budapest, Hungary.

Shankar Kumar, Wolfgang Macherey, Chris Dyer, and Franz Och. 2009. Efficient minimum error rate training and minimum Bayes-risk decoding for translation hypergraphs and lattices. In *Proceedings of the 47th Annual Meeting of the Association for Computational Linguistics and the 4th IJCNLP of the AFNLP (ACL-IJCNLP'09*, Suntec, Singapore.

Adam Lopez. 2007. Hierarchical phrase-based translation with suffix arrays. In *Proceedings of EMNLP-CoNLL*, Prague, Czech Republic.

André F. T. Martins, Noah A. Smith, Pedro M. Q. Aguiar, and Mário A. T. Figueiredo. 2011. Structured sparsity in structured prediction. In *Proceedings of the 2011 Conference on Empirical Methods in Natural Language Processing*, Edinburgh, Scotland.

Ryan McDonald, Keith Hall, and Gideon Mann. 2010. Distributed training strategies for the structured perceptron. In *Proceedings of Human Language Technologies: The 11th Annual Conference of the North American Chapter of the Association for Computational Linguistics (NAACL-HLT'10)*, Los Angeles, CA.

Preslav Nakov, Francisco Guzmán, and Stephan Vogel. 2012. Optimizing for sentence-level bleu+1 yields short translations. In *Proceedings of the 24th International Conference on Computational Linguistics (COLING 2012)*, Bombay, India.

Guillaume Obozinski, Ben Taskar, and Michael I. Jordan. 2010. Joint covariate selection and joint subspace selection for multiple classification problems. *Statistics and Computing*, 20:231–252.

Kishore Papineni, Salim Roukos, Todd Ward, and Wei-Jing Zhu. 2002. Bleu: a method for automatic evaluation of machine translation. In *Proceedings of the 40th Annual Meeting on Association for Computational Linguistics*, ACL '02, pages 311–318, Stroudsburg, PA, USA. Association for Computational Linguistics.

Ariadna Quattoni, Xavier Carreras, Michael Collins, and Trevor Darrell. 2009. An efficient projection for $\ell_{1,\infty}$ regularization. In *Proceedings of the 26th International Conference on Machine Learning (ICML'09)*, Montreal, Canada.

Frank Rosenblatt. 1958. The perceptron: A probabilistic model for information storage and organization in the brain. *Psychological Review*, 65(6).

Libin Shen and Aravind K. Joshi. 2005. Ranking and reranking with perceptron. *Journal of Machine Learning Research*, 60(1-3):73–96.

Patrick Simianer, Stefan Riezler, and Chris Dyer. 2012. Joint feature selection in distributed stochastic learning for large-scale discriminative training in SMT. In *Proceedings of the 50th Annual Meeting of the Association for Computational Linguistics (ACL 2012)*, Jeju, Korea.

Linfeng Song, Haitao Mi, Yajuan Lü, and Qun Liu. 2011. Bagging-based system combination for domain adaptation. In *Proceedings of MT Summit XIII*, Xiamen, China.

John Tinsley, Andy Way, and Paraic Sheridan. 2010. PLuTO: MT for online patent translation. In *Proceedings of the 9th Conference of the Association for Machine Translation in the Americas (AMTA 2010)*, Denver, CO.

Yoshimasa Tsuruoka, Jun'ichi Tsujii, and Sophia Ananiadou. 2009. Stochastic gradient descent training for ℓ_1-regularized log-linear models with cumulative penalty. In *Proceedings of the 47th Annual Meeting of the Association for Computational Linguistics (ACL-IJCNLP'09)*, Singapore.

Masao Utiyama and Hitoshi Isahara. 2007. A Japanese-English patent parallel corpus. In *Proceedings of MT Summit XI*, Copenhagen, Denmark.

Ulrike von Luxburg, Robert C. Williamson, and Isabelle Guyon. 2012. Clustering: Science or art? In *Proceedings of the ICML 2011 Workshop on Unsupervised and Transfer Learning*, Bellevue, WA.

Katharina Wäschle and Stefan Riezler. 2012a. Analyzing parallelism and domain similarities in the MAREC patent corpus. In *Proceedings of the 5th Information Retrieval Facility Conference (IRFC 2012)*, Vienna, Austria.

Katharina Wäschle and Stefan Riezler. 2012b. Structural and topical dimensions in multi-task patent translation. In *Proceedings of the 13th Conference of the European Chapter of the Association for Computational Linguistics*, Avignon, France.

Ming Yuan and Yi Lin. 2006. Model selection and estimation in regression with grouped variables. *J.R.Statist.Soc.B*, 68(1):49–67.

Peng Zhao, Guilherme Rocha, and Bin Yu. 2009. The composite absolute penalties family for grouped and hierarchical variable selection. *The Annals of Statistics*, 37(6A):3468–3497.

Online Learning Approaches in Computer Assisted Translation

Prashant Mathur‡†, Mauro Cettolo†, Marcello Federico†
‡ University of Trento
† FBK - Fondazione Bruno Kessler
Trento, Italy
{prashant, cettolo, federico}@fbk.eu

Abstract

We present a novel online learning approach for statistical machine translation tailored to the computer assisted translation scenario. With the introduction of a simple online feature, we are able to adapt the translation model on the fly to the corrections made by the translators. Additionally, we do online adaption of the feature weights with a large margin algorithm. Our results show that our online adaptation technique outperforms the static phrase based statistical machine translation system by 6 BLEU points absolute, and a standard incremental adaptation approach by 2 BLEU points absolute.

1 Introduction

The growing needs of the localization and translation industry have recently boosted research around computer assisted translation (CAT) technology. The purpose of CAT is to increase the productivity of a human translator. A CAT tool comes as a package of a Translation Memory (TM), built-in spell checkers, a dictionary, a terminology list etc. which help the translator while translating a sentence. Recent research has led to the integration of CAT tools with statistical machine translation (SMT) engines. SMT makes use of a large available parallel corpus to generate statistical models for translation. Due to their generalization capability, SMT systems are a good fit in this scenario and a seamless integration of SMT engines in CAT have shown to increase translator's productivity (Federico et al., 2012).

Although automatic systems generate reliable translations they are not accurate enough to be used directly and need postedition by human translators. In state-of-the-art CAT tools, the SMT systems are static in nature and so they cannot adapt to these corrections. When a SMT system keeps repeating the same error, productivity of translators as well as their trust in SMT technology are negatively affected. As an example, technical documentation typically contains a lot of *repetitions* due to the employed writing style and pervasive use of terminology. Hence, in order to provide useful hints, SMT systems are expected to behave consistently regarding the translation of domain-specific terms. However, if the user edits the translation of a technical term in the target text, most current SMT systems are incapable to learn from those corrections.

Online learning is a machine learning task where a predictor iteratively: (1) receives an input and outputs a label, (2) receives the correct label from a human and if the two labels do not match, it learns from the mistake. The task of learning from user corrections at the sentence level fits well the online learning scenario, and its expected usefulness is clearly related to the amount of repetitions occurring in the text. The higher the number of repetitions in a document the more the SMT system has chances to translate consistently through the use of online learning.

In this paper, we implemented two online learning methods through which a phrase-based SMT system evolves over time, sentence after sentence, by taking advantage of the post-edition or translation of the previous sentence by the user.[1]

In the first approach, we focus on the translation model aspect of SMT which is represented by five conventional features, namely lexical and phrase translation probabilities in both directed and inverted directions, plus a phrase penalty score. Translation, language and reordering models are combined in a linear fashion to obtain a score for

[1]Moses code is available in the github repository. `https://github.com/mtresearcher/mosesdecoder/tree/moses_onlinelearning`

the translation hypothesis as shown in Equation 1.

$$score(e^*, f) = \Sigma_i \lambda_i h_i(e^*, f) \quad (1)$$

where $h_i(\cdot)$ are the feature functions representing the models and λ_i are the linear weights. The highest scored translation is the best hypothesis e^* output by the system. We extend the translation model with a new feature which provides extra phrase-pair scores changing according to the user feedback. The scores of the new feature are adapted in a discriminative fashion, by rewarding phrase-pairs observed in the search space and in the reference, and penalizing phrase-pairs observed in the search space but not in the reference.

In the second approach, we also adapt the model weights of the linear combination after each test sentence by using a margin infused relaxed algorithm (MIRA).

For assessing the robustness of our methods, we performed experiments on two datasets from different domains and language pairs (§6). Moreover, our online learning approaches are compared against a static baseline system and against the incremental adaptation approach proposed by Levenberg et. al. (2010) (§5).

2 Related Works

Several online adaptation strategies have been proposed in the past, only a few deal with adaptation of post-edited/evaluation data while most works are on adaptation over development data during tuning of parameters (Och and Ney, 2003).

2.1 Online Adaptation during Tuning

Liang et. al. (2006) improved SMT performance by online adaptation of scaling factors (λ in (1)) using averaged perceptron algorithm (Collins, 2002). They presented different strategies to update the SMT models towards reference or oracle translation: (1) aggressively updating towards reference, *bold update*; (2) update towards the oracle translation in N-Best list, *local update*; (3) a hybrid approach in which a *bold* update is performed when the reference is reachable, otherwise a *local* update is performed. Liang and Klein (2009) compared two online EM algorithms, *stepwise online EM* (Sato and Ishii, 2000; Cappé and Moulines, 2007) and *incremental EM* (Neal and Hinton, 1998) which they use to update the alignment models (the generative component of SMT) on the fly. However, stepwise EM is prone to failure if mini-batch size and stepsize parameters are not chosen correctly, while incremental EM requires substantial storage costs because it has to store sufficient statistics for each sample. Other works on online minimum error rate training in SMT (Och and Ney, 2003) that deserve mentioning are (Hopkins and May, 2011; Hasler et al., 2011).

2.2 Online Adaptation during Decoding

Cesa-Bianchi et. al. (2008) proposed an online learning approach during decoding. They construct a layer of online weights over the regular feature weights and update these weights at sentence level using margin infused relaxed algorithm (Crammer and Singer, 2003); to our knowledge, this is the first work on online adaptation during decoding. Martínez-Gómez et. al. (2011; 2012) presented a comparison of online adaptation techniques in post editing scenario. They compared different adaptation strategies on scaling factors and feature functions (respectively, λ and $h(\cdot)$ in (1)). However, they modified the feature values during adaptation without any normalization, which disregards the initial assumption of the feature values being probabilities.

In our approach, the value of the additional *online feature* can be modified during decoding without changing other feature values (probabilities) and thus preserving their probability distribution.

3 Feature Adaptation

In the CAT scenario, the user receives a translation suggestion for each source segment, post-edits it and finally approves it. From the SMT point of view, for each source segment the decoder explores a search space of possible translations and finally returns the best scoring one (*bestHyp*) to the user. The user possibly corrects this suggestion thus generating the final translation (*postedit*).

Our online learning procedure is based on the following idea. For each N-best translation (*candidate*) in the search space, we compute a similarity score against the *postedit* using the sentence-level BLEU metric (Lin and Och, 2004), a smoothed variant of the popular BLEU metric (Papineni et al., 2001). We hence compare the similarity score of each *candidate* against the similarity score achieved by the *bestHyp*, that was also computed against the *postedit*. If the *candidate* scores better than the *bestHyp*, then we promote the building blocks, i.e. phrase-pairs, of *candidate* that were not used in *bestHyp* and demote the phrase-pairs used in *bestHyp* that were not used for *candidate*. On the contrary, if the *candidate* scores worse than the *bestHyp*, we promote the building blocks of *bestHyp* that are not in *candidate* and demote those of *candidate* that are not in *bestHyp*.

Our promotion/demotion mechanism could be implemented by updating the features values of the phrase pairs used in the *candidate* and *bestHyp* translations. However, features in the translation models are conditional probabilities and perturbing a subset of them by also preserving their normalization constraints can be computationally expensive. Instead, we propose to introduce an additional *online feature* which represents a goodness score of each phrase-pair in the test set.

We call the set of phrase pairs used to generate a *candidate* as $candidate_{PP}$ and the set of phrase pairs used to generate the *bestHyp* as $best_{PP}$. The online feature value of each phrase-pair is initialized to a constant and is updated according to the perceptron update (Rosenblatt, 1958) method. In particular, the amount by which a current feature value is rewarded or penalized depends on a learning rate α and on the difference between the model scores (i.e. $h \cdot w$) of *candidate* and *bestHyp* as calculated by the MT system. A sketch of our online learning procedure is shown in Algorithm 1.

Algorithm 1: Online Learning

```
foreach sourceSeg do
    bestHyp = Translate(sourceSeg);
    postedit = Human(bestHyp);
    for i = 1 → iterations do
        N-best=Nbest(source);
        foreach candidate ∈ N-best do
            sign = sgn |sBLEU(candidate) -
            sBLEU(bestHyp)| ;
            foreach phrasePair ∈ candidate_PP do
                if phrasePair ∉ best_PP then
                    f^i = f^(i-1) + (α · (Δh · w) ·
                    sign);
                end
            end
            foreach phrasePair ∈ best_PP do
                if phrasePair ∉ candidate_PP then
                    f^i = f^(i-1) - (α · (Δh · w) ·
                    sign);
                end
            end
        end
    end
end
```

In Algorithm 1, $\Delta h \cdot w$ is the above mentioned score difference as computed by the decoder; multiplied by α, it is the *margin*, that is the value with which the online feature score (f) of the phrase pair under processing is modified. We can observe that the feature scores are unbounded and could lead to instability of the algorithm; therefore, we normalise the scores through the sigmoid function:

$$f(x) = \frac{2}{1 + exp(x)} - 1 \qquad (2)$$

4 Weight Adaptation

In addition to adapting the online feature values, we can also apply online adaptation on the feature weights of the linear combination (eq. 1). In particular, after translating each sentence we can adapt the parameters depending on how good the last translation was. A commonly used algorithm in this online paradigm for tuning of parameters is the Margin Infused Relaxed Algorithm (MIRA).

MIRA is an online large margin algorithm that updates the parameter $\hat{w}$ of a given model according to the loss that is occurred due to incorrect classification. In the case of SMT this margin can be coupled with the loss function, which in this case is the complement of the sentence level BLEU(sBLEU). Thus, the loss function can be formulated as:

$$l(\hat{y}) = sBLEU(y^*) - sBLEU(\hat{y}) \qquad (3)$$

where y^* is the $oracle$ (closest translation to the reference) and $\hat{y}$ is the $candidate$ being processed. Ideally, this loss should correspond to the difference between the model scores:

$$\Delta h \cdot \hat{w} = score(y^*) - score(\hat{y}) \qquad (4)$$

MIRA is an ultraconservative algorithm, meaning that the update of the current weight vector is the smallest possible value satisfying the constraint that the variation incurred by the objective function must not be larger than the variation incurred by the model (plus a non-negative slack variable ξ). Formally, weight update at i^{th} iteration is defined as:

$$w_i = \arg\min_{w} \frac{1}{2\eta} \underbrace{||w - w_{i-1}||^2}_{conservative} + \underbrace{C}_{aggressive} \sum_j \xi_j$$

subject to

$$l_j \leq \Delta h_j \cdot w + \xi_j \quad \forall j \in J \subseteq \{1 \dots N\} \qquad (5)$$

where j ranges over all *candidates* in the N-best list, l_j is the loss between *oracle* and the *candidate* j, and $\Delta h_j \cdot w$ is the corresponding difference in the model scores. C is an aggressive parameter which controls the size of the update, η is the learning rate of the algorithm and ξ is usually a very small value (in our experiments we kept it as 0.0001). After partial differentiation and linearizing the loss, equation 5 can be rewritten as:

$$w_i = w_{i-1} + \eta \cdot \sum_j \alpha_j \cdot \Delta h_j$$

where

$$\alpha_j = min\left\{C, \frac{l_j - \Delta h_j \cdot w}{||\Delta h_j||^2}\right\} \quad (6)$$

We solve equation 5, by computing α with the optimizer integrated in the Moses toolkit by (Hasler et al., 2011). Algorithm 2 gives an overview of the online margin infused relaxed algorithm we implemented in Moses.

Algorithm 2: Online Margin Infused Relaxed

```
foreach sourceSeg do
    bestHyp = Translate(sourceSeg);
    postedit = Human(bestHyp);
    w0 = w;
    for i = 1 → iterations do
        N-best=Nbest(sourceSeg,w_{i-1});
        foreach candidate_j ∈ N-best do
            if Δh_j · w + ξ_j ≥ l_j then
                α_j = Optimize(l_j, h_j, w, C);
                w_i = w_{i-1} + η · Σ_j α_j Δh_j;
            end
        end
    end
end
```

In the following section we overview a stream based adaptation method with which we experimentally compared our two online learning approaches as it well fits the framework we are working in.

5 Stream based adaptation

Continuously updating an SMT system to an incoming stream of parallel data comes under stream based adaptation. Levenberg et. al. (2010) proposed an incremental adaptation technique for the core generative component of the SMT system, word alignments and language models (Levenberg and Osborne, 2009). To get the word alignments on the new data they use a *Stepwise online EM* algorithm, where old counts (from previous alignment models) are interpolated with the new counts.

Since we work at the sentence level, on-the-fly computation of probabilities of translation and reordering models is expensive in terms of both computational and memory requirements. To save these costs, we prefer using dynamic suffix array approach described in (Levenberg et al., 2010; Callison-Burch et al., 2005; Lopez, 2008). They are used to efficiently store the source and the target corpus and alignments in efficient data structure, namely the suffix array. When a phrase translation is asked by the decoder, the corpus is searched, the counts are collected and its probabilities are computed on the fly. However, the current implementation in Moses of the stream based MT relying on the suffix arrays is severely limited as it allows the computation of only three translation features, namely the two direct translation probabilities and the phrase penalty. This results in a significant degradation of performance.

6 Experiments

6.1 Datasets

We compared our online learning approaches (Sections 3 and 4) and the stream based adaptation method (Section 5) on two datasets from different domains, namely Information Technology (IT) and TED talks, and two different language pairs. The IT domain dataset is proprietary, it involves the translation of technical documents from English to Italian and has been used in the field test carried out under the MateCat project[2]. Experiments are also conducted on English to French TED talks dataset (Cettolo et al., 2012) to assess the robustness of the proposed approaches in a different scenario and to provide results on a publicly available dataset for the sake of reproducibility. The training, development (`dev2010`) and evaluation (`tst2010`[3]) sets are the same as used in the last IWSLT last evaluation campaigns. In experiments on TED data, we considered the human reference translations as post edits, even if they were

[2] www.matecat.com

[3] As the size of evaluation set in TED data is too large with respect to the current implementation of our algorithms, we performed evaluation on the first 200 sentences only.

actually generated from scratch.

In our experiments, the extent of usefulness of online learning highly depends on the amount of repetition of text. A reasonable way to measure the quantity of repetition in each document is through the *repetition rate* (Bertoldi et al., 2013). It computes the rate of non-singleton n-grams, n=1...4, averaging the values over sub-samples `S` of thousand words from the text, and then combining the rate of each n-gram to a single score by using the geometric mean. Equation 7 shows the formula for calculating the repetition rate of a document, where `dict(n)` represents the total number of different n-grams and n_r is the number of different n-grams occurring exactly `r` times:

$$RR = \left(\prod_{n=1}^{4} \frac{\sum_S dict(n) - n_1}{\sum_S dict(n)} \right)^{1/4} \quad (7)$$

Statistics of the parallel sets and their repetition rate on both sides are reported in Table 1.

Domain	Set	#srcTok	srcRR	#tgtTok	tgtRR
$IT_{en \to it}$	Train	57M	na	60M	na
	Dev	3.3k	12.03	3.5k	11.87
	Test	3.3k	15.00	3.3k	14.57
$TED_{en \to fr}$	Train	2.6M	na	2.8M	na
	Dev	20k	3.43	20k	5.27
	Test	32k	4.08	34k	3.57

Table 1: Statistics of the parallel data along with the corresponding repetition rate (RR).

It can be noted that the repetition rates of IT and TED sets are significantly different, particularly high in IT documents, much lower in the TED talks.

6.2 Systems

The SMT systems were built using the Moses toolkit (Koehn et al., 2007). Training data in each domain was used to create translation and lexical reordering models. We created a 5-gram LM for TED talks and a 6-gram LM for the IT domain using IRSTLM (Federico et al., 2008) with improved Kneser-Ney smoothing (Chen and Goodman, 1996) on the target side of the training parallel corpora. The log linear weights for the baseline systems are optimized using MERT (Och, 2003) provided in the Moses toolkit. To counter the instability of MERT, we averaged the weights of three MERT runs in each case. Performance is measured in terms of BLEU and TER (Snover et al., 2006) computed using the MultEval script (Clark et al., 2011). Since the implementations of standard Giza and of incremental Giza combined with dynamic suffix arrays are not comparable, we constructed two baselines, a standard phrase based SMT system and an incremental Giza baseline (§5). Details on experimental SMT systems we built follow.

Baseline This system was built on the parallel training data for each domain. We run 5 iterations of model 1, 5 of HMM (Vogel et al., 1996), 3 of model 3, 3 of model 4 (Brown et al., 1993) using MGiza (Gao and Vogel, 2008) toolkit to align the parallel corpus at word level. Translation and reordering models were built using Moses, while log-linear weights were optimized with MERT on the corresponding development sets. The same IT baseline system was used in the field test of MateCat and the references in the IT data are actual postedits of its translation.

IncGiza Baseline We trained alignment models with incGiza++[4] with 5 iterations of model 1 and 10 iterations of the HMM model. To build incremental Giza baselines, we used dynamic suffix arrays as implemented in Moses which allow the addition of new parallel data during decoding. In the incremental Giza baseline, once a sentence of the test set is translated, the sentence pair (source and target post-edit/reference) along with the alignment provided by incGiza are added to the models.

Online learning systems We developed several online systems on top of the two aforementioned baseline systems: (1) +O employ the additional online feature (Section 3) updated with Algorithm 1; (2) +O+NS as (1) but with the online feature normalized with the sigmoid function; (3) +W weights updated (Section 4) with Algorithm 2; (4) +O+W combination of online feature and weight update; (5) +O+NS+W as system (4) with normalized online feature score.

In the online learning system we have three additional parameters: a weight for the online feature, a learning rate for features (used in the perceptron update), and a learning rate for feature weights used by MIRA. These additional parameters were optimized by maximizing the BLEU

[4]http://code.google.com/p/inc-giza-pp/

score on the devset and on top of already optimized feature weights. For practical reasons, optimization of the parameters was run with the Simplex algorithm (Nelder and Mead, 1965).

7 Results and Discussion

Tables 2 and 3 collect results by the systems described in Section 6.2 on the IT and TED translation tasks, respectively.

In Table 2, the online system (1st block "+O+NS+W" system with 10 iterations of online learning) shows significant improvements, over 6 BLEU points absolute above the baseline. In this case the online feature can clearly take advantage of the high repetition rates observed in the IT dev and test sets (Table 1). Similarly, in the second block, the online system (2nd block "+O+NS+W" with 10 iterations of online learning) outperforms IncGiza baseline, too. It is interesting to note that by continuously updating the baseline system after each translation step, even the plain translation models are capable to learn from the correction in the post-edited text.

Figure 1 depicts learning curve of *Baseline* system, "+O+NS" (referred as *+online feature*) and "+O+NS+W" (referred as *+MIRA*). We plotted incremental BLEU scores after translation of each sentence, thereby the last point on the plot shows the corpus level BLEU on the whole test set.

In Table 3, from the first block we can observe that online learning systems perform only slightly better than the baseline systems, the main reason being the low repetition rate observed in the evaluation set (as shown in Table 1). The positive results observed in the second block ("+O+W" with 10 iterations) are probably due to the larger room for improvement available for translation models implemented with dynamic suffix arrays, as they only incorporate 3 features instead of 5. Sometimes, online learning systems show worse results with higher numbers of iterations, which seems due to overfitting. It is also interesting to notice that after optimization the weight value of the online feature was 0.509 for the IT task and 0.072 for the TED talk task. This confirms the different use and potential assigned to the online feature by the SMT systems in the two tasks.

8 Conclusion

We have shown a new way to update the translation model on the fly without changing the original probability distribution. We empirically proved that this method is robust and works for different domain datasets be it Information Technology or TED talks. In addition, if the repetition rate is high in the text, online learning works much better than if the rate is low. We tested both with an unbounded and a bounded range on the online feature and found out that bounded values produce more stable and consistent results. From previous works, it has been proven that MIRA works well with sparse features too, so, as for the future plan we would like to treat each phrase pair as a sparse feature and tune the sparse weights using MIRA. From the results, it is evident that we have not used any sort of stopping criterion for online learning; a random of 1, 5 and 10 iterations were chosen in a naive way. Our future plan will extend to working on finding a stopping criterion for online learning process.

Acknowledgements

This work was supported by the MateCat project, which is funded by the EC under the 7th Framework Programme.

References

N. Bertoldi, M. Cettolo, and M. Federico. 2013. Cache-based online adaptation for machine translation enhanced computer assisted translation. In *Proc. of MT Summit*, Nice, France.

P. F. Brown, S. A. Della Pietra, V. J. Della Pietra, and R. L. Mercer. 1993. The mathematics of statistical machine translation: Parameter estimation. *Computational Linguistics*, 19(2):263–312.

C. Callison-Burch, C. Bannard, and J. Schroeder. 2005. Scaling phrase-based statistical machine translation to larger corpora and longer phrases. In *Proc. of ACL*, pages 255–262, Ann Arbor, US-MI.

O. Cappé and E. Moulines. 2009. Online EM algorithm for latent data models. *Journal of the Royal Statistical Society Series B (Statistical Methodology)*, 71(3):593–613.

N. Cesa-Bianchi, G. Reverberi, and S. Szedmak. 2008. Online learning algorithms for computer-assisted translation. Technical report, SMART project (`www.smart-project.eu`).

M. Cettolo, C. Girardi, and M. Federico. 2012. WIT^3: web inventory of transcribed and translated talks. In *Proc. of EAMT*, Trento, Italy.

S. F. Chen and J. Goodman. 1996. An empirical study of smoothing techniques for language modeling. In *Proc. of ACL*, pages 310–318, Santa Cruz, US-CA.

System	Bleu (σ)			TER (σ)		
	1 Iter	5 Iter	10 Iter	1 Iter	5 Iter	10 Iter
Baseline	38.46(1.79)	-	-	39.98(1.35)	-	-
+O	39.88(1.77)	41.22(1.80)	41.16(1.74)	38.69(1.30)	37.78(1.32)	38.37(1.30)
+O+NS	39.91(1.80)	40.54(1.79)	40.71(1.76)	38.67(1.31)	38.21(1.29)	38.17(1.31)
+W	39.76(1.76)	38.16(1.77)	37.57(1.82)	38.58(1.27)	39.53(1.30)	39.93(1.30)
+O+W	41.23(1.66)	40.29(1.54)	29.36(1.45)	37.53(1.26)	38.03(1.24)	49.08(1.25)
+O+NS+W	41.19(1.86)	43.07(1.87)	**45.13(1.74)**	37.60(1.35)	36.43(1.43)	**34.53(1.36)**
IncGiza Baseline	28.48(1.50)	-	-	49.23(1.43)	-	-
+O	29.34(1.51)	27.80(1.49)	27.52(1.38)	47.86(1.41)	48.20(1.30)	51.01(1.53)
+O+NS	28.69(1.53)	29.68(1.45)	29.36(1.49)	48.21(1.45)	47.51(1.45)	47.92(1.45)
+W	28.25(1.56)	27.68(1.53)	27.57(1.50)	49.05(1.43)	48.74(1.36)	48.10(1.23)
+O+W	29.36(1.61)	29.94(1.64)	25.95(1.25)	47.15(1.41)	46.56(1.31)	50.31(1.15)
+O+NS+W	29.76(1.49)	30.28(1.54)	**30.83(1.60)**	46.62(1.39)	45.60(1.28)	**46.54(1.31)**

Table 2: Result on the IT domain task (EN>IT). Baseline is a standard phrase based SMT system, +O has the online feature, +NS adds normalization of online feature, +W has online weight adaptation.

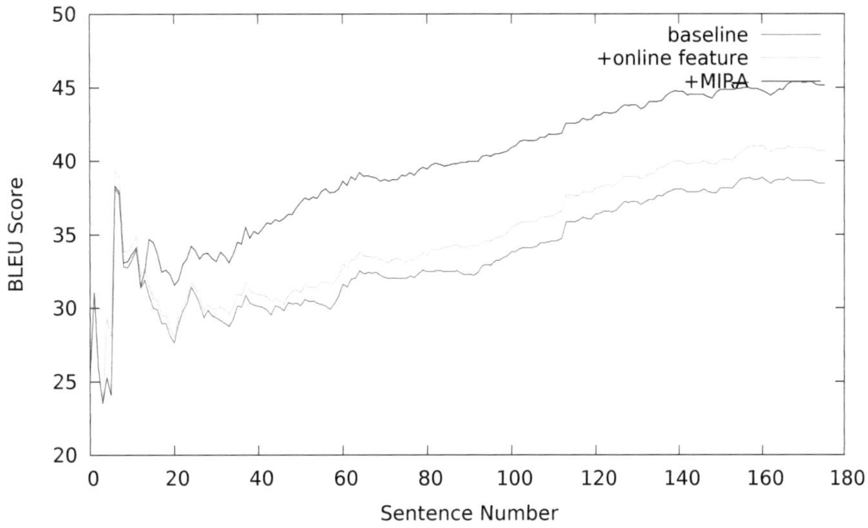

Figure 1: Incremental BLEU vs. evaluation test size on the information-technology task. Three systems are tracked: Baseline, +online feature, +MIRA

System	Bleu (σ)			TER (σ)		
	1 Iter	5 Iter	10 Iter	1 Iter	5 Iter	10 Iter
Baseline	22.18(1.23)	-	-	58.70(1.38)	-	-
+O	22.17(1.19)	21.85(1.25)	21.51(1.23)	58.75(1.35)	59.22(1.36)	60.48(1.35)
+O+NS	21.97(1.20)	22.37(1.20)	22.24(1.22)	58.86(1.37)	58.75(1.37)	59.09(1.40)
+W	22.39(1.23)	21.44(1.20)	21.00(1.13)	58.96(1.40)	58.73(1.34)	58.71(1.28)
+O+W	22.33(1.21)	22.11(1.22)	21.54(1.20)	58.63(1.37)	58.31(1.38)	58.70(1.36)
+O+NS+W	22.34(1.23)	22.09(1.21)	21.62(1.18)	58.60(1.37)	58.48(1.36)	58.40(1.33)
IncGiza Baseline	15.04(1.08)	-	-	72.64(1.34)	-	-
+O	15.30(1.08)	15.47(1.10)	15.86(1.11)	72.33(1.35)	71.68(1.37)	71.09(1.36)
+O+NS	15.21(1.09)	15.48(1.12)	15.48(1.11)	72.19(1.33)	72.06(1.36)	71.65(1.33)
+W	14.81(1.08)	14.61(1.07)	14.73(1.08)	73.03(1.37)	74.69(1.48)	74.28(1.46)
+O+W	15.08(1.08)	15.59(1.09)	**16.42(1.11)**	72.55(1.33)	70.98(1.32)	**70.07(1.27)**
+O+NS+W	15.09(1.08)	15.64(1.08)	**16.15(1.10)**	72.57(1.34)	71.13(1.31)	**70.61(1.33)**

Table 3: Result on the TED talk task (EN>FR). Baseline is a standard phrase based SMT system, +O has the online feature, +NS adds normalization of online feature, +W includes online weight adaptation.

J. Clark, C. Dyer, A. Lavie, and N. Smith. 2011. Better hypothesis testing for statistical machine translation: Controlling for optimizer instability. In *Proc. of ACL*, Portland, US-OR.

M. Collins. 2002. Discriminative training methods for hidden markov models: Theory and experiments with perceptron algorithms. In *Proc. of EMNLP*, Philadelphia, US-PA.

Koby Crammer and Yoram Singer. 2003. Ultraconservative online algorithms for multiclass problems. *Journal of Machine Learning Research*, 3:951–991.

M. Federico, N. Bertoldi, and M. Cettolo. 2008. IRSTLM: an open source toolkit for handling large scale language models. In *Proc. of Interspeech*, pages 1618–1621, Brisbane, Australia.

M. Federico, A. Cattelan, and M. Trombetti. 2012. Measuring user productivity in machine translation enhanced computer assisted translation. In *Proc. of AMTA*, Bellevue, US-WA.

Q. Gao and S. Vogel. 2008. Parallel implementations of word alignment tool. In *Proc. of SETQA-NLP*, pages 49–57, Columbus, US-OH.

E. Hasler, B. Haddow, and P. Koehn. 2011. Margin infused relaxed algorithm for Moses. *The Prague Bulletin of Mathematical Linguistics*, 96:69–78.

M. Hopkins and J. May. 2011. Tuning as ranking. In *Proc. of EMNLP*, pages 1352–1362, Edinburgh, UK.

P. Koehn, H. Hoang, A. Birch, C. Callison-Burch, M. Federico, N. Bertoldi, B. Cowan, W. Shen, C. Moran, R. Zens, C. Dyer, O. Bojar, A. Constantin, and E. Herbst. 2007. Moses: open source toolkit for statistical machine translation. In *Proc. of ACL Companion Volume of the Demo and Poster Sessions*, pages 177–180, Prague, Czech Republic.

A. Levenberg and M. Osborne. 2009. Stream-based randomised language models for SMT. In *Proc. of EMNLP*, pages 756–764, Singapore.

A. Levenberg, C. Callison-Burch, and M. Osborne. 2010. Stream-based translation models for statistical machine translation. In *Proc. of HLT-NAACL*, Los Angeles, US-CA.

P. Liang and D. Klein. 2009. Online EM for unsupervised models. In *Proc. of NAACL*, pages 611–619, Boulder, US-CO.

P. Liang, A. Bouchard-Côté, D. Klein, and B. Taskar. 2006. An end-to-end discriminative approach to machine translation. In *Proc. of ACL*, pages 761–768, Sydney, Australia.

C.-Y. Lin and F. J. Och. 2004. Orange: a method for evaluating automatic evaluation metrics for machine translation. In *Proc. of COLING*, pages 501–507, Geneva, Switzerland.

A. Lopez. 2008. Tera-scale translation models via pattern matching. In *Proc. of COLING*, pages 505–512, Manchester, UK.

P. Martínez-Gómez, G. Sanchis-Trilles, and F. Casacuberta. 2011. Online learning via dynamic reranking for computer assisted translation. In *Proc. of CICLing*, pages 93–105, Tokyo, Japan.

P. Martínez-Gómez, G. Sanchis-Trilles, and F. Casacuberta. 2012. Online adaptation strategies for statistical machine translation in post-editing scenarios. *Pattern Recogn.*, 45(9):3193–3203.

R. Neal and G. E. Hinton. 1998. A view of the EM algorithm that justifies incremental, sparse, and other variants. In *Learning in Graphical Models*, pages 355–368. Kluwer Academic Publishers.

J. A. Nelder and R. Mead. 1965. A simplex method for function minimization. *The Computer Journal*, 7(4):308–313.

F.J. Och and H. Ney. 2003. A systematic comparison of various statistical alignment models. *Computational Linguistics*, 29(1):19–51.

F. J. Och. 2003. Minimum error rate training in statistical machine translation. In *Proc. of ACL*, pages 160–167, Sapporo, Japan.

K. Papineni, S. Roukos, T. Ward, and W.-J. Zhu. 2001. Bleu: a method for automatic evaluation of machine translation. Research Report RC22176, IBM Research Division, Thomas J. Watson Research Center.

F. Rosenblatt. 1958. The Perceptron: a probabilistic model for information storage and organization in the brain. *Psychological Review*, 65:386–408.

M.-A. Sato and S. Ishii. 2000. On-line EM algorithm for the normalized Gaussian network. *Neural Comput.*, 12(2):407–432.

M. Snover, B. Dorr, R. Schwartz, L. Micciulla, and J. Makhoul. 2006. A study of translation edit rate with targeted human annotation. In *Proc. of AMTA*, Boston, US-MA.

S. Vogel, H. Ney, and C. Tillmann. 1996. HMM-based word alignment in statistical translation. In *Proc. of COLING*, pages 836–841, Copenhagen, Denmark.

Length-incremental Phrase Training for SMT

Joern Wuebker and Hermann Ney
Human Language Technology and Pattern Recognition Group
RWTH Aachen University
Aachen, Germany
{wuebker,ney}@cs.rwth-aachen.de

Abstract

We present an iterative technique to generate phrase tables for SMT, which is based on force-aligning the training data with a modified translation decoder. Different from previous work, we completely avoid the use of a word alignment or phrase extraction heuristics, moving towards a more principled phrase generation and probability estimation. During training, we allow the decoder to generate new phrases on-the-fly and increment the maximum phrase length in each iteration. Experiments are carried out on the IWSLT 2011 Arabic-English task, where we are able to reach moderate improvements on a state-of-the-art baseline with our training method. The resulting phrase table shows only a small overlap with the heuristically extracted one, which demonstrates the restrictiveness of limiting phrase selection by a word alignment or heuristics. By interpolating the heuristic and the trained phrase table, we can improve over the baseline by 0.5% BLEU and 0.5% TER.

1 Introduction

Most state-of-the-art SMT systems get the statistics from which the different component models are estimated via heuristics using a Viterbi word alignment. The word alignment is usually generated with tools like GIZA++ (Och and Ney, 2003), that apply the EM algorithm to estimate the alignment with the HMM or IBM-4 translation models. This is also the case for the phrases or rules which serve as translation units for the decoder. All phrases that do not violate the word alignment are extracted and their probabilities are estimated as relative frequencies (Koehn et al., 2003).

A number of different approaches have tried to do away with the heuristics and close this gap between the phrase table generation and translation decoding. However, most of these approaches either fail to achieve state-of-the-art performance or still make use of the word alignment or the extraction heuristics, e.g. as a prior in discriminative training or to initialize a generative or generatively inspired training procedure and are thus biased by their weaknesses. Here, we aim at moving towards the ideal situation, where a unified framework induces the phrases based on the same models as in decoding.

We train the phrase table without using a word alignment or the extraction heuristics. Different from previous work, we are able to generate all possible phrase pairs on-the-fly during the training procedure. A further advantage of our proposed algorithm is that we use basically the same beam search as in translation. This makes it easy to re-implement by modifying any translation decoder, and makes sure that training and translation are consistent. In principle, we apply the forced decoding approach described in (Wuebker et al., 2010) with cross-validation to prevent over-fitting, but we initialize the phrase table with IBM-1 lexical probabilities (Brown et al., 1993) instead of heuristically extracted relative frequencies. The algorithm is extended with the concept of *backoff phrases*, so that new phrase pairs can be generated at training time. The size of the newly generated phrases is incremented over the training iterations. By introducing *fallback decoding runs*, we are able to successfully align the complete training data. *Local language models* are used for better phrase pair pre-selection.

The experiments are carried out on the IWSLT 2011 Arabic-English shared task. We are able to show that it is possible and feasible to reach state-of-the-art performance without the need to word-align the bilingual training data. The small overlap of 18.5% between the trained and the heuristically extracted phrase table demonstrates the limitations of previous work, where training is initialized by the baseline phrase table or phrase selection is restricted by a word alignment. With a linear interpolation of phrase tables an improvement of 0.5% BLEU and 0.5% TER over the baseline can be achieved. The result in BLEU is statistically significant on the test set with 90% confidence. Further, we can confirm the observation of previous work, that phrases with near-zero entropies seem to be a disadvantage for translation quality. Although we use a phrase-based decoder here, the principles of our work can be applied to any statistical machine translation paradigm. The software used for our experiments is available under a non-commercial open source licence.

The paper is organized as follows. We review related work in Section 2. The decoder and its features are described in Section 3 and we give an overview of the training procedure in Section 4. The complete algorithm is described in Section 5 and experiments are presented in Section 6. We conclude with Section 7.

2 Related Work

Marcu and Wong (2002) present a joint probability model, which is trained with a hill-climbing technique based on break, merge, swap and move operations. Due to the computational complexity they are only able to consider phrases, which appear at least five times in the data. The model is shown to slightly underperform heuristic extraction in (Koehn et al., 2003). For higher efficiency, it is constrained by a word alignment in (Birch et al., 2006). DeNero et al. (2008) introduce a different training procedure for this model based on a Gibbs sampler. They make use of the word alignment for initialization.

A generative phrase model trained with the Expectation-Maximization (EM) algorithm is shown in (DeNero et al., 2006). It also does not reach the same top performance as heuristic extraction. The authors identify the hidden segmentation variable, which results in over-fitting, as the main problem.

Liang et al. (2006) present a discriminative translation system. One of the proposed strategies for training, which the authors call bold updating, is similar to our training scheme. They use heuristically extracted phrase translation probabilities as blanket features in all setups.

Another iteratively-trained phrase model is described by Moore and Quirk (2007). Their model is segmentation-free and, confirming the findings in (DeNero et al., 2006), can close the gap to phrase tables induced from surface heuristics. It relies on word alignment for phrase selection.

Mylonakis and Sima'an (2008) present a phrase model, whose training procedure uses prior probabilities based on Inversion Transduction Grammar and smoothing as learning objective to prevent over-fitting. They also rely on the word alignment to select phrase pairs.

Blunsom et al. (2009) perform inference over latent synchronous derivation trees under a non-parametric Bayesian model with a Gibbs sampler. Training is also initialized by extracting rules from a word alignment, but the authors let the sampler diverge from the initial value for 1000 passes over the data, before the samples are used. However, as the model is to weak for actual translation, the usual extraction heuristics are applied on the hierarchical alignments to infer a distribution over rule tables.

Wuebker et al. (2010) use a forced decoding training procedure, which applies a leave-one-out technique to prevent over-fitting. They are able to show improvements over a heuristically extracted phrase table, which is used for initialization of the training.

In (Saers and Wu, 2011), the EM algorithm is applied for principled induction of bilexica based on linear inversion transduction grammar. The model itself underperforms the baseline, but the authors show moderate improvements by combining it with the baseline phrase table, which is similar to our results.

(Neubig et al., 2011) also propose a probabilistic model based on inversion transduction grammar, which allows for direct phrase table extraction from unaligned data. They show results similar to the heuristic baseline on several tasks.

A number of different models that can be trained from forced derivation trees are shown in (Duan et al., 2012), including a re-estimated translation model, two reordering models and a rule sequence model. For inference, they optimize their parameters towards alignment F-score. The forced derivations are initialized with the standard heuristic extraction scheme.

He and Deng (2012) describe a discriminative phrase training procedure, where n-best translations are produced by the decoder on the whole training data. The heuristically extracted relative frequencies serve as a prior, and the probabilities are updated with a maximum BLEU criterion based on the n-best lists.

3 Translation Model

We use the standard phrase-based translation decoder from the open source toolkit *Jane 2* (Wuebker et al., 2012a) for both the training procedure and the translation experiments. It makes use of the usual features: Translation channel models in both directions, lexical smoothing models in both directions, an n-gram language model (LM), phrase and word penalty and a jump-distance-based distortion model. Formally, the best translation $\hat{e}_1^{\hat{I}}$ as defined by the models $h_m(e_1^I, s_1^K, f_1^J)$ can be written as (Och and Ney, 2004)

$$\hat{e}_1^{\hat{I}} = \arg\max_{I, e_1^I} \left\{ \sum_{m=1}^{M} \lambda_m h_m(e_1^I, s_1^K, f_1^J) \right\}, \quad (1)$$

where $f_1^J = f_1 \ldots f_J$ is the source sentence, $e_1^I = e_1 \ldots e_I$ the target sentence and $s_1^K = s_1 \ldots s_K$ their phrase segmentation and alignment. We define $s_k := (i_k, b_k, j_k)$, where i_k is the last position of kth target phrase, and (b_k, j_k) are the start and end positions of the source phrase aligned to the kth target phrase. Different from many standard systems, the lexical smoothing scores are not estimated by extracting counts from a word alignment, but with IBM-1 model scores trained on the bilingual data with GIZA++. They are computed as (Zens, 2008)

$$h_{lex}(e_1^I, s_1^K, f_1^J) = \sum_{k=1}^{K} \sum_{j=b_k}^{j_k} log \left(p(f_j|e_0) + \sum_{i=i_{k-1}+1}^{i_k} p(f_j|e_i) \right) \quad (2)$$

Here, e_0 denotes the empty target word. The lexical smoothing model for the inverse direction is computed analogously. The log-linear feature weights λ_m are optimized on a development data set with minimum error rate training (MERT) (Och, 2003). As optimization criterion we use BLEU (Papineni et al., 2001).

4 Training

4.1 Overview

In this work we employ a training procedure inspired by the Expectation-Maximization (EM) algorithm.

The **E-step** corresponds to force-aligning the training data with a modified translation decoder, which yields a distribution over possible phrasal segmentations and their alignment. Different from original EM, we make use of not only the two translation channel models that are being learned, but the full log-linear combination of models as in translation decoding. Formally, we are searching for the best phrase segmentation and alignment for the given sentence pair, which is defined by

$$\hat{s}_1^{\hat{K}} = \arg\max_{K, s_1^K} \left\{ \sum_{m=1}^{M} \lambda_m h_m(e_1^I, s_1^K, f_1^J) \right\} \quad (3)$$

To force-align the training data, the translation decoder is constrained to the given target sentence. The translation candidates applicable for each sentence pair are selected through a bilingual phrase matching before the actual search.

In the **M-step**, we re-estimate the phrase table from the phrase alignments. The translation probability of a phrase pair $(\tilde{f}, \tilde{e})$ is estimated as

$$p_{FA}(\tilde{f}|\tilde{e}) = \frac{C_{FA}(\tilde{f}, \tilde{e})}{\sum_{\tilde{f}'} C_{FA}(\tilde{f}', \tilde{e})} \quad (4)$$

where $C_{FA}(\tilde{f}, \tilde{e})$ is the count of the phrase pair $(\tilde{f}, \tilde{e})$ in the phrase-aligned training data.

In contrast to original EM, this is done by taking the phrase counts from a uniformly weighted n-best list. The limitation to n phrase alignments helps keeping the number of considered phrases reasonably small. Because the log-linear feature weights have been tuned in a discriminative fashion to optimize the ranking of translation hypotheses, rather than their probability distribution, posterior probabilities received by exponentiation and renormalization need to be scaled similar to (Wuebker et al., 2012b). Uniform weights can alleviate this mismatch between the discriminatively trained log-linear feature weights and the actual probability distribution, without having to resort to an arbitrarily chosen global scaling factor. This corresponds to the *count model* in (Wuebker et al., 2010) and was shown by the authors to perform similar or better than using actual posterior probabilities. In our experiments, we set the size of the n-best list to $n = 1000$.

The first iteration of phrase training is initialized with an empty phrase table. We use the notion of *backoff phrases* to generate new phrase pairs on-the-fly. To avoid over-fitting, we apply the cross-validation technique presented in (Wuebker et al., 2010) with a batch-size of 2000 sentences. This means that for each batch the phrase and marginal counts from the full phrase table are reduced by the statistics taken from the same batch in the previous iteration. The phrase translation probabilities are then estimated from these updated counts. Phrase pairs only appearing in a single batch are assigned a fixed penalty.

4.2 Backoff Phrases

Backoff phrases are phrase pairs that are generated on-the-fly by the decoder at training time. When aligning a sentence pair, for a given maximum phrase length m, the decoder inserts all combinations of source m_s-grams and target m_t-grams into the translation options, that are present in the sentence pair and with $m_s, m_t \leq m$. Formally, for the sentence pair (f_1^J, e_1^I), $f_1^J = f_1 \ldots f_J$, $e_1^I = e_1 \ldots e_I$, and maximum length m, we generate all phrase pairs $(\tilde{f}, \tilde{e})$ where

$$\begin{aligned}
&\exists m_s, m_t, j, i : \\
&1 \leq m_s, m_t \leq m \wedge 1 \leq j \leq J - m_s + 1 \\
&\wedge 1 \leq i \leq I - m_t + 1 \\
&\wedge \tilde{f} = f_j^{(j+m_s-1)} \wedge \tilde{e} = e_i^{(i+m_t-1)}. \qquad (5)
\end{aligned}$$

These generated phrase pairs are given a fixed penalty pen_p per phrase, pen_s per source word and pen_t per target word, which are summed up and substituted for the two channel models. The lexical smoothing scores are computed in the usual way based on an IBM-1 table. Note that this table is not extracted from a word alignment, but contains the real probabilities trained with the IBM-1 model by GIZA++.

We use backoff phrases in two different contexts. In the first $m_{max} = 6$ iterations, they are applied as a means to generate new phrase pairs on the fly. We increase the maximum phrase length m in each iteration and always generate all possible backoff phrases before aligning each sentence. Later, when a sufficient number of phrases have been generated in the previous iterations, they are used as a last resort in order to avoid alignment failures.

At the later stage of the length-incremental training, we also make use of a modified version, where we only allow new phrase pairs $(\tilde{f}, \tilde{e})$ to be generated, if no translation candidates exist for $\tilde{f}$ after the bilingual phrase matching. However, in this case, backoff phrases are only used if a first decoding run fails and we have to resort to *fallback runs*, which are described in the next Section.

4.3 Fallback Decoding Runs

To maximize the number of successfully aligned sentences, we allow for *fallback decoding runs* with slightly altered parameterization, whenever constrained decoding fails. In this work, we only change the parameterization of the backoff phrases. After $m_{max} = 6$ iterations, we no longer generate any backoff phrases in the first decoding run. If it fails, a second run is performed, where we allow to generate backoff phrases for all source phrases, which have no target candidates after the bilingual phrase matching. Finally, if this one also fails, all possible phrases are generated in the third run. Here, the maximum backoff phrase length is fixed to $m = 1$. We denote the number of fallback runs with $n_{fb} = 2$. In our experiments, the two fallback runs enable us to align every sentence pair of the training data after the sixth iteration.

4.4 Local Language Models

To make the training procedure feasible, it is parallelized by splitting the training data into batches of 2000 sentences. The batches are aligned independently. For each batch, we produce a *local language model*, which is a unigram LM trained on the target side of the current batch. We presort the phrases before search by their log-linear model score, which uses the phrase-internal unigram LM costs as one feature function. One effect of this is that the order in which phrase candidates are considered is adjusted to the local part of the data, which has a positive effect on decoding speed. Secondly, we limit the number of translation candidates for each source phrase to the best scoring 500 before the bilingual phrase matching.

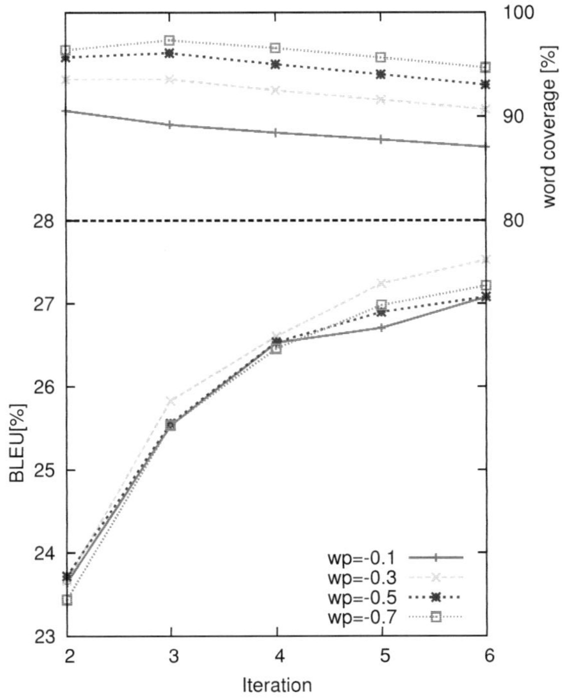

Figure 1: BLEU scores and word coverages on dev over the first 6 training iterations with different word penalties (wp).

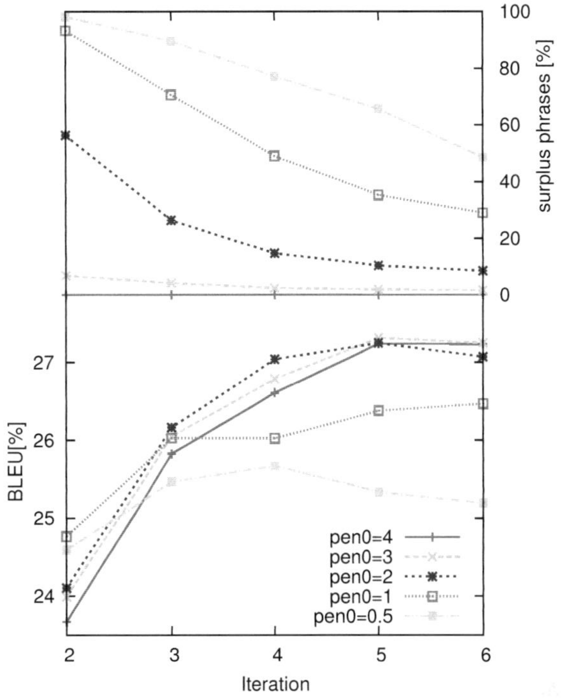

Figure 2: BLEU scores and percentage of surplus phrases on dev over the first 6 training iterations with different backoff phrase penalties pen_0.

Using the local LM for this means that the preselection better suits the current data batch. As a result, the number of phrases remaining after the phrase matching is increased as compared to the same setup without a local language model.

4.5 Parameterization

The training procedure has a number of hyper parameters, most of which do not seem to have a strong impact on the results. This section describes the parameters that have to be chosen carefully. To successfully align a sentence pair, our decoder is required to fully cover the source sentence. However, in order to achieve a good success rate in terms of number of aligned sentence pairs, we allow for incompletely aligned target sentences. We denote the percentage of successfully aligned sentence pairs as *sentence coverage*. Note that we count a sentence pair as successfully aligned, even if the target sentence is not fully covered. the **word penalty** (wp) feature weight λ_{wp} needs to be adjusted carefully. A high value leads to a high sentence coverage, but many of their target sides may be incompletely aligned. A low word penalty can decrease the sentence coverage, while aligning larger parts of the target sentences. We denote the total percentage of successfully aligned target words as *word coverage*. Please note the distincton to the sentence coverage, which is defined above. Figure 1 shows the word coverages and BLEU scores for training iterations 2 through 6 with different word penalties. In the first iteration, the results are identical, as only one-to-one phrases are allowed and the number of aligned target words is therefore predetermined. For $\lambda_{wp} = -0.1$, the word coverages are continuously decreasing with each iteration, although not by much. For $\lambda_{wp} = -0.3$ to $\lambda_{wp} = -0.7$ the word coverage slightly increases from iteration 2 to 3 and then decreases again. In terms of BLEU score, $\lambda_{wp} = -0.3$ has a slight advantage over the other values and we decided to continue using this value in all subsequent experiments.

The **backoff phrase penalties** directly affect the learning rate of the training procedure. With low penalties, only few, very good phrases get an advantage over the ones generated on-the-fly, which corresponds to a slow learning rate. In-

1. Initialize with empty phrase table
2. Set backoff phrase penalties to $pen_0 = 3$ and $m = 1$
3. Until $m = m_{max}$, iterate:
   - If iteration > 1: set
     $m = m + 1$
     $\lambda_{s2t} = \lambda_{s2t} + \delta$
     $\lambda_{t2s} = \lambda_{t2s} + \delta$
   - Force-align training data and re-estimate phrase table
4. Set $m = 1$ and $n_{fb} = 2$
5. Iterate:
   - Force-align training data and re-estimate phrase table

Figure 3: The complete training algorithm.

creasing the penalties means that a larger percentage of the phrase pairs generated in the previous iterations will be favored over new backoff phrases, which corresponds to a faster learning rate. We denote phrase pairs that are more expensive than their backoff phrase counterparts as *surplus phrases*. Figure 2 shows the behavior over the training iterations 2 through 6 with different penalties pen_0 in terms of percentage of surplus phrase pairs and BLEU score. Here we set $pen_s = pen_t = pen_0$ and $pen_p = 5pen_0$. We can see that $pen_0 = 4$ yields less than 0.1% surplus phrases through all iterations, whereas $pen_0 = 0.5$ starts off with 98.2% surplus phrases and goes down to 55.9% in iteration 6. In terms of BLEU, a fast learning rate seems to be preferable. The best results are achieved with $pen_0 = 3$, where the rate of surplus phrases starts at 6.8% and decreases to 1.7% until iteration 6. In all subsequent experiments, we set $pen_0 = 3$.

5 Length-incremental Training

In this section we describe the complete training algorithm. The first training iteration is initialized with an empty phrase table. The phrases used in alignment are backoff phrases, which are generated on-the-fly. The maximum backoff phrase length is set to $m = 1$. Then the forced alignment is iterated, increasing m by 1 in each iteration, up to a maximum of $m_{max} = 6$.

After $m_{max} = 6$ iterations, we have created a sufficient number of phrase pairs and continue iterating the training procedure with new parameters. Now, we do not allow usage of any backoff phrases in the first decoding run. If the first run fails, we allow a fallback decoding run, where backoff phrases are generated only for source phrases without translation candidates. If this one also fails, in a final fallback run all possible phrases are generated. Here we allow a maximum backoff phrase length of $m = 1$.

The log-linear feature weights λ_i used for training are mostly standard values. Only λ_{wp} for the word penalty is adjusted as described in Section 4.5, and λ_{s2t},λ_{t2s} for the two phrasal channel models are incremented with each iteration. We start off with $\lambda_{s2t} = \lambda_{t2s} = 0$ and increment the weights by $\delta = 0.02$ in each iteration, until the standard value $\lambda_{s2t} = \lambda_{t2s} = 0.1$ is reached in iteration 6, after which the values are kept fixed. MERT is not part of the training procedure, but only used afterwards for evaluation. The full algorithm is illustrated in Figure 3.

		Arabic	English
train	Sentences	305K	
	Running Words	6.5M	6.5M
	Vocabulary	104K	74K
dev	Sentences	934	
	Run. Words	19K	20K
	Vocabulary	4293	3182
	OOVs (run. words)	445	182
test	Sentences	1664	
	Run. Words	31K	32K
	Vocabulary	5415	3650
	OOVs (run. words)	658	159

Table 1: Statistics for the IWSLT 2011 Arabic-English data. The out-of-vocabulary words are denoted as OOVs.

6 Experiments

6.1 Data

We carry out our experiments on the IWSLT 2011 Arabic-English shared task[1]. It focuses on the translation of TED talks, a collection of lectures on a variety of topics ranging from science to culture. Our bilingual training data is composed of all available in-domain (TED) data and a selection of the out-of-domain MultiUN data provided for the evaluation campaign. The bilingual data selection

[1] www.iwslt2011.org

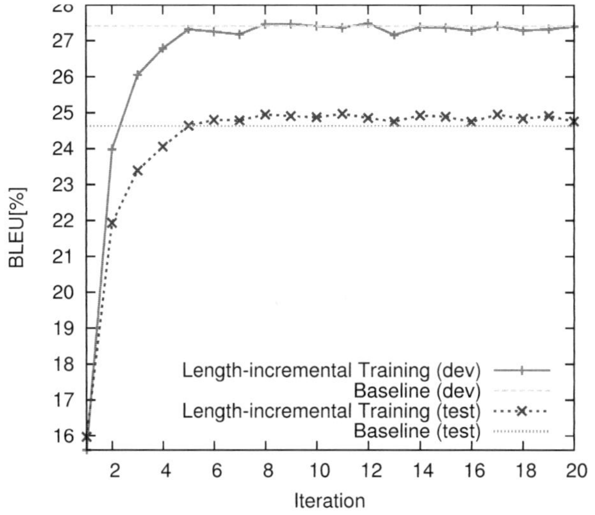

Figure 4: BLEU scores on `dev` and `test` over 20 training iterations.

is based on (Axelrod et al., 2011). Data statistics are given in Table 1. The language model is a 4-gram LM trained on all provided in-domain monolingual data and a selection based on (Moore and Lewis, 2010) of the out-of-domain corpora. To account for statistical variation, all reported results are average scores over three independent MERT runs.

6.2 Results

To build the baseline phrase table, we perform the standard phrase extraction from a symmetrized word alignment created with the IBM-4 model by GIZA++. The length of the extracted phrases is limited to a maximum of six words. The lexical smoothing scores are computed from IBM-1 probabilities. We run MERT on the development set (`dev`) and evaluate on the test set (`test`). A second baseline is the technique described in (Wuebker et al., 2010), which we denote as *leave-one-out*. It is initialized with the heuristically extracted table and run for one iteration, which the authors have shown to be sufficient.

Length-incremental training is performed as described in Section 5. After each iteration, we run MERT on `dev` using the resulting phrase table and evaluate. The set of models used here is identical to the baseline.

The results in BLEU are plotted in Figure 4. We can see that the performance increases up to iteration 5, after which only small changes can be observed. The performance on `dev` is similar to the baseline, on `test` the trained phrase tables are consistently slightly above the baseline. The optimum on `dev` is reached in iteration 12. Exact BLEU and TER (Snover et al., 2006) scores of the optimum on `dev` and the baseline are given in Table 2. The phrase table trained with leave-one-out (Wuebker et al., 2010) performs simlar to the heuristic baseline. Length-incremental training is slightly superior to the baseline, yielding an improvement of 0.3% BLEU and 0.4% TER on `test`. Similar to results observed in (DeNero et al., 2006) and (Wuebker et al., 2010), a linear interpolation with the baseline containing all phrase pairs from either of the two tables yields a moderate improvement of 0.5% BLEU and 0.5% TER both data sets. The BLEU improvement on `test` is statistically significant with 90% confidence based on bootstrap resampling as described by Koehn (2004).

	`dev`		`test`	
	BLEU [%]	TER [%]	BLEU [%]	TER [%]
baseline	27.4	54.0	24.6	57.8
leave-one-out	27.3	54.2	24.6	57.7
length-increm.	27.5	53.8	24.9	57.4
lin. interp.	**27.9**	**53.5**	**25.1**†	**57.3**

Table 2: BLEU and TER scores of the baseline, phrase training with leave-one-out and length-incremental training after 12 iterations, as well as a linear interpolation of the baseline with length-incremental phrase table. Results marked with † are statistically significant with 90% confidence.

6.3 Analysis

In Figure 5 we plot the number of phrase pairs present in the phrase tables after each iteration. In the first 6 iterations, we keep generating new phrase pairs via backoff phrases. The maximum of 14.4M phrase pairs is reached after three iterations. For comparison, the size of the heuristically extracted table is 19M phrase pairs. Afterwards, backoff phrases are only used in fallback decoding runs, which leads to drop in the number of phrase pairs that are being used. It levels out at 10.4M phrases.

When we take a look at the phrase length distributions in both the baseline and the trained phrase table shown in Figure 6, we can see that in the latter the phrases are generally shorter, which con-

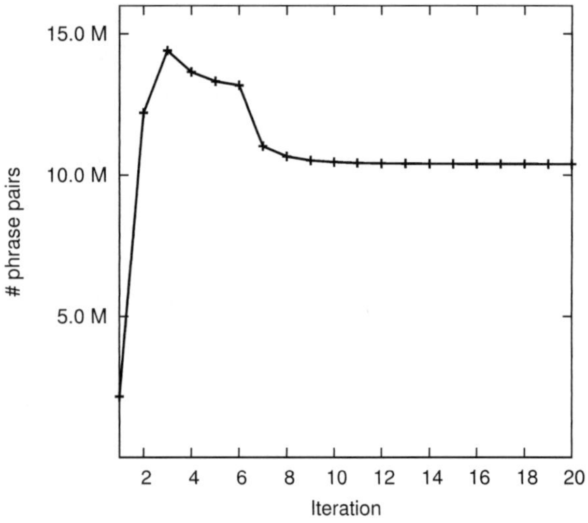

Figure 5: Number of generated phrase pairs over 20 training iterations.

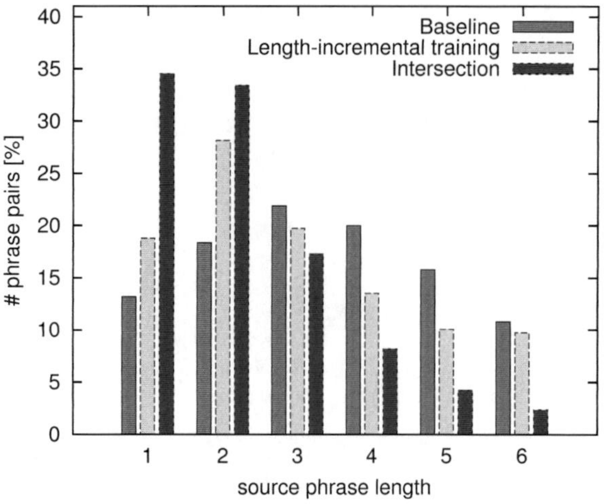

Figure 6: Histogram of the phrase lengths present in the phrase tables.

firms observations from previous work. In the trained phrase table, phrases of length one and two make up 47% of all phrases. In the heuristically extracted table it is only 32%. This is even more pronounced in the intersection of the two tables, where 68% of the phrases are of length one and two.

Interestingly, the total overlap between the two phrase tables is rather small. Only about 18.5% of the phrases from the trained table also appear in the heuristically extracted one. This shows that, by generating phrases on-the-fly without restrictions based on a word alignment or a bias from intialization, our training procedure strongly diverges from the baseline phrase table. We conclude that most previous work in this area, which adhered to the above mentioned restrictions, was only able to explore a fraction of the full potential of real phrase training.

Following (DeNero et al., 2006), we compute the entropy of the distributions within the phrase tables to quantify the 'smoothness' of the distribution. For a given source phrase $\tilde{f}$, it is defined as

$$H(\tilde{f}) = \sum_{\tilde{e}} p(\tilde{e}|\tilde{f}) log(p(\tilde{e}|\tilde{f})). \qquad (6)$$

A flat distribution with a high level of uncertainty yields a high entropy, whereas a peaked distribution with little uncertainty produces a low entropy. We analyze the phrase tables filtered towards the `dev` and `test` sets. The average entropy, weighted by frequency, is 3.1 for the table learned with length-incremental training, compared to 2.7 for the heuristically extracted one. However, the interpolated table, which has the best performance, lies in between with an average entropy of 2.9. When we consider the histogram of entropies for the phrase tables in Figure 7, we can see that in the baseline phrase table 3.8% of the phrases haven an entropy below 0.5, compared to 0.90% for length-incremental training and 0.16% for the linear interpolation. Therefore, we can confirm the observation in (DeNero et al., 2006), that phrases with a near-zero entropy are undesirable for decoding. The distribution of the higher entropies, however, does not seem to matter for translation quality. This also gives us a handle for understanding, why phrase table interpolation often improves results: It largely seems to eliminate near-zero entropies from either table.

6.4 Training time

The training was not run under controlled conditions, so we can only give a rough estimate of how the training times between the different methods compare. Also, some of the steps were parallelized while others are not. To account for the computational resources needed, we report the trainig times on a single machine by summing the times for all parallel and sequential processes.

Heuristc phrase extraction from the word alignment took us about 1.7 hours. A single iteration of standard phrase training (leave-one-out) needs about 24 hours. The first iteration of length-

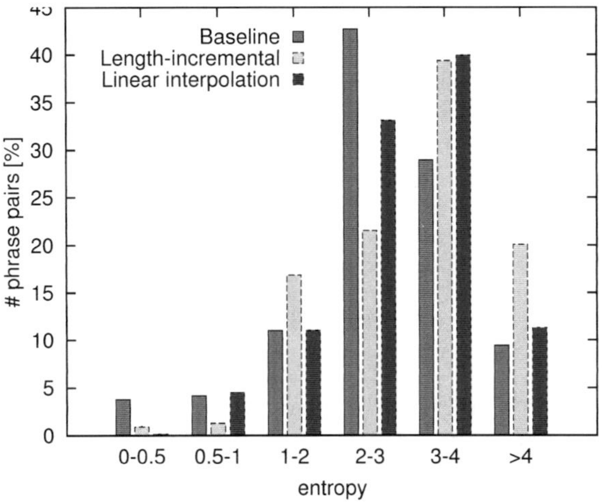

Figure 7: Histogram of entropies present in the phrase tables.

incremental training as well as all iterations after the sixth also took roughly 24 hours. The iterations two through six of length-incremental training are considerably more expensive due to the larger size of backoff phrases. Iteration six, with a maximum backoff phrase size of six words on source and target side, was the slowest with around 740 hours.

7 Conclusion

In this work we presented a training procedure for phrase or rule tables in statistical machine translation. It is based on force-aligning the training data with a modified version of the translation decoder. Different from previous work, we completely avoid the use of a word alignment on the bilingual training corpus. Instead, we initialize the procedure with an empty phrase table and generate all possible phrases on-the-fly through the concept of *backoff phrases*. Starting with a maximum phrase length of $m = 1$, we increment m in each iteration, until we reach m_{max}. Then, we continue training in a more conventional fashion, allowing creation of new phrases only in fallback runs. As additional extensions to previous work we introduce *fallback decoding runs* for higher coverage of the data and *local language models* for better pre-selection of phrases. The effects of the most important hyper parameters of our procedure are discussed and we show how they were selected in our setup. The experiments are carried out with a phrase-based decoder on the IWSLT 2011 Arabic-English shared task. The trained phrase table slightly outperforms our state-of-the-art baseline and a linear interpolation yields an improvement of 0.5% BLEU and 0.5% TER. The BLEU improvement on `test` is statistically significant with 90% confidence. The small overlap of 18.5% between the trained and the heuristically extracted phrase table shows how initialization or restrictions based on word alignments would have biased the training procedure. We also analyzed the distribution of entropies within the phrase tables, confirming the previous observation that fewer near-zero entropy phrases are advantageous for decoding. We also showed that, in our setup, near-zero entropies are largely eliminated by phrase table interpolation.

In future work we plan to apply this technique as a more principled way to train a wider range of models similar to (Duan et al., 2012). But even for the phrase models, we have only scratched the surface of its potential. We hope that by finding a meaningful way to set the hyper parameters of our training procedure, better and smaller phrase tables can be created.

Acknowledgments

This work was partially realized as part of the Quaero Programme, funded by OSEO, French State agency for innovation. The material is also partially based upon work supported by the DARPA BOLT project under Contract No. HR0011- 12-C-0015. Any opinions, findings and conclusions or recommendations expressed in this material are those of the authors and do not necessarily reflect the views of DARPA.

References

Amittai Axelrod, Xiaodong He, and Jianfeng Gao. 2011. Domain adaptation via pseudo in-domain data selection. In *Proceedings of the 2011 Conference on Empirical Methods in Natural Language Processing*, pages 355–362, Edinburgh, Scotland, UK., July. Association for Computational Linguistics.

Alexandra Birch, Chris Callison-Burch, Miles Osborne, and Philipp Koehn. 2006. Constraining the Phrase-Based, Joint Probability Statistical Translation Model. In *Human Language Technology Conf. (HLT-NAACL): Proc. Workshop on Statistical Machine Translation*, pages 154–157, New York City, NY, June.

Phil Blunsom, Trevor Cohn, Chris Dyer, and Miles Osborne. 2009. A gibbs sampler for phrasal synchronous grammar induction. In *Proceedings of the Joint Conference of the 47th Annual Meeting of the ACL and the 4th International Joint Conference on Natural Language Processing of the AFNLP: Volume 2 - Volume 2*, ACL '09, pages 782–790, Stroudsburg, PA, USA. Association for Computational Linguistics.

Peter F. Brown, Stephen A. Della Pietra, Vincent J. Della Pietra, and Robert L. Mercer. 1993. The Mathematics of Statistical Machine Translation: Parameter Estimation. *Computational Linguistics*, 19(2):263–311, June.

John DeNero, Dan Gillick, James Zhang, and Dan Klein. 2006. Why Generative Phrase Models Underperform Surface Heuristics. In *Proceedings of the Workshop on Statistical Machine Translation*, pages 31–38, New York City, June.

John DeNero, Alexandre Buchard-Côté, and Dan Klein. 2008. Sampling Alignment Structure under a Bayesian Translation Model. In *Proceedings of the 2008 Conference on Empirical Methods in Natural Language Processing*, pages 314–323, Honolulu, October.

Nan Duan, Mu Li, and Ming Zhou. 2012. Forced derivation tree based model training to statistical machine translation. In *Proceedings of the 2012 Joint Conference on Empirical Methods in Natural Language Processing and Computational Natural Language Learning*, pages 445–454, Jeju Island, Korea, July. Association for Computational Linguistics.

Xiaodong He and Li Deng. 2012. Maximum Expected BLEU Training of Phrase and Lexicon Translation Models. In *Proceedings of the 50th Annual Meeting of the Association for Computational Linguistics (ACL)*, pages 292–301, Jeju, Republic of Korea, Jul.

P. Koehn, F. J. Och, and D. Marcu. 2003. Statistical Phrase-Based Translation. In *Proceedings of the 2003 Meeting of the North American chapter of the Association for Computational Linguistics (NAACL-03)*, pages 127–133, Edmonton, Alberta.

Philipp Koehn. 2004. Statistical Significance Tests for Machine Translation Evaluation. In *Proc. of the Conf. on Empirical Methods for Natural Language Processing (EMNLP)*, pages 388–395, Barcelona, Spain, July.

Percy Liang, Alexandre Buchard-Côté, Dan Klein, and Ben Taskar. 2006. An End-to-End Discriminative Approach to Machine Translation. In *Proceedings of the 21st International Conference on Computational Linguistics and the 44th annual meeting of the Association for Computational Linguistics*, pages 761–768, Sydney, Australia.

Daniel Marcu and William Wong. 2002. A Phrase-Based, Joint Probability Model for Statistical Machine Translation. In *Proc. of the Conf. on Empirical Methods for Natural Language Processing (EMNLP)*, pages 133–139, Philadelphia, PA, July.

Robert C. Moore and William Lewis. 2010. Intelligent selection of language model training data. In *Proceedings of the ACL 2010 Conference Short Papers*, pages 220–224, Uppsala, Sweden, July. Association for Computational Linguistics.

Robert C. Moore and Chris Quirk. 2007. An Iteratively-Trained Segmentation-Free Phrase Translation Model for Statistical Machine Translation. In *Proceedings of the Second Workshop on Statistical Machine Translation*, pages 112–119, Prague, June.

Markos Mylonakis and Khalil Sima'an. 2008. Phrase Translation Probabilities with ITG Priors and Smoothing as Learning Objective. In *Proceedings of the 2008 Conference on Empirical Methods in Natural Language Processing*, pages 630–639, Honolulu, October.

Graham Neubig, Taro Watanabe, Eiichiro Sumita, Shinsuke Mori, and Tatsuya Kawahara. 2011. An unsupervised model for joint phrase alignment and extraction. In *Proceedings of the 49th Annual Meeting of the Association for Computational Linguistics: Human Language Technologies - Volume 1*, HLT '11, pages 632–641, Stroudsburg, PA, USA. Association for Computational Linguistics.

Franz Josef Och and Hermann Ney. 2003. A Systematic Comparison of Various Statistical Alignment Models. *Computational Linguistics*, 29(1):19–51, March.

Franz Josef Och and Hermann Ney. 2004. The alignment template approach to statistical machine translation. *Computational Linguistics*, 30(4):417–449, December.

Franz J. Och. 2003. Minimum Error Rate Training for Statistical Machine Translation. In *Proc. of the 41th Annual Meeting of the Association for Computational Linguistics (ACL)*, Sapporo, Japan, July.

Kishore Papineni, Salim Roukos, Todd Ward, and Wei-Jing Zhu. 2001. Bleu: a Method for Automatic Evaluation of Machine Translation. IBM Research Report RC22176 (W0109-022), IBM Research Division, Thomas J. Watson Research Center, P.O. Box 218, Yorktown Heights, NY 10598, September.

Markus Saers and Dekai Wu. 2011. Principled induction of phrasal bilexica. In *Proceedings of the 15th International Conference of the European Association for Machine Translation*, pages 313–320, May.

Matthew Snover, Bonnie Dorr, Richard Schwartz, Linnea Micciulla, and John Makhoul. 2006. A Study of Translation Edit Rate with Targeted Human Annotation. In *Proceedings of the 7th Conference of the Association for Machine Translation in the Americas*, pages 223–231, Cambridge, Massachusetts, USA, August.

Joern Wuebker, Arne Mauser, and Hermann Ney. 2010. Training phrase translation models with leaving-one-out. In *Proceedings of the 48th Annual Meeting of the Assoc. for Computational Linguistics*, pages 475–484, Uppsala, Sweden, July.

Joern Wuebker, Matthias Huck, Stephan Peitz, Malte Nuhn, Markus Freitag, Jan-Thorsten Peter, Saab Mansour, and Hermann Ney. 2012a. Jane 2: Open source phrase-based and hierarchical statistical machine translation. In *International Conference on Computational Linguistics*, pages 483–491, Mumbai, India, December.

Joern Wuebker, Mei-Yuh Hwang, and Chris Quirk. 2012b. Leave-One-Out Phrase Model Training for Large-Scale Deployment. In *Proceedings of the NAACL 2012 Seventh Workshop on Statistical Machine Translation*, pages 460–467, Montreal, Canada, June.

Richard Zens. 2008. *Phrase-based Statistical Machine Translation: Models, Search, Training*. Ph.D. thesis, Computer Science Department, RWTH Aachen – University of Technology, Germany, February.

Positive Diversity Tuning for Machine Translation System Combination

Daniel Cer, Christopher D. Manning and Daniel Jurafsky
Stanford University
Stanford, CA 94305, USA
{danielcer,manning,jurafsky}@stanford.edu

Abstract

We present Positive Diversity Tuning, a new method for tuning machine translation models specifically for improved performance during system combination. System combination gains are often limited by the fact that the translations produced by the different component systems are too similar to each other. We propose a method for reducing excess cross-system similarity by optimizing a joint objective that simultaneously rewards models for producing translations that are similar to reference translations, while also punishing them for translations that are too similar to those produced by other systems. The formulation of the Positive Diversity objective is easy to implement and allows for its quick integration with most machine translation tuning pipelines. We find that individual systems tuned on the *same data* to Positive Diversity can be even more diverse than systems built using different data sets, while still obtaining good BLEU scores. When these individual systems are used together for system combination, our approach allows for significant gains of 0.8 BLEU even when the combination is performed using a small number of otherwise identical individual systems.

1 Introduction

The best performing machine translation systems are typically not individual decoders but rather are ensembles of two or more systems whose output is then merged using system combination algorithms. Since combining multiple distinct equally good translation systems reliably produces gains over any one of the systems in isolation, it is widely used in situations where high quality is essential.

Exploiting system combination brings significant cost: Macherey and Och (2007) showed that successful system combination requires the construction of multiple systems that are simultaneously diverse and well-performing. If the systems are not distinct enough, they will bring very little value during system combination. However, if some of the systems produce diverse translations but achieve lower overall translation quality, their contributions risk being ignored during system combination.

Prior work has approached the need for diverse systems by using different system architectures, model components, system build parameters, decoder hyperparameters, as well as data selection and weighting (Macherey and Och, 2007; DeNero et al., 2010; Xiao et al., 2013). However, during tuning, each individual system is still just trained to maximize its own isolated performance on a tune set, or at best an error-driven reweighting of the tune set, without explicitly taking into account the diversity of the resulting translations. Such tuning does not encourage systems to rigorously explore model variations that achieve both good translation quality and diversity with respect to the other systems. It is reasonable to suspect that this results in individual systems that under exploit the amount of diversity possible, given the characteristics of the individual systems.

For better system combination, we propose building individual systems to attempt to simultaneously maximize the overall quality of the individual systems and the amount of diversity across systems. We operationalize this problem formulation by devising a new heuristic measure called Positive Diversity that estimates the potential usefulness of individual systems during system combination. We find that optimizing systems toward Positive Diversity leads to significant performance gains during system combination even when the combination is performed using a small number of otherwise identical individual translation systems.

The remainder of this paper is organized as follows. Section 2 and 3 briefly review the tuning of individual machine translation systems and how system combination merges the output of multiple systems into an improved combined translation. Section 4 introduces our Positive Diversity measure. Section 5 introduces an algorithm for training a collection of translation systems toward Positive Diversity. Experiments are presented in sections 6 and 7. Sections 8 and 9 conclude with discussions of prior work and directions for future research.

2 Tuning Individual Translation Systems

Machine translation systems are tuned toward some measure of the correctness of the translations produced by the system according to one or more manually translated references. As shown in equation (1), this can be written as finding parameter values Θ that produce translations sys_Θ that in turn achieve a high score on some correctness measure:

$$\arg\max_{\Theta} \ \texttt{Correctness(ref[],sys}_\Theta\texttt{)} \quad (1)$$

The correctness measure that systems are typically tuned toward is BLEU (Papineni et al., 2002), which measures the fraction of the n-grams that are both present in the reference translations and the translations produced by a system. The BLEU score is computed as the geometric mean of the resulting n-gram precisions scaled by a brevity penalty.

The most widely used machine translation tuning algorithm, minimum error rate training (MERT) (Och, 2003), attempts to maximize the correctness objective directly. Popular alternatives such as pairwise ranking objective (PRO) (Hopkins and May, 2011), MIRA (Chiang et al., 2008), and RAMPION (Gimpel and Smith, 2012) use surrogate optimization objectives that indirectly attempt to maximize the correctness function by using it to select targets for training discriminative classification models. In practice, either optimizing correctness directly or optimizing a surrogate objective that uses correctness to choose optimization targets results in roughly equivalent translation performance (Cherry and Foster, 2012).

Even when individual systems are being built to be used in a larger combined system, they are still usually tuned to maximize their isolated individual system performance rather than to maximize the potential usefulness of their contribution during system combination.[1] To our knowledge, no effort has been made to explicitly tune toward criteria that attempts to simultaneously maximize the translation quality of individual systems and their mutual diversity. This is unfortunate since the most valuable component systems for system combination should not only obtain good translation performance, but also produce translations that are different from those produced by other systems.

3 System Combination

Similar to speech recognition's Recognizer Output Voting Error Reduction (ROVER) algorithm (Fiscus, 1997), machine translation system combination typically operates by aligning the translations produced by two or more individual translation systems and then using the alignments to construct a search space that allows new translations to be pieced together by picking and choosing parts of the material from the original translations (Bangalore et al., 2001; Matusov et al., 2006; Rosti et al., 2007a; Rosti et al., 2007b; Karakos et al., 2008; Heafield and Lavie, 2010a).[2] The alignment of the individual system translations can be performed using alignment driven evaluation metrics such as invWER, TERp, METEOR (Leusch et al., 2003; Snover et al., 2009; Denkowski and Lavie, 2011). The piecewise selection of material from the original translations is performed using the combination model's scoring features such as n-gram language models, confidence models over the individual systems, and consensus features that score a combined translation using n-grams matches to the individual system translations (Rosti et al., 2007b; Zhao and He, 2009; Heafield and Lavie, 2010b).

Both system confidence model features and n-gram consensus features score contributions based in part on how confident the system combination model is in each individual machine translation system. This means that little or no gains will typically be seen when combining a good system with poor performing systems even if the systems col-

[1] The exception being Xiao et al. (2013)'s work using boosting for error-driven reweighting of the tuning set

[2] Other system combination techniques exist such as candidate selection systems, whereby the combination model attempts to find the best single candidate produced by one of the translation engines (Paul et al., 2005; Nomoto, 2004; Zwarts and Dras, 2008), decoder chaining (Aikawa and Ruopp, 2009), re-decoding informed by the decoding paths taken by other systems (Huang and Papineni, 2007), and decoding model combination (DeNero et al., 2010).

```
Input  : systems [], tune(), source, refs [], α, EvalMetric(), SimMetric()
Output: models []
// start with an empty set of translations from prior iterations
other_sys [] ← []
for i ← 1 to len(systems []) do
    // new Positive Diversity measure using prior translations
    PD_{α,i}() ← new PD(α, EvalMetric(), SimMetric(), refs [], other_sys [])
    // tune a new model to fit PD_{α,i}
    // e.g., using MERT, PRO, MIRA, RAMPION, etc.
    models [i] ← tune(systems [i], source, PD_{α,i}())
    // Save translations from tuned model_i for use during
    // the diversity computation for subsequent systems
    push(other_sys [], translate(systems [i], models [i], source))
end
return models []
```

Algorithm 1: Positive Diversity Tuning (PDT)

lectively produce very diverse translations.[3]

The requirement that the systems used for system combination be both of high quality and diverse can be and often is met by building several different systems using different system architectures, model components or tuning data. However, as will be shown in the next few sections, by explicitly optimizing an objective that targets both translation quality and diversity, it is possible to obtain meaningful system combination gains even using a single system architecture with identical model components and the same tuning set.

4 Positive Diversity

We propose Positive Diversity as a heuristic measurement of the value of potential contributions from an individual system to system combination. As given in equation (2), Positive Diversity is defined as the correctness of the translations produced by a system minus a penalty term that scores how similar the systems translations are with those produced by other systems:

$$PD_\alpha = \alpha \ \texttt{Correctness}(\texttt{ref[]}, \texttt{sys}_\Theta) - (1-\alpha) \ \texttt{Similarity}(\texttt{other\_sys[]}, \texttt{sys}_\Theta) \tag{2}$$

The hyperparameter α explicitly trades-off the preference for a well performing individual system with system combination diversity. Higher α values result in a Positive Diversity metric that mostly favors good quality translations. However, even for large α values, if two translations are of approximately the same quality, the Positive Diversity metric will prefer the one that is the most diverse given the translations being produced by other systems.

The `Correctness()` and `Similarity()` measures are any function that can score translations from a single system against other translations. This includes traditional machine translation evaluation metrics (e.g, BLEU, TER, METEOR) as well as any other measure of textual similarity.

For the remainder of this paper, we use BLEU to measure both correctness and the similarity of the translations produced by the individual systems. When tuning individual translation systems toward Positive Diversity, our task is then to maximize equation (3) rather than equation (1):

$$\arg\max_\Theta \ \alpha \ \texttt{BLEU}(\texttt{ref[]}, \texttt{sys}) - (1-\alpha) \ \texttt{BLEU}(\texttt{other\_sys[]}, \texttt{sys}) \tag{3}$$

Since this learning objective is simply the difference between two BLEU scores, it should be easy to integrate into most existing machine translation tuning pipelines that are already designed to optimize performance on translation evaluation metrics.

[3] The machine learning theory behind boosting suggests that it should be possible to combine a very large number of poor performing systems into a single good system. However, for machine translation, using a very large number of individual systems brings with it difficult computational challenges.

PDT Individual System Diversity										
System \ Iteration	1	2	3	4	5	6	7	8	9	10
$\alpha = 0.95$	36.6	32.0	19.0	13.6	11.9	8.2	15.9	8.7	7.3	2.3
$\alpha = 0.97$	32.9	21.7	17.7	10.4	2.7	7.4	2.3	7.3	2.1	2.9
$\alpha = 0.99$	23.9	13.1	7.9	2.3	3.2	2.6	2.2	1.5	3.4	0.7

Table 1: Diversity scores for PDT individual systems on BOLT dev12 dev. Individual systems are tuned to Positive Diversity on GALE dev10 web tune. A system's diversity score is measured as its 1.0−BLEU score on the translations produced by PDT systems from earlier iterations. Higher scores mean more diversity.

Diversity of Baseline System vs. Individual PDT Systems Available at Iteration i											
PDT Systems \ Iteration	0	1	2	3	4	5	6	7	8	9	10
$\alpha = 0.95$	27.3	20.4	16.8	14.9	12.8	11.4	9.4	8.6	8.3	8.1	7.9
$\alpha = 0.97$	28.4	21.3	15.8	14.7	13.3	13.0	12.5	12.2	10.3	10.0	9.7
$\alpha = 0.99$	27.5	22.6	18.5	17.1	16.8	15.9	15.4	14.6	14.3	13.5	13.4

Table 2: Diversity scores of a baseline system tuned to BOLT dev12 tune, a different tuning set than what was used for the PDT individual systems. The baseline system diversity is scored against all of the PDT individual systems available at iteration i for a given α value and over translations of BOLT dev12 dev.

5 Tuning to Positive Diversity

To tune a collection of machine translation systems using Positive Diversity, we propose a staged process, whereby systems are tuned one-by-one to maximize equation (2) using the translations produced by previously trained systems to compute the diversity term, `Similarity(other_sys[], sys`$_\Theta$`)`.

As shown in Algorithm 1, Positive Diversity Tuning (PDT) takes as input: a list of machine translation systems, `systems[]`; a tuning procedure for training individual systems, `tune()`; a tuning data set with source and reference translations, `source` and `refs`; a hyperparameter α to adjust the trade-off between fitting the reference translations and diversity between the systems; and metrics to measure correctness and cross-system similarity, `Correctness()` and `Similarity()`.

The list of systems can contain any translation system that can be parameterized using `tune()`. This can be a heterogeneous collection of substantially different systems (e.g., phrase-based, hierarchical, syntactic, or tunable hybrid systems) or even multiple copies of a single machine translation system. In all cases, systems later in the list will be trained to produce translations that both fit the references and are encouraged to be distinct from the systems earlier in the list.

During each iteration, the system constructs a new Positive Diversity measure $\texttt{PD}_{\alpha,i}$ using the translations produced during prior iterations of training. This $\texttt{PD}_{\alpha,i}$ measure is then given to `tune()` as the the training criteria for $\texttt{model}_i$ of $\texttt{system}_i$. The function `tune()` is any algorithm that allows a translation system's performance to be fit to an evaluation metric. This includes both minimum error rate training algorithms (MERT) that attempt to directly optimize a system's performance on a metric, as well as other techniques such as Pairwaise Ranking Objective (PRO), MIRA, and RAMPION that optimize a surrogate loss based on the preferences of an evaluation metric.

After training a model for each system, the resulting model-system pairs can be combined using any arbitrary system combination strategy.

6 Experiments

Experiments are performed using a single phrase-based Chinese-to-English translation system, built with the Stanford Phrasal machine translation toolkit (Cer et al., 2010). The system was built using all of the parallel data available for Phase 2 of the DARPA BOLT program. The Chinese data was segmented to the Chinese TreeBank (CTB) standard using a maximum match word segmenter, trained on the output of a CRF segmenter (Xiang et al., 2013). The bitext was word aligned using the Berkeley aligner (Liang et al., 2006). Standard phrase-pair extraction heuris-

	BLEU scores from individual systems tuned during iteration i of PDT										
PDT System	0	1	2	3	4	5	6	7	8	9	10
$\alpha = 0.95$	16.2	16.0	15.7	15.9	16.1	16.1	15.9	15.4	16.1	15.9	16.2
$\alpha = 0.97$	16.4	15.8	15.8	15.9	16.0	16.2	16.1	16.2	16.2	16.4	16.1
$\alpha = 0.99$	16.3	16.1	16.2	15.9	16.3	16.4	16.4	16.3	16.4	16.5	16.3

Table 3: BLEU scores on BOLT dev12 dev achieved by the individual PDT systems tuned on GALE dev10 web tune. Scores report individual system performance before system combination.

tics were used to extract a phrase-table over word alignments symmetrized using grow-diag (Koehn et al., 2003). We made use of a hierarchical reordering model (Galley and Manning, 2008) as well as a 5-gram language model trained on the target side of the bi-text and smoothed using modified Kneeser-Ney (Chen and Goodman, 1996).

Individual PDT systems were tuned on the GALE dev10 web tune set using online-PRO (Green et al., 2013; Hopkins and May, 2011) to the Positive Diversity Tuning criterion.[4] The Multi-Engine Machine Translation (MEMT) package was used for system combination (Heafield and Lavie, 2010a). We used BOLT dev12 dev as a development test set to explore different α parameterizations of the Positive Diversity criteria.

7 Results

Table 1 illustrates the amount of diversity achieved by individual PDT systems on the BOLT dev12 dev evaluation set for α values 0.95, 0.97, and 0.99.[5] Using different tuning sets is one of the common strategies for producing diverse component systems for system combination. Thus, as a baseline, Table 2 gives the diversity of a system tuned to BLEU using a different tuning set, BOLT dev12 tune, with respect to the PDT systems available at each iteration. As in Table 1, the diversity computation is performed using translations of BOLT dev12 dev.

Like the cross-system diversity term in the formulation of Positive Diversity using BLEU in equation (3), we measure the diversity of translations produced by an individual system as the negative BLEU score of the translations with respect to the translations from systems built during prior iterations. For clarity of presentation, these diversity scores are reported as $1.0-\text{BLEU}$. Using $1.0-\text{BLEU}$ to score cross-system diversity, means that the reported numbers can be roughly interpreted as the fraction of n-grams from the individual systems built during iteration i that have not been previously produced by other systems built during any iteration $< i$.[6]

In our experiments, we find that for $\alpha \leq 0.97$, during the first three iterations of PDT, *there is more diversity among the PDT systems tuned on a single data set (GALE dev10 web tune) than there is between systems tuned on different datasets (BOLT dev12 tune vs. GALE dev10 wb tune)*. This is significant since using different tuning sets is a common strategy for increasing diversity during system combination. These results suggest PDT is better at producing additional diversity than using different tuning sets. The PDT systems also achieve good coverage of the n-grams present in the baseline system that was tuned using different data. At iteration 10 and using $\alpha = 0.95$, the baseline systems receive a diversity score of *only 7.9%* when measured against the PDT systems.[7]

As PDT progresses, it becomes more difficult to tune systems to produce high quality translations that are substantially different from those already being produced by other systems. This is seen in the per iteration diversity scores, whereby during iteration 5, the individual PDT translation systems have a $1.0-\text{BLEU}$ diversity score with prior systems ranging from 11.9%, when using an α value

[4] Preliminary experiments performed using MERT to train the individual systems produced similar results to those seen here. However, we switched to online-PRO since it dramatically reduced the amount time required to train each individual system. We expect similar results when using other tuning algorithms for the individual systems, such as MIRA or RAMPION.

[5] Due to time constraints, we were not able to try additional α values. Given that our results suggest the lowest α value from the ones we tried works best (i.e., $\alpha = 0.95$), it would be worth trying additional smaller α values such as 0.90

[6] This intuitive interpretation assumes a brevity penalty that is approximately 1.0.

[7] For this diversity score, the brevity penalty is 1.0, meaning the diversity score is based purely on the n-grams present in the baseline system that are not present in translations produced by one or more of the PDT systems

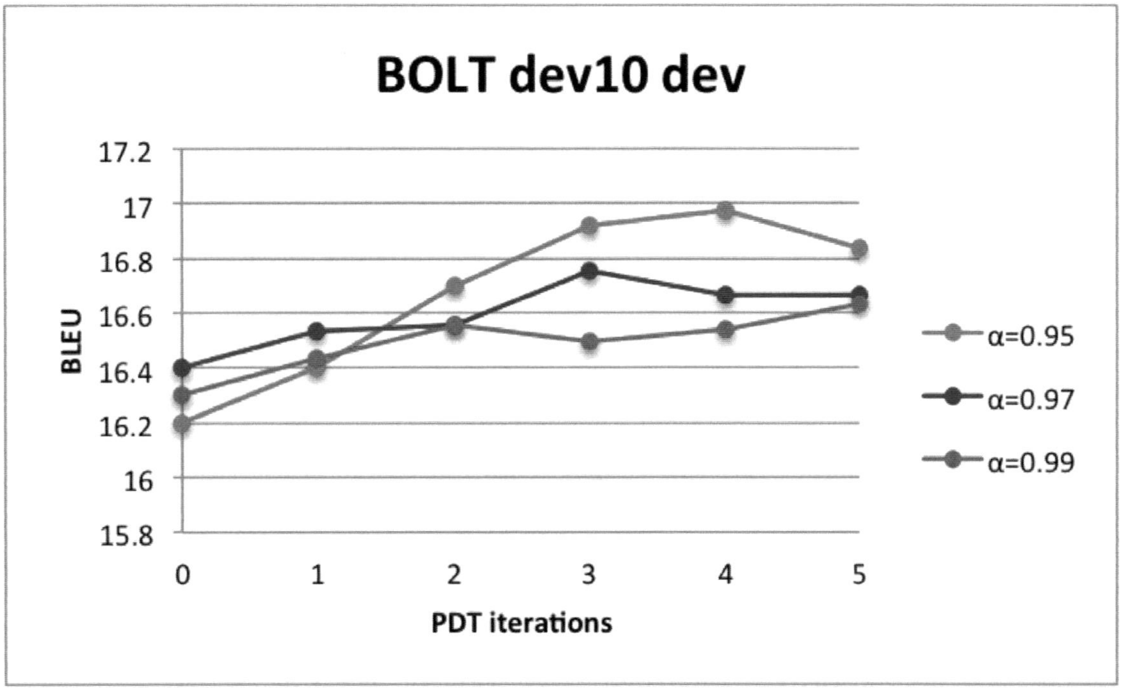

Figure 1: System combination BLEU score achieved using Positive Diversity Tuning with the α values 0.95, 0.97, and 0.99. Four iterations of PDT with $\alpha = 0.95$ results in a 0.8 BLEU gain over the initial BLEU tuned system. We only examine combinations of up to 6 systems (i.e., iterations 0-5), as the time required to tune MEMT increases dramatically as additional systems are added.

of 0.95, to 3.2% when using an α value of 0.99. A diversity score of 3.2% when using $\alpha = 0.99$ suggests that by iteration 5, very high α values put insufficient pressure on learning to find models that produce diverse translations. When using an α of 0.95, a sizable amount of diversity still exists across the systems translations all the way to iteration 7. By iteration 10, only a small amount of additional diversity is contributed by each additional system for all of the alpha values ($< 3\%$).[8]

Table 3 shows the BLEU scores obtained on the BOLT dev12 dev evaluation set by the *individual systems* tuned during each iteration of PDT. The 0th iteration for each α value has an empty set of translations for the diversity term. This means the resulting systems are effectively tuned to just maximize BLEU. Differences in system performance during this iteration are only due to differences in the random seeds used during training. Starting at iteration 1, the individual systems are optimized to produce translations that both score well on BLEU and are diverse from the systems produced during prior iterations. It is interesting to note that the systems trained during these subsequent iterations obtain BLEU scores that are usually competitive with those obtained by the iteration 0 systems. Taken together with the diversity scores in Table 1, this strongly suggests that PDT is succeeding at increasing diversity while still producing high quality individual translation systems.

Figure 1 graphs the system combination BLEU score achieved by using varying numbers of Positive Diversity Tuned translation systems and different α values to trade-off translation quality with translation diversity. After running 4 iterations of PDT, the best configuration, $\alpha = 0.95$, achieves a BLEU score that is 0.8 BLEU higher than the corresponding BLEU trained iteration 0 system.[9]

From the graph, it appears that PDT performance initially increases as additional systems are added to the system combination and then later plateaus or even drops after too many systems are included. The combinations using PDT systems

[8] We speculate that if heterogeneous translation systems were used with PDT, it could be possible to run with higher α values and still obtain diverse translations after a large number of PDT iterations

[9] Recall that the iteration 0 system is effectively just tuned to maximize BLEU since we have an empty set of translations from other systems that are used to compute diversity

built with higher α values reach the point of diminishing returns faster than combinations using systems built with lower alpha values. For instance, $\alpha = 0.99$ plateaus on iteration 2, while $\alpha = 0.95$ peaks on iteration 4. It might be possible to identify the point at which additional systems will likely not be useful by using the diversity scores in Table 1. Scoring about 10% or less on the 1−BLEU diversity measure, with respect to the other systems being used within the system combination, seems to suggest the individual system will not be very helpful to add into the combination.

8 Related Work

While the idea of encouraging diversity in individual systems that will be used for system combination has been proven effective in speech recognition and document summarization (Hinton, 2002; Breslin and Gales, 2007; Carbonell and Goldstein, 1998; Goldstein et al., 2000), there has only been a modest amount of prior work exploring such approaches for machine translation. Prior work within machine translation has investigated adapting machine learning techniques for building ensembles of classifiers to translation system tuning, encouraging diversity by varying both the hyperparameters and the data used to build the individual systems, and chaining together individual translation systems.

Xiao et al. (2013) explores using boosting to train an ensemble of machine translation systems. Following the standard Adaboost algorithm, each system was trained in sequence on an error-driven reweighting of the tuning set that focuses learning on the material that is the most problematic for the current ensemble. They found that using a single system to tune a large number of decoding models to different Adaboost guided weightings of the tuning data results in significant gains during system combination.

Macherey and Och (2007) investigated system combination using automatic generation of diverse individual systems. They programmatically generated variations of systems using different build and decoder hyperparameters such as choice of word-alignment algorithm, distortion limit, variations of model feature function weights, and the set of language models used. Then, in a process similar to forward feature selection, they constructed a combined system by iteratively adding the individual automatically generated system that produced the largest increase in quality when used in conjunction with the systems already selected for the combined system. They also explored producing variation by using different samplings of the the training data. The individual and combined systems produced by sampling the training data were inferior to systems that used all of the available data. However, the experiments facilitated insightful analysis on what properties an individual system must have in order to be useful during system combination. They found that in order to be useful within a combination, individual systems need to produce translations of similar quality to other individual systems within the system combination while also being as uncorrelated as possible from the other systems. The Positive Diversity Tuning method introduced in our work is an explicit attempt to build individual translation systems that meet this criteria, while being less computationally demanding than the diversity generating techniques explored by Macherey and Och (2007).

Aikawa and Ruopp (2009) investigated building machine translations systems specifically for use in sequential combination with other systems. They constructed chains of systems whereby the output of one decoder is feed as input to the next decoder in the pipeline. The downstream systems are built and tuned to correct errors produced by the preceding system. In this approach, the downstream decoder acts as a machine learning based post editing system.

9 Conclusion

We have presented Positive Diversity as a new way of jointly measuring the quality and diversity of the contribution of individual machine translation systems to system combination. This method heuristically assesses the value of individual translation systems by measuring their similarity to the reference translations as well as their dissimilarity from the other systems being combined. We operationalize this metric by reusing existing techniques from machine translation evaluation to assess translation quality and the degree of similarity between systems. We also give a straightforward algorithm for training a collection of individual systems to optimize Positive Diversity. Our experimental results suggest that tuning to Positive Diversity leads to improved cross-system diversity and system combination performance even when combining otherwise identical machine translation systems.

The Positive Diversity Tuning method explored in this work can be used to tune individual systems for any ensemble in which individual models can be fit to multiple extrinsic loss functions. Since Hall et al. (2011) demonstrated the general purpose application of multiple extrinsic loss functions to training structured prediction models, Positive Diversity Tuning could be broadly useful within natural language processing and for other machine learning tasks.

In future work within machine translation, it may prove fruitful to examine more sophisticated measures of dissimilarity. For example, one could imagine a metric that punishes instances of similar material in proportion to some measure of the expected diversity of the material. It might also be useful to explore joint rather than sequential training of the individual translation systems.

Acknowledgments

We thank the reviewers and the members of the Stanford NLP group for their helpful comments and suggestions. This work was supported by the Defense Advanced Research Projects Agency (DARPA) Broad Operational Language Translation (BOLT) program through IBM and a fellowship to one of the authors from the Center for Advanced Study in the Behavioral Sciences. Any opinions, findings, and conclusions or recommendations expressed in this material are those of the author(s) and do not necessarily reflect the view of DARPA or the US government.

References

Takako Aikawa and Achim Ruopp. 2009. Chained system: A linear combination of different types of statistical machine translation systems. In *Proceedings of MT Summit XII*.

S. Bangalore, G. Bordel, and Giuseppe Riccardi. 2001. Computing consensus translation from multiple machine translation systems. In *ASRU*.

C. Breslin and M. J F Gales. 2007. Complementary system generation using directed decision trees. In *ICASSP*.

Jaime Carbonell and Jade Goldstein. 1998. The use of MMR, diversity-based reranking for reordering documents and producing summaries. In *SIGIR*.

Daniel Cer, Michel Galley, Daniel Jurafsky, and Christopher D. Manning. 2010. Phrasal: A statistical machine translation toolkit for Exploring new model features. In *NAACL/HLT*.

Stanley F. Chen and Joshua Goodman. 1996. An empirical study of smoothing techniques for language modeling. In *ACL*.

Colin Cherry and George Foster. 2012. Batch tuning strategies for statistical machine translation. In *NAACL/HLT*.

David Chiang, Yuval Marton, and Philip Resnik. 2008. Online large-margin training of syntactic and structural translation features. In *EMNLP*.

John DeNero, Shankar Kumar, Ciprian Chelba, and Franz Och. 2010. Model combination for machine translation. In *NAACL/HLT*.

Michael Denkowski and Alon Lavie. 2011. Meteor 1.3: Automatic Metric for Reliable Optimization and Evaluation of Machine Translation Systems. In *Proceedings of the EMNLP 2011 Workshop on Statistical Machine Translation*.

J.G. Fiscus. 1997. A post-processing system to yield reduced word error rates: Recognizer output voting error reduction (ROVER). In *ASRU*.

Michel Galley and Christopher D. Manning. 2008. A simple and effective hierarchical phrase reordering model. In *Proceedings of the Conference on Empirical Methods in Natural Language Processing*.

Kevin Gimpel and Noah A. Smith. 2012. Structured ramp loss minimization for machine translation. In *NAACL/HLT*.

J. Goldstein, V. Mittal, J. Carbonell, and M. Kantrowitz. 2000. Multi-document summarization by sentence extraction. In *ANLP/NAACL Workshop on Automatic Summarization*.

Spence Green, Sida Wang, Daniel Cer, and Christopher D. Manning. 2013. Fast and adaptive online training of feature-rich translation models. In *(to appear) ACL*.

Keith Hall, Ryan McDonald, and Slav Petrov. 2011. Training structured prediction models with extrinsic loss functions. In *Domain Adaptation Workshop at NIPS*.

Kenneth Heafield and Alon Lavie. 2010a. CMU multi-engine machine translation for WMT 2010. In *WMT*.

Kenneth Heafield and Alon Lavie. 2010b. Voting on n-grams for machine translation system combination. In *AMTA*.

Geoffrey E. Hinton. 2002. Training products of experts by minimizing contrastive divergence. *Neural Comput.*, 14(8):1771–1800, August.

Mark Hopkins and Jonathan May. 2011. Tuning as ranking. In *EMNLP*.

Fei Huang and Kishore Papineni. 2007. Hierarchical system combination for machine translation. In *EMNLP-CoNLL*.

Damianos Karakos, Jason Eisner, Sanjeev Khudanpur, and Markus Dreyer. 2008. Machine translation system combination using ITG-based alignments. In *ACL/HLT*.

Philipp Koehn, Franz Josef Och, and Daniel Marcu. 2003. Statistical phrase-based translation. In *NAACL*.

Gregor Leusch, Nicola Ueffing, and Hermann Ney. 2003. A novel string-to-string distance measure with applications to machine translation evaluation. In *MT Summit*.

Percy Liang, Ben Taskar, and Dan Klein. 2006. Alignment by agreement. In *NAACL/HLT*.

Wolfgang Macherey and Franz J. Och. 2007. An empirical study on computing consensus translations from multiple machine translation systems. In *EMNLP/CoNLL*.

Evgeny Matusov, Nicola Ueffing, and Hermann Ney. 2006. Computing consensus translation from multiple machine translation systems using enhanced hypotheses alignment. In *EMNLP*.

Tadashi Nomoto. 2004. Multi-engine machine translation with voted language model. In *ACL*.

Franz Josef Och. 2003. Minimum error rate training in statistical machine translation. In *ACL*.

Kishore Papineni, Salim Roukos, Todd Ward, and Wei-Jing Zhu. 2002. Bleu: a method for automatic evaluation of machine translation. In *ACL*.

Michael Paul, Takao Doi, Youngsook Hwang, Kenji Imamura, Hideo Okuma, and Eiichiro Sumita. 2005. Nobody is perfect: ATR's hybrid approach to spoken language translation. In *IWSLT*.

Antti-Veikko Rosti, Necip Fazil Ayan, Bing Xiang, Spyros Matsoukas, Richard Schwartz, and Bonnie Dorr. 2007a. Combining outputs from multiple machine translation systems. In *NAACL/HLT*.

Antti-Veikko Rosti, Spyros Matsoukas, and Richard Schwartz. 2007b. Improved word-level system combination for machine translation. In *ACL*.

Matthew Snover, Nitin Madnani, Bonnie J. Dorr, and Richard Schwartz. 2009. Fluency, adequacy, or HTER?: exploring different human judgments with a tunable MT metric. In *WMT*.

Bing Xiang, Xiaoqiang Luo, and Bowen Zhou. 2013. Enlisting the ghost: Modeling empty categories for machine translation. In *ACL*.

Tong Xiao, Jingbo Zhu, and Tongran Liu. 2013. Bagging and boosting statistical machine translation systems. *Artif. Intell.*, 195:496–527, February.

Yong Zhao and Xiaodong He. 2009. Using n-gram based features for machine translation system combination. In *NAACL/HLT*.

Simon Zwarts and Mark Dras. 2008. Choosing the right translation: A syntactically informed classification approach. In *CoLING*.

Machine learning methods for comparative and time-oriented Quality Estimation of Machine Translation output

Eleftherios Avramidis and Maja Popović
German Research Center for Artificial Intelligence (DFKI GmbH)
Language Technology Lab
Alt Moabit 91c, 10559 Berlin
eleftherios.avramidis@dfki.de and maja.popovic@dfki.de

Abstract

This paper describes a set of experiments on two sub-tasks of Quality Estimation of Machine Translation (MT) output. *Sentence-level ranking* of alternative MT outputs is done with pairwise classifiers using Logistic Regression with black-box features originating from PCFG Parsing, language models and various counts. *Post-editing time prediction* uses regression models, additionally fed with new elaborate features from the Statistical MT decoding process. These seem to be better indicators of post-editing time than black-box features. Prior to training the models, feature scoring with ReliefF and Information Gain is used to choose feature sets of decent size and avoid computational complexity.

1 Introduction

During the recent years, Machine Translation (MT) has reached levels of performance which allow for its integration into real-world translation workflows. Despite the high speed and various advantages of this technology, the fact that the MT results are rarely perfect and often require manual corrections has raised a need to assess their quality, predict the required post-editing effort and compare outputs from various systems on application time. This has been the aim of current research on *Quality Estimation*, which investigates solutions for several variations of such problems.

We describe possible solutions for two problems of MT Quality Estimation, as part of the 8th Shared Task on Machine Translation: **(a) sentence-level quality ranking** (1.2) of multiple translations of the same source sentence and **(b) prediction of post-editing time** (1.3). We present our approach on acquiring (section 2.1) and selecting features (section 2.2), we explain the generation of the statistical estimation systems (section 2.3) and we evaluate the developed solutions with some of the standard metrics (section 3).

2 Methods: Quality Estimation as machine learning

These two Quality Estimation solutions have been seen as typical supervised machine learning problems. MT output has been given to humans, so that they perform either (a) ranking of the multiple MT system outputs in terms of meaning or (b) post-editing of single MT system output, where time needed per sentence is measured. The output of these tasks has been provided by the shared task organizers as a training material, whereas a small keep-out set has been reserved for testing purposes.

Our task is therefore to perform automatic quality analysis of the translation output and the translation process in order to provide features for the supervised machine learning mechanism, which is then trained over the corresponding to the respective human behaviour. The task is first optimized in a *development* phase in order to produce the two best shared task submissions for each task. These are finally tested on the keep-out set so that their performance is compared with the ones submitted by all other shared-task participants.

2.1 Feature acquisition

We acquire two types of sentence-level features, that are expected to provide hints about the quality of the generated translation, depending on whether they have access to internal details of the MT decoding process (*glass-box*) or they are only derived from characteristics of the processed and generated sentence text (*black-box*).

2.1.1 Black-box features

Features of this type are generated as a result of automatic analysis of both the source sentence and the MT output (when applicable), whereas many of them are already part of the baseline infrastructure. For all features we also calculate the ratios of the source to the target sentence. These features include:

PCFG Features: We parse the text with a PCFG grammar (Petrov et al., 2006) and we derive the counts of all node labels (e.g. count of VPs, NPs etc.), the parse log-likelihood and the number of the n-best parse trees generated (Avramidis et al., 2011).

Rule-based language correction is a result of hand-written controlled language rules, that indicate mistakes on several pre-defined error categories (Naber, 2003). We include the number of errors of each category as a feature.

Language model scores include the smoothed n-gram probability and the n-gram perplexity of the sentence.

Count-based features include count and percentage of tokens, unknown words, punctuation marks, numbers, tokens which do or do not contain characters "a-z"; the absolute difference between number of tokens in source and target normalized by source length, number of occurrences of the target word within the target hypothesis averaged for all words in the hypothesis (type/token ratio).

Source frequency: A set of eight features includes the percentage of uni-grams, bi-grams and tri-grams of the processed sentence in frequency quartiles 1 (lower frequency words) and 4 (higher frequency words) in the source side of a parallel corpus (Callison-Burch et al., 2012).

Contrastive evaluation scores: For the ranking task, each translation is scored with an automatic metric (Papineni et al., 2002; Lavie and Agarwal, 2007), using the other translations as references (Soricut et al., 2012).

2.1.2 Glass-box features

Glass-box features are available only for the time-prediction task, as a result of analyzing the verbose output of the Minimum Bayes Risk decoding process.

Counts from the best hypothesis: Count of phrases, tokens, average/minimum/maximum phrase length, position of longest and shortest phrase in the source sentence; count of **words unknown** to the phrase table, average number of unknown words first/last position of an unknown word in the sentence normalized to the number of tokens, variance and deviation of the position of the unknown words.

Log probability (pC) and **future cost estimate** (c) of the phrases chosen as part of the best translation: minimum and maximum values and their position in the sentence averaged to the number of sentences, and also their average, variance, standard deviation; count of the phrases whose probability or future cost estimate is lower and higher than their standard deviation; the ratio of these phrases to the total number of phrases.

Alternative translations from the search path of the decoder: average phrase length, average of the average/variance/standard deviation of phrase log probability and future cost estimate, count of alternative phrases whose log probability or future cost estimate is lower and higher than their standard deviation.

2.2 Feature selection

Feature acquisition results in a huge number of features. Although the machine learning mechanisms already include feature selection or regularization, huge feature sets may be unusable for training, due to the high processing needs and the sparsity or noise they may infer. For this purpose we first reduce the number of features by scoring them with two popular correlation measurement methods.

2.2.1 Information gain

Information gain (Hunt et al., 1966) estimates the difference between the prior entropy of the classes and the posterior entropy given the attribute values. It is useful for estimating the quality of each attribute but it works under the assumption that features are independent, so it is not suitable when strong feature inter-correlation exists. Information gain is only used for the sentence ranking task after discretization of the feature values.

2.2.2 ReliefF

ReliefF assesses the ability of each feature to distinguish between very similar instances from different classes (Kononenko, 1994). It picks up a number of instances in random and calculates a feature *contribution* based on the nearest hits and misses. It is a robust method which can deal with incomplete and noisy data (Robnik-Šikonja and Kononenko, 2003).

2.3 Machine learning algorithms

Machine learning is performed for the two sub-tasks using common *pairwise classification* and *regression* methods, respectively.

2.3.1 Ranking with pairwise binary classifiers

For the sub-task on sentence-ranking we used pairwise classification, so that we can take advantage of several powerful binary classification methods (Avramidis, 2012). We used **logistic regression**, which optimizes a logistic function to predict values in the range between zero and one (Cameron, 1998), given a feature set X:

$$P(X) = \frac{1}{1 + e^{-1(a+bX)}} \quad (1)$$

The logistic function is fitted using the Newton-Raphson algorithm to iteratively minimize the least squares error computed from training data (Miller, 2002). Experiments are repeated with two variations of Logistic Regression concerning internal features treatment: *Stepwise Feature Set Selection* (Hosmer, 1989) and *L2-Regularization* (Lin et al., 2007).

2.3.2 Regression

For the sub-task on post-editing time prediction, we experimented with several regression methods, such as *Linear Regression*, *Partial Least Squares* (Stone and Brooks, 1990), *Multivariate Adaptive Regression Splines* (Friedman, 1991), *LASSO* (Tibshirani, 1996), *Support Vector Regression* (Basak et al., 2007) and Tree-based regressors. Indicatively, Linear regression optimizes coefficient β for predicting a value y, given a feature vector X:

$$y = \mathrm{X}\beta + \varepsilon \quad (2)$$

2.4 Evaluation

The ranking task is evaluated by measuring correlation between the predicted and the human ranking, with the use of Kendall tau (Kendall, 1938) including penalization of ties. We additionally consider two more metrics specialized in ranking tasks: Mean Reciprocal Rank - MRR (Voorhees, 1999) and Normalized Discounted Cumulative Gain - NDGC (Järvelin and Kekäläinen, 2002), which give better scores to models when higher ranks (i.e. better translations) are ordered correctly, as these are more important than lower ranks.

The regression task is evaluated in terms of Root Mean Square Error (RMSE) and Mean Average Error (MAE).

3 Experiment and Results

3.1 Implementation

Relieff is implemented for k=5 nearest neighbours sampling m=100 reference instances. Information gain is calculated after discretizing features into n=100 values

N-gram features are computed with the SRILM toolkit (Stolcke, 2002) with an order of 5, based on monolingual training material from Europarl (Koehn, 2005) and News Commentary (Callison-Burch et al., 2011). PCFG parsing features are generated on the output of the Berkeley Parser (Petrov and Klein, 2007) trained over an English, a German and a Spanish treebank (Taulé et al., 2008). The open source *language tool*[1] is used to annotate source and target sentences with language suggestions. The annotation process is organised with the Ruffus library (Goodstadt, 2010) and the learning algorithms are executed using the Orange toolkit (Demšar et al., 2004).

3.2 Sentence-ranking

The sentence-ranking sub-task has provided training data for two language pairs, German-English and English-Spanish. For both sentence pairs, we train the systems using the provided annotated data sets WMT2010, WMT2011 and WMT2012, while the data set WMT2009 is used for the evaluation during the development phase. Data sets are analyzed with black-box feature generation. For each language pair, the two systems with the highest correlation are submitted.

We start the development with two feature sets that have shown to perform well in previous experiments: #24 (Avramidis, 2012) including features from PCFG parsing, and #31 which is the baseline feature set of the previous year's shared task (Callison-Burch et al., 2012) and we combine them (#33). Additionally, we create feature sets by

[1]Open source at http://languagetool.org

id	feature-set	de-en tau	de-en MRR	de-en NDGC	en-es tau	en-es MRR	en-es NDGC
#24	previous (Avramidis, 2012)	**0.28**	**0.57**	**0.78**	0.09	**0.52**	**0.75**
#31	baseline WMT2012	0.04	0.51	0.74	-0.16	0.43	0.69
#32	vanilla WMT2013	0.04	0.51	0.74	-0.13	0.45	0.70
#33	combine #24 and #31	**0.29**	**0.57**	**0.78**	0.10	**0.53**	**0.75**
#41	ReliefF 15 best	0.20	0.56	0.77	0.02	0.48	0.72
#411	ReliefF 5 best	0.22	0.53	0.76	**0.19**	0.49	0.73
#42	InfGain 15 best	0.15	0.53	0.75	-0.14	0.43	0.69
#43	combine #41 and #42	0.22	0.56	0.77	-0.12	0.44	0.70
#431	combine #41, #42 and #24	**0.27**	**0.60**	**0.80**	**0.11**	**0.54**	**0.75**

Table 1: Development experiments for task 1.2, reporting correlation and ranking scores, tested on the development set WMT2009.

target feature	β
avg target word occurrence	2.18
pseudoMETEOR	0.71
count of unknown words	0.55
count of dots	-0.25
count of commas	0.15
count of tokens	-0.13
count of VPs	-0.06
PCFG_{log}	-0.02
lm_{prob}	0.01

Table 3: Beta coefficients of the best fitted logistic regression on the German-English data set (set #33 with Stepwise Feature Set Selection)

target feature	β
count of unknown words	-0.55
count of VPs	0.19
count of of PCFG parse trees	-0.16
count of tokens	0.15
% of tokens with only letters	-0.07
lm_{prob}	-0.06
pseudoMETEOR precision	-0.05
source/target ratio of parse trees	-0.03

Table 4: Most indicative beta coefficients of the best fitted logistic regression on the English-Spanish data set (set #431 with L2-regularization)

scoring features with ReliefF (features #41x) and Information Gain (#42). Many combinations of all the above feature-sets are tested and the most important of them are shown in Table 1. Feature sets are described briefly in Table 2.

For **German-English**, we experiment with 14 feature sets, using both variations of Logistic Regression. The two highest tau scores are given by Stepwise Feature Set Selection using feature sets #33 and #24. We see that although baseline features #31 alone have very low correlation, when combined with previously successful #24, provide the best system in terms of tau. Feature set #431 (which combines the 15 features scored higher with ReliefF, the 15 features scored higher with Information Gain and the feature set #24) succeeds pretty well on the additional metrics MRR and NDGC, but it provides slightly lower tau correlation.

For **English-Spanish**, the correlation of the produced systems is significantly lower and it appears that the L2-regularized logistic regression performs better as classification method. We experiment with 24 feature sets, after more scoring with ReliefF and Inf. Gain. Surprisingly enough, Kendall tau correlation indicates that the best model is trained only with features based on counts of numbers and punctuation, combined with *contrastive BLEU score*. This seems to rather overfit a peculiarity of the particular development set and indeed performs much lower on the final test set of the shared task (tau=0.04). The second best feature set (#431) has been described above and luckily generalizes better on an unknown set. It is interesting to see that this issue would have been avoided, if the decision was taken based on the ranking metrics MRR and NDGC, which prioritize other feature sets. We assume that further work is needed to see whether these measures are more expressive and reliable than Kendall tau for similar tasks.

The fitted β coefficients (in tables 3 and 4) give an indication of the importance of each feature (see equation 1), for each language pair. In both language pairs, target-side features prevail upon other features. On the comparison of the models for the two language pairs (and the β coefficients as well) we can see that the model settings and performance may vary from one language pair to another. This also requires further investigation, given that Kendall tau and the other two metrics indicate different models as the best ones.

The fact that the German-English set is better fitted with Stepwise Feature Set Selec-

set	features
#24	From previous work (Avramidis, 2012): **[s+t]**: PCFG_{log}, count of: unknown words, tokens, PCFG trees, VPs **[t]**: pseudoMETEOR
#31	Baseline from WMT12 (Callison-Burch et al., 2012) **[s+t]**: tokens_{avg}, lm_{prob}, count of: commas, dots, tokens, avg translations per source word **[s]**: avg freq. of low and high freq. bi-grams/tri-grams, % of distinct uni-grams in the corpus **[t]**: type/token radio
#32	All 50 "vanilla" features provided by shared-task baseline software "Quest"
#411	ReliefF best 5 features **[s+t]**: % of numbers, difference between periods of source and target (plain and averaged) **[t]**: pseudoBLEU

Table 2: Description of most important feature sets for task 1.2, before internal feature selection of Logistic Regression is applied. [s] indicates source, [t] indicates target

	de-en		en-es	
set	StepFSS	L2reg	StepFSS	L2reg
#24	0.28	0.25	0.09	0.09
#33	0.29	0.26	0.08	0.10
#411	0.22	0.17	-0.25	0.19
#431	0.27	0.25	0.09	0.11

Table 5: Higher Kendall tau correlation (on the dev. set) is achieved on German-English by using Stepwise Feature Set Selection, whereas on English-Spanish by using L2-regularization

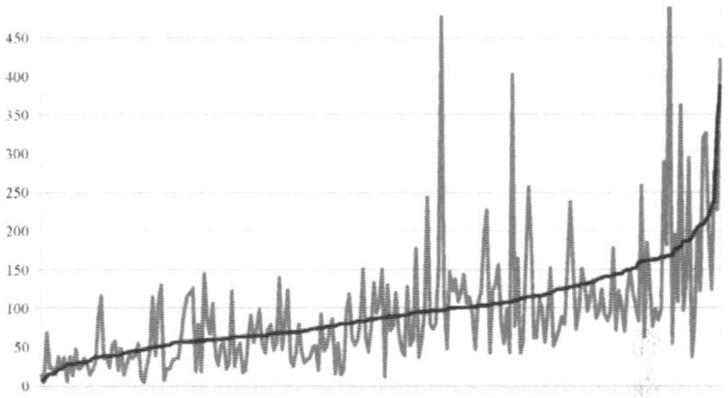

Figure 1: Graphical representation of the values predicted by the linear regression model with feature set #6 (blue) against the actual values of the development set (red)

tion, whereas the English-Spanish one with L2-Regularization (table 5) may be explained by the statistical theory about these two methods: The Stepwise method has has been proven to be too bound to particular characteristics of the development set (Flom and Cassell, 2007). L2-Regularization has been suggested as an alternative, since it generalizes better on broader data sets, which is probably the case for English-Spanish.

Our method also seems to perform well when compared to evaluation metrics which have access to reference translations, as shown in this year's Metrics Shared Task (Macháček and Ondřej, 2013).

3.3 Post-editing time prediction

The training for the model predicting post-editing time is performed over the entire given data set and the evaluation is done with 10-fold cross-validation. We evaluated 8 feature sets with 6 regression methods each, ending up with 48 experiments.

The evaluation of the most indicative regression models (two best performing ones per feature set) can be seen in Table 6. We start with a glass-box feature set, scored with ReliefF and consequently add black-box features. We note the models that have the lowest Root Mean Square Error and Mean Average Error.

Our best model seems to be the one built linear regression using feature set #6. This feature set is chosen by collecting the 17 best features as scored by ReliefF and includes both black-box and glass-box features. How well this model fits the development test is represented in Figure 1.

The second best feature set (#8) includes 29 glass-box features with the highest absolute ReliefF, joined with the black-box features of the successful feature set #6.

More details about the contribution of the most important features in the linear regression (equation 2) can be seen in table 7, where the fitted β coefficients of each feature are given. The vast majority of the best contributing features are glass-box features. Some draft conclusions out of the coefficients may be that post-editing time is lower when:

id	feature set	method	RMSE	MAE
#1	20 glass-box features with highest absolute ReliefF	MARS	91.54	59.07
		SVR	93.57	55.87
#2	9 glass-box features with highest positive ReliefF	Lasso	83.20	51.57
		Linear	83.32	51.72
#3	16 glass-box features with highest positive ReliefF	Lasso	77.54	47.16
		Linear	77.60	47.27
#4	22 glass-box features with highest positive ReliefF	Lasso	76.05	46.37
		Linear	76.17	46.48
#5	Combination of feature sets #1 and #2	MARS	91.54	59.07
		SVR	93.57	55.87
#6	17 features of any type with highest positive ReliefF	**Linear**	**74.70**	45.20
		Lasso	74.75	**44.99**
#8	Combination of #5 and #6 + counts of tokens	**Lasso**	75.14	**44.99**
		PLS	77.63	47.48
#6	First submission	Linear	84.27	52.41
#8	Second submission	PLS	88.34	53.49
	Best models		82.60	47.52

Table 6: Development and submitted experiments for task 1.3

- the longest of the source phrases used for producing the best hypothesis appears closer to the end of the sentence
- the phrases with the highest and the lowest probability appear closer to the end of the translated sentence
- there are more determiners in the source and/or less determiners in the translation
- there are more verbs in the translation and/or less verbs in the source
- there are fewer alternative phrases with very high probability

Further conclusions can be drawn after examining these observations along with the exact operation of the statistical MT system, which is subject to further work.

4 Conclusion

We describe two approaches for two respective problems of quality estimation, namely sentence-level ranking of alternative translations and prediction of time for post-editing MT output. We present efforts on compiling several feature sets and we examine the final contribution of the features after training Machine Learning models. Elaborate decoding features seem to be quite helpful for predicting post-editing time.

feature	β
best hyp: position of the longest aligned phrase in the source sentence averaged to the number of phrases	-16.652
best hyp: position of phrase with highest prob. averaged to the num. of phrases	-14.824
source: number of determiners	-9.312
best hyp: number of determiners	6.189
best hyp: position of phrase with lowest prob. averaged to the num. of phrases	-5.261
best hyp: position of phrase with lowest future cost estimate averaged to the number of phrases	-4.282
best hyp: number of verbs	-2.818
best hyp: position of phrase with highest future cost estimate averaged to the number of phrases	1.002
search: number of alternative phrases with very low future cost est.	-0.528
source: number of verbs	0.467
search: number of alternative phrases with very high probability	0.355
search: total num. of translation options	-0.153
search: number of alternative phrases with very high future cost estimate	-0.142
best hyp: number of parse trees	0.007
source: number of parse trees	0.002
search: total number of hypotheses	0.001

Table 7: Linear regression coefficients for feature set #6 indicate the contribution of each feature in the fitted model

Acknowledgments

This work has been developed within the TaraXŰ project, financed by TSB Technologiestiftung Berlin – Zukunftsfonds Berlin, co-financed by the European Union – European fund for regional development. Many thanks to Prof. Hans Uszkoreit for the supervision, Dr. Aljoscha Burchardt, and Dr. David Vilar for their useful feedback and to Lukas Poustka for his technical help on feature acquisition.

References

Avramidis, E. (2012). Comparative Quality Estimation: Automatic Sentence-Level Ranking of Multiple Machine Translation Outputs. In *Proceedings of 24th International Conference on Computational Linguistics*, pages 115–132, Mumbai, India. The COLING 2012 Organizing Committee.

Avramidis, E., Popovic, M., Vilar, D., and Burchardt, A. (2011). Evaluate with Confidence Estimation : Machine ranking of translation outputs using grammatical features. In *Proceedings of the Sixth Workshop on Statistical Machine Translation*, pages 65–70, Edinburgh, Scotland. Association for Computational Linguistics.

Basak, D., Pal, S., and Patranabis, D. C. (2007). Support vector regression. *Neural Information Processing-Letters and Reviews*, 11(10):203–224.

Callison-Burch, C., Koehn, P., Monz, C., Post, M., Soricut, R., and Specia, L. (2012). Findings of the 2012 Workshop on Statistical Machine Translation. In *Proceedings of the Seventh Workshop on Statistical Machine Translation*, pages 10–51, Montréal, Canada. Association for Computational Linguistics.

Callison-Burch, C., Koehn, P., Monz, C., and Zaidan, O. (2011). Findings of the 2011 Workshop on Statistical Machine Translation. In *Proceedings of the Sixth Workshop on Statistical Machine Translation*, pages 22–64, Edinburgh, Scotland. Association for Computational Linguistics.

Cameron, A. (1998). *Regression analysis of count data*. Cambridge University Press, Cambridge UK; New York NY USA.

Demšar, J., Zupan, B., Leban, G., and Curk, T. (2004). Orange: From Experimental Machine Learning to Interactive Data Mining. In *Principles of Data Mining and Knowledge Discovery*, pages 537–539.

Flom, P. L. and Cassell, D. L. (2007). Stopping stepwise: Why stepwise and similar selection methods are bad, and what you should use. In *NorthEast SAS Users Group Inc 20th Annual Conference*, Baltimore, Maryland. 2007.

Friedman, J. H. (1991). Multivariate Adaptive Regression Splines. *The Annals of Statistics*, 19(1):1–67.

Goodstadt, L. (2010). Ruffus: a lightweight Python library for computational pipelines. *Bioinformatics*, 26(21):2778–2779.

Hosmer, D. (1989). *Applied logistic regression*. Wiley, New York [u.a.], 8th edition.

Hunt, E., Martin, J., and Stone, P. (1966). Experiments in Induction. Academic Press, New York.

Järvelin, K. and Kekäläinen, J. (2002). Cumulated gain-based evaluation of IR techniques. *ACM Trans. Inf. Syst.*, 20(4):422–446.

Kendall, M. G. (1938). A New Measure of Rank Correlation. *Biometrika*, 30(1-2):81–93.

Koehn, P. (2005). Europarl: A parallel corpus for statistical machine translation. *Proceedings of the tenth Machine Translation Summit*, 5:79–86.

Kononenko, I. (1994). Estimating attributes: analysis and extensions of RELIEF. In *Proceedings of the European conference on machine learning on Machine Learning*, pages 171–182, Secaucus, NJ, USA. Springer-Verlag New York, Inc.

Lavie, A. and Agarwal, A. (2007). METEOR: An Automatic Metric for MT Evaluation with High Levels of Correlation with Human Judgments. In *Proceedings of the Second Workshop on Statistical Machine Translation*, pages 228–231, Prague, Czech Republic. Association for Computational Linguistics.

Lin, C.-J., Weng, R. C., and Keerthi, S. S. (2007). Trust region Newton methods for large-scale logistic regression. In *Proceedings of the 24th international conference on Machine learning - ICML '07*, pages 561–568, New York, New York, USA. ACM Press.

Macháček, M. . and Ondřej, B. (2013). Results of the WMT13 Metrics Shared Task. In *Proceedings of the 8th Workshop on Machine Translation*, Sofia, Bulgaria. Association for Computational Linguistics.

Miller, A. (2002). *Subset Selection in Regression*. Chapman & Hall, London, 2nd edition.

Naber, D. (2003). A rule-based style and grammar checker. Technical report, Bielefeld University, Bielefeld, Germany.

Papineni, K., Roukos, S., Ward, T., and Zhu, W.-J. (2002). BLEU: a Method for Automatic Evaluation of Machine Translation. In *Proceedings of the 40th Annual Meeting of the Association for Computational Linguistics*, pages 311–318, Philadelphia, Pennsylvania, USA. Association for Computational Linguistics.

Petrov, S., Barrett, L., Thibaux, R., and Klein, D. (2006). Learning Accurate, Compact, and Interpretable Tree Annotation. In *Proceedings of the 21st*

International Conference on Computational Linguistics and 44th Annual Meeting of the Association for Computational Linguistics, pages 433–440, Sydney, Australia. Association for Computational Linguistics.

Petrov, S. and Klein, D. (2007). Improved inference for unlexicalized parsing. In *Proceedings of the 2007 Annual Conference of the North American Chapter of the Association for Computational Linguistics*, Rochester, New York. Association for Computational Linguistics.

Robnik-Šikonja, M. and Kononenko, I. (2003). Theoretical and Empirical Analysis of ReliefF and RReliefF. *Machine Learning*, 53(1-2):23–69.

Soricut, R., Wang, Z., and Bach, N. (2012). The SDL Language Weaver Systems in the WMT12 Quality Estimation Shared Task. In *Proceedings of the Seventh Workshop on Statistical Machine Translation*, pages 145–151, Montréal, Canada. Association for Computational Linguistics.

Stolcke, A. (2002). SRILM – An Extensible Language Modeling Toolkit. In *Proceedings of the Seventh International Conference on Spoken Language Processing*, pages 901–904. ISCA.

Stone, M. and Brooks, R. J. (1990). Continuum regression: cross-validated sequentially constructed prediction embracing ordinary least squares, partial least squares and principal components regression. *Journal of the Royal Statistical Society Series B Methodological*, 52(2):237–269.

Taulé, M., Martí, A., and Recasens, M. (2008). AnCora: Multilevel Annotated Corpora for Catalan and Spanish. In *Proceedings of the Sixth International Conference on Language Resources and Evaluation (LREC'08)*, Marrakech, Morocco. European Language Resources Association (ELRA).

Tibshirani, R. (1996). Regression shrinkage and selection via the lasso. Series B:267–288.

Voorhees, E. (1999). TREC-8 Question Answering Track Report. In *8th Text Retrieval Conference*, pages 77–82, Gaithersburg, Maryland, USA.

SHEF-Lite: When Less is More for Translation Quality Estimation

Daniel Beck and **Kashif Shah** and **Trevor Cohn** and **Lucia Specia**
Department of Computer Science
University of Sheffield
Sheffield, United Kingdom
{debeck1,kashif.shah,t.cohn,l.specia}@sheffield.ac.uk

Abstract

We describe the results of our submissions to the WMT13 Shared Task on Quality Estimation (subtasks 1.1 and 1.3). Our submissions use the framework of Gaussian Processes to investigate lightweight approaches for this problem. We focus on two approaches, one based on feature selection and another based on active learning. Using only 25 (out of 160) features, our model resulting from feature selection ranked 1st place in the scoring variant of subtask 1.1 and 3rd place in the ranking variant of the subtask, while the active learning model reached 2nd place in the scoring variant using only $\sim$25% of the available instances for training. These results give evidence that Gaussian Processes achieve the state of the art performance as a modelling approach for translation quality estimation, and that carefully selecting features and instances for the problem can further improve or at least maintain the same performance levels while making the problem less resource-intensive.

1 Introduction

The purpose of machine translation (MT) quality estimation (QE) is to provide a quality prediction for new, unseen machine translated texts, without relying on reference translations (Blatz et al., 2004; Specia et al., 2009; Callison-burch et al., 2012). A common use of quality predictions is the decision between post-editing a given machine translated sentence and translating its source from scratch, based on whether its post-editing effort is estimated to be lower than the effort of translating the source sentence.

The WMT13 QE shared task defined a group of tasks related to QE. In this paper, we present the submissions by the University of Sheffield team. Our models are based on Gaussian Processes (GP) (Rasmussen and Williams, 2006), a non-parametric probabilistic framework. We explore the application of GP models in two contexts: 1) improving the prediction performance by applying a feature selection step based on optimised hyperparameters and 2) reducing the dataset size (and therefore the annotation effort) by performing Active Learning (AL). We submitted entries for two of the four proposed tasks.

Task 1.1 focused on predicting HTER scores (Human Translation Error Rate) (Snover et al., 2006) using a dataset composed of 2254 English-Spanish news sentences translated by Moses (Koehn et al., 2007) and post-edited by a professional translator. The evaluation used a blind test set, measuring MAE (Mean Absolute Error) and RMSE (Root Mean Square Error), in the case of the scoring variant, and DeltaAvg and Spearman's rank correlation in the case of the ranking variant. Our submissions reached 1st (feature selection) and 2nd (active learning) places in the scoring variant, the task the models were optimised for, and outperformed the baseline by a large margin in the ranking variant.

The aim of task 1.3 aimed at predicting post-editing time using a dataset composed of 800 English-Spanish news sentences also translated by Moses but post-edited by five expert translators. Evaluation was done based on MAE and RMSE on a blind test set. For this task our models were not able to beat the baseline system, showing that more advanced modelling techniques should have been used for challenging quality annotation types and datasets such as this.

2 Features

In our experiments, we used a set of 160 features which are grouped into *black box* (BB) and *glass box* (GB) features. They were extracted using the open source toolkit QuEst[1] (Specia et al., 2013). We briefly describe them here, for a detailed description we refer the reader to the lists available on the QuEst website.

The 112 BB features are based on source and target segments and attempt to quantify the source **complexity**, the target **fluency** and the source-target **adequacy**. Examples of them include:

- Word and n-gram based features:
  - Number of tokens in source and target segments;
  - Language model (LM) probability of source and target segments;
  - Percentage of source 1–3-grams observed in different frequency quartiles of the source side of the MT training corpus;
  - Average number of translations per source word in the segment as given by IBM 1 model with probabilities thresholded in different ways.
- POS-based features:
  - Ratio of percentage of nouns/verbs/etc in the source and target segments;
  - Ratio of punctuation symbols in source and target segments;
  - Percentage of direct object personal or possessive pronouns incorrectly translated.
- Syntactic features:
  - Source and target Probabilistic Context-free Grammar (PCFG) parse log-likelihood;
  - Source and target PCFG average confidence of all possible parse trees in the parser's n-best list;
  - Difference between the number of PP/NP/VP/ADJP/ADVP/CONJP phrases in the source and target;
- Other features:
  - Kullback-Leibler divergence of source and target topic model distributions;
  - Jensen-Shannon divergence of source and target topic model distributions;
  - Source and target sentence intra-lingual mutual information;
  - Source-target sentence inter-lingual mutual information;
  - Geometric average of target word probabilities under a global lexicon model.

[1] `http://www.quest.dcs.shef.ac.uk`

The 48 GB features are based on information provided by the Moses decoder, and attempt to indicate the **confidence** of the system in producing the translation. They include:

- Features and global score of the SMT model;
- Number of distinct hypotheses in the n-best list;
- 1–3-gram LM probabilities using translations in the n-best to train the LM;
- Average size of the target phrases;
- Relative frequency of the words in the translation in the n-best list;
- Ratio of SMT model score of the top translation to the sum of the scores of all hypothesis in the n-best list;
- Average size of hypotheses in the n-best list;
- N-best list density (vocabulary size / average sentence length);
- Fertility of the words in the source sentence compared to the n-best list in terms of words (vocabulary size / source sentence length);
- Edit distance of the current hypothesis to the centre hypothesis;
- Proportion of pruned search graph nodes;
- Proportion of recombined graph nodes.

3 Model

Gaussian Processes are a Bayesian non-parametric machine learning framework considered the state-of-the-art for regression. They assume the presence of a latent function $f : \mathbb{R}^F \rightarrow \mathbb{R}$, which maps a vector $\mathbf{x}$ from feature space F to a scalar value. Formally, this function is drawn from a GP prior:

$$f(\mathbf{x}) \sim \mathcal{GP}(\mathbf{0}, k(\mathbf{x}, \mathbf{x}'))$$

which is parameterized by a mean function (here, $\mathbf{0}$) and a covariance kernel function $k(\mathbf{x}, \mathbf{x}')$. Each response value is then generated from the function evaluated at the corresponding input, $y_i = f(\mathbf{x}_i) + \eta$, where $\eta \sim \mathcal{N}(0, \sigma_n^2)$ is added white-noise.

Prediction is formulated as a Bayesian inference under the posterior:

$$p(y_*|\mathbf{x}_*, \mathcal{D}) = \int_f p(y_*|\mathbf{x}_*, f)p(f|\mathcal{D})$$

where $\mathbf{x}_*$ is a test input, y_* is the test response value and $\mathcal{D}$ is the training set. The predictive posterior can be solved analitically, resulting in:

$$y_* \sim \mathcal{N}(\mathbf{k}_*^T(K + \sigma_n^2 I)^{-1}\mathbf{y},\\ k(x_*, x_*) - \mathbf{k}_*^T(K + \sigma_n^2 I)^{-1}\mathbf{k}_*)$$

where $\mathbf{k}_* = [k(\mathbf{x}_*, \mathbf{x}_1)k(\mathbf{x}_*, \mathbf{x}_2) \dots k(\mathbf{x}_*, \mathbf{x}_d)]^T$ is the vector of kernel evaluations between the training set and the test input and K is the kernel matrix over the training inputs.

A nice property of this formulation is that y_* is actually a probability distribution, encoding the model uncertainty and making it possible to integrate it into subsequent processing. In this work, we used the variance values given by the model in an active learning setting, as explained in Section 4.

The kernel function encodes the covariance (similarity) between each input pair. While a variety of kernel functions are available, here we followed previous work on QE using GP (Cohn and Specia, 2013; Shah et al., 2013) and employed a squared exponential (SE) kernel with automatic relevance determination (ARD):

$$k(\mathbf{x}, \mathbf{x}') = \sigma_f^2 \exp\left(-\frac{1}{2}\sum_{i=1}^{F}\frac{x_i - x_i'}{l_i}\right)$$

where F is the number of features, σ_f^2 is the covariance *magnitude* and $l_i > 0$ are the feature *length scales*.

The resulting model hyperparameters (SE variance σ_f^2, noise variance σ_n^2 and SE length scales l_i) were learned from data by maximising the model likelihood. In general, the likelihood function is non-convex and the optimisation procedure may lead to local optima. To avoid poor hyperparameter values due to this, we performed a two-step procedure where we first optimise a model with all the SE length scales tied to the same value (which is equivalent to an isotropic model) and we used the resulting values as starting point for the ARD optimisation.

All our models were trained using the GPy[2] toolkit, an open source implementation of GPs written in Python.

3.1 Feature Selection

To perform feature selection, we followed the approach used in Shah et al. (2013) and ranked the features according to their learned length scales (from the lowest to the highest). The length scales of a feature can be interpreted as the relevance of such feature for the model. Therefore, the outcome of a GP model using an ARD kernel can be viewed as a list of features ranked by relevance, and this information can be used for feature selection by discarding the lowest ranked (least useful) ones.

For task 1.1, we performed this feature selection over all 160 features mentioned in Section 2. For task 1.3, we used a subset of the 80 most general BB features as in (Shah et al., 2013), for which we had all the necessary resources available for the extraction. We selected the top 25 features for both models, based on empirical results found by Shah et al. (2013) for a number of datasets, and then retrained the GP using only the selected features.

4 Active Learning

Active Learning (AL) is a machine learning paradigm that let the learner decide which data it wants to learn from (Settles, 2010). The main goal of AL is to reduce the size of the dataset while keeping similar model performance (therefore reducing annotation costs). In previous work with 17 baseline features, we have shown that with only ~30% of instances it is possible to achieve 99% of the full dataset performance in the case of the WMT12 QE dataset (Beck et al., 2013).

To investigate if a reduced dataset can achieve competitive performance in a blind evaluation setting, we submitted an entry for both tasks 1.1 and 1.3 composed of models trained on a subset of instances selected using AL, and paired with feature selection. Our AL procedure starts with a model trained on a small number of randomly selected instances from the training set and then uses this model to query the remaining instances in the training set (our query pool). At every iteration, the model selects the more "informative" instance, asks an oracle for its true label (which in our case is already given in the dataset, and therefore we

[2] `http://sheffieldml.github.io/GPy/`

only simulate AL) and then adds it to the training set. Our procedure started with 50 instances for task 1.1 and 20 instances for task 1.3, given its reduced training set size. We optimised the Gaussian Process hyperparameters every 20 new instances, for both tasks.

As a measure of informativeness we used Information Density (ID) (Settles and Craven, 2008). This measure leverages between the variance among instances and how dense the region (in the feature space) where the instance is located is:

$$ID(x) = Var(y|\mathbf{x}) \times \left(\frac{1}{U}\sum_{u=1}^{U} sim(\mathbf{x}, \mathbf{x}^{(u)})\right)^{\beta}$$

The β parameter controls the relative importance of the density term. In our experiments, we set it to 1, giving equal weights to variance and density. The U term is the number of instances in the query pool. The variance values $Var(y|\mathbf{x})$ are given by the GP prediction while the similarity measure $sim(\mathbf{x}, \mathbf{x}^{(u)})$ is defined as the cosine distance between the feature vectors.

In a real annotation setting, it is important to decide when to stop adding new instances to the training set. In this work, we used the confidence method proposed by Vlachos (2008). This is an method that measures the model's confidence on a held-out non-annotated dataset every time a new instance is added to the training set and stops the AL procedure when this confidence starts to drop. In our experiments, we used the average test set variance as the confidence measure.

In his work, Vlachos (2008) showed a correlation between the confidence and test error, which motivates its use as a stop criterion. To check if this correlation also occurs in our task, we measure the confidence and test set error for task 1.1 using the WMT12 split (1832/422 instances). However, we observed a different behaviour in our experiments: Figure 1 shows that the confidence does not raise or drop according to the test error but it *stabilises* around a fixed value at the same point as the test error also stabilises. Therefore, instead of using the confidence *drop* as a stop criterion, we use the point where the confidence stabilises. In Figure 2 we can observe that the confidence curve for the WMT13 test set stabilises after $\sim$580 instances. We took that point as our stop criterion and used the first 580 selected instances as the AL dataset.

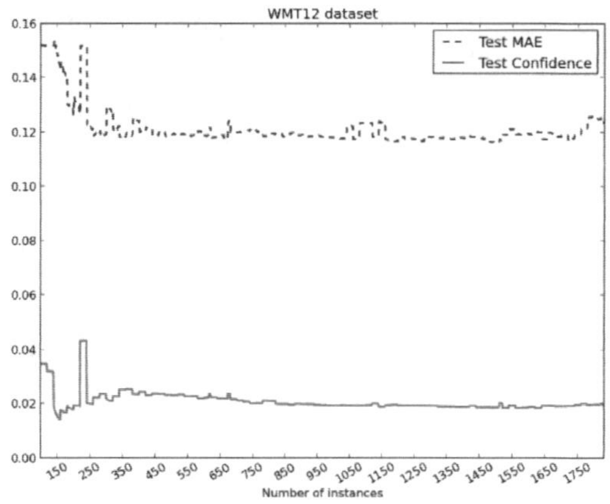

Figure 1: Test error and test confidence curves for HTER prediction (task 1.1) using the WMT12 training and test sets.

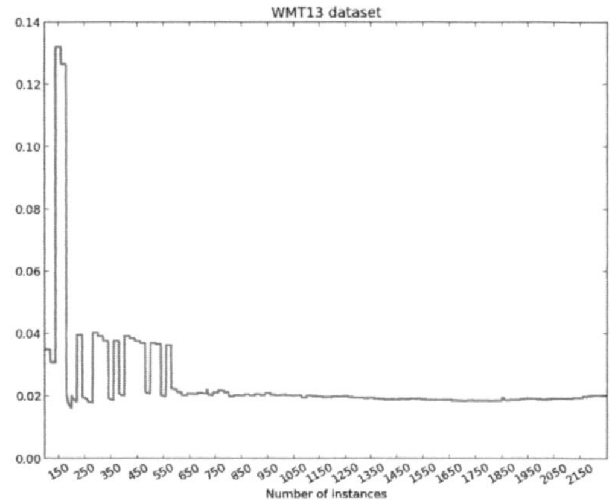

Figure 2: Test confidence for HTER prediction (task 1.1) using the official WMT13 training and test sets.

We repeated the experiment with task 1.3, measuring the relationship between test confidence and error using a 700/100 instances split (shown on Figure 3). For this task, the curves did not follow the same behaviour: the confidence do not seem to stabilise at any point in the AL procedure. The same occurred when using the official training and test sets (shown on Figure 4). However, the MAE curve is quite flat, stabilising after about 100 sentences. This may simply be a consequence of the fact that our model is too simple for post-editing time prediction. Nevertheless, in order to analyse the performance of AL for this task we submitted an entry using the first 100 instances chosen by the AL procedure for training.

The observed peaks in the confidence curves re-

	Task 1.1 - Ranking		Task 1.1 - Scoring		Task 1.3	
	DeltaAvg ↑	Spearman ↑	MAE ↓	RMSE ↓	MAE ↓	RMSE ↓
SHEF-Lite-FULL	9.76	0.57	**12.42**	15.74	55.91	103.11
SHEF-Lite-AL	8.85	0.50	13.02	17.03	64.62	99.09
Baseline	8.52	0.46	14.81	18.22	51.93	93.36

Table 1: Submission results for tasks 1.1 and 1.3. The bold value shows a winning entry in the shared task.

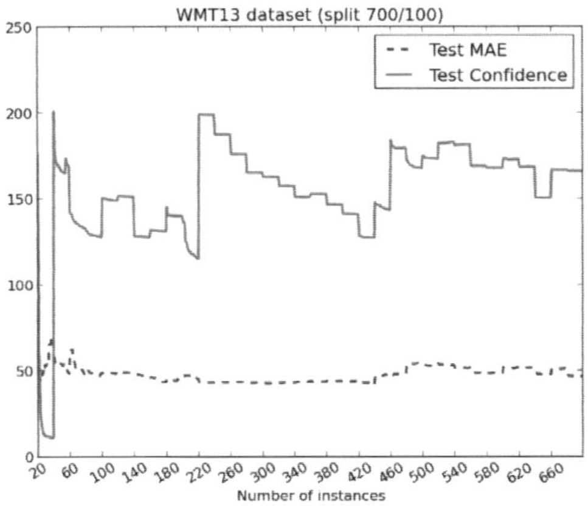

Figure 3: Test error and test confidence curves for post-editing time prediction (task 1.3) using a 700/100 split on the WMT13 training set.

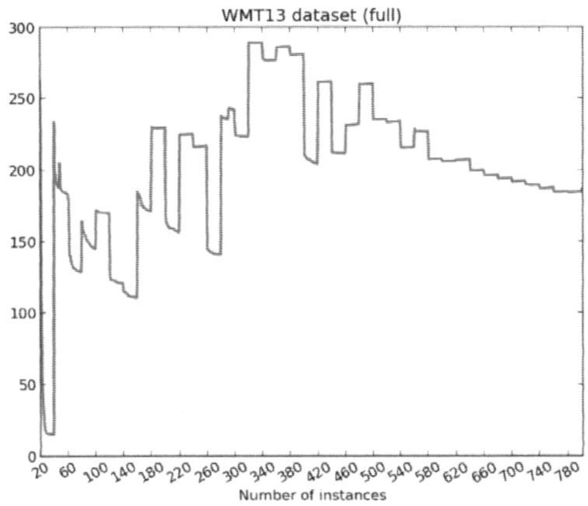

Figure 4: Test confidence for post-editing time prediction (task 1.3) using the official WMT13 training and test sets.

sult from steps where the hyperparameter optimisation got stuck at bad local optima. These degenerated results set the variances (σ_f^2, σ_n^2) to very high values, resulting in a model that considers all data as pure noise. Since this behaviour tends to disappear as more instances are added to the training set, we believe that increasing the dataset size helps to tackle this problem. We plan to investigate this issue in more depth in future work.

For both AL datasets we repeated the feature selection procedure explained in Section 3.1, retraining the models on the selected features.

5 Results

Table 1 shows the results for both tasks. SHEF-Lite-FULL represents GP models trained on the full dataset (relative to each task) with a feature selection step. SHEF-Lite-AL corresponds to the same models trained on datasets obtained from each active learning procedure and followed by feature selection.

For task 1.1, our submission SHEF-Lite-FULL was the winning system in the scoring subtask, and ranked third in the ranking subtask. These results show that GP models achieve the state of the art performance in QE. These are particularly positive results considering that there is room for improvement in the feature selection procedure to identify the optimal number of features to be selected. Results for task 1.3 were below the baseline, once again evidencing the fact that the noise model used in our experiments is probably too simple for post-editing time prediction. Post-editing time is generally more prone to large variations and noise than HTER, especially when annotations are produced by multiple post-editors. Therefore we believe that kernels that encode more advanced noise models (such as the multi-task kernel used by Cohn and Specia (2013)) should be used for better performance. Another possible reason for that is the smaller set of features used for this task (black-box features only).

Our SHEF-Lite-AL submissions performed better than the baseline in both scoring and ranking in task 1.1, ranking 2nd place in the scoring subtask. Considering that the dataset is composed by only ~25% of the full training set, these are very encouraging results in terms of reducing data annotation needs. We note however that these results are below those obtained with the full training set, but Figure 1 shows that it is possible to achieve the same or even better results with an AL dataset. Since the curves shown in Figure 1 were obtained using the full feature set, we believe that advanced feature selection strategies can help AL datasets to achieve better results.

6 Conclusions

The results obtained by our submissions confirm the potential of Gaussian Processes to become the state of the art approach for Quality Estimation. Our models were able to achieve the best performance in predicting HTER. They also offer the advantage of inferring a probability distribution for each prediction. These distributions provide richer information (like variance values) that can be useful, for example, in active learning settings.

In the future, we plan to further investigate these models by devising more advanced kernels and feature selection methods. Specifically, we want to employ our feature set in a multi-task kernel setting, similar to the one proposed by Cohn and Specia (2013). These kernels have the power to model inter-annotator variance and noise, which can lead to better results in the prediction of post-editing time.

We also plan to pursue better active learning procedures by investigating query methods specifically tailored for QE, as well as a better stop criteria. Our goal is to be able to reduce the dataset size significantly without hurting the performance of the model. This is specially interesting in the case of QE, since it is a very task-specific problem that may demand a large annotation effort.

Acknowledgments

This work was supported by funding from CNPq/Brazil (No. 237999/2012-9, Daniel Beck) and from the EU FP7-ICT QTLaunchPad project (No. 296347, Kashif Shah and Lucia Specia).

References

Daniel Beck, Lucia Specia, and Trevor Cohn. 2013. Reducing Annotation Effort for Quality Estimation via Active Learning. In *Proceedings of ACL (to appear)*.

John Blatz, Erin Fitzgerald, and George Foster. 2004. Confidence estimation for machine translation. In *Proceedings of the 20th Conference on Computational Linguistics*, pages 315–321.

Chris Callison-burch, Philipp Koehn, Christof Monz, Matt Post, Radu Soricut, and Lucia Specia. 2012. Findings of the 2012 Workshop on Statistical Machine Translation. In *Proceedings of 7th Workshop on Statistical Machine Translation*.

Trevor Cohn and Lucia Specia. 2013. Modelling Annotator Bias with Multi-task Gaussian Processes: An Application to Machine Translation Quality Estimation. In *Proceedings of ACL (to appear)*.

Philipp Koehn, Hieu Hoang, Alexandra Birch, Chris Callison-Burch, Marcello Federico, Nicola Bertoldi, Brooke Cowan, Wade Shen, Christine Moran, Richard Zens, Chris Dyer, Ondrej Bojar, Alexandra Constantin, and Evan Herbst. 2007. Moses: Open source toolkit for statistical machine translation. In *Proceedings of the 45th Annual Meeting of the ACL on Interactive Poster and Demonstration Sessions*, pages 177–180.

Carl Edward Rasmussen and Christopher K. I. Williams. 2006. *Gaussian processes for machine learning*, volume 1. MIT Press Cambridge.

Burr Settles and Mark Craven. 2008. An analysis of active learning strategies for sequence labeling tasks. In *Proceedings of the Conference on Empirical Methods in Natural Language Processing*, pages 1070–1079.

Burr Settles. 2010. Active learning literature survey. Technical report.

Kashif Shah, Trevor Cohn, and Lucia Specia. 2013. An Investigation on the Effectiveness of Features for Translation Quality Estimation. In *Proceedings of MT Summit XIV (to appear)*.

Matthew Snover, Bonnie Dorr, Richard Schwartz, Linnea Micciulla, and John Makhoul. 2006. A study of translation edit rate with targeted human annotation. In *Proceedings of Association for Machine Translation in the Americas*.

Lucia Specia, Craig Saunders, Marco Turchi, Zhuoran Wang, and John Shawe-Taylor. 2009. Improving the confidence of machine translation quality estimates. In *Proceedings of MT Summit XII*.

Lucia Specia, Kashif Shah, José G. C. De Souza, and Trevor Cohn. 2013. QuEst - A translation quality estimation framework. In *Proceedings of ACL Demo Session (to appear)*.

Andreas Vlachos. 2008. A stopping criterion for active learning. *Computer Speech & Language*, 22(3):295–312, July.

Referential Translation Machines for Quality Estimation

Ergun Biçici
Centre for Next Generation Localisation,
Dublin City University, Dublin, Ireland.
ergun.bicici@computing.dcu.ie

Abstract

We introduce referential translation machines (RTM) for quality estimation of translation outputs. RTMs are a computational model for identifying the translation acts between any two data sets with respect to a reference corpus selected in the same domain, which can be used for estimating the quality of translation outputs, judging the semantic similarity between text, and evaluating the quality of student answers. RTMs achieve top performance in automatic, accurate, and language independent prediction of sentence-level and word-level statistical machine translation (SMT) quality. RTMs remove the need to access any SMT system specific information or prior knowledge of the training data or models used when generating the translations. We develop novel techniques for solving all subtasks in the WMT13 quality estimation (QE) task (QET 2013) based on individual RTM models. Our results achieve improvements over last year's QE task results (QET 2012), as well as our previous results, provide new features and techniques for QE, and rank 1st or 2nd in all of the subtasks.

1 Introduction

Quality Estimation Task (QET) (Callison-Burch et al., 2012; Callison-Burch et al., 2013) aims to develop quality indicators for translations and predictors without access to the references. Prediction of translation quality is important because the expected translation performance can help in estimating the effort required for correcting the translations during post-editing by human translators.

Bicici et al. (2013) develop the Machine Translation Performance Predictor (MTPP), a state-of-the-art, language independent, and SMT system extrinsic machine translation performance predictor, which achieves better performance than the competitive QET baseline system (Callison-Burch et al., 2012) by just looking at the test source sentences and becomes the 2nd overall after also looking at the translation outputs in QET 2012.

In this work, we introduce referential translation machines (RTM) for quality estimation of translation outputs, which is a computational model for identifying the acts of translation for translating between any given two data sets with respect to a reference corpus selected in the same domain. RTMs reduce our dependence on any task dependent resource. In particular, we do not use the baseline software or the SMT resources provided with the QET 2013 challenge. We believe having access to glass-box features such as the phrase table or the n-best lists is not realistic especially for use-cases where translations may be provided by different MT vendors (not necessarily from SMT products) or by human translators. Even the prior knowledge of the training corpora used for building the SMT models or any other model used when generating the translations diverges from the goal of independent and unbiased prediction of translation quality. Our results show that we do not need to use any SMT system dependent information to achieve the top performance when predicting translation output quality.

2 Referential Translation Machine (RTM)

Referential translation machines (RTMs) provide a computational model for quality and semantic similarity judgments using retrieval of relevant training data (Biçici and Yuret, 2011a; Biçici, 2011) as interpretants for reaching shared semantics (Biçici, 2008). RTMs achieve very good performance in judging the semantic similarity of sentences (Biçici and van Genabith, 2013a) and we can also use RTMs to automatically assess the correctness of student answers to obtain better results (Biçici and van Genabith, 2013b) than the state-of-the-art (Dzikovska et al., 2012).

RTM is a computational model for identifying the acts of translation for translating between any given two data sets with respect to a reference corpus selected in the same domain. RTM can be used for predicting the quality of translation outputs. An RTM model is based on the selection of common training data relevant and close to both the training set and the test set of the task where the selected relevant set of instances are called the interpretants. Interpretants allow shared semantics to be possible by behaving as a reference point for similarity judgments and providing the context. In semiotics, an interpretant I interprets the signs used to refer to the real objects (Biçici, 2008). RTMs provide a model for computational semantics using interpretants as a reference according to which semantic judgments with translation acts are made. Each RTM model is a data translation model between the instances in the training set and the test set. We use the FDA (Feature Decay Algorithms) instance selection model for selecting the interpretants (Biçici and Yuret, 2011a) from a given corpus, which can be monolingual when modeling paraphrasing acts, in which case the MTPP model (Section 2.1) is built using the interpretants themselves as both the source and the target side of the parallel corpus. RTMs map the training and test data to a space where translation acts can be identified. We view that acts of translation are ubiquitously used during communication:

Every act of communication is an act of translation (Bliss, 2012).

Translation need not be between different languages and paraphrasing or communication also contain acts of translation. When creating sentences, we use our background knowledge and translate information content according to the current context. Given a training set `train`, a test set `test`, and some monolingual corpus $\mathcal{C}$, preferably in the same domain as the training and test sets, the RTM steps are:

1. $T = \texttt{train} \cup \texttt{test}$.
2. select$(T, \mathcal{C}) \rightarrow \mathcal{I}$
3. MTPP$(\mathcal{I}, \texttt{train}) \rightarrow \mathcal{F}_{\texttt{train}}$
4. MTPP$(\mathcal{I}, \texttt{test}) \rightarrow \mathcal{F}_{\texttt{test}}$
5. learn$(M, \mathcal{F}_{\texttt{train}}) \rightarrow \mathcal{M}$
6. predict$(\mathcal{M}, \mathcal{F}_{\texttt{test}}) \rightarrow \hat{q}$

Step 2 selects the interpretants, $\mathcal{I}$, relevant to the instances in the combined training and test data. Steps 3 and 4 use $\mathcal{I}$ to map `train` and `test` to a new space where similarities between translation acts can be derived more easily. Step 5 trains a learning model M over the training features, $\mathcal{F}_{\texttt{train}}$, and Step 6 obtains the predictions. RTM relies on the representativeness of $\mathcal{I}$ as a medium for building translation models for translating between `train` and `test`.

Our encouraging results in the QET challenge provides a greater understanding of the acts of translation we ubiquitously use when communicating and how they can be used to predict the performance of translation, judging the semantic similarity between text, and evaluating the quality of student answers. RTM and MTPP models are not data or language specific and their modeling power and good performance are applicable across different domains and tasks. RTM expands the applicability of MTPP by making it feasible when making monolingual quality and similarity judgments and it enhances the computational scalability by building models over smaller but more relevant training data as interpretants.

2.1 The Machine Translation Performance Predictor (MTPP)

In machine translation (MT), pairs of source and target sentences are used for training statistical MT (SMT) models. SMT system performance is affected by the amount of training data used as well as the *closeness* of the test set to the training set. MTPP (Biçici et al., 2013) is a state-of-the-art and top performing machine translation performance predictor, which uses machine learning models over features measuring how well the test set matches the training set to predict the quality of a translation without using a reference translation. MTPP measures the coverage of individual test sentence features and syntactic structures found in the training set and derives feature functions measuring the closeness of test sentences to the available training data, the difficulty of translating the sentence, and the presence of acts of translation for data transformation.

2.2 MTPP Features for Translation Acts

MTPP uses n-gram features defined over text or common cover link (CCL) (Seginer, 2007) structures as the basic units of information over which similarity calculations are made. Unsupervised parsing with CCL extracts links from base words to head words, resulting in structures representing the grammatical information instantiated in the training and test data. Feature functions use statistics involving the training set and the test sentences to determine their closeness. Since they are language independent, MTPP allows quality estimation to be performed extrinsically.

We extend MTPP (Biçici et al., 2013) in its learning module, the features included, and their representations. Categories for the 308 features (S for source, T for target) used are listed below where the number of features are given in {#} and the detailed descriptions for some of the features are presented in (Biçici et al., 2013).

- *Coverage* {*110*}: Measures the degree to which the test features are found in the training set for both S ({56}) and T ({54}).
- *Synthetic Translation Performance* {*6*}: Calculates translation scores achievable according to the n-gram coverage.
- *Length* {*7*}: Calculates the number of words and characters for S and T and their average token lengths and their ratios.
- *Feature Vector Similarity* {*16*}: Calculates similarities between vector representations.
- *Perplexity* {*90*}: Measures the fluency of the sentences according to language models (LM). We use both forward ({30}) and backward ({15}) LM features for S and T.
- *Entropy* {*9*}: Calculates the distributional similarity of test sentences to the training set over top N retrieved sentences.
- *Retrieval Closeness* {*24*}: Measures the degree to which sentences close to the test set are found in the selected training set, $\mathcal{I}$, using FDA (Biçici and Yuret, 2011a).
- *Diversity* {*6*}: Measures the diversity of co-occurring features in the training set.
- *IBM1 Translation Probability* {*16*}: Calculates the translation probability of test sentences using the selected training set, $\mathcal{I}$, (Brown et al., 1993).
- *IBM2 Alignment Features* {*11*}: Calculates the sum of the entropy of the distribution of alignment probabilities for S ($\sum_{s \in S} -p \log p$ for $p = p(t|s)$ where s and t are tokens) and T, their average for S and T, the number of entries with $p \geq 0.2$ and $p \geq 0.01$, the entropy of the word alignment between S and T and its average, and word alignment log probability and its value in terms of bits per word.
- *Minimum Bayes Retrieval Risk* {*4*}: Calculates the translation probability for the translation having the minimum Bayes risk among the retrieved training instances.
- *Sentence Translation Performance* {*3*}: Calculates translation scores obtained according to $q(T, R)$ using BLEU (Papineni et al., 2002), NIST (Doddington, 2002), or F_1 (Biçici and Yuret, 2011b) for q.
- *Character n-grams* {*4*}: Calculates cosine between character n-grams (for n=2,3,4,5) obtained for S and T (Bär et al., 2012).
- *LIX* {*2*}: Calculates the LIX readability score (Wikipedia, 2013; Björnsson, 1968) for S and T. [1]

For retrieval closeness, we use FDA instead of dice for sentence selection. We also improve FDA's instance selection score by scaling with the length of the sentence (Biçici and Yuret, 2011a). IBM2 alignments and their probabilities are obtained by first obtaining IBM1 alignments and probabilities, which become the starting point for the IBM2 model. Both models are trained for 25 to 75 iterations or until convergence.

3 Quality Estimation Task Results

We participate in all of the four challenges of the quality estimation task (QET) (Callison-Burch et al., 2013), which include English to Spanish (en-es) and German to English translation directions. There are two main categories of challenges: sentence-level prediction (Task 1.*) and word-level prediction (Task 2). Task 1.1 is about predicting post-editing effort (PEE), Task 1.2 is about ranking translations from different systems, Task 1.3 is about predicting post-editing time (PET), and Task 2 is about binary or multi-class classification of word-level quality.

For each task, we develop RTM models using the parallel corpora and the LM corpora distributed by the translation task (WMT13) (Callison-Burch et al., 2013) and the LM corpora provided by LDC for English and Spanish [2]. The parallel corpora contain 4.3M sentences for de-en with 106M words for de and 111M words for en and 15M sentences for en-es with 406M words for en and 455M words for

[1] LIX=$\frac{A}{B} + C\frac{100}{A}$, where A is the number of words, C is words longer than 6 characters, B is words that start or end with any of ".", ":", "!", "?" similar to (Hagström, 2012).

[2] English Gigaword 5th, Spanish Gigaword 3rd edition.

es. We do not use any resources provided by QET including data, software, or baseline features since they are SMT system dependent or language specific. Instance selection for the training set and the language model (LM) corpus is handled by a parallel implementation of FDA (Biçici, 2013). We tokenize and true-case all of the corpora. The true-caser is trained on all of the training corpus using Moses (Koehn et al., 2007). We prepare the corpora by following this procedure: tokenize $\rightarrow$ train the true-caser $\rightarrow$ true-case. Table 1 lists the statistics of the data used in the training and test sets for the tasks.

	Task	1.1	1.2 (de-en)	1.2 (en-es)	1.3 & 2
Train	sents	2254	32730	22338	803
	words	63K (en)	762K (de)	528K (en)	18K (en)
		67K (es)	786K (en)	559K (es)	20K (es)
Test	sents	500	1810	1315	284

Table 1: Data statistics for different tasks. The number of words is listed after tokenization.

Since we do not know the best training set size that will maximize the performance, we rely on previous SMT experiments (Biçici and Yuret, 2011a; Biçici and Yuret, 2011b) and quality estimation challenges (Biçici and van Genabith, 2013a; Biçici and van Genabith, 2013b) to select the proper training set size. For each training and test sentence provided in each subtask, we choose between 65 and 600 sentences from the parallel training corpora to be added to the training set, which creates roughly 400K sentences for training. We add the selected training set to the 8 million sentences selected for each LM corpus. The statistics of the training data selected by the parallel FDA and used as interpretants in the RTM models is given in Table 2.

Task	1.1	1.2 (de-en)	1.2 (en-es)	1.3	2
sents	406K	318K	299K	398K	397K
words	6.3M (en)	4.8M (de)	4.3M (en)	6.6M (en)	6.6M (en)
	6.9M (es)	4.9M (en)	4.6M (es)	7.2M (es)	7.2M (es)

Table 2: Statistics of the training data used as interpretants in the RTM models in thousands (K) of sentences or millions (M) of words.

3.1 Evaluation

In this section, we describe the metrics we use to evaluate the learning performance. Let y_i represent the actual target value for instance i, $\bar{y}$ the mean of the actual target values, $\hat{y}_i$ the value estimated by the learning model, and $\bar{\hat{y}}$ the mean of the estimated target values, then we use the following metrics to evaluate the learning models:

- *Mean Absolute Error (MAE):* $|\bar{\epsilon}| = \frac{\sum_{i=1}^{n} |\hat{y}_i - y_i|}{n}$
- *Relative Absolute Error (RAE) :* $|\overrightarrow{\epsilon}| = \frac{\sum_{i=1}^{n} |\hat{y}_i - y_i|}{\sum_{i=1}^{n} |\bar{y} - y_i|}$
- *Root Mean Squared Error:* RMSE $= \sqrt{\frac{\sum_{i=1}^{n} (\hat{y}_i - y_i)^2}{n}}$
- *DeltaAvg:* $\bar{\Delta}(V, S) = \frac{1}{|S|/2-1} \sum_{n=2}^{|S|/2} \left(\sum_{k=1}^{n-1} \frac{\sum_{s \in \bigcup_{i=1}^{k} q_i} V(s)}{|\bigcup_{i=1}^{k} q_i|} \right)$
- *Correlation:* $r = \frac{\sum_{i=1}^{n} (\hat{y}_i - \bar{\hat{y}})(y_i - \bar{y})}{\sqrt{\sum_{i=1}^{n} (\hat{y}_i - \bar{\hat{y}})^2} \sqrt{\sum_{i=1}^{n} (y_i - \bar{y})^2}}$

DeltaAvg (Callison-Burch et al., 2012) calculates the average quality difference between the scores for the top $n - 1$ quartiles and the overall quality for the test set. Relative absolute error measures the error relative to the error when predicting the actual mean. We use the coefficient of determination, $R^2 = 1 - \sum_{i=1}^{n} (\hat{y}_i - y_i)^2 / \sum_{i=1}^{n} (\bar{y} - y_i)^2$, during optimization where the models are regression based and higher R^2 values are better.

3.2 Task 1: Sentence-level Prediction of Quality

In this subsection, we develop techniques for the prediction of quality at the sentence-level. We first discuss the learning models we use and how we optimize them and then provide the results for the individual subtasks and the settings used.

3.2.1 Learning Models and Optimization

The learning models we use for predicting the translation quality include the ridge regression (RR) and support vector regression (SVR) with RBF (radial basis functions) kernel (Smola and Schölkopf, 2004). Both of these models learn a regression function using the features to estimate a numerical target value such as the HTER score, the F_1 score (Biçici and Yuret, 2011b), or the PET score. We also use these learning models after a feature subset selection with recursive feature elimination (RFE) (Guyon et al., 2002) or a dimensionality reduction and mapping step using partial least squares (PLS) (Specia et al., 2009), both of which are described in (Biçici et al., 2013). The learning parameters that govern the behavior of RR and SVR are the regularization λ for RR and the C, ε, and γ parameters for SVR. We optimize the learning parameters, the number of features to select, and the number of dimensions used for PLS. More detailed description of the optimization process is given in (Biçici et al., 2013). In our submissions, we only used the results we obtained from SVR and SVR after PLS (SVRPLS) since they perform the best during training.

Optimization can be a challenge for SVR due to the large number of parameter settings to search. In this work, we decrease the search space by selecting ε close to the theoretically optimal values. We select ε close to the standard deviation of the noise in the training set since the optimal value for ε is shown to have linear dependence to the noise level for different noise models (Smola et al., 1998). We use RMSE of RR on the training set as an estimate for the noise level (σ of noise) and the following formulas to obtain the ε with $\tau = 3$:

$$\varepsilon = \tau\sigma\sqrt{\frac{\ln n}{n}} \quad (1)$$

and the C (Cherkassky and Ma, 2004; Chalimourda et al., 2004):

$$C = \max(|\bar{y} + 3\sigma_y|, |\bar{y} - 3\sigma_y|) \quad (2)$$

Since the C obtained could be low (Chalimourda et al., 2004), we use a range of C values in addition to the obtained C value including C values with a couple of σ_y values larger.

Table 3 lists the RMSE of the RR model on the training set and the corresponding ε and C values for different subtasks. We also present the optimized parameter values for SVR and SVRPLS. Table 3 shows that, empirically, Equation 1 and Equation 2 gives results close to the best parameters found after optimization.

Task	1.1	1.2 (de-en)	1.2 (en-es)	1.3
RMSE RR	.1397	.1169	.1569	68.06
ε	.0245	.0062	.01	18.64
C	.8398	.8713	1.02	371.28
$\hat{C}$ (SVR)	.8398	.5	.5	100
γ (SVR)	.0005	.001	.0001	.0005
$\hat{C}$ (SVRPLS)	1.5	.8713	1.02	100
γ (SVRPLS)	.0001	.0001	.0001	.001
# dim (SVRPLS)	60	60	60	60

Table 3: Optimal parameters predicted by Equation 1 and Equation 2 and the optimized parameter values, $\hat{C}$ and γ for SVR and SVRPLS and the number of dimensions (# dim) for SVRPLS.

3.2.2 Task 1.1: Scoring and Ranking for Post-Editing Effort

Task 1.1 involves the prediction of the case insensitive translation edit rate (TER) scores obtained by TERp (Snover et al., 2009) and their ranking. In contrast, we derive features over sentences that are true-cased. We obtain the rankings by sorting according to the predicted TER scores.

Task 1.1	R^2	r	RMSE	MAE	RAE
RR	0.3510	0.5965	0.1393	0.1086	0.7888
RR PLS	0.4232	0.6509	0.1313	0.1023	0.7430
SVR	0.4394	0.6647	0.1295	0.0967	0.7023
SVR PLS	0.4305	0.6569	0.1305	0.1003	0.7284

Table 4: Task1.1 results on the training set.

Table 4 presents the learning performance on the training set using the optimized parameters. We are able to significantly improve the results when compared with the QET 2012 (Callison-Burch et al., 2012) and our previous results (Biçici et al., 2013) especially in terms of MAE and RAE.

The results on the test set are given in Table 5. Rank lists the overall ranking in the task. RTMs with SVR PLS learning is able to achieve the top rank in this task.

Ranking	DeltaAvg	r	Rank
CNGL SVRPLS	11.09	0.55	1
CNGL SVR	9.88	0.51	4
Scoring	MAE	RMSE	Rank
CNGL SVRPLS	13.26	16.82	3
CNGL SVR	13.85	17.28	8

Table 5: Task1.1 results on the test set.

3.2.3 Task 1.2: Ranking Translations from Different Systems

Task 1.2 involves the prediction of the ranking among up to 5 translation outputs produced by different MT systems. Evaluation is done against the human rankings using the Kendall's τ correlation (Callison-Burch et al., 2013): $\tau = (c - d)/\frac{n(n-1)}{2} = \frac{c-d}{c+d}$ where a pair is concordant, c, if the ordering agrees, discordant, d, if their ordering disagrees, and neither concordant nor discordant if their rankings are equal.

We use sentence-level F_1 scores (Biçici and Yuret, 2011b) as the target to predict. We use F_1 because it can be easily interpreted and it correlates well with human judgments (more than TER) (Biçici and Yuret, 2011b; Callison-Burch et al., 2011). We also found that the τ of the rankings obtained according to the F_1 score over the training set (0.2040) is better than BLEU (Papineni et al., 2002) (0.1780) and NIST (Doddington, 2002) (0.1907) for de-en. Table 6 presents the learning performance on the training set using the optimized parameters. Learning F_1 becomes an easier task than learning TER as observed from the results but we have significantly more training instances. We use the SVR model for predicting the F_1 scores on the training set and the test set. MAE is a more important performance metric here since we want to be as precise as possible when predicting the actual performance.

	Task 1.2	R^2	r	RMSE	MAE	RAE
de-en	RR	0.6320	0.7953	0.1169	0.0733	0.5535
	SVR	0.7528	0.8692	0.0958	0.0463	0.3494
en-es	RR	0.5101	0.7146	0.1569	0.1047	0.6323
	SVR	0.4819	0.7018	0.1613	0.0973	0.5873

Table 6: Task1.2 results on the training set.

Our next goal is to learn a threshold for judging if two translations are equal over the predicted F_1 scores. This threshold is used to determine whether we need to alter the ranking. We try to mimic the human decision process when determining whether two translations are equivalent. On some occasions where the sentences are close enough, humans give them equal ranking. This is also related to the granularity of the differences visible with a 1 to 5 ranking schema.

We compared different threshold formulations and used the following condition in our submissions to decide whether the ranking of item i in a set S of translations, $i \in S$, should be different:

$$\sum_{j \neq i} \frac{F_1(j) - F_1(i)}{|j - i|} / |S| > t, \quad (3)$$

where t is the optimized threshold minimizing the following loss for n training instances:

$$\sum_{i=1}^{n} \tau(f(t, q_i), r_i) \quad (4)$$

where $f(t, q_i)$ is a function returning rankings based on the threshold t and the quality scores for instance i, q_i and $\tau(r_j, r_i)$ calculates the τ score based on the rankings r_j and r_i.

For both de-en and en-es subtasks, we found the thresholds obtained to be very similar or the same. The optimized values are given in Table 7. On the test set, we used the same threshold, $t = 0.00275$ for both de-en and en-es, which is a little higher than the optimal t to prevent overfitting.

Task 1.2	τ	t	# same	# all
de-en	.2339	.00013	236	25644
	.2287	.00275	494	
en-es	.2801	.00073	136	17752
	.2764	.00275	233	

Table 7: Task1.2 optimized thresholds and the corresponding comparisons that were found to be equal (# same) over all comparisons (# all).

We believe that human judgments of linguistic equality and the corresponding thresholds we learned in this work can be useful for developing better automatic evaluation metrics and can improve the correlation of the scores obtained with human judgments (as we did here). The results on the test set are given in Table 8. We are also able to achieve the top ranking in this task.

Ties penalized	model	τ	Rank
de-en	CNGL SVRPLS F_1	0.17	3
	CNGL SVR F_1	0.17	4
en-es	CNGL SVRPLS F_1	0.15	1
	CNGL SVR F_1	0.13	2
Ties ignored	model	τ	Rank
de-en	CNGL SVRPLS F_1	0.17	3
	CNGL SVR F_1	0.17	4
en-es	CNGL SVRPLS F_1	0.16	2
	CNGL SVR F_1	0.13	3

Table 8: Task1.2 results on the test set.

3.2.4 Task 1.3: Predicting Post-Editing Time

Task 1.3 involves the prediction of the post-editing time (PET) for a translator to post-edit the MT output. Table 9 presents the learning performance on the training set using the optimized parameters.

Task 1.3	R^2	r	RMSE	MAE	RAE
RR	0.4463	0.6702	68.0628	39.5250	0.6694
RR PLS	0.5917	0.7716	58.4464	35.8759	0.6076
SVR	0.4062	0.6753	70.4853	36.5132	0.6184
SVR PLS	0.5316	0.7604	62.6031	33.5490	0.5682

Table 9: Task1.3 results on the training set.

The results on the test set are given in Table 10. We are able to become the 2nd best system according to MAE in this task.

3.3 Task 2: Word-level Prediction of Quality

In this subsection, we develop a learning model, global linear models with dynamic learning rate (GLMd), for the prediction of quality at the word-level where the word-level quality is a binary (K: keep, C: change) or multi-class classification problem (K: keep, S: substitute, D: delete). We first discuss the GLMd learning model, then we present

Task 1.3	MAE	Rank
CNGL SVR	49.2121	3
CNGL SVRPLS	49.6161	4
	RMSE	Rank
CNGL SVRPLS	86.6175	4
CNGL SVR	90.3650	7

Table 10: Task1.3 results on the test set.

the word-level features we use, and then present our results on the test set.

3.3.1 Global Linear Models with Dynamic Learning (GLMd)

Collins (2002) develops global learning models (GLM), which rely on Viterbi decoding, perceptron learning, and flexible feature definitions. We extend the GLM framework by parallel perceptron training (McDonald et al., 2010) and dynamic learning with adaptive weight updates in the perceptron learning algorithm:

$$\mathbf{w} = \mathbf{w} + \alpha \left(\Phi(\mathbf{x}_i, \mathbf{y}_i) - \Phi(\mathbf{x}_i, \hat{\mathbf{y}}) \right), \quad (5)$$

where Φ returns a global representation for instance i and the weights are updated by $\alpha = \exp(\log_{10}(3\epsilon_{-1}/\epsilon_0))$ with ϵ_{-1} and ϵ_0 representing the error of the previous and first iteration respectively. α decays the amount of the change during weight updates at later stages and prevents large fluctuations with updates. We used both the GLM model and the GMLd models in our submissions.

3.3.2 Word-level Features

We introduce a number of novel features for the prediction of word-level translation quality. In broad categories, these word-level features are:

- *CCL:* Uses CCL links.
- *Word context:* Surrounding words.
- *Word alignments:* Alignments, their probabilities, source and target word contexts.
- *Length:* Word lengths, n-grams over them.
- *Location:* Location of the words.
- *Prefix and Suffix:* Word prefixes, suffixes.
- *Form:* Capital, contains digit or punctuation.

We found that CCL links are the most discriminative feature among these. In total, we used 511K features for binary and 637K for multi-class classification. The learning curve is given in Figure 1.

The results on the test set are given in Table 11. P, R, and A stand for precision, recall, and accuracy respectively. We are able to become the 2nd according to A in this task.

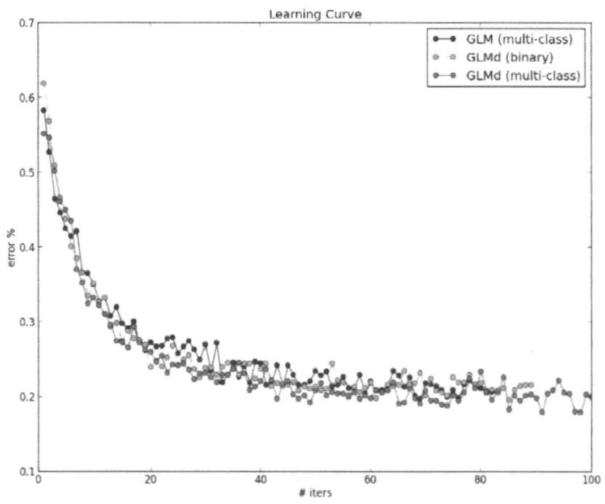

Figure 1: Learning curve with the parallel GLM and GLMd models.

Binary	A	P	R	F_1	Rank (A)
CNGL dGLM	.7146	.7392	.9261	.8222	2
CNGL GLM	.7010	.7554	.8581	.8035	5
Multi-class	A	Rank			
CNGL dGLM	.7162	3			
CNGL GLM	.7116	4			

Table 11: Task 2 results on the test set.

4 Contributions

Referential translation machines achieve top performance in automatic, accurate, and language independent prediction of sentence-level and word-level statistical machine translation (SMT) quality. RTMs remove the need to access any SMT system specific information or prior knowledge of the training data or models used when generating the translations. We develop novel techniques for solving all subtasks in the quality estimation (QE) task (QET 2013) based on individual RTM models. Our results achieve improvements over last year's QE task results (QET 2012), as well as our previous results, provide new features and techniques for QE, and rank 1st or 2nd in all of the subtasks.

Acknowledgments

This work is supported in part by SFI (07/CE/I1142) as part of the Centre for Next Generation Localisation (www.cngl.ie) at Dublin City University and in part by the European Commission through the QTLaunchPad FP7 project (No: 296347). We also thank the SFI/HEA Irish Centre for High-End Computing (ICHEC) for the provision of computational facilities and support.

References

Daniel Bär, Chris Biemann, Iryna Gurevych, and Torsten Zesch. 2012. Ukp: Computing semantic textual similarity by combining multiple content similarity measures. In **SEM 2012: The First Joint Conference on Lexical and Computational Semantics – Volume 1: Proceedings of the main conference and the shared task, and Volume 2: Proceedings of the Sixth International Workshop on Semantic Evaluation (SemEval 2012)*, pages 435–440, Montréal, Canada, 7-8 June. Association for Computational Linguistics.

Ergun Biçici and Josef van Genabith. 2013a. CNGL-CORE: Referential translation machines for measuring semantic similarity. In **SEM 2013: The Second Joint Conference on Lexical and Computational Semantics*, Atlanta, Georgia, USA, 13-14 June. Association for Computational Linguistics.

Ergun Biçici and Josef van Genabith. 2013b. CNGL: Grading student answers by acts of translation. In **SEM 2013: The Second Joint Conference on Lexical and Computational Semantics and Proceedings of the Seventh International Workshop on Semantic Evaluation (SemEval 2013)*, Atlanta, Georgia, USA, 14-15 June. Association for Computational Linguistics.

Ergun Biçici and Deniz Yuret. 2011a. Instance selection for machine translation using feature decay algorithms. In *Proceedings of the Sixth Workshop on Statistical Machine Translation*, pages 272–283, Edinburgh, Scotland, July. Association for Computational Linguistics.

Ergun Biçici and Deniz Yuret. 2011b. RegMT system for machine translation, system combination, and evaluation. In *Proceedings of the Sixth Workshop on Statistical Machine Translation*, pages 323–329, Edinburgh, Scotland, July. Association for Computational Linguistics.

Ergun Biçici, Declan Groves, and Josef van Genabith. 2013. Predicting sentence translation quality using extrinsic and language independent features. *Machine Translation.*

Ergun Biçici. 2011. *The Regression Model of Machine Translation.* Ph.D. thesis, Koç University. Supervisor: Deniz Yuret.

Ergun Biçici. 2013. Feature decay algorithms for fast deployment of accurate statistical machine translation systems. In *Proceedings of the Eighth Workshop on Statistical Machine Translation*, Sofia, Bulgaria, August. Association for Computational Linguistics.

Ergun Biçici. 2008. Consensus ontologies in socially interacting multiagent systems. *Journal of Multiagent and Grid Systems.*

Carl Hugo Björnsson. 1968. *Läsbarhet.* Liber.

Chris Bliss. 2012. Comedy is translation, February. http://www.ted.com/talks/chris_bliss_comedy_is_translation.html.

Peter F. Brown, Stephen A. Della Pietra, Vincent J. Della Pietra, and Robert L. Mercer. 1993. The mathematics of statistical machine translation: Parameter estimation. *Computational Linguistics*, 19(2):263–311, June.

Chris Callison-Burch, Philipp Koehn, Christof Monz, and Omer F. Zaidan. 2011. Findings of the 2011 Workshop on Statistical Machine Translation. In *Proceedings of the Sixth Workshop on Statistical Machine Translation*, Edinburgh, England, July. Association for Computational Linguistics.

Chris Callison-Burch, Philipp Koehn, Christof Monz, Matt Post, Radu Soricut, and Lucia Specia. 2012. Findings of the 2012 workshop on statistical machine translation. In *Proceedings of the Seventh Workshop on Statistical Machine Translation*, pages 10–51, Montréal, Canada, June. Association for Computational Linguistics.

Chris Callison-Burch, Philipp Koehn, Christof Monz, Matt Post, Radu Soricut, and Lucia Specia. 2013. Findings of the 2013 workshop on statistical machine translation. In *Proceedings of the Eighth Workshop on Statistical Machine Translation*, pages 10–51. Association for Computational Linguistics, August.

Athanassia Chalimourda, Bernhard Schölkopf, and Alex J. Smola. 2004. Experimentally optimal ν in support vector regression for different noise models and parameter settings. *Neural Networks*, 17(1):127–141, January.

Vladimir Cherkassky and Yunqian Ma. 2004. Practical selection of svm parameters and noise estimation for svm regression. *Neural Netw.*, 17(1):113–126, January.

Michael Collins. 2002. Discriminative training methods for hidden markov models: theory and experiments with perceptron algorithms. In *Proceedings of the ACL-02 conference on Empirical methods in natural language processing - Volume 10*, EMNLP '02, pages 1–8, Stroudsburg, PA, USA. Association for Computational Linguistics.

George Doddington. 2002. Automatic evaluation of machine translation quality using n-gram co-occurrence statistics. In *Proceedings of the second international conference on Human Language Technology Research*, pages 138–145, San Francisco, CA, USA. Morgan Kaufmann Publishers Inc.

Myroslava O. Dzikovska, Rodney D. Nielsen, and Chris Brew. 2012. Towards effective tutorial feedback for explanation questions: A dataset and baselines. In *Proceedings of the 2012 Conference of the North American Chapter of the Association for*

Computational Linguistics: Human Language Technologies, pages 200–210, Montréal, Canada, June. Association for Computational Linguistics.

Isabelle Guyon, Jason Weston, Stephen Barnhill, and Vladimir Vapnik. 2002. Gene selection for cancer classification using support vector machines. *Machine Learning*, 46(1-3):389–422.

Kenth Hagström. 2012. Swedish readability calculator. https://github.com/keha76/Swedish-Readability-Calculator.

Philipp Koehn, Hieu Hoang, Alexandra Birch, Chris Callison-Burch, Marcello Federico, Nicola Bertoldi, Brooke Cowan, Wade Shen, Christine Moran, Richard Zens, Chris Dyer, Ondrej Bojar, Alexandra Constantin, and Evan Herbst. 2007. Moses: Open source toolkit for statistical machine translation. In *Annual Meeting of the Assoc. for Computational Linguistics*, pages 177–180, Prague, Czech Republic, June.

Ryan McDonald, Keith Hall, and Gideon Mann. 2010. Distributed training strategies for the structured perceptron. In *Human Language Technologies: The 2010 Annual Conference of the North American Chapter of the Association for Computational Linguistics*, pages 456–464, Los Angeles, California, June. Association for Computational Linguistics.

Kishore Papineni, Salim Roukos, Todd Ward, and Wei-Jing Zhu. 2002. BLEU: a method for automatic evaluation of machine translation. In *Proceedings of 40th Annual Meeting of the Association for Computational Linguistics*, pages 311–318, Philadelphia, Pennsylvania, USA, July. Association for Computational Linguistics.

Yoav Seginer. 2007. *Learning Syntactic Structure*. Ph.D. thesis, Universiteit van Amsterdam.

Alex J. Smola and Bernhard Schölkopf. 2004. A tutorial on support vector regression. *Statistics and Computing*, 14(3):199–222, August.

A. J. Smola, N. Murata, B. Schölkopf, and K.-R. Müller. 1998. Asymptotically optimal choice of ε-loss for support vector machines. In L. Niklasson, M. Boden, and T. Ziemke, editors, *Proceedings of the International Conference on Artificial Neural Networks*, Perspectives in Neural Computing, pages 105–110, Berlin. Springer.

Matthew Snover, Nitin Madnani, Bonnie J. Dorr, and Richard Schwartz. 2009. Fluency, adequacy, or hter?: exploring different human judgments with a tunable mt metric. In *Proceedings of the Fourth Workshop on Statistical Machine Translation*, StatMT '09, pages 259–268, Stroudsburg, PA, USA. Association for Computational Linguistics.

Lucia Specia, Nicola Cancedda, Marc Dymetman, Marco Turchi, and Nello Cristianini. 2009. Estimating the sentence-level quality of machine translation systems. In *Proceedings of the 13th Annual Conference of the European Association for Machine Translation (EAMT)*, pages 28–35, Barcelona, May. EAMT.

Wikipedia. 2013. Lix. http://en.wikipedia.org/wiki/LIX.

FBK-UEdin participation to the WMT13 Quality Estimation shared-task

José G. C. de Souza
FBK-irst
University of Trento
Trento, Italy
desouza@fbk.eu

Christian Buck
School of Informatics
University of Edinburgh
Edinburgh, UK
christian.buck@ed.ac.uk

Marco Turchi, Matteo Negri
FBK-irst
Trento, Italy
{turchi,negri}@fbk.eu

Abstract

In this paper we present the approach and system setup of the joint participation of Fondazione Bruno Kessler and University of Edinburgh in the WMT 2013 Quality Estimation shared-task. Our submissions were focused on tasks whose aim was predicting sentence-level Human-mediated Translation Edit Rate and sentence-level post-editing time (Task 1.1 and 1.3, respectively). We designed features that are built on resources such as automatic word alignment, n-best candidate translation lists, back-translations and word posterior probabilities. Our models consistently overcome the baselines for both tasks and performed particularly well for Task 1.3, ranking first among seven participants.

1 Introduction

Quality Estimation (QE) for Machine Translation (MT) is the task of evaluating the quality of the output of an MT system without relying on reference translations. The WMT 2013 QE Shared Task defined four different tasks covering both word and sentence level QE. In this work we describe the Fondazione Bruno Kessler (FBK) and University of Edinburgh approach and system setup of our participation to the shared task. We developed models for two sentence-level tasks: Task 1.1: Scoring and ranking for post-editing effort, and Task 1.3: Predicting post-editing time.

The first task aims at predicting the Human-mediated Translation Edit Rate (HTER) (Snover et al., 2006) between a suggestion generated by a machine translation system and its manually post-edited version. The data set contains 2,754 English-Spanish sentence pairs post-edited by one translator (2,254 for training and 500 for test). We participated only in the scoring mode of this task.

The second task requires to predict the time, in seconds, that was required to post edit a translation given by a machine translation system. Participants are provided with 1,087 English-Spanish sentence pairs, source and suggestion, along with their respective post-edited sentence and post-editing time in seconds (803 data points for training and 284 for test).

For both tasks we applied supervised learning methods and made use of information about word alignments, n-best diversity scores, word posterior probabilities, pseudo-references, and back translation to train our models. In the remainder of this paper we describe the features designed for our participation (Section 2), the learning methods used to build our models (Section 3), the experiments that led to our submitted systems (Section 4), and we briefly conclude our experience in this evaluation task (Section 5).

2 Features

2.1 Word Alignment

Information about word alignments is used to extract quantitative (amount and distribution of the alignments) and qualitative features (importance of the aligned terms) under the assumption that features that explore *what* is aligned can bring improvements to tasks where sentence-level semantic relations need to be identified. Among the possible applications, Souza et al. (2013) recently investigated with success their application in Cross-lingual Textual Entailment for content synchronization (Mehdad et al., 2012; Negri et al., 2013).

For our experiments in both tasks we built word alignment models using the resources made available for the evaluation campaign. To train the word alignment models we used the MGIZA++ implementation (Gao and Vogel, 2008) of the IBM models (Brown et al., 1993) and the concatenation of Europarl, News Commentary, MultiUN, parallel corpora made available for task 1.3. The training data comprises about 12.8 million sentence pairs.

The word alignment features are divided into three main groups: **AL**, **POS** and **IDF**. The **AL** group regards quantitative information about aligned and unaligned words between source sentence (src) and machine translation output (tgt). The features of this group are computed for both src and tgt:

- proportion of aligned words;
- number of contiguous unaligned words normalized by the length of the sentence;
- length of the longest sequence of aligned/unaligned words normalized by the length of the sentence;
- average length of aligned/unaligned sequences of words;
- position of the first/last unaligned word normalized by the length of the sentence;
- proportion of aligned n-grams in the sentence.

To compute the features of the **POS** group we use part-of-speech (PoS) information for each word in src and tgt. Training and test data for both tasks were preprocessed with the TreeTagger (Schmid, 1995) and mapped to a more coarse-grained set of part-of-speech tags (P) based on the universal PoS tag set by Petrov et al. (2012). In this group there are two different types of features: one is computed for the *alignments* (the mapping between a word in src and a word in tgt) and the other is computed for *aligned words* (words in src that are aligned to one or more words in tgt and vice-versa). The features computed over the alignments are:

- proportion of alignments connecting words with the same PoS tag;
- proportion of alignments connecting words with the same PoS tag for each tag $p \in P$.

The features implemented for aligned words are:

- proportion of aligned words tagged with p in the sentence ($p \in P$). This feature is processed for both src and tgt;
- proportion of words in src aligned with words in tgt that share the same PoS tag (and vice-versa);
- proportion of words tagged with p in src and that are aligned to words with the same tag p in tgt (and vice-versa). This is done for every $p \in P$.

The last group, **IDF**, is composed by one feature that explores the notion of inverse document frequency as another source of qualitative information. The idea is that rare words (with higher IDF) are more informative than frequent words. The IDF scores for each word are calculated for English and Spanish on each side of the parallel corpora used to build the alignment models. This feature is calculated for both src and tgt (at test stage, the average IDF value of each language is assigned to unseen terms):

- summation of the IDF scores of aligned words in src divided by the sum of IDF scores of the aligned words in tgt (and vice-versa).

Preliminary experiments have been executed to find the best word alignment algorithm for each task. We explored three different word alignment algorithms: the *hidden Markov model* (HMM) (Vogel et al., 1996) and *IBM models* 3 and 4 (Brown et al., 1993). We also tried three symmetrization models (Koehn et al., 2005): *union*, *intersection*, and *grow-diag-final-and*, a more complex symmetrization method which combines intersection with some alignments from the union. The best alignment and symmetrization combination found for Task 1.1 was IBM4 with intersection and for task 1.3 was HMM with intersection. These experiments were carried out in 10-fold cross-validation on the training set and used only the alignment features.

2.2 N-best Diversity scores

Our n-best diversity features are based on the intuition that a large number of possible choices generally leads to more errors. While a similar notion can be expressed locally by counting the translation options for each word or phrase, we consider n-best lists as a good approximation of the search space. This allows us to circumvent problems associated with the local measures, such as ambiguous alignment and segmentation, and limitations of using the search graph directly such as the inability compute edit distance between hypotheses.

Thus, to quantify the coherence of translation options we compute a (symmetrical) matrix of pairwise Levenshtein distances, either on token or character level, for n-best lists of size up to 100k[1] using the baseline system and the systems we describe in Section 2.4. For this matrix the following features are produced:

1. The index of the *central hypothesis*, *i.e.* the translation with the minimum average distance to all other entries.

2. The average edit distance between the central hypothesis and all other entries normalized by the length of top scoring hypothesis.

3. Edit distance between top scoring and central hypothesis

4. Number of hypotheses with an edit distance to the top-scoring hypothesis below a set threshold.

2.3 Word Posterior Probabilities

Following previous work on word posterior probabilities (WPPs) (Ueffing et al., 2003) we computed the sequence of edit operations needed to transform the MT suggestion into all entries of an n-best list in which we normalized the logarithmic model scores to resemble probabilities. Tokens are considered incorrect is the operation is either *insert* or *substitute*, otherwise the probability of the hypothesis counts towards the correctness of the word. These word-level features were then normalized by taking the geometric mean of the individual probabilities. We did this for all systems described in Section 2.4 and varying sizes of n between 10 and 100k.

2.4 Pseudo-references and back-translation

Motivated by the success of pseudo-reference features (Soricut et al., 2012) we employed three additional MT systems: one similar to the original system but trained on more data, a hierarchical phrase-based system, and a Spanish-English system to translate back into English. All models have been estimated using publicly available software (SRILM (Stolcke, 2002), Moses (Koehn et al., 2007)), and corpora (Europarl, News Commentary, MultiUN, Gigaword). Using the predictions of the English-Spanish systems as pseudo-references and likewise the original source as reference for the back-translation system we computed a number of automatic metrics including BLEU (Papineni et al., 2002), GTM (Turian et al., 2003), PER (Tillmann et al., 1997), TER (Snover et al., 2006) and Meteor (Denkowski and Lavie, 2011).

3 Learning algorithms

To build our models using the features presented in Section 2 we tried different learning algorithms. After some preliminary experiments for both tasks we decided to use mainly two: support vector machines (SVM) and extremely randomized trees (Geurts et al., 2006). For all experiments presented in this paper we use the Scikit-learn (Pedregosa et al., 2011) implementations of the above algorithms.

In preliminary experiments we noticed that the number of features that we were using for both tasks was leading to poor results when using the SVM regression (SVR) models. In order to cope with this problem we performed feature selection prior to the SVM regression training. For that we used Randomized Lasso, or stability selection (Meinshausen and Bühlmann, 2010). It resamples the training data several times and fits a Lasso regression model on each sample. Features that appear in a given number of samples are retained. Both the fraction of the data to be sampled and the threshold to select the features can be configured. In our experiments we set the sampling fraction to 75%, the selection threshold to 25% and the number of re-samples to 200.

To optimize the SVR with radial basis function (RBF) kernel hyper-parameters we used random search (Bergstra and Bengio, 2012) instead of the traditional grid search procedure. We found random search to be as efficient or better than grid search and it drastically reduced the time required to compute the best parameter combination.

Finally, we trained an extremely randomized forest, i.e. an ensemble of extremely randomized trees. Each tree can be parameterized differently. The results of the individual trees are combined by averaging their predictions. When a tree is built,

[1] Computing the pair-wise edit-distances between all 100k entries is computationally expensive. However, we found the n-best lists to be highly repetitive, so that on average only 3.7% of the values had to be computed. The computation is also trivially parallel.

System	Features	MAE	RMSE	Predict. Interval	Parameters
SVR	Base	0.127	0.163	[0.046, 0.671]	347.5918, 0.001, 0.0001
SVR	Base + All	0.121	0.155	[0.090, 0.714]	0.4052, 0.0753, 0.0010
RL + SVR	Sel(Base + All)	0.119	0.1534	[0.084, 0.745]	40.5873, 0.0484, 0.0002
ET	Base + All	0.123	0.156	[0.142, 0.708]	100
ET	Base + All	0.122	0.155	[0.164, 0.712]	1000

Table 1: Experiments results for Task 1.1 on 10-fold cross-validation. "Base" are the 17 baseline features. "All" corresponds to all the features described in Section 2 in a total of 141 features. "SVR" is support vector regression, "RL" is randomized Lasso and "ET" is extremely randomized trees. MAE stands for the average mean absolute error and RMSE is the root mean squared error. Parameters for SVR are C, ϵ, γ and for ET is the number of estimators.

the node splitting step is done at random by picking the best split among a random subset of the input features.

4 Experiments

For both tasks we set up a baseline system that uses the same 17 black box "baseline" features provided for the WMT 2012 QE shared task (Callison-Burch et al., 2012). The baseline model is trained with an SVM regression with RBF kernel and optimized parameters. Parameter optimization for SVM regression models was performed with 1000 iterations of random search for which the process was set to minimize the mean absolute error (MAE)[2]. The parameters of SVR with RBF kernel (the penalty parameter C, the width of the insensitivity zone ϵ, and the RBF parameter γ) are sampled from an exponential distribution.

Experiments for both tasks were run using 10-fold cross-validation on the training set. In Task 1.3 some data points were annotated by 2 or more post-editors and, in a normal cross-validation scheme, the same data point might appear in the training and test set but annotated by different post-editors. To address this characteristic we implemented a cross-validation that divides along source sentences, so that all translations of a source segment end up in either the training or test portion of a split. The number of features available for both tasks is not the same (112 for Task 1.1 and 141 for Task 1.3) because there were fewer n-best diversity, pseudo-references and word posterior probability based features developed with different parameters due to time constraints.

During our experiments with the training set, the best model for **Task 1.1** was the combination of randomized Lasso feature selection with SVR (0.119 MAE). The extremely randomized trees presented results around 0.12 MAE worse than the figures obtained by the SVR models. Results obtained for Task 1.1 are summarized in Table 1.

As for **Task 1.3**, training results are presented in Table 2. The best model combines feature selection (randomized Lasso) with SVR. During training it obtained the lowest average MAE (38.6). Compared to the models built with extremely randomized trees, the prediction interval of this system is narrower. This indicates that the tree-based models cover a wider range of data points than the SVR-based models.

In the official results released by the organizers our submissions had close performances for Task 1.1. The difference between the SVR and the extremely randomized tree models is very small (around 0.0012 MAE points). For Task 1.3 our best submission is the one based on ensembles of trees, a trend that was not observed during training. Our hypothesis is that the tree-based ensemble model was capable of generalizing the training data better than the SVR-based ones and that despite the low number of employed features the latter was prone to overfitting.

Table 3 presents the official evaluation numbers for both tasks.

4.1 Feature analysis

To gain some insight about the relevance of the features we explored in our submissions, we compared the output of the randomized Lasso with the most important features computed by the extremely randomized tree algorithm. Below we present the features that appear in the intersection

[2]Given by $MAE = \frac{\sum_{i=1}^{N} |H(s_i)-V(s_i)|}{N}$, where $H(s_i)$ is the hypothesis score for the entry s_i and $V(s_i)$ is the gold standard value for s_i in a dataset with N entries.

System	Features	MAE	RMSE	Predict. Interval	Parameters
SVR	Base	41.3	69.2	[5.6, 315.7]	138.7359, 2.3331, 0.0185
SVR	Base + All	40.2	70.6	[8.6, 335.6]	308.3817, 0.2194, 0.0009
RL + SVR	Sel(Base + All)	38.6	69.1	[11.5, 332.0]	161.5705, 7.3370, 0.0460
ET	Base + All	44.1	72.2	[11.9, 446.2]	100
ET	Base + All	43.7	72.0	[12.6, 446.2]	1000

Table 2: Experiments results for Task 1.3 on 10-fold cross-validation. "Base" are the 17 baseline features. "All" corresponds to all the features described in Section 2 in a total of 141 features. "SVR" is support vector regression, "RL" is randomized Lasso and "ET" is extremely randomized trees. MAE stands for the average mean absolute error and RMSE is the root mean squared error. Parameters for SVR are C, ϵ, γ and for ET is the number of estimators.

System	MAE	RMSE
Task 1.1		
Official Baseline	0.1491	0.1822
RL + SVR	0.1450	0.1773
ET	0.1438	0.1768
Task 1.3		
Official Baseline	51.93	93.35
RL + SVR	47.92	86.66
ET	47.52	82.60

Table 3: Official results for tasks 1.1 and 1.3 on the test set.

of these two sets for each task.

In Task 1.1, the feature selection algorithm retained 29 out of 112 features. We take the intersection of this set with the 29 most relevant features computed by the ensemble tree-based method. This selection comes from features based on different resources:

- proportion of words in `src` aligned with words in `tgt` that share the same PoS tag;
- average number of translations per source word according to IBM Model 1 thresholded $P(t|s) > 0.01$;
- average number of translations per source word according to IBM Model 1 thresholded $P(t|s) > 0.2$;
- average source sentence token length;
- number of times the top-scoring hypothesis is repeated in an 10k-best list;
- position of the first unaligned word normalized by the length of the sentence for `src` and `tgt`;
- position of the last unaligned word normalized by the length of the sentence for `src` and `tgt`;
- summation of the IDF scores of aligned words in `tgt` divided by the summation of IDF scores of the aligned words in `src`;
- length of the longest sequence of unaligned words normalized by the length of the `src`;
- percentage of bigrams in the 4th quartile of frequency of the source language corpus;
- percentage of trigrams in the 4th quartile of frequency of the source language corpus;
- proportion of alignments connecting words with the same PoS tag;
- proportion of aligned words in `src`.

For Task 1.3, the randomized Lasso selection reduced the input feature vector from 141 features to 19. We compared these features with the 19 most important features computed by the extremely randomized tree algorithm. As above the intersection of both sets utilizes many resources:

- proportion of aligned words in `src` with the adjective PoS tag.
- rank of *central hypothesis* (see Section 2.2) and average edit distance to all other entries in 10k-best list of Spanish-English backtranslation system;
- language model probability for `tgt`;
- length of the longest sequence of aligned words in `tgt`;

- number of occurrences of the target word within the target hypothesis averaged for all words in the hypothesis;
- percentage of bigrams in the 4th quartile of frequency of the source language corpus;
- percentage of trigrams in the 4th quartile of frequency of the source language corpus;
- number of contiguous unaligned words in `tgt` normalized by the length of `tgt`.

5 Conclusion

This paper presented the participation of FBK and University of Edinburgh to the WMT 2013 Quality Estimation shared task. Our approach explored features based on word alignment, n-best diversity scores, pseudo-references and back-translations, and word posterior probabilities. We experimented with two different learning methods, SVR and extremely randomized trees for predicting sentence-level post-editing time and HTER.

Our submitted systems were particularly successful for predicting sentence-level post-editing time, ranking 1st among seven participants. The submitted models for predicting HTER consistently overcome the baseline for the task. In addition to the description of our approach and system setup, we presented a first analysis of the features used in our models with the objective of assessing the importance of the features used either for predicting time or HTER.

6 Acknowledgments

This work was partially funded by the European Commission under the project MateCat, Grant 287688. The authors want to thank Philipp Koehn for training two of the models used in Section 2.2.

References

James Bergstra and Yoshua Bengio. 2012. Random Search for Hyper-Parameter Optimization. *Journal of Machine Learning Research*, 13:281–305, March.

Peter F. E Brown, Stephen A. Della Pietra, Vincent J. Della Pietra, and Robert L. Mercer. 1993. The Mathematics of Statistical Machine Translation : Parameter Estimation. *Computational Linguistics*, 19(2):263–311.

Chris Callison-Burch, Philipp Koehn, Christof Monz, Matt Post, Radu Soricut, and Lucia Specia. 2012. Findings of the 2012 Workshop on Statistical Machine Translation. In *Proceedings of the 7th Workshop on Statistical Machine Translation*, pages 10–51, Montreal, Canada, June. Association for Computational Linguistics.

Michael Denkowski and Alon Lavie. 2011. Meteor 1.3: Automatic Metric for Reliable Optimization and Evaluation of Machine Translation Systems. In *Proceedings of the EMNLP 2011 Workshop on Statistical Machine Translation*.

Qin Gao and Stephan Vogel. 2008. Parallel implementations of word alignment tool. In *Software Engineering, Testing, and Quality Assurance*, SETQA-NLP '08, pages 49–57, Stroudsburg, PA, USA.

Pierre Geurts, Damien Ernst, and Louis Wehenkel. 2006. Extremely randomized trees. *Machine Learning*, 63(1):3–42, March.

Philipp Koehn, Amittai Axelrod, Alexandra Birch Mayne, Chris Callison-Burch, Miles Osborne, and David Talbot. 2005. Edinburgh system description for the 2005 IWSLT speech translation evaluation. In *Proceedings of the International Workshop on Spoken Language Translation*.

Philipp Koehn, Hieu Hoang, Alexandra Birch, Chris Callison-Burch, Marcello Federico, Nicola Bertoldi, Brooke Cowan, Wade Shen, Christine Moran, Richard Zenz, Chris Dyer, Ondřej Bojar, Alexandra Constantin, and Evan Herbst. 2007. Moses: Open source toolkit for statistical machine translation. In *ACL 2007 Demo and Poster Sessions*, pages 177–180, June.

Yashar Mehdad, Matteo Negri, and Marcello Federico. 2012. Detecting Semantic Equivalence and Information Disparity in Cross–lingual Documents. In *Proceedings of the 50th Annual Meeting of the Association for Computational Linguistics (ACL'12)*, pages 120–124, Jeju Island, Korea.

Nicolai Meinshausen and Peter Bühlmann. 2010. Stability selection. *Journal of the Royal Statistical Society: Series B (Statistical Methodology)*, 72(4):417–473, July.

Matteo Negri, Alessandro Marchetti, Yashar Mehdad, Luisa Bentivogli, and Danilo Giampiccolo. 2013. Semeval-2013 Task 8: Cross-lingual Textual Entailment for Content Synchronization. In *Proceedings of the 7th International Workshop on Semantic Evaluation (SemEval 2013)*.

Kishore Papineni, Salim Roukos, Todd Ward, and Wei-jing Zhu. 2002. BLEU: a Method for Automatic Evaluation of Machine Translation. In *Proceedings of the 40th Annual Meeting of the Association for Computational Linguistics (ACL)*, pages 311–318, July.

F. Pedregosa, G. Varoquaux, A. Gramfort, V. Michel, B. Thirion, O. Grisel, M. Blondel, P. Prettenhofer, R. Weiss, V. Dubourg, J. Vanderplas, A. Passos, D. Cournapeau, M. Brucher, M. Perrot, and

E. Duchesnay. 2011. Scikit-learn : Machine Learning in Python. *Journal of Machine Learning Research*, 12:2825–2830.

Slav Petrov, Dipanjan Das, and Ryan McDonald. 2012. A Universal Part-of-Speech Tagset. In *Proceedings of the Eight International Conference on Language Resources and Evaluation (LREC'12)*, Istanbul, Turkey, May. European Language Resources Association (ELRA).

Helmut Schmid. 1995. Improvements in Part-of-Speech Tagging with an Application to German. In *Proceedings of the ACL SIGDAT-Workshop*.

Matthew Snover, Bonnie Dorr, Richard Schwartz, Linnea Micciulla, and John Makhoul. 2006. A Study of Translation Edit Rate with Targeted Human Annotation. In *Association for Machine Translation in the Americas*, pages 223–231.

Radu Soricut, Nguyen Bach, and Ziyuan Wang. 2012. The SDL Language Weaver Systems in the WMT12 Quality Estimation Shared Task. In *Proceedings of the 7th Workshop on Statistical Machine Translation*, pages 145–151.

José G. C. de Souza, Miquel Esplà-Gomis, Marco Turchi, and Matteo Negri. 2013. Exploiting qualitative information from automatic word alignment for cross-lingual nlp tasks. In *The 51st Annual Meeting of the Association for Computational Linguistics - Short Papers (ACL Short Papers 2013)*.

Andreas Stolcke. 2002. SRILM - an extensible language modeling toolkit. In *Proceedings of ICSLP*, pages 901–904, Denver, Colorado.

Christoph Tillmann, Stephan Vogel, Hermann Ney, Alex Zubiaga, and Hassan Sawaf. 1997. Accelerated DP Based Search for Statistical Translation. In *Proceedings of the Fifth European Conference on Speech Communication and Technology*, pages 2667–2670, Rhodos, Greece.

Joseph P. Turian, Luke Shen, and I. Dan Melamed. 2003. Evaluation of machine translation and its evaluation. In *In Proceedings of MT Summit IX*, pages 386–393, New Orleans, LA, USA.

Nicola Ueffing, Klaus Macherey, and Hermann Ney. 2003. Confidence measures for statistical machine translation. In *In Procedings of Machine Translation Summit IX*.

Stephan Vogel, Hermann Ney, and Christoph Tillmann. 1996. HMM-based word alignment in statistical translation. In *Proceedings of the 16th conference on Computational linguistics-Volume 2*, pages 836–841, Morristown, NJ, USA. Association for Computational Linguistics.

The TALP-UPC Approach to System Selection: ASIYA Features and Pairwise Classification using Random Forests

Lluís Formiga[1], **Meritxell Gonzàlez**[1], **Alberto Barrón-Cedeño**[1,2]
José A. R. Fonollosa[1] and **Lluís Màrquez**[1]
[1] TALP Research Center, Universitat Politècnica de Catalunya, Spain
[2] Facultad de Informática, Universidad Politécnica de Madrid, Spain
{lluis.formiga, jose.fonollosa}@upc.edu, {mgonzalez, albarron, lluism}@lsi.upc.edu

Abstract

This paper describes the TALP-UPC participation in the WMT'13 Shared Task on Quality Estimation (QE). Our participation is reduced to task 1.2 on *System Selection*. We used a broad set of features (86 for German-to-English and 97 for English-to-Spanish) ranging from standard QE features to features based on pseudo-references and semantic similarity. We approached system selection by means of pairwise ranking decisions. For that, we learned Random Forest classifiers especially tailored for the problem. Evaluation at development time showed considerably good results in a cross-validation experiment, with Kendall's τ values around 0.30. The results on the test set dropped significantly, raising different discussions to be taken into account.

1 Introduction

In this paper we discuss the TALP-UPC[1] participation in the WMT'13 Shared Task on Quality Estimation (QE). Our participation is circumscribed to task 1.2, which deals with System Selection. Concretely, we were required to rank up to five alternative translations for the same source sentence produced by multiple MT systems, in the absence of any reference translation.

We used a broad set of features; mainly available through the last version of the ASIYA toolkit for MT evaluation[2] (Giménez and Màrquez, 2010). Concretely, we derived 86 features for the German-to-English subtask and 97 features for English-to-Spanish. These features cover different approaches and include standard Quality Estimation features, as provided by the above mentioned ASIYA toolkit and *Quest* (Specia et al., 2010), but also a variety of features based on *pseudo-references* (Soricut and Echihabi, 2010), explicit semantic analysis (Gabrilovich and Markovitch, 2007) and specialized language models. See section 3 for details.

In order to model the ranking problem associated to the system selection task, we adapted it to a classification task of pairwise decisions. We trained Random Forest classifiers (and compared them to SVM classifiers), expanding the work of Formiga et al. (2013), from which a full ranking can be derived and the best system per sentence identified.

Evaluation at development time, using cross-validation, showed considerably good and stable results for both language pairs, with correlation values around 0.30 (Kendall τ coefficient) classification accuracies around 52% (pairwise classification) and 41% (best translation identification). Unfortunately, the results on the test set were significantly lower. Current research is devoted to explain the behavior of the system at testing time. On the one hand, it seems clear that more research regarding the assignment of ties is needed in order to have a robust model. On the other hand, the release of the gold standard annotations for the test set will facilitate a deeper analysis and understanding of the current results.

The rest of the paper is organized as follows. Section 2 describes the ranking models studied for the system selection problem. Section 3 describes the features used for learning. Section 4 presents the setting for parameter optimization and feature selection and the results obtained. Finally, Section 5 summarizes the lessons learned so far and outlines some lines for further research.

2 Ranking Model

We considered two learning strategies to obtain the best translation ranking model: SVM and Random

[1]Center for Language and Speech Technologies and Applications (TALP), Technical University of Catalonia (UPC).

[2]http://asiya.lsi.upc.edu

Forests. Both strategies were based on predicting pairwise quality ranking decisions by means of supervised learning. These decision was motivated from our previous work (Formiga et al., 2013) were we learned that they were more consistent to select the best system (according to human and automatic metrics) compared to absolute regression approaches. In that work we used only the subset of features 1, 2, 3 and 8 described in Section 3. For this shared task we have introduced additional similarity measures (subsets 4 to 7) that feature semantic analysis and automatic alignments between the source and the translations.

The rationale for transforming a ranking problem to a pairwise classification problem has been described previously in several work (Joachims, 2002; Burges et al., 2005). The main idea is to ensemble the features of both individuals and assign a class {-1,1} which tries to predict the pairwise relation among them. For linear based approach this adaptation is as simple to compute the difference between features between all the pairs of the training data.

We used two different learners to perform that task. First, we trained a Support Vector Machine ranker by means of pairwise comparison using the SVM^{light} toolkit (Joachims, 1999), but with the "`-z p`" parameter, which can provide system rankings for all the members of different groups. The learner algorithm was run according to the following parameters: RBF-kernel, expanding the working set by 9 variables at each iteration, for a maximum of 50,000 iterations and with a cache size of 100 for kernel evaluations. The trade-off parameter was empirically set to 0.001. This implementation ignores the ties for the training step as it only focuses in better than/ worse than relations.

Secondly, we used Random Forests (Breiman, 2001), the rationale was the same as ranking-to-pairwise implementation from SVM^{light}. However, SVM^{light} considers two different data preprocessing methods depending on the kernel of the classifier: LINEAR and RBF-Kernel. We used the same data-preprocessing algorithm from SVM^{light} in order to train a Random Forest classifier with ties (three classes: {0,-1,1}) based upon the pairwise relations. We used the Random Forests implementation of scikit-learn toolkit (Pedregosa et al., 2011) with 50 estimators.

Once the classes are given by the Random Forest, we build a graph by means of the adjacency matrix of the pairwise decision. Once the adjacency matrix has been built, we assign the final ranking through a dominance scheme similar to Pighin et al. (2012). In that case, however, there are not topological problems as the pairwise relations are complete across all the edges.

3 Features Sets

We considered a broad set of features: 97 and 86 features for English-to-Spanish (*en-es*) and German-to-English (*de-en*), respectively. We grouped them into the following categories: *baseline QE metrics*, *comparison against pseudo-references*, *source-translation*, and *adapted language models*. We describe them below. Unless noted otherwise, the features apply to both language pairs.

3.1 Baseline Features

The baseline features are composed of well-known quality estimation metrics:

1. *Quest Baseline (QQE)*
   Seventeen baseline features from Specia et al. (2010). This set includes token counts (and their ratio), LM probabilities for source and target sentences, percentage of n-grams in different quartiles of a reference corpus, number of punctuation marks, and fertility ratios. We used these features in the *en-es* partition only.

2. ASIYA*'s QE-based features (AQE)*
   Twenty-six QE features provided by ASIYA (Gonzàlez et al., 2012), comprising bilingual dictionary ambiguity and overlap; ratios concerning chunks, named-entities and PoS; source and candidate LM perplexities and inverse perplexities over lexical forms, chunks and PoS; and out-of-vocabulary word indicators.

3.2 Pseudo-Reference-based Features

Soricut and Echihabi (2010) introduced the concept of pseudo-reference-based features (PR) for translation ranking estimation. The principle is that, in the lack of human-produced references, automatic ones are still good for differentiating good from bad translations. One or more secondary MT systems are required to generate translations starting from the same input, which are taken as pseudo-references. The similarity towards the pseudo-references can be calculated with any evaluation measure or text similarity function, which gives us all feature variants in this group. We consider the following PR-based features:

3. *Derived from* ASIYA*'s metrics (APR)*
   Twenty-three PR features, including GTM-l ($l \in \{1,2,3\}$) to reward different length matching (Melamed et al., 2003), four variants of ROUGE (-L, -S*, -SU* and -W) (Lin and Och, 2004), WER (Nießen et al., 2000), PER (Tillmann et al., 1997), TER, and TER_{base} (i.e., without stemming, synonymy look-up, nor paraphrase support) (Snover et al., 2009), and all the shallow and full parsing measures (i.e., constituency and dependency parsing, PoS, chunking and lemmas) that ASIYA provides either for Spanish or English as target languages.

4. *Lexical similarity (NGM)*
   Cosine and Jaccard coefficient similarity measures for both token and character n-grams considering $n \in [2, 5]$ (i.e., sixteen features). Additionally, one Jaccard-based similarity measure for "pseudo-prefixes" (considering only up to four initial characters for every token).

5. *Based on semantic information (SEM)*
   Twelve features calculated with named entity- and semantic role-based evaluation measures (again, provided by ASIYA). Sentences are automatically annotated using SwiRL (Surdeanu and Turmo, 2005) and BIOS (Surdeanu et al., 2005). We used these features in the *de-en* subtask only.

6. *Explicit semantic analysis (ESA)*
   Two versions of explicit semantic analysis (Gabrilovich and Markovitch, 2007), a semantic similarity measure, built on top of Wikipedia (we used the opening paragraphs of $100k$ Wikipedia articles as in 2010).

3.3 Source-Translation Extra Features

Source-translation features include explicit comparisons between the source sentence and its translation. They are meant to measure how *adequate* the translation is, that is, to what extent the translation expresses the same meaning as the source. Note that a considerable amount of the features described in the *baseline* group (*QQE* and *AQE*) fall in this category. In this subsection we include some extra features we devised to capture source–translation dependencies.

7. *Alignment-based features (ALG / ALGPR)*
   One measure calculated over the aligned words between a candidate translation and the source *(ALG)*; and two measures based on the comparison between these alignments for two different translations (e.g., candidate and pseudo-reference) and the source *(ALGPR)*.[3]

8. *Length model (LeM)*
   A measure to estimate the quality likelihood of a candidate sentence by considering the "expected length" of a proper translation from the source. The measure was introduced by (Pouliquen et al., 2003) to identify document translations. We estimated its parameters over standard MT corpora, including Europarl, Newswire, Newscommentary and UN.

3.4 Adapted Language-Model Features

We interpolated different language models comprising the WMT'12 Monolingual corpora (EPPS, News, UN and Gigafrench for English). The interpolation weights were computed as to minimize the perplexity according to the WMT Translation Task test data (2008-2010)[4]. The features are as follow:

9. *Language Model Features (LM)*
   Two log-probabilities of the translation candidate with respect to the above described interpolated language models over word forms and PoS labels.

4 Experiments and Results

In this section we describe the experiments carried out to select the best feature set, learner, and learner configuration. Additionally, we present the final performance within the task. The setup experiments were addressed doing two separate 10-fold cross validations on the training data and averaging the final results. We evaluated the results through three indicators: Kendall's τ with no

[3] Alignments were computed with the Berkeley aligner https://code.google.com/p/berkeleyaligner/

[4] http://www.statmt.org/wmt13/translation-task.html

penalization for the ties, accuracy in determining the pairwise relationship between candidate translations, and global accuracy in selecting the best candidate for each source sentence.

First, we compared our SVM learner against Random Forests with the two variants of data preprocessing (LINEAR and RBF). In terms of Kendall's τ, we found that the Random Forests (RF) were clearly better compared to SVM implementation. Concretely, depending on the final feature set, we found that RF achieved a τ between 0.23 and 0.29 while SVM achieved a τ between 0.23 and 0.25. With respect to the accuracy measures we did not find noticeable differences between methods as their results moved from 49% to 52%. However, considering the accuracy in terms of selecting only the best system there was a difference of two points (42.2% vs. 40.0%) between methods, being RF again the best system. Regarding the pairwise preprocessing the results between RBF and LINEAR based preprocessing were comparable, being RBF slightly better than LINEAR. Hence, we selected Random Forests with RBF pairwise preprocessing as our final learner.

de-en	τ with ties		*Accuracy*	
	Ignored	*Penalized*	*All*	*Best*
AQE+LeM+ALGPR+LM	***33.70***	***15.72***	***52.56***	***41.57***
AQE+SEM+LM	***32.49***	***14.61***	***52.72***	***40.92***
AQE+LeM+ALGPR+ESA+LM	32.08	13.81	52.71	41.37
AQE+ALG+ESA+SEM+LM	32.06	13.96	52.20	40.64
AQE+ALG+LM	31.97	14.29	52.00	40.83
AQE+LeM+ALGPR+SEM+LM	31.93	13.57	52.52	40.98
AQE+ESA+SEM+LM	31.79	13.68	52.50	40.76
AQE+LeM+ALGPR+ESA+SEM+LM	31.72	14.01	52.65	40.83
AQE+ALG+SEM+LM	31.17	12.86	52.18	40.51
AQE+ALG+SEM	30.72	12.58	51.75	39.66
AQE+LeM+ALGPR+ESA+SEM	30.47	11.79	51.85	39.58
AQE+ESA+LM	30.31	12.23	52.60	40.69
AQE+ALG+ESA+LM	30.26	12.40	52.03	40.99
AQE+LeM+ALGPR	30.24	11.83	51.96	40.42
AQE+LeM+ALGPR+SEM	30.23	11.84	52.10	40.32
AQE+LeM+ALGPR+ESA	29.89	11.87	51.83	40.07
AQE+ALG+ESA	29.81	11.30	51.37	39.47
AQE+SEM	29.80	12.06	51.75	39.52
AQE+NGM+APR+ESA+SEM+LM	29.34	10.58	51.33	38.55
AQE+ESA+SEM	29.31	11.46	51.66	39.24
AQE+ESA	29.13	11.12	51.82	39.90
AQE+ALG+ESA+SEM	28.35	10.32	51.37	38.98
AQE+NGM+APR+ESA+SEM	27.55	9.22	51.01	38.12

Table 1: Set-up results for *de-en*

For the feature selection process, we considered the most relevant combinations of feature groups. Table 1 shows the set-up results for the *de-en* subtask and Table 2 shows the results for the *en-es* subtask.

In terms of τ we observed similar results between the two language pairs. However accuracies for the *de-en* subtask were one point above the ones for *en-es*. Regarding the features used, we found that the best feature combination to use was composed of: *i*) a baseline QE feature set (Asiya or Quest) but not both of them, *ii*) Length Model, *iii*) Pseudo-reference aligned based features and the use of *iv*) adapted language models. However, within the *de-en* subtask, we found that substituting Length Model and Aligned Pseudo-references by the features based on Semantic Roles (SEM) could bring marginally better accuracy. We also noticed that the learner was sensitive to the features used so selecting the appropriate set of features was crucial to achieve a good performance.

en-es	τ with ties		*Accuracy*	
	Ignored	*Penalized*	*All*	*Best*
QQE+LeM+ALGPR+LM	***33.81***	***15.87***	***51.66***	***41.01***
AQE+LeM+ALGPR+LM	***33.75***	***16.44***	***51.56***	***41.52***
QQE+AQE+LM	32.71	14.59	51.18	41.02
QQE+AQE+LM+ESA	32.69	15.30	51.48	41.30
QQE+AQE+LeM+ALGPR+LM+ESA	32.63	13.64	51.39	40.48
QQE+AQE+LeM+ALGPR+LM	32.41	14.06	51.43	40.49
QQE+LeM+ALGPR+LM+ESA	31.66	13.39	51.37	41.05
QQE+AQE+ALG+LM	31.46	13.62	51.28	41.29
AQE+LeM+ALGPR+LM+ESA	31.29	14.10	51.55	41.43
QQE+AQE+ALG+LM+ESA	31.25	13.58	51.64	41.66
QQE+AQE+NGM+APR+LM+ESA	30.58	12.48	50.93	40.66
QQE+AQE+NGM+APR+LM	29.94	12.54	50.95	40.25
QQE+AQE	28.98	10.92	49.97	39.65
QQE+AQE+LeM+ALGPR	28.94	10.48	49.99	39.71
QQE+AQE+NGM+ESA+LM	28.85	11.88	50.90	40.22
AQE+LeM+ALGPR	28.81	10.11	50.06	40.01
QQE+AQE+ESA	28.68	10.31	49.96	39.27
AQE+ESA	28.67	10.81	50.35	39.18
AQE	28.65	10.68	49.76	38.90
QQE+AQE+ALG	28.47	9.63	49.67	39.66
QQE+AQE+NGM+APR+ESA	28.43	9.75	49.67	38.74
QQE+AQE+NGM	27.23	9.10	49.44	38.98
QQE+AQE+ALG+ESA	27.08	7.93	50.26	39.71
QQE+AQE+LeM+ALGPR+ESA	27.03	8.65	50.35	40.49
AQE+LeM+ALGPR+ESA	26.96	8.26	50.30	39.47
QQE+AQE+NGM+ESA	26.59	7.56	49.52	38.62
QQE+AQE+NGM+APR	25.39	6.97	49.90	39.53

Table 2: Setup results for *en-es*

de-en	**τ (ties penalized,**
ID	**non-symmetric between [-1,1])**
Best	0.31
UPC AQE+SEM+LM	0.11
UPC AQE+LeM+ALGPR+LM	0.10
Baseline Random-ranks-with-ties	-0.12
Worst	-0.49

Table 3: Official results for the *de-en* subtask (ties penalized)

en-es	**τ (ties penalized,**
ID	**non-symmetric between [-1,1])**
Best	0.15
UPC QQE+LeM+ALGPR+LM	-0.03
UPC AQE+LeM+ALGPR+LM	-0.06
Baseline Random-ranks-with-ties	-0.23
Worst	-0.63

Table 4: Official results for the *en-es* subtask (ties penalized)

In Tables 3, 4, 5 and 6 we present the official results for the WMT'13 Quality Estimation Task, in all evaluation variants. In each table we compare to the best/worst performing systems and also to the official baseline.

We can observe that in general the results on the test sets drop significantly, compared to our

de-en ID	τ (ties ignored, symmetric between [-1,1])	Non-ties / (882 dec.)
Best	0.31	882
UPC AQE+SEM+LM	0.27	768
UPC AQE+LeM+ALGPR+LM	0.24	788
Baseline Random-ranks-with-ties	0.08	718
Worst	-0.03	558

Table 5: Official results for the *de-en* subtask (ties ignored)

en-es ID	τ (ties ignored, symmetric between [-1,1])	Non-ties / (882 dec.)
Best	0.23	192
UPC QQE+LeM+ALGPR+LM	0.11	554
UPC AQE+LeM+ALGPR+LM	0.08	554
Baseline Random-ranks-with-ties	0.03	507
Worst	-0.11	633

Table 6: Official results for the *en-es* subtask (ties ignored)

set-up experiments. Restricting to the evaluation setting in which ties are not penalized (i.e., corresponding to our setting during system and parameter tuning), we can see that the results corresponding to *de-en* (Table 5) are comparable to our set-up results and close to the best performing system. However, in the *en-es* language pair the final results are comparatively much lower (Table 6). We find this behavior strange. In this respect, we analyzed the inter-annotator agreement within the gold standard. Concretely we computed the Cohen's κ for all overlapping annotations concerning at least 4 systems for both language pairs. The results of our analysis are presented in Table 7 and therefore it confirms our hypothesis that en-es annotations had more noise providing an explanation for the accuracy decrease of our QE models and setting the subtask into a more challenging scenario. However, further research will be needed to analyze other factors such as oracles and improvement on automatic metrics prediction and reliability compared to linguistic expert annotators.

Another remaining issue for our research concerns investigating better ways to deal with ties, as their penalization lowered our results dramatically. In this direction we plan to work further on

# of systems	Lang	Cohen's κ	# of elements
4	en-es	0.210	560
	de-en	0.369	640
5	en-es	0.211	130
	de-en	0.375	145

Table 7: Golden standard test set agreement coefficients measured by Cohen's κ

the adjacency matrix reconstruction heuristics and presenting the features to the learner in a structured form.

5 Conclusions

This paper described the TALP-UPC participation in the WMT'13 Shared Task. We approached the Quality Estimation task based on system selection, where different systems have to be ranked according to their quality. We derive a full ranking and identify the best system per sentence on the basis of Random Forest classifiers.

After the model set-up, we observed considerably good and robust results for both translation directions, German-to-English and English-to-Spanish: Kendall's τ around 0.30 as well as accuracies around 52% on pairwise classification and 41% on best translation identification. However, the results over the official test set were significantly lower. We have found that the low inter-annotator agreement between users on that set might provide an explanation to the poor performance of our QE models.

Our current efforts are centered on explaining the behavior of our QE models when facing the official test sets. We are following two directions: *i*) studying the ties' impact to come out with a more robust model and *ii*) revise the English-to-Spanish gold standard annotations in terms of correlation with automatic metrics to facilitate a deeper understanding of the results.

Acknowledgments

Acknowledgements

This work has been partially funded by the Spanish *Ministerio de Economía y Competitividad*, under contracts TEC2012-38939-C03-02 and TIN2009-14675-C03, as well as from the European Regional Development Fund (ERDF/FEDER) and the European Community's FP7 (2007-2013) program under the following grants: 247762 (FAUST, FP7-ICT-2009-4-247762) and 246016 (ERCIM "Alain Bensoussan" Fellowship).

References

Leo Breiman. 2001. Random forests. *Machine Learning*, 45(1):5–32.

Chris Burges, Tal Shaked, Erin Renshaw, Ari Lazier, Matt Deeds, Nicole Hamilton, and Greg Hullender.

2005. Learning to rank using gradient descent. In *Proceedings of the 22nd international conference on Machine learning*, pages 89–96. ACM.

Lluís Formiga, Lluís Màrquez, and Jaume Pujantell. 2013. Real-life translation quality estimation for mt system selection. In *Proceedings of 14th Machine Translation Summit (MT Summit)*, Nice, France, September. EAMT.

Evgeniy Gabrilovich and Shaul Markovitch. 2007. Computing Semantic Relatedness Using Wikipedia-based Explicit Semantic Analysis. In *Proceedings of the 20th International Joint Conference on Artificial Intelligence*, pages 1606–1611, San Francisco, CA, USA. Morgan Kaufmann Publishers Inc.

Jesús Giménez and Lluís Màrquez. 2010. Asiya: An Open Toolkit for Automatic Machine Translation (Meta-)Evaluation. *The Prague Bulletin of Mathematical Linguistics*, (94):77–86.

Meritxell Gonzàlez, Jesús Giménez, and Lluís Màrquez. 2012. A graphical interface for mt evaluation and error analysis. In *Proceedings of the ACL 2012 System Demonstrations*, pages 139–144, Jeju Island, Korea, July. Association for Computational Linguistics.

Thorsten Joachims, 1999. *Advances in Kernel Methods – Support Vector Learning*, chapter Making large-Scale SVM Learning Practical. MIT Press.

Thorsten Joachims. 2002. Optimizing search engines using clickthrough data. In ACM, editor, *Proceedings of the ACM Conference on Knowledge Discovery and Data Mining (KDD)*.

Chin-Yew Lin and Franz Josef Och. 2004. Automatic evaluation of machine translation quality using longest common subsequence and skip-bigram statistics. In *Proceedings of the 42nd Meeting of the Association for Computational Linguistics (ACL'04), Main Volume*, pages 605–612, Barcelona, Spain, July.

I. Dan Melamed, Ryan Green, and Joseph P. Turian. 2003. Precision and recall of machine translation. In *HLT-NAACL*.

Sonja Nießen, Franz Josef Och, Gregor Leusch, and Hermann Ney. 2000. An evaluation tool for machine translation: Fast evaluation for mt research. In *Proceedings of the 2nd Language Resources and Evaluation Conference (LREC 2000)*.

F. Pedregosa, G. Varoquaux, A. Gramfort, V. Michel, B. Thirion, O. Grisel, M. Blondel, P. Prettenhofer, R. Weiss, V. Dubourg, J. Vanderplas, A. Passos, D. Cournapeau, M. Brucher, M. Perrot, and E. Duchesnay. 2011. Scikit-learn: Machine Learning in Python . *Journal of Machine Learning Research*, 12:2825–2830.

Daniele Pighin, Lluís Formiga, and Lluís Màrquez. 2012. A graph-based strategy to streamline translation quality assessments. In *Proceedings of the Tenth Conference of the Association for Machine Translation in the Americas (AMTA'2012)*, San Diego, USA, October. AMTA.

Bruno Pouliquen, Ralf Steinberger, and Camelia Ignat. 2003. Automatic Identification of Document Translations in Large Multilingual Document Collections. In *Proceedings of the International Conference on Recent Advances in Natural Language Processing (RANLP-2003)*, pages 401–408, Borovets, Bulgaria.

Matthew G. Snover, Nitin Madnani, Bonnie Dorr, and Richard Schwartz. 2009. TER-Plus: Paraphrase, Semantic, and Alignment Enhancements to Translation Edit Rate. *Machine Translation*, 23(2):117–127.

Radu Soricut and Abdessamad Echihabi. 2010. Trustrank: Inducing trust in automatic translations via ranking. In *Proceedings of the 48th Annual Meeting of the Association for Computational Linguistics*, pages 612–621, Uppsala, Sweden, July. Association for Computational Linguistics.

Lucia Specia, Dhwaj Raj, and Marco Turchi. 2010. Machine Translation Evaluation Versus Quality Estimation. *Machine Translation*, 24:39–50, March.

Mihai Surdeanu and Jordi Turmo. 2005. Semantic Role Labeling Using Complete Syntactic Analysis. In *Proceedings of CoNLL Shared Task*.

Mihai Surdeanu, Jordi Turmo, and Eli Comelles. 2005. Named Entity Recognition from Spontaneous Open-Domain Speech. In *Proceedings of the 9th International Conference on Speech Communication and Technology (Interspeech)*.

C. Tillmann, S. Vogel, H. Ney, A. Zubiaga, and H Sawaf. 1997. Accelerated dp based search for statistical translation. In *Proceedings of European Conference on Speech Communication and Technology*.

Quality Estimation for Machine Translation Using the Joint Method of Evaluation Criteria and Statistical Modeling

Aaron Li-Feng Han
hanlifengaaron@gmail.com

Yi Lu
mb25435@umac.mo

Derek F. Wong
derekfw@umac.mo

Lidia S. Chao
lidiasc@umac.mo

Liangye He
wutianshui0515@gmail.com

Junwen Xing
mb15470@umac.mo

Natural Language Processing & Portuguese-Chinese Machine Translation Laboratory
Department of Computer and Information Science
University of Macau, Macau S.A.R. China

Abstract

This paper is to introduce our participation in the WMT13 shared tasks on Quality Estimation for machine translation without using reference translations. We submitted the results for Task 1.1 (sentence-level quality estimation), Task 1.2 (system selection) and Task 2 (word-level quality estimation). In Task 1.1, we used an enhanced version of BLEU metric without using reference translations to evaluate the translation quality. In Task 1.2, we utilized a probability model Naïve Bayes (NB) as a classification algorithm with the features borrowed from the traditional evaluation metrics. In Task 2, to take the contextual information into account, we employed a discriminative undirected probabilistic graphical model Conditional random field (CRF), in addition to the NB algorithm. The training experiments on the past WMT corpora showed that the designed methods of this paper yielded promising results especially the statistical models of CRF and NB. The official results show that our CRF model achieved the highest F-score 0.8297 in binary classification of Task 2.

1 Introduction

Due to the fast development of Machine translation, different automatic evaluation methods for the translation quality have been proposed in recent years. One of the categories is the lexical similarity based metric. This kind of metrics includes the edit distance based method, such as WER (Su et al., 1992), Multi-reference WER (Nießen et al., 2000), PER (Tillmann et al., 1997), the works of (Akiba, et al., 2001), (Leusch et al., 2006) and (Wang and Manning, 2012); the precision based method, such as BLEU (Papineni et al., 2002), NIST (Doddington, 2002), and SIA (Liu and Gildea, 2006); recall based method, such as ROUGE (Lin and Hovy 2003); and the combination of precision and recall, such as GTM (Turian et al., 2003), METEOR (Lavie and Agarwal, 2007), BLANC (Lita et al., 2005), AMBER (Chen and Kuhn, 2011), PORT (Chen et al., 2012b), and LEPOR (Han et al., 2012).

Another category is the using of linguistic features. This kind of metrics includes the syntactic similarity, such as the POS information used by TESLA (Dahlmeier et al., 2011), (Liu et al., 2010) and (Han et al., 2013), phrase information used by (Povlsen, et al., 1998) and (Echizen-ya and Araki, 2010), sentence structure used by (Owczarzak et al., 2007); the semantic similarity, such as textual entailment used by (Mirkin et al., 2009) and (Castillo and Estrella, 2012), Synonyms used by METEOR (Lavie and Agarwal, 2007), (Wong and Kit, 2012), (Chan and Ng, 2008); paraphrase used by (Snover et al., 2009).

The traditional evaluation metrics tend to evaluate the hypothesis translation as compared to the reference translations that are usually offered by human efforts. However, in the practice, there is usually no golden reference for the translated documents, especially on the internet works. How to evaluate the quality of automatically translated documents or sentences without using the reference translations becomes a new challenge in front of the NLP researchers.

ADJ	ADP	ADV	CONJ	DET	NOUN	NUM	PRON	PRT	VERB	X	.
ADJ	PREP, PREP/DEL	ADV, NEG	CC, CCAD, CCNEG, CQUE, CSUBF, CSUBI, CSUBX	ART	NC, NMEA, NMON, NP, PERCT, UMMX	CARD, CODE, QU	DM, INT, PPC, PPO, PPX, REL	SE	VCLIger, VLfin, VCLIinf, VLger, VCLIfin, VLinf, VEadj, VMadj, VEfin, VMfin, VEger, VMger, VEinf, VMinf, VHadj, VSadj, VHfin, VSfin, VHger, VSger, VHinf, VSinf VLadj,	ACRNM, ALFP, ALFS, FO, ITJN, ORD, PAL, PDEL, PE, PNC, SYM	BACKSLASH, CM, COLON, DASH, DOTS, FS, LP, QT, RP, SEMICO-LON, SLASH

Table 1: Developed POS mapping for Spanish and universal tagset

2 Related Works

Gamon et al. (2005) perform a research about reference-free SMT evaluation method on sentence level. This work uses both linear and non-linear combinations of language model and SVM classifier to find the badly translated sentences. Albrecht and Hwa (2007) conduct the sentence-level MT evaluation utilizing the regression learning and based on a set of weaker indicators of fluency and adequacy as pseudo references. Specia and Gimenez (2010) use the Confidence Estimation features and a learning mechanism trained on human annotations. They show that the developed models are highly biased by difficulty level of the input segment, therefore they are not appropriate for comparing multiple systems that translate the same input segments. Specia et al. (2010) discussed the issues between the traditional machine translation evaluation and the quality estimation tasks recently proposed. The traditional MT evaluation metrics require reference translations in order to measure a score reflecting some aspects of its quality, e.g. the BLEU and NIST. The quality estimation addresses this problem by evaluating the quality of translations as a prediction task and the features are usually extracted from the source sentences and target (translated) sentences. They also show that the developed methods correlate better with human judgments at segment level as compared to traditional metrics. Popović et al. (2011) perform the MT evaluation using the IBM model one with the information of morphemes, 4-gram POS and lexicon probabilities. Mehdad et al. (2012) use the cross-lingual textual entailment to push semantics into the MT evaluation without using reference translations. This evaluation work mainly focuses on the adequacy estimation. Avramidis (2012) performs an automatic sentence-level ranking of multiple machine translations using the features of verbs, nouns, sentences, subordinate clauses and punctuation occurrences to derive the adequacy information. Other descriptions of the MT Quality Estimation tasks can be gained in the works of (Callison-Burch et al., 2012) and (Felice and Specia, 2012).

3 Tasks Information

This section introduces the different sub-tasks we participated in the Quality Estimation task of WMT 13 and the methods we used.

3.1 Task 1-1 Sentence-level QE

Task 1.1 is to score and rank the post-editing effort of the automatically translated English-Spanish sentences without offering the reference translation.

Firstly, we develop the English and Spanish POS tagset mapping as shown in Table 1. The 75 Spanish POS tags yielded by the Treetagger (Schmid, 1994) are mapped to the 12 universal tags developed in (Petrov et al., 2012). The English POS tags are extracted from the parsed sentences using the Berkeley parser (Petrov et al., 2006).

Secondly, the enhanced version of BLEU (EBLEU) formula is designed with the factors of modified length penalty (MLP), precision, and recall, the h and s representing the lengths of hypothesis (target) sentence and source sentence respectively. We use the harmonic mean of precision and recall, i.e. $H(\alpha R_n, \beta P_n)$. We assign the weight values $\alpha = 1$ and $= 9$, i.e. higher weight value is assigned to precision, which is different with METEOR (the inverse values).

$$EBLEU = 1 - MLP \times exp(\sum w_n log(H(\alpha R_n, \beta P_n))) \quad (1)$$

$$MLP = \begin{cases} e^{1-\frac{s}{h}} & if\ h < s \\ e^{1-\frac{h}{s}} & if\ h \geq s \end{cases} \quad (2)$$

$$P_n = \frac{\#common\ ngram\ chunk}{\#\ ngram\ chunk\ in\ target\ sentence} \quad (3)$$

$$R_n = \frac{\#common\ ngram\ chunk}{\#\ ngram\ chunk\ in\ source\ sentence} \quad (4)$$

Lastly, the scoring for the post-editing effort of the automatically translated sentences is performed on the extracted POS sequences of the source and target languages. The evaluated performance of EBLEU on WMT 12 corpus is shown in Table 2 using the Mean-Average-Error (MAE), Root-Mean-Squared-Error (RMSE).

	Precision	Recall	MLP	EBLEU
MAE	0.17	0.19	0.25	0.16
RMSE	0.22	0.24	0.30	0.21

Table 2: Performance on the WMT12 corpus

The official evaluation scores of the testing results on WMT 13 corpus are shown in Table 3. The testing results show similar scores as compared to the training scores (the MAE score is around 0.16 and the RMSE score is around 0.22), which shows a stable performance of the developed model EBLEU. However, the performance of EBLEU is not satisfactory currently as shown in the Table 2 and Table 3. This is due to the fact that we only used the POS information as linguistic feature. This could be further improved by the combination of lexical information and other linguistic features such as the sentence structure, phrase similarity, and text entailment.

	MAE	RMSE	DeltaAvg	Spearman Corr
EBLEU	16.97	21.94	2.74	0.11
Baseline SVM	14.81	18.22	8.52	0.46

Table 3: Performance on the WMT13 corpus

3.2 Task 1-2 System Selection

Task 1.2 is the system selection task on EN-ES and DE-EN language pairs. Participants are required to rank up to five alternative translations for the same source sentence produced by multiple translation systems.

Firstly, we describe the two variants of EBLEU method for this task. We score the five alternative translation sentences as compared to the source sentence according to the closeness of their POS sequences. The German POS is also extracted using Berkeley parser (Petrov et al., 2006). The mapping of German POS to universal POS tagset is using the developed one in the work of (Petrov et al., 2012). When we convert the absolute scores into the corresponding rank values, the variant EBLEU-I means that we use five fixed intervals (with the span from 0 to 1) to achieve the alignment as shown in Table 4.

[1,0.4)	[0.4, 0.3)	[0.3, 0.25)	[0.25, 0.2)	[0.2, 0]
5	4	3	2	1

Table 4: Convert absolute scores into ranks

The alignment work from absolute scores to rank values shown in Table 4 is empirically determined. We have made a statistical work on the absolute scores yielded by our metrics, and each of the intervals shown in Table 4 covers the similar number of sentence scores.

On the other hand, in the metric EBLEU-A, "A" means average. The absolute sentence edit scores are converted into the five rank values with the same number (average number). For instance, if there are 1000 sentence scores in total then each rank level (from 1 to 5) will gain 200 scores from the best to the worst.

Secondly, we introduce the NB-LPR model used in this task. NB-LPR means the Naïve Bayes classification algorithm using the features of Length penalty (introduced in previous section), Precision, Recall and Rank values. NB-LPR considers each of its features independently. Let's see the conditional probability that is also known as Bayes' rule. If the $p(x|c)$ is given, then the $p(c|x)$ can be calculated as follows:

$$p(c|x) = \frac{p(x|c)p(c)}{p(x)} \quad (5)$$

Given a data point identified as $X(x_1, x_2, \dots, x_n)$ and the classifications $C(c_1, c_2, \dots, c_n)$, Bayes' rule can be applied to this statement:

$$p(c_i|x_1, x_2, \dots, x_n) = \frac{p(x_1, x_2, \dots, x_n|c_i)p(c_i)}{p(x_1, x_2, \dots, x_n)} \quad (6)$$

As in many practical applications, parameter estimation for NB-LPR model uses the method of maximum likelihood. For details of Naïve Bayes algorithm, see the works of (Zhang, 2004) and (Harrington, 2012).

Thirdly, the SVM-LPR model means the support vector machine classification algorithm using the features of Length penalty, Precision, Recall and Rank values, i.e. the same features as in NB-LPR. SVM solves the nonlinear classification problem by mapping the data from a low dimensional space to a high dimensional space using the Kernel methods. In the projected high dimensional space, the problem usually becomes a linear one, which is easier to solve. SVM is also called maximum interval classifier because it tries to find the optimized hyper plane that separates different classes with the largest margin, which is usually a quadratic optimization problem. Let's see the formula below, we should find the points with the smallest margin to the hyper plane and then maximize this margin.

$$arg\,max_{w,b}\left\{min_n(label \cdot (w^T x + b)) \cdot \frac{1}{\|w\|}\right\} \quad (7)$$

where $\boldsymbol{w}$ is normal to the hyper plane, $||\boldsymbol{w}||$ is the Euclidean norm of $\boldsymbol{w}$, and $|b|/||\boldsymbol{w}||$ is the perpendicular distance from the hyper plane to the origin. For details of SVM, see the works of (Cortes and Vapnik, 1995) and (Burges, 1998).

EN-ES					
NB-LPR			SVM-LPR		
MAE	RMSE	Time	MAE	RMSE	Time
.315	.399	.40s	.304	.551	60.67s
DE-EN					
NB-LPR			SVM-LPR		
MAE	RMSE	Time	MAE	RMSE	Time
.318	.401	.79s	.312	.559	111.7s

Table 5: NB-LPR and SVM-LPR training

In the training stage, we used all the officially released data of WMT 09, 10, 11 and 12 for the EN-ES and DE-EN language pairs. We used the WEKA (Hall et al., 2009) data mining software to implement the NB and SVM algorithms. The training scores are shown in Table 5. The NB-LPR performs lower scores than the SVM-LPR but faster than SVM-LPR.

Methods	DE-EN		EN-ES	
	Tau(ties penalized)	|Tau|(ties ignored)	Tau(ties penalized)	|Tau|(ties ignored)
EBLEU-I	-0.38	-0.03	-0.35	0.02
EBLEU-A	N/A	N/A	-0.27	N/A
NB-LPR	-0.49	0.01	N/A	**0.07**
Baseline	-0.12	0.08	-0.23	0.03

Table 6: QE Task 1.2 testing scores

The official testing scores are shown in Table 6. Each task is allowed to submit up to two systems and we submitted the results using the methods of EBLEU and NB-LPR. The performance of NB-LPR on EN-ES language pair shows higher Tau score (0.07) than the baseline system score (0.03) when the ties are ignored. Because of the number limitation of submitted systems for each task, we did not submit the SVM-LPR results. However, the training experiments prove that the SVM-LPR model performs better than the NB-LPR model though SVM-LPR takes more time to run.

3.3 Task 2 Word-level QE

Task 2 is the word-level quality estimation of automatically translated news sentences from English to Spanish without given reference translations. Participants are required to judge each translated word by assigning a two- or multi-class labels. In the binary classification, a good or a bad label should be judged, where "bad" indicates the need for editing the token. In the multi-class classification, the labels include "keep", "delete" and "substitute". In addition to the NB method, in this task, we utilized a discriminative undirected probabilistic graphical model, i.e. Conditional Random Field (CRF).

CRF is early employed by Lefferty (Lefferty et al., 2001) to deal with the labeling problems of sequence data, and is widely used later by other researchers. As the preparation for CRF definition, we assume that X is a variable representing the input sequence, and Y is another variable representing the corresponding labels to be attached to X. The two variables interact as conditional probability $p(Y|X)$ mathematically. Then the definition of CRF: Let a graph model $G = (V, E)$ comprise a set V of vertices or nodes together with a set E of edges or lines and $Y = \{Y_v | v \in V\}$, such that Y is indexed by the vertices of G, then (X, Y) shapes a CRF model. This set meets the following form:

$$P_\theta(Y|X) \propto exp \left(\textstyle\sum_{e\in E,k} \lambda_k f_k(e, Y|_e, X) + \sum_{v\in V,k} \mu_k g_k(v, Y|_v, X)\right) \quad (8)$$

where X and Y represent the data sequence and label sequence respectively; f_k and g_k are the features to be defined; λ_k and μ_k are the parameters trained from the datasets. We used the tool CRF++[1] to implement the CRF algorithm. The features we used for the NB and CRF are shown in Table 7. We firstly trained the CRF and NB models on the officially released training corpus (produced by Moses and annotated by computing TER with some tweaks). Then we removed the truth labels in the training corpus (we call it pseudo test corpus) and labeled each word using the derived training models. The test results on the pseudo test corpus are shown in Table 8,

[1] https://code.google.com/p/crfpp/

which specifies CRF performs better than NB algorithm.

$U_n, n \in (-4,3)$	Unigram, from antecedent 4th to subsequent 3rd token
$B_{n-1,n}, n \in (-1,2)$	Bigram, from antecedent 2nd to subsequent 2nd token
$B_{-1,1}$	Jump bigram, antecedent and subsequent token
$T_{n-1,n,n+1}, n \in (-1,1)$	Trigram, from antecedent 2nd to subsequent 2nd token

Table 7: Developed features

Binary			
CRF		NB	
Training	Accuracy	Training	Accuracy
Itera=108 Time=2.48s	0.944	Time=0.59s	0.941
Multi-classes			
CRF		NB	
Training	Accuracy	Training	Accuracy
Itera=106 Time=3.67s	0.933	Time=0.55s	0.929

Table 8: Performance on pseudo test corpus

The official testing scores of Task 2 are shown in Table 9. We include also the results of other participants (CNGL and LIG) and their approaches.

	Binary			Multiclass
Methods	Pre	Recall	F1	Acc
CNGL-dMEMM	0.7392	0.9261	0.8222	0.7162
CNGL-MEMM	0.7554	0.8581	0.8035	0.7116
LIG-All	N/A	N/A	N/A	0.7192
LIG-FS	0.7885	0.8644	0.8247	**0.7207**
LIG-BOOSTING	0.7779	0.8843	0.8276	N/A
NB	**0.8181**	0.4937	0.6158	0.5174
CRF	0.7169	**0.9846**	**0.8297**	0.7114

Table 9: QE Task 2 official testing scores

The results show that our method CRF yields a higher recall score than other systems in binary judgments task, and this leads to the highest F1 score (harmonic mean of precision and recall). The recall value reflects the loyalty to the truth data. The augmented feature set designed in this paper allows the CRF to take the contextual information into account, and this contributes much to the recall score. On the other hand, the accuracy score of CRF in multiclass evaluation is lower than LIG-FS method.

4 Conclusions

This paper describes the algorithms and features we used in the WMT 13 Quality Estimation tasks. In the sentence-level QE task (Task 1.1), we develop an enhanced version of BLEU metric, and this shows a potential usage for the traditional evaluation criteria. In the newly proposed system selection task (Task 1.2) and word-level QE task (Task 2), we explore the performances of several statistical models including NB, SVM, and CRF, of which the CRF performs best, the NB performs lower than SVM but much faster than SVM. The official results show that the CRF model yields the highest F-score 0.8297 in binary classification judgment of word-level QE task.

Acknowledgments

The authors are grateful to the Science and Technology Development Fund of Macau and the Research Committee of the University of Macau for the funding support for our research, under the reference No. 017/2009/A and RG060/09-10S/CS/FST. The authors also wish to thank the anonymous reviewers for many helpful comments.

References

Akiba, Yasuhiro, Kenji Imamura, and Eiichiro Sumita. 2001. Using Multiple Edit Distances to Automatically Rank Machine Translation Output. In *Proceedings of the MT Summit VIII*, Santiago de Compostela, Spain.

Albrecht, Joshua, and Rebecca Hwa. 2007. Regression for sentence-level MT evaluation with pseudo references. *ACL*. Vol. 45. No. 1.

Avramidis, Eleftherios. 2012. Comparative quality estimation: Automatic sentence-level ranking of multiple machine translation outputs. In *Proceedings of 24th International Conference on Computational Linguistics* (COLING), pages 115–132, Mumbai, India.

Burges, Christopher J. C. 1998. A Tutorial on Support Vector Machines for Pattern Recognition. J. *Data Min. Knowl. Discov.* Volume 2 Issue 2, June 1998, 121-167. Kluwer Academic Publishers Hingham, MA, USA.

Callison-Burch, Chris, Philipp Koehn, Christof Monz, Matt Post, Radu Soricut, and Lucia Specia. 2012. Findings of the 2012 workshop on statistical machine translation. In *Proceedings of the Seventh*

Workshop on Statistical Machine Translation, pages 10–51, Montréal, Canada, June.

Castillo, Julio and Paula Estrella. 2012. Semantic Textual Similarity for MT evaluation, *Proceedings of the 7th Workshop on Statistical Machine Translation* (WMT2012), pages 52–58, Montre´al, Canada, June 7-8. Association for Computational Linguistics.

Chan, Yee Seng and Hwee Tou Ng. 2008. MAXSIM: A maximum similarity metric for machine translation evaluation. In *Proceedings of ACL 2008: HLT*, pages 55–62. Association for Computational Linguistics.

Chen, Boxing and Roland Kuhn. 2011. Amber: A modified bleu, enhanced ranking metric. In *Proceedings of the Sixth Workshop on Statistical Machine translation of the Association for Computational Linguistics(ACL-WMT)*, pages 71-77, Edinburgh, Scotland, UK.

Chen, Boxing, Roland Kuhn and Samuel Larkin. 2012. PORT: a Precision-Order-Recall MT Evaluation Metric for Tuning, *Proceedings of the 50th Annual Meeting of the Association for Computational Linguistics*, pages 930–939, Jeju, Republic of Korea, 8-14 July.

Cortes, Corinna and Vladimir Vapnik. 1995. Support-Vector Networks, J. *Machine Learning*, Volume 20, issue 3, pp 273-297. Kluwer Academic Publishers, Boston. Manufactured in The Netherlands.

Dahlmeier, Daniel, Chang Liu, and Hwee Tou Ng. 2011. TESLA at WMT2011: Translation evaluation and tunable metric. In *Proceedings of the Sixth Workshop on Statistical Machine Translation, Association for Computational Linguistics* (ACL-WMT), pages 78-84, Edinburgh, Scotland, UK.

Doddington, George. 2002. Automatic evaluation of machine translation quality using n-gram cooccurrence statistics. In *Proceedings of the second international conference on Human Language Technology Research* (HLT '02). Morgan Kaufmann Publishers Inc., San Francisco, CA, USA, 138-145.

Echizen-ya, Hiroshi and Kenji Araki. 2010. Automatic evaluation method for machine translation using noun-phrase chunking. In *Proceedings of ACL 2010*, pages 108–117. Association for Computational Linguistics.

Gamon, Michael, Anthony Aue, and Martine Smets. 2005. Sentence-level MT evaluation without reference translations: Beyond language modeling. *Proceedings of EAMT*.

Hall, Mark, Eibe Frank, Geoffrey Holmes, Bernhard Pfahringer, Peter Reutemann, Ian H. Witten. 2009. The WEKA data mining software: An update. *SIGKDD Explorations*, 11.

Han, Aaron Li-Feng, Derek F. Wong and Lidia S. Chao. 2012. LEPOR: A Robust Evaluation Metric for Machine Translation with Augmented Factors. *Proceedings of the 24th International Conference on Computational Linguistics* (COLING 2012: Posters), Mumbai, India.

Han, Aaron Li-Feng, Derek F. Wong, Lidia S. Chao, Liangye He, Yi Lu, Junwen Xing and Xiaodong Zeng. 2013. Language-independent Model for Machine Translation Evaluation with Reinforced Factors. *Proceedings of the 14th International Conference of Machine Translation Summit* (MT Summit 2013), Nice, France.

Harrington, Peter. 2012. Classifying with probability theory: naïve bayes. *Machine Learning in Action*, Part 1 Classification. Page 61-82. Publisher: Manning Publications. April.

Lafferty, John, McCallum Andrew, and Pereira C.N. Ferando. 2001. Conditional random fields: Probabilistic models for segmenting and labeling sequence data. In *Proceeding of 18th International Conference on Machine Learning*. 282-289.

Lavie, Alon and Abhaya Agarwal. 2007. METEOR: An Automatic Metric for MT Evaluation with High Levels of Correlation with Human Judgments, *Proceedings of the ACL Second Workshop on Statistical Machine Translation*, pages 228-231, Prague, June.

Leusch, Gregor, Nicola Ueffing, and Hermann Ney. 2006. CDer: Efficient MT Evaluation Using Block Movements. In *Proceedings of the 13th Conference of the European Chapter of the Association for Computational Linguistics* (EACL-06), 241-248.

Lin, Chin-Yew and Eduard Hovy. 2003. Automatic Evaluation of Summaries Using N-gram Cooccurrence Statistics. In *Proceedings of 2003 Language Technology Conference (HLT-NAACL 2003)*, Edmonton, Canada, May 27 - June 1.

Lita, Lucian Vlad, Monica Rogati and Alon Lavie. 2005. BLANC: Learning Evaluation Metrics for MT, *Proceedings of Human Language Technology Conference and Conference on Empirical Methods in Natural Language Processing (HLT/EMNLP)*, pages 740–747, Vancouver, October. Association for Computational Linguistics.

Liu, Chang, Daniel Dahlmeier and Hwee Tou Ng. 2010. TESLA: Translation evaluation of sentences with linear-programming-based analysis. In *Proceedings of the Joint Fifth Workshop on Statistical Machine Translation and MetricsMATR*.

Liu, Ding and Daniel Gildea. 2006. Stochastic iterative alignment for machine translation evaluation. Sydney. *ACL06*.

Mariano, Felice and Lucia Specia. 2012. Linguistic Features for Quality Estimation. *Proceedings of the 7th Workshop on Statistical Machine Translation*, pages 96–103.

Mehdad, Yashar, Matteo Negri, and Marcello Federico. 2012. Match without a referee: evaluating MT adequacy without reference translations. *Proceedings of the Seventh Workshop on Statistical Machine Translation. Association for Computational Linguistics*.

Mirkin, Shachar, Lucia Specia, Nicola Cancedda, Ido Dagan, Marc Dymetman, and Idan Szpektor. 2009. Source-Language Entailment Modeling for Translating Unknown Terms, *Proceedings of the Joint Conference of the 47th Annual Meeting of the ACL and the 4th International Joint Conference on Natural Language Processing of the AFNLP*, pages 791–799, Suntec, Singapore, 2-7. ACL and AFNLP.

Nießen, Sonja, Franz Josef Och, Gregor Leusch, and Hermann Ney. 2000. A Evaluation Tool for Machine Translation: Fast Evaluation for MT Research. In *Proceedings of the 2nd International Conference on Language Resources and Evaluation* (LREC-2000).

Owczarzak, Karolina, Josef van Genabith and Andy Way. 2007. Labelled Dependencies in Machine Translation Evaluation, *Proceedings of the ACL Second Workshop on Statistical Machine Translation*, pages 104-111, Prague.

Papineni, Kishore, Salim Roukos, Todd Ward, and Wei-Jing Zhu. 2002. BLEU: a method for automatic evaluation of machine translation. In *Proceedings of the 40th Annual Meeting on Association for Computational Linguistics* (ACL '02). Association for Computational Linguistics, Stroudsburg, PA, USA, 311-318.

Petrov, Slav, Leon Barrett, Romain Thibaux, and Dan Klein. 2006. Learning accurate, compact, and interpretable tree annotation. In *Proceedings of the 21st International Conference on Computational Linguistics and the 44th annual meeting of the Association for Computational Linguistics* (ACL-44). Association for Computational Linguistics, Stroudsburg, PA, USA, 433-440.

Popovic, Maja, David Vilar, Eleftherios Avramidis, Aljoscha Burchardt. 2011. Evaluation without references: IBM1 scores as evaluation metrics. In *Proceedings of the Sixth Workshop on Statistical Machine Translation, Association for Computational Linguistics* (ACL-WMT), pages 99-103, Edinburgh, Scotland, UK.

Povlsen, Claus, Nancy Underwood, Bradley Music, and Anne Neville. 1998. Evaluating Text-Type Suitability for Machine Translation a Case Study on an English-Danish System. *Proceedings of the First Language Resources and Evaluation Conference, LREC-98*, Volume I. 27-31. Granada, Spain.

Schmid, Helmut. 1994. Probabilistic Part-of-Speech Tagging Using Decision Trees. In *Proceedings of International Conference on New Methods in Language Processing*, Manchester, UK.

Snover, Matthew G., Nitin Madnani, Bonnie Dorr, and Richard Schwartz. 2009. TER-Plus: paraphrase, semantic, and alignment enhancements to Translation Edit Rate. J. *Machine Tranlslation*, 23: 117-127.

Specia, Lucia and Gimenez, J. 2010. Combining Confidence Estimation and Reference-based Metrics for Segment-level MT Evaluation. The *Ninth Conference of the Association for Machine Translation in the Americas* (AMTA).

Specia, Lucia, Dhwaj Raj, and Marco Turchi. 2010. Machine Translation Evaluation Versus Quality Estimation. *Machine Translation*, 24:39–50.

Su, Keh-Yih, Wu Ming-Wen and Chang Jing-Shin. 1992. A New Quantitative Quality Measure for Machine Translation Systems. In *Proceedings of the 14th International Conference on Computational Linguistics*, pages 433–439, Nantes, France, July.

Tillmann, Christoph, Stephan Vogel, Hermann Ney, Arkaitz Zubiaga, and Hassan Sawaf. 1997. Accelerated DP Based Search For Statistical Translation. In *Proceedings of the 5th European Conference on Speech Communication and Technology* (EUROSPEECH-97).

Turian, Joseph P., Luke Shen, and I. Dan Melamed. 2003. Evaluation of Machine Translation and its Evaluation. In *Machine Translation Summit IX*, pages 386–393. International Association for Machine Translation.

Wang, Mengqiu and Christopher D. Manning. 2012. SPEDE: Probabilistic Edit Distance Metrics for MT Evaluation, *WMT2012*, 76-83.

Wong, Billy T. M. and Chunyu Kit. 2012. Extending Machine Translation Evaluation Metrics with Lexical Cohesion to Document Level. *Proceedings of the 2012 Joint Conference on Empirical*

Methods in Natural Language Processing and Computational Natural Language Learning, pages 1060–1068, Jeju Island, Korea, 12–14 July. Association for Computational Linguistics.

Zhang, Harry. 2004. The Optimality of Naive Bayes. *Proceedings of the Seventeenth International Florida Artificial Intelligence Research Society Conference*, Miami Beach, Florida, USA. AAAI Press.

MT Quality Estimation: The CMU System for WMT'13

Almut Silja Hildebrand
Carnegie Mellon University
Pittsburgh, USA
silja@cs.cmu.edu

Stephan Vogel
Qatar Computing Research Institute
Doha, Qatar
svogel@qf.org.qa

Abstract

In this paper we present our entry to the WMT'13 shared task: Quality Estimation (QE) for machine translation (MT). We participated in the 1.1, 1.2 and 1.3 sub-tasks with our QE system trained on features from diverse information sources like MT decoder features, n-best lists, mono- and bi-lingual corpora and giza training models. Our system shows competitive results in the workshop shared task.

1 Introduction

As MT becomes more and more reliable, more people are inclined to use automatically translated texts. If coming across a passage that is obviously a mistranslation, any reader would probably start to doubt the reliability of the information in the whole article, even though the rest might be adequately translated. If the MT system had a QE component to mark translations as reliable or possibly erroneous, the reader would know to use information from passages marked as bad translations with caution, while still being able to trust other passages. In post editing a human translator could use translation quality annotation as an indication to whether editing the MT output or translating from scratch might be faster. Or he could use this information to decide where to start in order to improve the worst passages first or skip acceptable passages altogether in order to save time. Confidence scores can also be useful for applications such as cross lingual information retrieval or question answering. Translation quality could be a valuable ranking feature there.

Most previous work in the field estimates confidence on the sentence level (e.g. Quirk et al. (2004)), some operate on the word level (e.g. Ueffing and Ney (2007), Sanchis et al. (2007), and Bach et al. (2011)), whereas Soricut and Echihabi (2010) use the document level.

Various classifiers and regression models have been used in QE in the past. Gandrabur and Foster (2003) compare single layer to Multi Layer Perceptron (MLP), Quirk et al. (2004) report that Linear Regression (LR) produced the best results in a comparison of LR, MLP and SVM, Gamon et al. (2005) use SVM, Soricut and Echihabi (2010) find the M5P tree works best among a number of regression models, while Bach et al. (2011) define the problem as a word sequence labeling task and use MIRA.

The QE shared task was added to the WMT evaluation campaign in 2012 (Callison-Burch et al., 2012), providing standard training and test data for system development.

2 WMT'13 Shared Task

In this WMT Shared Task for Quality Estimation[1] there were tasks for sentence and word level QE. We participated in all sub-tasks for Task 1: Sentence-level QE.

Task 1.1: Scoring and ranking for post-editing effort focuses on predicting HTER per segment for the translations of one specific MT system. Task 1.2: System selection/ranking required to predict a ranking for up to five translations of the same source sentence by different MT systems. The training data provided manual labels for ranking including ties. Task 1.3: Predicting post-editing time participants are asked to predict the time in seconds a professional translator will take to post edit each segment.

[1] http://www.statmt.org/wmt13/quality-estimation-task.html

Besides the training data with labels, for each of these tasks additional resources were provided. These include bilingual training corpora, language models, 1000-best lists, models from giza and moses training and various other statistics and models depending on task and language pair.

3 Features

3.1 Language Models

To calculate language model (LM) features, we train traditional n-gram language models with n-gram lengths of four and five using the SRILM toolkit (Stolcke, 2002). We calculate our features using the KenLM toolkit (Heafield, 2011). We normalize all our features with the target sentence length to get an average word feature score, which is comparable for translation hypotheses of different length. In addition to the LM probability we record the average n-gram length found in the language model for the sentence, the total number of LM OOVs and OOVs per word, as well as the maximum and the minimum word probability of the sentence, six features total.

We use language models trained on source language data and target language data to measure source sentence difficulty as well as translation fluency.

3.2 Distortion Model

The moses decoder uses one feature from a distance based reordering model and six features from a lexicalized reordering model: Given a phrase pair, this model considers three events Monotone, Swap, and Discontinuous in two directions Left and Right. This results in six events: LM (left-monotone), LS (left-swap), LD (left-discontinuous) and RM (right-monotone), RS, RD.

These distortion features are calculated for each phrase. For a total sentence score we normalize by the phrase count for each of the seven features.

3.3 Phrase Table

From the phrase table we use the features from the moses decoder output: inverse phrase translation probability, inverse lexical weighting, direct phrase translation probability and direct lexical weighting. For a total sentence score we normalize by the phrase count. We use the number of phrases used to generate the hypothesis and the average phrase length as additional features, six features total.

3.4 Statistical Word Lexica

From giza training we use IBM-4 statistical word lexica in both directions. We use six probability based features as described in Hildebrand and Vogel (2008): Normalized probability, maximum word probability and word deletion count from each language direction.

To judge the translation difficulty of each word in the source sentence we collect the number of lexicon entries for each word similar to Gandrabur and Foster (2003). The intuition is, that a word with many translation alternatives in the word-to-word lexicon is difficult to translate while a word with only a few translation choices is easy to translate.

In fact it is not quite this straight forward. There are words in the lexicon, which have many lexicon entries, but the probability for them is not very equally distributed. One entry has a very high probability while all others have a very low one - not much ambiguity there. Other words on the other hand have several senses in one language and therefore are translated frequently into two or three different words in the target language. There the top entries in the lexicon might each have about 30% probability. To capture this behavior we do not only count the total number of entries but also the number of entries with a probability over a threshold of 0.01.

For example one word with a rather high number of different translations in the English-Spanish statistical lexicon is the period (.) with 1570 entries. It has only one translation with a probability over the threshold which is the period (.) in Spanish at a probability of 0.9768. This shows a clear choice and rather little ambiguity despite the high number of different translations in the lexicon.

For each word we collect the number of lexicon entries, the number of lexicon entries over the threshold, the highest probability from the lexicon and whether or not the word is OOV. If a word has no lexicon entry with a probability over the threshold we exclude the word from the lexicon for this purpose and count it as an OOV. As sentence level features we use the sum of the word level features normalized by the sentence length as well as the total OOV count for the sentence, which results in five features.

3.5 Sentence Length Features

The translation difficulty of a source sentence is often closely related to the sentence length, as longer sentences tend to have a more complex structure. Also a skewed ratio between the length of the source sentence and its translation can be an indicator for a bad translation.

We use plain sentence length features, namely the source sentence length, the translation hypothesis length and their ratio as introduced in Quirk (2004).

Similar to Blatz et al. (2004) we use the n-best list as an information source. We calculate the average hypothesis length in the n-best list for one source sentence. Then we compare the current hypothesis to that and calculate both the diversion from that average as well as their ratio. We also calculate the source-target ratio to this average hypothesis length.

To get a representative information on the length relationship of translations from the source and target languages in question, we use the parallel training corpus. We calculate the overall language pair source to target sentence length ratio and record the diversion of the current hypothesis' source-target ratio from that.

The way sentences are translated from one language to another might differ depending on how complex the information is, that needs to be conveyed, which in turn might be related to the sentence length and the ratio between source and translation. As a simple way of capturing this phenomenon we divide the parallel training corpus into three classes (short, medium, long) by the length of the source language sentence. The boundaries of these classes are the mean 26.84 plus and minus the standard deviation 14.54 of the source sentence lengths seen in the parallel corpus. We calculate the source/target length ratio for each of the three classes separately. The resulting statistics for the parallel training corpora can be found in Table 1. For English - Spanish the ratio for all classes is close to one, for other language pairs these differ more clearly.

As features for each hypothesis we use a binary indicator for its membership to each class and its deviation from the length ratio of its class. This results in 12 sentence length related features in total.

	En train
number of sentences	1,714,385
average length	26.84
standard deviation	14.54
class short	0 - 12.29
class medium	12.29 - 41.38
class long	41.38 - 100
s/t ratio overall	0.9624
s/t ratio for short	0.9315
s/t ratio for medium	0.9559
s/t ratio for long	0.9817

Table 1: Sentence Length Statistics for the English-Spanish Parallel Corpus

3.6 Source Language Word and Bi-gram Frequency Features

The length of words is often related to whether they are content words and how frequently they are used in the language. Therefore we use the maximum and average word length as features.

Similar to Blatz et al. (2004) we sort the vocabulary of the source side of the training corpus by occurrence frequency and then divide it into four parts, each of which covers 25% of all tokens. As features we use the percentage of words in the source sentence that fall in each quartile. Additionally we use the number and percentage of source words in the source sentence that are OOV or very low frequency, using count 2 as threshold. We also collect all bigram statistics for the corpus and calculate the corresponding features for the source sentence based on bigrams. This adds up to fourteen features from source word and corpus statistics.

3.7 N-Best List Agreement & Diversity

We use the three types of n-best list based features described in Hildebrand and Vogel (2008): Position Dependent N-best List Word Agreement, Position independent N-best List N-gram Agreement and N-best List N-gram Probability.

To measure n-best list diversity, we compare the top hypothesis to the 5th, 10th, 100th, 200th, 300th, 400th and 500th entry in the n-best list (where they exist) to see how much the translation changes throughout the n-best list. We calculate the Levenshtein distance (Levenshtein, 1966) between the top hypothesis and the three lower ranked ones and normalize by the sentence length of the first hypothesis. We also record the n-best list size and the size of the vocabulary in the n-best list for each source sentence normalized by the source sentence length.

Fifteen agreement based and nine diversity based features add up to 24 n-best list based features.

3.8 Source Parse Features

The intuition is that a sentence is harder to translate, if its structure is more complicated. A simple indicator for a more complex sentence structure is the presence of subclauses and also the length of any clauses and subclauses. To obtain the clause structure, we parse the source language sentence using the Stanford Parser[2] (Klein and Manning, 2003). Features are: The number of clauses and subclauses, the average clause length, and the number of sentence fragments found. If the parse does not contain a clause tag, it is treated as one clause which is a fragment.

3.9 Source-Target Word Alignment Features

A forced alignment algorithm utilizes the trained alignment models from the MT systems GIZA (Och and Ney, 2003) training to align each source sentence to each translation hypothesis.

We use the score given by the word alignment models, the number of unaligned words and the number of NULL aligned words, all normalized by the sentence length, as three separate features. We calculate those for both language directions. Hildebrand and Vogel (2010) successfully applied these features in n-best list re-ranking.

3.10 Cohesion Penalty

Following the cohesion constraints described in Bach et al. (2009) we calculate a cohesion penalty for the translation based on the dependency parse structure of the source sentence and the word alignment to the translation hypothesis. To obtain these we use the Stanford dependency parser (de Marneffe et al., 2006) and the forced alignment from Section 3.9.

For each head word we collect all dependent words and also their dependents to form each complete sub-tree. Then we project each sub-tree onto the translation hypothesis using the alignment. We test for each sub-tree, whether all projected words in the translation are next to each other (cohesive) or if there are gaps. From the collected gaps we subtract any unaligned words. Then we count the number of gaps as cohesion violations as well as how many words are in each gap. We go recursively up the tree, always including all sub-trees for each head word. If there was a violation in one of the sub-trees it might be resolved by adding in its siblings, but if the violation persists, it is counted again.

4 Classifiers

For all experiments we used the Weka[3] data mining toolkit described in Hall et. al. (2009) to compare four different classifiers: Linear Regression (LR), M5P tree (M5Ptree), Multi Layer Perceptron (MLP) and Support Vector Machine for Regression (SVM). Each of these has been identified as effective in previous publications. All but one of the Weka default settings proved reliable, changing the learning rate for the MLP from default: 0.3 to 0.01 improved the performance considerably. We report Mean Absolute Error (MAE) and Root Mean Squared Error (RMSE) for all results.

5 Experiment Results

For Tasks 1.1 and 1.3 we used the 1000-best output provided. As first step we removed duplicate entries in these n-best list. This brought the size down to an average of 152.9 hypotheses per source sentence for the Task 1.1 training data, 172.7 on the WMT12 tests set and 204.3 hypotheses per source sentence on the WMT13 blind test data. The training data for task 1.3 has on average 129.0 hypothesis per source sentence, the WMT13 blind test data 129.8.

In addition to our own features described above we extracted the 17 features used in the WMT12 baseline for all sub-tasks via the software provided for the WMT12-QE shared task.

5.1 Task 1.1

Task 1.1 is to give a quality score between 0 and 1 for each segment in the test set, predicting the HTER score for the segment and also to give a rank for each segment, sorting the entire test set from best quality of translation to worst.

For Task 1.1 our main focus was the scoring task. We did submit a ranking for the blind test

[2] http://nlp.stanford.edu/software/lex-parser.shtml

[3] http://www.cs.waikato.ac.nz/ml/weka/

wmt12-test: WMT12 manual quality labels					
WMT12 best system: Language Weaver			0.61 - 0.75		
WMT12 baseline system			0.69 - 0.82		
feat. set	#feat	LR	M5Pt	MLP	SVM
full	117	0.617 - 0.755	0.618 - 0.756	0.619 - 0.773	0.609 - 0.750
no WMT12-base	100	0.618 - 0.766	0.618 - 0.767	0.603 - 0.757	0.611 - 0.761
slim	69	0.621 - 0.767	0.621 - 0.766	0.614 - 0.768	0.627 - 0.773
wmt12-test: HTER					
full	117	0.125 - 0.162	0.126 - 0.163	**0.122 - 0.156**	0.121 - 0.156
no WMT12-base	100	0.124 - 0.160	0.123 - 0.159	0.125 - 0.159	**0.121 - 0.155**
slim	69	0.125 - 0.161	0.126 - 0.161	0.124 - 0.159	0.123 - 0.158
wmt13-test: HTER					
WMT12 baseline system			0.148 - 0.182		
full	117	0.146 - 0.183	0.147 - 0.185	0.156 - 0.199	0.142 - 0.180
no WMT12-base	100	0.144 - 0.180	0.144 - 0.180	0.156 - 0.203	0.139 - 0.176
slim	69	0.147 - 0.182	0.147 - 0.181	0.153 - 0.194	0.142 - 0.177

Table 2: Task 1.1: Results in MAE and RMSE on the WMT12 test set for WMT12 manual labels as well as WMT13 HTER as target class and the WMT13 test set for HTER

set as well, which resulted from simply sorting the test set by the estimated HTER per segment.

In Table 2 we show the results for some experiments comparing the performance of different feature sets and classifiers. For development we used the WMT12-QE test set and both the WMT12 manual labels as well as HTER as target class. We compared the impact of removing the 17 WMT12-baseline features "no WMT12-base" and training a "slim" system by removing nearly half the features, which showed to have a smaller impact on the overall performance in preliminary experiments. Among the removed features are n-best list based features, redundant features between ours, the moses based and the base17 features and some less reliable features like e.g. the lexicon deletion features, who's thresholds need to be calibrated carefully for each new language pair. We submitted the full+MLP and the no-WMT12-base+SVM output to the shared task, shown in bold in the table.

The official result for our system for task 1.1 on the WMT13 blind data is MAE 13.84, RMSE 17.46 for the no-WMT12-base+SVM system and MAE 15.25 RMSE 18.97 for the full+MLP system. Surprising here is the fact that our full system clearly outperforms the 17-feature baseline on the WMT12 test set, but is behind it on the WMT13 blind test set. (Baseline bb17 SVM: MAE 14.81, RMSE 18.22) Looking at the WMT13 test set results, we should have chosen the slim+SVM system variant.

5.2 Task 1.2

Task 1.2 asks to rank different MT systems by translation quality on a segment by segment basis.

Since the manually annotated ranks in task 1.2 allowed ties, we treated them as quality scores and ran the same QE system on this data as we did for task 1.1. We submitted the full-MLP output with the only difference that for this data set the decoder based features were not available. We rounded the predicted ranks to integer. Since the training data contains many ties we did not employ a strategy to resolve ties.

As a contrastive approach we ran the hypothesis selection system described in Hildebrand and Vogel (2010) using the BLEU MT metric as ranking criteria. For this system it would have been very beneficial to have access to the n-best lists for the different system's translations. The BLEU score for the translation listed as the first system for each source sentence would be 30.34 on the entire training data. We ran n-best list re-ranking using MERT (Och, 2003) for two feature sets: The full feature set, 100 features in total and a slim feature set with 59 features. For the slim feature set we removed all features that are solely based on the source sentence, since those have no impact on re-ranking an n-best list. The BLEU score for the training set improved to 45.25 for the full feature set and to 45.76 for the slim system. Therefore we submitted the output of the slim system to the shared task. This system does not predict ranks directly, but estimates ranking according to BLEU gain on the test set. Therefore the new ranking is always ranks 1-5 without ties.

The official result uses Kendalls tau with and without ties penalized. Our two submissions score: -0.11 / -0.11 for the BLEU optimized system and -0.63 / 0.23 for the classifier system. The classifier system is the best submission in the "ties ignored" category.

5.3 Task 1.3

Task 1.3 is to estimate post editing time on a per segment basis.

In absence of a development test set we used 10-fold cross-validation on the training data to determine the best feature set and classifier for the two submissions. Table 3 shows the results on our preliminary tests for four classifiers and three feature sets. The "no pr." differs from the full feature set only by removing the provided features, in this case the 17 WMT12-baseline features and the "translator ID" and "nth in doc" features. For the "slim" system run the feature set size was cut in half in order to prevent overfitting to the training data since the training data set is relatively small. We used the same criteria as in Task 1.1. For the shared task we submitted the full+SVM and slim+LR variants, shown in bold in the table.

The official result for our entries on the WMT13 blind set in MAE and RMSE are: 53.59 - 92.21 for the full system and 51.59 - 84.75 for the slim system. The slim system ranks 3rd for both metrics and outperforms the baseline at 51.93 - 93.36.

6 Conclusions

In this WMT'13 QE shared task we submitted to the 1.1, 1.2 and 1.3 sub-tasks. In development we focused on the scoring type tasks.

In general there don't seem to be significant differences between the different classifiers.

Surprising is the fact that our full system for task 1.1 clearly outperforms the 17-feature baseline on the WMT12 test set, but is behind it on the WMT13 blind test set. This calls into question whether the performance on the WMT12 test set was the right criterium for selecting a system variant for submission.

The relative success of the "slim" system variant over the full feature set shows that our system would most likely benefit from a sophisticated feature selection method. We plan to explore this in future work.

References

Nguyen Bach, Stephan Vogel, and Colin Cherry. 2009. Cohesive constraints in a beam search phrase-based decoder. In *HLT-NAACL (Short Papers)*, pages 1–4.

Nguyen Bach, Fei Huang, and Yaser Al-Onaizan. 2011. Goodness: A method for measuring machine translation confidence. In *Proceedings of the 49th Annual Meeting of the Association for Computational Linguistics: Human Language Technologies*, pages 211–219, Portland, Oregon, USA, June. Association for Computational Linguistics.

John Blatz, Erin Fitzgerald, George Foster, Simona Gandrabur, Cyril Goutte, Alex Kulesza, Alberto Sanchis, and Nicola Ueffing. 2004. Confidence estimation for machine translation. Technical report, Final report JHU / CLSP 2003 Summer Workshop, Baltimore.

Chris Callison-Burch, Philipp Koehn, Christof Monz, Matt Post, Radu Soricut, and Lucia Specia. 2012. Findings of the 2012 workshop on statistical machine translation. In *Proceedings of the Seventh Workshop on Statistical Machine Translation*, pages 10–51, Montréal, Canada, June. Association for Computational Linguistics.

Marie-Catherine de Marneffe, Bill MacCartney, and Christopher D. Manning. 2006. Generating typed dependency parses from phrase structure parses. In *LREC-06*.

Michael Gamon, Anthony Aue, and Martine Smets. 2005. Sentence-level mt evaluation without reference translations: Beyond language modeling. In *In European Association for Machine Translation (EAMT*.

Simona Gandrabur and George Foster. 2003. Confidence estimation for translation prediction. In *In Proceedings of CoNLL-2003*, page 102.

Mark Hall, Eibe Frank, Geoffrey Holmes, Bernhard Pfahringer, Peter Reutemann, and Ian H. Witten. 2009. The WEKA data mining software: an update. *SIGKDD Explorations*, 11(1):10–18.

Kenneth Heafield. 2011. KenLM: Faster and Smaller Language Model Queries. In *Proceedings of the Sixth Workshop on Statistical Machine Translation*, pages 187–197, Edinburgh, Scotland, July. Association for Computational Linguistics.

feat. set	#feat	class.	10-fold cross	train	WMT13 test
full	119	LR	45.73 - 73.52	39.74 - 63.92	54.45 - 88.68
full	119	M5Pt	44.49 - 74.05	35.81 - 57.36	50.05 - 85.22
full	119	MLP	48.05 - 75.68	41.03 - 68.70	54.38 - 88.93
full	119	SVM	**40.88 - 73.61**	34.70 - 69.69	53.74 - 92.26
no pr	100	LR	46.06 - 74.94	40.39 - 66.00	52.13 - 86.68
no pr	100	M5Pt	43.80 - 74.30	36.80 - 59.47	50.86 - 87.42
no pr	100	MLP	47.70 - 75.41	39.85 - 68.30	52.39 - 87.93
no pr	100	SVM	41.35 - 74.68	35.59 - 70.99	52.87 - 92.22
slim	59	LR	**44.72 - 73.86**	41.14 - 67.44	51.71 - 84.83
slim	59	M5Pt	43.77 - 74.43	35.26 - 56.84	57.75 - 102.68
slim	59	MLP	46.98 - 74.38	40.35 - 69.79	51.06 - 85.48
slim	59	SVM	40.42 - 74.47	36.88 - 71.59	51.09 - 90.18

Table 3: Task 1.3: Results in MAE and RMSE for 10-fold cross validation and the whole training set as well as the WMT13 blind test set

Almut Silja Hildebrand and Stephan Vogel. 2008. Combination of machine translation systems via hypothesis selection from combined n-best lists. In *MT at work: Proceedings of the Eighth Conference of the Association for Machine Translation in the Americas*, pages 254–261, Waikiki, Hawaii, October. Association for Machine Translation in the Americas.

Almut Silja Hildebrand and Stephan Vogel. 2010. CMU system combination via hypothesis selection for WMT'10. In *Proceedings of the Joint Fifth Workshop on Statistical Machine Translation and MetricsMATR*, pages 307–310. Association for Computational Linguistics.

Dan Klein and Christopher D. Manning. 2003. Accurate unlexicalized parsing. In Erhard Hinrichs and Dan Roth, editors, *Proceedings of the 41st Annual Meeting of the Association for Computational Linguistics*, pages 423–430.

Vladimir Iosifovich Levenshtein. 1966. Binary codes capable of correcting deletions, insertions, and reversals. *Soviet Physics Doklady*, 10(8):707–710.

Franz Josef Och and Hermann Ney. 2003. A systematic comparison of various statistical alignment models. *Computational Linguistics*, 29(1):19–51.

Franz Josef Och. 2003. Minimum error rate training in statistical machine translation. In *Proceedings of the 41st Annual Meeting of the Association for Computational Linguistics*, pages 160–167, Sapporo, Japan, July. Association for Computational Linguistics.

Christopher B. Quirk. 2004. Training a sentence-level machine translation confidence measure. In *Proceedings of the Fourth International Conference on Language Resources and Evaluation*, pages 825–828, Lisbon, Portugal, May. LREC.

Alberto Sanchis, Alfons Juan, Enrique Vidal, and Departament De Sistemes Informtics. 2007. Estimation of confidence measures for machine translation. In *In Procedings of Machine Translation Summit XI*.

Radu Soricut and Abdessamad Echihabi. 2010. Trustrank: Inducing trust in automatic translations via ranking. In *Proceedings of the 48th Annual Meeting of the Association for Computational Linguistics*, pages 612–621, Uppsala, Sweden, July. Association for Computational Linguistics.

Andreas Stolcke. 2002. Srilm - an extensible language modeling toolkit. In *Proceedings International Conference for Spoken Language Processing*, Denver, Colorado, September.

Nicola Ueffing and Hermann Ney. 2007. Word-level confidence estimation for machine translation. *Computational Linguistics*, 33(1):9–40.

LORIA System for the WMT13 Quality Estimation Shared Task

Langlois David
LORIA
(Université de Lorraine, INRIA, CNRS)
615 rue du Jardin Botanique,
54602 Villers les Nancy, France
david.langlois@loria.fr

Smaïli Kamel
LORIA
(Université de Lorraine, INRIA, CNRS)
615 rue du Jardin Botanique,
54602 Villers les Nancy, France
kamel.smaili@loria.fr

Abstract

In this paper we present the system we submitted to the WMT13 shared task on Quality Estimation. We participated in the Task 1.1. Each translated sentence is given a score between 0 and 1. The score is obtained by using several numerical or boolean features calculated according to the source and target sentences. We perform a linear regression of the feature space against scores in the range [0..1]. To this end, we use a Support Vector Machine with 66 features. In this paper, we propose to increase the size of the training corpus. For that, we use the post-edited and reference corpora during the training step. We assign a score to each sentence of these corpora. Then, we tune these scores on a development corpus. This leads to an improvement of 10.5% on the development corpus, in terms of Mean Average Error, but achieves only a slight improvement on the test corpus.

1 Introduction

In the scope of Machine Translation (MT), Quality Estimation (QE) is the task consisting to evaluate the translation quality of a sentence or a document. This process may be useful for post-editors to decide or not to revise a sentence produced by a MT system (Specia, 2011; Specia et al., 2010). Moreover, it can be useful to decide if a translated document can be broadcasted or not (Soricut and Echihabi, 2010). The most obvious way to give a score to a translated sentence consists in using a machine learning approach. This approach is supervised: experts are asked to score translated sentences and with the obtained material, one learns a prediction model of scores. The main drawback of the machine learning approach is that it is supervised and requires huge data. To score a sentence is time-consuming. Moreau et al. in (Moreau and Vogel, 2012) dealt with this issue by proposing unsupervised similarity measures. In fact, the score of a translated sentence is defined by a measure giving the distance between it and the contents of an external corpus. The authors improve the results of the supervised approach but this method can be used only in the ranking task. Raybaud et al. (Raybaud et al., 2011) proposed a method to add errors in reference sentences (deletion, substitution, insertion). By this way, they build additional corpus in which each word can be associated with a label correct/not correct. But, it is not possible to predict the translation quality of sentences including these erroneous words.

In this paper, we propose to increase the size of the training corpus. For that, we use the score given by experts to evaluate additional sentences from the post-edited and reference corpora. Practically, we extract from source and target sentences numerical vectors (features) and we learn a prediction model of the scores. Then, we apply this model to predict the scores of the post-edited and the reference sentences. And finally, we tune the predicted scores on a development corpus.

The article is structured as follows. In Section 2, we give an overview of our machine learning approach and of the features we use. Then, in Sections 3 and 4 we describe the corpora and how we increase the size of the training corpus by a partly-unsupervised approach. In section 5, we give results about this method and we end by a conclusion and perspectives.

2 Overview of our quality estimation submission

We submit a system for the task 1.1: one has to evaluate each translated sentence with a score between 0 and 1. This score is read as the HTER between the translated sentence and its post-edited version. Each translated sentence is assigned a score between 0 and 1. The score is calculated using several numerical or boolean features extracted according to the source and target sentences. We perform a regression of the feature space against [0..1]. To this end, we use the Support Vector Machine algorithm (LibSVM toolkit (Chang and Lin, 2011)). We experimented only the linear kernel because our experience from last year (Langlois et al., 2012) showed that its performance are yet good while no parameters have to be tuned on a development corpus.

2.1 The baseline features

The QE shared task organizers provided a baseline system including the same features as last year: source and target sentences lengths; average source word length; source and target likelihood computed with 3-gram (source) and 5-gram (target) language models; average number of occurrences of the words within the target sentence; average number of translations per source word in the sentence, using IBM1 translation table (only translations higher than 0.2); weighted average number of translations per source word in the sentence (similar to the previous one, but a frequent word is given a low weight in the averaging); distribution by frequencies of the source n-gram into the quartiles; match between punctuation in source and target. Overall, the baseline system proposes 17 features. We remark that only 5 features take into account the target sentence.

2.2 The LORIA features

In previous works (Raybaud et al., 2011; Langlois et al., 2012), we tested several confidence measures. As last year (Langlois et al., 2012), we use the same features. We extract information by the way of language model (perplexity, level of back-off, intra-lingual triggers) and translation table (IBM1 table, inter-lingual triggers). The features are defined at word level, and the features at sentence level are computed by averaging over each word in the sentence. In our system, we use, in addition to baseline features, ratio of source and target lengths; source and target likelihood computed with 5-gram language models (Duchateau et al., 2002) (in addition to 3-gram features from baseline); level of backoff n-gram based features (Uhrik and Ward, 1997). This feature indicates if the 3-gram, the 2-gram or the unigram corresponding to the word is in the language model. For likelihoods and levels of backoff, we use models trained on corpus read from left to right (classical way), and from right to left (sentences are reversed before training language models). This leads to two language models, and therefore to two values for each feature and side (source and target). Moreover, a common property of all n-gram and backoff based features is that a word can get a low score if it is actually correct but its neighbours are wrong. To compensate for this phenomenon we took into account the average score of the neighbours of the word being considered. More precisely, for every relevant feature $x_.$ defined at word level we also computed:

$$\begin{aligned} x_.^{left}(w_i) &= x_.(w_{i-2}) * x_.(w_{i-1}) * x_.(w_i) \\ x_.^{centred}(w_i) &= x_.(w_{i-1}) * x_.(w_i) * x_.(w_{i+1}) \\ x_.^{right}(w_i) &= x_.(w_{i)} * x_.(w_{i+1}) * x_.(w_{i+2}) \end{aligned}$$

The other features are intra-lingual features: each word is assigned its average mutual information with the other words in the sentence; inter-lingual features: each word in target sentence is assigned its average mutual information with the words in source sentence; IBM1 features: contrary to IBM1 based baseline features which take into account the number of translations, we use the probability values in the translation table between source and target words; basic parser (correction of bracketing, presence of end-of-sentence symbol); number and ratio of out-of-vocabulary words in source and target sentences. This leads to 49 features. A few ones are equivalent to or are strongly correlated to baseline ones. We remark that 27 features take into account the target sentence.

The union of the both sets baseline+loria improved slightly the baseline system on the test set provided by the QE Shared Task 2012 (Callison-Burch et al., 2012).

3 Corpora

The organizers provide a set of files for training and development. We list below the ones we used:

- source.eng: 2,254 source sentences taken from three WMT data sets (English): news-test2009, news-test2010, and news-test2012. In the following, this file is named `src`
- target_system.spa: translations for the source sentences (Spanish) generated by a PB-SMT system built using Moses. In the following, this file is named `syst`

- target_system.HTER_official-score: HTER scores between MT and post-edited version, to be used as the official score in the shared task. In the following, this file is named `hteroff`
- target_reference.spa: reference translation (Spanish) for source sentences as originally given by WMT; In the following, this file is named `ref`
- target_postedited.spa: human post-edited version (Spanish) of the machine translations in target_system.spa. In the following, this file is named `post`

We split these files into two parts: a training part made up of the 1,832 first sentences, and a development part made up of the 442 remaining sentences. This choice is motivated by the fact that in the previous evaluation campaign we had exactly the same experimental conditions.
For each given file `f`, we use therefore a part named `f.train` for training and a part named `f.dev` for development.

4 Training Algorithm

This section describes the approach we propose to increase the size of the training corpus.

We have to train the prediction model of scores from the source and target sentences.

The common way to train such a prediction model consists in extracting a features vector for each couple `(source,target)` from the `(src.train,syst.train)` corpus. For each vector, the score associated by experts to the corresponding sentence is assigned. Then, we use a machine learning approach to learn the regression between the vectors and the scores. And finally, we use the triplet `(src.dev,syst.dev,hteroff.dev)` to tune parameters.

With machine learning approach, the number of examples is crucial for a relevant training, but unfortunately the evaluation campaign provides a training corpus of only 1,832 examples.

To increase the training corpus, we propose to use the `ref` and `post` files. But for that, we have to associate a score to these new target sentences. One way could be to calculate the HTER score between each sentence and its corresponding sentence in the post edited file. But this leads to a drawback: all the couples `(src,post)` would have a score equal to 0, and then there is a risk of overtraining on the 0 value. To prevent this problem, we preferred to learn a prediction model from the `(src.train,-syst.train,hteroff.train)` triplet. Then we apply this prediction model to the `(src.train,post.train)` and to the `(src.train,ref.train)`. By this way, we get a training corpus made up of $1,832 \times 3 = 3,696$ examples with their scores. Consequently, it is possible to learn a prediction model from this new training corpus. These scores are not optimal because the features cannot describe all the information from sentences, and a machine learning approach is limited if data are not sufficiently huge. Therefore, we propose an anytime randomized algorithm to tune the reference and post-edited scores on the development corpus. We give below the algorithm we propose.

1. **Prediction model**
   (a) Learn the prediction model using only features from `(src.train,syst.train)` and HTER target scores from experts
2. **Predict initial scores for postedited and reference sentences**
   (a) Use this model to predict the scores associated to the features from `(src.train,post.train)` and `(src.train,ref.train)`. The predicted scores for `(src.train,post.train)` are called `post_best` and the ones for `(src.train,ref.train)` are called `ref_best`
3. **Learn initial prediction model using the 3 trains (system part, post-edited part and reference part)**
   (a) Learn the prediction model using features from the three sets of features and the scores associated to these sets (experts scores, `post_best` and `ref_best`)
   (b) Evaluate this model. This leads to a performance equal to `best`
4. **Tune scores for postedited and reference sentences**
   (a) Repeat the following steps until stop

(b) Build a new set of scores named post_new (resp. ref_new) by disturbing each score of post_best (resp. ref_best) with a probability equal to pdisturb. A modified score is shifted by a value randomly chosen in [-disturb, +disturb]

(c) Learn the prediction model using features from the three sets of features and the new scores associated to these sets (experts scores for system set, post_new and ref_new for the post-edited and reference sets)

(d) Evaluate this model. This leads to a performance equal to perf

(e) If perf<best then replace best by perf, post_best by post_new and ref_best by ref_new.

To evaluate a model, we use it to predict the scores on the development corpus. Then we compare the predicted scores to the expert scores and we compute the Mean Average Error (MAE) given by the formula $MAE(s, r) = \frac{\sum_{i=1}^{n} |s_i - r_i|}{n} \times 100$ where s and r are two sets of n scores.

5 Results

We used the data provided by the shared task on QE, without additional corpus. This data is composed of a parallel English-Spanish training corpus. This corpus is made of the concatenation of europarl-v5 and news-commentary10 corpora (from WMT-2010), followed by tokenization, cleaning (sentences with more than 80 tokens removed) and truecasing. It has been used for baseline models provided in the baseline package by the shared task organizers. We used the same training corpus to train additional language models (5-gram with kneyser-ney discounting, obtained with the SRILM toolkit) and triggers required for our features. For feature extraction, we used the files provided by the organizers: 2,254 source english sentences, their translations by the baseline system, and the score of these translations. This score is the HTER between the proposed translation and the post-edited sentence. We used the train part to perform the regression between the features and the scores. Therefore, the system we propose in this campaign is the same as the one we presented for the previous campaign in terms of features. But, we only use a SVM with a linear kernel and we do not use any feature selection. The added value of the new system is the fact that we increase the size of the training corpus.

To evaluate the different configurations, we used the MAE measure. The performance of our system with only the classical train set (src.train, syst.train) are given in Table 1. In this table, BASELINE+LORIA use both features BASELINE and LORIA (Section 2). We remark that, contrary to last year, the BASELINE+LORIA do not improve the performance of the BASELINE features on the development set.

Set of features	Dev
BASELINE	13.46
LORIA	14.04
BASELINE+LORIA	13.88

Table 1: Performance in terms of MAE without increasing the training corpus

Now, we increase the training corpus with the method described in previous section. First, we use the system trained on (src.train, syst.train) to predict scores for the sentences in post.train and ref.train. We know that these scores should represent the HTER score, then a well translated sentence should be assigned a higher score. Therefore, we can make the hypothesis that sentences from post.train and ref.train are better than those in syst.train. We check this hypothesis by comparing the distributions of HTER scores in the three files (true HTER scores in syst.train, and predicted scores in the two other files). We present in Table 2 the Minimum, Maximum, Mean and Standard Deviation of this score for the three corpora. We remark that the scores are not well predicted because some of them are negative while all scores in syst.train are between 0 and 1. This is due to the fact that the constraint of HTER in terms of limit values is not explicitly taken into account by SVM. We give more details about these scores out of [0..1] in Table 3. For post.train, 2 scores are under 0 with a mean value equal to -0.123, and no scores are higher than 1. For ref.train, 4 scores are under 0 with a mean value equal to -3.023, and 26 scores are higher than 1 with a mean equal to 1.126. Comparing to the 1,832 sentences in the training corpus, we can conclude that the 'outliers' are very rare. In Table 2 Mean and Standard Deviation are computed only for scores predicted between 0 and 1. The obtained mean values are quite similar, but the standard deviation is very low for predicted scores.

This configuration leads to a performance equal to 13.88 on the development corpus, which is slightly worse than the BASELINE system but slightly better than the BASELINE+LORIA system.

Because, SVM predicts scores which do not represent exactly HTER and because the model is learnt on a relatively small corpus (1,832 sentences), we decided to modify randomly some scores. This operation is called in the following the tuning process.

Set	Min	Max	Mean	SD
`syst.train`	0	1	0.317	0.169
`post.train`	-0.147	0.708	0.315	0.083
`ref.train`	-11.314	0.746	0.329	0.081

Table 2: Statistics on HTER for the three sets of sentences used in the training corpus

	lower than 0		higher than 1	
Set	**Nb**	**Mean**	**Nb**	**Mean**
`syst.train`	0	-	0	-
`post.train`	2	-0.123	0	-
`ref.train`	4	-3.023	26	1.126

Table 3: Statistics on HTER for the three sets of sentences used in the training corpus. Nb is the number of sentences

For the tuning process, after several tests, we fixed to 0.1 the probability `pdisturb` to modify the score of a sentence. Then, the score is modified by randomly shifting it in $[-0.01... + 0.01]$. We start with the initial predicted scores (MAE = 13.88). Then we randomly modify a subset of scores and keep a new configuration if its MAE is improved. The process is stopped when MAE converges. Figure 1 presents the evolution of MAE on the development corpus.

The process stopped after $22,248$ iterations. Only 274 (1.2%) iterations led to an improvement. We present the results of this approach on the development corpus and on the official test set of the campaign (500 sentences). We group in Table 4 the results on development and test corpus for the BASELINE features and the BASELINE+LORIA features with and without using the post-edited and reference sentences. Finally, we achieve a MAE of 12.05 on the development set. This constitutes an improvement of 10.5% in comparison to the BASELINE system. But we improve only slightly the performance of the baseline system on the test set. We conclude that there is an overtraining on the development corpus. In order to prevent from this problem, we could use a leaving-one-out approach on training and development corpora.

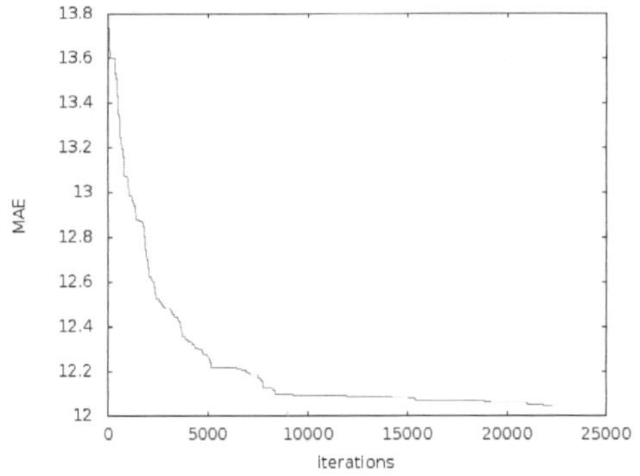

Figure 1: Evolution of the MAE on the development corpus

With the tuned values of scores, we calculated the same statistics as in Tables 2 and 3. We present these statistics in Tables 5 and 6. As we can see, the tuning process leads to an increasing of the mean value of the scores. Moreover, the number of scores out of range increases. This analysis reinforces our conclusion about overtraining: predicted scores may be strongly modified to obtain a good performance on the development corpus.

Set of features	Dev	Test
BASELINE	13.46	14.81
BASELINE+LORIA	13.88	nc
+ postedited + ref	13.78	nc
+ tuning	12.05	14.79

Table 4: Performance in terms of MAE of the features with and without increasing the training corpus

To conclude the experiments, we try to fix the problem of scores predicted out of range. For that, we set to 0 the scores lower than 0 and to 1 the

Set	Min	Max	Mean	SD
post. train	-0.811	1.322	0.407	0.235
ref. train	-10.485	1.320	0.409	0.242

Table 5: Statistics on HTER for the post and ref sets of sentences used in the training corpus, after tuning

	lower than 0		higher than 1	
Set of sentences	**Nb**	**Mean**	**Nb**	**Mean**
post.train	318	-0.164	29	1.118
ref.train	282	-0.205	28	1.123

Table 6: Statistics on HTER for the post and ref sets of sentences used in the training corpus, after tuning. Nb is the number of sentences.

ones greater than 1. Then we learn a new SVM model using these new scores. This leads to a MAE equal to 12.18 on the development corpus and 14.83 on the test corpus, which is worse than the performance without correction. This is for us a drawback of the machine learning approach. For this approach, the scores have no semantic. SVM do not "know" that the scores are HTER between 0 and 1. Then, if tuning leads to no reasonable values, this is not a problem if it increases the performance. Moreover, maybe the features do not extract from all sentences information representative of their quality, and this quality is overestimated: then the tuning system has to lower strongly the corresponding scores to counteract this problem.

6 Conclusion and perpespectives

In this paper we propose a method to increase the size of the training corpus for QE in the scope of Task 1.1. We add to the initial training corpus (sentences translated by a machine translation system) the post-edited and the reference sentences. We associate to these sentences scores predicted by using a model learnt on the system sentences. Then we tune the predicted scores on the development corpus. This method leads to an improvement of 10.5% on the development corpus in terms of MAE, but achieves only a slight improvement on the test corpus. A statistical study shows that tuning scores leads to out of range values. This surprising behavior have to be investigated. In addition, we will test another machine learning tools (neural networks for example). Another point is that, contrary to last year, the whole set of features leads to worse performance than baseline features. This could be explained by the fact that no selecting algorithm has been used to choose the best features. In fact, we preferred, this year to investigate the underlying knowledge on the post-edited and reference corpora. Last, we conclude that the good improvement on the development corpus is not reproduced on the test corpus. In order to prevent from this problem, we will use a leaving-one-out approach on the training.

References

C. Callison-Burch, P. Koehn, C. Monz, M. Post, R. Soricut, and L. Specia. 2012. Findings of the 2012 workshop on statistical machine translation. In *Proceedings of the Seventh Workshop on Statistical Machine Translation*, pages 10–51.

C.-C. Chang and C.-J. Lin. 2011. LIBSVM: A library for support vector machines. *ACM Transactions on Intelligent Systems and Technology*, 2:27:1–27:27. Software available at http://www.csie.ntu.edu.tw/ cjlin/libsvm.

J. Duchateau, K. Demuynck, and P. Wambacq. 2002. Confidence scoring based on backward language models. In *Proceedings of IEEE International Conference on Acoustics, Speech, and Signal Processing*, volume 1, pages 221–224.

D. Langlois, S. Raybaud, and Kamel Smaïli. 2012. Loria system for the WMT12 quality estimation shared task. In *Proceedings of the Seventh Workshop on Statistical Machine Translation*, pages 114–119.

E. Moreau and C. Vogel. 2012. Quality estimation: an experimental study using unsupervised similarity measures. In *Proceedings of the Seventh Workshop on Statistical Machine Translation*, pages 120–126.

S. Raybaud, D. Langlois, and K. Smaïli. 2011. "This sentence is wrong." Detecting errors in machine-translated sentences. *Machine Translation*, 25(1):1–34.

R. Soricut and A. Echihabi. 2010. Trustrank: Inducing trust in automatic translations via ranking. In *Proceedings of the 48th Annual Meeting of the Association for Computational Linguistics*, pages 612–621.

L. Specia, N. Hajlaoui, C. Hallett, and W. Aziz. 2010. Predicting machine translation adequacy. In *Proceedings of the Machine Translation Summit XIII*, pages 612–621.

L. Specia. 2011. Exploiting objective annotations for measuring translation post-editing effort. In *Proceedings of the 15th Conference of the European Association for Machine Translation*, pages 73–80.

C. Uhrik and W. Ward. 1997. Confidence metrics based on n-gram language model backoff behaviors. In *Fifth European Conference on Speech Communication and Technology*, pages 2771–2774.

LIG System for WMT13 QE Task: Investigating the Usefulness of Features in Word Confidence Estimation for MT

Ngoc-Quang Luong **Benjamin Lecouteux** **Laurent Besacier**
LIG, Campus de Grenoble
41, Rue des Mathématiques,
UJF - BP53, F-38041 Grenoble Cedex 9, France
{ngoc-quang.luong,laurent.besacier,benjamin.lecouteux}@imag.fr

Abstract

This paper presents the LIG's systems submitted for Task 2 of WMT13 Quality Estimation campaign. This is a word confidence estimation (WCE) task where each participant was asked to label each word in a translated text as a binary (Keep/Change) or multi-class (Keep/Substitute/Delete) category. We integrate a number of features of various types (system-based, lexical, syntactic and semantic) into the conventional feature set, for our baseline classifier training. After the experiments with all features, we deploy a "Feature Selection" strategy to keep only the best performing ones. Then, a method that combines multiple "weak" classifiers to build a strong "composite" classifier by taking advantage of their complementarity is presented and experimented. We then select the best systems for submission and present the official results obtained.

1 Introduction

Recently Statistical Machine Translation (SMT) systems have shown impressive gains with many fruitful results. While the outputs are more acceptable, the end users still face the need to post edit (or not) an automatic translation. Then, the issue is to be able to accurately identify the correct parts as well as detecting translation errors. If we focus on errors at the word level, the issue is called Word-level Confidence Estimation (WCE).

In WMT 2013, a shared task about quality estimation is proposed. This quality estimation task is proposed at two levels: word-level and sentence-level. Our work focuses on the word-level quality estimation (named Task 2). The objective is to highlight words needing post-edition and to detect parts of the sentence that are not reliable. For the task 2, participants produce for each token a label according to two sub-tasks:

- a binary classification: good (keep) or bad (change) label
- a multi-class classification: the label refers to the edit action needed for the token (i.e. keep, delete or substitute).

Various approaches have been proposed for WCE: Blatz et al. (2003) combine several features using neural network and naive Bayes learning algorithms. One of the most effective feature combinations is the Word Posterior Probability (WPP) as proposed by Ueffing et al. (2003) associated with IBM-model based features (Blatz et al., 2004). Ueffing and Ney (2005) propose an approach for phrase-based translation models: a phrase is a sequence of contiguous words and is extracted from word-aligned bilingual training corpus. The confidence value of each word is then computed by summing over all phrase pairs in which the target part contains this word. Xiong et al. (2010) integrate target word's Part-Of-Speech (POS) and train them by Maximum Entropy Model, allowing significative gains compared to WPP features. Other approaches are based on external features (Soricut and Echihabi, 2010; Felice and Specia, 2012) allowing to deal with various MT systems (e.g. statistical, rule based etc.).

In this paper, we propose to use both internal and external features into a conditionnal random fields (CRF) model to predict the label for each word in the MT hypothesis. We organize the article as follows: section 2 explains all the used features. Section 3 presents our experimental settings and the preliminary experiments. Section 4 explores a feature selection refinement and the section 5 presents work using several classifiers associated with a boosting decision. Finally we present our systems submissions and propose some conclusions and perspectives.

2 Features

In this section, we list all 25 types of features for building our classifier (see a list in Table 3). Some of them are already used and described in detail in our previous paper (Luong, 2012), where we deal with French - English SMT Quality Estimation. WMT13 was a good chance to re-investigate their usefulness for another language pair: English-Spanish, as well as to compare their contributions with those from other teams. We categorize them into two types: the **conventional features**, which are proven to work efficiently in numerous CE works and are inherited in our systems, and the **LIG features** which are more specifically suggested by us.

2.1 The conventional features

We describe below the conventional features we used. They can be found in some previous papers dealing with WCE.

- Target word features: the target word itself; the bigram (trigram) it forms with one (two) previous and one (two) following word(s); its number of occurrences in the sentence.

- Source word features: all the source words that align to the target one, represented in BIO[1] format.

- Source alignment context features: the combinations of the target word and one word before (left source context) or after (right source context) the source word aligned to it.

- Target alignment context features: the combinations of the source word and each word in the window ± 2 (two before, two after) of the target word.

- Target Word's Posterior Probability (WPP).

- Backoff behaviour: a score assigned to the word according to how many times the target Language Model has to back-off in order to assign a probability to the word sequence, as described in (Raybaud et al., 2011).

- Part-Of-Speech (POS) features (using TreeTagger[2] toolkit): The target word's POS; the source POS (POS of all source words aligned to it); bigram and trigram sequences between its POS and the POS of previous and following words.

- Binary lexical features that indicate whether the word is a: *stop word* (based on the stop word list for target language), *punctuation* symbol, *proper name* or *numerical*.

2.2 The LIG features

- Graph topology features: based on the N-best list graph merged into a confusion network. On this network, each word in the hypothesis is labelled with its WPP, and belongs to one *confusion set*. Every completed path passing through all nodes in the network represents one sentence in the N-best, and must contain exactly one link from each confusion set. Looking into a confusion set, we find some useful indicators, including: the *number of alternative paths* it contains (called *Nodes*), and the distribution of posterior probabilities tracked over all its words (most interesting are *maximum and minimum probabilities*, called *Max* and *Min*).

- Language Model (LM) features: the *"longest target n-gram length"* and *"longest source n-gram length"*(length of the longest sequence created by the current target (source aligned) word and its previous ones in the target (source) LM). For example, with the target word w_i: if the sequence $w_{i-2}w_{i-1}w_i$ appears in the target LM but the sequence $w_{i-3}w_{i-2}w_{i-1}w_i$ does not, the n-gram value for w_i will be 3.

- The *word's constituent label* and *its depth in the tree* (or the distance between it and the tree root) obtained from the constituent tree as an output of the Berkeley parser (Petrov and Klein, 2007) (trained over a Spanish treebank: AnCora[3]).

- Occurrence in Google Translate hypothesis: we check whether this target word appears in the sentence generated by Google Translate engine for the same source.

[1]http://www-tsujii.is.s.u-tokyo.ac.jp/GENIA/tagger/

[2]http://www.ims.uni-stuttgart.de/projekte/corplex/TreeTagger/

[3]http://clic.ub.edu/corpus/en/ancora

- Polysemy Count: the *number of senses* of each word given its POS can be a reliable indicator for judging if it is the translation of a particular source word. Here, we investigate the polysemy characteristic in both target word and its aligned source word. For source word (English), the number of senses can be counted by applying a Perl extension named Lingua::WordNet[4], which provides functions for manipulating the WordNet database. For target word (Spanish), we employ BabelNet[5] - a multilingual semantic network that works similarly to WordNet but covers more European languages, including Spanish.

3 Experimental Setting and Preliminary Experiment

The WMT13 organizers provide two bilingual data sets, from English to Spanish: the training and the test ones. The training set consists of 803 MT outputs, in which each token is annotated with one appropriate label. In the binary variant, the words are classified into *"K"* (Keep) or *"C"* (Change) label, meanwhile in the multi-class variant, they can belong to *"K"* (Keep), *"S"* (Substitution) or *"D"* (Deletion). The test set contains 284 sentences where all the labels accompanying words are hidden. For optimizing parameters of the classifier, we extract 50 sentences from the training set to form a development set. Since a number of repetitive sentences are observed in the original training set, the dev set was carefully chosen to ensure that there is no overlap with the new training set (753 sentences), keeping the tuning process accurate. Some statistics about each set can be found in Table 1.

Motivated by the idea of addressing WCE as a sequence labeling task, we employ the *Conditional Random Fields* (CRF) model (Lafferty et al., 2001) and the corresponding WAPITI toolkit (Lavergne et al., 2010) to train our classifier. First, we experiment with the combination of all features. For the multi-class system, WAPITI's default configuration is applied to determine the label, i.e. label which has the highest score is assigned to word. In case of the binary system, the classification task is then conducted multiple times, corresponding to a threshold increase from 0.300 to 0.975 (step = 0.025). When threshold = α, all words in the test set which the probability of *"K"* class $\geqslant \alpha$ will be labelled as *"K"*, and otherwise, *"C"*. The values of Precision (Pr), Recall (Rc) and F-score (F) for *K* and *C* label are tracked along this threshold variation, allowing us to select the optimal threshold that yields the highest $F_{avg} = \frac{F(K)+F(C)}{2}$.

Results for the all-feature binary system (*ALL_BIN*) at the optimal threshold (0.500) and the multi-class one (*ALL_MULT*) at the default threshold, obtained on our dev set, are shown in Table 2. We can notice that with *ALL_BIN*, *"K"* label scores are very promising and *"C'* label reaches acceptable performance. In case of *ALL_MULT* we obtain the almost similar above performance for *"K"* and *"S"*, respectively, except the disappointing scores for *"D"* (which can be explained by the fact that very few instances of *"D"* words (4%) are observed in the training corpus).

Data set	**Train**	**Dev**	**Test**
#segments	753	50	284
#distinct segments	400	50	163
#words	18435	1306	7827
%K : %C	70: 30	77: 23	-
%K: %S: %D	70:26:4	77:19:4	-

Table 1: Statistics of training, dev and test sets

System	**Label**	**Pr(%)**	**Rc(%)**	**F(%)**
ALL_BIN	K	85.79	84.68	85.23
	C	50.96	53.16	52.04
ALL_MULT	K	85.30	84.00	84.65
	S	43.89	49.00	46.31
	D	7.90	6.30	7.01

Table 2: Average Pr, Rc and F for labels of all-feature binary and multi-class systems, obtained on dev set.

4 Feature Selection

In order to improve the preliminary scores of all-feature systems, we conduct a feature selection which is based on the hypothesis that some features may convey "noise" rather than "information" and might be the obstacles weakening the other ones. In order to prevent this drawback, we propose a method to filter the best features

[4]http://search.cpan.org/dist/Lingua-Wordnet/Wordnet.pm
[5]http://babelnet.org

based on the "Sequential Backward Selection" algorithm[6]. We start from the full set of N features, and in each step sequentially remove the most useless one. To do that, all subsets of (N-1) features are considered and the subset that leads to the best performance gives us the weakest feature (not involved in the considered set). This procedure is also called "leave one out" in the literature. Obviously, the discarded feature is not considered in the following steps. We iterate the process until there is only one remaining feature in the set, and use the following score for comparing systems: $F_{avg}(all) = \frac{F_{avg}(K)+F_{avg}(C)}{2}$, where $F_{avg}(K)$ and $F_{avg}(C)$ are the averaged F scores for *K* and *C* label, respectively, when threshold varies from 0.300 to 0.975. This strategy enables us to sort the features in descending order of importance, as displayed in Table 3. Figure 1 shows the evolution of the performance as more and more features are removed.

Rank	Feature name	Rank	Feature name
1	Source POS	14*	Distance to root
2*	Occur in Google Trans.	15	Backoff behaviour
3*	Nodes	16*	Constituent label
4	Target POS	17	Proper name
5	WPP	18	Number of occurrences
6	Left source context	19*	Min
7	Right target context	20*	Max
8	Numeric	21	Left target context
9*	Polysemy (target)	22*	Polysemy (source)
10	Punctuation	23*	Longest target gram length
11	Stop word	24*	Longest source gram length
12	Right source context	25	Source Word
13	Target Word		

Table 3: The rank of each feature (in term of usefulness) in the set. The symbol "*" indicates our proposed features.

Observations in 10-best and 10-worst performing features in Table 3 suggest that numerous features extracted directly from SMT system itself (source and target POS, alignment context information, WPP, lexical properties: numeric, punctuation) perform very well. Meanwhile, opposite from what we expected, those from word statistical knowledge sources (target and source language models) are likely to be much less beneficial. Besides, three of our proposed features appear in top 10-best. More noticeable, among them, the first-time-experimented feature "Occurrence in Google Translation hypothesis" is the most prominent (rank 2), implying that such an online MT system can be a reliable reference channel for predicting word quality.

[6]http://research.cs.tamu.edu/prism/lectures/pr/pr_l11.pdf

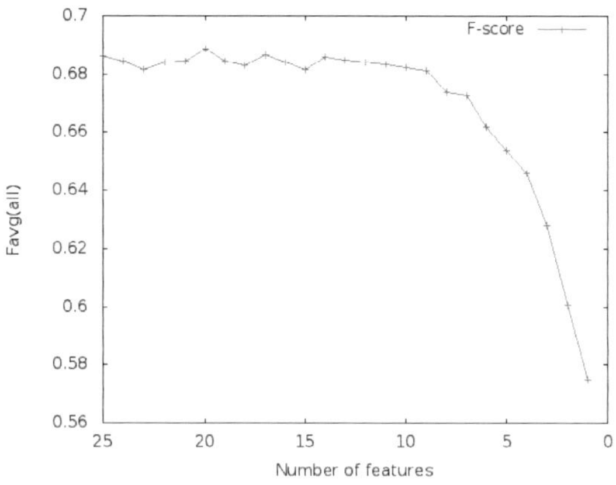

Figure 1: Evolution of system performance ($F_{avg}(all)$) during Feature Selection process, obtained on dev set

The above selection process also brings us the best-performing feature set (Top 20 in Table 3). The binary classifier built using this optimal subset of features (*FS_BIN*) reaches the optimal performance at the threshold value of 0.475, and slightly outperforms *ALL_BIN* in terms of F scores (0.46% better for *"K"* and 0.69% better for *"C"*). We then use this set to build the multi-class one (*FS_MULT*) and the results are shown to be a bit more effective compare to *ALL_MULT* (0.37% better for *"K"*, 0.80% better for *"S"* and 0.15% better for *"D"*). Detailed results of these two systems can be found in Table 4.

In addition, in Figure 1, when the size of feature set is small (from 1 to 7), we can observe sharply the growth of system scores for both labels. Nevertheless the scores seem to saturate as the feature set increases from the 8 up to 25. This phenomenon raises a hypothesis about the learning capability of our classifier when coping with a large number of features, hence drives us to an idea for improving the classification scores. This idea is detailed in the next section.

System	Label	Pr(%)	Rc(%)	F(%)
FS_BIN	K	85.90	85.48	85.69
	C	52.29	53.17	52.73
FS_MULT	K	85.05	85.00	85.02
	S	45.36	49.00	47.11
	D	9.1	5.9	7.16

Table 4: The Pr, Rc and F for labels of binary and multi-class system built from Top 20 features, at the optimal threshold value, obtained on dev set

5 Using Boosting technique to improve the system's performance

In this section, we try to answer to the following question: if we build a number of "weak" (or "basic") classifiers by using subsets of our features and a machine learning algorithm (such as *Boosting*), would we get a single "strong" classifier? When deploying this idea, our hope is that multiple models can complement each other as one feature set might be specialized in a part of the data where the others do not perform very well.

First, we prepare 23 feature subsets $(F_1, F_2, ..., F_{23})$ to train 23 basic classifiers, in which: F_1 contains all features, F_2 is the Top 20 in Table 3 and F_i $(i = \overline{3..23})$ contains 9 randomly chosen features. Next, a 7-fold cross validation is applied on our training set. We divide it into 7 subsets (S_1, S_2, ..., S_7). Each S_i $(i = \overline{1..6})$ contains 100 sentences, and the remaining 153 sentences constitute S_7. In the loop i $(i = \overline{1..7})$, S_i is used as the test set and the remaining data is trained with 23 feature subsets. After each loop, we obtain the results from 23 classifiers for each word in S_i. Finally, the concatenation of these results after 7 loops gives us the training data for Boosting. Therefore, the Boosting training file has 23 columns, each represents the output of one basic classifier for our training set. The detail of this algorithm is described below:

Algorithm to build Boosting training data

for i :=1 **to** 7 **do**
begin
    TrainSet(i) := $\cup S_k$ $(k = \overline{1..7}, k \neq i)$
    TestSet(i) := S_i
    for j := 1 **to** 23 **do**
    begin
        Classifier C_j := Train TrainSet(i) with F_j
        Result R_j := Use C_j to test S_i
        Column P_j := Extract the *"probability of word to be G label"* in R_j
    end
    Subset D_i (23 columns) := $\{P_j\}$ $(j = \overline{1..23})$
end
Boosting training set $D := \cup D_i$ $(i = \overline{1..7})$

Next, the Bonzaiboost toolkit[7] (which implements Boosting algorithm) is used for building Boosting model. In the training command, we invoked: algorithm = "AdaBoost", and number of iterations = 300. The Boosting test set is prepared as follows: we train 23 feature subsets with the **training set** to obtain 23 classifiers, then use them to test our **dev set**, finally extract the 23 probability columns (like in the above pseudo code). In the testing phase, similar to what we did in Section 4, the Pr, Rc and F scores against threshold variation for *"K"* and *"C"* labels are tracked, and those corresponding to the optimal threshold (0.575 in this case) are represented in Table 5.

System	Label	Pr(%)	Rc(%)	F(%)
BOOST_BIN	K	86.65	84.45	85.54
	C	51.99	56.48	54.15

Table 5: The Pr, Rc and F for labels of Boosting binary classifier (BOOST_BIN)

The scores suggest that using Boosting algorithm on our CRF classifiers' output accounts for an efficient way to make them predict better: on the one side, we maintain the already good achievement on *K* class (only 0.15% lost), on the other side we gain 1.42% the performance in *C* class. It is likely that Boosting enables different models to better complement each other, in terms of the later model becomes experts for instances handled wrongly by the previous ones. Another advantage is that Boosting algorithm weights each model by its performance (rather than treating them equally), so the strong models (come from all features, top 20, etc.) can make more dominant impacts than the rest.

6 Submissions and Official Results

After deploying several techniques to improve the system's prediction capability, we select two bests of each variant (binary and multi-class) to submit. For the binary task, the submissions include: the Boosting (BOOST_BIN) and the Top 20 (FS_BIN) system. For the multi-class task, we submit: the Top 20 (FS_MULT) and the all-feature (ALL_MULT) one. Before the submission, the training and dev sets were combined to re-train the prediction models for FS_BIN, FS_MULT and ALL_MULT. Table 6 reports the official results obtained by LIG at WMT 2013, task 2. We obtained the best performance among 3 participants. These results confirm that the feature selection strategy is efficient (FS_MULT slightly better than ALL_MULT) while the contribution of Boosting is unclear (BOOST_BIN better than FS_BIN if F-measure is considered but worse if Accuracy is considered - the difference is not significant).

[7]http://bonzaiboost.gforge.inria.fr/x1-20001

System	Pr	Rc	F	Acc
BOOST_BIN	0.777882	0.884325	0.827696	0.737702
FS_BIN	0.788483	0.864418	0.824706	0.738213
FS_MULT	-	-	-	0.720710
ALL_MULT	-	-	-	0.719177

Table 6: Official results of the submitted systems, obtained on test set

7 Discussion and Conclusion

In this paper, we describe the systems submitted for Task 2 of WMT13 Quality Estimation campaign. We cope with the prediction of quality at word level, determining whether each word is "good" or "bad" (in the binary variant), or is "good", or should be "substitute" or "delete" (in the multi-class variant). Starting with the existing word features, we propose and add various of novel ones to build the binary and multi-class baseline classifier. The first experiment's results show that precision and recall obtained in *"K"* label (both in binary and multi-class systems) are very encouraging, and *"C"* (or *"S"*) label reaches acceptable performance. A feature selection strategy is then deployed to enlighten the valuable features, find out the best performing subset. One more contribution we made is the protocol of applying Boosting algorithm, training multiple "weak" classifiers, taking advantage of their complementarity to get a "stronger" one. These techniques improve gradually the system scores (measure with F score) and help us to choose the most effective systems to classify the test set.

In the future, this work can be extended in the following ways. Firstly, we take a deeper look into linguistic features of word, such as the grammar checker, dependency tree, semantic similarity, etc. Besides, we would like to reinforce the segment-level confidence assessment, which exploits the context relation between surrounding words to make the prediction more accurate. Moreover, a methodology to evaluate the sentence confidence relied on the word- and segment- level confidence will be also deeply considered.

References

John Blatz, Erin Fitzgerald, George Foster, Simona Gandrabur, Cyril Goutte, Alex Kulesza, Alberto Sanchis, and Nicola Ueffing. Confidence estimation for machine translation. Technical report, JHU/CLSP Summer Workshop, 2003.

John Blatz, Erin Fitzgerald, George Foster, Simona Gandrabur, Cyril Goutte, Alex Kulesza, Alberto Sanchis, and Nicola Ueffing. Confidence estimation for machine translation. In *Proceedings of COLING 2004*, pages 315–321, Geneva, April 2004.

Mariano Felice and Lucia Specia. Linguistic features for quality estimation. In *Proceedings of the 7th Workshop on Statistical Machine Translation*, pages 96–103, Montreal, Canada, June 7-8 2012.

John Lafferty, Andrew McCallum, and Fernando Pereira. Conditional random fields: Probabilistic models for segmenting et labeling sequence data. In *Proceedings of ICML-01*, pages 282–289, 2001.

Thomas Lavergne, Olivier Cappé, and François Yvon. Practical very large scale crfs. In *Proceedings of the 48th Annual Meeting of the Association for Computational Linguistics*, pages 504–513, 2010.

Ngoc-Quang Luong. Integrating lexical, syntactic and system-based features to improve word confidence estimation in smt. In *Proceedings of JEP-TALN-RECITAL*, volume 3 (RECITAL), pages 43–56, Grenoble, France, June 4-8 2012.

Slav Petrov and Dan Klein. Improved inference for unlexicalized parsing. In *Proceedings of NAACL HLT 2007*, pages 404–411, Rochester, NY, April 2007.

S. Raybaud, D. Langlois, and K. Smaï li. "this sentence is wrong." detecting errors in machine - translated sentences. In *Machine Translation*, pages 1–34, 2011.

Radu Soricut and Abdessamad Echihabi. Trustrank: Inducing trust in automatic translations via ranking. In *Proceedings of the 48th ACL (Association for Computational Linguistics)*, pages 612–621, Uppsala, Sweden, July 2010.

Nicola Ueffing and Hermann Ney. Word-level confidence estimation for machine translation using phrased-based translation models. In *Proceedings of Human Language Technology Conference and Conference on Empirical Methods in Natural Language Processing*, pages 763–770, Vancouver, 2005.

Nicola Ueffing, Klaus Macherey, and Hermann Ney. Confidence measures for statistical machine translation. In *Proceedings of the MT Summit IX*, pages 394–401, New Orleans, LA, September 2003.

Deyi Xiong, Min Zhang, and Haizhou Li. Error detection for statistical machine translation using linguistic features. In *Proceedings of the 48th Association for Computational Linguistics*, pages 604–611, Uppsala, Sweden, July 2010.

DCU-Symantec at the WMT 2013 Quality Estimation Shared Task

Raphael Rubino[†⋆], Joachim Wagner[†‡], Jennifer Foster[†],
Johann Roturier[⋆] Rasoul Samad Zadeh Kaljahi[†⋆] and Fred Hollowood[⋆]
[†]NCLT, School of Computing, Dublin City University, Ireland
[‡]Center for Next Generation Localisation, Dublin, Ireland
[⋆]Symantec Research Labs, Dublin, Ireland
[†]{rrubino, jwagner, jfoster}@computing.dcu.ie
[⋆]{johann_roturier, fhollowood}@symantec.com

Abstract

We describe the two systems submitted by the *DCU-Symantec* team to Task 1.1. of the WMT 2013 Shared Task on Quality Estimation for Machine Translation. Task 1.1 involve estimating post-editing effort for English-Spanish translation pairs in the news domain. The two systems use a wide variety of features, of which the most effective are the word-alignment, n-gram frequency, language model, POS-tag-based and pseudo-references ones. Both systems perform at a similarly high level in the two tasks of scoring and ranking translations, although there is some evidence that the systems are over-fitting to the training data.

1 Introduction

The WMT 2013 Quality Estimation Shared Task involve both sentence-level and word-level quality estimation (QE). The sentence-level task consist of three subtasks: scoring and ranking translations with regard to post-editing effort (Task 1.1), selecting among several translations produced by multiple MT systems for the same source sentence (Task 1.2), and predicting post-editing time (Task 1.3). The DCU-Symantec team enter two systems to Task 1.1. Given a set of source English news sentences and their Spanish translations, the goals are to predict the HTER score of each translation and to produce a ranking based on HTER for the set of translations. A set of 2,254 sentence pairs are provided for training.

On the ranking task, our system `DCU-SYMC alltypes` is second placed out of thirteen systems and our system `DCU-SYMC combine` is ranked fifth, according to the Delta Average metric. According to the Spearman rank correlation, our systems are the joint-highest systems. In the scoring task, the `DCU-SYMC alltypes` system is placed sixth out of seventeen systems according to Mean Absolute Error (MAE) and third according to Root Mean Squared Error (RMSE). The `DCU-SYMC combine` system is placed fifth according to MAE and second according to RMSE.

In this system description paper, we describe the features, the learning methods used, the results for the two submitted systems and some other systems we experiment with.

2 Features

Our starting point for the WMT13 QE shared task was the feature set used in the system we submitted to the WMT12 QE task (Rubino et al., 2012). This feature set, comprising 308 features in total, extended the 17 baseline features provided by the task organisers to include 6 additional surface features, 6 additional language model features, 17 additional features derived from the MT system components and the n-best lists, 138 features obtained by part-of-speech tagging and parsing the source sentences and 95 obtained by part-of-speech tagging the target sentences, 21 topic model features, 2 features produced by a grammar checker[1] and 6 pseudo-source (or back-translation) features.

We made the following modifications to this 2012 feature set:

- The pseudo-source (or back-translation) features were removed, as they did not contribute useful information to our system last year.
- The language model and n-gram frequency feature sets were extended in order to cover 1 to 5 gram sequences, as well as source and target ratios for these feature values.
- The word-alignment feature set was also extended by considering several thresholds

[1] http://www.languagetool.org/

when counting the number of target words aligned with source words.

- We extracted 8 additional features from the decoder log file, including the number of discarded hypotheses, the total number of translation options and the number of nodes in the decoding graph.
- The set of topic model features was reduced in order to keep only those that were shown to be effective on three quality estimation datasets (the details can be found in (Rubino et al. (to appear), 2013)). These features encode the difference between source and target topic distributions according to several distance/divergence metrics.
- Following Soricut et al. (2012), we employed pseudo-reference features. The source sentences were translated with three different MT systems: an in-house phrase-based SMT system built using Moses (Koehn et al., 2007) and trained on the parallel data provided by the organisers, the rule-based system Systran[2] and the online, publicly available, Bing Translator[3]. The obtained translations are compared to the target sentences using sentence-level BLEU (Papineni et al., 2002), TER (Snover et al., 2006) and the Levenshtein distance (Levenshtein, 1966).
- Also following Soricut et al. (2012), one-to-one word-alignments, with and without Part-Of-Speech (POS) agreement, were included as features. Using the alignment information provided by the decoder, we POS tagged the source and target sentences with TreeTagger (Schmidt, 1994) and the publicly available pre-trained models for English and Spanish. We mapped the tagsets of both languages by simplifying the initial tags and obtain a reduced set of 8 tags. We applied that simplification on the tagged sentences before checking for POS agreement.

3 Machine Learning

In this section, we describe the learning algorithms and feature selection used in our experiments, leading to the two submitted systems for the shared task.

3.1 Primary Learning Method

To estimate the post-editing effort of translated sentences, we rely on regression models built using the Support Vector Machine (SVM) algorithm for regression ϵ-SVR, implemented in the LIBSVM toolkit (Chang and Lin, 2011). To build our final regression models, we optimise SVM hyper-parameters (C, γ and ϵ) using a grid-search method with 5-fold cross-validation for each parameter triplet. The parameters leading to the best MAE, RMSE and Pearson's correlation coefficient (r) are kept to build the model.

3.2 Feature Selection on Feature Types

In order to reduce the feature and obtain more compact models, we apply feature selection on each of our 15 feature types. Examples of feature types are *language model features* or *topic model features*. For each feature type, we apply a feature subset evaluation method based on the wrapper paradigm and using the best-first search algorithm to explore the feature space. The M5P (Wang and Witten, 1997) regression tree algorithm implemented in the Weka toolkit (Hall et al., 2009) is used with default parameters to train and evaluate a regression model for each feature subset obtained with best-first search. A 10-fold cross-validation is performed for each subset and we keep the features leading to the best RMSE. We use M5P regression trees instead of ϵ-SVR because grid-search with the latter is too computationally expensive to be applied so many times. Using feature selection in this way, we obtain 15 reduced feature sets that we combine to form the `DCU-SYMC alltypes` system, containing 102 features detailed in Table 1.

3.3 Feature Binarisation

In order to aid the SVM learner, we also experiment with binarising our feature set, i.e. converting our features with various feature value ranges into features whose values are either 1 or 0. Again, we employ regression tree learning. We train regression trees with M5P and M5P-R[4] (implemented in the Weka toolkit) and create a binary feature for each regression rule found in the trees (ignoring the leaf nodes). For example, a binary feature indicating whether the Bing TER score is less than or equal to 55.685 is derived from the

[2] Systran Enterprise Server version 6

[3] http://www.bing.com/translator

[4] We experiment with J48 decision trees as well, but this method did not outperform regression tree methods.

Backward LM
Source 1-gram perplexity.
Source & target 1-grams perplexity ratio.
Source & target 3-grams and 4-gram perplexity ratio.
Target Syntax
Frequency of tags: ADV, FS, DM, VLinf, VMinf, semicolon, VLger, NC, PDEL, VEfin, CC, CCNEG, PPx, ART, SYM, CODE, PREP, SE and number of ambiguous tags
Frequency of least frequent POS 3-gram observed in a corpus.
Frequency of least frequent POS 4-gram and 6-gram with sentence padding (start and end of sentence tags) observed in a corpus.
Source Syntax
Features from three probabilistic parsers. (Rubino et al., 2012).
Frequency of least frequent POS 2-gram, 4-gram and 9-gram with sentence padding observed in a corpus.
Number of analyses found and number of words, using a Lexical Functional Grammar of English as described in Rubino et al. (2012).
LM
Source unigram perplexity.
Target 3-gram and 4-gram perplexity with sentence padding.
Source & target 1-gram and 5-gram perplexity ratio.
Source & target unigram log-probability.
Decoder
Component scores during decoding.
Number of phrases in the best translation.
Number of translation options.
N-gram Frequency
Target 2-gram in second and third frequency quartiles.
Target 3-gram and 5-gram in low frequency quartiles.
Number of target 1-gram seen in a corpus.
Source & target 1-grams in highest and second highest frequency quartile.
One-to-One Word-Alignment
Count of O2O word alignment, weighted by target sentence length.
Count of O2O word alignment with POS agreement, weighted by count of O2O, by source length, by target length.
Pseudo-Reference
Moses translation TER score.
Bing translation number of words and TER score.
Systran sBLEU, number of substitutions and TER score.
Surface
Source number of punctuation marks and average words occurrence in source sentence.
Target number of punctuation marks, uppercased letters and binary value if the last character of the sentence is a punctuation mark.
Ratio of source and target sentence lengths, average word length and number of punctuation marks over sentence lengths.
Topic Model
Cosine distance between source and target topic distributions.
Jensen-Shannon divergence between source and target topic distributions.
Word Alignment
Averaged number of source words aligned per target words with $p(s\|t)$ thresholds: 1.0, 0.75, 0.5, 0.25, 0.01
Averaged number of source words aligned per target words with $p(s\|t) = 0.01$ weighted by target words frequency
Averaged number of target words aligned per source word with $p(t\|s) = 0.01$ weighted by source words frequency
Ratio of source and target averaged aligned words with thresholds: 1.0 and 0.1, and with threshold: 0.75, 0.5, 0.25 weighted by words frequency

Table 1: Features selected with the wrapper approach using best-first search and M5P. These features are included in the submitted system *alltypes*.

Feature to which threshold t is applied	t ($\leq$)
Target 1-gram backward LM log-prob.	-35.973
Target 3-gram backward LM perplexity	7144.99
Probabilistic parsing feature	3.756
Probabilistic parsing feature	57.5
Frequency of least frequent POS 6-gram	0.5
Source 3-gram LM log-prob.	65.286
Source 4-gram LM perplexity with padding	306.362
Target 2-gram LM perplexity	176.431
Target 4-gram LM perplexity	426.023
Target 4-gram LM perplexity with padding	341.801
Target 5-gram LM perplexity	112.908
Ratio src&trg 5-gram LM log-prob.	1.186
MT system component score	-50
MT system component score	-0.801
Source 2-gram frequency in low quartile	0.146
Ratio src&trg 2-gram in high freq. quartile	0.818
Ratio src&trg 3-gram in high freq. quartile	0.482
O2O word alignment	15.5
Pseudo-ref. Moses Levenshtein	19
Pseudo-ref. Moses TER	21.286
Pseudo-ref. Bing TER	16.905
Pseudo-ref. Bing TER	23.431
Pseudo-ref. Bing TER	37.394
Pseudo-ref. Bing TER	55.685
Pseudo-ref. Systran sBLEU	0.334
Pseudo-ref. Systran TER	36.399
Source average word length	4.298
Target uppercased/lowercased letters ratio	0.011
Ratio src&trg average word length	1.051
Source word align., $p(s\|t) > 0.75$	11.374
Source word align., $p(s\|t) > 0.1$	485.062
Source word align., $p(s\|t) > 0.75$ weighted	0.002
Target word align., $p(t\|s) > 0.01$ weighted	0.019
Word align. ratio $p > 0.25$ weighted	1.32

Table 2: Features selected with the M5P-R $M50$ binarisation approach. For each feature, the corresponding rule indicates the binary feature value. These features are included in the submitted system *combine* in addition to the features presented in Table 1.

regression rule *Bing TER score* ≤ 55.685.

The primary motivation for using regression tree learning in this way was to provide a quick and convenient method for binarising our feature set. However, we can also perform feature selection using this method by experimenting with various minimum leaf sizes (Weka parameter M). We plot the performance of the M5P and M5P-R (optimising towards correlation) over the parameter M and select the best three values of M. To experiment with the effect of smaller and larger feature sets, we further include parameters of M that (a) lead to an approximately 50% bigger feature set and (b) to an approximately 50% smaller feature set.

Our `DCU-SYMC combine` system was built by combining the `DCU-SYMC alltypes` feature set, reduced using the best-first M5P wrapper approach as described in subsection 3.2, with a binarised set produced using an M5P regression tree with a minimum of 50 nodes per leaf. This latter configuration, containing 34 features detailed in Table 2, was selected according to the evaluation scores obtained during cross-validation on the training set using ϵ-SVR, as described in the next section. Finally, we run a greedy backward feature selection algorithm wrapping ϵ-SVR on both `DCU-SYMC alltypes` and `DCU-SYMC combine` in order to optimise our feature sets for the SVR learning algorithm, removing 6 and 2 features respectively.

4 System Evaluation and Results

In this section, we present the results obtained with ϵ-SVR during 5-fold cross-validation on the training set and the final results obtained on the test set. We selected two systems to submit amongst the different configurations based on MAE, RMSE and r. As several systems reach the same performance according to these metrics, we use the number of support vectors (noted *SV*) as an indicator of training data over-fitting. We report the results obtained with some of our systems in Table 3.

The results show that the submitted systems `DCU-SYMC alltypes` and `DCU-SYMC combine` lead to the best scores on cross-validation, but they do not outperform the system combining the 15 feature types without feature selection (`15 types`). This system reaches the best scores on the test set compared to all our systems built on reduced feature sets. This indicates that we over-fit and fail to generalise from the training data.

Amongst the systems built using reduced feature sets, the `M5P-R M80` system, based on the tree binarisation approach using M5P-R, yields the best results on the test set on 3 out of 4 official metrics. These results indicate that this system, trained on 16 features only, tends to estimate HTER scores more accurately on the unseen test data. The results of the two systems based on the M5P-R binarisation method are the best compared to all the other systems presented in this Section. This feature binarisation and selection method leads to robust systems with few features: 31 and 16 for `M5P-R M50` and `M5P-R M80` respectively. Even though these systems do not lead to the best results, they outperform the two submitted systems on one metric used to evaluate the

System	nb feat	Cross-Validation MAE	RMSE	r	SV	Test MAE	RMSE	DeltaAvg	Spearman
15 types	442	0.106	0.138	0.604	1194.6	**0.126**	**0.156**	**0.108**	**0.625**
M5P $M50$	34	0.106	0.138	0.600	1417.8	0.135	0.167	0.102	0.586
M5P $M130$	4	0.114	0.145	0.544	750.6	0.142	0.173	0.079	0.517
M5P-R $M50$	31	0.106	0.137	0.610	655.4	0.135	0.166	0.100	0.591
M5P-R $M80$	16	0.107	0.139	0.597	570.6	0.134	0.165	0.106	0.597
alltypes*	96	**0.104**	0.135	0.624	1130.6	0.135	0.171	0.101	0.589
combine*	134	**0.104**	**0.134**	**0.629**	689.8	0.134	0.166	0.098	0.588

Table 3: Results obtained with different regression models, during cross-validation on the training set and on the test set, depending on the feature selection method. Systems marked with * were submitted for the shared task.

scoring task and two metrics to evaluate the ranking task.

On the systems built using reduced feature sets, we observe a difference of approximately 0.03pt absolute between the MAE and RMSE scores obtained during cross-validation and those on the test set. Such a difference can be related to training data over-fitting, even though the feature sets obtained with the tree binarisation methods are small. For instance, the system `M5P M130` is trained on 4 features only, but the difference between cross-validation and test MAE scores is similar to the other systems. We see on the final results that our feature selection methods is an over-fitting factor: by selecting the features which explain well the training set, the final model tends to generalise less. The selected features are suited for the specificities of the training data, but are less accurate at predicting values on the unseen test set.

5 Discussion

Training data over-fitting is clearly shown by the results presented in Table 3, indicated by the performance drop between results obtained during cross-validation and the ones obtained on the test set. While this drop may be related to data over-fitting, it may also be related to the use of different machine learning methods for feature selection (M5P and M5P-R) and for building the final regression models (ϵ-SVR). In order to verify this aspect, we build two regression models using M5P, based on the feature sets `alltypes` and `combine`. Results are presented in Table 4 and show that, for the `alltypes` feature set, the RMSE, DeltaAvg and Spearman scores are improved using M5P compared to SVM. For the `combine` feature set, the scoring results (MAE and RMSE) are better using SVM, while the ranking results are similar for both machine learning methods.

The performance drop between the results on the training data (or a development set) and the test data was also observed by the highest ranked participants in the WMT12 QE shared task. To compare our system without feature selection to the winner of the previous shared task, we evaluate the `15 types` system in Table 3 using the WMT12 QE dataset. The results are presented in Table 5. We can see that similar MAEs are obtained with our feature set and the WMT12 QE winner, whereas our system gets a higher RMSE (+0.01). For the ranking scores, our system is worse using the DeltaAvg metric while it is better on Spearman coefficient.

6 Conclusion

We presented in this paper our experiments for the WMT13 Quality Estimation shared task. Our approach is based on the extraction of a large initial feature set, followed by two feature selection methods. The first one is a wrapper approach using M5P and a best-first search algorithm, while the second one is a feature binarisation approach using M5P and M5P-R. The final regression models were built using ϵ-SVR and we selected two systems to submit based on cross-validation results.

We observed that our system reaching the best scores on the test set was not a system trained on a reduced feature set and it did not yield the best cross-validation results. This system was trained using 442 features, which are the combination of 15 different feature types. Amongst the systems built on reduced sets, the best results are obtained

System	nb feat	MAE	RMSE	DeltaAvg	Spearman
alltypes	96	0.135	0.165	0.104	0.604
combine	134	0.139	0.169	0.098	0.587

Table 4: Results obtained with the two feature sets contained in our submitted systems using M5P to build the regression models instead of ϵ-SVR.

System	nb feat	MAE	RMSE	DeltaAvg	Spearman
WMT12 winner	15	0.61	0.75	0.63	0.64
15 types	442	0.61	0.76	0.60	0.65

Table 5: Results obtained on WMT12 QE dataset with our best system (*15 types*) compared to WMT12 QE highest ranked team, in the Likert score prediction task.

using the feature binarisation approach `M5P-R 80`, which contains 16 features selected from our initial set of features. The tree-based feature binarisation is a fast and flexible method which allows us to vary the number of features by optimising the leaf size and leads to acceptable results with a few selected features.

Future work involves a deeper analysis of the over-fitting effect and an investigation of other methods in order to outperform the non-reduced feature set. We are also interested in finding a robust way to optimise the leaf size parameter for our tree-based feature binarisation method, without using cross-validation on the training set with an SVM algorithm.

Acknowledgements

The research reported in this paper has been supported by the Research Ireland Enterprise Partnership Scheme (EPSPG/2011/102 and EPSPD/2011/135) and Science Foundation Ireland (Grant 12/CE/I2267) as part of the Centre for Next Generation Localisation (`www.cngl.ie`) at Dublin City University.

References

Chih-Chung Chang and Chih-Jen Lin. 2011. LIBSVM: A Library for Support Vector Machines. *ACM Transactions on Intelligent Systems and Technology*, 2:27:1–27:27. Software available at `http://www.csie.ntu.edu.tw/~cjlin/libsvm`.

Mark Hall, Eibe Frank, Geoffrey Holmes, Bernhard Pfahringer, Peter Reutemann, and Ian H Witten. 2009. The WEKA Data Mining Software: an Update. *ACM SIGKDD Explorations Newsletter*, 11(1):10–18.

Philipp Koehn, Hieu Hoang, Alexandra Birch, Chris Callison-Burch, Marcello Federico, Nicola Bertoldi, Brooke Cowan, Wade Shen, Christine Moran, Richard Zens, et al. 2007. Moses: Open source toolkit for statistical machine translation. In *ACL*, pages 177–180.

Vladimir I Levenshtein. 1966. Binary codes capable of correcting deletions, insertions and reversals. In *Soviet physics doklady*, volume 10, page 707.

Kishore Papineni, Salim Roukos, Todd Ward, and Wei-Jing Zhu. 2002. Bleu: a method for automatic evaluation of machine translation. In *ACL*, pages 311–318.

Raphael Rubino, Jennifer Foster, Joachim Wagner, Johann Roturier, Rasul Samad Zadeh Kaljahi, and Fred Hollowood. 2012. DCU-Symantec Submission for the WMT 2012 Quality Estimation Task. In *Proceedings of the Seventh WMT*, pages 138–144.

Raphael Rubino et al. (to appear). 2013. Topic Models for Translation Quality Estimation for Gisting Purposes. In *Proceeding of MT Summit XIV*.

Helmut Schmidt. 1994. Probabilistic part-of-speech tagging using decision trees. In *Proceedings of the International Conference on New Methods in Natural Language Processing*.

Matthew Snover, Bonnie Dorr, Richard Schwartz, Linnea Micciulla, and John Makhoul. 2006. A study of translation edit rate with targeted human annotation. In *AMTA*, pages 223–231.

Radu Soricut, Nguyen Bach, and Ziyuan Wang. 2012. The SDL Language Weaver Systems in the WMT12 Quality Estimation Shared Task. In *Proceedings of the Seventh WMT*, pages 145–151.

Yong Wang and Ian H Witten. 1997. Inducing Model Trees for Continuous Classes. In *Proceedings of ECML*, pages 128–137. Prague, Czech Republic.

LIMSI Submission for the WMT'13 Quality Estimation Task: an Experiment with n-gram Posteriors

Anil Kumar Singh
LIMSI
Orsay, France
anil@limsi.fr

Guillaume Wisniewski
Université Paris Sud
LIMSI
Orsay, France
wisniews@limsi.fr

François Yvon
Université Paris Sud
LIMSI
Orsay, France
yvon@limsi.fr

Abstract

This paper describes the machine learning algorithm and the features used by LIMSI for the Quality Estimation Shared Task. Our submission mainly aims at evaluating the usefulness for quality estimation of n-gram posterior probabilities that quantify the probability for a given n-gram to be part of the system output.

1 Introduction

The dissemination of statistical machine translation (SMT) systems in the professional translation industry is still limited by the lack of reliability of SMT outputs, the quality of which varies to a great extent. In this context, a critical piece of information would be for MT systems to assess their output translations with automatically derived quality measures. This problem is the focus of a shared task, the aim of which is to predict the quality of a translation without knowing any human reference(s).

To the best of our knowledge, all approaches so far have tackled quality estimation as a supervised learning problem (He et al., 2010; Soricut and Echihabi, 2010; Specia et al., 2010; Specia, 2011). A wide variety of features have been proposed, most of which can be described as loosely 'linguistic' features that describe the source sentence, the target sentence and the association between them (Callison-Burch et al., 2012). Surprisingly enough, information used by the decoder to choose the best translation in the search space, such as its internal scores, have hardly been considered and never proved to be useful. Indeed, it is well-known that these scores are hard to interpret and to compare across hypotheses. Furthermore, mapping scores of a linear classifier (such as the scores estimated by MERT) into consistent probabilities is a difficult task (Platt, 2000; Lin et al., 2007).

This work aims at assessing whether information extracted from the decoder search space can help to predict the quality of a translation. Rather than using directly the decoder score, we propose to consider a finer level of information, the *n-gram posterior probabilities* that quantifies the probability for a given n-gram to be part of the system output. These probabilities can be directly interpreted as the confidence the system has for a given n-gram to be part of the translation. As they are directly derived from the number of hypotheses in the search space that contains this n-gram, these probabilities might be more reliable than the ones estimated from the decoder scores.

We first quickly review, in Section 2, the n-gram posteriors introduced by (Gispert et al., 2013) and explain how they can be used in the QE task; we then describe, in Section 3 the different systems that have developed for our participation in the WMT'13 shared task on Quality Estimation and assess their performance in Section 4.

2 n-gram Posterior Probabilities in SMT

Our contribution to the WMT'13 shared task on quality estimation relies on n-gram posteriors. For the sake of completeness, we will quickly formalize this notion and summarize the method proposed by (Gispert et al., 2013) to efficiently compute them. We will then describe preliminary experiments to assess their usefulness for predicting the quality of a translation hypothesis.

2.1 Computing n-gram Posteriors

For a given source sentence F, the n-gram posterior probabilities quantifies the probability for a given n-gram to be part of the system output. Their computation relies on all the hypotheses considered by a SMT system during decoding: intuitively, the more hypotheses a n-gram appears in, the more confident the system is that this n-gram is part of the 'correct' translation, and the higher its posterior probability is. Formally, the posterior of a given n-gram u is defined as:

$$P(u|\mathcal{E}) = \sum_{(A,E)\in\mathcal{E}} \delta_u(E) \cdot P(E, A|F)$$

where the sum runs over the translation hypotheses contained in the search space $\mathcal{E}$ (generally represented as a lattice); $\delta_u(E)$ has the value 1 if u occurs in the translation hypothesis E and 0 otherwise and $P(E, A|F)$ is the probability that the source sentence F is translated by the hypothesis E using a derivation A. Following (Gispert et al., 2013), this probability is estimated by applying a soft-max function to the score of the decoder:

$$P(A, E|F) = \frac{\exp\left(\alpha \times H(E, A, F)\right)}{\sum_{(A',E')\in\mathcal{E}} \exp\left(H(E', A', F)\right)}$$

where the decoder score $H(E, A, F)$ is typically a linear combination of a handful of features, the weights of which are estimated by MERT (Och, 2003).

n-gram posteriors therefore aggregate two pieces of information: first, the number of paths in the lattice (i.e. the number of translation hypotheses of the search path) the n-gram appears in; second, the decoder scores of these paths that can be roughly interpreted as a quality of the path.

Computing $P(u|\mathcal{E})$ requires to enumerate all n-gram contained in $\mathcal{E}$ and to count the number of paths in which this n-gram appears at least once. An efficient method to perform this computation in a single traversal of the lattice is described in (Gispert et al., 2013). This algorithm has been reimplemented[1] to generate the posteriors used in this work.

2.2 Analysis of n-gram Posteriors

Figure 1 represents the distribution of n-gram posteriors on the training set of the task 1-1. This distribution is similar to the ones observed for task 1-3 and for higher n-gram orders. It appears that, the distribution is quite irregular and has two modes. The minor modes corresponds to n-grams that appear in almost every translation hypotheses and have posterior probability close to 1. Further analyses show that these n-grams are mainly made of stop words and of out-of-vocabulary words. The major mode corresponds to very small n-gram posteriors (less than 10^{-1}) that the system has only a very small confidence in producing. The number of n-grams that have such a small posterior suggests that most n-grams occur only in a small number of paths.

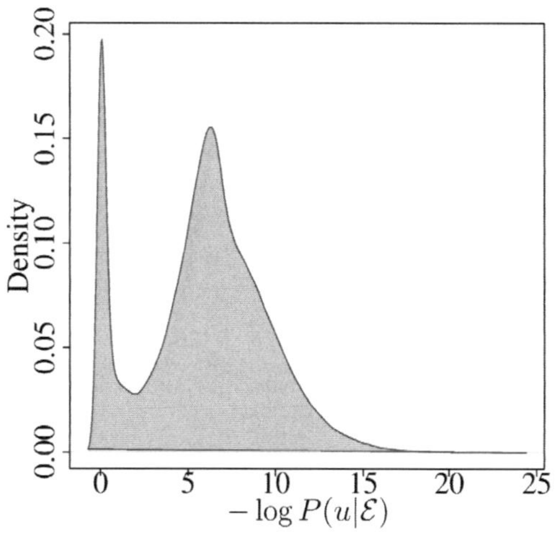

Figure 1: Distribution of the unigram posteriors observed on the training set of the task 1-1

Using n-gram posteriors to predict the quality of translation raises a representation issue: the number of n-grams contained in a sentence varies with the sentence length (and hence with the number of posteriors) but this information needs to be represented in a fixed-length vector describing the sentence. Similarly to what is usually done in the quality estimation task, we chose to represent posteriors probability by their histogram: for a given n-gram order, each posterior is mapped to a bin; each bin is then represented by a feature equal to the number of n-gram posteriors it contains. To account for the irregular distribution of posteriors, bin breaks are chosen on the training set so as to ensure that each bin contains the same number of examples. In our experiments, we considered a partition of the training data into 20 bins.

3 Systems Description

LIMSI has participated to the tasks 1-1 (prediction of the hTER) and 1-3 (prediction of the post-edition time). Similar features and learning algorithms have been considered for the two tasks. We will first quickly describe them before discussing the specific development made for task 1-3.

[1] Our implementation can be downloaded from http://perso.limsi.fr/Individu/wisniews/.

3.1 Features

In addition to the features described in the previous section, 176 'standard' features for quality estimation have been considered. The full list of features we have considered is given in (Wisniewski et al., 2013) and the features set can be downloaded from our website.[2] These features can be classified into four broad categories:

- **Association Features**: Measures of the quality of the 'association' between the source and the target sentences like, for instance, features derived from the IBM model 1 scores;
- **Fluency Features**: Measures of the 'fluency' or the 'grammaticality' of the target sentence such as features based on language model scores;
- **Surface Features**: Surface features extracted mainly from the source sentence such as the number of words, the number of out-of-vocabulary words or words that are not aligned;
- **Syntactic Features**: some simple syntactic features like the number of nouns, modifiers, verbs, function words, WH-words, number words, etc., in a sentence;

These features sets differ, in several ways, from the baseline feature set provided by the shared task organizers. First, in addition to features derived from a language model, it also includes several features based on large span continuous space language models (Le et al., 2011). Such language models have already proved their efficiency both for the translation task (Le et al., 2012) and the quality estimation task (Wisniewski et al., 2013). Second, each feature was expanded into two 'normalized forms' in which their value was divided either by the source length or the target length and, when relevant, into a 'ratio form' in which the feature value computed on the target sentence is divided by its value computed in the source sentence. At the end, when all possible feature expansions are considered, each example is described by 395 features.

[2] `http://perso.limsi.fr/Individu/wisniews/`

3.2 Learning Methods

The main focus of this work is to study the relevance of features for quality estimation; therefore, only very standard learning methods were used in our work. For this year submission both random forests (Breiman, 2001) and elastic net regression (Zou and Hastie, 2005) have been used. The capacity of random forests to take into account complex interactions between features has proved to be a key element in the results achieved in our experiments with last year campaign datasets (Zhuang et al., 2012). As we are considering a larger features set this year and the number of examples is comparatively quite small, we also considered elastic regression, a linear model trained with L_1 and L_2 priors as regularizers, hoping that training a sparse model would reduce the risk of overfitting.

In this study, we have used the implementation provided by `scikit-learn` (Pedregosa et al., 2011). As detailed in Section 4.1, cross-validation has been used to choose the hyper-parameters of all regressors, namely the number of estimators, the maximal depth of a tree and the minimum number of examples in a leaf for the random forests and the importance of the L_1 and the L_2 regularizers for the elastic net regressor.

3.3 System for Task 1-3

Like task 1-1, task 1-3 is a regression task that aims at predicting the time needed to post-edit a translation hypothesis. From a machine learning point of view, this task differs from task 1-1 in three aspects. First, the distributed training set is much smaller: it is made of only 803 examples, which increases the risk of overfitting. Second, contrary to hTER scores, post-edition time is not normalized and the label of this task can take any positive value. Finally and most importantly, as shown in Figure 2, the label distributions estimated on the training set has a long tail which indicates the presence of several outliers: in the worse case, it took more than 18 minutes to correct a single sentence made of 35 words! Such a long post-edition time most certainly indicates that the corrector has been distracted when post-editing the sentence rather than a true difficulty in the post-edition.

These outliers have a large impact on training and on testing, as their contributions to both MAE

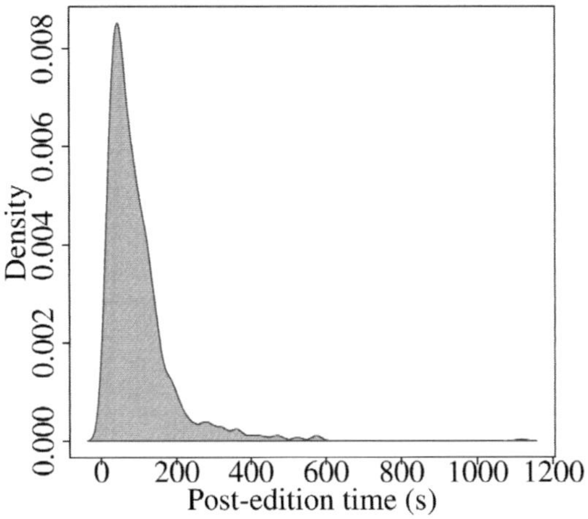

Figure 2: Kernel density estimate of the post-edition time distribution used as label in task 1-3.

and MSE,[3] directly depends on label values and can therefore be very large in the case of outliers. For instance, a simple ridge regression with the baseline features provided by the shared task organizer achieves a MAE of 42.641 ± 2.126 on the test set. When all the examples having a label higher than 300 are removed from the training set, the MAE drops to 41.843 ± 4.134. When outliers are removed from *both* the training and the test sets, the MAE further drops to 32.803 ± 1.673. These observations indicate that special care must be taken when collecting the data and that, maybe, post-edition times should be clipped to provide a more reliable estimation of the predictor performance.

In the following (and in our submission) only examples for which the post-edition time was less than 300 seconds were considered.

4 Results

4.1 Experimental Setup

We have tested different combinations of features and learning methods using a standard metric for regression: *Mean Absolute Error* (MAE) defined by:

$$\text{MAE} = \frac{1}{n} \sum_{i=1}^{n} |\hat{y}_i - y_i|$$

where n is the number of examples, y_i and $\hat{y}_i$ the true label and predicted label of the ith example. MAE can be understood as the averaged error made in predicting the quality of a translation.

Performance of both task 1-1 and task 1-3[4] was also evaluated by the Spearman rank correlation coefficient ρ that assesses how well the relationship between two variables can be described using a monotonic function. While the value of the correlation coefficient is harder to interpret as it not directly related to the value to predict, it can be used to compare the performance achieved when predicting different measures of the post-editing effort. Indeed, several sentence-level (or document level) annotation types can be used to reflect translation quality (Specia, 2011), such as the time needed to post-edit a translation hypothesis, the hTER, or qualitative judgments as it was the case for the shared task of WMT 2012. Comparing directly these different settings is complicated, since each of them requires to optimize a different loss, and even if the losses are the same, their actual values will depend on the actual annotation to be predicted (refer again to the discussion in (Specia, 2011, p5)). Using a metric that relies on the predicted rank of the example rather than the actual value predicted allows us to directly compare the performance achieved on the two tasks.

As the labels for the different tasks were not released before the evaluation, all the reported results are obtained on an 'internal' test set, made of 20% of the data released by the shared task organizers as 'training' data. The remaining data were used to train the regressor in a 10 folds cross-validation setting. In order to get reliable estimate of our methods performances, we used bootstrap resampling (Efron and Tibshirani, 1993) to compute confidence intervals of the different scores: 10 random splits of the data into a training and sets were generated; a regressor was then trained and tested for each of these splits and the resulting confidence intervals at 95% computed.

4.2 Results

Table 1and Table 2 contain the results achieved by our different conditions. We used, as a baseline, the set of 17 features released by the shared task organizers.

It appears that the differences in MAE between

[3] The two standard loss functions used to train and evaluate a regressor

[4] The Spearman ρ was an official metric only for task 1-1. For reasons explained in this paragraph, we also used it to evaluate our results for task 1-3.

the different configurations are always very small and hardly significant. However, the variation of the Spearman ρ are much larger and the difference observed are practically significant when the interpretation scale of (Landis and Koch, 1977) is used. We will therefore mainly consider ρ in our discussion.

For the two tasks 1-1 and 1-3, the features we have designed allow us to significantly improve prediction performance in comparison to the baseline. For instance, for task 1-1, the correlation is almost doubled when the features described in Section 3.1 are used. As expected, random forests are overfitting and did not manage to outperform a simple linear classifier. That is why we only used the elastic net method for our official submission. Including posterior probabilities in the feature set did not improve performance much (except when only the baseline features are considered) and sometimes even hurt performance. This might be caused by an overfitting problem, the training set becoming too small when new features are added. We are conducting further experiments to explain this paradoxical observation.

Another interesting observation that can be made looking at the results of Table 1 and Table 2 is that the prediction of the post-edition time seems to be easier than the prediction of the hTER: using the same classifiers and the same features, the performance for the former task is always far better than the performance for the latter.

5 Conclusion

In this paper, we described our submission to the WMT'13 shared task on quality estimation. We have explored the use of posteriors probability, hoping that information about the search space could help in predicting the quality of a translation. Even if features derived from posterior probabilities have shown to have only a very limited impact, we managed to significantly improve the baseline with a standard learning method and simple features. Further experiments are required to understand the reasons of this failure.

Our results also highlight the need to continue gathering high-quality resources to train and investigate quality estimation systems: even when considering few features, our systems were prone to overfitting. Developing more elaborated systems will therefore only be possible if more training resource is available. Our experiments also stress that both the choice of the quality measure (i.e. the quantity to predict) and of the evaluation metrics for quality estimation are still open problems.

6 Acknowledgments

This work was partly supported by ANR projects Trace (ANR-09-CORD-023) and Transread (ANR-12-CORD-0015).

References

Leo Breiman. 2001. Random forests. *Mach. Learn.*, 45(1):5–32, October.

Chris Callison-Burch, Philipp Koehn, Christof Monz, Matt Post, Radu Soricut, and Lucia Specia. 2012. Findings of the 2012 workshop on statistical machine translation. In *Proceedings of the Seventh Workshop on Statistical Machine Translation*, pages 10–51, Montréal, Canada, June. Association for Computational Linguistics.

B. Efron and R. Tibshirani. 1993. *An Introduction to the Bootstrap*. Chapman and Hall/CRC Monographs on Statistics and Applied Probability Series. Chapman & Hall.

Adrià Gispert, Graeme Blackwood, Gonzalo Iglesias, and William Byrne. 2013. N-gram posterior probability confidence measures for statistical machine translation: an empirical study. *Machine Translation*, 27(2):85–114.

Yifan He, Yanjun Ma, Josef van Genabith, and Andy Way. 2010. Bridging smt and tm with translation recommendation. In *Proceedings of the 48th Annual Meeting of the Association for Computational Linguistics*, pages 622–630, Uppsala, Sweden, July. Association for Computational Linguistics.

R. J. Landis and G. G. Koch. 1977. The measurement of observer agreement for categorical data. *Biometrics*, 33(1):159–174.

Hai Son Le, Ilya Oparin, Alexandre Allauzen, Jean-Luc Gauvain, and François Yvon. 2011. Structured Output Layer Neural Network Language Model. In *Proceedings of IEEE International Conference on Acoustic, Speech and Signal Processing*, pages 5524–5527, Prague, Czech Republic.

Hai-Son Le, Thomas Lavergne, Alexandre Allauzen, Marianna Apidianaki, Li Gong, Aurélien Max, Artem Sokolov, Guillaume Wisniewski, and François Yvon. 2012. Limsi @ wmt12. In *Proceedings of the Seventh Workshop on Statistical Machine Translation*, pages 330–337, Montréal, Canada, June. Association for Computational Linguistics.

	MAE		ρ	
	train	test	train	test
Baseline Features				
RandomForest	0.109 ± 0.013	0.130 ± 0.004	0.405 ± 0.008	0.314 ± 0.016
Elastic	0.127 ± 0.001	0.129 ± 0.003	0.336 ± 0.004	0.319 ± 0.015
'Linguistic' Features				
RandomForest	0.082 ± 0.019	0.118 ± 0.003	0.689 ± 0.003	0.625 ± 0.009
Elastic	0.107 ± 0.004	0.115 ± 0.003	0.705 ± 0.009	0.660 ± 0.009
'Linguistic' Features + posteriors				
RandomForest	0.088 ± 0.017	0.116 ± 0.003	0.694 ± 0.003	0.615 ± 0.014
Elastic	0.105 ± 0.006	0.114 ± 0.002	0.699 ± 0.007	0.662 ± 0.011

Table 1: Results for the task 1-1

	MAE		ρ	
	train	test	train	test
Baseline Features				
RandomForest	25.145 ± 3.745	33.279 ± 1.687	0.669 ± 0.007	0.639 ± 0.017
Elastic	32.776 ± 0.795	33.702 ± 2.328	0.678 ± 0.006	0.657 ± 0.018
Baseline Features + Posteriors				
RandomForest	33.707 ± 0.309	35.646 ± 0.889	0.674 ± 0.004	0.637 ± 0.017
Elastic	31.487 ± 0.261	32.922 ± 0.789	0.698 ± 0.004	0.681 ± 0.016
'Linguistic' Features				
RandomForest	25.236 ± 4.400	33.017 ± 1.582	0.735 ± 0.007	0.666 ± 0.023
Elastic	28.706 ± 1.273	31.630 ± 1.612	0.760 ± 0.006	0.701 ± 0.017
'Linguistic' Features + Posteriors				
RandomForest	22.951 ± 3.903	33.013 ± 1.514	0.741 ± 0.003	0.695 ± 0.013
Elastic	28.911 ± 1.020	31.865 ± 1.636	0.761 ± 0.008	0.710 ± 0.017

Table 2: Results for the task 1-3

Hsuan-Tien Lin, Chih-Jen Lin, and Ruby C. Weng. 2007. A note on platt's probabilistic outputs for support vector machines. *Mach. Learn.*, 68(3):267–276, October.

Franz Josef Och. 2003. Minimum error rate training in statistical machine translation. In *Proceedings of the 41st Annual Meeting of the Association for Computational Linguistics*, pages 160–167, Sapporo, Japan.

F. Pedregosa, G. Varoquaux, A. Gramfort, V. Michel, B. Thirion, O. Grisel, M. Blondel, P. Prettenhofer, R. Weiss, V. Dubourg, J. Vanderplas, A. Passos, D. Cournapeau, M. Brucher, M. Perrot, and E. Duchesnay. 2011. Scikit-learn: Machine Learning in Python . *Journal of Machine Learning Research*, 12:2825–2830.

John C. Platt, 2000. *Probabilities for SV Machines*, pages 61–74. MIT Press.

Radu Soricut and Abdessamad Echihabi. 2010. Trustrank: Inducing trust in automatic translations via ranking. In *Proceedings of the 48th Annual Meeting of the Association for Computational Linguistics*, pages 612–621, Uppsala, Sweden, July. Association for Computational Linguistics.

Lucia Specia, Dhwaj Raj, and Marco Turchi. 2010. Machine translation evaluation versus quality estimation. *Machine Translation*, 24(1):39–50, March.

Lucia Specia. 2011. Exploiting objective annotations for measuring translation post-editing effort. In *Proceedings of the 15th conference of EAMT*, pages 73–80, Leuven, Belgium.

Guillaume Wisniewski, Anil Kumar Singh, and François Yvon. 2013. Quality estimation for machine translation: Some lessons learned. *Machine Translation*. accepted for publication.

Yong Zhuang, Guillaume Wisniewski, and François Yvon. 2012. Non-linear models for confidence estimation. In *Proceedings of the Seventh Workshop on Statistical Machine Translation*, pages 157–162, Montréal, Canada, June. Association for Computational Linguistics.

Hui Zou and Trevor Hastie. 2005. Regularization and variable selection via the elastic net. *Journal of the Royal Statistical Society, Series B*, 67:301–320.

Ranking Translations using Error Analysis and Quality Estimation

Mark Fishel
Institute of Computational Linguistics
University of Zurich, Switzerland
fishel@cl.uzh.ch

Abstract

We describe TerrorCat, a submission to this year's metrics shared task. It is a machine learning-based metric that is trained on manual ranking data from WMT shared tasks 2008–2012. Input features are generated by applying automatic translation error analysis to the translation hypotheses and calculating the error category frequency differences. We additionally experiment with adding quality estimation features in addition to the error analysis-based ones. When evaluated against WMT'2012 rankings, the system-level agreement is rather high for several language pairs.

1 Introduction

Recently a couple of methods of automatic analysis of translation errors have been described (Zeman et al., 2011; Popović and Ney, 2011). Both of these compare a hypothesis translation to a reference and draw detailed conclusions from the differences between the two.

TerrorCat, a metric submitted to the metrics shared task of WMT'2012 (Callison-Burch et al., 2012) used the output of those two error analysis methods as input features, which yielded mildly promising results (Fishel et al., 2012). However the submitted version of TerrorCat was language pair-specific, which means that the classifier model used by the metric has to be retrained on new manual pairwise ranking data for every new language pair. This in turn complicates its usage.

Our main aim in this work is to make TerrorCat usable out-of-the-box. We compare models specific to the language pair (baseline), target language and a universal model for all languages. The updated metric is applied to the WMT'13 metrics shared task.

An additional modification to the metric uses input features from quality estimation. Using the resources of the quality estimation shared task of WMT'13 the modified model is applied to the English–Spanish language pair.

We start by briefly re-introducing the TerrorCat metric.

2 Baseline

The baseline TerrorCat metric is a machine learning-based metric: it uses manually ranked translation hypothesis pairs to train a classifier model. The trained model is then used to predict a ranking for new sentence pairs that have not been ranked yet.

To convert the binary comparisons between translation hypothesis pairs into a numeric score per translation hypothesis the wins per hypothesis are summed together. Previous year's work has shown (Fishel et al., 2012) that weighting the wins with the classifier's confidence for the summed score improves agreement with human judgements.

The input features for learning and classification are obtained by

1. applying translation error analysis software to the compared hypotheses,
2. getting the frequencies of every error type, i.e. the ratio of words marked with that error type to the hypothesis sentence length,
3. and using each error type's frequency differences between the two hypotheses as input features.

Relative frequencies are used on both system and segment level: i.e. the ratios of words marked with a particular error type to the hypothesis translation length. This guarantees that feature values lie in the $[-1, 1]$ range.

Translation error analysis is done with two tools: Addicter (Zeman et al., 2011) and Hjerson (Popović and Ney, 2011). Both perform error analysis by comparing the hypothesis and reference translations on word level and treating each difference as an error of one or the other kind. Translation error taxonomies as well as the way word differences and their contexts are interpreted differ between the two tools. In order to enable independent input from both tools the feature vectors obtained from them both tools are concatenated.

To increase the level of detail the frequencies of each error category are counted separately for each part-of-speech separately. As a result, e.g. instead of having the information of order errors having a particular frequency, the classifier will separately see the frequencies of misplaced nouns, adjectives, particles, etc.

3 Experiments

The usage of part-of-speech tags improves agreement with human judgements (Fishel et al., 2012); however, it also introduces language dependency for the metric. In the first set of experiments we try to remove this imposed dependency without losing the achieved benefit.

3.1 Common Settings

We focused on six language pairs: between English and German, French and Spanish. Manual ranking data for training was taken from WMT shared task evaluations 2008–2011; data from WMT'2012 was used as a development set to assess the performance of metric variations.

Final models for the WMT'2013 shared task were re-trained on the whole set of manual rankings, from WMT 2008–2012.

The classifier used by TerrorCat is an SVM with a linear kernel; more powerful kernels, such as radial basis function-based ones scaled poorly to the high number of features and thus were not tested.

PoS-tagging was done using TreeTagger (Schmid, 1995) with the pre-trained models for English, German, French and Spanish.

3.2 Language Independence

It is natural to expect error categories to have varying importance on the quality comparison between two translation candidates. For instance, one might expect order differences between translations into functional languages (e.g. English, Chinese) to have a greater importance than in case of languages with a more flexible word order (e.g. German, Russian); on the other hand inflection errors are likely to do more damage to the meaning in morphologically complex languages (e.g. Russian, Finnish) than in languages with simpler morphology (e.g. English, French). However, we want to see whether we can train a classifier that would generalize over all language pairs.

The main obstacle for training a general model on all language pairs are the different taxonomies of part-of-speech tags for different target languages: the arity of the input feature vectors is different for different target languages, which makes the data incompatible between them.

To overcome the difference we define a mapping from every used taxonomy to a common general set of PoS-tags, which is supposed to cover any language. It consists of general part-of-speech categories (such as noun, verb, particle, etc., a total of 15), without any morphological information (tense, case, person, etc.).

By using the same set of generalized PoS-tags for every language we ensure that the used TerrorCat classifier model is language-independent; the PoS-tagging step is naturally language-dependent still.

Tables 1 and 2 present system-level and segment-level correlations of TerrorCat based on this common PoS-tag set and three models, specific to the language pair, target language only and a general model for any language. Both sets of results show that using a language-independent model neither improves nor worsens the performance.

3.3 Quality Estimation for Ranking

To further improve the agreement between TerrorCat and human assessment we experimented with adding input features from quality estimation.

The input features were adopted from this year's shared task on quality estimation. We selected the smaller set of black-box features, which included the sentence lenghts, their language model probabilities, average numbers of translations per word, percentages of uni-, bi- and tri-grams in the different frequency quartiles, etc. All resources were taken from the shared task, which also meant that this modified model was applied only to English–Spanish.

	de-en	en-de	es-en	en-es	fr-en	en-fr
Language pair-specific	0.94	0.56	0.94	0.59	0.85	0.82
Target language-specific	0.92	0.56	0.97	0.59	0.84	0.82
Language-independent	0.93	0.71	0.94	0.66	0.84	0.88
BLEU	0.67	0.22	0.87	0.40	0.81	0.71
METEOR	0.89	0.18	0.95	0.45	0.84	0.82
TER	0.62	0.41	0.92	0.45	0.82	0.66

Table 1: System-level correlation between TerrorCat and human ranking. Correlations of BLEU, METEOR and TER scores are given for comparison.

	de-en	en-de	es-en	en-es	fr-en	en-fr
Language pair-specific	0.31	0.18	0.24	0.21	0.23	0.20
Target language-specific	0.31	0.18	0.28	0.21	0.23	0.20
Language-independent	0.28	0.20	0.27	0.22	0.24	0.21

Table 2: Segment-level correlation between TerrorCat and human ranking.

Training the model on quality estimation features alone yields a system-level score of 0.56. Although this is lower than the TerrorCat baseline, it beats the correlations of BLEU, TER and METEOR (see Table 1). The segment-level correlation is -0.01.

Next we combined features from error analysis and quality estimation by concatenating them into a single input feature vector. As a result system-level correlation improved to 0.72, which is higher than all TerrorCat variants so far (best correlation: 0.66). Segment-level correlation remained practically the same (0.22).

4 Conclusion

We have applied TerrorCat to the shared metrics task of WMT'2013. Just like last year, the results are mildly promising.

We were successful at achieving language independence, provided that PoS-tagging is done before applying the metric.

The trained model as well as the metric implementation with all the necessary scripts is available online[1].

It remains to be tested, whether quality estimation features fit well with the language-independent models. As the extracted feature values are based on completely different, language-specific resources, this does not seem to be a likely outcome.

[1] https://github.com/fishel/TerrorCat

References

Chris Callison-Burch, Philipp Koehn, Christof Monz, Matt Post, Radu Soricut, and Lucia Specia. 2012. Findings of the 2012 workshop on statistical machine translation. In *Proceedings of the Seventh Workshop on Statistical Machine Translation*, pages 10–51, Montréal, Canada.

Mark Fishel, Rico Sennrich, Maja Popović, and Ondřej Bojar. 2012. Terrorcat: a translation error categorization-based mt quality metric. In *Proceedings of the Seventh Workshop on Statistical Machine Translation*, pages 64–70, Montréal, Canada.

Maja Popović and Hermann Ney. 2011. Towards automatic error analysis of machine translation output. *Computational Linguistics*, 37(4):657–688.

Helmut Schmid. 1995. Improvements in part-of-speech tagging with an application to german. In *Proceedings of the ACL SIGDAT-Workshop*, Dublin, Ireland.

Daniel Zeman, Mark Fishel, Jan Berka, and Ondřej Bojar. 2011. Addicter: What is wrong with my translations? *The Prague Bulletin of Mathematical Linguistics*, 96:79–88.

Are ACT's scores increasing with better translation quality?

Najeh Hajlaoui
Idiap Research Institute
Rue Marconi 19
CH-1920 Martigny Switzerland
Najeh.Hajlaoui@idiap.ch

Abstract

This paper gives a detailed description of the ACT (Accuracy of Connective Translation) metric, a reference-based metric that assesses only connective translations. ACT relies on automatic word-level alignment (using GIZA++) between a source sentence and respectively the reference and candidate translations, along with other heuristics for comparing translations of discourse connectives. Using a dictionary of equivalents, the translations are scored automatically or, for more accuracy, semi-automatically. The accuracy of the ACT metric was assessed by human judges on sample data for English/French, English/Arabic, English/Italian and English/German translations; the ACT scores are within 2-5% of human scores.

The actual version of ACT is available only for a limited language pairs. Consequently, we are participating only for the English/French and English/German language pairs. Our hypothesis is that ACT metric scores increase with better translation quality in terms of human evaluation.

1 Introduction

Discourse connectives should preserve their sense during translation, as they are often ambiguous and may convey more than one sense depending on the inter-sentential relation (causality, concession, contrast or temporal). For instance, *since* in English can express temporal simultaneity, but also a causal sense.

In this paper, we present results of different Machine Translation systems for English-to-French and English-to-German pairs. More specifically, we measure the quality of machine translations of eight English discourse connectives: *although, even though, meanwhile, since, though, while, however*, and *yet*, adopting different approaches. This quality is measured using a dedicated metric named ACT (Accuracy of Connective Translation), a reference-based metric that assesses only connective translations.

The paper is organized as follows. In Section 2, we present the ACT metric and its error rate. In section 3, we compare the ACT metric to previous machine translation evaluation metrics. Finally, we present the results of the different English-to-German and English-to-French MT systems (Section 4).

2 ACT Metric

We described the ACT metric in (Hajlaoui and Popescu-Belis, 2013) and (Hajlaoui and Popescu-Belis, 2012). Its main idea is to detect, for a given explicit source discourse connective, its translation in a reference translation and in a candidate translation. ACT then compares and scores these translations. To identify the translations, ACT first uses a dictionary of possible translations of each discourse connective type, collected from training data and validated by humans. If a reference or a candidate translation contains more than one possible translation of the source connective, alignment information is used to detect the correct connective translation. If the alignment information is irrelevant (not equal to a connective), it then compares the word position (word index) of the source connective alignment with the index in the translated sentence (candidate or reference) and the set of candidate connectives to disambiguate the connective's translation. Finally, the nearest connective to the alignment is taken.

ACT proceeds by checking whether the reference translation contains one of the possible translations of the connective in question. After that, it similarly checks if the candidate translation contains a possible translation of the connective. Finally, it checks if the reference connective found is equal (case 1), synonymous (case 2) or incompatible [1](case 3) to the candidate connective. Discourse relations can be implicit in the candidate (case 4), or in the reference (case 5) translation or in both of them (case 6). These different comparisons can be represented by the following 6 cases:

- Case 1: same connective in the reference (Ref) and candidate translation (Cand).
- Case 2: synonymous connective in Ref and Cand.
- Case 3: incompatible connective in Ref and Cand.
- Case 4: source connective translated in Ref but not in Cand.
- Case 5: source connective translated in Cand but not in Ref.
- Case 6: the source connective neither translated in Ref nor in Cand.

Based on the connective dictionary categorised by senses, ACT gives one point for identical (case 1) and equivalent translations (case 2), otherwise zero. ACT proposes a semi-automatic option by manually checking instances of case 5 and case 6[2].

ACT returns the ratio of the total number of points to the number of source connectives according to the three versions: (1) ACTa counts only case 1 and case 2 as correct and all others cases as wrong, (2) ACTa5+6 excludes case 5 and case 6 and (3) ACTm considers the correct translations found by manual scoring of case 5 and case 6 noted respectively case5corr and case6corr to better consider these implicit cases.

$$ACTa = (| case1 | + | case2 |)/ \sum_{i=1}^{6} | casei | \quad (1)$$

$$ACTa5+6 = (| case1 | + | case2 |)/ \sum_{i=1}^{4} | casei | \quad (2)$$

$$ACTm = ACTa + (| case5corr | + | case6corr | / \sum_{i=1}^{6} | casei |) \quad (3)$$

[1]In terms of connective sense.

[2]We do not check manually case 4 because we observed that its instances propose generally explicit translations that do not belong to our dictionary, it means the SMT system tends to learn explicit translations for explicit source connective.

2.1 Configurations of ACT metric

As shown in Figure 1, ACT can be configured to use an optional disambiguation module. Two versions of this disambiguation module can be used: (1) without training, which means without saving an alignment model and only using GIZA++ as alignment tool; (2) with training and saving an alignment model using MGIZA++ (a multi-threaded version of GIZA++) trained on an external corpus to align the (Source, Reference) and the (Source, Candidate) data.

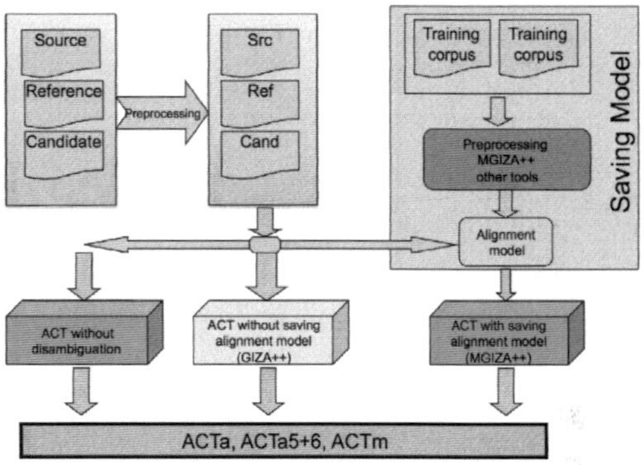

Figure 1: ACT architecture

ACT is more accurate using the disambiguation module. We encourage to use the version without training since it only requires the installation of the GIZA++ tool. Based on its heuristics and on its connective dictionaries categorised by senses, ACT has a higher precision to detect the right connective when more than one translation is possible. The following example illustrates the usefulness of the disambiguation module when we have more than one possible translation of the source connective. Without disambiguation, ACT detects the same connective **si** in both target sentences (wrong case 1), while the right translation of the source connective **although** is **bien que** and **même si** respectively in the reference and the candidate sentence (case 2).

Without disambiguation, case 1: Csrc= although, Cref = si, Ccand = si

With disambiguation, case 2: Csrc= although (concession), Cref = bien que, Ccand = même si

- SOURCE: *we did not have it so bad in ireland this time* ***although*** *we have had many serious wind storms on the atlantic .*

- REFERENCE: *cette fois-ci en irlande . ce n' était pas* **si** *grave .* **bien que** *de nombreuses tempêtes violentes aient sévi dans l' atlantique .*
- CANDIDATE: *nous n' était pas* **si** *mauvaise en irlande . cette fois .* **même si** *nous avons eu vent de nombreuses graves tempêtes sur les deux rives de l' atlantique .*

In the following experiments, we used the recommended configuration of ACT (without training).

2.2 Error rate of the ACT metric

ACT is a free open-source Perl script licensed under GPL v3[3]. It has a reasonable and acceptable error score when comparing its results to human judgements (Hajlaoui and Popescu-Belis, 2013). Its accuracy was assessed by human judges on sample data for English-to-French, English-to-Arabic, English-to-Italian and English-to-German translations; the ACT scores are within 2-5% of human scores.

2.3 Multilingual architecture of ACT Metric

The ACT architecture is multilingual: it was initially developed for the English-French language pair, then ported to English-Arabic, English-Italian and English-German.

The main resource needed to port the ACT metric to another language pair is the dictionary of connectives matching possible synonyms and classifying connectives by sense. To find these possible translations of a given connective, we proposed an automatic method based on a large corpus analysis (Hajlaoui and Popescu-Belis, 2012). This method can be used for any language pair.

Estimating the effort that would have to be taken to port the ACT metric to new language pairs focusing on the same linguistic phenomena mainly depends on the size of parallel data sets containing the given source connective. The classification by sense depends also on the number of possible translations detected for a given source connective. This task is sometimes difficult, as some translations (target connectives) can be as ambiguous as the source connective. Native linguistic knowledge of the target language is therefore needed in order to complete a dictionary with the main meanings and senses of the connectives.

[3]Available from `https://github.com/idiap/act`.

We think that the same process and the same effort can be taken to adapt ACT to new linguistic phenomena (verbs, pronouns, adverbs, etc).

3 Related works

ACT is different from existing MT metrics. The METEOR metric (Denkowski and Lavie, 2011) uses monolingual alignment between two translations to be compared: a system translation and a reference one. METEOR performs a mapping between unigrams: every unigram in each translation maps to zero or one unigram in the other translation. Unlike METEOR, the ACT metric uses a bilingual alignment (between the source and the reference sentences and between the source and the candidate sentences) and the word position information as additional information to disambiguate the connective situation in case there is more than one connective in the target (reference or candidate) sentence. ACT may work without this disambiguation.

The evaluation metric described in (Max et al., 2010) indicates for each individual source word which systems (among two or more systems or system versions) correctly translated it according to some reference translation(s). This allows carrying out detailed contrastive analyses at the word level, or at the level of any word class (e.g. part of speech, homonymous words, highly ambiguous words relative to the training corpus, etc.). The ACT metric relies on the independent comparison of one system's hypothesis with a reference. An automatic diagnostics of machine translation and based on linguistic checkpoints (Zhou et al., 2008), (Naskar et al., 2011) constitute a different approach from our ACT metric. The approach essentially uses the BLEU score to separately evaluate translations of a set of predefined linguistic checkpoints such as specific parts of speech, types of phrases (e.g., noun phrases) or phrases with a certain function word. A different approach was proposed by (Popovic and Ney, 2011) to study the distribution of errors over five categories (inflectional errors, reordering errors, missing words, extra words, incorrect lexical choices) and to examine the number of errors in each category. This proposal was based on the calculation of Word Error Rate (WER) and Position-independent word Error Rate (PER), combined with different types of linguistic knowledge (base forms, part-of-speech tags, name entity tags, compound words, suffixes, prefixes). This approach does not allow checking synonym words having the same meaning like the case of discourse connectives.

4 ACT-based comparative evaluation

We used the ACT metric to assess connective translations for 21 English-German systems and 23 English-French systems. It was computed on tokenized and lower-cased text using its second configuration "without training" (Hajlaoui and Popescu-Belis, 2013).

Table 1 shows only ACTa scores for the English-to-German translation systems since ACTa5+6 gives the same rank as ACTa. Table 2 present the same for the English-to-French systems. We are not presenting ACTm either because we didn't check manually case 5 and case 6.

Metric	System	Value	Avg	SD
ACTa	cu-zeman.2724	0.772	0.697	0.056
	rbmt-3	0.772		
	TUBITAK.2633	0.746		
	KITprimary.2663	0.737		
	StfdNLPG.2764	0.733		
	JHU.2888	0.728		
	LIMSI-N-S-p.2589	0.720		
	online-G	0.720		
	Shef-wproa.2748	0.720		
	RWTHJane.2676	0.711		
	uedin-wmt13.2638	0.707		
	UppslaUnv.2698	0.707		
	online-A	0.698		
	rbmt-1	0.694		
	online-B	0.677		
	uedin-syntax.2611	0.672		
	online-C	0.664		
	FDA.2842	0.664		
	MES-reorder.2845	0.664		
	PROMT.2789	0.621		
	rbmt-4	0.513		

Table 1: Metric scores for all En-De systems: ACTa and ACTa5+6 scores give the same rank; ACT V1.7. SD is the Standard Deviation.

5 Conclusion

The connective translation accuracy of the candidate systems cannot be measured correctly by current MT metrics such as BLEU and NIST. We therefore developed a new distance-based metric, ACT, to measure the improvement in connective translation. ACT is a reference-based metric that only compares the translations of discourse connectives. It is intended to capture the improvement of an MT system that can deal specifically with discourse connectives.

Metric	System	Value	Avg	SD
ACTa	cu-zeman.2724	0.772	0.608	0.04
	online-B	0.647		
	LIMSI-N-S.2587	0.647		
	MES.2802	0.647		
	FDA.2890	0.638		
	KITprimary.2656	0.638		
	cu-zeman.2728	0.634		
	online-G	0.634		
	PROMT.2752	0.634		
	uedin-wmt13.2884	0.634		
	MES-infl-pr.2672	0.629		
	StfdNLPGPTP.2765	0.629		
	DCUprimary.2827	0.625		
	JHU.2683	0.625		
	online-A	0.621		
	OmniFTEn-to-Fr.2647	0.616		
	RWTHph-Janepr.2639	0.612		
	OFITEnFr.2645	0.591		
	rbmt-1	0.586		
	Its-LATL.2667	0.565		
	rbmt-3	0.565		
	rbmt-4	0.543		
	Its-LATL.2652	0.543		
	online-C	0.500		

Table 2: Metric scores for all En-Fr systems: ACTa and ACTa5+6 scores give the same rank; ACT V1.7. SD is the Standard Deviation.

ACT can be also used semi-automatically. Consequently, the scores reflect more accurately the improvement in translation quality in terms of discourse connectives.

Theoretically, a better system should preserve the sense of discourse connectives. Our hypothesis is thus that ACT scores are increasing with better translation quality. We need access the human rankings of this task to validate if ACT's scores indeed correlate with overall translation quality rankings.

Acknowledgments

We are grateful to the Swiss National Science Foundation for its support through the COMTIS Sinergia Project, n. CRSI22_127510 (see www.idiap.ch/comtis/).

References

Marine Carpuat and Dekai Wu. 2005. Word sense disambiguation vs. statistical machine translation. In *Proceedings of the 43rd Annual Meeting on Association for Computational Linguistics (ACL)*, pages 387–394, Sydney, Australia.

Marine Carpuat, Yihai Shen, Xiaofeng Yu, and Dekai Wu. 2006. Toward integrating word sense and entity disambiguation into statistical machine translation. In *Proceedings of the 3rd International Workshop on Spoken Language Translation (IWSLT)*, pages 37–44, Kyoto, Japan.

Bruno Cartoni and Thomas Meyer. 2012. Extracting Directional and Comparable Corpora from a Multilingual Corpus for Translation Studies. In *Proceedings of the eighth international conference on Language Resources and Evaluation (LREC)*, Istanbul, Turkey.

Yee Seng Chan, Hwee Tou Ng, and David Chiang. 2007. Word sense disambiguation improves statistical machine translation. In *Proceedings of the 45th Annual Meeting of the Association of Computational Linguistics (ACL)*, pages 33–40, Prague, Czech Republic.

Jonathan Clark, Chris Dyer, Alon Lavie, and Noah Smith. 2011. Better hypothesis testing for statistical machine translation: Controlling for optimizer instability. In *Proceedings of ACL-HLT 2011 (46th Annual Meeting of the ACL: Human Language Technologies)*, Portland, OR.

Laurence Danlos and Charlotte Roze. 2011. Traduction (automatique) des connecteurs de discours. In *Actes de la 18è Conférence sur le Traitement Automatique des Langues Naturelles (TALN)*, Montpellier, France.

Laurence Danlos, Diégo Antolinos-Basso, Chloé Braud, and Charlotte Roze. 2012. Vers le fdtb : French discourse tree bank. In *Actes de la conférence conjointe JEP-TALN-RECITAL 2012, volume 2: TALN*, pages 471–478, Grenoble, France.

Michael Denkowski and Alon Lavie. 2011. Meteor 1.3: Automatic Metric for Reliable Optimization and Evaluation of Machine Translation Systems. In *Proceedings of the EMNLP 2011 Workshop on Statistical Machine Translation*, Edinburgh, UK.

Marcello Federico, Nicola Bertoldi, and Mauro Cettolo. 2008. IRSTLM: an open source toolkit for handling large scale language models. In *Proceedings of Interspeech*, Brisbane, Australia.

Najeh Hajlaoui and Andrei Popescu-Belis. 2012. Translating english discourse connectives into arabic: A corpus-based analysis and an evaluatoin metric. In *Proceedings of the 4th Workshop on Computational Approaches to Arabic Script-based Languages (CAASL) at AMTA 2012*, San Diego, CA.

Najeh Hajlaoui and Andrei Popescu-Belis. 2013. Assessing the accuracy of discourse connective translations: Validation of an automatic metric. In *Proceedings of the 14th International Conference on Intelligent Text Processing and Computational Linguistics*, Samos, Greece.

Hugo Hernault, Danushka Bollegala, and Ishizuka Mitsuru. 2010a. A semi-supervised approach to improve classification of infrequent discourse relations using feature vector extension. In *Proceedings of the 2010 Conference on Empirical Methods in Natural Language Processing (EMNLP)*, pages 399–409, Cambridge, MA.

Hugo Hernault, Helmut Prendinger, David A. duVerle, and Mitsuru Ishizuka. 2010b. HILDA: A discourse parser using Support Vector Machine classification. *Dialogue and Discourse*, 3(1):1–33.

Alistair Knott and Chris Mellish. 1996. A feature-based account of the relations signalled by sentence and clause connectives. *Language and Speech*, 39(2–3):143–183.

Philipp Koehn and Hieu Hoang. 2007. Factored Translation Models. In *Proceedings of the Joint Conference on Empirical Methods in Natural Language Processing (EMNLP) and Computational Natural Language Learning (CONLL)*, pages 868–876, Prague, Czech Republic.

Philipp Koehn, Hieu Hoang, Alexandra Birch, Chris Callison-Burch, Marcello Federico, Nicola Bertoldi, Brooke Cowan, Wade Shen, Christine Moran, Richard Zens, Chris Dyer, Ondrej Bojar, Alexandra Constantin, and Evan Herbs. 2007. Moses: Open Source Toolkit for Statistical Machine Translation. In *Proceedings of 45th Annual Meeting of the Association for Computational Linguistics (ACL), Demonstration Session*, pages 177–180, Prague, Czech Republic.

Philipp Koehn. 2005. Europarl: A Parallel Corpus for Statistical Machine Translation. In *Proceedings of MT Summit X*, pages 79–86, Phuket, Thailand.

S. Kolachina, R. Prasad, D. Sharma, and A. Joshi. 2012. Evaluation of discourse relation annotation in the hindi discourse relation bank. In *Proceedings of the eighth international conference on Language Resources and Evaluation (LREC)*, Instanbul, Turkey.

A. Max, J. M. Crego, and Yvon F. 2010. Contrastive lexical evaluation of machine translation. In *Proceedings of the International Conference on Language Resources and Evaluation (LREC)*, Valletta, Malta.

K. Naskar, S., A. Toral, F. Gaspari, and A. Way. 2011. A framework for diagnostic evaluation of mt based on linguistic checkpoints. In *Proceedings of MT Summit XIII*, Xiamen, China.

Franz Josef Och. 2003. Minimum Error Rate Training in Statistical Machine Translation. In *Proceedings of the 41st Annual Meeting of the Association for Computational Linguistics (ACL)*, pages 160–167, Sapporo, Japan.

M. Popovic and H. Ney. 2011. Towards automatic error analysis of machine translation output. *Computational Linguistics*, 37(4):657–688.

M. Zhou, B. Wang, S. Liu, M. Li, D. Zhang, and T. Zhao. 2008. Diagnostic evaluation of machine translation systems using automatically constructed linguistic check-points. In *Proceedings of the 22rd International Conference on Computational Linguistics (COLING)*, pages 1121–1128, Manchester, UK.

A Description of Tunable Machine Translation Evaluation Systems in WMT13 Metrics Task

Aaron L.-F. Han
hanlifengaaron@gmail.com

Derek F. Wong
derekfw@umac.mo

Lidia S. Chao
lidiasc@umac.mo

Yi Lu
mb25435@umac.mo

Liangye He
wutianshui0515@gmail.com

Yiming Wang
mb25433@umac.mo

Jiaji Zhou
mb25473@uamc.mo

Natural Language Processing & Portuguese-Chinese Machine Translation Laboratory
Department of Computer and Information Science
University of Macau, Macau S.A.R. China

Abstract

This paper is to describe our machine translation evaluation systems used for participation in the WMT13 shared Metrics Task. In the Metrics task, we submitted two automatic MT evaluation systems nLEPOR_baseline and LEPOR_v3.1. nLEPOR_baseline is an n-gram based language independent MT evaluation metric employing the factors of modified sentence length penalty, position difference penalty, n-gram precision and n-gram recall. nLEPOR_baseline measures the similarity of the system output translations and the reference translations only on word sequences. LEPOR_v3.1 is a new version of LEPOR metric using the mathematical harmonic mean to group the factors and employing some linguistic features, such as the part-of-speech information. The evaluation results of WMT13 show LEPOR_v3.1 yields the highest average-score 0.86 with human judgments at system-level using Pearson correlation criterion on English-to-other (FR, DE, ES, CS, RU) language pairs.

1 Introduction

Machine translation has a long history since the 1950s (Weaver, 1955) and gains a fast development in the recent years because of the higher level of computer technology. For instances, Och (2003) presents Minimum Error Rate Training (MERT) method for log-linear statistical machine translation models to achieve better translation quality; Menezes et al. (2006) introduce a syntactically informed phrasal SMT system for English-to-Spanish translation using a phrase translation model, which is based on global reordering and the dependency tree; Su et al. (2009) use the Thematic Role Templates model to improve the translation; Costa-jussà et al. (2012) develop the phrase-based SMT system for Chinese-Spanish translation using a pivot language. With the rapid development of Machine Translation (MT), the evaluation of MT has become a challenge in front of researchers. However, the MT evaluation is not an easy task due to the fact of the diversity of the languages, especially for the evaluation between distant languages (English, Russia, Japanese, etc.).

2 Related works

The earliest human assessment methods for machine translation include the intelligibility and fidelity used around 1960s (Carroll, 1966), and the adequacy (similar as fidelity), fluency and comprehension (improved intelligibility) (White et al., 1994). Because of the expensive cost of manual evaluations, the automatic evaluation metrics and systems appear recently.

The early automatic evaluation metrics include the word error rate WER (Su et al., 1992) and position independent word error rate PER (Tillmann et al., 1997) that are based on the Levenshtein distance. Several promotions for the MT and MT evaluation literatures include the ACL's annual workshop on statistical machine translation WMT (Koehn and Monz, 2006; Callison-Burch et al., 2012), NIST open machine translation (OpenMT) Evaluation series (Li, 2005) and the international workshop of spoken language translation IWSLT, which is also organized annually from 2004 (Eck and Hori, 2005;

Paul, 2008, 2009; Paul, et al., 2010; Federico et al., 2011).

BLEU (Papineni et al., 2002) is one of the commonly used evaluation metrics that is designed to calculate the document level precisions. NIST (Doddington, 2002) metric is proposed based on BLEU but with the information weights added to the n-gram approaches. TER (Snover et al., 2006) is another well-known MT evaluation metric that is designed to calculate the amount of work needed to correct the hypothesis translation according to the reference translations. TER includes the edit categories such as insertion, deletion, substitution of single words and the shifts of word chunks. Other related works include the METEOR (Banerjee and Lavie, 2005) that uses semantic matching (word stem, synonym, and paraphrase), and (Wong and Kit, 2008), (Popovic, 2012), and (Chen et al., 2012) that introduces the word order factors, etc. The traditional evaluation metrics tend to perform well on the language pairs with English as the target language. This paper will introduce the evaluation models that can also perform well on the language pairs that with English as source language.

3 Description of Systems

3.1 Sub Factors

Firstly, we introduce the sub factor of modified length penalty inspired by BLEU metric.

$$LP = \begin{cases} e^{1-\frac{r}{c}} & if\ c < r \\ 1 & if\ c = r \\ e^{1-\frac{c}{r}} & if\ c > r \end{cases} \quad (1)$$

In the formula, LP means sentence length penalty that is designed for both the shorter or longer translated sentence (hypothesis translation) as compared to the reference sentence. Parameters c and r represent the length of candidate sentence and reference sentence respectively.

Secondly, let's see the factors of n-gram precision and n-gram recall.

$$P_n = \frac{\#ngram_{matched}}{\#ngram\ chunks\ in\ hypothesis} \quad (2)$$

$$R_n = \frac{\#ngram_{matched}}{\#ngram\ chunks\ in\ reference} \quad (3)$$

The variable $\#ngram_{matched}$ represents the number of matched *n*-gram chunks between hypothesis sentence and reference sentence. The *n*-gram precision and *n*-gram recall are firstly calculated on sentence-level instead of corpus-level that is used in BLEU (P_n). Then we define the weighted *n*-gram harmonic mean of precision and recall (*WNHPR*).

$$WNHPR = exp(\sum_{n=1}^{N} w_n logH(\alpha R_n, \beta P_n)) \quad (4)$$

Thirdly, it is the *n*-gram based position difference penalty (*NPosPenal*). This factor is designed to achieve the penalty for the different order of successfully matched words in reference sentence and hypothesis sentence. The alignment direction is from the hypothesis sentence to the reference sentence. It employs the n-gram method into the matching period, which means that the potential matched word will be assigned higher priority if it also has nearby matching. The nearest matching will be accepted as a backup choice if there are both nearby matching or there is no other matched word around the potential pairs.

$$NPosPenal = e^{-NPD} \quad (5)$$

$$NPD = \frac{1}{Length_{hyp}} \sum_{i=1}^{Length_{hyp}} |PD_i| \quad (6)$$

$$|PD_i| = |MatchN_{hyp} - MatchN_{ref}| \quad (7)$$

The variable $Length_{hyp}$ means the length of the hypothesis sentence; the variables $MatchN_{hyp}$ and $MatchN_{ref}$ represent the position number of matched words in hypothesis sentence and reference sentence respectively.

3.2 Linguistic Features

The linguistic features could be easily employed into our evaluation models. In the submitted experiment results of WMT Metrics Task, we used the part of speech information of the words in question. In grammar, a part of speech, which is also called a word class, a lexical class, or a lexical category, is a linguistic category of lexical items. It is generally defined by the syntactic or morphological behavior of the lexical item in question. The POS information utilized in our metric LEPOR_v3.1, an enhanced version of LEPOR (Han et al., 2012), is extracted using the Berkeley parser (Petrov et al., 2006) for English, German, and French languages, using COMPOST Czech morphology tagger (Collins, 2002) for Czech language, and using TreeTagger (Schmid, 1994) for Spanish and Russian languages respectively.

Ratio	other-to-English				English-to-other			
	CZ-EN	DE-EN	ES-EN	FR-EN	EN-CZ	EN-DE	EN-ES	EN-FR
HPR:LP:NPP(word)	7:2:1	3:2:1	7:2:1	3:2:1	7:2:1	1:3:7	3:2:1	3:2:1
HPR:LP:NPP(POS)	NA	3:2:1	NA	3:2:1	7:2:1	7:2:1	NA	3:2:1
$\alpha:\beta$ (word)	1:9	9:1	1:9	9:1	9:1	9:1	9:1	9:1
$\alpha:\beta$ (POS)	NA	9:1	NA	9:1	9:1	9:1	NA	9:1
$w_{hw}:w_{hp}$	NA	1:9	NA	9:1	1:9	1:9	NA	9:1

Table 1. The tuned weight values in LEPOR_v3.1 system

System	Correlation Score with Human Judgment								
	other-to-English				English-to-other				Mean
	CZ-EN	DE-EN	ES-EN	FR-EN	EN-CZ	EN-DE	EN-ES	EN-FR	score
LEPOR_v3.1	0.93	0.86	0.88	0.92	0.83	0.82	0.85	0.83	**0.87**
nLEPOR_baseline	0.95	0.61	0.96	0.88	0.68	0.35	0.89	0.83	0.77
METEOR	0.91	0.71	0.88	0.93	0.65	0.30	0.74	0.85	0.75
BLEU	0.88	0.48	0.90	0.85	0.65	0.44	0.87	0.86	0.74
TER	0.83	0.33	0.89	0.77	0.50	0.12	0.81	0.84	0.64

Table 2. The performances of nLEPOR_baseline and LEPOR_v3.1 systems on WMT11 corpora

3.3 The nLEPOR_baseline System

The nLEPOR_baseline system utilizes the simple product value of the factors: modified length penalty, *n*-gram position difference penalty, and weighted *n*-gram harmonic mean of precision and recall.

$$nLEPOR = LP \times PosPenalty \times WNHPR \quad (8)$$

The system level score is the arithmetical mean of the sentence level evaluation scores. In the experiments of Metrics Task using the nLEPOR_baseline system, we assign *N*=1 in the factor WNHPR, i.e. weighted unigram harmonic mean of precision and recall.

3.4 The LEPOR_v3.1 System

The system of LEPOR_v3.1 (also called as hLEPOR) combines the sub factors using weighted mathematical harmonic mean instead of the simple product value.

$$hLEPOR = \frac{w_{LP}+w_{NPosPenal}+w_{HPR}}{\frac{w_{LP}}{LP}+\frac{w_{NPosPenal}}{NPosPenal}+\frac{w_{HPR}}{HPR}} \quad (9)$$

Furthermore, this system takes into account the linguistic features, such as the POS of the words. Firstly, we calculate the hLEPOR score on surface words $hLEPOR_{word}$ (the closeness of the hypothesis translation and the reference translation). Then, we calculate the hLEPOR score on the extracted POS sequences $hLEPOR_{POS}$ (the closeness of the corresponding POS tags between hypothesis sentence and reference sentence). The final score $hLEPOR_{final}$ is the combination of the two sub-scores $hLEPOR_{word}$ and $hLEPOR_{POS}$.

$$hLEPOR_{final} = \frac{1}{w_{hw}+w_{hp}}(w_{hw}hLEPOR_{word} + w_{hp}hLEPOR_{POS}) \quad (10)$$

4 Evaluation Method

In the MT evaluation task, the Spearman rank correlation coefficient method is usually used by the authoritative ACL WMT to evaluate the correlation of different MT evaluation metrics. So we use the Spearman rank correlation coefficient ρ to evaluate the performances of nLEPOR_baseline and LEPOR_v3.1 in system level correlation with human judgments. When there are no ties, ρ is calculated using:

$$\rho = 1 - \frac{6\sum d_i^2}{n(n^2-1)} \quad (11)$$

The variable d_i is the difference value between the ranks for $system_i$ and n is the number of systems. We also offer the Pearson correlation coefficient information as below. Given a sample of paired data (X, Y) as (x_i, y_i), $i = 1\ to\ n$, the Pearson correlation coefficient is:

$$\rho_{XY} = \frac{\sum_{i=1}^{n}(x_i-\mu_x)(y_i-\mu_y)}{\sqrt{\sum_{i=1}^{n}(x_i-\mu_x)^2}\sqrt{\sum_{i=1}^{n}(y_i-\mu_y)^2}} \quad (12)$$

where μ_x and μ_y specify the mean of discrete random variable X and Y respectively.

Directions	EN-FR	EN-DE	EN-ES	EN-CS	EN-RU	Av
LEPOR_v3.1	*.91*	*.94*	*.91*	*.76*	***.77***	***.86***
nLEPOR_baseline	*.92*	*.92*	*.90*	***.82***	*.68*	*.85*
SIMP-BLEU_RECALL	**.95**	.93	.90	**.82**	.63	.84
SIMP-BLEU_PREC	.94	.90	.89	**.82**	.65	.84
NIST-mteval-inter	.91	.83	.84	.79	.68	.81
Meteor	.91	.88	.88	**.82**	.55	.81
BLEU-mteval-inter	.89	.84	.88	.81	.61	.80
BLEU-moses	.90	.82	.88	.80	.62	.80
BLEU-mteval	.90	.82	.87	.80	.62	.80
CDER-moses	.91	.82	.88	.74	.63	.80
NIST-mteval	.91	.79	.83	.78	.68	.79
PER-moses	.88	.65	.88	.76	.62	.76
TER-moses	.91	.73	.78	.70	.61	.75
WER-moses	.92	.69	.77	.70	.61	.74
TerrorCat	.94	**.96**	**.95**	na	na	.95
SEMPOS	na	na	na	.72	na	.72
ACTa	.81	-.47	na	na	na	.17
ACTa5+6	.81	-.47	na	na	na	.17

Table 3. System-level Pearson correlation scores on WMT13 English-to-other language pairs

5 Experiments

5.1 Training

In the training stage, we used the officially released data of past WMT series. There is no Russian language in the past WMT shared tasks. So we trained our systems on the other eight language pairs including English to other (French, German, Spanish, Czech) and the inverse translation direction. In order to avoid the overfitting problem, we used the WMT11 corpora as training data to train the parameter weights in order to achieve a higher correlation with human judgments at system-level evaluations. For the nLEPOR_baseline system, the tuned values of α and β are 9 and 1 respectively for all language pairs except for ($\alpha = 1, \beta = 9$) for CS-EN language pair. For the LEPOR_v3.1 system, the tuned values of weights are shown in Table 1. The evaluation scores of the training results on WMT11 corpora are shown in Table 2. The designed methods have shown promising correlation scores with human judgments at system level, 0.87 and 0.77 respectively for nLEPOR_baseline and LEPOR_v3.1 of the mean score on eight language pairs. As compared to METEOR, BLEU and TER, we have achieved higher correlation scores with human judgments.

5.2 Testing

In the WMT13 shared Metrics Task, we also submitted our system performances on English-to-Russian and Russian-to-English language pairs. However, since the Russian language did not appear in the past WMT shared tasks, we assigned the default parameter weights to Russian language for the submitted two systems. The officially released results on WMT13 corpora are shown in Table 3, Table 4 and Table 5 respectively for system-level and segment-level performance on English-to-other language pairs.

Directions	EN-FR	EN-DE	EN-ES	EN-CS	EN-RU	Av
SIMP-BLEU_RECALL	.92	.93	.83	.87	.71	**.85**
LEPOR_v3.1	*.90*	*.9*	*.84*	*.75*	***.85***	***.85***
NIST-mteval-inter	**.93**	.85	.80	.90	.77	**.85**
CDER-moses	.92	.87	.86	.89	.70	**.85**
nLEPOR_baseline	*.92*	*.90*	*.85*	*.82*	*.73*	*.84*
NIST-mteval	.91	.83	.78	.92	.72	.83
SIMP-BLEU_PREC	.91	.88	.78	.88	.70	.83
Meteor	.92	.88	.78	**.94**	.57	.82
BLEU-mteval-inter	.92	.83	.76	.90	.66	.81
BLEU-mteval	.89	.79	.76	.90	.63	.79
TER-moses	.91	.85	.75	.86	.54	.78
BLEU-moses	.90	.79	.76	.90	.57	.78
WER-moses	.91	.83	.71	.86	.55	.77
PER-moses	.87	.69	.77	.80	.59	.74
TerrorCat	**.93**	**.95**	**.91**	na	na	.93
SEMPOS	na	na	na	.70	na	.70
ACTa5+6	.81	-.53	na	na	na	.14
ACTa	.81	-.53	na	na	na	.14

Table 4. System-level Spearman rank correlation scores on WMT13 English-to-other language pairs

Table 3 shows LEPOR_v3.1 and nLEPOR_baseline yield the highest and the second highest average Pearson correlation score 0.86 and 0.85 respectively with human judgments at system-level on five English-to-other language pairs. LEPOR_v3.1 and nLEPOR_baseline also yield the highest Pearson correlation score on English-to-Russian (0.77) and English-to-Czech (0.82) language pairs respectively. The testing results of LEPOR_v3.1 and nLEPOR_baseline show better correlation scores as compared to METEOR (0.81), BLEU (0.80) and TER-moses (0.75) on English-to-other language pairs, which is similar with the training results.

On the other hand, using the Spearman rank correlation coefficient, SIMPBLEU_RECALL yields the highest correlation score 0.85 with human judgments. Our metric LEPOR_v3.1 also yields the highest Spearman correlation score on English-to-Russian (0.85) language pair, which is similar with the result using Pearson correlation and shows its robust performance on this language pair.

Directions	EN-FR	EN-DE	EN-ES	EN-CS	EN-RU	Av
SIMP-BLEU_RECALL	**.16**	**.09**	**.23**	**.06**	**.12**	**.13**
Meteor	.15	.05	.18	**.06**	.11	.11
SIMP-BLEU_PREC	.14	.07	.19	**.06**	.09	.11
sentBLEU-moses	.13	.05	.17	.05	.09	.10
LEPOR_v3.1	*.13*	*.06*	*.18*	*.02*	*.11*	*.10*
nLEPOR_baseline	*.12*	*.05*	*.16*	*.05*	*.10*	*.10*
dfki_logregNorm-411	na	na	.14	na	na	.14
TerrorCat	.12	.07	.19	na	na	.13
dfki_logregNormSoft-431	na	na	.03	na	na	.03

Table 5. Segment-level Kendall's tau correlation scores on WMT13 English-to-other language pairs

However, we find a problem in the Spearman rank correlation method. For instance, let two evaluation metrics MA and MB with their evaluation scores $\overrightarrow{MA} = \{0.95, 0.50, 0.45\}$ and $\overrightarrow{MB} = \{0.77, 0.75, 0.74\}$ respectively reflecting three MT systems $\vec{M} = \{M_1, M_2, M_3\}$. Before the calculation of correlation with human judgments, they will be converted into $\overleftrightarrow{MA} = \{1,2,3\}$ and $\overleftrightarrow{MB} = \{1,2,3\}$ with the same rank sequence using Spearman rank method; thus, the two evaluation systems will get the same correlation with human judgments whatever are the values of human judgments. But the two metrics reflect different results indeed: MA gives the outstanding score (0.95) to M_1 system and puts very low scores (0.50 and 0.45) on the other two systems M_2 and M_3 while MB thinks the three MT systems have similar performances (scores from 0.74 to 0.77). This information is lost using the Spearman rank correlation methodology.

The segment-level performance of LEPOR_v3.1 is moderate with the average Kendall's tau correlation score 0.10 on five English-to-other language pairs, which is due to the fact that we trained our metrics at system-level in this shared metrics task. Lastly, the officially released results on WMT13 other-to-English language pairs are shown in Table 6, Table 7 and Table 8 respectively for system-level and segment-level performance.

Directions	FR-EN	DE-EN	ES-EN	CS-EN	RU-EN	Av
Meteor	**.98**	.96	.97	**.99**	**.84**	**.95**
SEMPOS	.95	.95	.96	**.99**	.82	.93
Depref-align	.97	.97	.97	.98	.74	.93
Depref-exact	.97	.97	.96	.98	.73	.92
SIMP-BLEU_RECALL	.97	.97	.96	.94	.78	.92
UMEANT	.96	.97	**.99**	.97	.66	.91
MEANT	.96	.96	**.99**	.96	.63	.90
CDER-moses	.96	.91	.95	.90	.66	.88
SIMP-BLEU_PREC	.95	.92	.95	.91	.61	.87
LEPOR_v3.1	*.96*	*.96*	*.90*	*.81*	*.71*	*.87*
nLEPOR_baseline	*.96*	*.94*	*.94*	*.80*	*.69*	*.87*
BLEU-mteval-inter	.95	.92	.94	.90	.61	.86
NIST-mteval-inter	.94	.91	.93	.84	.66	.86
BLEU-moses	.94	.91	.94	.89	.60	.86
BLEU-mteval	.95	.90	.94	.88	.60	.85
NIST-mteval	.94	.90	.93	.84	.65	.85
TER-moses	.93	.87	.91	.77	.52	.80
WER-moses	.93	.84	.89	.76	.50	.78
PER-moses	.84	.88	.87	.74	.45	.76
TerrorCat	**.98**	**.98**	.97	na	na	.98

Table 6. System-level Pearson correlation scores on WMT13 other-to-English language pairs

METEOR yields the highest average correlation scores 0.95 and 0.94 respectively using Pearson and Spearman rank correlation methods on other-to-English language pairs. The average performance of nLEPOR_baseline is a little better than LEPOR_v3.1 on the five language pairs of other-to-English even though it is also moderate as compared to other metrics. However, using the Pearson correlation method, nLEPOR_baseline yields the average correlation score 0.87 which already wins the BLEU (0.86) and TER (0.80) as shown in Table 6.

Directions	FR-EN	DE-EN	ES-EN	CS-EN	RU-EN	Av
Meteor	.98	.96	**.98**	.96	.81	**.94**
Depref-align	**.99**	**.97**	.97	.96	.79	**.94**
UMEANT	**.99**	.95	.96	**.97**	.79	.93
MEANT	.97	.93	.94	**.97**	.78	.92
Depref-exact	.98	.96	.94	.94	.76	.92
SEMPOS	.94	.92	.93	.95	**.83**	.91
SIMP-BLEU_RECALL	.98	.94	.92	.91	.81	.91
BLEU-mteval-inter	**.99**	.90	.90	.94	.72	.89
BLEU-mteval	**.99**	.89	.89	.94	.69	.88
BLEU-moses	**.99**	.90	.88	.94	.67	.88
CDER-moses	**.99**	.88	.89	.93	.69	.87
SIMP-BLEU_PREC	**.99**	.85	.83	.92	.72	.86
nLEPOR_baseline	*.95*	*.95*	*.83*	*.85*	*.72*	*.86*
LEPOR_v3.1	*.95*	*.93*	*.75*	*0.8*	*.79*	*.84*
NIST-mteval	.95	.88	.77	.89	.66	.83
NIST-mteval-inter	.95	.88	.76	.88	.68	.83
TER-moses	.95	.83	.83	0.8	0.6	0.80
WER-moses	.95	.67	.80	.75	.61	.76
PER-moses	.85	.86	.36	.70	.67	.69
TerrorCat	.98	.96	.97	na	na	.97

Table 7. System-level Spearman rank correlation scores on WMT13 other-to-English language pairs

Once again, our metrics perform moderate at segment-level on other-to-English language pairs due to the fact that they are trained at system-level. We notice that some of the evaluation metrics do not submit the results on all the language pairs; however, their performance on submitted language pair is sometimes very good, such as the dfki_logregFSS-33 metric with a segment-level correlation score 0.27 on German-to-English language pair.

6 Conclusion

This paper describes our participation in the WMT13 Metrics Task. We submitted two systems nLEPOR_baseline and LEPOR_v3.1. Both of the two systems are trained and tested using the officially released data. LEPOR_v3.1 yields the highest Pearson correlation average-score 0.86 with human judgments on five English-to-other language pairs, and nLEPOR_baseline yields better performance than LEPOR_v3.1 on other-to-English language pairs. Furthermore, LEPOR_v3.1 shows robust system-level performance on English-to-Russian language pair, and nLEPOR_baseline shows best system-level performance on English-to-Czech language pair using Pearson correlation criterion. As compared to nLEPOR_baseline, the experiment results of LEPOR_v3.1 also show that the proper use of linguistic information can increase the performance of the evaluation systems.

Directions	FR-EN	DE-EN	ES-EN	CS-EN	RU-EN	Av
SIMP-BLEU_RECALL	**.19**	**.32**	**.28**	.26	.23	**.26**
Meteor	.18	.29	.24	**.27**	**.24**	.24
Depref-align	.16	.27	.23	.23	.20	.22
Depref-exact	.17	.26	.23	.23	.19	.22
SIMP-BLEU_PREC	.15	.24	.21	.21	.17	.20
nLEPOR_baseline	*.15*	*.24*	*.20*	*.18*	*.17*	*.19*
sentBLEU-moses	.15	.22	.20	.20	.17	.19
LEPOR_v3.1	*.15*	*.22*	*.16*	*.19*	*.18*	*.18*
UMEANT	.10	.17	.14	.16	.11	.14
MEANT	.10	.16	.14	.16	.11	.14
dfki_logregFSS-33	na	.27	na	na	na	.27
dfki_logregFSS-24	na	.27	na	na	na	.27
TerrorCat	.16	.30	.23	na	na	.23

Table 8. Segment-level Kendall's tau correlation scores on WMT13 other-to-English language pairs

Acknowledgments

The authors wish to thank the anonymous reviewers for many helpful comments. The authors are grateful to the Science and Technology Development Fund of Macau and the Research Committee of the University of Macau for the funding support for our research, under the reference No. 017/2009/A and RG060/09-10S/CS/FST.

References

Banerjee, Satanjeev and Alon Lavie. 2005. METEOR: An Automatic Metric for MT Evaluation with Improved Correlation with Human Judgments. In *Proceedings of the 43th Annual Meeting of the*

Association of Computational Linguistics (ACL- 05), pages 65–72, Ann Arbor, US, June. Association of Computational Linguistics.

Callison-Burch, Chris, Philipp Koehn, Christof Monz, and Omar F. Zaidan. 2011. Findings of the 2011 Workshop on Statistical Machine Translation. In *Proceedings of the Sixth Workshop on Statistical Machine Translation* (WMT '11). Association for Computational Linguistics, Stroudsburg, PA, USA, 22-64.

Callison-Burch, Chris, Philipp Koehn, Christof Monz, Matt Post, Radu Soricut, and Lucia Specia. 2012. Findings of the 2012Workshop on Statistical Machine Translation. In *Proceedings of the Seventh Workshop on Statistical Machine Translation*, pages 10–51, Montreal, Canada. Association for Computational Linguistics.

Carroll, John B. 1966. An Experiment in Evaluating the Quality of Translations, *Mechanical Translation and Computational Linguistics*, vol.9, nos.3 and 4, September and December 1966, page 55-66, Graduate School of Education, Harvard University.

Chen, Boxing, Roland Kuhn and Samuel Larkin. 2012. PORT: a Precision-Order-Recall MT Evaluation Metric for Tuning, *Proceedings of the 50th Annual Meeting of the Association for Computational Linguistics*, pages 930–939, Jeju, Republic of Korea, 8-14 July 2012.

Collins, Michael. 2002. Discriminative Training Methods for Hidden Markov Models: Theory and Experiments with Perceptron Algorithms. In *Proceedings of the ACL-02 conference on Empirical methods in natural language processing*, Volume 10 (EMNLP 02), pages 1-8. Association for Computational Linguistics, Stroudsburg, PA, USA.

Costa-jussà, Marta R., Carlos A. Henríquez and Rafael E. Banchs. 2012. Evaluating Indirect Strategies for Chinese-Spanish Statistical Machine Translation. *Journal of artificial intelligence research*, Volume 45, pages 761-780.

Doddington, George. 2002. Automatic evaluation of machine translation quality using n-gram co-occurrence statistics. In *Proceedings of the second international conference on Human Language Technology Research* (HLT '02). Morgan Kaufmann Publishers Inc., San Francisco, CA, USA, 138-145.

Eck, Matthias and Chiori Hori. 2005. Overview of the IWSLT 2005 Evaluation Campaign. *Proceedings of IWSLT 2005.*

Federico, Marcello, Luisa Bentivogli, Michael Paul, and Sebastian Stiiker. 2011. Overview of the IWSLT 2011 Evaluation Campaign. In *Proceedings of IWSLT 2011*, 11-27.

Han, Aaron Li-Feng, Derek F. Wong and Lidia S. Chao. 2012. LEPOR: A Robust Evaluation Metric for Machine Translation with Augmented Factors. *Proceedings of the 24th International Conference on Computational Linguistics* (COLING 2012: Posters), Mumbai, India.

Koehn, Philipp and Christof Monz. 2006. Manual and Automatic Evaluation of Machine Translation between European Languages. *Proceedings of the ACLWorkshop on Statistical Machine Translation*, pages 102–121, New York City.

Li, A. (2005). Results of the 2005 NIST machine translation evaluation. In *Machine Translation Workshop.*

Menezes, Arul, Kristina Toutanova and Chris Quirk. 2006. Microsoft Research Treelet Translation System: NAACL 2006 Europarl Evaluation, *Proceedings of the ACLWorkshop on Statistical Machine Translation*, pages 158-161, New York City.

Och, Franz Josef. 2003. Minimum Error Rate Training for Statistical Machine Translation. In *Proceedings of the 41st Annual Meeting of the Association for Computational Linguistics* (ACL-2003). pp. 160-167.

Papineni, Kishore, Salim Roukos, Todd Ward, and Wei-Jing Zhu. 2002. BLEU: a method for automatic evaluation of machine translation. In *Proceedings of the 40th Annual Meeting on Association for Computational Linguistics* (ACL '02). Association for Computational Linguistics, Stroudsburg, PA, USA, 311-318.

Paul, Michael. 2008. Overview of the IWSLT 2008 Evaluation Campaign. *Proceeding of IWLST 2008*, Hawaii, USA.

Paul, Michael. 2009. Overview of the IWSLT 2009 Evaluation Campaign. In *Proc. of IWSLT 2009*, Tokyo, Japan, pp. 1–18.

Paul, Michael, Marcello Federico and Sebastian Stiiker. 2010. Overview of the IWSLT 2010 Evaluation Campaign, *Proceedings of the 7th International Workshop on Spoken Language Translation*, Paris, December 2nd and 3rd, 2010, page 1-25.

Petrov, Slav, Leon Barrett, Romain Thibaux, and Dan Klein. 2006. Learning accurate, compact, and interpretable tree annotation. In *Proceedings of the 21st International Conference on Computational Linguistics and the 44th annual meeting of the Association for Computational Linguis-*

tics (ACL-44). Association for Computational Linguistics, Stroudsburg, PA, USA, 433-440.

Popovic, Maja. 2012. Class error rates for evaluation of machine translation output. *Proceedings of the 7th Workshop on Statistical Machine Translation*, pages 71–75, Canada.

Schmid, Helmut. 1994. Probabilistic Part-of-Speech Tagging Using Decision Trees. In *Proceedings of International Conference on New Methods in Language Processing*, Manchester, UK.

Snover, Matthew, Bonnie J. Dorr, Richard Schwartz, Linnea Micciulla, and John Makhoul. 2006. A Study of Translation Edit Rate with Targeted Human Annotation. In *Proceedings of the 7th Conference of the Association for Machine Translation in the Americas (AMTA-06)*, pages 223–231, USA. Association for Machine Translation in the Americas.

Su, Hung-Yu and Chung-Hsien Wu. 2009. Improving Structural Statistical Machine Translation for Sign Language With Small Corpus Using Thematic Role Templates as Translation Memory, *IEEE TRANSACTIONS ON AUDIO, SPEECH, AND LANGUAGE PROCESSING*, VOL. 17, NO. 7.

Su, Keh-Yih, Wu Ming-Wen and Chang Jing-Shin. 1992. A New Quantitative Quality Measure for Machine Translation Systems. In *Proceedings of the 14th International Conference on Computational Linguistics*, pages 433–439, Nantes, France.

Tillmann, Christoph, Stephan Vogel, Hermann Ney, Arkaitz Zubiaga, and Hassan Sawaf. 1997. Accelerated DP Based Search For Statistical Translation. In *Proceedings of the 5th European Conference on Speech Communication and Technology* (EUROSPEECH-97).

Weaver, Warren. 1955. Translation. In William Locke and A. Donald Booth, editors, *Machine Translation of Languages: Fourteen Essays*. John Wiley & Sons, New York, pages 15–23.

White, John S., Theresa O'Connell, and Francis O'Mara. 1994. The ARPA MT evaluation methodologies: Evolution, lessons, and future approaches. In *Proceedings of the Conference of the Association for Machine Translation in the Americas* (AMTA 1994). pp193-205.

Wong, Billy and Chunyu Kit. 2008. Word choice and word position for automatic MT evaluation. In Workshop: *MetricsMATR of the Association for Machine Translation in the Americas (AMTA)*, short paper, Waikiki, Hawai'I, USA. Association for Machine Translation in the Americas.

MEANT at WMT 2013: A tunable, accurate yet inexpensive semantic frame based MT evaluation metric

Chi-kiu LO and **Dekai WU**
HKUST
Human Language Technology Center
Department of Computer Science and Engineering
Hong Kong University of Science and Technology
{jackielo|dekai}@cs.ust.hk

Abstract

The linguistically transparent MEANT and UMEANT metrics are tunable, simple yet highly effective, fully automatic approximation to the human HMEANT MT evaluation metric which measures semantic frame similarity between MT output and reference translations. In this paper, we describe HKUST's submission to the WMT 2013 metrics evaluation task, MEANT and UMEANT. MEANT is optimized by tuning a small number of weights—one for each semantic role label—so as to maximize correlation with human adequacy judgment on a development set. UMEANT is an unsupervised version where weights for each semantic role label are estimated via an inexpensive unsupervised approach, as opposed to MEANT's supervised method relying on more expensive grid search. In this paper, we present a battery of experiments for optimizing MEANT on different development sets to determine the set of weights that maximize MEANT's accuracy and stability. Evaluated on test sets from the WMT 2012/2011 metrics evaluation, both MEANT and UMEANT achieve competitive correlations with human judgments using nothing more than a monolingual corpus and an automatic shallow semantic parser.

1 Introduction

We evaluate in the context of WMT 2013 the MEANT (Lo *et al.*, 2012) and UMEANT (Lo and Wu, 2012) semantic machine translation (MT) evaluation metrics—tunable, simple yet highly effective, fully-automatic semantic frame based objective functions that score the degree of similarity between the MT output and the reference translations via semantic role labels (SRL). Recent studies (Lo *et al.*, 2013; Lo and Wu, 2013) show that tuning MT systems against MEANT more robustly improves translation adequacy, compared to tuning against BLEU or TER.

In the past decade, the progress of machine translation (MT) research is predominantly driven by the fast and cheap n-gram based MT evaluation metrics, such as BLEU (Papineni *et al.*, 2002), which assume that a good translation is one that shares the same lexical choices as the reference translation. Despite enforcing fluency, it has been established that these metrics do not enforce translation utility adequately and often fail to preserve meaning closely (Callison-Burch *et al.*, 2006; Koehn and Monz, 2006). Unlike BLEU, or other n-gram based MT evaluation metrics, MEANT adopts at outset the principle that a good translation is one from which the human readers may successfully understand at least the central meaning of the input sentence as captured by the basic event structure—*"who did what to whom, when, where and why"*(Pradhan *et al.*, 2004).

Lo *et al.* (2012) show that MEANT correlates better with human adequacy judgment than other commonly used automatic MT evaluation metrics, such as BLEU (Papineni *et al.*, 2002), NIST (Doddington, 2002), METEOR (Banerjee and Lavie, 2005), CDER (Leusch *et al.*, 2006), WER (Nießen *et al.*, 2000), and TER (Snover *et al.*, 2006). Recent studies (Lo *et al.*, 2013; Lo and Wu, 2013) also show that tuning MT system against MEANT produces more robustly adequate translations on both formal news text genre and informal web forum or public speech genre compared to tuning against BLEU or TER. These studies show that MEANT is a tunable and highly-accurate MT evaluation metric that drives MT system development towards higher utility.

As described in Lo and Wu (2011a), the parameters in MEANT, i.e. the weight for each semantic role label, could be estimated using simple grid search to optimize the correlation with human adequacy judgments. Later, Lo and Wu (2012) described an unsupervised approach for estimating the parameters of MEANT using relative frequency of each semantic role label in the reference translations under the situation when the human judgments for the development set are unavailable. In this paper, we refer the version of MEANT using the unsupervised approach of weight estimation as UMEANT.

In this paper, we present a battery of experiments for optimizing MEANT on different development sets to determine the set of weights that maximizes MEANT's accuracy and stability. Evaluated on the test sets of WMT 2012/2011 metrics evaluation, MEANT and UMEANT achieve a competitive correlation score with human judgments by nothing more than a monolingual corpus and an automatic shallow semantic parser.

2 Related work

2.1 Lexical similarity based metrics

N-gram or edit distance based metrics such as BLEU (Papineni *et al.*, 2002), NIST (Doddington, 2002), METEOR (Banerjee and Lavie, 2005), CDER (Leusch *et al.*, 2006), WER (Nießen *et al.*, 2000), and TER (Snover *et al.*, 2006) do not correctly reflect the similarity of the basic event structure— *"who did what to whom, when, where and why"*— of the input sentence. In fact, a number of large scale meta-evaluations (Callison-Burch *et al.*, 2006; Koehn and Monz, 2006) report cases where BLEU strongly disagrees with human judgments of translation adequacy.

Although AMBER (Chen *et al.*, 2012) shows a high correlation with human adequacy judgment (Callison-Burch et al., 2012) and claims to preserve the simplicity of BLEU, the modifications it incurred on BLEU through four different n-gram matching strategies and several different penalties makes it very hard to interpret and indicate what errors the MT systems are making.

2.2 Linguistic feature based metrics

ULC (Giménez and Màrquez, 2007, 2008) is an automatic metric that incorporates several semantic similarity features and shows improved correlation with human judgement of translation quality (Callison-Burch *et al.*, 2007; Giménez and Màrquez, 2007; Callison-Burch *et al.*, 2008; Giménez and Màrquez, 2008) but no work has been done towards tuning an SMT system using a pure form of ULC perhaps due to its expensive run time. Lambert *et al.* (2006) did tune on QUEEN, a simplified version of ULC that discards the semantic features of ULC and is based on pure lexical similarity. Therefore, QUEEN suffers from the problem of failing to reflect translation adequacy similar to other n-gram based metrics.

Similarly, SPEDE (Wang and Manning, 2012) is an integrated probabilistic FSM and probabilistic PDA model that predicts the edit sequence needed for the MT output to match the reference. Sagan (Castillo and Estrella, 2012) is a semantic textual similarity metric based on a complex textual entailment pipeline. These aggregated metrics require sophisticated feature extraction steps; contain several dozens of parameters to tune and employ expensive linguistic resources, like WordNet and paraphrase table. Like ULC, these matrices are not useful in the MT system development cycle for tuning due to expensive running time. The metrics themselves are also expensive in training and tuning due to the large number of parameters to be estimated. Although ROSE (Song and Cohn, 2011) is a weighted linear model of shallow linguistic features which is cheaper in run time but it still contains several dozens of weights that need to be tuned which affects the portability of the metric for evaluating translations across domains.

Rios *et al.* (2011) introduced TINE, an automatic recall-oriented evaluation metric which aims to preserve the basic event structure, but no work has been done toward tuning an SMT system against it. TINE performs comparably to BLEU and worse than METEOR on correlation with human adequacy judgment.

3 MEANT and UMEANT

MEANT (Lo *et al.*, 2012), which is the weighted f-measure over the matched semantic role labels of the automatically aligned semantic frames and role fillers, outperforms BLEU, NIST, METEOR, WER, CDER and TER. Recent studies (Lo *et al.*, 2013; Lo and Wu, 2013) also show that tuning MT system against MEANT produces more robustly adequate translations than the common practice of tuning against BLEU or TER across different data genres, such as formal newswire text, informal web forum text and informal public speech. Pre-

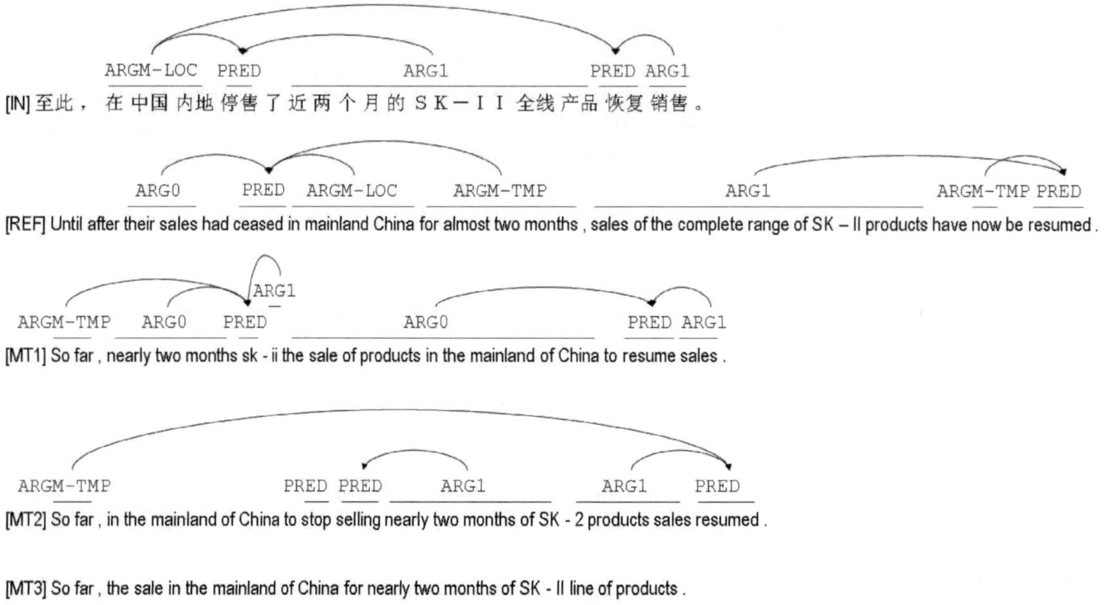

Figure 1: Examples of automatic shallow semantic parses. The input is parsed by a Chinese automatic shallow semantic parser. The reference and MT output are parsed by an English automatic shallow semantic parser. There are no semantic frames for MT3 since there is no predicate.

cisely, MEANT is computed as follows:

1. Apply an automatic shallow semantic parser on both the references and MT output. (Figure 1 shows examples of automatic shallow semantic parses on both reference and MT output.)

2. Apply maximum weighted bipartite matching algorithm to align the semantic frames between the references and MT output by the lexical similarity of the predicates.

3. For each pair of aligned semantic frames,

   (a) Lexical similarity scores determine the similarity of the semantic role fillers.

   (b) Apply maximum weighted bipartite matching algorithm to align the semantic role fillers between the reference and MT output according to their lexical similarity.

4. Compute the weighted f-measure over the matching role labels of these aligned predicates and role fillers.

$$
\begin{aligned}
M_{i,j} &\equiv \text{total \# ARG j of aligned frame i in MT} \\
R_{i,j} &\equiv \text{total \# ARG j of aligned frame i in REF} \\
S_{i,\text{pred}} &\equiv \text{similarity of predicate in aligned frame i} \\
S_{i,j} &\equiv \text{similarity of ARG j in aligned frame i} \\
w_{\text{pred}} &\equiv \text{weight of similarity of predicates} \\
w_j &\equiv \text{weight of similarity of ARG j}
\end{aligned}
$$

$$
\begin{aligned}
m_i &\equiv \frac{\text{\#tokens filled in aligned frame i of MT}}{\text{total \#tokens in MT}} \\
r_i &\equiv \frac{\text{\#tokens filled in aligned frame i of REF}}{\text{total \#tokens in REF}} \\
\text{precision} &= \frac{\sum_i m_i \frac{w_{\text{pred}} S_{i,\text{pred}} + \sum_j w_j S_{i,j}}{w_{\text{pred}} + \sum_j w_j M_{i,j}}}{\sum_i m_i} \\
\text{recall} &= \frac{\sum_i r_i \frac{w_{\text{pred}} S_{i,\text{pred}} + \sum_j w_j S_{i,j}}{w_{\text{pred}} + \sum_j w_j R_{i,j}}}{\sum_i r_i}
\end{aligned}
$$

where m_{i} and r_{i} are the weights for frame, i, in the MT/REF respectively. These weights estimate the degree of contribution of each frame to the overall meaning of the sentence. $M_{\text{i,j}}$ and $R_{\text{i,j}}$ are the total counts of argument of type j in frame i in the MT and REF respectively. $S_{i,\text{pred}}$ and $S_{i,j}$ are the lexical similarities of the predicates and role fillers of the arguments of type j between the reference translations and the MT output. w_{pred} and w_j are the weights of the lexical similarities of the predicates and role fillers of the arguments of type j between the reference translations and the MT output. There are in total 12 weights for the set of semantic role labels in MEANT as defined in Lo and Wu (2011b).

For MEANT, w_{pred} and w_j are determined using supervised estimation via a simple grid search to optimize the correlation with human adequacy judgments (Lo and Wu, 2011a). For UMEANT, w_{pred} and w_j are estimated in an unsupervised manner using relative frequency of each semantic role label in the reference translations when the human judgments on adequacy of the development set were unavailable (Lo and Wu, 2012).

In this experiment, we use a MEANT / UMEANT implementation along the lines described in Lo *et al.* (2012) and Tumuluru *et al.* (2012) but we incorporate a variant of the aggregation function proposed in Mihalcea *et al.* (2006) for phrasal similarity of role fillers as it normalizes the phrase length better than geometric mean as described in Tumuluru *et al.* (2012). In case there is no semantic frame in the sentence, we treat the whole sentence as a phrase and calculate the phrasal similarity, like the role fillers in step 3.1, as the MEANT score.

4 Experimental setup

We tune the 12 weights for the set of semantic role labels in MEANT using grid search to maximize the correlation with human judgment on 6 development sets. Following the protocol in WMT12 metrics evaluation task (Callison-Burch *et al.*, 2012), we use Kendall's correlation coefficient for the sentence-level correlation with human judgments.

The GALE development set consists of 40 sentences randomly drawn from the DARPA GALE P2.5 Chinese-English evaluation set along with the outputs from 3 participating MT systems and the corresponding human adequacy judgments. The WMT12-A development set consists of 800 sentences randomly drawn from the Czech-English test set in WMT12 metrics evaluation task along with the output from 5 participating systems and the corresponding human judgments. Similarly, each of the WMT12-B, WMT12-C and WMT12-D development sets consists of 800 randomly drawn sentences from the WMT12 metrics evaluation test set on German-English, Spanish-English and French-English respectively. The WMT12-E development set consists of 800 sentences out of which 200 sentences were randomly drawn from each of WMT12-A, WMT12-B, WMT12-C and WMT12-D data set.

We evaluated MEANT and UMEANT on 3 groups of test sets. The first group is the original (without partition) test data for each language pair (translated in English) in WMT12. This group of test sets is used for comparing MEANT's performance with the reported results from other participants of WMT12. The second group is the held out subset of the test data for each language pair in WMT12. The third group is the original set of test data for each language pair in WMT11. The latter 2 groups are used for determining which set of tuned weights maximize the accuracy and stability of MEANT.

5 Results

Table 1 shows that the best and the worst sentence-level correlations reported in Callison-Burch *et al.* (2012) on the original WMT12 test sets (without partitioning) for translations into English, together the sentence-level correlation of MEANT tuned on different development sets and UMEANT. The grey boxes mark the results of experiments in which there was an overlap between parts of the development data and the test data. A study of the values for the 12 weights associated with the semantic role labels show that a general trend of the importance of different labels in MEANT: ”who” is always the most important; ”did”, ”what”, ”where”, ”why”, ”extent”, ”modal” and ”other” are quite important too; ”when”, ”manner” and ”negation” fluctuate where they are quite important in some development sets but not quite important in some development sets; ”whom” is usually not important. Given the fact that MEANT employs significantly less expensive linguistic resources and less sophisticated machine learning algorithm in tuning the parameters, the performance of MEANT is very competitive with other participants last year.

Table 2 shows the sentence-level correlation on the WMT12 held-out test sets and the original WMT11 test sets of MEANT tuned on different development sets and UMEANT together with the average sentence-level correlation on all test sets. The results show that MEANT tuning on WMT12-C development set achieve the highest sentence-level correlation with human judgments on average. UMEANT, the unsupervised wight estimated version of MEANT, achieves a very competitive correlation score when compared with MEANT tuned on different development sets. As a result,

Table 1: The best and the worst sentence-level correlation reported in Callison-Burch *et al.* (2012) on the original WMT12 test sets (without partitioning) for translations into English together the sentence-level correlation of MEANT tuned on different development sets and UMEANT. The grey box marked results of experiments in which parts of the development data and the test data are overlapped.

	WMT12 cz-en	WMT12 de-en	WMT12 es-en	WMT12 fr-en
Best reported	0.21	0.28	0.26	0.26
MEANT (GALE)	0.13	0.16	0.15	0.15
MEANT (WMT12-A)	0.12	0.17	0.16	0.15
MEANT (WMT12-B)	0.11	0.18	0.15	0.14
MEANT (WMT12-C)	0.12	0.17	0.17	0.15
MEANT (WMT12-D)	0.12	0.17	0.16	0.16
MEANT (WMT12-E)	0.12	0.17	0.17	0.15
UMEANT	0.12	0.17	0.16	0.14
Worst reported	0.06	0.08	0.08	0.07

Table 2: Sentence-level correlation on the WMT12 held-out test sets and the original WMT11 test sets of MEANT tuned on different development sets and UMEANT together with the average sentence-level correlation on all test sets.

	WMT12 held-out				WMT11				Average
	cz-en	de-en	es-en	fr-en	cz-en	de-en	es-en	fr-en	-
MEANT (GALE)	0.0657	0.1251	0.1762	**0.1719**	0.3460	0.1123	0.2416	0.1913	0.1788
MEANT (WMT12-A)	0.0652	0.1117	0.1663	0.1540	0.3764	0.1101	0.2314	0.1944	0.1762
MEANT (WMT12-B)	0.0458	0.1294	0.1556	0.1548	**0.3992**	**0.1479**	0.2571	**0.2037**	0.1867
MEANT (WMT12-C)	**0.0746**	0.1278	**0.1833**	0.1592	0.3764	0.1324	0.2674	0.1882	**0.1887**
MEANT (WMT12-D)	0.0628	0.1164	0.1826	0.1655	0.3802	0.1168	0.2339	0.1975	0.1820
MEANT (WMT12-E)	0.0496	**0.1353**	0.1791	0.1619	0.3840	0.1101	0.2596	0.1851	0.1831
UMEANT	0.0477	0.1333	0.1606	0.1548	0.3764	0.1257	**0.2828**	0.1913	0.1841

we submitted two metrics to WMT 2013 metrics evaluation task. One is MEANT with weights learned from tuning on WMT12-C development sets and the other submission is UMEANT.

6 Conclusion

In this paper, we have evaluated in the context of WMT2013 the MEANT and UMEANT metrics, which are tunable, accurate yet inexpensive fully automatic machine translation evaluation metrics that measure similarity between the MT output and the reference via semantic frames. Recent studies show that tuning MT system against MEANT produces more robustly adequate translations than the common practice of tuning against BLEU or TER across different data genres, such as formal newswire text, informal web forum text and informal public speech. The weight for each semantic role label in MEANT is estimated by maximizing the correlation with human adequacy judgment on a development set. UMEANT is a version of MEANT in which weight for each semantic role label is estimated in an unsupervised fashion using the relative frequency of the semantic role labels in the reference. We present the experimental results for determining the set of weights that maximize MEANT's accuracy and stability by optimizing MEANT on different development sets.

We disagree with the notion "a good evaluation metric is not necessarily a good tuning metric, and vice versa" (Chen *et al.*, 2012). Instead, we believe that a good evaluation metric should be one that is a good objective function to drive the development of MT systems towards higher utility. In other words, a good evaluation metric should correlate well with human adequacy judgment and at the same time, be inexpensive in running time so as to fit into the MT pipeline to improve MT quality. Our results shows that MEANT is a good evaluation/tuning metric because it achieves a competitive correlation score with human judgments by using less expensive linguistic resources and training algorithms making it possible to tune MT system against MEANT to improve MT quality.

7 Acknowledgment

This material is based upon work supported in part by the Defense Advanced Research Projects Agency (DARPA) under BOLT contract no. HR0011-12-C-0016, and GALE contract nos. HR0011-06-C-0022 and HR0011-06-C-0023; by the European Union under the FP7 grant agreement no. 287658; and by the Hong Kong Research Grants Council (RGC) research grants GRF620811, GRF621008, and GRF612806. Any opinions, findings and conclusions or recommendations expressed in this material are those of the authors and do not necessarily reflect the views of DARPA, the EU, or RGC.

References

Satanjeev Banerjee and Alon Lavie. METEOR: An automatic metric for MT evaluation with improved correlation with human judgments. In *Proceedings of the ACL Workshop on Intrinsic and Extrinsic Evaluation Measures for Machine Translation and/or Summarization*, pages 65–72, Ann Arbor, Michigan, June 2005.

Chris Callison-Burch, Miles Osborne, and Philipp Koehn. Re-evaluating the role of BLEU in Machine Translation Research. In *Proceedings of the 13th Conference of the European Chapter of the Association for Computational Linguistics (EACL-06)*, pages 249–256, 2006.

Chris Callison-Burch, Cameron Fordyce, Philipp Koehn, Christof Monz, and Josh Schroeder. (Meta-) evaluation of Machine Translation. In *Proceedings of the 2nd Workshop on Statistical Machine Translation*, pages 136–158, 2007.

Chris Callison-Burch, Cameron Fordyce, Philipp Koehn, Christof Monz, and Josh Schroeder. Further Meta-evaluation of Machine Translation. In *Proceedings of the 3rd Workshop on Statistical Machine Translation*, pages 70–106, 2008.

Chris Callison-Burch, Philipp Koehn, Christof Monz, Matt Post, Radu Soricut, and Lucia Specia. Findings of the 2012 Workshop on Statistical Machine Translation. In *Proceedings of the 7th Workshop on Statistical Machine Translation (WMT 2012)*, pages 10–51, 2012.

Julio Castillo and Paula Estrella. Semantic Textual Similarity for MT evaluation. In *Proceedings of the 7th Workshop on Statistical Machine Translation (WMT 2012)*, pages 52–58, 2012.

Boxing Chen, Roland Kuhn, and George Foster. Improving AMBER, an MT Evaluation Metric. In *Proceedings of the 7th Workshop on Statistical Machine Translation (WMT 2012)*, pages 59–63, 2012.

George Doddington. Automatic evaluation of machine translation quality using n-gram co-occurrence statistics. In *Proceedings of the 2nd International Conference on Human Language Technology Research*, pages 138–145, San Diego, California, 2002.

Jesús Giménez and Lluís Màrquez. Linguistic features for automatic evaluation of heterogenous MT systems. In *Proceedings of the Second Workshop on Statistical Machine Translation*, pages 256–264, Prague, Czech Republic, June 2007.

Jesús Giménez and Lluís Màrquez. A smorgasbord of features for automatic MT evaluation. In *Proceedings of the Third Workshop on Statistical Machine Translation*, pages 195–198, Columbus, Ohio, June 2008.

Philipp Koehn and Christof Monz. Manual and Automatic Evaluation of Machine Translation between European Languages. In *Proceedings of the Workshop on Statistical Machine Translation (WMT-06)*, pages 102–121, 2006.

Patrik Lambert, Jesús Giménez, Marta R Costa-jussá, Enrique Amigó, Rafael E Banchs, Lluıs Márquez, and JAR Fonollosa. Machine Translation system development based on human likeness. In *Spoken Language Technology Workshop, 2006. IEEE*, pages 246–249. IEEE, 2006.

Gregor Leusch, Nicola Ueffing, and Hermann Ney. CDer: Efficient MT Evaluation Using Block Movements. In *Proceedings of the 13th Conference of the European Chapter of the Association for Computational Linguistics (EACL-06)*, 2006.

Chi-kiu Lo and Dekai Wu. MEANT: An Inexpensive, High-Accuracy, Semi-Automatic Metric for Evaluating Translation Utility based on Semantic Roles. In *Proceedings of the Joint conference of the 49th Annual Meeting of the Association for Computational Linguistics : Human Language Technologies (ACL-HLT-11)*, 2011.

Chi-kiu Lo and Dekai Wu. SMT vs. AI redux: How semantic frames evaluate MT more accurately. In *Proceedings of the 22nd International Joint Conference on Artificial Intelligence (IJCAI-11)*, 2011.

Chi-kiu Lo and Dekai Wu. Unsupervised vs. supervised weight estimation for semantic MT evaluation metrics. In *Proceedings of the 6th Workshop on Syntax and Structure in Statistical Translation (SSST-6)*, 2012.

Chi-kiu Lo and Dekai Wu. Can informal genres be better translated by tuning on automatic semantic metrics? In *Proceedings of the 14th Machine Translation Summit (MTSummit-XIV)*, 2013.

Chi-kiu Lo, Anand Karthik Tumuluru, and Dekai Wu. Fully Automatic Semantic MT Evaluation. In *Proceedings of the Seventh Workshop on Statistical Machine Translation (WMT2012)*, 2012.

Chi-kiu Lo, Karteek Addanki, Markus Saers, and Dekai Wu. Improving machine translation by training against an automatic semantic frame based evaluation metric. In *Proceedings of the 51st Annual Meeting of the Association for Computational Linguistics (ACL-13)*, 2013.

Rada Mihalcea, Courtney Corley, and Carlo Strapparava. Corpus-based and knowledge-based measures of text semantic similarity. In *Proceedings of the national conference on artificial intelligence*, volume 21, page 775. Menlo Park, CA; Cambridge, MA; London; AAAI Press; MIT Press; 1999, 2006.

Sonja Nießen, Franz Josef Och, Gregor Leusch, and Hermann Ney. A Evaluation Tool for Machine Translation: Fast Evaluation for MT Research. In *Proceedings of the 2nd International Conference on Language Resources and Evaluation (LREC-2000)*, 2000.

Kishore Papineni, Salim Roukos, Todd Ward, and Wei-Jing Zhu. BLEU: a method for automatic evaluation of machine translation. In *Proceedings of the 40th Annual Meeting of the Association for Computational Linguistics*, pages 311–318, Philadelphia, Pennsylvania, July 2002.

Sameer Pradhan, Wayne Ward, Kadri Hacioglu, James H. Martin, and Dan Jurafsky. Shallow Semantic Parsing Using Support Vector Machines. In *Proceedings of the 2004 Conference on Human Language Technology and the North American Chapter of the Association for Computational Linguistics (HLT-NAACL-04)*, 2004.

Miguel Rios, Wilker Aziz, and Lucia Specia. Tine: A metric to assess MT adequacy. In *Proceedings of the Sixth Workshop on Statistical Machine Translation (WMT-2011)*, pages 116–122, 2011.

Matthew Snover, Bonnie Dorr, Richard Schwartz, Linnea Micciulla, and John Makhoul. A study of translation edit rate with targeted human annotation. In *Proceedings of the 7th Conference of the Association for Machine Translation in the Americas (AMTA-06)*, pages 223–231, Cambridge, Massachusetts, August 2006.

Xingyi Song and Trevor Cohn. Regression and Ranking based Optimisation for Sentence Level Machine Translation Evaluation. In *Proceedings of the 6th Workshop on Statistical Machine Translation (WMT 2011)*, pages 123–129, 2011.

Anand Karthik Tumuluru, Chi-kiu Lo, and Dekai Wu. Accuracy and robustness in measuring the lexical similarity of semantic role fillers for automatic semantic mt evaluation. In *Proceeding of the 26th Pacific Asia Conference on Language, Information, and Computation (PACLIC-26)*, 2012.

Mengqiu Wang and Christopher D. Manning. SPEDE: Probabilistic Edit Distance Metrics for MT Evaluation. In *Proceedings of the 7th Workshop on Statistical Machine Translation (WMT 2012)*, pages 76–83, 2012.

An approach using style classification features for Quality Estimation

Erwan Moreau
CNGL and Computational Linguistics Group
Centre for Computing and Language Studies
School of Computer Science and Statistics
Trinity College Dublin
Dublin 2, Ireland
`moreaue@cs.tcd.ie`

Raphael Rubino
NCLT
Dublin City University
Dublin 9, Ireland
`rrubino@computing.dcu.ie`

Abstract

In this paper we describe our participation to the WMT13 Shared Task on Quality Estimation. The main originality of our approach is to include features originally designed to classify text according to some author's style. This implies the use of reference categories, which are meant to represent the quality of the MT output.

Preamble

This paper describes the approach followed in the two systems that we submitted to subtask 1.3 of the WMT13 Shared Task on Quality Estimation, identified as `TCD-DCU-CNGL_1-3_SVM1` *and* `TCD-DCU-CNGL_1-3_SVM2`. *This approach was also used by the first author in his submissions to subtask 1.1, identified as* `TCD-CNGL OPEN` *and* `TCD-CNGL RESTRICTED`[1]. *In the remaining of this paper we focus on subtask 1.3, but there is very little difference in the application of the approach to task 1.1.*

1 Introduction

Quality Estimation (QE) aims to provide a quality indicator for machine translated sentences. There are many cases where such an indicator would be useful in a translation process: to compare different Machine Translation (MT) models on a given set of sentences, to tune automatically the parameters of a MT model, to select the bad sentences for human translation or post-editing, to select the good sentences for immediate publication and try to apply automatic post-editing to the others, or simply to provide users who are not fluent in the source language information about the fluency of the translated text they are reading. As long as machine translated text cannot be of reasonably consistent quality, QE is helpful in indicating linguistic quality variability.[2]

After focusing on automatic prediction of adhoc quality scores (as estimated by professional annotators) in the previous edition (Callison-Burch et al., 2012), the WMT Shared Task on Quality Estimation 2013 proposes several variants of the task. We participated in task 1.1 which aims to predict HTER scores (edit distance between the MT output and its manually post-edited version), and in task 1.3 which aims to predict the expected time needed to post-edit the MT output.

The originality of our participation lies in the fact that we intended to test "style classification" features for the task of QE: the idea is to select a set of n-grams which are particularly representative of a given level of quality. In practice we use only two levels which simply represent low and high quality. We explore various ways to build these two reference categories and to select the n-grams, as described in §2. The goal was to see if such features can contribute to the task of predicting quality of MT. As explained in §3, however, various constraints forced us to somehow cut corners in some parts of the features selection and training process; therefore we think that the modest results presented and discussed in §4 might not necessarily reflect the real contribution of these features.

2 Features

2.1 Classical features

We extract a set of features inspired by the ones provided by the shared task organisers in their 17 baseline feature set. Using the corpora provided for the task, we extract for each source and target

[1]The second author's submission to subtask 1.1 is independent from this approach and is described in a different paper in this volume.

[2]We focus on translation fluency rather than target language faithfulness to sources.

segments pair:

- 24 surface features, such as the segment length, the number of punctuation marks and uppercased letters, words with mixed case, etc.

- 30 language Model (LM) features, n-gram log-probability and perplexity (with and without start and end of sentence tags) with $n \in [1; 5]$.

- 30 backward LM features, n-gram log-probability and perplexity (with and without start and end of sentence tags) with $n \in [1; 5]$.

- 44 n-gram frequency features, with $n \in [1; 5]$, extracted from frequency quartiles.

- 24 word-alignment features according to the alignment probability thresholds: 0.01, 0.1, 0.25, 0.5, 0.75 and 1.0, with or without words frequency weighting.

For all these features, except the ones with binary values, we compute the ratio between the source and target feature values and add them to our feature set, which contains 223 classical features.

2.2 Style classification features

We call the features described below "style classification" features because they have been used recently in the context of author identification/profiling (Moreau and Vogel, 2013a; Moreau and Vogel, 2013b) (quite sucessfully in some cases). The idea consists in representing the n-grams which are very specific to a given "category", a category being a level of quality in the context of QE, and more precisely we use only the *"good"* and *"bad"* categories here.

Thus this approach requires the following parameters:

- At least two datasets used as reference for the categories;

- Various n-grams patterns, from which comparisons based on frequency can be done;

- One or several methods to compare a sentence to a category.

2.2.1 Reference categories

As reference categories we use both the training datasets provided for task 1.1 and 1.3: both are used in each task, that is, categories are extracted from subtasks 1.1 dataset and 1.3 dataset and used in task 1.1 and 1.3 as well. However we use only half of the sentences of task 1.1 in 1.1 and similarly in 1.3, in order to keep the other half for the classical training process. This is necessary to avoid using (even indirectly) a sentence as both a fixed parameter from which features are extracted (the category data) and an actual instance on which features are computed. In other words this simply follows the principle of keeping the training and test data independent, but in this case there are two stages of training (comparing sentences to a reference category is also a supervised process).

The two datasets are used in three different ways, leading to three distinct pairs of categories "*good/bad*":[3]

- The sentences for which the quality is below the median form the *"bad"* category, the one above form the *"good"* category;

- The sentences for which the quality is below the first quartile form the *"bad"* category, the one above the third quartile form the *"good"* category;

- The complete set of MT output sentences form the *"bad"* category, their manually post-edited counterpart form the *"good"* category.

We use these three different ways to build categories because there is no way to determine a priori the optimal choice. For instance, on the one hand the opposite quartiles probably provide more discriminative power than the medians, but on the other hand the latter contains more data and therefore possibly more useful cases.[4] In the last version the idea is to consider that, in average, the machine translated sentences are of poor quality compared to the manually post-edited sentences; in this case the categories contain more data, but it might be a problem that (1) some of the machine-translated sentences are actually good and (2) the

[3]Below we call "quality" the value given by the HTER score (1.1) or post-editing time (1.3), the level of quality being of course conversely proportional to these values.

[4]The datasets are not very big: only 803 sentences in task 1.3 and 2,254 sentences in task 1.1 (and we can only use half of these for categories, as explained above).

right translation of some difficult phrases in the post-edited sentences might never be found in MT output. We think that the availability of different categories built in various ways is potentially a good thing, because it lets the learning algorithm decide which features (based on a particular category) are useful and which are not, thus tuning the model automatically while possibly using several possibilities together, rather than relying on some predefined categories.

It is important to notice that the correspondence between an MT output and its post-edited version is not used[5]: in all categories the sentences are only considered as an unordered set. For instance it would be possible to use a third-party corpus as well (provided it shares at least a common domain with the data).

We use only the target language (Spanish) of the translation and not the source language in order not to generate too many categories, and because it has been shown that there is a high correlation between the complexity of the source sentence and the fluency of the translation (Moreau and Vogel, 2012). However it is possible to do so for the categories based on quantiles.

2.2.2 n-grams patterns, thresholds and distance measures

We use a large set of 30 n-grams patterns based on tokens and POS tags. POS tagging has been performed with TreeTagger (Schmid, 1995). Various combinations of n-grams are considered, including standard sequential n-grams, skip-grams, and combinations of tokens and POS tags.

Since the goal is to compare a sentence to a category, we consider the frequency in terms of number of sentences in which the n-gram appears, rather than the global frequency or the local frequency by sentence.[6]

Different frequency thresholds are considered, from 1 to 25. Additionally we can also filter out n-grams for which the relative frequency is too similar between the *"good"* and *"bad"* categories. For instance it is possible to keep only the n-grams for which 80% of the occurrencies belong to the *"bad"* category, thus making it a strong marker for low quality. Once again different thresholds are considered, in order to tradeoff between the amount of cases and their discriminative power.

We use only three simple distance/similarity measures when comparing a sentence to a category:

- Binary match: for each n-gram in the sentence, count 1 if it belongs to the category, 0 otherwise, then divide by the number of n-grams in the sentence;
- Weighted match: same as above but sum the proportion of occurrences belonging to the category instead of 1 (this way an n-gram which is more discriminative is given more weight);
- Cosine similarity.

Finally for every tuple formed by the combination of

- a category,
- a quality level (*"good/bad"*),
- an n-gram pattern,
- a frequency threshold,
- a threshold for the proportion of the occurrences in the given category,
- and a distance measure

a feature is created. For every sentence the value of the feature is the score computed using the parameters defined in the tuple. From our set of parameters we obtain approximately 35,000 features.[7] It is worth noticing that these features are not meant to represent the sentence entirely, but rather particularly noticeable parts (in terms of quality) of the sentence.

[5] in the categories used as reference data; but it is used in the final features during the (supervised) training stage (see §3).

[6] The frequency by sentence is actually also taken into account in the following way: instead of considering only the n-gram, we consider a pair (n-gram, local frequency) as an observation. This way if a particular frequency is observed more often in a given category, it can be interpreted as a clue in favor of this category. However in most cases (long n-grams sequences) the frequency by sentence is almost always one, sometimes two. Thus this is only marginally a relevant criterion to categorize a sentence.

[7] The number of features depends on the data in the category, because if no n-gram at all in the category satisfies the conditions given by the parameters (which can happen with very high thresholds), then the feature does not exist.

2.3 Features specific to the dataset

In task 1.3 we are provided with a translator id and a document id for each sentence. The distribution of the time spent to post-edit the sentence depending on these parameters shows some significant differences among translators and documents. This is why we add several features intended to account for these parameters: the id itself, the mean and the median for both the translator and the document.

3 Design and training process

The main difficulty with so many features (around 35,000) is of course to select a subset of reasonable size, in order to train a model which is not overfitted. This requires an efficient optimization method, since it is clearly impossible to explore the search space exhaustively in this case.

Initially it was planned to use an ad-hoc genetic algorithm to select an optimal subset of features. But unfortunately the system designed in this goal did not work as well as expected[8], this is why we had to switch to a different strategy: the two final sets of features were obtained through several stages of selection, mixing several different kinds of correlation-based features selection methods.

The different steps described below were carried out using the Weka Machine Learning toolkit[9] (Hall et al., 2009). Since we have used half of the training data as a reference corpus for some of the categories (see §2), we use the other half as training instances in the selection and learning process, with 10 folds cross-validation for the latter.

3.1 Iterative selection of features

Because of the failure of the initial strategy, in order to meet the time constraints of the Shared Task we had to favor speed over performance in the process of selecting features and training a model. This probably had a negative impact on the final results, as discussed in section §4.

In particular the amount of features was too big to be processed in the remaining time by a subset selection method. This is why the features were first ranked individually using the Relief attribute estimation method (Robnik-Sikonja and Kononenko, 1997). Only the 20,000[10] top features were extracted from this ranking and used further in the selection process.

From this initial subset of features, the following heuristic search algorithms combined with a correlation-based method[11] to evaluate subsets of features (Hall, 1998) are applied iteratively to a given input set of features:

- Best-first search (forward, backward, bi-directional);
- Hill-climbing search (forward and backward);
- Genetic search with Bayes Networks.

Each of these algorithms was used with different predefined parameters in order to trade off between time and performance. This selection process is iterated as long as the number of features left is (approximately) higher than 200.

3.2 Training the models

When less than 200 features are obtained, the iterative selection process is still applied but a 10 folds cross-validated evaluation is also performed with the following regression algorithms:

- Support Vector Machines (SVM) (Smola and Schölkopf, 2004; Shevade et al., 2000);
- Decision trees (Quinlan, 1992; Wang and Witten, 1996);
- Pace regression (Wang and Witten, 2002).

These learning algorithms are also run with several possible sets of parameters. Eventually the submitted models are chosen among those for which the set of features can not be reduced anymore without decreasing seriously the performance. Most of the best models were obtained with SVM, although the decision trees regression algorithm performed almost as well. It was not possible to decrease the number of features below 60 for task 1.3 (80 for task 1.1) without causing a loss in performance.

[8] At the time of writing it is still unclear if this was due to a design flaw or a bug in the implementation.

[9] Weka 3.6.9, `http://www.cs.waikato.ac.nz/ml/weka`.

[10] For subtask 1.3. Only the 8,000 top features for subtask 1.1.

[11] Weka class `weka.attributeSelection.CfsSubsetEval`.

4 Results and discussion

The systems are evaluated based on the Mean Average Error, and every team was allowed to submit two systems. Our systems ranked 10th and 11th among 14 for task 1.1, and 13th and 15th among 17 for task 1.1.

4.1 Possible causes of loss in performance

We plan to investigate why our approach does not perform as well as others, and in particular to study more exhaustively the different possibilities in the features selection process.[12] It is indeed very probable that the method can perform better with an appropriate selection of features and optimization of the parameters, in particular:

- The final number of features is too large, which can cause overfitting. Most QE system do not need so many features (only 15 for the best system in the WMT12 Shared Task on QE (Soricut et al., 2012)).
- We had to perform a first selection to discard some of the initial features based on their individual contribution. This is likely to be a flaw, since some features can be very useful in conjuction with other even if poorly informative by themselves.
- We also probably made a mistake in applying the selection process to the whole set of features, including both classical features and style classification features: it might be relevant to run two independent selection processes at first and then gather the resulting features together only for a more fine-grained final selection. Indeed, the final models that we submitted include very few classical features; we believe that this might have made these models less reliable, since our initial assumption was rather that the style classification features would act as secondary clues in a model primarily relying on the classical features.

4.2 Selected features

The following observations can be made on the final models obtained for task 1.3, keeping in mind that the models might not be optimal for the reasons explained above:

[12]Unfortunately the results of this study are not ready yet at the time of writing.

- Only 5% of the selected features are classical features;
- The amount of data used in the category seems to play an important role: most features correspond to categories built from the 1.1 dataset (which is bigger), and the proportions between the different kinds of categories are: 13% for first quartile vs. fourth quartile (smallest dataset), 25% for below median vs. above median, and 61% for MT output vs. postedited sentence (largest dataset);
- It seems more interesting to identify the low quality n-grams (i.e. errors) rather than the high quality ones: 76% of the selected features represent the *"bad"* category;
- 81% of the selected features represent an n-grams containing at least one POS tag, whereas only 40% contain a token;
- Most features correspond to selecting n-grams which are very predictive of the *"good/bad"* category (high difference of the relative proportion between the two categories), although a significant number of less predictive n-grams are also selected;
- The cosine distance is selected about three times more often than the two other distance methods.

5 Conclusion and future work

In conclusion, the approach performed decently on the Shared Task test data, but was outperformed by most other participants systems. Thus currently it is not proved that style classification features help assessing the quality of MT. However the approach, and especially the contribution of these features, have yet to be evaluated in a less constrained environment in order to give a well-argued answer to this question.

Acknowledgments

This research is supported by the Science Foundation Ireland (Grant 12/CE/I2267) as part of the Centre for Next Generation Localisation (`www.cngl.ie`) funding at Trinity College, University of Dublin.

References

Chris Callison-Burch, Philipp Koehn, Christof Monz, Matt Post, Radu Soricut, and Lucia Specia. 2012. Findings of the 2012 workshop on statistical machine translation. In *Proceedings of the Seventh Workshop on Statistical Machine Translation*, Montreal, Canada, June. Association for Computational Linguistics.

M. Hall, E. Frank, G. Holmes, B. Pfahringer, P. Reutemann, and I.H. Witten. 2009. The weka data mining software: an update. *ACM SIGKDD Explorations Newsletter*, 11(1):10–18.

M. A. Hall. 1998. *Correlation-based Feature Subset Selection for Machine Learning*. Ph.D. thesis, University of Waikato, Hamilton, New Zealand.

Erwan Moreau and Carl Vogel. 2012. Quality estimation: an experimental study using unsupervised similarity measures. In *Proceedings of the Seventh Workshop on Statistical Machine Translation*, pages 120–126, Montréal, Canada, June. Association for Computational Linguistics.

Erwan Moreau and Carl Vogel. 2013a. Participation to the pan author identification task. In *to appear in the proceeding of CLEF 2013*.

Erwan Moreau and Carl Vogel. 2013b. Participation to the pan author profiling task. In *to appear in the proceeding of CLEF 2013*.

J.R. Quinlan. 1992. Learning with continuous classes. In *Proceedings of the 5th Australian joint Conference on Artificial Intelligence*, pages 343–348. Singapore.

Marko Robnik-Sikonja and Igor Kononenko. 1997. An adaptation of relief for attribute estimation in regression. In Douglas H. Fisher, editor, *Fourteenth International Conference on Machine Learning*, pages 296–304. Morgan Kaufmann.

Helmut Schmid. 1995. Improvements in part-of-speech tagging with an application to german. In *Proceedings of the ACL SIGDAT-Workshop*, pages 47–50.

S.K. Shevade, SS Keerthi, C. Bhattacharyya, and K.R.K. Murthy. 2000. Improvements to the SMO algorithm for SVM regression. *Neural Networks, IEEE Transactions on*, 11(5):1188–1193.

A.J. Smola and B. Schölkopf. 2004. A tutorial on support vector regression. *Statistics and computing*, 14(3):199–222.

Radu Soricut, Nguyen Bach, and Ziyuan Wang. 2012. The SDL Language Weaver systems in the WMT12 Quality Estimation shared task. In *Proceedings of the Seventh Workshop on Statistical Machine Translation*, pages 145–151, Montréal, Canada, June. Association for Computational Linguistics.

Y. Wang and I.H. Witten. 1996. Induction of model trees for predicting continuous classes.

Y. Wang and I.H. Witten. 2002. Modeling for optimal probability prediction. In *Proceedings of the Nineteenth International Conference on Machine Learning*, pages 650–657. Morgan Kaufmann Publishers Inc.

DCU Participation in WMT2013 Metrics Task

Xiaofeng Wu[†], **Hui Yu**[⋆],**Qun Liu**[†]
[†]CNGL, Dublin City University, Ireland
[⋆]ICT, Chinese Academy of Sciences, China
[†]{xfwu, qliu}@computing.dcu.ie
[⋆]yuhui@ict.ac.cn

Abstract

In this paper, we propose a novel syntactic based MT evaluation metric which only employs the dependency information in the source side. Experimental results show that our method achieves higher correlation with human judgments than BLEU, TER, HWCM and METEOR at both sentence and system level for all of the four language pairs in WMT 2010.

1 Introduction

Automatic evaluation plays a more important role in the evolution of machine translation. At the earliest stage, the automatic evaluation metrics only use the lexical information, in which, BLEU (Papineni et al., 2002) is the most popular one. BLEU is simple and effective. Most of the researchers regard BLEU as their primary evaluation metric to develop and compare MT systems. However, BLEU only employs the lexical information and cannot adequately reflect the structural level similarity. Translation Error Rate (TER) (Snover et al., 2006) measures the number of edits required to change the hypothesis into one of the references. METEOR (Lavie and Agarwal, 2007), which defines loose unigram matching between the hypothesis and the references with the help of stemming and Wordnet-looking-up, is also a lexical based method and achieves the first-class human-evaluation-correlation score. AMBER (Chen and Kuhn, 2011; Chen et al., 2012) incorporates recall, extra penalties and some text processing variants on the basis of BLEU. The main weakness of all the above lexical based methods is that they cannot adequately reflect the structural level similarity.

To overcome the weakness of the lexical based methods, many syntactic based metrics were proposed. Liu and Gildea (2005) proposed STM, a constituent tree based approach, and HWCM, a dependency tree based approach.

Both of the two methods compute the similarity between the sub-trees of the hypothesis and the reference. Owczarzak et al (2007a; 2007b; 2007c) presented a method using the Lexical-Functional Grammar (LFG) dependency tree. MAXSIM (Chan and Ng, 2008) and the method proposed by Zhu et al (2010) also employed the syntactic information in association with lexical information.With the syntactic information which can reflect structural information, the correlation with the human judgments can be improved to a certain extent.

As we know that the hypothesis is potentially noisy, and these errors expand through the parsing process. Thus the power of syntactic information could be considerably weakened.

In this paper, we attempt to overcome the shortcoming of the syntactic based methods and propose a novel dependency based MT evaluation metric. The proposed metric only employs the reference dependency tree which contains both the lexical and syntactic information, leaving the hypothesis side unparsed to avoid the error propagation. In our metric, F-score is calculated using the string of hypothesis and the dependency based n-grams which are extracted from the reference dependency tree.

Experimental results show that our method achieves higher correlation with human judgments than BLEU, HWCM, TER and METEOR at both sentence level and system level for all of the four language pairs in WMT 2010.

2 Background: HWCM

HWCM is a dependency based metric which extracts the headword chains, a sequence of words which corresponds to a path in the dependency tree, from both the hypothesis and the reference dependency tree. The score of HWCM is obtained

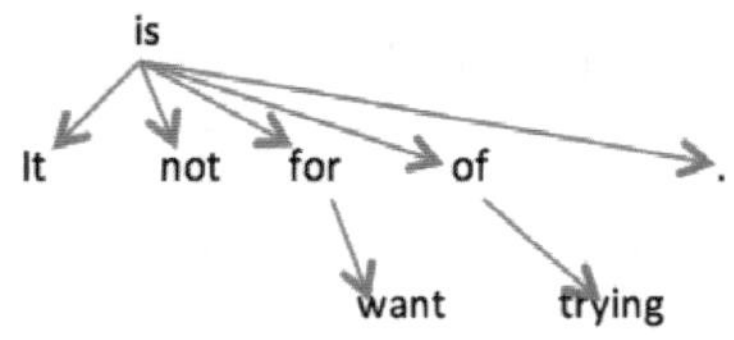

Figure 1: The dependency tree of the reference

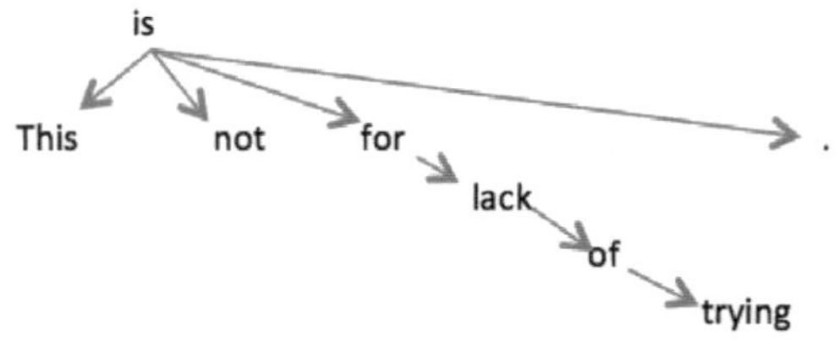

Figure 2: The dependency tree of the hypothesis

by formula (1).

$$HWCM = \frac{1}{D}\sum_{n=1}^{D}\frac{\sum_{g\in chain_n(hyp)} count_{clip}(g)}{\sum_{g\in chain_n(hyp)} count(g)} \quad (1)$$

In formula (1), D is the maximum length of the headword chain. $chain_n(hyp)$ denotes the set of the headword chains with length of n in the tree of hypothesis. $count(g)$ denotes the number of times g appears in the headword chain of the hypothesis dependency tree and $count_{clip}(g)$ denotes the clipped number of times when g appears in the the headword chain of the reference dependency trees. Clipped means that the count computed from the headword chain of the hypothesis tree should not exceed the maximum number of times when g occurs in headword chain of any single reference tree. The following are two sentences representing as reference and hypothesis, and Figure 1 and Figure 2 are the dependency trees respectively.

reference: It is not for want of trying .

hypothesis: This is not for lack of trying .

In the example above, there are 8 1-word, 7 2-word and 3 3-word headword chains in the hypothesis dependency tree. The number of 1-word and 2-word headword chains in the hypothesis tree which can match their counterparts in the reference tree is 5 and 4 respectively. The 3-word headword chains in the hypothesis dependency tree are *is for lack, for lack of* and *lack of trying*. Due to the difference in the dependency structures, they have no matches in the reference side.

3 A Novel Dependency Based MT Evaluation Method

In this new method, we calculate F-score using the string of hypothesis and the dep-n-grams which are extracted from the reference dependency tree. The new method is named DEPREF since it is a DEPendency based method only using dependency tree of REference to calculate the F-score. In DEPREF, after the parsing of the reference sentences, there are three steps below being carried out. 1) Extracting the dependency based n-gram (dep-n-gram) in the dependency tree of the reference. 2) Matching the dep-n-gram with the string of hypothesis. 3) Obtaining the final score of a hypothesis. The detail description of our method will be found in paper (Liu et al., 2013) . We only give the experiment results in this paper.

4 Experiments

Both the sentence level evaluation and the system level evaluation are conducted to assess the performance of our automatic metric. At the sentence level evaluation, Kendall's rank correlation coefficient τ is used. At the system level evaluation, the Spearman's rank correlation coefficient ρ is used.

4.1 Data

There are four language pairs in our experiments including German-to-English, Czech-to-English, French-to-English and Spanish-to-English, which are all derived from WMT2010. Each of the four language pairs consists of 2034 sentences and the references of the four language pairs are the same. There are 24 translation systems for French-to-English, 25 for German-to-English, 12 for Czech-to-English and 15 for Spanish-to-English. We parsed the reference into constituent tree by Berkeley parser and then converted the constituent tree into dependency tree by Penn2Malt [1]. Presumably, we believe that the performance will be even better if the dependency trees are manually revised.

In the experiments, we compare the performance of our metric with the widely used lexical based metrics BLEU, TER, METEOR and a dependency based metric HWCM. In order to make a fair comparison with METEOR which is known to perform best when external resources like stem and synonym are provided, we also provide results of DEPREF with external resources.

[1] http://w3.msi.vxu.se/ nivre/research/Penn2Malt.html

Metrics		Czech-English	German-English	Spanish-English	French-English
BLEU		0.2554	0.2748	0.2805	0.2197
TER		0.2526	0.2907	0.2638	0.2105
HWCM	N=1	0.2067	0.2227	0.2188	0.2022
	N=2	0.2587	0.2601	0.2408	0.2399
	N=3	0.2526	0.2638	0.2570	0.2498
	N=4	0.2453	0.2672	0.2590	0.2436
DEPREF		**0.3337**	**0.3498**	**0.3190**	**0.2656**

Table 1.A Sentence level correlations of the metrics without external resources.

Metrics	Czech-English	German-English	Spanish-English	French-English
METEOR	0.3186	0.3482	0.3258	0.2745
DEPREF	**0.3281**	**0.3606**	**0.3326**	**0.2834**

Table 1.B Sentence level correlations of the metrics with stemming and synonym.

Table 1: The sentence level correlations with the human judgments for Czech-to-English, German-to-English, Spanish-to-English and French-to-English. The number in bold is the maximum value in each column. N stands for the max length of the headword chains in HWCM in Table 1.A.

4.2 Sentence-level Evaluation

Kendall's rank correlation coefficient τ is employed to evaluate the correlation of all the MT evaluation metrics and human judgements at the sentence level. A higher value of τ means a better ranking similarity with the human judges. The correlation scores of the four language pairs and the average scores are shown in Table 1.A (without external resources) and Table 1.B (with stemming and synonym), Our method performs best when maximum length of dep-n-gram is set to 3, so we present only the results when the maximum length of dep-n-gram equals 3.

From Table 1.A, we can see that all our methods are far more better than BLEU, TER and HWCM when there is no external resources applied on all of the four language pairs. In Table 1.B, external resources is considered. DEPREF is also better than METEOR on the four language pairs. From the comparison between Table 1.A and Table 1.B, we can conclude that external resources is helpful for DEPREF on most of the language pairs. When comparing DEPREF without external resources with METEOR, we find that DEPREF obtains better results on Czech-English and German-English.

4.3 System-level Evaluation

We also evaluated the metrics with the human rankings at the system level to further investigate the effectiveness of our metrics. The matching of the words in DEPREF is correlated with the position of the words, so the traditional way of computing system level score, like what BLEU does, is not feasible for DEPREF. Therefore, we resort to the way of adding the sentence level scores together to obtain the system level score. At system level evaluation, we employ Spearman's rank correlation coefficient ρ. The correlations of the four language pairs and the average scores are shown in Table 2.A (without external resources) and Table 2.B (with stem and synonym).

From Table 2.A, we can see that the correlation of DEPREF is better than BLEU, TER and HWCM on German-English, Spanish-English and French-English. On Czech-English, our metric DEPREF is better than BLEU and TER. In Table 2.B (with stem and synonym), DEPREF obtains better results than METEOR on all of the language pairs except one case that DEPREF gets the same result as METEOR on Czech-English. When comparing DEPREF without external resources with METEOR, we can find that DEPREF gets better result than METEOR on Spanish-English and French-English.

From Table 1 and Table 2, we can conclude that, DEPREF without external resources can obtain comparable result with METEOR, and DEPREF with external resources can obtain better results than METEOR. The only exception is that at the system level evaluation, Czech-English's best score is abtained by HWCM. Notice that there are only 12 systems in Czech-English, which means there are only 12 numbers to be sorted, we believe

Metrics		Czech-English	German-English	Spanish-English	French-English
BLEU		0.8400	0.8808	0.8681	0.8391
TER		0.7832	0.8923	0.9033	0.8330
HWCM	N=1	0.8392	0.7715	0.7231	0.6730
	N=2	0.8671	0.8600	0.7670	0.8026
	N=3	**0.8811**	0.8831	0.8286	0.8209
	N=4	**0.8811**	0.9046	0.8242	0.8148
DEPREF		0.8392	**0.9238**	**0.9604**	**0.8687**

Table 2.A System level correlations of the metrics without external resources.

Metrics	Czech-English	German-English	Spanish-English	French-English
METEOR	**0.8392**	0.9269	0.9516	0.8652
DEPREF	**0.8392**	**0.9331**	**0.9692**	**0.8730**

Table 2.B System level correlations of the metrics with stemming and synonym.

Table 2: The system level correlations with the human judgments for Czech-to-English, German-to-English, Spanish-to-English and French-to-English. The number in bold is the maximum value in each column. N stands for the max length of the headword chains in HWCM in Table 2.A.

the spareness issure is more serious in this case.

5 Conclusion

In this paper, we propose a new automatic MT evaluation method DEPREF. The experiments are carried out at both sentence-level and system-level using four language pairs from WMT 2010. The experiment results indicate that DEPREF achieves better correlation than BLEU, HWCM, TER and METEOR at both sentence level and system level.

References

Yee Seng Chan and Hwee Tou Ng. 2008. Maxsim: A maximum similarity metric for machine translation evaluation. In *Proceedings of ACL-08: HLT*, pages 55–62.

Boxing Chen and Roland Kuhn. 2011. Amber: A modified bleu, enhanced ranking metric. In *Proceedings of the Sixth Workshop on Statistical Machine Translation*, pages 71–77, Edinburgh, Scotland, July. Association for Computational Linguistics.

Boxing Chen, Roland Kuhn, and George Foster. 2012. Improving amber, an mt evaluation metric. In *Proceedings of the Seventh Workshop on Statistical Machine Translation*, WMT '12, pages 59–63, Stroudsburg, PA, USA. Association for Computational Linguistics.

Alon Lavie and Abhaya Agarwal. 2007. Meteor: an automatic metric for mt evaluation with high levels of correlation with human judgments. In *Proceedings of the Second Workshop on Statistical Machine Translation*, StatMT '07, pages 228–231, Stroudsburg, PA, USA. Association for Computational Linguistics.

Ding Liu and Daniel Gildea. 2005. Syntactic features for evaluation of machine translation. In *Proceedings of the ACL Workshop on Intrinsic and Extrinsic Evaluation Measures for Machine Translation and/or Summarization*, pages 25–32.

Q. Liu, H. Yu, X. Wu, J. Xie, Y. Lu, and S. Lin. 2013. A Novel Dependency Based MT Evaluation Method. *Under Review*.

Karolina Owczarzak, Josef van Genabith, and Andy Way. 2007a. Dependency-based automatic evaluation for machine translation. In *Proceedings of the NAACL-HLT 2007/AMTA Workshop on Syntax and Structure in Statistical Translation*, SSST '07, pages 80–87, Stroudsburg, PA, USA. Association for Computational Linguistics.

Karolina Owczarzak, Josef van Genabith, and Andy Way. 2007b. Evaluating machine translation with lfg dependencies. *Machine Translation*, 21(2):95–119, June.

Karolina Owczarzak, Josef van Genabith, and Andy Way. 2007c. Labelled dependencies in machine translation evaluation. In *Proceedings of the Second Workshop on Statistical Machine Translation*, StatMT '07, pages 104–111, Stroudsburg, PA, USA. Association for Computational Linguistics.

K. Papineni, S. Roukos, T. Ward, and W.J. Zhu. 2002. BLEU: a method for automatic evaluation of machine translation. In *Proceedings of the 40th annual meeting on association for computational linguistics*, pages 311–318. Association for Computational Linguistics.

Matthew Snover, Bonnie Dorr, Richard Schwartz, Linnea Micciulla, and John Makhoul. 2006. A study of translation edit rate with targeted human annotation. In *Proceedings of Association for Machine Translation in the Americas*, pages 223–231.

Junguo Zhu, Muyun Yang, Bo Wang, Sheng Li, and Tiejun Zhao. 2010. All in strings: a powerful string-based automatic mt evaluation metric with multiple granularities. In *Proceedings of the 23rd International Conference on Computational Linguistics: Posters*, COLING '10, pages 1533–1540, Stroudsburg, PA, USA. Association for Computational Linguistics.

Efficient solutions for word reordering in German-English phrase-based statistical machine translation

Arianna Bisazza and **Marcello Federico**
Fondazione Bruno Kessler
Trento, Italy
{bisazza,federico}@fbk.eu

Abstract

Despite being closely related languages, German and English are characterized by important word order differences. Long-range reordering of verbs, in particular, represents a real challenge for state-of-the-art SMT systems and is one of the main reasons why translation quality is often so poor in this language pair. In this work, we review several solutions to improve the accuracy of German-English word reordering while preserving the efficiency of phrase-based decoding. Among these, we consider a novel technique to dynamically shape the reordering search space and effectively capture long-range reordering phenomena. Through an extensive evaluation including diverse translation quality metrics, we show that these solutions can significantly narrow the gap between phrase-based and hierarchical SMT.

1 Introduction

Modeling the German-English language pair is known to be a challenging task for state-of-the-art statistical machine translation (SMT) methods. A major factor of difficulty is given by word order differences that yield important long-range reordering phenomena.

Thanks to specific reordering modeling components, phrase-based SMT (PSMT) systems (Zens et al., 2002; Koehn et al., 2003; Och and Ney, 2002) are generally good at handling *local* reordering phenomena that are not captured inside phrases. However, they typically fail to predict long reorderings. On the other hand, hierarchical SMT (HSMT) systems (Chiang, 2005) can learn reordering patterns by means of discontinuous translation rules, and are therefore considered a better choice for language pairs characterized by massive and hierarchical reordering.

Looking at the results of the Workshop of Machine Translation's last edition (WMT12) (Callison-Burch et al., 2012), no particular SMT approach appears to be clearly dominating. In both language directions (official results excluding the online systems) the rule-based systems outperformed all SMT approaches, and among the best SMT systems we find a variety of approaches: pure phrase-based, phrase-based and hierarchical systems combination, n-gram based, a rich syntax-based approach, and a phrase-based system coupled with POS-based pre-ordering. This gives an idea of how challenging this language pair is for SMT and raises the question of which SMT approach is best suited to model it.

In this work, we aim at answering this question by focussing on the word reordering problem, which is known to be an important factor of SMT performance (Birch et al., 2008). We hypothesize that PSMT can be as successful for German-English as the more computationally costly HSMT approach, provided that the reordering-related parameters are carefully chosen and the best available reordering models are used. More specifically, our study covers the following topics: distortion functions and limits, and dynamic shaping of the reordering search space based on a discriminative reordering model.

We first review these topics, and then evaluate them systematically on the WMT task using both generic and reordering-specific metrics, with the aim of providing a reference for future system developers' choices.

2 Background

Word order differences between German and English are mainly found at the clause (global) level, as opposed to the phrase (local) level. We refer to Collins et al. (2005) and Gojun and Fraser (2012) for a detailed description of the German clause structure. To briefly summarize, we can say that the *verb-second order* of German main clauses contrasts with the rigid SVO structure of English, as does the clause-final verb position of German subordinate clauses. A further difficulty is given by the German *discontinuous* verb phrases, where the main verb is separated from the inflected auxiliary or modal. The distance between the two parts of a verb phrase can be arbitrarily long as shown in the following example:

[DE] Jedoch **konnten** sie Kinder in Teilen von Helmand und Kandahar im Süden aus Sicherheitsgrund **nicht erreichen**.

[EN] But they **could not reach** children in parts of Helmand and Kandahar in the south for security reasons.

Translating this sentence with a PSMT engine implies performing two very long jumps that are not even considered by typical systems employing a distortion limit of 6 or 8 words. At the same time, increasing the distortion limit to very high values is known to have a negative impact on both efficiency and translation quality (cf. results presented later in this paper).

Because reordering patterns of this kind are very common between German and English, this paper focuses on techniques that enable the PSMT decoder to explore long jumps and thus improve reordering accuracy without hurting efficiency nor general translation quality.

2.1 Alternative approaches

German-English reordering in SMT has been widely studied and is still an open topic. In this work, we only consider efficient solutions that are fully integrated into the decoding process, and that do not require syntactic parsers or manual reordering rules. Still, it has to be mentioned that several alternative solutions were proposed in the literature. A well-known strategy consists of pre-ordering the German sentence in an English-like order by applying a set of manually written rules to its syntactic parse tree (Collins et al., 2005).[1] Other approaches learn the pre-ordering rules automatically, from syntactic parses (Xia and McCord, 2004; Genzel, 2010) or from part-of-speech labels (Niehues and Kolss, 2009). In the former case, pre-ordering decisions are typically taken deterministically (i. e. one permuation per sentence), whereas in the latter, multiple alternatives are represented as word lattices, and the optimal path is selected by the decoder at translation time. In (Tromble and Eisner, 2009), pre-ordering is cast as a permutation problem and solved by a model that estimates the probability of reversing the relative order of any two input words.

In the field of tree-based SMT, positive results in German-English were achieved by combining syntactic translation rules with unlabeled hierarchical SMT rules (Hoang and Koehn, 2010). More recently, Braune et al. (2012) proposed to improve the long-range reordering capability of an HSMT system by integrating constraints based on clausal boundaries and by manually selecting the rule patterns applicable to long word spans. The paper did not analyse the impact of the technique on efficiency.

2.2 Evaluation methods

A large number of previous works on word reordering measured their success with general-purpose metrics such as BLEU (Papineni et al., 2001) or METEOR (Banerjee and Lavie, 2005). These metrics, however, are only indirectly sensitive to word order and do not sufficiently penalize long-range reordering errors, as demonstrated for instance by Birch et al. (2010). While BLEU remains a standard choice for many evaluation campaigns, we believe it is extremely important to complement it with metrics that are specifically designed to capture word order differences. In this work, we adopt two reordering-specific metrics in addition to BLEU and METEOR:

Kendall Reordering Score (KRS). As proposed by Birch et al. (2010), the KRS measures the similarity between the input-output reordering and the input-reference reordering. This is done by converting word alignments to permutations and computing a permutation distance among them. When interpolated with BLEU, this score is called LRscore.[2]

Verb-specific KRS (KRS-V). The ideal way to automatically evaluate our systems would be to use syntax- or semantics-based metrics, as the impact of long reordering errors is particularly important at these levels. As a light-weight alternative, we instead concentrate the evaluation on those word classes that are typically crucial to guess the general structure of a sentence. To this end, we adopt a word-weighted version of the

[1] A similar solution for the opposite translation direction (English-German) was proposed by Gojun and Fraser (2012).

[2] Thus, our KRS results correspond exactly to the LRscore(α=1) presented in other papers.

KRS and set the weights to 1 for verbs and 0 for all other words, so that only verb reordering errors are captured. We call the resulting metric KRS-V. The KRS-V rates a translation hypothesis as perfect (100%) when the translations of all source verbs are located in their correct position, regardless of the other words' ordering.

3 Early distortion cost

In its original formulation, the PSMT approach includes a basic reordering model, called **distortion cost**, that exponentially penalizes longer jumps among consecutively translated phrases simply based on their distance. Thus, a completely monotonic translation has a total distortion cost of zero.

A weakness of this model is that it penalizes long jumps only when they are performed, rather than accumulating their cost gradually. As an effect, hypotheses with gaps (i. e. uncovered input positions) can proliferate and cause the pruning of more monotonic hypotheses that could lead to overall better translations.

To solve this problem, Moore and Quirk (2007) proposed an improved version of the distortion cost function that anticipates the gradual accumulation of the total distortion cost, making hypotheses with the same number of covered words more comparable with one another. **Early distortion cost** (as called in Moses, or "distortion penalty estimation" in the original paper) is computed by a simple algorithm that keeps track of the uncovered input positions. Note that this option affects the distortion *feature function*, but not the distortion *limit*, which always corresponds to the maximum distance allowed between consecutively translated phrases.

Early distortion cost was shown by its authors to yield similar BLEU scores as the standard one but with stricter pruning parameters, i. e. faster decoding. Experiments were performed on an English-French task, with a fixed distortion limit of 5 and without lexicalized reordering models. Our study deals with a language pair that is arguably more difficult at the level of reordering. Moreover, we start from a stronger baseline and measure the impact of early distortion cost in various distortion limit settings, using also reordering-specific metrics. Results are presented in Section 6.2.

4 Word-after-word reordering modeling and pruning

Phrase orientation (lexicalized reordering) models (Tillmann, 2004; Koehn et al., 2005; Galley and Manning, 2008) have proven very useful for short and medium-range reordering and are probably the most widely used in PSMT nowadays. However, their coarse classification of reordering steps makes them unsuitable to capture long-range reordering phenomena, such as those attested in German-English. Indeed, Galley and Manning (2008) reported a decrease of translation quality when the distortion limit was set beyond 6 in Chinese-English and beyond 4 in Arabic-English.

To address this problem, we have developed a different reordering model that predicts what input word should be translated at a given decoding state (Bisazza, 2013; Bisazza and Federico, 2013). The model is similar to the one proposed by Visweswariah et al. (2011), however we use it differently: that is, not simply for data preprocessing but as an additional feature function fully integrated in the phrase-based decoder. More importantly, we propose to use the same model to dynamically shape the space of reorderings explored during decoding (cf. Section 4.2), which was never done before.

Another related work is the source-side decoding sequence model by Feng et al. (2010), that is a generative n-gram model trained on a corpus of pre-ordered source sentences. Although reminiscent of a source-side bigram model, our model has two important differences: (i) the discriminative modeling framework enables us to design a much richer feature set including, for instance, the context of the next word to pick; (ii) all our features are independent from the decoding history, which allows for an efficient decoder-integration with no effect on hypothesis recombination.

Finally, we have to mention the models by Al-Onaizan and Papineni (2006) and Green et al. (2010), who predict the direction and (binned) length of a jump to perform after a given input word. Those models too were only used as additional feature functions, and were not shown to maintain translation quality and efficiency at very high distortion limits.

4.1 The model

The Word-after-word (**WaW**) reordering model is trained to predict whether a given input position should be translated *right after* another, given the words at those positions and their contexts. It is based on the following maximum-entropy binary classifier:

$$P(R_{i,j}{=}Y|f_1^J,i,j) = \frac{exp[\sum_m \lambda_m h_m(f_1^J,i,j,R_{i,j}{=}Y)]}{\sum_{Y'} exp[\sum_m \lambda_m h_m(f_1^J,i,j,R_{i,j}{=}Y')]}$$

where f_1^J is a source sentence of J words, h_m are feature functions and λ_m the corresponding feature weights. The outcome Y can be either 1 or 0, with $R_{i,j}{=}1$ meaning that the word at position j is translated right after the word at position i.

Training examples are extracted from a corpus of reference reorderings, obtained by converting the word-aligned parallel data into a set of source sentence permutations. A heuristic similar to the one proposed by Visweswariah et al. (2011) is used to this end. For each input word, we generate: (i) one positive example for the word that should be translated right after it; (ii) negative examples for all the uncovered words that lie within a given *sampling window* or δ. The latter parameter serves to control the proportion between positive and negative examples.

The WaW model builds on binary features that are extracted from the local context of positions i and j, and from the words occurring between them. In addition to the actual words, the features may include POS tags and shallow syntax labels (i. e. chunk types and boundaries). For instance, one feature may indicate that the last translated word (w_i) is an adjective while the currently translated one (w_j) is a noun:

$$\text{POS}(w_i)\text{=adj} \wedge \text{POS}(w_j)\text{=noun}$$

Other features indicate that a given word or punctuation is found between w_i and w_j:

$$w_b\text{='jedoch'} \quad ... \quad w_b\text{='.'}$$

or that w_i and w_j belong to the same shallow syntax chunk.

The WaW reordering model can be seamlessy integrated into a standard phrase-based decoder that already includes phrase orientation models. When a partial hypothesis is expanded with a given phrase pair, the model returns the log-probability of translating its words in the order defined by the phrase-internal word alignment. Moreover, the global WaW score is independent from phrase segmentation, and normalized across outputs of different lengths.

The complete list of features, training data generation algorithm and other implementation details are presented in (Bisazza, 2013) and (Bisazza and Federico, 2013).

4.2 Early reordering pruning

Besides providing an additional feature function for the log-linear PSMT framework, the WaW model's predictions can be used as an early indication of whether or not a given reordering path should be further explored. In fact, we have mentioned that the existing reordering models are not capable of guiding the search through very large reordering search spaces. As a solution, we propose to decode with loose reordering constraints (i. e. high distortion limit) but only explore those long reorderings that are promising according to the WaW model.

More specifically, at each hypothesis expansion, we consider the set of input positions that are reachable within the fixed distortion limit. Only based on the WaW score, we apply histogram and threshold pruning to this set and then proceed to expand only the non-pruned positions.[3] Furthermore, it is possible to ensure that local reorderings are always allowed, by setting a so-called *non-prunable-zone* of width ϑ around the last covered input position.[4] In this way, we can ensure that the usual space of short to medium-range reordering is exhaustively explored in addition to few promising long-range reorderings.

The rationale of this approach is two-fold: First, to avoid costly hypothesis expansions for very unlikely reordering steps and thus speed up decoding under loose reordering constraints. Second, to decrease the risk of model errors by exploiting the fact that some components of the PSMT log-linear model are more important than others at different stages of the translation process.

The WaW model is not the only scoring function that can be used for early reordering pruning. In principle, even phrase orientation model scores could be used, but we expect them to perform poorly due to the coarse classification of reordering steps (all phrases that are not adjacent to the current one are treated as *discontinuous* steps).

[3]The idea is reminiscent of early pruning by Moore and Quirk (2007): an optimization technique that consists of discarding hypothesis extensions based on their estimated score *before* computing the exact language model score.

[4]See (Bisazza, 2013) for technical details on the integration of word-level pruning with phrase-level hypothesis expansion.

5 Reordering in hierarchical SMT

To allow for a fair evaluation of our systems, we also perform a contrastive experiment using a tree-based SMT approach: namely, **hierarchical phrase-based SMT (HSMT)** (Chiang, 2005).

Reordering in HSMT is not modeled separately but is embedded in the translation model itself, which contains lexicalized, non syntactically motivated rules that are directly learnt from word-aligned parallel text. The major strength of HSMT compared to PSMT, is the ability to learn discontinous phrases and long-range lexicalized reordering rules. However, this modeling power has a cost in terms of model size and decoding complexity.

To have a concrete idea, consider that the phrase-table trained on our SMT training data (cf. Section 6.1) with a maximum phrase length of 7 contains 127 million entries (before phrase table pruning). The hierarchical rule table trained on the same data with a comparable span constraint (10) contains instead 1.2 billion entries – one order of magnitude larger.

Furthermore, the HSMT decoder is based on a chart parsing algorithm, whose complexity is cubic in the input length, and even higher when taking into account the target language model. This issue can be partially addressed by different strategies such as cube pruning (Chiang, 2007), which reduces the LM complexity to a constant, or rule application constraints. One of such constraints is the maximum number of source words that may be covered by non-terminal symbols (span constraint). Setting a span constraint – which is essential to obtain reasonable decoding times – means preventing long-range reordering similarly to setting a distortion limit in PSMT. In our experiments, we consider two settings for this parameter: 10 to capture short to medium-range reorderings, and 20 to also capture long-range reorderings.

6 Experiments

In this section we evaluate the impact on translation quality and efficiency of the techniques presented above. Our main objective is to empirically verify the hypothesis that better reordering modeling and better reordering space definition can significantly improve the accuracy of PSMT in German-English without sacrificing its efficiency.

6.1 Experimental setup

We choose the WMT German-English news translation task as our case study. More specifically we use the WMT10 training data: Europarl (v.5) plus News-commentary-2010 for a total of 1.6M parallel sentences, 44M German tokens. The target LM is trained on the monolingual news data provided for the constrained track of WMT10 (1133M English tokens). For development we use the WMT08 news benchmark, while for testing we use the following data sets:

tests(09-11): the concatentation of three previous years' benchmarks from 2009 to 2011 (8017 sentences, 21K German tokens).

test12: the latest released benchmark (3003 sentences, 8K German tokens).

Each data set includes one reference translation. Note that our goal is not to reach the performance of the best systems participating at the last WMT edition, but rather to assess the usefulness of our techniques on a larger and therefore more reliable test set, while starting from a reasonable baseline.[5]

For German tokenization and compound splitting we use Tree Tagger (Schmid, 1994) and the Gertwol morphological analyser (Koskenniemi and Haapalainen, 1994).[6]

All our SMT systems are built with the Moses toolkit (Koehn et al., 2007; Hoang et al., 2009), and word alignments are generated by the Berkeley Aligner (Liang et al., 2006). The target language model is estimated by the IRSTLM toolkit (Federico et al., 2008) with modified Kneser-Ney smoothing (Chen and Goodman, 1999).

The **phrase-based** baseline decoder includes a phrase translation model (two phrasal and two lexical probability features), a lexicalized reordering model (six features), a 6-gram target language model, distortion cost, word and phrase penalties. As lexicalized reordering model, we use a hierarchical phrase orientation model (Galley and Manning, 2008) trained on all the parallel data using three orientation classes – *monotone, swap* or *discontinuous* – in bidirectional mode. Statistically

[5]Our results on test12 are not directly comparable to the WMT12 submissions due to the different training data: that is, the WMT12 parallel data includes 50M German tokens of Europarl data and 4M of news-commentary, as opposed to the 41M and 2.5M released for WMT10 and used in our experiments.

[6]http://www2.lingsoft.fi/cgi-bin/gertwol

improbable phrase pairs are pruned from the translation model as proposed by Johnson et al. (2007).

The **hierarchical** system is trained and tested using the standard Moses configuration which includes: a rule table (two phrasal and two lexical probability features), a 6-gram target language model, word and rule penalties. We set the span constraint (cf. Section 5) to the default value of 10 words for rule extraction, while for decoding we consider two different settings: the default 10 words and a large value of 20 to enable very long-range reorderings.

Feature weights for all systems are optimized by minimum BLEU-error training (Och, 2003) on test08. To reduce the effects of the optimizer instability, we tune each configuration four times and use the average of the resulting weight vectors for testing, as suggested by Cettolo et al. (2011).

The source-to-reference word alignments that are needed to compute the reordering scores are generated by the Berkeley Aligner previously trained on the training data. Source-to-output alignments are obtained from the decoder's trace.

6.2 Distortion function and limit

We start by measuring the difference between *standard* and *early* distortion cost.[7] Figure 1 shows the results in terms of BLEU and KRS, plotted against the distortion limit (DL).

Indeed, early distortion cost (Moore and Quirk, 2007) outperforms the standard one in all the tested configurations and according to both metrics. We can see that the quality of both systems deteriorates as the distortion limit increases, however the system with early distortion cost is more robust to this effect. In particular, when passing from DL=12 to DL=18, the baseline system loses 1.2 BLEU and no less than 6.8 KRS, whereas the system with early distortion cost loses 0.8 BLEU and 4.9 KRS. Given these results, we decide to use early distortion cost in all the remaining experiments.

6.3 WaW reordering pruning

We have seen that early distortion cost can effectively reduce the loss of translation quality, but cannot totally prevent it. Moreover, increasing the distortion limit means exploring many more hypotheses and, consequently, slowing down the decoding process. With our WaW model-based reordering pruning technique, we aim at solving both issues.

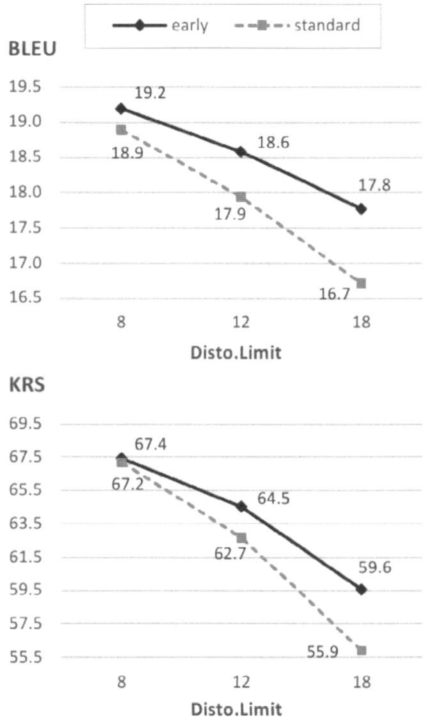

Figure 1: Standard *vs* early distortion cost performance measured in terms of BLEU and KRS on tests(09-11) under different distortion limits.

We generate the WaW training data from the first 30K sentences of the News-commentary-2010 parallel corpus, using a sampling window of width δ=10. This results in 8 million training samples, which are fed to the binary classifier implementation of the MegaM Toolkit[8]. Features with less than 20 occurrences are ignored and the maximum number of training iterations is set to 100.

Evaluated intrinsically on test08, the model achieves the following classification accuracy: 67.0% precision, 50.0% recall, 57.2% F-score. While these figures are rather low, we recall that the WaW model is not meant to be used as a stand-alone classifier, but rather as one of several SMT feature functions and as a way to detect very unlikely reordering steps. Hence, we also evaluate its ability to rank a typical set of reordering options during decoding: that is, we traverse the source words in target order and, for each of them, we ex-

[7]For this first series of experiments, feature weights are tuned in the DL=8 setting and the two resulting weight vectors (one for standard, one for early distortion) are re-used in the higher-DL experiments.

[8]http://www.cs.utah.edu/~hal/megam/ (Daumé III, 2004).

		tests(09-11)				test12				ms/
System	**DL**	**bleu**	**met**	**krs**	**krs-V**	**bleu**	**met**	**krs**	**krs-V**	**word**
Allowing only short to medium-range reordering:										
PSMT, early disto	8	19.2	28.1	67.4	65.4	19.0	28.1	67.8	66.1▲	202
+WaW (feature only)		19.4▲	28.2▲	67.6▲	65.5▲	19.5▲	28.3▲	67.8	66.2	212
HSMT, max.span=10		20.1▲	28.5▲	68.4▲	66.7▲	19.7△	28.4△	68.6▲	67.3▲	406
Allowing also long-range reordering:										
PSMT, early disto	18	18.2	28.0	62.9	62.0	18.2	28.1	63.4	62.5	408
+WaW (feature only)		18.4▲	28.0	61.8▼	61.3▼	18.1	28.1	62.2▼	61.7▼	428
+WaW reo.pruning (ϑ=5)		19.5▲	28.3▲	67.9▲	66.3▲	19.3▲	28.4▲	67.8▲	66.3▲	**142**
HSMT, max.span=20		20.0▲	28.5▲	68.1▲	66.7▲	19.7▲	28.4	68.2▲	67.1▲	706

Table 1: Effects of WaW reordering model and early reordering pruning on PSMT translation quality and efficiency, compared against a hierarchical SMT baseline. Translation quality is measured with % BLEU, METEOR, and Kendall Reordering Score: regular (KRS) and verb-specific (KRS-V). Statistically significant differences with respect to the previous row are marked with ▲▼ at the $p \leq .05$ level and △▽ at the $p \leq .10$ level. Decoding time is measured in milliseconds per input word.

amine the ranking of all words that may be translated next (i. e. the uncovered positions within a given DL). We find that, even when the DL is very high (18), the correct jump is ranked among the top 3 reachable jumps in the large majority of cases (81.4%). If we only consider long jumps – i. e. spanning more than 6 words – the Top-3 accuracy is 56.4% while that of a baseline that simply favors shorter jumps (as the distortion cost does) is only 26.5%.

For the early reordering pruning experiment, we set the pruning parameters to 2 for histogram and 0.25 for relative threshold.[9] A non-prunable-zone of width ϑ=5 is set around the last covered position. The resulting configuration is re-optimized by MERT on test08 for the final experiment.

Table 1 shows the effects of integrating the WaW reordering model into a PSMT decoder that already includes a state-of-the-art hierarchical phrase orientation model. The same table also presents the results of the HSMT constrastive experiments. Two scenarios are considered: in the first block, the PSMT distortion limit is set to a medium value (8) and the HSMT maximum span constraint is set to 10. Although not directly comparable, these settings have the same effect of disallowing long-range reorderings. In the second block, long-range reorderings are instead allowed with a DL of 18 and a HSMT span constraint of 20.

[9] Pruning parameters were optimized for BLEU with a grid search over the values (1, 2, 3, 4, 5) for histogram and (0.5, 0.25, 0.1) for threshold.

Feature weights are optimized for each experiment using the procedure described above (four averaged MERT runs). Statistical significance is computed for each experiment against the previous one (i. e. previous row), using approximate randomization as in (Riezler and Maxwell, 2005). Run times are obtained by an Intel Xeon X5650 processor on the first 500 sentences of tests(09-11), excluding loading time of all models.

Medium reordering space. Integrating the WaW model as an additional feature function yields small but consistent improvements (second row of Table 1). Concerning the run time, we notice just a small overload of about 5%: that is, from 202 to 212 ms/word.

In comparison, the tree-based system (third row) has almost double decoding time but achieves statistically significant higher translation quality, especially at the level of reordering.

Large reordering space. As expected, raising the DL to 18 with no special pruning (fourth row) results in much slower decoding (from 202 to 408 ms/word) but also in very poor translation quality. This loss is especially visible on the reordering scores: e. g. from 67.4 to 62.9 KRS on tests(09-11). Unfortunately, adding the WaW model as a feature function (fifth row) does not appear to be helpful under the high DL condition.

On the other hand, when using the WaW model

SRC (de)	adv. verb$_{mod}$ subj. obj. compl. Jedoch **konnten** sie Kinder in Teilen von Helmand und Kandahar im Süden aus Sicherheit∼ grund *however could they children in parts of Helmand and Kandahar in South for security reasons* neg verb$_{inf}$ **nicht erreichen** . *not reach*
REF	But they **could not reach** children in parts of Helm. and Kand. in the south for security reasons.
BASE-8	However, they **were** children in parts of Helm. and Kand. in the south, for security reasons.
HIER-10	However, they **were** children in parts of Helm. and Kand. in the south **not reach** for security reasons.
BASE-18	However, they **were** children in parts of Helm. and Kand. in the south **do not reach** for security reasons.
WAWP-18	However, they **could not reach** children in parts of Helm. and Kand. in the south for security reasons.
HIER-20	However, they **were** children in parts of Helm. and Kand. in the south **not reach** for security reasons.

Table 2: Long-range reordering example showing the behavior of different systems: [BASE-*] are phrase-based systems with a DL of 8 and 18 respectively; [WAWP-18] refers to the WaW-pruning PSMT system; [HIER-*] are hierarchical SMT systems with a span constraint of 10 and 20 words respectively.

also for reordering pruning (sixth row) we are able to recover the performance of the medium-DL baseline performance and even to slightly improve it. It is interesting to note that the largest improvement concerns the accuracy of verb reordering on tests(09-11): from 65.4 to 66.3 KRS-V. Although the other gains are rather small, we emphasize the fact that our solutions mostly affect rare and isolated events, which have a limited impact on the general purpose evaluation metrics but are are essential to produce readable translations. WaW reordering pruning has also a remarkable effect on efficiency, making decoding time decrease from 428 ms/word to 142 ms/word, that is even faster than a baseline that does not explore any long-range reordering at all (202 ms/word).

Finally, we can see from the last row of Table 1 that the gap between PSMT and HSMT has been narrowed significantly. While more work is needed to reach and outperform the quality of the HSMT system, we were able to closely approach it with five times lower decoding time (142 versus 706 ms/word) and about ten times smaller models (cf. Section 5). Comparing our best system with the best HSMT system (i. e. span constraint 10), we see that the gap in translation accuracy is slightly larger and that the decoding speed-up is smaller (142 versus 406 ms/word). However, the better performance and efficiency of HSMT-10 comes at the expense of all long-range reorderings.

Thus, our enhanced PSMT appears as an optimal choice in terms of trade-off between translation quality and efficiency.

Table 3 reports two kinds of decoding statistics that allow us to explain the very different decoding times observed, and to verify that the WaW-pruning system actually performs long-range reorderings: **#hyp/sent** is the average number of partial translation hypotheses created[10] per test sentence; **(#jumps/sent)×100** is the average number of phrase-to-phrase jumps included in the 1-best translation of every 100 test sentences. Only medium and long jumps are shown (distortion D≥6), divided into three distortion buckets.

System	DL	#hyp/sent	(#jumps/sent)×100 D: [6..8]	[9..12]	[13..18]
baseline	8	600K	90	–	–
baseline	18	1278K	88	61	48
+WaW r.prun.	18	364K	52	29	17

Table 3: Decoding statistics of three PSMT systems exploring different reordering search spaces for the translation of test12.

We can see that the early-pruning system indeed performed several long jumps but it explored a much smaller search space compared to the high-distortion baseline (364K versus 1278K partial hypotheses). As for the lower number of long jumps (e. g. 29 versus 61 with D in [9..12] and 17 versus 48 in [13..18]) it suggests that the early-pruning system is more precise, while the high-distortion baseline is over-reordering.

The output of different systems for our example sentence is shown in Table 2. In this sentence, a jump forward with D=12 and a jump backward with D=14 were necessary to achieve the correct reordering of the verb and its negation. Although

[10]That is, the hypotheses that were scored by all the PSMT model components and added to a hypothesis stack.

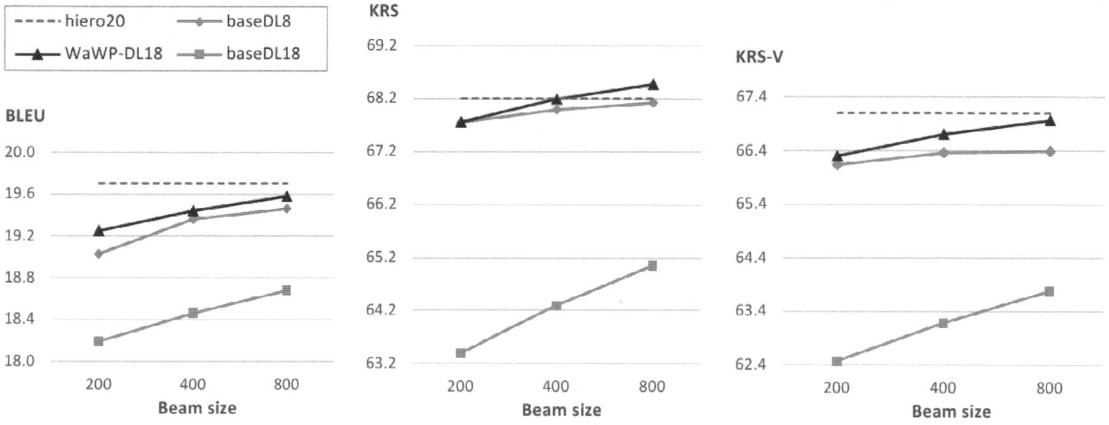

Figure 2: Effects of beam size on translation quality measured by BLEU, KRS and KRS-V, in two baseline PSMT systems (DL=8 and DL=18) and in the WaW early-pruning system (test12). For comparison, the hierarchical system performance (span constraint 20) is provided as a dotted line.

these jumps were reachable for both the [PSMT-18] and the [HSMT-20] systems, only the WaW-pruning PSMT system actually performed them.

6.4 Interaction with beam-search pruning

During the beam-search decoding process, early reordering pruning interacts with regular hypothesis pruning based on the weighted sum of all model scores. In particular, all the PSMT systems presented so far apply a default histogram threshold of 200 to each hypothesis stack. To examine this interaction, we increase the histogram threshold (beam size) from the default value of 200 up to 800, while keeping all other parameters and feature weights fixed. The results on test12 are plotted against the beam size and reported in Figure 2. The dotted line in each plot represents the performance of the hierarchical system presented in the last row of Table 1 (span constraint 20).

We can see that increasing the beam size is more beneficial for the high-DL baseline (baseDL18) than for the medium one (baseDL8). This is not surprising as the risk of search error is higher when a larger search space is explored with equal models and pruning parameters. Nevertheless, baseDL18 remains by far the worst performing system, even in our largest beam setting (800) corresponding to four times longer decoding time (1582 ms/word). What is remarkable, instead, is that the larger beam size also results in better performances by the WaW-pruning system, which is the PSMT system that explores by far the smallest search space (cf. Table 3). The superiority of the WaW-pruning system over the PSMT baselines is maintained in all tested settings and according to all metrics, which confirms the usefulness of our methods not only as optimization techniques, but also for reducing model errors of a baseline that already includes strong reordering models.

With a very large beam size (800) our enhanced PSMT system can closely approach the performance of HSMT-20 in terms of BLEU and KRS-V, and even surpass it in terms of KRS (statistically significant) while still remaining faster: that is, 554 versus 706 ms/word.

Overall HSMT-10 remains the best system, with slightly higher KRS and KRS-V and lower decoding time than our best enhanced PSMT system (406 versus 554 ms/word). However, we note once more that this performance comes at the expense of all long-range reorderings. For a completely fair comparison, the HSMT system should also be enhanced with similar reordering-pruning techniques – a research path that we plan to explore in the future, possibly inspiring from the approach of Braune et al. (2012).

7 Conclusions

We have presented a few techniques that can improve the accuracy of the word reordering performed by a German-English phrase-based SMT system. In particular, we have shown how long-range reorderings can be captured without worsening the general quality of translation and without renouncing to efficiency. Our best PSMT system is actually faster than a system that does not even attempt to perform long-range reordering, and it obtains significantly higher evaluation scores.

In comparison to a more computationally costly tree-based approach (hierarchical SMT), our enhanced PSMT system produces slightly lower translation quality but in five times lower decoding time when long-range reordering is allowed. Moreover, when a larger beam size is explored, the performance of our system can equal that of the long-reordering hierarchical system, but still with faster decoding.

In summary, we have shown that an appropriate modeling of the word reordering problem can lead to narrow or even fill the gap between phrase-based and hierarchical SMT in this difficult language pair. We have also disproved the common belief that sacrificing long-range reorderings by setting a low distortion limit is the only way to obtain well-performing PSMT systems.

Acknowledgments

This work was partially funded by the European Union under FP7 grant agreement EU-BRIDGE, Project Number 287658.

References

Yaser Al-Onaizan and Kishore Papineni. 2006. Distortion models for statistical machine translation. In *Proceedings of the 21st International Conference on Computational Linguistics and 44th Annual Meeting of the Association for Computational Linguistics*, pages 529–536, Sydney, Australia, July.

Satanjeev Banerjee and Alon Lavie. 2005. METEOR: An automatic metric for MT evaluation with improved correlation with human judgments. In *Proceedings of the ACL Workshop on Intrinsic and Extrinsic Evaluation Measures for Machine Translation and/or Summarization*, pages 65–72, Ann Arbor, Michigan, June.

Alexandra Birch, Miles Osborne, and Philipp Koehn. 2008. Predicting success in machine translation. In *Proceedings of the Conference on Empirical Methods in Natural Language Processing*, pages 745–754, Stroudsburg, PA, USA.

Alexandra Birch, Miles Osborne, and Phil Blunsom. 2010. Metrics for MT evaluation: evaluating reordering. *Machine Translation*, 24(1):15–26.

Arianna Bisazza and Marcello Federico. 2013. Dynamically shaping the reordering search space of phrase-based statistical machine translation. To appear in *Transactions of the ACL*.

Arianna Bisazza. 2013. *Linguistically Motivated Reordering Modeling for Phrase-Based Statistical Machine Translation*. Ph.D. thesis, University of Trento. http://eprints-phd.biblio.unitn.it/1019/.

Fabienne Braune, Anita Gojun, and Alexander Fraser. 2012. Long-distance reordering during search for hierarchical phrase-based SMT. In *Proceedings of the Annual Conference of the European Association for Machine Translation (EAMT)*, pages 28–30, Trento, Italy.

Chris Callison-Burch, Philipp Koehn, Christof Monz, Matt Post, Radu Soricut, and Lucia Specia. 2012. Findings of the 2012 workshop on statistical machine translation. In *Proceedings of the Seventh Workshop on Statistical Machine Translation*, pages 10–51, Montréal, Canada, June.

Mauro Cettolo, Nicola Bertoldi, and Marcello Federico. 2011. Methods for smoothing the optimizer instability in SMT. In *MT Summit XIII: the Thirteenth Machine Translation Summit*, pages 32–39, Xiamen, China.

Stanley F. Chen and Joshua Goodman. 1999. An empirical study of smoothing techniques for language modeling. *Computer Speech and Language*, 4(13):359–393.

David Chiang. 2005. A hierarchical phrase-based model for statistical machine translation. In *Proceedings of the 43rd Annual Meeting of the Association for Computational Linguistics (ACL'05)*, pages 263–270, Ann Arbor, Michigan, June.

David Chiang. 2007. Hierarchical phrase-based translation. *Computational Linguistics*, 33(2):201–228.

Michael Collins, Philipp Koehn, and Ivona Kucerova. 2005. Clause restructuring for statistical machine translation. In *Proceedings of the 43rd Annual Meeting of the Association for Computational Linguistics (ACL'05)*, pages 531–540, Ann Arbor, Michigan, June.

Hal Daumé III. 2004. Notes on CG and LM-BFGS optimization of logistic regression. Paper available at `http://pub.hal3.name`, implementation available at `http://hal3.name/megam`.

Marcello Federico, Nicola Bertoldi, and Mauro Cettolo. 2008. IRSTLM: an Open Source Toolkit for Handling Large Scale Language Models. In *Proceedings of Interspeech*, pages 1618–1621, Brisbane, Australia.

Minwei Feng, Arne Mauser, and Hermann Ney. 2010. A source-side decoding sequence model for statistical machine translation. In *Conference of the Association for Machine Translation in the Americas (AMTA)*, Denver, Colorado, USA.

Michel Galley and Christopher D. Manning. 2008. A simple and effective hierarchical phrase reordering model. In *EMNLP '08: Proceedings of the Conference on Empirical Methods in Natural Language Processing*, pages 848–856, Morristown, NJ, USA.

Dmitriy Genzel. 2010. Automatically learning source-side reordering rules for large scale machine translation. In *Proceedings of the 23rd International Conference on Computational Linguistics*, COLING '10, pages 376–384, Stroudsburg, PA, USA.

Anita Gojun and Alexander Fraser. 2012. Determining the placement of German verbs in English-to-German SMT. In *Proceedings of the 13th Conference of the European Chapter of the Association for Computational Linguistics*, pages 726–735, Avignon, France, April.

Spence Green, Michel Galley, and Christopher D. Manning. 2010. Improved models of distortion cost for statistical machine translation. In *Human Language Technologies: The 2010 Annual Conference of the North American Chapter of the Association for Computational Linguistics (NAACL)*, pages 867–875, Los Angeles, California.

Hieu Hoang and Philipp Koehn. 2010. Improved translation with source syntax labels. In *Proceedings of the Joint Fifth Workshop on Statistical Machine Translation and MetricsMATR*, pages 409–417, Uppsala, Sweden, July.

Hieu Hoang, Philipp Koehn, and Adam Lopez. 2009. A unified framework for phrase-based, hierarchical, and syntax-based statistical machine translation. In *International Workshop on Spoken Language Translation (IWSLT)*, pages 152–159, Tokyo, Japan.

H. Johnson, J. Martin, G. Foster, and R. Kuhn. 2007. Improving translation quality by discarding most of the phrasetable. In *In Proceedings of EMNLP-CoNLL 07*, pages 967–975.

Philipp Koehn, Franz Josef Och, and Daniel Marcu. 2003. Statistical phrase-based translation. In *Proceedings of HLT-NAACL 2003*, pages 127–133, Edmonton, Canada.

Philipp Koehn, Amittai Axelrod, Alexandra Birch Mayne, Chris Callison-Burch, Miles Osborne, and David Talbot. 2005. Edinburgh system description for the 2005 IWSLT speech translation evaluation. In *Proc. of the International Workshop on Spoken Language Translation*, October.

P. Koehn, H. Hoang, A. Birch, C. Callison-Burch, M. Federico, N. Bertoldi, B. Cowan, W. Shen, C. Moran, R. Zens, C. Dyer, O. Bojar, A. Constantin, and E. Herbst. 2007. Moses: Open Source Toolkit for Statistical Machine Translation. In *Proceedings of the 45th Annual Meeting of the Association for Computational Linguistics Companion Volume Proceedings of the Demo and Poster Sessions*, pages 177–180, Prague, Czech Republic.

Kimmo Koskenniemi and Mariikka Haapalainen, 1994. *GERTWOL – Lingsoft Oy*, chapter 11, pages 121–140. Roland Hausser, Niemeyer, Tübingen.

Percy Liang, Ben Taskar, and Dan Klein. 2006. Alignment by agreement. In *Proceedings of the Human Language Technology Conference of the NAACL, Main Conference*, pages 104–111, New York City, USA, June.

Robert C. Moore and Chris Quirk. 2007. Faster beam-search decoding for phrasal statistical machine translation. In *In Proceedings of MT Summit XI*, pages 321–327, Copenhagen, Denmark.

Jan Niehues and Muntsin Kolss. 2009. A POS-based model for long-range reorderings in SMT. In *Proceedings of the Fourth Workshop on Statistical Machine Translation*, pages 206–214, Athens, Greece.

F. Och and H. Ney. 2002. Discriminative training and maximum entropy models for statistical machine translation. In *Proceedings of the 40th Annual Meeting of the Association for Computational Linguistics (ACL)*, pages 295–302, Philadelhpia, PA.

Franz Josef Och. 2003. Minimum Error Rate Training in Statistical Machine Translation. In Erhard Hinrichs and Dan Roth, editors, *Proceedings of the 41st Annual Meeting of the Association for Computational Linguistics*, pages 160–167.

Kishore Papineni, Salim Roukos, Todd Ward, and Wei-Jing Zhu. 2001. Bleu: a method for automatic evaluation of machine translation. Research Report RC22176, IBM Research Division, Thomas J. Watson Research Center.

Stefan Riezler and John T. Maxwell. 2005. On some pitfalls in automatic evaluation and significance testing for MT. In *Proceedings of the ACL Workshop on Intrinsic and Extrinsic Evaluation Measures for Machine Translation and/or Summarization*, pages 57–64, Ann Arbor, Michigan, June.

Helmut Schmid. 1994. Probabilistic part-of-speech tagging using decision trees. In *Proceedings of International Conference on New Methods in Language Processing*.

Christoph Tillmann. 2004. A Unigram Orientation Model for Statistical Machine Translation. In *Proceedings of the Joint Conference on Human Language Technologies and the Annual Meeting of the North American Chapter of the Association of Computational Linguistics (HLT-NAACL)*.

Roy Tromble and Jason Eisner. 2009. Learning linear ordering problems for better translation. In *Proceedings of the 2009 Conference on Empirical Methods in Natural Language Processing*, pages 1007–1016, Singapore, August.

Karthik Visweswariah, Rajakrishnan Rajkumar, Ankur Gandhe, Ananthakrishnan Ramanathan, and Jiri Navratil. 2011. A word reordering model for improved machine translation. In *Proceedings of the 2011 Conference on Empirical Methods in Natural Language Processing*, pages 486–496, Edinburgh, Scotland, UK., July.

Fei Xia and Michael McCord. 2004. Improving a statistical MT system with automatically learned rewrite patterns. In *Proceedings of Coling 2004*, pages 508–514, Geneva, Switzerland, Aug 23–Aug 27. COLING.

R. Zens, F. J. Och, and H. Ney. 2002. Phrase-based statistical machine translation. In *25th German Conference on Artificial Intelligence (KI2002)*, pages 18–32, Aachen, Germany. Springer Verlag.

A Phrase Orientation Model for Hierarchical Machine Translation

Matthias Huck and **Joern Wuebker** and **Felix Rietig** and **Hermann Ney**
Human Language Technology and Pattern Recognition Group
Computer Science Department
RWTH Aachen University
D-52056 Aachen, Germany
{huck,wuebker,rietig,ney}@i6.informatik.rwth-aachen.de

Abstract

We introduce a lexicalized reordering model for hierarchical phrase-based machine translation. The model scores *monotone*, *swap*, and *discontinuous* phrase orientations in the manner of the one presented by Tillmann (2004). While this type of lexicalized reordering model is a valuable and widely-used component of standard phrase-based statistical machine translation systems (Koehn et al., 2007), it is however commonly not employed in hierarchical decoders.

We describe how phrase orientation probabilities can be extracted from word-aligned training data for use with hierarchical phrase inventories, and show how orientations can be scored in hierarchical decoding. The model is empirically evaluated on the NIST Chinese→English translation task. We achieve a significant improvement of +1.2 %BLEU over a typical hierarchical baseline setup and an improvement of +0.7 %BLEU over a syntax-augmented hierarchical setup. On a French→German translation task, we obtain a gain of up to +0.4 %BLEU.

1 Introduction

In hierarchical phrase-based translation (Chiang, 2005), a probabilistic synchronous context-free grammar (SCFG) is induced from bilingual training corpora. In addition to continuous *lexical* phrases as in standard phrase-based translation, *hierarchical* phrases with usually up to two non-terminals are extracted from the word-aligned parallel training data.

Hierarchical decoding is typically carried out with a parsing-based procedure. The parsing algorithm is extended to handle translation candidates and to incorporate language model scores via cube pruning (Chiang, 2007). During decoding, a hierarchical translation rule implicitly specifies the placement of the target part of a sub-derivation which is substituting one of its non-terminals in a partial hypothesis. The hierarchical phrase-based model thus provides an integrated reordering mechanism. The reorderings which are being conducted by the hierarchical decoder are a result of the application of SCFG rules, which generally means that there must have been some evidence in the training data for each reordering operation. At first glance one might be tempted to believe that any additional designated phrase orientation modeling would be futile in hierarchical translation as a consequence of this. We argue that such a conclusion is false, and we will provide empirical evidence in this work that lexicalized phrase orientation scoring can be highly beneficial not only in standard phrase-based systems, but also in hierarchical ones.

The purpose of a phrase orientation model is to assess the adequacy of phrase reordering during search. In standard phrase-based translation with continuous phrases only and left-to-right hypothesis generation (Koehn et al., 2003; Zens and Ney, 2008), phrase reordering is implemented by jumps within the input sentence. The choice of the best order for the target sequence is made based on the language model score of this sequence and a distortion cost that is computed from the source-side jump distances. Though the space of admissible reorderings is in most cases contrained by a maximum jump width or coverage-based restrictions (Zens et al., 2004) for efficiency reasons, the basic approach of arbitrarily jumping to uncovered positions on source side is still very permissive. Lexicalized reordering models assist the decoder in taking a good decision. Phrase-based decoding allows for a straightforward integration of lexicalized reordering models which assign different scores depending on how a currently translated phrase has been reordered with respect to its context. Popular lexicalized reordering models for phrase-based translation distinguish three orientation classes: *monotone*, *swap*, and *discontinuous* (Tillmann, 2004; Koehn et al., 2007; Galley and Manning, 2008). To obtain such a model, scores for the three classes are calculated from the counts of the respective orientation occurrences in the word-aligned training data for each extracted phrase. The left-to-right orientation of phrases during phrase-based search can be easily determined from the start and end positions of continuous phrases. Approximations may need to be adopted for the right-to-left scoring direction.

The utility of phrase orientation models in standard phrase-based translation is plausible and has been empirically established in practice. In hierarchical phrase-based translation, some other types of lexicalized reordering models have been investigated recently (He et al., 2010a; He et al., 2010b; Hayashi et al., 2010; Huck et al., 2012a), but in none of them are the orientation scores conditioned on the lexical identity of each phrase individually. These models are rather word-based and applied on block boundaries. Experimental results obtained with these other types of lexicalized reordering models have been very encouraging, though.

There are certain reasons why assessing the adequacy of phrase reordering should be useful in hierarchical search:

- Albeit phrase reorderings are always a result of the application of SCFG rules, the decoder is still able to choose from many different parses of the input sentence.

- The decoder can furthermore choose from many translation options for each given parse, which result in different reorderings and different phrases being embedded in the reordering non-terminals.

- All other models only weakly connect an embedded phrase with the hierarchical phrase it is placed into, in particular as the set of non-terminals of the hierarchical grammar only contains two generic non-terminal symbols.

We therefore investigate phrase orientation modeling for hierarchical translation in this work.

2 Outline

The remainder of the paper is structured as follows: We briefly outline important related publications in the following section. We subsequently give a summary of some essential aspects of the hierarchical phrase-based translation approach (Section 4). Phrase orientation modeling and a way in which a phrase orientation model can be trained for hierarchical phrase inventories are explained in Section 5. In Section 6 we introduce an extension of hierarchical search which enables the decoder to score phrase orientations. Empirical results are presented in Section 7. We conclude the paper in Section 8.

3 Related Work

Hierarchical phrase-based translation was proposed by Chiang (2005). He et al. (2010a) integrated a maximum entropy based lexicalized reordering model with word- and class-based features. Different classifiers for different rule patterns are trained for their model (He et al., 2010b). A comparable discriminatively trained model which applies a single classifier for all types of rules was developed by Huck et al. (2012a). Hayashi et al. (2010) explored the word-based reordering model by Tromble and Eisner (2009) in hierarchical translation.

For standard phrase-based translation, Galley and Manning (2008) introduced a hierarchical phrase orientation model. Similar to previous approaches (Tillmann, 2004; Koehn et al., 2007), it distinguishes the three orientation classes *monotone*, *swap*, and *discontinuous*. However, it differs in that it is not limited to model local reordering phenomena, but allows for phrases to be hierarchically combined into *blocks* in order to determine the orientation class. This has the advantage that probability mass is shifted from the rather uninformative default category *discontinuous* to the other two orientation classes, which model the location of a phrase more specifically. In this work, we transfer this concept to a hierarchical phrase-based machine translation system.

4 Hierarchical Phrase-Based Translation

The non-terminal set of a standard hierarchical grammar comprises two symbols which are shared by source and target: the initial symbol S and one generic non-terminal symbol X. The generic non-terminal X is used as a placeholder for the gaps

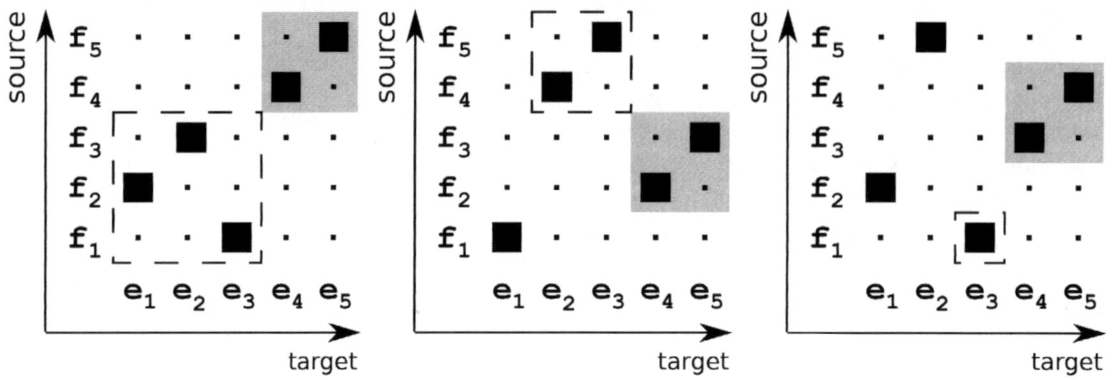

(a) Monotone phrase orientation. (b) Swap phrase orientation. (c) Discontinuous phrase orientation.

Figure 1: Extraction of the orientation classes *monotone*, *swap*, and *discontinuous* from word-aligned training samples. The examples show the left-to-right orientation of the shaded phrases. The dashed rectangles indicate how the predecessor words are merged into *blocks* with regard to their word alignment.

within the right-hand side of hierarchical translation rules as well as on all left-hand sides of the translation rules that are extracted from the parallel training corpus.

Extracted rules of a standard hierarchical grammar are of the form $X \rightarrow \langle \alpha, \beta, ^\sim \rangle$ where $\langle \alpha, \beta \rangle$ is a bilingual phrase pair that may contain X, i.e. $\alpha \in (\{X\} \cup V_F)^+$ and $\beta \in (\{X\} \cup V_E)^+$, where V_F and V_E are the source and target vocabulary, respectively. The non-terminals on the source side and on the target side of hierarchical rules are linked in a one-to-one correspondence. The $^\sim$ relation defines this one-to-one correspondence. In addition to the extracted rules, a non-lexicalized *initial rule*

$$S \rightarrow \langle X^{\sim 0}, X^{\sim 0} \rangle \quad (1)$$

is engrafted into the hierarchical grammar, as well as a special *glue rule*

$$S \rightarrow \langle S^{\sim 0} X^{\sim 1}, S^{\sim 0} X^{\sim 1} \rangle \quad (2)$$

that the system can use for serial concatenation of phrases as in monotonic phrase-based translation. The initial symbol S is the start symbol of the grammar.

Hierarchical search is conducted with a customized version of the CYK+ parsing algorithm (Chappelier and Rajman, 1998) and cube pruning (Chiang, 2007). A hypergraph which represents the whole parsing space is built employing CYK+. Cube pruning operates in bottom-up topological order on this hypergraph and expands at most k derivations at each hypernode.

5 Modeling Phrase Orientation for Hierarchical Machine Translation

The phrase orientation model we are using was introduced by Galley and Manning (2008). To model the sequential order of phrases within the global translation context, the three orientation classes *monotone* (M), *swap* (S) and *discontinuous* (D) are distinguished, each in both left-to-right and right-to-left direction. In order to capture the global rather than the local context, previous phrases can be merged into *blocks* if they are consistent with respect to the word alignment. A phrase is in monotone orientation if a consistent monotone predecessor block exists, and in swap orientation if a consistent swap predecessor block exists. Otherwise it is in discontinuous orientation.

Given a sequence of source words f_1^J and a sequence of target words e_1^I, a block $\langle f_{j_1}^{j_2}, e_{i_1}^{i_2} \rangle$ (with $1 \leq j_1 \leq j_2 \leq J$ and $1 \leq i_1 \leq i_2 \leq I$) is *consistent* with respect to the word alignment $A \subseteq \{1, ..., I\} \times \{1, ..., J\}$ *iff*

$$\begin{aligned} &\exists (i,j) \in A : i_1 \leq i \leq i_2 \wedge j_1 \leq j \leq j_2 \\ &\wedge \forall (i,j) \in A : i_1 \leq i \leq i_2 \leftrightarrow j_1 \leq j \leq j_2. \end{aligned} \quad (3)$$

Consistency is based upon two conditions in this definition: (1.) At least one source and target position within the block must be aligned, and (2.) words from inside the source interval may only be aligned to words from inside the target interval and vice versa. These are the same conditions as those that are applied for the extraction of

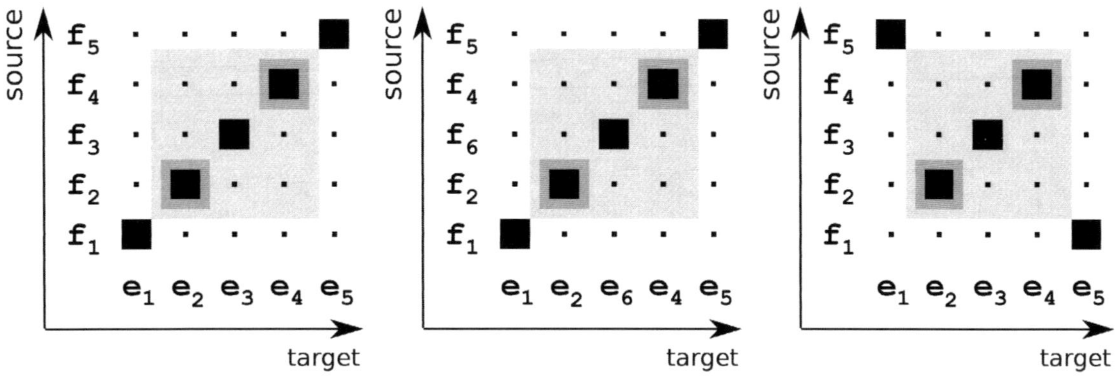

(a) A monotone orientation.

Left-to-right orientation counts:

$$N(M|f_2X^{\sim 0}f_4, e_2X^{\sim 0}e_4) = 1$$
$$N(S|f_2X^{\sim 0}f_4, e_2X^{\sim 0}e_4) = 0$$
$$N(D|f_2X^{\sim 0}f_4, e_2X^{\sim 0}e_4) = 0$$

(b) Another monotone orientation.

Left-to-right orientation counts:

$$N(M|f_2X^{\sim 0}f_4, e_2X^{\sim 0}e_4) = 2$$
$$N(S|f_2X^{\sim 0}f_4, e_2X^{\sim 0}e_4) = 0$$
$$N(D|f_2X^{\sim 0}f_4, e_2X^{\sim 0}e_4) = 0$$

(c) A swap orientation.

Left-to-right orientation counts:

$$N(M|f_2X^{\sim 0}f_4, e_2X^{\sim 0}e_4) = 2$$
$$N(S|f_2X^{\sim 0}f_4, e_2X^{\sim 0}e_4) = 1$$
$$N(D|f_2X^{\sim 0}f_4, e_2X^{\sim 0}e_4) = 0$$

Figure 2: Accumulation of orientation counts for hierarchical phrases during extraction. The hierarchical phrase $\langle f_2X^{\sim 0}f_4, e_2X^{\sim 0}e_4\rangle$ (dark shaded) can be extracted from all the three training samples. Its orientation is identical to the orientation of the continuous phrase (lightly shaded) which the sub-phrase is cut out of, respectively. Note that the actual lexical content of the sub-phrase may differ. For instance, the sub-phrase $\langle f_3, e_3\rangle$ is being cut out in Fig. 2a, and the sub-phrase $\langle f_6, e_6\rangle$ is being cut out in Fig. 2b.

standard continuous phrases. The only difference is that length constraints are applied to phrases, but not to blocks.

Figure 1 illustrates the extraction of monotone, swap, and discontinuous orientation classes in left-to-right direction from word-aligned bilingual training samples. The right-to-left direction works analogously.

We found that this concept can be neatly plugged into the hierarchical phrase-based translation paradigm, without having to resort to approximations in decoding, which is necessary to determine the right-to-left orientation in a standard phrase-based system (Cherry et al., 2012). To train the orientations, the extraction procedure from the standard phrase-based version of the reordering model can be used with a minor extension. The model is trained on the same word-aligned data from which the translation rules are extracted. For each training sentence, we extract all phrases of unlimited length that are consistent with the word alignment, and store their corners in a matrix. The corners are distinguished by their location: top-left, top-right, bottom-left, and bottom-right. For each bilingual phrase, we determine its left-to-right and right-to-left orientation by checking for adjacent corners.

The lexicalized orientation probability for the orientation $O \in \{M, S, D\}$ and the phrase pair $\langle\alpha, \beta\rangle$ is estimated as its smoothed relative frequency:

$$p(O) = \frac{N(O)}{\sum_{O' \in \{M,S,D\}} N(O')} \quad (4)$$

$$p(O|\alpha, \beta) = \frac{\sigma \cdot p(O) + N(O|\alpha, \beta)}{\sigma + \sum_{O' \in \{M,S,D\}} N(O'|\tilde{f}, \tilde{e})}. \quad (5)$$

Here, $N(O)$ denotes the global count and $N(O|\alpha, \beta)$ the lexicalized count for the orientation O. σ is a smoothing constant.

To determine the orientation frequency for a hierarchical phrase with non-terminal symbols, the orientation counts of all those phrases are accumulated from which a sub-phrase is cut out and replaced by a non-terminal symbol to obtain this hierarchical phrase. Figure 2 gives an example.

Negative logarithms of the values are used as costs in the log-linear model combination (Och and Ney, 2002). Cost 0 for all orientations is assigned to the special rules which are not extracted from the training data (initial and glue rule).

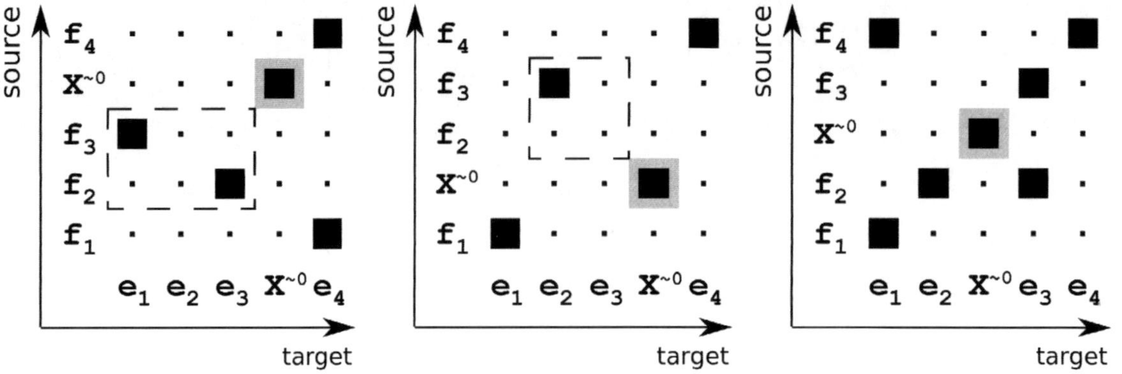

(a) Monotone non-terminal orientation. (b) Swap non-terminal orientation. (c) Discontinuous non-terminal orientation.

Figure 3: Scoring with the orientation classes *monotone*, *swap*, and *discontinuous*. Each picture shows exactly one hierarchical phrase. The block which replaces the non-terminal X during decoding is embedded with the orientation of this non-terminal X within the hierarchical phrase. The examples show the left-to-right orientation of the non-terminal. The left-to-right orientation can be detected from the word alignment of the hierarchical phrase, except for cases where the non-terminal is in boundary position on target side.

6 Phrase Orientation Scoring in Hierarchical Decoding

Our implementation of phrase orientation scoring in hierarchical decoding is based on the observation that hierarchical rule applications, i.e. the usage of rules with non-terminals within their right-hand sides, settle the target sequence order. Monotone, swap, or discontinuous orientations of blocks are each due to monotone, swap, or discontinuous placement of non-terminals which are being substituted by these blocks.

The problem of phrase orientation scoring can thus be mostly reduced to three steps which need to be carried out whenever a hierarchical rule is applied:

1. Determining the orientations of the non-terminals in the rule.

2. Retrieving the proper orientation cost of the topmost rule application in the sub-derivation which corresponds to the embedded block for the respective non-terminal.

3. Applying the orientation cost to the log-linear model combination for the current derivation.

The orientation of a non-terminal in a hierarchical rule is dependent on the word alignments in its context. Figure 3 depicts three examples.[1] We however need to deal with special cases where a non-terminal orientation cannot be established at the moment when the hierarchical rule is considered. We first describe the non-degenerate case (Section 6.1). Afterwards we briefly discuss our strategy in the special situation of *boundary non-terminals* where the non-terminal orientation cannot be determined from information which is inherent to the hierarchical rule under consideration (Section 6.3).

We focus on left-to-right orientation scoring; right-to-left scoring is symmetric.

6.1 Determining Orientations

In order to determine the orientation class of a non-terminal, we rely on the word alignments within the phrases. With each phrase, we store the alignment matrix that has been seen most frequently during phrase extraction. Non-terminal symbols on target side are assumed to be aligned to the respective non-terminal symbols on source

[1]Note that even maximal consecutive lexical intervals (either on source or target side) are not necessarily aligned in a way which makes them consistent bilingual blocks. In Fig. 3a, e_4 is for instance aligned both below and above the non-terminal. In Fig. 3c, neither $\langle f_1 f_2, e_1 e_2 \rangle$ nor $\langle f_1 f_2, e_3 e_4 \rangle$ would be valid continuous phrases (the same holds for $\langle f_3 f_4, e_1 e_2 \rangle$ and $\langle f_3 f_4, e_3 e_4 \rangle$). We actually need the generalization of the phrase orientation model to hierarchical phrases as described in Section 5 for this reason. Otherwise we would be able to just score neighboring consistent sub-blocks with a model that does not account for hierarchical phrases with non-terminals.

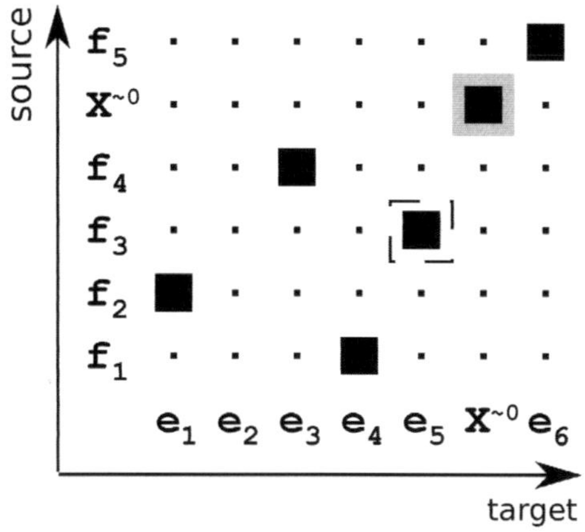

(a) Last previous aligned target position.

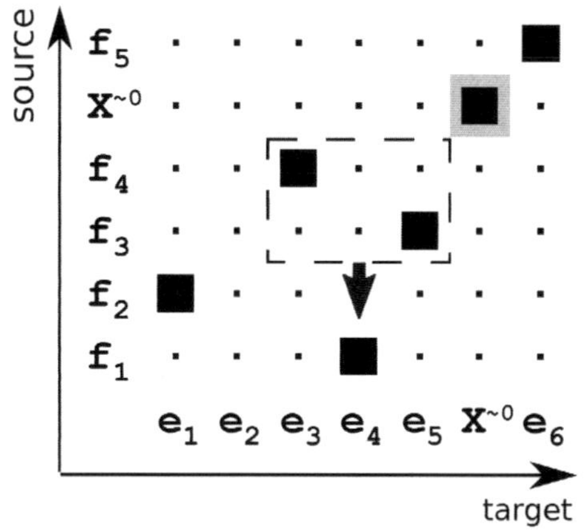

(b) Initial box.

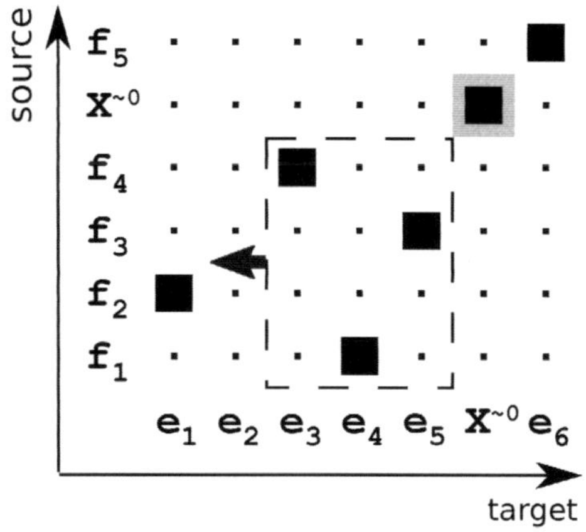

(c) Expansion of the initial box.

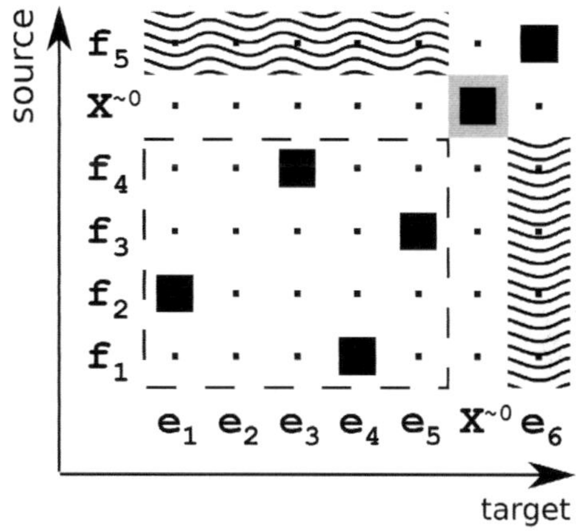

(d) The final box is a consistent left-to-right monotone predecessor block of the non-terminal.

Figure 4: Determining the orientation class during decoding. Starting from the last previous aligned target position, a box is spanned across the relevant alignment links onto the corner of the non-terminal. The box is then checked for consistency.

side according to the $\sim$ relation. In the alignment matrix, the rows and columns of non-terminals can obviously contain only exactly this one alignment link.

Starting from the last previous aligned target position to the left of the non-terminal, the algorithm expands a box that spans across the other relevant alignment links onto the corner of the non-terminal. Afterwards it checks whether the areas on the opposite sides of the non-terminal position are non-aligned in the source and target intervals of this box. The non-terminal is in discontinuous orientation if the box is not a consistent block. If the box is a consistent block, the non-terminal is in monotone orientation if its source-side position is larger than the maximum of the source-side interval of the box, and in swap orientation if its source-side position is smaller than the minimum of the source-side interval of the box.

Figure 4 illustrates how the procedure operates. In left-to-right direction, an initial box is spanned from the last previous aligned target position to the lower (monotone) or upper (swap) left corner of the non-terminal. In the example, starting from $\langle f_3, e_5 \rangle$ (Fig. 4a), this initial box is spanned to the lower left corner by iterating from f_3 to f_4 and expanding its target interval to the minimum aligned target position within these two rows of the alignment matrix. The initial box covers $\langle f_3 f_4, e_3 e_4 e_5 \rangle$ (Fig. 4b). The procedure then repeatedly checks whether the box needs to be expanded—alternating to the bottom (monotone) or top (swap) and to the left—until no alignment links below or to the left of the box break the consistency. Two box expansion are conducted in the example: the first one expands the initial box below, resulting in a larger box which covers $\langle f_1 f_2 f_3 f_4, e_3 e_4 e_5 \rangle$ (Fig. 4c); the second

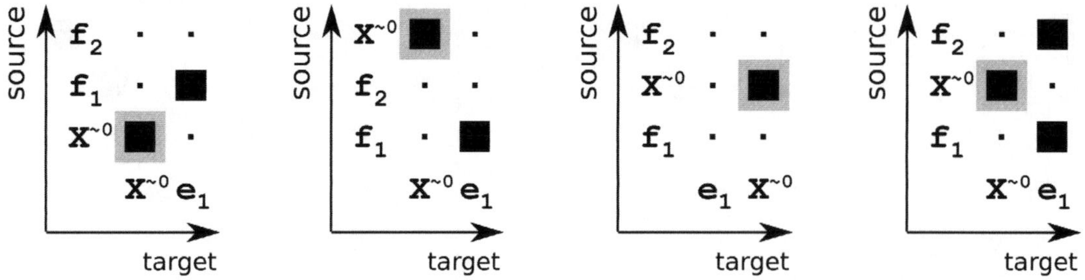

(a) Left boundary non-terminal that can be placed in left-to-right monotone or discontinuous orientation when the phrase is embedded into another one.

(b) Left boundary non-terminal that can be placed in left-to-right discontinuous or swap orientation when the phrase is embedded into another one.

(c) Left boundary non-terminal that can be placed in left-to-right monotone, swap, or discontinuous orientation when the phrase is embedded into another one.

(d) Left boundary non-terminal that can only be placed in left-to-right discontinuous orientation when the phrase is embedded into another one.

Figure 5: Left boundary non-terminal symbols. Orientations the non-terminal can eventually turn out to get placed in differ depending on existing alignment links in the rest of the phrase. Delayed left-to-right scoring is not required in cases as in Fig. 5d. Fractional costs for the possible orientations are temporarily applied in the other cases and recursively corrected as soon as an orientation is constituted in an upper hypernode.

one expands this new box to the left, resulting in a final box which covers $\langle f_1 f_2 f_3 f_4, e_1 e_2 e_3 e_4 e_5 \rangle$ (Fig. 4d) and does not need to be expanded towards the lower left corner any more. Afterwards the procedure examines whether the final box is a consistent block by inspecting whether the areas on the opposite side of the non-terminal position are non-aligned in the intervals of the box (areas with waved lines in the Fig. 4d). These areas do not contain alignment links in the example: the orientation class of the non-terminal is *monotone* as it has a consistent left-to-right monotone predecessor block. (Suppose an alignment link $\langle f_5, e_2 \rangle$ would break the consistency: the orientation class would then be *discontinuous* as the final box would not be a consistent block.)

Orientations of non-terminals could basically be precomputed and stored in the translation table. We however compute them on demand during decoding. The computational overhead did not seem to be too severe in our experiments.

6.2 Scoring Orientations

Once the orientation is determined, the proper orientation cost of the embedded block needs to be retrieved. We access the topmost rule application in the sub-derivation which corresponds to the embedded block for the respective non-terminal and read the orientation model costs for this rule. The special case of delayed scoring for boundary non-terminals as described in the subsequent section is recursively processed if necessary. The retrieved orientation costs of the embedded blocks of all non-terminals are finally added to the log-linear model combination for the current derivation.

6.3 Boundary Non-Terminals

Cases where a non-terminal orientation cannot be established at the moment when the hierarchical rule is considered arise when a non-terminal symbol is in a *boundary position* on target side. We define a non-terminal to be in (left or right) boundary position *iff* no symbols are aligned between the phrase-internal target-side index of the non-terminal and the (left or right) phrase boundary. Left boundary positions of non-terminals are critical for left-to-right orientation scoring, right boundary positions for right-to-left orientation scoring. We denote non-terminals in boundary position as *boundary non-terminals*.

The procedure as described in Section 6.1 is not applicable to boundary non-terminals because a last previous aligned target position does not exist. If it is impossible to determine the final non-terminal orientation in the hypothesis from information which is inherent to the phrase, we are forced to delay the orientation scoring of the embedded block. Our solution in these cases is to heuristically add fractional costs of all orientations the non-terminal can still eventually turn out to get placed in (cf. Figure 5). We do so because not adding an orientation cost to the derivation would give it an unjustified advantage over other ones. As soon as an orientation is constituted in an upper hypernode, any heuristic and actual orientation costs can be collected by means of a recursive call. Note that monotone or swap orientations in upper hypernodes can top-down transition into discontinuous orientations for boundary non-terminals, depending on existing phrase-internal alignment links in the context of the respective boundary non-terminal. In the derivation at the upper hypernode, the heuristic costs are subtracted and the correct actual costs added. Delayed scoring can lead to search errors; in order to keep them confined, the delayed scoring needs to be done separately for all derivations, not just for the first-best subderivations along the incoming hyperedges.

7 Experiments

We evaluate the effect of phrase orientation scoring in hierarchical translation on the Chinese→English 2008 NIST task[2] and on the French→German language pair using the standard WMT[3] newstest sets for development and testing.

7.1 Experimental Setup

We work with a Chinese–English parallel training corpus of 3.0 M sentence pairs (77.5 M Chinese / 81.0 M English running words). To train the German→French baseline system, we use 2.0 M sentence pairs (53.1 M French / 45.8 M German running words) that are partly taken from the Europarl corpus (Koehn, 2005) and have partly been collected within the Quaero project.[4]

Word alignments are created by aligning the data in both directions with GIZA++[5] and symmetrizing the two trained alignments (Och and Ney, 2003). When extracting phrases, we apply several restrictions, in particular a maximum length of ten on source and target side for lexical phrases, a length limit of five on source and ten on target side for hierarchical phrases (including non-terminal symbols), and no more than two non-terminals per phrase.

A standard set of models is used in the baselines, comprising phrase translation probabilities and lexical translation probabilities in both directions, word and phrase penalty, binary features marking hierarchical rules, glue rule, and rules with non-terminals at the boundaries, three simple count-based binary features, phrase length ratios, and a language model. The language models are 4-grams with modified Kneser-Ney smoothing (Kneser and Ney, 1995; Chen and Goodman, 1998) which have been trained with the SRILM toolkit (Stolcke, 2002).

Model weights are optimized against BLEU (Papineni et al., 2002) with MERT (Och, 2003) on 100-best lists. For Chinese→English we employ MT06 as development set, MT08 is used as unseen test set. For German→French we employ newstest2009 as development set, newstest2008, newstest2010, and newstest2011 are used as unseen test sets. During decoding, a maximum length constraint of ten is applied to all non-terminals except the initial symbol S. Translation quality is measured in truecase with BLEU and TER (Snover et al., 2006). The results on MT08 are checked for statistical significance over the baseline. Confidence intervals have been computed using bootstrapping for BLEU and Cochran's approximate ratio variance for TER (Leusch and Ney, 2009).

7.2 Chinese→English Experimental Results

Table 1 comprises all results of our empirical evaluation on the Chinese→English task.

We first compare the performance of the phrase orientation model in left-to-right direction only with the performance of the phrase orientation model in left-to-right and right-to-left direction (*bidirectional*). In all experiments, monotone, swap, and discontinuous orientation costs are treated as being from different feature functions in the log-linear model combination: we assign a separate scaling factor to each of the orientations. We have three more scaling factors than in the baseline for left-to-right direction only, and six more scaling factors for bidirectional phrase orientation scoring. As can be seen from the results table, the left-to-right model already yields a gain of 1.1 %BLEU over the baseline on the unseen test set (MT08). The bidirectional model performs just slightly better (+1.2 %BLEU over the baseline). With both models, the TER is reduced significantly as well (-1.1 / -1.3 compared to the baseline). We adopted the discriminative lexicalized reordering model (*discrim. RO*) that has been suggested by Huck et al. (2012a) for comparison purposes. The phrase orientation model provides clearly better translation quality in our experiments.

[2]http://www.itl.nist.gov/iad/mig/tests/mt/2008/

[3]http://www.statmt.org/wmt13/translation-task.html

[4]http://www.quaero.org

[5]http://code.google.com/p/giza-pp/

NIST Chinese→English	MT06 (Dev) BLEU [%]	MT06 (Dev) TER [%]	MT08 (Test) BLEU [%]	MT08 (Test) TER [%]
HPBT Baseline	32.6	61.2	25.2	66.6
+ discrim. RO	33.0	61.3	25.8	66.0
+ phrase orientation (left-to-right)	33.3	60.7	**26.3**	**65.5**
+ phrase orientation (bidirectional)	33.2	60.6	**26.4**	**65.3**
+ swap rule	32.8	61.7	25.8	66.6
+ discrim. RO	33.1	61.2	**26.0**	66.1
+ phrase orientation (bidirectional)	33.3	60.7	**26.5**	**65.3**
+ binary swap feature	33.2	61.0	25.9	66.2
+ discrim. RO	33.2	61.3	**26.2**	66.1
+ phrase orientation (bidirectional)	33.6	60.5	**26.6**	**65.1**
+ soft syntactic labels	33.4	60.8	**26.1**	66.4
+ phrase orientation (bidirectional)	33.7	60.1	**26.8**	**65.1**
+ phrase-level s2t+t2s DWL + triplets	34.3	60.1	**27.7**	**65.0**
+ discrim. RO	34.8	59.8	**27.7**	**64.7**
+ phrase orientation (bidirectional)	35.3	59.0	**28.4**	**63.7**

Table 1: Experimental results for the NIST Chinese→English translation task (truecase). On the test set, bold font indicates results that are significantly better than the baseline ($p < .05$).

As a next experiment, we bring in more reordering capabilities by augmenting the hierarchical grammar with a single *swap rule*

$$X \to \langle X^{\sim 0} X^{\sim 1}, X^{\sim 1} X^{\sim 0} \rangle \quad (6)$$

supplementary to the initial rule and glue rule. The swap rule allows adjacent phrases to be transposed. The setup with swap rule and bidirectional phrase orientation model is about as good as the setup with just the bidirectional phrase orientation model and no swap rule. If we furthermore mark the swap rule with a binary feature (*binary swap feature*), we end up at an improvement of +1.4 %BLEU over the baseline. The phrase orientation model again provides higher translation quality than the discriminative reordering model.

In a third experiment, we investigate whether the phrase orientation model also has a positive influence when integrated into a syntax-augmented hierarchical system. We configured a hierarchical setup with *soft syntactic labels* (Stein et al., 2010), a syntactic enhancement in the manner of preference grammars (Venugopal et al., 2009). On MT08, the syntax-augmented system performs 0.9 %BLEU above the baseline setup. We achieve an additional improvement of +0.7 %BLEU and -1.3 TER by including the bidirectional phrase orientation model. Interestingly, the translation quality of the setup with soft syntactic labels (but without phrase orientation model) is worse than of the setup with phrase orientation model (but without soft syntactic labels) on MT08. The combination of both extensions provides the best result, though.

In a last experiment, we finally took a very strong setup which improves over the baseline by 2.5 %BLEU through the integration of phrase-level discriminative word lexicon (*DWL*) models and *triplet* lexicon models in source-to-target (s2t) and target-to-source (t2s) direction. The models have been presented by Hasan et al. (2008), Bangalore et al. (2007), and Mauser et al. (2009). We apply them in a similar manner as proposed by Huck et al. (2011). In this strong setup, the discriminative reordering model gives gains on the development set which barely carry over to the test set. Adding the bidirectional phrase orientation model, in contrast, results in a nice gain of +0.7 %BLEU and a reduction of 1.3 points in TER on the test set, even on top of the DWL and triplet lexicon models.

7.3 French→German Experimental Results

Table 2 comprises the results of our empirical evaluation on the French→German task.

The left-to-right phrase orientation model boosts the translation quality by up to 0.3 %BLEU. The reduction in TER is in a similar order of magnitude. The bidirectional model performs a bit better again, with an advancement of up to 0.4 %BLEU and a maximal reduction in TER of 0.6 points.

French→German	newstest2008		newstest2009		newstest2010		newstest2011	
	BLEU [%]	TER [%]	BLEU [%]	TER [%]	BLEU [%]	TER [%]	BLEU [%]	TER [%]
HPBT Baseline	15.2	71.7	15.0	71.7	15.7	69.5	14.2	72.2
+ phrase orientation (left-to-right)	15.1	71.4	15.3	71.4	15.9	69.2	14.5	71.8
+ phrase orientation (bidirectional)	15.4	71.1	15.4	71.3	15.9	69.1	14.6	71.6

Table 2: Experimental results for the French→German translation task (truecase). newstest2009 is used as development set.

8 Conclusion

In this paper, we introduced a phrase orientation model for hierarchical machine translation. The training of a lexicalized reordering model which assigns probabilities for *monotone*, *swap*, and *discontinuous* orientation of phrases was generalized from standard continuous phrases to hierarchical phrases. We explained how phrase orientation scoring can be implemented in hierarchical decoding and conducted a number of experiments on a Chinese→English and a French→German translation task. The results indicate that phrase orientation modeling is a very suitable enhancement of the hierarchical paradigm.

Our implementation will be released as part of Jane (Vilar et al., 2010; Vilar et al., 2012; Huck et al., 2012b), the RWTH Aachen University open source statistical machine translation toolkit.[6]

Acknowledgments

This work was partly achieved as part of the Quaero Programme, funded by OSEO, French State agency for innovation. This material is also partly based upon work supported by the DARPA BOLT project under Contract No. HR0011-12-C-0015. Any opinions, findings and conclusions or recommendations expressed in this material are those of the authors and do not necessarily reflect the views of the DARPA. The research leading to these results has received funding from the European Union Seventh Framework Programme (FP7/2007-2013) under grant agreement n° 287658.

References

Srinivas Bangalore, Patrick Haffner, and Stephan Kanthak. 2007. Statistical Machine Translation through Global Lexical Selection and Sentence Reconstruction. In *Proc. of the Annual Meeting of the Assoc. for Computational Linguistics (ACL)*, pages 152–159, Prague, Czech Republic, June.

Jean-Cédric Chappelier and Martin Rajman. 1998. A Generalized CYK Algorithm for Parsing Stochastic CFG. In *Proc. of the First Workshop on Tabulation in Parsing and Deduction*, pages 133–137, Paris, France, April.

Stanley F. Chen and Joshua Goodman. 1998. An Empirical Study of Smoothing Techniques for Language Modeling. Technical Report TR-10-98, Computer Science Group, Harvard University, Cambridge, MA, USA, August.

Colin Cherry, Robert C. Moore, and Chris Quirk. 2012. On Hierarchical Re-ordering and Permutation Parsing for Phrase-based Decoding. In *Proc. of the Workshop on Statistical Machine Translation (WMT)*, pages 200–209, Montréal, Canada, June.

David Chiang. 2005. A Hierarchical Phrase-Based Model for Statistical Machine Translation. In *Proc. of the Annual Meeting of the Assoc. for Computational Linguistics (ACL)*, pages 263–270, Ann Arbor, MI, USA, June.

David Chiang. 2007. Hierarchical Phrase-Based Translation. *Computational Linguistics*, 33(2):201–228, June.

Michel Galley and Christopher D. Manning. 2008. A Simple and Effective Hierarchical Phrase Reordering Model. In *Proc. of the Conf. on Empirical Methods for Natural Language Processing (EMNLP)*, pages 847–855, Honolulu, HI, USA, October.

Saša Hasan, Juri Ganitkevitch, Hermann Ney, and Jesús Andrés-Ferrer. 2008. Triplet Lexicon Models for Statistical Machine Translation. In *Proc. of the Conf. on Empirical Methods for Natural Language Processing (EMNLP)*, pages 372–381, Honolulu, HI, USA, October.

Katsuhiko Hayashi, Hajime Tsukada, Katsuhito Sudoh, Kevin Duh, and Seiichi Yamamoto. 2010. Hierarchical Phrase-based Machine Translation with Word-based Reordering Model. In *Proc. of the Int. Conf. on Computational Linguistics (COLING)*, pages 439–446, Beijing, China, August.

[6] http://www.hltpr.rwth-aachen.de/jane/

Zhongjun He, Yao Meng, and Hao Yu. 2010a. Extending the Hierarchical Phrase Based Model with Maximum Entropy Based BTG. In *Proc. of the Conf. of the Assoc. for Machine Translation in the Americas (AMTA)*, Denver, CO, USA, October/November.

Zhongjun He, Yao Meng, and Hao Yu. 2010b. Maximum Entropy Based Phrase Reordering for Hierarchical Phrase-based Translation. In *Proc. of the Conf. on Empirical Methods for Natural Language Processing (EMNLP)*, pages 555–563, Cambridge, MA, USA, October.

Matthias Huck, Saab Mansour, Simon Wiesler, and Hermann Ney. 2011. Lexicon Models for Hierarchical Phrase-Based Machine Translation. In *Proc. of the Int. Workshop on Spoken Language Translation (IWSLT)*, pages 191–198, San Francisco, CA, USA, December.

Matthias Huck, Stephan Peitz, Markus Freitag, and Hermann Ney. 2012a. Discriminative Reordering Extensions for Hierarchical Phrase-Based Machine Translation. In *Proc. of the Annual Conf. of the European Assoc. for Machine Translation (EAMT)*, pages 313–320, Trento, Italy, May.

Matthias Huck, Jan-Thorsten Peter, Markus Freitag, Stephan Peitz, and Hermann Ney. 2012b. Hierarchical Phrase-Based Translation with Jane 2. *The Prague Bulletin of Mathematical Linguistics*, 98:37–50, October.

Reinhard Kneser and Hermann Ney. 1995. Improved Backing-Off for M-gram Language Modeling. In *Proc. of the Int. Conf. on Acoustics, Speech, and Signal Processing (ICASSP)*, volume 1, pages 181–184, Detroit, MI, USA, May.

Philipp Koehn, Franz Joseph Och, and Daniel Marcu. 2003. Statistical Phrase-Based Translation. In *Proc. of the Human Language Technology Conf. / North American Chapter of the Assoc. for Computational Linguistics (HLT-NAACL)*, pages 127–133, Edmonton, Canada, May/June.

Philipp Koehn, Hieu Hoang, Alexandra Birch, Chris Callison-Burch, Marcello Federico, Nicola Bertoldi, Brooke Cowan, Wade Shen, Christine Moran, Richard Zens, Chris Dyer, Ondřej Bojar, Alexandra Constantin, and Evan Herbst. 2007. Moses: Open Source Toolkit for Statistical Machine Translation. In *Proc. of the Annual Meeting of the Assoc. for Computational Linguistics (ACL)*, Demo and Poster Sessions, pages 177–180, Prague, Czech Republic.

Philipp Koehn. 2005. Europarl: A Parallel Corpus for Statistical Machine Translation. In *Proc. of the MT Summit X*, Phuket, Thailand, September.

Gregor Leusch and Hermann Ney. 2009. Edit distances with block movements and error rate confidence estimates. *Machine Translation*, 23(2):129–140, December.

Arne Mauser, Saša Hasan, and Hermann Ney. 2009. Extending Statistical Machine Translation with Discriminative and Trigger-Based Lexicon Models. In *Proc. of the Conf. on Empirical Methods for Natural Language Processing (EMNLP)*, pages 210–218, Singapore, August.

Franz Josef Och and Hermann Ney. 2002. Discriminative Training and Maximum Entropy Models for Statistical Machine Translation. In *Proc. of the Annual Meeting of the Assoc. for Computational Linguistics (ACL)*, pages 295–302, Philadelphia, PA, USA, July.

Franz Josef Och and Hermann Ney. 2003. A Systematic Comparison of Various Statistical Alignment Models. *Computational Linguistics*, 29(1):19–51, March.

Franz Josef Och. 2003. Minimum Error Rate Training for Statistical Machine Translation. In *Proc. of the Annual Meeting of the Assoc. for Computational Linguistics (ACL)*, pages 160–167, Sapporo, Japan, July.

Kishore Papineni, Salim Roukos, Todd Ward, and Wei-Jing Zhu. 2002. Bleu: a Method for Automatic Evaluation of Machine Translation. In *Proc. of the Annual Meeting of the Assoc. for Computational Linguistics (ACL)*, pages 311–318, Philadelphia, PA, USA, July.

Matthew Snover, Bonnie Dorr, Richard Schwartz, Linnea Micciulla, and John Makhoul. 2006. A Study of Translation Edit Rate with Targeted Human Annotation. In *Proc. of the Conf. of the Assoc. for Machine Translation in the Americas (AMTA)*, pages 223–231, Cambridge, MA, USA, August.

Daniel Stein, Stephan Peitz, David Vilar, and Hermann Ney. 2010. A Cocktail of Deep Syntactic Features for Hierarchical Machine Translation. In *Proc. of the Conf. of the Assoc. for Machine Translation in the Americas (AMTA)*, Denver, CO, USA, October/November.

Andreas Stolcke. 2002. SRILM – An Extensible Language Modeling Toolkit. In *Proc. of the Int. Conf. on Spoken Language Processing (ICSLP)*, volume 2, pages 901–904, Denver, CO, USA, September.

Christoph Tillmann. 2004. A Unigram Orientation Model for Statistical Machine Translation. In *Proceedings of HLT-NAACL 2004: Short Papers*, HLT-NAACL-Short '04, pages 101–104, Boston, MA, USA.

Roy Tromble and Jason Eisner. 2009. Learning Linear Ordering Problems for Better Translation. In *Proc. of the Conf. on Empirical Methods for Natural Language Processing (EMNLP)*, pages 1007–1016, Singapore, August.

Ashish Venugopal, Andreas Zollmann, Noah A. Smith, and Stephan Vogel. 2009. Preference Grammars:

Softening Syntactic Constraints to Improve Statistical Machine Translation. In *Proc. of the Human Language Technology Conf. / North American Chapter of the Assoc. for Computational Linguistics (HLT-NAACL)*, pages 236–244, Boulder, CO, USA, June.

David Vilar, Daniel Stein, Matthias Huck, and Hermann Ney. 2010. Jane: Open Source Hierarchical Translation, Extended with Reordering and Lexicon Models. In *Proc. of the Workshop on Statistical Machine Translation (WMT)*, pages 262–270, Uppsala, Sweden, July.

David Vilar, Daniel Stein, Matthias Huck, and Hermann Ney. 2012. Jane: an advanced freely available hierarchical machine translation toolkit. *Machine Translation*, 26(3):197–216, September.

Richard Zens and Hermann Ney. 2008. Improvements in Dynamic Programming Beam Search for Phrase-Based Statistical Machine Translation. In *Proc. of the Int. Workshop on Spoken Language Translation (IWSLT)*, pages 195–205, Waikiki, HI, USA, October.

Richard Zens, Hermann Ney, Taro Watanabe, and Eiichiro Sumita. 2004. Reordering Constraints for Phrase-Based Statistical Machine Translation. In *Proc. of the Int. Conf. on Computational Linguistics (COLING)*, pages 205–211, Geneva, Switzerland, August.

A Dependency-Constrained Hierarchical Model with Moses

Yvette Graham[†‡]
[†]Department of Computing and Information Systems, The University of Melbourne
[‡]Centre for Next Generation Localisation, Dublin City University
ygraham@unimelb.edu.au

Abstract

This paper presents a dependency-constrained hierarchical machine translation model that uses Moses open-source toolkit for rule extraction and decoding. Experiments are carried out for the German-English language pair in both directions for projective and non-projective dependencies. We examine effects on SCFG size and automatic evaluation results when constraints are applied with respect to projective or non-projective dependency structures and on the source or target language side.

1 Introduction

A fundamental element of natural language syntax is the dependency structure encoding the binary asymmetric head-dependent relations captured in dependency grammar theory. A main criteria for determining the dependency structure of a given sentence is the following: *The linear position of dependent, D, is specified with reference to its head, H* (Kübler et al., 2009). This runs in parallel with that which hierarchical machine translation SCFG rules encode: *The linear position of a translated phrase, X_i, is specified with reference to the lexicalised words in the rule.* Figure 1 shows de-

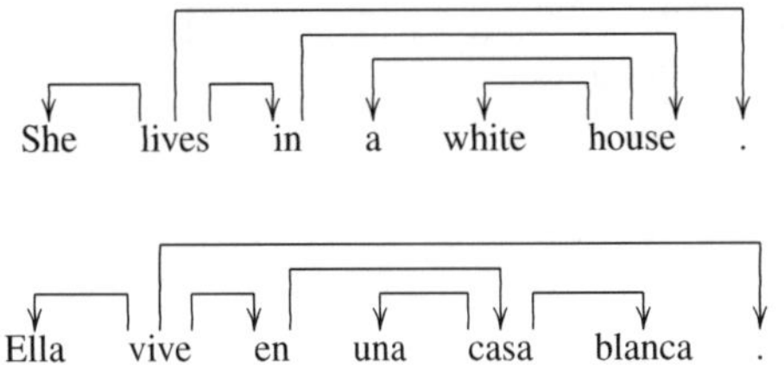

Figure 1: Projective Dependency Structures

pendency structures for *She lives in a white house* and its Spanish translation, with example SCFG

(1) $X \rightarrow <$ *white house , casa blanca* $>$
(2) $X \rightarrow <$ *white , blanca* $>$
(3) $X \rightarrow <$ *house , casa* $>$
(4) $X \rightarrow <$ X_0 *house , casa* X_0 $>$
(5) $X \rightarrow <$ *white* X_0 , X_0 *blanca* $>$

Figure 2: Initial rules (1), (2) and (3), with hierarchical rules (4) and (5)

rules shown in Figure 2. Given the existence of initial rules (1), (2) and (3), hierarchical rules (4) and (5) can be created. Rule (4) specifies the linear position of the translation of the English phrase that precedes *house* with reference to lexicalised *casa*.

For hierarchical machine translation models (Chiang, 2005), there is no requirement for a syntactic relationship to exist between the lexicalised words of a rule and the words replaced by non-terminals, the only requirement being that substituted words form an SMT phrase (Koehn et al., 2003). The dependency structure of either the source or target (or indeed both) can, however, be used to constrain rule extraction as to only allow hierarchical rules in which the linear position of dependents are specified with reference to the position of their lexicalised heads. For example, in the case of the hierarchical rules in Figure 2, rule (4) satisfies such a constraint according to both the source and target language dependency structures (since *white* is the dependent of *house* and *blanca* is the dependent of *casa*, and it is both *white* and *blanca* that are replaced by non-terminals while the heads remain lexicalised) and results in a synchronous grammar rule that positions a dependent relative to the position of its lexicalised head. Rule (5), on the other hand, does not satisfy such a constraint for either language dependency structure.

In this work, we examine a dependency-constrained model in which hierarchical rules are only permitted in which lexicalised heads specify the linear position of missing dependents, and examine the effects of applying such constraints across a variety of settings for German to English and English to German translation.

2 Related Work

The increased computational complexity introduced by hierarchical machine translation models (Chiang, 2005), has motivated techniques of constraining model size as well as decoder search. Among such include the work of Zollmann et al. (2008) and Huang and Xiang (2010), in which rule table size is vastly reduced by means of filtering low frequency rules, while Tomeh et al. (2009), Johnson et al. (2007) and Yang and Zheng (2009) take the approach of applying statistical significance tests to rule filtering, with Lee et al. (2012) defining filtering methods that estimate translational effectiveness of rules.

Dependency-based constraints have also been applied in a variety of settings to combat complexity challenges. Xie et al. (2011) use source side dependency constraints for translation from Chinese to English, while Shen et al. (2010) apply target-side dependency constraints for the same language pair and direction in addition to Arabic to English, Peter et al. (2011) also apply dependency constraints on the target side, but rather soft constraints that can be relaxed in the case that an ill-formed structure does in fact yield a better translation. Gao et al. (2011) similarly apply soft dependency constraints but to the source side for Chinese to English translation, and Galley and Manning (2009) show several advantages to using maximum spanning tree non-projective dependency parsing decoding for Chinese to English translation. Li et al. (2012), although not constraining with dependency structure, instead create non-terminals with part-of-speech tag combinations for Chinese words identified as heads for translation into English.

In this paper, we apply the same dependency constraint to SCFG rule extraction in a variety of configurations to investigate effects of applying constraints on the source or target side, to the language with most or least free word order, as well as constraining with non-projective dependency structures.

Non-Projective Dependencies	
German	38%
English	11%

Table 1: WMT Parallel Training Data

3 Non-Projective Dependencies

A non-projectivity structure is defined as follows: *A non-projective dependency structure is a dependency structure in which at least one dependency relation exists between a head, H, and its dependent, D, in which the directed path from H to D does not include at least one word positioned linearly in the surface form between H and D.* Figure 3 shows an example non-projective dependency structure arising from English *Wh-fronting*.

Non-projective dependencies occur frequently

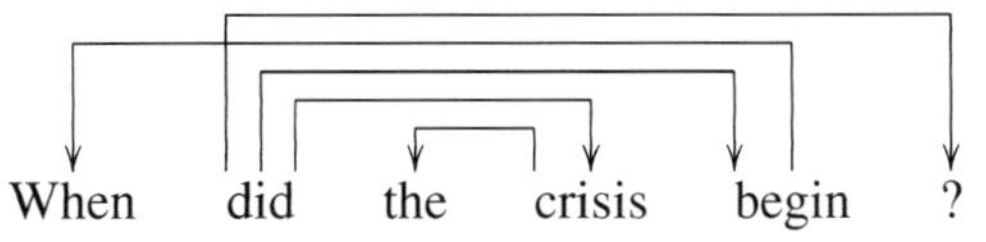

Figure 3: Non-projective Dependency Structure

for many languages, increasingly so for languages with high levels of free words order. An examination of Chinese treebanks, for example, reports that Chinese displays nine different kinds of non-projective phenomena (Yuelong, 2012) with reports of as many as one in four sentences in tree banks having non-projective dependency structures (Nivre, 2007). Even for a language with relatively rigid word order such as English non-projectivity is still common, due to Wh-fronting, topicalisation, scrambling and extraposition. Table 1 shows the frequency of non-projective dependency structures in WMT parallel data sets for German and English when parsed with a state-of-the-art non-projective dependency parser (Bohnet, 2010).

4 Constrained Model

We define the dependency constraint as follows: *to create a hierarchical rule by replacing a word or phrase with a non-terminal, all the words of that phrase must belong to a single complete dependency tree and its head must remain lexicalised in the rule.* In this way, the hierarchical rules of the SCFG position missing dependents relative to the position of lexicalised heads. Before extracting SCFG rules for the dependency-constrained models, we transform non-projective structures into projective ones, in order to allow the substitution of non-projective dependency trees by a single non-terminal. Although the transformation simplifies the dependency structure, it will introduce some dis-fluency to the training data, and we therefore include experiments to examine such effects.

Figure 4 shows a German-English translation constrained by means of the German dependency structure and Figure 5 shows the full set of dependency-constrained hierarchical SCFG rules, where dependents are specified with reference to lexicalised heads.

5 Implementation with Moses

For rule extraction we use Moses (Williams and Koehn, 2012) implementation of GHKM (Galley et al., 2004; Galley et al., 2006), which although is conventionally used to extract syntax-augmented SCFGs from phrase-structure parses (Zollmann and Venugopal, 2006), we apply the same rule extraction tool to dependency parses. Rule extraction is implemented in such a way as not to be restricted to any particular set of node labels. The conventional input format is for example:

```
<tree label="NP">
  <tree label="DET"> the </tree>
  <tree label="NN"> cat </tree>
</tree>
```

The dependency-constrained ruleset can be extracted with this implementation by arranging dependency structures into tree structures as follows:[1]

```
<tree label="X">
  <tree label="X">
    <tree label="X"> the </tree>
    <tree label="X"> black </tree>
    cat
  </tree>
  ate
  <tree label="X">
    <tree label="X"> the </tree>
    rat
  </tree>
</tree>
```

Since XML format requires nesting of substructures, only projective dependency structures can be input to the tool in the way we use it, as non-projectivity breaks nesting.

[1]Note that is is possible to replace X with dependency labels.

6 Non-Projectivity Transform

We therefore transform non-projective dependency structures into projective ones by relocating the dislocated dependent to a position closer to its head so that it no longer violates projectivity. We do this in such a way as not to break any of the existing dependency relations between pairs of words. Figure 6 shows an example non-projective structure (a) before and (b) after the transformation, where the transformation results in the constituent comprised of words *when* and *begin* forming a continuous string, making possible the substitution of this constituent with a non-terminal. The fact that one side of the training data from which hierarchical rules are extracted, however, is no longer guaranteed to be fluent, raises the question as to what effect this disfluency might have when the constraint is applied on the target side. We therefore include in our evaluation for both language directions (and for the case where the constraints are applied to the source) the effects of word reorder cause by the transformation. The

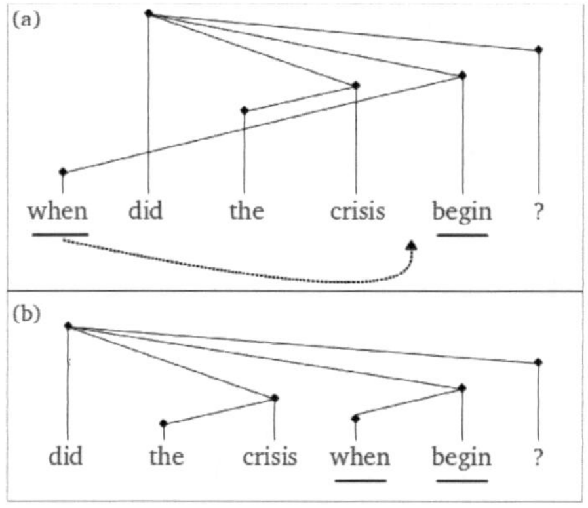

Figure 6: Non-Projectivity Transformation

algorithm for converting non-projective structures is an inorder traversal of the dependency structure as follows, where words are indexed according to their position in the original string prior to the transformation:

Algorithm 6.1: DEP_IN_ORD($root$)

for each $d \in D$ **and** $d.index < root.index$
  do $dep\_in\_ord(d)$
PRINT($root$)
for each $d \in D$ **and** $d.index > root.index$
  do $dep\_in\_ord(d)$

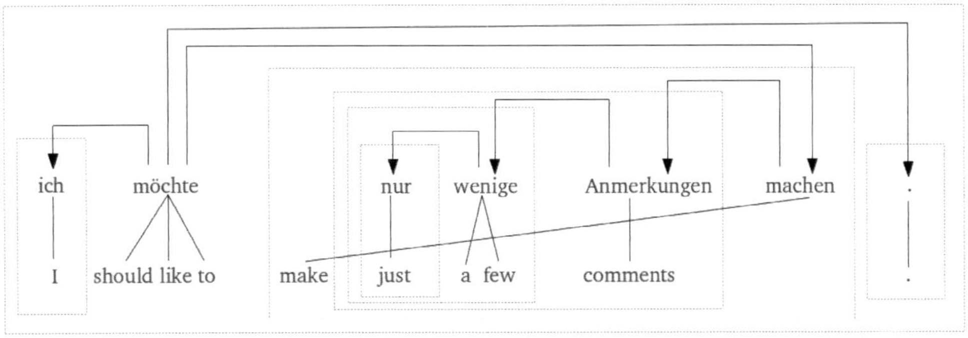

Figure 4: German English translation with German dependency structure, words surrounded by a dashed box form a complete dependency tree.

Rules spanning source words 0-6: ich möchte nur wenige anmerkungen machen .

X_0 möchte nur wenige anmerkungen machen .	X_0 should like to make just a few comments .
ich möchte X_0 .	i should like to X_0 .
ich möchte X_0 machen .	i should like to make X_0 .
ich möchte X_0 anmerkungen machen .	i should like to make X_0 comments .
ich möchte X_0 wenige anmerkungen machen .	i should like to make X_0 a few comments .
ich möchte nur wenige anmerkungen machen X_0	i should like to make just a few comments X_0
non-proj X_0 möchte X_1 .	X_0 should like to X_1 .
X_0 möchte X_1 machen .	X_0 should like to make X_1 .
X_0 möchte X_1 anmerkungen machen .	X_0 should like to make X_1 comments .
X_0 möchte X_1 wenige anmerkungen machen .	X_0 should like to make X_1 a few comments .
X_0 möchte nur wenige anmerkungen machen X_1	X_0 should like to make just a few comments X_1
ich möchte X_0 X_1	i should like to X_0 X_1
ich möchte X_0 machen X_1	i should like to make X_0 X_1
ich möchte X_0 anmerkungen machen X_1	i should like to make X_0 comments X_1
ich möchte X_0 wenige anmerkungen machen X_1	i should like to make X_0 a few comments X_1
X_0 möchte X_1 X_2	X_0 should like to X_1 X_2
X_0 möchte X_1 machen X_2	X_0 should like to make X_1 X_2
X_0 möchte X_1 anmerkungen machen X_2	X_0 should like to make X_1 comments X_2
X_0 möchte X_1 wenige anmerkungen machen X_2	X_0 should like to make X_1 a few comments X_2

Rules spanning source words 2-5: nur wenige anmerkungen machen

X_0 machen	make X_0
X_0 anmerkungen machen	make X_0 comments
X_0 wenige anmerkungen machen	X_0 a few comments

Rules spanning source words 2-4: nur wenige anmerkungen

X_0 anmerkungen	X_0 comments
X_0 wenige anmerkungen	X_0 a few comments

Rules spanning source words 2-3: nur wenige

X_0 wenige	X_0 a few

Figure 5: Complete set of dependency-constrained hierarchical SCFG rules for Figure 4

7 Experiments

WMT training data sets were used for both parallel (1.49 million German/English sentence pairs) and monolingual training (11.51 million English & 4.74 million German sentences). Mate non-projective dependency parser (Bohnet, 2010) was used for parsing both the German and English parallel data with standard pre-trained models, the same parser was used for projective parsing with non-projectivity turned off.[2] Parallel training data lines containing multiple sentences were merged into a single pseudo-dependency structure by adding an artificial root and head-dependent relation between the head of the initial sentence and any subsequent sentences. Non-projective dependencies were converted into projective structures using Algorithm 6.1.

Giza++ (Och et al., 1999) was employed for automatic word alignment, and Moses GHKM rule extraction (Williams and Koehn, 2012) was used for hierarchical rule extraction for the dependency-constrained models. Default settings were used for rule extraction for all models with the exception on non-fractional counting being used, as well as Good-turing discounting. Both the dependency-constrained and standard models use the same set of initial rules. For decoding, since only a single non-terminal, X, is present for all models, Moses hierarchical decoder (Koehn et al., 2007) was used with default settings with the exception of rule span limit being removed for all models. SRILM (Stolke, 2002) was used for 5-gram language modeling and Kneser-Ney smoothing (Kneser and Ney, 1995) for both German-to-English and English-to-German translation. MERT (Och, 2003) was carried out on WMT newstest2009 development set optimizing for BLEU, and final results are reported for held-out test sets, newstest2010 and newstest2011, with BLEU (Papineni et al., 2001) and LR-score (Birch and Osborne, 2010) for evaluation.

7.1 Results

Table 2 shows automatic evaluation results for both the dependency-constrained and standard hierarchical models for both language directions. Compared to the standard hierarchical model (orig), the best performing dependency-constrained models, sl_npr (de-en) and tl_npr (en-de), show significant decreases in mean BLEU score, -0.44 for German to English and -0.13 for English to German. However, there is a trade-off, as the dependency-constrained models achieve vast reductions in model size, approx. 93% for German to English and 89% for English to German in numbers of SCFG hierarchical rules. This results in decreased decoding times, with the best performing dependency-constrained models achieving a decrease of 26% for German to English and 34% for English to German in mean decoding times.

The decrease in BLEU scores is not likely to be attributed to less accurate long-distance reordering for German to English translation, as the Kendall Tau LR-scores for this language direction show an increase over the standard hierarchical models of +0.25 mean LR. Although this is not the case for English to German, as mean LR scores show a slight decrease (-0.11 LR).

The number of hierarchical rules (not including glue rules) employed during decoding provides a useful indication of to what degree each model actually uses hierarchical rules to construct translations, i.e. not simply concatenating phrases with glue rules. For English to German translation, while the number of hierarchical rules present in the SCFG is vastly reduced, the number of hierarchical rules used during decoding actually increases, with double the number of hierarchical rules used to translate test segments compared to the standard hierarchical model, from an average of only 0.58 hierarchical rules per segment for the standard model to 1.19 per segment. This indicates that the set of hierarchical rules is refined by the dependency constraint.

When the more linguistically valid non-projective dependency structure, as opposed to the projective dependency structure, is used to constrain rule extraction significant increases in BLEU scores are achieved for all configurations. The most significant gains in this respect occur when constraints are applied on the source side, +0.58 mean BLEU for German to English and +0.50 mean BLEU for English to German.

In general, when constraints are applied to the more free word order language, German, regardless of whether or not translation is *into* or *out of* German, marginally higher BLEU scores result, with an increase of +0.03 mean BLEU for German to English translation and similarly an increase of

[2] OpenNLP (Feinerer, 2012) sentence splitter is recommended with the parser we and was used for preprocessing.

			SCFG hier. rules (millions)	newstest 2010 BLEU	newstest 2010 LR-K	newstest 2011 BLEU	newstest 2011 LR-K	mean BLEU	mean hier. rules decoder	mean segment decode time (seconds)
de-en	hpb	orig	35.25	22.30	**71.86**	20.47	**70.55**	21.39	2.51	6.76
		tl_re	34.77	22.31	71.43	**20.49**	70.27	**21.40**	2.63	6.39
		tl_are	34.77	**22.41**	71.16	20.36	69.89	21.39	2.68	6.14
		sl_are	33.87	22.40	70.78	20.27	69.78	21.34	2.71	6.02
		sl_re	33.87	22.06	71.38	20.15	70.25	21.11	2.41	6.17
	dc	sl_npr	2.49	21.57	71.87	20.09	71.04	20.95	1.15	4.99
		tl_npr	1.45	21.88	72.20	19.95	71.36	20.92	2.85	4.62
		tl_pr	1.12	21.43	71.82	19.75	70.90	20.59	1.40	3.62
		sl_pr	0.34	21.05	72.20	19.69	71.36	20.37	1.10	1.98
en-de	hpb	orig	36.30	16.14	**70.24**	**15.05**	**69.91**	**15.60**	0.58	7.25
		tl_re	35.20	16.13	69.81	14.94	69.45	15.54	1.03	5.16
		tl_are	35.20	**16.15**	69.06	14.57	68.66	15.36	1.89	4.82
		sl_are	35.68	15.72	69.25	14.44	69.06	15.08	1.88	5.23
		sl_re	35.68	15.72	70.21	14.38	69.84	15.05	1.16	5.16
	dc	tl_npr	4.00	16.03	70.12	14.91	69.81	15.47	1.19	4.79
		sl_npr	1.09	15.94	70.07	14.85	69.69	15.40	1.78	3.46
		tl_pr	0.92	15.88	70.46	14.78	69.90	15.33	1.23	4.05
		sl_pr	0.88	15.58	70.18	14.22	69.80	14.90	1.19	2.90

Table 2: Effects of dependency constraints and dependency-based reordering on translation quality for German-to-English (de-en) and English to German (en-de), hpb=hierarchical phrase-based, orig=no reordering, *re=dependency-based word reordering where only hierarchical rules are extracted from reordered training data, *are=dependency-based word reordering where all SCFG rules extracted from reordered training data, dc=dependency-constrained, *pr=projective parse used for dependency constraint, *npr=non-projective parse used for dependency constraint, sl*=constraints or reordering for source language, tl*=constraints or reordering for target language, numbers of hierarchical rules reported do not include glue rules.

+0.07 mean BLEU for English to German, with the increase being statistically significant for German to English for the newstest2010 test set, but not statistically significant for newstest2011 test set or English to German (Koehn, 2004).

Overall the best performing dependency-constrained models are those that retain the highest numbers of hierarchical rules in the SCFG. This indicates that although the dependency-constrained models produce a refined ruleset, they nevertheless discard some SCFG rules that would be useful to translate the unseen test data. One possible reason is that although the non-projective dependency structures are significantly better, these high-quality linguistic structures may still not be optimal for translation. Another possibility is that a the GHKM rule extraction constraints combined with the dependency constraint is causing a small set of very useful rules to be discarded.

7.2 Dependency-based Reordering

We examine the effects of the non-projective transformation in isolation of any dependency-constraints by training a standard hierarchical model on the reordered corpus with no dependency constraints applied. We do this in two setups. First, we extract hierarchical rules from the reordered training corpus and initial rules from the original unaltered corpus (*_re in Table 2), as this is the set-up for the dependency-constrained models. Simply for interest sake, we repeat this experiment but extract all rules (hierarchical and initial rules) from the reordered corpus (*_are in Table 2).

Surprisingly, when non-projective reordering is carried out on the target side no significant decrease in BLEU scores occurs for both language directions. In fact, a minor increase in mean BLEU (+0.01) is observed for German to English translation, but this small increase is not statistically significant. For the English to German direction, a minor decrease of -0.06 mean BLEU occurs (not statistically significant).

Similarly for German to English, when reordering is applied to the source side, only a minor decrease (-0.05) results. Non-projective reordering causes the most significant reduction in performance for English to German when the English source is reordered, with a decrease of -0.52 mean BLEU.

Conclusions

This paper examines non-projectivity and language application for dependency-constrained hierarchical models using Moses open-source toolkit. Experiments show that when applied to English to German translation, vastly reduced model size and subsequently decreased decoding times result with only a minor decrease in BLEU. In addition, higher numbers of (non-glue) hierarchical rules are used to translate test segments. For German to English translation, similar decreases in model size and decoding times occur, but at the expense of a more significant decrease in BLEU.

In general, results for the dependency-constrained models show that applying constraints on the source or target side does not have a major impact on BLEU scores. Rather the use of high quality linguistic structures is more important, as significant improvements are made for all configurations when the non-projective dependency structure is used to constrain rule extraction.

Acknowledgments

Many thanks to the Moses developers, especially Hieu Hoang and Alexandra Birch. Thanks also to Tsuyoshi Okita and anonymous reviewers. This research was supported by the Australian Research Council, as well as Science Foundation Ireland as part of the Centre for Next Generation Localisation.

References

Alexandra Birch and Miles Osborne. 2010. Lrscore for evaluating lexical and reordering quality in mt. In *Proceedings of the Joint Fifth Workshop on Statistical Machine Translation and MetricsMATR*, pages 327–332, Uppsala, Sweden, July. Association for Computational Linguistics.

Bernd Bohnet. 2010. Very high accuracy and fast dependency parsing is not a contradiction. In *Proceedings of the 23rd International Conference on Computational Linguistics*, pages 89–97. Association for Computational Linguistics.

David Chiang. 2005. A hierarchical phrase-based model for statistical machine translation. In *Proceedings of the 43rd Annual Meeting on Association for Computational Linguistics*, pages 263–270. Association for Computational Linguistics.

Ingo Feinerer. 2012. tm: Text mining package. *R package version 0.5-7.1.*

Michel Galley and Christopher D Manning. 2009. Quadratic-time dependency parsing for machine translation. In *Proceedings of the Joint Conference of the 47th Annual Meeting of the ACL and the 4th International Joint Conference on Natural Language Processing of the AFNLP: Volume 2-Volume 2*, pages 773–781. Association for Computational Linguistics.

Michel Galley, Mark Hopkins, Kevin Knight, and Daniel Marcu. 2004. What's in a translation rule? In *HLT-NAACL*, pages 273–280.

Michel Galley, Jonathan Graehl, Kevin Knight, Daniel Marcu, Steve DeNeefe, Wei Wang, and Ignacio Thayer. 2006. Scalable inference and training of context-rich syntactic translation models. In *Proceedings of the 21st International Conference on Computational Linguistics and the 44th annual meeting of the Association for Computational Linguistics*, pages 961–968. Association for Computational Linguistics.

Yang Gao, Philipp Koehn, and Alexandra Birch. 2011. Soft dependency constraints for reordering in hierarchical phrase-based translation. In *Proceedings of the Conference on Empirical Methods in Natural Language Processing*, pages 857–868. Association for Computational Linguistics.

Fei Huang and Bing Xiang. 2010. Feature-rich discriminative phrase rescoring for smt. In *Proceedings of the 23rd International Conference on Computational Linguistics*, pages 492–500. Association for Computational Linguistics.

Howard Johnson, Joel Martin, George Foster, and Roland Kuhn. 2007. Improving translation quality by discarding most of the phrasetable. In *Proceedings of the 2007 Joint Conference on Empirical Methods in Natural Language Processing and Computational Natural Language Learning (EMNLP-CoNLL)*, pages 967–975.

Reinhard Kneser and Hermann Ney. 1995. Improved backing-off for m-gram language modeling. In *Proceedings of the IEEE International Conference on Accoustics, Speech and Signal Processing*, volume 1.

Philipp Koehn, Franz Josef Och, and Daniel Marcu. 2003. Statistical phrase based translation. In *Proceedings of the Joint Conference on Human Language Technologies and the Annual Meeting of the North American Chapter of the Association of Computational Linguistics (HLT-NAACL)*.

Philipp Koehn, Hieu Hoang, Alexandra Birch, Chris Callison-Burch, Marcello Federico, Nicola Bertoldi, Brooke Cowan, Wade Shen, Christine Moran, Richard Zens, Christopher J. Dyer, Ondřej Bojar, Alexandra Constantin, and Evan Herbst. 2007. Moses: Open source toolkit for statistical machine translation. In *Proceedings of the 45th Annual Meeting of the Association for Computational Linguistics Companion Volume Proceedings of the Demo and Poster Sessions*, pages 177–180, Prague, Czech Republic, June. Association for Computational Linguistics.

Philipp Koehn. 2004. Statistical significance tests for machine translation evaluation. In Dekang Lin and Dekai Wu, editors, *Proceedings of EMNLP 2004*, pages 388–395, Barcelona, Spain, July. Association for Computational Linguistics.

Sandra Kübler, Ryna McDonald, and Joakim Nivre. 2009. *Dependency Parsing*. Synthesis Lectures on Human Language Technologies. Morgan & Claypool.

Seung-Wook Lee, Dongdong Zhang, Mu Li, Ming Zhou, and Hae-Chang Rim. 2012. Translation model size reduction for hierarchical phrase-based statistical machine translation. In *Proceedings of the 50th Annual Meeting of the Association for Computational Linguistics (Volume 2: Short Papers)*, pages 291–295, Jeju Island, Korea, July. Association for Computational Linguistics.

Junhui Li, Zhaopeng Tu, Guodong Zhou, and Josef van Genabith. 2012. Using syntactic head information in hierarchical phrase-based translation. In *Proceedings of the Seventh Workshop on Statistical Machine Translation*, pages 232–242, Montréal, Canada, June. Association for Computational Linguistics.

Joakim Nivre. 2007. Incremental non-projective dependency parsing. In *Proceedings of Human Language Technologies: The Annual Conference of the North American Chapter of the Association for Computational Linguistics (NAACL-HLT)*, pages 396–403, Rochester, NY.

Franz Josef Och, Christoph Tillmann, and Hermann Ney. 1999. Improved alignment models for statistical machine translation. In *Proceedings of the Joint Conference of Empirical Methods in Natural Language Processing and Very Large Corpora (EMNLP-VLC)*, pages 20–28.

Franz Josef Och. 2003. Minimum error rate training in statistical machine translation. In Erhard Hinrichs and Dan Roth, editors, *Proceedings of the 41st Annual Meeting of the Association for Computational Linguistics*, pages 160–167.

Kishore Papineni, Salim Roukos, Todd Ward, and Wei-Jing Zhu. 2001. BLEU: a method for automatic evaluation of machine translation. Technical Report RC22176(W0109-022), IBM Research Report, September 17.

Jan-Thorsten Peter, Matthias Huck, Hermann Ney, and Daniel Stein. 2011. Soft string-to-dependency hierarchical machine translation. In Marcello Federico, Mei-Yuh Hwang, Margit Rödder, and Sebastian Stüker, editors, *Proceedings of the seventh International Workshop on Spoken Language Translation (IWSLT)*, pages 246–253.

Libin Shen, Jinxi Xu, and Ralph Weischedel. 2010. String-to-dependency statistical machine translation. *Computational Linguistics*, 36(4):649–671.

Andreas Stolke. 2002. SRILM - an extensible language modeling toolkit. In *Proceedings of the International Conference on Spoken Language Processing*, pages 577–585.

Nadi Tomeh, Nicola Cancedda, and Marc Dymetman. 2009. Complexity-based phrase-table filtering for statistical machine translation. In *Proceedings of the Twelfth Machine Translation Summit (MT Summit XII)*. International Association for Machine Translation.

Philip Williams and Philipp Koehn. 2012. GHKM rule extraction and scope-3 parsing in moses. In *Proceedings of the Seventh Workshop on Statistical Machine Translation*, pages 434–440, Montreal, Canada, June. Association for Computational Linguistics.

Jun Xie, Haitao Mi, and Qun Liu. 2011. A novel dependency-to-string model for statistical machine translation. In *Proceedings of the 2011 Conference on Empirical Methods in Natural Language Processing*, pages 216–226, Edinburgh, Scotland, UK., July. Association for Computational Linguistics.

Mei Yang and Jing Zheng. 2009. Toward smaller, faster, and better hierarchical phrase-based smt. In *Proceedings of the ACL-IJCNLP 2009 Conference Short Papers*, pages 237–240, Suntec, Singapore, August. Association for Computational Linguistics.

Wang Yuelong. 2012. *Edge-crossing Non-projective Phenomena in Chinese Language*. Ph.D. thesis, National University of Singapore.

Andreas Zollmann and Ashish Venugopal. 2006. Syntax augmented machine translation via chart parsing. In *Proceedings on the Workshop on Statistical Machine Translation*, pages 138–141, New York City, June. Association for Computational Linguistics.

Andreas Zollmann, Ashish Venugopal, Franz Josef Och, and Jay Ponte. 2008. A systematic comparison of phrase-based, hierarchical and syntax-augmented statistical MT. In *Proceedings of the 22nd International Conference on Computational Linguistics (Coling 2008)*, pages 1145–1152, Manchester, UK, August. Coling 2008 Organizing Committee.

Investigations in Exact Inference for Hierarchical Translation

Wilker Aziz[†], **Marc Dymetman**[‡], **Sriram Venkatapathy**[‡]

[†]University of Wolverhampton, Wolverhampton, UK

[‡]Xerox Research Centre Europe, Grenoble, France

[†]`w.aziz@wlv.ac.uk`, [‡]`{first.last}@xrce.xerox.com`

Abstract

We present a method for inference in hierarchical phrase-based translation, where both *optimisation* and *sampling* are performed in a common exact inference framework related to adaptive rejection sampling. We also present a first implementation of that method along with experimental results shedding light on some fundamental issues. In hierarchical translation, inference needs to be performed over a high-complexity distribution defined by the intersection of a translation hypergraph and a target language model. We replace this intractable distribution by a sequence of tractable upper-bounds for which exact optimisers and samplers are easy to obtain. Our experiments show that exact inference is then feasible using only a fraction of the time and space that would be required by the full intersection, without recourse to pruning techniques that only provide approximate solutions. While the current implementation is limited in the size of inputs it can handle in reasonable time, our experiments provide insights towards obtaining future speedups, while staying in the same general framework.

1 Introduction

In statistical machine translation (SMT), *optimisation* — the task of searching for an optimum translation — is performed over a high-complexity distribution defined by the intersection between a translation hypergraph and a target language model (LM). This distribution is too complex to be represented exactly and one typically resorts to approximation techniques such as beam-search (Koehn et al., 2003) and cube-pruning (Chiang, 2007), where maximisation is performed over a pruned representation of the full distribution.

Often, rather than finding a single optimum, one is really interested in obtaining a set of probabilistic *samples* from the distribution. This is the case for minimum error rate training (Och, 2003; Watanabe et al., 2007), minimum risk training (Smith and Eisner, 2006) and minimum risk decoding (Kumar and Byrne, 2004). Due to the additional computational challenges posed by sampling, n-best lists, a by-product of optimisation, are typically used as approximation to true probabilistic samples. A known issue with n-best lists is that they tend to be clustered around only one mode of the distribution. A more direct procedure is to attempt to directly draw samples from the underlying distribution rather than rely on n-best list approximations (Arun et al., 2009; Blunsom and Osborne, 2008).

OS* (Dymetman et al., 2012a) is a recent approach that stresses a unified view between the two types of inference, optimisation and sampling. In this view, rather than resorting to pruning in order to cope with the tractability issues, one upper-bounds the complex goal distribution with a simpler "proposal" distribution for which dynamic programming is feasible. This proposal is incrementally refined to be closer to the goal until the maximum is found, or until the sampling performance exceeds a certain level.

This paper applies the OS* approach to the problem of inference in hierarchical SMT (Chiang, 2007). In a nutshell, the idea is to replace the intractable problem of intersecting a context-free grammar with a full language model by the tractable problem of intersecting it with a simplified, optimistic version of this LM which "forgets" parts of n-gram contexts, and to incrementally add more context based on evidence of the need to do so. Evidence is gathered by optimising or sampling from the tractable proxy distribution and focussing on the most serious over-optimistic estimates relative to the goal distribution.

Our main contribution is to provide an exact optimiser/sampler for hierarchical SMT that is efficient in exploring only a small fraction of the space of n-grams involved in a full intersection. Although at this stage our experiments are limited to short sentences, they provide insights on the behavior of the technique and indicate directions towards a more efficient implementation within the same paradigm.

The paper is organized as follows: §2 provides background on OS* and hierarchical translation; §3 describes our approach to exact inference in SMT; in §4 the experimental setup is presented and findings are discussed; §5 discusses related work, and §6 concludes.

2 Background

2.1 OS*

The OS* approach (Dymetman et al., 2012a; Dymetman et al., 2012b) proposes a unified view of exact inference in sampling and optimisation, where the two modalities are seen as extremes in a continuum of inference tasks in L^p spaces (Rudin, 1987), with sampling associated with the L_1 norm, and optimisation with the L^∞ norm.

The objective function p, over which inference needs to be performed, is a complex non-negative function over a discrete or continuous space X, which defines an unnormalised distribution over X. The goal is to optimise or sample relative to p — where sampling is interpreted in terms of the normalised distribution $\bar{p}(.) = p(.)/\int_X p(x)dx$.

Directly optimising or sampling from p is unfeasible; however, it is possible to define an (unnormalized) distribution q of lower complexity than p, which upper-bounds p everywhere (ie. $p(x) \leq q(x), \forall x \in X$), and from which it is feasible to optimise or sample directly.

Sampling is performed through *rejection sampling*: first a sample x is drawn from q, and then x is accepted or rejected with probability given by the ratio $r = p(x)/q(x)$, which is less than 1 by construction. Accepted x's can be shown to produce an exact sample from p (Robert and Casella, 2004). When the sample x from q is rejected, it is used as a basis for "refining" q into a slightly more complex q', where $p \leq q' \leq q$ is still an upper-bound to p. This "adaptive rejection sampling" technique incrementally improves the rate of acceptance, and is pursued until some rate above a given threshold is obtained, at which point one stops refining and uses the current proposal to obtain further exact samples from p.

In the case of **optimisation**, one finds the maximum x relative to q, and again computes the ratio $r = p(x)/q(x)$. If this ratio equals 1, then it is easy to show that x is the actual maximum from p.[1] Otherwise we refine the proposal in a similar way to the sampling case, continuing until we find a ratio equal to 1 (or very close to 1 if we are willing to accept an approximation to the maximum). For finite spaces X, this optimisation technique is argued to be a generalisation of A^*.

An application of the OS^* technique to sampling/optimisation with High-Order HMM's is described in Carter et al. (2012) and provides background for this paper. In that work, while the high-order HMM corresponds to an intractable goal distribution, it can be upper-bounded by a sequence of tractable distributions for which optimisers and samplers can be obtained through standard dynamic programming techniques.

2.2 Hierarchical Translation

An abstract formulation of the decoding process for hierarchical translation models such as that of Chiang (2007) can be expressed as a sequence of three steps. In a first step, a translation model $\mathcal{G}$, represented as a weighted synchronous context-free grammar (SCFG) (Chiang, 2005), is applied to (in other words, intersected with) the source sentence f to produce a weighted context-free grammar $G(f)$ over the target language.[2] In a second step, $G(f)$ is intersected with a weighted finite-state automaton A representing the target language model, resulting in a weighted context-free grammar $G'(f) = G(f) \cap A$. In a final step, a dynamic programming procedure (see §2.4) is applied to find the maximum derivation x in $G'(f)$, and the sequence of leaves of yield(x) is the result translation.

While this formulation gives the general principle, already mentioned in Chiang (2007), most implementations do not exactly follow these steps or use this terminology. In practice, the closest approach to this abstract formulation is that of Dyer (2010) and the related system cdec (Dyer et al., 2010); we follow a similar approach here.

[1]This is because if x' was such that $p(x') > p(x)$, then $q(x') \geq p(x') > p(x) = q(x)$, and hence x would not be a maximum for q, a contradiction.

[2]$G(f)$ is thus a compact representation of a forest over target sequences, and is equivalent to a *hypergraph*, using different terminology.

Whatever the actual implementation chosen, all approaches face a common problem: the complexity of the intersection $G'(f) = G(f) \cap A$ increases rapidly with the order of the language model, and can become unwieldy for moderate-length input sentences even with a bigram model. In order to address this problem, most implementations employ variants of a technique called *cube-pruning* (Chiang, 2007; Huang and Chiang, 2007), where the cells constructed during the intersection process retain only a k-best list of promising candidates. This is an approximation technique, related to beam-search, which performs well in practice, but is not guaranteed to find the actual optimum.

In the approach presented here — described in detail in §3 — we do not prune the search space. While we do construct the full initial grammar $G(f)$, we proceed by incrementally intersecting it with simple automata associated with upper-bounds of A, for which the intersection is tractable.

2.3 Earley Intersection

In their classical paper Bar-Hillel et al. (1961) showed that the intersection of a CFG with a FSA is a CFG, and Billot and Lang (1989) were possibly the first to notice the connection of this construct with chart-parsing. In general, parsing with a CFG can be seen as a special case of intersection, with the input sequence represented as a "flat" (linear chain) automaton, and this insight allows to generalise various parsing algorithms to corresponding intersection algorithms. One such algorithm, for weighted context-free grammars and automata, inspired by the CKY parsing algorithm, is presented in Nederhof and Satta (2008). The algorithm that we are using is different; it is inspired by Earley parsing, and was introduced in chapter 2 of Dyer (2010). The advantage of Dyer's "Earley Intersection" algorithm is that it combines top-down predictions with bottom-up completions. The algorithm thus avoids constructing many non-terminals that may be justified from the bottom-up perspective, but can never be "requested" by a top-down derivation, and would need to be pruned in a second pass. Our early experiments showed an important gain in intermediary storage and in overall time by using this Earley-based technique as opposed to a CKY-based technique.

We do not describe the Earley Intersection algorithm in detail here, but refer to Dyer (2010), which we follow closely.

2.4 Optimisation and Sampling from a WCFG

Optimisation in a weighted CFG (WCFG)[3], that is, finding the maximum derivation, is well studied and involves a dynamic programming procedure that assigns in turn to each nonterminal, according to a bottom-up traversal regime, a maximum derivation along with its weight, up to the point where a maximum derivation is found for the initial nonterminal in the grammar. This can be seen as working in the max-times semiring, where the weight of a derivation is obtained through the product of the weights of its sub-derivations, and where the weight associated with a nonterminal is obtained by maximising over the different derivations rooted in that nonterminal.

The case of sampling can be handled in a very similar way, by working in the sum-times instead of the max-times semiring. Here, instead of maximising over the weights of the competing derivations rooted in the same nonterminal, one sums over these weights. By proceeding in the same bottom-up way, one ends with an accumulation of all the weights on the initial nonterminal (this can also be seen as the *partition function* associated with the grammar). An efficient exact sampler is then obtained by starting at the root nonterminal, randomly selecting an expansion proportionally to the weight of this expansion, and iterating in a top-down way. This process is described in more detail in section 4 of Johnson et al. (2007), for instance.

3 Approach

The complexity of building the full intersection $G(f) \cap A$, when A represents a language model of order n, is related to the fact that the number of states of A grows exponentially with n, and that each nonterminal N in $G(f)$ tends to generate in the grammar $G'(f)$ many indexed nonterminals of the form (i, N, j), where i, j are states of A and the nonterminal (i, N, j) can be interpreted as an N connecting an i state to a j state.

In our approach, instead of explicitly constructing the full intersection $G(f) \cap A$, which, using the notation of §2.1, is identified with the unnormalised goal distribution $p(x)$, we incrementally produce a sequence of "proposal" grammars $q^{(t)}$, which all upper-bound p, where $q^{(0)} = G(f) \cap A^{(0)}$, ..., $q^{(t+1)} = q^{(t)} \cap A^{(t)}$, etc. Here $A^{(0)}$ is

[3]Here the CFG is assumed to be acyclic, which is typically the case in translation applications.

an optimistic, low complexity, "unigram" version of the automaton A, and each increment $A^{(t)}$ is a small automaton that refines $q^{(t)}$ relative to some specific k-gram context (i.e., sequence of k words) not yet made explicit in the previous increments, where k takes some value between 1 and n. This process produces a sequence of grammars $q^{(t)}$ such that $q^{(0)}(.) \geq q^{(1)}(.) \geq q^{(2)}(.) \geq ... \geq p(.)$.

In the limit $\bigcap_{t=0}^{M} A^{(t)} = A$ for some large M, so that we are in principle able to reconstruct the full intersection $p(.) = q^{(M)} = G(f) \cap A^{(0)} \cap ... \cap A^{(M)}$ in finite time. In practice our actual process stops much earlier: in optimisation, when the value of the maximum derivation x_t^* relative to $q^{(t)}$ becomes equal to its value according to the full language model, in sampling when the acceptance rate of samples from $q^{(t)}$ exceeds a certain threshold. The process is detailed in what follows.

3.1 OS* for Hierarchical Translation

Our application of OS* to hierarchical translation is illustrated in Algorithm 1, with the two modes, optimisation and sampling, made explicit and shown side-by-side to stress the parallelism.

On line 1, we initialise the time step to 0, and for sampling we also initialise the current acceptance rate (AR) to 0. On line 2, we initialise the initial proposal grammar $q^{(0)}$, where $A^{(0)}$ is detailed in §3.2. On line 3, we start a loop: in optimisation we stop when we have found an x that is accepted, meaning that the maximum has been found; in sampling, we stop when the estimated acceptance rate (AR) of the current proposal $q^{(t)}$ exceeds a certain threshold (e.g. 20%) — this AR can be roughly estimated by observing how many of the last (say) one hundred samples from the proposal have been accepted, and tends to reflect the actual acceptance rate obtained by using $q^{(t)}$ without further refinements. On line 4, in optimisation, we compute the argmax x from the proposal, and in sampling we draw a sample x from the proposal.[4] On line 5, we compute the ratio $r = p(x)/q^{(t)}(x)$; by construction $q^{(t)}$ is an optimistic version of p, thus $r \leq 1$.

On line 6, in optimisation we accept x if the ratio is equal to 1, in which case we have found the maximum, and in sampling we accept x with probability r, which is a form of *adaptive rejection sampling* and guarantees that accepted samples form exact samples from p; see (Dymetman et al., 2012a).

If x was rejected (line 7), we then (lines 8, 9) refine $q^{(t)}$ into a $q^{(t+1)}$ such that $p(.) \leq q^{(t+1)}(.) \leq q^{(t)}(.)$ everywhere. This is done by defining the incremental automaton $A^{(t+1)}$ on the basis of x and $q^{(t)}$, as will be detailed below, and by intersecting this automaton with $q^{(t)}$

Finally, on line 11, in optimisation we return the x which has been accepted, namely the maximum of p, and in sampling we return the list of already accepted x's, which form an exact sample from p, along with the current $q^{(t)}$, which can be used as a sampler to produce further exact samples with an acceptance rate performance above the predefined threshold.

3.2 Incremental refinements

Initial automaton $A^{(0)}$ This deterministic automaton is an "optimistic" version of A which only records unigram information. $A^{(0)}$ has only one state q_0, which is both initial and final. For each word a of the target language it has a transition (q_0, a, q_0) whose weight is denoted by $w_1(a)$. This weight is called the "max-backoff unigram weight" (Carter et al., 2012) and it is defined as:

$$w_1(a) \equiv \max_h p_{lm}(a|h),$$

where $p_{lm}(a|h)$ is the conditional language model probability of a relative to the history h, and where the maximum is taken over all possible histories, that is, over all possible sequence of target words that might precede a.

Max-backoffs Following Carter et al. (2012), for any language model of finite order, the unigram max-backoff weights $w_1(a)$ can be precomputed in a "Max-ARPA" table, an extension of the ARPA format (Jurafsky and Martin, 2000) for the target language model, which can be precomputed on the basis of the standard ARPA table.

From the Max-ARPA table one can also directly compute the following "max-backoff weights": $w_2(a|a_{-1})$, $w_3(a|a_{-2}\,a_{-1})$, ..., which are defined by:

$$\begin{aligned} w_2(a|a_{-1}) &\equiv \max_h p_{lm}(a|h, a_{-1}) \\ w_3(a|a_{-2}\,a_{-1}) &\equiv \max_h p_{lm}(a|h, a_{-2}\,a_{-1}) \\ &\dots \end{aligned}$$

where the maximum is taken over the part of the history which is not explicitely indicated.

[4]Following the OS* approach, taking an argmax is actually assimilated to an extreme form of sampling, with an L_∞ space taking the place of an L_1 space.

Algorithm 1 OS* for Hierarchical Translation: Optimisation (left) and Sampling (right).

$t \leftarrow 0$	$t \leftarrow 0, AR \leftarrow 0$
$q^{(0)} \leftarrow G(f) \cap A^{(0)}$	$q^{(0)} \leftarrow G(f) \cap A^{(0)}$
while not an x has been accepted **do**	**while not** $AR > threshold$ **do**
Find maximum x in $q^{(t)}$	Sample $x \sim q^{(t)}$
$r \leftarrow p(x)/q^{(t)}(x)$	$r \leftarrow p(x)/q^{(t)}(x)$
Accept-or-Reject x according to r	Accept-or-Reject x according to r
if Rejected(x) **then**	**if** Rejected(x) **then**
define $A^{(t+1)}$ based on x and $q^{(t)}$	define $A^{(t+1)}$ based on x and $q^{(t)}$
$q^{(t+1)} \leftarrow q^{(t)} \cap A^{(t+1)}$	$q^{(t+1)} \leftarrow q^{(t)} \cap A^{(t+1)}$
$t \leftarrow t+1$	$t \leftarrow t+1$
return x	**return** already accepted x's along with $q^{(t)}$

Note that: (i) if the underlying language model is, say, a trigram model, then $w_3(a|a_{-2}\,a_{-1})$ is simply $p_{lm}(a|a_{-2}\,a_{-1})$, and similarly for an underlying model of order k in general, and (ii) $w_2(a|a_{-1}) = \max_{a_{-2}} w_3(a|a_{-2}\,a_{-1})$ and $w_1(a) = \max_{a_{-1}} w_2(a|a_{-1})$.

Incremental automata $A^{(t)}$ The weight assigned to any target sentence by $A^{(0)}$ is larger or equal to its weight according to A. Therefore, the initial grammar $q^{(0)} = G(f) \cap A^{(0)}$ is *optimistic* relative to the actual grammar $p = G(f) \cap A$: for any derivation x in p, we have $p(x) \leq q^{(0)}(x)$. We can then apply the OS* technique with $q^{(0)}$. In the case of **optimisation**, this means that we find the maximum derivation x from $q^{(0)}$. By construction, with $y = \text{yield}(x)$, we have $A^{(0)}(y) \geq A(y)$. If the two values are equal, we have found the maximum,[5] otherwise there must be a word y_i in the sequence $y_1^m = y$ for which $p_{lm}(y_i|y_1^{i-1})$ is strictly smaller than $w_1(y_i)$. Let us take among such words the one for which the ratio $\alpha = w_2(y_i|y_{i-1})/w_1(y_i) \leq 1$ is the smallest, and for convenience let us rename $b = y_{i-1}, a = y_i$. We then define the (deterministic) automaton $A^{(1)}$ as illustrated in the following figure:

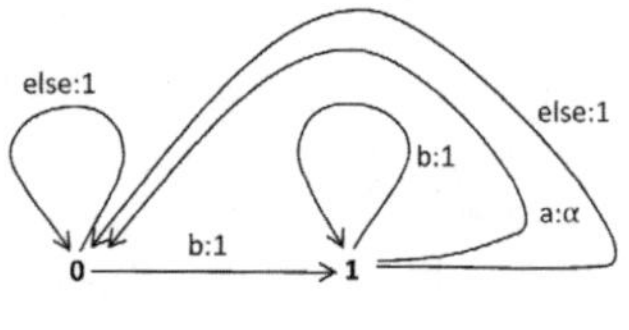

Here the state 0 is both initial and final, and the state 1 is final; all edges carry a (multiplicative) weight equal to 1, except edge $(1, a, 0)$, which carries the weight α. We use the abbreviation "else" to refer to any label other than b when starting from 0, and other than b or a when starting from 1.

[5]This case is very unlikely with $A^{(0)}$, but helps introduce the general case.

It is easy to check that this automaton assigns to any word sequence y a weight equal to α^k, where k is the number of occurrences of $b\,a$ in y. In particular, if y is such that $y_{i-1} = b, y_i = a$, then the transition in (the deterministic automaton) $A^{(0)} \cap A^{(1)}$ that consumes y_i carries the weight $\alpha\, w_1(a)$, in other words, the weight $w_2(a|b)$. Thus the new proposal grammar $q^{(1)} = q^{(0)} \cap A^{(1)}$ has now "incorporated" knowledge of the bigram a-in-the-context-b, at the cost of some increase in its complexity.[6]

The general procedure for choosing $A^{(t+1)}$ follows the same pattern. We find the max derivation x in $q^{(t)}$ along with its yield y; if $p(x) = q^{(t)}(x)$, we stop and output x; otherwise we find some subsequence $y_{i-m-1}, y_{i-m}, ..., y_i$ such that the knowledge of the n-gram $y_{i-m}, ..., y_i$ has already been registered in $q^{(t)}$, but not that of the n-gram $y_{i-m-1}, y_{i-m}, ..., y_i$, and we define an automaton $A^{(t+1)}$ which assign to a sequence a weight α^k, where

$$\alpha = \frac{w_{m+1}(y_i|y_{i-m-1}, y_{i-m}, ..., y_{i-1})}{w_m(y_i|y_{i-m}, ..., y_{i-1})},$$

and where k is the number of occurrences of $y_{i-m-1}, y_{i-m}, ..., y_i$ in the sequence.[7]

We note that we have $p \leq q^{(t+1)} \leq q^{(t)}$ everywhere, and also that the number of possible refinement operations is bounded, because at some point we would have expanded all contexts to their maximum order, at which point we would have reproduced $p(.)$ on the whole space X of possible

[6]Note that without further increasing $q^{(1)}$'s complexity one can incorporate knowledge about all bigrams sharing the prefix b. This is because $A^{(1)}$ does not need additional states to account for different continuations of the context b, all we need is to update the weights of the transitions leaving state 1 appropriately. More generally, it is not more costly to account for all n-grams prefixed by the same context of $n-1$ words than it is to account for only one of them.

[7]Building $A^{(t+1)}$ is a variant of the standard construction for a "substring-searching" automaton (Cormen et al., 2001) and produces an automaton with n states (the order of the n-gram). This construction is omitted for the sake of space.

derivations exactly. However, we typically stop much earlier than that, without expanding contexts in the regions of X which are not promising even on optimistic assessments based on limited contexts.

Following the OS* methodology, the situation with **sampling** is completely parallel to that of optimisation, the only difference being that, instead of finding the maximum derivation x from $q^{(t)}(.)$, we draw a sample x from the distribution associated with $q^{(t)}(.)$, then accept it with probability given by the ratio $r = p(x)/q^{(t)}(x) \leq 1$. In the case of a reject, we identify a subsequence $y_{i-m-1}, y_{i-m}, ..., y_i$ in yield(x) as in the optimisation case, and similarly refine $q^{(t)}$ into $q^{(t+1)} = q^{(t)} \cap A^{(t+1)}$. The acceptance rate gradually increases because $q^{(t)}$ comes closer and closer to p. We stop the process at a point where the current acceptance rate, estimated on the basis of, say, the last one hundred trials, exceeds a predefined threshold, perhaps 20%.

3.3 Illustration

In this section, we present a small running example of our approach. Consider the lowercased German source sentence: *eine letzte beobachtung .*

Table 1 shows the translation associated with the optimum derivation from each proposal $q^{(i)}$. The n-gram whose cost, if extended by one word to the left, would be increased by the largest factor is underlined. The extended context selected for refinement is highlighted in bold.

i	Rules	Optimum
0	311	**<s>** one last observation . </s>
1	454	<s> **one** last observation . </s>
2	628	<s> one **last** observation . </s>
3	839	<s> one final **observation** . </s>
4	1212	<s> one **final observation .** </s>
		...
12	3000	<s> **a final** observation . </s>
13	3128	<s> one final observation . </s>

Table 1: Optimisation steps showing the iteration (i), the number of rules in the grammar and the translation associated to the *optimum* derivation.

Consider the very first iteration ($i = 0$), at which point only unigram costs have been incorporated. The sequence *<s> one last observation . </s>* represents the translation associated to the best derivation x in $q^{(0)}$. We proceed by choosing from it one sequence to be the base for a refinement that will lower $q^{(0)}$ bringing it closer to p. Amongst all possible one-word (to the left) extensions, extending the unigram 'one' to the bigram '<s> one' is the operation that lowers $q^{(0)}(x)$ the most. It might be helpful to understand it as the bigram '<s> one' being associated to the largest LM gap observed in x. Therefore the context '<s>' is selected for refinement, which means that an automaton $A^{(1)}$ is designed to down-weight derivations compatible with bigrams prefixed by '<s>'. The proposal $q^{(0)}$ is intersected with $A^{(1)}$ producing $q^{(1)}$. We proceed like this iteratively, always selecting a context not yet accounted for until $q^{(i)}(x) = p(x)$ for the best derivation (13th iteration in our example), when the true optimum is found with a certificate of optimality.

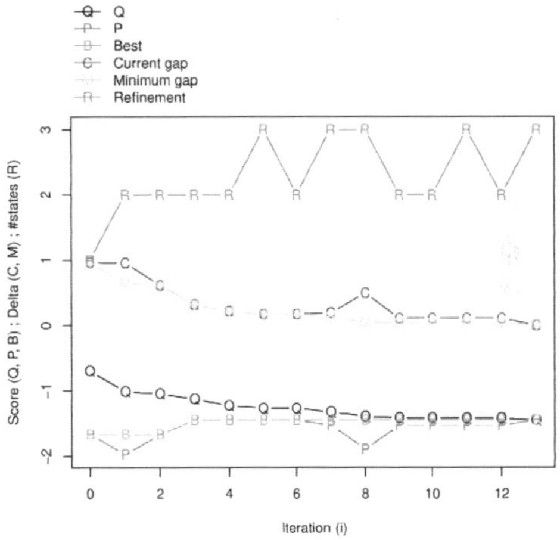

Figure 1: Certificate of optimality.

Figure 1 displays the progression of Q (score of the best derivation) and P (that derivation's true score). As guaranteed by construction, Q is always above P. B represents the score of the best derivation so far according to the true scoring function, that is, B is a lower-bound on the true optimum[8]. The optimal solution is achieved when $P = Q$.

Curve B in Figure 1 shows that the best scoring solution was found quite early in the search ($i = 3$). However, optimality could only be proven 10 iterations later. Another way of stating the convergence criterion $Q = P$ is observing a zero gap (in the log domain) between Q and P (see curve C – current gap), or a zero gap between Q and B (see curve M – minimum gap). Observe how M drops quickly from 1 to nearly 0, followed by a long tail where M

[8]This observation allows for error-safe pruning in *optimisation*: if x is a lower-bound on the true optimum, derivations in $q^{(i)}$ that score lower than $p(x)$ could be safely removed. We have left that possibility for future work.

decreases much slower. Note that if we were willing to accept an approximate solution, we could already stop the search if B remained unchanged for a predetermined number of iterations or if changes in B were smaller than some threshold, at the cost of giving up on the optimality certificate.

Finally, curve R shows the number of states in the automaton $A^{(i)}$ that refines the proposal at iteration i. Note how lower order n-grams (2-grams in fact) are responsible for the largest drop in the first iterations and higher-order n-grams (in fact 3-grams) are refined later in the long tail.

Figure 2 illustrates the progression of the sampler for the same German sentence. At each iteration a batch of 500 samples is drawn from $q^{(i)}$. The rejected samples in the batch are used to collect statistics about overoptimistic n-grams and to heuristically choose one context to be refined for the next iteration, similar to the optimisation mode. We start with a low acceptance rate which grows up to 30% after 15 different contexts were incorporated. Note how the L_1 norm of q (its partition function) decreases after each refinement, that is, q is gradually brought closer to p, resulting in the increased number of exact samples and better acceptance rate.

Note that, starting from iteration one, all refinements here correspond to 2-grams (i.e. one-word contexts). This can be explained by the fact that, in sampling, lower-order refinements are those that mostly increase acceptance rate (rationale: high-order n-grams are compatible with fewer grammar rules).

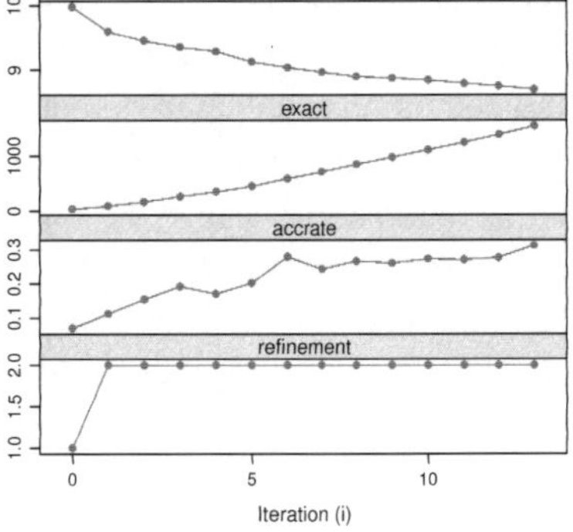

Figure 2: L_1 norm of q, the number of exact samples drawn, the acceptance rate and the refinement type at each iteration.

4 Experiments

We used the Moses toolkit (Koehn et al., 2007) to extract a SCFG following Chiang (2005) from the 6th version of the Europarl collection (Koehn, 2005) (German-English portion). We trained language models using lmplz (Heafield et al., 2013) and interpolated the models trained on the English monolingual data made available by the WMT (Callison-Burch et al., 2012) (i.e. *Europarl*, *newscommentaries*, *news-2012* and *commoncrawl*). Tuning was performed via MERT using *newstest2010* as development set; test sentences were extracted from *newstest2011*. Finally, we restricted our SCFGs to having at most 10 target productions for a given source production.

Figure 3 shows some properties of the initial grammar $G(f)$ as a function of the input sentence length (the quantities are averages over 20 sentences for each class of input length). The number of unigrams grows linearly with the input length, while the number of unique bigrams compatible with strings generated by $G(f)$ appears to grow quadratically[9] and the size of the grammar in number of rules appears to be cubic — a consequence of having up to two nonterminals on the right-hand side of a rule.

Figure 4 shows the number of refinement operations until convergence in optimisation and sampling, as well as the total duration, as a function of the input length.[10] The plots will be discussed in detail below.

4.1 Optimisation

In optimisation (Figures 4a and 4b), the number of refinements up to convergence appears to be linear with the input length, while the total duration grows much quicker. These findings are further discussed in what follows.

Table 2 shows some important quantities regarding optimisation with OS* using a 4-gram LM. The first column shows how many sentences we are considering, the second column shows the sentence length, the third column m is the average number of refinements up to convergence. Column $|A|$ refers to the refinement type, which is the number of states in the automaton A, that is, the order of

[9]The number of unique bigrams is an estimate obtained by combining the terminals at the boundary of nonterminals that may be adjacent in a derivation.

[10]The current implementation faces timeouts depending on the length of the input sentence and the order of the language model, explaining why certain curves are interrupted earlier than others in Figure 4.

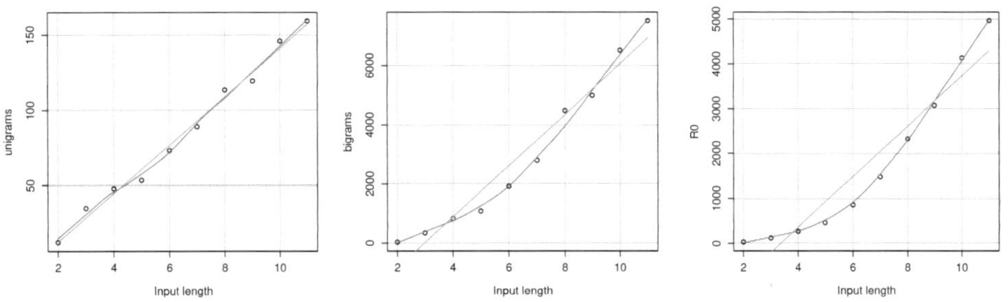

(a) Unigrams in $G(f)$ (b) Bigrams compatible with $G(f)$ (c) Number of rules in $G(f)$

Figure 3: Properties of the initial grammar as function of input length

S	Length	m	$\|A\|$	count	$\frac{\|R_f\|}{\|R_0\|}$
9	4	45.0	2	20.3	74.6 ± 53.9
			3	19.2	
			4	5.4	
10	5	62.3	2	21.9	145.4 ± 162.6
			3	32.9	
			4	7.5	
9	6	102.8	2	34.7	535.8 ± 480.0
			3	54.9	
			4	13.2	

Table 2: Optimisation with a 4-gram LM.

S	Input	m	$\|A\|$	count	$\frac{\|R_f\|}{\|R_0\|}$
10	5	1.0	2	1.0	1.9 ± 1.0
10	6	6.6	2	6.3	17.6 ± 13.6
			3	0.3	
10	7	14.5	2	12.9	93.8 ± 68.9
			3	1.5	
			4	0.1	

Table 3: Sampling with a 4-gram LM and reaching a 5% acceptance rate.

the n-grams being re-weighted (e.g. $|A| = 2$ when refining bigrams sharing a one-word context). Column *count* refers to the average number of refinements that are due to each refinement type. Finally, the last column compares the number of rules in the final proposal to that of the initial one.

The first positive result concerns how much context OS* needs to take into account for finding the optimum derivation. Table 2 (column m) shows that OS* explores a very reduced space of n-gram contexts up to convergence. To illustrate that, consider the last row in Table 2 (sentences with 6 words). On average, convergence requires incorporating only about 103 contexts of variable order, of which 55 are bigram (2-word) contexts (remember that $|A| = 3$ when accounting for a 2-word context). According to Figure 3b, in sentences with 6 words, about 2,000 bigrams are compatible with strings generated by $G(f)$. This means that only 2.75% of these bigrams (55 out of 2,000) need to be explicitly accounted for, illustrating how wasteful a full intersection would be.

A problem, however, is that the time until convergence grows quickly with the length of the input (Figure 4b). This can be explained as follows. At each iteration the grammar is refined to account for n-grams sharing a context of $(n-1)$ words. That operation typically results in a larger grammar: most rules are preserved, some rules are deleted, but more importantly, some rules are added to account for the portion of the current grammar that involves the selected n-grams. Enlarging the grammar at each iteration means that successive refinements become incrementally slower.

The histogram of refinement types of Table 2 highlights how efficient OS* is w.r.t. the space of n-grams it needs to explore before convergence. The problem is clearly not the number of refinements, but rather the relation between the growth of the grammar and the successive intersections. Controlling for this growth and optimising the intersection as to partially reuse previously computed charts may be the key for a more generally tractable solution.

4.2 Sampling

Figure 4c shows that sampling is more economical than optimisation in that it explicitly incorporates even fewer contexts. Note how OS* converges to acceptance rates from 1% to 10% in much fewer iterations than are necessary to find an optimum[11]. Although the convergence in sampling is

[11] Currently we use MERT to train the model's weight vector — which is normalised by its L_1 norm in the Moses implementation. While optimisation is not sensitive to the scale of the weights, in sampling the scale determines how flat or

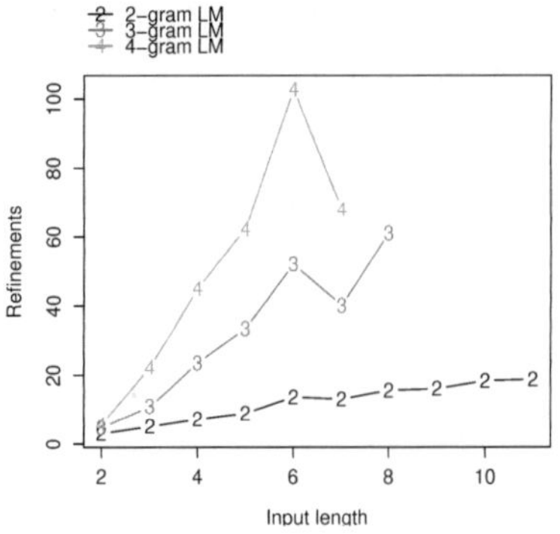

(a) Optimisation: number of refinements.

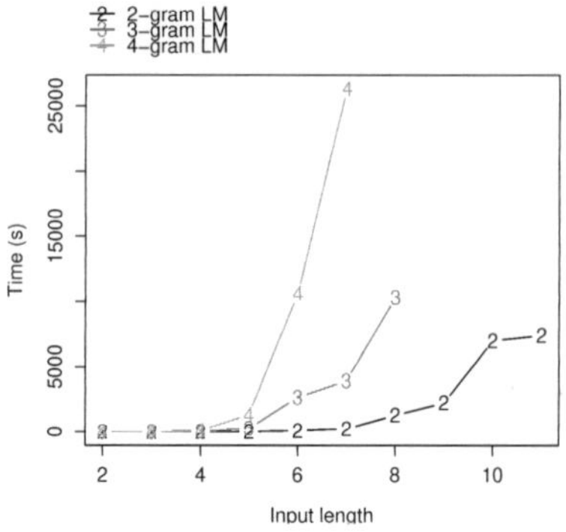

(b) Optimisation: time for convergence.

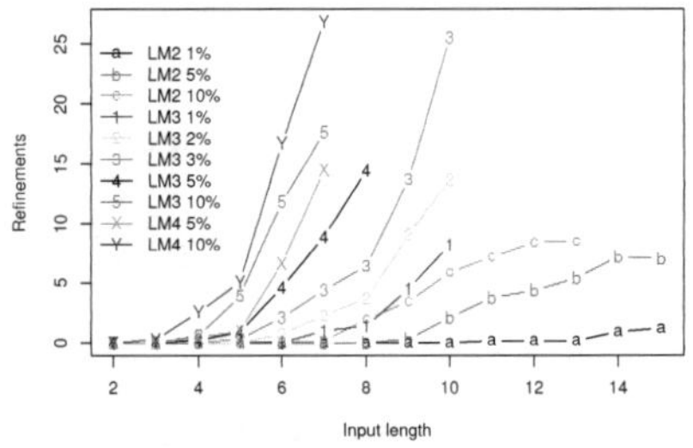

(c) Sampling: number of refinements.

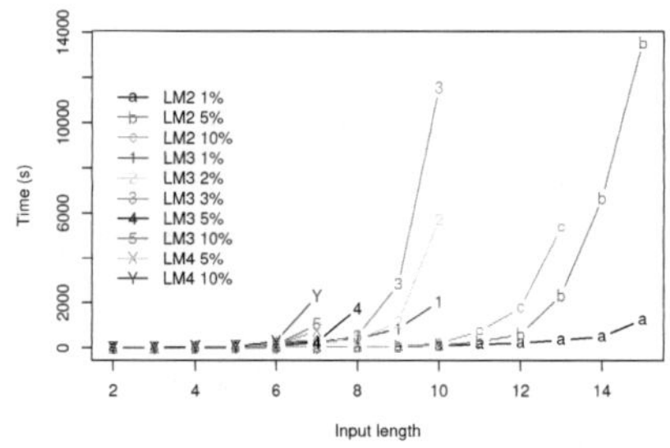

(d) Sampling: time for convergence.

Figure 4: Convergence for different LM order as function of the input length in optimisation (top) and sampling (bottom). We show the number of refinements up to convergence on the left, and the convergence time on the right. In optimisation we stop when the true optimum is found. In sampling we stop at different acceptance rate levels: (a, b and c) use a 2-gram LM to reach 1, 5 and 10% AR; (1-4) use a 3-gram LM to reach 2, 3, 5 and 10% AR; and (X, Y) use a 4-gram LM to reach 5 and 10% AR.

faster than in optimisation, the total duration is still an issue (Figure 4b).

Table 3 shows the same quantities as Table 2, but now for sampling. It is worth highlighting that even though we are using an upper-bound over a 4-gram LM (and aiming at a 5% acceptance rate), very few contexts are selected for refinement, most of them lower-order ones (one-word contexts — rows with $|A| = 2$).

Observe that an improved acceptance rate always leads to faster acquisition of exact samples after we stop refining our proxy distribution. However, Figure 4d shows for example that moving from 5% to 10% acceptance rate using a 4-gram LM (curves X and Y) is time-consuming. Thus there is a trade-off between how much time one spends improving the acceptance rate and how many exact samples one intends do draw. Figure 5 shows the average time to draw batches between one and one million samples from two exact samplers that were refined up to 5% and 10% acceptance rate respectively. The sampler at 5% AR (which is faster to obtain) turns out to be more efficient if we aim at producing less than 10K samples.

Finally, note that samples are independently

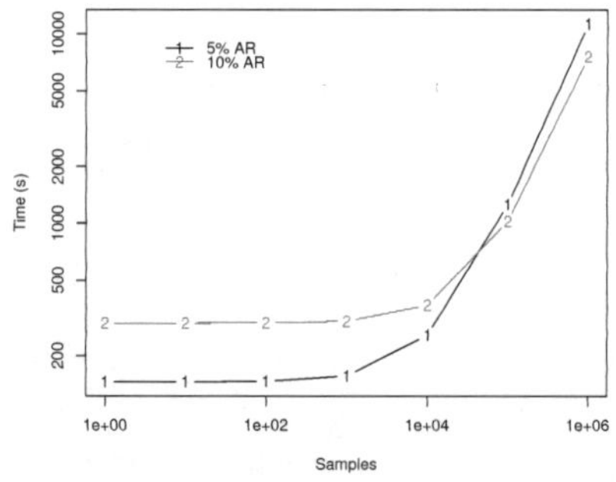

Figure 5: Average time to draw 1 to 1 million samples, for input sentences of length 6, using a 4-gram LM at 5% (curve 1) and 10% (curve 2) acceptance rate (including the time to produce the sampler).

peaked the distribution is. Arun et al. (2010) experiment with scaling MERT-trained weights as to maximise BLEU on held-out data, as well as with MBR training. A more adequate training algorithm along similar lines is reserved for future work.

drawn from the final proposal, making the approach an appealing candidate to parallelism in order to increase the effective acceptance rate.

5 Related Work

Rush and Collins (2011) do not consider sampling, but they address exact decoding for hierarchical translation. They use a Dual Decomposition approach (a special case of Lagrangian Relaxation), where the target CFG (hypergraph in their terminology) component and the target language model component "trade-off" their weights so as to ensure agreement on what each component believes to be the maximum. In many cases, this technique is able to detect the actual true maximum derivation. When this is not the case, they use a finite-state-based intersection mechanism to "tighten" the first component so that some constraints not satisfied by the current solution are enforced, and iterate until the true maximum is found or a time-out is met, which results in a high proportion of finding the true maximum.

Arun et al. (2009, 2010) address the question of sampling in a standard phrase-based translation model (Koehn et al., 2003). Contrarily to our use of rejection sampling (a Monte-Carlo method), they use a Gibbs sampler (a Markov-Chain Monte-Carlo (MCMC) method). Samples are obtained by iteratively re-sampling groups of well-designed variables in such a way that (i) the sampler does not tend to be trapped locally by high correlations between conditioning and conditioned variables, and (ii) the combinatorial space of possibilities for the next step is small enough so that conditional probabilities can be computed explicitly. By contrast to our exact approach, the samples obtained by Gibbs sampling are not independent, but form a Markov chain that only converges to the target distribution in the limit, with convergence properties difficult to assess. Also by contrast to us, these papers do not address the question of finding the maximum derivation directly, but only through finding a maximum among the derivations sampled so far, which in principle can be quite different.

Blunsom and Osborne (2008) address probabilistic inference, this time, as we do, in the context of hierarchical translation, where sampling is used both for the purposes of decoding and training the model. When decoding in the presence of a language model, an approximate sampling procedure is performed in two stages. First, cube-pruning is employed to construct a WCFG which generates a subset of all the possible derivations that would correspond to a full intersection with the target language model. In a second step this grammar is sampled through the same dynamic programming procedure that we have described in §2.4. By contrast to our approach, the paper does not attempt to perform exact inference. However it does not only address the question of decoding, but also that of training the model, which requires, in addition to sampling, an estimate of the model's partition function. In common with Arun et al. (2010), the authors stress the fact that a sampler of derivations is also a sampler of translations as strings, while a maximiser over derivations *cannot* be used to find the maximum translation string.

6 Conclusions

The approach we have presented is, to our knowledge, the first one to address the problem of exact sampling for hierarchical translation and to do that in a framework that also handles exact optimisation. Our experiments show that only a fraction of the language model n-grams need to be incorporated in the target grammar in order to perform exact inference in this approach. However, in the current implementation, we experience time-outs for sentences of even moderate length. We are working on improving this situation along three dimensions: (i) our implementation of the Earley Intersection rebuilds a grammar from scratch at each intersection, while it could capitalise on the charts built during the previous steps; (ii) the unigram-level max-backoffs are not as tight as they could be if one took into account more precisely the set of contexts in which each word can appear relative to the grammar; (iii) most importantly, while our refinements are "local" in the sense of addressing one n-gram context at a time, they still affect a large portion of the rules in the current grammar, even rules that have very low probability of being ever sampled by this grammar; by preventing refinement of such rules during the intersection process, we may be able to make the intersection more local and to produce much smaller grammars, without losing the exactness properties of the approach.

Acknowledgements

The first author wishes to thank the PASCAL-2 Visit to Industry programme for partially funding his visit to Xerox Research Centre Europe last Fall, which initiated this collaboration.

References

Abhishek Arun, Chris Dyer, Barry Haddow, Phil Blunsom, Adam Lopez, and Philipp Koehn. 2009. Monte carlo inference and maximization for phrase-based translation. In *Proceedings of the Thirteenth Conference on Computational Natural Language Learning*, CoNLL '09, pages 102–110, Stroudsburg, PA, USA. Association for Computational Linguistics.

Abhishek Arun, Barry Haddow, Philipp Koehn, Adam Lopez, Chris Dyer, and Phil Blunsom. 2010. Monte carlo techniques for phrase-based translation. *Machine Translation*, 24(2):103–121, June.

Yehoshua Bar-Hillel, Micha A. Perles, and Eli Shamir. 1961. On formal properties of simple phrase structure grammars. *Zeitschrift für Phonetik, Sprachwissenschaft und Kommunikationsforschung*, (14):143–172.

Sylvie Billot and Bernard Lang. 1989. The structure of shared forests in ambiguous parsing. In *Proceedings of the 27th Annual Meeting of the Association for Computational Linguistics*, pages 143–151, Vancouver, British Columbia, Canada, June. Association for Computational Linguistics.

Phil Blunsom and Miles Osborne. 2008. Probabilistic inference for machine translation. In *Proceedings of the Conference on Empirical Methods in Natural Language Processing*, EMNLP '08, pages 215–223, Stroudsburg, PA, USA. Association for Computational Linguistics.

Chris Callison-Burch, Philipp Koehn, Christof Monz, Matt Post, Radu Soricut, and Lucia Specia. 2012. Findings of the 2012 workshop on statistical machine translation. In *Proceedings of the Seventh Workshop on Statistical Machine Translation*, pages 10–51, Montréal, Canada, June. Association for Computational Linguistics.

Simon Carter, Marc Dymetman, and Guillaume Bouchard. 2012. Exact Sampling and Decoding in High-Order Hidden Markov Models. In *Proceedings of the 2012 Joint Conference on Empirical Methods in Natural Language Processing and Computational Natural Language Learning*, pages 1125–1134, Jeju Island, Korea, July. Association for Computational Linguistics.

David Chiang. 2005. A hierarchical phrase-based model for statistical machine translation. In *Proceedings of the 43rd Annual Meeting on Association for Computational Linguistics*, ACL '05, pages 263–270, Stroudsburg, PA, USA. Association for Computational Linguistics.

David Chiang. 2007. Hierarchical Phrase-Based Translation. *Computational Linguistics*, 33:201–228.

Thomas H. Cormen, Clifford Stein, Ronald L. Rivest, and Charles E. Leiserson. 2001. *Introduction to Algorithms*. McGraw-Hill Higher Education, 2nd edition.

Chris Dyer, Jonathan Weese, Hendra Setiawan, Adam Lopez, Ferhan Ture, Vladimir Eidelman, Juri Ganitkevitch, Phil Blunsom, and Philip Resnik. 2010. cdec: a decoder, alignment, and learning framework for finite-state and context-free translation models. In *Proceedings of the ACL 2010 System Demonstrations*, ACLDemos '10, pages 7–12, Stroudsburg, PA, USA. Association for Computational Linguistics.

Christopher Dyer. 2010. *A Formal Model of Ambiguity and its Applications in Machine Translation*. Ph.D. thesis, University of Maryland.

M. Dymetman, G. Bouchard, and S. Carter. 2012a. The OS* Algorithm: a Joint Approach to Exact Optimization and Sampling. *ArXiv e-prints*, July.

Marc Dymetman, Guillaume Bouchard, and Simon Carter. 2012b. Optimization and sampling for nlp from a unified viewpoint. In *Proceedings of the First International Workshop on Optimization Techniques for Human Language Technology*, pages 79–94, Mumbai, India, December. The COLING 2012 Organizing Committee.

Kenneth Heafield, Ivan Pouzyrevsky, Jonathan H. Clark, and Philipp Koehn. 2013. Scalable modified Kneser-Ney language model estimation. In *Proceedings of the 51st Annual Meeting of the Association for Computational Linguistics*, Sofia, Bulgaria, August.

Liang Huang and David Chiang. 2007. Forest rescoring: Faster decoding with integrated language models. In *Proceedings of the 45th Annual Meeting of the Association of Computational Linguistics*, pages 144–151, Prague, Czech Republic, June. Association for Computational Linguistics.

Mark Johnson, Thomas Griffiths, and Sharon Goldwater. 2007. Bayesian inference for PCFGs via Markov chain Monte Carlo. In *Human Language Technologies 2007: The Conference of the North American Chapter of the Association for Computational Linguistics; Proceedings of the Main Conference*, pages 139–146, Rochester, New York, April. Association for Computational Linguistics.

Daniel Jurafsky and James H. Martin. 2000. *Speech and Language Processing: An Introduction to Natural Language Processing, Computational Linguistics and Speech Recognition (Prentice Hall Series in Artificial Intelligence)*. Prentice Hall, 1 edition.

Philipp Koehn, Franz Josef Och, and Daniel Marcu. 2003. Statistical phrase-based translation. In *Proceedings of the 2003 Conference of the North American Chapter of the Association for Computational Linguistics on Human Language Technology - Volume 1*, NAACL '03, pages 48–54, Stroudsburg, PA, USA. Association for Computational Linguistics.

Philipp Koehn, Hieu Hoang, Alexandra Birch, Chris Callison-Burch, Marcello Federico, Nicola Bertoldi, Brooke Cowan, Wade Shen, Christine Moran, Richard Zens, Chris Dyer, Ondřej Bojar, Alexandra Constantin, and Evan Herbst. 2007. Moses: open source toolkit for statistical machine translation. In *Proceedings of the 45th Annual Meeting of the ACL on Interactive Poster and Demonstration Sessions*, ACL '07, pages 177–180, Stroudsburg, PA, USA. Association for Computational Linguistics.

Philipp Koehn. 2005. Europarl: A parallel corpus for statistical machine translation. In *Proceedings of Machine Translation Summit*, pages 79–86.

Shankar Kumar and William Byrne. 2004. Minimum Bayes Risk Decoding for Statistical Machine Translation. In *Joint Conference of Human Language Technologies and the North American chapter of the Association for Computational Linguistics (HLT-NAACL 2004)*.

Mark-Jan Nederhof and Giorgio Satta. 2008. Probabilistic parsing. In M. Dolores Jimnez-Lpez G. Bel-Enguix and C. Martn-Vide, editors, *New Developments in Formal Languages and Applications, Studies in Computational Intelligence*, volume 113, pages 229–258. Springer.

Franz Josef Och. 2003. Minimum error rate training in statistical machine translation. In *Proceedings of the 41st Annual Meeting on Association for Computational Linguistics*, volume 1 of *ACL '03*, pages 160–167, Stroudsburg, PA, USA. Association for Computational Linguistics.

Christian P. Robert and George Casella. 2004. *Monte Carlo Statistical Methods (Springer Texts in Statistics)*. Springer-Verlag New York, Inc., Secaucus, NJ, USA.

Walter Rudin. 1987. *Real and Complex Analysis*. McGraw-Hill.

Alexander M. Rush and Michael Collins. 2011. Exact decoding of syntactic translation models through lagrangian relaxation. In *Proceedings of the 49th Annual Meeting of the Association for Computational Linguistics: Human Language Technologies - Volume 1*, HLT '11, pages 72–82, Stroudsburg, PA, USA. Association for Computational Linguistics.

David A. Smith and Jason Eisner. 2006. Minimum risk annealing for training log-linear models. In *Proceedings of the COLING/ACL on Main conference poster sessions*, COLING-ACL '06, pages 787–794, Stroudsburg, PA, USA. Association for Computational Linguistics.

Taro Watanabe, Jun Suzuki, Hajime Tsukada, and Hideki Isozaki. 2007. Online large-margin training for statistical machine translation. In *Proceedings of the 2007 Joint Conference on Empirical Methods in Natural Language Processing and Computational Natural Language Learning (EMNLP-CoNLL)*, pages 764–773, Prague, Czech Republic, June. Association for Computational Linguistics.

Evaluating (and Improving) Sentence Alignment under Noisy Conditions

Omar Zaidan
Microsoft Research, USA
ozaidan@cs.jhu.edu

Vishal Chowdhary
Microsoft Research, USA
vishalc@microsoft.com

Abstract

Sentence alignment is an important step in the preparation of parallel data. Most aligners do not perform very well when the input is a noisy, rather than a highly-parallel, document pair. Evaluating aligners under noisy conditions would seem to require creating an evaluation dataset by manually annotating a noisy document for gold-standard alignments. Such a costly process hinders our ability to evaluate an aligner under various types and levels of noise. In this paper, we propose a new evaluation framework for sentence aligners, which is particularly suitable for noisy-data evaluation. Our approach is unique as it requires no manual labeling, instead relying on small parallel datasets (already at the disposal of MT researchers) to generate many evaluation datasets that mimic a variety of noisy conditions. We use our framework to perform a comprehensive comparison of three aligners under noisy conditions. Furthermore, our framework facilitates the fine-tuning of a state-of-the-art sentence aligner, allowing us to substantially increase its recall rates by anywhere from 5% to 14% (absolute) across several language pairs.

1 Introduction

Virtually all training pipelines of statistical machine translation systems expect training data to be in the form of a sequence of parallel sentence pairs. This means that a pair of parallel documents must first be segmented into a sequence of aligned sentence pairs, discarding or combining sentences when needed, and aligning sentences as appropriate. The performance and output of an SMT system is directly dependent on the amount and quality of available training data. Therefore, it is critical to perform this *sentence alignment* step properly, ensuring both high recall (to have as much training data as possible) and high precision (to avoid noisy training data).

While sentence aligners achieve excellent performance on highly-parallel, clean data, the task is much more difficult under noisy conditions. Some prior work has investigated evaluation under noisy conditions (see section 6), but the major focus of prior work has been the clean-data scenario, where accuracy rates exceed 98% (e.g. Simard et al. (1993), Moore (2002)). For one thing, this meant that the various sentence alignment algorithms differ only slightly in absolute terms. Similarly, fine-tuning any one of those algorithms might not seem to have an impact on performance. More importantly, this also meant that we do not have a clear understanding of how well these algorithms would perform under noisy conditions.

Arguably, there was little need to examine sentence alignment of noisy datasets in early MT research, since almost all training data came from high-quality, highly-parallel sources, such as UN documents or parliamentary proceedings.[1] However, recent efforts have attempted to utilize web resources and non-perfectly-parallel texts, such as Wikipedia articles and news stories (e.g. Resnik and Smith (2003), Utiyama and Isahara (2003), Munteanu and Marcu (2005), and Smith et al. (2010)). Such resources naturally contain significantly more noise, at a level that would render sentence alignment a much less straightforward task.

Because sentence alignment algorithms had usually been evaluated under a clean-data scenario, there are fewer empirical results to guide those who wish to extract parallel data from noisy

[1] Also, parallel datasets created explicitly for MT research (by having a source corpus translated into the target language) would be already sentence-aligned by mere construction if the source side is split into sentences beforehand.

sources. Furthermore, there is also no easy way to fine-tune an aligner of interest. For building the Microsoft Translation service, we are continuously mining inherently-noisy web resources, from which we extract MT training data for dozens of the world's languages. Therefore, having a principled method to evaluate and fine-tune our aligner was critical.

In this paper, we describe our framework for evaluating sentence alignment under noisy conditions. We use this framework to examine and evaluate the Moore alignment algorithm (Moore, 2002), which was empirically shown to be state-of-the-art under clean conditions, and which we regularly use to extract parallel data from web resources to create training data. We perform a comprehensive comparison of this aligner against two other algorithms, and furthermore use our framework to fine-tune the algorithm along dimensions of interest (such as the aligner's search parameters) by quantitatively evaluating how the aligner's performance is affected by such changes.

The paper is organized as follows. We briefly define sentence alignment and existing approaches in section 2. We then discuss the *evaluation* of alignment algorithms in section 3, and present our evaluation framework. In section 4, we perform a comparative assessment of three alignment algorithms using our framework, illustrating the differences between them under noisy conditions. In section 5, we present two additional applications of our framework, namely fine-tuning an aligner and performing training data cleanup. Finally, we give an overview in section 6 of prior work that has tackled the specific issue of evaluating sentence aligners.

2 Sentence Alignment

Sentence alignment is the process by which a pair of parallel documents lacking explicit sentence links are used to extract a parallel dataset consisting of sentence pairs that are translations of each other. Specifically, let S and T be the document pair to be aligned, with S composed of the sentence sequence $s_1, s_2, ..., s_m$, and T composed of the sentence sequence $t_1, t_2, ..., t_n$. A sentence alignment of S and T is a segmentation of each of S and T into p sequences $s'_1, s'_2, ..., s'_p$ and $t'_1, t'_2, ..., t'_p$ such that the following holds about the segmentation of S: (a similar set of conditions exist that correspond to T)

- $s'_i = C_S[a, b)$ for some $1 \leq a \leq b \leq m \; \forall i$
- $s'_1 = C_S[1, b)$ for some $b >= 1$
- $s'_p = C_S[a, m)$ for some $a <= m$
- If $s'_i = C_S[a, b)$, then $s'_{i+1} = C_S[b, c)$
- If $s'_i = C_S[x, x)$, then $t'_i = C_T[y, z)$ such that $y \neq z$

Above, $C_S[a, b)$ is the concatenation of $s_a, s_{a+1}, ..., s_{b-1}$, which indicates the possibility of aligning multiple source sentences to a single sentence (or combined sequence of sentences) on the target side. Note that $C_S[a, a)$ is the empty string, which indicates deletion on the target side (i.e. a target sentence is aligned to the empty string). The last condition disallows aligning an empty string to another empty string, thus eliminating the possibility for an infinite segmentation sequence.

Note that the result of this segmentation is q (non-empty) sentence pairs, where $q <= p$ (and naturally $q <= m$ and $q <= n$). The deleted sentences, each aligned with an empty string, are left out of the resulting parallel corpus.

2.1 Approaches to Sentence Alignment

Tiedemann (2007) and Santos (2011) each provide a broad overview of sentence alignment, giving a timeline of relevant research and discussing algorithms and performance metrics for sentence alignment. In general, there are two main approaches to sentence alignment: length-based and lexical-based.

In length-based alignment approaches (e.g. Brown et al. (1991), Gale and Church (1991), and Kay and Röscheisen (1993)), the aligner relies on a probabilistic model that describes the source-to-target sentence length ratio for a pair of corresponding sentences. Such a model would account both for the average or typical length ratio as well as its variance. The aligner proceeds to align sentence pairs such that the output would be highly likely under the length ratio model.

In lexical-based alignment approaches (e.g. Chen (1993), Melamed (1997), Simard and Plamondon (1998), Menezes and Richardson (2001), and the LDC alignment tool, *Champollion* (Ma, 2006)), the aligner relies on a probabilistic model that describes the lexical similarity between a pair of sentences. The model could either be a fully-trained translation model, or a simpler bilingual lexicon that finds corresponding word pairs. In contrast to length-based algorithms, lexical-based approaches typically require external bilingual resources, and usually perform better.

Previous work on sentence alignment varies across a few other dimensions as well. Some lexical-based algorithms build the needed bilingual resources from the very dataset that is to be aligned, whereas other approaches assume that such resources are externally provided. Another dimension is the need to provide anchor points within the text to be aligned, such as in the form of paragraph-level alignment. Such anchor points are typically needed to restrict the search space to a manageable size.

Another group of aligners take a hybrid approach, relying both on sentence length and lexical similarity (e.g. Zhao and Vogel (2002)). One notable example is the algorithm by Moore (2002), which has the benefit of relying only on the input data when training the lexical similarity model, rather than needing external resources (bilingual lexicon or parallel training data) for that purpose. The Moore algorithm is a state-of-the-art algorithm, and has been used, for example, to align the data for the Europarl corpus (Koehn, 2005), and is often a strong baseline in papers proposing new alignment algorithms (e.g. Braune and Fraser (2010)). In section 4, we use our proposed framework to evaluate Moore's algorithm, and compare it against two other aligners, illustrating our framework's utility as a comparative tool.

3 Evaluating Sentence Alignment Algorithms under Noisy Conditions

In much of the prior work mentioned above in 2.1, and in other comparative evaluation work (e.g. Simard et al. (1993), Langlais et al. (1998), and Véronis and Langlais (2000)), sentence alignment algorithms were evaluated using a manually-created gold-standard dataset. This is done by taking a parallel dataset, and manually annotating sentence pairs that are translations of each other (and should therefore be aligned). This evaluation dataset is provided as input to the aligner, which is evaluated based on the precision and recall of its output, as measured against the set of hand-annotated sentence pairs.

While this is a reasonable approach that mirrors the evaluation model in many other tasks within machine learning (i.e. to manually create an evaluation set with gold-standard labels, based on which the learner's output is judged), it suffers from some drawbacks.

For one thing, all the difficulties of creating an evaluation dataset apply here as well. Most significantly, manually labeling sentence pairs is costly and time-consuming. This problem is magnified in the context of machine translation, since one should ideally evaluate a sentence alignment algorithm under several language pairs, rather than a single one, requiring the creation of several evaluation sets, rather than a single one.

Furthermore, prior work usually used a fairly clean dataset to annotate, on which it is relatively easy for an aligner to achieve very high precision and recall rates. This means that differences between algorithms are sometimes fairly small in absolute terms, making it difficult to attribute such differences to the algorithms themselves or to statistical noise.

The noisy-data scenario is extremely important in the web domain. The web is a huge repository of parallel documents that machine translation systems leverage for training data, and we continually extract content from noisy online sources. Unlike the above evaluation setup, we are concerned with scenarios where the data has a relatively high degree of noise, where by 'noise' we mean both non-perfect translations but also additional content on one side that is not translated at all. Both kinds of noise should be dealt with appropriately: the first introduces imperfect training data, while the second could eliminate good translations, or might send word alignment into a frenzy.

Because prior work mostly focused on the clean-data scenario, it is unknown whether previous evaluations would hold for noisy input. This makes it difficult to judge how these algorithms would compare to each other under more noisy conditions, or when any other experimental dimension is varied, such as domain and the language pair in question.

3.1 Creating Noisy Datasets for Evaluation Purposes

How can we create a noisy-data scenario under which to evaluate a sentence alignment algorithm? One approach is to mimic prior work: in a dataset that is known to be noisy, have an annotator select the sentence pairs that should be aligned to each other. However, this approach would be expensive and time-consuming.

We propose a completely different approach. Rather than attempting to annotate corresponding sentences in a dataset that is known to be noisy, we deliberately introduce noise into a dataset that is already perfectly-aligned (and for which, as a consequence, we already know the sentence correspondence).

Specifically, we start with a parallel dataset D that we know to be perfectly-aligned. Such datasets are abundant and readily available for MT researchers in the form of a myriad of tuning and test datasets across many language pairs and domains. We introduce noise into D (using any of the methods described below and detailed in subsection 4.2) to obtain a modified dataset D'. The source side of D' is a subset of the source side of D (possibly reordered), and the same holds for the target side. Since we know what the correct sentence alignments are in D, we also know, by mere construction, what the correct alignments in D' are as well. This allows us to easily compute precision and recall of a sentence alignment algorithm when it is given D' as input, without the need to collect a single annotation.

We employ several methods to create a noisy dataset D' from a perfectly-aligned dataset D:[2]

- **Clean dataset.** The source and target sides of D' are exactly the unaltered source and target sides of D. This represents the easiest test set for a sentence aligner, as the test set consists entirely of 1-to-1 mappings, all of which fall exactly along the search matrix diagonal.

- **Random deletions.** The source side of D' is a subset of the source side of D, where the number of discarded sentences is determined by a source deletion rate del_s. For example, for a dataset D with 1000 sentences on the source side and $del_s = 0.10$, the source side of D' consists of 900 randomly-chosen sentences from the source side of D (with no reordering). The target side of D' is created similarly, using a target deletion rate del_t. Note that the deletion on the target side is done independently from the deletion on the source side. That is, the probability of deleting the ith sentence on the target side is del_t, regardless of whether the ith sentence on the source side was deleted or not.

- **Random combinations.** The source and target sides of D' are the same as those from D, but with random consecutive pairs of sentences combined into a single sentence. The degree to which sentences are combined is determined by source and target combination rates $comb_s$ and $comb_t$. For example, for a dataset D with 1000 sentences on the source side and $comb_s = 0.10$, 100 sentence pairs (each consisting of consecutive sentences) are chosen randomly, and each pair is combined into a single sentence, yielding a set of 900 source sentences in D'. The goal of this scenario is to test the aligner's ability to recover 1-to-many and many-to-1 mappings, rather than focusing solely on 1-to-1 mappings.[3] As with random deletions, the combination processes on the source side and on the target side are independent from each other.

- **Randomized order.** The source side of D' consists of the source side of D, but in random order. The target side of D is also randomized.

- **Length-aligned from same dataset.** The source side of D' is exactly the same as the source side of D. The noise is introduced into the target side, where all the target sentences from D are preserved, but they are reordered. The reordering is not completely stochastic. Rather, an attempt is made to have the sentences length-aligned as much as possible. This is somewhat of an adversarial scenario, since a length-based alignment method would align too many sentences that are completely unrelated to each other.

- **Different datasets.** The dataset D' is formed by taking two datasets D_1 and D_2, and aligning the source side of D_1 with the target side of D_2, and vice versa. A good sentence aligner would deem that the source and target sides are unrelated, yielding a very low alignment rate.

[2] In a few of our experiments, we make use of *two* datasets (that are non-overlapping and non-related), say D_1 and D_2, to create D'. The way we frame the creation of D', as a mapping from a single dataset D, still applies here: D is simply the concatenation of D_1 and D_2.

[3] With high enough combination rates, many-to-many mappings arise as well.

4 Experimental Results

Even though this paper is not mainly concerned with comparing aligners to each other, we utilize our proposed framework and apply it to three different aligners as a demonstration. In this section, we describe the aligners to be compared, and provide specific details about how our test sets were generated. We then describe the metrics we use, and present results based on these metrics.

4.1 Sentence Aligners

The first aligner (LEN) is a length-based aligner based on the algorithm described in Brown et al. (1991). It segments the source and target sides by finding the highest-likelihood segmentation according to a model describing the relationship between source sentence length and target sentence length. In particular, this relationship is modeled using a Poisson distribution that has as its mean the length ratio observed in the dataset to align.[4]

The second aligner (MRE) is based on Moore's algorithm (Moore, 2002), which makes use of the length-based aligner's output to build a tentative model 1. Moore's algorithm takes the output from this "first phase" and builds a bilingual lexicon that allows it to compute translation model scores. For a given pair of sentences, the likelihood that they are translations of each other is now computed based not only on their lengths, but also on their lexical similarity.

The third aligner (MRE+) is similar to the second aligner, but uses a much stronger translation model. The stronger translation model is simply the translation system that has already been built for that particular language pair and now helps aligning new data. While this requires the availability of external resources, this setup closely resembles the resources we have, given our parallel training datasets. We note here that our evaluation datasets have no overlap with the data used to train the translation models used by MRE+.

4.2 Noisy Dataset Generation

For random deletions, we use six different deletion rates (from 0.00 to 0.25, with 0.05 increments), both on the source side and the target side, for a total of 35 test sets. For random combinations, we use four different combination rates (from 0.00 to 0.15, with 0.05 increments), both on the source side and the target side, for a total of 15 test sets. Note that we do not consider the case when both deletion/combination rates are 0.00, since that mimics the clean-dataset scenario.

For the length-aligned scenario, we align each source sentence with a randomly-selected sentence from the target side that is closest in length to that source sentence. (We take the target-to-source length ratio into consideration, and multiply the source length by that ratio before trying to find the closest-length target sentence.) If several target sentences have lengths that are equally close to the desired length, we pick one at random.

We note here that if the source sentences are processed sequentially, there will be a clustering of overly long target sentences at the bottom of the dataset, since such sentences are never chosen based on length – they are simply too long. Therefore, we process the source sentences in random order rather than sequentially, to avoid this clustering of long sentences.

4.3 Performance Metrics

We report the following metrics for quantitatively evaluating and describing the output of the sentence aligner:

- **Precision**: of the sentence pairs produced by the aligner, what percentage are sentence pairs in the gold-standard dataset D?
- **Recall**: of the sentence pairs in the gold-standard dataset D, what percentage are produced by the aligner?
- **Alignment rate**: what proportion of the sentences in the input dataset D' were aligned by the aligner? Due to the possibility that the source and target sides of D' have different sizes, there are two alignment rates, and we report their average.[5]

Higher precision and higher recall are, by definition, indicators of better performance. This cannot be said of the alignment rate. For instance, consider the noisy deletion scenario of 3.1 above. By mere construction of D', there will be source (resp. target) sentences that should not be aligned to anything on the target (resp. source) side, since we deliberately deleted the corresponding sentence. In such cases, an alignment rate of 100%

[4]Note that we follow Moore (2002) in using a Poisson distribution instead of the Gaussian of Brown et al.

[5]Of course, the dataset returned by the aligner always has source and target sides of equal sizes.

Language Pair	Test Scenario	LEN	MRE	MRE+
EN-ES	Clean (no noise)	100%, 82%, 82%	100%, 85%, 85%	100%, 99%, 99%
	$del_s = del_t = 0.05$	100%, 46%, 44%	99%, 71%, 68%	100%, 96%, 91%
	$comb_s = comb_t = 0.05$	100%, 39%, 38%	99%, 66%, 64%	100%, 92%, 89%
	Randomized	0%, 0%, 1%	0%, 0%, 4%	34%, 1%, 4%
	Length-aligned	0%, 0%, 82%	0%, 0%, 15%	0%, 0%, 7%
EN-AR	Clean (no noise)	100%, 55%, 55%	100%, 60%, 60%	100%, 89%, 89%
	$del_s = del_t = 0.05$	99%, 27%, 26%	99%, 44%, 42%	100%, 82%, 78%
	$comb_s = comb_t = 0.05$	99%, 22%, 21%	99%, 41%, 39%	99%, 77%, 74%
	Randomized	N/A, 0%, 0%	17%, <1%, <1%	26%, <1%, 1%
	Length-aligned	0%, 0%, 59%	0%, 0%, 9%	5%, <1%, 2%
EN-CH	Clean (no noise)	100%, 66%, 66%	100%, 72%, 72%	100%, 97%, 97%
	$del_s = del_t = 0.05$	100%, 40%, 39%	99%, 56%, 55%	100%, 92%, 88%
	$comb_s = comb_t = 0.05$	99%, 35%, 34%	99%, 52%, 50%	99%, 87%, 82%
	Randomized	0%, 0%, <1%	0%, 0%, <1%	29%, <1%, 2%
	Length-aligned	0%, 0%, 62%	0%, 0%, 13%	2%, <1%, 5%
Average (over the 3 LP's)	Clean (no noise)	100%, 68%, 68%	100%, 72%, 72%	100%, 95%, 95%
	$del_s = del_t = 0.05$	100%, 38%, 36%	99%, 57%, 55%	100%, 90%, 86%
	$comb_s = comb_t = 0.05$	99%, 32%, 31%	99%, 53%, 51%	99%, 85%, 82%
	Randomized	0%, 0%, <1%	6%, <1%, 2%	30%, 1%, 2%
	Length-aligned	0%, 0%, 68%	0%, 0%, 12%	2%, <1%, 5%

Table 1: Results of the comparative experiment of the three aligners. For brevity, we report the results for only five scenarios (per language pair and aligner) out of the more than fifty scenarios we propose. Each cell contains three percentages: precision, recall, and alignment rate. The N/A precision value for LEN in the EN-AR randomized scenario indicates the aligner produced no output.

for example (i.e. all input sentences were aligned to some other sentence) is indicative of pervasive alignment rather than good performance.[6]

Hence, alignment rate is not a performance measure in the conventional sense, as it is not an objective to be maximized or minimized. Still, it is a useful descriptor that sheds light on the aligner's behavior, as we see in the next subsection.

4.4 Results

We carried out experiments covering three language pairs: English-Spanish, English-Arabic, and English-Chinese. The comparative experiment is quite telling, and the results (Table 1) point to consistent and noticeable differences between the three examined aligners. While all aligners have very high alignment precision rates in non-adversary scenarios, always exceeding 99%, the difference is in how well they recover sentence pairs that should be aligned to each other, illustrated by significant differences in recall rates.

The clearest trend is that the length-based algorithm (LEN) performs worse than Moore's algorithm (MRE), which in turn benefits quite a bit when it's aided by an external strong translation model (MRE+). It is worth pointing out that the gap between MRE and MRE+ is typically larger than the gap between LEN and MRE, suggesting the important of external bilingual resources to aid the sentence aligner.

The results of the adversary scenarios (randomized and length-aligned) are particularly interesting. Looking at precision and recall alone, it might seem that there is not much to separate the three algorithms. For example, they all have 0% precision and 0% recall in the length-aligned EN-ES scenario (fifth row of Table 1). However, looking at the alignment rate, we find that LEN was prone to over-aligning the data, having an (unnecessarily very high) alignment rate of 82%. On the other hand, MRE and MRE+, have much lower alignment rates of 15% and 7%, respectively. This means that they would introduce only a fraction of the

[6]Even an oracle aligner with perfect precision and recall will almost surely have an alignment rate less than 100% (or even 90%) when D' is constructed using high deletion rates.

bad data that LEN would, which is a great advantage for MRE and especially MRE+.

5 Applications of the Evaluation Framework

In the previous section, we utilized our framework to perform a comparison between three different aligners, by evaluating them under various noisy-data circumstances. In this section, we use our framework in two more applications relevant to sentence alignment and machine translation.

5.1 Fine-tuning Aligner Parameters

We explore using the evaluation setup to fine-tune the parameters of the MRE+ algorithm. Lacking a principled way to evaluate the aligner's output, it was not possible to fine-tune the aligner's various parameters. Now, equipped with our evaluation framework, it is possible to quantitatively determine the effect of changing the value of any parameter, and pick the best value. This is preferable to accepting whatever default parameters are in already place, which are more than likely suitable for a specific domain, dataset, or low-to-nonexistent noise.

5.1.1 Experimental Design

We fine-tune the parameters of the MRE+ algorithm by optimizing its performance on a tuning dataset generated using the noisy deletion setup, and then measure its performance on a different evaluation set that was also generated using the noisy deletion setup. We investigate two cases, one with $del_s = del_t = 0.05$, and one with $del_s = del_t = 0.20$, to examine the benefit of fine-tuning both under a relatively low noise level and under a relatively high noise level.

We optimize the performance of the MRE+ algorithm along three dimensions:

- **Prior probabilities (PRIOR).** As explained in section 2, sentence alignment is essentially a segmentation of the source and target sides of the parallel dataset. In addition to relying on length similarity and lexical correspondence, the MRE+ aligner also relies on a set of prior probabilities for each insert/delete/align action it could take. By default, the probability assigned to deletion and insertion was set at 0.02. It is reasonable to assume that this might be too low, especially for highly-noisy input data, and so this is the first dimension that we optimize.
- **Search beam size (SIZE).** The algorithm also pays attention to the location of a candidate sentence pair. While positional similarity does not play a direct role in computing the alignment probability, the aligner does prune the search space based on location. For example, when considering a sentence half-way through the source side, only sentences that are close to the half-way point in the target side will be considered. How far the aligner is willing to deviate from the diagonal[7] is a tunable parameter, making it our second dimension.
- **Alignment threshold (THRESHOLD).** The aligner assigns a probability to each sentence pair it considers for alignment, reflecting its confidence that the sentence pair should be aligned. By default, the aligner eliminates any sentence pair that fails to meet a threshold of 0.99. This alignment threshold is the third dimension we optimize, as it should be lowered or increased to reflect our confidence in the translation model and/or the variability of the length-correspondence model.

5.1.2 Experimental Results

The results in Tables 2 and 3 show the benefit of optimizing the aligner's parameters. It is beneficial to optimize the prior probabilities and the alignment threshold, as indicated by higher recall rates compared to the default values. On the other hand, the tuning of the search beam size had minimal impact. This indicates that the mistakes made by the sentence aligner are usually model errors rather than search error.

The effect of optimizing the prior probabilities is more pronounced in the high-noise scenario (Table 3), where it proves to provide the most gain over the baseline. Contrast this with the low-noise scenario (Table 2), where optimizing the alignment threshold is at least equally important, if not more so. This is to be expected, since the default prior of 0.02 in the high-noise scenario significantly underestimates the amount of deletion that has actually taken place, making the prior the most important parameter to optimize.

[7] If we were to create a grid of alignment probabilities, this pruning of the search space means that grid cells far off the *diagonal* of this grid are never considered.

Tuned parameter(s)	EN-ES	EN-AR	EN-CH
None	95.7%	82.4%	92.0%
PRIOR	96.2%	85.6%	93.5%
SIZE	95.8%	82.8%	92.0%
THRESHOLD	96.8%	86.7%	92.9%
All	97.1%	87.5%	93.7%

Table 2: Results of the MRE+ fine-tuning experiment for the 0.05 deletion rate scenario. For clarity, we show only recall rates – all precision rates are 99% or higher.

Tuned parameter(s)	EN-ES	EN-AR	EN-CH
None	87.8%	68.1%	81.9%
PRIOR	92.7%	81.5%	88.4%
SIZE	88.0%	68.8%	82.3%
THRESHOLD	89.3%	70.4%	84.3%
All	93.0%	82.8%	90.6%

Table 3: Results of the MRE+ fine-tuning experiment for the 0.20 deletion rate scenario. For clarity, we show only recall rates – all precision rates are 98% or higher.

It is worth pointing out the work of Yu et al. (2012), who perform a comparative study of sentence aligners, and show that Moore's algorithm does not perform as well as other aligners on a noisy dataset. As they provide no details regarding the values of the various parameters of Moore's algorithm, one can assume that they used default values and performed no tuning. Of course, such tuning would not have been easy to perform, given the lack of a tuning dataset. This is exactly why we propose our evaluation framework, so that future researchers would not have to guess parameter values or accept default values if they believe that would lead to suboptimal performance. Given the results of our experiments, it is conceivable that the performance of Moore's algorithm in Yu et al.'s work (and other algorithms they examined as well) might have been improved had their parameters been optimized.

5.2 Using Sentence Alignment to Filter Training Data

Much of our training data comes from noisy sources, both online and otherwise. Due to the vast amount of data, it is not possible to go through it to discard noisy sentence pairs. Now, equipped with a better understanding of our sentence aligner and its performance, we use it to trim down our training data by eliminating sentence pairs to which the aligner does not assign a high weight.

5.2.1 Experimental Design

We provide our current training data as input to the sentence aligner, and treat the output of the aligner as a filtered version of our data, since sentences that are discarded (not aligned) by the aligner tend to be noisy data. To evaluate the effectiveness of this process, we compare models trained with pre-filtered data vs. ones trained with the filtered data. We examine how the filtering affects the data and model size, since trimming those down would speed up training and translation. This is especially relevant for us given the large number of language pairs for which we train models. To ensure the translation quality doesn't degrade, we measure the effect on translation quality for two in-house evaluation datasets.

We consider three scenarios:

- **No filtering.** As a baseline, we use our training data as-is to train the MT system, without any filtering.
- **Uniform filtering.** We provide our training data as input to the sentence aligner, and use the aligner's output as the training data to train the MT system. (We refer to this as 'uniform' filtering in contrast to the next scenario.)
- **Filtering 'web' datasets.** Here, we apply sentence alignment filtering only to certain hand-picked datasets that we believe to contain a relatively high level of noise. The datasets are not picked by inspecting their content, but simply by deciding that any dataset that came from online sources (aka 'web' data) should undergo filtering.

5.2.2 Experimental Results

We performed our filtering experiments on two systems, Arabic-English and Urdu-English, with the results displayed in Tables 4 and 5, respectively. In all cases but one, the BLEU score went up or down by less than a quarter of a point, indicating general stability in performance quality.

This line of experiments is still in progress. We plan to carry out another set of experiments where

Scenario	Data Size	Model Size	Test1 BLEU	Test2 BLEU
No filtering	100%	100%	31.44	30.57
All filtered	94.8%	96.7%	31.29	30.34
Web only	96.6%	96.0%	31.54	30.52

Table 4: Results of the data filtering experiments for the Arabic-English system.

Scenario	Data Size	Model Size	Test1 BLEU	Test2 BLEU
No filtering	100%	100%	38.03	13.32
All filtered	81.6%	85.9%	38.19	13.13
Web only	99.1%	99.1%	37.80	12.78

Table 5: Results of the data filtering experiments for the Urdu-English system.

the prior deletion probability is customized for each portion of our training data, based on our belief of how noisy that portion of the dataset is. We are also expanding the experiments to include more language pairs.

6 Related Work

Singh and Husain (2005) evaluate several sentence alignment algorithms. Their work does have a hint of proposing a fuller evaluation framework, in that they have one test scenario where noise is added to their test set (in the form of adding sentences from another, unrelated dataset). Another major difference from our work is that they rely on manual evaluation of the output, as is the case for much of prior work.

Moore does point out that the error rates obtained by his algorithm are very low partly because the data being aligned is highly parallel, therefore making it "fairly easy data to align" (Moore (2002), p. 142). He therefore presents one additional experiment where a single block of sentences is deleted from one side of the input to mimic a noisy condition. While this is similar in spirit to our noisy deletions scenario, it introduces only a very small amount of noise in practice. This is because the deleted sentences are all sequential rather than being at different positions in the corpus, are all on one side of the corpus, and since the deletion rate was very low (varied up to only 3.0%). Case in point, the resulting dataset was still very easy to align, with error rates that remained below 2.0% even for the baseline aligner.

Yu et al. (2012) use the BAF dataset (Simard, 2006) as an evaluation dataset, since it is known to contain a relatively high degree of 0-1 and 1-0 beads (what they call "null links"), and use that dataset specifically to evaluate an alignment algorithm customized to handle noisy data. Similarly, Rosen (2005) evaluates several aligners using three datasets, one of which is characterized as being more noisy than the others.

Abdul-Rauf et al. (2012) compare several algorithms to each other, across several datasets, including the noisy BAF dataset. However, they do not propose a full framework for evaluating sentence alignment itself, and instead emphasize the differences in performance of MT systems trained on the aligned data.

There is a good amount of prior work dealing with filtering noisy data from parallel datasets. Taghipour et al. (2010) propose a discriminative framework to filter noisy sentence pairs from parallel data, and apply it to a Farsi-English dataset. Denkowski et al. (2012) briefly describe a filtering method to clean up training data for a French-English system submitted to WMT 2010, relying on deviations from typical values for certain statistical measures to identify noisy sentence pairs.

7 Conclusion

In this paper, we proposed a new evaluation framework for sentence aligners, which is specifically designed with noisy-data conditions in mind. Our approach is unique in that it requires absolutely no manual labeling, and relies on parallel datasets that are already in existence. We provide several methods to deliberately introduce noise into a dataset that is already perfectly-aligned, thus creating a whole host of evaluation test sets quickly and at no cost.

Our framework allows us and other researchers to easily compare and contrast several aligners to each other. Furthermore, our framework can be used to improve the performance of an aligner by facilitating the fine-tuning of any or all of its hyperparameters.

References

Sadaf Abdul-Rauf, Mark Fishel, Patrik Lambert, Sandra Noubours, and Rico Sennrich. 2012. Extrinsic evaluation of sentence alignment systems. In *Proceedings of LREC Workshop on Creating Cross-*

language Resources for Disconnected Languages and Styles, CREDISLAS, pages 6–10.

Fabienne Braune and Alexander Fraser. 2010. Improved unsupervised sentence alignment for symmetrical and asymmetrical parallel corpora. In *Proceedings of COLING: Poster Volume*, pages 81–89.

Peter F. Brown, Jennifer C. Lai, and Robert L. Mercer. 1991. Aligning sentences in parallel corpora. In *Proceedings of ACL*, pages 169–176.

Stanley F. Chen. 1993. Aligning sentences in bilingual corpora using lexical information. In *Proceedings of ACL*, pages 9–16.

Michael Denkowski, Greg Hanneman, and Alon Lavie. 2012. The CMU-Avenue French-English translation system. In *Proceedings of the NAACL Workshop on Statistical Machine Translation*, pages 261–266.

William A. Gale and Kenneth W. Church. 1991. A program for aligning sentences in bilingual corpora. In *Proceedings of ACL*, pages 177–184.

Martin Kay and Martin Röscheisen. 1993. Text-translation alignment. *Computational Linguistics*, 19(1):121–142.

Philipp Koehn. 2005. Europarl: A parallel corpus for statistical machine translation. In *Proceedings of MT Summit*, pages 79–86.

Philippe Langlais, Michel Simard, and Jean Véronis. 1998. Methods and practical issues in evaluating alignment techniques. In *ACL/COLING*, pages 711–717.

Xiaoyi Ma. 2006. Champollion: A robust parallel text sentence aligner. In *Proceedings of LREC*, pages 489–492.

I. Dan Melamed. 1997. A portable algorithm for mapping bitext correspondence. In *Proceedings of ACL*, pages 305–312.

Arul Menezes and Stephen D. Richardson. 2001. A best-first alignment algorithm for automatic extraction of transfer mappings from bilingual corpora. In *Proceedings of the ACL Workshop on Data-Driven Methods in Machine Translation*, pages 39–46.

Robert C. Moore. 2002. Fast and accurate sentence alignment of bilingual corpora. In Stephen D. Richardson, editor, *AMTA 2002: From Research to Real Users*, pages 135–144. Springer Berlin Heidelberg.

Dragos Stefan Munteanu and Daniel Marcu. 2005. Improving machine translation performance by exploiting non-parallel corpora. *Computational Linguistics*, 31(4):477–504.

Philip Resnik and Noah A. Smith. 2003. The web as a parallel corpus. *Computational Linguistics*, 29(3):349–380.

Alexandr Rosen. 2005. In search of the best method for sentence alignment in parallel texts. In *Proceedings of SLOVKO*.

André Santos. 2011. A survey on parallel corpora alignment. In *Proceedings of MI-Star*, pages 117–128.

Michel Simard and Pierre Plamondon. 1998. Bilingual sentence alignment: Balancing robustness and accuracy. *Machine Translation*, 13:59–80.

Michel Simard, George F. Foster, and Pierre Isabelle. 1993. Using cognates to align sentences in bilingual corpora. In *Proceedings of the Conference of the Centre for Advanced Studies on Collaborative Research: Distributed Computing - Volume 2*, pages 1071–1082.

Michel Simard. 2006. The BAF: A corpus of English-French bitext. In *Proceedings of LREC*, pages 489–494.

Anil Kumar Singh and Samar Husain. 2005. Comparison, selection and use of sentence alignment algorithms for new language pairs. In *Proceedings of the ACL Workshop on Building and Using Parallel Texts*, pages 99–106.

Jason R. Smith, Chris Quirk, and Kristina Toutanova. 2010. Extracting parallel sentences from comparable corpora using document level alignment. In *Proceedings of NAACL*, pages 403–411.

Kaveh Taghipour, Nasim Afhami, Shahram Khadivi, and Saeed Shiry. 2010. A discriminative approach to filter out noisy sentence pairs from bilingual corpora. In *Proceedings of International Symposium on Telecommunications*, pages 537–541.

Jörg Tiedemann. 2007. Improved sentence alignment for movie subtitles. In *Proceedings of Recent Advances in Natural Language Processing*.

Masao Utiyama and Hitoshi Isahara. 2003. Reliable measures for aligning japanese-english news articles and sentences. In *Proceedings of ACL*, pages 72–79.

Jean Véronis and Philippe Langlais. 2000. Evaluation of parallel text alignment systems: The ARCADE project. In Jean Véronis, editor, *Parallel Text Processing: Alignment and Use of Translation Corpora*, pages 369–388. Kluwer Academic Publishers.

Qian Yu, Aurélien Max, and François Yvon. 2012. Revisiting sentence alignment algorithms for alignment visualization and evaluation. In *Proceedings of the LREC Workshop on Building and Using Comparable Corpora*, pages 10–16.

Bing Zhao and Stephan Vogel. 2002. Adaptive parallel sentences mining from web bilingual news collection. In *IEEE International Conference on Data Mining*, pages 745–748.

Multi-rate HMMs for Word Alignment

Elif Eyigöz
Computer Science
University of Rochester
Rochester, NY 14627

Daniel Gildea
Computer Science
University of Rochester
Rochester, NY 14627

Kemal Oflazer
Computer Science
Carnegie Mellon University
PO Box 24866, Doha, Qatar

Abstract

We apply multi-rate HMMs, a tree structured HMM model, to the word-alignment problem. Multi-rate HMMs allow us to model reordering at both the morpheme level and the word level in a hierarchical fashion. This approach leads to better machine translation results than a morpheme-aware model that does not explicitly model morpheme reordering.

1 Introduction

We present an HMM-based word-alignment model that addresses transitions between morpheme positions and word positions simultaneously. Our model is an instance of a multi-scale HMM, a widely used method for modeling different levels of a hierarchical stochastic process. In multi-scale modeling of language, the deepest level of the hierarchy may consist of the phoneme sequence, and going up in the hierarchy, the next level may consist of the syllable sequence, and then the word sequence, the phrase sequence, and so on. By the same token, in the hierarchical word-alignment model we present here, the lower level consists of the morpheme sequence and the higher level the word sequence.

Multi-scale HMMs have a natural application in language processing due to the hierarchical nature of linguistic structures. They have been used for modeling text and handwriting (Fine et al., 1998), in signal processing (Willsky, 2002), knowledge extraction (Skounakis et al., 2003), as well as in other fields of AI such as vision (Li et al., 2006; Luettgen et al., 1993) and robotics (Theocharous et al., 2001). The model we propose here is most similar to multi-rate HMMs (Çetin et al., 2007), which were applied to a classification problem in industrial machine tool wear.

The vast majority of languages exhibit morphology to some extent, leading to various efforts in machine translation research to include morphology in translation models (Al-Onaizan et al., 1999; Niessen and Ney, 2000; Čmejrek et al., 2003; Lee, 2004; Chung and Gildea, 2009; Yeniterzi and Oflazer, 2010). For the word-alignment problem, Goldwater and McClosky (2005) and Eyigöz et al. (2013) suggested word alignment models that address morphology directly.

Eyigöz et al. (2013) introduced two-level alignment models (TAM), which adopt a hierarchical representation of alignment: the first level involves word alignment, the second level involves morpheme alignment. TAMs jointly induce word and morpheme alignments using an EM algorithm. TAMs can align rarely occurring words through their frequently occurring morphemes. In other words, they use morpheme probabilities to smooth rare word probabilities.

Eyigöz et al. (2013) introduced TAM 1, which is analogous to IBM Model 1, in that the first level is a bag of words in a pair of sentences, and the second level is a bag of morphemes. By introducing distortion probabilities at the word level, Eyigöz et al. (2013) defined the HMM extension of TAM 1, the TAM-HMM. TAM-HMM was shown to be superior to its single-level counterpart, i.e., the HMM-based word alignment model of Vogel et al. (1996).

The alignment example in Figure 1 shows a Turkish word aligned to an English phrase. The morphemes of the Turkish word are aligned to the English words. As the example shows, morphologically rich languages exhibit complex reordering phenomena at the morpheme level, which is left unutilized in TAM-HMMs. In this paper, we add morpheme sequence modeling to TAMs to capture morpheme level distortions. The example also shows that the Turkish morpheme or-

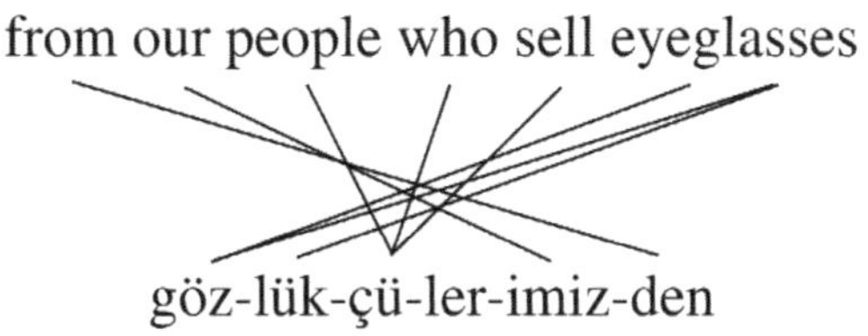

Figure 1: Turkish word aligned to an English phrase.

der is the reverse of the English word order. Because this pattern spans several English words, it can only be captured by modeling morpheme reordering across word boundaries. We chose multi-rate HMMs over other hierarchical HMM models because multi-rate HMMs allow morpheme sequence modeling across words over the entire sentence.

It is possible to model the morpheme sequence by treating morphemes as words: segmenting the words into morphemes, and using word-based word alignment models on the segmented data. Eyigöz et al. (2013) showed that TAM-HMM performs better than treating morphemes as words.

Since the multi-rate HMM allows both word and morpheme sequence modeling, it is a generalization of TAM-HMM, which allows only word sequence modeling. TAM-HMM in turn is a generalization of the model suggested by Goldwater and McClosky (2005) and TAM 1. Our results show that multi-rate HMMs are superior to TAM-HMMs. Therefore, multi-rate HMMs are the best two-level alignment models proposed so far.

2 Two-level Alignment Model (TAM)

The two-level alignment model (TAM) takes the approach of assigning probabilities to both word-to-word translations and morpheme-to-morpheme translations simultaneously, allowing morpheme-level probabilities to guide alignment for rare word pairs. TAM is based on a concept of alignment defined at both the word and morpheme levels.

2.1 Morpheme Alignment

A word alignment a_w is a function mapping a set of word positions in a target language sentence $\mathbf{e}$ to a set of word positions in a source language sentence $\mathbf{f}$, as exemplified in Figure 2. A morpheme alignment a_m is a function mapping a set of morpheme positions in a target language sentence to a set of morpheme positions in a source language sentence. A morpheme position is a pair of integers (j, k), which defines a word position j and a relative morpheme position k in the word at position j, as shown in Figure 3. The word and morpheme alignments below are depicted in Figures 2 and 3.

$$a_w(1) = 1 \quad a_m(2,1) = (1,1) \quad a_w(2) = 1$$

A morpheme alignment a_m and a word alignment a_w are *compatible* if and only if they satisfy the following conditions: If the morpheme alignment a_m maps a morpheme of e to a morpheme of f, then the word alignment a_w maps e to f. If the word alignment a_w maps e to f, then the morpheme alignment a_m maps at least one morpheme of e to a morpheme of f. If the word alignment a_w maps e to null, then all of its morphemes are mapped to null. Figure 3 shows a morpheme alignment that is compatible with, i.e., restricted by, the word alignment in Figure 2. The smaller boxes embedded inside the main box in Figure 3 depict the embedding of the morpheme level inside the word level in two-level alignment models (TAM).

2.2 TAM 1

We call TAM without sequence modeling TAM 1, because it defines an embedding of IBM Model 1 (Brown et al., 1993) for morphemes inside IBM Model 1 for words. In TAM 1, $p(\mathbf{e}|\mathbf{f})$, the probability of translating the sentence $\mathbf{f}$ into $\mathbf{e}$ is computed by summing over all possible word alignments and all possible morpheme alignments that are compatible with a given word alignment a_w:

$$\overbrace{R_w \prod_{j=1}^{|\mathbf{e}|} \sum_{i=0}^{|\mathbf{f}|}}^{\text{Word}} \left(t(e_j|f_i) \; \overbrace{R_m \prod_{k=1}^{|e_j|} \sum_{n=0}^{|f_i|} t(e_j^k|f_i^n)}^{\text{Morpheme}} \right) \tag{1}$$

where f_i^n is the nth morpheme of the word at position i. The probability of translating the word f_i into the word e_j is computed by summing over all possible morpheme alignments between the morphemes of e_j and f_i. R_w substitutes $\frac{P(l_\mathbf{e}|l_\mathbf{f})}{(l_\mathbf{f}+1)^{l_\mathbf{e}}}$ for easy readability.[1] R_m is equivalent to R_w except

[1] $l_\mathbf{e} = |\mathbf{e}|$ is the number of words in sentence $\mathbf{e}$ and $l_\mathbf{f} = |\mathbf{f}|$.

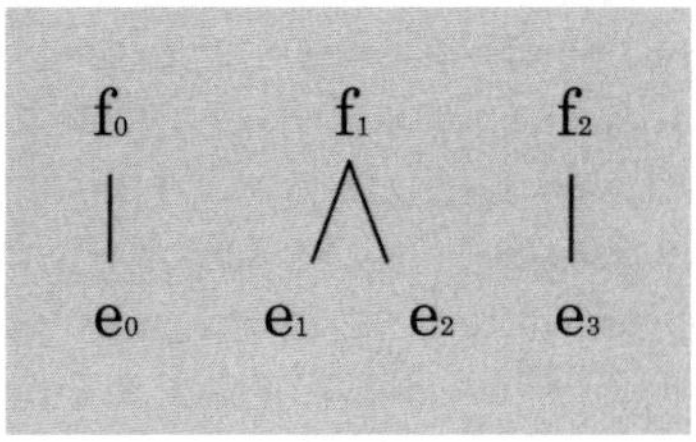

Figure 2: Word alignment

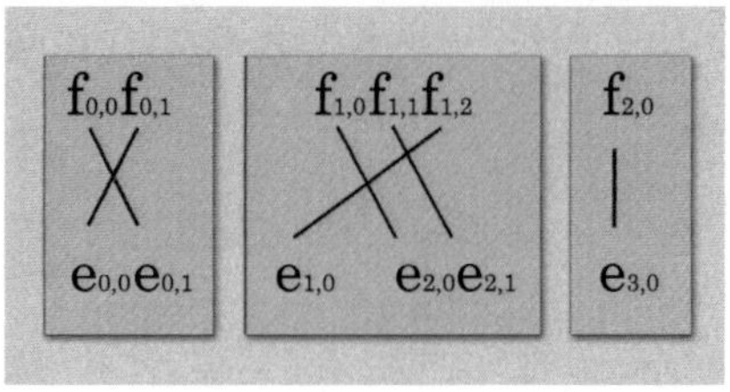

Figure 3: Morpheme alignment

for the fact that its domain is not the set of sentences but the set of words. The length of a word is the number of morphemes in the word. The length of words e_j and f_i in $R(e_j, f_i)$ are the number of morphemes of e_j and f_i. We assume that all unaligned morphemes in a sentence map to a special null morpheme.

TAM 1 with the contribution of both word and morpheme translation probabilities, as in Eqn. 1, is called 'word-and-morpheme' version of TAM 1. The model is technically deficient probabilistically, as it models word and morpheme translation independently, and assigns mass to invalid word/morpheme combinations. We can also define the 'morpheme-only' version of TAM 1 by canceling out the contribution of word translation probabilities and assigning 1 to $t(e_j|f_i)$ in Eqn. 1. Please note that, although this version of the two-level alignment model does not use word translation probabilities, it is also a word-aware model, as morpheme alignments are restricted to correspond to a valid word alignment. As such, it also allows for word level sequence modeling by HMMs. Finally, canceling out the contribution of morpheme translation probabilities reduces TAM 1 to IBM Model 1. Just as IBM Model 1 is used for initialization before HMM-based word-alignment models (Vogel et al., 1996; Och and Ney, 2003), TAM Model 1 is used to initialize its HMM extensions, which are described in the next section.

3 Multi-rate HMM

Like other multi-scale HMM models such as hierarchical HMM's (Fine et al., 1998) and hidden Markov trees (Crouse et al., 1998), the multi-rate HMM characterizes the inter-scale dependencies by a tree structure. As shown in Figure 5, scales are organized in a hierarchical manner from coarse to fine, which allows for efficient representation of both short- and long-distance context simultaneously.

We found that 51% of the dependency relations in the Turkish Treebank (Oflazer et al., 2003) are between the last morpheme of a dependent word and the first morpheme (the root) of the head word that is immediately to its right, which is exemplified below. The following examples show English sentences in Turkish word/morpheme order. The pseudo Turkish words are formed by concatenation of English morphemes, which are indicated by the '+' between the morphemes.

- – I will come from X.
  – X+ABL come+will+I
- – I will look at X.
  – X+DAT look+will+I

In English, the verb 'come' subcategorizes for a PP headed by 'from' in the example above. In the pseudo Turkish version of this sentence, 'come' subcategorizes for a NP marked with ablative case (ABL), which corresponds to the preposition 'from'. Similarly, 'look' subcategorizes for a PP headed by 'at' in English, and a NP marked with dative case (DAT) in Turkish. Just as the verb and the preposition that it subcategorizes for are frequently found adjacent to each other in English, the verb and the case that it subcategorizes for are frequently found adjacent to each other in Turkish. Thus, we have a pattern of three corresponding morphemes appearing in reverse order in English and Turkish, spanning two words in Turkish and three words in English. In order to capture such regularities, we chose multi-rate HMMs over other hierarchically structured HMM models because, unlike other models, multi-rate HMMs allow morpheme sequence modeling across words over the entire sentence. This allows us to capture morpheme-mediated syntactic relations between words (Eryiğit et al., 2008), as exemplified above.

Morpheme sequence modeling across words is shown in Figure 4 by the arrows after the nodes

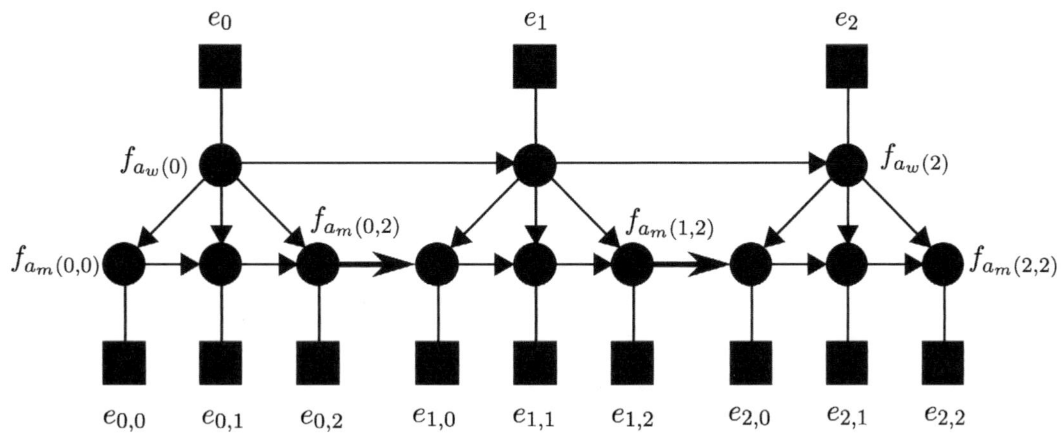

Figure 4: Multi-rate HMM graph.

representing $f_{a_m(0,2)}$ and $f_{a_m(1,2)}$. The circles represent the words and morphemes of the source language, the squares represent the words and morphemes of the target language. $e_{0,2}$ is the last morpheme of word e_0, and $e_{1,0}$ is the first morpheme of the next word e_1. $f_{a_m(1,0)}$ is conditioned on $f_{a_m(0,2)}$, which is in the previous word.

In order to model the morpheme sequence across words, we define the function $prev(j,k)$, which maps the morpheme position (j,k) to the previous morpheme position:

$$prev(j,k) = \begin{cases} (j, k-1) & \text{if } k > 1 \\ (j-1, |e_{j-1}|) & \text{if } k = 1 \end{cases}$$

If a morpheme is the first morpheme of a word, then the previous morpheme is the last morpheme of the previous word.

3.1 Transitions

3.1.1 Morpheme transitions

Before introducing the morpheme level transition probabilities, we first restrict morpheme level transitions according to the assumptions of our model. We consider only the morpheme alignment functions that are compatible with a word alignment function. If we allow unrestricted transitions between morphemes, then this would result in some morpheme alignments that do not allow a valid word alignment function.

To avoid this problem, we restrict the transition function as follows: at each time step, we allow transitions between morphemes in sentence $\mathbf{f}$ if the morphemes belong to the same word. This restriction reduces the transition matrix to a block diagonal matrix. The block diagonal matrix $\mathbf{A^b}$ below is a square matrix which has blocks of square matrices $\mathbf{A}_1 \cdots \mathbf{A}_n$ on the main diagonal, and the off-diagonal values are zero.

$$\mathbf{A^b} = \begin{bmatrix} \mathbf{A}_0 & 0 & \cdots & 0 \\ 0 & \mathbf{A}_1 & \cdots & 0 \\ \vdots & \vdots & \ddots & \vdots \\ 0 & 0 & \cdots & \mathbf{A}_n \end{bmatrix}$$

The square blocks $\mathbf{A}_0, \ldots, \mathbf{A}_n$ have the dimensions $|f_0|, \ldots, |f_n|$, the length of the words in sentence $\mathbf{f}$. In each step of the forward-backward algorithm, multiplying the forward (or backward) probability vectors with the block diagonal matrix restricts morpheme transitions to occur only within the words of sentence $\mathbf{f}$.

In order to model the morpheme sequence across words, we also allow transitions between morphemes across the words in sentence $\mathbf{f}$. However, we allow cross-word transitions only at certain time steps: between the last morpheme of a word in sentence $\mathbf{e}$ and the first morpheme of the next word in sentence $\mathbf{e}$. This does not result in morpheme alignments that do not allow a valid word alignment function. Instead of the block diagonal matrix $\mathbf{A^b}$, we use a transition matrix $\mathbf{A}$ which is not necessarily block diagonal, to model morpheme transitions across words.

In sum, we multiply the forward (or backward) probability vectors with either the transition matrix $\mathbf{A^b}$ or the transition matrix $\mathbf{A}$, depending on whether the transition is occurring at the last morpheme of a word in $\mathbf{e}$. We introduce the function $\delta(p,q,r,s)$ to indicate whether a transition is allowed from source position (p,q) to source position (r, s) when advancing one target position:

$$\delta(p,q,r,s) = \begin{cases} 1 & \text{if } p = r \text{ or } s = 1 \\ 0 & \text{otherwise} \end{cases}$$

Morpheme transition probabilities have four components. First, the δ function as described above. Second, the jump width:

$$\mathcal{J}(p,q,r,s) = abs(r,s) - abs(p,q)$$

where $abs(j,k)$ maps a word-relative morpheme position to an absolute morpheme position, i.e., to the simple left-to-right ordering of a morpheme in a sentence. Third, the morpheme class of the previous morpheme:[2]

$$\mathcal{M}(p,q) = Class(f_p^q)$$

Fourth, as the arrow from $f_{a_w(0)}$ to $f_{a_m(0,0)}$ in Figure 4 shows, there is a conditional dependence on the word class that the morpheme is in:

$$\mathcal{W}(r) = Class(f_r)$$

Putting together these components, the morpheme transitions are formulated as follows:

$$p(a_m(j,k) = (r,s) \mid a_m(prev(j,k)) = (p,q)) \propto p\big(\mathcal{J}(p,q,r,s) | \mathcal{M}(p,q), \mathcal{W}(r)\big)\ \delta(p,q,r,s) \quad (2)$$

The block diagonal matrix $\mathbf{A}^{\mathbf{b}}$ consists of morpheme transition probabilities.

3.1.2 Word transitions

In the multi-rate HMM, word transition probabilities have two components. First, the jump width:

$$\mathcal{J}(p,r) = r - p$$

Second, the word class of the previous word:

$$\mathcal{W}(p) = Class(f_p)$$

The jump width is conditioned on the word class of the previous word:

$$p(a_w(j) = r \mid a_w(j-1) = p) \propto p(\mathcal{J}(p,r) \mid \mathcal{W}(p)) \quad (3)$$

The transition matrix $\mathbf{A}$, which is not necessarily block diagonal, consists of values which are the product of a morpheme transition probability, as defined in Eqn. 2, and a word transition probability, as defined in Eqn. 3.

[2]We used the mkcls tool in GIZA (Och and Ney, 2003) to learn the word and the morpheme classes.

3.2 Probability of translating a sentence

Finally, putting together Eqn. 1, Eqn. 2 and Eqn. 3, we formulate the probability of translating a sentence $p(\mathbf{e}|\mathbf{f})$ as follows:

$$R_w \sum_{a_w} \prod_{j=1}^{|e|} \Bigg(t(e_j | f_{a_w(j)}) p(a_w(j) | a_w(j-1)) \; R_m \sum_{a_m} \prod_{k=1}^{|e_j|} t(e_{j,k} | f_{a_m(j,k)}) \; p(a_m(j,k) | a_m(prev(j,k))) \Bigg)$$

R_w is the same as it is in Eqn. 1, whereas $R_m = P(l_e|l_f)$. If we cancel out morpheme transitions by setting $p(a_m(j,k)|a_m(prev(j,k))) = 1/|f_{a_m(j,k)}|$, i.e., with a uniform distribution, then we get TAM with only word-level sequence modeling, which we call TAM-HMM.

The complexity of the multi-rate HMM is $O(m^3 n^3)$, where n is the number of words, and m is the number of morphemes per word. TAM-HMM differs from multi-rate HMM only by the lack of morpheme-level sequence modeling, and has complexity $O(m^2 n^3)$.

For the HMM to work correctly, we must handle jumping to and jumping from null positions. We learn the probabilities of jumping to a null position from the data. To compute the transition probability from a null position, we keep track of the nearest previous source word (or morpheme) that does not align to null, and use the position of the previous non-null word to calculate the jump width. In order to keep track of the previous non-null word, we insert a null word between words (Och and Ney, 2003). Similarly, we insert a null morpheme after every non-null morpheme.

3.3 Counts

We use Expectation Maximization (EM) to learn the word and morpheme translation probabilities, as well as the transition probabilities of the reordering model. This is done with forward-backward training at the morpheme level, collecting translation and transition counts for both the word and the morphemes from the morpheme-level trellis.

In Figure 5, the grid on the right depicts the morpheme-level trellis. The grid on the left is the abstraction of the word-level trellis over the

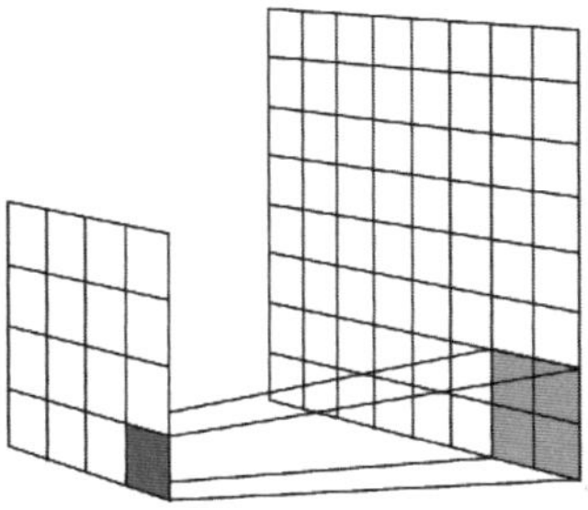

Figure 5: Multi-rate HMM trellis

morpheme-level trellis. For each target word e and for each source word f, there is a small HMM trellis with dimensions $|e| \times |f|$ inside the morpheme-level trellis, as shown by the shaded area inside the grid on the right. We collect counts for words by summing over the values in the small HMM trellis associated with the words.

3.3.1 Translation counts

Morpheme translation counts We compute expected counts over the morpheme-level trellis. The morpheme translation count function below collects expected counts for a morpheme pair (h, g) in a sentence pair $(\mathbf{e}, \mathbf{f})$:

$$c_m(h|g; \mathbf{e}, \mathbf{f}) = \sum_{\substack{(j,k) \\ \text{s.t.} \\ h=e_j^k}} \sum_{\substack{(p,q) \\ \text{s.t.} \\ g=f_p^q}} \gamma_{j,k}(p, q)$$

where $\gamma_{j,k}(p, q)$ stands for the posterior morpheme translation probabilities for source position (p, q) and target position (i, j) that are computed with the forward-backward algorithm.

Word translation counts For each target word e and source word f, we collect word translation counts by summing over posterior morpheme translation probabilities that are in the small trellis associated with e and f.

Since δ allows only within-word transitions to occur inside the small trellis, the posterior probability of observing the word e given the word f is preserved across time points within the small trellis associated with e and f. In other words, the sum of the posterior probabilities in each column of the small trellis is the same. Therefore, we collect word translation counts only from the last morphemes of the words in $\mathbf{e}$.

The word translation count function below collects expected counts from a sentence pair $(\mathbf{e}, \mathbf{f})$ for a particular source word f and target word e:

$$c_w(e|f; \mathbf{e}, \mathbf{f}) = \sum_{\substack{j \\ \text{s.t.} \\ e=e_j}} \sum_{\substack{p \\ \text{s.t.} \\ f=f_p}} \sum_{1 \leq q \leq |f|} \gamma_{j,|e|}(p, q)$$

3.3.2 Transition counts

Morpheme transition counts For all target positions (j, k) and all pairs of source positions (p, q) and (r, s), we compute morpheme transition posteriors:

$$\xi_{j,k}((p, q), (r, s))$$

using the forward-backward algorithm. These expected counts are accumulated to estimate the morpheme jump width probabilities $p(\mathcal{J}(p, q, r, s)|\mathcal{M}(p, q), \mathcal{W}(r))$ used in Eqn. 2.

Word transition counts We compute posterior probabilities for word transitions by summing over morpheme transition posteriors between the morphemes of the words f_l and f_n:

$$\xi_j(p, r) = \sum_{1 \leq q \leq |f_p|} \sum_{1 \leq s \leq |f_r|} \xi_{j,|e_j|}((p, q), (r, s))$$

Like the translation counts, the transition counts are collected from the last morphemes of words in $\mathbf{e}$. These expected counts are accumulated to estimate the word jump width probabilities $p(\mathcal{J}(p, r) \mid \mathcal{W}(p))$ used in Eqn. 3.

Finally, $R_m = P(l_e|l_f)$ does not cancel out in the counts of the multi-rate HMM. To compute the conditional probability $P(l_e|l_f)$, we assume that the length of word e varies according to a Poisson distribution with a mean that is linear with length of the word f (Brown et al., 1993).

3.4 Variational Bayes

In order to prevent overfitting, we use the Variational Bayes extension of the EM algorithm (Beal, 2003). This amounts to a small change to the M step of the original EM algorithm. We introduce Dirichlet priors α to perform an inexact normalization by applying the function $f(v) = \exp(\psi(v))$ to the expected counts collected in the E step, where ψ is the digamma function (Johnson, 2007). The M-step update for a multinomial parameter $\theta_{x|y}$ becomes:

$$\theta_{x|y} = \frac{f(E[c(x|y)] + \alpha)}{f(\sum_j E[c(x_j|y)] + \alpha)}$$

		Multi-rate HMM	TAM-HMM Word-Morph	TAM-HMM Morph only	WORD IBM 4	WORD Baseline
BLEU	TR to EN	**30.82**	29.48	29.98	29.13	27.91
	EN to TR	**23.09**	22.55	22.54	21.95	21.82
AER		0.254	0.255	0.256	0.375	0.370

Table 1: AER and BLEU Scores

We set α to 10^{-20}, a very low value, to have the effect of anti-smoothing, as low values of α cause the algorithm to favor words which co-occur frequently and to penalize words that co-occur rarely. We used Dirichlet priors on morpheme translation probabilities.

4 Experiments and Results

4.1 Data

We trained our model on a Turkish-English parallel corpus of approximately 50K sentences which have a maximum of 80 morphemes. Our parallel data consists mainly of documents in international relations and legal documents from sources such as the Turkish Ministry of Foreign Affairs, EU, etc. The Turkish data was first morphologically parsed (Oflazer, 1994), then disambiguated (Sak et al., 2007) to select the contextually salient interpretation of words. In addition, we removed morphological features that are not explicitly marked by an overt morpheme. For English, we use part-of-speech tagged data. The number of English words is 1,033,726 and the size of the English vocabulary is 28,647. The number of Turkish words is 812,374, the size of the Turkish vocabulary is 57,249. The number of Turkish morphemes is 1,484,673 and the size of the morpheme vocabulary is 16,713.

4.2 Experiments

We initialized our implementation of the single level 'word-only' model, which we call 'baseline' in Table 1, with 5 iterations of IBM Model 1, and further trained the HMM extension (Vogel et al., 1996) for 5 iterations. Similarly, we initialized TAM-HMM and multi-rate HMM with 5 iterations of TAM 1 as explained in Section 2.2. Then we trained TAM-HMM and the multi-rate HMM for 5 iterations. We also ran GIZA++ (IBM Model 1–4) on the data. We translated 1000 sentence test sets.

We used Dirichlet priors in both IBM Model 1 and TAM 1 training. We experimented with using Dirichlet priors on the HMM extensions of both IBM-HMM and TAM-HMM. We report the best results obtained for each model and translation direction.

We evaluated the performance of our model in two different ways. First, we evaluated against gold word alignments for 75 Turkish-English sentences. Table 1 shows the AER (Och and Ney, 2003) of the word alignments; we report the grow-diag-final (Koehn et al., 2003) of the Viterbi alignments. Second, we used the Moses toolkit (Koehn et al., 2007) to train machine translation systems from the Viterbi alignments of our various models, and evaluated the results with BLEU (Papineni et al., 2002).

In order to reduce the effect of nondeterminism, we run Moses three times per experiment setting, and report the highest BLEU scores obtained. Since the BLEU scores we obtained are close, we did a significance test on the scores (Koehn, 2004). In Table 1, the colors partition the table into equivalence classes: If two scores within the same row have different background colors, then the difference between their scores is statistically significant. The best scores in the leftmost column were obtained from multi-rate HMMs with Dirichlet priors only during the TAM 1 training. On the contrary, the best scores for TAM-HMM and the baseline-HMM were obtained with Dirichlet priors both during the TAM 1 and the TAM-HMM training. In Table 1, as the scores improve gradually towards the left, the background color gets gradually lighter, depicting the statistical significance of the improvements. The multi-rate HMM performs better than the TAM-HMM, which in turn performs better than the word-only models.

5 Conclusion

We presented a multi-rate HMM word alignment model, which models the word and the morpheme sequence simultaneously. We have tested our model on the Turkish-English pair and showed that our model is superior to the two-level word alignment model which has sequence modeling only at the word level.

Acknowledgments Partially funded by NSF award IIS-0910611. Kemal Oflazer acknowledges the generous support of the Qatar Foundation through Carnegie Mellon University's Seed Research program. The statements made herein are solely the responsibility of this author(s), and not necessarily that of Qatar Foundation.

References

Yaser Al-Onaizan, Jan Curin, Michael Jahr, Kevin Knight, John Lafferty, Dan Melamed, Franz-Josef Och, David Purdy, Noah A. Smith, and David Yarowsky. 1999. Statistical machine translation. Technical report, Final Report, JHU Summer Workshop.

Matthew J. Beal. 2003. *Variational Algorithms for Approximate Bayesian Inference*. Ph.D. thesis, University College London.

Peter F. Brown, Stephen A. Della Pietra, Vincent J. Della Pietra, and Robert L. Mercer. 1993. The mathematics of statistical machine translation: Parameter estimation. *Computational Linguistics*, 19(2):263–311.

Özgür Çetin, Mari Ostendorf, and Gary D. Bernard. 2007. Multirate coupled Hidden Markov Models and their application to machining tool-wear classification. *IEEE Transactions on Signal Processing*, 55(6):2885–2896, June.

Tagyoung Chung and Daniel Gildea. 2009. Unsupervised tokenization for machine translation. In *EMNLP*, pages 718–726.

Martin Čmejrek, Jan Cuřín, and Jiří Havelka. 2003. Czech-English dependency-based machine translation. In *EACL*, pages 83–90.

Matthew Crouse, Robert Nowak, and Richard Baraniuk. 1998. Wavelet-based statistical signal processing using Hidden Markov Models. *IEEE Transactions on Signal Processing*, 46(4):886–902.

Gülşen Eryiğit, Joakim Nivre, and Kemal Oflazer. 2008. Dependency parsing of Turkish. *Computational Linguistics*, 34(3):357–389.

Elif Eyigöz, Daniel Gildea, and Kemal Oflazer. 2013. Simultaneous word-morpheme alignment for statistical machine translation. In *NAACL*.

Shai Fine, Yoram Singer, and Naftali Tishby. 1998. The hierarchical Hidden Markov model: Analysis and applications. *Machine Learning*, 32(1):41–62, July.

Sharon Goldwater and David McClosky. 2005. Improving statistical MT through morphological analysis. In *HLT-EMNLP*.

Mark Johnson. 2007. Why doesn't EM find good HMM POS-taggers? In *EMNLP-CoNLL*, pages 296–305, Prague, Czech Republic, June. Association for Computational Linguistics.

Philipp Koehn, Franz Josef Och, and Daniel Marcu. 2003. Statistical phrase-based translation. In *HLT-NAACL*.

Philipp Koehn, Hieu Hoang, Alexandra Birch, Chris Callison-Burch, Marcello Federico, Nicola Bertoldi, Brooke Cowan, Wade Shen, Christine Moran, Richard Zens, Chris Dyer, Ondrej Bojar, Alexandra Constantin, and Evan Herbst. 2007. Moses: Open source toolkit for statistical machine translation. In *ACL*, pages 177–180.

Philipp Koehn. 2004. Statistical significance tests for machine translation evaluation. In *EMNLP*, pages 388–395.

Young-suk Lee. 2004. Morphological analysis for statistical machine translation. In *HLT-NAACL*, pages 57–60.

Jia Li, Robert Gray, and Richard Olshen. 2006. Multiresolution image classification by hierarchical modeling with two-dimensional Hidden Markov Models. *IEEE Transactions on Information Theory*, 46(5):1826–1841, September.

Mark R. Luettgen, William C. Karl, Alan S. Willsky, and Robert R. Tenney. 1993. Multiscale representations of Markov Random Fields. *IEEE Transactions on Signal Processing*, 41(12):3377–3396.

Sonja Niessen and Hermann Ney. 2000. Improving SMT quality with morpho-syntactic analysis. In *COLING*, pages 1081–1085.

Franz Josef Och and Hermann Ney. 2003. A systematic comparison of various statistical alignment Models. *Computational Linguistics*, 29(1):19–51.

Kemal Oflazer, Bilge Say, Dilek Z. Hakkani-Tür, and Gökhan Tür. 2003. Building a Turkish treebank. In A. Abeillé, editor, *Treebanks: Building and Using Parsed Corpora*, pages 261–277. Kluwer, London.

Kemal Oflazer. 1994. Two-level description of Turkish morphology. *Literary and Linguistic Computing*, 9(2).

Kishore Papineni, Salim Roukos, Todd Ward, and Wei-Jing Zhu. 2002. BLEU: A method for automatic evaluation of machine translation. In *Proceedings of the 40th Annual Conference of the Association for Computational Linguistics (ACL-02)*, pages 311–318.

Haşim Sak, Tunga Güngör, and Murat Saraçlar. 2007. Morphological disambiguation of Turkish text with perceptron algorithm. In *CICLing*, pages 107–118.

Marios Skounakis, Mark Craven, and Soumya Ray. 2003. Hierarchical Hidden Markov Models for information extraction. In *International Joint Conference on Artificial Intelligence*, volume 18, pages 427–433.

Georgios Theocharous, Khashayar Rohanimanesh, and Sridhar Maharlevan. 2001. Learning hierarchical observable Markov decision process Models for robot navigation. In *ICRA 2001*, volume 1, pages 511–516.

Stephan Vogel, Hermann Ney, and Christoph Tillmann. 1996. HMM-based word alignment in statistical translation. In *COLING*, pages 836–841.

Alan S. Willsky. 2002. Multiresolution Markov Models for signal and image processing. In *Proceedings of the IEEE*, pages 1396–1458.

Reyyan Yeniterzi and Kemal Oflazer. 2010. Syntax-to-morphology mapping in factored phrase-based statistical machine translation from English to Turkish. In *ACL 2010*, pages 454–464.

Hidden Markov Tree Model for Word Alignment

Shuhei Kondo **Kevin Duh** **Yuji Matsumoto**
Graduate School of Information Science
Nara Institute of Science and Technology
8916-5, Takayama, Ikoma, Nara, 630-0192, Japan
{shuhei-k,kevinduh,matsu}@is.naist.jp

Abstract

We propose a novel unsupervised word alignment model based on the Hidden Markov Tree (HMT) model. Our model assumes that the alignment variables have a tree structure which is isomorphic to the target dependency tree and models the distortion probability based on the source dependency tree, thereby incorporating the syntactic structure from both sides of the parallel sentences. In English-Japanese word alignment experiments, our model outperformed an IBM Model 4 baseline by over 3 points alignment error rate. While our model was sensitive to posterior thresholds, it also showed a performance comparable to that of HMM alignment models.

1 Introduction

Automatic word alignment is the first step in the pipeline of statistical machine translation. Translation models are usually extracted from word-aligned bilingual corpora, and lexical translation probabilities based on word alignment models are also used for translation.

The most widely used models are the IBM Model 4 (Brown et al., 1993) and Hidden Markov Models (HMM) (Vogel et al., 1996). These models assume that alignments are largely monotonic, possibly with a few jumps. While such assumption might be adequate for alignment between similar languages, it does not necessarily hold between a pair of distant languages like English and Japanese.

Recently, several models have focused on incorporating syntactic structures into word alignment. As an extension to the HMM alignment, Lopez and Resnik (2005) present a distortion model conditioned on the source-side dependency tree, and DeNero and Klein (2007) propose a distortion model based on the path through the source-side phrase-structure tree. Some supervised models receive syntax trees as their input and use them to generate features and to guide the search (Riesa and Marcu, 2010; Riesa et al., 2011), and other models learn a joint model for parsing and word alignment from word-aligned parallel trees (Burkett et al., 2010). In the context of phrase-to-phrase alignment, Nakazawa and Kurohashi (2011) propose a Bayesian subtree alignment model trained with parallel sampling. None of these models, however, can incorporate syntactic structures from both sides of the language pair and can be trained computationally efficiently in an unsupervised manner at the same time.

The Hidden Markov Tree (HMT) model (Crouse et al., 1998) is one such model that satisfies the above-mentioned properties. The HMT model assumes a tree structure of the hidden variables, which fits well with the notion of word-to-word dependency, and it can be trained from unlabeled data via the EM algorithm with the same order of time complexity as HMMs.

In this paper, we propose a novel word alignment model based on the HMT model and show that it naturally enables unsupervised training based on both source and target dependency trees in a tractable manner. We also compare our HMT word alignment model with the IBM Model 4 and the HMM alignment models in terms of the standard alignment error rates on a publicly available English-Japanese dataset.

2 IBM Model 1 and HMM Alignment

We briefly review the IBM Model 1 (Brown et al., 1993) and the Hidden Markov Model (HMM) word alignment (Vogel et al., 1996) in this section. Both are probabilistic generative models that factor as

$$p(\mathbf{f}|\mathbf{e}) = \sum_{\mathbf{a}} p(\mathbf{a}, \mathbf{f}|\mathbf{e})$$

$$p(\mathbf{a}, \mathbf{f}|\mathbf{e}) = \prod_{j=1}^{J} p_d(a_j|a_{j\_})p_t(f_j|e_{a_j})$$

where $\mathbf{e} = \{e_1, ..., e_I\}$ is an English (source) sentence and $\mathbf{f} = \{f_1, ..., f_J\}$ is a foreign (target) sentence. $\mathbf{a} = \{a_1, ..., a_J\}$ is an alignment vector such that $a_j = i$ indicates the j-th target word aligns to the i-th source word and $a_j = 0$ means the j-th target word is null-aligned. $j\_$ is the index of the last non null-aligned target word before the index j.

In both models, $p_t(f_j|e_{a_j})$ is the lexical translation probability and can be defined as conditional probability distributions. As for the distortion probability $p_d(a_j|a_{j\_})$, $p_d(a_j = 0|a_{j\_} = i') = p_0$ where p_0 is NULL probability in both models. $p_d(a_j = i|a_{j\_} = i')$ is uniform in the Model 1 and proportional to the relative count $c(i - i')$ in the HMM for $i \neq 0$. DeNero and Klein (2007) proposed a syntax-sensitive distortion model for the HMM alignment, in which the distortion probability depends on the path from the i-th word to the i'-th word on the source-side phrase-structure tree, instead of the linear distance between the two words.

These models can be trained efficiently using the EM algorithm. In practice, models in two directions (source to target and target to source) are trained and then symmetrized by taking their intersection, union or using other heuristics. Liang et al. (2006) proposed a joint objective of alignment models in both directions and the probability of agreement between them, and an EM-like algorithm for training.

They also proposed posterior thresholding for decoding and symmetrization, which take

$$\mathbf{a} = \{(i, j) : p(a_j = i|\mathbf{f}, \mathbf{e}) > \tau\}$$

with a threshold τ. DeNero and Klein (2007) summarized some criteria for posterior thresholding, which are

- Soft-Union

$$\sqrt{p_f(a_j = i|\mathbf{f}, \mathbf{e}) \cdot p_r(a_i = j|\mathbf{f}, \mathbf{e})}$$

- Soft-Intersection

$$\frac{p_f(a_j = i|\mathbf{f}, \mathbf{e}) + p_r(a_i = j|\mathbf{f}, \mathbf{e})}{2}$$

- Hard-Union

$$max(p_f(a_j = i|\mathbf{f}, \mathbf{e}), p_r(a_i = j|\mathbf{f}, \mathbf{e}))$$

- Hard-Intersection

$$min(p_f(a_j = i|\mathbf{f}, \mathbf{e}), p_r(a_i = j|\mathbf{f}, \mathbf{e}))$$

where $p_f(a_j = i|\mathbf{f}, \mathbf{e})$ is the alignment probability under the source-to-target model and $p_r(a_i = j|\mathbf{f}, \mathbf{e})$ is the one under the target-to-source model.

They also propose a posterior decoding heuristic called *competitive thresholding*. Given a $j \times i$ matrix of combined weights c and a threshold τ, it choose a link (j, i) only if its weight $c_{ji} \geq \tau$ and it is connected to the link with the maximum weight both in row j and column i.

3 Hidden Markov Tree Model

The Hidden Markov Tree (HMT) model was first introduced by Crouse et al. (1998). Though it has been applied successfully to various applications such as image segmentation (Choi and Baraniuk, 2001), denoising (Portilla et al., 2003) and biology (Durand et al., 2005), it is largely unnoticed in the field of natural language processing. To the best of our knowledge, the only exception is Žabokrtský and Popel (2009) who used a variant of the Viterbi algorithm for HMTs in the transfer phase of a deep-syntax based machine translation system.

An HMT model consists of an observed random tree $\mathbf{X} = \{x_1, ..., x_N\}$ and a hidden random tree $\mathbf{S} = \{s_1, ..., s_N\}$, which is isomorphic to the observed tree.

The parameters of the model are

- $P(s_1 = j)$, the initial hidden state prior
- $P(s_t = j|s_{\rho(t)} = i)$, transition probabilities
- $P(x_t = h|s_t = j)$, emission probabilities,

where $\rho()$ is a function that maps the index of a hidden node to the index of its parent node. These parameters can be trained via the EM algorithm.

The "upward-downward" algorithm proposed in Crouse et al. (1998), an HMT analogue of the forward-backward algorithm for HMMs, can be used in the E-step. However, it is based on the decomposition of joint probabilities and suffers from numerical underflow problems.

Durand et al. (2004) proposed a smoothed variant of the upward-downward algorithm, which is based on the decomposition of smoothed probabilities and immune to underflow. In the next section, we will explain this variant in the context of word alignment.

4 Hidden Markov Tree Word Alignment

We present a novel word alignment model based on the HMT model. Given a target sentence $\mathbf{f} = \{f_1, ..., f_J\}$ with a dependency tree $\mathbf{F}$ and a source sentence $\mathbf{e} = \{e_1, ..., e_I\}$ with a dependency tree $\mathbf{E}$, an HMT word alignment model factors as

$$p(\mathbf{f}|\mathbf{e}) = \sum_{\mathbf{a}} p(\mathbf{a}, \mathbf{f}|\mathbf{e})$$

$$p(\mathbf{a}, \mathbf{f}|\mathbf{e}) = \prod_{j=1}^{J} p_d(a_j|a_{j\_})p_t(f_j|e_{a_j}).$$

While these equations appear identical to the ones for the HMM alignment, they are different in that 1) $\mathbf{e}$, $\mathbf{f}$ and $\mathbf{a}$ are not chain-structured but tree-structured, and 2) $j\_$ is the index of the non null-aligned *lowest ancestor* of the j-th target word[1], rather than that of the last non null-aligned word preceding the j-th word as in the HMM alignment. Note that $\mathbf{A}$, the tree composed of alignment variables $\mathbf{a} = \{a_1, ..., a_J\}$, is isomorphic to the target dependency tree $\mathbf{F}$.

Figure 1 shows an example of a target dependency tree with an alignment tree, and a source dependency tree. Note that English is the target (or foreign) language and Japanese is the source (or English) language here. We introduce the following notations following Durand et al. (2004), slightly modified to better match the context of word alignment.

- $\rho(j)$ denotes the index of the head of the j-th target word.
- $c(j)$ denotes the set of indices of the dependents of the j-th target word.
- $\overline{\mathbf{F}}_j = \overline{\boldsymbol{f}}_j$ denotes the target dependency subtree rooted at the j-th word.

As for the parameters of the model, the initial hidden state prior described in Section 3 can be defined by assuming an artificial ROOT node for both dependency trees, forcing the target ROOT node to be aligned only to the source ROOT node and prohibiting other target nodes from being aligned to the source ROOT node. The lexical translation probability $p_t(f_j|e_{a_j})$, which corresponds to the emission probability, can be defined as conditional probability distributions just like in the IBM Model 1 and the HMM alignment.

The distortion probability $p_d(a_j = i|a_{j\_} = i')$, which corresponds to the transition probability, depends on the distance between the i-th source word and the i'-th source word on the source dependency tree $\mathbf{E}$, which we denote $d(i, i')$ hereafter. We model the dependence of $p_d(a_j = i|a_{j\_} = i')$ on $d(i, i')$ with the counts $c(d(i, i'))$.

In our model, $d(i, i')$ is represented by a pair of non-negative distances $(up, down)$, where up is the distance between the i-th word and the lowest common ancestor (*lca*) of the two words, $down$ is the one between the i'-th word and the *lca*. For example in Figure 1b, $d(0, 2) = (0, 4)$, $d(2, 5) = (2, 2)$ and $d(4, 7) = (3, 0)$. In practice, we clip the distance by a fixed window size w and store $c(d(i, i'))$ in a two-dimensional $(w + 1) \times (w + 1)$ matrix. When $w = 3$, for example, the distance $d(0, 2) = (0, 3)$ after clipping.

We can use the smoothed variant of upward-downward algorithm (Durand et al., 2004) for the E-step of the EM algorithm. We briefly explain the smoothed upward-downward algorithm in the context of tree-to-tree word alignment below. For the detailed derivation, see Durand et al. (2004).

In the smoothed upward-downward algorithm, we first compute the state marginal probabilities

$$p(a_j = i) = \sum_{i'} p(a_{\rho(j)} = i')p_d(a_j = i|a_{\rho(j)} = i')$$

for each target node and each state, where

$$p_d(a_j = i|a_{\rho(j)} = i') = p_0$$

if the j-th word is null-aligned, and

$$p_d(a_j = i|a_{\rho(j)} = i') = (1 - p_0) \cdot \frac{c(d(i', i))}{\sum_{i'' \neq 0} c(d(i', i''))}$$

if the j-th word is aligned. Note that we must artificially normalize $p_d(a_j = i|a_{\rho(j)} = i')$, because unlike in the case of the linear distance, multiple words can have the same distance from the j-th word on a dependency tree.

[1] This dependence on $a_{j\_}$ can be implemented as a first-order HMT, analogously to the case of the HMM alignment (Och and Ney, 2003).

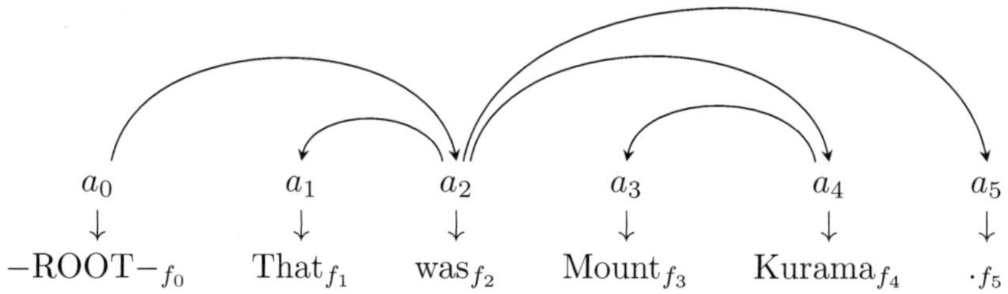

(a) Target sentence with its dependency/alignment tree. Target words $\{f_0, ..., f_5\}$ are emitted from alignment variables $\{a_0, ..., a_5\}$. Ideally, $a_0 = 0, a_1 = 1, a_2 = 7, a_3 = 5, a_4 = 4$ and $a_5 = 9$.

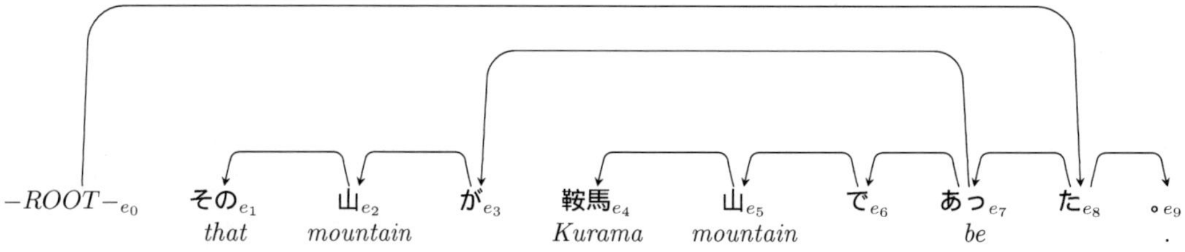

(b) Source sentence with its dependency tree. None of the target words are aligned to e_2, e_3, e_6 and e_8.

Figure 1: An example of sentence pair under the Hidden Markov Tree word alignment model. If we ignore the source words to which no target words are aligned, the dependency structures look similar to each other.

In the next phase, the upward recursion, we compute $p(a_j = i|\overline{\mathbf{F}}_j = \overline{\boldsymbol{f}}_j)$ in a bottom-up manner. First, we initialize the upward recursion for each leaf by

$$\begin{aligned}\beta_j(i) &= p(a_j = i|F_j = f_j) \\ &= \frac{p_t(f_j|e_i)p(a_j = i)}{N_j},\end{aligned}$$

where

$$N_j = p(F_j = f_j) = \sum_i p_t(f_j|e_i)p(a_j = i).$$

Then, we proceed from the leaf to the root with the following recursion,

$$\begin{aligned}\beta_j(i) &= p(a_j = i|\overline{\mathbf{F}}_j = \overline{\boldsymbol{f}}_j) \\ &= \frac{\{\prod_{j' \in c(j)} \beta_{j,j'}(i)\}p_t(f_j|e_i)p(a_j = i)}{N_j},\end{aligned}$$

where

$$\begin{aligned}N_j &= \frac{p(\overline{\mathbf{F}}_j = \overline{\boldsymbol{f}}_j)}{\prod_{j' \in c(j)} p(\overline{\mathbf{F}}_{j'} = \overline{\boldsymbol{f}}_{j'})} \\ &= \sum_i \{\prod_{j' \in c(j)} \beta_{j,j'}(i)\}p_t(f_j|e_i)p(a_j = i)\end{aligned}$$

and

$$\begin{aligned}\beta_{\rho(j),j}(i) &= \frac{p(\overline{\mathbf{F}}_j = \overline{\boldsymbol{f}}_j|a_{\rho(j)} = i)}{p(\overline{\mathbf{F}}_j = \overline{\boldsymbol{f}}_j)} \\ &= \sum_{i'} \frac{\beta_j(i')p_d(a_j = i'|a_{\rho(j)} = i)}{p(a_j = i')}.\end{aligned}$$

After the upward recursion is completed, we compute $p(a_j = i|\overline{\mathbf{F}}_0 = \overline{\boldsymbol{f}}_0)$ in the downward recursion. It is initialized at the root node by

$$\xi_0(i) = p(a_0 = i|\overline{\mathbf{F}}_0 = \overline{\boldsymbol{f}}_0).$$

Then we proceed in a top-down manner, computing

$$\begin{aligned}&\xi_j(i) = p(a_j = i|\overline{\mathbf{F}}_0 = \overline{\boldsymbol{f}}_0) \\ &= \frac{\beta_j(i)}{p(a_j = i)} \cdot \\ &\sum_{i'} \frac{p_d(a_j = i|a_{\rho(j)} = i')\xi_{\rho(j)}(i')}{\beta_{\rho(j),j}(i')}.\end{aligned}$$

for each node and each state.

The conditional probabilities

$$\begin{aligned}&p(a_j = i, a_{\rho(j)} = i'|\overline{\mathbf{F}}_0 = \overline{\boldsymbol{f}}_0) \\ &= \frac{\beta_j(i)p_d(a_j = i|a_{\rho(j)} = i')\xi_{\rho(j)}(i')}{p(a_j = i)\beta_{\rho(j),j}(i')},\end{aligned}$$

which is used for the estimation of distortion probabilities, can be extracted during the downward recursion.

In the M-step, the lexical translation model can be updated with

$$p_t(f|e) = \frac{c(f,e)}{c(e)},$$

just like the IBM Models and HMM alignments, where $c(f,e)$ and $c(e)$ are the count of the word pair (f,e) and the source word e. However, the update for the distortion model is a bit complicated, because the matrix that stores $c(d(i,i'))$ does not represent a probability distribution. To approximate the maximum likelihood estimation, we divide the counts $c(d(i,i'))$ calculated during the E-step by the number of distortions that have the distance $d(i,i')$ in the training data. Then we normalize the matrix by

$$c(d(i,i')) = \frac{c(d(i,i'))}{\sum_{i=0}^{\mathbf{W}} \sum_{i'=0}^{\mathbf{W}} c(d(i,i'))}.$$

Given initial parameters for the lexical translation model and the distortion counts, an HMT aligner collects the expected counts $c(f,e)$, $c(e)$ and $c(d(i,i'))$ with the upward-downward algorithm in the E-step and re-estimate the parameters in the M-Step. Dependency trees for the sentence pairs in the training data remain unchanged during the training procedure.

5 Experiment

We evaluate the performance of our HMT alignment model in terms of the standard alignment error rate[2] (AER) on a publicly available English-Japanese dataset, and compare it with the IBM Model 4 (Brown et al., 1993) and HMM alignment with distance-based (HMM) and syntax-based (S-HMM) distortion models (Vogel et al., 1996; Liang et al., 2006; DeNero and Klein, 2007).

We use the data from the Kyoto Free Translation Task (KFTT) version 1.3 (Neubig, 2011). Table 1 shows the corpus statistics. Note that these numbers are slightly different from the ones observed under the dataset's default training procedure because of the difference in the preprocessing scheme, which is explained below.

[2]Given sure alignments S and possible alignments P, the alignment error rate of alignments A is $1 - \frac{|A \cap S| + |A \cap P|}{|A| + |S|}$ (Och and Ney, 2003).

The tuning set of the KFTT has manual alignments. As the KFTT doesn't distinguish between sure and possible alignments, F-measure equals $1 - \text{AER}$ on this dataset.

5.1 Preprocessing

We tokenize the English side of the data using the Stanford Tokenizer[3] and parse it with the Berkeley Parser[4] (Petrov et al., 2006). We use the phrase-structure trees for the Berkeley Aligner's syntactic distortion model, and convert them to dependency trees for our dependency-based distortion model[5]. As the Berkeley Parser couldn't parse 7 (out of about 330K) sentences in the training data, we removed those lines from both sides of the data. All the sentences in the other sets were parsed successfully.

For the Japanese side of the data, we first concatenate the function words in the tokenized sentences using a script[6] published by the author of the dataset. Then we re-segment and POS-tag them using MeCab[7] version 0.996 and parse them using CaboCha[8] version 0.66 (Kudo and Matsumoto, 2002), both with UniDic. Finally, we modify the CoNLL-format output of CaboCha where some kind of symbols such as punctuation marks and parentheses have dependent words. We chose this procedure for a reasonable compromise between the dataset's default tokenization and the dependency parser we use.

As we cannot use the default gold alignment due to the difference in preprocessing, we use a script[9] published by the author of the dataset to modify the gold alignment so that it better matches the new tokenization.

5.2 Training

We initialize our models in two directions with jointly trained IBM Model 1 parameters (5 iterations) and train them independently for 5 iterations

[3]`http://nlp.stanford.edu/software/`

[4]We use the model trained on the WSJ portion of Ontonotes (Hovy et al., 2006) with the default setting.

[5]We use Stanford's tool (de Marneffe et al., 2006) with options `-conllx -basic -makeCopulaHead -keepPunct` for conversion.

[6]`https://github.com/neubig/util-scripts/blob/master/combine-predicate.pl`

[7]`http://code.google.com/p/mecab/`

[8]`http://code.google.com/p/cabocha/`

[9]`https://github.com/neubig/util-scripts/blob/master/adjust-alignments.pl`

	Sentences	English Tokens	Japanese Tokens
Train	329,974	5,912,543	5,893,334
Dev	1,166	24,354	26,068
Tune	1,235	30,839	33,180
Test	1,160	26,730	27,693

Table 1: Corpus statistics of the KFTT.

	Precision	Recall	AER
HMT (Proposed)	71.77	55.23	37.58
IBM Model 4	60.58	57.71	40.89
HMM	69.59	56.15	37.85
S-HMM	71.60	56.14	37.07

Table 2: Alignment error rates (AER) based on each model's peak performance.

with window size $w = 4$ for the distortion model. The entire training procedure takes around 4 hours on a 3.3 GHz Xeon CPU.

We train the IBM Model 4 using GIZA++ (Och and Ney, 2003) with the training script of the Moses toolkit (Koehn et al., 2007).

The HMM and S-HMM alignment models are initialized with jointly trained IBM Model 1 parameters (5 iterations) and trained independently for 5 iterations using the Berkeley Aligner. We find that though initialization with jointly trained IBM Model 1 parameters is effective, joint training of HMM alignment models harms the performance on this dataset (results not shown).

5.3 Result

We use posterior thresholding for the HMT and HMM alignment models, and the *grow-diag-final-and* heuristic for the IBM Model 4.

Table 2 and Figure 2 show the result. As the Soft-Union criterion performed best, we don't show the results based on other criteria. On the other hand, as the peak performance of the HMT model is better with competitive thresholding and those of HMM models are better without it, we compare Precision/Recall curves and AER curves both between the same strategy and the best performing strategy for each model.

As shown in Table 2, the peak performance of the HMT alignment model is better than that of the IBM Model 4 by over 3 point AER, and it was somewhere between the HMM and the S-HMM. Taking into account that our distortion model is simpler than that of S-HMM, these results seem natural, and it would be reasonable to expect that replacing our distortion model with more sophisticated one might improve the performance.

When we look at Precision/Recall curves and AER curves in Figures 2a and 2d, the HMT model is performing slightly better in the range of 50 to 60 % precision and 0.15 to 0.35 posterior threshold with the Soft-Union strategy. Results in Figures 2b and 2e show that the HMT model performs better around the range around 60 to 70 precision and it corresponds to 0.2 to 0.4 posterior threshold with the competitive thresholding heuristic. In addition, results on both strategies show that performance curve of the HMT model is more peaked than those of HMM alignment models.

We suspect that a part of the reason behind such behavior can be attributed to the fact that the HMT model's distortion model is more uniform than that of HMM models. For example, in our model, all sibling nodes have the same distortion probability from their parent node. This is in contrast with the situation in HMM models, where nodes within a fixed distance have different distortion probabilities. With more uniform distortion probabilities, many links for a target word may have a considerable amount of posterior probability. If that is true, too many links will be above the threshold when it is set low, and too few links can exceed the threshold when it is set high. More sophisticated distortion model may help mitigate such sensitivity to the posterior threshold.

6 Related Works

Lopez and Resnik (2005) consider an HMM model with distortions based on the distance in dependency trees, which is quite similar to our model's distance. DeNero and Klein (2007) propose another HMM model with syntax-based distortions based on the path through constituency trees, which improves translation rule extraction for tree-to-string transducers. Both models as-

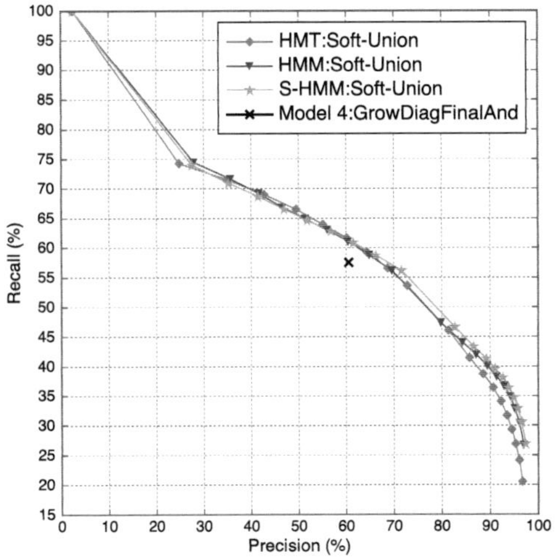

(a) Precision/Recall Curve with Soft-Union.

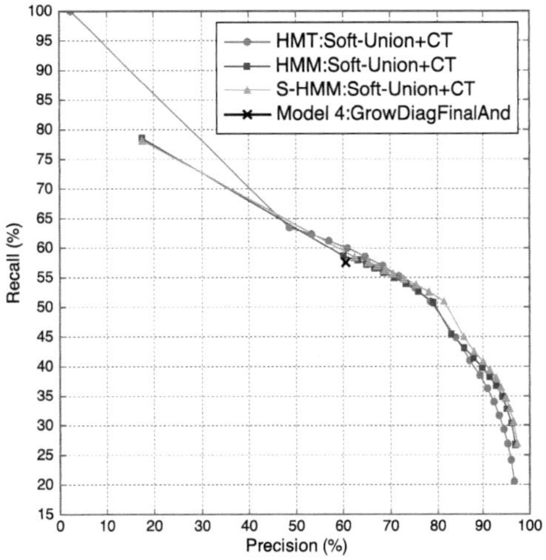

(b) Precision/Recall Curve with Soft-Union + Competitive Thresholding.

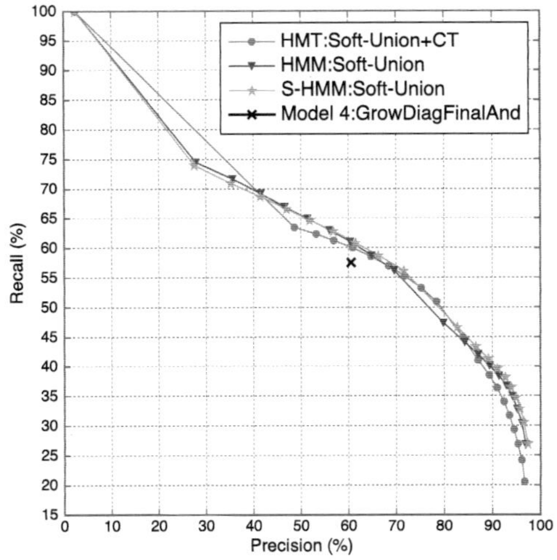

(c) Precision/Recall Curve with the Best Strategy.

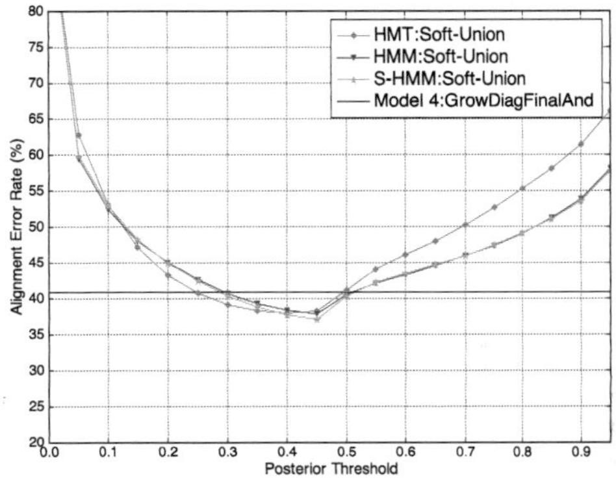

(d) Alignment Error Rate with Soft-Union.

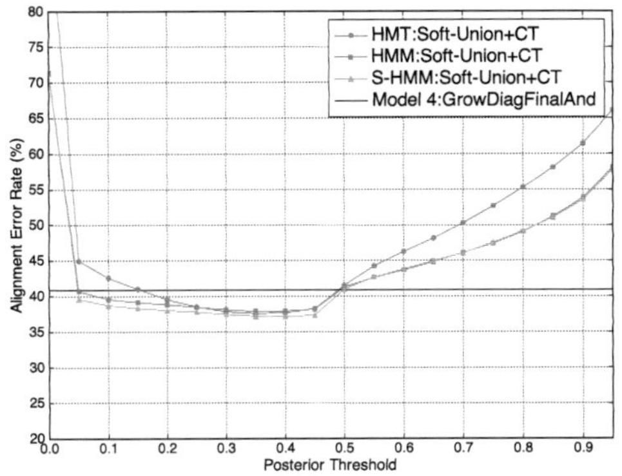

(e) Precision/Recall Curve with Soft-Union + Competitive Thresholding.

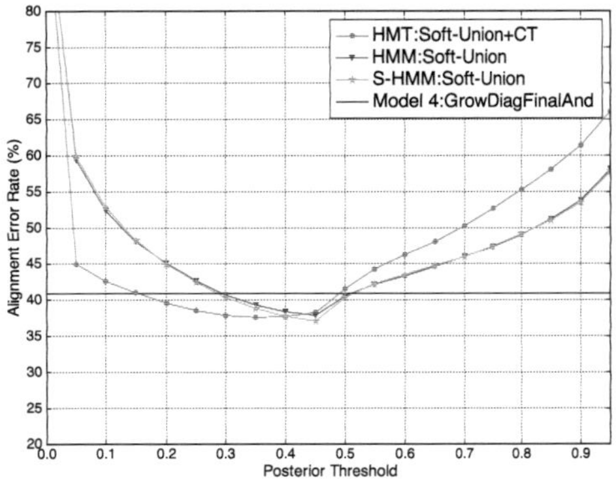

(f) Alignment Error Rate with with the Best Strategy.

Figure 2: Precision/Recall Curve and Alignment Error Rate with Different Models and Strategies.

sume a chain structure for hidden variables (alignment) as opposed to a tree structure as in our model, and condition distortions on the syntactic structure only in one direction.

Nakazawa and Kurohashi (2011) propose a dependency-based phrase-to-phrase alignment model with a sophisticated generative story, which leads to an increase in computational complexity and requires parallel sampling for training.

Several supervised, discriminative models use syntax structures to generate features and to guide the search (Burkett et al., 2010; Riesa and Marcu, 2010; Riesa et al., 2011). Such efforts are orthogonal to ours in the sense that discriminative alignment models generally use statistics obtained by unsupervised, generative models as features and can benefit from their improvement. It would be interesting to incorporate statistics of the HMT word alignment model into such discriminative models.

Žabokrtský and Popel (2009) use HMT models for the transfer phase in a tree-based MT system. While our model assumes that the tree structure of alignment variables is isomorphic to target side's dependency tree, they assume that the deep-syntactic tree of the target side is isomorphic to that of the source side. The parameters of the HMT model is given and not learned by the model itself.

7 Conclusion

We have proposed a novel word alignment model based on the Hidden Markov Tree (HMT) model, which can incorporate the syntactic structures of both sides of the language into unsupervised word alignment in a tractable manner. Experiments on an English-Japanese dataset show that our model performs better than the IBM Model 4 and comparably to the HMM alignment models in terms of alignment error rates. It is also shown that the HMT model with a simple tree-based distortion is sensitive to posterior thresholds, perhaps due to the flat distortion probabilities.

As the next step, we plan to improve the distortion component of our HMT alignment model. Something similar to the syntax-sensitive distortion model of DeNero and Klein (2007) might be a good candidate.

It is also important to see the effect of our model on the downstream translation. Applying our model to recently proposed models that directly incorporate dependency structures, such as string-to-dependency (Shen et al., 2008) and dependency-to-string (Xie et al., 2011) models, would be especially interesting.

Last but not least, though the dependency structures don't pose a hard restriction on the alignment in our model, it is highly likely that parse errors have negative effects on the alignment accuracy. One way to estimate the effect of parse errors on the accuracy is to parse the input sentences with inferior models, for example trained on a limited amount of training data. Moreover, preserving some ambiguities using k-best trees or shared forests might help mitigate the effect of 1-best parse errors.

Acknowledgments

We thank anonymous reviewers for insightful suggestions and comments.

References

Peter F. Brown, Vincent J. Della Pietra, Stephen A. Della Pietra, and Robert L. Mercer. 1993. The Mathematics of Statistical Machine Translation: Parameter Estimation. *Computational linguistics*, 19(2):263–311.

David Burkett, John Blitzer, and Dan Klein. 2010. Joint Parsing and Alignment with Weakly Synchronized Grammars. In *Proceedings of NAACL HLT 2010*, pages 127–135.

Hyeokho Choi and Richard G. Baraniuk. 2001. Multiscale Image Segmentation Using Wavelet-Domain Hidden Markov Models. *IEEE Transactions on Image Processing*, 10(9):1309–1321.

Matthew S. Crouse, Robert D. Nowak, and Richard G. Baraniuk. 1998. Wavelet-Based Statistical Signal Processing Using Hidden Markov Models. *IEEE Transactions on Signal Processing*, 46(4):886–902.

Marie-Catherine de Marneffe, Bill MacCartney, and Christopher D. Manning. 2006. Generating Typed Dependency Parses from Phrase Structure Parses. In *Proceedings of LREC'06*, pages 449–454.

John DeNero and Dan Klein. 2007. Tailoring Word Alignments to Syntactic Machine Translation. In *Proceedings of ACL 2007*, pages 17–24.

Jean-Baptiste Durand, Paulo Gonçalvès, and Yann Guédon. 2004. Computational Methods for Hidden Markov Tree Models-An Application to Wavelet Trees. *IEEE Transactions on Signal Processing*, 52(9):2551–2560.

J.-B. Durand, Y. Guédon, Y. Caraglio, and E. Costes. 2005. Analysis of the plant architecture via tree-structured statistical models: the hidden Markov tree models. *New Phytologist*, 166(3):813–825.

Eduard Hovy, Mitchell Marcus, Martha Palmer, Lance Ramshaw, and Ralph Weischedel. 2006. OntoNotes: The 90% Solution. In *Proceedings of HLT-NAACL 2006, Short Papers*, pages 57–60.

Philipp Koehn, Hieu Hoang, Alexandra Birch, Chris Callison-Burch, Marcello Federico, Nicola Bertoldi, Brooke Cowan, Wade Shen, Christine Moran, Richard Zens, Chris Dyer, Ondřej Bojar, Alexandra Constantin, and Evan Herbst. 2007. Moses: Open Source Toolkit for Statistical Machine Translation. In *Proceedings of ACL 2007, Demonstration Session*, pages 177–180.

Taku Kudo and Yuji Matsumoto. 2002. Japanese Dependency Analysis using Cascaded Chunking. In *Proceedings of CoNLL-2002*, pages 63–69.

Percy Liang, Ben Taskar, and Dan Klein. 2006. Alignment by Agreement. In *Proceedings of HLT-NAACL 2006*, pages 104–111.

Adam Lopez and Philip Resnik. 2005. Improved HMM Alignment Models for Languages with Scarce Resources. In *Proceedings of the ACL Workshop on Building and Using Parallel Texts*, pages 83–86.

Toshiaki Nakazawa and Sadao Kurohashi. 2011. Bayesian Subtree Alignment Model based on Dependency Trees. In *Proceedings of IJCNLP 2011*, pages 794–802.

Graham Neubig. 2011. The Kyoto Free Translation Task. http://www.phontron.com/kftt.

Franz Josef Och and Hermann Ney. 2003. A Systematic Comparison of Various Statistical Alignment Models. *Computational linguistics*, 29(1):19–51.

Slav Petrov, Leon Barrett, Romain Thibaux, and Dan Klein. 2006. Learning Accurate, Compact, and Interpretable Tree Annotation. In *Proceedings of COLING/ACL 2006*, pages 433–440.

Javier Portilla, Vasily Strela, Martin J. Wainwright, and Eero P. Simoncelli. 2003. Image Denoising Using Scale Mixtures of Gaussians in the Wavelet Domain. *IEEE Transactions on Image Processing*, 12(11):1338–1351.

Jason Riesa and Daniel Marcu. 2010. Hierarchical Search for Word Alignment. In *Proceedings of ACL 2010*, pages 157–166.

Jason Riesa, Ann Irvine, and Daniel Marcu. 2011. Feature-Rich Language-Independent Syntax-Based Alignment for Statistical Machine Translation. In *Proceedings of EMNLP 2011*, pages 497–507.

Libin Shen, Jinxi Xu, and Ralph Weischedel. 2008. A new string-to-dependency machine translation algorithm with a target dependency language model. In *Proceedings of ACL-08: HLT*, pages 577–585.

Stephan Vogel, Hermann Ney, and Christoph Tillmann. 1996. HMM-Based Word Alignment in Statistical Translation. In *Proceedings of COLING 1996*, pages 836–841.

Jun Xie, Haitao Mi, and Qun Liu. 2011. A Novel Dependency-to-String Model for Statistical Machine Translation. In *Proceedings of EMNLP 2011*, pages 216–226.

Zdeněk Žabokrtský and Martin Popel. 2009. Hidden Markov Tree Model in Dependency-based Machine Translation. In *Proceedings of ACL-IJCNLP 2009, Short Papers*, pages 145–148.

An MT Error-driven Discriminative Word Lexicon using Sentence Structure Features

Jan Niehues and Alex Waibel
Institute for Anthropomatics
Karlsruhe Institute of Technology, Germany
firstname.secondname@kit.edu

Abstract

The Discriminative Word Lexicon (DWL) is a maximum-entropy model that predicts the target word probability given the source sentence words. We present two ways to extend a DWL to improve its ability to model the word translation probability in a phrase-based machine translation (PBMT) system. While DWLs are able to model the global source information, they ignore the structure of the source and target sentence. We propose to include this structure by modeling the source sentence as a bag-of-n-grams and features depending on the surrounding target words. Furthermore, as the standard DWL does not get any feedback from the MT system, we change the DWL training process to explicitly focus on addressing MT errors.

By using these methods we are able to improve the translation performance by up to 0.8 BLEU points compared to a system that uses a standard DWL.

1 Introduction

In many state-of-the-art SMT systems, the phrase-based (Koehn et al., 2003) approach is used. In this approach, instead of building the translation by translating word by word, sequences of source and target words, so-called phrase pairs, are used as the basic translation unit. A table of correspondences between source and target phrases forms the translation model. Target language fluency is modeled by a language model storing monolingual n-gram occurrences. A log-linear combination of these main models as well as additional features is used to score the different translation hypotheses. Then the decoder searches for the translation with the highest score.

One problem of this approach is that bilingual context is only modeled within the phrase pairs. Therefore, different approaches to increase the context available during decoding have been presented (Haque et al., 2011; Niehues et al., 2011; Mauser et al., 2009). One promising approach is the Discriminative Word Lexicon (DWL). In this approach, a discriminative model is used to predict the probability of a target word given the words in the source sentence.

In contrast to other models in the phrase-based system, this approach is capable of modeling the translation probability using information from the whole sentence. Thus it is possible to model long-distance dependencies. But the model is not able to use the structure of the sentence, since the source sentence is modeled only as a bag-of-words. Furthermore, the DWL is trained to discriminate between all translation options without knowledge about the other models used in a phrase-based machine translation system such as the translation model, language model etc. In contrast, we try to feedback information about possible errors of the MT system into the DWL. Thereby, the DWLs are able to focus on improving the errors of the other models of an MT system.

We will introduce features that encode information about the source sentence structure. Furthermore, the surrounding target words will also be used in the model to encode information about the target sentence structure. Finally, we incorporate information from the other models into the creation of the training examples. We create the negative training examples using possible errors of the other models.

2 Related Work

Bangalore et al. (2007) presented an approach to machine translation using discriminative lexical selection. Motivated by their results, Mauser et al. (2009) integrated the DWL into the PBMT approach. Thereby, they are able to use global source information.

This was extended by Huck et al. (2010) by a feature selection strategy in order to reduce the number of weights. In Mediani et al. (2011) a first approach to use information about MT errors in the training of DWLs was presented. They select the training examples by using phrase table information also.

The DWLs are related to work that was done in the area of word sense disambiguation (WSD). Carpuat and Wu (2007) presented an approach to disambiguate between different phrases instead of performing the disambiguation at word level.

A different lexical model that uses target side information was presented in Jeong et al. (2010). The focus of this work was to model complex morphology on the target language.

3 Discriminative Word Lexicon

The DWL is a maximum entropy model used to determine the probability of using a target word in the translation. Therefore, we train individual models for every target word. Each model is trained to return the probability of this word given the input sentence.

The input of the model is the source sentence. Therefore, we need to represent the input sentence by features. In this approach this is done by using binary features. We use an indicator feature for every input word. Therefore, the sentence is modeled as a bag-of-words and the order of the words is ignored. More formally, a given source sentence $F = f_1 \ldots f_I$ is represented by the features $I(F) = \{i_f(F) : f \in SourceVocabulary\}$:

$$i_f(F) = \begin{cases} 1 & : f \in F \\ 0 & : f \notin F \end{cases} \quad (1)$$

The models are trained on examples generated by the parallel training data. The labels for training the classifier of target word e are defined as follows:

$$label_e(F, E) = \begin{cases} 1 & : e \in E \\ 0 & : e \notin E \end{cases} \quad (2)$$

We used the MegaM Toolkit[1] to train the maximum entropy models. This model approximates the probability $p(e_j|F)$ of a target word e_j given the source sentence F.

[1] http://www.umiacs.umd.edu/ hal/megam/index.html

When we have the probability for every word e_j given the source sentence F, we need to combine these probabilities into a probability of the whole target sentence $E = e_1 \ldots e_J$ given F. Making an assumption of independence on the target side as well, the models can be combined to the probability of E given F :

$$p(E|F) = \prod_{e_j \in e} p(e_j|F) \quad (3)$$

In this equation we multiply the probability of one word only once even if the word occurs several times in the sentence. Since we build the target sentence from left to right during decoding, we would need to change the score for this feature only if a new word is added to the hypothesis. If a word is added second time we do not want to change the feature value. In order to keep track of this, additional bookkeeping would be required. But the other models in our translation system will prevent us from using a word too often in any case. Therefore, we approximate the probability of the sentence differently as defined in Equation 4.

$$p(E|F) = \prod_{j=1}^{J} p(e_j|F) \quad (4)$$

In this case we multiply the probabilities of all word occurrences in the target sentence. Therefore, we can calculate the score for every phrase pair before starting with the translation.

4 Modeling Sentence Structure

As mentioned before one main drawback of DWLs is that they do not encode any structural information about the source or target sentence. We incorporated this information with two types of features. First, we tried to encode the information from the source sentence better by using a bag-of-n-grams approach. Secondly, we introduced new features to be able to encode information about the neighboring target words also.

4.1 Source Sentence Structure

In the default approach the sentence is represented as a bag-of-words. This has the advantage that the model can use a quite large context of the whole sentence. In contrast to the IBM models, where the translation probability only depends on the aligned source word, here the translation probability can be influenced by all words in the sentence.

On the other hand, the local context is ignored by the bag-of-words approach. Information about the word order get lost. No information about the previous and next word is available. The problem is illustrated in the example in Figure 1.

Figure 1: *Example for source structural information*

Source:	Die Lehrer wussten nicht, ...
Reference:	The teachers didn't know ...

The German word *Lehrer* (engl. *teacher*) is the same word for singular or plural. It is only possible to distinguish whether singular or plural is meant through the context. This can be determined by the plural article *die*. If only one teacher would be meant, the corresponding article would be *der*.

In order be able to use the DWL to distinguish between these two translations, we need to improve the representation of the input sentence. As shown in the example, it would be helpful to know the order of the words. If we know that the word *die* precedes *Lehrer*, it would be more probable that the word is translated into *teachers* rather than *teacher*.

Therefore, we propose to use a bag-of-n-grams instead of a bag-of-words to represent the input sentence. In this case we will use an indicator feature for every n-gram occurring in the input sentence and not only for every word. This way we are also able to encode the sequence of the words. For the example, we would have the input feature *die_Lehrer*, which would increase the probability of using *teachers* in the translation compared to *teacher*.

By increasing the order of the n-grams, we will also increase the number of features and run into data sparseness problems. Therefore, we used count filtering on the features for higher order n-grams. Furthermore, we combine n-grams of different orders to better handle the data sparseness problem.

4.2 Target Sentence Structure

In the standard DWL approach, the probability of the target word depends only on the source words in the input sentence. But this is a quite rough approximation. In reality, the probability of a target word occurring in the sentence also depends on the other target words in the sentence.

If we look at the word *langsam* (engl. *slow* or *slowly*) in the example sentence in Figure 2, we can only determine the correct translation by using the target context. The word can be translated as *slow* or *slowly* depending on how it is used in the English sentence.

In order to model the translation probability better we need structural information of the target side. For example, if the preceding word on the target side is *be*, the translation will be more probably *slow* than *slowly*.

We encoded the target context of the word by features indicating the preceding or next word. Furthermore, we extend the context to up to three words before and after the word. Therefore the following target features are added to the set of features for the classifier of word e:

$$i_{TC\_e'\_k}(E) = \begin{cases} 1 & : \exists j : e_j = e \wedge e_{j+k} = e' \\ 0 & : else \end{cases} \quad (5)$$

where $k \in \{-1, 1\}$ for a context of one word before and after.

5 Training

Apart from the missing sentence structure the DWL is not able to make use of feedback from the other models in the MT system. We try to incorporate information about possible errors introduced by the other models into the training of the DWL.

The DWL is trained on the parallel data that is available for the task $T = (F_1, E_1), \ldots, (F_M, E_M)$. In order to train it, we need to create positive and negative examples from this data. We will present different approaches to generate the training examples, which differ in the information used for creating the negative examples.

In the original approach, one training example is created for every sentence of the parallel data and for every DWL classifier. If the target word occurs in the sentence, we create a positive example and if not the source sentence is used as a negative example as described in Equation 2. For most words, this results in a very unbalanced set of training examples. Most words will only occur in quite few sentences and therefore, we have mostly negative examples.

Mediani et al. (2011) presented an approach to create the training examples that is driven by looking at possible errors due to the different

Figure 2: *Example for target structural information*

Source:	Die Anerkennung wird langsam sein in den Vereinigten Staaten ...
Reference:	The recognition is going to be slow in the United States, ...

translations in the phrase table (**Phrase pair approach**). Since a translation is generated always using phrase pairs $(\tilde{f}, \tilde{e})$ with matching source side, wrong words can only be generated in the translation if the word occurs in the target side words of those matching phrase pairs. Therefore, we can define the possible target vocabulary $TV(F)$ of a source sentence:

$$TV(F) = \{e | \exists(\tilde{f}, \tilde{e}) : \tilde{f} \subseteq F \land e \in \tilde{e}\} \quad (6)$$

As a consequence, we generate a negative training example for one target word only from those training sentences where the word is in the target vocabulary but not in the reference.

$$label_e(F, E) = \begin{cases} 1 : & e \in E \\ 0 : & e \notin E \land e \in TV(F) \end{cases} \quad (7)$$

All training sentences for which the label is not defined are not used in the training of the model for word e. Thereby, not only can we focus the classifiers on improving possible errors made by the phrase table, but also reduce the amount of training examples and therefore the time needed for training dramatically.

In the phrase pair approach we only use information about possible errors of the translation model for generating the negative training examples. But it would be preferable to consider possible errors of the whole MT system instead of only using the phrase table. Some of the errors of the phrase table might already be corrected by the language model. The possible errors of the whole system can be approximated by using the N-Best list.

We first need to translate the whole corpus and save the N-Best list for all sentences $NBEST(F) = \{E'_1 \dots E'_N\}$. Then we can approximate the possible errors of the MT system with the errors that occur in the N-Best list. Therefore, we create a negative example for a target word only if it occurs in the N-Best list and not in the reference. Compared to the phrase pair approach, the only difference is the definition of the target vocabulary:

$$TV(F) = \{e | e \in NBEST(F)\} \quad (8)$$

The disadvantage of the N-Best approach is, of course, that we need to translate the whole corpus. This is quite time consuming, but it can be parallelized.

5.1 Training Examples for Target Features

If we use target features, the creation of the training examples gets more difficult. When using only source features, we can create one example from every training sentence. Even if the word occurs in several phrase pairs or in several entries of the N-Best list, all of them will create the same training example, since the features only depend on the source sentence.

When we use target features, the features of the training example depend also on the target words that occur around the word. Therefore, we can only use the N-Best list approach to create the target features since previous approaches mentioned in the last part do not have the target context information. Furthermore, we can create different examples from the same sentence. If we have, for example, the N-Best list entries *I think* ... and *I believe* .., we can use the context *think* or the context *believe* for the model of *I*.

In the approach using all target features (**All TF**), we created one training example for every sentence where the word occurs. If we see the word in different target contexts, we create all the features for these contexts and use them in the training example.

$$I(F, E) = max(\quad I(F); I(E); \quad I(E') | E' \in NBEST(F)) \quad (9)$$

The maximum is defined component-wise. So all features, which have in $I(F)$,$I(E)$ or $I(E')$ the value one, also have the value one in $I(F, E)$. If we use the context that was given by the reference, this might not exist in the phrase-based MT system. Therefore, in the next approach (**N-Best TF**), we only used target features from the N-Best list.

$$I(F, E) = max(I(F); I(E') | E' \in NBEST(F)) \quad (10)$$

In both examples, we still have the problem that we can use different contexts in one training example. This condition can not happen when applying the DWL model. Therefore, we changed the set of training examples in the separate target features approach (**Separate TF**). We no longer create one training example for every training sentence (F, E), but one for every training sentence N-Best list translation (F, E, E'). We only considered the examples for the classifier of target word e, where e occurs in the N-Best list entry E'. If the word does not occur in any N-Best list entry of a training sentence, but in the reference, we created an additional example $(F, E, "")$. The features of this examples can then be created straight forward as:

$$I((F, E, E')) = max(I(F); I(E')) \quad (11)$$

If we have seen the word only in the reference, we create an training example without target features. Therefore, we have again a training example which can not happen when using the DWL model. Therefore, we removed these examples in the last method (**Restricted TF**).

6 Experiments

After presenting the different approaches to perform feature and example selection, we will now evaluate them. First, we will give a short overview of the MT system. Then we will give a detailed evaluation on the task of translating German lectures into English and analyze the influence of the presented approaches. Afterwards, we will present overview experiments on the German-to-English and English-to-German translation task of WMT 13 Shared Translation Task.

6.1 System Description

The translation system was trained on the EPPS corpus, NC corpus, the BTEC corpus and TED talks.[2] The data was preprocessed and compound splitting (Koehn and Knight, 2003) was applied for German. Afterwards the discriminative word alignment approach as described in Niehues and Vogel (2008) was applied to generate the alignments between source and target words. The phrase table was built using the scripts from the Moses package (Koehn et al., 2007). A 4-gram language model was trained on the target side of the parallel data using the SRILM toolkit (Stolcke, 2002). In addition we used a bilingual language model as described in Niehues et al. (2011).

[2]http://www.ted.com

Reordering was performed as a preprocessing step using part-of-speech information generated by the TreeTagger (Schmid, 1994). We used the reordering approach described in Rottmann and Vogel (2007) and the extensions presented in Niehues and Kolss (2009) to cover long-range reorderings, which are typical when translating between German and English.

An in-house phrase-based decoder was used to generate the translation hypotheses and the optimization was performed using MERT (Venugopal et al., 2005).

We optimized the weights of the log-linear model on a separate set of TED talks and also used TED talks for testing. The development set consists of 1.7k segments containing 16k words. As test set we used 3.5k segments containing 31k words. We will refer to this system as System 1.

In order to show the influence of the approaches better, we evaluated them also in a second system. In addition to the models used in the first system we performed a log-linear language model and phrase table adaptation as described in Niehues and Waibel (2012). To this system we refer as *System 2* in the following experiments.

6.2 German - English TED Experiments

6.2.1 Source Features

In a first set of experiments, we analyzed the different types of source structure features described in Section 4.1. In all the experiments, we generate the negative training examples using the candidate translations generated by the phrase pairs. The results can be found in Table 1.

First, we added the unigram DWL to the baseline system. The higher improvements for the System 1 is due to the fact that the DWL is only trained on the TED corpus and therefore also performs some level of domain adaptation. This is more important for the System 1, since System 2 is already adapted to the TED domain.

If we use features based on bigrams instead of unigrams, the number of features increases by a factor of eight. Furthermore, in both cases the translation quality drops. Especially for System 1, we have a significant drop in the BLEU score of the test set by 0.6 BLEU points. One problem might be that most of the bigrams occur quite rarely and therefore, we have a problem of data sparseness and generalization.

If we combine the features of unigram and bi-

Table 1: *Experiments using different source features*

System	FeatureSize	System 1		System 2	
		Dev	Test	Dev	Test
Baseline	0	26.32	24.24	28.40	25.89
Unigram	40k	27.46	25.56	28.58	26.15
Bigram	319k	27.34	24.92	28.53	25.82
Uni+bigram	359k	27.69	25.55	28.66	26.51
+ Count filter 2	122k	27.75	25.71	28.75	26.74
+ Count filter 5	63k	27.81	25.67	28.72	26.81
+ Trigram	77k	27.76	25.76	28.82	26.94

gram features, for System 1, we get an improvement of 0.2 BLEU points on the development data and the same translation quality on the test data as the baseline DWL system using only unigrams. For System 2, we can improve by 0.1 on the development data and 0.4 on the test data. So we can get a first improvement using these additional source features, but the number of features increased by a factor of nine.

In order to decrease the number of features again, we applied count filtering to the bigram features. In a first experiment we only used the bigram features that occur at least twice. This reduced the number of features dramatically by a factor of three. Furthermore, this even improved the translation quality. In both systems we could improve the translation quality by 0.2 BLEU points. So it seems to be quite important to add only the relevant bigram features.

If we use a minimum occurrence of five for the bigram features, we can even decrease the number of features further by a factor of two without losing any translation performance.

Finally, we added the trigram features. For these features we applied count filtering of five. For System 1, the translation quality stays the same, but for System 2 we can improve the translation quality by additional 0.2 BLEU points.

In summary, we could improve the translation quality by 0.2 for the System 1 and 0.8 BLEU points for the System 2 on the test set. Due to the count filtering, this is achieved by only using less than twice as many features.

6.3 Training Examples

In a next step we analyzed the different example selection approaches. The results are summarized in Table 2. In these experiments we used the source features using unigrams, bigrams and trigrams with count filtering in all experiments.

In the first experiment, we used the original approach to create the training examples. In this case, all sentences where the word does not occur in the reference generate negative examples. In our setup, we needed 8,461 DWL models to translate the development and test data. These are all target words that occur in phrase pairs that can be used to translate the development or test set.

In each of approaches we have 0.75M positive examples for these models. In the original approach, we have 428M negative examples. So in this case the number of positive and negative examples is very unbalanced. This training data leads to models with a total of 659M feature weights.

If we use the target side of the phrase pairs to generate our training examples, we dramatically reduce the number of negative training examples. In this case only 5M negative training examples are generated. The size of the models is reduced dramatically to 38M weights. Furthermore, we could improve the translation quality by 0.3 BLEU points on both System 1 and System 2.

If we use the 300-Best lists produced by System 1 to generate the training examples, we can reduce the model size further. This approach leads to models only half the size of the phrase pairs approach using only 1.59M negative examples. Furthermore, for System 1 the translation quality can be improved further to 25.87 BLEU points. For System 2 the BLEU score on the development data increases, but the score on the test sets drops by 0.4 BLEU points.

In the next experiment we used the N-Best lists generated by System 2. The results are shown in the line *N-Best list 2*. In this case, the model size is slightly reduced further. And on the adapted system a similar performance is achieved. But for

Table 2: *Experiments using different methods to create training examples*

System	#weight	#neg. Examples	System 1		System 2	
			Dev	Test	Dev	Test
Original Approach	659 M	428 M	27.39	25.44	28.64	26.63
Phrase pairs	38 M	5.26 M	27.76	25.76	28.82	26.94
N-Best list 1	16 M	1.59 M	27.93	25.87	29.07	26.57
N-Best list 2	11 M	1.22 M	27.46	25.37	28.79	26.59
N-Best list 1 nonUnique	16 M	1.41M	27.99	25.97	29.07	26.65

System 1 the performance of this approach drops.

Consequently, it seems to be fine to use an N-Best list of a more general system to generate the negative examples. But the N-Best list should not stem from an adapted system.

Finally, the phrase table was trained on the same corpus as the one that was used to generate the N-Best lists for DWL training. Since we have seen the data before, longer phrases can be used than in a real test scenario. To compensate partly for that, we removed all phrase pairs that occur only once in the phrase table. The results are shown in the last line. This approach could slightly improve the translation quality leading to a BLEU score of 25.97 for System 1 and 26.65 for the System 2.

6.4 Target Features

After evaluating the different approaches to generate the negative examples, we also evaluated the different approaches for the target features. The results are summarized in Table 3. In all these experiments we use the training examples generated by the N-Best list of System 1 using the phrase table without unique phrase pairs.

First, we tested the four different methods using a context of one word before and one word after the word.

In the experiments the first two methods, All TF and N-Best TF , perform worse than the last two approaches, Separate TF and Restricted TF. So it seems to be important to have realistic examples and not to mix different target contexts in one example. The Separate and Restricted approach perform similarly well. In both cases the performance can be improved slightly by using a context of three words before and after instead of using only one word.

If we look at the model size, the number of weights increases from 16M to 17M, when using a context of one word and to 21M using a context of three words.

If we compare the results to the systems using no target features in the first row, no or only slight improvements can be achieved. One reason might be that the morphology of English is not very complex and therefore, the target context is not as important to determine the correct translation.

6.4.1 Overview

In Table 4, we give an overview of the results using the different extensions to DWLs given in this paper. The baseline system does not use any DWL at all. If we use a DWL using only bag-of-words features and the training examples from the phrase pairs, we can improve by 1.3 BLEU points on System 1 and 0.3 BLEU points on System 2.

By adding the source-context features, the first system can be improved by 0.2 BLEU points and the second one by 0.8 BLEU points. If we use the training examples from the N-Best list instead of using the ones from the phrase table, we improve by 0.2 on System 1, but perform 0.3 worse on System 2. Adding the target context features does not improve System 1, but System 2 can be improved by 0.3 BLEU points. This system results in the best average performance. Compared to the baseline system with DWLs, we can improve by 0.4 and 0.8 BLEU points, respectively.

Table 4: *Overview of results for TED lectures*

System	System 1		System 2	
	Dev	Test	Dev	Test
Baseline	26.32	24.24	28.40	25.89
DWL	27.46	25.56	28.58	26.15
sourceContext	27.76	25.76	28.82	26.94
N-Best	27.99	25.97	29.07	26.65
TargetContext	28.15	25.91	29.12	26.90

6.5 German - English WMT 13 Experiments

In addition to the experiments on the TED data, we also tested the models in the systems for the

Table 3: *Experiments using different target features*

System	Context	System 1		System 2	
		Dev	Test	Dev	Test
No Target Features	0-0	27.99	25.97	29.07	26.65
All TF	1-1	27.80	25.48	28.80	26.38
N-Best TF	1-1	27.99	25.74	28.86	26.37
Separate TF	1-1	28.06	25.81	28.98	26.80
Restricted TF	1-1	28.13	25.84	28.94	26.68
Separate TF	3-3	27.87	25.90	28.99	26.75
Restricted TF	3-3	28.15	25.91	29.12	26.90

WMT 2013. The systems are similar to the one used before, but were trained on all available training data and use additional models. The systems were tested on newstest2012. The results for German to English are summarized in Table 5. In this case the DWLs were trained on the EPPS and the NC corpus. Since the corpora are bigger, we perform an additional weight filtering on the models.

The baseline system uses already a DWL trained with the bag-of-words features and the training examples were created using the phrase table. If we add the bag-of-n-grams features up to a n-gram length of 3, we cannot improve the translation quality on this task. But by additionally generating the negative training examples using the 300-Best list, we can improve this system by 0.2 BLEU points.

Table 5: *Experiments on German to English WMT 2013*

System	Dev	Test
Unigram DWL	25.79	24.36
+ Bag-of-n-gram	25.85	24.33
+ N-Best	25.84	24.52

6.6 English - German WMT 13 Experiments

We also tested the approach also on the reverse direction. Since the German morphology is much more complex than the English one, we hope that in this case the target features can help more. The results for this task are shown in Table 6. Here, the baseline system again already uses DWLs. If we add the bag-of-n-grams features and generate the training examples from the 300-Best list, we can again slightly improve the translation quality. In this case we can improve the translation quality by additional 0.1 BLEU points by adding the target features. This leads to an overall improvement by nearly 0.2 BLEU points.

Table 6: *Experiments on English to German WMT 2013*

System	Dev	Test
unigram DWL	16.97	17.41
+ Bag-of-n-gram	16.89	17.45
+ N-Best	17.10	17.47
+ Target Features	17.08	17.58

7 Conclusion

Discriminative Word Lexica have been recently used in several translation systems and have shown to improve the translation quality. In this work, we extended the approach to improve its modeling of the translation process.

First, we added features which represent the structure of the sentence better. By using bag-of-n-grams features instead of bag-of-words features, we are able to encode the order of the source sentence. Furthermore, we use features for the surrounding target words to also model the target context of the word. In addition, we tried to train the DWLs in a way that they help to address possible errors of the MT system by feeding information from the MT system back into the generation of the negative training examples. Thereby, we could reduce the size of the models and improve the translation quality. Overall, we were able to improve the translation quality on three different tasks in two different translation directions. Improvements of up to 0.8 BLEU points could be achieved.

8 Acknowledgements

This work was partly achieved as part of the Quaero Programme, funded by OSEO, French State agency for innovation. The research leading to these results has received funding from the European Union Seventh Framework Programme (FP7/2007-2013) under grant agreement n° 287658.

References

S. Bangalore, P. Haffner, and S. Kanthak. 2007. Statistical Machine Translation through Global Lexical Selection and Sentence Reconstruction. In *Annual Meeting-Association for Computational Linguistics*, volume 45, page 152.

M. Carpuat and D. Wu. 2007. Improving Statistical Machine Translation using Word Sense Disambiguation. In *In The 2007 Joint Conference on Empirical Methods in Natural Language Processing and Computational Natural Language Learning.*

R. Haque, S.K. Naskar, A. Bosch, and A. Way. 2011. Integrating source-language context into phrase-based statistical machine translation. *Machine Translation*, 25(3):239–285.

M. Huck, M. Ratajczak, P. Lehnen, and H. Ney. 2010. A Comparison of Various Types of Extended Lexicon Models for Statistical Machine Translation. In *Proc. of the Conf. of the Assoc. for Machine Translation in the Americas (AMTA).*

M. Jeong, K. Toutanova, H. Suzuki, and C. Quirk. 2010. A Discriminative Lexicon Model for Complex Morphology. In *Proceedings of the Ninth Conference of the Association for Machine Translation in the Americas (AMTA 2010).*

P. Koehn and K. Knight. 2003. Empirical Methods for Compound Splitting. In *EACL*, Budapest, Hungary.

P. Koehn, F.J. Och, and D. Marcu. 2003. Statistical Phrase-Based Translation. In *Proceedings of the 2003 Conference of the North American Chapter of the Association for Computational Linguistics on Human Language Technology*, pages 48–54, Edmonton, Canada.

P. Koehn, H. Hoang, A. Birch, C. Callison-Burch, M. Federico, N. Bertoldi, B. Cowan, W. Shen, C. Moran, R. Zens, C. Dyer, O. Bojar, A. Constantin, and E. Herbst. 2007. Moses: Open Source Toolkit for Statistical Machine Translation. In *ACL 2007, Demonstration Session*, Prague, Czech Republic.

A. Mauser, S. Hasan, and H. Ney. 2009. Extending Statistical Machine Translation with Discriminative and Trigger-based Lexicon Models. In *Proceedings of the 2009 Conference on Empirical Methods in Natural Language Processing: Volume 1 – Volume 1*, Emnlp'09, Singapore.

M. Mediani, E. Cho, J. Niehues, T. Herrmann, and A. Waibel. 2011. The KIT English-French Translation Systems for IWSLT 2011. *Proceedings of the eight International Workshop on Spoken Language Translation (IWSLT).*

Jan Niehues and Mutsin Kolss. 2009. A POS-Based Model for Long-Range Reorderings in SMT. *Fourth Workshop on Statistical Machine Translation (WMT 2009), Athens, Greece.*

J. Niehues and S. Vogel. 2008. Discriminative Word Alignment via Alignment Matrix Modeling. *Proceedings of the Third Workshop on Statistical Machine Translation*, pages 18–25.

J. Niehues and A. Waibel. 2012. Detailed Analysis of different Strategies for Phrase Table Adaptation in SMT. In *Proceedings of the Tenth Conference of the Association for Machine Translation in the Americas (AMTA).*

J. Niehues, T. Herrmann, S. Vogel, and A. Waibel. 2011. Wider Context by Using Bilingual Language Models in Machine Translation. *Sixth Workshop on Statistical Machine Translation (WMT 2011), Edinburgh, UK.*

K. Rottmann and S. Vogel. 2007. Word Reordering in Statistical Machine Translation with a POS-Based Distortion Model. In *TMI*, Skövde, Sweden.

H. Schmid. 1994. Probabilistic Part-of-Speech Tagging Using Decision Trees. In *International Conference on New Methods in Language Processing*, Manchester, UK.

A. Stolcke. 2002. SRILM – An Extensible Language Modeling Toolkit. In *Icslp*, Denver, Colorado, USA.

A. Venugopal, A. Zollman, and A. Waibel. 2005. Training and Evaluation Error Minimization Rules for Statistical Machine Translation. In *Workshop on Data-drive Machine Translation and Beyond (WPT-05)*, Ann Arbor, MI.

Author Index